J. Tyler Hodges

Hodges' New Bank Note Safe-Guard

J. Tyler Hodges

Hodges' New Bank Note Safe-Guard

ISBN/EAN: 9783741197512

Manufactured in Europe, USA, Canada, Australia, Japa

Cover: Foto ©knipser5 / pixelio.de

Manufactured and distributed by brebook publishing software
(www.brebook.com)

J. Tyler Hodges

Hodges' New Bank Note Safe-Guard

HODGES'

NEW BANK NOTE

SAFE-GUARD;

(Fourth Quarterly Edition.)

Giving Fac Simile Descriptions of Upwards of

TEN THOUSAND BANK NOTES

EMBRACING

EVERY GENUINE NOTE

ISSUED IN THE

UNITED STATES & CANADA.

THE MOST EFFECTUAL DETECTOR OF SPURIOUS, ALTERED AND COUNTERFEIT BILLS EVER PUBLISHED.

THE ONLY WORK OF THE KIND EXTANT.

ARRANGED AND PUBLISHED BY

J. TYLER HODGES, Banker,

No. 271 BROADWAY,

CORNER OF CHAMBERS STREET.

NEW-YORK:

1860.

THE SAFE-GUARD.

After years of toil and great expense, this work has at length been completed, and we may safely assert that no work was ever published in any language, or in any country, of greater utility for commercial purposes. It is of interest and importance to every individual, of every age, condition or sex, who handles a dollar of the miscellaneous and precarious paper currency of our country.

The paper money of the United States is of such infinite varieties of design and execution, that the artful and accomplished counterfeiter can sport upon and defy the perceptions of the great majority of our people. And the frequent and cruel impositions so repeatedly practised upon the honest and credulous, have derived their impunity from the fact that other works and Detectors have only attempted to direct attention to the spurious and counterfeit, while in our SAFE-GUARD ALONE, has the idea been developed of minutely describing the genuine Bank notes.

A new counterfeit or spurious Bank note is prepared by a rogue, who, with his numerous accomplices and confederates, distribute and circulate their issue simultaneously in different and distant localities. These notes (not being described in the Reporters and Detectors) being readily taken by the unsuspecting, and by the imperfect judges, in a short time obtain an extensive circulation; and days, weeks, and, in some instances, months have elapsed, before the VIGILANT Bank Note Reporters have informed the community that they have been fearfully victimized. Thus being at last exposed, but not until he has reaped a rich harvest from his first issue, the counterfeiter again takes the plate to his haunt and alters it to some other Bank or denomination, and may do the same thing again and again, and each time with impunity and profit, before the Detectors can act as an efficient check on his proceedings.

But the SAFE-GUARD always, and in every case, acts as a check and preventative against these impositions and frauds, by describing every GENUINE Bank note, and every part of every note, dissecting and analizing all denominations of all notes of every Bank organised and doing business in the United States and British North America, showing each note made up of different designs, vignettes, &c.; each denomination differing so materially, that no one of the notes could be altered to another and larger denomination, without the certainty of an immediate detection on reference to the fac-simile of the plates (in the SAFE-GUARD) of the particular Bank on which such fraud has been perpetrated. Herein is exemplified the great superiority of the SAFE-GUARD over all Reporters and other Bank Note Detectors.

Spurious or altered notes, are by far the most numerous class of bad money, and bear no resemblance to the genuine. They are detected at a glance by reference to the SAFE-GUARD, there being therein portrayed a perfect Daguerreotype of the genuine notes; the dress and design of which are as unlike the spurious as is light to darkness.

Counterfeits, or *fac simile* notes, are comparitively rare. They are intended to resemble and imitate the true, and calculated to circulate where the genuine are well-known, but can be more easily detected by close inspection than any other class of bad bills. Very few of this description are in circulation, as will be seen on reference to our Reporter.

In a word, THE SAFE-GUARD detects all PAST, PRESENT and FUTURE spurious and altered notes, and is of more value, protection and security to the commercial interests of the country, than all the Detectors, Bank Note Lists, and other works, which up to this time have been published. In fact THE SAFE-GUARD is almost indispensable, FOR IT GOES AHEAD OF, AND ANTICIPATES THE COUNTERFEITER, cutting off his success, while the Reporters and Bank Note Lists but follow AFTER, and to use a homely, but forcible expression, "can only lock the stable after the horse is stolen."

We have herein endeavored to show the utility and importance of this work, and with the promise *that it shall be always correct to the date of its issue*, we are satisfied to send it forth to the public on its own merits.

☞ Below will be found commendations from *all the First Class* BANK NOTE ENGRAVING COMPANIES in the Union, endorsing HODGES' NEW BANK NOTE SAFE-GUARD. This testimony, together with the approval and patronage of nearly every Banker and Broker in America, at once stamps it as the most valuable publication of the times—indispensable to every well regulated counting room or business place.

☞ No person is authorized to act as Agent, unless having the Publisher's printed Receipts, and written authority.

J. TYLER HODGES.

CERTIFICATES.

OFFICE OF DANFORTH, WRIGHT & CO.,
New York, March, 1858.

J. T. HODGES, Esq.:

SIR,—Your "Bank Note Safe-Guard" seems to possess unequalled merit, in the detailed description it gives of all Genuine Bank notes; and, combined with the "Journal of Finance and Bank Reporter," you certainly offer a work of great utility, as a protection against frauds in paper currency.

Respectfully yours,
DANFORTH, WRIGHT & Co.

OFFICE OF RAWDON, WRIGHT, HATCH & EDSON,
New York, March, 1858.

J. T. HODGES, Esq.:

SIR,—Having examined the plan proposed in your "Bank Note Safe Guard," for enabling the public to detect Spurious and Altered Bank notes, by furnishing accurate descriptions of the genuine notes of all the Banks of the country, we take pleasure in expressing our approval of the same, as affording a simple and effectual protection against that species of fraudulent paper money.

Respectfully yours
RAWDON, WRIGHT, HATCH & EDSON.

OFFICE OF WELLSTOOD, HAY & WHITING,
New York, March, 1858.

J. T. HODGES, Esq.:

SIR,—We regard your "Bank Note Safe Guard" as a work that should receive the most favorable attention from all who are accustomed to handle Bank notes. The facility with which Altered, Spurious, or Counterfeit notes can be detected, is such, that the most inexperienced can scarcely go astray. And we have no hesitation in commending the work to the public as one which is much required, and as fully accomplishing its object.

With best wishes for the success of your efforts to prevent imposition, through the medium of your publication.

We remain, truly yours,
WELLSTOOD, HAY & WHITING.

OFFICE OF THE NEW ENGLAND BANK NOTE CO.,
Boston, March, 1858.

J. T. HODGES, Esq.:

SIR,—Allow me to express to you my unqualified opinion in favor of your "Bank Note Safe-Guard." The simplicity of it is what I most admire; the most inexperienced of the great mass, who are in the habit of taking Paper Currency can at once detect an altered or spurious note, which are much more dangerous than counterfeits, and more numerously in circulation.

You have my best wishes for its success, believing it to be the best work of its character ever published.

ISAAC CARY, Agent.

New York, March, 1858.

J. T. HODGES, Esq.:

SIR,—We take great pleasure in endorsing Mr. Cary's opinion of your "Bank Note Safe-Guard," and in recommending it as a work of the greatest utility.

Respectfully yours,
TOPPAN, CARPENTER & CO.

OFFICE OF THE AMERICAN BANK NOTE COMPANY,
New York, March, 1858.

J. T. HODGES, Esq.:

SIR,—Attempts at literal imitation, or counterfeiting, in the present advanced state of Bank Note Engraving, are of unfrequent occurrence, most of the notes represented in Bank Note Detectors and Reporters being either Spurious or Altered Notes.

Spurious Bank Notes merely retain the name of the Bank and place of issue—not always using the true name of the President and Cashier, and are made up of devices unlike those of the genuine notes, a want of familiarity with which, on the part of the public, being counted on in perpetrating these frauds.

Your "Bank Note Safe-Guard," supplies a desideratum in a manner so simple and so easy of reference, that there can be no danger of suffering from Spurious or Altered Bank Notes, if brought to the test of comparison which it furnishes.

Respectfully yours,
JOCELYN, DRAPER, WELSH & CO.

TERMS.

The SAFE-GUARD sent by mail to all parts of the Country on receipt of............$2 00
The Journal of Finance and Bank Reporter, including Hodges' Gold and Silver Coin Chart Manual, and Safe-Guard, Weekly Issue............$4 00
Semi-Monthly............$3 00
Monthly............$2 50

INDEX TO THE SAFE-GUARD.

THE FIGURES ENCLOSED IN BRACKETS DENOTE THE DENOMINATION OF NOTES

IMITATED AND PHOTOGRAPHED.

MAINE.

Page
Alfred Bank, Alfred ... 285, 313
American ... 134
Atlantic ... 335
Auburn ... 224, 225
Augusta ... [1] ... 146
Bank of Commerce ... 238
Bank of Cumberland ... 252, 321
Bank of Hallowell ... 136, 324
Bank of Somerset ... 141
Bank of the State of Maine ... 141
Bank of Winthrop ... 163
Bath ... 163
Belfast ... 143
Biddeford ... 138
Bucksport ... 136, 137, 371
Calais ... 370
Canal ... 161, 162
Casco ... (5) ... 275, 334
City Bank, Bath ... 140
City Bank, Biddeford ... 40
Cobbosseecontee ... 149
Eastern ... [2] ... 136
Farmers' ... 134, 344
Freemans ... 141
Frontier ... [1] ... 182, 183
Gardiner ... 134
George's ... 143
Granite ... 134
Kenduskeag ... 146
Lewiston Falls ... 145
Lime Rock ... 149
Lincoln ... 186
Long Reach ... 333, 371
Lumberman's ... 142
Maine ... 349
Manufacturers' ... 232
Manufacturers' & Traders' ... 125, 249, 289
Marine ... 139
Market ... 212, 213
Mechanics' ... 298
Medomak ... (3) ... 228, 284
Merchants' Bank, Bangor ... 274
Merchants' Bank, Portland ... 137, 371
New Castle ... 140
Norombega ... 335, 346
North ... 136
Northern ... 251
Oakland ... 286
Ocean ... 227
Orono ... 137, 138
Pejepscot ... 233, 371
Peoples' ... 286, 316
Richmond ... 148
Rockland ... 366
Sagadahock ... 141
Sandy River ... 228
Searsport ... 135
Skowhegan ... 161
South Berwick ... 203, 204
State ... 227, 371
Thomaston ... 138, 341, 371
Ticonic ... 134
Traders' ... 140
Union ... 274, 284
Veazie ... 228, 229
Village ... 310, 371
Waldoboro ... 264
Waterville ... (20) ... 266
York ... 227

NEW-HAMPSHIRE.

Amoskeag Bank ... 168
Ashuelot ... 175
Bank of Lebanon ... 268
Bank of New Hampshire ... 201, 302, 334
Belknap Co. ... 275, 276
Carroll Co. ... 266, 371
Cheshire ... 168, 169
Cheshire Co. ... 296
Citizens' ... 225, 315
City ... 196
Claremont ... [5] ... 207
Cocheco ... 223, 371
Connecticut River ... 167, 315
Derry ... 292, 371
Dover ... 197, 198
Farmers' & Mechanics' ... 317
Farmington ... 144
Francestown ... 165
Granite State ... 231
Great Falls ... 148
Indian Head ... 144, 148
Lake ... 265
Lancaster ... 271
Langdon ... 172, 173
Manchester ... 145, 372
Mechanicks' ... (10) ... 275, 314, 371
Mechanics' & Traders' ... 203
Merrimack Co. ... 250
Merrimack River ... 293
Monadnock ... 211, 212
Nashua ... 171
New Ipswich ... 173, 372
New Market ... 308
Pawtuckaway ... 227
Pennichuck ... 299
Peterborough ... 172
Pine River ... 316
Piscataqua Exchange ... 256
Pittsfield ... 286
Rochester ... 166
Rockingham ... (3) ... 167
Salmon Falls ... 168
Somersworth ... 296
Souhegan ... 292
State Capitol ... 254
Strafford ... 167
Sugar River ... 242, 243
Union Bank, Concord ... (5) ... 237, 369
Warner ... 163
Weare ... 233
White Mountain ... 210, 344
Winchester ... 169, 170

VERMONT.

Ascutney ... 170
Bank of Bellows' Falls ... 242
" Black River ... 190, 191
" Brattleboro ... 3 ... 267, 268, 338, 355
" Burlington ... (2) ... 238
" Caledonia ... 231, 342, 372
" Castleton ... 168
" Lyndon ... 174
" Middlebury ... 276
" Montpelier ... (1. 3) ... 195
" Newbury ... 242
" Orange Co. ... 364
" Orleans ... 171, 175, 371
" Poultney ... 161
" Royalton ... 149
" Rutland ... 229, 289, 310, 325, 339, 371
" Vergennes ... 153
" Waterbury ... 147
" Woodstock ... 265
Battenkill ... 171, 172
Bradford ... (2) ... 261, 275
Brandon ... 175
Commercial ... 152
Exchange ... 167, 168
Farmers ... 172, 330
Farmers' & Mechanics ... 176
Franklin County ... 166
Lamoille County ... 149
Merchants ... 153
Missisquoi ... 236, 237, 311
Northfield ... 226, 313
Passumpsic ... 264
People's ... 173, 174, 372
St. Albans ... 256
State ... 362
Stark ... 239
Union ... 170, 289
Vermont ... 163
West River ... 154, 168
Windham Co. ... 326, 337
White River ... (8) ... 147, 371
Woodstock Bank ... 154, 313

MASSACHUSETTS.

BOSTON CITY BANKS.

Atlantic Bank ... 18
Atlas ... 19
Bank of Commerce ... 20, 331
Bank of North America ... 19
Bank of the Metropolis ... 361
Bank of Mutual Redemption ... 376
Blackstone ... 21, 301
Boston ... 19
Boylston ... (10) ... 21, 374
Broadway ... 20, 362
City ... 21
Columbian ... 21, 22
Eagle ... [2] ... 22
Eliot ... 20
Exchange ... 22
Faneuil Hall ... 24
Freeman's ... 26
Globe ... 320
Granite ... 24
Hamilton ... 29, 374
Hide and Leather ... 338, 343
Howard Bk., (formerly Howard Bk. Co.) ... 24, 374
Market ... 29, 30, 371
Massachusetts ... [2] ... 27, 344
Maverick ... [2] ... 100, 319, 374
Mechanics' ... 27
Merchants' ... (5) ... 20, 374
National ... 26, 374
New England ... 23
North ... (20) ... 23
Revere ... 373
Safety Fund ... 361, 371
Shawmut ... 26, 374
Shoe and Leather Dealers' ... 29, 344
State ... 25
Suffolk Bank ... (10) ... 27, 362
Traders' Bank ... 28
Tremont Bank ... 25
Union Bank ... [illegible]
Washington Bank ... 26, 37[illegible]
Webster Bank ... (5) ... 26, 341

COUNTRY BANKS.

Abington Bank ... 79, 80
Adams Bank ... 63, 158, 371
Agawam Bank ... 84
Agricultural Bank ... [1] ... 90, 91
Andover Bank ... 96, [illegible]
Appleton Bank ... [illegible]
Asiatic Bank ... 96, [illegible]
Attleborough Bank ... [illegible]
Bank of Brighton ... 85, 86, 311
Bank of Cape Ann ... [illegible]
Bank of Cape Cod ... [illegible]
Barnstable Bank ... 54, [illegible]
Bass River Bank ... 82, [illegible]
Bay State Bank ... [illegible]
Bedford Com. Bank ... 108, 312, 342
Beverly Bank ... 82, [illegible]
Blackstone Bank ... (5) ... 79, [illegible]
Blue Hill Bank ... 110, 311
Brighton Market Bank ... [100] ... 110, 204, [illegible]
Bristol County Bank ... [illegible]
Bunker Hill Bank ... 79, [illegible]
Cabot Bank ... 59
Cambridge Bank ... 60
Cambridge City Bank ... (2) ... [illegible]
Cambridge Market Bank ... 76, [illegible]
Central Bank ... [illegible]
Charles River Bank ... [illegible]
Chicopee Bank ... [illegible]
Citizens' Bank ... 77
City Bank, Lynn ... 98, 292
City Bank, Worcester ... 75, 305
Commercial Bank ... 2 ... 97, 347, [illegible]
Concord Bank ... [illegible]
Conway Bank ... 97, 371
Danvers Bank ... 97
Dedham Bank ... [illegible]
Essex Bank ... [illegible]
Exchange Bank ... 80
Fair Haven Bank ... 84, [illegible]
Falmouth Bank ... (5) ... 78, [illegible]
Fall River Bank ... 70, [illegible]
Fitchburg Bank ... 77, [illegible]
Framingham Bank ... 81
Franklin County ... 84
Gloucester ... [10] ... 81
Grafton ... 81, 371
Grand ... [20] ... 61, 82
Greenfield ... 103, 371
Hadley Falls ... [5, 10] ... 65, 311, [illegible]
Hampden ... 96, 300, 373, [illegible]
Hampshire Man. ... [illegible]
Haverhill ... 85, 288, 248, [illegible]
Hingham ... 65, 341, [illegible]
Holyoke ... 65, 99, 360
Holliston ... 100
Hopkinton ... [2] ... 120
Housatonic ... [5] ... 115, 116, [illegible]
John Hancock ... [1, 3] ... 106, 347
Leighton ... [5] ... 85, [illegible]
Lancaster ... 2 ... [illegible]
Lee ... 63, 331, 343, [illegible]
Leicester ... [5] ... 116, [illegible]
Lechmere ... 115, 374
Lowell ... 108, 347, 374
Lynn Mechanics ... [5] ... 62, 83, 265, [illegible]
Machinists ... 83, 84, [illegible]
Mahaiwe ... [10] ... 100, 101, [illegible]
Malden ... 101, [illegible]
Marblehead ... [illegible]
Marine ... [10] ... 101, 312
Martha's Vineyard ... 284, [illegible]
Massasoit ... 56, [illegible]
Mattapan ... 103, 104, [illegible]
Mechanicks' Newburyport ... 101
Mechanics', New Bedford ... 5 ... 105, 310
Mechanics', Worcester ... 1, 2] ... 115, 314
Mercantile ... 98, 343
Merchants', Lowell ... 102, [illegible]
Merchants', Newburyport ... 118, [illegible]
Merchants', New Bedford ... (1, 2) ... 107, 118, [illegible]
Merchants', Salem ... [illegible]
Merrimack ... 117
Metacomet ... 105, 106, 372
Milford ... 57
Millbury ... 99, 159
Millers' River ... [10] ... 99
Monson ... 66
Monument ... 137
Mount Wollaston ... [illegible]
Naumkeag ... [20] ... 97, 98, 342, 349, 361
Neponset ... 95
Newton ... 66
Northampton ... [5] ... 94, 338, 364
Northborough ... 130, 311, 372
North Bridgewater ... 116, 117
Ocean ... 121
Old Colony ... 117
Oxford ... [20] ... 117, 362
Pacific ... 102
Pemberton ... 105, [illegible]
Peoples' ... 102

INDEX TO THE NEW BANK NOTE SAFE-GUARD.

Page

Pittsfield (5) 113, 114, 355
Plymouth 102, 103
Powow River 113
Prescott 113, 349
Provincetown 124, 133
Pynchon 1 (3) 118
Quincy Stone 55, 373
Quinsigamond 57, 342
Railroad 121, 344, 358
Randolph 57, 344
Rockland 104, 158
Rockport 56, 314
Rollstone (5) 114
Salem 114, 115, 349, 367
Shelburne Falls 310
Southbridge 54, 120
South Reading 111, 112
Spicket Falls 104
Springfiled 112
Taunton 104, 105
Townsend 112, 133
Tradesman's 58
Union, Haverhill 55, 311
Union Bank of Weymouth 112, 112, 373
Village 109, 110, 334
Waltham 110, 261
Wamesit (2) 111, 143
Wamsutta 311
Wareham 111
Warren 108, 109
Western (1) 109
Westfield 105, 107
Woburn (5) 107
Worcester (2, 3, 5,) 109, 357
Worcester County (3) 110, 261, 354
Wrentham 3 110, 111

RHODE ISLAND.

PROVIDENCE CITY BANKS.

American 210, 316, 324
Arcade (3) 212
Atlantic 204, 365
Atlas 216
Bank of America 212
Bank of Commerce [3] 208, 209
Bank of North America 204, 300, 375
Blackstone Canal (2, 5) 206
Butchers' & Drovers 215
City 211
Commercial 250
Continental 205, 206
Eagle 207
Exchange [3] 216, 217
Globe 271, 272, 306, 350, 365
Grocers' and Producers 211
High Street 252, 253, 374
Jackson 215, 216
Liberty (3) 210, 211
Lime Rock Bank 5 374
Manufacturers 267, 324
Marine 321
Mech. & Man. 204, 205
Mechanics 215
Mercantile 217
Merchants 208
Mount Vernon 214
National [1, 3] 217, 324, [illegible], 356
Northern Bank 321
Pawtuxet Bank 210, 323
Phenix Bank 206, 207
Providence Bank 218, 219
Roger Williams' Bank 207, 208
Smithfield Lime Rock Bank 206
State Bank 213, 214, 374
Traders' Bank [1] 209, 376
Union Bank 209
Westminster Bank 214, 215
Weybosset Bank (1, 3) 218, 323
What Cheer Bank 209

COUNTRY BANKS.

Aquidneck Bank 219
Ashaway Bank 268, 374
Bank of Bristol 216
Bank of Kent [5] 251
Bank of Rhode Island 221
Bank of the South County [5] 180
Centerville Bank 173, 355
Citizens' Bank 248
Citizens' Union Bank 219, 375
Commercial Bank 220
Coventry Bank 275, 376
Cranston Bank 264
Cumberland Bank 265
Eagle Bank 218
Elmwood Bank 172, 331
Exeter Bank 234
Fall River Union Bank 221
Franklin Bank [10, 20] 258
Freemen's Bank 237
Globe Bank 270
Granite Bank 249
Greenwich Bank 253, 336
Hope Bank 217, 218, 246
Hopkinton Bank 231, 232
Landholders' Bank 201, 202, 375
Merchants' Bank 225, 313
Narragansett Bank 273
[illegible]land Commercial Bank 222
New-England Pacific Bank 267
Newport Bank 220
[illegible]change Bank 220, 221
[illegible] 223
North [illegible]on Bank 254, 362
North Providence Bank 266
Peoples' Bank 171
Peoples' Exchange Bank 262
Phenix Bank 262
Phenix Village Bank 230
Pomeset Bank 222
Producers' Bank 236
Railroad Bank 169
Rhode Island Exchange Bank 225, 323
Rhode Island Union Bank 220
Richmond Bank 247, 331
Slater Bank 198, 238
Smithfield Exchange Bank 264
Smithfield Union Bank 237
Sowamset Bank 271
Traders' Bank 219, 220
Village Bank 174
Wakefield Bank 125, 175, 176
Warren Bank 224, 342, 375

Page

Washington Do 212
Washington County Bank 316, 322
Woonsocket Falls Bank 211, 339, 376

CONNECTICUT.

Ætna Bank, Hartford 343, 380
Bank of Commerce 188, 189
Bank of Hartford County 194, 309
Bank of Litchfield County 201, 376
Bank of New-England 177
Bank of North America 199, 200
Bank of Norwalk 341, 345, 376
Bridgeport Bank 189
Bridgeport City Bank [2] 189
Central Bank 209
Charter Oak Bank 193, 194
Citizens' Bank 199, 326, 357
City Bank, Hartford 1 191, 192
City Bank of New Haven [5, 10] 196, 343
Clinton Bank 287, 325, 842
Connecticut Bank 187, 319
Conn. River Banking Co. 192
Danbury Bank 202
Deep River Bank 205
East Haddam Bank 199, 336
Elm City Bank 298
Exchange Bank 190
Fairfield County Bank [3] 192, 348
Farmers' Bank 188, 323
Farmers' & Mechanics' Bank 190
Hartford Bank [2, 5] 191, 312
Hatters' Bank 200
Home Bank 298
Hulbart Bank 199, 375
Iron Bank 201, 288, 326, 376
Jewett City Bank 260
Manufacturers' Bank (2) 244
Mechanics' Bank 5 197
Mercantile Bank 192, 291
Merchants' Bank, New Haven (10) 197
Merchants Bank, Norwich 194, 375
Merchants' & Manufact's Bank, Hartford 350, 380
Meriden Bank (5) 183
Middlesex County Bank 201
Middletown Bank [2 3] 234
Mystic Bank 186
Mystic River Bank 229
New Haven Bank [2, 5, 10] 195, 304, 313, 343
New Haven County Bank 196
New London Bank 189
Norwich Bank 193
Norfolk Bank 40
Ocean Bank [2] 187
Pahquioque Bank 202, 226, 289
Pawcatuck Bank 222
Pequonnock Bank 188
Phœnix Bank 192, 193, 331
Quinebaug Bank [2] 195
Quinnipiac Bank 197
Rockville Bank 293
Saugatuck Bank 202, 289
Saybrook Bank (3) 250
Shetucket Bank 195, 306, 375
Southport Bank (2) 200
Stafford Bank (20) 247, 336
Stamford Bank [2, 3, 5, 10] 201, 325, 336, 375
State Bank (5) 191
Stonington Bank (5) 187, 188, 347
Thames Bank 194, 326
Thompson Bank 274
Tolland County Bank [10] 278
Tradesmens' Bank 299
Uncas Bank 195, 336
Union Bank 186
Waterbury Bank 196, 199
Whaling Bank 186, 187
Windham Bank 184
Windham County Bank 182
Winsted Bank 199
Wooster Bank 205

NEW-YORK.

NEW-YORK CITY BANKS.

American Exchange Bank [2] 133, 319
Artisans' Bank 12
Atlantic Bank 9
Bank of America 4, 339
Bank of New York 2 (10) 11
Bank of North America [10] 6
Bank of the Commonwealth 6
Bank of the New York Dry Dock Company 16
Bank of the Republic 12
Bank of the State of New York (5) 5, 319
Bowery Bank 15
Broadway Bank 14
Bull's Head Bank 66
Butchers' & Drovers' Bank (5) 18, 291
Chatham Bank 7
Chemical Bank [5] 9, 354
Citizens Bank 13
Continental Bank 3
Corn Exchange Bank [10] 7
East River Bank 3 15, 356
Fulton Bank 10, 376
Greenwich Bank 15, 16
Grocers' Bank 319
Hanover Bank [2, 5] 14
Importers' & Traders' Bank 302
Irving Bank 10, 319
Leathern Manufacturers Bank 380
Manhattan Co. 5
Marine Bank 9
Market Bank (2) 11
Mechanics' Banking Association 8
Mechanics' Bank (2) 5
Mechanics' & Traders' Bank [3] 14, 15
Mercantile Bank 10
Merchants' Bank 319, 366
Merchants' Exchange Bank 14
Metropolitan Bank (5) 3
Nassau Bank 17
National Bank (1, 5, 10) 6
New York Co. Bank 1 284
New York Exchange Bank 8
North River Bank 4
Ocean Bank [5] 9
Oriental Bank 16
Pacific Bank 1 [2, 5] 13
Park Bank (2) 295
People's Bank 16

Page.

Phenix Bank [2] 4
Seventh Ward Bank [2] 7
Shoe & Leather Bank 12
St. Nicholas Bank 30, 31
Tradesmen's Bank (5) 12, 13
Union Bank 10

COUNTRY BANKS.

Addison Bank 61
Albany City Bank [5] 72, 336, 369
Albany Exchange Bank [1] 5 72, 336
Atlantic Bank 17
Auburn City Bank 68, 312, 370
Auburn Exchange Bank 304
Ballston Spa Bank [1] 73
Bank of Albany [5] 72, 350
Bank of Albion 60
Bank of Attica 78
Bank of Auburn 70, 177
Bank of Bath 62, 266
Bank of Binghampton 74, 283, 342
Bank of the Capitol 108, 357
Bank of Canandaigua 63
Bank of Cayuga Lake (1) 69
Bank of Cazenovia 306, 337
Bank of Central New York 5 70
Bank of Chemung (1, 2, 5) 69, 123
Bank of Chenango 52
Bank of Commerce 69, 314
Bank of Cooperstown 51
Bank of Corning [5] 69
Bank of Coxsackie 49, 90
Bank of Danseville [1, 3] 47, 341
Bank of Fishkill 74, 183
Bank of Fort Edward 64
Bank of Fayetteville 65
Bank of Geneseo 60
Bank of Geneva 67, 66, 359, 369
Bank of Havana [5] 89
Bank of the Interior 339
Bank of Kent 310
Bank of Kinderhook 45
Bank of Lansingburgh (5) 50
Bank of Lima 340
Bank of Lowville [2, 3] 69, 350
Bank of Malone 62
Bank of Newark 46, 340
Bank of Newburgh 67, 330
Bank of Newport 353, 380
Bank of Norwich 306, 370
Bank of Old Saratoga 304, 313
Bank of Orange Co. [10] 73, 376
Bank of Owego (5) 62, 65
Bank of Pawling 46
Bank of Port Jervis 125, 364, 365
Bank of Poughkeepsie 67
Bank of Rhinebeck 75, 342
Bank of Rondout (10) 46, 351
Bank of Rome 70
Bank of Salem 62
Bank of Salina 42
Bank of Saratoga Springs 73, 325
Bank of Seneca Falls 74, 340
Bank of Silver Creek 49
Bank of Sing Sing 50
Bank of Syracuse (2) 65, 71
Bank of Tioga 39
Bank of Troy [3] 315
Bank of Ulster 42
Bank of Utica [5] 74, 286, 335
Bank of Vernon 75, 157
Bank of Watertown 92
Bank of Waterville 42
Bank of West Troy 49
Bank of Westfield (2) 71, 350
Bank of Whitestown [1] 90, 289
Bank of Whitehall 2, 3, 5 71
Bank of Yonkers 131, 152
Black River Bank 47, 311
Briggs Bank of Clyde 300
Brockport Exchange Bk 41
Brooklyn Bank 18
Broome Co. Bank [1, 5, 10] 122, 123, 342
Burnett Bank 49, 121, 375
Buffalo City Bank 74
Cambridge Valley Bank 243
Canajoharie Bank (1, 3) 256
Canal Bank of Lockport 62
Canastota Bank 304
Cataract Bank 354
Catskill Bank [1, 10] 132
Cayuga County Bank [10] 92, 308, 350
Central Bank, Brooklyn 11
Central Bk, Cherry Valley 75
Central Bank, Troy 40
Central City Bank 341, 370
Chautauque County Bank 90
Chemung Canal Bank [10] 66, 268, 335
Chester Bank 90, 313
Chittenango Bank 44, 305
Citizens Bank 47, 323
City Bank of Brooklyn 18
City Bank of Oswego 88, 312, 359
Clinton Bank 70
Commercial Bank, Clyde 74, 315
Commercial Bank, Albany 132
Commercial Bank of Rochester 70, 71
Commercial Bank, Troy 3 [1, 5] 74, 291, 337, 343, 375
Commercial Bank of Whitehall 89, 174
Commercial Bank of Glenn's Falls 61, 305
Commercial Bank of Saratoga 304
Croton River Bank 1 303, 350
Crouse Bank 92
Cuba Bank 272
Cuylers Bank 54
Delaware Bank 3 [5] 44
Deposit Bank 52, 288
Dover Plains Bank 345
Eagle Bank, Rochester 53
Elmira Bank 51
Essex County Bank 91, 370
Exchange Bank, Lockport 53, 290
Fall Kill Bank 89
Farmers' Bank, Amsterdam 41, 258
Farmers' Bank, Attica 40
Farmers' Bank, Hudson 91
Farmers' Bank, Troy (3) 125, 129
Farmers' Bank of Lansingburgh (2) 89
Farmers' Bank of Saratoga Co. 119
Farmers Bank of Washington Co. 322, 376
Far. & Citizens' B'k, Williamsburgh 30
Farmers' & Drovers' Bank 3 (3) 87
Far. & Manufacturers' Bank (5) 10 60
Far. & Mechanics' Bank, Genesee (1) 85, 307

INDEX TO THE NEW BANK NOTE SAFE-GUARD.

Page

Farmers' & Mechanics' Bank, Rochester .. 71, 317
Flour City Bank .. 296
Fort Plain Bank .. 82
Fort Stanwix Bank .. 5 .. 42, 127
Frankfort Bank .. 66
Fredonia Bank .. 322
Frontier Bank .. [1, 2] .. 71
Fulton County Bank .. 122
Genesee County Bank .. 31
Genesee River Bank .. 68
Genesee Valley Bank .. 56, 376
George Washington Bank .. 62
Glenn's Falls Bank .. 63
Goshen Bank .. [20] .. 124, 125
H. J. Miner & Co.'s Bank .. 362
Hamilton Bank .. 81
Herkimer Co. Bank .. 88
Highland Bank .. 48
Hudson River Bank .. [3] .. 126, 133
Huguenot Bank .. [10] .. 124
Hungerford's Bank .. [2, 5] .. 91, 365
International Bank .. 54
Ilion Bank .. 75, 360
Iron Bank .. 119
Jamestown Bank .. 70
Jefferson County Bank .. 91, 146
J. N. Hungerford's Bank .. 362
J. T. Raplee's Bank .. 340, 376
Judson Bank .. 66
Kingston Bank .. 124, 324
Lake Mahopac Bank .. 121
Lake Ontario Bank .. 232
Lake Shore Bank .. 235, 375
Leonardsville Bank .. 139
Livingston Co. Bank .. 128, 342
Long Island Bank, Brooklyn .. 17
Lyons Bank .. 370
Madison County Bank .. 46
Manufacturers' Bank of Brooklyn .. 260
Manufacturers' Bank, Rochester .. 311
Manufacturers' Bank, Troy .. 126, 133
Man. & Traders' Bank .. 307
Marine Bank .. 95
Marine Bank, Oswego .. 307
Market Bank .. [1] .. 126, 291
Mechanics' Bank, Brooklyn .. 17, 184
Mechanics' Bank of Syracuse .. 43, 311
Mechanics' Bank, Williamsburgh .. [10] .. 301
Mech. & Farmers' Bank .. [5] .. 44, 288
Medina Bank .. 56
Mercantile Bank .. 63
Merchants' & Mechanics' Bank .. 46, 291, 35[illegible]
Merchant's Bank, Albany .. 52
Merchants' Bank, Lancaster .. 40
Merchants' Bank, Poughkeepsie .. 43
Merchants' Bank, Syracuse .. 41
Merchants' Bank of Westfield .. 95
Merchants' & Farmers' Bank, Ithica .. 1[illegible]
Middletown Bank of Orange Co. .. [5] .. 96
Mohawk Bank .. [1, 2, 5, 10] .. 128, 244, 342, 354
Mohawk River Bank .. 322
Mohawk Valley Bank .. 61, 62
Monroe County Bank .. 332
Montgomery Co. Bank .. 150, 355
Mutual Bank .. 87
Nassau Bank, Brooklyn .. 382
National Bank .. 302, 342
New York & Erie Bank .. 107
New York State Bank .. 180, 196, 356
Niagara Co. Bank .. 307
Niagara River Bank .. 65, 325
Ogdensburg Bank .. [3] .. 100
Oneida Bank .. [5, 20] .. 42, 375
Oneida Central Bank .. 61
Oneida County Bank .. [10] .. 50
Oneida Valley Bank .. [3] .. 46
Onondaga Bank .. [5] .. 120
Onondaga County Bank .. [3, 10] .. 47
Oswegatchie Bank .. 125
Oswego River Bank .. 307
Otsego County Bank .. 61
Palmyra Bank [now Lyons' Bank] .. 46
Prattin Bank .. [1] .. 300
Pulaski Bank .. 66
Quassiack Bank .. 89
Randall Bank .. 64
Rensselaer County Bank .. 60
R. M. Goddard & Co.'s Bank .. 369
Rochester Bank .. [10] .. 75
Rochester City Bank .. 65
Rome Exchange Bank .. 5 .. 45
Saratoga County Bank .. 41, 341
Salt Springs Bank .. 49
Schenectady Bank .. 131, 132
Schoharie County Bank .. 63
Security Bank .. [5] .. 130
Seneca County Bank .. [1, 10] .. 45, 270, 294, 376
Smith's Bank of Perry .. 2[illegible], 323
Sprakers Bank .. 63
State Bank, Troy .. [5, 20] .. 51, 375
State of New York Bank .. 95, 360
Steuben Co. Bank .. [2, 5] .. 121
Stissing Bank .. 307
Suffolk County Bank .. 93
Susquehanna Valley Bank .. 226
Syracuse City Bank .. 131
Tanners' Bank .. 120
Tompkins County Bank .. 130
Troy City Bank .. [10] .. 129, 291
Ulster City Bank .. [5] .. 67, 342
Unadilla Bank .. [1, 5] .. 125, 289, 291
Union Bank, Albany .. 87
Union Bank, Kinderhook .. 90
Union Bank, Monticello .. [3] .. 67, 127
Union Bank, Rochester .. 2 .. 127
Union Bank, Troy .. 53, 379
Union Bank, Watertown .. 2 .. 68
Utica City Bank .. 48
Wallkill Bank .. 332
Washington County Bank .. [2] .. 124
Watertown Bank & Loan Co. .. [2] .. 128, 318
Waverly Bank .. [1] .. 2[illegible], 315
Weedsport Bank .. 131, 287
Westchester County Bank .. 47
West Winfield Bank .. 96
White's Bank of Buffalo .. 128
Williamsburgh City Bank .. [1, 2, 10] .. 30
Wooster Sherman's Bank .. 87
Worthington Bank .. 234, 315
Wyoming County Bank .. 44

NEW-JERSEY.

Artisan Bank .. 280, 344
Bank of Jersey City .. 3[illegible]
Bank of New Jersey .. [illegible]
Bank of Trade .. 340
Belvidere Bank .. [1, 20] .. 263, 264
Bordentown Banking Co. .. 148
Burlington Bank .. [3, 5] .. 286, 336
Burlington County Bank .. 241, 367
Cataract City Bank .. 87, 325
Central Bank of N. J. .. 142
City Bank, Perth Amboy .. 308
Clinton Bank .. 303
Cumberland Bank of N. J. .. [1, 3] .. 258, 312, 342
Essex County Bank .. 353
Farmers' Bank of N. J. .. [5, 10] .. 261
Farmers' Bank of Wantage .. 148
Far. & Mech. Bank, Camden .. 301, 338, 364
Far. & Mech. Bank, Rahway .. 155, 156
Far. & Merchants' Bank .. [2, 5, 50] .. 271, 380
Freehold Banking Co. .. 310
Gloucester County Bank .. 294
Hackettstown Bank .. 293
Hoboken City Bank .. 328
Hudson Co. Bank .. (1) .. 39, 365
Hunterdon Co. Bank .. 151, 347
Iron Bank .. [5] .. 300, 342, 361, 376
Lambertville Bank .. 332
Mechanics' Bank, Burlington .. 258
Mechanics' Bank, Newark .. [2, 3] .. 286
Mech. & Manufacturers' Bank .. 147
Mech. & Traders' Bank .. 3 .. 89
Merchants' Bank of Paterson .. 348
Millville Bank .. 351
Mt. Holly Bank .. 330, 350
Morris County Bank .. [5] .. 152, 354
Newark Banking Co. .. 224, 230, 231, 378
Newark City Bank .. [2] .. 224, 231
Orange Bank .. [1, 2, 3] .. 146, 284, 339
Passaic County Bank .. 284, 289
Phillipsburgh Bank .. 40
Princeton Bank .. [5] .. 150
Rockaway Bank .. 348
Salem Banking Co. .. [5] .. 150, 151
Somerset County Bank .. 240
State Bank, Camden .. 255, 376
State Bank, Elizabethtown .. 156, 331
State Bank, Newark .. 232, 233
State Bank, N. Brunswick .. [2] .. 153
Stock Security Bank .. 349
Sussex Bank .. [10] .. 217, 310, 335
Trenton Banking Co. .. [1] .. 152, 384
Union Bank, Dover .. 152
Union Bank, Frenchtown .. 303

PENNSYLVANIA.

PHILADELPHIA CITY BANKS.

Bank of Commerce .. 5 .. 81
Bank of North America .. [5] .. 31
Bank of the Northern Liberties .. 82
Bank of Penn Township .. [5] .. 30
City Bank .. 255, 288, 310
Commercial Bank of Penn .. [5] .. 31
Commonwealth Bank .. 340
Consolidation Bank .. 259, 288
Corn Exchange Bank .. 337
Far. & Mech. Bank .. [5] .. 32, 377
Girard Bank .. [5, 10] .. 34
Kensington Bank .. 33
Man. & Mech. Bank .. 36
Mechanics' Bank .. [5] .. 38, 377
Philadelphia Bank .. 5, 50, 100 .. 34, 364
Southwark Bank .. [5, 10, 20] .. 35
Tradesmens' Bank .. 82, 83
Union Bank .. 368
Western Bank .. [5] .. 32, 367

COUNTRY BANKS.

Alleghany Bank .. 383
Allentown Bank .. 261
Anthracite Bank .. 262
Bank of Chambersburg .. [10] .. 129, 352
Bank of Beaver County .. 352
Bank of Catasauqua .. 339
Bank of Chester Co. .. 59, 60
Bank of Chester Valley .. 344
Bank of Commerce, Erie .. 359
Bank of Crawford County .. 335
Bank of Danville .. 128
Bank of Delaware Co. .. [10] .. 100, 377
Bank of Fayette County .. 357
Bank of Germantown .. 100, 339
Bank of Gettysburg .. 90
Bank of Lawrence Co. .. 363
Bank of Middletown .. [5] .. 119, 310, 312, 336
Bank of Montgomery Co. .. [5, 10] .. 128, 310
Bank of Northumberland .. [10] .. 119
Bank of Pittsburgh .. [5] .. 122
Bank of Pottstown .. 353
Bank of Phoenixville .. 366
Central Bank of Pennsylvania .. 347
Citizens' Bank, Pittsburg .. 346
Columbia Bank .. [10] .. 121
Doylestown Bank .. 64
Easton Bank .. [5, 10] .. 120
Exchange Bank .. [10] .. 64
Far. Bank of Buck's Co. .. 128
Farmers' Bank of Lancaster .. 78, 201
Farmers' Bank of Reading .. 63, 255
Farmers' Bank of Schuylkill Co. .. 107, 313
Farmers' & Drovers' Bank .. [5, 10, 20] .. 123, 124, 352
Far. & Mechanics' Bank, Easton .. [5] .. 118
Franklin Bank .. [5] .. 107
Harrisburg Bank .. [5, 10] .. 58
Honesdale Bank .. 64, 364
Iron City Bank .. 366
Jersey Shore Bank .. 337
Kittanning Bank .. 331
Lancaster Co. Bank .. 129
Lebanon Bank .. 128
Lebanon Valley Bank .. 359
Lewisburg Bank .. 352, 379
Lock Haven Bank .. 297
Mauch Chunk Bank .. 293
McKean County Bank .. 348
Mechanics' Bank, Pittsburgh .. 259, 333
Mer. & Man. Bank .. 132, 352, 359
Miners' Bank of Pottsville .. 93
Monongahela Bank .. 129
Monongahela Valley Bank .. 357
Octoraro Bank .. 360
Pittston Bank .. 376
Shamokin Bank .. 347
Stroudsburgh Bank .. 332
Union Bank of Reading .. 317, 370
Warren Co. Bank .. 151, 311
West Branch Bank .. [10] .. 151, 311
Wyoming Bank .. 107, 109
[illegible] .. [10] .. 1[illegible]
[illegible] .. [illegible]

DELAWARE.

Page

Bank of Delaware .. [1, 2, 5] .. 124, 205
Bank of Newark .. 3[illegible]
Bank of Smyrna .. 165, 306, 309
Bank of Wilm. & Brandywine .. [1, 5, 10] .. 207
Delaware City Bank .. [2, 3] .. 2[illegible]
Farmers' Bank .. [3] .. 237, 312
Mechanics' Bank .. [illegible]
New Castle County Bank .. 181
Union Bank .. 260

MARYLAND.

Bank of Baltimore .. [5, 100] .. 38, 39
Bank of Commerce .. 37
Bank of Westminster .. [10] .. 122
Cecil Bank .. 119, 377
Central Bank, Frederick .. 131
Chesapeake Bank .. 34
Citizens' Bank .. [5] .. 36
Cumberland City Bank .. 354
Commercial & Far. Bank .. [10] .. 37, 370
Cumberland Bank of Allegheny .. 119
Clinton Bank .. 378
Easton Bank .. 164
Farmers' Bank .. 285
Farmers' & Mech. Bank of Carroll Co. .. 64, 2[illegible]8, 314
Farmers & Mech. Bank of Kent Co. .. 323, 334, 370
Farmers' & Mech. Bank, Frederick .. 125
Farmers' & Mech. Bank, Baltimore .. 323, 340
Farmers' & Merchants' Bank, Greensboro' .. 1[illegible]
Farmers' & Planters' Bank .. 87
Fells' Point Savings Institution .. 8
Franklin Bank .. [5] .. 39
Frederick County Bank .. 63, 64
Fredericktown Savings' Institution .. 120, 321
Frostburg Bank .. 308
Hagerstown Bank .. 127
Hagerstown Savings Institution .. 87
Howard Bank .. 37, 38
Marine Bank .. [100] .. 38
Mechanics' Bank .. [10] .. 35, 36
Merchants' Bank .. 36
Peoples' Bank .. 365
Union Bank .. 35
Washington County Bank .. 122
Western Bank .. 36

DISTRICT OF COLUMBIA.

Bank of Commerce .. 18[illegible]
Bank of the Metropolis .. 255
Bank of Washington .. 18[illegible]
Corporation of Alex., &c. .. 290, 351
Far. & Mech. Bank .. 290, 370
Patriotic Bank .. [100] .. 161
United States Treasury Notes .. 35[illegible]

VIRGINIA.

Bank of Berkeley .. 146
Bank of Commerce .. 194, 342
Bank of Danville .. 360
Bank of Howardsville .. 301
Bank of Manassas .. 348
Bank of Philippi .. [5] .. 381
Bank of Roanoke .. 350
Bank of Rockbridge .. 325
Bank of Rockingham .. 162
Bank of Scottsville .. 146, 377
Bank of the Commonwealth .. 3[illegible]9
Bank of the Old Dominion .. [5] .. 170, 378
Bank of the Valley .. [10] .. 2[illegible]
Bank of Virginia .. 2[illegible]8
Bank of Weston .. 369
Bank of Wheeling .. 17[illegible]
Bank of Winchester .. 161
Central Bank of Virginia .. 282
Exchange Bank of Virginia .. [5, 10] .. 27[illegible]
Fairmont Bank .. 213
Far. Bank of Fincastle .. 309
Farmers' Bank of Virginia .. [10, 20, 30] .. 292, 342
Manufacturers' Bk. of Kanawha .. [illegible]
Man. & Farmers' Bank .. [5] .. 178
Merchants' Bank .. [20] .. 170, 325
Mer. & Mech. Bank .. [5] .. 177, 287, 38[illegible]
Monticello Bank .. 2[illegible]1, 28[illegible]
North-Western Bank of Va. .. [5, 10] .. 176, 312, 36[illegible]
Rappahannock Bank .. 34[illegible]
South Western Bank .. 351, [illegible]

NORTH CAROLINA.

Bank of Cape Fear .. [4, 10, 20] .. 281, 382
Bank of Charlotte .. [10, 20] .. 176, 37[illegible]
Bank of Clarendon .. 255, 314
Bank of Fayetteville .. 214, 323, 3[illegible]
Bank of Lexington .. 3[illegible]
Bank of State of N. C. .. [3, 4, 10, 20] .. 283, [illegible]
Bank of Wadesborough .. 278, 325, [illegible]
Bank of Washington .. [illegible]
Bank of Wilmington .. [5, 10] .. [illegible]
Bank of Yanceyville .. 2[illegible]
Commercial Bank .. 279, [illegible]
Farmers' Bank .. [100] .. 2[illegible]
Merchants' Bank .. [illegible]

SOUTH CAROLINA.

Bank of Camden .. [illegible]
Bank of Charleston .. [5, 20, 50] .. [illegible]
Bank of Chester .. [illegible]
Bank of Georgetown .. [3, 10, 20] .. 224, 323, 342
Bank of Hamburg .. [20] .. 177, [illegible]
Bank of Newberry .. 141
Bank of South Carolina .. [50] .. 27[illegible]
Bank of State of S. C. .. 1, 2, 4, 5 .. 279, 2[illegible]
Com. Bank of Columbia .. 161
Exchange Bank .. 256, 257
Far. & Exchange Bank .. 244, 244
Merchants' Bank .. [10] .. 323, 344, 377
Peoples' Bank .. 1[illegible]3
Planters' Bank of Fairfield .. 162, 163
Planters' and Mech. B'k .. [10] .. [illegible]
South Western R R B'k .. 176
State Bank .. [5, 20] .. 279
Union Bank .. 270

GEORGIA.

Aug. Ins. and Banking Co. .. 240
Bank of Athens .. 300
Bank of Augusta .. [10] .. 283
Bank of Columbus .. 3[illegible]
Bank of Commerce .. 309, 340
Bank of the Empire State .. 352
Bank of Fulton .. 279, 306, 340
Bank of Middle Georgia .. 303, 317
Bank of Savannah .. 162
Bank of the State of Geo. .. [10] .. 238, 240, 31[illegible]
Central R. R. & Bank Co. .. 107, 3[illegible]
City Bank .. [illegible]
[illegible] Bank [illegible] .. [50] .. [illegible]

INDEX TO THE NEW BANK NOTE SAFE-GUARD.

Page

La Grange Bank 248
Manufacturers' Bank 151, 306, 351, 380
Marine Bank .... [20] .. 229
Mechanics' Bank 213
Mechanics' Savings Bank 161
Mer. and Planters' Bank 306, 309
North Western Bank of Georgia 350
Planters' Bank 216
Timber Cutters' Bank 377
Union Bank 228, 291

ALABAMA.

Bank of Mobile .... [10, 20, 50, 100] .. 282, 290
Bank of Montgomery 272, 288
Central Bank 226, 260, 377
Commercial Bank 321
Eastern Bank 362
Northern B'k of Alabama 179
Southern B'k of Alabama 292

OHIO.

Bank of Commerce .... [10] .. 243
Bank of Delaware 363
Bank of Geauga .... [10] .. 262
Bank of Marion 229
Bank of the Ohio Valley 378
Champaign County Bank 224
City Bank, Cleveland .... [3, 10] .. 181
City Bank of Columbus 285
Com. Bank of Cincinnati .... [3] .. 258
Forest City Bank .... [10] .. 245
Franklin Bk of Portage Co. 181
Franklin Bk of Zanesville .... [3] 144
Iron Bank .... [5, 10] .. 241
Mahoning County Bank 184
Merchants' Bank 244
Miami Valley Bank .... [10] .. 285
Pickaway County Bank .... [10] .. 183
Sandusky City Bank .... [3, 5, 10, 20] .. 264
Springfield Bank .... [5] .. 166
Stark County Bank .... [10] .. 241
State Bk. Ohio [1, 2, 3, 5, 10, 20] 241, 267, 323, 325, 362
Union Bank 178
Western Reserve Bank 263

INDIANA.

Bank of Elkhart 158
Bank of Goshen 236
Bank of Mount Vernon 169
Bank of the State of Indiana 329, 346, 372
Bloomington Bank 378
Cambridge City Bank 135
Exchange Bank 300
Farmers' Bank, Westfield 265
Indiana Bank 227
Indiana Farmers Bank 303
Kentucky Stock Bank 238, 273
La Grange Bank 188
Parke Co. Bank 300
Prairie City Bank 135
Salem Bank 169
Southern Bank of Ind 189
Union Plank Road Co 160

ILLINOIS.

Agricultural Bank .... [2, 5]. 302
Alton 229, 372
American Exchange 166
Bank of Albion 346
Bank of America 378
Bank of Aurora 5 143
Bank of Bloomington 345
Bank of Carmi 2 356
Bank of Chester 142
Bank of Commerce 350
Bank of the Commonwealth 350, 366
Bank of Elgin 167
Bank of Federal Union 356
Bank of Galena 186
Bank of Geneseo 377
Bank of Illinois 370
Bank of Indemnity 367
Bank of Kewanee 163
Bank of LaSalle 350
Bank of Metropolis 377
Bank of Naperville 156
Bank of Northern Ills 169
Bank of Peru 156
Bank of Pike Co 169
Bank of Quincy 308
Bank of Raleigh 208
Bank of the Republic .... [5] .. 353, 378
Bank of Southern Ills 287, 289
Bank of the State 379
Belvidere Bank 283
Bull's Head Bank 357
Central Bank 157
Citizens Bank 356
City Bank of Cairo 359
Columbian Bank 379
Kane Co. Bank 368
City Bank of Cairo 366
City Bank, Ottawa 337
Continental Bank 300
Corn Exchange Bank 302
Edgar County Bank 291
E. I. Tinkham & Co.'s Bank 297
Farmers & Traders's Bank 167
Frontier Bank 356
Garden State Bank 365
Grayville Bank 241
Grand Prairie Bank 297
Highland Bank 356
Illinois Central Bank 355
Illinois State Bank 369
Illinois State Security Bank 365
International Bank .... [10] .. 277
Kankakee Bank 305
Lafayette Bank 5 255
Lake Michigan 367
Lancaster Bank 365
Marine Bank 158
Merchants Bank Carmi 356
Mer. and Drovers' Bank 166
Mississippi River Bank 237
M'Lean County Bank 157
Morgan County Bank 308
Narragansett Bank 122
National Bank 307
Ohio River Bank 379
Patriotic Bank 379
Pittsfield Bank 378
Prairie State Bank 335
Railroad Bank 251
Reapers' Bank 379
Reed's Bank 326
Southern Bank of Ills .... [5] .. 355
State Bank of Illinois 158, 377
Union County Bank 364
Warren County Bank 287

KENTUCKY.

Bank of Ashland .... 10, 20 .. 321
Bank of Kentucky .. [all denominations] .. 277
Bank of Louisville [5, 10, 20, 50] 276, 320, 324, 351, 362
Commercial Bank of Kentucky 277, 325, 377, 379
Farmers' Bank .... [1, 2, 5, 10] .. 185
Northern Bank ... [all denominations] ... 230, 345
Peoples' Bank 146, 367
Southern Bank .... [1, 2, 3, 5, 10] 180, 341, 367, 377

TENNESSEE.

Agricultural Bank 249, 262
Bank of Chattanooga 246, 334, 325
Bank of Commerce 293
Bank of Knoxville 261, 325
Bank of Memphis 246, 253
Bank of Middle Tennes 245, 288
Bank of Nashville 247, 246
Bank of Paris 297
Bank of Tennessee [2, 10, 20, 50.] .. 323, 325, 342, 377
Bank of the Union 302
Bank of West Tennessee 324
Buck's Bank 363
City Bank 298
Commercial Bank of Tennessee 246
Exchange Bank 286, 287, 315
Farmers' Bank 180, 308
Merchants' Bank 300, 367
Northern Bank .... [5] .. 299
Ocoee Bank 237, 377
Planters' Bank .... [20] .. 181, 182, 287, 289
River Bank 160
Shelbyville Bank 309, 351
Traders Bank 292
Union Bank .... [1, 20.] .. 184, 186

LOUISIANA.

Bank of America 353
Bank of Louisiana 283, 290, 377
Bank of New Orleans .... [5] .. 179, 180
Canal Bank .... 20 .. [20] .. 287, 290
Citizens' Bank .... [10, 50, 100] .. 283, 290
Crescent City Bank 353
Louisiana State Bank .... [10, 20] 100 .. 253
Mechanics and Traders Bank 251
Merchants' Bk. (formerly Bk. Jas. Robb. 341, 377
Southern Bank 284
Union Bank .... [50] .. 261

FLORIDA.

Bank of Commerce 360
Bank of St. Johns 360
State Bank of Florida 358

MICHIGAN.

Bank of Tecumseh 328
Farmers' and Mech 162, 343
Michigan Ins. Co 184
Peninsular 251
State Bank of Michigan 363

WISCONSIN.

Arctic Bank 327
Bank of Appleton 329
" Albany 366
" Beloit 233, 318
" Columbus .... [5] .. 317
" Commerce 182
" Eau Claire 340
" Fond du Lac 342
" Fox Lake 330
" Green Bay 365
" Horicon 368
" Jefferson 359
" La Pointe 347
" Manitowoc 328
" Milwaukee 184
" Moneka 346
" Monroe 369
" Monticello 330
" New London 346
" North America 364
" Oconto 328
" Oshkosh 49
" Portage 328
" Prairie du Chein 318
" Racine 184
" Ripon 318
" Sheboygan 229
" Sparta 354
" Superior 329
" the Capitol 318
" the Interior .... [5] .. 346
" the North West 240
" Watertown 167
" Whitewater 330
" Wisconsin 329
Beloit Savings' Bank 366
Brown Co 318
Central 299
Chippewa 128
Citizens' Bank of Oshkosh 329
City Bank, Beaver Dam 329, 378
City Bank, Kenosha 144
City Bank of Prescott 330
City Bank, Racine 184
Clark County 328
Columbia County 260
Commercial 317
Corn Exchange 268
Corn Planters 358
Dane County 155, 189
Dodge County 241
E. J. Hinckley's Bank of Grant Co 246
Elkhorn 48
Exchange Bank of Darling & Co 187
Farmers' Bank of Chippewa 366
Farmers' & Mech. Bank, Fond-du-Lac 359
Farmers' & Millers' 167
Forest City 49
Fox River 140
Frontier 346
German 306
Green Bay 355
Hall & Bros. Bank 327
Howard Bank 364
Hudson City 318
Jefferson Co 168
Juneau 329
Katanyan 318
Kenosha Co 291
Kokomo 328
Koshkonong Bank 366
Laborers' 347
LaCrosse County 328
Lake Shore 367
Lumbermen's 129
Manitowoc Co 328
Marathon City Bank 378
Marine 294
Mechanics' 354
Menomonee 329
Mercantile 337
Mer. & Mech. Bank, Whitewater 327
Monroe Co 354
Northern 291, 330
North Western 318
Oakwood 292
Oconto Co 328
Oneida Bank, Berlin 346
Osborn Bank of New London 347
Oshkosh Commercial 166
Portage County Bank 366
Racine County 184
Reedsburgh 358
Richland County Bank 364
Rock Co 296
Rock River 144
Sauk Co 327
Sauk City Bank 362
Shawanaw 328
State Stock 329
Second Ward 308
Southern 267
State Bank, Madison 182
State Bank of Wisconsin 164
St. Croix River 169
St. Croix Valley 327
St. Louis 328
Tradesmen's 328
Union Bank, Milwaukee 346
Walworth County 296
Waukesha County 261, 366
Waupacca County 346
Waupun 318
Winnebago Co 277
Wisconsin Bank 327
Wisconsin Marine & Fire Ins Co .. [10] .. 164
Wisconsin Pinery 348
Wisconsin Valley 330
Wood Co. Bank 364

MISSOURI.

Bk. of the State of Missouri .... [20] .. 180, 345
Bank of S Louis 340, 367
Exchange Bank of St. Louis 362
Farmers' Bank of Mo 361
Mechanics' Bank 346 349, 357
Merchants' Bank of St. Louis 355
Southern Bank 341

MINNESOTA.

Bank of Owatonna 351
Bank of Rochester 367
Bank of Saint Paul 369
Bank of the State 368
Chisago Co. Bank 366, 372
Exchange 369
Farmers' Bank 358
Goodhue County Bank 358
Nicollet Co. Bank 367
State Bank of Minn 359
Winona Co. Bank 358

KANSAS.

Kansas Valley Bank 372

IOWA.

State Bank of Iowa 367

TEXAS.

Commercial and Agricultural Bank 183, 313

NEBRASKA.

Western Exchange Fire & Marine Ins. Co .. 261, 297

CANADA.

☞ The notes of the Branches of the Bank of British North America, are all alike, with but little difference on the ends.

Bank of B. N. A., Hamilton 273
Bank of B. N. A., Kingston 263
Bank of B. N. A., Montreal 263
Bank of B. N. A., Toronto 269
Bank of Montreal .... [5] .. 180, 181
Bank of Toronto 341
Bank of the County of Elgin 322
Banque Du Peuple 372
Bank of Upper Canada .... 5 .. [10] .. 269 341
City Bank 164, 166
Colonial Bank 370
Com. Bank M. D Kingston 259, 337
Com Bank M. D. Montreal 259
Eastern Township Bank 379
Gore Bank .... (10) .. 273
Grenville County Bank 290
International Bank of Canada 360
Molsons' Bank 180, 323
Niagara District Bank 235, 289
Ontario Bank 344, 378
Provincial Bank 306
Quebec Bank 180, 341
St. Francis Bank 345

NEW-BRUNSWICK.

Bank of B. N. America 249
Bank of New Brunswick 217
Central Bank 242
Charlotte County Bank 242
Commercial Bank 230
Saint Stephens' Bank 233, 234
Westmoreland Bank 178

PRINCE EDWARD'S ISLAND.

Bank of Prince Edward Island .... [illegible]

1 Compt's die. METROPOLITAN BK New York City. Words "one dollar" over portrait of Washington in large die. 1 Die.	Compt's die. ONE Male portrait 1 Indian princess, fig. 1, shield, water fall and rainbow. 1 CONTINENTAL BK., New York City. City Arms. ONE Female erect; ship in distance.	1000 Washington and other military officers. Compt's die. Vig. The Globe. CONTINENTAL BK., New York City. 1000 Head of Washington.
2 Compt's die. METROPOLITAN BK New York City. Words "two dollars" over a male portrait in large die. 2 Die.	Compt's die. TWO Male portrait 2 Female seated on either side of a fig. 2. 2 CONTINENTAL BK., New York City. City Arms. TWO Spread eagle Male portrait	1 ONE Compt's die. ISLAND CITY BANK, New York City. Tram of cars, men, etc. 1 Eagle on a shield.
3 Compt's die. METROPOLITAN BK New York City. Words "three dollars" over a male portrait in large die. 3 3	Compt's die. 3 Male portrait Three females and fig. 3; buildings in distance. 3 CONTINENTAL BK., New York City. View of sunrise. Male portrait THREE Male portrait	2 Locomotive and tender. ISLAND CITY BANK, New York City. Ship building. TWO 2 Compt's die.
5 Compt's die. METROPOLITAN BK New York City. Vig. Three females representing the Arts and Sciences; building in distance. 5 FIVE	Male portrait 5 Male portrait Compt's die. Five females and fig. 5; shipping, cars and buildings in distance. 5 CONTINENTAL BK., New York City. Eagle. Male portrait Male portrait Male portrait	3 Compt's die. ISLAND CITY BANK, New York City. Ships, schooner, steamboat, etc 3 Two females; one kneeling.
Compt's die. 10 METROPOLITAN BK New York City. Vig. Three females in clouds. 10 X	10 Continental officer. Compt's die. Signing Declaration of Independence. CONTINENTAL BK., New York City. 10 Female with pole, cap, shield and Declaration of Independence.	FIVE Female drawing water from well. Cattle; farming scene in distance. ISLAND CITY BANK, New York City. Eagle. 5 Compt's die.
Compt's die. Figure of [illegible], globe, etc. 50 View of a building. 50 METROPOLITAN BK New York City. FIFTY DOLLARS	TWENTY Two females representing Liberty and Justice. Compt's die. Male portrait 20 CONTINENTAL BK., New York City. Winged female erect; female seated with pole, cap, eagle and cornucopia.	Full length figure of Liberty with pole, cap, shield, eagle, etc. TEN Spread eagle; vessels in distance. ISLAND CITY BANK, New York City. 10 Compt's die.
100 Female seated with pole and cap; flowers, etc. Compt's Die. Female reclining on a part of City Arms; vessels in distance. 100 METROPOLITAN BK New York City. ONE HUNDRED	FIFTY Male portrait Compt's die. 50 Steamer at sea. CONTINENTAL BK., New York City. Shield. 50 Sailor with quadrant, globe, etc.	XX Compt's die. Steamship, ship, row-boat, view of city and fort. ISLAND CITY BANK, New York City. 20 Male portrait
500 Female erect and flowers. 500 Vig. Female reclining with pole, cap, eagle, drapery, &c.; vessels in distance. METROPOLITAN BK New York City. View of sunrise. 500 Compt's die.	100 Compt's die. 100 Female on either side of a shield, surmounted by an eagle; steamboat, vessels, cars and buildings in distance. CONTINENTAL BK., New York City. Cornucopia and anvil. 100 Male portrait 100	FIFTY View of a large public building. ISLAND CITY BANK, New York City. 50 Compt's die.
1000 Female with spear and shield; owl, globe, &c. Compt's die. Female reclining with scroll, globe, etc.; ship and steamer in distance. METROPOLITAN BK New York City. View of sunrise 1000	Female erect; an eagle in act of drinking from urn. 500 500 Compt's die. CONTINENTAL BK., New York City. 500 Male portrait	100 Compt's die. 100 C Signing the Declaration of Independence. ISLAND CITY BK., New York City. 100 Washington.

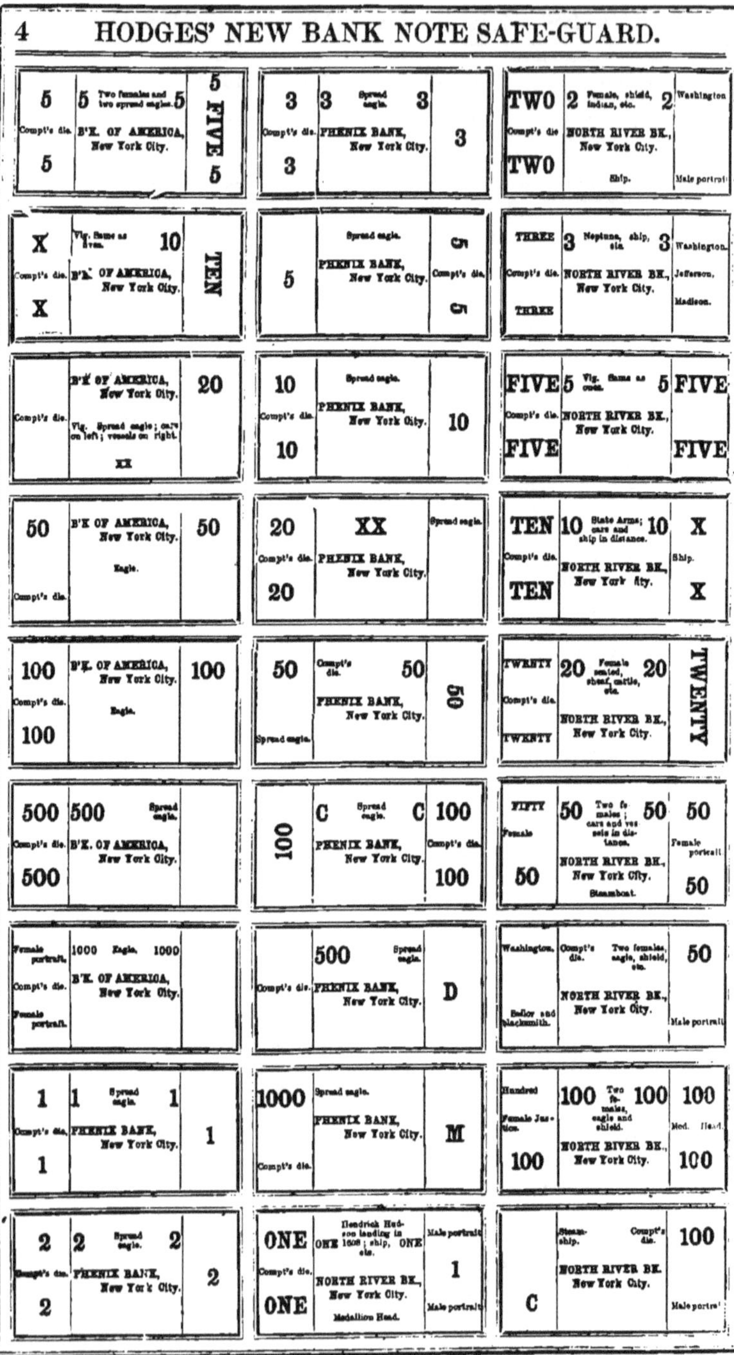

5 | 5 Two females and two spread eagles. 5 | 5
Compt's die. | B'K. OF AMERICA, New York City. | FIVE
5 | | 5

3 | 3 Spread eagle. 3 |
Compt's die. | PHENIX BANK, New York City. | 3
3 | |

TWO | 2 Female, shield, indian, etc. 2 | Washington
Compt's die | NORTH RIVER BK., New York City. |
TWO | Ship. | Male portrait

X | Vig. Same as fives. 10 |
Compt's die. | B'K. OF AMERICA, New York City. | TEN
X | |

| Spread eagle. | 5
5 | PHENIX BANK, New York City. | Compt's die.
| | 5

THREE | 3 Neptune, ship, etc. 3 | Washington.
Compt's die. | NORTH RIVER BK., New York City. | Jefferson.
THREE | | Madison.

| B'K OF AMERICA, New York City. | 20
Compt's die. | Vig. Spread eagle; cars on left; vessels on right. |
| XX |

10 | Spread eagle. |
Compt's die. | PHENIX BANK, New York City. | 10
10 | |

FIVE | 5 Vig. Same as ones. 5 | FIVE
Compt's die. | NORTH RIVER BK., New York City. |
FIVE | | FIVE

50 | B'K OF AMERICA, New York City. | 50
| Eagle. |
Compt's die. | |

20 | XX | Spread eagle.
Compt's die. | PHENIX BANK, New York City. |
20 | |

TEN | 10 State Arms; cars and ship in distance. 10 | X
Compt's die. | NORTH RIVER BK., New York City. | Ship.
TEN | | X

100 | B'K. OF AMERICA, New York City. | 100
Compt's die. | Eagle. |
100 | |

50 | Compt's die. 50 |
| PHENIX BANK, New York City. | 50
Spread eagle. | |

TWENTY | 20 Female seated, sheaf, cattle, etc. 20 | TWENTY
Compt's die. | NORTH RIVER BK., New York City. |
TWENTY | |

500 | 500 Spread eagle. |
Compt's die. | B'K. OF AMERICA, New York City. |
500 | |

| C Spread eagle. C | 100
100 | PHENIX BANK, New York City. | Compt's die.
| | 100

FIFTY | 50 Two females; cars and vessels in distance. 50 | 50
Female | NORTH RIVER BK., New York City. | Female portrait
50 | Steamboat. | 50

Female portrait. | 1000 Eagle. 1000 |
Compt's die. | B'K. OF AMERICA, New York City. |
Female portrait. | |

| 500 Spread eagle. |
Compt's die. | PHENIX BANK, New York City. | D

Washington. | Compt's die. Two females, eagle, shield, etc. | 50
Sailor and blacksmith. | NORTH RIVER BK., New York City. | Male portrait

1 | 1 Spread eagle. 1 |
Compt's die. | PHENIX BANK, New York City. | 1
1 | |

1000 | Spread eagle. |
| PHENIX BANK, New York City. | M
Compt's die. | |

Hundred | 100 Two females, eagle and shield. 100 | 100
Female Justice. | NORTH RIVER BK., New York City. | Med. Head.
100 | | 100

2 | 2 Spread eagle. 2 |
Compt's die. | PHENIX BANK, New York City. | 2
2 | |

ONE | ONE Hendrick Hudson landing in 1608; ship, etc. ONE | Male portrait
Compt's die. | NORTH RIVER BK., New York City. | 1
ONE | Medallion Head. | Male portrait

| Steamship. Compt's die. | 100
| NORTH RIVER BK. New York City. |
C | | Male portrait

5 | 5 Two females; steamboat and sail vessels in distance. 5 | FIVE
Compt's die. | BK. OF THE STATE, New York City. | Female representing Justice.
5 | Eagle and shield. | FIVE

3 | 3 Archimedes raising the world. | 3
Compt's die. | MECHANICS' BANK, New York City.
3 | Arm.

2 | Vig. Same as ones. 2 | TWO
Compt's die. | MANHATTAN CO., New York City. | Indian with bow.
2 | Man reclining.

10 | X Vig. Same as fives. X | 10
Compt's die. | BK. OF THE STATE, New York City. | Cupid.
10 | Canal Lock. | X

5 | 5 Vig. Same as threes. | V
Compt's die. | MECHANICS' BANK, New York City.
5 | Arm.

3 | Vig. Same as ones. 3 | THREE
Compt's die. | MANHATTAN CO., New York City. | Indian with bow.
3 | Man reclining.

20 | 20 Vig. Same as fives. 20 | XX
Compt's die | BK. OF THE STATE, New York City. | Justice.
20 | Eagle on view of rising sun. | TWENTY

10 | MECHANICS' BANK, New York City. | 10
Compt's die. | Mechanic with hammer and anvil; buildings in distance. Red figs 10 on either side.

FIVE | V Title of Bank. Vig. Same as ones. | 5
Compt's die.
5 | Head of Indian.

50 | L Vig. Same as fives. L | 50
Compt's die. | BK. OF THE STATE, New York City. | Steamboat and sail vessels.
50 | Eagle, &c. | 50

Medallion head and word twenty. | 20 Vig. Same as threes. | 20
MECHANICS' BANK, New York City.
Compt's die. | Arm.

TEN | Compt's die. MANHATTAN CO., New York City. | TEN
X
Head of Indian. | Vig. Same as ones. | 10

100 | C Vig. Same as fives. C | 100
Compt's die. | BK. OF THE STATE, New York City. | Sail Vessel.
100 | Eagle, &c. | 100

50 | MECHANICS' BANK, New York City. | Compt's die.
Arm and hammer.
50 | | 50

TWENTY | Vig. Female reclining with jar of water; Indian in canoe, trees, etc. in distance. Compt's die. | Indian in act of drawing arrow.
MANHATTAN CO., New York City.
20 | Man reclining.

500 | 500 Vig. Same as fives. | Die.
BK. OF THE STATE, New York City. | Compt's die.
Eagle, sunrise, etc. | Die.

100 | MECHANICS' BANK, New York City. | 100
Arm and hammer.
Compt's die. | | 100

FIFTY | MANHATTAN CO., New York City. | FIFTY
Compt's die.
Head of Indian. | 50 Vig. Same as 20s. 50
Man reclining.

1000 | Vig. Same as fives. 1000 | Die.
BK. OF THE STATE, New York City. | Compt's die.
Eagle, sunrise, etc. | Die.

500 | MECHANICS' BANK, New York City. | Arm and hammer.
500 Female reclining.
FIVE HUNDRED

100 | MANHATTAN CO., New York City. | 100
Compt's die. | C Vig. Same as twenties. | Head of Indian
100 | Man reclining. | 100

1 Male and female; mechanical implements; ship, cars and bridge in distance. 1 | Female.
Arm. | MECHANICS' BANK, New York City. | Compt's die.
ONE | Horse. | Female.

1000 | 1000 Vig. Same as threes. | Arm and hammer.
MECHANICS' BANK, New York City.
ONE THOUSAND.

500 | Vig. Same as twenties. | 500
Compt's die. | MANHATTAN CO., New York City.
D | Man reclining. | 500

TWO | 2 Vig. Same as ones. 2 | Washington.
Cooper at work. | MECHANICS' BANK, New York City. | Compt's die.
TWO | Locomotive. | Male portrait.

1 | 1 Male figure and Indian on either side of a shield, on which is a view of N. Y. harbor; female raising drapery from shield. | ONE
Compt's die. | MANHATTAN CO., New York City.
1 | Man reclining. | Indian erect.

1000 | Compt's die. Vig. Same as twenties. | 1000
MANHATTAN CO., New York City. | Letter M, and words "one thousand" around it.
Head of Indian.

1 · Spread eagle; steamer and buildings in distance. · 1 · Compt's die. · BK. OF NORTH AM., New York City. · Female with ear of corn and fig. 1. · ONE · Sheaf, plow, etc.	500 · Vig. Same as ones. · 500 · Compt's die. · BK. OF NORTH AM., New York City. · Female with flag, and three cupids in clouds. · 500 · Safe.	100 · 100 Compt's die. 100 · Statue of Washington. · Female feeding an eagle. · NATIONAL BANK, New York City. · Eagle.
Compt's die. · 2 Vig. Same as ones. · TWO · BK. OF NORTH AM., New York City. · Two females. · Indian princess. · City Arms. · TWO	1000 · Compt's die. Vig. Same as ones. · 1000 · BK. OF NORTH AM., New York City. · Female, eagle, wreath, shield, etc. · Arms.	1000 1000 · 1000 · Female feeding an eagle. · NATIONAL BANK, New York City. · Statue of Washington. · Compt's die.
THREE · 3 Vig. Same as ones. · 3 · Compt's die. · BK. OF NORTH AM., New York City. · Two males bearing aloft a female. · THREE · Cog-wheel, etc.	1 · 1 Male portrait. 1 · Compt's die. · NATIONAL BANK, New York City. · Statue of Washington. · 1	One and fig. 1 across. · BANK OF THE COMMONWEALTH, New York City. · One and fig. 1 across. · Female seated with eagle, shield, etc. · Large die on which is words "one dollar" and Compt's die. · Sailor at wheel.
Compt's die. · 5 Vig. Same as ones. · FIVE · BK. OF NORTH AM., New York City. · Indian with bow, arrow and belt. · Steamboat. · Squaw and pappoose.	2 · 2 Male portrait. 2 · Compt's die. · NATIONAL BANK, New York City. · Statue of Washington. · 2	Man plowing. · Large die and word two repeated. · BANK OF THE COMMONWEALTH, New York City. · Same as on left. · Compt's die.
Compt's die. · Vig. Same as ones. 10 · TEN · 10 · BK. OF NORTH AM., New York City. · Helmeted female with spear and shield. · Steamship. · Arms. · TEN	3 · THREE Male portrait. THREE · 3 · Compt's die. · NATIONAL BANK, New York City. · Eagle. · 3 · 3	Bank of the · Large die with female portrait, words three dollars, and Compt's die at bottom. · Commonw'th · Die with fig. 3, and word three. · Same as on left.
Compt's die. · TEN Washington. X · TEN · 10 · BK. OF NORTH AM., New York City. · Helmeted female with spear and shield. · Steamer. · Arms. · TEN	Statue of Washington. · 5 Compt's die. Male portrait. · 5 · NATIONAL BANK, New York City. · FIVE · Female feeding an eagle.	Milkmaids and cows; in distance on right, canal scene; on left house. · Figure 3, and two trains of cars. · BANK OF THE COMMONWEALTH, New York City. · Figure 5 full length of the note; view of city at top, and wharf scene and shipping at bottom. · Compt's die.
20 · Compt's die. Vig. Same as ones. · XX · BK. OF NORTH AM., New York City. · Female seated with spear and shield. · Machinery. · Female with vase of flowers, etc.	10 · TEN TEN · Two Dollars · Compt's die. · NATIONAL BANK, New York City. · Statue of Washington. · 10 · Vig. Female feeding an eagle.	TEN · The arms of each State of the Union in miniature casing, completely surrounding the whole note. · TEN · BANK OF THE COMMONWEALTH, New York City. · 10 · Compt's die. · 10
50 · Compt's die. Vig. Same as ones. · 50 · Female with flag and balloon; buildings in distance. · BK. OF NORTH AM., New York City. · Female with spear and shield. · FIFTY · Steamship.	20 · Female feeding an eagle. · 20 · Compt's die. · NATIONAL BANK, New York City. · Statue of Washington. · 20	Compt's die. · Steamship, sail vessels, view of city, etc. · 50 · Sailor leaning on capstan. · BANK OF THE COMMONWEALTH, New York City. · Blacksmith, anvil, forge, etc.
100 · Compt's die. Vig. Same as ones. · 100 · Helmeted female with spear and shield. · BK. OF NORTH AM., New York City. · Merchandise. · Female erect.	50 · 50 50 · Female feeding an eagle. · Compt's die. · NATIONAL BANK, New York City. · 50 · Eagle.	100 · BANK OF THE COMMONWEALTH, New York City. · 100 · View of New York harbor and city life scenery generally. · Male portrait. · Compt's die. · Male portrait.

ONE | 1 Firemen, fire engine, buildings, etc. | 1 Compt's die. | CHATHAM BANK, New York City. | Secured, &c. ONE | Male portrait | ONE	Large figure of Mercury with bag of coin and wand. 1000 | Portrait of Washington. CHATHAM BANK, New York City. Compt's die. | Female with sickle and sheaf. 1000	FIVE HUNDRED | Compt's die. Vig. Same as fives. SEVENTH WARD BK New York City. | 500 Launch of a vessel.
2 | Female seated surrounded by mechanical implements. | 2 Compt's die. | CHATHAM BANK, New York City. | Secured, &c. TWO | Male portrait | TWO	Goddess of Liberty. Compt's die. | 1 Female seated with frame on which is agricultural implements, &c.; shipping in distance. SEVENTH WARD BK New York City. Vessels. | 1 Steamer. ONE	Compt's die. Launch of a vessel. | Vig. Same as fives. SEVENTH WARD BK New York City. 1000 | 1000 Launch of a vessel.
Sailor seated on Compt's die; vessel below | 3 Female seated on left of City Arms. 3 CHATHAM BANK, New York City. Male portrait | Ship. 3	2 Compt's die. TWO | Female seated with mechanical implements; on right in distance cars and bridge; on left ship building. SEVENTH WARD BK New York City. Steamship. | 2 Man-of-war. TWO	1 Compt's die. | CORN EX. BANK, New York City. Two male figures; sheafs; house and ship in distance. ONE | 1 ONE
Sailor erect, leaning on bale. Compt's die. | 5 Steamship and other vessels. CHATHAM BANK, New York City. Male portrait | Large 5, cars, bridge, falls, Indians, etc. 5	3 Compt's die. THREE | Male and female in sea car drawn by horses; man and female on left of car; steamship and steamboat in distance. SEVENTH WARD BK New York City. Steamship. | 3 Ship building THREE	2 | CORN EX. BANK, New York City. Vig. Same as ones. Compt's die. | 2 2
10 Compt's die. 10 | Female seated on left of shield, sheafs of grain; cars and bridge in distance. CHATHAM BANK, New York City. Male portrait | 10 City Arms. 10	5 5 | Title of Bank. 5 Female seated receiving horn of gold from Mercury; eagle on right of female. Eagle. | 5 Compt's die. 5	3 | Vig. Same as ones. CORN EX. BANK, New York City. THREE | THREE Compt's die. 3
Female seated on Compt's die. TWENTY | 20 Sailor and female seated; steamer on left in distance; on right farming scene. CHATHAM BANK, New York City. Male portrait | 20 Secured, etc. Female seated.	10 Jefferson. 10 | Launch of a vessel. Title of Bank. Launch of a vessel. Vig. Same as fives. | 10 Compt's die. 10	FIVE Compt's die. | CORN EX. BANK, New York City. Female with pole, cap, eagle, etc. | 5
50 Compt's die. 50 | Two females on right of shield; eagle and vessel on left. CHATHAM BANK, New York City. Male portrait | 50 Steamboat FIFTY	20 Female with book, torch, eagle and portrait. XX | XX Vig. Same as fives. XX SEVENTH WARD BK New York City. | 20 Compt's die. 20	10 TEN | CORN EX. BANK, New York City. Vig. Same as fives. | 10 Compt's die.
100 Compt's die. | Spread eagle. CHATHAM BANK, New York City. Male portrait | 100 Female with sledge.	50 Compt's die. 50 | 50 Vig. Same as fives. 50 SEVENTH WARD BK New York City. | New York Safety Fund. Same as on left of 20s. 50	Compt's die. 50 | Male portrait CORN EX. BANK, New York City. | 50 Four females representing Agriculture, Merchandise, etc.
500 Compt's die. | Portrait of Washington, with flags and cannon on each side. CHATHAM BANK, New York City. Male portrait | 500 City Arms. 500	100 Compt's die. 100 | Washington. Title of Bank. Male portrait. Vig. Same as fives. | 100 Launch of a vessel. 100	Compt's die. C | CORN EX. BANK, New York City. Vig. Four females, representing Agriculture, Merchandise, etc. | 100 Male portrait

Left end	Centre	Right end
Compt's die on a large fig. 1.	ONE Two mechanics, anvil, etc.; cars and ship in distance. ONE MECHANICS' BANKING ASSOCIATION, New York City. Steamship.	Washington on a large figure 1.
TWO Compt's die Carpenter at his bench.	Figure 2 with portrait of Washington and word two. Title of Bank.	Stone cutter seated. 2
Two females; figure 3 between them.	3 Indian princess, surrounded by flags, drums, cannon, etc. Title of Bank. Arm.	3
5 Female, eagle safe, etc. FIVE	V Three females and a fig. 5; cars, shipping, etc., in distance. V Title of Bank. Arm.	5 Med. Head. FIVE
10 Same as fives TEN	Two females on either side of a shield; cars, buildings, canal, shipping, &c., in distance Title of Bank. Arm.	10 Two females, eagle etc. TEN
TWENTY Same as fives TWENTY	20 Female seated at table; scientific apparatus on her right; steamer in distance. 20 Title of Bank. Arm.	Die. XX Die.
FIFTY Female seated; steamboat on right. 50	Two Indians, and white man with gun. Medallion head and word fifty on either side of vig. Title of Bank. Arm.	FIFTY Female seated; house in distance. 50
HUNDRED Figure of Justice. 100	Two females on either side of a shield, surmounted by an eagle. Shipping in distance. Med. head and figs. 100 on either side of vig. Title of Bank Arm.	ONE HUNDRED
500 Same as fives 500	500 Train of cars, steamboat and other vessels in distance. Title of Bank. Arm.	500

Left end	Centre	Right end
1000 Same as fives 1000	1000 Steamship, row-boat, other vessels and view of city. Title of Bank. Arm.	ONE THOUSAND
1 Female reclining on scroll, globe, pole, cap, etc.	N. Y. EX. BANK, New York City. Vig. Female seated, with pole and cap; Compt's die on her left.	1 Female seated with balance.
TWO Male erect; female seated.	N. Y. EX. BANK, New York City. 2 2 Compt's die.	TWO Male erect; female seated.
3 Female reclining on a view of cars, mountain, &c.	N. Y. EX. BANK, New York City. Compt's die.	3 Female seated in oval frame.
5 Compt's die. FIVE	N. Y. EX. BANK, New York City. Females and Cupids surrounding figure 5.	5 Male bust. FIVE
TEN Compt's die TEN	N. Y. EX. BANK, New York City. Steamship and other vessels.	10 Washington.
20 Compt's die. TWENTY	N. Y. EX. BANK, New York City. Train of cars; buildings, etc.	20 Female portrait.
50 Compt's die. FIFTY	N. Y. EX. BANK, New York City. Drover and cattle.	50 Female portrait.
100 Compt's die. 100	N. Y. EX. BANK, New York City. Vessels, harbor, city, etc.	100 Head of little girl.

Left end	Centre	Right end
1 ONE Compt's die.	1 Neptune, steamship, and other vessels. OCEAN BANK, New York City.	Ship. ONE
II Man and female in row-boat.	OCEAN BANK, New York City. Vig. Same as ones.	II Compt's die Sailor seated
III 3 Female seated.	OCEAN BANK, New York City. Vig. Same as ones.	Die. 3 Die.
5 Sailor at wheel.	Ship loading; dray, boxes; sailor with glass; steamer and other vessels in distance. OCEAN BANK, New York City.	5 Compt's die 5
5 Compt's die. Word five and figure 5 across.	Vig. Neptune, steamship, &c. OCEAN BANK, New York City.	FIVE Female erect on a rock; lighthouse, etc. FIVE
Sailor and letter X. Compt's die.	OCEAN BANK, New York City. Vig. Same as ones. Ship.	10 10
20 Compt's die. TWENTY	OCEAN BANK, New York City. Vig. Same as ones. Ship.	20 Dolphin. TWENTY
50 Compt's die. 50	Vig. Same as ones. OCEAN BANK, New York City.	View of the bank building. FIFTY
C Compt's die.	Vig. Same as ones. OCEAN BANK, New York City.	Indian. 100

1 Male portrait. Spread eagle; ship on either side. ATLANTIC BANK, New York City. 1 Compt's die.	TWO Indian on his knees with gun. 2 MARINE BANK, New York City. Compt's die. Red figure 2. Ship under full sail.	2 Compt's die. TWO CHEMICAL BANK, New York City. Vig. Same as ones. 2 Two females; one kneeling.
2 Compt's die. Steamship and other vessels. ATLANTIC BANK, New York City. 2 Male portrait.	3 View of a ship-wreck, mariners, etc. Compt's die. MARINE BANK, New York City. 3 Male portrait.	Female with pole and cap. 5 Female reclining with cornucopia. CHEMICAL BANK, New York City. 5 Compt's die.
Large steamship and other vessels. THREE Male portrait. ATLANTIC BANK, New York City. 3 Compt's die.	FIVE Mechanic seated and sailor with flag and quadrant. Compt's die. Male portrait. MARINE BANK, New York City. 5 V	5 Red figure 5. CHEMICAL BANK, New York City. Female. Word five and fig. 5. Female. Compt's die. 5 Red fig. 5.
5 Compt's die. Three females and cupid in water. ATLANTIC BANK, New York City. Fire Engine. 5 Henry Clay.	Sailor seated with nautical implements, &c.; shipping in distance. X X Compt's die. MARINE BANK, New York City. TEN Male portrait.	TEN Compt's die TEN X Spread eagle. CHEMICAL BANK, New York City. X Female with shield, eagle, pole and cap.
10 Anchor, bales, &c. Steamship and other vessels. ATLANTIC BANK, New York City. Secured, etc. 10 Compt's die.	20 Male portrait. Female reclining on bales of goods. MARINE BANK, New York City. XX XX Compt's die. 20	TWENTY Compt's die. 20 Two females, shield, cars, etc.; ship in distance. CHEMICAL BANK, New York City. TWENTY Washington.
20 Portrait of Webster. ATLANTIC BANK, New York City. Sailor erect; vessels in distance. 20 Compt's die.	L Ship under full sail. Compt's die. MARINE BANK, New York City. 50 Male portrait.	Compt's die, fig. 50 on either side. Female seated with fig. 50. CHEMICAL BANK, New York City. Secured, &c. 50
50 Male portrait. ATLANTIC BANK, New York City. Female with pole, cap, eagle, &c. 50 Compt's die.	100 Ship wreck scene. MARINE BANK, New York City. Compt's die. C Male portrait.	100 Female with shield. C CHEMICAL BANK, New York City. 100 Compt's die 100
C Male portrait. Vessels, view of city, &c. ATLANTIC BANK, New York City. 100 Compt's die.	ONE Two sailors and females. Compt's die. Vig. Forest scene; dogs in pursuit of game. CHEMICAL BANK, New York City. 1	D Compt's die. 500 CHEMICAL BANK, New York City. Three females; building in background. 500
ONE Male portrait. Compt's die. Steamship. MARINE BANK, New York City. 1 1	TWO Compt's die. TWO Two females and sheaf; ship in the distance. Medallion head and 2 on either side. CHEMICAL BANK, New York City. Female bust. Male portrait. Female bust.	M CHEMICAL BANK, New York City. Figures 1000 and words one thousand across. Compt's die. 1000

1 Steamship. Compt's die. | 1 Head of Irving. 1 IRVING BANK, New York City | 1 Steamboat ONE	THREE Female with wheat in hand. | Cupid and fig. 3. Compt's die. Cupid and fig. 3. MERCANTILE B'K., New York City. | THREE Same as 2s.	Steamboat. | 50 Vig. Same as ones. FULTON BANK, New York City. Female and ship. | 50
Ship. Compt's die. | 2 Head of Irving. 2 IRVING BANK, New York City. | Female with sheaf. TWO	FIVE | 5 Female reclining with shield, anchor, and the word "Hope"; cars and building in distance. Compt's die. MERCANTILE B'K., New York City. Mechanic with hammer. | 5 V 5	Steamboat. | 100 Title of Bank. Vig. Same as ones. Wheat and plow. | 100
Compt's die. Dolphin. THREE | 3 Indian reclining, and another approaching IRVING BANK, New York City. | 3 Male portrait 3	10 Mechanic with hammer. 10 | X Emblematic group of females in clouds; one with keys. Compt's die. MERCANTILE B'K., New York City. | TEN	5 Compt's die. 5 | V Female reclining; vase of flowers, eagle, etc. V UNION BANK, New York City. Secured, etc. | FIVE Figure 5 and a female. FIVE
Compt's die. | Old man seated with gun. 5 Male portrait IRVING BANK, New York City. | 5 Milkmaid seated.	50 | Female with eagle, shield, portrait of Washington, etc. Compt's die. MERCANTILE B'K., New York City. | 50 Human figure with spear and shield.	10 Compt's die. 10 | 10 Vig. Same as fives. UNION BANK, New York City. Secured, etc. | 10 Female seated. TEN
10 Compt's die. 10 | View of a cottage covered with vines. 10 IRVING BANK, New York City. | Ten Dollars Female with sword. Male portrait	100 Figure of Justice. | Compt's die. Female with pole, cap and eagle; letter C on shield. MERCANTILE B'K., New York City. | 100	20 Female seated. TWENTY | Compt's die. 20 Vig. Same as ones. UNION BANK, New York City. Secured, etc. | 20 Female seated. TWENTY
Female. Compt's die. | 50 Eagle and shield. IRVING BANK, New York City. | 50	Steamboat. | 1 1 FULTON BANK, New York City. Bust of Fulton, mechanic seated on right; cars and steamship in distance. | ONE One Dollar Sailor erect; vessel in distance. One Dollar ONE	50 Compt's die. 50 | 50 Vig. Same as fives. 50 UNION BANK, New York City. Secured, etc. | 50 Female in oval frame. 50
Compt's die. | Eagle, shield, &c. IRVING BANK, New York City. | 100 Male portrait 100	Steamboat. | 2 Vig. Same as ones. FULTON BANK, New York City. | 2 Female with sheaf and sickle. TWO	C Compt's die. C | 100 Vig. Same as fives. UNION BANK, New York City. Secured, etc. | 100
ONE Female holding fig. 1, leaning on bale of merchandise. | Cupid. Compt's die. 1 MERCANTILE B'K., New York City. | ONE Female holding flag with emblematic figures around her.	Steamboat. | 5 Vig. Same as ones. FULTON BANK, New York City. Eagle. | 5 Female with trident. 5	Die work. Compt's die. Die work | D Female seated feeding an eagle; clouds, etc. D UNION BANK, New York City. Secured, &c. | 500
TWO Indian female holding spear and bow | 2 Compt's die. Cupid and fig. 2 MERCANTILE B'K., New York City. | TWO Female with fruit and flowers.	Steamboat. | 10 Vig. Same as ones. FULTON BANK, New York City. | X Boy in cornfield.	Die work Compt's die. Die work | M Female seated with pole and cap on her right shield with the words "Manufacturers and Commerce," over it; cornucopia at her feet; steamboat and cars in distance. M Title of Bank. Secured, etc. | 1000

1 | Bee hive surrounded by flowers. Large red fig. 1 across face of bill. | 1
Compt's die | BK. OF NEW YORK, New York City. | 1
Eagle.

2 | Bee hive surrounded by flowers. Red fig. 2 across face of bill. | 2
Compt's die. | BK. OF NEW YORK, New York City. Female head.

Compt's die. | Bee hive surrounded by flowers. Red figure 3 across face of bill. | 3
3 | BK. OF NEW YORK, New York City. Head of Indian.

Female portrait. | View of N. Y. harbor, shipping, etc. Word Five in red letters across face of bill. | 5
5 | BK. OF NEW YORK, New York City. | Compt's die.

Sailor with flag; female reclining at his feet; anchor, bale, &c. | 10 Shipping. Word Ten in red letters across face of bill. | 10
BK. OF NEW YORK, New York City. | Compt's die.

20 | Male portrait. Eagle on rock; shipping. | 20
Compt's die. | Word Twenty in red letters across face of bill.
20 | BK. OF NEW YORK, New York City.

50 | Winged female seated on flags; globe, eagle, etc. Word Fifty in red letters across face of bill. | 50
Compt's die.
50 | BK. OF NEW YORK, New York City. Secured, etc.

C | Female seated on bales, pointing with wand to shipping in distance; lighthouse on left of note. | 100
Compt's die. | BK. OF NEW YORK, New York City. Secured, etc. | Male portrait

Shipping. | Compt's die. | 300
BK. OF NEW YORK, New York City.
300 | Portrait of J. Q. Adams.

400 | Spread eagle on rock; shipping. | 400
BK. OF NEW YORK, New York City.
Male portrait | Compt's die.

500 | Two females seated on either side of a frame, surmounted by an eagle, in which is a view of sunrise, and word "Excelsior;" shipping in distance. | 500
Med. head of Washington. | BK. OF NEW YORK, New York City. | Compt's die.

ONE THOUSAND | View of New York harbor, with shipping, city, &c. | 1000
BK. OF NEW YORK, New York City. | Compt's die.

1 | Drovers and cattle; cars, bridge, buildings, &c., in distance. | 1
MARKET BANK, New York City.
Female with flowers. | Dog, key and safe. | Compt's die.

TWO | Steamship and other vessels. | 2
Male and female seated; anvil, &c. | MARKET BANK, New York City.
2 | Eagle. | Compt's die.

Three females; anchor, etc. | 3 Millmaid and cattle; houses and trees in distance. 3 | 3
MARKET BANK, New York City.
THREE | Steamboat. | Compt's die.

5 | Female reclining on bale of merchandise; ships in distance. | Female seated, holding out fig. 5; ship in distance.
MARKET BANK, New York City.
Female portrait. | Compt's die.

10 | Train of cars; in distance two other trains; water scene, houses; trees, etc. | 10
MARKET BANK, New York City.
Female bust. | Compt's die.

Henry Clay seated; dog by his side. | Spread eagle. | 20
MARKET BANK, New York City.
20 | Compt's die.

Cattle and sheep. Female portrait. | 50
MARKET BANK, New York City.
50 | Compt's die.

100 | Three females in clouds; ships on right. | 100
Sailor with flag, bbl. anchor, bale and quadrant | MARKET BANK, New York City. | Compt's die.

1 | CENTRAL BANK, Brooklyn, N. Y. | 1
Compt's die. | Farmer and farm scene; boy with horse and sledge.
ONE | Male portrait

2 | Santa Claus drawn by reindeer. Compt's die. | TWO
2 | CENTRAL BANK, Brooklyn, N. Y. | Male portrait

3 | CENTRAL BANK, Brooklyn, N. Y. | 3
3 | Female reclining on bale of goods; sail vessel on right, and steamboat on left. | Compt's die.

5 | CENTRAL BANK, Brooklyn, N. Y. | 5
Compt's die. | View of the Brooklyn City Hall.
V | Male portrait

10 | CENTRAL BANK, Brooklyn, N. Y. | TEN
Compt's die. | X Ship under sail. X
X | Male portrait

50 | Goddess of Liberty and female representing Agriculture. | 50
Compt's die. | CENTRAL BANK, Brooklyn, N. Y.
L | Male portrait

100 | CENTRAL BANK, Brooklyn, N. Y. | C
Compt's die. Male portrait. | Three men at work.

1 | Men on horses catching wild cattle with lasso. | 1
SHOE & LEATH. BK. New York City.
Female Portrait. | Spread Eagle. | Compt's die.

2 TWO | ARTIZANS BANK, New York City. | 2 TWO
Compt's die. Two black-smiths; one with hammer. 2

10 | Shipping and view of city on right in distance. | 10
BK of the REPUBLIC, New York City.
Compt's die. | Building. | Eagle on a shield

Compt's die. | SHOE & LEATH. BK. New York City. | 2
Vig. Same as ones.
2 | Steamboat. | Female Portrait.

3 | Compt's die. Black-smith and hammer. 3 | Two males and a female; buildings in distance.
THREE | ARTIZANS BANK, New York City.

20 | View of steamship and other vessels. | 20
BK of the REPUBLIC, New York City.
Compt's die. | Dog, key and safe. | Agricultural implements.

Men carrying leather. | 3 Vig. Same as ones. | 3
SHOE & LEATH. BK. New York City.
Compt's die. | Steamship. | Female portrait.

5 | ARTIZANS BANK, New York City. | FIVE
Portrait of a boy. | 5 Stone cutter at work 5 | Compt's die
FIVE | FIVE

FIFTY | Eagle on limb of tree; cars and canal scene in distance. | 50
Compt's die. | BK of the REPUBLIC, New York City. | Female leaning on a column; two females in background.
50 | Shield.

5 | SHOE & LEATH. BK. New York City. | 5
FIVE | Vig. Same as ones.
Male head. | Compt's die.

X | Male portrait. Three men looking at plans on a table; shipping in distance | 10
TEN | ARTIZANS BANK, New York City. | Compt's die.

100 | Two females and bust of Washington on shield in centre; shipping, etc. 100 | Merchandise
Compt's die. | Female portrait.
100 | BK of the REPUBLIC, New York City. | Train of cars.
Shield.

Vig. Same as ones. Portrait of Washington. | 10
SHOE & LEATH. BK. New York City.
10 | Bee hive. | Compt's die

TWENTY | ARTIZANS BANK, New York City. | XX
Three females with male bust in centre.
Twenty Compt's die. Dollars | Male portrait

1 | TRADESMEN'S B'K., New York City. | 1
Farmer with bundle under his arm, dog, horse, etc. | Blacksmith shoeing horse; man seated on log; man in background. | Compt's die.

Mercury with bag of coin. | Vig. Same as ones. | 20
SHOE & LEATH. BK. New York City.
20 | Compt's die.

Vig. Same as 20s. Fifty Dollars. | 50
ARTIZANS BANK, New York City.
50 | Compt's die. | Liberty surrounded by stars.

2 | Portrait of boy. 2 Portrait of girl. | 2
TRADESMEN'S B'K., New York City.
Blacksmith's boy at forge. | Compt's die.

50 | SHOE & LEATH. BK. New York City. | 50
Vig. Same as ones.
Male head. | Compt's die.

NEW-YORK | ARTIZANS BANK, New York City.
100 C | Vig. Same as 20s. | 100 C
Compt's die.
One Hundred Dollars

3 | Compt's die. Sailor seated on anchor smoking pipe, and apparently conversing with two others; ship in distance. | 3
Two men at work on frame of cart. | TRADESMEN'S B'K., New York City. | Portrait of little girl.

Male head. | SHOE & LEATH. BK. New York City. | 100
ONE HUNDRED | Vig. Same as ones.
100 | Compt's die.

Sailor with spy-glass | BK of the REPUBLIC, New York City. | 3
3 | 3 Ship under full sail; steamboat on left. 3 | Female with eagle and shield.
Compt's die.

5 | Sailor reclining against bale of goods, supporting flag; vessels and light-house in distance. | Figure 5, and large letter V, on this end.
Compt's die. | TRADESMEN'S B'K., New York City.

1 | ARTIZANS BANK, New York City. | 1
Blacksmith and anvil.
Compt's die. | Portrait of a boy.

5 | BK of the REPUBLIC, New York City. | 5
V View of shipping. V
Compt's die. | Female and anchor. | Sailor with flag in left hand, and hat in right.

X | Stone cutter seated with mallet, chisel, etc. | Figs. 10, and large letter X on this end.
TRADESMEN'S B'K., New York City.
Compt's die.

TWENTY Compt's die.	Eagle and figs. 20 on shield. Bull's head; horse, shipping, etc. TRADESMEN'S B'K., New York City.	TWENTY

50 Med. head.	Compt's die. Female with globe, chart, quadrant, book, ink stand, pen, &c.; cars, shipping, factory, etc., in distance. CITIZENS BANK, New York City. Anchor, bale, &c.	50 Two females

100 Compt's die 100	C Two females leaning on a view of drovers and cattle. C Title of Bank. Ship.	Female erect with sheaf and sickle. 100

Compt's die. 50	50 Vig. Same as twenties. TRADESMEN'S B'K., New York City.	FIFTY

100 Med. head. 100	Compt's die. Female with eagle, shield, safe, cap, harrow, sheaf, etc. CITIZENS BANK, New York City. Dog, key and safe.	100 Female with fruit leaning on anchor

1 Compt's die. Dolphin.	Female reclining holding a fig. 1; cars and steamboat in distance. PACIFIC BANK, New York City. City Arms.	1 Steamship. ONE

ONE HUNDRED	100 Vig. Same as 20s. 100 TRADESMEN'S B'K., New York City.	Med. head. Compt's die. Med. head.

1 Compt's die. 1	BUTCHERS' & DROVERS' BANK, New York City. 1 Drovers and cattle in a frame. 1	ONE DOLLAR

Figure 2 supported by two mythological figures. Steamship.	Compt's die. Train of cars. PACIFIC BANK, New York City. City Arms.	2 Two dolphins

1 Compt's die. ONE	Drover and cattle. CITIZENS BANK, New York City. City Arms.	1 Female portrait ONE

2 Compt's die. 2	2 Vig. Same as 1s. 2 Title of Bank.	2 Female 2

THREE 3 Compt's die.	Ship under full sail; vessels in distance. PACIFIC BANK, New York City. City Arms.	Shell. 3 Steamship and dolphin.

TWO Compt's die. TWO	Farmer with basket of corn; farmers gathering corn; cars in distance. CITIZENS BANK, New York City. Bbls., boxes, etc.	2 Two females

3 Compt's die 3	3 Vig. Same as ones. 3 Title of Bank.	3 Female bathing 3

5 FIVE Compt's die.	Sailor reclining with spy-glass in his hand; shipping in distance. PACIFIC BANK, New York City. City Arms.	FIVE Steamship. 5 Shipping and wharf.

3 Compt's die.	Farmer reclining on sheafs, with pitcher, dog, basket, &c. CITIZENS BANK, New York City. Cog wheel, box, &c.	3 Med. Head. THREE

5 Compt's die. 5	5 Cattle and sheep. 5 Title of Bank. Die.	5 Four females 5

TEN Compt's die. TEN	10 Two females, one crowning bust of Washington with wreath; bales, sheaf, etc. PACIFIC BANK, New York City. City Arms.	TEN Boy holding a shell, his foot on a dolphin. TEN

5 Compt's die. V	Blacksmith reclining on anvil, hammer in his hand; factory, cars, &c., in distance. CITIZENS BANK, New York City. Cog wheel, bales, &c.	5 Med. head and word five. FIVE

10 Compt's die. 10	Cattle and sheep lying on the ground. 10 Title of Bank.	TEN

XX Compt's die. 20	Female reclining, right arm on a view of steamboat, &c.; cornucopia, safe, etc.; cars and steamship in distance. PACIFIC BANK, New York City. City Arms.	20 Vessel. TWENTY

10 Compt's die	Sailor with glass in hand, reclining on bales, etc.; shipping in distance. CITIZENS BANK, New York City. City Arms.	10 Med. head. TEN

20 Compt's die. 20	20 Vig. Same as tens. 20 Title of Bank. Ship.	TWENTY Female bust TWENTY

50 Two dolphins Compt's die.	Female with globe, quadrant, chart, book, pen and ink; shipping and factory in distance. 50 PACIFIC BANK, New York City. Steamship.	Bale of goods. City Arms. Train of cars.

20 Compt's die. XX	Washington. Female with cap, shield, grain, etc. Franklin. CITIZENS BANK, New York City. Female.	20 Female between 2 and 0.

50 Compt's die. 50	50 Female with sheaf; cars and factory in distance. 50 Title of Bank. Ship.	50 FIFTY Drovers and cattle. DOLLARS 50

100 Compt's die. Two ornamental male and female figures.	Female with eagle, shield, safe, &c; agricultural implements in background. 100 PACIFIC BANK, New York City. City Arms.	Ship. Shell. 100

1 — MER. EX. BANK, New York City. — 1
Compt's die. — Female seated with cornucopia and wand; bbls., quadrant, etc.; in distance vessels, buildings, cars, canal, &c.
ONE — Ship and other vessels.

Compt's die. — 2 Female seated with pole, cap, fig. 2, and eagle. — 2
Female portrait.
Indian princess erect. — HANOVER BANK, New York City. — TWO
Sailor reclining.

THREE — 3 Two females seated, ship between; on left steamboat and ship; on right in distance, cars, schooner, etc. — 3
Building, street, etc. — BROADWAY BANK, New York City. — Mechanic in frame; cars in distance.
Compt's die.
Sheaf, plow, &c.

MER. EX. BANK, New York City. — 2
Vig. Same as ones. — Compt's die. — Female seated; buildings in distance.
TWO

3 — Winged female and cupid in act of raising drapery from shield on which is an eagle. — 3
Compt's die.
HANOVER BANK, New York City. — Female seated.
THREE — City Arms.

FIVE — Two females seated on either side of shield, surmounted by an eagle; miniature view of sunrise and river; on right, cars; on left steamboat. — 5
5 — BROADWAY BANK, New York City. — Figure of Justice in clouds.
Compt's die.
Cog-wheels, etc.

Compt's die. — MER. EX. BANK, New York City. — 3
Vig. Same as ones. — Mercury with wand, bag of coin and cornucopia.
THREE

5 — Female with shield, pole and cap. — Washington. — 5
HANOVER BANK, New York City. — Sailor erect, leaning on capstan.
Compt's die.
Safe.

Compt's die. — 10 Female reclining on merchandise; on left, cars, canal scene; on right ships and city.
Female seated with spear and head on shield. — BROADWAY BANK, New York City. — 10
Safe.

Vig. Same as ones. — Compt's die. — 5
MER. EX. BANK, New York City. — Sailor leaning on capstan; masts in background.
FIVE

Female seated; vessel & steamer in distance. — 10 Female, shield and eagle soaring in clouds. — 10
Franklin.
HANOVER BANK, New York City.
Compt's die. — TEN
Boxes, bbls., &c.

Two females representing Liberty and Justice. — 20 Female seated with sheaf; cars and canal scene. In distance. — 20
BROADWAY BANK, New York City. — Female seated between a 2 and 0.
Compt's die.
Boxes, bbls., bales, etc.

Steamship and other vessels. — Compt's die. — 10
MER. EX. BANK, New York City. — Female with flag, and 3 cupids.
10

20 — Compt's die. — Two females, bust and shield between them; ship in distance. — 20
HANOVER BANK, New York City.
Mercury seated between a 2 and 0. — Jefferson.
Bbls., bales, etc.

50 — Female with pole, cap and shield. — 50 — FIFTY
Compt's die. — BROADWAY BANK, New York City.
FIFTY — Winged female seated.
State Arms.

Compt's die. — Spread eagle; steamship and other vessels in distance. — 20
MER. EX. BANK, New York City.
Mercury seated between 2 and 0. — Female seated between a 2 and 0.

50 — Compt's die. — Female reclining on a view of sunrise; cars, steamer, &c., in distance. — 50
City Arms. — Female, horn of plenty, etc.
50 — HANOVER BANK, New York City.
Dragon and key. — FIFTY

100 — Vessels and view of city. — 100
Compt's die. — BROADWAY BANK, New York City.
100 — Female erect with right hand on capstan.
Steamship.

50 — Compt's die. — Female crowning eagle with wreath, right hand on portrait of Washington; in distance, vessels, cars, buildings, etc. — 50
Female with spear and twig and a shield. — MER. EX. BANK, New York City. — Ship and other vessels.

100 — Compt's die. — Female and cupid on either side of a view of sunrise. — 100
Female with pole, cap and shield. — HANOVER BANK, New York City. — Ship and other vessels.
Sailor reclining.

1 — ONE — Blacksmith with hammer and anvil, female with bag of money and barrels; shipping in background. — ONE — 1
Compt's die. — Clock.
1 — MECHANICS' & TRADERS' BANK, New York City. — 1

Compt's die. — Female, eagle, safe, balances, etc.; cars, buildings, and vessels. — 100
MER. EX. BANK, New York City. — Female seated; building in distance.
100

ONE — 1 Spread eagle; steamer, ships, etc. — ONE
Building, street, &c. — BROADWAY BANK, New York City.
Compt's die. — Female and fig. 1.
Implements.

2 — 2 Vig. Same as ones. — 2
Compt's die — Title of Bank.
2 — 2

1 — Ship and other vessels. — 1ONE
HANOVER BANK, New York City. — Female head
Horses with wings.
Compt's die. — Bbls. and bales.

TWO — 2 Female, shield, eagle, portrait of Washington; cars, vessels and buildings in distance. — 2
Building, street, etc.
BROADWAY BANK, New York City. — Female seated; building, etc.
Compt's die. — Arms.

3 — Vig. Same as ones. — 3 — 3
Compt's die. — Title of Bank. — Clock.
3 — 3

Vulcan with anvil and hammer and two females. V	5 Five Dollars Figure of Justice with scales; shipping in distance. MECHANICS' & TRADERS' BANK, New York City. Ship.	5 Compt's die 5

Compt's die. Female Portrait.	Female seated within an ornamental fig. 5, cupids around her. BOWERY BANK, New York City.	5 Female resting on a fig. 5; men in background; money at her feet.

TEN Dogs head.	Compt's die. Two blacksmiths in shop; one shoeing horse, the other blowing forge. EAST RIVER BANK, New York City.	X

5 Compt's die. 5	5 5 Title of Bank. Vig. Same as ones.	FIVE Female leaning on an urn 5

Deer. Compt's die. Bison	Female seated on an iron chest between 1 and 0. BOWERY BANK, New York City.	10 Female holding an ear of corn and X.

20 Sailor with spy glass, quadrant and compass.	Compt's die. Steamboat, wharf, etc. EAST RIVER BANK, New York City.	XX

10 Compt's die. 10	Blacksmith with hammer and anvil. 10 Title of Bank.	Female with liberty cap, leaning on cornucopia. X

20 Compt's die.	Female seated between a 2 and 0; grain around her BOWERY BANK, New York City.	20 Stone cutter with mallet and chisel.

50 Compt's die.	Steamship. Portrait of Franklin. EAST RIVER BANK, New York City.	50 Female portrait. L

20 Compt's die 20	Male and female figure with frame between them enclosing three cupids. Title of Bank.	20 Mercury reclining on a bale. 20

Female Portrait. 50	50 Compt's die. 50 BOWERY BANK, New York City.	50 Female raking hay.

C	Sailor seated on ground with quadrant, telescope, compass, &c., boxes, bbls.; shipping in distance. Compt's die. EAST RIVER BANK, New York City.	100 Arm and hammer.

50 Compt's die. 50	50 Two Cupids with globe and chart. 50 Title of Bank.	50 FIFTY 50

Farmer sharpening scythe. 100	100 Compt's die. 100 BOWERY BANK, New York City.	100 Male portrait

ONE Compt's die. ONE	1 Winged female with sword and scales, holding fig. 1. 1 GREENWICH BANK, New York City.	ONE Female with flowers. ONE

100 Compt's die. 100	100 Title of Bank.	Male and female; male with sickle.

1 Compt's die. 1	View of buildings in course of erection; laborers, horse, truck, &c. EAST RIVER BANK, New York City.	ONE Sailor leaning on capstan with quadrant in hand.

2 Compt's die.	Ship carpenter at work, with axe lying beside him; ship in background. GREENWICH BANK, New York City.	2 Two Cupids holding an ornamental figure 2.

Soldier with wooden leg. Compt's die.	1 Female reclining and holding an ornamental fig. 1. BOWERY BANK, New York City.	1 Female churning.

TWO Female sewing on a cap.	Train of cars passing a railroad station; ladies on platform. EAST RIVER BANK, New York City.	2 Compt's die TWO

3 Compt's die.	Three females representing Agriculture, Manufacturers and Commerce. GREENWICH BANK, New York City.	THREE Three Cupids supporting a fig. 3. THREE

2 Compt's die. TWO	Farmer on the left, and milkmaid on the right, holding between them a frame, with a landscape view on it. BOWERY BANK, New York City.	2 Vessel.

3 Female portrait.	EAST RIVER BANK, New York City. Faust, Guttenburg and Schoeffer, chests, wheels, books, etc.	3 III Compt's die.

FIVE Full length female figure	Compt's die. Figure of Justice. FIVE GREENWICH BANK, New York City. Steamboat.	FIVE DOLLARS

Compt's die. Blacksmith with hammer and anvil.	3 Female reclining with sheaf and sickle; steamboat in background. BOWERY BANK, New York City.	3 Drove of cattle.

5 FIVE	View of ship yard, three ships on ways; factory to left; men at work, &c. EAST RIVER BANK, New York City.	V Compt's die. V

10 Washington. 10	Compt's die. Eagle on City Arms. TEN GREENWICH BANK, New York City.	X Male portrait X

20 Compt's die. 20 — 20 Figure of Justice with sword and scales on left, on right Goddess of Liberty with pole and cap; between them an eagle surmounting frame on which is a view of sunrise. Title of Bank running around them. 20 — 20 Ship. 20	50 Compt's die. — Spread eagle, his feet on an olive branch and Am. shield. Title of Bank running over the shield. Horse. — 50 Male portrait.	100 Compt's die. Female swimming with arm around neck of swan — Female reclining against box, bale and bbl.; shipping in distance. ORIENTAL BANK, New York City. Bird. — 100 Same as ones.
50 Compt's die. 50 — 50 Female representing Commerce, [illegible] 50 GREENWICH BANK, New York City. Eagle. — 50 Male portrait. 50	100 Male portrait. — Large steamship with shipping on right and left. Title of Bank running over the vignette. — 100 Compt's die.	ONE Compt's die. ONE — 1 Neptune and female in a shell, drawn by two horses on the sea. 1 BANK OF THE NEW YORK DRY DOCK CO. New York City. Ship. — ONE
100 Compt's die. 100 — 100 Female seated on the base of a column pointing to a sloop in the distance; sheaf and rake. 100 GREENWICH BANK, New York City. Steamboat. — Male portrait. 100 Male portrait.	1 Compt's die. — ORIENTAL BANK, New York City. Wood cutter seated, gold dollar on right; house, wagon, trees, etc in distance. Bird. — ONE Oriental female reclining, playing with a bird, a fan in her right hand, fountain in background.	2 Compt's die 2 — 2 Female with safe and key, bird perched on safe, female in background. 2 Title of Bank. Ship. — TWO Female with sheaf in her hand. TWO
ONE Compt's die. Word one and fig. 1. — Train of cars passing under a bridge. PEOPLE'S BANK. New York City. — 1 Portrait of Taylor.	2 Same as on right of 1s. — ORIENTAL BANK, New York City. Compt's die. Farmer and milkmaid seated; two gold dollars, house cattle and trees in distance. Bird. — 2	3 Compt's die. 3 — 3 Goddess of Liberty with pole and cap, flag around her, leaning on a shield, money flowing from the base of the shield. 3 Title of Bank. Ship. — THREE Female with sheaf. 3
TWO Compt's die TWO — View of the bank building with sign on top. PEOPLES BANK, New York City. — 2 Male portrait.	3 Compt's die THREE — ORIENTAL BANK, New York City. Farmer, sailor and mechanic; three gold dollars on the ground. Bird. — 3 Same as one.	5 Compt's die 5 — 5 Neptune in a sea car drawn by two horses, raising his arms towards a winged female. 5 Title of Bank. Ship. — FIVE Franklin. 5
3 Compt's die THREE — Mechanic seated on machinery with hammer on his shoulder; cars and factory in distance. Title of Bank running around the vignette. — 3 Male portrait.	5 Two Elephants. Compt's die. — Indian female, hunter with gun, five gold dollars and three cupids. ORIENTAL BANK, New York City Bird. — 5 Same as one.	10 Compt's die. 10 — X Vig. Same as fives. X Title of Bank running around the vig. Ship. — Female with pole leaning on an anchor 10
FI V VE Compt's die. FI V VE — One of the Peoples Line of steamers, with flag on it and words "Peoples Line" Dock on the right. PEOPLES BANK, New York City. — FIVE Portrait of Franklin.	10 Machinists at work, ship and factory. Compt's die. — ORIENTAL BANK, New York City. Machinist resting against piece of machinery with tools in his hand. Bird. — TEN Same as one.	20 Compt's die 20 — XX Vig. Same as fives, with title running around it. XX Red figures 20. Ship. — Female with scroll in her hand. 20
TEN Compt's die. 10 — Female and Goddess of Liberty seated; ship on left; cars, sheaf, &c., on right. Title of Bank running around vignette. — X Head of Washington.	XX Female portrait. Compt's die. — ORIENTAL BANK, New York City. View of ship yard, with two vessels on weighs. Bird. — 20 Same as ones.	50 Compt's die. — Female seated with sheaf and sickle; steamboat in distance. 50 Title of Bank. — Sailor with coil of rope on his shoulder looking at female sitting with hand raised.
20 Compt's die — Female representing Commerce, resting right arm on a bale of goods; shipping on the right. PEOPLES BANK, New York City. Eagle. — 20 Male portrait.	50 Compt's die FIFTY — Architect lying against fallen column with plans before him, compass in his hand; in the background, piece of architecture, two men, man with truck and horses. ORIENTAL BANK, New York City. Bird. — 50 Same as ones.	100 Compt's die. — Female seated with pole, cap and key, eagle, safe etc. Title of Bank. — 100 Female, horn of plenty, etc.

1 — Faust, Guttenberg and Schoeffer, chests, wheels, books, etc. — ONE
Compt's die.
NASSAU BANK, New York City.
Franklin. — 1

2 — TWO Same vig. as ones. Title running around the vig. 2 — TWO
Compt's die.
2 — Fish.

5 — 5 Neptune riding in a sea shell on the sea drawn by two horses, female by his side. 5 — FIVE
Compt's die. — Ships.
ATLANTIC BANK, Brooklyn, N. Y.
5 — Sea shell. — FIVE

2 — Steamer at sea. — TWO
Compt's die.
NASSAU BANK, New York City. — Female portrait with grain.
TWO — 2

3 — 3 Vig. Same as ones. — THREE
Compt's die
LONG ISLAND B'K., Brooklyn, N. Y.
3 — Chicken.

10 — X Vig. Same as fives. X — TEN
Compt's die. — Shipping.
ATLANTIC BANK, Brooklyn, N. Y.
10 — Sea shell. — TEN

3 — Five persons representing Agriculture, Manufactures and Commerce. — THREE
Compt's die — Full length female figure with sickle and cornucopia; sheaf by her side.
NASSAU BANK, New York City.
3

5 — Male figure seated on rock in clouds; buildings in background. 5 — FIVE
Compt's die.
LONG ISLAND B'K., Brooklyn, N. Y.
5 — Deer.

20 — XX Vig. Same as 5s. XX — 20
Compt's die. — Shipping.
ATLANTIC BANK, Brooklyn, N. Y.
20 — Sea shell. — XX

5 — Compt's die. View of the N. Y. Crystal Palace. — FIVE
NASSAU BANK, New York City.
Stone cutter at work. — V

X — 10 Title of Bank. — TEN
Compt's die. — Vig. Same as fives.
X — Fish.

50 — ATLANTIC BANK, Brooklyn, N. Y. — 50
Compt's die. — Vig. Same as 5s
50 — Letter L in med. die work — 50

TEN — View of the Battery, Castle Garden and Governor's Island, New York city. — X
NASSAU BANK, New York City.
Compt's die — X

50 — Indian standing beside block of stone, in his right hand a sword; in background an ox with plow. 50 — Die Work.
Franklin.
LONG ISLAND B'K., Brooklyn, N. Y.
Compt's die. — Deer. — Die Work.

Compt's die. — 100 Vig. Same as fives. — 100
ATLANTIC BANK, Brooklyn, N. Y.
100 — Sea shell. — 100

20 — Vig. Same as tens. — XX
NASSAU BANK, New York City.
Compt's die

100 — 100 Vig. Same as fifties, with the Title running around it. 100 — Med. head.
Washington.
Compt's die. — Med. head.

Compt's die. — 500 Vig. Same as fives.
ATLANTIC BANK, Brooklyn, N. Y. — 500
500

Female reclining on a bale of merchandise; steamship and yacht in distance. — 50
NASSAU BANK, New York City.
L — Compt's die.

1 — 1 Shipping. 1
Compt's die. — ATLANTIC BANK, Brooklyn, N. Y. — Full length female on a large figure 1.
1 — Shield with anchor on it.

1000 — Vig. Same as fives. 1000 — Compt's die
ATLANTIC BANK, Brooklyn, N. Y
1000

100 — Hunter with dog and gun warming himself by a fire, enclosed in a large ornamental letter C. — C
One hundred — Dollars
NASSAU BANK, New York City.
Compt's die.

2 — 2 Shipping. 2
Compt's die. — ATLANTIC BANK, Brooklyn, N. Y. — Liberty with cap, pole and cornucopia, standing in a large ornamental fig. 2.
2 — Shield with anchor on it

1 — Blacksmith shoeing horse. — 1
MECHANICS' BANK, Brooklyn, N. Y.
Compt's die. — Squaw and papoose

Soldier on a galloping horse. ONE — Washington.
LONG ISLAND B'K., Brooklyn, N. Y.
Compt's die. — Deer. — Female reclining on a rock.

3 — 3 Vig. Same as 1s 3
Compt's die. — ATLANTIC BANK, Brooklyn, N. Y. — Female with flowers standing in a large ornamental fig. 3.
3 — Shield with anchor on it.

2 — Stone cutters at work. — 2
Title of Bank. Female portrait
Compt's die. — Franklin.

3 Compt's die Carpenter at work; Head tools lying on the of bench. Washington. MECHANICS' BANK, Brooklyn, N. Y. 3 Mechanics' arm, with hammer, anvil, and cog-wheel.	10 Compt's die. 10 Archimedes raising the world. 10 BROOKLYN BANK, Brooklyn, N. Y. Female with grain. Horse. TEN	20 View of the City Hall. TWENTY Compt's die. Female seated between a 2 and 0. Title of Bank. Same as threes. 20 Female seated between, and holding a 2 and 0.
5 Compt's die. MECHANICS' BANK, Brooklyn, N. Y. Three Cupids with press and levers trying to raise a large stone. 5 Locomotive and tender.	20 Compt's die. 20 Horse with Title of Bank running around him. Archimedes raising the world. Female with grain. 20 XX	Neptune with trident. Compt's die. 50 Female on right of shield crowning bust of Washington with wreath; Goddess of Liberty and sheaf; on the left bbls., bales and ship on right. Title of Bank. Same as threes. 50 Portrait of a child.
10 Compt's die. Masons working on scaffold, building a house, man coming up a ladder with hod. MECHANICS' BANK, Brooklyn, N. Y. 10 Jenny Lind.	50 Compt's die. 50 Title of Bank. 50 FIFTY DOLLARS. 50 Horse. FIFTY	100 Compt's die. 100 Female seated on either side of view of ship and water, surmounted by an eagle; bale of goods, cars, steamboat, &c. Title of Bank. Same as threes. 100 Female Portrait.
50 Compt's die. Two females reclining inside a kind of shell, with bee hive between them; female on left has sword and scales. MECHANICS' BANK, Brooklyn, N. Y. 50 Blacksmith resting on hammer and anvil; female in background.	100 Compt's die. 100 100 Archimedes raising the world; Title of Bank running around the vig. 100 Lion guarding safe. Female with sword and scales; eagle with portrait of Washington on his breast.	1 Portrait of Taylor on large 1 ATLANTIC BANK, Boston, Mass. Spread eagle and ships above Title. 1 Female with spy-glass.
100 Compt's die. 100 View of the Brooklyn City Hall. 100 MECHANICS' BANK, Brooklyn, N. Y. C Female seat with Am. shield beside her.	Word one and fig. 1. Compt's die. ONE View of Atlantic Basin, Brooklyn. CITY BANK OF BROOKLYN, Brooklyn, N. Y. Female with scales and money. 1 Female resting on a large fig. 1; shield by her side.	2 Portrait of Taylor. TWO Steamship and other vessels. ATLANTIC BANK, Boston, Mass. TWO Female with spy glass. TWO
1 Compt's die. 1 1 Three small male figures with compass, charts, globe, &c.; shipping on right. 1 BROOKLYN BANK, Brooklyn, N. Y. Female seated. ONE	TWO Compt's die. TWO 2 Female with sickle and grain. Title of Bank. Female with scales. 2 Female raking hay.	Female with spy glass. 3 3 Indian with gun and female with sickle. THREE between and eagle at top. ATLANTIC BANK, Boston, Mass. 3 Sailor seated on a bale.
2 Compt's die 2 Two Dollars Two Dollars 2 Female on either side of a shield, on which is a fig. 2. 2 BROOKLYN BANK, Brooklyn, N. Y. Human figure astride a deer. Head laughing. TWO Head laughing.	Ship under sail. Compt's die. 3 Train of cars. Title of Bank. Female with scales and money. 3 Ship on the stocks. THREE	FIVE Winged female with trumpet. Portrait of Taylor with Title on right. V FIVE Male and female. 5
3 Compt's die. 3 3 Female seated with sickle, sheaf and plough; cattle lying on the ground. 3 BROOKLYN BANK, Brooklyn, N. Y. Spread eagle. Female with sickle. THREE	Merchandise and anchor. Compt's die. Train of cars. FIVE Female and eagle on either side of a shield with fig. 5 on it. Title of Bank. Same as threes. 5 Female with fig. 5 on a safe; warrior with shield and spear in background.	Female. X Portrait of Taylor. ATLANTIC BANK, Boston, Mass. TEN Female with spy-glass.
5 Compt's die. 5 5 Archimedes raising the world. 5 BROOKLYN BANK, Brooklyn, N. Y. Steamboat. FIVE Winged female beside an urn; one with trumpet. V	TEN View of the Ship houses at the Navy Yard; ships. TEN Compt's die. Female seated between a 1 and 0. Title of Bank. Same as threes. 10 Two females; one with spear and shield, the other with sword and scales.	The 20s, 50s, 100s, 500s and 1000s, are of the Perkins' Stereotype Plate, which has the denomination printed in fine letters all over the bill.

Atlas Bank	Boston Bank	Bk. of North Am.
1 ONE 1 — ONE Atlas supporting the globe on his shoulders. 1 — ATLAS BANK, Boston, Mass. — ONE DOLLAR	1 Indian with bow. ONE — 1 Shipping, etc. 1 BOSTON BANK, Boston, Mass. — 1 Ship. ONE	1 — Female seated and leaning on a bale; cars and canal; shipping in distance. 1 BK. OF NORTH AM., Boston, Mass. — Female and 1 ONE
2 TWO 2 — TWO Vig. Same as ones. 2 — ATLAS BANK, Boston, Mass. — TWO DOLLARS	2 Mercury. TWO — 2 Shipping, etc. 2 BOSTON BANK, Boston, Mass. — 2 State Arms. TWO	2 — Sailor and shipping. 2 BK. OF NORTH AM., Boston, Mass. — 2 State Arms.
3 THREE 3 — THREE Vig. Same as ones. 3 — ATLAS BANK, Boston, Mass. — THREE DOLLARS	3 Justice. Female. — 3 Shipping, etc. 3 BOSTON BANK, Boston, Mass. — 3 Shield with fig. 3 on it. Female.	THREE — Two female figures and bust of Washington. 3 on right BK. OF NORTH AM., Boston, Mass. — 3 Female holding flag and 2 cupids
5 FIVE 5 — V Vig. Same as ones. 5 — ATLAS BANK, Boston, Mass. — FIVE DOLLARS	5 Reapers. FIVE — 5 Shipping, etc. 5 BOSTON BANK, Boston, Mass. — 5 Shipping. FIVE	FIVE Female. — Spread Eagle. Cupid either side holding fig. 5. BK. OF NORTH AM., Boston, Mass. — FIVE Female.
10 TEN 10 — X Vig. Same as ones. — ATLAS BANK, Boston, Mass. — TEN DOLLARS	10 — Female and X on shield X BOSTON BANK, Boston, Mass. — 10	TEN — Train of cars. 10 BK. OF NORTH AM., Boston, Mass. State Arms — TEN Squaw with bow and spear.
20 TWENTY 20 — XX Vig. Same as ones. 20 — ATLAS BANK, Boston, Mass. — TWENTY	20 — Deck of a ship; sailor at the wheel 20 on right BOSTON BANK, Boston, Mass. — TWENTY	20 Female. — Two female figures either side of shield BK. OF NORTH AM., Boston, Mass. — 20 Sailor.
50 FIFTY 50 — FIFTY Vig. Same as ones. 50 — ATLAS BANK, Boston, Mass. — FIFTY DOLLARS	The 50s and 100s, are of the Perkins' Stereotype Plate, which has the denomination printed in fine letters all over the bill.	Male and female. — 50 Female, eagle and shield. 50 BK. OF NORTH AM., Boston, Mass. — Sailor and female.
100 100 100 — C Vig. Same as ones. 100 — ATLAS BANK, Boston, Mass. — ONE HUNDRED	D Sailor standing by capstan. — 500 BOSTON BANK, Boston, Mass. — Shipping. 500	100 Female. — Steamship and vessels. BK. OF NORTH AM., Boston, Mass. — 100 Female.
This Bank also issues 500s and 1000s; they have the same vignette as all other denominations.	M Female, eagle, wreath and scales. — 1000 BOSTON BANK, Boston, Mass. — Shipping. 1000	500 Female, eagle and shield. — BK. OF NORTH AM., Boston, Mass. FIVE HUNDRED Female, eagle and shield. — 500 Squaw and papoose.

1 Portrait. / Train of cars. BK. OF COMMERCE, Boston, Mass. Indian c'l / 1 Portrait.	Female reclining; shipping scene. 1000 / Male portrait. BK. OF COMMERCE, Boston, Mass. Steamship. / 1000	100 inverted. Indian erect, with bow and arrow / Indians on cliff contemplating the progress of civilization. ELIOTT BANK, Boston, Mass. / 100 C
2 Portrait. / Spread eagle and shipping. BK. OF COMMERCE, Boston, Mass. Ship / 2 Female portrait	1 / Eliott preaching to the Indians. Portrait of Pierce. ELIOT BANK, Boston, Mass. Female head / ONE Dog's head ONE	D / Wreckers scene; ship wrecked in distance. ELIOTT BANK, Boston, Mass. / 500 D
3 Portrait. / Spread eagle with view of State street and Faneuil Hall. BK. OF COMMERCE, Boston. Mass. Arms / 3 Female figure.	2 / ELIOT BANK, Boston, Mass. Eliott preaching to the Indians. 2 / TWO Sailors on board of a ship.	1 / Machinery, etc. BROADWAY BANK, Boston, Mass. / 1 Indian female.
5 Male Portrait. / Spread eagle with view of State street, and the Market House. BK. OF COMMERCE, Boston, Mass. Steamer / 5 Male Portrait	3 Boston Female. / Vig. Same as ones. ELIOT BANK, Boston, Mass. / 3 Portrait of Webster	2 / BROADWAY BANK, Boston, Mass. Machinery, etc. / 2 Wheels, bale TWO
Three female figures TEN / Steamship and sailing vessels. BK. OF COMMERCE, Boston, Mass. Female, etc. / 10 Male Portrait.	FIVE Boston Indian. / Female head Vig. Same as ones. ELIOT BANK, Boston, Mass. / 5 5	3 Female THREE / BROADWAY BANK, Boston, Mass. Machinery, etc. / 3
Male Portrait. 20 / View of the Boston Custom House. BK. OF COMMERCE, Boston, Mass. Vessels / 20 Goddess of Liberty.	TEN Hunter seated by a fire in the woods / TEN X X Title of Bank. / TEN Hunter washing in a brook.	5 / BROADWAY BANK, Boston, Mass. Machinery, etc. / 5 Female and State Arms.
50 Sailor with flag. / Female with trumpet eagle, globe, etc. BK. OF COMMERCE, Boston, Mass. Locomotive and tender. / 50 Washington.	20 / Ship under full sail. Portrait of Webster. ELIOT BANK, Boston, Mass. / 20 Female with sickle and sheaf.	X Female and State Arms. / BROADWAY BANK, Boston, Mass. Machinery, etc. / X X
Male Portrait. C / Three female figures vessels, etc. BK. OF COMMERCE, Boston, Mass. Ship / 100 Female portrait	FIFTY Sailor and mechanic. / L Portrait of J. Q. Adams. 50 ELIOT BANK, Boston, Mass. / FIFTY Three females.	50 Ship, and bales. FIFTY / BROADWAY BANK, Boston, Mass. Machinery, etc. / 50
Male portrait D / Squaw reclining; shield, eagle and flags; steamship in distance. BK. OF COMMERCE, Boston, Mass. Bee-hive / 500 Female.	Indian with bow. / C Large Steamship. ELIOT BANK, Boston, Mass.	C / BROADWAY BANK, Boston, Mass. Machinery, etc. / 100 Sailor seated on a bale.

Left	Centre	Right
1	View of Haymarket Square. 1 on 1 on right. BLACKSTONE BANK Boston, Mass.	ONE Indian female with bow and spear.
TWO	Vig. Same as ones. 2 BLACKSTONE BANK Boston, Mass.	2 Sailor.
3	Vig. Same as ones. 3 BLACKSTONE BANK Boston, Mass.	3 Ship under full sail.
FIVE	Vig. Same as ones. 5 BLACKSTONE BANK Boston, Mass.	5 State Arms.
10	Vig. Same as ones. Head of female on X on right. BLACKSTONE BANK Boston, Mass.	10 Female.
20 Female, eagle and shield.	Vig. Same as ones. BLACKSTONE BANK Boston, Mass.	20
50	Vig. Same as ones. 50; Cupid with Lee shield on right. BLACKSTONE BANK Boston, Mass.	FIFTY Female.
Female. 100	Vig. Same as ones. BLACKSTONE BANK Boston, Mass.	100 Female.
Same as right ONE	Portrait of Washington; steamer and locomotive. BOYLSTON BANK, Boston, Mass.	Female on 1 ONE

Left	Centre	Right
TWO Eagle on fig. 2. TWO	Vulcan. BOYLSTON BANK, Boston, Mass.	TWO Eagle on fig. 2. TWO
Eagle on 3 THREE	Steamship and sailing vessels. BOYLSTON BANK, Boston, Mass.	THREE Indian and 3
V on Five Same as right	Eagle. BOYLSTON BANK, Boston, Mass.	5 Man, boy and sheep on V.
X Farming scene.	Portrait of Columbus. X Portrait of Washington. BOYLSTON BANK, Boston, Mass.	10 Wharves, carmen and horses.
20 Female seated.	XX Eagle. XX BOYLSTON BANK, Boston, Mass.	20 Ship.
FIFTY Female. FIFTY	50 Man and horse. 50 BOYLSTON BANK, Boston, Mass.	FIFTY Female. FIFTY
Words one hundred and figs. 100. Male portrait	Wharf scene—loading wagon, men, horses, shipping, &c. BOYLSTON BANK, Boston, Mass.	Words one hundred and figures 100. Male portrait
1 Steamship.	View of Boston and the harbor. CITY BANK, Boston, Mass.	1 Ship under full sail.
2 Medallion.	Vig. Same as ones. CITY BANK. Boston, Mass.	2 Medallion.

Left	Centre	Right
3 Medallion. 3	Vig. Same as ones. CITY BANK, Boston, Mass.	3 Medallion.
5 Med head FIVE	Vig. Same as ones. CITY BANK, Boston, Mass. Indian on shield	5 Medallion.
TEN Word Ten on med. head.	Vig. Same as ones. CITY BANK, Boston, Mass.	10 Medallion.
	The 20s, 50s, 100s, and 500s, are of the Perkins' Stereotype Plate, which has the denomination printed in fine letters all over the bill.	
1 Washington. 1	COLUMBIAN BANK, Boston, Mass. 1 Two blacksmiths, anvil, &c. 1	1 Female. 1
Female bust. 1	COLUMBIAN BANK, Boston, Mass. Female; ONE on 1 either side.	1 Male Portrait.
2 Female. 2	COLUMBIAN BANK, Boston, Mass. 2 Harvest scene. 2	2 Female. 2
Indian. 2	COLUMBIAN BANK, Boston, Mass. TWO Ships. DOLL'S	2 Male Portrait.
3 Harvest scene. 3	COLUMBIAN BANK, Boston, Mass. 3 Female, eagle, &c. 3	3 Sailor, coil of rope, &c. 3

Female. THREE | 3 COLUMBIAN BANK, Boston, Mass. 3 3 Portrait. 3 | Female. THREE	1 Interior of a blacksmith's shop. ONE | Spread eagle. 1 EAGLE BANK, Boston, Mass. | 1 Man and horse. ONE	2 | Steamship. Female on 2 EXCHANGE BANK, Boston, Mass. | 2 Female.
5 Washington. 5 | COLUMBIAN BANK, Boston, Mass. 5 Female, Landing of Columbus; city in distance. 5 | 5 Male portrait. 5	2 Flower girl. TWO | Spread Eagle. TWO EAGLE BANK, Boston, Mass. | 2 TWO Female with sickle.	3 Eagle at its bottom. THREE | Steamship and sailing vessels. EXCHANGE BANK, Boston, Mass. | 3 Sailor. THREE
Portrait. 5 | Ship building. COLUMBIAN BANK, Boston, Mass. | 5 Female in 5	5 | Spread Eagle. V, cupid either side. EAGLE BANK, Boston, Mass. Grain | FIVE Female.	5 Female. | Spread eagle. EXCHANGE BANK, Boston, Mass. | Female and cupid on V. 5
10 Portrait of Washington. 10 | COLUMBIAN BANK, Boston, Mass. Ten, large X, Ten across the note. | 10 Portrait of Columbus. 10	X | Spread eagle, building, safe, dog and key. EAGLE BANK, Boston, Mass. | 10 Female at well.	10 | Female figures, horses and chariot. X EXCHANGE BANK, Boston, Mass. | 10 Steamship. TEN
Three females with anchor. TEN | Two females tending looms. COLUMBIAN BANK, Boston, Mass. | 10 Male portrait	20 | Spread eagle Cupid either side of XX. EAGLE BANK, Boston, Mass. | 20 Female.	Twenty on 20 Portrait of Columbus. | Female with scales, shipping, locomotive and State Arms cupid, etc. EXCHANGE BANK, Boston, Mass. | Twenty on 20 Portrait of Washington.
20 Female. | Spread eagle and ships. COLUMBIAN BANK, Boston, Mass. | 20 Female.	L Steamboat. 50 | Spread eagle; bust of female. EAGLE BANK, Boston, Mass. | 50 Reapers. L	FIFTY on 50 | View of the Boston Custom House. 50 EXCHANGE BANK, Boston, Mass. | 50 Franklin.
50 Female 50 | Steamship. COLUMBIAN BANK, Boston, Mass. Imp. and products. | 50	100 Female. 100 | Spread eagle. EAGLE BANK, Boston. Mass. | 100 Female. 100	100 | Female, canal, train of cars and shipping. EXCHANGE BANK, Boston, Mass. | Hundred on 100
C Portrait of Washington. | Female, eagle, shield and liberty cap. COLUMBIAN BANK, Boston, Mass. | 100 Portrait of Columbus.	The 50ths, are of the Perkins' Stereotype Plate, which has the denomination printed in fine letters all over the bill.	500 | Steamship and other vessels. EXCHANGE BANK, Boston, Mass. Dog's head. | 500 Female.
500 Man with cornucopia. 500 | Landing of Columbus. COLUMBIAN BANK, Boston, Mass. FIVE HUNDRED | 500 DOLLARS	1 | State Arms. 1 EXCHANGE BANK, Boston, Mass. | 1 Girl.	EXCHANGE BANK Boston, Mass. Female seated by horn of plenty and shield; ships, steamship, cars, bridge and city in distance. | 1000 1000

1 on large 1 | Stone cutter. NEW ENGLAND BK. Boston, Mass. Eagle | Same as left.

Justice seated. 1000 | Various vessels; city in distance. NEW ENGLAND BK. Boston, Mass. Locomotive. | 1000 Portrait of Washington.

10 10 | Ship. Female, spear and shield. Vig. Same as old ones. NORTH BANK, Boston, Mass. | 10 Agricultural implements.

2 | Portrait of Washington and Franklin on large 2. NEW ENGLAND BK. Boston, Mass. | 2

1 Female and 1. | (New Plate.) Female, electric machine and portrait of Franklin; Franklin drawing lightning from the clouds with a kite; telegraph, train of cars and State House in distance. NORTH BANK, Boston, Mass. | 1 Female with sickle and fig 1.

10 inverted Portrait of Fillmore. | Vig. Same as new ones. NORTH BANK, Boston, Mass. | 10 inverted Sailor boy.

Title and locomotive on large 3. | Female with a roll of cloth; factories and steamboat in distance. Indian head | 3 Ship.

1 Female. 1 | (Old Plate.) View of the State House and Boston Common. NORTH BANK, Boston, Mass. | 1 Ship. 1

20 Female erect with eagle and shield. | Vig. Same as ones new plates. NORTH BANK, Boston, Mass. | 20 Female portrait.

5 | Female seated on bale; city in distance. Fig. 5 running the entire length of the note. NEW ENGLAND BK. Boston, Mass. Female head | 5

TWO Female feeding an eagle from cup. | Vig. Same as new plate of ones. NORTH BANK, Boston, Mass. | 2 Washington

20 Female seated. | XX Eagle. XX NORTH BANK, Boston, Mass. | 20 Ship.

TEN DOLLARS | Ten Dollars Spread eagle on rock, overlooking the sea; ship in distance. NEW ENGLAND BK. Boston, Mass. | 10 Female with spear and shield.

2 Ship. 2 | Female. Three females. Vig. Same as old ones. NORTH BANK, Boston, Mass. | 2 Ship. 2

Steamboat. XX Train of cars. | 20 Three females; one with liberty cap; one with scales and the other with book; eagle and shield; ship in distance. NORTH BANK, Boston, Mass. | XX Milkmaid with pail and stool.

20 TWENTY DOLLARS 20 | Twenty Dollars. Vig. Same as tens. NEW ENGLAND BK. Boston, Mass. | 20 Female and 20 on shield

3 Eagle and shield. THREE | Vig. Same as ones, new plate. NORTH BANK, Boston, Mass. | 3 Female.

50 Female portrait. | Vig. Same as ones, new plate. NORTH BANK, Boston, Mass. | 50 Female.

Indian in canoe. 50 | Fifty Dollars 50 NEW ENGLAND BK. Boston, Mass. | FIFTY

3 Reapers. 3 | Vig. Same as old ones with word three on either side. NORTH BANK, Boston, Mass. | 3 3

C Female with scales and sheaf. | Vig. Same as ones, new plate. NORTH BANK, Boston, Mass. | 100 Female.

100 | ONE HUNDRED 100 Indian in a canoe; mountains in distance on upper left. NEW ENGLAND BK. Boston, Mass. | 100

5 Male portrait | Vig. Same as ones, new plate. NORTH BANK, Boston, Mass. | 5 Five females and 5.

D inverted Sailor erect, leaning on capstan. | Vig. Same as ones, new plate. NORTH BANK, Boston, Mass. | 500 inverted Female erect with cornucopia.

FIVE HUN. D | FIVE HUNDRED DOLL'S Title of Bank. Female seated; boxes and bales at her back; ships in distance. | 500 NEW ENGLAND BK

5 Ship. 5 | FIVE FIVE Vig. Same as ones, old plate. NORTH BANK, Boston, Mass. | 5 Female. 5

M Female seated with trident. | Vig. Same as ones, new plate. NORTH BANK, Boston, Mass. | 1000 Female portrait. 1000

1 — View of Faneuil Hall and other buildings. — 1 FANEUIL HALL BK. Boston, Mass. Female and 1. — Female with dog and cupid.	Female giving eagle drink. — Indian, shield, eagle, deer. — 1 HOWARD BANKING COMPANY, Boston, Mass. 1 — Male portrait.	1 on ONE — Female with scales, and motto, "Industry the means, plenty the result;" shipping and railroad in distance. ONE — 1 on ONE Ship. — Bee hive. ONE — GRANITE BANK, Boston, Mass. — ONE
2 — Vig. Same as ones. — 2 FANEUIL HALL BK. Boston, Mass. Washington. — Female.	TWO — HOWARD BANKING COMPANY, Boston, Mass. — 2 Sailor hoisting the Am. flag. — Female, eagle and globe; ships in distance. — Female with spear and shield and fig. 2.	2 — Vig. Same as ones. TWO — 2 Ship. — GRANITE BANK, Boston, Mass. — Bee hive. TWO — TWO
3 — Vig. Same as ones. — 3 FANEUIL HALL BK. Boston, Mass. Female — Mechanic, sailor and farmer and fig. 3.	Female reclining; locomotive, ship, factory, &c. — 3 HOWARD BANKING COMPANY, Boston, Mass. 3 — Cupid holding figure 3.	3 — Vig. Same as ones. THREE — 3 Ship. — GRANITE BANK, Boston, Mass. — Bee hive. THREE — THREE
Vig. Same as ones, with Cupid on V on right. — 5 FANEUIL HALL BK. Boston, Mass. — Five female figures and 5 5	Male portrait — HOWARD BANKING COMPANY, Boston, Mass. — 5 Five female figures and fig. 5. 5 — Santa Claus in sleigh drawn by reindeers on top of houses.	5 — Vig. Same as ones. FIVE, vessels, 5 on right; 5, merchandise, etc., on left. — 5 Ship. — GRANITE BANK, Boston, Mass. — Bee hive. FIVE — FIVE
View of Quincy Market. X — X FANEUIL HALL BK. Boston, Mass. — Drove of cattle. TEN	Ship and two steamships. — X HOWARD BANKING COMPANY, Boston, Mass. X — Male portrait.	10 — Vig. Same as ones. TEN, vessels, 10 on right; 10, merchandise etc., on left. — 10 Ship. — GRANITE BANK, Boston, Mass. — Bee hive. TEN — TEN
Ship. — Milkmaid and cows. — 20 FANEUIL HALL BK. Boston, Mass. 20 — Female.	Steamship and six sailing vessels. — 20 HOWARD BANKING COMPANY, Boston, Mass. 20 — Male portrait.	20 — Vig. Same as ones. TWENTY — 20 Ship. — GRANITE BANK, Boston, Mass. — Bee hive. TWENTY — TWENTY
50 — Cows and sheep. — 50 FANEUIL HALL BK. Boston, Mass. Female. — State Arms.	50 — Shipping and view of city in distance. — 50 HOWARD BANKING COMPANY, Boston, Mass. L — Indian female	FIFTY — 50 Man and horse. 50 — FIFTY Female. — GRANITE BANK, Boston, Mass. — Female. FIFTY — FIFTY
100 — Farming scene. — 100 FANEUIL HALL BK. Boston, Mass. Train of cars. — Drove of cattle.	100 — HOWARD BANKING COMPANY, Boston, Mass. — C Large steamship and sail vessels.	100 — Spread eagle on branch of tree; cars and canal in distance. — 100 GRANITE BANK, Boston, Mass. Vulcan seated. — Female seated.
500 — Female reclining on bale with distaff in her hand; ships, city, canal, boats, sail lock, cars, &c., in distance. — 500 Washington and his horse — FANEUIL HALL BK. Boston, Mass. 500 — 500	500 — Title of Bank. — 500 Neptune, ship, globe, &c. — FIVE HUNDRED DOLL'S 500 — Boston, — Female leaning on a book reading.	Words one hundred and figs. 100. — Scene on a wharf. — Same as on left. GRANITE BANK, Boston, Mass. Portrait of Harrison. — Portrait of Columbus

Left	Centre	Right
ONE Liberty. ONE	Neptune; on right Boston in 1852; on left Boston in 1630. TREMONT BANK, Boston, Mass.	1 Female
1 ONE 1	View of Street. TREMONT BANK, Boston, Mass	Word one, fig. 1 and 6 mark. Male portrait
Female surrounded by the names of the States. TWO	Vig. Same as first ones. TREMONT BANK, Boston, Mass.	2 Two females
2	View of a street. 2 TREMONT BANK, Boston, Mass.	Word two and fig 2 and II. Two females
3 Female seated on a barrel.	Vig. Same as first ones. TREMONT BANK, Boston, Mass.	3 Blacksmith, sailor and farmer.
3 THREE 3	3 View of a street. TREMONT BANK, Boston, Mass.	Word three and fig. 3 and III. Three females.
	All other notes of the Tremont Bank are of the Perkins' Stereotype Plate, which has the denomination printed in fine letters all over the bill.	
1 Ship.	Winged female with scales and sword and fig. 1. STATE BANK, Boston, Mass. Steamer	1 State Arms.
2 State Arms.	Female and child, bale and birds; steamboat on right, and vessels on left. STATE BANK, Boston, Mass. Machinery	2 Cupids and 2.

Left	Centre	Right
3 Cupids and 3	Spread eagle and ships. STATE BANK, Boston, Mass. Steamer	3 State Arms.
Female. 5	Female portrait. 5 Female portrait STATE BANK, Boston, Mass.	5 State Arms.
10 Portrait of Washington.	State Arms; female and factories on right; female and shipping on left. X on right. STATE BANK, Boston, Mass.	10 State Arms.
20 State Arms.	Two females; shipping railroad and canal. STATE BANK, Boston, Mass. Dog's head	20 Med. head.
State Arms 50	Three females. STATE BANK, Boston, Mass. Horse	50 Sailor with telescope.
State Arms. 100	Female seated on a bale; ships and lighthouse in distance. STATE BANK, Boston, Mass.	100 Two females, eagle and globe.
500 Med. head. 500	STATE BANK, Boston, Mass. Female seated representing Commerce; ship and rainbow in distance. Steamship.	500 State Arms. 500
Justice seated. 1000	Spread eagle on limb of tree; ships in distance. STATE BANK, Boston, Mass. Ships	1000 State Arms.
Bunker Hill Monument. ONE	WEBSTER BANK, Boston, Mass. Portrait of Webster. ONE DOLLAR	1

Left	Centre	Right
Bunker Hill Monument. TWO	WEBSTER BANK, Boston, Mass. Portrait of Webster. TWO DOLLARS	2
Bunker Hill Monument. THREE	WEBSTER BANK, Boston, Mass. Portrait of Webster. 3 DOLLARS	3
Bunker Hill Monument. FIVE	WEBSTER BANK, Boston, Mass. Portrait of Webster. FIVE DOLLARS	5
Bunker Hill Monument. X on left TEN	WEBSTER BANK, Boston, Mass. Portrait of Webster. TEN DOLLARS	10 X
XX Twenty on XX	WEBSTER BANK, Boston, Mass. Portrait of Webster. TWENTY DOLLARS	20 View of Faneuil Hall.
50 FIFTY	WEBSTER BANK, Boston, Mass. Portrait of Webster. FIFTY DOLLARS	50 View of Faneuil Hall.
100 100	WEBSTER BANK, Boston, Mass. Portrait of Webster. ONE HUNDRED DOLLA'S	C View of Faneuil Hall.
500 500	WEBSTER BANK, Boston, Mass. Portrait of Webster.	500 View of Faneuil Hall.
M 1000	WEBSTER BANK. Boston, Mass. Portrait of Webster.	1000 View of Faneuil Hall.

1 Washington.	Spread eagle; capitol at Washington on right; steamboat on left. WASHINGTON B'K., Boston, Mass.	Merchandise 1 Train of cars

100 Washington and his horse	100 Sailor seated on the ground. WASHINGTON B'K., Boston, Mass.	100 100

C View of Boston from the harbor. C	Vig. Same as ones. SHAWMUT BANK, Boston, Mass.	100 View of Merchants' Row. 100

ONE Washington and his horse ONE	1 Indian in a canoe. 1 WASHINGTON B'K., Boston, Mass.	ONE Bust of Washington. ONE

	☞ The Washington Bank formerly used the Perkins' Stereotype Plate.	

ONE Sailing vessel 1	Battle of Bunker Hill. ONE on right. FREEMANS' BANK, Boston, Mass. Sloop, etc.	1 Female. ONE

2 Portrait of Washington.	View of the State House. WASHINGTON B'K., Boston, Mass.	2 State Arms.

ONE View of Merchants' Row. 1	Indian seated on a rock; ship in distance. SHAWMUT BANK, Boston, Mass. Boat and men	1 View of Boston from the harbor. ONE

TWO Girl. 2	Washington on horseback—ship builders. FREEMANS' BANK, Boston, Mass. Imp. and products	2 Franklin. TWO

TWO TWO	2 Shipping. 2 WASHINGTON B'K., Boston, Mass.	TWO Washington and his horse TWO

2 Same as ones TWO	Vig. Same as ones. SHAWMUT BANK, Boston, Mass. Men in boat, etc.	2 Same as ones TWO

THREE Female. 3	Steamboat landing and sailing vessels. THREE FREEMANS' BANK, Boston, Mass. Sloop	3 Washington and horse THREE

Female THREE	Large steamships and sail vessels. WASHINGTON B'K., Boston, Mass. Washington	3 Sailor.

THREE Same as ones on right and THREE	Vig. Same as ones. SHAWMUT BANK, Boston, Mass. Eagle	3 View of Merchants' Row

5 Wharf and shipping. FIVE	View of Quincy Market. FREEMANS' BANK, Boston, Mass. Dog	5 Female.

5 Washington and his horse	View of the State House. WASHINGTON B'K., Boston, Mass.	5 Female.

5 View of Boston from the harbor. FIVE	Vig. Same as ones. SHAWMUT BANK, Boston, Mass Anchor, etc	5 Same as 5s.

TEN Interior of a blacksmith's shop. 10	X Ships TEN FREEMANS' BANK, Boston, Mass.	10 Male and female. TEN

TEN Washington and his horse	Train of cars. WASHINGTON B'K., Boston, Mass. State Arms	10 Steamship. TEN

10 Same as fives 10	Vig. Same as ones. SHAWMUT BANK, Boston, Mass. 10	10 Same as fives 10

XX Female. 20	Cows. Female making hay. FREEMANS' BANK, Boston, Mass.	20 Ships. XX

TWENTY Squaw with bow and spear.	XX Spread eagle and shield; Capitol at Washington on right; steamship on left. WASHINGTON B'K., Boston, Mass. Washington	20

View of Merchants' Row. XX	Vig. Same as ones. SHAWMUT BANK, Boston, Mass.	20 View of Boston from the harbor. 20

FIFTY Female. FIFTY	50 Man and horse. 50 FREEMANS' BANK, Boston, Mass.	FIFTY Female. FIFTY

50 Washington.	Female seated, leaning on a bale; ships on right; railroad and canal on left. WASHINGTON B'K., Boston, Mass. Shell	50 50

50 Same as 20s. 50	Vig. Same as ones. SHAWMUT BANK, Boston, Mass.	50 Same as 20s. 50

Words one hundred and figs. 100. Male portrait	Wharf scene—loading wagon, men, horses, shipping, &c. FREEMANS' BANK, Boston, Mass.	Words one hundred and figures 100. Male portrait

1 MECHANICS' BANK, Boston, Mass. 1 Wood cutter; gold dollar; log hut and wagon in distance. Vulcan seated with anvil and hammer. Ships.	XX Man on horseback, and man on foot; cattle, sheep and dogs. Cars 20 Female with pail and stool. MECHANICS' BANK, Boston, Mass. Boy and girl sailing boat in tub.	MASSACHUSETTS BANK 100 100 ONE HUNDRED State Arms. MASS. BANK, Boston, Mass. 100 100 100 ONE HUNDRED
Fishing vessels. Female 1 MECHANICS' BANK, Boston, Mass. ONE Statue of Washington 1	FIFTY 50 Man and horse. 50 FIFTY Female. MECHANICS' BANK, Boston, Mass. Female. FIFTY FIFTY	FIVE HUNDRED Five Hundred Dollars Indian on shield, farming utensils around; ship in distance MASS. BANK, Boston, Mass. 500
2 MECHANICS' BANK, Boston, Mass. 2 Farmer boy with rake; milkmaid with pail; two gold dollars; farm house and cows in distance. Blacksmith anvil and forge. Locomotive.	Words one hundred and figs. 100. Scene on a wharf. Same as on left. MECHANICS' BANK, Boston, Mass. Portrait of Harrison. Portrait of Columbus.	MASSACHUSETTS BANK 1000 1000 1000 ONE THOUSAND State Arms. Title of Bank. 1000 1000 MASSACHUSETTS BANK
2 TWO Interior of a blacksmith's shop. TWO 2 MECHANICS' BANK, Boston, Mass. Female portrait. 2	1 on Med. head. Indian sitting on the ground; mountains in distance. ONE MASSACHUSETTS BANK, Boston, Mass. 1 on med head Same as left	1 Female portrait. 1 Female portrait ONE SUFFOLK BANK, Boston, Mass. Eagle. Washington and his horse ONE
3 MECHANICS' BANK, Boston, Mass. 3 Farmer with scythe, sailor with spy-glass, blacksmith, hammer and anvil; three gold dollars. Female. Stone cutter.	TWO Ships. MASS. BANK, Boston, Mass. TWO	TWO 2 2 2 TWO Washington and his horse Female. SUFFOLK BANK, Boston, Mass. TWO TWO
THREE Ship building. Steamboat. 3 Washington and staff on Dorchester Heights. MECHANICS' BANK, Boston, Mass. Man on horseback; cattle. THREE THREE	V State Arms. 5 Washington. MASS. BANK, Boston, Mass. Male portrait. 5 V	THREE 3 THREE 3 SUFFOLK BANK, Boston, Mass. Female. Dog, safe and building. 3
FIVE MECHANICS' BANK, Boston, Mass. 5 Female with pole and cap; shield at her feet. Indian female on left, hunter on right, three cupids in centre; five gold dollars; cars in distance. Portrait of Webster.	X State Arms. 10 Washington MASS. BANK, Boston, Mass. Male portrait 10 X	5 Winged female with trumpet. On right portrait of Columbus. On left portrait of Washington. 5 Two females State Arms. V SUFFOLK BANK, Boston, Mass. V Eagle
FIVE Washington and staff on Dorchester Heights; evacuation of Boston, 1776. 5 MECHANICS' BANK, Boston, Mass. Washington.	MASSACHUSETTS BANK 20 20 TWENTY State Arms. DOLL'S MASS. BANK, Boston, Mass. 20 20 TWENTY	10 Female, eagle and shield. 10 SUFFOLK BANK, Boston, Mass. Washington Bust. Building
Wharf and shipping. Steamboat landing and sail vessels Washington on horse on right. 10 MECHANICS' BANK, Boston, Mass. Train of cars. 10 TEN Shipping scene	MASSACHUSETTS BANK 50 Fifty Dollars State Arms. 50 50 MASS. BANK, Boston, Mass. 50 50 FIFTY DOLLARS.	☞ The Suffolk Bank formerly used the Perkins' Stereotype Plate, and still continue to use it for 50s and 100s, 500s and 1000s.

ONE Sailor hoisting a flag. Wood cutter, gold dollar; house and wagon in distance. NATIONAL BANK, Boston, Mass. 1 Female and fig. 1.	1 Ship building ONE Wharf and shipping; view of Boston in distance. 1 on right. TRADERS' BANK, Boston, Mass. 1 Male and female. ONE	1 Portrait of Fillmore. State Arms; female and cars on right; female and steamboat on left. UNION BANK, Boston, Mass. Female and 1. ONE
Female. 2 Man with rake, female with pail; two gold dollars; house, barn and cows NATIONAL BANK, Boston, Mass. 2 Sailor with spy glass.	2 Boy and girl sailing boats in a tub. TWO Vig. Same as ones. 2 TRADERS' BANK, Boston, Mass. 2 Girl. TWO	TWO Indian female with bow and spear. Female seated, leaning on bale; railroad, ships and city in distance. UNION BANK, Boston, Mass. 2 Gen. Taylor.
3 Mermaid and merman. Steamer. Farmer with scythe, sailor with telescope and blacksmith with sledge, also three gold dollars. NATIONAL BANK, Boston, Mass. 3 Washington	3 Interior of a blacksmith's shop. THREE Vig. Same as ones. 3 TRADERS' BANK, Boston, Mass. 3 Female in a forest THREE	3 Female Spread eagle and ships. UNION BANK, Boston, Mass. 3 Webster
FIVE Liberty. Three Cupids, five gold dollars, hunter and Indian female. NATIONAL BANK, Boston, Mass. 5 Capitol at Washington	FIVE Justice. Vig. Same as ones. 5 TRADERS' BANK, Boston, Mass. 5 Portrait of Webster. FIVE	5 Washington Three females. Figure 5 running the entire length of the bill. UNION BANK, Boston, Mass. 5
X Capitol at Washington. NATIONAL BANK, Boston, Mass. 10 Franklin.	TEN Female. Vig. Same as ones. X TRADERS' BANK, Boston, Mass. 10 Female. TEN	10 10 Sailor with flag; ships Letter X running the entire length of the bill. UNION BANK, Boston, Mass. 10 10
Female giving eagle a drink. XX View of building NATIONAL BANK, Boston, Mass. 20 Female feeding a horse.	20 Female. XX Vig. Same as ones. TRADERS' BANK, Boston, Mass. 20 Justice. XX	XX State Arms. 20 Female and eagle. 20 UNION BANK, Boston, Mass. Steamer XX Portrait. XX
Fountain. 50 Ship and two steamships NATIONAL BANK, Boston, Mass. 50 Female bust	50 Vig. Same as ones. 50 TRADERS' BANK, Boston, Mass. 50 Covered wagon and merchandise.	50 Indian female with bow and arrow. State Arms with female on each side. UNION BANK, Boston, Mass. Clasped hands 50 Portrait of J. Q. Adams.
100 Female with spear and shield. Spread eagle and shield; capitol at Washington on right; steamship on left NATIONAL BANK, Boston, Mass. C Portrait.	Vig. Same as ones. 100 ONE HUND TRADERS' BANK, Boston, Mass. Hundred on 100 Washington	100 State Arms. Portrait of Washington surrounded by arms of the States. UNION BANK, Boston, Mass. Steamer 100 Cupid in a sail boat. 100
D Female seated by shield; steamship, cars, bridge and city in distance. NATIONAL BANK, Boston, Mass. 500 Female portrait.	500 Vig. Same as ones. 500 TRADERS' BANK, Boston, Mass. 500 Eagle and shield.	The Union Bank also used the Stereotype Plate for 1s, 2s, and 3s, and still use it for 500s.

ONE Bust ONE	Eagle. 1 Eagle. HAMILTON BANK, Boston, Mass.	ONE Male Portrait. ONE
Female sickle and sheaf 100	Vig. Same as fives. MERCHANTS BANK, Boston, Mass. Steamer	C State Arms.
Horses and cart. ONE Farming scene.	1 Indian on 1 1 MARKET BANK, Boston, Mass.	Man on horseback; cattle. ONE Horses and trucks with view of Quincy Market.
2 Male Portrait. TWO	Ship. 2 Ship. HAMILTON BANK, Boston, Mass.	2 Male Portrait TWO
1 Men dressing leather. ONE	Shoe and Leather Dealers Store, horses, wagon, wharf and shipping. SHOE & LEATHER DEALERS' BANK, Boston, Mass.	1 Interior of shoemaker's shop. ONE
Vase of flowers. 2	TWO 2 TWO MARKET BANK, Boston, Mass.	Ship. 2
THREE Male Portrait. THREE	Washington on his horse. 3 Washington on his horse. HAMILTON BANK, Boston, Mass.	THREE Male Portrait. THREE
2 Interior of a shoemaker's shop. TWO	Vig. Same as ones. Title of Bank.	2 Morocco dressing. TWO
3 Vase of flowers.	Bust of Washington. 3 Female. MARKET BANK, Boston, Mass.	3 Vase of flowers
	The 5s, 10s, 50s, and 100s, are of the Perkins' Stereotype Plate, which has the denomination printed in fine letters all over the bill.	
3 Cows THREE	Vig. Same as ones. Title of Bank.	3 Interior of a shoemaker's shop. THREE
Train of cars FIVE	Portrait of Lady Washington. 5 Portrait of Washington. MARKET BANK, Boston, Mass. Bull	5 Eagle and five on shield.
20 Male Portrait. XX	XX Portrait. XX HAMILTON BANK, Boston, Mass.	20 Male Portrait. XX
5 Morocco dressing.	Vig. Same as ones. Title of Bank.	5 Justice.
5 FIVE	Merchandise, shipping and Quincy Market V MARKET BANK, Boston, Mass.	5 Cows. FIVE
5 Portrait of Franklin. V	View of the Merchants Bank and other buildings. V and cupid either side. MERCHANTS BANK, Boston, Mass. Cupid on V.	FIVE Female, eagle, Washington, on 5. FIVE
10 Washington and his horse TEN	Vig. Same as ones. Title of Bank.	10 Shipping. TEN
X	Ship under full sail. X MARKET BANK, Boston, Mass. Bull	10 Female Portrait. TEN
Medallion head. X	10 Boston custom House. 10 MERCHANTS BANK, Boston, Mass. 10	TEN Female, with spear and shield. TEN
XX Indian with bow. 20	Vig. Same as ones. Title of Bank.	20 Eagle. XX
10 Female. TEN	X Merchandise, shipping and Quincy Market. X MARKET BANK, Boston, Mass.	10 Ship. TEN
20 Female with flag. TWENTY	Ship of war and sail boats. MERCHANTS BANK, Boston, Mass. Washington.	20 Spread eagle and shield. TWENTY
FIFTY Washington 50	Vig. Same as ones. Title of Bank. Some have fig. 50 on vig.	50 Franklin. FIFTY
20 Washington TWENTY	Spread eagle on branch of tree; cars and canal in distance. MARKET BANK, Boston, Mass. Steamship.	20 Male portrait TWENTY
Female in kneeling position. 50	Female, sickle and sheaf of wheat; factory and Railroad in distance. MERCHANTS BANK, Boston, Mass. Cornucopia, etc.	L Cupid in sail boat. 50
Words one hundred and figs. 100. Male portrait	Wharf scene—loading wagon, men, horses, shipping, &c. Title of Bank.	Words one hundred and figures 100. Male portrait
50	Steamship. 50 MARKET BANK, Boston, Mass.	FIFTY Portrait of Columbus. FIFTY

100 Neptune. 100 Steamship. MARKET BANK, Boston, Mass. 100 Franklin. 100	100 Female reclining with sheaf and sickle. Cattle and stream of water. MECHANICS' BANK, Williamsburg, N. Y. 100 Compt's die.	Sailor with flag; anchor, bbl., quadrant and bale. ONE State building; view of city in distance. WILLIAMSBURG CITY BANK, Williamsburg, N. Y. Sloop. 1 Compt's die
500 Nat. bond. 500 Female seated with sheaf; boat and cars in distance. MARKET BANK, Boston, Mass. 500 Portrait of Washington	Compt's die. Land scene, drovers and cattle, load of hay, etc 1 Female with ears of corn; vessels and city in distance. FARMERS' & CITIZENS' BK OF LONG ISLAND, Williamsburg, N. Y. Agricultural Implements. 1 Train of cars; houses, etc in distance	Female portrait. TWO 2 Female seated, eagle, etc., in distance cars, city, vessels, &c. Title of Bank. Eagle. 2 Compt's die.
1 Female with pen and tablets. Sailor steering ship. MECHANICS' BANK OF WILLIAMSBURG, N. Y. 1 Compt's die.	2 Compt's die TWO Shipwright at work; vessels, men, etc. Title of Bank. Steamship. 2 Female seated with tablets.	Indian on cliff. 3 Female seated with shield; falls in the distance. Title of Bank. Bee hive. 3 Compt's die
Indian on cliff. 2 MECHANICS' BANK, Williamsburg, N. Y. Mechanic with anvil, hammer, cog wheel, etc. 2 Compt's die.	3 Horses drinking from trough, man seated; female feeding hogs, buildings, etc. Compt's die. Title of Bank. Eagle. 3 Female with shield, etc.	Female seated holding a figure 5. FIVE Vessels and view of city. Title of Bank. Head of Indian. Female seated holding a 5; masts in background Compt's die
THREE View of wharves, vessels, etc THREE Milkmaids and cows; house in distance. MECHANICS' BANK, Williamsburgh, N. Y. 3 Compt's die	Three females, one above the other. FIVE Title of Bank. Female with trident seated in a shell; vessels in distance. 5 Compt's die	10 Female with flowers in her apron. Female reclining on bales; vessels in distance. Title of Bank. Locomotive and tender. 10 Compt's die.
5 Female portrait. MECHANICS' BANK, Williamsburg, N. Y. Mechanic erect between a letter V; anvil, hammer, cog wheel, etc.; buildings, &c., in distance. 5 Compt's die.	10 Female portrait. Steamship and other vessels. Title of Bank. Eagle. 10 Compt's die.	50 Drovers and cattle, load of hay, etc.; and scene in general. Farmers at rest and nooning; loading hay in distance. Title of Bank. Yacht Una. 50 Compt's die.
10 Spread eagle; buildings, street, etc. Female portrait MECHANICS' BANK, Williamsburg, N. Y. 10 Compt's die	Female seated with sword, etc. TWENTY Title of Bank. Milkmaid seated, cows; house in distance. Steamboat. 20 Compt's die	Spread eagle. 100 Compt's die. Title of Bank. Dog, key and safe. 100
20 Arm and hammer. 20 MECHANICS' BANK, Williamsburg, N. Y. Figures 20 winged female on either side: two cupids between 2 and 0. 20 TWENTY Compt's die	Sailor erect flag; female reclining. FIFTY Title of Bank. Female with pole, cap and shield; buildings in distance. 50 Compt's die	ONE Male portrait Compt's die. 1 View of the St. Nicholas Hotel. 1 ST. NICHOLAS B'K., New York City. Game Cock. ONE Santa Claus filling the stockings. ONE
50 50 Three females and winged cupid floating in water. Compt's die. MECHANICS' BANK, Williamsburg, N. Y. 50 Female with compass, etc	Mercury with wand and bag of coin. 100 Title of Bank. Indian, shield, eagle, female and letter C. 100 Compt's die	TWO Male portrait Compt's die. 2 Santa Claus riding over tops of houses. 2 ST. NICHOLAS B'K., New York City. Game Cock. Merchandise City Arms. Merchandise.

THREE	View of the St. Nicholas Hotel. 3 on left.	3
Male portrait	ST. NICHOLAS B'K., New York City.	Santa Claus filling the stockings.
Compt's die.	Cock	

Die Work.	50 Female seated on anchor, right arm resting on shield with 50 on it; sheaf, ship, &c. 50	Die Work.
Franklin.	Title of Bank.	Male portrait
Die Work.		Die Work.

Ornamental work.	500 Ship with sails set. 500	Ornamental work.
Dog and safe.	BK OF NORTH AM., Philadelphia, Pa.	Sailor with telescope.
Ornamental work.	Spread eagle.	Ornamental work.

	Santa Claus in sleigh drawn by reindeers.	5
	ST. NICHOLAS B'K., New York City.	
Compt's die.	Eagle.	Male portrait

Die Work.	100 Female seated, eagle beside; shipping in distance. 100	Die Work.
Male portrait	Title of Bank.	Male portrait
Die Work.	Sword.	Die Work.

Ornamental work.	1000 Ship with sails set. 1000	Ornamental work.
Dog and safe.	BK OF NORTH AM., Philadelphia, Pa.	Sailor with telescope.
Ornamental work.	Spread eagle.	Ornamental work.

10	Santa Claus with sleigh and reindeer.	10
	ST. NICHOLAS B'K., New York City.	
Compt's die.	Bee hive.	Bank building.

Figures 500 written with a pen.	Med. head. Female reclining with sprig and wand; shipping in distance. Med. head.	
Med. head.	Title of Bank.	Same as on left.
Figures 500 written with a pen.		

Three females with anchor.	V Steamship and sail vessels.	5
	B'K. OF COMMERCE, Philadelphia, Pa.	Female seated with spy glass; ship in distance.
FIVE		

20	ST. NICHOLAS B'K., New York City.	20
Children asleep in bed; Santa Claus entering from chimney.	Compt's die.	Male portrait

Figs. 1000 written with a pen.	Med. head. Vig. Same as 500s. Med. head.	
Med. Head.	Title of Bank.	Same as on left.
Figs. 1000 written with a pen.		

TEN	10 Shipping; storehouse on right; city on left.	10
Sailor with flag and female at his feet: cornucopia, anchor bales, barrels, &c.	B'K. OF COMMERCE, Philadelphia, Pa.	Liberty with pole, cap and shield.
		TEN

50	ST. NICHOLAS B'K., New York City.	50
Compt's die	Children asleep in bed; Santa Claus entering from chimney.	Male portrait

5	BK OF NORTH AM., Philadelphia, Pa.	5
Word Five and fig. 5.	Portrait of Franklin. Indian female in the centre of a V; eagle, shield, pole and cap. Female portrait.	Locomotive.
5		5

	20 Shipping. 20	20
Statue of Liberty with pole and cap.	B'K. OF COMMERCE, Philadelphia, Pa.	Artist seated with brush and canvass.
		20

	U. S. Capitol; pedestrians, horses, carriages, etc.	100
	ST. NICHOLAS B'K., New York City.	
Compt's die.	Gamecock.	Male portrait

10	Female and Indian on either side of a frame enclosing ship, plough and sheafs; cattle and factory in background.	10
Portrait of Wm. Penn.	BK OF NORTH AM., Philadelphia, Pa.	Franklin.
TEN	Dog, key and safe.	TEN

	Med head with 50 on it. Female seated with eagle perched on shield on right; ship on left. Med. head with 50 on it.	50
FIFTY	B'K. OF COMMERCE, Philadelphia, Pa.	Cupid seated with pencil and paper.
		50

FIVE	Shipping; schooner on the right with figure 5 on the sail; on left small steamboat.	5
	COMMERCIAL BANK OF PENNSYLVANIA, Philadelphia, Pa.	Locomotive.
Sailor with flag.		Landscape, etc.

20	Female seated on bale; shield, barrel, sheaf, &c.	20
Male portrait	BK OF NORTH AM., Philadelphia, Pa.	Female with arms extended resting on anchor; shipping in background.
20		

100 C 100	100 Female seated and giving eagle drink. 100	100 C 100
	B'K. OF COMMERCE, Philadelphia, Pa.	

10	Sailor on deck of ship with quadrant; shipping in background. Title of Bank running over the vignette.	10
Anchor and bale of goods.		Female Portrait.

50	Female reclining; on left eagle, shield, flags, etc.; on right, shipping.	50
Lafayette.	BK OF NORTH AM., Philadelphia, Pa.	Justice.
50	Sheaf, plow, &c.	50

500	Female seated on bale of goods with wand in her right hand; shipping on left.	500
Neptune with trident, seated in sea shell.	B'K. OF COMMERCE, Philadelphia, Pa.	Ship under full sail.
	Medallion head.	

Die Work.	20 Two females representing Agriculture and Manufacturers; between them shield with 20 on it; ships on left, and sheep on right. 20	Die Work
Washington	Title of Bank.	LaFayette
Die Work.	Spread eagle.	Die Work.

100	Eagle on a rock; shipping on either side.	100
Washington	BK OF NORTH AM., Philadelphia, N. Y.	Liberty with pole and cap.
100	Dog, key and safe.	100

POST	Neptune with trident seated in a shell on the sea.	POST
Ship in a storm.	B'K. OF COMMERCE. Philadelphia, Pa.	Med. head.
NOTE		NOTE

Left	Centre	Right
5 FIVE	WESTERN BANK, Philadelphia, Pa. Indian, squaw and pa poose; buildings, etc. FIVE	5 Female kneeling; buildings and spire.
5 Med. Head and word five. V	Eagle mounted on escutcheon; group of persons representing various pursuits—Agriculture, Commerce, Manufactures, Justice, Liberty, and so on; ship on right. B'K. OF NORTHERN LIBERTIES, Philadelphia, Pa.	V Med. head and word five. 5
20 Farmer leaning against a tree; female seated. 20	Two cupids, flag, vessel; &c., word Twenty and Medallion head each side FAR. & MECH. B'K., Philadelphia, Pa.	XX Blacksmith at forge. XX
5 Boy gathering corn. Med. head.	5 Farmers reposing beneath a tree and enjoying their dinner; basket, horses, etc. WESTERN BANK, Philadelphia, Pa. Agricultural Implements.	5 Female rep- [illegible] figure 5. 5
10 Washington X	Vig. Same as 5ves. B'K. OF NORTHERN LIBERTIES, Philadelphia, Pa.	X Med. head and word ten 10
50 Female seated; house in distance. FIFTY	Blacksmith, farmer, horses, farming utensils, &c., spire in distance. FAR. & MECH. B'K., Philadelphia, Pa. Bee-hive.	50 Sailor seated, vessel, &c. FIFTY
Two Indians, one erect the other kneeling; wigwam &c.	WESTERN BANK, Philadelphia, Pa. 10 Female representing agriculture; cars crossing bridge in distance. Mechanics arm.	Letter X and word Ten. Female reclining.
20 Med head; 20	Vig. Same as 5ves. B'K. OF NORTHERN LIBERTIES, Philadelphia, Pa.	20 Washington 20
Female erect with shield and spear. 100	FAR. & MECH. B'K., Philadelphia, Pa. 100 Female, harvest scene, vessel, houses, &c. 100	100 Word hundred on Med head. 100
X Med. Head. X	10 Female with trumpet, globe and eagle. 10 WESTERN BANK, Philadelphia, Pa. Steamship.	X Med. head X
FIFTY Group of persons, Liberty, Justice, spear horse, eagle, &c. FIFTY	Med. head and 50 on it. State Arms. Med. head and 50 on it. B'K. OF NORTHERN LIBERTIES, Philadelphia, Pa.	50 Washington 50
FIVE HUNDRED	Female seated; anvil, screw, hammer, &c. Steamboat in distance. FAR. & MECH. BANK, Phila. Pa	Female erect Sheaf, plow and ship. 500
Female seated on bale. 20	WESTERN BANK, Philadelphia, Pa. Two females seated; ship, steamboat and small sail vessel on left; cars on right. Med. head and word Twenty on either side of vignette. Steamboat and sail vessel	20 Med. head. 20
100 Washington 100	Female with babe in arms shipping and sheafs; life boat; steamboat in distance. Med head and 100 on it, on either side of the vignette. Title of Bank.	100 Same as on left of 50s. 100
ONE THOUSAND	FAR. & MECH. B'K., Philadelphia, Pa. 1000 Vulcan.	ONE THOUSAND
Human figure reclining 50	WESTERN BANK, Philadelphia, Pa. Portrait of Washington. Instructor and pupil; house on right. Med. head figs. 50 on it. Dog's head.	50 Med. head. 50
500 Med. head. 500	Liberty and Justice on either side of escutcheon, surmounted by eagle; ship and plow in centre; heads of two horses. 500 Title of Bank. State Arms	Escutcheon, mounted eagle and group of persons.
FIVE Blacksmith and female seated. 5	5 Female seated, supporting urn; vessels on right. 5 TRADESMEN'S B'K., Philadelphia, Pa. Steamship.	FIVE Blacksmith erect. FIVE
100 Med. head. 100	WESTERN BANK, Philadelphia, Pa. C Eagle; ship and other small sail vessel. C Steamboat and life-boat.	Female erect with horn of plenty. 100
	1000 Escutcheon, mounted eagle, Goddess of Liberty, Justice, female with horn of plenty, and other persons; ship on right and two horses on left. Vig. on left end of note. Title of Bank.	POST Child's head NOTE
Female encircled by heavy folds of dress, left arm extended.	10 Goddess of Liberty and spread eagle. TRADESMEN'S B'K., Philadelphia, Pa. X	10 Franklin. TEN
500 Female representing Agriculture. 500	Indian seated; grain, agricultural implements, etc.; house seen amid the wood. WESTERN BANK, Philadelphia, Pa. Female bathing.	500 Liberty reclining.
5 Sailor seated.	FAR. & MECH. B'K., Philadelphia, Pa. Blacksmith, farmer and horses; spire in distance.	5 Female seated; house in background.
TWENTY Bust of Penn TWENTY	20 Two females; one reclining on cornucopia, the other apparently elevated in the air. XX TRADESMEN'S B'K., Philadelphia, Pa.	
1000 Med. head. 1000	Goddess of Liberty and two other females; eagle surmounted; ship and cars in distance. WESTERN BANK, Philadelphia, Pa. Spread eagle.	1000 Milkmaid erect
X Female portrait. 10	Female seated between 1 and 0; agricultural scenery, house, &c. 10 on right. FAR. & MECH. B'K., Philadelphia, Pa. Arm, anvil and hammer	X Female portrait. 10
50 Canal scene; bridge, houses and spire. FIFTY	Female with right arm leaning on hogshead; cars and vessel on left; house on right. Portrait of female on either side of the vignette. TRADESMEN'S B'K., Philadelphia, Pa.	50 Ship. FIFTY

100 Indian squaw and papoose. 100 C Group of three mechanics; vessel on right; man and horses on left. TRADESMEN'S B'K., Philadelphia, Pa. 100 Med. head. 100	500 MECHANICS' BANK, Philadelphia, Pa. 500 View of the building formerly occupied by the Bank. 500 FIVE HUNDRED	5 Female bust. V Vessels; ship building and houses in distance. Double med. head on either side of vig. KENSINGTON B'K., Philadelphia, Pa. V Female portrait. 5
500 Washington 500 Spread eagle; houses on right; cars on left. TRADESMEN'S B'K., Philadelphia, Pa. Female bathing. Two females one standing the other kneeling. 500	1000 MECHANICS' BANK, Philadelphia, Pa. 1000 Vig. Same as 500s. 1000 ONE THOUSAND	10 Female erect and vessel in distance. X Med. head. Rafts, boats, and other water craft; mountain scenery, houses, etc. Med. head. KENSINGTON B'K., Philadelphia, Pa. X Female and spinning wheel. 10
5 Sailor leaning on capstan. MECHANICS' BANK, Philadelphia, Pa. Mechanic, letter V and mechanical implements, factories in distance; FIVE across V on left; on right DOLLARS across V. 5 Female head.	5 Bust of Penn FIVE Agricultural scene; group of five persons. BANK OF PENN TOWNSHIP, Philadelphia, Pa. 5 Washington on horseback	Die. Columbus. Die. 20 The Old Elm Tree; harbor or city in distance. 20 KENSINGTON B'K., Philadelphia, Pa. Sword. Die. Wm. Penn. Die.
Bank building. 5 5 Portrait of a female; globe, &c. 5 MECHANICS' BANK, Philadelphia, Pa. Blacksmith's arm. Washington and horse. 5	Goddess of Liberty. Wm. Penn. Goddess of Liberty. 10 Female seated, sickle, cornucopia, farming implements, house, etc. 10 Title of Bank. Spread eagle. Washington Spread eagle	20 Indians contemplating the progress of civilization. KENSINGTON B'K., Philadelphia, Pa. Vig. Same as 20s above. Large red 20 in centre of bill. XX XX 20 Portrait of Wm. Penn.
TEN Female with cornucopia. TEN 10 Blacksmith reclining on anvil; house in distance. 10 MECHANICS' BANK, Philadelphia, Pa. Liberty. TEN	20 Franklin. 20 Title of Bank. Portrait of Penn. Two females embracing each other; safe in foreground; ship in background; steamboat on left. Washington 20	Die Work. Male portrait Die Work. 50 Two females seated; escutcheon between; eagle and ship; ship in distance. 50 KENSINGTON B'K., Philadelphia, Pa. Eagle. Die Work. Washington Die Work.
TWENTY Miniature view of female reclining on hogshead, etc.; locomotive in distance. MECHANICS' BANK, Philadelphia, Pa. 20 Spread eagle on trunk of fallen tree; cars on left; depot on right. Mechanics' Arm. 20	50 Locomotive and cars; Train of cars ascending hill. 50 Portrait of Penn. Female seated on bale of goods; houses and spires in distance. Portrait of Washington. Title of Bank. 50 Franklin. 50	50 Franklin. KENSINGTON B'K., Philadelphia, Pa. Female seated in a letter L with machinery, etc.; cars on left; factory on right. Female in water. 50 Washington
50 MECHANICS' BANK, Philadelphia, Pa. Train of cars crossing bridge; vessel at the farther end; trees, wagon, horses, etc. Goddess of Liberty. 50 Vessels and harbor.	100 Washington 100 Title of Bank. Portrait of Penn. Milkmaid erect; cottage in distance. 100	Justice and head of Washington 100 Female seated and cupids; cattle, harvest scene, houses, agricultural implements, &c. Title of Bank on either side of vig. 100 Male figure. Die Work. Lafayette. Die Work.
50 Male portrait Die. Two females representing Agriculture and Commerce. MECHANICS' BANK, Philadelphia, Pa. Mechanics' Arm. 50 Washington Die.	Die. FIVE HUNDRED Die. Three females seated; cornucopias, etc. Figs. 500 on either side of vig Title of Bank. Eagle. Die. Head of Penn Die.	C 100 C KENSINGTON B'K., Philadelphia, Pa. View of ship yard, three vessels on stocks. Large red C. 100 PENNSYLVANIA 100 100 Female with sheaf and sickle.
100 Mechanics' arm. 100 MECHANICS' BANK, Philadelphia, Pa. Agricultural implements. ONE HUNDRED	Die. POST 1000 NOTE Die. 1000 Washington and others on horseback; soldiers and cannon. 1000 Title of Bank. Spread eagle. Die. Wm. Penn. Die.	500 Interior of a rolling mill. KENSINGTON B'K. Philadelphia, Pa. Steamship at sea; large red letter D. PENNSYLVANIA. 500 Factory and creek.

FIVE. Justice. 5 — Med. head and fig. 5 on it. State Arms. Med. head, and fig. 5 on it. BANK OF PENNSYLVANIA, Philadelphia, Pa. Male portrait — FIVE. Female erect. 5	Med. head. 500. Med. head. — State Arms. 500. BK OF PENNSYL'IA, Philadelphia, Pa. — Med. head. 500. Med. head.	500. Head of Girard. 500 — View of the Bank building. Figures 500 on either side of vig. GIRARD BANK, Philadelphia, Pa. — 500. Head of Girard. 500
5. Male portrait — BK OF PENNSYL'IA, Philadelphia, Pa. State Arms; building, bridge, &c., in distance. Boy's head. — 5. Male portrait	Med. head. 1000. Med. head. — 1000. State Arms. BK OF PENNSYL'IA, Philadelphia, Pa. — Med. head. 1000. Med. Head.	1000. Head of Girard. 1000 — Female seated representing Commerce, Manufactures and Arts; ship and engine in distance. Word Thousand on either side of vignette. GIRARD BANK, Philadelphia, Pa. — 1000. Head of Girard. 1000
10. Male portrait — BK OF PENNSYL'IA, Philadelphia, Pa. State Arms. — 10. Male portrait	5000 — State Arms. 5000. BK OF PENNSYL'IA, Philadelphia, Pa. — FIVE THOUSAND	Two females and Goddess of Liberty. 5 — PHILADELPHIA BK, Philadelphia, Pa. 5 — FIVE. Female seated with bird, globe and spear.
20. Male portrait. XX — 20 on Med. head. State Arms. 20 on Med. head. BK OF PENNSYL'IA, Philadelphia, Pa. — XX. Washington. 20	5. Female portrait. — GIRARD BANK, Philadelphia, Pa. Goddess of Liberty and eagle. — 5. Female portrait.	TEN. Female portrait. TEN — Female seated on bales of goods; shipping and lighthouse. Figs. 10 on either side of vignette. PHILADELPHIA BK, Philadelphia, Pa. Dog's head. — TEN. Female portrait. TEN
20. State Arms. — BK OF PENNSYL'IA, Philadelphia, Pa. Male portrait — 20. Male portrait	10. Male portrait. X — 10. Market scene; wagons, horses, pedestrians, &c. 10. GIRARD BANK, Philadelphia, Pa. — X. Male portrait. 10	20. Wm. Penn. 20 — Female on either side of escutcheon; vessels and houses in distance. Portrait on either side of vignette. PHILADELPHIA BK, Philadelphia, Pa. Spread eagle. — 20. Franklin. 20
Die Work. Washington. Die Work. — State Arms, with two double med. heads with word Fifty on each, on either side of vignette. BK OF PENNSYL'IA, Philadelphia, Pa. State Arms. — Die Work. Male portrait. Die Work.	10. Washington — GIRARD BANK, Philadelphia, Pa. Portrait of Girard; plow and ship. Word Ten on either side. — 10. Male portrait	50. Franklin. 50 — PHILADELPHIA BK, Philadelphia, Pa. Vig. Same as 20s. Washington — 50. Wm. Penn. 50
50. Male portrait — BK OF PENNSYL'IA, Philadelphia, Pa. State Arms; building on left; steamboat on right. — 50. Male portrait	20. Head of Girard. XX — 20. Female reclining; anvil and hammer; cars in distance. 20. GIRARD BANK, Philadelphia, Pa. — XX. Head of Girard. 20	100. Male portrait. 100 — PHILADELPHIA BK, Philadelphia, Pa. Vig. Same as 20s. Bee-hive. — 100. Male portrait. 100
Die. Wm. Penn. Die. — State Arms; Two double medallion heads with figs. 100 on them, on either side of vig. BK OF PENNSYL'IA, Philadelphia, Pa. State Arms. 100 — Die. Washington. Die.	L. Head of Girard. 50 — Two females seated on bale of goods; shipping, &c. Word Fifty on either side of vig. GIRARD BANK, Philadelphia, Pa. — 50. Head of Girard. L	Med. head. Female erect. — View of impending cliff; locomotive, omnibuses, forest trees, &c. Figures 500 on either side of vig. PHILADELPHIA BK, Philadelphia, Pa. Ship. — Med. head. Three females.
Male portrait. 100 — 100 Title of Bank. 100. State Arms. — Male portrait. 100	100 HUNDRED 100 — Female seated in chariot drawn by sea horses. Head of Girard on either side of vignette. GIRARD BANK, Philadelphia, Pa. — 100 HUNDRED 100	Female statue. 1000 — PHILADELPHIA BK, Philadelphia, Pa. Female seated and raising lid of chest; cars in distance. Figures 1000 on either side of vignette. Male reclining. — Female erect with horn of plenty. 1000

5 | MAN. & MECH. B'K Philadelphia, Pa. | 5
Portrait of little girl. | Vig. Two horses; houses, shrubberry &c. in background. 5 |

10 | Two females reclining; city, vessels and light-house in distance. | 10
Indian on rock with bow and arrow. | SOUTHWARK BANK Philadelphia, Pa. | Female with eagle and portrait of Washington. TEN

50 | Female seated with pen and chart; Mercury flying toward her with wand and bag of coin; Neptune with sea horses on right, ship on right. | 50
Female erect with sword and scales. | Title of Bank. 50 | Male portrait. 50

10 | MAN. & MECH. B'K Philadelphia, Pa. | 10
Female and cows: farm scene. | Large 10 and words ten dollars. X | Log-rolling, forest, yoke of oxen, &c.

X on a med. head. Justice and head of Washington on breast of eagle. | SOUTHWARK BANK Philadelphia, Pa. Female representing the Arts, angel; sea horses and car and man therein; Vessel on left. | TEN Indian with bow and arrow. TEN

Die Work. Male portrait. Die Work. | 100 Title of Bank. Female holding scales, with shield beside her. Words one hundred on the left, and on right word dollars. | ONE HUNDRED

20 | MAN. & MECH. B'K Philadelphia, Pa. | 20
Canal scene, men unloading wood and coal from canal boats; men, horse and cart, &c., city in distance. The vig. extends across the whole lower part of note.

20 Indian with bow and arrow. | SOUTHWARK BANK Philadelphia, Pa. Two females representing Agriculture and Commerce. 20 | Justice and head of Washington on breast of eagle. Washington

500 Med. head. 500 | Spread eagle holding in his beak a shield, with 500 on it. Title of Bank. | 500 Med. head. 500

50 | MAN. & MECH. B'K Philadelphia, Pa. | 50
City Arms, with female on either side; train of cars and sheaf on right; steamboat and barrel on left. The vig. extends across the whole lower part of note.

Indian with bow and arrow. 50 | SOUTHWARK BANK Philadelphia, Pa. Two females reclining; cars and vessels in distance. 50 | Same as 20s. Female portrait.

1000 1000 Med. head. 1000 | Three figures representing Agriculture, Manufactures and Commerce. Title of Bank. | 1000 Med head 1000

100 | MAN. & MECH. B'K Philadelphia, Pa. | 100
C | Train of cars, bridge, factory, &c.; cars, hills and houses in distance. | C

Same as 50s. 100 | SOUTHWARK BANK Philadelphia, Pa. Goddess of Liberty and eagle; vessels, etc. Figs 100 on either side of vig. Steamboat | Same as 20s. C

FIVE Blacksmith with implements. 5 | 5 Washington penning his Farewell Address. 5 MECHANICS' BANK, Baltimore, Md. Justice. | FIVE Ship at sea. 5

500 | MAN. & MECH. BK, Philadelphia, Pa. | 500
Male portrait | Five Hundred Dollars in ornamental die work. Red letter D. The State House as it looked in 1776.

Indian with bow and arrow. | SOUTHWARK BANK Philadelphia, Pa. 500 Steamboat. |

Letter X between two females. | 10 Ship carpenter at work; ship on way in background. MECHANICS' BANK, Baltimore, Md. | TEN Ship under full sail. TEN

1000 | MAN. & MECH. BK, Philadelphia, Pa. | 1000
M | Frame enclosing view of shipping. M M | M

5 Milkmaid with pail on her head, and stool in hand. 5 | 5 Male seated at a table, with pens and chart on it; column in back. 5 UNION BANK OF MARYLAND, Baltimore, Md. Cars. | 5 Reaper with sickle. 5

Ornamental scroll work. Stone cutter seated with tools. Ornamental scroll work. | 20 Archimedes raising the world with lever; cars on right, steamboat on left. MECHANICS' BANK, Baltimore, Md. | 20 Female with sword and scales. 20

Justice eagle and head of Washington | SOUTHWARK BANK Philadelphia, Pa. 5 Large fig. 5, two females, cupid and eagle. 5 Eagle. | Die. Wm. Penn. Die.

10 Washington 10 | Title of Bank. Female on either side of a Male portrait in a frame. Title of Bank. Vessel. | 10

FIFTY | 50 Steamboat on the water; men in a small boat in foreground; shop on the right in background. 50 MECHANICS' BANK, Baltimore, Md. FIFTY | 50 Head of Indian 50

5 Portrait of Buchanan. | Spread eagle on a rock; ship and steamboat in distance. Large V and two figure 5s in red ink. SOUTHWARK BANK Philadelphia, Pa. | 5 Wm. Penn.

20 | Portrait of Washington with female seated on either side. Title of Bank. Steamship. | 20 Male portrait 20

100 Landscape, arched bridge in background. 100 | Old fashioned train of cars; rocks, trees, &c. MECHANICS' BANK, Baltimore, Md. | 100 Train of cars crossing an arched bridge. 100

Left	Centre	Right
500 Cut through a rock with rail track. 500	Male figure seated with pole; machinery; ship in distance on left. Figs. 500 on either side. MECHANICS' BANK, Baltimore, Md. Head of Indian.	View of a monument.
Same as on right of 5s. 20	20 Ship at sea. 20 CITIZENS' BANK, Baltimore, Md. Clasped hands.	20 Female with scales; on right eagle on shield; bbls., bales, &c. 20
100	C Vig. Same as fives. C MERCHANTS' BANK Baltimore, Md. ONE HUNDRED	100
1000 Statue of Washington	Female seated her left arm resting on a large cog-wheel; on her left base and part of a column MECHANICS' BANK, Baltimore, Md. Spread eagle.	1000 Car track, rocks, trees, &c. 1000
Same as on right of 5s. 50	50 Female seated; her left arm resting on a shield on which is a building. CITIZENS' BANK, Baltimore, Md.	L Female with torch; eagle with portrait of Washington on its breast.
500	500 Vig. Same as fives. 500 MERCHANTS' BANK Baltimore, Md. FIVE HUNDRED	500
5 Train of cars; bridge with cars passing over. 5	V View of a harbor with shipping. V CHESAPEAKE B'K Baltimore, Md.	5 Washington 5
C Same as on right of 10s.	Vig. Same as 50s. 100 CITIZENS' BANK, Baltimore, Md.	Same as on right of 5s. 100
1000	1000 Vig. Same as fives. 1000 MERCHANTS' BANK Baltimore, Md. ONE THOUSAND	1000
TEN Jackson. 10	CHESAPEAKE B'K, Baltimore, Md. 10 Female seated; Mercury approaching with cornucopia; spread eagle with scroll. 10 Eagle.	TEN Van Buren 10
Same as on right of 5s. 500	D 500 CITIZENS' BANK, Baltimore, Md. Clasped hands.	500
5 Med head. 5	5 Mercury seated with globe, wand, cornucopia, &c.; safe, scales, lion, etc. 5 WESTERN BANK, Baltimore, Md. Dog's head.	Washington in a large fig. 5.
20 Jackson. 20	20 Indian and Sailor on either side of a shield surmounted by an eagle; schooner on right. 20 CHESAPEAKE B'K., Baltimore, Md. Ship.	20 Van Buren. 20
1000	1000 M CITIZENS' BANK, Baltimore, Md. Clasped hands.	Same as on right of 5s. 1000
Male and female reapers, dog, etc. TEN	X Vig. Same as fives. WESTERN BANK, Baltimore, Md. Dog's head.	X Med. head. 10
Female feeding an eagle. 50	Male portrait 50 Male portrait CHESAPEAKE B'K., Baltimore, Md. Schooner.	Indian with bow and arrow. 50
V Shipping, harbor, city in distance. V	5 Female seated with key in her hand; Phoenix on a safe; Mercury approaching with cornucopia of money; coin at side of female. 5 MERCHANTS' BANK Baltimore, Md.	FIVE Schooner. FIVE
Winged head surrounded by flags, anchor, etc.; eagle at top. XX Head of Vulcan with hammer.	20 Farmers mowing; female with rake; sheafs, etc. WESTERN BANK, Baltimore, Md. Dog's head.	20
Male portrait 100 Male portrait	Female with torch seated on a globe; on her left eagle with Washington on its breast. Figures 100 on each side of the vig. CHESAPEAKE B'K Baltimore, Md. Schooner.	Female with sea horses at her feet; cupid in the air. 100
10 Female seated with wand anchor on shield beside her. 10	X Vig. Same as fives. X MERCHANTS' BANK Baltimore, Md.	10 Female seated with a torch; eagle with portrait of Washington on his breast. 10
50 Canal scene. FIFTY	WESTERN BANK, Baltimore, Md. L Village with men, teams, cattle, &c. L Sheafs.	50 Female representing Commerce. FIFTY
V Female seated with rake in right hand shield, etc. V	5 Wharf scene—bales, barrels, boxes, &c., steamboat, shipping, &c. 5 CITIZENS' BANK, Baltimore, Md. Clasped hands.	Female representing Agriculture. Vulcan with hammer and anvil; Mercury with a bag. V
20 Female with scales; eagle on shield; bbls., bales, &c. 20	XX Vig. Same as fives. XX MERCHANTS' BANK Baltimore, Md.	20 Schooner. 20
100 Sloop; city in distance. 100	WESTERN BANK, Baltimore, Md. C Female seated; eagle on right, with medal in his beak; bbls., bales, boxes, etc. C 100	100 Female seated representing Art, carrying a male bust. 100
Same as on upper right [illegible] of the fives. 10	10 Same as fives. 10 CITIZENS' BANK, Baltimore, Md. Clasped hands.	10 Franklin seated with pen and book; book at his feet with motto on it. 10
50 Cupid on one knee looking at scroll with the words, "Capital $2,000,000." 50	L Vig. Same as fives. L MERCHANTS' BANK Baltimore, Md.	50
500	Cupid. 500 Cupid. WESTERN BANK, Baltimore, Md. Ship.	500

FIVE
Three females over figures.
B'K OF COMMERCE,
Baltimore, Md.
5
Female head

5
Schooner.
5
Cars. Two females; wagon and four horses on right; building on left. Cars.
COMMERCIAL AND FARMERS' BANK,
Baltimore, Md.
5
Female with rake and pitcher.
5

TWENTY
XX Female erect with bundle of grain, another seated with rake; shield with plow on it. XX
Title of Bank.
Schooner.
Manufacturing house in distance.
Man ploughing with two horses.

5
Ship at sea.
Sailor seated and two standing; cannon, boxes, barrels, &c., on left; and a ship on right.
B'K OF COMMERCE,
Baltimore, Md.
5
Squaw seated with cap, pole and shield.

10
Ship.
10
X Sailor and farmer with hands clasped; landscape in distance. X
Title of Bank.
10
Eagle on a shield.
10

FIFTY
50 Same as tens. 50
Title of Bank.
Schooner.
Man ploughing with two horses.
Men farming with two horses; in distance houses.

10
Female head
X
Harvest scene; four men, etc.
B'K OF COMMERCE,
Baltimore, Md.
X
Sailor.

20
Schooner.
20
Med. head. Two females with shield between them with XX on it, and surmounted by an eagle. Med. head
Title of Bank.
20
Agricultural implements.
20

ONE HUNDRED
100 Same as fives. 100
Title of Bank.
Schooner.
Man gathering corn.
100

10
Male portrait
Large vessel; steamship and another vessel in the distance. Title of bank running around vignette
10
Portrait of a girl.

50
Ship.
FIFTY
Med. head. Female seated with sickle; vessels on right; plow, bales, boxes, trees, etc., on left. Med. head
Title of Bank.
50
Statue of female with sheaf and sickle.

500
500 Same as 20s. 500
Title of Bank.
Schooner
Milkmaid churning in dairy.

20
Mechanic reclining on a boiler; cog-wheel; foundry in distance.
Large steamship; vessels in distance.
B'K OF COMMERCE,
Baltimore, Md.
Female head.
20
Sailor seated; box, bales and barrels

100
Female seated with cornucopia, cap money, wand and book.
100
Med. head. Shipping; sheaf on right; plow on left. Med. head.
Title of Bank.
100
Female seated with chart.
100

1000
Two females soaring with wand, bag, grain and sickle; figures 1000 each side.
Title of Bank.
Schooner.
Female erect with scroll.
1000

Ship.
50
B'K OF COMMERCE,
Baltimore, Md.
50 Portrait of Henry Clay. 50
FIFTY
Female erect with sword and shield; fruit and flowers at her feet.

500
Med. head.
500
Female seated on a bale surrounded by boxes, bales, &c.; anchor and shipping. Title of Bank.
Five Hundred Dollars
500
Justice.

5
Male portrait
FIVE
Male portrait; female on left with pole and cap; on right two females reclining.
HOWARD BANK,
Baltimore, Md.
Spread eagle.
F I V V E
Milkmaid and pail; house on the right.

Blacksmith erect with hammer and anvil.
100
B'K OF COMMERCE,
Baltimore, Md.
C Portrait of Washington. C
100
Locomotive.

1000
Female seated, bales, shipping, etc.
1000
Title of Bank
Three females representing Agriculture Manufactures and Commerce.
ONE THOUSAND.
1000
Female seated with sickle.
1000

10
Clay.
10
Female on either side of portrait of Washington; sheaf, farmers, etc.
HOWARD BANK,
Baltimore, Md.
Locomotive.
X
Med head and word Ten.

D
Portrait of a girl.
B'K OF COMMERCE,
Baltimore, Md.
Three females representing Agriculture, Commerce and Manufactures.
500
Sailor with quadrant; steamship in distance.

FIVE
5 Female representing Agriculture with sheaf and sickle; cattle on left. 5
FARMERS' AND PLANTERS' BANK,
Baltimore, Md.
Schooner.
Statue of Washington.
FIVE

20
J. Q. Adams.
TWENTY
Steamship, vessel, fort, etc.; city in distance.
HOWARD BANK,
Baltimore, Md.
Anvil.
20
Portrait of a Sailor.

View of a depot, buildings, factories, &c., cars, docks, drays, steamboat, vessels, boxes, bales, men, &c.
M
Male portrait
B'K OF COMMERCE,
Baltimore, Md.
1000
Vessel, houses, &c.

TEN
X Two men cradling; houses in distance. X
Title of Bank.
Vessel.
Female with sheaf and sickle; reapers in distance.
Drovers and cattle.

50
Franklin.
Female seated; safe, money bags, etc.; on her right shield with view of Monument; sheep, grain, fruit, etc.
HOWARD BANK,
Baltimore, Md.
Ship.
50
Interior of blacksmith's shop; smith resting.

Left end	Centre	Right end
100 Female leaning on a railing.	[illegible] harbor; on right schooner with letter C on the sail; city in distance. HOWARD BANK, Baltimore, Md. Shells.	100 Jackson.
Female seated representing Manufactures. 500	500 Franklin. 500 FRANKLIN BANK, Baltimore, Md. Justice.	Female seated with scroll; bridge and wagon in distance. 500
20 Med head. 20	Med. head. Sailor with flag; warehouses, bales boxes, shipping, dock, &c. Med. head. MARINE BANK, Baltimore, Md.	XX Med. head. XX
5 Franklin. FIVE	Shield with figure of Justice on it; on left Indian, squaw and papoose; on right female instructing children with globe. FRANKLIN BANK, Baltimore, Md. Head of female.	5 Milkmaid.
Three females grouped, one in centre has helmet; grain on the ground. 1000	1000 Franklin 1000 FRANKLIN BANK, Baltimore, Md. Justice.	Same as on left. 1000
50 Med. head 50	50 Female seated 50 with anchor; shipping in distance. MARINE BANK, Baltimore, Md. Dog, and safe.	50 Med. Head with 50 on it FIFTY
TEN Franklin. TEN	X Milkmaid seated; cattle, etc. FRANKLIN BANK, Baltimore, Md.	TEN
5 Clay.	FELLS POINT SAVINGS INSTITUTION of Baltimore, Md. Two sailors, one seated on merchandise, the other smoking a pipe; coil of rope, anchor, trumpet, bbls, bales, sails, etc.; steamship, schooner and brig in distance.	5 Washington
Med. head with 100 on it Male portrait. Med. head with 10 on it.	Med. head with 100 on it. Female with wand representing Commerce seated on bales, shipping on left. Med. head with 100 on it. MARINE BANK, Baltimore, Md. Two cherubs in a boat.	Full length portrait of Lafayette.
20 Ship. 20	Female with quadrant, chart, globe, compass, &c., fruit at her feet; man in the water. Franklin on either side of vig. FRANKLIN BANK, Baltimore, Md Steamboat.	20 Ship. 20
Female with flowers. TEN	10 Large steamship at sea; ship in the distance. Title of Bank.	TEN
5 Med. head. V	Med. head with 5 on it. Sailor and farmer on either side of shield eagle at the top. Med. head with 5 on it. BK OF BALTIMORE, Baltimore, Md.	5 Med. head. V
XX 20	FRANKLIN BANK, Baltimore, Md. Portrait of Franklin; on right sailor; farmer on left.	20 20
20 Ship under full sail.	Three men with plans on a table; ship yard scene, man and two horses; on right steamship. Title of Bank.	20 Female seated representing Commerce.
10 Med. head. 10	Med. head with Ten on it. Same as fives. Med. head with Ten on it. BK OF BALTIMORE, Baltimore, Md.	10 Med head. 10
50 50	Ship. Franklin. Ship. FRANKLIN BANK, Baltimore, Md. Man reclining.	50 50
50 Webster.	Three vessels; lighthouse on right in distance. Title of Bank.	FIFTY Sailor with telescope, leaning on capstan. FIFTY
20 Portrait of Z. Taylor. 20	BANK OF BALTIMORE, Baltimore, Md, Head of Indian female.	Same as vig. of fives. 20
50 Franklin.	FRANKLIN BANK, Baltimore, Md. Figure 50 and words Fifty Dollars on three large red dies.	50 Female feeding fowls.
100 Child with hen and sod chickens in her arms.	View of the Capitol at Washington. Title of Bank.	100 Sailor with telescope seated on a bale; capstan vessel, etc.
50 Portrait of D. Webster. 50	Same as fives. BK OF BALTIMORE, Baltimore, Md.	50 Female with flag and shield
100 Franklin. 100	Female representing Agriculture; farmers mowing in distance. Eagle on either side of vig. FRANKLIN BANK, Baltimore, Md. Dog, key and safe.	100 Franklin. 100
Die Work. Male portrait Die Work.	5 Ornamental figure 5 and two females with trident and figure 5; cupid, scales and eagle. MARINE BANK, Baltimore, Md. Sword and scales.	Justice; part of column, shield, anchor, &c. FIVE
100 Male portrait 100	Same as fives. 100 BK OF BALTIMORE, Baltimore, Md.	ONE HUNDRED
100 Female with [illegible]	FRANKLIN BANK, Baltimore, Md. Portrait of Franklin. ONE HUNDRED	100 Female seated; two men, [illegible] wheel, buildings, etc.
10 Sailor with flag; bales, shipping, &c. 10	X on med. head. Neptune in a shell with trident; ship on right. X on med. head. MARINE BANK, Baltimore, Md.	X Ship under full sail. X
FIVE HUNDRED	500 Same as fives 500 Med. head. Med. head. BK OF BALTIMORE, Baltimore, Md.	Female representing Agriculture. 500

Female erect with wand, shield, pillar and medallion head. 1000. 1000. Three females seated with grain, sickle, quadrant, &c.; ship in distance. BK OF BALTIMORE, Baltimore, Md. ONE THOUSAND. ONE THOUSAND.

ONE. Compt's die. ONE. Masons at work building a house. MECHANICS' AND TRADERS' BANK, Jersey City, N. J. ONE. 1. Blacksmith with sledge.

3. Compt's die. 3. Locomotive and cars; factory on left. HUDSON CO. BANK, Jersey City, N. J. Schooner. THREE. Steamer. 3.

ONE. 1. Blacksmith shoeing horse, man looking on, another by anvil. BK OF JERSEY CITY, Jersey City, N. J. 1. Compt's die.

Blacksmith shoeing a horse. 2. Compt's die. Title of Bank. TWO. 2. Sailor with telescope.

State Arms. FIVE. 5. Same as ones. HUDSON CO. BANK, Jersey City, N. J. Sea monster. 5. Locomotive. 5.

2. TWO. Female portrait. Ship under sail. Compt's die. Two on 2. Title of Bank. 2. TWO.

THREE. Title of Bank. Carpenter at work. THREE. 3. Compt's die.

X, 10; two sailors, boat, telescope and light house, &c. Compt's die. 10. View of a large building, &c. HUDSON CO. BANK, Jersey City, N. J. Shells. 10. Mechanic seated on a boiler; cars in distance.

3. THREE. THREE. Eagle on shield; female seated with anchor and quadrant. 3. Title of bank on right of vignette. 3. Compt's die.

FIVE. Mechanic, sailor and farmer making offering to winged female. Compt's die. Title of Bank. 5. 5.

Compt's die. Female instructing children. Steamship and sail-vessel; city in distance. HUDSON CO. BANK, Jersey City, N. J. Bales of goods. 20. Locomotive.

5. FIVE. V. BK OF JERSEY CITY, Jersey City, N. J. Locomotive and cars. 5. 5. Compt's die. FIVE.

X. Compt's die. Title of Bank. Locomotive and cars. TEN. 10. TEN.

FIFTY. Two males and two females with tablets and quadrant; city in distance. HUDSON CO. BANK, Jersey City, N. J. Compt's die. FIFTY. Male, two females, dog and cattle.

X. TEN. BK OF JERSEY CITY, Jersey City, N. J. Female with cornucopia. American shield; female instructing children on right; Indian, squaw and papoose, on left. TEN. TEN. 10. Compt's die.

L. Compt's die. Die Work. Title of Bank. Portrait of Washington. Figures 50, letter L and words FIFTY each side. L. L. L. 50. Die Work.

Indian family on cliff contemplating the progress of civilization. HUDSON CO. BANK, Jersey City, N. J. Compt's die. 100. Mechanic seated with hammer; factory in distance.

XX. Female with wheat. BK OF JERSEY CITY, Jersey City, N. J. XX. Compt's die. XX. 20. Female with flowers in her apron.

100. Compt's die. ONE HUNDRED surrounded by ornamental die work. Title of Bank. 100. C. 100.

1. Compt's die. Train of cars, trees, houses, chimney, sloop, hills, &c. BANK OF TIOGA, Owego, N. Y. Secured &c. 1. Webster.

50. Ship. BK OF JERSEY CITY, Jersey City, N. J. Red letter L on a shield; sailor, ship in distance on right; farmer with scythe on left. 50. Compt's die.

1. Compt's die. 1. Jersey City ferry landing; ferry boat "Aressoch" coming in the slip. HUDSON CO. BANK, Jersey City, N. J. Steamship. 1. Blacksmith with anvil and hammer.

2. Compt's die. TWO. Portrait of Daniel Webster; female, cornucopia, scythe and cars on right; female, distaff, bale, men anchor and steamship on left. BANK OF TIOGA, Owego, N. Y. Secured &c. 2. Cattle, telegraph and railroad.

100. Steamboat, hills and raft. BK OF JERSEY CITY, Jersey City, N. J. 100. C. Compt's die.

2. Compt's die. Farmer with two horses and a plough. HUDSON CO. BANK, Jersey City, N. J. Implements of war. 2. Man with basket of corn.

FIVE. 5. FIVE. Portrait of Henry Clay; milkmaid and cows on right; two females and sheaf on left. BANK OF TIOGA, Owego, N. Y. Secured &c. 5. Compt's die. F I V V E.

ONE Female feeding fowls.	ONE on fig. 1. CITY BANK, Biddeford, Me. Cherub rolling silver dollar; cars and bridge in distance.	ONE on fig. 1 Female and figure 1.
2	NORFOLK BANK, Norfolk, Conn. Drove of cattle, drover on horseback, boy in water; trees and farmhouse in distance.	2 2 TWO
3	PHILLIPSB'RGH BK Phillipsburgh, N. J. Bull's head on a shield; men dressing leather on right and female sewing shoes on left.	3 Milkmaid with pail.
TWO Female with flowers.	Boot and shoe manufactory; man at work. CITY BANK, Biddeford, Me.	2 Santa Claus.
3 Man dressing leather.	NORFOLK BANK, Norfolk, Conn. Two horses frightened at train of cars.	3 3 3
Female with flowers. 5	PHILLIPSB'RGH BK Phillipsburgh, N. J. Bridge, (two men on a raft; trees, houses and a raft in distance. 5 5	V Locomotive.
3 Washington	View of U. S. Capitol. CITY BANK, Biddeford, Me.	THREE on 3 Female seated by shield and fig. 3.
5, V & FIVE. Six men at work in an iron mill.	NORFOLK BANK, Norfolk, Conn.	5 5 5
Female with cornucopia. 10	PHILLIPSB'RGH BK Phillipsburgh, N. J. Men at work in a glass manufactory; horse in distance.	10 Blacksmith; anvil hammer and houses.
5 Portrait of a female.	CITY BANK, Biddeford, Me, Five cherubs and five silver dollars.	5 Sailor with quadrant; globe, bales, &c.
5	State arms; eagle at top; two females, cars and trees on right; female and ship on left. NORFOLK BANK, Norfolk, Conn.	FIVE FIVE 5
Indian family contemplating the progress of civilization. 20	Figure 20 with word Twenty, six times, around it on red die, PHILLIPSB'RGH BK Phillipsburgh, N. J.	20 Mechanic and implements.
X State Arms. Sailor and farmer.	CITY BANK, Biddeford, Me. Nine cherubs, ten gold dollars, female, shield and cornucopia.	10 Portrait of a female.
TEN on X. TEN	Female with cornucopia. Female with wings NORFOLK BANK, Norfolk, Conn.	10 Female with quadrant.
50 Female with cornucopia.	Fig. 50 and words Fifty dollars on three red dies. PHILLIPSB'RGH BK Phillipsburgh, N. J. Spread eagle.	50 Female with quadrant.
20 Two children	Cattle, sheep, horse, dog and two men. CITY BANK, Biddeford, Me.	XX Female representing Agriculture.
XX 20	NORFOLK BANK, Norfolk, Conn. State Arms with eagle at top and horse each side; cars, bridge and city in distance, on right and a building on left.	20
ONE HUNDRED Female erect.	PHILLIPSB'RGH BK Phillipsburgh, N. J. Fig. 100 and words One hundred dollars on three red dies.	Helmeted female. ONE HUNDRED
Fountain 50	CITY BANK, Biddeford, Me. Three female representing Agriculture, Commerce and Manufactures; ship in distance.	50 Female churning.
L FIFTY	NORFOLK BANK Norfolk, Conn. Portrait of Washington.	50 Male, two females, dog, cattle and sheaves.
1 ONE Compt's die.	Drove of cattle, four drovers on horseback; town in distance. FARMERS' BANK OF ATTICA, N. Y.	1 Female.
C Female portrait.	CITY BANK, Biddeford, Me. Large spread eagle.	C Female portrait.
ONE	Train of cars coming through arch; two laborers. PHILLIPSB'RGH BK Phillipsburgh, N. J.	1 Puddling in an iron-mill
2 Compt's die. 2	Mechanic, sailor and farmer; man and horse in distance. FARMERS' BANK OF ATTICA, N. Y.	2 Female with bundle on her head
1	NORFOLK BANK, Norfolk, Conn. Drove of cattle, horses and sheep; trees, barn, fence and boy in distance.	1 1 ONE
2 TWO	Female feeding fowls. 2 Six men at work in an iron mill. PHILLIPSB'RGH BK Phillipsburgh, N. J.	2 TWO
5 Farmer drinking.	FARMERS' BANK OF ATTICA, N. Y. 5 Male portrait 5	5 Compt's die. 5

1 — Plank road scene.
BROCKPORT EXCHANGE BANK. Vig. Female sitting with basket and fruit; vessels at a distance. Bee-hive.
1 — Superintendent's die.

ONE — Compt's die. — ONE
1 Cupid with silver dollar. 1
LUTHER WRIGHT'S BANK, Oswego, N. Y.
ONE

ONE DOLLAR
SARATOGA CO. BK. Vig. Oxen, plough, man, &c. 1 ONE 1 Female sitting, shield.
1 — Compt's die — 1

TWO — Flower girl.
BROCKPORT EXCHANGE BANK. Vig. Two mechanics at work on iron boiler. Eagle.
2 — Superintendent's die.

TWO — Compt's die. — TWO
2 Female, eagle, etc. 2
Title of Bank.
TWO — Female with wand. — TWO

---

2 — Compt's die — 2
2 Harvest scene; reapers; farming utensils and beehive. 2
SARATOGA CO. BK., Waterford, N. Y. TWO
TWO DOLLARS

---

5 — Female representing America.
Milkmaid and cows; agricultural scene. BROCKPORT EX. BK Brockport, N. Y. Farming utensils.
5 — Compt's die.

---

5 — Compt's die. — 5
Title of Bank. 5 Female, eagle, etc.
5 — Female portrait. — FIVE

---

3 — Compt's die. — 3
Vig. Sheaf, two youths, steamboat, vessels, &c. SARATOGA CO. BK. Portrait.
THREE

Female reaper. — Superintendent's die.
10 BROCKPORT EXCHANGE BANK. Head of Franklin. Bee-hive.
X — Train of cars.

---

10 — Compt's die. — TEN
X LUTHER WRIGHT'S BANK, Oswego. Vignette in centre at top. Goddess of Ocean in car on water, drawn by horses; figures in water at side; figure in front of car.
10 — Female.

---

5 — Compt's die. — FIVE
SARATOGA CO. BK. Portrait. Vig. Eagle drinking; female with pitcher; arms. Fire engine.
5 — Figure of Justice.

---

1 — Compt's die. — 1
Man plowing with two horses. MERCHANTS' BANK Syracuse, N. Y.
1 — Haymakers.

---

20 — Compt's die. — TWENTY
LUTHER WRIGHT'S BANK, Oswego. Vignette in centre at top. Shield; farmer with rake on left; female with bucket, &c. on right.
20 — Two male figures carrying female on shoulders.

---

10 — Compt's die.
SARATOGA CO. BK. Portrait, Vig. Head of Washington, female with Liberty cap and wreath in hand; eagle and shield. Fire engine.
10

---

2 — Compt's die.
Three females; setting sun; ship in distance. MERCHANTS' BANK Syracuse, N. Y.
2 — Female portrait. — TWO

ONE
FARMERS' BANK, Amsterdam. 1 Vig. Female and child standing, female with rod and scroll, and child with horn of plenty; small anchor; cogwheel; ship in the distance. Man on horseback, whip in hand.
ONE — Female in sitting posture.

---

50 — Compt's die. — 50
SARATOGA CO. BK. Vig. Two females. 50 Small die.
50 — Likeness. — 50

---

5 — Compt's die.
Female reclining; ship, sheaf, plough, sheep, etc. MERCHANTS' BANK Syracuse, N. Y.
5 — Female portrait.

TWO — Female with balance. — Eagle. — TWO
Title under vig. 2 Vig. Female with sickle in right hand; mill, sheaf of wheat, &c. Two cattle, two trees, plough, sheaf of wheat.
Two ears of corn. Man sitting in undress with horn of plenty. Two ears of corn.

State Arms. — Figure of a blacksmith, hammer and anvil.
PRATT BANK, Buffalo. Vig. A wide spread eagle and a female with a key in her hand; scales, &c.
1 — Figure of female with a rake in her hand

Ship. — Compt's die.
10 Female reclining on cornucopia. MERCHANTS' BANK Syracuse, N. Y. Still here.
X — Female portrait.

---

5 — Female with scales; eagle, key, safe, &c. — FIVE
Title under vig. V Vig. Three females in sitting posture; implements of agriculture, steamship, railroad cars, &c. V Two cattle, two trees, plough, sheaf of wheat.
5 — Med. head. — FIVE

State Arms. — Figure of a sculptor, with his mallet and chisel.
Male figure. Farming utensils. Female figure. PRATT BANK.
2 — Figure of a sailor boy.

20
MERCHANTS' BK. Syracuse. Vig. Three females, cornucopia, anchor, cars crossing bridge, trees, water, &c.; State arms, ship, city in distance.
20 — Ocean ship.

---

10 — Female with scales; key, safe, &c. — TEN
Title of Bank under vig. Vig. Two females; one on each side of a circle, one holding a sickle; implements of agriculture, steamship, casks, &c. Two cattle, two trees, plough, sheaf of wheat.
10 — Two females, eagle, Liberty staff, cap, &c. — TEN

Compt's die. — Farmer with scythe.
Neptune and Venus in a car drawn by sea horses. PRATT BANK, Buffalo, N. Y.
5 — Roman soldier, and female holding figure 5.

Compt's die. Water scene, bridge, boat, etc.	1 Indian seated; agricultural scene. FORT STANWIX BK Rome, N. Y.	ONE Female with grain and sickle. ONE

Med head and TWO. Compt's die.	Man plowing with two horses. FORT STANWIX BK Rome, N. Y. Locomotive.	2 Female head. TWO

Portrait of Wm. Penn. Compt's die.	FIVE on med. head. Signing the Declaration of Independence. FORT STANWIX BK Rome, N Y.	5 FIVE on Med. head. 5

TEN on med. head. Compt's die.	Goddess of Justice, Liberty and Truth. FORT STANWIX BK Rome, N. Y.	X TEN on med. head. 10

1 Compt's die 1	BANK OF SALINA. 1 Female standing. Indian sitting. 1 Shield. 1 1	1 Eagle. 1

2 Compt's. die. 2	BANK OF SALINA. Eagle on a rock. Female filling goblet from a pitcher. Indian in a canoe between sigs	TWO Archimedes with lever and globe TWO

3 Compt's. die. 3	BANK OF SALINA. 3 Man lying and vase. Pump-house & saltworks. 3	THREE Portrait. 3

5 Compt's. die. 5	BANK OF SALINA. FIVE Vig. lady in chariot drawn by three lions; key in uplifted hand. FIVE on right Lion's head.	5 Portrait. 5

10 Compt's. die 10	Title under vig. 10 Vig. Female resting one arm on shield; 10 male riding in car and looking suspiciously at female. Cupid on a deer.	TEN Female & X

TWENTY	BANK OF SALINA. 20 Vig. Woman with left arm on a pedestal; lion by her side. 20	20 Compt's. die. 20

50 Man sitting. 50	BANK OF SALINA. Face. Eagle. Face.	50 Compt's. die 50

Portrait. Compt's die.	ONE ONE POWELL BANK, Newburgh. Vig. Landscape; house; Liberty Pole at top; a flag.	1

2 State Arms.	POWELL BANK, Newburgh. Vig. Landscape; house; Liberty Pole; flag at top.	2 Portrait.

5 State Arms.	Portrait. POWELL BANK, Newburgh.	5 Landscape; house; Liberty Pole; flag at top, &c.

State Arms. 10	POWELL BANK, Newburgh. Portait. X X	10 Landscape; house; Liberty Pole; flag at top.

20 State Arms	POWELL BANK, Newburgh. Portrait.	20 Landscape; house; Liberty Pole; flag at top.

1 Washington	Signing Declaration of Independence. Compts die BK of WATERVILLE Waterville, N. Y.	1 Female.

TWO Compt's die. TWO	2 Female with sickle, grain, plow, etc. 2 BK of WATERVILLE Waterville, N. Y. Eagle.	Ears of corn Male figure with hammer. Ears of corn.

5 Compt's die. 5	V Three females with fig. 5 in centre. V BK of WATERVILLE Waterville, N. Y. Eagle.	5 Med head. FIVE

10 Compt's die. 10	10 Two females representing Agriculture and Commerce. BK of WATERVILLE Waterville, N. Y. Eagle and X.	10 State Arms. TEN

20 Compt's die. TWENTY	BK of WATERVILLE Waterville, N. Y. Cattle, cows, &c. 20 Dog and safe. 20	20 on med. head. Fillmore.

50 50	BK of WATERVILLE Waterville, N. Y. Indian, squaw and papoose; shield; female instructing children. Compt's die.	50 50

1 ONE Compt's die.	Puddling iron from mill. BANK OF ULSTER, Saugerties, N. Y.	1 Clay.

Portrait of Jackson. TWO State Arms.	BANK OF ULSTER, Saugerties. Vig. Local view of an iron mill and stream of water.	2 Woman in a shell, with trident in right hand.

3 Supported by three female figures.	BANK OF ULSTER, Saugerties. THREE DOLLARS. Vig. Female figure in a reclining position, with bales of goods, &c.; a ship to the right in distance.	3 State Arms.

5 Compt's. die. FIVE	Tit ' Bank under vig. Vig ridge and Falls; woman itting posture, holding undle of sticks, left arm ,esting on a shield.	5 Portrait of female.

Three female figures representing Faith, Hope, and Charity. TEN	BANK OF ULSTER, Saugerties. TEN DOLLARS Vig. Woman reclining on a bale of goods; two ships to the right and one to the left.	10 State Arms

1 State Arms. STATE BANK, Saugerties. Vig. A horse in front of a pair of oxen with a load of grain, on which a man is pitching more sheaves. 1 Washington.	ONE Compt's. die. ONE ONEIDA BANK, Utica. Vig. Dairy scene, cows, milk maid and pail. ONE Canal boat and sloop. ONE	TEN 10 Compt's. die. Vig. Female, horn of plenty, key, and eagle. MINER'S BANK. Iron safe. 10 One female holding a flag, horn of plenty and three cupids, &c. &c.
2 Compt's die. Three mechanics at a bench; vessel, etc. on the right; man and horses on left. STATE BANK, Saugerties, N. Y. 2 on shield. Female with cap; cars in distance.	TWO Compt's die. TWO 2 Train of cars, steamboat, etc. ONEIDA BANK, Utica, N. Y. II Canal boat and sloop.	ONE Compt's. die. ONE Vig. Female, shield in left hand; cornucopia beneath; ship in distance. MERCHANTS' B'K, Poughkeepsie, N. Y. 1 ONE
FIVE Water scene, boats, farms, &c. STATE BANK, Saugerties. Vig. Indian squaw and papoose. Compt's. die. 5 Female with Liberty cap; eagle standing on shield.	3 Compt's die. 3 3 Three females and an iron chest guarded by a dragon. ONEIDA BANK, Utica, N. Y. III Train of cars	TWO Compt's. die. 2 Title under vig. Vig. Female sitting, globe on her left, and pen in her right hand; ship in the distance. 2 Female head.
Compt's die. ONE 1 Man seated on a boiler, with sledge in right hand. 1 MECHANICS' BANK, Syracuse, N. Y. Man bearing a hide. ONE	5 Compt's die. 5 Title of Bank. 5 Female, Cupids and a figure 5. FIVE Female portrait. 5	3 Compt's die THREE 3 Female seated with pole, twig and shield; steamboat and sheep in distance. MERCHANTS' BANK Poughkeepsie, N. Y. 3 Female head THREE
II Compt's die Female seated; boiler, anvil, etc.; ship in distance. MECHANICS' BANK, Syracuse, N. Y. II Blacksmith with forge and anvil.	10 Compt's die. 10 X Train of cars; building with cupola. X ONEIDA BANK, Utica, N. Y. Canal Locks 10 Female. 10	V 5 Title of Bank under vig. Vig. Female holding stalk of corn in right hand and sickle in left; grain and ripe fruits at her feet, left of the centre. Canal and railroad in the distance. No margin at the left. 5 Compt's die. 5 Wm. Penn. FIVE
3 Compt's. die. 1 1 1 MECHANICS' BK. Syracuse. Vig. Two females sitting; factory, canal, cars steamboat, &c., in the distance. 3 Indian viewing a ship.	20 Portrait of a female. 20 ONEIDA BANK, Utica. XX XX Vig. Reapers with sickles and sheaf of wheat. 20 20	10 Head of Female. TEN Compt's. die. 10 Eagle, etc. Title of Bank. X 10
5 Compt's die 5 MECHANICS' BANK, Syracuse, N. Y. Two Indians one with gun and the other lying down. Secured, etc. FIVE 5 Cars. Waterfall. FIVE	1 Compt's die. ONE Female with eagle, shield and head of Washington. MINERS' BANK, Fredonia, N. Y. Machinery. ONE Female and fig. 1.	20 Female standing. MERCHANTS' BK. Poughkeepsie. Compt's. die. 20 Male figure; hammer in hand. Steamship in the distance. 20
X Sailor, light-house, etc. Compt's die. Locomotive and cars. MECHANICS' BANK, Syracuse, N. Y. 10 Female and anvil. 10	2 Compt's die TWO Female and Liberty cap. 2 Justice with scales. MINERS' BANK. Sheaf of wheat. 2 Female on bale of goods scales, &c.	50 Compt's. die. 50 MERCHANTS' BK. Poughkeepsie. Vig. Infant figure holding shield with figure 50; cask and cornucopia on the left; money chest and dollars on the right. 50
Female with sword in right hand. Compt's. die. TWENTY MECHANICS' BK. Syracuse. Vig. Female sitting; two sheafs of wheat, scroll and globe; car in distance. 20 Canal view	FIVE 5 Compt's. die. Title of Bank under vig Vig. Large female holding Mercury wand and resting on bale of goods. Small motto. 5 Male and female; figure 5 holding scales, &c.	100 Compt's. die 100 MERCHANTS' BK. Poughkeepsie. Vig. Goddess of Liberty, eagle and shield, with letter C in centre of it. 100

ONE Woman with a sickle in her hand. ONE	DELAWARE BANK. Vig. An eagle resting on a broken tree-top	1 Enclosing full length female with distaff in one hand and wand in the other.

V 5 V State Arms.	Vig. Liberty with a sheaf of wheat in right hand, sickle in left; men cradling grain; farm-house in distance; train of cars crossing a viaduct. WYOMING CO. B'K.	FIVE Head of Seward.

XX Indian with lance and bow in right hand.	CHITTENANGO BK. Vig. Comptroller's die; Indian reclining on a shield, bow and arrow in right hand; eagle flying above him, water on his right and left; on his right deer and canoe in water; on his left three deers, one lying down and two standing. Safe.	20 Portrait of D'l Webster TWENTY

TWO Compt's die. TWO	2 Female with sickle and wand sheafs, mill, canal, railroad, etc. 2 DELAWARE BANK, Delhi, N. Y. TWO Agricultural scene.	Ears of corn. Man surrounded by devices. Ears of corn.

TEN State Arms.	Vig. Portage Bridge, and train of cars passing over. WYOMING CO. B'K.	10 X Indian bow and arrows slung at his side.

50 Portrait of Franklin Pierce. Compt's. die.	CHITTENANGO BK. Vig. Commercial scene; vessels and houses in background; in foreground female sitting; cornucopia in right hand, sceptre in left, and sheaf of wheat on her right; cornucopia of coin on left; also, barrels, boxes, &c. Steamboat.	Angel, or Cupid holding shield with 50 on it. Female standing.

THREE Liberty leaning on one side, and Justice sitting on the other. 1 1 1	DELAWARE BANK. Vig. Female Indian in frame of State arms; on each side figures representing Agriculture and Commerce. Cows and sheep.	3

Head of Washington. ONE	Female sitting. Eagle, cap, shield. Female with staff standing. BK. OF THE PEOPLE, Lowville. Deer.	1 Compt's. die.

1 Compt's. die. 1	1 Vig. Female, male, grain, farmers' and mechanics' tools, &c. 1 MECHANICS' AND FARMERS' BANK, Albany.	ONE Head of Washington ONE

5 Compt's. die. FIVE	DELAWARE BANK. Vig. Female figures representing Agriculture and Commerce, on each side of a large 5, in which a woman is seated; railroad, canals, &c. in the background. V each side. Agricultural scene.	5 Medallion head. FIVE

Eagle, cap, shield and female. Compt's. die.	BK. OF THE PEOPLE, Lowville. 3 Head of Washington. Agricultural implements, sheaf of wheat, &c.	3 1 1 1

2 Compt's die. 2	2 Title of Bank. II Vig. Same as ones.	2 Washington 2

10 Compt's. die. TEN	DELAWARE BANK. Vig. Figures Agriculture and Commerce on each side of a shield; ships, railroad, canals, &c. in the distance. Agricultural scene.	10 Medallion work. TEN

5 Compt's. die.	Vig. Large spread eagle and shield. 5 BK. OF THE PEOPLE, Lowville.	FIVE Head of Washington. FIVE

3 Compt's die. 3	3 Title of Bank. 3 Vig. Same as ones.	3 Washington 3

TWENTY Compt's. die. TWENTY	Title of Bank under vig. Vig. Female seated at a table, on which is a map, quadrant, compasses, &c.; scientific apparatus near her, and globe behind. Steamship in the distance. 20 each side Agricultural scene.	Die work. XX Die work.

1 Female with Liberty cap in left hand.	CHITTENANGO BK. Vig. Comptroller's die; landscape in the back ground; wood chopper with left foot and axe on stump; one dollar leaning against another stump; wagon, house, &c. Sheaf of wheat, plough, shovel, rakes, sickle.	ONE Two females one with rake, the other turning hay with a fork.

5 Compt's. die	Title of Bank under vig. FIVE DOLLARS Vig Female, male, grain, farmers' and mechanics' tools, &c. 5 on right	FIVE A female standing, upwards, and resting her right hand upon a shield, upon which is a 5.

1 ONE State Arms	Vig. Two horse team; boy on one horse; man attaching team to plough. WYOMING CO. BK.	ONE Head of Franklin.

2 Portrait of female. TWO	Title under vig. Vig. Compt's die; cows lying and standing; milk maid sitting, pail on right arm; farmer with rake lying down, hat in left hand; two gold dollars before him. Dog, his name, "Wave," on collar.	2 Two females.

X Compt's. die.	MECHANICS' AND FARMERS' BANK, Albany. Vig. Female, male, grain, farmers' and mechanics' tools, &c.	X TEN

2 State Arms.	Vig. Train of railroad cars passing under bridge; also, telegraph posts; stage coach crossing a bridge. WYOMING CO. BK.	TWO Head of Washington TWO

5 FIVE Compt's. die.	Title under vig. Vig. Indian reclining on left; hunter on right, sitting, gun in right hand resting on ground, and pointing left hand at train of cars; five gold dollars at feet. Smith reclining on anvil. bet. sigs.	FIVE Figure 5 embellished so as to show an eagle; battle-axe, woman sitting, head of Washington. FIVE

50 FIFTY 50	MECHANICS' AND FARMERS' BANK, Albany. Vig. Mechanic seated. FIFTY DOLLARS 50	

3 State Arms.	Vig. Blacksmith shop; smith shoeing horse, and another at the bellows. WYOMING CO. BK.	3 Head of Webster.

Female with balances; sheaf of wheat, etc. Compt's die.	10 Harvest scene; farmers nooning; loading wagon, etc. CHITTENANGO BK., Chittenango, N. Y. Female reclining.	10 Squaw and papoose.

ONE HUNDRED	MECHANICS' AND FARMERS' BANK, Albany. Vig. Mechanic seated, ONE HUNDRED 100	

1 — Figure of Knicker-bocker on his travels. — Compt's die. | Vig. Sheep washing; man with staff, dog, &c.; man ploughing in the distance. Fig. 1 with letter ONE running across it. BANK OF KINDER HOOK. ONE | The word NEW YORK is printed on a large figure 1

20 | Vig. Female reclining, holding in right hand a sledge hammer; in left, a pair of compasses; vessel under sail in the distance; four men working with horse on right in the distance. State Arms with Cupid on either side. CITIZENS' BANK, Fulton. | TWENTY — Portrait of female. — 20

5 — Two females sitting, eagle and balances between | Sheaf of wheat, sickle, basket and child. Child in sail vessel; an angel above. SENECA CO. BANK | 5 — Medallion head.

TWO — Justice with scales and sword; eagle, safe, key &c. — TWO | 2 2 Vig. Female holding sickle in right hand, and extending sceptre with left hand; sheaf of wheat, horn of plenty. In the distance a mill and stream, canal, train of cars, &c. BANK OF KINDER HOOK. Anchor between sigs. | Ears of corn. — Blacksmith with his implements.

1 — 1 | ROME EXCHANGE BANK. Vig. Locomotive with train of cars. 1 | ONE — Female with sheaf, and mechanic. — Compt's die.

10 — Two females sitting, &c. — 10 | 10 Vig. Man reclining; left arm on vessel containing fluid, which is running out. SENECA CO. BANK. Eagle. | 10

---

5 — Justice with scales and sword; eagle, safe, key, &c. — FIVE | Vig. Group of four figures, two horses, chariot, plough and rake, horn of plenty; ships in distance. BANK OF KINDER-HOOK. Anchor between sigs. | 5 — Minerva with head of Medusa on a shield; reapers in the distance. — FIVE

2 — Compt's die. | Vig. Watering horses. 2 ROME EXCHANGE BANK. | 2 — Female gleaner.

20 — Two females sitting, &c. — 20 | SENECA CO. BANK. XX Indian full length. XX | Gentleman, with hat and cane in hand.

---

10 — Justice with scales and sword; eagle, safe, key, &c. — TEN | Vig. Shield bearing coat of arms of the several States; female on either side; rake, plough, sickle, barrels; steamship, factory, train of cars, and city in the distance. BANK OF KINDER-HOOK. Anchor between sigs. | 10 — State Arms. — TEN

5 — Compt's die. | Milking scene 5 5 ROME EXCHANGE BANK. | FIVE — Female with scales and sword.

FIFTY | SENECA CO. BANK. 50 Indian full length. Two females sitting, eagle and balances. | FIFTY

TWENTY — Compt's die — Man whetting scythe. | 20 Cattle, sheep, two men, horse and Dog. BANK OF KINDER-HOOK. Kindertook, N. Y. Bee hive. | Twenty across the Bill on either side of 20

10 — Compt's die. | Vig. Falls of Niagara in the distance; female figure in foreground. X ROME EXCHANGE BANK. | 10 — Head of Washington.

Indian. | 100 C Two females sitting; eagle, balances, &c. SENECA CO. BANK. | C — 100

ONE — State Arms — ONE | Portrait and flag. Female in sitting posture, staff in left hand. 1 A CITIZENS' BANK, Fulton. | ONE — Female in standing position, left hand resting on ledge of rock, right arm elevated; monument in view. — ONE

20 — Compt's die. | ROME EXCHANGE BANK. XX Reaping scene | 20 — Female head

ONE — State Arms. — ONE | MERCHANTS' BK. Lancaster. Title under vig. Vig. Spread eagle, cask, bale, shield, &c.; village, stars, cars, &c. in background | 1 — Female reading book, guard chain on her neck chin resting on hand, in circle. — ONE

TWO — Human figure seated, left foot slightly elevated, right arm extended. — State Arms. | 2 Vig. Female resting, flag, &c CITIZENS' BANK, Fulton. Sail vessel. | Large 2, word TWO twice, and portrait.

1 — Two females sitting, with eagle and balances between. — 1 | SENECA CO. BANK. Vig. Locomotive and train of cars. Machine. | Shield with large figure 1 on it. — Medallion head. — ONE

TWO — State Arms. — TWO | MERCHANTS' BK. Lancastor. 2 Vig. Female and spread eagle, in clouds; one hand holds horn of plenty and the other over eagle's neck; shield in eagle's talons. | 2 — Half nude female sitting, scroll overreaching her. — TWO

---

5 | Vig. Female in sitting position, left arm reclining upon shield; motto of U. S. inscribed; eagle, &c. Figure 5 with re-presentations of cupid. B CITIZENS' BANK, Fulton. | FIVE — State Arms. — FIVE

2 — Two females sitting, eagle and balances between. — TWO | Vig. Farmer ploughing with team of horses 2 SENECA CO BANK | Female with Liberty Cap

5 — State Arms. — FIVE | MERCHANTS' BK. Lancaster. Vig. An old gentleman, two young men, and one lad, washing sheep; trees, dog, and water factories in the background. | 5 — Female standing with wreath in right hand and leaning other arm on large figure 5, with Liberty Cap.

State Arms. — Monument. X Woman with [illegible]; boy in ship. | 10 Vig. Two human figures—male and female; female holding sickle and sheaf of wheat; house and farm scene to the right in the distance; vessel under sail to the left. CITIZENS' BANK. Fulton. | 10 — Portrait. — 10

3 — Two females sitting; eagle and balances between. — 3 | SENECA CO. BANK. 3 Females reclining on monument; bunch of grain in hand; vessel in distance 3 Canoe. | 3 — 3

10 — State Arms. — TEN | MERCHANTS' BK. Lancaster. Vig. An old man sitting nearly naked, sledge in right hand, chin on the left; shield with letter X on it; anvil, anchor, &c. Water, steamship, vessel, cars, &c in the background | 10 — Female standing, right hand on capstan and left hand hold of her dress.

ONE	PALMYRA BANK, Lyons, N. Y.	
Female with sickle in right hand, and grain in left hand.	1 Eagle standing on the bare limb of a tree. 1	Large figure 1, in the centre of which is a female.
ONE		

100	BANK OF PAWLING	100 on head.
Compt's die.	Goddess, American eagle and flag.	Man with scythe.
100		

5	MADISON CO. BANK	5
Compt's die.	5 Female upright in ellipsis. 5	Drovers and cattle in circular frame.
5		5

TWO	PALMYRA BANK.	Vulcan with forge: in right hand hammer resting on anvil; in left hand horn of plenty, &c.
Justice sitting, sword in right hand and scales in left; safe, eagle, key, &c	2 Female sitting; in right hand sickle, grain, plough, mills, canal, road, &c. in the distance. 2	
TWO	Farmer cradling grain.	

1	View of harbor of New York, with steamship Pacific and ship.	1
ONE	BANK OF NEWARK.	Wayne co.
Compt's die.	ONE	Cattle, telegraph and railroad.
	Female bathing.	

10	X Two figures seated, one on scroll, and the other on globe. Box between figures. X	10
Compt's die.		Male portrait
10	MADISON CO. BANK	10

5	PALMYRA BANK.	5
	V Female. 5 Female. V Female.	
Justice.	Rake, plough, farmers, reapers, mill, railroad, building, &c. — Steamship, bale, bbls, &c	Med head.
FIVE	Farmer cradling.	FIVE

TWO	Railroad trains coming out of a tunnel; two laborers standing looking on.	2
	BANK OF NEWARK	Compt's die.
Two Indian chiefs with bows.	TWO	TWO

20	MADISON CO. BANK	XX
		Female in frame.
Compt's die.	Female, spear in right hand; Eagle on fig. 20; Figs. 20 each side.	X X
		Horn of plenty.
20		XX

1	1 Three cows and two females. 1	1
Compt's die.		Franklin.
ONE	BK OF PAWLING, Pawling, N. Y.	1

Compt's die.	Three female figures seated, with shield in centre and eagle perched on it.	5
	BANK OF NEWARK	
Five, V, 5.	Locomotive.	Squaw and child seated.

50	MADISON CO. BANK	50
Compt's die.	50 Woman standing upright in canoe. 50	Male portrait
50		50

2		2
Wm. Penn	Vig. Spread eagle. Compt's die.	Spotted heifer.
2	BK OF PAWLING	2

TEN	Vig. Mechanic, sailor, and farmer making offerings to Goddess of Liberty, with eagle seated above the Goddess.	10
	BANK OF NEWARK.	Railroad with locomotive.

One on 1	Female seated; sheafs, vessels, etc. 1 on med. head on each side.	ONE
Med. head.	MERCHANTS' AND MECHANICS' BANK Troy, N. Y.	Compt's die.
1		ONE

5	Compt's die. BANK OF PAWLING	5
Compt's die.		
Washington.	Vig. Wagon and oxen, two men loading hay, four men and scythes, and female with child.	
5	Secured, etc.	FIVE

TWENTY	BANK OF NEWARK.	20
Eagle on shield, female with quadrant seated.	Vig. Ploughman and horses, with houses in distance.	
TWENTY		

TWO	Blacksmiths at work; one at anvil and one at bellows. 2 on med head on either side.	TWO
Justice.	Title of Bank.	Compt's die
TWO		TWO

X		10
Compt's die.	Vig. Drove of cattle and sheep; driver on horse with arms and whip extended.	Goddess with Liberty pole and cap and small eagle.
10	B'NK OF PAWLING.	

1		1
Compt's die.	1 Vig. Woman standing upright in canoe. 1	Profile of Canova.
1	MADISON CO. BANK	1

3	Title of Bank under vig.	THREE
Washington.	3 Vig. Female sitting on bale of goods; in background, on left, vessels, &c.; in background, on right, cars, &c. 3	
3		State Arms.

	Compt's die.	20
	Vig. Drove of cattle and sheep; driver on horse with arms and whip extended.	Female in an oval circle, dark ground.
20	B'NK OF PAWLING.	

2		2
Compt's die.	2 Building. 1st. Building. 2d. Building. 3d. 2	Profile of Canova.
2	MADISON CO. BANK.	2

5	Title of Bank under vig.	5
	5 Medallion head. Medallion head. 5	Ile 5 ad.
State Arms.	Vig. Signing Declaration of Independence. Steamboat	5

FIFTY		50
Female with sickle and sheaf of wheat on back.	Vig. Two females, one holding Liberty pole and cap; horse's head and neck between them.	Female in circle, with Duchess co. over.
Compt's die.	B'NK OF PAWLING.	

3		3
Compt's die.	3 Vig. Drovers and cattle in circular frame. 3	Profile of Linckiaen.
3	MADISON CO. BANK.	3

TEN	Water scene, vessels, steamboats, etc. Ten on med head either side.	X
Compt's die	Title of Bank.	TEN and med. head.
TEN	Eagle	10

ONE State Arms. ONE Vig. Milkmaid sitting with pail, cattle, &c. 1 BLACK RIVER B' Watertown. N. Y. 1 Boy and anvil. ONE	3 State Arms 3 WESTCHE TER CO. BANK. 3 Capture of Andre. 3 THREE 3 THREE	20 Compt's die. Vig. Dairy scene, with maid in midst of cows, in sitting posture, with pail. BK. OF DANSVILLE. Machine 20 Banking house.
TWO Compt's die. TWO Two females; one with sickle; sheaf; ship in distance. 2 on med. head. BLACK RIVER BK., Watertown, N. Y. Female. Portrait. Female.	5 State Arms. 5 WESTCHESTER CO. BANK. Capture of Andre. Woman. FIVE Sheaves of wheat. FIVE	50 Compt's. die. Vig. Indian sitting, bow in left hand, and viewing agricultural scene, chin resting on hand, elbow on words BK. OF DANSVILLE. Eagle 50 Portrait of Gov. Hunt.
Female with Liberty Cap. State Arms. BLACK RIVER BK. Watertown. Vig. Female with cornucopia; on right, female with shield, on which is inscribed the figure 3; to the left, an eagle soaring, with figure 3 under eagle. 3	10 State Arms. 10 X TEN WESTCHESTER CO. BANK. Capture of Andre. Barrels, ships, &c. TEN Gold Dollars TEN	ONE Compt's die 1 1 Wheat, fruits, and Agricultural implements. 1 ONONDAGA CO. B'K, Syracuse, N. Y. ONE ONE
FIVE Female with sickle and grain. FIVE 5 Man plowing with two horses. BLACK RIVER BK., Watertown, N. Y. 5 Compt's die	20 State Arms. 20 XX XX WESTCHESTER CO. BANK. Barrels, ships, &c. Capture of Andre. 20	2 Compt's. die. 2 ONONDAGO CO. BK. Vig. Figure of Justice in an oval TWO. Figure of Justice in an oval TWO TWO
TEN Compt's die. TEN X Two females; cars, vessels, etc. BLACK RIVER BK., Watertown, N. Y. 10 Boy and anvil. X	Capture of Andre. 50 WESTCHESTER CO. DANK. 50 50 State Arms. 50	3 Compt's die. 3 ONONDAGO CO. BK. 3 Vig. Syracuse House. 3 THREE THREE
20 Forest, and cars crossing bridge. BLACK RIVER BK Watertown Vig. Three females representing Hope, Industry, and Charity Compt's die. 20 City, shipping, &c.	100 State Arms. 100 WESTCHESTER CO. BANK. Capture of Andre. Portrait of Lieut. Gov. Van Cortlandt. 100	5 Compt's die. 5 5 Vig. State Arms, and large letter V 5 ONONDAGO CO. BK. FIVE FIVE Portrait of DeWitt Clinton. FIVE
FIFTY Female with Liberty Cap and shield. BLACK RIVER BK. Watertown. State Arms. Angel and female on right receiving a ball, and one on left, extending hand to angel. 50	1 Compt's die. ONE Vig. Man and two boys washing sheep, and dog. fig. 1 on left. BK. OF DANSVILLE. ONE DOLLAR. Banking house. NEW YORK on fig. 1.	10 Compt's die. 10 ONONDAGA CO. B'K, Syracuse, N. Y. 10 Three Females with agricultural implements. 10 TEN TEN
1 ONE WESTCHESTER CO. BANK. under vig. Vig. Goddess of Liberty seated; ship in the distance. State Arms. Sloop. ONE Capture of Andre. ONE	2 Die TWO Vig. Agricultural scene, family group; horses and man in the distance. BK. OF DANSVILLE. TWO DOLLARS. Banking house. 2 Two female figures.	TWENTY Compt's die. 20 ONONDAGO CO. BK. Vig. Woman, shield, and Indian. XX Female with sheaf of wheat. 20
Capture of Andre. 2 2 Compt's die. WESTCHESTER CO. BANK, Peekskill, N. Y. Steamboat. TWO Female and sheafs. TWO	3 Die. THREE Vig. Three figures, two male, one female, and a dog. BK. OF DANSVILLE. THREE DOLLARS. Banking house. 3 Three men, one embracing or holding up figure 3.	FIFTY Compt's die. 50 ONONDAGO CO. BK. 50 50 Vig. Cattle. Indian shooting. 50

Left end	Centre	Right end
ONE Child's head.	State Arms. View of Rondout. BANK OF RONDOUT.	1
Compt's die Female bust.	Vig. Goddess lifting drapery from an eagle. X ONEIDA VALLEY BK Safe.	Harvest scene. TEN
100 Compt's. die. 100	Vig. Washington's head quarters. HIGHLAND BANK, Newburgh. ONE HUNDRED DOLLARS	100 Head of De Witt Clinton C
Blacksmith and anvil. TWO	2 State Arms. BANK OF RONDOUT The letters TWO, with the words Two Dollars running across.	TWO Two female heads.
Compt's die Mermaid and Neptune blowing sea horn. Ship.	20 Baronial coat of arms. ONEIDA VALLEY BK Female in sitting posture.	20
1 Compt's. die.	FOREST CITY BANK Waukesha, Wis. Load of hay, men, horses, barn, etc. Dog's head.	ONE 1
Farmer and milkmaid.	3 State Arms. BANK OF RONDOUT. The letters THREE, with the words Three Dollars running across.	THREE Head of Washington
1 Compt's. die. 1	HIGHLAND BANK, Newburgh. 1 1 Vig. Entrance to the Highlands from Newburgh Bay; steamboat under way, with ship at dock in foreground; mountains in distance, with schooner under way in left of vig. ONE DOLLAR.	1 Head of Gen. Jas Clinton. ONE
2 Compt's die.	FOREST CITY BANK Waukesha Wis. Liberty, eagle and shield, on half globe. Shield.	TWO Female and fig. 2.
Two females supporting a figure 5 with three Cupids around them.	State Arms. BANK OF RONDOUT. The letters FIVE, with the word Five Dollars running across.	5 Portrait.
2 Compt's. die. 2	HIGHLAND BANK, Newburgh. Portrait of Washington. Head of Clinton. Vig. Same as above. TWO DOLLARS. 2	2 A man gathering corn.
Compt's die. 3	FOREST CITY BANK Waukesha, Wis. Ship and other vessels at sea. Hands.	3 Sailor at wheel.
Two females supporting a shield, on which is a small view of Rondout. 10	State Arms. BANK OF RONDOUT. TEN DOLLARS.	10 Portrait.
3 Compt's. die. 3	HIGHLAND BANK, Newburgh. 3 Head of Clinton. Vig. Same as above. THREE DOLLARS.	3 3
1 Compt's. die.	UTICA CITY BANK. Vig. Head of Martha Washington.	1 Head of a girl.
ONE Squaw State Arms.	ONEIDA VALLEY BK 1 Vig. Female, eagle, smie, key, &c. Sheaf of wheat, plough, &c.	1 Female resting on figure 1, and holding ear of corn.
5 Compt's. die. 5	5 5 Vig. Same as above. HIGHLAND BANK, Newburgh. FIVE. Head of Washington.	Head of Lafayette. Washington on horseback.
Compt's die. Mower sharpening scythe.	Vig. Liberty and Ceres; shield with crest of the head of a horse; iron chest, vessels, &c.; horn of plenty, sheaf of wheat, &c. UTICA CITY BANK.	TWO Blacksmith at a forge.
Indian with bow and arrows, &c. Compt's die.	ONEIDA VALLEY BK 2 Vig. Female, eagle, Cap of Liberty. Title to the right. State Arms.	2 Two females with spear, sword and scales. TWO
10 Compt's. die. 10	10 10 Vig. Washington's head-quarters at Newburgh. HIGHLAND BANK, Newburgh. TEN DOLLARS. X	TEN Same as the vig. of 1s, 2s, 3s, and 5s, except the schooner, which is not seen. TEN
Compt's die. Head of Franklin on dark ground.	Vig. Indian and woodman; shield. UTICA CITY BANK. Secured, etc.	5 Girl with a hay rake. V
Indian with bow and arrows in right hand and a compass belt in left.	ONEIDA VALLEY BK 3 Vig. Female, shield; staff with Cap of Liberty. Steamboat and railroad in the distance. Dog and safe.	3 Female, sword and scales.
20 Compt's. die. 20	20 Vig. Washington's head quarters at Newburgh. HIGHLAND BANK, Newburgh. TWENTY DOLLARS. Head of Washington.	XX Head of Jas. Clinton 20
Compt's die. Head of Washington on dark ground.	UTICA CITY BANK. Vig. Two half length female figures.	10 Female with ear of corn in right hand and figure X in left.
5 Med. head. FIVE	Compt's die. Shield surmounted by an eagle; man on right; female with sword and scales on left. ONEIDA VALLEY BK Oneida, N. Y. Compt's die.	5 Female with flowers and anchor.
50 Compt's. die. 50	Vig. Washington's head quarters. HIGHLAND BANK, Newburgh. FIFTY DOLLARS.	50 Head of De Witt Clinton. 50
Compt's die. 20	Female with the wand of Mercury; factory, viaduct, cars, steam vessels, etc. UTICA CITY BANK, Utica, N. Y. XX XX Secured, etc.	20 State of New York. Female seated between 2 and 0.

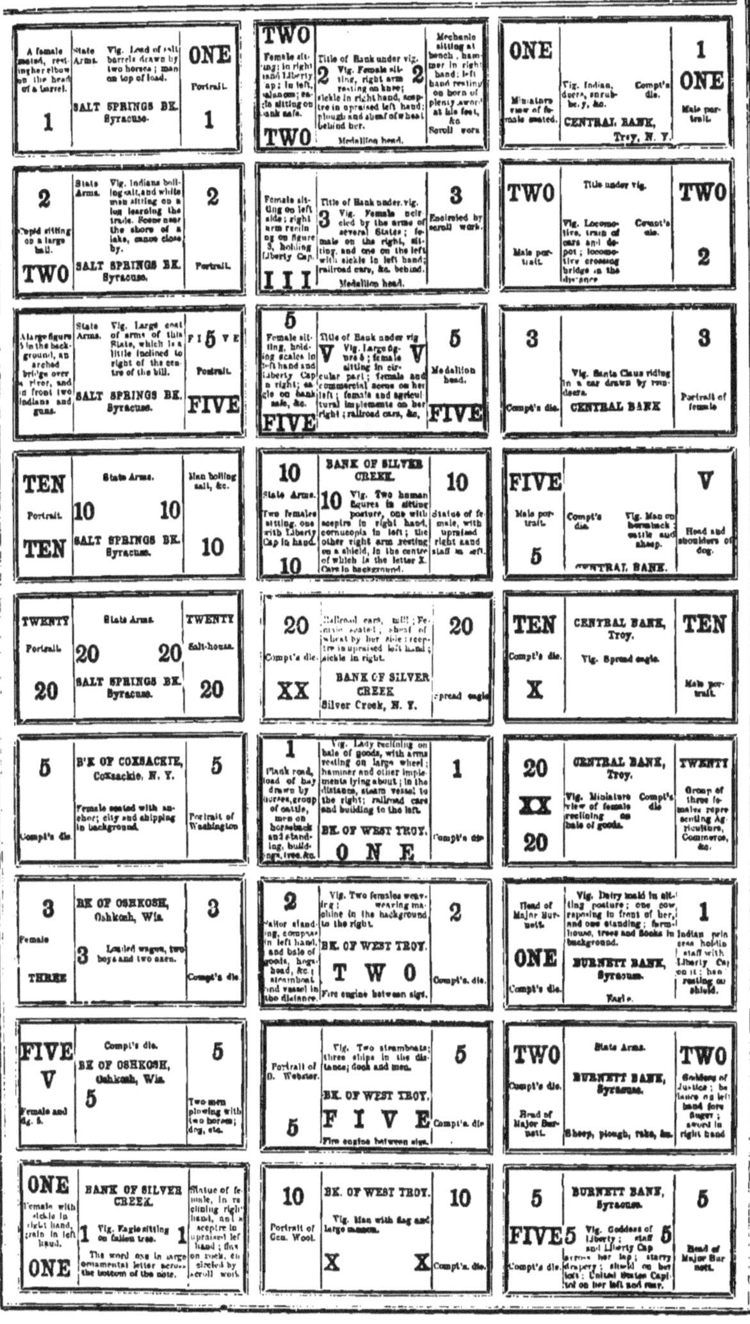

A female seated, resting her elbow on the head of a barrel. 1 — State Arms. Vig. Load of salt barrels drawn by two horses; man on top of load. SALT SPRINGS BK. Syracuse. — ONE Portrait. 1

TWO Female sitting; in right hand Liberty cap; in left, balances; eagle sitting on bank safe. TWO — Title of Bank under vig. 2 Vig. Female sitting, right arm resting on knee; sickle in right hand, sceptre in upraised left hand; plough and sheaf of wheat behind her. 2 Medallion head. — Mechanic sitting at bench, hammer in right hand; left hand resting on horn of plenty, sword at his feet, &c. Scroll work.

ONE Miniature view of female seated. — Vig. Indian, deers, shrubbery, &c. Compt's die. CENTRAL BANK, Troy, N. Y. — 1 ONE Male portrait.

2 Cupid sitting on a large ball. TWO — State Arms. Vig. Indians boiling salt, and white man sitting on a log learning the trade. Scene near the shore of a lake, canoe close by. SALT SPRINGS BK. Syracuse. — 2 Portrait.

Female sitting on left side; right arm resting on figure 3, holding Liberty Cap. III — Title of Bank under vig. 3 Vig. Female encircled by the arms of several States; female on the right, sitting, and one on the left with sickle in left hand; railroad cars, &c. behind. Medallion head. — 3 Encircled by scroll work.

TWO Male portrait. — Title under vig. Vig. Locomotive, train of cars and depot; locomotive crossing bridge in the distance. Compt's die. — TWO 2

A large figure 5 in the background, an arched bridge over a river, and in front two Indians and guns. — State Arms. Vig. Large coat of arms of this State, which is a little inclined to right of the centre of the bill. SALT SPRINGS BK. Syracuse. — FI 5 VE Portrait. FIVE

5 Female sitting, holding scales in left hand and Liberty Cap in right; eagle on bank safe, &c. FIVE — Title of Bank under vig V Vig. Large figure 5; female sitting in circular part; female and commercial scene on her left; female and agricultural implements on her right; railroad cars, &c. V — 5 Medallion head. FIVE

3 Compt's die. — Vig. Santa Claus riding in a car drawn by reindeers. CENTRAL BANK — 3 Portrait of female.

TEN Portrait. TEN — State Arms. 10 10 SALT SPRINGS BK. Syracuse. — Man boiling salt, &c. 10

10 State Arms. Two females sitting, one with Liberty Cap in hand. 10 — BANK OF SILVER CREEK. 10 Vig. Two human figures in sitting posture, one with sceptre in right hand, cornucopia in left; the other right arm resting on a shield, in the centre of which is the letter X. Cars in background. — 10 Statue of female, with upraised right hand staff in left.

FIVE Male portrait. 5 — Compt's die. Vig. Man on horseback, cattle and sheep. CENTRAL BANK. — V Head and shoulders of dog.

TWENTY Portrait. 20 — State Arms. 20 20 SALT SPRINGS BK. Syracuse. — TWENTY Salt-house. 20

20 Compt's die. XX — Railroad cars, mill; Female seated, sheaf of wheat by her side; sceptre in upraised left hand; sickle in right. BANK OF SILVER CREEK Silver Creek, N. Y. — 20 Spread eagle.

TEN Compt's die. X — CENTRAL BANK, Troy. Vig. Spread eagle. — TEN Male portrait.

5 Compt's die. — B'K OF COXSACKIE, Coxsackie, N. Y. Female seated with anchor; city and shipping in background. — 5 Portrait of Washington.

1 Plank road, load of hay drawn by horses, group of cattle, men on horseback and standing, buildings, trees, &c. — Vig. Lady reclining on bale of goods, with arms resting on large wheel; hammer and other implements lying about; in the distance, steam vessel to the right; railroad cars and building to the left. BK. OF WEST TROY. O N E — 1 Compt's die.

20 XX 20 — CENTRAL BANK, Troy. Vig. Miniature view of female reclining on bale of goods. Compt's die. — TWENTY Group of three females representing Agriculture, Commerce, &c.

3 Female THREE — BK OF OSHKOSH, Oshkosh, Wis. 3 Loaded wagon, two boys and two oxen. — 3 Compt's die.

2 Sailor standing, compass in left hand, and bale of goods, hogshead, &c.; steamboat and vessel in the distance. — Vig. Two females weaving; wearing machine in the background to the right. BK. OF WEST TROY. T W O Fire engine between sigs. — 2 Compt's. die.

Head of Major Burnett. ONE Compt's die. — Vig. Dairy maid in sitting posture; one cow reposing in front of her, and one standing; farm-house, trees and flocks in background. BURNETT BANK, Syracuse. Eagle. — 1 Indian princess holding staff with Liberty Cap on it; hand resting on shield.

FIVE V Female and fig. 5. — Compt's die. BK OF OSHKOSH, Oshkosh, Wis. 5 — 5 Two men plowing with two horses; dog, etc.

Portrait of D. Webster. 5 — Vig. Two steamboats; three ships in the distance; dock and men. BK. OF WEST TROY. F I V E Fire engine between sigs. — 5 Compt's. die.

TWO Compt's die. Head of Major Burnett. — State Arms. BURNETT BANK, Syracuse. Sheep, plough, rake, &c. — TWO Goddess of Justice; balance in left hand fore finger; sword in right hand.

ONE Female with sickle in right hand, grain in left hand. ONE — BANK OF SILVER CREEK. 1 Vig. Eagle sitting on fallen tree. 1 The word one in large ornamental letter across the bottom of the note. — Statue of female, in reclining right hand, and a sceptre in upraised left hand; flag on rock, encircled by scroll work.

10 Portrait of Gen. Wool. X — BK. OF WEST TROY. Vig. Man with dog and large mansion. X — 10 Compt's. die.

5 FIVE 5 Compt's die. — BURNETT BANK, Syracuse. Vig. Goddess of Liberty; staff and Liberty Cap across her lap; starry drapery; shield on her left; United States Capitol on her left and rear. 5 — 5 Head of Major Burnett.

Left	Centre	Right
ONE Webster. ONE	1 Two milkmaids, one erect, the other seated. 1 BANK OF LANSINGBURGH, Lansingburgh, N. Y. Horse's head.	Franklin. Compt's die. Male portrait.
TWO Male portrait TWO	2 Three reapers at work in field. 2 BANK OF LANSINGBURGH, Lansingburgh, N. Y.	Female head. Compt's die. Male portrait.
FIVE V A female sitting on the point of the 5. 5	BANK OF LANSING BURGH. 5 Vig. Two men on horseback, driving cattle and sheep; dog; barn. In the distance, a small sloop. 5	Head of Washington. State Arms. Chief Justice Marshall.
10 on med. head. Washington	Compt's die. Eagle; light house, vessels, man plowing, etc., in distance. BANK OF LANSINGBURGH, Lansingburgh, N. Y. TEN	10 on med. head. Martha Washington
20 State Arms. 20	BANK OF LANSING BURGH. 20 Vig. Two children; one astride 20 a fish, surmounted with an eagle; one lying down; a steamboat in the distance.	20 Figure of Justice with scales; American eagle head of Washington. 20
50 State Arms. 50	BANK OF LANSINGBURGH. 50 Vig. Three females sitting; 50 sheaf of wheat, sickle, plough handle; hay-stack in rear.	50 Cattle and two men. 50
1 With two small images on either side. Compt's die. ONE	ONEIDA CO. BANK. Vig. Three small figures with scythe, anvil, and capstan; ship and railroad cars in the distance. Gold dollar between sigs.	1 Man clasping ornamental figure 1.
2 Compt's die. TWO	ONEIDA CO. BANK. Vig. Two females with man reclining on anvil and safe; steamship and railroad cars in the distance.	Large figure 2, with man whetting scythe. TWO
V With word Five running across. Compt's die. 5	ONEIDA CO. BANK. Vig. Shield, Indian and farmer on either side; canoe, Indian tents, and railroad cars in the distance. Dog between signatures	FIVE Portrait of a female,

Left	Centre	Right
10 Compt's die.	ONEIDA CO. BANK. Vig. Drover with cattle and sheep.	10 Female reclining with pen and book.
[illegible] ing frame, on which is mechanic, anvil and hammer; locomotive, steamship and vessel in the distance. 20	Comptroller's die. ONEIDA CO. BANK	Shepherd reclining, with dog and flock around him; cars in distance. 20 TWENTY
ONE Portrait of male. ONE	Vig. Female reclining on bale of goods. BK. OF SING SING	1 Compt's die.
2 2	Vig. Santa Claus riding in car drawn by reindeers. Comp's die. BK OF SING SING	TWO Portrait of Peter Stuyvesant.
3	BK. OF SING SING. Vig. Herd of cattle. 3	3 Compt's die.
V Miniature view of female representing Agriculture.	BK. OF SING SING. Vig. Steamboat under way; locomotive in distance on right; schooner and lighthouse on left in distance.	5 Compt's die
Compt's die. TEN	BK. OF SING SING. Bust of Webster. Vig. Spread eagle, with flag and talons.	X X
20 Male portrait	Vig. Locomotive and train of cars; steamer in distance, crossing bridge. BK. OF SING SING.	XX Compt's die 20
L Compt's die.	BK. OF SING SING. Vig. Group of three females representing Agriculture, Commerce, &c.	50 Male portrait.

Left	Centre	Right
C	BK. OF SING SING. Vig. Water-fall, rural scenery, house on right. Portrait of female.	100 Compt's die.
1 Compt's die. 1	1 Eagle. 1 FARMERS AND MANUFACTURES BK Poughkeepsie, N. Y. Head of horse.	ONE Portrait 1
2 Compt's die. 2	Title under vig. Male Portrait. Portrait of Washington. Arm	2 Farmer with cradle. TWO
3 Compt's die. 3	FARMERS' AND MANUFACT'RS' BK. Poughkeepsie. 3 Vig. Ship and other smaller vessels. 3	THREE Portrait. 3
5 Compt's die. 5	Title under vig. 5 Vig. Two human figures, male erect; female reclining. 5	FIVE 5 FIVE
Male and female, male erect, female reclining. 10	10 Compt's die. FARMERS' AND MANUFACT'RS BK. Poughkeepsie.	TEN 10 TEN
TWENTY	XX Compt's die. XX FARMERS' AND MANUFACT'RS' BK. Poughkeepsie.	Male and female; the one reclining, the other erect. XX
Male and female; male standing, female reclining. 50	FIFTY FARMERS' AND MANUFAC'TRS BK. Poughkeepsie. Eagle between signatures.	Compt's die 50
Male and female; the one reclining, the other erect. 100	ONE HUNDRED FARMERS' AND MANUFACT'RS' BK. Poughkeepsie. Eagle between signatures.	Compt's die. 100

1	BANK OF COOPERS-TOWN.	1
Portrait of Daniel Webster.	Vig. Woodchopper, gold dollar; farm house and waggon in distance.	Goddess of liberty supporting figure one.
Compt's die.	Shield, etc.	

2	BANK OF COOPERS-TOWN.	2
Portrait of Franklin.	Vig. Farmer, milk maid, two gold dollars, and cattle. Farm house in distance.	
Compt's. die.	Dog.	Indian with bow, spear, and arrows.

3	BANK OF COOPERS-TOWN. 3	THREE
Portrait.	Vig. Farmer, mechanic and sailor, seated, holding implements; three gold dollars lapped.	Full length female.
Compt's. die.	Goddess of liberty.	

FIVE	BANK OF COOPERS TOWN.	5
Washington.	Vig. Five figures and five gold dollars lapped.	Female holding balances; small figure 5; safe; soldier in armor.
Compt's die.	Safe.	FIVE

10	BANK OF COOPERS-TOWN.	10
Compt's die.	Vig. Two females seated, hogshead and bale of goods; farmer plowing; cars and steamship in the distance.	Female Indian holding ear of corn and small X
TEN	Safe.	

1	Vig. Milk maid and cows; farm house in distance.	1
Female leaning on pedestal with tablet in hand.	STATE BANK, Troy.	
	Grain and farming implements.	Compt's die.

Portrait of female.	Vig. Iron works with forges and workmen.	2
TWO	STATE BANK Troy.	
2	Steamboat.	Compt's die.

3	Vig. Cattle standing in water. Sheep grazing.	3
Mason at work.	STATE BANK Troy.	
	Eagle	Compt's die

5	Vig. Shield, females on either side with liberty cap and balances; ship and steamboat in distance	5
Female sitting on anvil; mechanical tools, &c.	STATE BANK Troy.	
	Farming implements.	Compt's die

Female with sickle.	10 Vig. Female 10 reclining on bale of goods barrels, &c.; house and ship in distance.	Female sitting on bale of goods.
10	STATE BANK Troy.	
	Eagle.	Compt's die.

20	STATE BANK Troy.	20
Portrait of Benjamin Franklin.	Vig. Female seated in shell with trident in hand; ship in distance.	
		Compt's die.

1	Vig. Three horses prancing; farm houses in distance.	1
	ELMIRA BANK.	Female portrait.
Compt's die.		

2	Vig. Three females bathing; cupid in centre.	2
	ELMIRA BANK.	
Compt's die,		Female portrait.

3	ELMIRA BANK.	3
	Vig. Male and female with little child.	Female portrait.
Compt's die,		

5	Vig. Raft, two men polling; female seated with child in arms.	5
	ELMIRA BANK.	Female portrait.
Compt's die.		

	Vig. Two trains of railroad cars; water and small vessel on the left; mountains in the distance. X	10
Compt's die.	ELMIRA BANK.	Portrait of Daniel Webster.

Male portrait	Vig. Train of cars, canal boat passing thro' lock; farmers at work.	20
20	ELMIRA BANK.	
		Compt's die

ONE	1 Vig. Goddess of Industry, child, bale of goods, anchor, plow, &c. Ship in distance,	ONE
Compt's die.		
ONE	GENESEE CO. BK. Leroy.	Female seated; railroad cars, &c.

TWO	2 Vig. Female 2 seated, sickle in hand, plow and grain house; cars and canal boat in distance.	Mechanic seated; hammer and cornucopia in his hands; die surrounded by corn.
Compt's die.	GENESSE CO. BK. Leroy.	
TWO	Trees and cattle.	

3	Compt's. die. Vig. Farmer plowing.	3
Franklin.	GENESEE CO. BK. Leroy.	Female with sickle and grain in each hand.
3		3

5	V Vig. Three V female figures; middle one surrounded by ornamental figure 5; steamer in distance, on right; cars on left.	5
Compt's die.	GENESEE CO. BK. Leroy.	Medallion head.
FIVE	Trees and cattle.	FIVE

X	Compt's die. Goddess of Liberty. Vig. Signing declaration of independence.	X
Male portrait.	GENESEE CO. BK. Leroy.	Male portrait.
TEN		TEN

ONE	1 Vig. Eagle. 1	Large ornamental figure one; full length female figure.
Female bust with sickle.	EXCHANGE BANK, Lockport.	
ONE	ONE in large ornamental letters.	

TWO	2 Vig. Female 2 seated; farming implements; grain; factory on left, canal boat on left.	Mechanic; die surrounded with corn.
Compt's die.	EXCHANGE BANK. Lockport.	
TWO	Eagle and safe.	

Compt's die	3 Vig. Female 3 portrait surrounded by state arms; two females on either side.	3
111	EXCHANGE BANK, Lockport.	
	Eagle and safe.	

5	V 5 Vig. Two figures, one holding key; the other cornucopia; winged monster standing upon a safe.	FIVE
Compt's die		Full length female with balances and sword.
5	EXCHANGE BANK, Lockport.	FIVE

10	Vig. Male figure soaring in clouds with cornucopia in arms. 10	X
Compt's die		Eagle perched upon a shield.
10	EXCHANGE BANK, Lockport.	TEN

1 — Head of De Witt Clinton. | MERCHANTS' BK. Albany. Vig. Scene on the Erie Canal; railroad with train of cars crossing a bridge over the canal, farmers loading hay on the left. | 1 — State Arms

TEN | X Vig. Female holding an eagle; horn of plenty at her feet; ships in distance. X BANK OF OWEGO. Compt's die. | 10 — Female with arm resting on shield; anchor on it. 10

2 — Compt's die. | DEPOSIT BANK. Vig. Drove of cattle and sheep; drover on horseback; train of cars in distance. 2 on either side. | 2 — Male portrait.

2 — Head of Washington. | Vig. Female figure representing Agriculture in the foreground; Hudson River in the distance. MERCHANTS' BK. Albany. | 2 — State Arms.

TWENTY | 20 Vig. Female holding an eagle; horn of plenty at her feet; ships in distance. 20 BANK OF OWEGO. Raft. | TWENTY — Cars passing over aqueduct; houses in distance. XX

5 — Compt's die. | Vig. Train of cars, houses in background; small sail-boat on right. DEPOSIT BANK. | 5 — Drove of cattle, drovers, dog, telegraph wires, &c.

Head of female. 3 | Vig. Three female figures supporting the figure of Cupid. MERCHANTS' BK. Albany. | 3 — State Arms

Two females with sickle and grain; mechanics, sledge, anvil and safe. Compt's. die. | BANK OF SALEM. O N E Vig. Train of cars; cattle drinking; steamship and vessel in distance. Gold dollar. | 1 — Farmer in cornfield, supporting ornamental figure 1.

Full length male portrait. ONE | 1 Vig. Canal boat and locks. Compt's die. BK. OF CHENANGO, Norwich. Canal locks. | ONE — Female, sheaf of wheat and cattle. 1

5 — Head of John Hancock. | Vig. Railroad scene on the Susquehanna River; train of cars in the foreground; bridge over the river in the distance. MERCHANTS' BK. Albany. | 5 — State Arms

2 — Compt's. die. | Vig. Female reclining on bale of goods, with Liberty cap, &c.; cars, steamship and vessel in distance. BANK OF SALEM. T W O Two gold dollars. | 2 — Farmer in cornfield with basket of corn.

2 — Canal boats and locks. 2 | Vig. Cupid inscribing on rocks. BK. OF CHENANGO, Norwich. Canal locks. | Full length figure with shield and spear. TWO

X 10 | Vig. Very fine view of one of the Collins' line of steamers at sea, under both sails and steam. Head of John Jay. MERCHANTS' BK. Albany. | 10 — State Arms.

5 — Indians, locomotive and cars. Compt's. die. | Vig. Drover on horseback; cattle and sheep. BANK OF SALEM. Five gold dollars. | 5 — Milkmaid seated; farm house in distance.

3 — Female. THREE | Vig. Female with arm resting on wheel. BK. OF CHENANGO, Norwich. Canal locks. | Full length male figure. THREE

20 — Female figure. TWENTY | MERCHANTS' BK. Albany. Vig. Goddess of Liberty; eagle to the left of the figure. | 20 — State Arms.

Compt's die. Female seated; horn of plenty and Liberty cap; village in distance. | Vig. Three figures, mechanic, farmer and sailor, implements, &c.; steamship and vessel in distance. BANK OF SALEM. | 10 — Female seated with balance and sword; locomotive in distance.

5 Compt's die. 5 | 5 Vig. Female seated. 5 BK. OF CHENANGO, Norwich. | Female seated, holding an eagle; three vessel on left in distance. V

ONE — Compt's. die. Male portrait. | Vig. Portrait with females on either side, farmers at work; ship and steamboat in distance. BANK OF OWEGO. Wheelbarrow, &c. | ONE — Female with sickle and grain. ONE

TWENTY — Goddess of Liberty. | TWENTY DOLLARS. Compt's die. BANK OF SALEM. | Female soaring in the air with garland of flowers in either hand; train of cars and houses in distance. 20

10 Compt's die. 10 | Vig. Atlas supporting globe; cars and village in distance. 10 each side. BK. OF CHENANGO, Norwich. Cupid riding deer. | Full length female. X

TWO — Compt's. die. Portrait of Taylor. | Vig. Three females surrounding frame, on which is perched an eagle; ship and cars in distance. BANK OF OWEGO. Locomotive. | TWO — Two Indians. TWO

50 — Female with sword in one hand, shield and branch in other. | BANK OF SALEM. FIFTY DOLLARS. Railroad depot. Compt's die. | 50 — Three figures, farmer, mechanic and sailor supporting die 50, with implements.

Full length female. 20 | Vig. Two female figures soaring in the air. BK. OF CHENANGO, Norwich. Canal locks. | Full length male figure. 20

5 Compt's. die. 5 | 5 Vig. Female holding an eagle; horn of plenty at her feet; ships in distance. 5 BANK OF OWEGO. Raft. | V — Female, eagle, &c. V

ONE on fig. 1. Three woodmen, one seated; team of oxen and driver in distance. | DEPOSIT BANK. 1 | 1 — Compt's. die

FIFTY | Vig. Cupid inscribing on rock. BK. OF CHENANGO, Norwich. Canal locks. | FIFTY

1 Compt's die. ONE ELKHORN BANK, Elkhorn, Wis. Elk's head. ONE Cupid. ONE Cupid. 1 Female and figure 1.	ONE Female portrait. ONE Vig. Eagle on branch of tree. PINE PLAINS BANK, Pine Plains. Cupid. Large figure one, and full length female.	ONE Compt's die. ONE Vig. Indian and squaws in canoe. BANK OF CANANDAGUIA. Canandaguia. Fowls 1 Male portrait.
TWO Female portrait. Compt's die. ELKHORN BANK, Elkhorn, Wis. Lovers at a well; barn in distance. Man. 2 Elk's head.	TWO Compt's die. TWO Vig. Female sitting, sickle in hand; canal boat and rail road cars on right; large building, plow and grain on left. 2 each side of Vig. PINE PLAINS BANK, Pine Plains. Sheaf wheat, beehive, &c. Mechanic seated with implements, die surrounded by corn	TWO Compt's die. Vig. Wild horses. BANK OF CANANDAGUIA. Canandaguia. T W O Dog. 2 Male portrait.
THREE Female portrait. Compt's die. ELKHORN BANK, Elkhorn, Wis. Train of cars; hills and village in distance. Beaver. 3 Elk's head. THREE	5 Compt's die. FIVE Vig. Four female; the centre one holding globe; lions crouching at her feet; steamer and ship on right. PINE PLAINS BANK Pine Plains. 5 Circular die; female seated, and farmer at work. FIVE	V Railroad; train of cars. BANK OF CANANDAGUIA. Canandaguia. Compt's die Vig. Female seated, arm resting on bale of goods; steamboat on left; vessel on right. 5 FIVE
Merchandise Compt's die Train of cars 1 Female with horn of plenty; bundle of sheafs at her feet. UNION BANK, Troy, N. Y. Wheels, tale, etc One on 1 Female with fig. 1.	10 Compt's die. TEN Vig. Two females and State Arms in centre, sickle and balances, barrels and steamship on right; cars and houses on left. PINE PLAINS BANK, Pine Plains. 10 Circular die goddess of liberty, and Justice. TEN	TEN Female in field of grain. Vig. Train of cars passing under bridge. Telegraph, &c. BANK OF CANANDAGUIA, Canandaguia. Dog. X Compt's die
Female standing. Compt's die. Vig. Farmer with basket of corn. 2 on left. UNION BANK, Troy. Barrels and boxes between signatures. 2 Drove of cattle TWO	1 Compt's die. Dog, safe and scales. Eagle; female reclining on anchor. EAGLE BANK, Rochester, N. Y. 1 Arm, hammer, and anvil. 1 1 Eagle and shield. ONE	FIVE Two male figures; two females seated; light house and city in distance. HARRISBURG BK. Harrisburg, Pa. 5 State House. 5 Male figure; two female sitting; yoke of oxen and dog.
THREE Female surrounded by circle with names of the different states inscribed thereon. Compt's die Vig. Locomotive and cars; depot in distance. fig. 3 on left UNION BANK, Troy. Steamboat between signatures THREE Figure three with blacksmith, sailor and farmer THREE	2 Compt's die. Vig. Female with liberty cap and shield; spread eagle. EAGLE BANK, Rochester. 2 Machinery. 2 2 Steamboat and rowboat TWO	10 Two females seated; vessel in distance. 10 Female seated with liberty cap and book in lap; houses on left. TEN on either side of vig. HARRISBURG B'K., Harrisburg, Pa. X Same as left X
5 FIVE Compt's die. Vig. Figures of females, one holding wreath over head of Washington. UNION BANK, Troy. Wheels, tale, etc FIVE 5 surrounded by females.	FIVE Compt's die. Vig. Spread eagle with scroll, E Pluribus Unum; plowman, lighthouse and ship in distance. EAGLE BANK, Rochester. 5 Steamboat. 5 5 Female portrait. FIVE	Indian. 20 20 Vig. State House. HARRISBURG BK. Harrisburg, Pa. Eagle. 20 Wash'gton. 20
10 Two male and female figures, lower extremities like a fish. Steamer Compt's die. Vig. Eagle on branch; canal locks on right, and railroad cars on left. UNION BANK, Troy. Sailor TEN 10 Sea horses	10 Compt's die. Vig. Spread eagle standing on a shield; scroll in mouth; railroad cars and vessels in distance. X EAGLE BANK, Rochester. 10 Female with sheaf of grain.	50 Female with sword and balances. 50 Vig. Female in stooping posture; man in boat and houses on right in distance. HARRISBURG BK. Harrisburg, Pa.
XX Male portrait. Compt's die. Vig. Two females on either side of shield; eagles perched on top in centre; hogshead and bale on left; cars and steamship on right. UNION BANK, Troy. Safe. 20 Vessel in circular die. TWENTY	20 Compt's die. XX Spread eagle; shield. EAGLE BANK, Rochester. Portrait. 20 Washington. TWENTY	100 Cupid reading; plow, sheaf of wheat, &c. 100 Vig. Female sitting holding liberty cap; horses in distance on right. HARRISBURG BK. Harrisburg, Pa. 100 Cupid scale-holding bust. 100

Left end	Centre	Right end
1 Surrounded by ornamental die work.	1 Compt's die. 1 CUTLER'S BANK, Palmyra.	1 Female with scales and sword.
20 Suspension bridge, two steamboats and falls. TWENTY	Compt's die. Vig. Female figure seated, three cupids riding sea animal. INTERNATIONAL BANK Buffalo. Goddess of liberty.	20 Portrait of Male
1	Vig. A man ploughing with two horses, and another sowing, two or three baskets in the fore ground; cars in the distance. 1 SOUTHBRIDGE BK, Southbridge, Mass.	1 Spread Eagle. ONE
2 Surrounded by ornamental die work.	2 Compt's die. 2 CUTLER'S BANK, Palmyra.	2 Man with sheaf of wheat.
Compt's die. Male portrait	50 INTERNATIONAL BANK Buffalo. Vig. Steamship on left ship on right, ship and steamer in distance.	50 Male portrait
2	Vig. A large building; train of cars, man with wheelbarrow, and church in the distance. 2 SOUTHBRIDGE BK, Southbridge, Mass.	2 Man pitching hay
5 Surrounded by ornamental die work.	5 Compt's die. 5 CUTLER'S BANK, Palmyra.	5 Portrait of Lady Washington.
ONE Female reclining on a fence, apron full of wheat ONE	Ship. Ship cutting in a whale. Vig. Eagle standing on shield, bundle of arrows in talons. 1 1 BARNSTABLE BK, Yarmouth, Mass.	ONE Vessel and lighthouse. ONE
3	Vig. Train of cars, church and village at the left in the distance; and a building with cupola. 3 SOUTHBRIDGE BK, Southbridge, Mass.	3 Female with a basket in her hands
10 Ornamental die work.	X Compt's die. X CUTLER'S BANK, Palmyra.	10 Portrait of Washington
2 Sailor seated on bale of goods. TWO	Eagle on cliff. TWO Eagle on cliff. 2 2 BARNSTABLE BK, Yarmouth, Mass.	2 Ship and stern of another.
FIVE	Vig. Female sitting; a hand spinning wheel on the right of the scene, factory buildings; in the distance. 5 SOUTHBRIDGE BK, Female head	5 Bust of a female FIVE
Goddess of Liberty. Compt's die.	1 Vig. Male portrait; female with trumpet and wreath of flowers on left; Cupid on right. 1 INTERNATIONAL BANK, Buffalo. Shield.	1 Female, Falls, rainbow and figure 1.
FIVE Sailor one hand on an anchor ships masts seen in back ground FIVE	Vig train of cars; church on left; factory on right in distance. V V BARNSTABLE BK, Yarmouth, Mass.	5 Schooner discharging barrels into a flat boat. 5
TEN	Vig. A female sitting between the digits 1 & 0, holding key in her left hand a cornucopia at her right hand. X SOUTHBRIDGE BK, Southbridge, Mass. Shield.	10 General Taylor. TEN
2 Male portrait.	Compt's die. Vig. 4 figures, sailor, Indian, Goddess of Liberty and Justice head in centre. INTERNATIONAL BANK Buffalo. Mechanic reclining on anvil.	2 Male Portrait.
10 Jackson 10	TEN TEN Vig. Steamboat: ship on right, schooner on left X X BARNSTABLE BK, Yarmouth, Mass.	10 Sailor at helm 10
20 Female sitting.	XX Eagle XX SOUTHBRIDGE BK, Southbridge, Mass.	20 Ship
3 Male Portrait THREE	Compt's die. Vig. Two men and horse, dog, cattle and sheep. INTERNATIONAL BANK. Buffalo. Two horses.	3 Male portrait THREE
XX Sailor leaning against anchor stock smoking. stern of vessel on left. XX	Vig. Ship and brig in foreground, pilot boat on left, and one on extreme right; two ships in the distance, between ship and brig. BARNSTABLE BK, Yarmouth, Mass. Anchor and fish gear	20 Steamboat, and ship behind 20
FIFTY Large female figure wreath in right hand FIFTY	50 50 Vig. A man holding a horse which is apparently trying to break away. SOUTHBRIDGE BK, Southbridge Mass.	FIFTY Female standing, left elbow resting on a column. FIFTY
FIVE Male portrait. Compt's die.	5 Vig R R depot, locomotive, dray-man loading goods harbor and ships INTERNATIONAL BANK Buffalo. Canal locks.	Five human figures surrounding ornamental figure 5. FIVE
FIFTY	L L Vig. Female leaning on anchor by sea-side; ship in distance wrecked. BARNSTABLE BK, Yarmouth, Mass. Boats and two men	50 50
Words one hundred across the figure 100. Bust of Gen. Harrison.	Market waggon men and team. SOUTHBRIDGE BK, Southbridge, Mass.	Words one hundred across the figure 100. Bust of Kosciusko
10 Portrait of male.	Compt's die. 10 Vig Female seated bale of goods, shipping &c; lighthouse and canal boat. INTERNATIONAL BANK Buffalo. Farmers loading hay.	Two female figures one erect, the other seated, liberty cap and eagle.
ONE HUNDRED	BARNSTABLE BK, Yarmouth, Mass. C C Vig. Female with grain on left, offering a part to a figure sitting on right with liberty pole and cap; ship in distance. Anchor and fish gear.	100 Two ships and a part of another seen on right. 100
500	Vig. Agricultural scene, female among sheaves, men in the distance reaping. 500 and D on right. SOUTHBRIDGE BK, Southbridge, Mass.	500

ONE State Arms supported by two females. 1 Head of Franklin UNION BANK, Haverhill, Mass. Eagle 1 Female. ONE	Laocoon and serpents. 1000 THOUSAND Cars Title of Bank. 1000 Ship. 1000	ONE Eagle with shield in talons; and ONE on shield. Vig. Blacksmith blowing at forge, wheel behind him; anvil in front. 1 APPLETON BANK, Lowell, Mass. 1 Farmer with sickle and bundle of grain.
TWO Farming scene; female and four males prominent; load of hay. 2 UNION BANK, Haverhill, Mass. Clasped hands 2 Boy.	1 Head of John Adams. ONE Vig. A scene in Quincy; horses, teams, stream of water, and sloops. QUINCY STONE BK. Quincy, Mass. 1 Head of John Hancock. ONE	2 Vig. Sheep washing scene. 2 APPLETON BANK, Lowell, Mass. Cow and fence. 2 Locomotive and cars.
THREE Female with horn of plenty, ships on left in distance; on right manufacturing scene. 3 UNION BANK, Haverhill, Mass. Wheels, bale, etc 3 Squaw and child.	TWO Head of John Hancock. 2 Vig. Same as ones. QUINCY STONE BK Quincy, Mass. 2 Head of John Adams. TWO	3 Vig. Blacksmith's shop, man and horse, smith at anvil; dog at his feet, and boy at forge 3 APPLETON BANK, Lowell, Mass. Dog 3 Male portrait.
5 Two females supporting an oval, with head of female enclosed, eagle on top; head of Washington on right hand corner, enclosed in large fig. 5. 5 UNION BANK, Haverhill, Mass. Imp. and products. 5	THREE John Adams 3 Vig Same as ones. QUINCY STONE BK. Quincy, Mass. 3 John Hancock. THREE	5 Vig. A person driving horses in chariot, accompanied by train of people; an angel above horses, 5 APPLETON BANK. Lowell, Mass. FIVE Medallion head 5
TEN Horse shoeing scene. Female on X. UNION BANK, Haverhill, Mass. State arms 10 Female and three children.	5 John Hancock. FIVE Vig. Same as ones. QUINCY STONE BK. Quincy, Mass. 5 John Adams FIVE	X Vig. Large house, train of cars; man with wheelbarrow; and steeple of church in distance. X APPLETON BANK, Lowell, Mass. TEN Indian female. TEN
20 Female with helmet and spear. 2 Female. 0 UNION BANK, Haverhill, Mass. XX 20 Female, globe and horn of plenty. 20	X John Hancock. TEN Vig. Same as ones. QUINCY STONE BK. Quincy, Mass. 10 John Adams TEN	20 Woman sitting, with left hand on an open book XX Eagle XX APPLETON BANK, Lowell, Mass. 20 Ship.
50 Female. Male and female. UNION BANK, Haverhill, Mass. 50 50 Cupid in boat 50	20 John Adams. TWENTY Vig. Same as ones. QUINCY STONE BK. Quincy, Mass. 20 John Hancock. TWENTY	FIFTY A woman with a wreath in her left hand. FIFTY 50 Vig. A man with his right hand on the mane of a wild horse. 50 APPLETON BANK, Lowell, Mass. FIFTY A woman with a bunch of flowers in her left hand FIFTY
100 Male seated Eagle on limb of tree cars and canal scene in distance. UNION BANK, Haverhill, Mass. 100 100 Female seated.	FIFTY Female with wreath in hand. FIFTY 50 Vig. Man and horse. 50 QUINCY STONE BK. Quincy, Mass. FIFTY Female with horn of plenty. FIFTY	Same as right Portrait of Harrison. Vig. A wharf with a large covered waggon, into which two men are rolling a hogshead. APPLETON BANK, Lowell, Mass. One Hundred and 100, Male portrait.
Agricultural scene; female prominent. 500 500 D UNION BANK, Haverhill, Mass. 500	100 Eagle. 100 C Vig. Horses, car man with truck, &c 100 QUINCY STONE BK. Quincy, Mass. C Head of Washington C	500 Vig. Woman sitting, pointing with her left hand to men reaping, and a man on horseback. 500 D APPLETON BANK, Lowell, Mass. 500

ONE 1 / Vig. Wood scene, man sowing grain; ox team. 1 ROCKPORT BANK, Rockport, Mass. / 1 Full rigged ship. ONE	2 Figure 2; spread eagle. / Steam-boat. Bust of Indian. Loco-motive. MASSASOIT BANK, Fall River, Mass. / 2 Figure 2 and spread eagle.	3 / Vig. Same as ones. 3 NEWTON BANK, Newton Agricultural implements, and horn of plenty. / 3 Female holding bow, arrows and quiver. THREE
TWO 2 / Vig. Spread eagle, cannon balls; cog wheels; train of cars. 2 ROCKPORT BANK. Rockport, Mass. / 2 TWO Schooner and sloop in a storm.	Indian, dog, and dead deer 5 / V MASSASOIT BANK, Fall River, Mass. / Eagle. 5 FIVE	5 / Vig. Same as ones, on right med. head and 5. NEWTON BANK, Newton. Engine, tender, and car. / 5 Cattle, sheep and swine. FIVE
THREE 3 / Vig. Sailor, bales of goods, shipping; houses, horse, dray, &c. 3 ROCKPORT BANK, Rockport, Mass. / 3 THREE Train of cars.	X Washington, and his horse / Female head X Female head. MASSASOIT BANK, Fall River. / 10 Indian springing bow.	10 / Vig. Same as ones. X NEWTON BANK. Newton. Farmer sitting on plough. / 10 Female Indian, left hand resting on an X
FIVE / Vig. Eagle standing on shield and anchor; town in distance; foundries, &c. Female and child in large figure five. ROCKPORT BANK, Rockport. Mass. / FIVE Girl holding basket.	Two Indians, and a steam-boat. 20 / 20 MASSASOIT BANK, Fall River. / XX Female with basket on her head.	Female seated, holding horn of plenty; shield with the word TWENTY on it. 20 / Vig. Same as ones. NEWTON BANK, Newton. Engine and cars. / 20 State Arms.
TEN / Vig. Man sitting holding sledge; train of cars crossing bridge. X ROCKPORT BANK, Rockport, Mass. / 10 Man holding sickle and sheaf of grain	FIFTY Female figure. FIFTY / 50 Horse and groom. 50 MASSASOIT BANK, Fall River. / FIFTY Female figure. FIFTY	50 Female holding spear in right hand. / Vig. Male and female figures seated with horn of plenty; rake, anchor, &c., representing Agriculture, Commerce, &c. NEWTON BANK, Newton. 50 / 50 Cupid in a sail boat; using an oar as a rudder. 50
20 Female sitting, book in her lap. / XX Eagle. XX ROCKPORT BANK, Rockport, Mass. / 20 Full rigged ship.	The figures 100, with the words one hundred across. Portrait. / Vig. Baggage waggon, and men loading it. MASSASOIT BANK, Fall River. / The figures 100, with the words one hundred Portrait.	100 Male figure seated, representing Commerce, &c. / Vig. Eagle on a branch of tree over canal, on which are loaded boats; train of cars in backgr'nd NEWTON BANK, Newton. C 100 C / 100 Female figures seated, representing agriculture.
FIFTY Female. / 50 Vig. Man training horse. 50 ROCKPORT BANK, Rockport, Mass. / FIFTY Female. FIFTY	Indian in a canoe. 500 / 500 MASSASOIT BANK, Fall River. / 500 Female with scales.	500 / Vig. Female seated, sheafs at her feet; farmers reaping and loading grain in the distance. 500 D NEWTON BANK, Newton. / 500
The figures 100, with the words one hundred across. Portrait of Harrison. / Vig. Loading covered waggons with merchandise. ROCKPORT BANK. Rockport, Mass. / The figures 100, with the words one hundred across. Fancy portrait.	1 / Vig. The apostle "Eliot" attended by three others, with bible in hand, preaching to seven Indians on a hill. Head of Franklin. 1 NEWTON BANK, Newton, Mass. Cog wheels resting on bale of cotton / 1 Head of J. Q Adams, ONE	5 Female FIVE / Vig. Female seated; beneath her, upon which she is gazing, train of cars steamboat, and canal boat; town in distance. CUMBERLAND SAVINGS BANK. Maryland. Female in water. / FIVE Female FIVE
Large figure 1, in the centre of which is an Indian. ONE / Vig. A large factory, and train of cars. MASSASOIT BANK, Fall River, Mass. / Large figure 1, in the centre of which is an Indian ONE	2 / Vig. Same as ones. 2 NEWTON BANK, Newton. State Arms. / 2 Head of Washington. TWO	X Cattle. TEN / Vig. Female holding sickle, sheaf of wheat; steamboat surrounded with ornamental work. CUMBERLAND SAVINGS BANK. Maryland. Locomotive. / Medallion head with 10 upon it. Two smiths at work.

Head of female. 1	Vig. Church, court-houses, dwellings, trees, men on horseback, carriages, &c., which is a view of Main street, Worcester QUINSIGAMOND BANK, Worcester, Mass.	1 Portrait of male.	1 A female. ONE	Vig. Interior of boot shop, with men at work. ONE on 1 on right MILFORD BANK, Milford, Mass. Locomotive and tender.	1 Washington on horseback	Two farmers, one tying up grain. 1	1 Bee hive. RANDOLPH BANK, Randolph, Mass.	1 Boots and shoes. ONE
2 Plank road scene.	Vig. Same as ones QUINSIGAMOND BANK, Worcester, Mass. Female head.	2 Houses in distance; railroad train &c.	Portrait of Henry Clay.	Vig. Same as ones. MILFORD BANK, Milford, Mass. Job waggon and two horses	2 Portrait of Gen. Taylor	TWO Boots and shoes. 2	2 Vig. Drover on horseback, cattle dogs, &c.; cattle lying down RANDOLPH BANK, Randolph, Mass. Dog and safe.	2 Portrait of Franklin.
Mason at work. 3	Vig. Same as ones. QUINSIGAMOND BANK, Worcester, Mass. Eagle.	3 Female with bundle of grain under her arm.	Portrait of Gen. Jackson	Vig. Dairy scene, maid milking, female looking on, &c. MILFORD BANK, Milford, Mass.	3 Large figure three, and three cupids.	THREE Portrait of Jefferson. 3	THREE Spr'd THREE eagle. RANDOLPH BANK, Randolph, Mass. Farmer's reaping.	3 Washington, and his horse. THREE
5	Vig Same as ones. Male Portrait. QUINSIGAMOND BANK, Worcester, Mass.	5 Female with flowers.	FIVE Male and female, FIVE	MILFORD BANK, Milford Mass. Vig. Girl with a sheaf of grain in large V.	5 Portrait of Daniel Webster.	5 Female child.	Vig. Three females, one with liberty pole and cap; Eagle on left of vig; and ship on right. V RANDOLPH BANK, Randolph, Mass. Dog and safe.	5 Boot and shoes. FIVE
10 X 10	Vig. Cincinnatus at his plough, oxen &c. 10 QUINSIGAMOND BANK, Worcester, Mass.	TEN Full length female an horn of plenty.	X Portrait of female. 10	Vig. Large spread eagle. X MILFORD BANK, Milford, Mass. Job waggon and two horses.	10 Male portrait	TEN Female in the act of pouring water from a pitcher.	10 Vig. Blacksmith shoeing horse, and man holding horse by the head. X RANDOLPH BANK, Randolph, Mass. Bundles of grain.	10 Boots and shoes.
State Arms. 20	Vig. Female figure with wings, blowing trumpet; eagle with arrows, &c. in his talons. QUINSIGAMOND BANK. Worcester, Mass.	20 Portrait of J. Q. Adams.	20 Railroad depot and locomotive and tender.	Vig. Female, arms extended; cupids on either side. MILFORD BANK, Milford, Mass. Ship and steamboat.	20 Girl with a sickle in her hand and a sheaf of straw.	20 Minerva	2 Female figure with rake. 0 RANDOLPH BANK, Randolph, Mass. XX	20 Female with horn of plenty; globe and trident. 20
50 Head of Washington.	QUINSIGAMOND BANK Worcester, Mass. Vig. Two cows in water, one lying down; two sheep resting and one standing.	50	50 Portrait of female. 50	Vig. Two females sitting; ship on left, and houses on right. MILFORD BANK, Milford, Mass. Locomotive and tender.	50 Boy picking cotton.	50 Minerva.	Vig. State Arms. Male and female figure; horn of plenty between them; rake on female's right, grain on left. RANDOLPH BANK, Randolph, Mass. 50	50 Cupid afloat. 50
100 Figure of justice with scales and sword.	Vig. House and cattle in distance; dairy maid, pail and two cows QUINSIGAMOND BANK, Worcester, Mass.	100 Head of Franklin.	100 Sailor with flag.	MILFORD BANK, Milford, Mass. Vig. Female and Cupid hovering over city.	100 Vessel under sail 100	100 Male sitting, with scroll in right hand.	Vig. Spread eagle on branch; canal boats and lock; railroad train in distance. RANDOLPH BANK, Randolph, Mass. 100	100 Female sitting with rule in right hand, and grain in left, resting on horn of plenty.
500 Three horses, balances, female, dog, basket, cattle, &c.	QUINSIGAMOND BANK, Worcester.	500 Medallion head of Washington.	500 Portrait of female.	MILFORD BANK, Milford, Mass. Vig. Three females, and Railroad train. Eagle	500 Barrel and ship 500	Female figure; reapers; team ladened with grain. 500	500 D RANDOLPH BANK, Randolph, Mass.	500

Bay State Bank	Central Bank	Tradesman's Bank
ONE State Arms. Vig. Female reclining; on her left ships; on right houses, hills, &c. BAY STATE BANK, Lawrence, Mass. 1 Indian with liberty cap, shield and quiver on back.	Female sitting with pen and scroll. ONE Vig. Female, dog and child; plough, sheaf, &c; railroad and vessels. CENTRAL BANK, Worcester, Mass. 1 Head of female.	Female with a spear and shield, holding a pillar in the form of a figure one ONE Vig. View of Chelsea; ferry boat going into slip. TRADESMAN'S BK. Chelsea, Mass. 1 State Arms.
TWO State Arms. Vig. Dog and safe; bags of specie, &c. BAY STATE BANK, Lawrence, Mass. 2 TWO 2	Indian sitting on rock; waterfall. TWO Vig. Mechanic sitting with one hand resting on wheel; female standing; mechanical implements scattered around; ship on right. CENTRAL BANK, Worcester, Mass. 2 Female with sheaf on shoulder.	TWO Vig. Same as ones. 2 TRADESMAN'S BK. Chelsea, Mass. 2 Figure of Justice.
THREE State Arms. Vig. Mechanics at work, one with sledge upraised, and the other holding chisel; steam mill and other buildings in back-ground, BAY STATE BANK, Lawrence, Mass. 3 Medallion head.	Female with flowers in her apron. 3 Title of Bank. Female sitting, sickle in hand; shield on her right, fruit, flowers &c on the ground; railroad bridge on the right. 3 Female head.	THREE Vig. Same as ones. 3 TRADESMAN'S BK. Chelsea, Mass. 3 Blacksmith and anvil.
FIVE State Arms. Portrait BAY STATE BANK, Lawrence Mass. Vig. Commercial scene; boxes and men at work; horse and dray with a load of barrels; ferry boat crossing river; houses and hills in the back-ground. 5	Female with sickle, holding figure 5. FIVE 5 CENTRAL B'K. 5 Worcester, Mass. Horse at full speed; train of cars in the distance. Female sitting on bales holding the figure 5. FIVE	Figure 5 formed by an eagle and horn of plenty; likeness of Washington in the scroll or finish. Same as ones. TRADESMAN'S BK. Chelsea, Mass. FIVE 5 Portrait of Gen. Taylor.
10 Medallion head. BAY STATE BANK, Lawrence, Mass. Vig. Carpenter at his bench, plane behind him on bench. 10 State Arms	10 Vig. Three female figures, one on the left with horn of plenty; ship on the extreme right. Title of Bank. TEN Female with sickle and sheaf.	TEN Vig. Same as ones. X TRADESMAN'S BK. Chelsea, Mass. 10 Female with horn of plenty, in right hand, left hand on anchor.
20 Mechanic with sledge on his shoulder, anvil at his side. BAY STATE BANK, Lawrence, Mass. State Arms. 20 Indian with liberty cap, shield and quiver on his back.	20 CENTRAL BANK, Worcester, Mass. Winged figures supporting the figures 20 20	20 Indian girl with bow and and arrows. Vig. Same as ones. TRADESMAN'S BK. Chelsea, Mass. TWENTY Machinery. 20 Female with 2 in right hand, and on her knee, and 0 under her left.
FIFTY State Arms. BAY STATE BANK, Lawrence, Mass. Vig. Horses and chariots; men holding horses, and one horse drinking; persons on the right. 50	50 Vig. Cows standing in water, sheep on the bank lying down. CENTRAL BANK, Worcester, Mass. Small female head. 50 Head of Washington.	50 Female in the act of stepping into the water, an urn in her left hand. Vig. Same as ones. TRADESMAN'S BK. Chelsea, Mass. FIFTY 50 Female holding a flag; three children representing Agriculture &c. all floating in the air.
100 State Arms. BAY STATE BANK, Lawrence, Mass. Spread eagle. 100	100 Vig. Female with shield; capitol in the distance. Title of Bank. Horses at water trough. 100 Head of Webster.	100 Sailor and ship in the distance. Vig. Same as ones, TRADESMAN'S BK. Chelsea, Mass. 100 100 Figure of a Stone cutter
D BAY STATE BANK, Lawrence, Mass. Vig. Female with shield, sitting on bale of goods; barrel on right, sheaf of wheat on left. 500 in dead letters. 500 State Arms.	D Vig. Female leaning on bale; ship on right. CENTRAL BANK, Worcester, Mass. 500 Eagle and shield.	500 Ship on stocks. 500 Vig. Same as ones. TRADESMAN'S BK. Chelsea, Mass. 500 State Arms 500 Steamboat. 500

Left end	Centre	Right end
ONE Man and boy driving sheep	Vig. Blacksmith shop; three men, horse, dog, &c 1 CABOT BANK, Chicopee. Mass.	1 Man whet'ng scythe.
Female rest-ing on figure 2, with sheaf.	Vig. Man watching sheep 2 CABOT BANK, Chicopee, Mass.	2 Beehive, flowers, &c.
THREE Man holding sheafs and sickle. 3	Eagle. 3 CABOT BANK, Chicopee, Mass.	3 Indian enclosed in a shield
FIVE 5	Vig. Cars, &c V CABOT BANK, Chicopee, Mass.	FIVE Blacksmith with hammer resting on figure 5. FIVE
10	Vig. Spread eagle, canal boats, and cars. X CABOT BANK, Chicopee, Mass.	TEN Cars. TEN
20 Female with chest and money bags.	XX Eagle. XX CABOT BANK, Chicopee, Mass.	20 Ship.
FIFTY Female with flowers. FIFTY	50 Man holding a horse. 50 CABOT BANK, Chicopee, Mass.	FIFTY Female with flowers. FIFTY
The words one hundred with the figures 100 running across. Male portrait.	Vig. Wharf scene; men loading waggon; ships, &c. CABOT BANK, Chicopee, Mass.	The words one hundred with the figures 100 running across. Male portrait.
1	Vig. Locomotive and train of cars; village in the distance. 1 ATTLEBOROUGH BANK, Attleborough, Mass.	1 Drover and cattle. ONE
2	Vig. Farmer on horseback; load of hay entering barn; hay-makers, cattle, &c. 2 ATTLEBOROUGH BANK, Attleborough, Mass.	2 Female with bundle of grain and sickle. TWO
3	Female with grain under left arm; reapers, dwelling house and mill in the background. 3 ATTLEBOROUGH BANK, Attleborough, Mass.	3 Spread eagle. THREE
5 Reaper sitting with a sickle in his hand. 5	Medallion head. Vig. Two females and three cherubs surrounding the figure 5. ATTLEBOROUGH BANK, Attleborough, Mass.	5 Man harvesting corn.
10 Portrait of J. Q. Adams.	Vig. Female and Eagle. ATTLEBOROUGH BANK, Attleborough, Mass. Man at work; house and bridge in background.	10 Farmer cradling grain.
20 Spread eagle. XX	Vig. Two females sitting, plough and eagle between them; factory, man ploughing, steamboat and train of cars in the distance. ATTLEBOROUGH BANK, Attleborough, Mass. Dog.	20 Male portrait. XX
50 Female bust. 50	ATTLEBOROUGH BANK, Attleborough, Mass. Vig. Eagle bearing aloft person with arms extended; cherub under each arm. State Arms.	50 Female sitting. 50
Female sitting.	100 Vig. Male and female sitting; horn of plenty between 100 ATTLEBOROUGH BANK, Attleborough Mass. A deer.	Reaper with sickle and grain.
FIVE Three females over figure 5.	B'K OF COMMERCE, Baltimore, Md.	5 Female figure head.
10 Head of female. X	Vig. Harvest scene; four men. B'K OF COMMERCE, Baltimore, Md.	X Sailor.
20 Machinist.	Steamship and ship. B'K OF COMMERCE, Baltimore, Md.	20 Sailor sitting; ship back.
Ship sailing. 50	50 Henry Clay. 50 B'K OF COMMERCE, Baltimore, Md.	FIFTY Female with dagger in right hand.
Blacksmith leaning against anvil 100	C Head of Washington C B'K OF COMMERCE, Baltimore. Md.	100 Locomotive under way.
Medallion portrait of late Cashier of the bank. 5	Vig. Female seated on ground, with right hand on a milking pail. Cows near; cottage and cattle in the distance. BANK OF CHESTER COUNTY, Westchester, Penn.	5 Male portrait.
10 Half length figure of a city lady, with basket of flowers in her hand. TEN	Vig. Farmer with scythe in hand seated on ground, dinner basket beside him; haymakers, acqueduct, and warehouses in background. BANK OF CHESTER COUNTY, Westchester, Penn.	10 Country girl with sheaf of wheat on her shoulder. TEN
20 Drove of cattle, waggon load of hay, and travelers on a plank road.	Vig. Female seated on ground; basket of corn, melons, grapes, &c., at her side; hay, vessels, town and mountains in the distance. BANK OF CHESTER COUNTY, Westchester, Penn.	20 Locomotive. 20
50 Daniel Boone and dog.	Vig. Female seated on the ground, left arm resting on shield; both hands holding a bundle of lances; Niagara falls in distance. BANK OF CHESTER COUNTY, Westchester, Penn.	50 Indian seated gun in hand.
100 Portrait of lady.	Vig. Female figure seated on a chair; eagle on shield at her feet, miner's pick and rocker behind her; viaduct and cars, city, bay, and mountains in the distance. BANK OF CHESTER COUNTY, Westchester, Penn.	100 Two cows, one standing and one lying down; milk maid sitting
500 Medallion head of Washington. 500	Vig. Two men standing and one seated on a stone in the foreground; railroad, viaduct, and city in the background; mountains in the distance. 500 on Medallion head BANK OF CHESTER COUNTY, Westchester, Penn.	Full length figure in Roman toga. 500

Female head. 1000 Female head. | Vig. Locomotive and train of passenger cars, coming round a rocky bank; city and mountains in distance. BANK OF CHESTER COUNTY, Westchester, Penn. | 1000 Medallion head of Washington. 1000

Secured by pledge, &c. ONE | 1 Vig. Female Die. with sword child, cornucopia, anchor, agricultural implements, &c; ship in distance, BANK OF ALBION, Albion, N. Y. Dog's head. | ONE Female seated, cars and vessel in distance.

10 Compt's die. 10 | TEN TEN Vig. Agricultural implements, sheaf wheat, trees. BANK OF GENESSE, Batavia, N. Y. | 10 Male portrait 10

Female portrait. Compt's die. Female portrait. | 1 Vig. Eagle on branch of tree; canal boats; train of cars. BANK OF ORLEANS, Albion, N. Y. Horse. | 1 Female; sheaf of wheat and sickle. ONE

TWO Compt's die. TWO | 2 Vig. Female seated; agricultural implements 2 factory on left; canal boat and cars on right; steamboat in distance. BANK OF ALBION, Albion, N. Y. Female reclining. | Mechanic seated, tools, horn of plenty, &c, surrounded with corn.

Female seated, holding frame, on which is man chopping; locomotive, steamship and vessel in distance. 1 | Vig. Male portrait in frame, cupids on either side. RENSSALAER COUNTY BANK, Lansingburgh, N. Y. Gold dollar. | 1 Compt's die. ONE

---

2 Compt's die. 2 | 2 Farmers harvesting, female carrying grain; barn on right in distance. BANK OF ORLEANS, Albion, N. Y. Dog's head. | 2 Female, cupid, horn of plenty.

Secured by pledge, &c. Male and female, figure 3 in centre. Compt's die. | 3 Vig. Female portrait in frame, surrounded by flags, drum, cannon, &c. BANK OF ALBION, Albion, N. Y. Female reclining. | 3

2 Compt's die. TWO | RENSSALAER COUNTY BANK, Lansingburgh, N. Y Vig. Two females holding liberty cap sword and balances, two gold dollar and eagle mounted between them; cars on left; village on right. | 2 Portrait of Washington.

---

3 Compt's die. 3 | 3 Vig. Child, dog, key and safe BANK OF ORLEANS, Albion, N. Y. Sheaf of wheat, agricultural implements. | 3 Ornamental 3 surrounding female 3

5 Compt's die. FIVE | Vig. Group of persons, centre female holding globe in one hand, key in the other, seated in chariot; lions at her feet; vessel and steamship in the distance BANK OF ALBION, Albion, N. Y. Female. | 5 Female pointing towards cars in the distance; man cradling FIVE

3 Squaw seated holding bow and spear; two Indians in canoe, and wigwams in distance. | III Compt's die. III RENSSELEAR COUNTY BANK, Lansingburgh, N. Y. Three gold dollars. Male Portrait. Three gold dollars. | 3 Female seated, holding pen and book; cars, &c., in distance.

---

5 Compt's die. 5 | 5 Vig. Portrait of Jackson in square frame. 5 BANK OF ORLEANS, Albion, N. Y. Eagle. | 5 Two men cradling; house in distance. FIVE

X Washington. 10 | Vig. Signing Declaration of Independence Compt's die BANK OF ALBION, Albion, N. Y. Mechanics arm, hammer, anvil, &c. | X Martha Washington. 10

FIVE Compt's. die. 5 | Male portrait in frame, Cupid on either side. RENSSELAER COUNTY BANK, Lansingburg, N. Y. Five gold dollars lapped. | Vig. Boy seated, basket and dog beside him; flock of sheep, cars in distance. 5 FIVE

---

10 Compt's die. 10 | 10 Vig. Two females on either side of farmer holding rake and sheaf of wheat; steamboat in distance 10 BANK OF ORLEANS, Albion. N Y. Eagle. | TEN Female soaring in air. 10

1 Compt's die. 1 | Vig. Two females ONE with sword balances, & spear; eagle mounted over a figure 1. ONE BANK OF GENESEE, Batavia, N. Y. | 1 Portrait of Washington ONE

Compt's die. Light house, large X small 10 on it, two sailors, one in boat, the other standing with glass in hand. | RENSSELAER COUNTY BANK, Lansingburgh, N. Y. Vig. Drover on horseback; drove cattle and sheep. | TEN Male portrait. 10

XX Compt's die. 20 | Vig. Vig Indian and sailor seated, the latter on cannon; 20 between them; eagle mounted, ship in full sail on right. BANK OF ORLEANS, Albion, N. Y. Canal locks. | XX Canal boat and locks. 20

2 Compt's die. 2 | 2 BANK OF GENESEE, Batavia, N. Y. Two dollars on die work. | Vig. Two females on either side figure 2; liberty cap, beehive, and flowers. TWO

20 Compt's die. | RENSSELEAR COUNTY BANK, Lansingburgh, N. Y. Vig. Two females reclining, with liberty cap, sword and balances; sun rise, eagle and vessel in distance. | 20 Male portrait.

Female, horses and chariot; cupid soaring in air Compt's die. | 50 Man cradling; farm house in distance. 50 BANK OF ORLEANS, Albion, N. Y. | Two females, book; two cupids soaring in air. 50

3 Compt's die. 3 | 3 Vig. Neptune in his car; female on left; ship in distance on right; canal on left. 3 BANK OF GENESEE Batavia, N. Y. Die | Full length Male portrait. THREE

Male figure pouring coin from horn of plenty. FIFTY | RENSSELAER COUNTY BANK, Lansingburgh, N. Y. 50 Male portrait 50 Compt's die. | Female soaring in the clouds, right arm extended over title of bank; sickle in one hand, sheaf of wheat in the other. FIFTY

---

100 | Two males, one, Neptune seated in his chariot; ship in distance. Compt's die. BANK OF ORLEANS, Albion, N. Y. | Female with balances, harbor and shipping; barrels and bales of goods. 100

5 Compt's die. 5 | 5 Vig. Three females; agricultural implements; sheaf of wheat, bee hive, &c. 5 BANK OF GENESEE, Batavia, N. Y. Die. | 5 Male Portrait 5

Male portrait 100 | RENSSELEAR COUNTY BANK, Lansingburgh, N. Y. Vig. Mechanic resting on anvil and safe, rule in one hand, hammer in the other, square, tongs, &c., beside him; two females; steamship on right, cars on left. | 100 Compt's die.

Compt's die. 1 Vig. Load of barrels. ONE
Mechanic, safe, and anvil; two females; steamship in distance.
Washington.
COMMERCIAL B'K. Glenns Falls, N. Y. ONE

---

1 Vig. Three females seated, agricultural implements, beehive, sheaf of wheat, &c. 1
Compt's die.
1 OTSEGO COUNTY B'K Cooperstown, N. Y.
Eagle.
ONE DOLLAR.

1, with letters one running across. ONEIDA CENTRAL BANK, Rome, N. Y. 1
Vig. Cattle, man plowing. Compt's die. Henry Clay.

Compt's die. Vig. Two female figures, Justice and Liberty; village on right, cars on left; eagle mounted between the two. TWO
2
Cupid on a fish. COMMERCIAL BK. Glenns Falls, N. Y. TWO

---

2 Female with scroll in each hand, on which is two dollars. 2
Deer in frame surmounted with eagle; female on either side, with sword, spear and balances.
Compt's. die.
2 OTSEGO COUNTY B'K Cooperstown, N. Y. 2

---

2 ONEIDA CENTRAL BANK, Rome, N. Y. 2
Compt's die
2 Vig. Blacksmith shop; smith shoeing horse. 2

Compt's die. Vig. Goddess of Liberty on globe; eagle and shield. THREE
3
3 COMMERCIAL B'K. Glenns Falls, N. Y. Lighthouse, and female seated.

---

3 3 Vig. Man seated within large figure 3; spears, gun, battle axe, &c. 3
3
Female with sword and balances; portrait of Washington.
Compt's die.
3 OTSEGO COUNTY B'K Cooperstown, N. Y. 3

FIVE Vig. Two females with sword and balances; beehive, &c. 5
Compt's die.
Man and woman; two boys and sheep. ONEIDA CENTTAL BANK, Rome, N.Y. 5

Compt's die. V with letters FIVE running across. Female portrait. Cupid on side. V with letters FIVE running across. 5
Squaw; Indians in canoe; wigwam in distance. COMMERCIAL B'K. Glenns Falls, N. Y. Female seated with book and pen.

FIVE 5 Vig. Pillar on which is the word Otsego and V, male and female on either side; implements of war, science and arts. Compt's die. FIVE
FIVE
OTSEGO COUNTY B'K Cooperstown, N. Y.
Fish.
FIVE
FIVE FIVE

TEN X Vig. Group of ten figures; ten gold dollars; steamboat in distance. 10
Compt's die.
10 ONEIDA CENTRAL BANK, Rome, N.Y. X

Compt's. die. COMMERCIAL B'K. Glenns Falls, N. Y. X, letters ten running across.
Mechanic seated on a boiler.
Light house; large X; sailors, glass and boat. Vig. Three figures, farmer, mechanic and sailor; implements, &c. TEN

X 10 Vig. circular die on which is X surmounted with scroll on which is Otsego; male and female on either side implements of war, science and arts. Compt's die. X
Male portrait.
TEN 10 TEN
10 OTSEGO COUNTY B'K Cooperstown, N. Y. X
Fish.

---

20 Vig. Female sitting; three cupids sporting on water. XX
Female portrait.
Compt's die. ONEIDA CENTRAL BANK, Rome, N.Y. 20

ONE Compt's die. Vig. Wood chopper seated on fallen log; horse and waggon in back ground; gold dollar on left. 1
Two large buildings; shade trees, cattle, &c.
Female erect holding figure one.
ONE HAMILTON BANK, Hamilton, N. Y.
Dog.

ONE on med. head. Spread eagle on shield in clouds. 1
ONE ADDISON BANK, Addison, N. Y.
Compt's die. One Dollar One Dollar Female.

ONE Compt's die. ONE
1 Cupid.
Female seated, holding figure one.
ONE MOHAWK VALLEY BANK, Mohawk, N. Y. Indian with bow and spear.

---

2 Compt's die. Vig. Man and woman; rake and pail; two gold dollars; cattle and farm house. 2
Two large buildings; shade trees, cattle &c.
TWO HAMILTON BANK. Hamilton, N. Y. Female raking.
Mechanic.

TWO TWO TWO 2 Rafting scene—men in boat with two birds; five males, female and child on raft; another raft in distance. 2 TWO TWO TWO
Compt's die.
TWO ADDISON BANK, Addison, N. Y. TWO on med. head.
Two Dollars Two Dollars

Indian drawing bow. 2 Vig. Farmers harvesting; two seated at lunch; female holding rake, and pouring drink. 2
Female portrait surrounded by corn.
Compt's die. MOHAWK VALLEY BANK, Mohawk, N. Y.

FIVE Vig. Five human figures; five gold dollars lapped. 5
Female portrait.
HAMILTON BANK, Hamilton, N. Y. Ornamental 5 surrounded by five human figures.
Compt's die. Farming tools.

F I V V E ADDISON BANK, Addison, N. Y. 5
Three females with sickle, quadrant, cornucopia and compass.
Compt's die.
Portrait of Martha Washington
Five Dollars Five Dollars FIVE

Indian drawing bow. 3 Vig. Female portrait in frame, surmounted with eagle; antelopes, on either side. Vessel in distance. 3
Compt's die. MOHAWK VALLEY BANK, Mohawk, N. Y.

---

10 Vig. Female reclining upon a chest; locomotive on left, female and cattle on right. 10
Compt's die. Female portrait.
TEN HAMILTON BANK. Hamilton, N. Y. TEN
Anvil and horn of plenty.

---

10 on med. head. ADDISON BANK, Addison, N. Y. 10
Portrait of Washington; female, train of cars, scythe and grain on right; female, anchor, barrels, men and ship on left.
Male portrait Compt's die.
Ten Dollars Ten Dollars

Indian drawing bow. 5 Vig. Deer and Indians in canoe hunting them. FIVE
Compt's die. MOHAWK VALLEY BANK, Mohawk, N. Y. Full length male figure.

10 10
Indian drawing bow.
Two females seated; shield between them; sickle and balances; barrels and steamship on right; train of cars and houses on left.
Eagle and deer.
Secured, etc.
Compt's die.
MOHAWK VALLEY BANK, Mohawk, N. Y.
Deer.

5
Train of cars.
Compt's die.
BANK OF MALONE, Malone, N. Y.
Large ornamental 5; waterfall, cars, Indians &c.
V

50
FORT PLAIN BANK, Fort Plain, N. Y.
50
Compt's die.
Farmers at lunch, loading hay, &c.
Full length female Indian.
FIFTY

50 50 Vig. Farmer plowing
50
Compt's die.
MOHAWK VALLEY BANK, Mohawk, N. Y.
Female portrait.
50

10
Vig. Female seated; globe and cars behind her; wheat, &c, on right.
10
Compt's die.
Franklin.
10
BANK OF MALONE, Malone, N. Y.
10

100
FORT PLAIN BANK, Fort Plain, N. Y.
100
Spread eagle.
Full length female; liberty pole and cap.
Compt's die.
Cattle and sheep; drover on horse back.

100
Vig. Indian seated, canoe on right, deer on left, letter C.
100
Reaper with sheaf of wheat and sickle.
Compt's die.
100
MOHAWK VALLEY BANK, Mohawk, N. Y.
100

20
BANK OF MALONE, Malone, N. Y.
20
Compt's die.
Male Portrait.
Vig. Cattle and sheep; farm house in distance.
TWENTY
TWENTY

1
Female portrait in centre; angel on left, cupid on right.
1
Compt's die.
GEORGE WASHINGTON BANK, Corning, N. Y.
ONE
Wheat, plow, anvil &c.
Washington.

Compt's die.
1 Vig. Female, sword, and child, anchor on left; emblems of agriculture on right.
ONE
CANAL BANK, Lockport, N. Y.
Locks
ONE
Female seated.

1
Compt's die.
Vig. Milkmaid seated, and cattle.
ONE on fig. 1
Female with spear, figure one at her feet.
Female portrait.
FORT PLAIN BANK, Fort Plain, N. Y.
Dog.
ONE

2
Vig. Washington.
2
GEORGE WASHINGTON BANK, Corning, N. Y.
Compt's die.
TWO
TWO
Shield.
Lady Washington.

TWO 2 Vig. Female seated, sickle in hand; houses, plow and wheat on left; canal and cars on right. 2
Compt's die.
CANAL BANK, Lockport, N. Y.
Mechanic in round frame, implements, &c.
TWO
Man on horseback, shrubbery &c.

TWO 2 Vig. Female; sheaf of wheat, plow, canal, rail-road cars &c. 2
Compt's die.
Mechanical tools, and horn of plenty surrounded with corn.
FORT PLAIN BANK, Fort Plain, N. Y.
TWO
Round building, &c.

5
V Vig. Indian seated beside slain deer.
5
GEORGE WASHINGTON BANK. Corning, N. Y.
Male portrait.
Female portrait.
Compt's die.

5
V Vig. Three females, centre one seated in large figure 5; barrels, steamship, &c. on the right; cars, buildings, &c, on left.
5
Compt's die.
Medallion head.
CANAL BANK, Lockport, N. Y.
Same as twos
FIVE
FIVE

3 Vig. Three females; one in frame.
3
Compt's die.
FORT PLAIN BANK, Fort Plain, N. Y.
Round building.

TEN X Vig. Sailor, Indian, Justice and liberty.
10
GEORGE WASHINGTON BANK, Corning, N. Y.
Full length Washington.
Dogs head.
Compt's die.

10
Vig. Two females, rake, plow, canal, cars, &c., on left; barrels, bales and steamship on right.
10
Compt's die.
CANAL BANK. Lockport, N. Y.
Two females in round frame.
TEN
Man horseback, locks, &c.
TEN

5
Vig. Group of females; centre one in car; lions at her feet; key in one hand; globe in other.
5
Compt's die.
Female seated; one at feet; man [illegible]
FORT PLAIN BANK, Fort Plain, N. Y.
Round building.
FIVE
FIVE

ONE and 1
BANK OF BATH, Bath, N. Y.
1
Vig. Blacksmith shop; smiths shoeing horse; one dollar.
Compt's die.
Male portrait.
ONE

ONE 1 Vig. Man on horseback watering his horse; drover and cattle.
1
Compt's die.
BANK OF MALONE, Malone, N. Y.
ONE
Franklin.

10
Vig. Two females, cars and houses on left; steamship, barrels and bales on right.
10
Compt's die.
Two females in round frame.
FORT PLAIN BANK, Fort Plain, N. Y.
TEN
Round building.
TEN

2
Vig. Drover; Cattle and sheep, cars in distance.
TWO and 2
TWO
2 2
TWO
BANK OF BATH, Bath, N. Y.
Male portrait.
Compt's die.
TWO TWO

2
Saw mill, horses and waggon; yoke of oxen; men at work, &c.
2
Compt's die.
Train of cars.
BANK OF MALONE, Malone, N. Y.
TWO
TWO

Man seated, holding C and bag of coin.
FORT PLAIN BANK, Fort Plain, N. Y.
20
Vig. Steamboats; cars; female seated, holding balances, &c; safe, steamship coin, &c.
Compt's die.
Female portrait.
TWENTY

5
Vig. Harvest scene.
5
5 5
FIVE
BANK OF BATH, Bath, N. Y.
Male portrait.
Compt's die.
FIVE FIVE

Male Portrait ONE Compt's die. MERCANTILEBANK Plattsburgh, N.Y. Vig. Two Indians in the forest—one reclining on the ground, the other in the back ground. 1 Male figure clasping ornamental figure 1.	1 Female with sheaf of wheat on her shoulder. Vig. Milk maids—one milking cow; farm house on right, vessel on left. GLENN'S FALLS BK. Glenn's Falls, N.Y. Bee-hive. 1 Compt's die.	100 Medallion Head, and figure 100 inscribed. 100 Head of Washington. Vig. Three horses. Head of Lafayette. FARMER'S [illegible]K, Reading, Penn. 100 Medallion Head, and figure 100 inscribed. 100
Compt's die. Male Portrait MERCANTILEBANK Plattsburgh, N.Y. Vig. Steamer coming into the dock. Small vessel on left. TWO Large 2. Man sharpening scythe.	2 Hunter, dog and gun. Vig. Female seated; eagle at her feet; bags of coin and pick-axe on her right; vessels in distance on left; cars on right end. GLENN'S FALLS BK. Glenn's Falls, N.Y. Agricultural implements. 2 Compt's die.	Female seated, wheat and balances. Compt's die. 1 Vig. Farmers sitting at lunch; female children and dog; team of horses. SCHOHARIE CO. BK. Schoharie, N.Y. 1 ONE Female holding rake.
Male Portrait Compt's die. MERCANTILEBANK Plattsburgh, N.Y. Vig. Mechanics at work, machinery, &c. THREE Large 3. Female seated. Man in small boat.	3 Man, woman, and child. Vig. 3 females,—one holding sword and balances; ship on right. GLENN'S FALLS BK. Glenn's Falls, N.Y. Eagle. 3 Compt's die	Indian with bow and arrows. Compt's die. 2 Vig. Gathering corn; church and cars in back ground. SCHOHARIE CO. BK. Schoharie, N.Y. Building. 2 Female portrait. TWO
5 Male Portrait MERCANTILE BANK Plattsburgh, N.Y. Vig. Train of cars. Cattle drinking Large 5. Indians, and train of cars. Compt's die.	Female with liberty cap; large building in back ground. 5 GLENN'S FALLS BK. Glenn's Falls, N.Y. Male Portrait. 5 5 Indian. 5 Compt's die.	FIVE FIVE Compt's die. Vig. Cattle, &c. SCHOHARIE CO. BK. Schoharie, N.Y. Building. 5 5, five figures around, and balances, &c.
ONE Compt's die. SPRAKER BANK, Montgomery Co., N.Y. 1 Vig. Man and boy at work; horse and sled. 1 1 Portrait of Gen. Cass.	10 Indian, gun and waterfall Vig. Spread eagle. GLENN'S FALLS BK. Glenn's Falls, N.Y. 10 Compt's die.	Vig. Spread Eagle,—flags on either side. TEN Male Portrait, SCHOHARIE CO. BK. Schoharie, N.Y. Dog. X Compt's die.
2 Indian; small vessel in distance. TWO SPRAKER BANK, Montgomery Co., N.Y. 2 2 Compt's die. 2 Waterfall hunter on his knees drinking.	FIVE Portrait of female, with sickle and sheaf. V Vig. Milkmaid and cows. 5 FARMER'S BANK, Reading, Penn. Wagon load of hay. 5 Child in imitation of blacksmith. 5	5 Portrait of Washington. 5 Head of Clay. Vig. Female resting on anchor; harbor and shipping. Head of Cass. FREDERICK CO. BK. Frederick, Md. Bee-hive. 5 3 Females supporting globe. FIVE
3 Compt's die. Vig. Two females; cars on right, vessels on left. SPRAKER BANK, Montgomery Co., N.Y. Large red 3 lengthwise. THREE Portrait of Webster.	TEN Two females in round miniature; agriculture and commerce. TEN X Vig. City Hall and scenery. FARMER'S BANK, Reading, Penn. X Farming implements. X X Portrait of female. 10	10 Dog. 10 Train of cars. Large X with heads of ten of the Presidents. Farmers loading hay. FREDERICK CO. BK. Frederick, Md. 10 TEN 10
Hunter warming himself at fire; dog and gun. V Compt's die. SPRAKER BANK, Montgomery Co., N.Y. Large figure 5 lengthwise of note. 5 Male portrait	Female reclining, shield, &c. 20 20 Vig. Farmer ploughing. FARMER'S BANK. Reading, Penn. Dog and safe. 20 medallion head. 20	XX 20 Vig. Female with sword and balances; farmer ploughing, &c. FREDERICK CO. BK. Frederick, Md. MARYLAND.
TEN Male Portrait Vig. Spread eagle with U. S. flag in talons. SPRAKER BANK. Montgomery Co., N.Y. X Compt's die. TEN	50 Double medallion head. 50 Male Portrait. Male Portrait. Vig. Large house, with cupalo, spire, and smaller house in back ground. FARMER'S BANK, Reading, Penn. 50 Double medallion head. 50	Franklin. 50 50 Vig. Female on either side of 50; sheep; spinning wheel; ship in distance, &c. FREDERICK CO. BK. Frederick, Md. Female and sheep. Washington

Male head. Full length figure with spear and shield. 100 100 Vig. Female sitting on plough; child; agricultural implements; oxen, &c. FREDERICK CO. BK. Frederick, Md. Spread Eagle. Washington.	5 Male portrait. 5 Vig. View of the city of Pittsburgh; spread eagle on the other side of the river. EXCHANGE BANK, Pittsburgh, Penn. State Arms. 5 Portrait of Millard Fillmore. 5	20 Blacksmith. 20 Vig. Female sitting, haymakers; railroad in the distance. DOYLESTOWN B'K. Doylestown, Penn. Eagle. 20 Portrait of Chief Justice Marshall.
5 Franklin. 5 Vig. Milkmaid seated. 5 FARMERS AND MECHANICS' B[illegible] of Carroll County, Westminister, Md. Horses and Waggon. FIVE Female portrait. FIVE	10 Figure of Wm. Penn standing. Female portrait. Vig. View of the interior of a rolling mill; men at work. EXCHANGE BANK, Pittsburgh, Penn. Steamer. 10 Male portrait. TEN	50 Head of female. 50 50 Vig. Female, plough oxen, two children, anvil, &c. 50 DOYLESTOWN B'K. Doylestown, Penn. 50 Head of female. 50
TEN Women drawing water from a well. Vig. Man on horse; farmer harvesting. FARMERS' AND MECHANICS' BANK, of Carroll County, Westminister, Md. X Washington. TEN	20 Portrait of Gen. Scott. TWENTY Title of Bank. Vig. Train of cars. 20 Female with sheaf. TWENTY	100 Drove of cattle. 100 100 Vig. View of Fairmount water works, female, two trains. 100 DOYLESTOWN B'K. Doylestown, Penn. 100 Drove of cattle. 100
20 Washington. TWENTY FARMERS AND MECHANICS' BANK, of Carroll County, Westminister, Md. Vig. Cattle; farmer plowing in distance. Medallion head with figure 20 on it. Male portrait.	50 Male portrait. State arms. EXCHANGE BANK, Pittsburgh, Penn. Goddess with horn of plenty in the clouds over landscape. 50	5 Farmer sitting, woman with rake and pitcher, dog behind her. FIVE Vig. Boy plowing with two horses; boy by his side with shovel on his shoulder. YORK COUNTY B'K. York, Penn. Female with sickle. 5 Wm. Penn. 5
50 Two male portraits. FIFTY Vig. Farmer plowing. FARMERS' AND MECHANICS' BANK of Carroll County, Westminister, Md. Spread eagle. 50 Ship.	100 Male portrait. 100 Vig. Eagle standing on a shield. EXCHANGE BANK, Pittsburgh, Penn. 100 Male portrait. 100	Female with grain and sickle. 10 Vig. Two boys on horseback, driving cattle and sheep; boy sitting beside a tree, dog behind him. YORK COUNTY B'K. York, Penn. Farming utensils. 10 Portrait. 10
V Female sitting; arm resting on shield. V 5 Vig. Three human figures; winged monster standing upon safe; cars in distance on right; vessel on left. 5 HONESDALE BANK, Honesdale, Pa. Dog. V Female seated; book, portrait, eagle, &c. V	500 Female holding a medallion head on a pedestal, in left a staff with two serpents coiled around it. Medallion head. Vig. A female sitting with a plant in her hand; steamboat in the distance. Medallion head. EXCHANGE BANK, Pittsburgh, Penn. A figure in the act of pouring a liquid from a vessel. 500	XX Portrait. XX Vig. Blacksmith shop; one smith at work on anvil, another shoeing horse, man standing in door. YORK COUNTY B'K. York, Penn. Farming utensils. 20 Washington.
TEN X Vig. Male and female seated; Jupiter in rear, anvil, hammer, &c. X HONESDALE BANK, Honesdale, Pa, X	Small medallion head. 1000 Small medallion head. Infant figure. Vig. Eagle standing on a log; steamer in the distance. Infant figure. EXCHANGE BANK, Pittsburgh, Penn. Small medallion head. 1000 Small medallion head.	1 Male portrait. Compt's die. Vig. Milk maid seated, cattle, &c. RANDALL BANK, Cortland, N. Y. ONE Female, sword and balances.
Female seated; ship on left; State Arms on right. XX 20 Vig. Cupid soaring in clouds. XX HONESDALE BANK Honesdale, Pa. Eagle. TWENTY	5 FIVE on figure 5 5 William Penn. A large V and a female between the heavy part of the letter and the light part. Franklin. DOYLESTOWN B'K. Doylestown, Penn. 5 Man sharpening scythe 5	2 Male portrait Vig. Three females, sword, balances, horn of plenty, &c.; vessels on right. Compt's die. RANDALL BANK, Cortland, N. Y. 2 Full length female.
FIFTY 50 L on circular die. HONESDALE BANK, Honesdale, Pa. Head of dog. Vig. Female seated, arm resting on bale of goods; Jupiter and eagle with scroll in mouth. 50	10 Female and scales. Vig. Haymakers, agricultural scene. DOYLESTOWN B'K. Doylestown, Penn. State Arms. 10 Female Indian sitting.	5 Male portrait FIVE Vig. Train of cars; group of persons; some seated; most prominent one holding gun; hat in hand extended. Compt's die. RANDALL BANK, Cortland, N. Y. 5 Female portrait.

1 | Vig. Female seated, clasping large figure one. | 1 ONE | Compt's die. | ROCHESTER CITY BANK, Rochester, N. Y. | Full length squaw, holding bow and spear. | ONE

2 | Vig. Two women over wash tub; mechanic at work, machinery, &c. | 2 | Compt's die. | PULASKI BANK, Pulaski, N. Y. | 2, with letters TWO running across. | 2 | 2 2 | 2

20 | BANK OF FAYETTEVILLE, Fayetteville, N. Y. | 20 | Indian woman, bow and spear. | Compt's die. | Vig. Train cars, village; female holding book and pen.

2 | Vig. Mechanic seated, with tools around him cars and steam factory in distance. | 2 | Compt's die | TWO | ROCHESTER CITY BANK, Rochester, N. Y. | Two females with spear, balances, &c.

3 | PULASKI BANK, Pulaski, N. Y. | 3 | Compt's die. | Vig. Three men, one holding pole. | THREE | THREE | 3 3 | 3

ONE | 1 Vig. Eagle on branch. 1 | Female portrait. | BANK OF SYRACUSE Syracuse, N. Y. | Full length female, on large 1 | ONE | Cupid and ONE running across.

3 | Vig. Farmer; team of horses and plow; steam boat in distance. | 3 | Compt's die | ROCHESTER CITY BANK, Rochester, N. Y. | Female seated. | THREE

5 | PULASKI BANK, Pulaski, N. Y. | 5 | Vig. Two horses; female mounted; figure 5 in centre; steam boat on right, cars, &c, on left. | 5, with letters FIVE running across it. | Compt's die. | 5 5 | 5

TWO | 2 Vig. Female seated; canal and cars on right; plow, wheat on left. 2 | Compt's die. | Mechanic; frame surrounded by corn. | TWO | BANK OF SYRACUSE Syracuse, N. Y. | Canal locks.

5 | Vig. Female reclining on bale of goods; shipping in distance on right; canal locks and boat on left; cars, &c. | 5 | Compt's die. | FIVE | ROCHESTER CITY BANK, Rochester, N. Y. | Male portrait.

X | Vig. Woman reclining on chest male portrait, horn of plenty, sheep, &c. | 10 | Compt's die. | X | TEN | PULASKI BANK, Pulaski, N. Y. | X X | 10

Two females, ornamental figure 3. | 3 Vig. Three females; centre one in frame. | 3 | BANK OF SYRACUSE Syracuse, N. Y. | III | Locks.

10 | Vig. Female seated, holding horn of plenty, &c; steam ship and shipping on right; canal boat, town on left. | 10 | Compt's die. | TEN | ROCHESTER CITY BANK, Rochester, N. Y. | Male portrait.

Female seated, holding spear and branch; and large figure 1. | Female portrait; cupids on either side. | ONE | Vig. Female soaring; sword in one hand, branch in the other eagle; steam ship and vessels. | BANK OF FAYETTEVILLE, Fayetteville, N. Y. | Compt's die. | 1

5 | V Vig. Three females; centre one seated with in large figure 5. V | 5 | Compt's die. | Medallion head. | BANK OF SYRACUSE Syracuse, N. Y. | Locks. | FIVE | FIVE

Compt's die. | 20 Washington. | XX | Man seated, holding 0, and bag of coin. | ROCHESTER CITY BANK, Rochester, N. Y. | Female portrait. | 20 | Columns.

Female holding figure 2. | Male portrait; cupids on either side. | 2 | BANK OF FAYETTEVILLE, Fayetteville, N. Y. | Vig. Two females; mechanic reclining against safe; implements, cars, steamship, &c. | Compt's die. | TWO

10 | Vig. Two females holding sickle and balances; steamship, barrels, &c., on right; cars, implements of agriculture, &c., on left. | 10 | Compt's die. | Liberty and Justice. | TEN | BANK OF SYRACUSE Syracuse, N. Y. | Locks. | TEN

50 | Vig. Eagle on limb of tree, railroad cars, canal boats, &c. | 50 | Compt's die. | Male portrait. | ROCHESTER CITY BANK, Rochester, N. Y. | Columns. | 50 | FIFTY

Female holding figure 3. | Franklin; cupids on either side. | III | Compt's die. | BANK OF FAYETTEVILLE, Fayetteville, N. Y. | Vig. Boy plowing; Farm house, steamboat. | THREE | 3

TWENTY | 20 Vig. Female seated globe, chemical instruments, steamship. 20 | Die. | Compt's die. | BANK OF SYRACUSE Syracuse, N. Y. | XX | TWENTY | Locks. | Die.

Compt's die. | ROCHESTER CITY BANK, Rochester, N. Y. | 100 | 100 Vig. Female holding liberty cap and pole; spread eagles, C between them. | Female seated. | Benjamin Franklin. | Columns.

FIVE | Compt's die. Cupids on either side. | FIVE | Girl. | BANK OF FAYETTEVILLE, Fayetteville, N. Y. | Flower girl with basket of flowers. | 5 | FIVE | 5

FIFTY | L L | BANK OF OWEGO, Owego, N. Y. | 50 | Vig. Female seated on rock, with eagle in left hand; horn of plenty at her feet. | Cattle. | Canal boat. | 50

1 with letters one running across it. | PULASKI BANK, Pulaski, N. Y. 1 1 | 1 | Compt's die | Female portrait. | One dollar in part circle | Male portrait. | Large figure 1 and one dollar.

X with letters TEN running across it. | BANK OF FAYETTEVILLE, Fayetteville, N. Y. | 10 | Vig. Farmer, sailor, and mechanic; implements, &c. Two vessels, cars, &c, in back ground. | Female, liberty pole cap, &c. | Farm house and boat. | Compt's die.

ONE HUNDRED | 100 100 | BANK OF OWEGO, Owego, N. Y. | Vig. Same as 50s. | Canal locks. | ONE HUNDRED

1 Compt's die. ONE Vig. Cupid rolling gold piece; locomotive in distance. FRANKFORT BANK Frankfort, N. Y. Dog. 1 Female seated with shield and figure 1.	ONE Full length female figure with sword. MONSON BANK, Monson, Mass. A 1 Vig. Indian seated looking down upon a city; bow and arrows in hand 1 1 Female portrait.	50 Medallion head. 50 MONSON BANK, Monson, Mass. Vig. Dogs chasing an elk. 50 Franklin.
2 Compt's die. TWO Vig. Two children fencing, with gold pieces for shields, one standing; locomotive in distance. FRANKFORT BANK, Frankfort, N. Y. 2 Female seated with figure 2.	ONE Girl with sheaf of grain on her head. ONE 1 ONE Harvest field, farmers at work. B MONSON BANK, Monson, Mass. Vig. Female kneeling, holding shield, barrels and bales cars and ship in back ground. 1 Locomotive horse, &c.	1 with ONE running across it. Telegraph, road and cows BULLS HEAD BANK, New York City. Vig. Bull's head with title of Bank running around it. 1, one running across it. 1, one running across it. 1 with ONE running across it. Compt's die
3 Compt's die. THREE Vig. Three children with three gold pieces. FRANKFORT BANK, Frankfort, N. Y. Loading bay. 3 Large figure 3 with three men, one in centre, and one on either side.	Female portrait. 2 Vig. Two men, one a farmer holding horse under a tree, factories several tall chimneys. MONSON BANK, Monson, Mass. 2 Shield, scroll E Pluribus Unum.	2 Compt's die. Vig. Same as One. BULL'S HEAD BANK New York City. 2 with Two running across it. 2 with word dollars running across it. 2 TWO 2
5 Compt's die. FIVE Vig. Five children with 5 gold pieces. FRANKFORT BANK, Frankfort, N. Y. Oxen. 5 Female seated with scale and figure 5.	3 Male portrait MONSON BANK, Monson, Mass. 3 Vig. Three figures, liberty pole and cap; cornucopia, anvil and hammer 3 3 Blacksmith making horse shoe.	3 Compt's die. THREE Vig. Same as ones. BULL'S HEAD BANK New York City. 3 3 3 THREE 3
10 Compt's die. TEN Vig. Sailor, Indian, and two females with eagle, liberty pole and cap, bust, &c. FRANKFORT BANK, Frankfort, N. Y. Bee hive. 10 Female portrait.	5 MONSON BANK. A Monson, Mass. Vig. Train of cars. FIVE 5 FIVE Female Indian standing	5 Compt's die. BULL'S HEAD BANK New York City. Vig. Horses and tree. 5 Bull's head. FIVE
20 Compt's die. TWENTY Vig. Oxen, sheep, farmers, &c. FRANKFORT BANK, Frankfort, N. Y. Two horses. 20 Female portrait.	5 B Portrait of Washington. Vig. Locomotive and train of cars also second train going towards village in distance. MONSON BANK, Monson, Mass. 5 5	10 Bull's head. 10 Vig. Agricultural scene; oxen in foreground BULL'S HEAD BANK New York City. 10 with TEN running across it. Compt's die
1 Compt's die. ONE Vig. Am. eagle, E Pluribus Unum; shipping &c. JUDSON BANK, Ogdensburgh, N. Y. 1 Female portrait.	FIVE C Farmer seated, sheaf of grain on either side, sickle in right hand. MONSON BANK, Monson, Mass. 5 Vig. Two Females, one spinning. Train of cars in distance. 5	XX Compt's die. BULL'S HEAD BANK New York City. Vig. Mill, drove of sheep and man on horseback in foreground. 20 Bull's head. 20
2 Locomotive. JUDSON BANK, Ogdensburgh, N. Y. Vig. Indians feeding horse. Compt's die 2	Vig. Train of oxen, horses in front Farmers loading wheat. 10 MONSON BANK, Monson, Mass. X X X Justice leaning on shield, scroll at feet; vessel, cars and houses.	50 Bull's head. BULL'S HEAD BANK New York City. Vig. Two horses. State Arms. 50
Locomotive and cars. FIVE JUDSON BANK, Ogdensburgh, N. Y. 5 Compt's die. FIVE	Full length female holding cornucopia. TWENTY Vig. Two cows; mill, water, &c, in distance. MONSON BANK, Monson, Mass. 20 Male portrait	ONE HUNDRED. Bull's head. Compt's die. ONE HUNDRED DOLLARS. BULL'S HEAD BANK New York City. 100

Compt's die. 1 | Vig. Train of cars, &c. BK OF NEWBURGH Newburgh, N. Y. Large figure 1 running lengthwise of the note. | ONE 1

2 Compt's die. 2 | ULSTER COUNTY BK Kingston, N. Y. Vig. Three children with hammer, lever, and wedge, millstones screw &c. steamboat in distance. 2 Steamboat. | TWO Male Portrait TWO

10 Compt's die. 10 | Vig. Large X in centre, Portrait on either side, the whole surrounded by scroll work, within which is seated cupids. BANK OF POUGH-KEEPSIE Poughkeepsie, N. Y. Building. | 10 Washington

2 Compt's die. 2 | 2 Vig. Female seated sickle in hand Wheat & cattle on either side. 2 BK OF NEWBURGH Newburgh, N. Y. Steamboat. | TWO Cupid engraving. TWO

3 Compt's die. 3 | Vig. Female in skiff. 3 ULSTER COUNTY BK Kingston, N. Y. Steamboat. | Man seated within large ornamental figure 3. 3

50 Steamboats shipping and harbor. 50 | 50 Compt's die. Vig. Harvest field laborers at work man and woman in fore-ground, dog at their feet. BANK OF POUGH-KEEPSIE Poughkeepsie N. Y. Dog, key, and safe. | 50 Indian in canoe

3 Compt's die. 3 | 3 Vig. Blacksmith at work. two females. 3 BK OF NEWBURGH Newburgh, N. Y. Steamboat. | THREE Full length male figure. THREE

5 Compt's die. 5 | 5 Vig. Female in square frame with balances &c. ship in full sail on right. ULSTER COUNTY BK Kingston, N. Y. Engine. | FIVE

Artist seated 100 | BANK OF POUGH-KEEPSIE Poughkeepsie, N. Y. Compt's die. 100 Vig. Cupid in clouds. Dog, key, and safe. | Artist. 100

5 Compt's die. 5 | 5 Vig. Female leaning on a wheel, monument behind her. 5 BK OE NEWBURGH Newburgh, N. Y. Steamboat. | V Female seated one arm around a column the other extended. V

10 Compt's die. 10 | ULSTER COUNTY BK Kingston, N. Y. 10 Vig. Female in square frame with spear, implements of agriculture, grain, beehive, horn of plenty on each side. Male portrait. | 10

ONE Compt's die. 1 | Vig. Boy ploughing, steamboat on left; Farm house on right. UNION BANK Monticello, N. Y. | 1 Man dressing leather.

Compt's die. 10 | BK OF NEWBURGH Newburgh, N. Y. X Vig. Two females seated, cask and bales in rear, canal boat in distance. |

50 Compt's die. 50 | 50 Vig. Knight on horseback. 50 ULSTER COUNTY BK Kingston, N. Y. | New York Safety Fund.

2 Compt's die. TWO | Vig. Cattle and sheep, farm house in distance. UNION BANK Monticello N. Y. | 2 Blacksmith at work.

Compt's die. XX | Vig. Mechanic seated leaning on anvil hammer on his shoulder, cars on right, &c. BK OF NEWBURGH Newburgh, N. Y. | 20

1 Female seated, eagle sword, balances, &c. | Vig. Milk maids cows, &c. Farm house in distance. BANK OF POUGH-KEEPSIE Poughkeepsie, N. Y. Building. | 1 Compt's die.

Large ornamental 5 car, &c. Compt's die. | Vig. Sailor and female seated. UNION BANK Monticello, N. Y. | 5 Man carrying basket of corn.

FIFTY | 50 BK OF NEWBURGH Newburgh, N. Y. Title of bank on each side of vignette. Vig. Female seated holding balances, anchor and small sail vessel. Compt's stamp on back of note. |

2 Compt's die. 2 | Small port. of Jefferson. Small port. of Washington Vig. Female seated on plough holding sickle and grain; steamboat and cars in distance. BANK OF POUGH-KEEPSIE Poughkeepsie, N. Y. Building. | TWO Female Indian, liberty cap and pole. TWO

X Compt's die. X | Vig. Two females, sword ballances &c. eagle on left. UNION BANK Monticello, N. Y. | 10 Cars. 10

HUNDRED | 100 BK OF NEWBURGH Newburgh, N. Y. Title of bank on each side of vignette. Vig. Female seated holding balances, sickle, wheat and small vessel. Compt's stamp on back of note. | 100

3 Female holding aloft file with fig. on it, ship in background | 3 Vig. Female leaning upon anchor, shipping and harber in distance. 3 BANK OF POUGH-KEEPSIE Poughkeepsie, N. Y. Building. | Female with wheat in her arms. Compt's die

20 Compt's die. 20 | 20 Vig. Public buildings &c. man on horseback and one on foot. UNION BANK Monticello, N. Y. | Female with sword and balances. Locomotive TWENTY

1 Compt's die. 1 | 1 Vig. Two females hands clasped, harvest field on left, cars on right in distance. 1 ULSTER COUNTY BK Kingston, N. Y. Female reclining. | 1 Horse. 1

Compt's die. 5 | Vig. Spread eagle. BANK OF POUGH-KEEPSIE Poughkeepsie, N. Y Building. | 5 Washington on horseback

1 Compt's die. | Vig. Female seated sickle grain, reapers at work. Portrait of Washington BANK OF GENEVA Geneva, N. Y. | 1 Female, ship in distance. ONE

2	Vig. Angel blowing trumpet. Male portrait.	2
Compt's die.	BANK OF GENEVA, Geneva, N. Y.	Two cupids seated on large figure 2

Compt's die.	Vig. Cattle and sheep, some standing and some lying down.	5
5	GENESEE RIVER BANK, Mount Morris, N. Y.	Indian reclining.

2	Vig. Female with liberty pole and cap, shield, banners, cannon and drum.	2
Compt's die. TWO	BANK OF FORT EDWARD, Fort Edward, N. Y.	Male portrait.

Portrait of male. Compt's die.	5 Vig. Man standing with flag and sword, others kneeling around.	5 Male portrait.
	BANK OF GENEVA, Geneva, N. Y.	V

10	GENESEE RIVER BANK, Mount Morris, N. Y.	10
Compt's die.		Man felling a tree; oxen; children seated on ground.

3	Vig. Drover, cattle and sheep; man on horseback watering his horse.	3
Compt's die. 3	BANK OF FORT EDWARD, Fort Edward, N. Y.	Male portrait. 3

X	Vig. Harvest scene.	10
Compt's die. 10	BANK OF GENEVA, Geneva, N. Y. Locomotive.	Goddess of Liberty.

20	Vig. Indian seated, gun in right hand; city in distance, and steamship.	20
Compt's die.	GENESEE RIVER BANK, Mount Morris, N. Y.	Female with tablet, resting on column.

FIVE	5 Vig. Two females, one reclining; liberty pole and cap, balances, sword, shield and eagle, ship in distance.	5
Compt's die. FIVE	BANK OF FORT EDWARD, Fort Edward, N. Y.	Franklin.

	Vig. Female seated, leaning on rock, canal boats, steamboat &c., village in distance. Compt's die.	1
1	NIAGARA RIVER BANK, Buffalo N. Y.	Canal boat and bridge.

	Vig. Indian and sailor seated on either side of frame, surmounted by an eagle. Compt's die	1
1	UNION BANK, Watertown, N. Y.	Female emperor.

Compt's die.	Male portrait. 10	TEN
Female, liberty pole in one hand, the other resting on X.	BANK OF FORT EDWARD, Fort Edward, N. Y.	Two Indians, female kneeling between them, 10

TWO	Vig. Anchor, word Hope above in scroll, cars, factories, &c., on right; steamboat and harbor on left.	2
Compt's die. TWO	NIAGARA RIVER BANK,	Drove cattle cars, &c.

	Vig. Three mechanics; on right, bridge, factory, &c., in the distance. Compt's die.	2
2	UNION BANK, Watertown, N. Y.	Locomotive and tender.

Compt's die.	Male portrait. 20	
Two Indians and female. TWENTY	BANK OF FORT EDWARD, Fort Edward, N. Y.	Vig. Canal boat, and cars crossing bridge; house

3	Vig. Ship and schooner under full sail; steamboats and cars in distance.	3
Train cars. 3	NIAGARA RIVER BANK,	Compt's die. THREE

	Vig. Three females, two seated, and the other reclining. Compt's die.	5
5	UNION BANK, Watertown, N. Y.	Two females, one with arm resting on shield.

ONE	Compt's die. Rain bow and falls; female seated, with one hand on figure 1; U.S. shield, &c.	1
Full length female.	AUBURN CITY BANK, Auburn, N. Y. Emblems of commerce and agriculture.	Female portrait.

FIVE	NIAGARA RIVER BANK,	V with letters Five running across it.
Indian with bow and tomahawk.	Compt's die. Vig. Vessels, steamboat and harbor. Large 5 across note.	

Compt's die	UNION BANK, Watertown, N. Y.	TEN
10	Vig. Man, woman, girl, boy and dog, rural scenery, &c.	Sailor in the act of hoisting a flag.

TWO	Compt's die. Vig. Two females, figure 2 between them liberty pole, cap and balances.	2
Female holding liberty pole and cap; eagle feeding, horn of plenty.	AUBURN CITY BANK, Auburn, N. Y. Female seated.	Female portrait.

Female holding figure 1.	Vig. Female seated, with basket of corn; river and vessels in distance.	1
Compt's die.	GENESEE RIVER BANK, Mount Morris, N. Y. Sheaf of wheat and agricultural implements	Female Indian with shield and pole.

20	UNION BANK, Watertown, N. Y.	20
Compt's die	Vig. Spread eagle, seated on the globe.	20

5	Vig. Ornamental 5 in centre; five females, sword, balances, &c.; horn of plenty, locomotive and building, in background; shipping in distance.	5
Compt's die FIVE	AUBURN CITY BANK, Auburn, N. Y.	Washington.

2	Vig. Locomotive and cars going over bridge; canal boats and hay makers,	Compt's die.
Portrait of female.	GENESEE RIVER BANK, Mount Morris, N. Y.	2

1	Vig. Locomotive and train of cars; canal boat and village in distance.	1
Compt's die.	BANK OF FORT EDWARD, Fort Edward, N. Y.	Male portrait.

TEN	Compt's die. Vig. Female reclining, eagle at her back, globe and liberty cap; shipping in distance.	10 Male portrait.
Full length Indian, with bow, arrows and spear.	AUBURN CITY BANK, Auburn, N. Y.	TEN

Secured by pledge, &c. 1 Vig. Female with child; ship in distance ONE B'K OF LOWVILLE, Lowville, N. Y. Female seated, cars in distance. ONE Dog's head.	Male portrait Vig. Female seated by safe; picture; sheep to the right. 10 Compt's die. BANK OF CHEMUNG Elmira, N. Y. Locomotive	TWO 2 Vig. Oxen and cart, man with pitchfork, and boy asleep on top of load of hay. 2 Two females with a large bundle of grain over their heads. B'K OF HORNELLS-VILLE, Hornellsville, N. Y. Compt's die
TWO 2 Vig. Female reaper 2 Compt's die. B'K OF LOWVILLE, Lowville, N. Y. Artisan pouring gold out of horn. TWO Dog's head.	1 Vig. Female seated, with mirror, &c.; cars on right, steamer and ship on left. ONE Compt's die. B'K OF COMMERCE, Carmel, N. Y. Reaper clasping figure 1	FIVE 5 Compt's die. 5 FIVE Hunter and dog, seated by fire. B'K OF HORNELLS-VILLE, Hornellsville, N. Y. Hunter kneeling and drinking from brook.
3 Vig. Female portrait, with female on either side. 3 Large figure 3 with female on either side B'K OF LOWVILLE, Lowville, N. Y. Dog's head.	2 Vig. Crystal Palace, N. Y. B'K OF COMMERCE, Carmel, N. Y. Female seated in large figure 2. Compt's die. 2 TWO	10 X Compt's die. X 10 Man and boy with guns in hands. B'K OF HORNELLS-VILLE, Hornellsville, N. Y. Fowls. Man standing with gun, and a man seated with gun and pipe
5 V Vig. Female in figure 5; female on either side. V 5 Compt's die. B'K OF LOWVILLE, Lowville, N. Y. Bust FIVE Dog's head. FIVE	3 Vig. Artisans; vessel, cars and factory in distance. 111 B'K OF COMMERCE, Carmel, N. Y. Fig. 3 and Female seated on rocks. Compt's die. 3	Mechanic at bench. BANK OF HAVANA, Havana, N. Y. 1 Compt's die. 1 Male portrait. 1 Female seated; houses in distance.
10 Vig. Wreath with female on either side; shipping, cars and buildings in distance. 10 Compt's die. State Arms. TEN B'K OF LOWVILLE, Lowville, N. Y. Dog's head TEN	FIVE BK OF COMMERCE, Carmel, N. Y. 5 Large V with FIVE running across it. Goddess of Liberty. Vig. Locomotive and cars, oxen and water in foreground. Compt's die	2 Male portrait Vig. Female kneeling, with pail; cattle lying down, &c. 2 Compt's die. 2 BANK OF HAVANA, Havana, N. Y. Male portrait
Vig. Road, load of hay, canal boat, &c. B'K OF LOWVILLE, Lowville, N. Y. 25 Compt's die Male portrait. 25 Cornucopia, bales, &c. 25	ONE 1 Female seated with grain, plow, etc.; cars, bridge, canal, &c., in distance. Mill on right. ONE Compt's die. ONE BANK OF CORNING, Corning, N. Y. Secured, etc. Reaper.	Compt's die. 5 Portrait of Washington. 5 FIVE BANK OF HAVANA, Havana, N. Y. Female standing, canal lock in distance. Male portrait Canal boat.
1 Vig. Man loading hay. 1 Compt's die. Bridge and canal boat. ONE BANK OF CHEMUNG Elmira, N. Y. Wheelbarrow ONE	3 Vig. Female portrait, American flags on either side. 3 Female on either side of figure 3. BANK OF CORNING, Corning, N. Y.	1 Vig. Locomotive and cars. 1 Portrait of Washington. BANK OF CAYUGA LAKE, Painted Post, N. Y. ONE Compt's die
TWO Vig. Female seated in figure 2. 2 Compt's die. BANK OF CHEMUNG Elmira, N. Y. Female with wheat. TWO Load of hay. 2	5 5 Vig. Female reapers, cars and buildings in distance. 5 5 Compt's die. Female seated in circular die. 5 BANK OF CORNING, Corning, N. Y. 5	TWO Medallion head, with TWO on it. Compt's die. Medallion head, with TWO on it. TWO Farmers loading grain Female seated in large figure 2 TWO BANK OF CAYUGA LAKE, Painted Post, N. Y.
5 Vig. Oxen. 5 Compt's die. BANK OF CHEMUNG Elmira, N. Y. FIVE Deer. Fillmore.	Circular die, with the word one dollar running partly around. Vig. Female with sheaf of grain in hand; cars crossing bridge; on left reapers; houses on right. 1 ONE Compt's die Indian, etc. B'K OF HORNELLS-VILLE, Hornellsville, N. Y.	5 Medallion head. Vig. Signing the declaration of independence. FIVE Male portrait BANK OF CAYUGA LAKE, Painted Post, N. Y. Compt's die.

1 ONE Compt's die.
Vig. Country scene; female figure, farm house and water mill in back ground.
BANK OF AUBURN, Auburn, N. Y.
1 Female figure. 1

1 Compt's die.
Female reclining, eagle behind; train of cars, bridge and city in distance. 1
CLINTON BANK, Buffalo, N. Y.
Horse.
Statue of DeWitt Clinton.

20 TWENTY 20
20 20
BANK OF ROME, Rome, N. Y.
Vig. Two females holding State Arms between; liberty pole and cap, sword and balances.
Round building with flag flying; view of cultivated fields, &c.

2 Compt's die. 2
Vig. Female seated with cap and liberty pole.
BANK OF AUBURN, Auburn, N. Y.
2 Female figure. 2

2 Compt's die. TWO
Portrait of Clinton; city, steamboat, bridge and cars on right; farm scene on left.
CLINTON BANK, Buffalo, N. Y.
2 2
2 Two cherubs soaring with distaff and sheaf.

Female with sheaf of wheat and sickle in her hand. ONE
JAMESTOWN BANK, Jamestown, N. Y.
Vig. Farmer, sailor, and mechanic; city, locomotive and ship in distance.
1 Compt's die ONE

5 Compt's die. 5
Vig. Medallion head, supported on left by female figure of art and science, and on right by female figure of commerce.
BANK OF AUBURN, Auburn, N. Y.
5 Medallion head. 5

Compt's die. 3
CLINTON BANK, Buffalo, N. Y.
Three females reclining, representing Liberty, Agriculture and Manufactures.
3 3
THREE Justice erect and a female seated.

2 Compt's die.
JAMESTOWN BANK, Jamestown, N. Y.
Vig. Two females seated; steamboat, factory, cars, canal, &c., in the distance.
TWO Female seated in large figure 2.

Compt's die.
Vig. Eagle on rock, shipping, &c, on left. 10
BANK OF AUBURN, Auburn, N. Y.
TEN

V Fillmore. FIVE
CLINTON BANK, Buffalo, N. Y.
Truth reclining on safe looking at shield on which is ship on stocks and rising sun; sheep and sheaf on right.
5 5
5 Compt's die. V across five.

FIVE Franklin Pierce. FIVE
Compt's die.
Vig. Farmer and Indian seated on either side of frame; Indian huts on left; cars and canal on right.
JAMESTOWN BANK, Jamestown, N. Y.
V

1 Compt's die.
ONE ONE
Vig. Train of cars.
BANK OF CENTRAL NEW YORK, Utica, N. Y.
Building.
1 Portrait of female.

X Justice seated.
Shield on which is word Hope and anchor; cars crossing bridge and factories on right; ship, steamboat and city on left. Webster.
CLINTON BANK, Buffalo, N. Y.
TEN
10 Compt's die

1 Washington. 1
1 Compt's die.
Vig. Female leaning on rock, looking down on steamboat, &c.
COMMERCIAL B'K. Rochester, N. Y.
Plow, &c.
1 Female with liberty pole, U. S. shield, &c.

TWO Compt's die. TWO
2 2
Vig. Female seated, with sickle in right hand, trident in left; canal, railroad, &c, on left, mill on right
BANK OF CENTRAL NEW YORK, Utica, N. Y.
Building.
Ears of corn, man seated with implements around him.

ONE Man soaring holding horn of plenty and wand, vessel in distance. Compt's die
Vig. Winged female, kneeling in front of large one, sword and balances.
BANK OF ROME, Rome, N. Y.
Indian.
1

TWO Compt's die. TWO
2 2
Vig. Female with wings, sword, sickle, &c. cars on right, agricultural implements, &c, on left
COMMERCIAL B'K. Rochester, N. Y.
Mechanic seated; cornucopia; implements &c surrounded with corn.

5 Compt's die. FIVE
V V
Vig. Three females, one seated in a large figure 5, cars, canal, waterfall, &c, on left; steamship &c on right in the distance.
BANK OF CENTRAL NEW YORK, Utica, N. Y.
Building.
5 Medallion head. FIVE

TWO Compt's die. TWO
2 2
Vig. Farm house milk maids, cows Barn, &c.
BANK OF ROME, Rome, N. Y.
Indian's bust.
TWO Two cupids, surrounded by large ornamental figure 2. TWO

3 Male portrait 3
Vig. Female, bales, &c.; cars and ship in distance. 3
COMMERCIAL B'K. Rochester, N. Y.
Eagle.
Compt's die 3 Female seated.

10 Compt's die. TEN
Vig. Two females on either side of a frame containing the arms of the different states; steamship on right; cars, houses, factory, canal, &c, on left in distance.
BANK OF CENTRAL NEW YORK, Utica, N.Y.
Deer.
10 Two females with liberty pole and cap, horn of plenty, in a circular die. TEN

THREE Compt's die. THREE
3 3
Vig. Spread eagle on bow; canal boat, locks and train of cars.
BANK OF ROME, Rome, N. Y.
Horse.
3 Three females standing.

FIVE Female holding cap, eagle, ship, and U. S. flag Compt's die.
Vig. Shield with 5 in centre; Indians on left; female teaching children on right.
COMMERCIAL B'K. Rochester, N. Y.
Female.
5 Male portrait

TWENTY Compt's die. TWENTY
20 20
Vig. Female seated at table, pointing to large steamship on left.
BANK OF CENTRAL NEW YORK, Utica, N.Y.
House
XX

5 Compt's die 5
5
Vig. Five figures surrounding ornamental figure 5, vessel in distance.
BANK OF ROME, Rome, N. Y.
V
5 Female holding aloft figure 5. 5

TEN Female portrait. Compt's die.
COMMERCIAL B'K. Rochester, N. Y.
Vig. Three females, cornucopia, anchor, &c.
Propeller
10 Male portrait TEN

20 · Compt's die. XX · Vig. Three females, shield and eagle mounted in centre; cars on right, ship on left. · COMMERCIAL BK, Rochester, N. Y. Full length female standing on globe with word TWENTY on it.	10 · Compt's die. · TEN Vig. Female, key in one hand, liberty pole in other; balances on safe; spread eagle, ships, and cars in distance, · B'K OF WHITEHALL Whitehall, N. Y. · Locomotive and cars. 10 · Female churning.	Female with hammer and anvil. · Compt's die. 1 · Portrait of Washington. · FRONTIER BANK Potsdam, N. Y. 1 · Female seated with sheaf of wheat.
50 · Compt's die. · 50 Vig. Two females, bales and bbls behind them; ship in the distance. · 50 · COMMERCIAL BK, Rochester, N. Y. FIFTY · Sailor leaning on a capstan, telescope in his hand, anchor behind him · FIFTY	20 · Farmer sharpening scythe. Compt's die. · Vig. Female holding liberty pole, seated between figures 2 and 0. · B'K OF WHITEHALL Whitehall, N. Y. 20 · Female raking hay.	Child standing. · Compt's die. 2 · Male portrait. · FRONTIER BANK Potsdam, N. Y. 2 · Female portrait.
Three females, anchor. · 100 COMMERCIAL BK, Rochester, N. Y. · Vig. Steamship and vessels. 100 · Compt's die.	50 · Head of McDonough. · 50 50 · Washington on horseback. · 50 · BK OF WHITEHALL Whitehall, N. Y. FIFTY DOLLARS	Large figure 5 with Indian at the bottom. · Compt's die. 5 · Male portrait. · 5 · FRONTIER BANK Potsdam, N. Y. Sailor standing. · 5
1 · Compt's die, · 1 1 · Vig. Urn with eagle on top; angel, female with liberty cap and pole. · 1 · B'K OF WHITEHALL Whitehall, N. Y. 1 · Clock. Child on either side. · 1	ONE · Compt's die. · ONE 1 · Vig. Female and child, ship in distance. · Oval die, · FARMERS AND MECHANICS' BANK, Rochester, N. Y. · Anvil, etc ONE · Female seated, cars in distance.	Large X, figure 10, sailor looking through a telescope and a sailor in a boat. · Compt's die. 10 · Male portrait · 10 · FRONTIER BANK Potsdam, N. Y. TEN · Ship at sea. · TEN
2 · Compt's die. · 2 2 · Vig. Mechanic at work, tools, &c, anchor; two females, ship in distance. · 2 · B'K OF WHITEHALL Whitehall, N. Y. · Steamboat. 2 · Ship on stocks. · 2	TWO · Compt's die. · TWO 2 · Vig. Female reaper seated. · 2 · FARMERS' AND MECHANICS' BANK, Rochester, N. Y. · Farmer gathering corn. Artisan with horn of plenty.	Female sharpening scythe. · Compt's die. 1 · Vig. Female reaper seated. · B'K OF WESTFIELD Westfield, N. Y. ONE · Ship.
3 · Compt's die, · 3 3 · Vig. Shield surmounted with eagle, female on either side; balances, ship, &c. · 3 · B'K OF WHITEHALL Whitehall, N. Y. · Locomotive. 3 · Male portrait · 3	Female on either side of figure 3. · III 3 · Vig. Portrait of female in wreath, with flags, drum, &c. · FARMERS' & MECHANICS' BANK, Rochester, N. Y. · Farmer gathering corn. 3	Compt's die. · Pigs. 2 · Vig. male ploughing. · B'K OF WESTFIELD Westfield, N. Y. 2 · Female, churning.
5 · Compt's die. · FIVE Vig. Female seated; plow, sickle, wheat, &c. canal boat, cars, &c, · B'K OF WHITEHALL Whitehall, N. Y. · Anchor, horn of plenty, &c. 5 · Sailor leaning against capstan, glass in hand.	5 · Compt's die. · FIVE Vig. Female with lions, key, &c. · Title of Bank. · Farmer gathering corn. 5 · Portrait of female. · FIVE	Compt's die. · Artisan. 5 · Vig. Washing sheep. · B'K OF WESTFIELD Westfield. N. Y. 5 · Female standing by figure 5.
FIVE (Old Plate.) · 5 · Vig. Three females seated; agricultural implements, &c. · B'K OF WHITEHALL Whitehall, N. Y. · Steamboat. 5 · Cattle and sheepdrovers · 5	10 · Compt's die. · TEN Vig. Wreath with female on either side, cars, shipping, &c., in the distance. · Title of Bank. · Arm 10 · State Arms. · TEN	Compt's die. · Female, Minerva and shield. 25 · Vig. Man seated, mechanic's tools and steam manufactory. · BANK OF SYRACUSE Syracuse, N. Y. 25 · Iron safe. · 25
Full length male portrait. (Old Plate.) · X · Vig. Two females with liberty cap, pole, balances, &c; shield surmounted with eagle in centre. · X · B'K OF WHITEHALL Whitehall, N. Y. · Steamboat 10 · TEN 10 TEN · 10	TWENTY · Compt's die. · TWENTY 20 · Vig. Female with chemical apparatus, pointing to steamer in distance. · 20 · Title of Bank. · Arm XX	ONE HUNDRED Vig. Female seated leaning on cask and bales; ship in distance on one side; canal boat on the other. · BANK OF SYRACUSE Syracuse, N. Y. 100 · Compt's' die

1; Compt's die.; ONE Vig. Farmer plowing.; CAMDEN BANK, Camden, N. Y, Wheelbarrow ONE; Male portrait	5 in circular die. Vig. Same as ones; BANK OF ALBANY, Albany, N. Y.; Beaver; FIVE FIVE 5; Compt's die; 5	1; Compt's die.; 1 ALBANY CITY B'K. Albany, N. Y.; 1 1; Vig. Artisan with two females.; City Hall ONE
2; Compt's die.; TWO CAMDEN BANK, Camden, N. Y.; Vig. Farmers loading wheat. TWO; Female seated within large ornamental figure 2.	10 Vig. Same as ones.; BANK OF ALBANY, Albany, N. Y.; Drover; TEN TEN X; Compt's die.; 10	Compt's die.; Portrait of female. Vig. Indian and female with American eagle on the world over capitol.; ALBANY CITY B'K. Albany, N. Y. 2
THREE; Compt's die.; THREE 3 Vig. Drover, sheep and dog; mill in distance. 3; CAMDEM BANK, Camden, N. Y.; Female. THREE; Full length mechanic.; THREE	1; Male portrait Vig. Three artisans, shipping in distance. 1; ALBANY EXCHANGE BANK, Albany, N. Y.; Female portrait ONE; Compt's die.; Female portrait.	3; Compt's die. Vig. Female pointing to shipping in distance.; ALBANY CITY B'K. Albany, N. Y. 3
5; Compt's die Vig. Interior of blacksmith shop, mechanics at work; CAMDEN BANK, Camden, N. Y. 5; Female portrait, wheat, &c.	2; Male portrait ALBANY EXCHANGE BANK, Albany, N. Y.; Female seated representing Commerce; fort'ts. On right is Compt's die, and word 2 on large. 2 2; Female portrait.	5; Compt's die.; 5 5 5; Vig. Same as ones; ALBANY CITY B'K Albany, N. Y. Capitol.; 5; Dwelling with trees.
TEN; Compt's die.; TEN CAMDEN BANK, Camden, N. Y.; Vig. Three females seated, cornucopia, anchor, &c.; 10 TEN; Franklin.; TEN	5; Compt's die.; FIVE V Vig. Female seated in figure 5, females on either side. V; ALBANY EXCHANGE BANK, Albany, N. Y.; Building. 5; Medallion head.; FIVE	10; Compt's die.; 10 ALBANY CITY B'K. Albany, N. Y.; X X; Vig. Same as ones. X in wreath.; Capitol.; 10
20; Compt's die Vig. Eagle on branch; houses on right, cars on left.; CAMDEN BANK, Camden, N. Y. 20; Washington.	10; Compt's die.; TEN Vig. Shield with female on either side, cars, shipping and buildings in distance.; ALBANY EXCHANGE BANK, Albany, N. Y.; Building. 10; State Arms.; TEN	20; Compt's die.; 20 20 20; ALBANY CITY B'K. Albany, N. Y.; Vig. Female with wheat; cars in distance.; Capitol. 20; Medallion head.; 20
ONE; Portrait of S. Van Rensselaer.; 1 1 Male erect with sickle in hand; Indian seated gazing at him; shield surmounted by a sloop. 1; BANK OF ALBANY, Albany, N. Y.; ONE Secured, etc. ONE 1; Compt's die.; 1	Compt's die.; ONE 1 Vig. Portrait of Washington. 1; B'K OF CARTHAGE, Jefferson Co, N. Y. Blacksmith.; ONE	1; Compt's die.; ONE 1; Vig. Two females seated.; B'K OF THE EMPIRE STATE, Burton, N. Y. Justice.; ONE
2; Portrait of A. Van Vechten; 2 2 Vignette same as ones. 2; BANK OF ALBANY, Albany, N. Y.; TWO Beaver. TWO 2; Compt's die.; 2	Female artisan.; Compt's die. 2 Vig. Male portrait. 2; B'K OF CARTHAGE, Jefferson Co, N. Y. Female.; TWO; from work.	Compt's die.; Two females. Vig. Indian handing ear of corn to woodman.; B'K OF THE EMPIRE STATE, Burton, N. Y 2; Oxen and pigs.
Portrait of J. Bleecker.; THREE; Portrait of S Van Rensselaer. 3 Vignette same as ones. 3; BANK OF ALBANY, Albany, N. Y.; Three Beaver. Three 3; Compt's die; 3	FIVE; Barge.; Compt's die. 5 Male portrait.; B'K OF CARTHAGE, Jefferson Co. N. Y. 5; Artist.	5; Compt's die. Vig. Female with eagle.; B'K OF THE EMPIRE STATE, Burton, N. Y. 5; Female holding figure 5.

Secured, &c. 1 Female with child ONE BALLSTON SPA B'K. Ballston, N. Y. ONE House. Female seated.	TEN 10 Farmer ploughing, with two horses. 10 Public building, street, omnibus and people. Compt's die. BANK OF ATTICA, Buffalo, N. Y. Oxen and pigs.	Male portrait. Vig. Female seated, holding one. 1 B'K OF LAKE ERIE, Frankfort, N. Y. Compt's die. Secured, &c. Sailor standing.
TWO 2 Female reaper seated. 2 Compt's die. BALLSTON SPA B'K. Ballston, N. Y. Artisan. TWO Public building.	TWENTY 20 Vig. Agricultural scene. 20 reaper sharpening scythe Compt's die. BANK OF ATTICA, Buffalo, N. Y. Female seated, holding 2 in right hand, 0 in left.	Male portrait. Vig. Shipping. 2 Compt's die, with cupids on either side. B'K OF LAKE ERIE, Frankfort, N. Y. Female standing.
5 V Female seated in figure 5; female on both sides. V 5 Compt's die. BALLSTON SPA B'K. Ballston, N. Y. Medallion head. FIVE Building. FIVE	1 Vig. Wreath with Indian on left, sailor on right. ONE Compt's die. B'K OF THE UNION, Belfast, N. Y. Female with shield.	Male portrait. Vig. Female seated with shield. 5 Compt's die. B'K OF LAKE ERIE, Frankfort, N. Y. Two females, one holding figure 5.
10 Shield, with female on either side. 10 Compt's die. BALLSTON SPA B'K, Ballston, N. Y. State Arms. TEN Building. TEN	3 Vig. Mirror with goddess of liberty on right; two females on left. THREE Compt's die. B'K OF THE UNION Belfast, N. Y. Goddess of liberty.	Male portrait. Vig. Two men with mirror; shipping in distance. 10 TEN Compt's die. B'K OF LAKE ERIE Frankfort, N. Y. Sailor standing over female seated.
TWENTY 20 Vig. Female seated with electrical apparatus, pointing to shipping in distance. 20 Compt's die. BALLSTON SPA B'K. Ballston, N. Y. XX TWENTY Building.	Medallion head. 1 Vig. Dairy maid with oxen. 1 ONE Compt's die. B'K OF ORANGE CO. Goshen, N. Y. Female portrait. Medallion head. Dog's head. ONE	Female. 1 Vig. Goddess of liberty with eagle. ONE Compt's die. B'K OF SARATOGA SPRINGS, Saratoga, N. Y. Female standing.
Secured, &c 1 Female with child. ONE ONE BANK OF ATTICA, Buffalo, N. Y. Female seated.	Female portrait. 2 Vig. Farmer with drove of cattle. TWO Compt's die. B'K OF ORANGE CO. Goshen, N. Y. Locomotive and cars. Female portrait. Eagle. TWO	Two men holding females in their arms. 2 Vig. Mirror, with farmer on left, dairymaid on right. 2 B'K OF SARATOGA SPRINGS, Saratoga, N. Y. Compt's die. Locomotive and cars.
TWO 2 Vig. Female reaper. 2 Corn Compt's die. BANK OF ATTICA, Buffalo, N. Y. Artisan in circular die. TWO Drover and oxen. Corn	Female portrait. 5 Vig. Locomotive and cars. FIVE Compt's die. Male portrait. Female portrait. B'K OF ORANGE CO. Goshen, N. Y. FIVE	Female seated in figure 5 Cupids. Vig. Portrait of female. 5 B'K OF SARATOGA SPRINGS, Saratoga, N. Y. Compt's die. Two females, one holding figure 5.
Secured, etc. 3 Vig. Portrait of female in oval die, with flags on either side. 3 Figure 3, female on either side. BANK OF ATTICA, Buffalo, N. Y. III Oxen and trees.	TEN 10 Female churning. X 1 B'K OF ORANGE CO. Goshen, N. Y. Compt's die Agricultural implements. 0	TEN 1 Female. 0 10 Building. Compt's die. B'K OF SARATOGA SPRINGS. Saratoga, N.Y. Female standing.
5 Vig. Group of females; plough, wheel, key, &c. &c. &c. 5 Compt's die. BANK OF ATTICA, Buffalo, N. Y. Female with shield reaper in distance. FIVE Oxen and trees. FIVE	TWENTY 20 Female churning. 20 Compt's die. B'K OF ORANGE CO. Goshen, N. Y. Farming tools	20 2 Female. 0 20 Building and street. B'K OF SARATOGA SPRINGS, Saratoga, N. Y. Female holding 2 in right and 0 in left hand. TWENTY

ONE Fillmore. Compt's die. Vig. Female seated, holding figure one, cars in distance. BANK OF BINGHAMPTON. Binghampton, N. Y. Female standing in large figure 1.	3 Franklin. THREE Vig. Farmer pulling corn. BANK OF UTICA, Utica, N. Y. 3 3 Compt's die. THREE	2 Farmer ploughing. Female portrait. BANK OF FISHKILL Fishkill Village, N. Y. Secured, &c. 2 Compt's die.
3 Female portrait. Compt's die. Vig. Farmers at dinner. BANK OF BINGHAMPTON, Binghampton, N. Y. 3 Artisan in figure 3, art on either side. THREE	5 FIVE 5 5 Compt's die. Vig. Artisan painting. BANK OF UTICA, Utica, N. Y. 5 FIVE DOLLARS	THREE Compt's die. Vig. Horses drinking, pigs on right. 3 BANK OF FISHKILL, Fishkill Village, N. Y. Secured, &c. 3 Washington on horseback.
FIVE FIVE Compt's die. 5 Locomotive and cars. BANK OF BINGHAMPTON, Binghampton, N. Y. Safe. FIVE Large figure and five females.	TEN DOLLARS 10 Vig. Indian standing. Compt's die. BANK OF UTICA, Utica, N. Y. X 10 TEN 10	5 Compt's die. 5 Large ornamental figure 5, with word five on it. Vig. Artisans at work. BANK OF FISHKILL, Fishkill Village, N. Y. Secured, &c. 5 Portrait of Washington
Compt's die. Male portrait TEN 10 Vig. 3 females. BANK OF BINGHAMPTON, Binghampton, N. Y. American Shield. 10 Goddess of Liberty in wreath, with name of States and territories.	ONE Compt's die. ONE COMMERCIAL BK. Clyde, N. Y. 1 Vig. Female seated, ship in distance. 1 Ox. 1	20 Female Indian. BANK OF FISHKILL Fishkill Village, N. Y. X Vig. Eagle. X 20 Compt's die. Secured, &c.
1 Compt's die 1 Vig. Sailor with shipping in distance. BUFFALO CITY B'K. Buffalo, N. Y. 1 ONE Canal boat under bridge	II Compt's die. II 2 Vig. Female seated on bale, &c. 2 COMMERCIAL BK, Clyde, N. Y. Female seated holding two. TWO	1 Female with wheat. 1 COMMERCIAL B'K, Troy, N. Y. 1 Female with pail on head cows, &c. 1 1 Compt's die.
2 Compt's die. Vig. Indian female overlooking City in distance. BUFFALO CITY B'K. Buffalo, N. Y. 2 Sailor seated.	5 Compt's die. 5 5 Vig. Neptune seated with eagle, ship and cars in distance. 5 COMMERCIAL BK. Clyde, N. Y. Vessels. Eagle. FIVE	2 Compt's die. TWO Male portrait. Female seated on bales steamer in distance. COMMERCIAL B'K, Troy, N. Y. 2 2
FIVE Vig. Three artisans, one holding wheel to goddess of liberty on throne, with eagle. Compt's die. BUFFALO CITY B'K. Buffalo, N. Y. 5 5	Compt's die. Country road with oxen, load of hay, &c. Vig. Locomotive and cars crossing bridge, canal boats, &c. BANK OF SENECA FALLS, N. Y. Fire Engine. 1 Portrait of female.	TWO Compt's die. TWO 2 Female seated with wheat, &c. 2 COMMERCIAL B'K, Troy, N. Y. Washington. Artisan with gold.
X Bridge. BUFFALO CITY B'K. Buffalo, N. Y. Vig. Three females seated. Compt's die 10 Shipping.	2 Compt's die. Ocean steamer. Portrait of Washington. BANK OF SENECA FALLS, N. Y. Eagle. 2 Female.	3 Vig. 3 figures with printing press, &c., Faust, Guttenburg and Schoeffer. COMMERCIAL B'K. Troy, N. Y. Compt's die. 3 Male portrait 3
1 Drover and cattle. ONE Vig. Female, &c. BANK OF UTICA, Utica, N. Y. Dogs Head. 1 Compt's die. ONE	5 Compt's die. Vig. Locomotive and cars. BANK OF SENECA FALLS, N. Y. Wheel and rollers. 5 Portrait of female.	5 Compt's die. FIVE Five females with lions, keys, &c. COMMERCIAL B'K. Troy, N. Y. Coach. 5 Female with shield. FIVE

1 Vig. Female looking at shipping in distance. 1 Lewis Cass. B'K OF RHINEBECK, Rhinebeck, N. Y. 1 Compt's die.	ONE 1 Vig. Farmer ploughing. 1 BANK OF VERNON, Vernon Village N. Y. Female seated. Compt's die. Secured, &c. ONE	5 Washington Jefferson Vig: Female with sheaf of wheat. 5 Compt's die. Locomotive ROCHESTER BANK, Rochester, N. Y. 5 5
Vig. Farmers at dinner; hay making in backgro'd. Portrait of Franklin. 2 B'K OF RHINEBECK, Rhinebeck, N. Y. 2 Compt's die	2 Vig. Dairymaid seated, cattle in distance. 2 TWO Compt's die. BANK OF VERNON, Vernon Village, N. Y. Reaper with bundle of wheat. TWO	X Vig. Male portrait, with female on each side. TEN ROCHESTER BANK, Rochester, N. Y. Male portrait Compt's die. Eagle. TEN
3 Vig. Farmer with two horses; locomotive and cars in background. 3 B'K OF RHINEBECK, Rhinebeck, N. Y. Male portrait Compt's die.	THREE 3 Vig. Female with wheat. 3 Secured, &c. Female seated. BANK OF VERNON, Vernon Village, N. Y. Portrait of Female. Compt's die THREE Wheat, &c. THREE	20 Vig. Male portrait, with female on left, with liberty pole; two females on right. 20 ROCHESTER BANK, Rochester, N. Y. Compt's die. Locomotive. Portrait of Fillmore.
Portrait of Henry Clay. B'K OF RHINEBECK, Rhinebeck, N. Y. 5 5 Vig. Farmer with oxen and sheep. 5 5 Compt's die.	5 FIVE FIVE Vig. Same as 3. 5 Compt's die. BANK OF VERNON, Vernon Village, N. Y. Female with shield, reaper in background. FIVE Dog. FIVE	Medallion head. One on medallion head. Vig. Farmer with oxen and sheep. One on medallion head. 1 Compt's die. CENTRAL BANK, Cherry Valley, N. Y. Female with rake. Medallion head. Loading hay. 1
1 Vig. Dairy maid, cows, &c. 1 ONE ILLION BANK, Illion, N. Y. Compt's die Dog. Artisan.	10 Vig. Mirror, with female on either side, shipping, cars, &c. in distance. 10 Compt's die. BANK OF VERNON, Vernon Village, N. Y. State Arms. TEN Dog. TEN	Med. head 2 on medallion head. Vig. Female seated in figure 2; two farmers in background. 2 on medallion head. TWO Compts die CENTRAL BANK, Cherry Valley, N. Y. Female seated in figure 2 with balances and sword. Med. head Dog's head. TWO
Indian standing. 2 Mirror, female with pail on right; man with rake on left. 2 ILLION BANK, Illion, N. Y. Compt's die. Two females. Dog.	Compt's die. Vig. Farmer ploughing, two horses. 50 BANK OF VERNON, Vernon Village, N. Y. Reaper sharpening sythe. Secured, &c. Female with rake.	3 CENTRAL BANK, Cherry Valley, N. Y. Female standing. Medallion head. THREE, on medallion head. Vig. Two females with liberty pole and cap. THREE, on medallion head. 3 Wheat, &c. 3
3 Compt's die. Vig. Three females seated. 3 ILLION BANK, Illion, N. Y. Figure 3 and three men. Medallion head. Dog. THREE	Figure 1 with ONE running across it. Vig. Female seated, farmers loading hay in background. 1 ROCHESTER BANK, Rochester, N. Y. Washington Compt's die.	FIVE 5 Vig. Large figure 5, females on either side. 5 FIVE Compt's die. CENTRAL BANK, Cherry Valley, N. Y. Female. FIVE Female with anchor. FIVE
Compt's die. 5 Female with mirror, liberty pole and cap, motto Agriculture and Commerce. FIVE Large V and females, sailor and two men. ILLION BANK, Illion, N. Y. Figure 5 and five females.	2 Vig. Dog and safe. Compt's die. 2 ROCHESTER BANK, Rochester, N. Y. Goddess of liberty. Female seated.	X Medallion head, with TEN on it. Female holding 1 in right, and 0 in left. X Compt's die. Portrait of female. 10 CENTRAL BANK, Cherry Valley, N. Y. 10
10 Female seated with scales, and sword; ship, house, trees, sun and cupid. X Deer. Eagle. 10 ILLION BANK, Illion, N. Y. Compt's die. Dog's head. Buffalo.	3 Vig. Female seated on safe, with dog and child. Portrait of female. THREE ROCHESTER BANK, Rochester, N. Y. Female reaper. Compt's die.	20 Vig. Female looking at sea. 20 Female with sickle and sheep. 20 Medallion head. Medallion head. 20 CENTRAL BANK, Cherry Valley, N. Y. 20

Female and fig. 1
1
CAMBRIDGE CITY BANK,
Cambridgep't, Mass.
Man chopping trees, cabin and waggon. one gold dollar.
ONE
1

Female feeding an Eagle from a Cup
2
CAMBRIDGE CITY BANK.
Cambridgeport, Mass.
Farmer with rake, milk maid and cows, farm-house in back ground
Two gold dollars.
TWO TWO
2
Two Dollars
Train of Cars

3
Farmer, Sailor, and Mechanic, Female
3 gold dollars.
CAMBRIDGE CITY BANK.
Cambridgeport, Mass.
3
Farmer, Sailor, and Mechanic, and figure three

5
Men with gun, Steamship
a dian woman, 3 cupids and 5 gold dollars.
CAMBRIDGE CITY BANK.
Cambridgeport, Mass.
5
Group of Females, and figure five.

X
X
CAMBRIDGE CITY BANK.
Cambridgeport, Mass.
Train of cars.
TEN TEN
X
Load of Grain.

XX
Man holding figs. 20.
CAMBRIDGE CITY BANK.
Cambridgeport, Mass.
Female in foreground, R. R. and steamboat in background.
Twenty Twenty
20

50
Female.
Spread eagle, capitol at Washington and steam ship in background.
CAMBRIDGE CITY BANK.
Cambridgeport, Mass.
Fifty Fifty
50

Femal, spear and shield,
Hundred
CAMBRIDGE CITY BANK.
Cambridgeport, Mass.
Female, Eagle and globe shipping in the back-grounds.
One Hundred
100
A hunter.

1
Bull's head.
Figure 1 and cupid.
Cows and sheep.
CAMBRIDGE MARKET BANK.
Cambridgeport, Mass.
ONE
Female

TWO
Female.
Figure 2 and cupid
Cows and sheep.
CAMBRIDGE MARKET BANK,
Cambridge, Mass.
2
Cattle and hogs.

Female.
THREE
Man on horseback, cattle and sheep.
CAMBRIDGE MARKET BANK,
Cambridge, Mass.
3
Farmer, sailor, Mechanic and figure three.

Eagle.
Female figure
FIVE
Man on horseback, cattle and sheep.
CAMBRIDGE MARKET BANK,
Cambridge, Mass.
FIVE
5
Man.
Spread Eagle.
FIVE

Man plowing with horses.
X
10
CAMBRIDGE MARKET BANK,
Cambridge, Mass.
TEN
Female with scales.

20
Cattle.
Train of cars.
CAMBRIDGE MARKET BANK,
Cambridge, Mass.
20
Female.

50
Female figure.
Cattle, houses in the distance.
CAMBRIDGE MARKET BANK,
Cambridge Mass.
50

1
ONE
1
Steam Boat. Steam Boat.
1 Blacksmith. anvil and forge 1
Factory and Railroad in background
One.
FALL RIVER BANK
Fall River Mass.
1
Bee Hive.
ONE

1
Female figure and ship.
Females weaving at factory looms
FALL RIVER BANK
Fall River Mass.
1
Portrait of female.

TWO
Female with rake.
TWO
2 Steamboat. 2
FALL RIVER BANK
Fall River, Mass.
TWO
Female with sword and scales
TWO

2
Men, cattle and horses on a plank road.
Female leaning on a bale; ships in back ground,
FALL RIVER BANK
Fall River Mass.
Steam boat
2
Train of cars,

THREE
Portrait of Washington.
THREE
Factories and machinery. Steam boat.
Farming scene.
FALL RIVER BANK
Fall River, Mass.
3
Eagle.
3

3
Anchor.
FALL RIVER BANK,
Fall River, Mass.
Sailor, shipping in background.
3
Portrait of female

FIVE
Female.
5
Shipping. Interior of a blacksmith shop. Train of cars.
FALL RIVER BANK,
Fall River, Mass.
5
Female.
5

5
Blacksmith anvil &c.
FALL RIVER BANK.
Fall River, Mass.
Shipping.
5
Portrait of Female.

TEN
Female.
Shipping. Farming scene.
FALL RIVER BANK.
Fall River, Mass.
10
Female.

10
Sailor.
Steamship.
FALL RIVER BANK.
Fall River. Mass.
10
Female figure.

20
Female with spear.
2 Female. 0
FALL RIVER BANK,
Fall River, Mass.
XX
20
Female.
20

100
Vulcan the blacksmith.
Spread eagle, R. R. and canal.
FALL RIVER BANK,
Fall River, Mass.
100
100
Female.

1 — Train of cars. House and 1. — 1 — Spread Eagle — CHICOPEE BANK, Springfield Mass. — 1 — ONE

2 — Farmer, horses, & harrow & old Pynchon house. 2 — 2 — Loading hay. — CHICOPEE BANK, Springfield Mass. — 2 — TWO

3 — Medallion Head — Vulcan the blacksmith. 3 — Three and 3. — CHICOPEE BANK, Springfield, Mass. — Gen. Washington. — THREE

5 — Large V and reaper. CHICOPEE BANK, Springfield, Mass. — 5 — Female. — Portrait of Washington. — 5

X — Female. — Man ploughing with horses. — 10 — State arms with female on either side. — CHICOPEE BANK, Springfield, Mass. — TEN — TEN

Goddess of liberty eagle & shield. — XX Signing the declaration of independence. — 20 — CHICOPEE BANK, Springfield, Mass. — 20 — 20

50 — Man on horse back, flock of sheep. — 50 — Medallion head. — CHICOPEE BANK, Springfield, Mass. — Medallion head. — 50 50

100 — Female reclining and horn of plenty. — 100 — Medallion head. — CHICOPEE BANK, Springfield, Mass. — Medallion head. — 100

Female figure and 1. — Female supporting the figure 1. Railroad & Steamboat. — 1 — ONE — CITIZENS BANK, Worcester, Mass. — Blacksmith & anvil.

2 — Farmer, dog & grain. — 2 — Cherub and dolphin — Portrait of Z. Taylor. — CITIZENS BANK, Worcester, Mass. — TWO

3 — Sea monsters — Man resting a sledge upon his shoulder, factories & stream of water in the background. — 3 — Steamship. — CITIZENS BANK. Worcester Mass. — State arms.

FIVE — 5 Juno & Mercury, also a griffin standing upon a safe. — V — 5 on right — Female with a rake. — CITIZENS BANK, Worcester, Mass. — Canal Locks — V

TEN — X Cupid. X — Jupiter Juno and Mercury. — CITIZENS BANK, Worcester, Mass. — 10

TWENTY — 20 Female & eagle, portrait of Washington, 20 — Jupiter. — CITIZENS BANK, Worcester, Mass. — Cars — 20

Female warrior. — L Train of cars. L — 2 Female figures. — 50 — CITIZENS BANK, Worcester, Mass. — 50

Indian shooting an arrow. — 100 Neptune. 100 — Statue of Washington. — CITIZENS BANK. Worcester Mass. — 100 — 100

Train of cars. 1 — ONE — Medallion head. — 1 — FITCHBURG BANK, Fitchburg, Mass. — ONE

Spread eagle, railroad and canal. 2 — TWO — Female. — 2 — FITCHBURG BANK, Fitchburg, Mass. — TWO

Man on horse back, and drove of cattle. 3 — 3 — 3 — FITCHBURG BANK, Fitchburg, Mass. — Blacksmith, anvil and forge.

Female. — Canal and inclined railway, buildings on each side. Train of cars. — 5 — Portrait. — FIVE — FITCHBURG BANK, Fitchburg, Mass. — Agricultural implements — FIVE

TEN — State arms. Wharf, shipping and merchandise. Sailor in fore ground. — 10 — Portrait, Mr. Van Buren. — 10 — FITCHBURG BANK, Fitchburg, Mass. — Milk maid.

(New Plate.) FITCHBURG BANK, Fitchburg, Mass. — 20 — XX — Female seated on a bale, holding a sheaf of wheat. — Female.

20 — (1st. Plate.) XX Eagle. XX — 20 — Female. — FITCHBURG BANK. Fitchburg, Mass. — Ship.

20 — (2d. Plate.) 2 Female. 0 — 20 — Female. — Female with spear and shield. — FITCHBURG BANK, Fitchburg, Mass. — XX — 20

FIFTY — 50 Man and horse. 50 — FIFTY — Female. — Female. — FIFTY — FITCHBURG BANK, Fitchburg, Mass. — FIFTY

100 — (Old Plate.) C Phaeton in the car of the Sun. 100 — C — Eagle. — Portrait of Washington. — 100 — FITCHBURG BANK, Fitchburg, Mass. — C

Same as right — Scene on a wharf. — One hundred and 100. — Portrait of Harrison. — FITCHBURG BANK, Fitchburg, Mass. — Portrait of Columbus.

FIVE — Man on horseback talking with a farmer. — FIVE
Vig. Farmers at lunch. Female with basket seated, load of hay, and farm houses in distance. 5
FARMERS BANK OF LANCASTER, Pa.
Dog, key, and Safe.
Pennsylvania. Two females, one standing, sickle, wheat &c. — FIVE

10 — [illegible] in circle. — 10
Medallion head with ten across. Medallion head with ten across.
Vig. Female seated, [illegible] in front of her, wheat in rear.
FARMERS BANK OF LANCASTER, Pa.
10 — Boy with spade and basket of [illegible] spring. — 10

20 — Female with rake; load of hay, &c. — 20
Med. head with twenty across it. Med. head with twenty across it.
Vig. Woodman seated, dog, and axe beside him.
FARMERS BANK OF LANCASTER, Pa.
Same as left.

50 — Man and dog. — 50
Med. head with fifty across it. Med. head with fifty across it.
Vig. Medallion head, cupids on either side, spinning wheels, &c
FARMERS BANK OF LANCASTER, Pa.
50 — Man and dog. — 50

100 — Washington.
FARMERS BANK OF LANCASTER, Pa.
Vig. Harvest field farmers at work
100 — Female, U. S shield, eagle and liberty pole and cap.

1 — Portrait of Washington.
Female. 1 Female.
FALMOUTH BANK, Falmouth, Mass.
1 — Portrait of Franklin.

2 — Portrait of Columbus.
Female. 2 Female.
FALMOUTH BANK. Falmouth, Mass.
2 — Portrait.

3 — Genl. Washington.
Female. 3 Female.
FALMOUTH BANK Falmouth, Mass.
3 — Vulcan the blacksmith.

Female with sword and scales. — FIVE
FIVE Female and cherubs.
FALMOUTH BANK, Falmouth, Mass.
Ship
5 — Female.

10 — Two female figures.
1 Female, chest and key. 0
FALMOUTH BANK, Falmouth, Mass.
10 — 2 females

20 — Female.
Eagle and shield, factories and falls in back ground.
FALMOUTH BANK, Falmouth, Mass.
20 — Female.

100 — Female. — 100
C Shipping. C
FALMOUTH BANK, Falmouth, Mass.
100 — Female. — 100

1 — ONE
View of Harvard College.
CHARLES RIVER BANK, Cambridge, Mass.
1 — Portrait of Judge Story. — ONE

2 — Genl. Washington. — TWO
View of Harvard College.
CHARLES RIVER BANK, Cambridge, Mass.
2 — Portrait of Judge Story. — TWO

3 — Female with sword and scales. — THREE
View of Harvard College.
CHARLES RIVER BANK. Cambridge, Mass.
3 — Portrait of Judge Story. — THREE

Female. — FIVE
View of Harvard College.
CHARLES RIVER BANK. Cambridge, Mass.
5 — Portrait of Judge Story. — FIVE

10 — Portrait of Franklin. — TEN
View of Harvard College.
CHARLES RIVER BANK. Cambridge, Mass.
Male seated
10 — Portrait of Judge Story. — TEN

20 — Female.
Spread eagle; shipping and R. R., in background.
CHARLES RIVER BANK. Cambridge, Mass.
Female with sheaf of wheat. — 20

Medallion head. — 50
State arms, female on either side, also spread eagle on the top.
CHARLES RIVER BANK, Cambridge Mass.
50 — Medallion head.

Female. — 100
CHARLES RIVER BANK. Cambridge, Mass
Horses, chariot and female figure.
100

1 — View of a large building.
CITY BANK, Worcester, Mass.
Mechanic at work in machine shop.
Word one and figure 1 — Same as above.

2 — Same as on ones.
CITY BANK Worcester, Mass.
Three farmers loading wheat, one on top of load another pitching up sheaf and the other holding horse.
TWO
Word two and figure 2 — 2

3 — Same as on ones.
Female reclining machine in centre of ring; sheep and sheafs of wheat on right, safe on left.
CITY BANK Worcester, Mass.
3 — Large figure 3

Word five and letter V
A Bull head man dressing leather and female sewing boots.
CITY BANK Worcester, Mass.
V — 5

Male portrait — X on Ten
CITY BANK, Worcester, Mass.
Worcester city seal.
10 — City bank building

XX — 20
CITY BANK, Worcester, Mass.
Three females.
20 — City Bank building.

50 — 50
CITY BANK, Worcester, Mass.
Portrait of J. C. Calhoun.
50 — City bank building.

1	Female. 1 Female.	1
Portrait of Washington.	BLACKSTONE BANK Uxbridge, Mass.	Portrait of Franklin.

2 TWO	Portrait Female Portrait, sickle and sheaf of wheat.	2 TWO
on med. head 2	BRISTOL COUNTY BANK, Taunton, Mass.	on med head 2

3	BUNKER HILL B'K.	3
Gen. Warren	3 Bunker hill Monument. 3	Eagle and shield.
THREE	Charlestown, Mass.	3

2	Female. 2 Female.	2
Portrait of Columbus.	BLACKSTONE BANK Uxbridge, Mass.	Portrait

TWO	Iron workers; factory in background.	2
Male and female. 2	BRISTOL COUNTY BANK, Taunton, Mass. Eagle	Portrait of Filmore.

FIVE	BUNKER HILL B'K.	5
	Bunker hill Monument.	Gen. Warren.
Female.	Charlestown Mass.	FIVE

3	Female. 3 Female.	3
Washington.	BLACKSTONE BANK Uxbridge, Mass.	Vulcan the Blacksmith.

3	Portrait. Three Portrait Females figures.	3
Medallion head. 3	BRISTOL COUNTY BANK, Taunton, Mass.	Medallion head. 3

X	BUNKER HILL B'K.	10
Gen. Warren.	Bunker hill Monument.	
X	Charlestown Mass.	Female.

Spread eagle.	V	5
FIVE	BLACKSTONE BANK Uxbridge, Mass.	Girl.

3	View of Taunton green.	3
3 Cupids and fig 3	BRISTOL COUNTY BANK. Taunton, Mass. Agricultural implements	Portrait of Clay.

20	XX Eagle XX	20
Female.	BUNKER HILL B'K Charlestown, Mass.	Ship.

Vulcan the blacksmith, train of cars, factories in the backgr'd	X	10
TEN	BLACKSTONE BANK Uxbridge, Mass.	Reaper.

5	Interior of an iron foundry.	5
Female.	BRISTOL COUNTY BANK, Taunton, Mass.	Train of cars

FIFTY	50 Man and horse. 50	FIFTY
Female.	BUNKER HILL B'K.	Female.
FIFTY	Charlestown, Mass.	FIFTY

20	XX Eagle. XX	20
Female.	BLACKSTONE BANK Uxbridge, Mass.	Ship.

10	River, Railroad and train of cars.	10
Anchor and merchandise.	BRISTOL COUNTY BANK. Taunton, Mass.	Portrait of Webster.

Same as right	Scene on a wharf.	One Hundred and 100.
Portrait of Harrison.	BUNKER HILL B'K. Charlestown, Mass.	Portrait of Columbus.

Same as right	Scene on a wharf.	One Hundred and 100.
Portrait.	BLACKSTONE BANK Uxbridge, Mass.	Portrait of Columbus.

	This bank also uses the old Perkins stereotype plates for 5s and 10s. It is used expressly now for 20s 50s and 100s.	

	Train of cars. 1	1
	ABINGTON BANK.	
1	Abington, Mass. State Arms	Female figure and cherubs.

1 on med. head.	Portrait. Shipping. Portrait.	1 on med. head.
ONE	BRISTOL CO. BANK, Taunton, Mass.	ONE
1 on medallion head.		1 on med. head.

1	BUNKER HILL B'K.	1
Female resting her arm upon an urn, bearing the inscription of "Washington."	1 Bunker Hill Monument. 1	Gen. Washington
ONE	Charlestown Mass.	ONE

	Cattle, village and train of cars in the background. 2	2
	ABINGTON BANK.	
2	Abington, Mass. Female head.	State arms.

1	View of Taunton green.	1
Blacksmith, anvil, hammer, &c.	BRISTOL COUNTY BANK, Taunton, Mass.	Female.

2	BUNKER HILL B'K.	2
Female.	2 Bunker hill Monument. 2	Gen. Warren
TWO	Charlestown, Mass.	TWO

	State arms with a female on either side. Cupid and 3.	THREE
	ABINGTON BANK.	Female.
THREE	Abington, Mass. Wheels, bale, etc.	THREE

5. Female eagle and shield. V. Female and sheaf of wheat. FIVE. Female and 5. ABINGTON BANK. Abington, Mass. Wheels, bale, ect	10. Portrait of Fisher Ames. TEN. Train of cars passing through a gap. Female with horn of plenty. DEDHAM BANK, Dedham, Mass. Dog, key, safe. 10. Portrait of Washington. TEN	100. Vulcan the blacksmith. Spread eagle, rail road and canal. ESSEX BANK, Haverhill, Mass. 100. Female.
10. Female, eagle and safe. X. TEN. Portrait of Adams. ABINGTON BANK. Abington, Mass	20. Female and a chest. XX Eagle XX. DEDHAM BANK. Dedham, Mass. 20. Ship.	1. Portrait. ONE. 1 Female seated upon a rostrum with spear and shield, water, vessels, and mountains, in the background. 1. EXCHANGE BANK. Salem, Mass. 1. Female. 1
20. Female. 2 Female with rake. 0. ABINGTON BANK, Abington, Mass. XX. 20. Female. 20	FIFTY. Female. FIFTY. 50 Man and horses. 50. DEDHAM BANK. Dedham, Mass. FIFTY. Female. FIFTY	2. Female spear and shield. TWO. 2 Same Vig., as above. 2. EXCHANGE BANK. Salem, Mass. TWO. Female and ships. 2
50. Female figure. Male and female. ABINGTON BANK, Abbington, Mass. 50. 50. Cupid in a sail boat. 50	One Hundred and 100. Portrait of Harrison. House on a wharf. DEDHAM BANK. Dedham, Mass. Same as left. Portrait of Columbus.	3. Justice. THREE. 3 Same Vig., as above. 3. EXCHANGE BANK. Salem, Mass. III. Female and ship in distance. 3
100. Vulcan. Eagle, train of cars and canal. ABINGTON BANK, Abington, Mass. 100. 100. Female.	Female sitting on the ground supporting the figure 1, train of cars and steamboat. 1. 1. ESSEX BANK. Haverhill, Mass. 1. Female.	5. Female. V. 5 Same Vig. 5. EXCHANGE BANK. Salem, Mass. FIVE. Female with scales and sword. 5
1. Portrait of Fisher Ames. ONE. ONE Interior of a blacksmith shop. ONE. DEDHAM BANK. Dedham, Mass. 1. Portrait of Washington. ONE	2. Two female figures, steamboat in the distance. 2. ESSEX BANK, Haverhill, Mass. 2. Female.	10. Portrait of Washington. TEN. Same Vig. EXCHANGE BANK. Salem, Mass. TEN. Portrait. 10
2. Portrait of Fisher Ames. TWO. TWO Spread eagle. TWO. DEDHAM BANK. Dedham, Mass. 2. Portrait of Washington. TWO	Train of cars. THREE. 3. ESSEX BANK, Haverhill, Mass. 3. Blacksmith and sailor, and figure 3	20. Female. XX Eagle XX. EXCHANGE BANK. Salem, Mass. 20. Ship
3. Portrait of Fisher Ames. THREE. Female seated, farmers gathering grain. Factories and a machine. DEDHAM BANK. Dedham, Mass. 3. Portrait of Washington. THREE	5. Two females and motto "Prosperity and liberty," factory, steamship and train of cars in the distance. 5. ESSEX BANK, Haverhill, Mass. 5. Group of females, and figure 5	Also 20s old Perkins stereotype plate.
5. Portrait of Fisher Ames. FIVE. Man on horseback, cars, and on foot. Train of Cattle. DEDHAM BANK. Dedham, Mass. Dog, key, safe. 5. Portrait of Washington. FIVE	TEN. Two females, bust and shield, ship in the distance. X. ESSEX BANK. Haverhill, Mass. 10. State arms	CAMBRIDGE BANK, Cambridge Mass. This Bank uses the Perkin's stereotype Plate, which is the denomination printed in 9ns letters all over the bill.

ONE Cows, farmer ploughing and train of cars. 1 Portrait of Webster. FRAMINGHAM B'K Framingham, Mass. 1 2 females.	FIFTY Female. FIFTY 50 Man and horse. 50 FRAMINGHAM B'K Framingham, Mass. FIFTY Female. FIFTY	Farmers and load of hay. Portrait. 1 ONE GRAFTON BANK, Grafton, Mass. Female bathing Portrait of H. Clay.
1 Female figure. 1 ONE Female ONE sitting on a bale with a horn of plenty. Shipping in backg round. FRAMINGHAM B'K, Framingham, Mass. 1 Eagle. 1	ONE Wharfs and shipping. ONE GLOUCESTER BANK Gloucester, Mass. Horses and dray 1 Sailing vessel. ONE	TWO Portrait of Webster. Female weaving at factory looms. GRAFTON BANK, Grafton, Mass. Dog TWO Portrait.
Female with sickle and sheaf of wheat. Factory and train of cars. TWO 2 Cattle and hogs. FRAMINGHAM B'K. Framingham, Mass. 2 2 Blacksmith, anvil and forge.	2 TWO 2 Wharfs and shipping. TWO GLOUCESTER BANK Gloucester, Mass. Ship, bbls., etc 2 Horse, cart, and barrels 2	Female blowing a horn, also farmers and load of hay. GRAFTON BANK, Grafton, Mass. THREE 3 Portrait.
2 Female and eagle. 2 2 Female sitting on a bale with horn of plenty. 2 Shipping in background. FRAMINGHAM B'K Framinzham, Mass 2 Female figure. 2	THREE Wharfs and shipping. GLOUCESTER BANK, Gloucester, Mass. 3 Ship.	V Interior of a shoemakers shop. GRAFTON BANK, Grafton, Mass. Portrait. V Portrait. 5 Female sewing boot, child resting upon her lap.
3 Farming scene. 3 FRAMINGHAM B'K Framingham, Mass. Machinery and bale 3 Portrait of Washington.	FIVE Wharfs and shipping. GLOUCESTER BANK Gloucester, Mass. 5 FIVE Horses and waggon. Merchandise.	X Portrait of W. Penn. Wild horses running across a plain. GRAFTON BANK, Grafton, Mass. 10 Portrait.
3 Eagle standing upon a rock overlooking the sea. 3 3 Female sitting upon a bale with 3 horn of plenty. Shipping in background. FRAMINGHAM B'K Framingham, Mass. 3 Female figure. 3	TEN Wharf's and shipping. GLOUCESTER BANK, Gloucester, Mass. 10 Sail boat. X	Farmer sowing seed. FIFTY L Milk maid and cows. GRAFTON BANK, Grafton, Mass. 50 Portrait.
5 Farmers gathering corn. 5 FRAMINGHAM B'K Framingham, Mass. FIVE 3 male and 2 female figures and a large V.	20 Eagle. Wharf's and shipping. 20 GLOUCESTER BANK Gloucester, Mass. XX Sail vessels. 20	1 Male and female. ONE 1 Steamboat and sailing vessels. 1 GRAND BANK, Marblehead, Mass. 1 Female figure. ONE
5s. 10s, 20s, 50s, and 100s old plate of Perkins stereotype.	50 Wharf's and shipping. 50 GLOUCESTER BANK, Gloucester, Mass. 50 Sailor, merchandise and shipping. FIFTY	2 Ship. 2 Female resting her arm upon fence; dog. 2 GRAND BANK, Marblehead, Mass. 2 Agricultural implements 2
X Milk maid and cows. Ten [illegible] FRAMINGHAM B'K Framingham, Mass 10 Female with dog, and 3 cherubs.	100 Wharf's and shipping. GLOUCESTER BANK, Gloucester, Mass. 100 Sail vessels	Eagle. FIVE 5 6 [illegible] figures 5 GRAND BANK, Marblehead, Mass. Statue of Washington.

10 Sailor, his foot resting on a cannon. 10 X Ship. X GRAND BANK, Marblehead Mass. 10 Bee hive. 10	50 Female. BASS RIVER BANK Beverly Mass. Shipping. 50 Sailor with chart &c.	Vulcan the the blacksmith. TEN X BEVERLY BANK, Beverly Mass. 10 Reaper.
20 Female figure. 2 Female. 0 GRAND BANK, Marblehead, Mass. XX 20 Female. 20	1 Female, train of cars and canal. BEVERLY BANK, Beverly, Mass. 1 Female.	10 Female merchandise and shipping BEVERLY BANK, Beverly, Mass. TEN X 10 Cupid.
Steamboat XX Train of cars. 3 female figures, eagle and shield. 20 GRAND BANK, Marblehead, Mass. XX Milk maid.	Female One, cupid. BEVERLY BANK, Beverly, Mass. Shipping. 1 Female.	20 Female. XX Eagle XX BEVERLY BANK, Beverly, Mass. 20 Ship.
ONE Sailor and merchandise. 1 View of Beverly bridge and Beverly in the back ground. BASS RIVER BANK, Beverly Mass. Man ,rowing 1 Steam ship. ONE	Farmers washing sheep. 2 2 BEVERLY BANK, Beverly Mass. TWO Females. TWO	FIFTY Female. FIFTY 50 Man and house 50 BEVERLY BANK. Beverly, Mass. FIFTY Female. FIFTY
2 Horses. 2 BASS RIVER BANK. Beverly Mass. Same vig. as ones Loading hay 2 Cows. 2	2 2 BEVERLY BANK, Beverly, Mass. Female and eagle ships in distance. 2 2 Two females.	1 Portrait of Washington. Female. 1 Female. LYNN MECHANICS' BANK, Lynn, Mass. 1 Portrait of Franklin.
3 Female. 3 Vig. Same as ones. BASS RIVER BANK. Beverly Mass. 3 Farmer sailor and Blacksmith. and fig. 3	Farming scene. 3 BEVERLY BANK, Beverly, Mass. 3 Female. THREE	2 Portrait of Columbus. Female. 2 Female. LYNN MECHANICS' BANK, Lynn, Mass. 2 Portrait.
Female. 5 BASS RIVER BANK. Beverly Mass. Bust of Webster also sailor, Indian, and two females. 5 Group of females and figure 5.	Three female figures. 3 Portrait of Webster. BEVERLY BANK, Beverly. Mass. 3 Shipping.	3 Gen. Washington. Female. 3 Female. LYNN MECHANICS' BANK, Lynn, Mass. 3 Vulcan the blacksmith.
10 Female also farmer with rake, house and barn. BASS RIVER BANK. Beverly Mass. TEN X Fountain.	Spread eagle. FIVE V and female. BEVERLY BANK. Beverly Mass. 5 Girl	FIVE Female. V LYNN MECHANICS' BANK, Lynn, Mass. 5 Ship.
TWENTY 20 TWENTY Female, R. R. and steam ship in back-ground. BASS RIVER BANK. Beverly Mass. 20 XX	FIVE Sailor and flag. BEVERLY BANK Beverly, Mass. Group of females factory and shipping. 5 Portrait of Washington	10 X 10 Man, and yoke of oxen. 10 LYNN MECHANICS' BANK, Lynn, Mass. TEN Female.

20 XX Eagle. XX 20 LYNN MECHANICS' BANK, Lynn, Mass. Female. Ship.	20 2 Female. 0 20 Female. LAIGHTON BANK. Lynn, Mass. Female. 20 XX	(New Plate.) 10 X 10 LEE BANK, Lee, Mass. Female. Square Beehive
FIFTY 50 Man and horse. 50 FIFTY Female. Female. LYNN MECHANICS' BANK. Lynn, Mass. FIFTY FIFTY	50 Male and female. 50 Cupid in a sailboat. LAIGHTON BANK. Lynn. Mass. Female, 50 50	20 XX Eagle. XX 20 LEE BANK, Lee, Mass. Female. Ship.
100 C Phoebus in the chariot of the sun. 100 C Eagle. Portrait of Washin ton LYNN MECHANICS, BANK, Lynn, Mass. 100 C	100 Spread eagle, railroad and canal. 100 LAIGHTON BANK, Lynn, Mass. Male figure. Female. 100	FIFTY 50 Man and horse. 50 FIFTY Female. Female. LEE BANK, Lee, Mass. FIFTY FIFTY
Same as right One Hundred and 100. Scene on a wharf. LYNN MECHANICS' BANK, Lynn, Mass. Portrait of Harrison. Portrait of Columbus.	ONE 1 Female, also eagle and shield surrounded by the several state arms; ship in distance. 1 ONE Female. Portrait of Washington. ONE LEE BANK, Lee, Mass. ONE State Arms	Female. Male and female. 1 1 ONE MACHINISTS' BANK Taunton, Mass. Female with scales. Man seated on plow
Female sitting on the ground supporting the figure 1. 1 Portrait of Franklin. 1 ONE LAIGHTON BANK, Lynn, Mass. Portrait of a boy. 1	TWO 2 Female each side of figure 2 in centre; city in background. 2 Female, Female figure, and large figure 2. TWO LEE BANK, Lee, Mass. State Arms	Female, anvil, wheel &c.; ship building and train of cars in background. 2 2 TWO MACHINISTS' BANK Taunton, Mass. Reaper. Indian in canoe
Blacksmith shoeing a horse. 2 2 2 LAIGHTON BANK, Lynn, Mass. Female. State Arms	5 Male figure and anchor, shipping and a city in background. V 5 Blacksmith, anvil and forge. Girl. FIVE LEE BANK, Lee, Mass. FIVE	Female with a pen in her right hand, her left resting on a globe. 3 3 THREE MACHINISTS' BANK Taunton, Mass. 2 females. Indian
Female and eagle. 3 Portrait of Washington. THREE 3 LAIGHTON BANK, Lynn, Mass. Indian woman and child.	5 Female, 5 Female. 5 Cupid in a cloud, with a basket of flowers upon his head. 5 LEE BANK, Lee, Mass. State Arms	Train of cars. Large V with female in the centre. 5 FIVE MACHINISTS' BANK Taunton, Mass. Female.
State arms, female on each side. 5 5 5 LAIGHTON BANK, Lynn, Mass. Portrait of Webster. Wheels, bales, etc.	5 5 5 LEE BANK, Lee, Mass. Female. Female	Spread eagle, railroad and canal. 10 TEN MACHINISTS' BANK Taunton, Mass. Female.
TEN Farming scene. 10 Female. LAIGHTON BANK, Lynn, Mass. Portrait of Adams. Wheels bales, ect.	10 Man and yoke of oxen. 10 TEN X 10 LEE BANK, Lee, Mass. Female.	Blacksmith, anvil and forge. 2 Female. 0 20 20 MACHINISTS' BANK Taunton, Mass. Spread eagle and shield. XX

50 | Male and Female. | 50 Female figure. | MACHINISTS' BANK Taunton, Mass. 50 | Cupid in a sailboat. 50	100 | Spread eagle, R. R., and canal. | 100 Vulcan the blacksmith. | FRANKLIN, Co. BANK. Greenfield, Mass. 100 | Female with with rake.	Two males and female. ONE | Female supporting the figure 1. 1 AGAWAM BANK, Springfield, Mass. Deer | 1 Portrait of a female
100 Vulcan the blacksmith. | Spread eagle, railroad and canal. MACHINISTS' BANK Taunton, Mass. 100 | 100 Female.	Large figure 1 across each end of bill with a female on the body of it. ONE | Ships and steamboat. FAIRHAVEN BANK. Fairhaven, Mass. | Justice on a fig. 1. ONE	2 | Indian with figure 2, deer and canoe. AGAWAM BANK. Springfield, Mass. State Arms. | 2 Reaper.
ONE | Cattle, farmer ploughing, train of cars in the distance. 1 FRANKLIN Co. BANK. Greenfield, Mass. 1 | 1 Portrait of Washington	Large 2 and female bust. TWO | Whale fishing. FAIRHAVEN BANK. Fairhaven, Mass. | Same as left. TWO	Two females. 3 | 3 AGAWAM BANK. Springfield, Mass. Cow | 3 Portrait of a boy.
Farmer ploughing, with horses, steamboat in the distance. TWO | 2 FRANKLIN Co. BANK, Greenfield, Mass. 2 | 2 Portrait of Franklin.	3 Sailor and capstan. | Female and motto "Enterprise." FAIRHAVEN BANK. Fairhaven, Mass. THREE THREE | 3 Farmer, sailor and mechanic, and figure 3	A party of Indians receiving a company of white men. 5 | V and female. AGAWAM BANK. Springfield. Mass. | FIVE Female. 5
Farmer, sailor and mechanic, 3 gold dollars. 3 | FRANKLIN Co. BANK. Greenfield, Mass. | 3 Portrait of Webster.	5 Female 5 | Eagle and shield. V FAIRHAVEN BANK. Fairhaven, Mass. | FIVE Medallion head. 5	Female with sickle and sheaf of wheat. X | X AGAWAM BANK. Springfield Mass. Products and implements | 10 Portrait of a girl.
Farming scene. 5 | 5 FRANKLIN, Co. BANK, Greenfield, Mass. Imp. and products | FIVE Female. FIVE	Female, grain &c., rail road and canal in background. X | 10 FAIRHAVEN BANK. Fairhaven, Mass. | TEN Medallion head. 10	20 Cupid in a sail boat. 20 | Steamship. AGAWAM BANK. Springfield, Mass. Products and implements | 20 Spread eagle and shield.
Female, eagle and shield, portrait of Washington. TEN | X FRANKLIN Co. BANK. Greenfield, Mass. | 10 2 females.	20 Female with spear. | 2 Female. 0 FAIRHAVEN BANK. Fairhaven, Mass. XX | 20 Female. 20	50 Indian girl with bow and arrows. | Female and eagle on shield. AGAWAM BANK. Springfield, Mass. Cow | 50 Female.
20 Female figure. | 2 Female. 0 FRANKLIN Co. BANK, Greenfield, Mass. XX | 20 Female sitting on the ground. 20	50 Female with spear. | Male and female. FAIRHAVEN BANK Fairhaven, Mass. 50 | 50 Cupid in a sail boat. 50	100 Female resting her hand upon a capstan. | Load of grain crossing a bridge. 100 AGAWAM BANK. Springfield, Mass. Deer | 100 Milk maid.
50 Female figure resting her arm upon a pillar. | Male with hammer, female with rake. FRANKLIN, Co. BANK, Greenfield, Mass. 50 | 50 Cupid in a sail boat. 50	100 Vulcan the blacksmith. | Spread eagle, R. R. and canal. FAIRHAVEN BANK. Fairhaven, Mass. 100 | 100 Female.	CONCORD BANK, Concord, Mass. This Bank uses the old Perkin's sterrotype plate, which is the denomination printed in fine letters all over the bill.

1 | Portrait of female. | Female sitting on a bale also two cherubs, shipping and train of cars in background. 1 | HADLEY FALLS BANK, Holyoke, Mass. | 1 | Indian woman and child.	3 | Ship building. | THREE | Farmer sowing seed. Cattle | HAVERHILL BANK, Haverhill, Mass. | 3 | Indian. | THREE	Spread eagle shield and anchor, village and shipping in background. Large V with female within. | FIVE | HINGHAM, BANK Hingham, Mass. | 5 | Girl.
2 | American flag and shield surmounted by an eagle, at right is female instructing children; at left an Indian woman and child 2 on right. | HADLEY FALLS BANK. Holyoke, Mass. | TWO 2 | Anvil and hammer.	FIVE | Milk maid. | State arms. Farming scene. State arms. | HAVERHILL BANK, Haverhill, Mass. | 5 | Female. | FIVE	Vulcan the blacksmith. | TEN | X | HINGHAM, BANK Hingham, Mass. | 10 | Reaper.
THREE | Female feeding an eagle from a cup | THREE | 3 Three men. 3 | HADLEY FALLS BANK, Holyoke, Mass. | 3 | Sailor and flag, shipping in background.	10 | Female. | TEN | TEN Cattle, man on horseback. TEN | HAVERHILL, BANK Haverhill, Mass. | 10 | Female. | 10	20 | Female. | XX Eagle. XX | HINGHAM, BANK Hingham, Mass. | 20 | Ship.
FIVE | Female drawing water from a well. | FIVE | 5 Machinery. | HADLEY FALLS BANK, Holyoke, Mass. FIVE | 5	20 | Female figure. | 2 Female 0 | HAVERHILL, BANK Haverhill, Mass. | 20 | Female. | 20	1 on medallion head. | Portrait of Washington. | Train of cars and two horses. Medallion head. | HOLYOKE BANK, Northampton, Mass. | 1 Eagle 1 | 1 | Sailor.
10 | X | HADLEY FALLS BANK, Holyoke, Mass. | View of Hadley Falls; mountains in background | 10 | X	50 | Female figure. | Male and female. | HAVERHILL, BANK Haverhill, Mass. | 50 | Cupid in a sailboat. | 50	2 | Portrait of J. Q. Adams. | HOLYOKE BANK, Northampton, Mass. Female portrait. Female, shield and merchandise, steamboat in background. Locomotive | 2 | Portrait of J. Hancock.
XX | Female with scales and sword. | State arms and two horses, Factory, train of cars and steamboat. | HADLEY FALLS BANK, Holyoke, Mass. | 20 | Female.	100 | Vulcan the blacksmith. | Spread eagle. R. R. and canal. | HAVERHILL, BANK Haverhill. Mass. | 100 | Female.	5 | Indians upon a precipice, overlooking a city. | Female. | HOLYOKE BANK, Northampton, Mass | V Female V | 5 | Female, eagle and shield.
C | River, train of cars crossing a bridge; city in distance. | HADLEY FALLS BANK Holyoke, Mass. | Three female figures. | 100 | Ship; city in distance.	ONE | Steamboat and sail vessels. 1 | HINGHAM. BANK Hingham, Mass. | ONE | Indian girl with bow and arrows | ONE	10 | Portrait of Franklin. | Portrait of female. Winged female and horn of plenty | HOLYOKE BANK, Northampton. Mass. | X Female. X | 10 | Female receiving an apple from female above.
1 | Children sailing boats in a tub. | ONE | Steamboat, sail vessels | Plough and sheaf of wheat | HAVERHILL BANK Haverhill, Mass. | 1 | Blacksmith, anvil and forge. | ONE	2 | TWO | 2 | Ships 2 | HINGHAM, BANK Hingham, Mass. | TWO | Female drawing water from a well | TWO	Milk Maid. | 1 | (Old Plate.) Cattle, sheep and hogs; scene in Brighton on a market day. | B'K OF BRIGHTON, Briguton, Mass. | 1 | General Washington | ONE
2 | Indian with bow. | TWO | Train of cars passing through a gap. Female and shield. | HAVERHILL BANK, Haverhill, Mass. | 2 | Vessel. | TWO	THREE | Reapers. 3 | HINGHAM, BANK Hingham, Mass. | THREE | Steamboat. | 3	1 | ONE | 1 | View of Cattle fair hotel. | B'K OF BRIGHTON, Brighton, Mass. | 1 | A bulls head. | ONE

TWO	(Old Plate.)	2
Female.	Cattle, sheep and hogs; a scene in Brighton on a market day.	
2	B'K OF BRIGHTON, Brighton, Mass.	TWO

2	(New Plate.	TWO on 2.
TWO	View of cattle fair hotel.	
2	B'K OF BRIGHTON, Brighton, Ma s.	Yoke of oxen

3	(Old Plate.)	3
Portrait.	Cattle, sheep and hogs; a scene in Brighton on a market day.	Cattle.
3	B'K OF BRIGHTON, Brighton. N. Y.	THREE

3	(New Plate.)	3
THREE	View of Cattle fair hotel.	THREE
3	B'K OF BRIGHTON, Brighton, Mass.	Cattle.

5	(Old Plate.)	5
Portrait of Franklin.)	Cattle, sheep and hogs; scene in Brighton on a market day.	Female.
5	B'K OF BRIGHTON, Brighton. Mass.	V

5	(New Plate.)	FIVE, 5, V.
V and FIVE	View of Cattle fair hotel.	
5	B'K OF BRIGHTON, Brighton, N. Y.	Cattle and sheep.

10	(Old Plate.)	10
Portrait of Washington.	Cattle, sheep and hogs; a scene in Brighton on a market day.	Female.
10	B'K OF BRIGHTON, Brighton, Mass.	TEN

X	(New Plate.)	10
Portrait of Webster.	View of cattle fair hotel.	
TEN	B'K OF BRIGHTON, Brighton, Mass.	Locomotive.

TWENTY	(Old Plate.)	20
	Cattle, sheep, and hogs; a scene in Brighton on a market day.	Train of cars
Female.	B'K OF BRIGHTON, Brighton, Mass	XX

XX	(New Plate	20
	View of cattle fair hotel.	
Portrait of Washington	B'K OF BRIGHTON, Brighton, Mass.	Female and shield.

Portrait of Washington.	Drove of cattle.	50
50	B'K OF BRIGHTON, Brighton, Mass.	Locomotive.

Female.	Drove of cattle.	100
100	B'K OF BRIGHTON, Brighton, Mass.	Portrait of Franklin.

ONE	1 Vig. Head of Washington. 1	ONE
Compt's die.	OLIVER LEE & Co.'s BANK	
ONE	Buffalo, N. Y. Secured &c.	

2	2 Vig. A Buffalo in foreground (large,) smaller one in distance. 2	TWO
Compt's die.	OLIVER LEE & Co.'s BANK	
2	Buffalo N. Y. Secured &c.	

3	3 Vig. Marine view, Ships, vessels, and a steamboat. 3	THREE
Compt's die	OLIVER LEE & Co.'s BANK	
3	Buffalo N. Y. Secured, &c.	

5	5 Vig. A large buffalo in foreground smaller in distance.	FIVE
Compt's die	OLIVER LEE & Co.'s BANK	Large figure 5 female and head of Washington.
5	Buffalo N. Y. Secured, &c,	FIVE

10	10 Vig. Nautical view, ship, steamboat and other vessels.	TEN
Compt's die.	OLIVER LEE & Co.'s BANK	A female in Roman costume, with helmet and spear.
10	Buffalo N. Y. Secured, &c.	TEN

20	20 Vig. Nautical view, ship steamboat, and other vessels. 20	20
Compt's die.	OLIVER LEE & Co.'s BANK	Female with sheaf under her arm.
20	Buffalo N. Y Secured, &c.	20

50	50 Vig. Nautical view, ships, and vessels, foam dashing up about the bows of foremost ship. 50	50
Compt's die	OLIVER LEE & Co.'s BANK,	Medallion head of Liberty.
50	Buffalo N. Y. Secured, &c.	50

C	100 Vig. Nautical view, same as fifty.	100
Compt's die.	OLIVER LEE & Co.'s BANK	Farmer with agricultural implements.
C	Buffalo N.Y. Secured, &c	100

1	Female bathing. Vig. Female seated on rock over-looking city. ONE	1
	MEDINA BANK Medina, N. Y.	
Compt's die.	Locomotive.	ONE

2	Compt's die. Vig. Two females with frame, in which is agricultural implements, houses on right, train of cars on left.	2
	MEDINA BANK Medina, N. Y.	2
	Horse.	

5	Vig. Portrait of Jefferson with two females on either side, nautical view on left. Compt's die.	5
	MEDINA BANK Medina, N. Y.	V
	Building.	

Female with rake.	1 Vig. Female seated with oxen.	1
Compt's die.	GENESEE VALLEY BANK. Genesee, N. Y.	Cows, and pigs.
	Safe.	

2	Vig. Farmer seated with jug, basket, dog, &c.	2
Compt's die.	GENESEE VALLEY BANK	Two Females standing
TWO	Genesee' N. Y. Wheat.	

5	Vig. Oxen and sheep.	5
Spread eagle	GENESEE VALLEY BANK,	
Compt's die	Genesee, N. Y. Ox	Female leaning on figure 5.

Indian.	10 Vig. Farmers at dinner, loading hay, &c.	10
	GENESEE VALLEY BANK,	
Compt's die	Genesee, N Y. State Arms.	Male portrait

ONE 1 Vig. Eagle on branch of tree. 1
Female portrait. ONE
FARMER'S & DROVER'S BANK, Somers, N Y.
View of Croton dam between signatures.
Female in standing position, figure 1 full width of note.

ONE 1 Vig. Eagle on a branch. 1
Female portrait. ONE
WOOSTER SHERMAN'S BANK, Watertown, N. Y.
Male portrait
Female standing in large figure one.

ONE MUTUAL BANK, Troy, N. Y. 1
Vig. Artisans at work
Compt's die. Male portrait

TWO 2 Vig. Female seated; agricultural implements, factory on left; canal boat and cars on right; steamboat in distance. 2
Compt's die TWO
FARMER'S & DROVER'S BANK, Somers, N Y. Men and cattle.
Mechanic seated, tools, horn of plenty, &c., surrounded with corn.

TWO 2 Female seated with wheat &c. 2
Compt's die. TWO
WOOSTER SHERMAN'S BANK, Watertown, N. Y.
Artisan with horn of plenty.

2 Compt's die Vig. Artisans at work. 2
Female portrait.
MUTUAL BANK, Troy, N. Y.
TWO

3 3 Vig. Female portrait in frame, surrounded by flags, drum, cannon, &c. 3
Compt's die III
FARMER'S & DROVER'S BANK, Somers, N. Y. Men and cattle.

Figure 3 with female on either side. 3 Female portrait, female on either side. 3
III
WOOSTER SHERMAN'S BANK, Watertown, N. Y.

Vig. Artisans at work. 3 Compt's die. 3
3
MUTUAL BANK, Troy, N. Y.
Male portrait

5 V Vig. Three females seated; surrounded by ornamental figure 5. V 5
Female seated, balances, eagle, key, safe, &c. FIVE
FARMER'S & DROVER'S BANK, Somers, N Y. Men and cattle.
Medallion head. FIVE

5 V Female seated in large figure 5, female on either side V 5
Compt's die. FIVE
WOOSTER SHERMAN'S BANK, Watertown, N. Y
Male portrait.
Medallion head. FIVE

V MUTUAL BANK, Troy, N Y 5
Male portrait.
Compt's die. 5
Vig. Old man seated talking to children.

10 Vig. Two females representing agriculture, &c., spread eagle in min. case, farming implements, locomotive and cars, houses &c. on left; steamship, barrels, &c. on right. 10
Female adjusting scales, eagle, key, safe, &c. TEN
FARMER'S & DROVER'S BANK, Somers, N. Y. Men and cattle.
Two females, liberty cap, mounted eagle, vase of flowers, &c. TEN

ONE Vig. Building, load of hay, &c. ONE
1 Compt's die.
UNION BANK, Albany, N. Y.
Canal boat
1 Male portrait.

TEN 10 Vig. Old man seated talking to children. 10 X
Male portrait.
MUTUAL BANK, Troy, N. Y. TEN
Compt's die

TWENTY 20 Vig. Female in sitting posture, globe by her side, steamship in the distance. 20
Same as tens. TWENTY
FARMER'S & DROVER'S BANK, Somers, N. Y. Men and cattle.
XX

TWO Vig. Buildings, street, &c. 2
2 Compt's die.
UNION BANK, Albany, N. Y.
Beaver.
Male portrait.

XX Old man seated talking to children. XX 20
Compt's die
MUTUAL BANK, Troy, N. Y. XX
Male portrait.

5 HAGERSTOWN SAVINGS BANK, Hagerstown, Md. 5, V & FIVE.
Two females on either side of bee hive in mark to rest.
Large V, on which is Five Dollars on lathe strip.
Bust of Blacksmith.

FIVE Vig. Male portrait, with locomotive on left factory on right FIVE
5 Compt's die
UNION BANK, Albany, N. Y.
Secured, etc
5 Portrait of Washington.

ONE ONE Pig pen, pigs and chickens. 1
CATARACT CITY BK Paterson, N. J.
ONE
Treas. die.

X American shield; on right is female instructing children; on left is Indian, squaw and papoose. 10
Washington
Title of Bank.
Female runner.

TEN UNION BANK, Albany, N. Y.
Male portrait. 10
X Vig. Cupids with wheat. X
Large X with the word "TEN" running across it and 10. Compt's die.
10

2 Title of Bank. TWO 2
TWO
Treas. die. View of horse shoe falls and tower at Niagara Falls. 2
TWO
TWO

20 Title of Bank. 20
Cows; men mowing and house on right; man plowing on left. XX
XX
Woodcutter.

TWENTY 20 Vig. Female with shield, American eagle, &c. XX
Male portrait. 20
UNION BANK, Albany, N. Y.
Secured, etc.
Compt's die XX

3 THREE CATARACT CITY BK Paterson, N. J. 3
THREE
Indian female contemplating the progress of civilization. THREE
THREE
Treas. die.

Left end	Centre	Right end
1 Compt's die. ONE	Vig. Female with mirror; shipping and cars in distance. WESTERN BANK, Lockport, N. Y. Barrel and bales.	1 Female seated. ONE
10 Eagle. Compt's die.	(New Plate.) Vig. Female seated, with shipping in the distance. CHEMUNG CANAL BANK, Elmira, N. Y. Wheat &c.	Bale of goods &c. 10 Train of cars
Large figure 5, cars crossing bridge; Indians. Compt's die.	Vig. Female seated on bales; cars and shipping in distance. CITY BANK, Oswego, N. Y.	5 FIVE 5
2 Compt's die.	Vig. Oxen, men fishing on right; farmer ploughing, locomotive and cars on left. WESTERN BANK, Lockport, N. Y Man shearing sheep.	2 Milk maid seated.
1 Female portrait.	Vig. Harvest scene with man on horseback. MONROE BANK OF ROCHESTER, Cuba, N. Y.	1 Compt's die
TEN Sailor seated Compt's die.	10 Amer. eagle. CITY BANK, Oswego, N. Y	TEN Female seated. 10
5 FIVE Compt's die.	Vig. Locomotive and cars. WESTERN BANK, Lockport, N. Y. Man and plough.	5 Two females are seated holding figure 5.
Female portrait. 2	MONROE BANK OF ROCHESTER, Cuba, N. Y. Female seated by a shield; waterfall in front. 2	2 Compt's die
20 Compt's die.	Vig. Two females with mirror, eagle, &c. CITY BANK, Oswego, N. Y.	20 Portrait of Washington
10 Compt's die.	Vig. Eagle, shipping in distance. WESTERN BANK, Lockport, N. Y. Safe.	10 Female standing with flowers and anchor.
3 Three females.	Vig. Cows and sheep. MONROE BANK OF ROCHESTER, Cuba, N. Y. 3 3	3 Compt's die
1 Compt's die. 1	HERKIMER Co. B'K, Little Falls, N. Y. 1 Portrait of child with wheat and sickle. 1	Female seated with wheat. 1
Compt's die. Steamer.	1 Vig. Locomotive and cars. CHEMUNG CANAL BANK, Elmira, N. Y. Farmer, plow, &c.	Figure 1 with "ONE" running across it. Female leaning on figure 1.
FIVE Two Indians with bows, one seated the other standing.	Compt's die. MONROE BANK OF ROCHESTER, Cuba, N. Y.	5 Female seated by a shield.
2 Compt's die. 2	HERKIMER Co. B'K, Little Falls, N. Y. 2 Vig. Female seated with sheaf of wheat. 2	Female standing in large figure 2.
Female Indian. Compt's die.	2 Vig. Dairy maid, oxen, &c. CHEMUNG CANAL BANK, Elmira, N. Y. Dogs head.	2 Child with shell, &c. TWO
10 Compt's die.	Vig. Indian holding horse with left hand spear in right hand; train of railroad cars. MONROE BANK OF ROCHESTER, Cuba, N. Y. X	TEN Female and child seated at foot of a tree. 10
3 Compt's die. 3	Title of Bank 3 Vig. Eagle on branch of tree; train of cars. 3 TH 3 REE	THREE Portrait of child. THREE
Compt's die. Portrait of female.	3 Vig. Farmer with oxen and sheep. CHEMUNG CANAL BANK, Elmira. N. Y. Wand and flowers.	3 Two females standing.
XX Compt's die.	Vig. Drove of wild horses, two more prominent than others. MONROE BANK OF ROCHESTER, Cuba, N. Y. Female bust.	TWENTY Indian woman with bow and arrows, and female kneeling with sickle and grain. 20
5 Compt's die. 5	HERKIMER Co. B'K. Little Falls, N. Y. 5 Vig. Oxen, sheep, &c 5 5	FIVE Female seated in large figure 5. FIVE
FIVE FIVE Compt's die.	5 Vig. Two females with the bust of Washington, and American shield. CHEMUNG CANAL BANK, Elmira, N. Y. Locomotive and cars.	FIVE Female seated in a large figure 5. FIVE
1 Compt's die.	Vig. Woodman kneeling, &c. Gold dollar. CITY BANK, Oswego, N. Y. State Arms.	1 Public building. ONE
10 Compt's die. 10	TEN TEN HERKIMER Co. B'K, Little Falls, N. Y. Vig. Female seated with eagle, &c.	TEN State arms. X
10 Male portrait. 10	X Vig. Compt's die. X CHEMUNG CANAL BANK, Elmira, N. Y. Head of horse	Female holding the word "TEN." 10
TWO Compt's die. TWO	2 Vig. Ship in die. 2 CITY BANK, Oswego, N. Y.	Sailor. 2
100 Goddess of liberty with eagle; Union is strength; E Pluribus Unum. 100	HERKIMER Co. B'K. Little Falls, N. Y. Male portrait. Male portrait. Vig. Man killing snakes with clubs.	100 Female churning.

Left end	Centre	Right end
1 Compt's die. 1	State arms. FALL KILL BANK, Poughkeepsie, N. Y.	1 View of falls.
TWO TWO	Vig. Drove of cattle, 2 men, one on horse back, and horse drinking from trough at a pump. Compt's die. FARMERS' BANK OF LANSINGBURGH, N. Y. 2	TWO Large figure 2, and a female with pail behind her.
100 Man and boy with guns.	Compt's die. Vig. Buildings, viaduct, locomotive and train of cars on right; Indians and wigwams on left. QUASSIACK BANK, Newburgh, N. Y.	100 C
Justice. Compt's die.	2 Drover watering his horse. FALL KILL BANK. Poughkeepsie, N. Y.	2 Falls.
Vig. Sailor, female, mechanic, ship and steamer on left; buildings, viaduct &c., on right. Three females and a large [illegible]	Compt's die. FARMERS' BANK OF LANSINGBURGH, N. Y. 5	FIVE Large figure 5, two Indians, viaduct, train of cars, water fall, and rural scenery.
ONE Compt's die.	Farmer ploughing. COMMERCIAL B'K, Whitehall, N. Y.	ONE Female.
3 Compt's die.	3 Boiler maker seated on boiler. FALL KILL BANK. Poughkeepsie, N. Y.	3 Falls.
Sailor, mechanic and farmer holding aloft a wreath on which is figures 10.	FARMERS' BANK OF LANSINGBURGH, N. Y. Vig. Two horses and a plow, man engaged in fastening the traces to plough, horse on right; steamboat on left.	Large X with ten across it, milkmaid with pail, cow, viaduct, train of cars, &c. Compt's die.
2 Compt's die. TWO	Sailor. Portrait of Washington. Female reaper. COMMERCIAL B'K. Whitehall, N. Y.	2 Compt's die. TWO
Falls. 5	Two female figures emblematic of manufactures. FALL KILL BANK, Poughkeepsie, N. Y.	5 Compt's die.
1 Train of cars, boys, telegraph wires, Washington's head quarters, &c.	QUASSIACK BANK, Newburgh, N. Y. Bust in oval. Compt's die.	1 Scene on a plank road, carriage, man on horse back, sheep, omnibus, load of hay, &c.
Compt's die. 3 State arms.	Steamboat leaving wharf. COMMERCIAL B'K, Whitehall, N. Y. Schooner.	3 Cupid. THREE
TEN Female TEN	FALL KILL BANK. Poughkeepsie, N. Y. 10 Falls. 10	Liberty and large X. Compt's die.
2 Same as on ones.	QUASSIACK BANK, Newburgh, N. Y. Bust in oval. Compt's die.	TWO Same as on ones.
Female with sword. Compt's die.	5 Vig. Female seated with artisans tools, steamer in distance. COMMERCIAL B'K, Whitehall, N. Y.	5 Male with basket of corn.
Falls. 20	FALL KILL BANK. Poughkeepsie, N. Y. 20 Washington. Compt's die.	TWENTY Liberty, science, globe, &c.
V Same as on 1s and 2s.	QUASSIACK BANK, Newburgh, N. Y. Bust in oval. Compt's die.	V Man and merchandise on wharf; steamboat, barges, vessels, &c.
1 Compt's die. 1	DAIRYMENS' B'K. Newport, N. Y. Vig. Female with pail on head, cows, &c.	ONE Male portrait. ONE
50 Falls.	Female portrait. Compt's die. FALL KILL BANK. Poughkeepsie, N. Y.	FIFTY Railroad. FIFTY
X Vig. Indian with gun, behind a ledge of rocks, watching deer.	QUASSIACK BANK, Newburgh, N. Y. Compt's die.	TEN Bust in oval.
2 Compt's die. TWO	Loading hay. DAIRYMENS, B'K, Newport, N. Y.	TWO Female reaper.
C 100	FALL KILL BANK. Poughkeepsie, N. Y. View of falls, American and Indian female on either side. Steamship.	Compt's die. 100
XX Vig. Same as tens.	QUASSIACK BANK, Newburgh, N. Y. Compt's die.	20 Bust in oval.
5 Female reaper.	Vig. Canal boat. DAIRYMENS' B'K. Newport, N. Y.	5 Compt's die.
ONE Compt's die.	FARMERS' BANK OF LANSINGBURGH, N. Y. Vig. Train of cars, bridge, canal boat; village in background, rural scenery, &c.	ONE Female and large figure 1.
FIFTY DOLLARS. Two Continental soldiers, one sitting with pipe in hand—the other standing and reclining on his gun.	Compt's die. Vig. Indians in a canoe, rocks, trees, and mountains. QUASSIACK BANK, Newburgh, N. Y.	50 Little girl sitting at a table, with left hand over left eye to protect it from the light.
TEN Horse and cow. X	DAIRYMENS' B'K. Newport, N. Y. Compt's die.	X Three females with anchor, wheat, &c.

5 Female head. FIVE | Vig. American shield in centre containing figures of ship, plough, and sheafs of wheat. On left two Indians male and female with child, mountains in distance. On right female with three children, sheaf of wheat, trees and farm houses in distance. BK OF GETTYSBURG Gettysburg, Pa. Loading hay. | 5 Female head. FIVE

2 2 | Vig. Female reclining, factories in an oval frame, sheep, grain, &c. Compts die. UNION BANK Kinderhook, N. Y. | 2 Two females one standing and the other kneeling.

10 Compt's die. 10 | Vig. Farmers mowing CHAUTAUQUE Co. BANK Jamestown, N. Y. | Oxen. Female. Portrait. 10

TEN head. X | Vig. Two females supporting shield, containing the arms of the different states, with a representation of an eagle. BK OF GETTYSBURG Gettysburg, Pa. Female bathing. | TEN head 10

3 Compts die | UNION BANK Kinderhook, N. Y. 3 3 Vig. Eagle on branch of a tree, cars, &c., in the distance. | The word "Three" with the figure 3 running across. Female walking with pail.

Two males with females on shoulders. Compt's die. | 1 Vig. Female seated holding figure 1. CHESTER BANK, Chester, N. Y. | 1 Female churning.

---

20 Female. holding cup, eagle in the act of drinking. XX | Vig. Washington surmounted by an eagle, on the left female seated having in right hand pole with liberty cap, on the right, two females, one reclining and the other kneeling behind her; ship on the left, and railroad bridge on right in distance. Title of bank. Agricultural implements. | XX Female head. 20

5 Compts die. | UNION BANK, Kinderhook, N. Y V Vig. Three females sitting, the middle one a little above the others one with a quadrant, another with a pair of compasses and the middle one with sickle. V | 5 Man driving cattle; trees, bridge, telegraph poles &c.

2 Compt's die TWO | Vig. Mirror with male on right, female on left. CHESTER BANK, Chester, N. Y. | 2 Locomotive and cars.

L 50 L | Vig. Three farmers harvesters in fore-ground; town and water on right in distance trees and hay stacks on left. BK OF GETTYSBURG Gettysburg, Pa. Eagle. | Medallion head of female with 50 on it. 50

Female standing, and resting on her left elbow. TEN | UNION BANK Kinderhook, N. Y. Compts die Three females seated, one of whom is reclining, and a pair of compasses in her hand | 10

5 Compt's die. FIVE | Vig. Female with liberty pole, seated by American eagle with figure 5. CHESTER BANK, Chester, N. Y. | 5 Figure of Justice standing.

---

1 Compt's die ONE | Vig. male ploughing. BANK OF COXSACKIE. Coxsackie, N. Y. | 1 Indian seated with gun in hand.

XX Man talking to a boy who is sitting on the ground. | UNION BANK Kinderhook, N. Y. Compts die. | 20 Mechanic sitting with hammer in right hand; factories &c.

Vig. Female holding 2 on right, and 0 in left hand. 20 | Compt's die. CHESTER BANK. Chester, N. Y | 20 Female portrait.

Female. holding figure 2. Compt's die. | Vig. Horse running from locomotive in distance. BANK OF COXSACKIE. Coxsackie, N. Y. | 2 Female milking cows

1 Compt's die. 1 | 1 Vig. Man seated by die with 1 on it, an eagle on top with motto—"Internal improvements." 1 CHAUTAUQUE Co. BANK. Jamestown, N. Y. | 1 Oxen. 1

1 Compt's die. | Vig. Farmers at lunch loading hay in distance BANK OF WHITESTOWN, Whitestown, N. Y. | 1 Goddess of liberty.

---

3 Portrait of Female. 3 | BANK OF COXSACKIE. Coxsackie. N. Y. Vig. Female seated on safe, with dog and child. | 3 Compt's die.

2 Compt's die. 2 | 2 Vig. Oxen in small die. 2 CHAUTAUQUE Co. BANK Jamestown, N. Y. | 2 Vessel ready to launch. 2

TWO Compt's die. TWO | 2 Vig. Female seated with sickle, wheat, &c. 2 BANK OF WHITESTOWN, Whitestown, N. Y. Trees &c. | Artisan with horn of plenty

---

State Arms. 10 | Male portrait. BANK OF COXSACKIE. Coxsackie, N Y. | 10 Compt's die.

3 Compt's die 3 | 3 Vig. Oxen in small die. 3 CHAUTAUQUE Co. BANK Jamestown, N. Y. | 3 Male portrait. 3

Washington and horse. Compt's die. | Vig. Oxen, sheep &c. BANK OF WHITESTOWN, Whitestown, N. Y. | FIVE Female with wheat. 5

Compts die. Figure 1 and the words one dollar. | One Vig. Female sitting with pail on her lap, cows, &c., UNION BANK Kinderhook, N. Y. | 1 Bust of female with sheaf of grain; man in oval frame

5 Compt's die. 5 | CHAUTAUQUE Co. BANK Jamestown, N. Y. Vig. Indian springing bow | FIVE Female Portrait. V

10 Compt's die TEN | Vig. Mirror with female on either side; shipping and cars in distance. BANK OF WHITESTOWN, Whitestown, N. Y. Trees, ox, &c. | 10 State arms. TEN

ONE figure 1 on shield. Female milking cows 1
Female with rake.
Compts die. HUNGERFORD'S. BK Adams, N. Y. 1

5 Vig. farmer and female seated, agricultural implements &c. Landscape view between them. 5
Compts die Female portrait
FIVE AGRICULTURAL BK Herkimer. N. Y. Dog's head FIVE

3 3 Vig. female seated by furnace with pestle and mortar. 3 3
3 Compts die.
3 ESSEX CO., BANK Keeseville, N. Y. steamer. 3

Figure 2 on shield. Compts die. Loading hay. 2
HUNGERFORD'S B'K Adams, N. Y.
Male portrait. Female portrait.

10 Vig. Female seated between 1 0 key in one hand, horn of plenty in the other. Safe X 10
Compts die AGRICULTURAL BK Herkimer, N. Y. Female churning.

5 5 Female seated; Eagle. 5
Compt's die. ESSEX CO., BANK Keeseville, N. Y. FIVE
5 cupid riding a deer.

3 HUNGERFORD'S BK Adams, N. Y. 3 on medallion head.
Compts die. 3 Vig female with shield; steamer in distance. 3 female portrait.

ONE JEFFERSON CO. BK Watertown, N. Y. 1
Male portrait
Compts die. Vig. Locomotive and cars.

10 10 Vig 10
Compts die. Eagle Goddess of liberty mechanics' arm and justice. TEN
10 ESSEX CO., BANK Keeseville. N. Y.

5 Vig. horses, colt, trees, &c. 5
Canal boat and bridge.
Compt's die. HUNGERFORD'S BK Adams, N. Y. 5

3 3 Female with an Eagle and shield 3
Compts die. JEFFERSON CO., BK Watertown, N. Y. Female portrait.
3 American eagle.

TWENTY 20 Vig. Archimedes raising the world with lever resting on mountain. 20 TWENTY
ESSEX CO., BANK Keeseville, N. Y. Artisan at work.

TEN Compts die. Vig. drove of sheep man on horse; mill in background. X on shield.
HUNGERFORD'S BK Adams. N. Y. Wheat, plough, &c.
male portrait.

Compts die. Farmer seated with sickle loading hay in distance 3
JEFFERSON CO., BK Watertown. N. Y.
large figure 3 and three cupids. Female portrait.
Secured, etc.

Secured &c. 1 Vig. Female with child, sheaf of wheat on right; ship in distance on left. Ornamental die. ONE
ONE FARMERS BANK Hudson, N. Y. Man, dog and birds. Female seated.

Female with arm resting on large figure 1 1 Vig cattle, and train of cars in the distance. Figure 1 with One running across.
AGRICULTURAL BK Herkimer, N. Y.
Compts die. Safe. Milkmaid seated.

5 Shipping, steamer &c. 5
Compt's die. JEFFERSON CO., BK Watertown, N. Y. Engine Female with wheat.

TWO 2 Vig. Female seated with sickle and grain factory on left, and canal boat, Locomotive and cars on right in distance. 2 Man seated with mechanical implements.
Compts die.
TWO FARMERS BANK, Hudson, N. Y. Cattle.

Secured &c. 1 Vig. Female and child wheat, anchor, &c; ship in the distance. ONE
AGRICULTURAL BK Herkimer, N. Y.
ONE Sheaf of wheat, &c. Female, cars in distance.

10 X Two females with safe key horn of plenty &c X TEN
Compt's die. JEFFERSON CO., BK. Watertown. N. Y. Farmer ploughing
10 Locomotive and cars. 10

5 Vig. Group of females, holding globe; dragon and lions. Steamship, and ship on right. 5
Compts die. FARMERS BANK Hudson, N. Y. cattle. Female seated resting on shield, man mowing in distance.
FIVE FIVE

TWO 2 Vig female seated on plow, wheat sickle &c. 2
Compts die.
TWO AGRICULTURAL BK Herkimer, N. Y. Dogs head. Female portrait surrounded with corn.

ONE 1 Vig female seated with wheat. 1 1
Indian head. ESSEX CO., BANK. Keeseville, N. Y. Compts die.
ONE Eagle. 1

10 Vig. Two females seated resting on shield, steamship on right locomotive, factory, cars on left in distance. 10
Compts die State arms
TEN FARMERS BANK Hudson, N. Y. cattle. TEN

3 Female with liberty pole and cap shield with 3 on it eagle, cask, bale &c. 3
AGRICULTURAL BK Herkimer, N. Y.
Compts die. dogs head.

2 TWO 2 2
Female 2 Indian Compts die
2 ESSEX CO., BANK Keeseville. N. Y. Mechanics' arm. 2

20 Compts die. Vig. Oxen, waggon and, farmers loading grain. TWENTY
Full length female.
Male portrait. FARMERS BANK Hudson, N. Y. TWENTY

ONE Compt's die 1 Vig. Portrait of Washington. 1 CAYUGA Co. BANK. Auburn, N. Y. ONE Child seated. ONE DOLLAR. DOLLAR. ONE Figure standing.	FIVE Washington. FIVE 5 Vig. Man seated by water, ship pitching. 5 BANK OF TROY, Troy, N. Y. 5 Compt's die 5	Compt's die. Portrait of girl. 2 Vig. Farmers at lunch. CROUSE BANK. Syracuse, N. Y. Wheat &c. 2 Girl with wheat.
TWO Compt's die. 2 Vig. Male portrait; shipping and cars in background. Bee hive. CAYUGA Co. BANK, Auburn, N. Y. Man's head. TWO Figure standing.	X Male portrait X 10 Vig. Female seated, with mirror, eagle, &c. 10 BANK OF TROY, Troy, N. Y. 10 Compt's die. 10	5 Eagle. Compt's die. Vig. Female, eagle, shield, portrait of Washington &c. CROUSE BANK, Syracuse, N. Y. Wheat &c. FIVE Five female with large figure 5.
Compt's die. THREE 3 Vig. Portrait of Andrew Jackson, female on either side. CAYUGA Co. BANK, Auburn, N. Y. Eagle. 3 Indian in canoe. THREE	XX 20 Vig. Locomotive and cars. 20 BANK OF TROY, Troy, N. Y. Female standing. XX	10 Compt's die. TEN Vig. Artisans. CROUSE BANK. Syracuse. N. Y. Dog. 10 Female portrait. TEN
5 Compt's die. 5 Public building. Vig. Figure standing. Wheat &c CAYUGA Co. BANK. Auburn, N. Y. FIVE FIVE 5 FIVE	Secured &c. ONE 1 Female and child; ship in distance. Die. BANK OF WATERTOWN, Washington, N. Y. Anvil and hammer. ONE Female seated.	Female seated on wheat with scales. Compt's die. 20 Vig. Shipping; city in distance. CROUSE BANK, Syracus N. Y. Female seated. TWENTY Sailor hoisting American FLAG.
10 Compt's die. 10 Locomotive and cars. Vig. Figure standing. Canal scene. CAYUGA Co. BANK, Auburn, N. Y. Indian in canoe, TEN X TEN	TWO Compt's die. TWO 2 Female reaper. 2 BANK OF WATERTOWN. Washington, N. Y. Wheat &c. Artisan with horn of plenty.	5 Washington. 5 Vig. Train of cars, village in the distance. MINERS BANK OF POTTSVILLE, Pa. Eagle. 5 Female. 5
50 Compt's die. 50 L Portrait of Washington. L CAYUGA Co. BANK, Auburn, N. Y. Sampson and lion. Female with eagle. 50	Secured &c. Figure 3, female on either side, I I I 3 Female. Portrait of female. Female. BANK OF WATERTOWN, Washington, N. Y. Wheat &c. 3	10 Webster. TEN Head of Randolph. Vt. Eagle on branch of tree; train of cars and canal and boats in the distance. MINERS BANK OF POTTSVILLE PA. 10 Fillmore. TEN
1 Compt's die. 1 1 Vig. Female with horn of plenty; liberty pole, cap, &c. 1 BANK OF TROY, Troy, N. Y. ONE	5 Compt's die. FIVE V Females with large figure 5. V BANK OF WATERTOWN, Washington, N. Y. FIVE Wheat, etc. 5 Med. Head. FIVE	20 Female. 20 Columbus. Vig. Winged female blowing a trumpet, globe, eagle, flags &c. Washington. MINERS BANK OF POTTSVILLE, PA. Dogs Head. 20 Female 20
2 Compt's die. 2 Vig. Two cupids riding two whales. BANK OF TROY, Troy, N. Y. TWO	10 Compt's die. TEN Vig. Mirror with female on either side; cars and shipping in distance. BANK OF WATERTOWN, Washington, N. Y. Wheat &c 10 State arms. TEN	50 Female 50 Franklin. Vig. A female seated between 5 and 0, barrel, bales, &c. ship on left. Fulton. MINERS BANK OF POTTSVILLE, PA. Eagle. 50 Female. 50
3 Compt's die. 3 3 Vig. Female seated holding figure 3. 3 BANK OF TROY, Troy, N. Y. 3 Portrait of female, 3	ONE Stone cutter at work. ONE Compt's die. Vig. Man shoeing horse. CROUSE BANK, Syracuse, N. Y. 1 Artisan. ONE	C Portrait of Washington. Vig. Eagle on branch of tree; view of Niagara Falls, in the background. MINERS BANK OF POTTSVILLE PA. Horse 100 Franklin.

Goddess of Liberty. 1 Whaling scene; two ships, whale and whale boat. ONE Bust of female. Compt's die. SUFFOLK CO. BANK Sag Harbor, N. Y. ONE	10 View of Lynn Common. 10 CITY B'K OF LYNN Mass. X State arms 10	3 Portrait of female. 3 Portrait of female. 3 Gen. Washington. ADAMS BANK. North Adams, Mass Man with sledge.
TWO Vig. Two females, box, barrel, sheaf of wheat; on left female with sickle in hand, and ship in distance. 2 2 Compt's die. Medallion head of female. TWO SUFFOLK CO. BANK Sag Harbor, N. Y. 2	20 CITY B'K OF LYNN Mass. TWENTY 20 State Arms. Female on each side TWENTY	Indian with bow. 5 Vulcan and two female figures. 5 V Train of cars V ADAMS BANK, North Adams, Mass. V
3 Eagle Large figure 3 with Female on right and female in clouds on left. Compt's die. SUFFOLK CO. BANK Sag Harbor, N. Y.	Train of cars. 50 CITY B'K OF LYNN Mass. 50 Portrait of Webster.	10 X Archimides. X Female Train of cars. ADAMS BANK. North Adams, Mass 10 10
FIVE Ship under sail. 5 FIVE Vig. Three females sitting; box; compass and sheaf of wheat the female on left is pointing to ship. Medallion head. Compt's die. SUFFOLK Co. BANK Sag Harbor. N. Y. FIVE	C CITY B'K OF LYNN Mass. 100 Three cherubs, one turning a screw, one splitting a block with wedge, the other lifting rock with lever. Ship C 100 C	20 Female between figures 2 and 0. 20 Female. Female with spear. ADAMS BANK, North Adams, Mass 20 XX
10 Vig. Steamboat; ship under full sail leaving port, ship in distance 10 Full length female. Compt's die. SUFFOLK Co. BANK Sag Harbor. N. Y.	ONE Farmer sowing grain. 1 1 Ship. 1 ADAMS BANK, North Adams. Mass. ONE	50 Male and female. 50 Cupid in a sail boat. Female figure. ADAMS BANK. North Adams. Mass 50 50
TWENTY 20 Female, Eagle sitting; and ship in distance at shield left of female. 20 Compt's die SUFFOLK Co. BANK Sag Harbor, N. Y.	1 Female. 1 Female. 1 Portrait of Washington. ADAMS BANK. North Adams. Mass. Portrait of Franklin.	ONE (Old Plate.) 1 Train of cars. 1 ONE Drove of cattle. AGRICULTURAL BANK, Pittsfield, Mass. ONE
View of Lynn Common. ONE on 1 Figure 1 with one running across it CITY B'K OF LYNN Mass. portrait.	TWO Spread Eagle 2 2 2 ADAMS BANK, North Adams, Mass. Sail boats	ONE on 1 (New Plate.) 1 Farming scene. Female instructing children. AGRICULTURAL BANK, Pittsfield, Mass. Indian woman and child.
View of Lynn Common. 2 CITY B'K OF LYNN Mass 2 Sailor on shipboard.	2 Female. 2 Female. 2 Portrait of Columbus. ADAMS BANK. North Adams, Mass. Portrait.	(Old Plate.) TWO 2 Milk maids; vessels in the distance. 2 AGRICULTURAL BANK. Pittsfield. Mass. Man ploughing with horse. State Arms.
FIVE View of Lynn Common. 5 5 CITY B'K OF LYNN Mass. The word "FIVE" with a large V running across. FIVE 5	THREE Wharf and shipping. 3 on right 3 ADAMS BANK. North Adams, Mass. 3 Train of cars	(New Plate.) Farming scene; female in foreground. TWO in 2 on right 2 Two female figures. AGRICULTURAL BANK. Pittsfield. Mass. State arms.

Left	Centre	Right
Female with sickle and horn of plenty; ship in distance. Three on 3	AGRICULTURAL BK, Pittsfield, Mass. Vig. White and black horse facing each other, Indian on shield surmounted with eagle between them, at right of black horse a steamboat, on left of white horse canal boat, cars and manufacturing establishment.	3 Milk maid; cars and house in distance.
TWO Female. 2	2 Farming scene 2 NORTHAMPTON BK, Northampton, Mass.	TWO Female. 2
State arms. ONE	Milk maid and cows Cupid and 1 on right. LANCASTER BANK Lancaster, Mass.	ONE Female figure
Female with sickle 3	State arms and 2 horses; factories, railroad and steamboat in distance. AGRICULTURAL BANK, Pittsfield, Mass.	3 [illegible]
2 Portrait.	Female. 2 Female. NORTHAMPTON BK, Northampton, Mass.	2 Portrait.
Female. TWO	Female sitting upon the ground leaning upon a bale, factory, village in background. LANCASTER BANK Lancaster, Mass.	2 Indian woman and child.
FIVE Man and agricultural implements. 5	5 View of Pittsfield. 5 AGRICULTURAL BANK, Pittsfield, Mass. State Arms	FIVE
THREE Man sharpening a scythe. 3	3 Female and eagle. 3 NORTHAMPTON BK, Northampton, Mass.	THREE Sailor. 3
FIVE	Female figure. V LANCASTER BANK Lancaster, Mass.	5 Ship.
FI V VE Train of cars passing under a bridge.	Female reclining with her arm upon a chest; factories in background. AGRICULTURAL BK, Pittsfield, Mass.	5 Wood cutter.
5 FIVE 5	V Spread eagle; shipping in background. V NORTHAMPTON BK, Northampton, Mass.	5 FIVE 5
FIVE Female sitting on a bale.	5 Cupid Cows, farmer ploughing also a train of cars. LANCASTER BANK Lancaster, Mass.	FIVE Indian girl with bow spear and arrows
10 X 10	Man and oxen. Large 10 at the right of Vig. AGRICULTURAL BANK, Pittsfield, Mass.	TEN Female figure.
FIVE	Spread eagle and shield; village in distance. Large V, female and cupid. NORTHAMPTON BK, Northampton, Mass.	5 Girl.
10 X 10	10 Man an oxen. LANCASTER BANK Lancaster, Mass.	TEN Female figure.
10 Portrait of Webster.	Train of cars. AGRICULTURAL BK, Pittsfield, Mass.	Ten, X, 10. Hay makers.
10 X 10	Man and oxen. 10 NORTHAMPTON BK, Northampton, Mass.	TEN Female.
10 Female figure.	Farming scene. LANCASTER BANK Lancaster, Mass.	TEN A bulls head.
20 Female.	XX Eagle. XX AGRICULTURAL BANK, Pittsfield, Mass.	20 Ship
TEN	Vulcan the blacksmith; train of cars and factories in the background. X NORTHAMPTON BK, Northampton, Mass.	10 Reaper.
20 Female.	XX Eagle. XX LANCASTER BANK Lancaster, Mass.	20 Ship.
ONE Bust. ONE	1 Interior of a blacksmith's shop. 1 NORTHAMPTON BK, Northampton, Mass.	ONE Female. ONE
20 Female.	XX Eagle. XX NORTHAMPTON BK, Northampton, Mass.	20 Ship.
FIFTY Female. FIFTY	50 Man and horse. 50 LANCASTER BANK Lancaster, Mass.	FIFTY Female. FIFTY
1 Portrait of Washington.	Female. 1 Female. NORTHAMPTON BK, Northampton, Mass.	1 Portrait of Franklin.
FIFTY Female. FIFTY	50 Man and horse. 50 NORTHAMPTON BK, Northampton, Mass.	FIFTY Female. FIFTY
Same as right Portrait of Harrison	Scene on a wharf. LANCASTER BANK Lancaster, Mass.	One Hundred and 100. Portrait of Columbus

ONE — Female. — Compt's die.
MERCHANTS' BANK OF WESTFIELD N.Y.
Vig. Female seated, leaning on a shield; ship and steamboat in the distance on the left.
1 — Portrait of Daniel Webster.

Female. — Compt's die.
Vig. Locomotive and train of cars.
MERCHANTS' BANK OF WESTFIELD, N.Y.
II — 2 — TWO

5 — Compt's die — FIVE
Vig. Cattle and sheep
MERCHANT'S BANK OF WESTFIELD, N.Y.
5 — Portrait of Washington

ONE — Compt's die — ONE
Vig. Farmer and Indian on either side of a shield.
STATE OF NEW YORK BANK, Kingston, N. Y.
Gold dollar.
1 — Man dressing leather.

Compt's die — 2
State Arms.
STATE OF NEW YORK BANK, Kingston, N. Y.
Schooner.
2 — Stone cutter at work.

3 — Portrait of Dewitt Clinton.
STATE OF NEW YORK BANK, Kingston, N. Y.
Vig. Sailor, woman, mechanic; ship and steamboat in the distance.
3 — Compt's die

V — Compt's die.
Vig. Kingston Academy, with wagon hauled with flag stone, horses, and driver.
STATE OF NEW-YORK BANK, Kingston, N. Y.
Clasped hands.
FIVE — 5 — Male portrait.

Figure 10 with cupids on either side — View of Washington Irving's residence.
STATE OF NEW YORK BANK, Kingston, N. Y.
Letter X with Ten running across it. — Compt's die.

50 — Squaw in a resting posture, wigwams in distance.
STATE OF NEW YORK BANK, Kingston, N. Y.
Compt's die.
50 — Woman with pen in hand, resting on a book.

Secured by pledge of &c. — ONE
1 Vig. Female with sword, child, cornucopia, anchor, agricultural implements, &c; ship in distance.
FARMERS & MECHANICS' BANK OF GENESEE, Buffalo, N. Y.
ONE — Female seated, cows, and vessel in distance.

TWO — Compt's die. — TWO
2 Vig. Female seated, agricultural implements factory, canal boat and cars; steamboat in distance. 2
FARMERS' AND MECHANICS' BANK OF GENESEE, Buffalo, N. Y.
Mechanic seated, tools, horn of plenty, &c. surrounded with corn.

5 — Compt's die. — FIVE
V FI 5 VE V
Vig. Three females, centre one seated in large figure 5; factories, cars, and agricultural implements on the left, vessels and articles of commerce on the right, wheat, &c.
FARMERS' & MECHANICS' BANK OF GENESEE, Buffalo, N. Y.
5 — Medallion head. — FIVE

ONE — Ship in full sail.
Compt's die, 1
Vig. Houses and shipping, sailor in foreground.
MARINE BANK, Buffalo, N. Y.
ONE — Ship in full sail.

2 — Compt's die.
TWO TWO
Shipping and marine view.
MARINE BANK, Buffalo, N. Y.
2 — Sailor holding flag.

5 — Compts die.
FIVE FIVE
Marine view.
MARINE BANK, Buffalo, N. Y.
5 — Canal boat passing under a bridge

X — Compts die.
X Whaling scene. X
MARINE BANK, Buffalo, N. Y.
10 — Ship in full sail

1 — Load of hay, drove of cattle &c.
Vig. Cows, three sheep reclining.
WEST WINDFIELD, West Windfield, N. Y
1 — Compts die

2
Drove of cattle and sheep. — Compt's die.
WEST WINDFIELD, West Windfield, N. Y.
Locomotive.
2 — Female.

5 — 5
WEST WINDFIELD BANK, West Windfield, N. Y.
Locomotive and cars crossing bridge; mountains in distance.
5 — Compt's die.

Compts die. — Sailor, bbl. bale of cotton &c.
Steamship.
WEST WINDFIELD BANK, West Windfield, N. Y.
10 — Blacksmith, forge an anvil, anchor, &c.

Compts die. — Portrait of Jackson.
Vig. Capitol at Washington.
WEST WINDFIELD BANK, West Windfield, N. Y.
20 — Portrait of Webster.

ONE — Female with sickle and sheaf of wheat. — ONE
1 Hampden bank building, store and Hotel. 1
HAMPDEN BANK, Westfield, Mass.
ONE — Farmers mowing. — 1

2 — Female and sheaf of wheat.
2 Same vignette as above 2
HAMPDEN BANK, Westfield, Mass.
Steamboat
2 — Train of cars.

THREE — Female figure. — THREE
3 Same as above. 3
HAMPDEN BANK, Westfield, Mass.
Ship
3 — Man and sheep. — THREE

FIVE — Milk maid. — FIVE
Same as above
HAMPDEN BANK, Westfield, Mass.
FIVE — Eagle and &.

TEN — Portrait of [illegible] — TEN
Same as above
HAMPDEN BANK, Westfield, Mass.
10 — Female with wreaths.

FIFTY — Medallion Head. — 50
Same vig. as the others
HAMPDEN BANK, Westfield, Mass.
50 — Portrait. — FIFTY

Female.	View in Essex street, Salem.	1
		Elephants.
ONE	ASIATIC BANK Salem Mass.	ONE

TWO	View in Essex street, Salem.	TWO
Elephants		Female.
TWO	ASIATIC BANK Salem, Mass.	TWO

THREE	View in Essex street, Salem.	3
Female.		Elephants.
THREE	ASIATIC BANK Salem, Mass.	THREE

Female.	View in Essex street, Salem.	V
		Elephants.
FIVE	ASIATIC BANK. Salem, Mass.	FIVE

TEN	10 View in Essex street, Salem X	10
	ASIATIC BANK Salem, Mass.	Female.

20	20 Party of milk maids.	20
Man ploughing with horses.		Ship.
20	ASIATIC BANK Salem, Mass.	XX

20	XX Eagle XX	20
Female.	ASIATIC BANK Salem, Mass	Ship

FIFTY	50 Man and horse. 50	FIFTY
Female with wreath.		Female.
FIFTY	ASIATIC BANK Salem, Mass.	FIFTY

50	Male and female.	50
		Cupid in sail boat.
Female figure.	ASIATIC BANK Salem Mass. 50	50

Same as right	Scene on a wharf.	One Hundred and 100.
Portrait of Harrison.	ASIATIC BANK Salem, Mass.	Portrait of Columbus

100	Spread Eagle train of cars and canal.	100
Vulcan	ASIATIC BANK Salem Mass. 100	Female

1	Train of cars.	1
Female with scales.	ANDOVER BANK Andover Mass. Eagle	Portrait of Samuel Farrar.

TWO	Three female figures.	2
Female with the American flag.	ANDOVER BANK Andover, Mass. Indian head	Portrait of Samuel Farrar.

3	Three female figures.	3
State arms	ANDOVER BANK Andover, Mass. Cog-wheels, etc.	Portrait of Samuel Farrar.

Three female figures.	Spread eagle.	5
FIVE	ANDOVER BANK Andover, Mass. Girl's head.	Portrait of Samuel Farrar.

10	Winged female blowing a trumpet.	10
Portrait of Samuel Farrar.	ANDOVER BANK Andover. Mass. Imp. and products	Female holding scales.

20	Farming scene.	20
Portrait of Samuel Farrar.	ANDOVER BANK Andover, Mass	Female.

Female with sheaf of wheat.	Landing of Columbus	50
50	ANDOVER BANK Andover Mass.	Portrait of Female.

Female seated.	Vig. Harbor scene, ships, steamers, &c.; buildings in the distance	5
5	ERIE CITY BANK, Erie, Pa.	
FIVE		Locomotive

X	Vig. Female sitting on a log, grain, farm-house to the left, and rail cars in the distance.	10
TEN	ERIE CITY BANK, Erie, Pa.	Two farmers with rakes, dog, &c.

20	Vig. Eagle, three females sitting; ship on the left, &c.	20
Male portrait.	ERIE CITY BANK. Erie, Pa.	
XX	Female in water.	Two men.

50	Vig. Arms of state, factory, railway, canal, steamer, &c.	50
Medallion head	ERIE CITY BANK. Erie, Pa.	Portrait of Washington.
50		

Secured by pledge, &c.	1 Vig. Female with sword Die child, cornucopia, anchor, agricultural implements, &c; ship in distance.	ONE
ONE	MIDDLETOWN B'K. OF ORANGE CO. Middletown, N. Y. Girl milking.	Female seated, cars and vessel in distance.

TWO	2 Vig. Female seated; agricultural implements; factory on left; canal boat and cars on right; steamboat in distance. 2	Mechanic seated, tools, horn of plenty, surrounded by ears of corn
Compt's die.		
TWO	Title of Bank. Female milking.	

5	Vig. Group of persons, centre female holding a globe in one hand, key in the other seated in chariot; lions at her feet; vessel and steamship in the distance.	Female pointing towards cars in the distance; man cradling.
Compt's die.		
FIVE	Title of Bank. Female milking.	FIVE

10	Vig. Two females seated, shield, balances and sickle between them; mill, agricultural implements, cars, steamboat, barrels, &c.	10
Compt's die.	MIDDLETOWN BK. OF ORANGE CO. Middletown, N Y.	State die.
TEN	Female milking.	TEN

TWENTY	20 Vig. Female seated, left hand extended towards steamboat, chemical apparatus, table and writing implements, globe, &c. 20	
Compt's die.		XX
TWENTY	Title of Bank. Female milking	

1 Eagle and shipping. ONE 1 Female. COMMERCIAL B'K. Salem, Mass. Female. ONE ONE	(New Plate.) 100 Spread eagle, railroad, and canal. 100 Vulcan the blacksmith. COMMERCIAL B'K, Salem, Mass. Female.	1 Farmer eating dinner in the open field 1 Portrait. DANVERS BANK. Danvers, Mass. Portrait.
TWO 2 Female, merchandise, and a ship in distance. 2 TWO Ship. COMMERCIAL B'K. Salem Mass. Head of an Indian. TWO TWO	(Old Plate.) 100 C Phœbus in the chariot of the sun. 100 C Eagle. COMMERCIAL B'K, Salem, Mass. Portrait of Washington. 100 C	2 Milk maid and cows. 2 Portrait. DANVERS BANK. Danvers, Mass. Portrait.
3 THREE Indian seated on a rock. THREE 3 Male figure. COMMERCIAL B'K. Salem, Mass. Ship. THREE THREE	Farmer sowing seed. ONE Man on horseback, flock of sheep. 1 ONE CONWAY BANK. Conway, Mass. Female. Ducks	3 Female resting upon a bale; manufacturing village in distance. 3 Portrait. DANVERS BANK. Danvers, Mass. Portrait.
5 Female. River, steamboat, ship and bridge. V 5 Cattle. COMMERCIAL B'K, Salem Mass. Cattle. FIVE FIVE	2 CONWAY BANK. Conway, Mass. TWO Mechanic and sailor. TWO DOLLARS. Two females supporting a sheaf of wheat.	5 Farmer ploughing with horses. 5 Portrait. DANVERS BANK. Danvers, Mass. Portrait.
10 10 Whale ships. Large X, female and horn of plenty. 10 Ship. COMMERCIAL B'K. Salem, Mass. Ship. TEN TEN	Men driving a drove of cattle across a river. 3 3 3 CONWAY BANK, Conway, Mass. 3 females and sheaf of wheat.	10 Spread eagle, capitol at Washington, and steam ship in distance. 10 Portrait. DANVERS BANK. Danvers, Mass. Portrait.
(Old Plate.) 20 XX 20 · 20 Female, merchandise, ship in distance. 20 · TWENTY COMMERCIAL B'K Salem, Mass.	V CONWAY BANK. Conway, Mass. 5 Females weaving at factory looms. Negro with a basket of cotton. Portrait.	20 TWENTY TWENTY Portrait surmounted by an eagle, female on either side. Portrait. DANVERS BANK. Danvers Mass. 20
(New Plate.) 20 2 Female. 0 20 Female, spear, and globe. COMMERCIAL B'K. Salem. Mass. Female. 20	TEN Three Indians in a canoe 10 Indian. CONWAY BANK. Conway, Mass. Portrait of a boy.	Portrait. DANVERS BANK, Danvers, Mass. 50 50 FIFTY State arms. DOLLARS. Portrait.
(New Plate.) 50 Male and female. 50 Female figure. COMMERCIAL B'K. Salem, Mass. Cupid in a sail boat. 50	XX Santa Claus in a sleigh drawn by reindeers over the roofs of houses. 20 Indian. CONWAY BANK. Conway, Mass. Fancy piece.	100 100 Three female figures. 100 100 Portrait. DANVERS BANK. Danvers, Mass. Portrait.
(Old Plate.) FIFTY FIFTY Female. 50 Man and horse. 50 Female. FIFTY COMMERCIAL B'K Salem. Mass. FIFTY	C Man cutting timber in a forest. 100 CONWAY BANK. Conway, Mass. Rip Van Winkle smoking a pipe. Portrait.	ONE 1 Street in Salem. 1 1 Interior of railroad depot. NAUMKEAG BANK, Salem. Mass. Indians. ONE Cars. ONE

TWO	Street in Salem	2
Indians.	NAUMKEAG BANK, Salem, Mass.	Man smoking, and shipping.
2	Shipping scene.	TWO

ONE	(New Plate.) Farming scene.	1
Female figure.	NEPONSET BANK, Canton, Mass.	Spread eagle and shield
		ONE

Same as right	Horses, waggons and shipping.	One Hundred and 100.
Portrait.	NEPONSET BANK, Canton, Mass.	Portrait.

THREE	3 Street in Salem. 3	3
Ships.	NAUMKEAG BANK, Salem, Mass.	Indian and female.
3	Vessels.	THREE

ONE	(Old Plate.) 1 Interior of a blacksmith's shop. 1	ONE
Bust.	NEPONSET BANK, Canton, Mass.	Female.
ONE		ONE

ONE	Farmer sowing seed. 1	1
	MERCANTILE B'K, Salem, Mass.	Ship.
1		ONE

V	5 Street in Salem.	5
Ships.	NAUMKEAG BANK, Salem, Mass.	Man with dog and gun
V	Vessels	

Female figure.	(New Plate.) Female, train of cars, and steamship in background.	2
TWO	NEPONSET BANK, Canton, Mass.	2 females.

TWO	Spread eagle. 2	2
	MERCANTILE B'K, Salem, Mass.	TWO
2		Sail boat.

Ship building.	Street in Salem.	10
Sampson distroying a lion.	NAUMKEAG BANK, Salem, Mass.	Train of cars.
	Anchor, &c	10

TWO	(Old Plate.) 2 Farming scene. 2	TWO
Female.	NEPONSET BANK, Canton, Mass.	Female
2		2

THREE	Sailor, wharf and shipping. 3	3
	MERCANTILE B'K, Salem, Mass.	THREE
3		Train of cars

Steamboat.	(Old Plate.) Three female figures and eagle. 20	XX
XX	NAUMKEAG BANK, Salem, Mass.	Milk maid.
Train of cars.		

3	Cattle and sheep, man on horseback.	3
Female portrait.	NEPONSET BANK, Canton, Mass.	Blacksmith, farmer and sailor
THREE		THREE

	Female, also emblems of agriculture, commerce &c. Large V and Indian girl.	5
The word five with large V across	MERCANTILE B'K, Salem, Mass.	Portrait of Washington.

20	(New Plate.) XX Eagle. XX	20
Female.	NAUMKEAG BANK, Salem, Mass	Ship.

FIVE	Viaduct of the Boston & Providence railroad.	5
Stone cutter.	NEPONSET BANK, Canton, Mass.	Indian.
5		FIVE

	Vulcan the blacksmith. X	10
TEN	MERCANTILE B'K, Salem, Mass.	Reaper.

FIFTY	50 Man and horse. 50	FIFTY
Female.	NAUMKEAG BANK, Salem, Mass.	Female.
FIFTY		FIFTY

10	Viaduct of the Boston & Providence railroad.	10
Portrait of Washington.	NEPONSET BANK, Canton, Mass.	Portrait.
X		TEN

20	XX Eagle. XX	20
Female.	MERCANTILE B'K, Salem, Mass.	Ship.

100	(Old Plate.) C Phœbus in the chariot of the sun, 100	C
Eagle.	NAUMKEAG BANK, Salem, Mass.	Portrait of Washington
100		C

20	XX Eagle. XX	20
Female,	NEPONSET BANK, Canton, Mass.	Ship,

FIFTY	50 Man and horse. 50	FIFTY
Female.	MERCANTILE B'K, Salem, Mass.	Female.
FIFTY		FIFTY

Same as right	(New Plate.) Horses, waggons, and shipping.	One Hundred and 100.
Portrait.	NAUMKEAG BANK, Salem, Mass.	Portrait.

FIFTY	50 Man and horse 50	FIFTY
Female.	NEPONSET BANK, Canton, Mass.	Female.
FIFTY		FIFTY

Same as right	Horses, waggons, wharf and shipping.	One Hundred and 100.
Portrait.	MERCANTILE B'K, Salem, Mass.	Portrait.

Two females. | MILLERS' RIVER BANK, Athol, Mass. ONE DOLLAR. | 1 ONE 1

2 Stream of water, bridge and train of cars. | MILLERS' RIVER BANK, Athol, Mass. TWO DOLLARS. | 2 Indian woman and child.

3 Male, female and children. | MILLERS' RIVER BANK, Athol, Mass. THREE | 3 THREE 3

FIVE 5 FIVE | MILLERS' RIVER BANK, Athol, Mass. Blacksmith's shop. FIVE DOLLARS. | V

10 | MILLERS' RIVER BANK, Athol, Mass. Two females. | 10 Portrait of Washington.

TWENTY Farmer, mechanic and sailor. | Female and eagle. Portrait of female. MILLERS' RIVER BANK, Athol, Mass. | 20 Train of cars.

FIFTY Group of females. | MILLERS' RIVER BANK, Athol, Mass. L | 50 Spread eagle.

ONE Portrait of Washington ONE | 1 Interior of blacksmith's shop. 1 MILLBURY BANK, Millbury, Mass. | ONE Female. ONE

2 | (New Plate.) Farmers driving sheep across a brook. 2 and 3 men MILLBURY BANK, Millbury, Mass. | TWO Female. TWO

TWO Female. 2 | (Old Plate.) 2 Farming scene. 2 MILLBURY BANK, Millbury, Mass. | TWO Female. 2

3 | Farming scene. 3 MILLBURY BANK, Millbury, Mass. | 3 Female. THREE

FIVE Female crowning a bust of Washington. Eagle. 5 | 5 Interior of a blacksmith's shop. V MILLBURY BANK, Millbury, Mass. | 5 Ship building.

TEN Washington and horse. 10 | X Farming scene. 10 MILLBURY BANK, Millbury, Mass. Canal Locks | TEN Portrait full length.

20 XX 20 | 20 Female holding scales; ship in background. 20 MILLBURY BANK, Millbury, Mass. | TWENTY

50 Female. 50 | FIFTY DOLLARS. 50 MILLBURY BANK, Millbury, Mass. | FIFTY

1 ONE Portrait of J. Q. Adams | MOUNT WOLLASTON BANK, Quincy, Mass. Interior of a shoe makers shop. | 1 Dog. ONE

2 Portrait of J. Q. Adams TWO | MOUNT WOLLASTON BANK, Quincy, Mass. Stone cutters. | TWO Church.

3 3 | Portrait of Cha's F. Adams. Stone cutter. MOUNT WOLLASTON BANK, Quincy, Mass. | 3 3

V Church. | View of the old mansion of J. Q. Adams. MOUNT WOLLASTON BANK, Quincy, Mass. | 5 Portrait of C. F. Adams.

TEN Dog. TEN | Sailing vessel. MOUNT WOLLASTON BANK, Quincy, Mass. | X Church.

XX Hunter warming himself by a fire in the woods. | House. Female. House. MOUNT WOLLASTON BANK, Quincy, Mass. | 20 Portrait of J. Q. Adams.

50 Dog. L | Train of cars. MOUNT WOLLASTON BANK, Quincy, Mass. | 50 Female.

C | Spread eagle and American flag. MOUNT WOLLASTON BANK, Quincy, Mass. | 100 Indian.

Female with liberty cap and pole. | (New Plate.) 5 Female sitting on the ground with horn of plenty. HOLYOKE BANK Northampton, Mass. | 5 State arms.

Female with liberty cap and pole. | 20 Female sitting on the ground with horn of plenty HOLYOKE BANK Northampton, Mass. Eagle | XX Female figure flying in the air.

Female eagle and shield. | HOLYOKE BANK Northampton, Mass. 50 Three female figures. on med head Yacht and steamer | 50

100 on med head River, train of cars cross a bridge, city in distance | HOLYOKE BANK Northampton, Mass. Three females. 100 | 100 on med head Ships and city in the distance.

5 — Medallion head. — V | Pat Lyon at forge. Five on used. head each side. BANK OF DELAWARE CO. Chester, Pa. Locomotive and cars. | 5 — Medallion head. — V

10 — Head of Washington. — 10 | Vig. Harvest scene; three men seated, taking lunch, hat and basket, house in the distance. BANK OF GERMANTOWN, Philadelphia, Pa. Agricultural implements. | 10 — Head of Penn. — 10

1 — Compt's die. — 1 | 1 Vig. Agricultural implements, bee hive, and wheat. 1 OGDENSBURGH BK. Ogdensburgh, N. Y. Shield, plough, key, wheat. | ONE

10 — Double Medallion head, and TEN — X | View of sea with ships, &c. BANK OF DELAWARE CO. Chester, Pa. | X — Double Medallion head, and TEN — 10

20 — Medallion head of female. — 20 | Vig. Man representing the mechanic arts; wheel sledge hammer, compass and square; two men and house in the distance. BANK OF GERMANTOWN, Philadelphia, Pa. | 20 — Female seated, holding sheaf and sickle on right shoulder, left hand extended up wards. — 20

2 — Compt's die. — 2 | 2 OGDENSBURGH BK 2 Ogdensburgh, N. Y. Vig. Female with left arm on shield, Neptune in car drawn by sea horses. Spread Eagle. | TWO DOLLARS.

20 — Medallion head. — 20 | (Old Plate.) Title of Bk. 20 Vig. Harvest field, farmer under tree, house in distance. | 20 — Medallion head. — 20

50 — Head of Marshall — 50 | Vig. Female in sitting posture, holding a sheaf of grain in her right hand, reclining on a bale of cotton; tobacco stalk and hogshead, farm scene in the distance. BANK OF GERMANTOWN, Philadelphia, Pa. | 50 — Washington on horseback — 50

3 — Compt's die. — 3 | OGDENSBURG BK. Ogdensburg, N. Y. 3 Vig. A man reclining on the bottom part of a large figure 3; gun, spear and flag behind. 3 Spread eagle. | 3 — Three cupids in round die — 3

20 — Head of Wm. Penn. | (New Plate.) Vig. View of Upland, a manufacturing village. BANK OF DELAWARE CO. Chester, Pa. | 20 — Head of female

100 — Head of Layfayette. — 100 | Vig. Dairy scene, female in sitting posture, and woman holding little girl in sitting posture; rail and farm house in distance. BANK OF GERMANTOWN, Philadelphia, Pa. | 100 — Head of Gen. Taylor — 100

FIVE | Vig. A female sitting; key in right hand, left hand extended to another female figure 5 in clouds 5 with horn of plenty on her knees, a third face seen between the two, on the right of them a griffin on chest. Title of Bank. Steamboat. | V — Locomotive and cars crossing a viaduct. — V

Female with rake. — FIFTY — Female with rake. | Vig. Female reclining under sheaf of wheat. BANK OF DELAWARE CO. Chester, Pa. | Female with rake. — FIFTY — Female with rake.

500 | BANK OF GERMAN. TOWN, Philadelphia, Pa. Vig. Eagle on globe, with female holding stalk of grain in her right hand on right; and Indian with rifle on left. Five Hundred 500 Dols | 500

TEN | X Vig. Two females sitting; X on right of Vig. a steamboat running, on left vessel at the dock with sails, ship in the rear with sails partly seen. OGDENSBURG BK. Ogdensburg, N. Y. Locomotive and cars. | TEN — Schooner sailing. — 10

100 — Medallion head. — 100 | Vig. Female figures of Justice and Liberty with shield between them, also eagle and ships. BANK OF DELAWARE CO. Chester, Pa. | 100 — Medallion head. — 100

ONE — Indian and family viewing city shipping, &c. | HAMILTON EXCHANGE BANK, Greene, N. Y. Head of Columbus. Compt's die. Mechanics' arm. | 1

Full length statue of Washington. | 20 Vig. Figure of Liberty 20 leaning on a cornucopia, her left hand on a shield. OGDENSBURG BK. Ogdensburg, N. Y. | XX — Female reclining on a cornucopia, holding a shield. — XX

500 — Head of Wm. Penn — D | Vig. Eagle in the right, factory to the left; locomotive and train of cars. BANK OF DELAWARE CO. Chester, Pa. Steamship. | 500 — Female head.

2 — Compt's die. — TWO | HAMILTON EXCHANGE BANK, Greene, N. Y. Female portrait. Agricultural scene, men loading grain on waggon, oxen and horse harnessed to it. Female portrait. | 2 — Female portrait.

50 — Female seated. — 50 | Vig. Two cupids, one with wand in left hand, sitting on a porpoise, the other reclining on a porpoise. OGDENSBURG BK. Ogdensburg, N. Y. | 50 — Liberty leaning on a cornucopia, her left hand on a shield. — 50

5 — Head of Wm. Penn. — 5 | Vig. Boy and man on horseback; drove of sheep and cattle; boy reclining at foot of tree, farmer, &c. in the distance. BANK OF GERMANTOWN, Philadelphia, Pa. | 5 — Head of Franklin. — 5

FIVE — Compt's die — FIVE | Vig. Portrait of Washington with female on each side; shipping on the right, harvest scene on left. HAMILTON EXCHANGE BANK, Greene, N. Y. Eagle. | FIVE — Statute of Penelope. — FIVE

ONE — Female. | Female sitting on the ground supporting the figure one. MAHAIWE BANK, Gt. Barrington, Mass. State Arms. | 1 — Cattle and hogs.

Female representing Agriculture, with sickle in hand. — TEN | 10 Vig. Harvest scene, farmers reclining; female seated with child in arms, basket and pitcher by her side. BANK OF GERMANTOWN, Philadelphia, Pa. | 10 — Head of J. Q. Adams. — TEN

10 | Title of Bank. Female portrait. Two winged females, one in the right with right arm extended over horn of plenty, left arm extended with sickle towards female on left. Compt's die. | 10

2 — Female. | Men driving sheep across a brook. MAHAIWE BANK, Gt. Barrington, Mass. State Arms. | 2 — Stonecutter

Female borne in the arms of 2 males. THREE	Train of cars. 3 MAHAIWE BANK, Gt. Barrington, N. Y State Arms.	THREE Female figure. THREE

Wharf and shipping. 5	V MARINE BANK, New Bedford, Mass.	5 Sailor, merchandise and shipping. FIVE

Train of cars 5	V full length MECHANICKS B'K Newburyport, Mass.	5 Portrait of Franklin.

Two Indian women, one of them stepping from a precipice into ravine below	Five, V, 5 State Arms MAHAIWE BANK, Gt. Barrington, Mass.	5 Five female figures and 5

Female, eagle and State Arms, shipping and train of cars in background. TEN	X MARINE BANK, New Bedford, Mass.	10 Female.

Ship and steamship. 10	MECHANICKS B'K Newburyport, Mass	10 Portrait of Washington.

Deer. 10 Farmer sitting upon a plough.	TEN TEN Female sitting upon a bale with sickle and sheaf of wheat; train of cars and factory in background MAHAIWE BANK, Gt. Barrington, Mass. State Arms.	10 Indian woman, holding X

X Indian with bow	Shipping and wharf MARINE BANK, New Bedford, Mass.	10 Female and sheaf of wheat.

20 Female.	XX Eagle XX MECHANICKS B'K Newburyport, Mass.	20 Ship.

20 Female figure.	2 Female. 0 MAHAIWE BANK, Gt. Barrington, Mass. XX	20 Female. 20

20	Vig. Female, train of cars and canal in background. 20 MARINE BANK, New Bedford, Mass.	XX Portrait of Columbus.

FIFTY Female. FIFTY	50 Man and horse 50 MECHANICKS B'K Newburyport, Mass.	FIFTY Female. FIFTY

50 Female figure.	Male and female. MAHAIWE BANK, Gt. Barrington Mass. 50	50 Cupid in a sailboat. 50

50 FIFTY	Spread eagle, Railroad and canal. 50 MARINE BANK, New Bedford, Mass.	50 Ship.

On Hundred and 100. Portrait.	Scene on a wharf. MECHANICKS B'K Newburyport, Mass.	same as left. Portrait of Columbus.

1	Shipping 1 MARINE BANK, New Bedford, Mass.	1 Female.

100 Portrait of Washington.	Ship and steamship. MARINE BANK, New Bedford, Mass.	100 Large C with female within it.

1 Female.	Train of cars. MALDEN BANK Malden, Mass. Arm and hammer	1 State arms

2	Shipping Female and 2. MARINE BANK, New Bedford, Mass.	2 Whale fishing.

Train of cars and factory. 1	MECHANICKS B'K Newburyport. Mass.	1 Sailor at the wheel.

Indian girl with bow and spear. TWO	Man sitting upon the ground, anvil hammer &c., factory and train of cars in background. MALDEN BANK Malden Mass. Wheels bale, ect,	2 Child and dolphin. TWO

Steamship and sail vessels. THREE 3	MARINE BANK, New Bedford, Mass. 3 THREE	3 Girl.

Shipping and ship building. 2	2 and female head MECHANICKS B'K Newburyport, Mass.	2 Large figure 2 and eagle.

Female. THREE	Farming Scene. MALDEN BANK Malden, Mass.	3 Female and cherubs

5 FIVE 5	V Eagle, anchor, merchandise, &c shipping in back-groud. V MARINE BANK, New Bedford, Mass	5 FIVE 5

Ships steam boat and landing. 3	MECHANICKS B'K Newburyport. Mass.	3 Blacksmith and forge.

5 Portrait of female. FIVE	Female leaning upon a bale, factory village in background. MALDEN BANK Malden, Mass. State Arms	FIVE Portrait of Z Taylor. FIVE

10 Blacksmith anvil and forge. · 1 Female key and horn of plenty. 0 MALDEN BANK Malden, Mass. Cars. · 10 Female.	20 Cupid in a sail boat. 20 · Medallion. Neptune. Medallion. PACIFIC BANK Nantucket, Mass. · 20 Female.	20 Female. · XX Eagle. XX PEOPLES BANK Roxbury, Mass. · 20 Ship.
20 Female. · Female, Eagle, and shield, factory, and ships in background. MALDEN BANK Malden, Mass. · 20 2 Female. 0	50 Medallion. 50 · Medallion. Neptune. Medallion. female figure. PACIFIC BANK Nantucket, Mass. · 50 Portrait of a girl. FIFTY	FIFTY Female. FIFTY · 50 Man and horse. 50 PEOPLES BANK Roxbury, Mass. · FIFTY Female. FIFTY
50 Female figure. · Male and Female. MALDEN BANK Malden, Mass. 50 · 50 Cupid in a sail boat. 50	100 Ship building. 100 · C Two females shipping in background. C PACIFIC BANK Nantucket, Mass. · 100 Ships.	One Hundred and 100 Portrait. · Horses, wagons, shipping &c. PEOPLES BANK Roxbury, Mass. · Same as left Portrait.
100 Vulcan the blacksmith · Spread Eagle R. R. and Canal. MALDEN BANK Malden, Mass. 100 · 100 Female.	The Pacific Bank also use the Perkins Stereotype plate.	Cupids supporting the fig. 1 · Landing of the pilgrims 1620. PLYMOUTH BANK Plymouth, Mass. · 1 Female. Some have ships under sail.
Ships and steamboats. 1 · PACIFIC BANK Nantucket, Mass. · ONE Whale, fishing. ONE	ONE Female. ONE · Farming scene. PEOPLES BANK Roxbury, Mass. · Large figure one, female within. ONE	2 Portrait of Franklin. · Landing of the pilgrims 1620. PLYMOUTH BANK Plymouth, Mass. · 2 Two cupids.
Whale fishing. 2 · PACIFIC BANK Nantucket, Mass. · 2 Ship.	TWO Female. · Train of cars. PEOPLES BANK Roxbury, Mass. · TWO 2	5 Portrait of Washington. FIVE · Landing of the pilgrims 1620. PLYMOUTH BANK Plymouth, Mass. Indian · 5 Female sickle and sheaf of wheat. In fig. 5. FIVE
Ships. 3 · PACIFIC BANK Nantucket, Mass. · 3 Farmers and sheep.	THREE Indian girl with bow and arrow. THREE · Spread eagle R. R. and canal. PEOPLES BANK Roxbury, Mass. · THREE General Washington THREE	10 10 · Landing of the pilgrims 1620. X PLYMOUTH BANK Plymouth, Mass. · 10 Female.
5 Female. FIVE · Neptune and three female figures. PACIFIC BANK Nantucket, Mass. · 5 Sailor.	FIVE Female. · Eagle and steamship. V PEOPLES BANK Roxbury, Mass. · 5 Portrait.	20 20 · Landing of the Pilgrims, 1620. XX PLYMOUTH BANK. Plymouth, Mass. · 20 Twenty on Medallion. Head.
10 Sea nymphs Steamship · Spread eagle, ships in distance. PACIFIC BANK Nantucket, Mass. State Arms · 10 Female. TEN	Horses, chariot and a group of female figures. 10 · PEOPLES BANK Roxbury, Mass. · TEN Portrait of Washington TEN	Female sickle and sheaf of wheat. · 50 PLYMOUTH BANK Plymouth, Mass. Landing of the Pilgrims, 1620. · 50

The figures 100 with the words one hundred running across. Female; ship in distance. — Landing of the pilgrims 1620. PLYMOUTH BANK Plymouth, Mass. Vegle — 100 100

1 — Female leaning upon a bale; stream of water, factories, railroad and shipping in background. 1 MERCHANTS BANK. Lowell, Mass. — 1 Female.

TWO Ship. 2 — Two females. 2 MERCHANTS BANK. Lowell, Mass. — 2 Female and figure 2.

Female. 3 — Large figure 3 and Three female figures; factory in background 3 on right. MERCHANTS BANK. Lowell, Mass. — 3 Portrait.

5 Female and ship. 5 — Female and eagle: ship in distance 5 MERCHANTS BANK. Lowell, Mass. — 5 Ship FIVE

10 Bales and barrels. TEN — Female, eagle and globe; ships in background. MERCHANTS BANK. Lowell, Mass. — 10 Female.

20 XX — XX Portrait of female. XX MERCHANTS BANK. Lowell, Mass. — 20 XX

50 Female. — Shipping; city in the background. MERCHANTS BANK Lowell, Mass. — 50 Portrait of Washington.

100 Portrait. C — Railroad depot, train of cars, wharfs, shipping, merchandise &c. MERCHANTS BANK, Lowell, Mass. — 100 C

ONE Large figure 1 with female on it. — Farmers driving sheep across a stream of water. GREENFIELD BANK Greenfield, Mass. — ONE Large figure 1 with female on it.

Factory and train of cars. 2 — Large figure 2 with Indian. GREENFIELD BANK Greenfield, Mass. — 2 Female with fruit basket upon her arm.

State arms 3 — Train of cars. GREENFIELD BANK Greenfield, Mass. — THREE Portrait Z. Taylor THREE

FIVE Farmer sowing seed. 5 — 5 Cluster of buildings. 5 GREENFIELD BANK Greenfield, Mass. — FIVE Vulcan the blacksmith and fig. 5.

TEN Cattle. TEN — 10 Cluster of buildings. 10 GREENFIELD BANK Greenfield, Mass. — X Female raking hay

20 Female. — 2 Female. 0 GREENFIELD BANK Greenfield, Mass XX — 20 Female. 20

50 Female. — Male and female. GREENFIELD BANK Greenfield, Mass. 50 — 50 Cupid in a sail boat. 50

1 — 1 Child, dog, and safe; ship in distance. 1 BEDFORD COMMERCIAL B'K, New Bedford, Mass. — ONE

2 — 2 Female and anchor, ship in the distance. 2 BEDFORD COMMERCIAL B'K, New Bedford. Mass. — TWO

THREE Female. — Spread eagle, capital at Washington and steamship. BEDFORD COMMERCIAL, B'K, New Bedford. Mass. — 3

5 Indian sitting under a tree. FIVE — 5 Spread eagle, canal and rail road. 5 BEDFORD COMMERCIAL B'K. New Bedford, Mass. Female — FIVE

10 Medallion head. 10 — X Spread eagle and ship. X BEDFORD COMMERCIAL B'K, New Bedford. Mass. — TEN DOLLARS

20 Portrait of Wm. Penn. 20 — (Old Plate.) 20 Female sitting on a bale, ship in distance. BEDFORD COMMERCIAL B'K. New Bedford, Mass Horse — 20

20 Cupid. — (New Plate.) Ship and steamship. BEDFORD COMMERCIAL B'K. New Bedford, Mass. Wheels — 20

FIFTY Female. FIFTY — Female, child and merchandise; ship in distance. BEDFORD COMMERCIAL B'K, New Bedford, Mass. Building — 50

100 Fancy piece, Steamship. — Ships, city in the distance. BEDFORD COMMERCIAL B'K, New Bedford, Mass Justice — 100

Female. ONE — Steamship and sail vessels. MATTAPAN BANK, Dorchester, Mass. — 1 Sailor.

Two Indian women, one stepping from a precipice into a ravine below. TWO — Train of cars. MATTAPAN BANK. Dorchester, Mass. — 2 Female.

Left	Centre	Right
3 Large figure 3 Mechanic, farmer and sailor.	Man sitting upon the ground, with a hammer upon his shoulder; train of cars and factory in the background. MATTAPAN BANK. Dorchester, Mass	3 Female.
5 Female sewing.	Interior of a shoemakers shop. SPICKET FALLS B'K. Methuen, Mass.	V Dog
X Two females.	ROCKLAND BANK, Roxbury, Mass. Farming scene.	X Portrait of Washington.
Indian FIVE	Ships and steamship. MATTAPAN BANK, Dorchester, Mass. Wheels, bale, etc	5 Two female figures and 5.
TEN Indian.	Farmers, and horse and sled gathering grain. SPICKET FALLS B'K, Methuen, Mass.	X X
State Arms. XX	Farmer ploughing, cattle and horses in pasture; city in distance. ROCKLAND BANK, Roxbury, Mass.	20 Portrait.
10 Stone cutter.	Spread eagle, ship and Steamship. MATTAPAN BANK. Dorchester, Mass.	10 Indian woman.
XX A hunter warming himself by a fire.	20 SPICKET FALLS B'K. Methuen, Mass.	20 Portrait of Lewis Cass.
50 L and Cupid	ROCKLAND BANK, Roxbury, Mass. Ships, and city in the background.	50 50
20 Female figure.	2 Female. 0 MATTAPAN BANK. Dorchester, Mass. XX	20 Female. 20
50	Cattle. SPICKET FALLS B'K. Methuen, Mass.	50 Female with sickle and sheaf of wheat.
C Fountain.	ROCKLAND BANK, Roxbury, Mass. Farming scene, men women and children.	100 Portrait of Jefferson.
50 Female figure	Male and female. MATTAPAN BANK. Dorchester, Mass. 50	50 Cupid in a sail boat. 50
100	Santa Claus in sleigh drawn over roofs of houses by a reindeer. SPICKET FALLS B'K. Methuen, Mass.	C Santa Claus sitting at a fire place.
1 Reaper. ONE	Reaper gath ering grain. 1 Shipping. TAUNTON BANK, Taunton, Mass	1 Vulcan the blacksmith.
100 Vulcan the blacksmith.	Spread eagle, railroad and canal MATTAPAN BANK. Dorchester, Mass. 100	100 Female
1	Oval die, through is seen a female, train of cars and city in distance; a female each side of the die, steamboat and train of cars in the background. ROCKLAND BANK. Roxbury, Mass.	1 Farmer, plough and rake and ONE on half shield.
TWO Indian 2	Eagle. 2 Washington on horseback. TAUNTON BANK. Taunton, Mass.	2 Train of cars
ONE The arm of a man holding a hammer.	Factory. SPICKET FALLS B'K. Methuen, Mass.	1 Portrait of Webster.
Portrait of female. 2	Farmers and sheep. ROCKLAND BANK, Roxbury, Mass.	2 Female and 2
THREE.	Female with a sheaf of wheat, reapers in the background. TAUNTON BANK, Taunton, Mass.	3 Male figure.
TWO	Factory. Portrait of J. Q. Adams SPICKET FALLS B'K, Methuen, Mass.	2 2
3	ROCKLAND BANK, Roxbury, Mass. Farmer with scythe, sailor with spy glass, and mechanic, anvil, hammer &c., also three gold dollars. THREE	3 A dog's head
5	Female seated; railroad and canal in background. V TAUNTON BANK, Taunton, Mass	FIVE Five and Eagle FIVE

20	2 Female. 0	20
Female figure.	TAUNTON BANK, Taunton Mass.	Female.
	XX	20

50	Male and female.	50
Female figure.	TAUNTON BANK, Taunton, Mass.	Cupid in a sail boat.
	50	50

One Hundred and 100.	Horses, waggons, shipping &c.	Same as left.
Portrait.	TAUNTON BANK, Taunton, Mass.	Portrait.

1	Stream of water R. R. train of cars.	1
Portrait of female.		Portrait of Webster.
ONE	PEMBERTON BANK Lawrence, Mass.	ONE

2	PEMBERTON BANK Lawrence, Mass.	2
Female.	Female weaving at factory looms.	Portrait of Washington.

3	Three female figures and cupid upon the water.	3
		Portrait of Jackson.
Female.	PEMBERTON BANK Lawrence, Mass.	THREE

	White men in a boat and Indians on shore receiving them.	5
FIVE	PEMBERTON BANK Lawrence, Mass.	Portrait of Calhoun.

X	Female, state arms and ships in background.	10
Three female figures.		Blacksmith anvil &c.
TEN	PEMBERTON BANK Lawrence, Mass.	

20	Men and cattle.	20
Sailor leaning upon a capstan	PEMBERTON BANK Lawrence, Mass.	Washington on horse back.

50	PEMBERTON BANK Lawrence, Mass.	50
Portrait of Clay.	Female and shield; capitol in distance.	Portrait of Female.

1	Whale fishing.	1
	MECHANICS BANK New Bedford, Mass.	
	Indian head	

2	Sailor, merchandise, and ship in distance.	2
Stone cutter.	MECHANICS BANK New Bedford, Mass.	Dog and safe.
	Cars	

5	Whale fishing.	5
	MECHANICS BANK New Bedford, Mass.	
	Three female figures	

10	City, R. R. Station and train of cars.	10
Blacksmith anvil and forge.	MECHANICS BANK New Bedford, Mass.	Sailor with spy glass.
	Ship.	

20	20 Child dog and safe.	20
Medallion.	MECHANICS BANK New Bedford, Mass.	
20	Ships.	

50	New Bedford City Hall.	50
Medallion	50	
50	MECHANICS BANK New Bedford, Mass. Head	

1	Blacksmith anvil and forge.	ONE and 1.
Portrait of Washington.		Female, eagle and shield.
ONE	MECHANICS BANK Worcester, Mass. Machine.	ONE

TWO	Female Man on Female horse back; flock of sheep.	2
Portrait of Franklin.		Female.
TWO	MECHANICS BANK Worcester, Mass. 2 Arm 2	TWO on med head

THREE	State arms surmounted by an eagle; three females	3
Portrait of John Adams.		Girl.
THREE	MECHANICS BANK Worcester, Mass 3 Female 3	3

5	MECHANICS BANK Worcester, Mass.	5
Female sickle and sheaf of wheat.	State arms Boys, sheaf of wheat, and sheep, ship in background Female	
5	5 Eagle. 5	Portrait of Webster.

	10 Man and anvil, train of cars and village in background.	10
Female, eagle and shield.		
	MECHANICS BANK Worcester, Mass. X Arm. X	Portrait of Z. Taylor.

XX	MECHANICS BANK Worcester, Mass	20
Portrait of J. Q. Adams.	Three female figures.	
	Female.	

	50 Farmer ploughing.	50
Two males and two females.	MECHANICS BANK Worcester, Mass.	

100	State arms, Two horses, factories, and train of cars and steamboat	100
Portrait.		Portrait.
100	MECHANICS BANK Worcester, Mass.	100

ONE	Indian, Indian woman and child in a canoe, the Indian throwing a harpoon at a fish.	1
Indian.	METACOMET BANK Fall River, Mass.	Portrait.

TWO	Steam boat and sail vessels.	2
Portrait.	METACOMET BANK Fall River, Mass.	Indian.

3	Steamboat and sail vessels.	3
Portrait.	METACOMET BANK Fall River, Mass.	Indian in a canoe.

V METACOMET BANK Fall River, Mass. Same vig as one's. 5 FIVE Portrait.	ONE Milk maid and cows. 1 Portrait. HOLLISTON B'K Holliston, Mass. Portrait of Clay.	2 JOHN HANCOCK B'K Springfield, Mass. 2 Portrait of female. View of the U. S. Armory at Springfield also spread eagle.
10 Same vig as ones. X 10 METACOMET BANK Fall River, Mass. Portrait.	TWO HOLLISTON BANK Holliston, Mass. 2 Two females supporting a sheaf of wheat above their heads. Portrait. Female.	3 JOHN HANCOCK B'K Springfield, Mass. 3 Train of cars. Females Female.
XX Steamboat and sail vessels. 20 XX METACOMET BANK Fall River, Mass. Indian in a canoe.	3 HOLLISTON BANK Holliston, Mass. 3 Portrait of Charles Sumner. Females weaving at factory looms Boy.	5 JOHN HANCOCK B'K Springfield, Mass. 5 Female eagle and shield, steamer in distance. Portrait of J. Hancock. Female and 5 on a shield
L Same vig as ones. L 50 METACOMET BANK Fall River, Mass. Portrait	V HOLLISTON BANK Holliston, Mass. V 5 V Portrait. Train of cars. Portrait of Webster.	Female sickle and sheaf of wheat. 10 Three female figures ships in the distance. 10 JOHN HANCOCK B'K Springfield, Mass TEN Eagle Female.
1 View of Ware village Cupids supporting the fig. 1 Portrait of female. ONE HAMPSHIRE MANUFACTURERS' BANK Ware, Mass. ONE	TEN Spread Eagle. X Portrait of General Cass. HOLLISTON BANK Holliston, Mass. Portrait.	50 Scene in a farm yard. 50 JOHN HANCOCK B'K Springfield, Mass. Female and factories. Female and shield.
Large figure 2, Portrait of Washington, and Portrait of Franklin. View of Ware village 2 HAMPSHIRE MANUFACTURERS BANK Ware, Mass. Eagle Indian girl with bow and arrows	20 Train of cars and railroad station. 20 Portrait of J. Q. Adams. HOLLISTON BANK Holliston, Mass. Female and child.	ONE Indian sitting on a rock, also plough and log cabin. 1 1 Portrait of Z. Taylor. 1 WESTFIELD BANK Westfield, Mass. Female. ONE on Medallion head. ONE
3 View of Ware village, HAMPSHIRE MANUFACTURERS' BANK Ware, Mass. 3 Female. Clay Cupids in large 3.	50 Cattle. 50 Portrait of Charles Sumner. HOLLISTON BANK Holliston, Mass. Portrait of Washington	2 Two females; farming scene in background. TWO 2 State arms. Indians. TWO WESTFIELD BANK Westfield, Mass. Fish. TWO
5s 10s 20s 50s all of the Perkins Patent Stereotype steel plate.	C Indians in a canoe. 100 Farmer sowing seed. HOLLISTON BANK Holliston, Mass. Portrait of Charles Sumner.	THREE WESTFIELD BANK Westfield, Mass. 3 Dogs. Three men. Female teaching children. THREE THREE Dog, key and safe.
100 C Phoebus in the car of the sun. 100 C Eagle. Portrait of Washington. 100 HAMPSHIRE MANUFACTURERS BANK Ware, Mass. C	1 JOHN HANCOCK B'K Springfield, Mass. 1 View of the U. S. armory at Springfield also spread eagle. Portrait of female.	Two males and three females. FIVE Westfield Green. WESTFIELD BANK Westfield, Mass. 5

Left	Centre	Right
10 Train of cars and vessel.	Westfield Green. WESTFIELD BANK Westfield, Mass. Locomotive	X Medallion head. 10
50	WOBURN BANK Woburn, Mass. Two females, factories steamship and train of cars in background.	50 Female, vessel, etc. FIFTY
20 Portrait of Wm. Penn.	Vig. Female sitting on a log with hands resting on a pail; cottage, steamboat, &c. FARMERS BANK OF SCHUYLKILL CO. Pottsville, Pa. Safe; dog with key in left paw.	20 Portrait of Ben. Frank lin.
TWENTY Female drawing water at a well.	Westfield Green. WESTFIELD BANK Westfield, Mass. Load of hay.	20 on med head Black smith shop.
100 State Arms	WOBURN BANK Woburn, Mass. 100 Capitol at Washington.	100
500 Portrait of Washington. 500	Vig. Female sitting on a plough, left hand with sickle resting on sheaf of wheat, right hand uplifted with stems of wheat. 500 FARMERS BANK OF SCHUYLKILL CO. Pottsville, Pa.	500 Portrait of Marshall. 500
50 Cattle.	WESTFIELD BANK Westfield, Mass. West field Green.	50 Female and whip machine.
1 Compt's die. 1	Vig. Large steamboat. NEW YORK & ERIE BANK, Buffalo, N. Y.	1 Portrait of Franklin.
5 Head of Ben Franklin. FIVE	FRANKLIN BANK. Washington, Pa. Vig. Men loading hay on waggon; oxen. Head of female.	5 Washington. FIVE
1 1	WOBURN BANK Woburn, Mass. Female reclining, train of cars, milk maids and cars in background. Wheels, bale, etc.	1 Child and Dolphin.
2 Compt's die. TWO	Vig. Female with sheaf of wheat and sickle; farm house, viaduct with train of cars passing over it in the distance. NEW YORK & ERIE BANK, Buffalo, N. Y.	2 Locomotive
10 Franklin. TEN	Man on horse, sheep, dog and m ill. Washington. FRANKLIN BANK, Washington, Pa. Eagle.	TEN Milkmaid. TEN
Farmer, milk maid and cows 2	Train of cars. WOBURN BANK Woburn, Mass.	2 Females raking hay.
5 Compt's die. FIVE	Vig. Locomotive and train of cars passing under a bridge. NEW YORK & ERIE BANK, Buffalo, N. Y.	V Portrait of Washington
20 Franklin XX	Harvest scene; man with fork, female with rake; men loading wagon with hay. 20 on med. head on either side. FRANKLIN BANK, Washington, Pa.	XX Washington 20
Female, eagle, and ships. 3	WOBURN BANK Woburn, Mass.	3 Cupid and figure 3.
Vig. Cattle and sheep, some lying down. TEN	Compt's die. NEW YORK & ERIE BANK, Buffalo, N. Y.	X Portrait of Webster.
50 Fifty on medallion head. 50	Wash-ington. Vig. Harvest scene, reapers man standing by a tree, with arms folded, sickle in his hand, female sitting, child on her lap, baskets, &c. Frank-lin. FRANKLIN BANK, Washington, Pa.	50 FIFTY on med head 50
Female feeding an eagle from a cup. 5	WOBURN BANK Woburn, Mass. FIVE	5 Five females and fig. 5.
20 Portrait of Gen. Taylor.	Vig. Spread eagle, holding the American flag in its talons. NEW YORK & ERIE BANK, Buffalo, N. Y.	20 Compt's die.
5 Franklin. V	(Old Plate.) 5 Vig. Female with sheaf of wheat, pole boat with two men in distance. 5 WYOMING BANK, Wilkes Barre, Pa. State Arms.	5 Jackson; V
TEN Female.	WOBURN BANK Woburn, Mass. Train of cars. TEN	10 Horses and load of hay
5 Male portrait FIVE	5 5 Vig. Two females, shield, mansion, cars, &c. in distance. FARMERS BANK OF SCHUYLKILL CO. Pottsville, Pa.	V and Five Male portrait FIVE
5 head of Ben Franklin. FIVE	(New Plate.) WYOMING BANK, Wilkes Barre, Pa. Agricultural implements.	Large V a figure 5. and FIVE. Male portrait.
20	Portrait of Washington. WOBURN BANK Woburn, Mass. Spread eagle, Capitol at Washington and steamship in background. TWENTY	20
TEN Female. TEN	X Vig. Female in a sitting posture with a sickle and sheaf. X FARMERS BANK OF SCHUYLKILL CO. Pottsville, Pa. Locomotive.	10 Bridge, boat, horse, house &c. in distance. TEN
X Mars. X	(Old Plate.) Vig. Female with rake sitting on plough, and 10 small figures working at forge. 10 Title of Bank. State Arms.	Canal locks, boats passing through.

Left	Centre	Right
10 Two Indians in front of tent, one standing, the other on right knee.	(New Plate.) WYOMING BANK, Wilkes Barre, Pa. Girl bathing	10 Male portrait. TEN
Female ONE	View of the city of Lowell LOWELL BANK, Lowell, Mass Dog and safe.	Female. 1
Farmers and sheep. 2	(Old Plate.) 2 WARREN BANK, Danvers, Mass.	TWO Females. TWO
Canal, lock, and boats passing through.	20 Female on either side of a shield, surmounted by an eagle. 20 WYOMING BANK, Wilkesbarre, Pa. State Arms.	20 Washington. 20
TWO Female. 2	Same Vig. as ones. LOWELL BANK, Lowell, Mass Bales, bbls., etc.	TWO Female. 2
Fema . 3	(New Plate.) WARREN BANK, Danvers, Mass. Large Portrait.	3 Indian, woman.
50 Canal scene 50	50 on medallion head. State Arms 50 on medallion head. WYOMING BANK, Wilkes Barre, Pa.	Female with sickle and wheat. 50
THREE Female. 3 on THREE	Same Vig. as ones. LOWELL BANK, Lowell, Mass. Men and horses	THREE Female 3 on THREE
Farming scene. 3	(Old Plate.) 3 WARREN BANK, Danvers, Mass.	3 Female. THREE
100 Portrait of Washington. 100	100 on medallion head. Signing of Declaration of Independence. 100 on medallion head. WYOMING BANK, Wilkes Barre, Pa.	100 Portrait of DeWitt Clinton. 100
	5s, 10s, all of the Perkins Stereotype Steel Plate	
5 Two females	(New Plate) WARREN BANK, Danvers, Mass. Large portrait.	5 Portrait.
ONE Female. Compt's die.	Vig. Woodchopper kneeling on one knee; farm house and waggon in distance. 1 BK OF THE CAPITOL Albany, N. Y. Plough and shield.	ONE Female Indian with bow and quiver.
FIFTY Female. FIFTY	50 Man and horse. 50 LOWELL BANK, Lowell, Mass.	FIFTY Female. FIFTY
Spread eagle. FIVE	(Old Plate.) Large V, female and cupid. WARREN BANK, Danvers, Mass.	5 Girl.
Compt's die Eagle. 2	2 Vig. Male and female seated, two gold dollars, oxen and building in background. BK OF THE CAPITOL Albany, N. Y. Shield.	2 Female portrait
One Hundred and 100. Portrait of Harrison.	Scene on a wharf. LOWELL BANK, Lowell, Mass.	Same as left. Portrait of Columbus.
10 Indian, woman.	(New Plate.) WARREN BANK, Danvers, Mass. Large Portrait.	10 Female.
3 Compt's die THREE	Vig. Artisans reclining with three gold dollars. BK OF THE CAPITOL Albany, N. Y. Shield.	3 Male portrait.
Female, railroad, shipping and canal in background. 1	(Old Plate.) 1 WARREN BANK, Danvers, Mass.	1 Female
Vulcan the blacksmith. TEN	(Old Plate.) X WARREN BANK, Danvers, Mass.	10 Reaper.
5 FIVE Compt's die.	Vig. Male and female with three cupids between them; five gold dollars. BK OF THE CAPITOL Albany, N. Y. Shield	FIVE Large figure 5, and five females
Portrait 1	(New Plate.) WARREN BANK, Danvers, Mass. Large portrait. ONE	1 Female
20 Female.	2 Female 0 WARREN BANK, Danvers, Mass. XX	20 Female. 20
Goddess of liberty with eagle. Compt's die.	10 Vig. A public building. BK OF THE CAPITOL Albany, N. Y. Shield	10 Male portrait. TEN
Portrait. 2	(New Plate.) WARREN BANK, Danvers, Mass. Large portrait. TWO	2 Female and fig. 2.
50 Female.	Male and female. WARREN BANK, Danvers, Mass. 50	50 Cupid in a sailboat. 50

100 Vulcan the blacksmith.	Spread eagle, railroad and canal. WARREN BANK, Danvers, Mass. 100	100 Female.
1	Blacksmith, anvil, hammer, &c., train of cars and factories in background 1 WESTERN BANK, Springfield, Mass. 1	1 Bull's head.
One on 1.	Ship building and city in distance. MAVERICK BANK, Boston, Mass.	1 Female.
1 Female.	Large figure 1 with portrait of Washington. WORCESTER BANK, Worcester, Mass.	1 Carpenter at his bench.
2	Cattle, farmers ploughing, and train of cars in distance. 2 WESTERN BANK, Springfield, Mass.	2 Cattle and hogs.
2 TWO 2	MAVERICK BANK, Boston, Mass. Ship building and city in distance.	2 Sailor.
2 Farmer sharpening a scythe.	Portrait of Washington, and large figure 2. WORCESTER BANK, Worcester, Mass.	2 Dog and safe.
Farmers and sheep. 3	3 WESTERN BANK, Springfield, Mass. THREE Cars. THREE	3 Female and chests.
3 Ship, bales, cars, etc. 3	MAVERICK BANK, Boston, Mass. Ship building and city in distance. Three 3 Three	3
3 Portrait.	Large figure 3 and portrait. WORCESTER BANK, Worcester, Mass.	3 Female.
5 Medallion head. FIVE	V Wild horses. V WESTERN BANK, Springfield, Mass. 5 5	5 Goddess of Liberty, and fig. 5.
5 V	East Boston ferry landing. MAVERICK BANK, Boston, Mass.	5 Portrait of Webster.
5 Female Indian.	Portrait of female 5 Portrait of female. WORCESTER BANK, Worcester, Mass.	5 Female.
FIVE	Farming scene. 5 WESTERN BANK, Springfield, Mass. Wheels, bales, &c.	5 Female.
10 X	East Boston Ferry Landing. MAVERICK BANK, Boston, Mass.	10 Sailor and Indian Ten on shield between.
10 Blacksmith.	Female; farmers loading hay; train of cars. WORCESTER BANK, Worcester, Mass. 10	10 Stone cutter.
TEN	Female riding upon a reindeer. X WESTERN BANK, Springfield, Mass.	10 Blacksmith, anvil and forge.
XX	MAVERICK BANK, Boston, Mass. Winthrop block and street in East Boston.	20 Sailor.
Female with sheaf of wheat. 20	Indian and female. WORCESTER BANK, Worcester, Mass.	20 Farmer sowing seed.
20 Portrait of Webster. 20	Female with horn of plenty, and merchandise, factories and shipping in background. WESTERN BANK, Springfield, Mass.	20 2 Female. 0
50 FIFTY	MAVERICK BANK, Boston, Mass. Winthrop block and street in East Boston.	50 Ship and ship houses in Navy Yard.
L 50	Shepherd boy and sheep. WORCESTER BANK, Worcester, Mass.	50 Female.
50 Female.	WESTERN BANK, Springfield, Mass. Blacksmith shoeing a horse. State Arms.	50 Indian woman and child.
100 Female. HUNDRED	Winthrop block and street in East Boston. MAVERICK BANK, Boston, Mass.	100 Female and ship.
100 Female, sickle and sheaf of wheat.	Vig. Winged female with a trumpet, also globe and eagle. WORCESTER BANK, Worcester, Mass.	C Female. C
100 Portrait of Franklin. 100	State Arms, female each side. WESTERN BANK, Springfield, Mass.	100 Portrait of Washington. 100
1	Cattle and hogs; village in the background. 1 VILLAGE BANK, North Danvers, Mass.	ONE Female.

2 Ships and steamship. 2 VILLAGE BANK, North Danvers, Mass Female. TWO	Female. 5 WALTHAM BANK, Waltham Mass. Men, women and children; farming scene. 5 Female.	3 (Old Plate.) Farming scene 3 WORCESTER CO. B'K Blackstone, Mass. 3 Female. THREE
3 Portrait of Fillmore. Train of cars. VILLAGE BANK, North Danvers, Mass 3 Female.	10 Female. WALTHAM BANK, Waltham, Mass Indian; river, canoe, deer in background. 10 Female.	5 Train of cars. (New Plate.) WORCESTER CO. B'K Blackstone, Mass Female reclining, train of cars, shipping, mill, mills and cars in background. 5 Arms.
Female and sickle. FIVE 5 VILLAGE BANK, Danvers, Mass Female and wheel, train of cars and steamship in background. 5 Female.	20 Female figure. 2 Female 0 WALTHAM BANK, Waltham, Mass XX 20 Female 20	FIVE (Old Plate.) Spread eagle and shield. Large V; Female and cupid. WORCESTER CO. B'K Blackstone, Mass. 5 Girl.
Female with sheaf of wheat. X Cattle and sheep, man on horseback. VILLAGE BANK, North Danvers, Mass. 10 Washington on horseback	50 Female. Male and female. WALTHAM BANK, Waltham, Mass 50 50 Cupid in a sailboat. 50	TEN Vulcan the blacksmith. X WORCESTER CO. B'K Blackstone, Mass. 10 Reaper.
20 Female, eagle, chest, &c. Female figure and two cherubs. VILLAGE BANK, North Danvers, Mass 20 Female.	100 Vulcan the blacksmith Spread eagle, railroad and canal. WALTHAM BANK, Waltham, Mass. 100 100 Female.	20 Female. 2 Female. 0 WORCESTER CO. B'K Blackstone, Mass. XX 20 Female. 20
50 Female with sickle. 50 Two females; factories and ship in background. VILLAGE BANK, North Danvers, Mass. 50 Farmer gathering corn.	1 Portrait of Webster. (New Plate.) Man sitting on the ground, anvil, hammer &c. Factories and train of cars in background. WORCESTER CO. B'K Blackstone, Mass. 1 Indian woman.	50 Female. Male and female. WORCESTER CO B'K Blackstone, Mass. 50 50 Cupid in sail boat. 50
100 Sailor and flag. VILLAGE BANK, North Danvers, Mass. Female and cupid floating in the air, over a city. 100 Portrait of female. 100	Female, Railroad and canal. 1 (Old Plate.) 1 WORCESTER CO B'K Blackstone, Mass 1 Female.	100 Vulcan the black smith. Spread eagle, Railroad and canal. WORCESTER CO. B'K Blackstone, Mass. 100 100 Female.
Sailor holding a flag. WALTHAM BANK, Waltham, Mass. Female reclining, locomotive and factories, mill, mills and cows in background. 1 Cupid. 1	2 Farmers and sheep; stream of water. 2 WORCESTER CO. B'K Blackstone, Mass. TWO Female. TWO	1 Female, train of cars and canal in background. 1 WRENTHAM BANK Wrentham, Mass. 1 Female.
2 Females raking hay. WALTHAM BANK, Waltham, Mass. A mechanic designing; also stone cutting. 2 Farmer, rake and plough.	2 Female. (New Plate.) WORCESTER CO. B'K Blackstone, Mass. Two females, and bust of Washington, ship in distance 2 Portrait of Washington	2 Farmer and sheep, stream of water. 2 WRENTHAM BANK Wrentham, Mass. TWO Female. TWO

3 Farming scene. 3 WRENTHAM BANK Wrentham, Mass. 3 Female. THREE	TWO, 2, 2 Indians. Carpenter at work. 2 WAMESIT BANK Lowell, Mass. Female bathing 2 Man sitting on the ground, factories in back ground.	FIVE Spread eagle and shield; village in distance. Large V; female and cupid within. WAREHAM BANK Wareham, Mass. 5 Girl.
Large V with five running across. (New Plate.) Female with sickle rake &c, shipping in background. Large V with Indian girl. WRENTHAM BANK Wrentham, Mass. 5 Portrait of Washington.	3 Indians upon a cliff overlooking a city. THREE Large figure 3 with State Arms top—Title across 3. 3 Hay makers.	X Signing of the de- ration of independence. X WAREHAM BANK Wareham, Mass. 10 Train of cars.
FIVE (Old Plate.) Female. 5 WRENTHAM BANK Wrentham, Mass. 5 Ship.	FIVE Train of cars passing under a bridge. Large V with five at top, Man with sickle and sheaf of wheat, at bottom. WAMESIT BANK Lowell, Mass. 5 Cattle, train of cars in distance.	TEN Vulcan the blacksmith. X WAREHAM BANK Wareham, Mass. 10 Reaper.
X (New Plate.) Signing of the declaration of independence. X WRENTHAM BANK Wrentham, Mass. 10 Train of cars	TEN Two males and two females, city in background. 10 WAMESIT BANK Lowell, Mass. TEN TEN A male and two females, also a yoke of oxen.	20 Female. XX Eagle. XX WAREHAM BANK Wareham, Mass. 20 Ship.
10 X 10 (Old Plate.) Man and oxen. 10 WRENTHAM BANK Wrentham, Mass. TEN Female.	20 Male, female, two children and a dog. State arms. 20 WAMESIT BANK Lowell, Mass. Female. TWENTY	FIFTY Female. FIFTY 50 Man and horse. 50 WAREHAM BANK Wareham, Mass. FIFTY Female. FIFTY
20 Female. XX Eagle. XX WRENTHAM BANK Wrentham, Mass. 20 Ship.	FIFTY DOLLARS 50 Four female figures so arranged as to extend across the entire length of the bill. WAMESIT BANK Lowell, Mass. Female bathing 50	One Hundred And 100. Portrait. Horses, waggons, shipping, &c. WAREHAM BANK Wareham, Mass Same as left Portrait.
50 Steamboat and sail-vessel. Farming scene. 50 WRENTHAM BANK Wrentham, Mass. L Female.	1 Female Railroad and shipping. 1 WAREHAM BANK Wareham, Mass. 1 Female.	Female and fig. 1. 1 Cupid rolling a silver dollar upon a Railroad track, train of cars and village in the distance. SOUTH READING BK South Reading, Mass 1 Portrait.
One Hundred and 100. Portrait. Horses, wagons, shipping &c. WRENTHAM BANK Wrentham, Mass. Same as left Portrait.	2 Farmers and sheep. 2 WAREHAM BANK Wareham, Mass. TWO Female. TWO	Female. 2 Two cherubs and two silver dollars, train of cars and cattle in the background. SOUTH READING BK South Reading, Mass. 2 Portrait.
1 Indian with bow and hatchet. Brick layers. 1 WAMESIT BANK Lowell, Mass. 1 Stone cutter.	3 Farming scene. 3 WAREHAM BANK Wareham, Mass. 3 Female. T HREE	3 Portrait. Three cherubs and three silver dollars. SOUTH READING B'K South Reading, Mass. 3 Blacksmith anvil and forge.

5 Portrait. 5	Five cherubs and five silver dollars. SOUTH READING BK South Reading, Mass.	5 Female and fig. 5
2 Two females and eagle.	Two cupids and two silver dollars. TOWNSEND BANK, Townsend, Mass.	2 Female and large figure 2.
TWO Female. 2	(Old Plate.) 2 Farming scene. 2 UNION BANK OF WEYMOUTH AND BRAINTREE, Weymouth, Mass.	TWO Female. 2
Farmer with basket of fruit and a cradle 10	Portrait. SOUTH READING BK South Reading, Mass.	X Female and anchor.
3 Portrait. 3	TOWNSEND BANK, Townsend, Mass Three cupids and three silver dollars. Mechanic seated	3 Female reading.
I I I 3	(New Plate.) UNION BANK OF WEYMOUTH AND BRAINTREE, Weymouth, Mass. Two females, train of cars and ship in background.	3 Portrait of J. Q. Adams.
XX Female.	Female reclining, locomotive and factory, milk maids and cows in background. SOUTH READING BK South Reading, Mass.	20 Portrait.
Female feeding an eagle from a cup. 5	Five cupids and five silver dollars. TOWNSEND BANK, Townsend, Mass.	5 Group of females and large figure 5
THREE Farmer sharpening his scythe. 3	(Old Plate.) 3 Female and eagle. 3 UNION BANK OF WEYMOUTH AND BRAINTREE, Weymouth, Mass.	THREE Sailor. 3
Girl with sheaf of grain. 50	Female sitting on a rock, and cupids sporting with a dolphin in the water. SOUTH READING BK South Reading, Mass.	50 Portrait.
10 X	TOWNSEND BANK, Townsend, Mass. Farming scene	X Female.
FIVE V	(New Plate.) UNION BANK OF WEYMOUTH AND BRAINTREE, Weymouth, Mass. A street in Weymouth.	V Webster V
Female, feeding an eagle from a cup. 100	Capitol at Washington. SOUTH READING BK South Reading, Mass.	100 Portrait.
TWENTY Indian woman with bow and spear.	TOWNSEND BANK. Townsend. Mass. Indian sitting on the ground beside a slain deer.	20 Farmer-boy and XX on half shield.
5 FIVE 5	(Old Plate.) V Eagle and shipping. V UNION BANK OF WEYMOUTH AND BRAINTREE, Weymouth, Mass.	5 FIVE 5
1 Cattle. ONE	Man and dog in a forest. SPRINGFIELD B'K Springfield, Mass. Vessel.	1 Portrait of Jenny Lind.
50 Female.	Capitol at Washington. TOWNSEND BANK. Townsend, Mass.	50 Female feeding a horse.
TEN	(New Plate.) UNION BANK OF WEYMOUTH AND BRAINTREE, Weymouth, Mass. A street in Weymouth.	X Portrait of Washington.
Female. TWO	Man and dog in a forest. SPRINGFIELD B'K Springfield, Mass. Bales and boxes.	TWO 2 Hay makers.
1 Female with sickle and sheaf of wheat; reapers and farm house in background.	(New Plate.) UNION BANK OF WEYMOUTH AND BRAINTREE, Weymouth, Mass. Portrait of Washington. Train of cars.	ONE 1
10 X 10	(Old Plate.) Man and oxen. 10 UNION BANK OF WEYMOUTH AND BRAINTREE, Weymouth, Mass.	TEN Female.
	The Springfield Bank uses the old sterotype plate for all other denominations.	
ONE Bust of Washington. ONE	(Old Plate.) 1 Interior of a blacksmith's shop. 1 UNION BANK OF WEYMOUTH AND BRAINTREE, Weymouth, Mass.	ONE Female. ONE
XX Portrait of Franklin.	(New Plate.) UNION BANK OF WEYMOUTH AND BRAINTREE, Weymouth, Mass. A street in Weymouth.	20
ONE and 1 Merchandise. 1	TOWNSEND BANK, Townsend, Mass. Cupid rolling a silver dollar upon the railroad track, train of cars and city in distance. Farmer cradling	1 Two females.
TWO TWO	(New Plate.) UNION BANK OF WEYMOUTH AND BRAINTREE. Weymouth. Mass. Spread eagle and several flags bearing the names of the States.	2 Portrait of Z. Taylor.
20 Female.	(Old Plate.) XX Eagle. XX UNION BANK OF WEYMOUTH AND BRAINTREE, Weymouth, Mass.	20 Ship.

FIFTY 50 Man and horse. 50 FIFTY Female. UNION BANK OF WEYMOUTH AND BRAINTREE, Weymouth, Mass. Female. FIFTY FIFTY	Two females, train of cars and steamboat in background. 1 1 1 PRESCOTT BANK, Lowell, Mass. Female.	2 on TWO Female; farming scenes in the background. 2 TWO Old Pynchon House. PYNCHON BANK, Springfield, Mass. Female. TWO
100 across One Hundred. Horses, waggons, shipping &c. 100 across One Hundred. Portrait. UNION BANK OF WEYMOUTH AND BRAINTREE, Weymouth, Mass. Portrait.	Man sitting on the ground with hammer on his shoulder; factory and train of cars in background. Cupid and figure 2. TWO 2 PRESCOTT BANK, Lowell, Mass. Female.	3 Two horses and eagle; train of cars, factory and steamboat in background. 3 THREE A bull's head. PYNCHON BANK, Springfield, Mass. THREE
View in the streets of Salisbury. 1 ONE POWOW RIVER B'K, Salisbury, Mass. Farmers and sheep.	Farmers ploughing, man on horseback, train of cars running under a bridge. 3 THREE 3 PRESCOTT BANK, Lowell, Mass. Two females.	Large figure 5, female and shield. PYNCHON BANK, Springfield, Mass. 5 Old Pynchon House. FIVE 5 Three boys and ship. 5 5
2 View in the streets of Salisbury. 2 Interior of blacksmiths shop. POWOW RIVER B'K, Salisbury, Mass. Sail boats. TWO TWO	Female reclining; a stream of water and factories in background. 5 FIVE 5 PRESCOTT BANK, Lowell, Mass. Female. Mon shield.	X, 10, Ten Man ploughing with yoke of oxen and horse. 10 Old Pynchon House. PYNCHON BANK, Springfield, Mass. Two females. TEN X
5 View of the town of Salisbury. 5 Indian. POWOW RIVER B'K, Salisbury, Mass. Farmers mowing. FIVE FIVE	Female, eagle and shield, also portrait of Washington. X 10 TEN PRESCOTT BANK, Lowell, Mass. State Arms.	20 Indian and plough, log cabin &c. 20 on right. XX [illegible] of Webster. PYNCHON BANK, Springfield, Mass. Female. XX
Signing the Declaration of Independence. X 10 X POWOW RIVER B'K, Salisbury, Mass. Train of cars.	20 2 Female. 0 20 Female. PRESCOTT BANK, Lowell, Mass. Female. XX 20	50 Signing of the Declaration of Independence. 50 Female. PYNCHON BANK, Springfield, Mass. Portrait of Washington.
20 XX Eagle. XX 20 Female. POWOW RIVER B'K, Salisbury, Mass. Ship.	50 Male and female. 50 PRESCOTT BANK, Lowell, Mass. Cupid in a sail boat. Female. 50 50	100 PYNCHON BANK, Springfield, Mass. 100 Female. C Female leaning upon a chest; old Pynchon House in the distance.
FIFTY 50 Man and horse. 50 FIFTY Female. POWOW RIVER B'K, Salisbury, Mass. Female. FIFTY FIFTY	100 Spread eagle, railroad and canal. 100 Vulcan the blacksmith. PRESCOTT BANK, Lowell, Mass. Female. 100	1 PITTSFIELD BANK, Pittsfield, Mass. ONE Stone cutters. Portrait
One Hundred and 100. Horses, waggons, shipping &c. Same as left Portrait. POWOW RIVER B'K, Salisbury, Mass. Portrait.	Train of cars. 1 1 ON 1 E PYNCHON BANK, Springfield, Mass. Head and shoulders of a man with hammer. 1	TWO Interior of a shoe makers shop 2 Portrait. PITTSFIELD BANK, Pittsfield, Mass. 2

FIVE V Spread eagle and flags bearing the name of each State in the Union PITTSFIELD BANK, Pittsfield, Mass. 5 Portrait.	L Portrait of female. Female seated on a bale; steamship and sail vessels in the distance. PROVINCETOWN BANK, Provincetown, Mass. 50	100 Vulcan the blacksmith. Spread eagle, railroad and canal. ROLLSTONE BANK, Fitchburg, Mass 100 100 Female
X Indian. Portrait. Steamship PITTSFIELD BANK. Pittsfield, Mass. X TEN	C Large Ship. PROVINCETOWN BANK, Provincetown, Mass. Large C in the middle of the bill printed in red. 100 Sailor leaning upon a capstan.	1 Three female figures 1 Machinery and factories. Ship. Bee hive. SALEM BANK, Salem. Mass. 1 Portrait of Washington 1
20 Indian. Santa Claus in sleigh, drawn by reindeer over roofs of houses. PITTSFIELD BANK, Pittsfield, Mass. 20 Portrait.	ONE Female seated on the ground; factory village in the distance 1 on right. ROLLSTONE BANK, Fitchburg, Mass. Wheels, bale, etc 1 Female and 3 cherubs.	2 Masts, cars, bbls., fruit &c. 2 TWO Shipping. Female figure. Farming scene. SALEM BANK, Salem. Mass. 2 Female crowning a bust of Washington. 2
L PITTSFIELD BANK, Pittsfield, Mass. Faust, Guttenberg and Scheffer. 50 Portrait.	2 Female riding upon the back of a reindeer. 2 ROLLSTONE BANK. Fitchburg, Mass. Cars TWO Two females	THREE Female sitting on the ground, also anchor and bale; ship in distance. 3 Female, anchor, merchandise and ships. SALEM BANK, Salem, Mass 3 Portrait of Washington 3
1 Man chopping down a tree. ONE Ships. PROVINCETOWN BANK, Provincetown, Mass. 1 Girl.	3 Milk maid and cows. 3 ROLLSTONE BANK. Fitchburg, Mass 3 Portrait of female. THREE	5 Female. 5 5 Female figure and ship. 5 FIVE SALEM BANK, Salem, Mass 5 Female and sickle. 5
2 Church. Ships. PROVINCETOWN BANK, Provincetown, Mass. 2 TWO	5 Train of cars. Female in large V ROLLSTONE BANK. Fitchburg, Mass. State Arms 5 Females, chest and horn of plenty and 5.	10 X 10 (Old Plate.) Man and oxen. 10 SALEM BANK, Salem. Mass. TEN Female
Female and eagle. V Portrait of Webster. PROVINCETOWN BANK, Provincetown, Mass. FIVE Boy.	TEN Female with sickle, farmers gathering grain in the background. X ROLLSTONE BANK, Fitchburg, Mass. Female head 10 Female figure.	10 Portrait of female. TEN (New Plate.) 1 Female with key and horn of plenty. 0 SALEM BANK, Salem, Mass. TEN 10 Portrait of female. TEN
Female. TEN Ships. PROVINCETOWN BANK, Provincetown, Mass 10 X	20 Female. 2 Female. 0 ROLLSTONE BANK. Fitchburg, Mass. XX 20 Female. 20	20 Female. 2 Female. 0 SALEM BANK, Salem, Mass. XX 20 Female. 20
XX Portrait of J. Q. Adams. PROVINCETOWN BANK, Provincetown, Mass. Sailors on shore, throwing a rope with a mortar to a ship wrecked in the sea. XX 20	50 Female. Male and female. ROLLSTONE BANK, Fitchburg, Mass 50 50 Cupid in a sail boat. 50	50 Female figure Male and female. SALEM BANK, Salem, Mass. 50 50 Cupid in a sail boat. 50

100 — Vulcan the blacksmith.
Spread eagle, railroad and canal. SALEM BANK, Salem, Mass. 100
100 — Female.

1 — 1
State arms with female on each side, steamboat and train of cars in background. 1 — LEICESTER BANK Leicester, Mass.
1 — Female.

TWO — 2 — Portrait of Fillmore.
Female with sword and scales also shipping and boy 2 — LEICESTER BANK Leicester, Mass.
2 — Portrait of Webster.

3 — THREE — Clay.
Farmer and milk maid. 3 — LEICESTER BANK, Leicester, Mass.
3 — Taylor.

5 — Portrait of Washington.
Reindeer running across a plain bearing a female upon his back. Large V, female within — LEICESTER BANK Leicester, Mass.
5 — Female with a flag also three cherubs.

Large X; with figure 10 running across.
Female with horn of plenty and key sitting, figures 1 and 0. LEICESTER BANK Leicester, Mass.
X — Female.

20 — Female.
(Old Plate.) XX Eagle. XX — LEICESTER BANK Leicester, Mass.
20 — Ship.

20 — Female.
(New Plate) 2 Female. 0 — LEICESTER BANK Leicester, Mass. XX
20 — Female. 20

ONE — Female.
Railroad, and Cambridge bridge, train of cars, vessels, and East Cambridge in distance. LECHMERE BANK East Cambridge, Mass.
1 — Portrait of Winchester

2 — Portrait of female.
LECHMERE BANK East Cambridge Mass. Same vig.
2 — Portrait of Winchester.

3 — Same Vig.
LECHMERE BANK East Cambridge, Mass.
3 — Portrait of Winchester

5
Same vig. Portrait of female. LECHMERE BANK East Cambridge Mass
5 — Portrait of Winchester

Female 10 — TEN
LECHMERE BANK East Cambridge Mass. Portrait of Winchester.
10 Female — TEN

20 — Sailor leaning upon a capstan.
LECHMERE BANK East Cambridge, Mass. Blacksmith shoeing a horse
20 — Portrait of Winchester

50 — State arms.
LECHMERE BANK East Cambridge Mass. Capitol at Washington, female and shield in fore ground.
50 — Portrait of John Hancock.

100 — Portrait of female.
Three female figures, LECHMERE BANK East Cambridge, Mass
100 — Portrait of Winchester

1 — Portrait of Washington.
Female 1 Female — MARBLEHEAD B'K Marblehead, Mass
1 — Franklin.

2 — Portrait of Columbus.
Female 2 Female — MARBLEHEAD B'K Marblehead, Mass.
2 — Portrait

3 — General Washington, and horse.
Female 3 Female — MARBLEHEAD B'K Marblehead, Mass.
3 — Vulcan the black smith

Spread eagle — FIVE
Large V; Female and Cupid. MARBLEHEAD B'K Marblehead, Mass.
5 — Girl.

Vulcan the black smith. — TEN
X — MARBLEHEAD B'K Marblehead, Mass.
10 — Reaper.

20 — Female.
XX Eagle. XX — MARBLEHEAD B'K Marblehead, Mass.
20 — Ship.

FIFTY — Female — FIFTY
50 Man and horse. 50 — MARBLEHEAD B'K Marblehead, Mass.
FIFTY — Female. — FIFTY

1 — Medallion head. — 1
(Old Plate.) 1 Indian woman and canoe. 1 — HOUSATONIC B'K Stockbridge, Mass.
ONE — Female. — ONE

ONE — Portrait of Taylor. — ONE
(New Plate.) Man with an axe and Indian with an ear of corn. Figure 1 each side. HOUSATONIC B'K Stockbridge, Mass. Safe.
1 — Stone cutter

2 — Female. — 2
(Old Plate.) 2 Female, anchor, and spinning wheel. factories and train of cars in background. HOUSATONIC B'K Stockbridge, Mass.
2 — Medallion head.

TWO — Farmer sharpening a scythe.
(New Plate.) Two female figures and bust, ship in distance. fig 2 each side. HOUSATONIC B'K Stockbridge, Mass. Wheat, &c.
2 — Female — TWO

FIVE DOLLARS
(Old Plate.)
5 Female feeding an eagle from a cup. 5
Indian.
HOUSATONIC B'K.
Stockbridge, Mass.
Drovers, cattle, &c.
5

FIVE
(New Plate.)
5
V Train of cars. V
HOUSATONIC B'K
Stockbridge, Mass.
Mechanics arm.
Indian.
Two female figures fig. 5, scales, safe, etc.

(Old Plate.)
10
X Archimedes raisin the world with a lever. X
TEN
Portrait of Washington.
Portrait.
HOUSATONIC B'K
Stockbridge, Mass.
Female with wheat
10
TEN

[illegible]emale and eagle.
(New Plate.)
10 Farmers and cattle.
10
TEN
HOUSATONIC B'K
Stockbridge, Mass.
Horses
Indian woman and X

Two female figures
20 Female sitting upon a rock also three cupids sporting with a dolphin in the water.
20
HOUSATONIC B'K
Stockbridge, Mass.
2 Female 0

1
Street in Brighton; drovers of cattle.
1
Female
BRIGHTON MARKET BANK.
Brighton, Mass.
ONE
Female and shield and fig. 1

Two female figures.
Street in Brighton; droves of cattle.
2
BRIGHTON MARKET BANK.
Brighton, Mass.
2
Sailor and Indian and TWO on shield.

3
Same as above.
3
Cattle.
BRIGHTON MARKET BANK
Brighton, Mass.
THREE
Man plowing
Farmer sailor and blacksmith and fig. 3

5
Same as above.
5
Portrait of female
BRIGHTON MARKET BANK.
Brighton, Mass.
5
Female shield and globe.

Farmers washing sheep.
Farming scene.
10
BRIGHTON MARKET BANK,
Brighton, Mass.
X
Loading hay
Train of cars.

Female.
Farming scene
20
BRIGHTON MARKET BANK.
Brighton, Mass.
20
Farmer cradling
Cattle.

Female with a rake.
BRIGHTON MARKET BANK,
Brighton, Mass.
50
Cattle.
50
Imp. and products.
Female and churn.

C
BRIGHTON MARKET BANK
Brighton, Mass.
100
Female reclining locomotive, factories, shipping and cattle in background.
Portrait of Webster.
C
Two horses
100

ONE
Farmer sowing seed.
1
1
Ship.
BLUE HILL BANK
Dorchester, Mass
1
ONE

TWO
Spread eagle.
2
2
BLUE HILL BANK
Dorchester, Mass.
TWO
2
Sailboats.

THREE
Wharf and shipping.
3
3
BLUE HILL BANK
Dorchester, Mass.
THREE
3
Train of cars.

Spread eagle.
Large V near the centre.
5
BLUE HILL BANK
Dorchester, Mass.
Girl.
FIVE

Vul[illegible]n the blacksmith; train of cars and factories in the background.
Large X near the centre
10
TEN
BLUE HILL BANK
Dorchester, Mass.
Reaper.

20
2 Female. 0
20
BLUE HILL BANK
Dorchester, Mass.
Female figure.
20

50
Farming scene
50
L
BLUE HILL BANK
Dorchester, Mass.
Steamboat and sail vessel.
Female, sword and scales.

100
Spread eagle, Railroad and canal.
100
BLUE HILL BANK
Dorchester, Mass.
Vulcan the blacksmith.
Female.

1
NORTH BRIDGEWATER BANK.
N. Bridgewater, Mass.
1
A street in N. Bridgewater.
Portrait.

A street in North Bridgewater.
Train of cars.
2
NORTH BRIDGEWATER BANK,
N. Bridgewater, Mass.
2
Female
Portrait.

Female.
Street in North Bridgewater.
3
NORTH BRIDGEWATER BANK,
N. Bridgewater, Mass.
3
Cow and calf
Portrait.

5
NORTH BRIDGEWATER BANK.
N. Bridgewater, Mass.
FIVE
A group of females; ships and factories in background.
Portrait.
Group of females and large figure 5.

TEN inverted
Train of cars.
10
NORTH BRIDGEWATER BANK.
N. Bridgewater, Mass.
10
Loading hay
Female and X

Female with a basket of fruit and flowers.
Female reclining; milk maids, cows, locomotive and factory in background.
20
NORTH BRIDGEWATER BANK,
N. Bridgewater, Mass
2 Female 0
XX
Female
TWENTY

Female. 50 50 NORTH BRIDGEWATER BANK. N. Bridgewater, Mass. State arms, eagle and two females; steamboat and train of cars in the background. Female.	100 Reaper. Landing of the Pilgrims in 1620. OLD COLONY BANK, Plymouth, Mass. 100 Female and eagle.	ONE Phœbus in the chariot of the Sun. Dog, safe and building. MERRIMACK B'K. Haverhill, Mass. 1 Female.
Portrait of female. 100 View of the capitol at Washington. NORTH BRIDGEWATER BANK. N. Bridgewater, Mass. 100 Blacksmith, anvil and forge. 100	ONE Eagle. ONE 1 Farming scene. ONE OXFORD BANK, Oxford, Mass. 1 Female figures 1	2 TWO 2 Female figure and cupid. TWO MERRIMACK BANK, Haverhill, Mass. 2 Ship building.
1 Female figure holding scales and sword. ONE 1 Landing of the Pilgrims in 1620. 1 OLD COLONY BANK, Plymouth, Mass. 1 Portrait of Washington. ONE	2 Female with scales and sword. 2 Cattle and sheep, man on horseback. 2 OXFORD BANK, Oxford, Mass. TWO General Washington. 2	THREE Horses, wagons, wharf and shipping. 3 MERRIMACK BANK, Haverhill, Mass. Female.
TWO Female with scales and sword. TWO 2 Landing of the Pilgrims in 1620. 2 OLD COLONY BANK, Plymouth, Mass. 2 Female figure. TWO	3 Female. 3 THREE Surrender of Lord Cornwallis. 3 OXFORD BANK, Oxford, Mass. THREE Agricultural implements. 3	5 FIVE Female. Train of cars. MERRIMACK BANK, Haverhill, Mass. 5 Fancy piece
3 Portrait of Washington. 3 THREE Landing of the Pilgrims in 1620. 3 OLD COLONY BANK, Plymouth, Mass. THREE	FIVE Female. V Battle of Bunker Hill. 5 OXFORD BANK, Oxford, Mass. FIVE Portrait of Washington. 5	X Steamboat. Men on horseback, cattle and sheep. MERRIMACK BANK Haverhill, Mass. 10 Female. X
Statue of Washington. 5 Landing of the Pilgrims in 1620. 5 OLD COLONY BANK, Plymouth, Mass. Eagle standing upon a rock overlooking the sea. FIVE	Statue of Washington. 10 Washington crossing the Delaware. 10 OXFORD BANK, Oxford, Mass. TEN Portrait. X	20 Female. XX Eagle XX MERRIMACK BANK, Haverhill, Mass. 20 Ship.
Eagle standing upon a rock overlooking the sea. TEN 10 Landing of the Pilgrims in 1620. X OLD COLONY BANK, Plymouth, Mass. Female figure. TEN	Steamboat. XX Train of cars. Three female figures and eagle. 20 OXFORD BANK. Oxford. Mass. XX Milk maid.	FIFTY Female. FIFTY 50 Man and horse. 50 MERRIMACK BANK, Haverhill, Mass. FIFTY Female. FIFTY
20 Indian. Landing of the Pilgrims in 1620. OLD COLONY BANK, Plymouth, Mass. 20 Portrait of Washington. XX	50 Steamboat and sail boat. Farming scene. 50 OXFORD BANK, Oxford, Mass. L Female with scales and sword.	One Hundred and 100. Portrait. Horses, waggons, wharf, shipping, &c. MERRIMACK BANK. Haverhill. Mass. Same as left Portrait.
Indians. Landing of the Pilgrims in 1620. OLD COLONY BANK. Plymouth, Mass. 50 Train of cars. FIFTY	100 Eagle. 100 C Phaeton in the car of the sun. 100 OXFORD BANK, Oxford, Mass. C Portrait of Washington. C	ONE State Arms. Male and female; train of cars and ship in background. MERCHANTS BANK, New Bedford, Mass. Locomotive 1 Female.

2 Female. TWO	Female sitting on bale; factory in background. MERCHANTS BANK, New Bedford, Mass. Steamboat	2 Ship. TWO
1 Ships. ONE	ONE Whale ships and a whale. 1 Female MERCHANTS BANK, Newburyport, Mass.	1 Ship. ONE
TWENTY Female figure, one arm resting on a pedestal, the other on shield.	20 on medallion head. Vig. Female seated, leaning against safe; sheep on right, church in centre, cornucopia, &c. FARMERS AND MECHANICS BANK OF EASTON, Pa.	XX 20
3	Two females in foreground; shipping, train of cars in background. 3 on right. MERCHANTS BANK, New Bedford, Mass. Beehive	3 Portrait of female.
TWO Train of cars. TWO	2 Ships. 2 MERCHANTS BANK, Newburyport, Mass.	2 Male figure 2
Goddess of Liberty; fifty on shield and eagle.	50 on medallion head. FARMERS AND MECHANICS BANK OF EASTON, Pa. Vig. Milkmaid seated on a log, farm house on left, steamboat on right.	50 50
5 Female.	MERCHANTS BANK, New Bedford, Mass Female sitting on a bale; ships and light house in background. 5 each side. Wheat, &c.	5 Female.
THREE Steamboat. THREE	Female Ship-building. Sailor MERCHANTS BANK, Newburyport. Mass.	3 Ship. 3
100 on medallion head. Farmers going to work house in the distance.	FARMERS AND MECHANICS BANK OF EASTON, Pa. Vig. Mechanic seated, sledge in hand, viewing factories and train of cars, &c. 100	Two females, one seated with sickle and bunch of grain. C
TEN Ship building 10	(Old Plate.) 10 Interior of blacksmith shop. X MERCHANTS BANK, New Bedford, Mass	10 Whale ship. TEN
Eagle. FIVE	Ship Washington and his troops crossing the Delaware. 5 MERCHANTS BANK, Newburyport, Mass.	Ships and merchandise FIVE
FIVE Public buildings. FIVE	5 Female portrait. Vig. Public building with spire and clock. LANCASTER BANK Lancaster, Pa. Dog, safe and scales.	FIVE Building. FIVE
10 State arms	(New Plate.) Female, child, dog, and safe. 10 MERCHANTS BANK New Bedford, Mass Eagle	TEN Female with sheaf of wheat. 10
10 Surrender of Lord Cornwallis. TEN	Ship. Phœbus in the car of the Sun. Ship. MERCHANTS BANK, Newburyport, Mass.	10 Washington crossing the Delaware. TEN
10 Female head. 10	LANCASTER BANK, Lancaster, Pa. Vig. Eagle on shield; buildings in background. Sheaf of grain and agricultural implements.	10 Female leaning on, liberty pole, cap &c TEN
20 Female.	(Old Plate.) XX Eagle. XX MERCHANTS BANK, New Bedford. Mass. 20 State Arms 20	20 Ship.
FIFTY Male figure. 50	FIFTY Steamboat; city in the distance. Female. MERCHANTS BANK, Newburyport, Mass	50 Bust. FIFTY
Female with sword and balances. 20	20 20 LANCASTER BANK. Lancaster, Pa. Vig. Washington, female on either side. Mail turning.	Female with grain, &c 20
TWENTY Female with sickle and sheaf of wheat.	(New Plate.) Eagle. Indian, female and public building. MERCHANTS BANK, New Bedford. Mass. Female and ship	20 Ship.
100 Statue of Washington.	Battle of Bunker Hill. Three female figures. MERCHANTS BANK, Newburyport, Mass	100 Female.
50 Two females, liberty pole and cap, balances, &c. 50	LANCASTER BANK. Lancaster, Pa. Vig. Female seated, eagle, shield, safe, sword; banners, &c., in the distance, ships Bee Hive.	Washington on horse-back FIFTY
Portrait of female. 50	Three females, train of cars and ship in background. MERCHANTS BANK New Bedford, Mass. Building	50 Portrait of female.
5 Small head. FIVE	Vig. Harvest scene four human figures, cradler sharpening his scythe. 5 FARMERS & MECHANICS BANK OF EASTON, Pa.	FIVE Mechanic, anvil, tools &c, FIVE
100	Vig. C on shield in centre surmounted with eagle; Indian and female on either side. One Hundred Dollars on Scroll. LANCASTER BANK, Lancaster, Pa.	100
100 Portrait of Washington. 100	Female sitting on a bale. MERCHANTS BANK, New Bedford, Mass House	100 Female and anchor; city in the background.
Full length female with shield, wand, &c. TEN	10 on medallion head. Vig. Public buildings. FARMERS AND MECHANICS BANK OF EASTON, Pa.	10 Male portrait
500	LANCASTER BANK. Lancaster, Pa. Vig. D. Five Hundred Dollars on scroll above female seated on bale of goods; barrel, grain, &c.	500

1 Compt's die. ONE Vig. Harvest scene; female seated, child in her arms; loading hay in distance. FARMERS' BANK OF SARATOGA CO., Half Moon Village N Y 1 Female head. 1	5 V Vig. Indian hunting deer. Compt's die IRON BANK. Plattsburgh, N. Y. 5 Female seated in harvest field.	A 5 Female with horn of plenty. 5 CUMBERLAND B'K. OF ALLEGHANY, Md Vig. View of Cumberland with drover and cattle; road waggon in front; medallion head on each side. FIVE Female with horn of plenty. FIVE
2 Female head. TWO Vig. Milk maids milking, cars in distance. FARMERS' BANK OF SARATOGA CO., Half Moon Village N Y Secured, etc. TWO Female, grain and sickle. Compt's die	TEN Compt's die IRON BANK, Plattsburgh, N Y. Vig. Steamboat and vessel; train of cars, light house &c. in distance. X	5 Indian seated. 5 D Vig. Same as above CUMBERLAND B'K. OF ALLEGHANY, Md 5 Indian seated. 5
5 Compt's die. 5 Man's head. Vig. Harvest scene; farmer seated, scythe and lunch beside him; houses and train of cars in the distance. FARMERS' BANK OF SARATOGA CO., Half Moon Village N Y 5 Washington on horseback	5 Female head 5 V Two females, eagle, &c. V BANK OF MIDDLETOWN, Pa. 5 Female head with grain, &c. 5	5 Drove of cattle 5 C Vig. Same as above CUMBERLAND B'K OF ALLEGHANY, Md. FIVE Reaper lying down. FIVE
10 Male head. Compt's die. Vig. Female seated, bale and cask behind her, farmer loading hay, cars in distance. FARMERS' BANK OF SARATOGA CO. Half Moon Village N Y 10 Dog and safe	10 Ten on Medallion 10 10 on medal-lion Vig. Two horses, shield in centre, surmounted with eagle, scroll with virtue, liberty and independence. 10 on medal-lion BANK OF MIDDLETOWN, Pa. TEN	10 Drove of Cattle 10 Medallion of Franklin. Medallion of Franklin CUMBERLAND B'K. OF ALLEGHANY, Md Vig. Blacksmith sitting on his anvil. 10 Waggon unloading near a market woman 10
The new Plate (10) have the head on the right of Vig. instead of left,	20 Medallion head, twenty across it. 20 20 Vig. Female seated with sickle grain, &c.; house, &c. in distance. 20 BANK OF MIDDLETOWN, Pa. XX Twenty on Medallion head. XX	20 Female with horn of plenty. Vig. Female seated with a sheaf of wheat, bridge in background and medallions on either side. CUMBERLAND B'K OF ALLEGHANY, Md 20 Same as other end.
50 Compt's die. 50 FARMERS' BANK OF SARATOGA CO., Half Moon Village N Y Vig. Eagle on limb of tree, canal, boats, railroad cars, locomotive &c. Secured by pledge, &c, 50 Male head.	50 Artist seated at work. 50 50 Vig. Cupids at work at press, lever and sledge. 50 BANK OF MIDDLETOWN, Pa. 50 50 across medallion head. 50	50 Female seated, sheaf of wheat in her lap. L Vig. Reaper, male and female, seated on a rock in the woods. Medallion on either side. CUMBERLAND B'K. OF ALLEGHANY, Md L Female seated, sheaf of wheat in her lap. 50
1 Compt's die. Vig. Santa Claus in sledge drawn by reindeers. IRON BANK, Plattsburgh, N. Y. ONE Smith with hammer on his shoulder	5 Female head. BANK OF NORTHUMBERLAND, Pa. Vig. Farmers loading hay, canal and boat, train of cars. 5 Girls head	Female with sword. FIVE 5 Female with shield. 5 CECIL BANK. Port Deposit Md. Raft and timber. FIVE Female with horn of plenty. FIVE
TWO Compt's die. IRON BANK, Plattsburgh, N. Y. Large red 2. Vig. Female seated on bale; steamboat in distance. 2 2	Three female figures, anchor, &c. TEN BANK OF NORTHUMBERLAND, Pa. Vig. Female seated, scythe, sickle and pitcher, train of cars in distance, grain and implements. 10 Male head. TEN	TEN Justice. 10 10 Reapers. CECIL BANK, Port Deposit. Md. Raft and timber. 10 Female with sling.
3 Mechanic and sailor. 3 Compt's die. IRON BANK, Plattsburgh, N. Y. Large red 3 length wise of note. 3 Dog's head	20 Dog. 20 Vig. Spread eagle on rock; ship on either side. BANK OF NORTHUMBERLAND, Pa. Female with grain. 20	Full length figure of an Indian drawing bow. 20 Vig. Two females, steamboat on the right and vessel on left of them. CECIL BANK, Port Deposit, Md Raft and timber. 20 Head of Washington. TWENTY

1 Interior of a boot manufactory. 1	HOPKINTON BANK Hopkinton, Mass. Large figure 1 with words "ONE DOLLAR" running across. Dog's head.	1 Portrait of Lee Claflin.

2 Interior of a boot manufactory. 2	HOPKINTON BANK Hopkinton, Mass. Large figure 2, with the words "TWO DOLLARS" running across. Dog's head	2 Portrait of J. P. Hale.

5 Same as ones and twos. 5	HOPKINTON BANK Hopkinton, Mass. Large figure 5, with the words "FIVE DOLLARS" running across. Dog's head	5 Portrait of Lee Claflin.

X Same as ones twos and fives. 10	HOPKINTON BANK Hopkinton, Mass. Large X, with the words "TEN DOLLARS" running across. Dog's head	X Portrait of J. P. Hale.

50 Male head.	HOPKINTON BANK Hopkinton, Mass. Boot makers at work.	50

C Boot makers at work.	HOPKINTON BANK Hopkinton, Mass.	100 Wheels, bale, etc.

1 Compt's die. 1	1 Vig. Male and female, most prominent figures group in rear, also train of cars. TANNERS BANK Catskill, N. Y. Cars.	1 Cattle. 1

2 Compt's die. 2	Vig. same as ones. 2 TANNERS BANK Catskill, N. Y.	TWO

FIVE	5 Vig. same as ones and twos 5 TANNERS BANK Catskill, N. Y. Steamboat.	5 Compt's die. 5

10 Female, liberty pole and cap. 10	Vig. frame with vessel surmounted with eagle, female on either side, cars on right, shipping on left. 10 TANNERS BANK Catskill, N. Y. Steamboat.	10 Compt's die. 10

5 Hunter with rifle. 5	Medallion head, 5 on it. Vig. wood chopper, seated, dog and axe beside him, cabin in distance. Medallion head, 5 on it. EASTON BANK Easton, Pa.	5 Male Portrait. 5

10 Male portrait. 10	Medallion head ten across it. Vig. Indian seated bow and arrow, canoe in distance. Medallion head ten across it. EASTON BANK Easton, Pa.	10 Medallion head. 10

20 Washington. 20	Child seated reading. Vig. child in canoe plow and wheat. Child seated house in distance, artists tools in hand, &c. EASTON BANK Easton, Pa. Locomotive and cars.	20 Male Portrait. 20

50 Male portrait. FIFTY	Vig. Female seated. agricultural implements wheat, &c., cars locks, &c., in distance. Female portrait EASTON BANK Easton, Pa.	50 Male portrait. FIFTY.

100 Head of male 100	Vig. Female seated, shield, sickle, &c., two Indians on right. Female portrait on right. EASTON BANK Easton, Pa.	100 Head of male 100

Blacksmith.	FIVE'S FREDERICK TOWN SAVING INSTITUTION, Md. Vig. ploughman and two horses; laborer with shovel on his shoulder.	Carpenter sawing; another resting his right foot on the plank.

Portrait of Franklin.	TEN'S FREDERICK TOWN SAVING INSTITUTION, Md. Vig. harvest scene, harvesting wheat, &c.	Justice with scales.

Medallion head of Washington.	MONONGAHELA B'K Brownsville, Pa. 5 Vig. Large V, with female and sheaf of wheat in centre of V. 5	Fame blowing a trumpet, and holding pole with liberty cap. 5

X Medallion head. X	10 Vig. Harvest scene, and farmers taking lunch. MONONGAHELA BK Brownsville, Pa.	Large X with persons supporting it on either side; sledge and anvil at bottom.

Female portrait.	20 Vig. Goddess of Liberty, with pole and cap, reclining against U. S. Coat of Arms. MONONGAHELA BK Brownsville, Pa.	20 Portrait of Washington

Male head.	ONONDAGA BANK Syracuse, N. Y. Vig. Cattle standing in water.	1 Compt's die.

Compt's die. Plank road, cattle, &c	Vig. Indian on rock and city in distance. ONONDAGA BANK Syracuse, N. Y. Beehive.	2 Male head.

3	Vig. Blacksmith shoeing horses, &c. ONONDAGA BANK Syracuse, N. Y.	3 Sea nymph in shell

Compt's die. Indian looking over a rock.	ONONDAGA BANK Syracuse, N. Y. Vig. Drover selling oxen to Farmer.	5

10 Compt's die.	ONONDAGA BANK Syracuse, N. Y. Three sea nymphs supporting Cupid in water.	10 Female head.

Boys head. Compt's die.	Vig. Horses running, prominent feature, three horses. ONONDAGA BANK Syracuse, N. Y.	50 Female head.

Female head.	Vig. Capitol at Washington. ONONDAGA BANK Syracuse, N. Y.	100 Male head.

ONE 1 Vig. Female, soaring eagle, shield, liberty cap and pole, cornucopia &c. 1 Full length portrait of an officer. Compt's die. ONE STEUBEN CO. BANK. Bath, N. Y. Cornucopia, anchor &c. ONE

20 COLUMBIA BANK Columbia, Pa. Goddess of liberty. Franklin. Medallion head. Vig. Rott and train of cars. Medallion head. 20 20

5 LAKE MAHOPAC B'K Carmel, N. Y. 5 Large V, with five running across. Compt's die. Indian scene. Large figure 5 with cars on bridge.

TWO 2 Vig. Female seated on bale, train of cars, sickle, grain &c.; factory in distance. 2 Same as one's. Compt's die. TWO STEUBEN CO. BANK. Bath, N. Y. Agricultural implements TWO

50 50 on medallion head. Vig. Pat. Lyon in his shop. 50 on medallion head. 50 Waggon, horses, bales, unloading on skids. Cattle; landscape in distance. COLUMBIA BANK, Columbia Pa. 50 50

1 Vig. Portrait of H. Clay. ONE HOLISTER BANK Buffalo, N. Y. Female seated. Compt's die. Secured by pledge &c. ONE

---

3 3 Vig. Farmer at lunch. 3 Same as one's. Compt's die. STEUBEN CO. BANK, Bath, N. Y. 3 Agricultural implements THREE

Medallion head. 100 Medallion head. COLUMBIA BANK, Columbia, Pa. Female figure seated on bale of merchandise, right arm resting on a shield, with plough in centre and ship above it. 100 on medallion head. HUNDRED Female standing, her right hand over shield resting on a pedestal, head of mars on shield. HUNDRED ONE HUNDRED.

Female 2 Vig. Boiler maker seated on boiler. 2 Two dollars. HOLISTER BANK Buffalo, N. Y. Portrait of Clay. Compt's die Secured &c. Two dollars.

V 5 Vig. Large ornamental 5, female on either side, cupids &c. 5 Same as one's. Compt's die. STEUBEN CO. BANK, Bath, N. Y. V Dog and safe. FIVE

Compt's die. 1 Vig. Female, one hand extended over child's head, agricultural implements, anchor &c.; sail vessel in distance. Die. ONE MERCHANTS' AND FARMERS' BANK. Ithica, N. Y. Building. ONE Female seated, liberty pole and cap.

5 Vig. Train of cars large house in distance. 5 Portrait of H. Clay. Compt's die HOLISTER BANK Buffalo, N. Y. FIVE Secured &c. FIVE

---

10 Vig. Female portrait in frame, surrounded by banners, drum, cannon &c. 10 Same as one's. Compt's die. STEUBEN CO. BANK, Bath, N. Y. 10 Agricultural implements and wheat. TEN

TWO 2 Vig. Female seated, wand in left hand extended, sickle, wheat &c.; houses and railroad in distance. 2 Compt's die. Mechanic seated, horn of plenty &c. MERCHANTS' AND FARMERS' BANK, Ithica, N. Y. TWO Steamboat.

TEN 10 Vig. Drovers driving sheep and watering a horse. TEN Compt's die HOLISTER BANK Buffalo, N. Y. Portrait of H. Clay. 10 Secured, &c. 10

---

20 20 Vig. Spread eagle on bale and shield, cask, anchor; falls and train of cars in distance. 20 Same as one's. Compt's die. STEUBEN CO. BANK, Bath, N. Y. 20 Agricultural implements and wheat. TWENTY

5 V Vig. Female seated within large 5, female on either side; implements of agriculture, barrels, bales, steamboat &c. V 5 Compt's die. Medallion head. MERCHANTS' AND FARMERS' BANK. Ithica, N. Y. Die. FIVE FIVE

TWENTY Vig. Steamship under way and vessels in distance. TWENTY Compt's die. HOLISTER BANK Buffalo, N. Y. Portrait of H. Clay. 20 Secured &c. 20

---

50 STEUBEN CO. BANK. Bath, N. Y. Full length portrait of a military officer. Female seated, key and wand. Vig. Horse. 50 50

10 Vig. Two females, shield between them, sickle, balances, implements of agriculture, barrels, bales, shipping, manufactories &c. 10 Compt's die. Two females, horn of plenty, liberty pole, cap &c. MERCHANTS' AND FARMERS' BANK. Ithica. N. Y. Steamboat. TEN TEN

10 Male portrait. Male portrait 10 BURNET BANK, Syracuse, N. Y. TEN Soldiers seated; one with drum. Compt's die.

---

5 COLUMBIA BANK, Columbia, Pa. 5 Washington. Vig. Female and cupid with wand seated, vessel in distance. 5 on medallion head. Train of cars. V V

Compt's die. LAKE MAHOPAC B'K Carmel, N. Y. ONE Female seated holding a Bucket. Figure 1, with one running across; long train of cars houses, hills &c in distance. Female seated.

OCEAN BANK, Newburyport, Mass. This Bank uses Perkins' Patent Stereotype plate, which is the denomination printed in fine letters all over the bill.

---

10 COLUMBIA BANK. Columbia, Pa. X Male portrait Vig. Wood chopper seated, dog and axe beside him. Medallion head with ten across it. 10

TWO LAKE MAHOPAC B'K Carmel, N. Y. TWO Com pt's die. Vig. Indians on horses, train of cars in distance. Female seated, in figure 2 2 2

RAILROAD BANK, Lowell, Mass. This Bank uses Perkins' Patent Stereotype plate, which is the denomination printed in fine letters all over the bill.

Left end	Centre	Right end
5 Female and sheaf of wheat, sickle in left hand, grain in right. FIVE	Vig. Three artisans with implements, ship yard factory and bridge in distance. BANK OF PITTSBURG, Pa.	5 Train of cars. FIVE
Two females with American flag and eagle beneath.	20 Vig. Washington on horse with staff, artillery, river, &c. in distance. 20 WASHINGTON CO. BANK, Williamsport, Md. Locomotive and cars	Blacksmith and forge.
X Auditor's die	Title of Bank. TEN Liberty surrounded by stars. TEN	10 Squaw and papoose.
X Locomotive and tender. TEN	Vig. Blacksmith in sitting posture hammer in right hand, anvil, train of cars crossing a bridge in distance, workshops; river and hills in distance. BANK OF PITTSBURG, Pa	10 Head of Washington X
FIFTY	50 Vig. Female sitting at table, reading the "Farewell Address", large mill, water, &c. in the distance. 50 WASHINGTON CO. BANK, Williamsport, Mass.	Full length portrait of Washington in citizens dress.
5 Clay. FIVE	Washington; two females on left; sheafs, female, etc., on right. FARMERS' AND MERCHANTS' BANK Greensborough, Md.	5 Jackson. FIVE
20 Head of Dewitt Clinton. 20	20 Vig. Black smith sitting with forearm and anvil to right cars crossing bridge in distance. 20 BANK OF PITTSBURG, Pa.	20 Head of Jefferson, 20
Indian with bow and arrow.	Vig. Fox chase. BANK OF WESTMINSTER, Md.	5 Indian squaw.
10 Head of Jackson.	Vig. Reaping machine at work. FARMERS' AND MERCHANTS BANK Greensborough, Md	10 Head of Clay
50 Medallion head 50	50 Vig. Female reclining with stacks of grain in left hand, ship, pier and farm house in distance. 50 BANK OF PITTSBURGH, Pa.	Die Figure of Justice. Die
10 10	Vig. Blacksmith shoeing a horse. 10 BANK OF WESTMINISTER, Md.	Female with wreath of flowers.
Mechanic at work. Compt's die	FULTON CO. BANK Gloversville, N. Y. 1 Vig. Male portrait. 1	1 Vase. ONE
Female with harp.	100 Vig. Female 100 sitting on a bale; Mercury descending; shipping in distance. BANK OF PITTSBURG, Pa	Figure of Justice.
20 20	20 Vig. Female sitting on a rock, bag of coin, mile stone, 23 miles to B. 20 BANK OF WESTMINSTER, Md	Female head.
2 Deer.	Compt's die. Vig. Mechanics at work. FULTON CO. BANK, Gloversville, N. Y. Bale of goods.	2 Female seated.
Artisan and sailor standing, two females sitting, spinning wheel and capstan to right, view of city in distance.	D Vig. Shield on which is a view of a city Indian, squaw, and child on left; female teaching group of children on right. BANK OF PITTSBURG, Pa.	500
50 50	50 Vig. Female with sickle in hand inclined on mile stone, marked 23 miles to B. 50 BANK OF WESTMINSTER, Md.	50
5 Female seated.	FULTON CO. BANK Gloversville, N. Y. Compt's die. Vig. Mechanics at work Bales of goods.	5 Portrait of George Washington
1000 Two blacksmiths at work.	Vig. Group of three, farmer and two artisans, half length figures BANK OF PITTSBURG, Pa.	1000 Female standing among grain, sickle in right hand 1000
2 TWO	Female Hunter shooting a deer; dog, trees and stream of water. NARRAGANSETT BANK, Vienna, Ills. Auditor's die. TWO	2 2 TWO
TEN Geo. Washington. Compt's die	Vig. Large eagle resting on liberty cap. X FULTON CO BANK, Gloversville, N. Y. Bales of goods.	10 Mechanic at work TEN
5 Spread eagle on shield 5	Train of cars. Vig. Female seated on a plough, with sickle, &c., reaping scene on her right hand; mill scene on her left. Canal boats, country scene. WASHINGTON CO. BANK, Williamsport, Md.	5 Bust of Washington. 5
3 THREE	Indian seated; plow, house, sheaves, hills, &c. 3 Title of Bank.	3 Auditor's die
ONE Compt's die. Female head.	Vig. Harvest scene; Lunch time. 1 BROOME CO. B'K. Binghampton, N. Y.	1 Female 1
TEN Justice with sword and scales, scroll with inscription under figure. TEN	10 Bust of Washington surmounted by an eagle, female on either side. 10 WASHINGTON CO. BANK, Williamsport, Md.	TEN Female and dog.
5 Indian head	Title of Bank. 5 Three females with cornucopia quadrant sickle and compass. 5	5 Auditors' die
2 Compt's die. 2	Vig. Spread eagle on branch, cars, &c. 2 BROOME CO. B'K. Binghampton, N. Y.	2 Female, sickle, &c. TWO

5 — BROOME CO. BANK, Binghampton, N. Y. — Figure 5 with Cupid on left.
Compt's die. Vig. Farmer about to sharpen his scythe, canal and cars in distance.
FIVE — Franklin.

100 — Vig. Spread eagle on branch of tree; train of cars, canal boat, &c. — 100
Male figure, cog wheel, &c. — LEICESTER BANK, Leicester, Mass. — Female with rake, fruit, &c.

Female, sheaf of wheat and plough. — 3 Compt's die. — THREE
ONTARIO BANK, Utica, N. Y.
3 — Train of cars — Female holding scales.

10 — Vig. Harvest scene, female seated with infant. — 10
Compt's die. — BROOME CO. BANK, Binghampton, N. Y.
10 — Female, artist tools, &c.

One Hundred and 100. — Vig. Shipping, buggy, waggon and merchandise. — Same as left
LEICESTER BANK, Leicester, Mass.
Portrait of Harrison. — Portrait of Columbus.

5 — 5 Vig. Canal boats and houses. 5 — V
Compt's die. — ONTARIO BANK, Utica, N. Y. — Female holding a rake.
5 — Boquet of flowers. — V

Secured &c. — 1 Vig. Female standing erect, child, ship in distance. — ONE
EXCHANGE BANK OF GENESEE, Batavia, N. Y.
ONE — Safe. — Female

Female standing erect holding a shield. — State arms. Vig. Capitol building. — 20
BANK OF CHEMUNG, Elmira, N. Y.
TWENTY — Medallion head.

5 Compt's die. — FIVE
Train of cars. — ONTARIO BANK, Utica, N. Y.
Vig. Female eagle &c.
Farming implements.

TWO — 2 Vig. Female with sickle sheaf of wheat, and cars crossing a bridge in distance. 2
Compt's die. — EXCHANGE BANK OF GENESEE, Batavia, N. Y. — Chemist seated surrounded with corn.
TWO — State Arms.

1 — ONTARIO BANK, Canandaigua, N. Y. — 1
Vig. Shepherd watching his sheep.
Medallion work. — Farming implements. — Compt's die.

10 — X Vig. Houses, train of cars, &c. X — 10
Compt's die. — ONTARIO BANK, Utica, N. Y. — Man shearing sheep.
10 — An arm holding a hammer. — 10

5 — V Vig. three females resting on figure 5, on right barrels and steamship, and on left rake plough &c, and cars in distance. V — 5
Compt's die. — EXCHANGE BANK OF GENESEE, Batavia, N. Y. — Medallion head.
FIVE — State arms. — FIVE

2 — ONTARIO BANK, Canandiagua, N. Y. — 2
Vig. Shepherd watching the sheep.
Medallion work. — Farming implements. — Compt's die.

20 — XX Vig. Houses, cars &c. XX — 20
Farmers at work. — ONTARIO BANK, Utica, N. Y. — Farmers ploughing.
20 — Female laying down holding a sheaf of wheat. — 20

10 — Vig. Two females seated on each side of shield, scales &c. on right barrels and steamship on left, agricultural implements houses and cars in distance. — 10
Compt's die. — EXCHANGE BANK OF GENESEE, Batavia, N. Y. — State arms.
TEN — State arms. — TEN

5 — ONTARIO BANK, Canandiagua, N. Y. — 5
Vig. Female and large V.
Eagle and shield. — Compt's die.

FIFTY DOLLARS — 50 Vig. Three females, one standing and the other reclining, the one on right holding a child. L — STATE OF NEW YORK
ONTARIO BANK, Utica, N. Y.

50 — Vig. Sailor and Indian on either side of a shield, shipping in distance; two females on either side of shield, surmounted by an eagle, canal boats and locks in distance. — Winged female with trumpet, another female at her feet with pole and cap; eagle and cornucopia.
Portrait of female. — HOUSATONIC BANK, Stockbridge, Mass.
Landing hay.

10 — ONTARIO BANK, Canandaigua, N. Y. — TEN
Vig. Eagle standing on shield, on right vessels and steamboat, on left cars and farmers at work. — Female holding a sheaf of wheat.
Compt's die. — Horse. — 10

ONE HUNDRED — 100 Vig. Female with mantel around her, left hand resting on a plough; two ships on the left foundering on the rocks. C — STATE OF NEW YORK
ONTARIO BANK, Utica, N. Y.

50 — Vig. Two figures a male and female, the female holding a rake in one hand and in the other a handful of grain, male figure with a scroll in hand, his feet resting on an anchor, cog wheel, &c. — Cupid in a boat.
Figure of Liberty. — LEICESTER BANK, Leicester, Mass. — 50

Two men carrying a female. — 1 Compt's die — 1
ONTARIO BANK, Utica, N. Y.
ONE — Cow. — Man with spear.

(1st. Plate.)
5 — Medallion head. Vig. Farmer leaning against a tree, female sitting along side of him; farmers reaping on right, also farm house. Medallion head. — FIVE
Cattle. — Cattle.
5 — FARMERS & DROVERS BANK Waynesburg, Pa. — FIVE

FIFTY — 50 Vig. A wild horse. 50 — FIFTY
LEICESTER BANK Leicester, Mass.
Female figure. FIFTY — Female figure. FIFTY

Farmer holding a rake. — TWO — 2
Vig. Train of cars. — Compt's die.
ONTARIO BANK, Utica, N. Y.
Female portrait. — Deer. — Cattle &c.

(2d. Plate.)
5 — Vig. Cattle; farmers reaping on right; and farmer ploughing with oxen and horse on left. — 5
Portrait of Washington. — Female.
FIVE — FARMERS & DROVERS BANK, Waynesburg, Pa. — FIVE

FIVE Female with sheaf of wheat and sickle. (3d. Plate) Vig. Farmer and boy loading hay oxen and horse before cart. FARMERS & DROVERS BANK, Waynesburg, Pa. 5 Female portrait.	Secured by pledge &c. ONE 1 Vig. Female and child; on left an anchor and vessel in distance. Die. WASHINGTON CO. BANK Greenwich, N. Y. Portrait of Washington. ONE Female seated.	10 Compt's die. X Vig. Females and males; on right, houses and load of hay. HUGUENOT BANK New Platz, N. Y. Sheaf of wheat plough &c. 10 Book torch and staff. TEN
10 Farmer and dog. 10 (Old Plate.) X on med. head Vig. Male and female with pitchfork in right hand, farmers loading hay, &c. X on med. head. FARMERS & DROVERS BANK, Waynesburg, Pa. X Farmer and dog. X	TWO Female seated with scales. TWO 2 Vig. Female seated holding sickle, on right bridge &c.; left sheaf of wheat and mill in distance. 2 WASHINGTON CO BANK Greenwich, N. Y. Man at work. Female seated.	XX Portrait of Washington. Compt's die. Vig. Female seated, goods and boats on right, cars and vessels on left. HUGUENOT BANK New Platz, N. Y. Female seated. 20 Book torch and staff. TWENTY
X Bulls head TEN (New Plate.) Vig. Man on horseback, another holding pitchfork in hand, and another tying up bundle of grain. X FARMERS & DROVERS BANK, Waynesburg, Pa. Two females, one with sickle and sheaf of wheat. TEN	Secured &c. THREE Two females, one on left holding scales. Compt's die. 3 Vig. Two Females and in centre a female portrait, on left cars in distance. WASHINGTON CO. BANK, Greenwich, N. Y. Man at work. 3	ONE Female reclining. 1 Vig. female seated on safe, Dog and child; ship in distance on right, plough on left. KINGSTON BANK Kingston, N. Y. Park. 1 Compt's die.
20 Female with pitchfork. 20 (Old Plate.) Vig. Country wagon with four horses and drove of cattle crossing a stream of water; bridge, houses mail coach, wharf, &c in background. med. head. FARMERS & DROVERS BANK. Waynesburg, Pa. 20 Female with pitchfork 20	5 Female holding scales, eagle safe and key FIVE V Three females and in centre figure 5, on right barrels, and steamship in distance, on left a plough sickle and cars in distance. V WASHINGTON CO. BANK. Greenwich, N. Y. Man at work. 5 Medallion head. FIVE	THREE 3 Vig. Three females seated on a shield, ship on right, sheaf of wheat and cars, on left Compt's die KINGSTON BANK Kingston, N. Y. 3 A park. 3 3 Steamboat.
XX Milkmaid. TWENTY New Plate. Vig. Drover on horseback, dog and flock of sheep; mill in background on left. FARMERS & DROVERS BANK, Waynesburg, Pa. 20 Female seated.	10 Female with scales, eagle, safe and key. TEN Vig. Two females, in centre a shield with scales at top, on right barrels and steamship in distance, on left houses and cars in distance. WASHINGTON CO. BANK, Greenwich, N. Y. Man at work. 10 State arms. TEN	FIVE DOLLARS 5 Vig. State arms ship on right, cars on left. 5 KINGSTON BANK Kingston, N. Y. Hands joined together. V Compt's die. V
Female erect ONE Scene at sea; lighthouse and vessels. 1 on med. head on either side. BK. OF DELAWARE Wilmington, Del. ONE DOLLAR	TWENTY Female with scales eagle safe &c. TWENTY 20 Vig. Female seated steamship on right and globe on left. 20 WASHINGTON CO. BANK Greenwich, N. Y. Man at work. XX	TEN Cupid, grind stone &c. 10 X Vig. Female; sheaf of wheat and plough, and cattle on left. X KINGSTON BANK Kingston, N. Y Steamboat. 10 Female and wheel. 10
TWO Washington TWO Shipping scene, houses, etc.; 2 on med head on each side. BK OF DELAWARE Wilmington, Del. TWO DOLLARS	Female and eagle. Compt's die. 1 Vig. White men trading with Indians. HUGUENOT BANK New Platz, N Y Shield. 1 Book staff and torch. ONE	1 Female seated. 1 Compt's die. 1 Female seated on sheaf of wheat cars on right and steam boat on left. GOSHEN BANK Goshen, N Y 1 Female erect.
Compt's die. Sailor with implements. TEN Cars; horse: house in distance. COMMERCIAL BK of Whitehall, N. Y. 10 Female seated. TEN	TWO Book staff and torch. Compt's die. 2 Vig. White men trading with Indians. HUGUENOT BANK New Platz, N. Y. Dog. 2 Two females standing erect.	2 Compt's die. TWO Vig. Farming scene; on right men loading hay. GOSHEN BANK Goshen, N. Y. Sheaf of wheat plough &c. 2 Female seated, bucket on each side.
Compt's die. Sailor with quadrant; ship in distance. Spread eagle on shield; cars and house in distance. 50 COMMERCIAL BK of Whitehall, N. Y. Female seated on bale. 50	Compt's die. Book staff and torch. FIVE Vig. Group of children white man with gun on right, and Indian on left cars on right in distance. HUGUENOT BANK New Platz, N. Y. 5 Group of females with scales shield &c, large figure 5.	FIVE Compt's die. FIVE Vig. Drove of cattle and man on horse. GOSHEN BANK Goshen, N. Y. Female. 5 5, and group of females

TEN 10 Vig. Train of cars, house and steam boat on left. 10
Compt's die. GOSHEN BANK Goshen, N. Y. Female erect shield on left.
X Ox.

V Vig. Train of cars, bridge and telegraph poles. 5
BANK OF PORT JERVIS, Port Jervis, N. Y.
Male portrait. Compt's die.

5 CHIPPEWA BANK, Pepin, Wis. 5
Two horses frightened at cars.
Compt's die. Indian

20 XX Vig. Female seated, safe, sheaf of wheat, farming implements and cars on right, steamship on left 20
Eagle, shield &c. GOSHEN BANK Goshen, N. Y. 2 Female seated. 0
Compt's die Man shearing a sheep.

X Vig. Female reclining on bale of goods, barrels and ships, in distance on right steamship on left. TEN
BANK OF PORT JERVIS, Port Jervis, N. Y
Compt's die. Male portrait.

ONE 1 Vig. Female in the air and figure 1. 1 1
Compt's die. UNADILLA BANK, Unadilla, N. Y. Female seated, resting on shield
ONE Secured, &c. 1

ONE Vig. Female resting on a safe, on right females, cattle &c, on left locomotive. 1
Compt's die. OSWEGATCHIE B'K Ogdensburgh, N. Y.
1 Blacksmith. Female Portrait.

Female with scales, portrait of Washington and anchor, ship masts seen in distance.
5 Vig. Two females one with helmet on her head, and the other a [illegible] female with wand, ship on right. V
FARMERS & MECHANICS BANK OF FREDERICK CO., Md.
FIVE

TWO 2 Vig. Two females seated, on right plough and sheaf of wheat, on left ships in distance. 2 2
Compt's die. UNADILLA BANK, Unadilla, N. Y. Man with an axe in right hand; cows &c. in distance.
TWO Secured, &c.

Vig. Water scene, female and children. Compt's die. 2
2 OSWEGATCHIE B'K Ogdensburgh, N. Y. Female Portrait.

TEN 10 Vig. Female with sickle cornucopia, &c. clouds back of female. 10
Portrait of Washington. Male portrait.
TEN FARMERS AND MECHANICS BANK OF FREDERICK CO. Md.

5 5 Vig. Female seated, in right hand a sickle, sheafs of wheat and house on right, on left cars. 5 5
Compt's die. Female portrait, in left hand a sickle.
5 UNADILLA BANK, Unadilla, N. Y. V

FIVE Vig. Female seated on right, bales of goods, steamship and ship, and on left vessels &c. in distance. 5
Compt's die. OSWEGATCHIE B'K Ogdensburgh, N. Y.
V Male Portrait.

20 Vig. Drover and cattle, drover on horseback. 20
Male portrait. Male portrait.
FARMERS AND MECHANICS BANK OF FREDERICK CO., Md

1 1 Vig. Male and female erect, female has a wreath in left hand, on left a sheaf of wheat, on right an anvil. 1
Female erect with staff, shield and eagle on left.
Compt's die. FARMERS' BANK, Troy, N. Y.
1 Female reclining with sheaf of wheat. ONE

TEN 10 Vig. Train of cars leaving depot; people &c. 10
Compt's die. OSWEGATCHIE B'K Ogdensburgh, N. Y. Male portrait.
10 TEN

50 Vig. Female, child, and another child stirring fire, yoke of oxen, plough, anvil, rake, &c. 50
Portrait of Lafayette. Portrait of Washington.
FARMERS & MECHANICS BANK OF FREDERICK CO., Md

2 2 Vig. Two females, shield and figure 2, one on left holds scales, one on right a sickle, on right a sheaf of wheat, on left a ship in distance. 2
Female erect with staff, shield and eagle on left
Compt's die. FARMERS' BANK, Troy, N. Y
2 2 2

XX Vig. Large eagle on which a female is reclining with an American flag around her. 20
Compt's die. OSWEGATCHIE B'K Ogdensburgh, N. Y.
20 Men loading hay. Male portrait.

100 Vig. Female seated on bales, barrels, sheaf of grain, cornucopia, rake, &c. two houses and a man in the distance on left. 100
Portrait of Washington. Portrait of Jefferson.
FARMERS & MECHANICS BANK OF FREDERICK CO., Md.

3 3 Man erect with mantel around him, a plough on right, shield, cap and spear on left. 3
Female erect with staff, shield and eagle on left.
Compt's die. FARMERS' BANK, Troy, N. Y.
3 Female reclining. 3

ONE Vig. Canal and boats hills on either side 1
BANK OF PORT JERVIS. Compt's die.

ONE on fig. 1 Two females with cornucopia; anvil between them; factory in distance 1
ONE WAKEFIELD BK., Wakefield, R. I.

5 FIVE Vig. Man FIVE erect and oxen; on left in distance. 5
Compt's die. FARMERS' BANK, Large vase.

ONE Compt's die. ONE 1 Vig. Indians hunting buffaloes. 1 WHITE'S BANK OF BUFFALO, N. Y. Secured, &c. 1 Female 1	1 Compt's die 1 1 Vig. Farmers at work in field; bee hive, plough, rake &c. 1 HUDSON RIVER B'K, Hudson, N. Y. Steamboat. ONE	1 Compt's die. 1 1 Vig. Indian seated in canoe going through rapids. 1 MOHAWK BANK, Schenectady, N. Y Locomotive and cars. 1 Female seated. 1
TWO Compt's die TWO 2 Vig. Female reclining, shield &c in centre, on right train of cars, on left steamboat. 2 WHITE'S BANK OF BUFFALO, N. Y. Secured, &c. 2	2 Compt's die. 2 2 Vig. Two children seated, in centre sheaf of wheat, on right ships in distance, on left steamboat. 2 HUDSON RIVER B'K, Hudson N. Y. Steamboat. TWO	2 Compt's die. 2 MOHAWK BANK. Schenectady, N. Y. 2 Vig. Indian seated in canoe going through rapids. 2 TWO TWO
5 Compt's die. 5 5 Vig. Steamboat and vessels. 5 WHITE'S BANK OF BUFFALO, N. Y. Secured, &c. FIVE 5 female, etc. FIVE	3 Compt's die 3 Two children seated, sheaf of wheat in centre, on right a ship, on left a steamboat. 3 HUDSON RIVER B'K, Hudson, N. Y. Steamboat. THREE	3 Compt's die. MOHAWK BANK, Schenectady, N. Y. 3 Vig. Indian seated in canoe going through rapids, 3 Secured, &c. THREE Female, sheaf of wheat, sickle &c. 3
TEN Male and female figures. Compt's die. Vig. Female holding a vase, steamship on right, sheaf, canal, cars and mills on left WHITE'S BANK OF BUFFALO, N. Y. Safe. 10 Sailor and Indian, in centre a shield. X	5 Compt's die. 5 5 Male and female reclining, monument &c. 5 HUDSON RIVER B'K, Hudson, N. Y. Portrait of Washington. FIVE	5 Female portrait. MOHAWK BANK, Schenectady, N. Y. 5 Indian seated in canoe going through rapids. 5 Canal lock. FIVE Compt's die. 5
Medallion head and ONE Compt's die. Vig. Three blacksmiths at work. WATERTOWN B'K, AND LOAN CO. Watertown, N. Y. Female in water. 1 Medallion head. ONE	10 Compt's die. 10 10 Vig. Large ship under sail, small boat and whale on left in distance, vessels in distance on right. 10 HUDSON RIVER B'K, Hudson, N. Y Male portrait. TEN	10 Compt's die. 10 Title of Bank Vig. Indian seated in canoe going through rapids. X 10 Male portrait, 10
TWO Compt's die Vessels and cars Three females reclining, two on left and one on right, eagle and shield in centre, ships on left in distance, bridge and cars on right. WATERTOWN B'K AND LOAN CO., Watertown, N. Y. Female in water. 2 Train of cars. TWO	Female and figure 1. Compt's die. Mechanics at work in an iron mill; large wheel in distance. 1 MANUFACTURERS' BANK, Troy, N. Y. Secured, &c. ONE Female seated. ONE	1 Compt's die ONE Vig. Farmers at work; cars in distance. MARKET BANK, Troy, N. Y. 1 Female, sheaf of wheat and sickle.
FIVE Compt's die. Male portrait. Vig. Train of cars; in the background large rocks and a man on right, houses and hills in distance. WATERTOWN B'K AND LOAN CO., Watertown, N. Y. Female in water. 5 Female portrait, 5	TWO Compt's die. 2 Vig. Train of cars; steamboat on right, trees and rocks on left. MANUFACTURERS' BANK, Troy, N. Y Secured, &c. TWO Boiler makers seated on boiler. TWO	Compt's die. 2 Vig. Two farmers and man on horse, sheaf of wheat on right, and trees on left. MARKET BANK, Troy, N. Y. 2 Female portrait.
TEN Compt's die. Portrait of Washington, Vig Signing of the Declaration of Independence. WATERTOWN B'K AND LOAN CO., Watertown, N. Y. Eagle. 10 Male portrait. TEN	Compt's die Cupid and dolphin. THREE Vig. Sailor seated holding a quadrant; female with sheaf of wheat and sickle, on right sheaf of wheat and men at work in distance, on left steamship in distance. MANUFACTURERS' BANK, Troy, N. Y. Secured, &c. THREE Female portrait. 3	Compt's die. 5 Vig. Man on horse, cattle and sheep, houses and waggons on right. MARKET BANK, Troy, N. Y. 5 Group of children with shield and spear.
Compt's die. 25 Vig. Mechanic seated hammer in hand, anvil; factories and cars in distance. WATERTOWN B'K AND LOAN CO., Watertown, N. Y. Deer 25 Two females, one blind folded holding balances, the other seated playing on harp	FIVE Male portrait. Compt's die. Vig. Large iron mill and houses, large house in distance on a hill, on left waggon, on right houses in distance. MANUFACTURERS' BANK, Troy, N. Y. Secured, &c. Blacksmith at work. FIVE	X Bull's head. X MARKET BANK, Troy, N. Y. Three females, two seated and one in centre erect, one on right is drawing, on left playing a harp; house in background. 10 Compt's die. X

Female with sheaf. | 1 Franklin. 1 | Farmer with basket of corn.
PUTNAM VALLEY BANK, Putnam Valley, N. Y.
Compt's die. | Secured &c. | ONE

100 | Vig. Female with staff and shield; ship in distance on left. | C | ONE HUNDRED
Female with key.
YATES CO. BANK. Pen Yan. N. Y.
100 | Antelope.

100 | 100 on medallion head. | Vig. Female with liberty pole and cap, eagle, and shield; vessels in distance on either side. | 100 on medallion head. | 100
Female with sickle on sheaf of wheat | Male with tablet.
HAGERSTOWN BK, Hagerstown. Md.
100 | 100

Man, two horses and a plough. | 2 on large 2. | TWO
Title of Bank.
Female representing Agriculture.
Compt's die. | 2 | Secured, etc. | TWO

TWENTY on med. head. | FORT STANWIX BK, Rome, N. Y. | 20 on med. head.
Indian family contemplating the progress of civilization. | Two females. | Compt's die.

Female standing resting on shield. | 1 | Vig. Female seated, shield &c. figure 1, and falls on left. | 1
Eagle and shield
UNION BANK OF ROCHESTER, N. Y.
Compt's die. | ONE

Female seated; factory in distance. | 5 | Mechanic seated on a boiler; cars in distance | 5 | FIVE
Large 5, two indians, water fall, cars and bridge.
Title of Bank.
Compt's die. | Secured, etc. | FIVE

L on med. head. | FORT STANWIX BK, Rome, N. Y. | 50 on med. head.
Scene in the battle of New Orleans.
Compt's die. | Male portrait.

2 | Compt's die. | Vig. Seven females, each side a female, and the one on right holding scales, and one on left a spear. | 2
Male and female figure and steamship | Two females standing erect.
UNION BANK OF ROCHESTER

[illegible] | 1 | Vig. [illegible] on right in distance. | 1 | ONE
Compt's die. | Medallion head [illegible]
Medallion head | YATES CO. BANK Pen Yan. N Y | ONE

1 | ONE ONE ONE ONE ONE | 1
Female, right arm resting on a fence; men and a mill in distance.
ONE | BANK OF AUBURN, Auburn, N. Y. | Female and fig. 1, with one on it.
Compt's die. | ONE ONE ONE ONE ONE | 1

5 | Compt's die. | Vig. figure 5, five females on [illegible] scales, on [illegible] large [illegible] locomotive [illegible] | 5
Group of males and females, and large V. | Portrait of Washington.
UNION BANK OF ROCHESTER, N Y. | FIVE

2 | Medallion head and figure 2. | Vig. Portrait of Washington. [illegible] | 2
Compt's die.
2 | YATES CO BANK Pen Yan, N Y | Female; on left a train [illegible]

Compt's die. | THREE THREE | 3
Shield, eagle at top; on right two females with scales, cars in distance; on left, Liberty, ship in distance.
Med head | Female with flowers.
3 | BANK OF AUBURN, Auburn, N. Y. | 3
The word Three five times.

10 | Vig. Two females liberty cap and eagle in centre on right cars and steamship in distance, on left a man ploughing, ship and mill in distance. | 10
Compt's die. | Male portrait.
10 | UNION BANK OF ROCHESTER N. Y. | TEN
Wheels and bale of goods

Medallion head. | 3 | Vig. Milk maid, churn, cabin, horse | 3 | 3
Compt's die. | Portrait of Washington.
Medallion head. | YATES CO. BANK, Pen Yan, N. Y | 3

5 | 5 Vig. Two females in the clouds one with rake, sickle, spade and pitchfork. 5 | 5
5 on medallion head. | 5 on medallion head.
HAGERSTOWN B'K, Hagerstown. Md.
5 | 5

20 | Vig. Female with scales in centre, fort vessels and steamboat, in distance, on right cupid. | 20
Compt's die. | UNION BANK OF ROCHESTER. N. Y.
XX | Sheaf of wheat rake plough and shovel. | Female eagle and money.

5 | Vig. A man ploughing. | FIVE
YATES CO BANK Pen Yan N Y. | Compt's die.
Male portrait. | Farming implements. | 5

X | 10 on medallion head. | Vig. Two boys carrying a basket of flowers on a pole across their shoulders, another boy in the act of twining flowers around a pole another with sickle in left hand and sheaf of wheat on his head | 10 on medallion head. | Female with sickle and sheaf of wheat.
Another medallion head.
10 | TITLE OF BANK. | X

FIFTY | Vig. Female reclining in ge eagle and glow, on left steamships and ship in distance. | 50
Female standing erect with looking glass in right hand.
UNION BANK OF ROCHESTER. N. Y.
Shield. | Compt's die.

10 | Vig. Large eagle standing on shield; on left a ship in distance | TEN
YATES CO. BANK Pen Yan, N. Y. | Compt's die.
Female, sheaf of wheat &c. | X

20 | Medallion head. | Vig. Two females, ships in distance on right. | Medallion head. | 20
Female with babe in her arms. | Man and cattle.
20 | HAGERSTOWN B'K. Hagerstown. Md. | 20

100 | UNION BANK OF ROCHESTER, N. Y. | 100
Vig. Two females seated, eagle and shield in centre; cars and steamboat in distance.
Female resting on anchor. | Shield. | Compt's die.

50 | Vig. Female seated on plough, cornucopia and wing'd wand sail vessels &c.; farming scene in distance. | 50 | FIFTY
Full length male figure.
YATES CO BANK. Pen Yan, N. Y.
Deer

50 | Medallion head. | Vig. Boy in boat, with cupid soaring over him; another boy in the act of [illegible] | Medallion head. | 50
Portrait of Washington. | Female with rake and sheaf of wheat.
50 | HAGERSTOWN B'K. Hagerstown. Md. | 50

3 | Vig. Saw mill and men at work. | 3
Compt's die. | UNION BANK OF MONTICELLO, N. Y. | Female with sheaf of wheat.
Secured, &c.

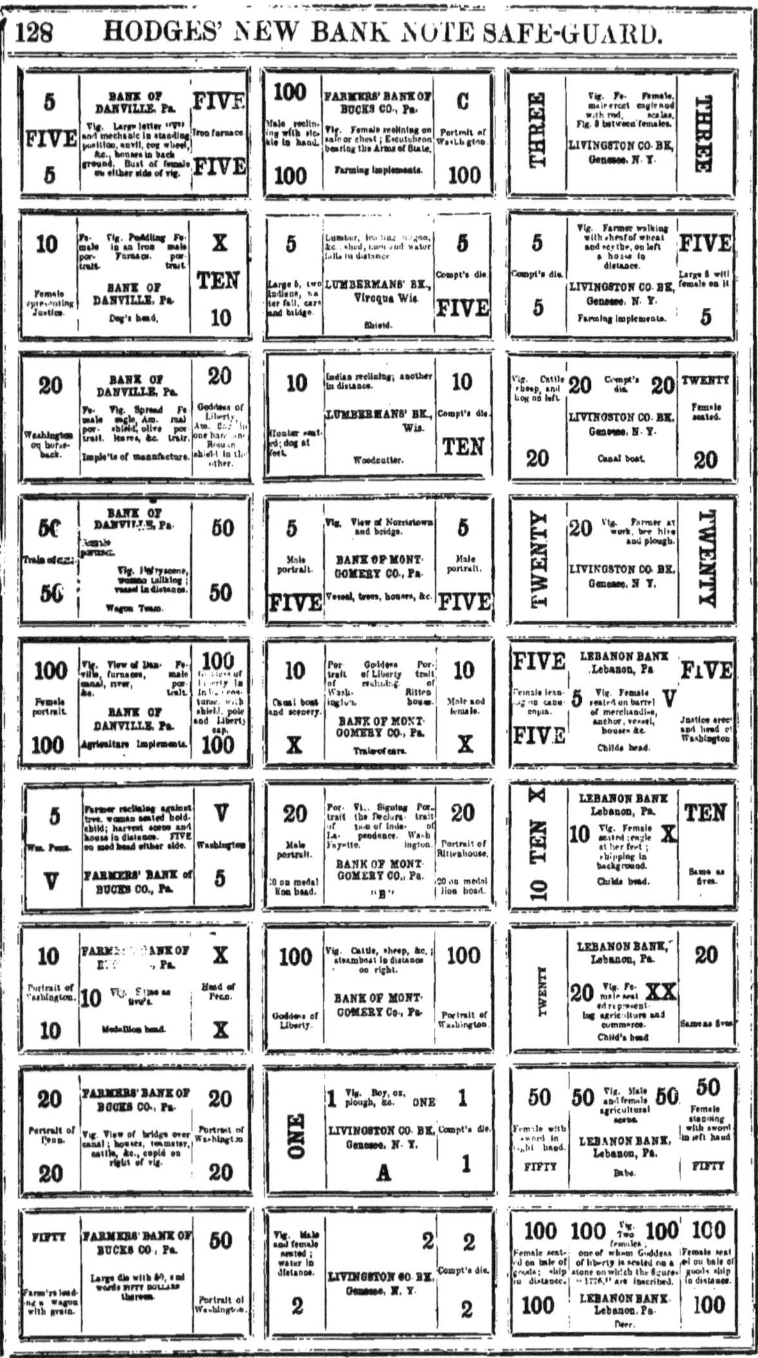

5 / FIVE / 5 — BANK OF DANVILLE, Pa. Vig. Large letter "Five" and mechanic in standing position, anvil, cog wheel, &c., houses in back ground. Bust of female on either side of vig. — FIVE / Iron furnace / FIVE	100 / Male reclining with sickle in hand. / 100 — FARMERS' BANK OF BUCKS CO., Pa. Vig. Female reclining on safe or chest; Escutcheon bearing the Arms of State. Farming implements. — C / Portrait of Washington. / 100	THREE — Vig. Fe- Female, male erect eagle and with rod, scales, Fig. 3 between females. LIVINGSTON CO. BK, Genesee, N. Y. — THREE
10 / Female representing Justice. — Fe- Vig. Puddling Fe- male in an iron male por- Furnace. por- trait. trait. BANK OF DANVILLE, Pa. Dog's head. — X / TEN / 10	5 / Large 5, two Indians, water fall, cars and bridge. — Lumber, loading wagon, &c., shed, men and water falls in distance. LUMBERMANS' BK., Viroqua Wis. Shield. — 5 / Compt's die. / FIVE	5 / Compt's die. / 5 — Vig. Farmer walking with sheaf of wheat and scythe, on left a house in distance. LIVINGSTON CO. BK, Genesee, N. Y. Farming implements. — FIVE / Large 5 with female on it / 5
20 / Washington on horse-back. — BANK OF DANVILLE, Pa. Fe- Vig. Spread Fe- male eagle, Am. male por- shield, olive por- trait. leaves, &c. trait. Imple'ts of manufacture. — 20 / Goddess of Liberty, Am. flag in one hand, on Roman shield in the other.	10 / Hunter seated; dog at feet. — Indian reclining; another in distance. LUMBERMANS' BK., Wis. Woodcutter. — 10 / Compt's die. / TEN	Vig. Cattle sheep, and hog on left. / 20 — 20 Compt's die. 20 LIVINGSTON CO. BK, Genesee, N. Y. Canal boat. — TWENTY / Female seated. / 20
50 / Train of cars. / 50 — BANK OF DANVILLE, Pa. Female portrait. Vig. Hayscene, woman talking; vessel in distance. Wagon Team. — 50 / 50	5 / Male portrait. / FIVE — Vig. View of Norristown and bridge. BANK OF MONTGOMERY CO., Pa. Vessel, trees, houses, &c. — 5 / Male portrait. / FIVE	TWENTY — 20 Vig. Farmer at work, bee hive and plough. LIVINGSTON CO. BK, Genesee, N. Y. — TWENTY
100 / Female portrait. / 100 — Vig. View of Danville, furnaces, canal, river, &c. Female portrait. BANK OF DANVILLE, Pa. Agriculture Implements. — 100 / Goddess of Liberty in Indian costume, with shield, pole and Liberty cap. / 100	10 / Canal boat and scenery. / X — Portrait of Washington. Goddess of Liberty reclining. Portrait of Rittenhouse. BANK OF MONTGOMERY CO., Pa. Train of cars. — 10 / Male and female. / X	FIVE / Female leaning on cornucopia. / FIVE — LEBANON BANK Lebanon, Pa 5 Vig. Female seated on barrel of merchandise, anchor, vessel, houses &c. V Childs head. — FIVE / Justice erect and head of Washington
5 / Wm. Penn. / V — Farmer reclining against tree, woman seated holding child; harvest scene and house in distance. FIVE on seed head either side. FARMERS' BANK of BUCKS CO., Pa. — V / Washington / 5	20 / Male portrait. / 20 on medal lion head. — Portrait of Lafayette. Vig. Signing the Declaration of Independence. Portrait Washington. BANK OF MONTGOMERY CO., Pa. "B" — 20 / Portrait of Rittenhouse. / 20 on medal lion head.	X TEN 10 — LEBANON BANK Lebanon, Pa. 10 Vig. Female seated; eagle at her feet; shipping in background. X Childs head. — TEN / Same as five.
10 / Portrait of Washington. / 10 — FARMERS' BANK OF BUCKS CO., Pa. 10 Vig. Same as five's. Medallion head. — X / Head of Penn. / X	100 / Goddess of Liberty. — Vig. Cattle, sheep, &c.; steamboat in distance on right. BANK OF MONTGOMERY Co., Pa. — 100 / Portrait of Washington.	TWENTY — LEBANON BANK, Lebanon, Pa. 20 Vig. Female seated representing agriculture and commerce. XX Child's head — 20 / Same as fives
20 / Portrait of Penn. / 20 — FARMERS' BANK OF BUCKS CO., Pa. Vig. View of bridge over canal; houses, teamster, cattle, &c., cupid on right of vig. — 20 / Portrait of Washington / 20	ONE — 1 Vig. Boy, ox, plough, &c. ONE LIVINGSTON CO. BK, Genesee, N. Y. A — 1 / Compt's die. / 1	50 / Female with sword in right hand. / FIFTY — 50 Vig. Male and female agricultural scene. 50 LEBANON BANK, Lebanon, Pa. Babe. — 50 / Female standing with sword in left hand / FIFTY
FIFTY / Farmer's leading a wagon with grain. — FARMERS' BANK OF BUCKS CO., Pa. Large die with 50, and words FIFTY DOLLARS thereon. — 50 / Portrait of Washington.	Vig. Male and female seated; water in distance. / 2 — 2 LIVINGSTON CO. BK, Genesee, N. Y. — 2 / Compt's die. / 2	100 / Female seated on bale of goods; ship in distance. / 100 — 100 100 Vig. Two females, one of whom Goddess of liberty is seated on a stone on which the figures "1776," are inscribed. 100 LEBANON BANK. Lebanon, Pa. Deer. — 100 / Female seated on bale of goods, ship in distance. / 100

Portrait of Washington. 5 Male portrait.	5 Vig. Two female reclining, farming implements, &c. 5 BANK OF CHAMBERSBURG, Pa.	Male portrait. 5 Male portrait.

100 Allegorical figure representing manufactures; water in distance. 100	Vig. Landscape, load of hay drawn by oxen, man on horseback, mill, viaduct, train of cars &c in distance. LANCASTER CO., BANK. Pa. Dogs head.	100 Farmer ploughing.

20 Compt's die. 20	Vig. Man on horseback; cattle, &c. FARMERS' BANK, Troy, N. Y. Farmers at work.	Female portrait. 20 Cars and man with wheelbarrow 20

X Medallion head and word "TEN" 10	Med. head TEN on it. Vig. Instructor and pupil; house in distance on right. Med head TEN on it. BANK OF CHAMBERSBURG, Pa.	Female representing Agriculture X

1 Compt's die. 1	1 Vig. Two females one seated and other erect holding a sheaf of wheat figure 1, in centre, on right plough rake &c. 1 TROY CITY BANK Troy, N. Y. Steamboat.	1 Male portrait. ONE

L Compt's die. 50	Vig. Man on horseback; cattle, sheep, &c. FARMERS' BANK, Troy N. Y. Dog, safe and key.	FIFTY Female standing holding scales.

20 Bust of Penn XX	Med. head. Vig. Spread eagle. Med. head. BANK OF CHAMBERSBURG, Pa.	XX Bust of Washington 20

2 Compt's die. 2	TROY CITY BANK Troy, N. Y. 2 Vig. Female standing erect and Indian seated holding a gun in left hand Vessel.	TWO 2

1 Compt's die. 1	SACKETTS HARBOR BANK Buffalo, N. Y. 1 Vig. Sea dragon, and water scene. 1	1 Male portrait ONE

50 Med. head. 50	Vig. Female reclining on safe; commerce and agriculture; two sheep on right. BANK OF CHAMBERSBURG, Pa.	50 Male portrait FIFTY

3 Compt's die. 3	3 Vig. Large steamboat under way. 3 TROY CITY BANK Troy, N. Y. Female reclining.	THREE Female standing erect with scales in right hand. 3

2 Compt's die. 2	SACKETTS HARBOR BANK Buffalo, N. Y. 2 Vig. Man on horse, dragon. 2	2 Ship; and city in distance.

100 Male portrait 100	Vig. Wild horses. BANK OF CHAMBERSBURG, Pa.	Med. head and figures "100" on it 100

5 Compt's die. 5	V Vig. Female seated holding scales in left hand, on right ships barrels and male at work. V TROY CITY BANK Troy, N. Y. Steamboat.	5 Female erect with grain in left hand V

3 Compt's die. 3	3 Man reclining on right; water on left; male figures. 3 Title of Bank. Eagle.	THREE Female seated, and man in the left. THREE

FIVE Reaping scene. FIVE	5 Vig. Farm scene, harvesters at lunch LANCASTER CO. BANK, Pa. Dogs head.	5 V 5

5 Male portrait.	Vig. Large eagle resting on tree; falls in background. TROY CITY BANK Troy, N. Y. Horse	Compt's die. 5

5 Compt's die.	5 Water and vessels; steamboat and house in distance. 5 Title of Bank. 5	5 General and horse.

Female and churn. 10	Vig. Female representing a flax spinner. X LANCASTER CO., BANK, Pa. Dogs head.	Agricultural scene. TEN

X Male portrait. 10	X Vig. Female seated with key in left hand X TROY CITY BANK Troy, N. Y. Steamboat.	TEN Two females one on right holding a sheaf of wheat on left a rake. 10

10 Compt's die.	SACKETTS HARBOR BANK Buffalo, N. Y. TEN TEN Vig. A General erect and his horse. X	10 Cattle &c.

XX Farmer gathering corn. 20	Med head. 20 Med head. LANCASTER CO. BK. Lancaster, Pa. Eagle.	Head of female surmounted by an eagle. XX Bust of a mechanic.

10 Male portrait.	Vig. Large eagle and shield on right a vessel under sail, on left a vessel. TROY CITY BANK. Troy, N. Y. Farm implements.	Compt's die. TEN X

FIVE	(Old Plate.) FIVE Two female figures and eagle; train of cars and ship in background. FIVE SOUTHBRIDGE B'K, Southbridge. Mass.	5 Portrait. FIVE

50 Medallion head. 50	Vig. Farmers cradling grain; houses in back ground. L LANCASTER CO. BK. Lancaster, Pa. Dogs head.	50 surrounded by the words fifty dollars. Farmer sowing grain, another harrowing.

TWENTY Female with trumpet and staff. 20	Vig. Two females and two children, supporting the figures 20. TROY CITY BANK. Troy, N. Y. Eagle.	20 Female. Compt's die

10 Portrait. 10	(Old Plate.) X Spread eagle. X SOUTHBRIDGE B'K, Southbridge. Mass.	10 Female.

1 Compt's die. Vig. A female looking over a precipice; steamboat, cars and canal in distance on right. Female portrait. SECURITY BANK, Huntsville, N. Y. 1 ONE ONE

3 Compt's die. Vig. Portrait of Washington, and female on either side; sheaf of wheat on left. SECURITY BANK, Huntsville, N. Y. Female portrait and large 3.

5 Compt's die. Vig. Three females, two of which is on the right side, one on left, shield and eagle in center. SECURITY BANK, Huntsville, N. Y. Large 5 with FIVE at the top.

1 Portrait. ONE. Train of cars. NORTHBOROUGH BANK Northborough, Mass. 1 Female seated on plough with sickle &c.

2 Portrait. Female reclining, train of cars factories, and shipping, milk maids and cows in background. NORTHBOROUGH BANK Northborough, Mass. Man plowing. 2 Interior of boat makers shop.

5 Farmer with scythe. Portrait, a winged female with trumpet at the left of portrait and cupid at the right. NORTHBOROUGH BANK Northborough, Mass. Implements. 5 Group of females, large figure 5.

10 Portrait. A female figure and nine cherubs. NORTHBOROUGH BANK. Northborough, Mass. X Female globe and shield.

XX Portrait of Washington. Female reclining also eagle and globe, ships in distance. NORTHBOROUGH BANE Northborough, Mass. Imp. and products. 20 Cattle.

1 Compt's die. Female portrait. Female with spear; bales on left; quadrant, urn, pallet, etc., on right. TOMPKINS CO. BK Ithaca, N. Y. ONE Female 1 ONE

2 Compt's die 2 Vig. Female reclining liberty cap and safe. TOMPKINS CO., B'K Ithica, N. Y. TWO Large figure 2 and female standing. TWO

Female sitting on shield 5 Vig. Large figure 5, with five at top, female at each side. TOMPKINS CO., B'K Ithica, N. Y. 5 Compt's die

10 Female in ... with vase ... left hand ships in distance. TEN Female portrait X Female portrait TOMPKINS, CO., B'K Ithica, N. Y. Bee Hive. 10 Compt's die

20 Medallion head. 20 20 on med head. Vig. Female, shield and sheaf of wheat; ship in distance. 20 on med head. TOMPKINS CO. BK. Ithica, N. Y. B 20 Medallion head. 20

100 Medallion head and figures, 100. C Medallion head and fig 100. Vig. Eagle standing on a log on the left a steamboat. Medallion head and fig. 100. TOMPKINS CO. B'K Ithica, N. Y. Letter A. 100 Medallion head and figure, 100. C

1 Compt's die. 1 Vig. Female seated with bucket and dog at her feet, cattle on either side. 1 MONTGOMERY CO BANK Johnstown, N. Y. Farming implements. Large house. 1 Church.

3 Compt's die. Vig. Farmers washing sheep. 3 MONTGOMERY CO BANK Johnstown, N. Y. 3 sheafs of wheat and rake. 3 Large house.

5 Compt's die. Vig. Farmers ploughing, large V with five running across. MONTGOMERY CO. BANK Johnstown, N. Y. 5 Large house. 5 5 Church.

10 Compt's die. Vig. Farmers at work. 10 MONTGOMERY CO BANK Johnstown, N. Y. X House X Church.

50 Female seated with eagle. 50 MONTGOMERY CO. BANK. Johnstown, N. Y. L Vig. Female erect and large eagle. L 50 Female, shield and anchor. 50

100 ... sculptor on his knees 100 C Vig. Female and two males; canal, locks, cars and houses in distance. C MONTGOMERY CO. BANK, Johnstown, N. Y. Female erect and large eagle. 100

1 Compt's die. 1 NEW YORK STATE BANK Albany, N. Y. 1 Vig. State arms. 1 Male portrait. ONE

2 Compt's die 2 2 NEW YORK STATE BANK. Albany, N. Y. Vig. Two females ... &c. female on left holding scales, on right ship in distance. Male portrait. 2 2

3 Compt's die. 3 3 Vig. State arms 3 NEW YORK STATE BANK Albany, N. Y. Male portrait THREE

Die Work Compt's die Die work 5 Vig. State arms 5 NEW YORK STATE BANK Albany, N. Y. Secured &c. Die Work 5 Die Work

Med. work Compt's die. Med. work 10 Vig. State arms. 10 NEW YORK STATE BANK Albany, N. Y. Secured, &c. Medallion work.

50 State Arms 50 50 Vig. Two Females with scales &c. on right a ship in distance. 50 N. Y. STATE BANK Albany, N. Y. Secured, etc FIFTY

50 Female and anchor; steamboat in distance. 50 FIFTY DOLLARS 50 SOUTHBRIDGE B'K, Southbridge, Mass. FIFTY

5 head of female. CENTRAL BK OF FREDERIC, Md. Vig. Female seated with pail, two cows, farm house and trees in the background. 5 head of Webster.	Compt's die. Load of hay &c. ONE Vig. Female resting on sheaf of wheat, and on left a dancing scene. fig. 1 on left. SYRACUSE CITY B'K Syracuse, N. Y. Dogs head. ONE Female standing erect. and fig. 1.	5 Justice reclining. Vig. View of a public building, miniature view of female on right of vig. WEST BRANCH BK. Williamsport. Pa. Dog and safe. 5 Sailor and shipping in background.
10 10 CENTRAL BK OF FREDERIC, Md. Vig. Female with sheaf of wheat in left hand, sickle in right; a cow and grain field in background. Medallions of Clay and Chief Justice Marshall on either side of vig. 10 10	Compt's die. Indian standing erect. 2 Vig. Indians and white men holding a council. SYRACUSE CITY B'K Syracuse, N. Y. Deer. 2 Indian female and pappoose. TWO	10 Medallion head. 10 Vig. Spread eagle poised on trunk of tree; locomotive and cars in background 10 WEST BRANCH BK. Williamsport, Pa. Arms of Pa. Portrait of Washington TEN Portrait of Harrison.
20 Medallion portrait. Vig. Three nymphs swimming, supporting a winged cupid. CENTRAL BANK OF FREDERIC, Md. 20 Milkmaid, child, two cows.	Female seated on rock. Compt's die. 5 Vig. Water scene water gods &c. SYRACUSE CITY B'K Syracuse, N. Y. Train of cars. 5 Female standing erect.	XX Miniature view of farm girl drawing pail of water from well. Vig. Iron furnace, locomotive and cars, forest scenery in back ground; locomotive and cars on left of vig in fore ground. WEST BRANCH BK. Williamsport, Pa. Indian padling canoe. 20 Portrait of Lafayette. 20
50 Medallion portrait of Pierce. CENTRAL BANK OF FREDERICK, Md. Vig. Cattle, stream of water; three sheep in background. 50 Medallion portrait of Fillmore.	Compt's die. Indian with bow and spear in right hand. TEN Vig. Deer and water scene. SYRACUSE CITY B'K Syracuse, N. Y. A Buffalo. 10 Female standing holding an ear of corn X	5 Male portrait. FIVE Vig. Public buildings, stage coach, teamsters, shrubberry, &c. YORK BANK. York, Pa. 5 Male portrait. FIVE
Am shield surmounted by eagle. C Vig. Medallion portrait of Washington. CENTRAL BANK OF FREDERICK, Md. 100	V Train of cars, house on right and telegraph poles and man on right Vig. Large Eagle standing on globe with shield and arrows, and the flags of different states on either side. WARREN Co. BANK Warren, Pa. 5 Male Portrait.	10 Male portrait. TEN Vig. Daguerreotype view of York. YORK BANK. York, Pa. 10 TEN Male portrait.
1 Compt's die. 1 1 Vig. Indian drawing his bow. 1 SCHENECTADY B'K Schenectady, N. Y. ONE Houses &c. ONE	X Male portrait WARREN Co. BANK Warren. Pa. Vig. Woodsmen at work, three in centre rolling a log, two on right one chopping, yoke of oxen on left and hut in background. Dog laying down. 10 TEN	1 Comps die. Female portrait, Vig. Female and figure 1. BK OF YONKERS, Yonkers. N. Y. Secured, &c. 1 Bee hive.
Compt's die. 2 2 Vig. train of cars. 2 SCHENECTADY B'K Schenectady, N. Y. Canal locks. Indian drawing his bow 2	Male portrait. Compt's die. WEEDSPORT BANK, Weedsport, N. Y. 1 Vig. Five boys sporting in wheat. 1 ONE Large build'g One with figure 1 across.	2 Female portrait. Vig. Three females and a child in water, the females are holding up the child. BK OF YONKERS, Yonkers, N Y. Secured, &c. 2 Compt's die.
5 Compt's die. 5 Vig. Indian drawing his bow. 5 SCHENECTADY B'K Schenectady, N. Y. FIVE Indian drawing his bow	TWO Female erect with right hand resting on Compt's die. WEEDSPORT BANK, Weedsport, N. Y. Male portrait with female on either side; buildings on right in distance. Canal locks. 2 Portrait of Washington.	Compt's die. Female portrait. BK OF YONKERS, Yonkers, N Y. 5 Vig. A view of Yonkers; train of cars, sloops, etc. Secured, etc. 5 5
X Compt's die. 10 Vig. Indian drawing his bow. X SCHENECTADY B'K Schenectady. N. Y. Canal locks. Houses &c. 10 Train of cars.	FIVE 5 Compt's die Vig. Frame surmounted by an eagle, on either side is a female. WEEDSPORT BANK, Weedsport, N Y. Canal boat. 5 Male portrait	10 Compt's die. TEN Vig. View of Yonkers, train of cars, sloops &c. BK OF YONKERS Yonkers, N. Y. Secured, &c. 10 Female Portrait.

Compt's die. BK OF YONKERS Yonkers, N. Y. 20
Vig. Cattle, three of which are standing up and one laying down three sheep on left.
20 Secured, &c. Childs Portrait.

5 Vig. Group of three. Farmer and two artisans; half length figures. FIVE
Canal boat passing under a bridge. MERCHANTS AND MANUFACTURERS BANK, Pittsburgh, Pa. Medallion head.
FIVE Blacksmith's arm, hammer and anvil. FIVE

THREE CATSKILL BANK, Catskill, N. Y. THREE
Sheaf of grain. 3 Vig. Large ship, female seated in representation of commerce. 3 Figure of Liberty erect supporting vase of flowers.
THREE Ferry boat.

1 1 Vig. Three females seated, sheaf of wheat, and quadrant on right, trees in distance on left, ship in distance. 1 ONE
Compt's die. Male portrait.
1 COMMERCIAL BANK Albany, N. Y. 1 Secured, &c. 1 ONE

10 MERCHANTS AND MANUFACTURERS BANK, Pittsburg, Pa. 10
Blacksmith with hammer in right hand resting on anvil. Vig. Female figure, left hand resting on a vase Pitcher in right hand, pouring water into a vase out of which an eagle is drinking. Blacksmith with right hand resting on an anvil.
10 10

5 V Vig. Female and eagle, female holds a goblet. V FIVE
Compt's die
5 CATSKILL BANK, Catskill, N. Y. Eagle.

2 TWO on Med. head. Vig. Female looking over a rock, cars, steamboat and canal on right. TWO
Compt's die. Franklin.
2 COMMERCIAL BANK Albany, N. Y. 2 Secured, &c. 2 TWO

20 MERCHANTS AND MANUFACTURERS BANK, Pittsburg, Pa. 20
Farmer cleaning scythe. Railroad bridge, locomotive and cars in background. Vig. Three female figures. Right end figure of Justice with sword and scales. Centre figure with wand of Mercury in left hand; left end figure with basket of fruit. Machinery XX
20

10 Vig. Female with bucket; sheep on right, and cattle on left. X Female reclining, and word TEN.
Compt's die.
10 CATSKILL BANK, Catskill, N. Y. 10

3 3 on Med. head. 3 on Med. head. THREE
Compt's die. Vig. Two females and shield, one on right holds a sickle. Portrait of Jackson.
3 COMMERCIAL BANK Albany, N. Y. 3 Secured, &c. 3. THREE

50 Med. head. Vig. Female sitting on a rock of Franklin, sketching, anvil and hammer at her feet. Railroad bridge locomotive and cars in the background. Med. head of Franklin. 50
Female with hands on spinning wheel. Female with hands on spinning wheel.
50 Title of bank. 50

FIFTY 50 Vig. A Female seated working a spinning wheel. 50 FIFTY DOLLARS.
CATSKILL BANK, Catskill, N. Y.

5 Med. head and word five. Compt's die. 5
Portrait of Washington. Vig. Three females seated, sheaf of wheat, and quadrant, on right trees in distance on left ship in distance. Male portrait
V COMMERCIAL BANK Albany, N. Y. V

100 Medallion head. Vig. Mercury with wand pointing to a steamboat female with right arm resting on bale of goods. In the background Neptune drawn by horses. Medallion head. 100
Steamboat. Canal boat
100 Title of Bank. 100

ONE HUNDRED 100 and medallion head. 100 Vig. A female seated large eagle and figures 100. ONE HUNDRED
CATSKILL BANK, Catskill, N. Y.

10 Med. head and word Ten. Compt's die. 10
Male portrait Vig. Three females seated sheaf of wheat, and quadrant on right trees in distance, on left ship in distance. Portrait of Washington.
10 COMMERCIAL BANK Albany, N. Y. 10

500 Vig. Locomotive and train of cars. 500
Franklin. MERCHANTS AND MANUFACTURERS BANK, Pittsburg, Pa. Figure resting on shield sextant and compass at her feet, in right hand a bow.
D Safe.

20 SCHENECTADY B'K Schenectady, N. Y. 20
Female with torch, eagle and medallion head of Washington. XX XX Female with torch, eagle and medallion head of Washington
20 Vig. Indian with bow and arrow. 20

20 20 Vig. Two females reclining, ships in distance on right, and shield on left. Compt's die. 20
Male portrait. Portrait of Washington.
20 COMMERCIAL BK. Albany N. Y. Secured, etc. 20

1000 Vig. Blacksmith seated, left arm resting on an anvil; Factories, ships, &c. in the background. Med head on right 1000
Washington. Female head and bust.
1000 MERCHANTS AND MANUFACTURERS BANK, Pittsburg, Pa. M

50 Vig. Female with torch, and medallion head of Washington. Indian with bow and arrow.
Buildings L L
50 SCHENECTADY B'K Schenectady, N. Y. Eagle. 50

50 Vig. Three females seated, representing agriculture and commerce. Medallion head and figure 50 on left of Vig. State Arms on right. 50
Portrait Male portrait
50 COMMERCIAL BK. Albany, N. Y. 50

1 ONE Vig. Female, ONE shield and eagle; wheel and anvil on right; ships in distance on the left. Steamboat.
Compt's die. 1
1 CATSKILL BANK, Catskill, N. Y. Steamboat. Steamboat.

Vig. Indian with bow and arrow. 100 N. Y. Safety Fund.
100 SCHENECTADY B'K Schenectady, N. Y. Female with torch, eagle and medallion head of Washington.
Eagle. 100

100 100 Vig. Three females seated, sheaf of wheat on right, and quadrant and ship on left in distance. Compt's die. 100
Portrait of Washington. Male portrait
100 COMMERCIAL BK. Albany, N. Y. Secured, etc. 100

2 2 Vig. Ship and small boat, and hills in background. 2 TWO DOLLARS.
Compt's die.
2 CATSKILL BANK, Catskill, N. Y. Steamboat.

100 100 N. Y. STATE BANK, Albany, N. Y.
Compt's die.
100 100 Vig. Liberty and Justice seated; eagle mounted on a miniature view of sunrise. 100

Word ONE and fig. 1.
Man on horseback, with cattle, sheep and colt. 1 on right.
Indian on cliff.
ONE
COLCHESTER BANK Colchester, Conn.
Word ONE and fig. 1.
ONE

Male portrait
Vig. A farmer buying cattle of drover; cattle on right, sheep on left.
2
AM. EX BANK, New York.
2
Steamboat
Compt's die.

100
CITY BANK Bangor, Me.
100
Female portrait.
Sailor with American flag.
Vig. Female and cherub soaring in the air over city, water, vessels, &c.
100

2
COLCHESTER BANK Colchester, Conn.
TWO
TWO
Train of cars crossing a bridge; drove of cattle, &c. passing under.
Farmer seated on plow; men reaping and loading wagon with hay, steamer, vessels and house in distance.
TWO

3
AM. EX BANK. New York.
3
Vig. Drove of horses, fences, trees, etc., in background.
Male portrait
Eagle.
Compt's die.

X
[New Plate.] Vig. Farmers at work loading hay horse and ox for the team on right hay steer & trees on left large trees.
X
TEN
Female blowing dinner horn, table &c., farmers and load of hay.
FARMERS BANK OF LANCASTER, Pa.
X

3
COLCHESTER BANK, Colchester, Conn.
Word Three and fig. 3.
Farmer seated with scythe; houses in distance.
Female seated, dog, cows, etc.
Train of cars, houses, etc. in distance.

1
Vig. Train of cars, water, rural scene; on right train of cars, on left trees, vessel, &c.
1
Female with arms uplifted.
CITY BANK Bangor, Me.
1
Indian seated.

ONE
Vig. Train of cars; village in distance on left, steamboat on right.
1
Large figure 1 with portrait of Washington.
BANK OF FISHKILL Fishkill Village, N. Y.
Secured, &c.
Compt's die

5
COLCHESTER BANK Colchester, Conn.
5
Female with flowers.
Farmer with scythe; loading hay on left; buildings on right.
Female with flowers in her apron.

Washington and his horse.
Vig. Drove of cattle and drover.
2
CITY BANK Bangor, Me.
2
Eagle.
Male portrait.

3
PROVINCETOWN BANK
3
Sailor erect and mechanic seated on bale of goods his hand resting on sledge hammer.
Provincetown, Mass
Vig. Large ship and small boats in distance on right is a steamship, and ships on left.
Ornamental figure 3

X
COLCHESTER BANK, Colchester, Conn.
10
Girls with sheafs of grain.
TEN
Man shearing sheep.

3
Vig. Vessels, steamship; on left city.
Three females supporting frame with 3 on it.
Male portrait.
CITY BANK Bangor, Me.
3
Indian.
THREE

20
TWENTY
Vig. Male portrait with female on the right and male on left.
20
HUDSON RIVER B'K Hudson, N. Y.
20
20

TWENTY
Males and females trimming poles with flowers from a box on left; on right, child and dog.
20
COLCHESTER BANK, Colchester, Conn.
XX

FIVE
Male portrait.
5
CITY BANK Bangor, Me.
Steamship vessels, &c.
Female seated, with basket of fruit.

L
50 Vig. Three females, liberty pole and cap, beehive on left. 50
50
Female standing erect.
Portrait of Washington.
L
HUDSON RIVER B'K Hudson, N. Y.
50

TEN
MANUFACTURERS' BANK, Troy, N. Y.
Man with scythe.
Liberty by X
Large steamboat leaving wharf.
Compt's die.
Secured &c.
10

X
Vig. Female seated with wheel, &c.; steamship on right, train of cars and buildings on left.
10
Country road drover and cattle, load of hay, &c.
CITY BANK Bangor, Me.
Male portrait

D
Vig. View of the Capitol at Washington.
500
LECHMERE BANK East Cambridge, Mass.
Portrait of Washington.
Eagle.
Male portrait

20
Two females seated; factory in distance.
20
MANUFACTURERS' BANK, Troy, N. Y.
Compt's die.
Female seated on bale.
Secured, etc.

Female seated on bale of merchandise vessels in background.
Portrait of Washington.
20
CITY BANK Bangor, Me.
Sailor, steamer on left, ship on right.
20
Beehive.

C
TOWNSENDS BANK Townsends, Mass.
100
Vig. Blacksmith shoeing a horse.
Female, arm resting on a tub.
Farming scene; load of grain, trees &c.

1
Vig. Steamship under way, vessels in distance.
1
AM. EX. BANK, New York.
Male portrait
Locomotive.
Compt's die.

50
Vig. Two females seated, on right a train of cars crossing a bridge, factories; on left a ship.
50
Female with sickle.
CITY BANK Bangor, Me.
50
Engine and tender.
Boy plucking ears of corn.

100
Man watering three horses at trough, sheep, &c.; house and trees in distance.
100
FARMER'S BK. OF SCHUYLKILL CO. Pottsville, Pa.
Male portrait
100
Male portrait

1 — Female Portrait. — Two farmers, one seated, apparently eating, the other smoking and holding a jug. — 1 — FARMERS BANK, Bangor, Me. — Train of cars. — 1	Vessels under sail; steamboat, &c. 1 — 1 — GARDINER BANK, Gardiner, Me. — Man and sheep. — 1	Vig. Female on either side of a shield; steamboat on left, train of cars on right. 1 — 1 — AMERICAN BANK Hallowell, Me. — Female Portrait. — 1
2 — Man ploughing; village on right; on left steamboat in distance. — 2 — FARMER'S BANK, Bangor. Me — Ships, &c. — Bee-Hive — Female Portrait.	State Arms. 2 — 2 — GARDINER BANK, Gardiner, Me. — Ship under sail. — 2	2 — AMERICAN BANK Hallowell, Me. — 2 — Ship building. 2 — 2 — Locomotive and car. — Cupid and a sea monster.
3 — Cattle and sheep, (two cows standing in water. — 3 — FARMER'S BANK, Bangor. Me. — Large figure 3, and three Cupids — Agricultural Implements. — Female seated with flowers.	Train of Cars, &c. 3 — 3 — Female. — 3 — GARDINER BANK, Gardiner, Me — THREE	3 — AMERICAN BANK, Hallowell, Me — 3 — Female with balances in one hand, wreath in other, eagle by her side. — Female and swan in water. 3 — Two females.
5 — Drove of cattle and hogs, two men on horseback; train of cars, village &c, in background — 5 — Ship, steamer; lighthouse, &c., in distance. — FARMER'S BANK, Bangor. Me. — Large figure 5, & female. — Locomotive.	This Bank has also the Perkin's Stereotype Plate for all denominations except 500s.	Female reclining; eagle, globe, &c., steamer and ship on left. — 5 — 5 — AMERICAN BANK, Hallowell, Me — 5 — Figure 5 and two females.
Milkmaid seated, & two cows; cows, house, trees, &c in distance. — Female Portrait — 10 — FARMER'S BANK, Bangor, Me — 10 — Steamboat. — Man sharpening scythe.	20 — 2 Female. 0 — 20 — Female. — Figure with helmet and spear. — GARDINER BANK, Gardiner Me — XX — 20	Female feeding an eagle from cup. — Spread eagle, steamer on left; public building on right. — 10 — X — AMERICAN BANK, Hallowell, Me — Portrait of Washington.
20 — Female sitting with arms extended, scales in right hand, cap & pole in left; naked boy on one side and one partially draped on the other. — 20 — Female with scales and sword; eagle, key &c. — FARMER'S BANK, Bangor, Me. — Female with sheaf of wheat. — Steamship.	50 — Male and Female Seated. — 50 — Cupid in a sail boat. — Minerva. — GARDINER BANK, Gardiner, Me. — 50 — 50	Female. — Vig. Capitol at Washington. — 20 — XX — AMERICAN BANK, Hallowell, Me — Man beside a capstan and bbls. behind.
50 — Two females seated with pieces of machinery, factories on right; ship in distance on the left. — 50 — Female with sickle. — FARMER'S BANK, Bangor, Me — Farmer gathering corn. — 50 — Engine & Tender.	100 — Spread eagle; train of cars, canal, &c., in background. — 100 — Vulcan — GARDINER BANK, Gardiner, Me — Female seated. — 100	50 — Female. State Arms. Female. — 50 — Man; capstan behind. — AMERICAN BANK, Hallowell, Me — Female with pole, cap, shield, etc.
100 — FARMER'S BANK Bangor, Me — 100 — Female reclining with One Cupid Hundred scattering fruits over a city in foreground. — Portrait of female. — Sailor supporting a flag staff. — Machines. — 100	Indians in canoe, trees and mountainous scenery in background. — 500 — 500 — 500 — GARDINER BANK, Gardiner Me. — Female holding scales.	100 — Vig. Ships, steamboats, vessels, &c., city in distance. — 100 — Men with grain cradle. — AMERICAN BANK, Hallowell, Me. — Female, with rake.
500 — FARMER'S BANK, Bangor, Me. — 500 — Female with receiver arms and Coat of Arms of the different States. — Three females, one seated the others reclining; train of cars & ship in the distance. — 500 — Eagle.	GRANITE BANK. Augusta, Me. This Bank uses the old Perkin's Stereotype plate, which has the denomination printed in fine letters all over the bill.	TICONIC BANK, Waterville, Me This Bank uses the old Perkins Stereotype Plate, which has the denomination printed in fine letters all over the bill.

1 Washington	Female. 1 Female. MAN. & TRADERS' BANK, Portland, Me.	1 Portrait.
ONE	Water scene, ships, &c. 1 MAN. & TRADERS' BANK, Portland, Me.	ONE Female. ONE
2 TWO 2	Water scene, ships, &c. 2 MAN. & TRADERS' BANK, Portland, Me.	TWO Female. TWO
2 Portrait.	Female with cornucopia. 2 Female with balances. MAN. & TRADERS' BANK, Portland, Me.	2 Portrait.
THREE	Female with hat in hand, man reaping and another carrying grain. 3 MAN. & TRADERS' BANK, Portland, Me.	THREE Ship. The word three and figure 3.
3 Washington and his horse.	Portrait of Female. 3 Portrait of Female. MAN. & TRADERS' BANK, Portland, Me.	3 Blacksmith, anvil, &c.
FIVE	Female, &c. V MAN. & TRADERS' BANK, Portland, Me.	5 Ship.
Spread eagle. FIVE	Female with sceptre and horn of plenty, figure 5 and angel. MAN. & TRADERS' BANK, Portland, Me.	5 Female with hat and wreath in hands.
10 X 10	Oxen and man. 10 MAN. & TRADERS' BANK, Portland, Me.	TEN Female with horn of plenty, &c.

TEN	Blacksmith seated, sledge in right hand resting on anvil; block and wheel behind him. X MAN. & TRADERS' BANK, Portland, Me.	10 Farmer with sheaf of grain and sickle.
TWENTY Female seated.	XX Eagle. XX MAN. & TRADERS' BANK, Portland, Me.	20 Ship.
FIFTY Female. FIFTY	50 Man and horse. 50 MAN. & TRADERS' BANK, Portland, Me.	FIFTY Female. FIFTY
The words one hundred and figures 100. Harrison.	Wharf scene, market wagon, drays, horses, men, vessels, &c. MAN. & TRADERS' BANK, Portland, Me.	Same as on left. Columbus.
1 Head of Female.	Ship-yard — two ships on the stocks —City in distance. SEARSPORT BANK, Searsport, Me.	1 Ship under full sail.
2 Washington.	SEARSPORT BANK, Searsport Me. Steamship.	2 Female leaning on bale.
THREE Sailor seated holding Am. flag.	3 Man on horse back, drove o cattle & sheep SEARSPORT BANK, Searsport, Me.	3 Female with spy-glass.
5 5	Spread eagle on rock; ship at right, and ship under sail on left. Head of Female. SEARSPORT BANK, Searsport, Me. Head of Indian	5 Bale of goods & anchor.
Group of 3 Females, the one above apparently supported by the others. TEN	Ship under sail; in distance steamship and sail ship. SEARSPORT BANK, Searsport, Me.	10 Female with spear seated in car of Neptune.

1 Male Portrait.	Vig. Train of Cars; on left in distance village; on right steamboat and sloop. PRAIRIE CITY B'K, Terre Haute, Ind.	1 Woodman in the act of cutting; buffalo.
Female with sheaf of grain on right shoulder.	Vig. Man seated on trough; three horses, one drinking; girl feeding swine; houses in background. PRAIRE CITY B'K. Terre Haute, Ind.	2 Same as Ones.
3 Female with flowers.	Vig. Three females in clouds; flowers, &c.; on right train of cars, canal lock, boat, &c. PRAIRE CITY B'K. Terre Haute, Ind.	3 Same as Ones.
Male Portrait. 5	Vig. Steamship, and four ships under sail PRAIRIE CITY B'K, Terre Haute, Ind.	5 Same as Ones.
Three females, one above the other; anchor, sheaf of grain, &c. TEN	Vig. Four cows and three sheep; stream of water, trees, &c. PRAIRIE CITY B'K. Terre Haute, Ind.	10 Same as Ones.
5 Male Portrait.	Vig. Female soaring in clouds, eagle, shield, &c. CAMBRIDGE CITY BANK. Cambridge City, Ind. Eagle.	5 Male Portrait.
5 Male Portrait. 5	5 Farmer feeding hogs in pen; two horses looking over bars. CAMBRIDGE CITY BANK. Cambridge City, Ind.	5 Male Portrait. 5
FIVE Male Portrait. FIVE	5 Vig. Female seated on barrel, holding a pitcher; mechanical implements laying around; ships on right in distance. 5 CAMBRIDGE CITY BANK, Cambridge City, Ind.	FIVE Male Portrait. FIVE
10 Male Portrait. 10	10 Vig. A large X. with portraits of ten of the Presidents of the United States thereon. 10 CAMBRIDGE CITY BANK, Cambridge City, Ind. Eagle.	10 Male Portrait. 10

1 — Vig. Farmer and sailor on either side of a shield on which is a deer and tree; on right, ships; on left, mill, &c. — 1
Indian female seated, with shield, &c.
EASTERN BANK, Bangor, Me. Spread eagle.
Female seated with pen and tablet.

Man ploughing with two horses; train of cars on the right. — Large figure 2 and a child. — 2
2
LINCOLN BANK, Bath, Me.
Female reclining.

---

3 — Three silver dollars and three Cupids. — 3
Female with wreath and scales; eagle and shield.
NORTH BANK, Rockland, Me.
Female seated; globe, shield, and "Declaration of Independence."

---

2 — Vig. Farmer and sailor on either side of a shield on which is a deer and tree; on right, ships; on left, mill, &c. — 2
Female portrait.
EASTERN BANK, Bangor, Me. Spread Eagle.
Female portrait.

Steamship; ships lying too. — 3
LINCOLN BANK, Bath, Me.
3
Ship under full sail.

Sailor and Indian with word FIVE between them; two females seated on either side of a frame, surmounted by an eagle; bust between Indian and female, steamer, ship and canal lock in distance. — Five at top of large figure 5. — 5
5
Title of Bank.
Female with pole and cap, and shield.

---

3 — Vig. Farmer and sailor on either side of a shield on which is a deer and tree; on right, ships; on left, mill &c. — 3
Mechanic seated with mallet and chisel in right and left hand.
EASTERN BANK. Bangor, Me. Spread eagle.
3

---

5 — Schooner lying too; ship and brig. — Large V, female and Cupid. — 5
5
LINCOLN BANK, Bath, Me.
Female with basket of flowers.

Female seated on rocks, three Cupids sporting with sea monster in water. — Large X & male Portrait. — X
10
NORTH BANK, Rockland Me.
Female Portrait.

---

5 — Vig. Female leaning on anchor, merchandise, &c.; on right, sloop of war; on left, city, vessels, &c. — 5
Spread eagle
EASTERN BANK. Bangor. Me. Horse.
Steamboat.

TEN — Pilot boat, steamboat, shipping and a small boat with four men in it. — 10
Ship under full sail.
TEN
LINCOLN BANK, Bath, Me.
Large X and a female.

ONE — Drove of wild horses, two more prominent than others. — 1
Indian kneeling on the bank of river with gun in his hand.
ONE
BUCKSPORT BANK Bucksport, Me.
Portrait of a boy.

---

10 — Vig. Spread eagle, ships, &c. — 10
Portrait of Washington
EASTERN BANK, Bangor, Me. Dog, key and safe.
Two females seated, one with scales and sword.

XX — Depot with engine and tender, man with wheelbarrow, steamboat at wharf, and also boat with two men. — 20
Steamship.
LINCOLN BANK, Bath, Me.
Ship under full sail.

TWO — BUCKSPORT BANK. Bucksport, Me. — 2
Two females holding a bundle of grain over their heads, a sickle in the bundle.
2 TWO 2
Ship; light-house and vessels seen in the distance.

Female with sheaf of grain. — Vig. Spread eagle on rocks; man-of-war on right, b.y on left — 20
TWENTY
EASTERN BANK, Banger, Me. Female seated, ship, &c.

---

50 — Farm house and out buildings, load of hay, two persons on top; man with rake in right hand, pail in left. — L
Steamboat and pilot boat.
LINCOLN BANK. Bath. Me.
Female with sword in right hand.

Spread eagle over the banners of the different States. — Head of a dog. — 3
THREE
BUCKSPORT BANK. Bucksport. Me.
Portrait of girl resting on right arm, left hand over her eyes to shield from light.

---

50 — Female reclining, shield, eagle, cornucopia, liberty pole and cap, &c. — 50
Medallion Head.
EASTERN BANK. Bangor, Me. Agricultural implements.
Medallion head.

---

100 — C Neptune in car drawn by three horses. 100 — C
Eagle.
100
LINCOLN BANK, Bath, Me.
Head of Washington.
C

FIVE — Fleet of Vessels; light-house in the distance. — 5
Sailor erect and blacksmith seated
BUCKSPORT BANK, Bucksport, Me.
V

---

100 — Vig. Female seated; on right men loading wagon with hay; ship, steam boat, &c. — 100
Female portrait.
EASTERN BANK. Bangor, Me. Head of Indian.
Female Indian princess

ONE — Cupid & Figure 1 — Cupid & Figure 1 — ONE
Vig. Female seated, ship on right in distance
Female seated.
Female.
ONE
NORTH BANK. Rockland, Me.
ONE

TEN — Three ships on the stocks, steam mill, &c. — X
Female with a sickle in right hand, left hand holding a bundle of grain on her shoulder.
BUCKSPORT BANK. Bucksport, Me.
State Arms.

Train of cars; house on right. — 1
LINCOLN BANK Bath, Me.
1
Man in his shirt sleeves, with tools at his feet.

Female seated with Portrait of Washington and eagle; steamer ship &c, on right large building and train of cars on left. — 2 — 2
2
NORTH BANK. Rockland. Me.
Figure of Justice.

Light-house, small vessels, steam boat, and train of cars. — 20
20
BUCKSPORT BANK, Bucksport, Me. Bee hive
Sailor with quadrant in right hand.

L Three dogs. BUCKSPORT BANK. Bucksport, Me. Santa Claus riding over the top of houses by moon light. Dogs. 50 Indian.	20 Portrait of Fillmore. Spread Eagle, houses, &c. MERCHANT'S BANK Portland, Me. Indian Head. 20 Portrait of Washington.	C Bunker Hill Monument. MONUMENT BANK, Charlestown, Mass. Spread eagle on shield; on the left is Charlestown with a view of the monument; on right schooners sailing. Rail cars in front. 100 Portrait of Webster.
100 Man with his gun and dog in the woods by the side of a fire. 100 Indian, white man, woman and child in a canoe. BUCKSPORT BANK. Bucksport, Me. Head of Washington. 100 C	50 Female with scales. MERCHANT'S BANK Portland, Me. Steamship, man-of-war, and brig. 50 Female leaning on a pedestal; harp at her feet.	FIVE HUNDRED MONUMENT BANK, Charlestown, Mass. Vig. Two angels, one woman and little boy scattering gold coin on city below. 500 Bunker Hill Monument.
Sailor seated and holding flag. 1 View of the Custom House, Portland. MERCHANT'S BANK Portland, Me. 1 Ship under full sail.	C 100 C MERCHANT'S BANK Portland, Me. Female figure holding shield, pole and cap; on right, Capitol at Washington C 100 C	1 Blacksmith seated, implements around him. Three females reclining and cupid OMONO BANK, Orono, Me. 1 Portrait of General Taylor.
1 Train of cars crossing a bridge; mountains in the distance; boat on river and three figures in the foreground reclining. MERCHANT'S BANK Portland, Me. 1 Female Portrait.	1 Drummer boy and two soldiers seated. Vig. Battle of Bunker Hill. Scene is the death of Warren. MONUMENT BANK, Charlestown, Mass. 1 1 Bunker Hill Monument.	2 Female with basket of flowers. Female, horn of plenty, shield, eagle, colors, &c.; [illegible] and steam boat in the distance ORONO BANK, Orono, Me. 2 Portrait of Jackson.
Figure with shield, pole and cap. 2 Spread Eagle; on right, man-of-war, and on left, a brig. MERCHANT'S BANK Portland, Me. Locomotive. 2 Female gathering flowers, &c.	2 Portrait of Warren. MONUMENT BANK, Charlestown, Mass. Vig. Same as ones. TWO Bunker Hill Monument.	3 Indian resting, his gun reclining. State arms; ships in distance. ORONO BANK, Orono, Me. 3 Portrait of Henry Clay.
Goddess of Liberty. 2 View of the Portland Custom House. MERCHANT'S BANK Portland Me. 2 Washington and his horse.	THREE Bunker Hill Monument. MONUMENT BANK, Charlestown, Mass. 3 Vig. Same as ones. 3	5 Female seated. Curved rail road track. Cars in the foreground and in the distance near bridge; also further in the distance, cars going out of sight. ORONO BANK, Orono, Me. 5 Man erect with whip in hand. [illegible] farmer in distance.
3 Large figure 3, and three Cupids. Portrait of Daniel Webster; ship, steamship, &c. MERCHANT'S BANK Portland, Me. Agricultural implements. 3 Cooper at work.	5 5 Vig. Same as ones MONUMENT BANK, Charlestown, Mass. 5 Bunker Hill Monument.	10 Same as threes. Heads of Washington and Franklin in frame; four cupids and X. ORONO BANK, Orono, Me. Steamboat. 10 Portrait of W. H. Seward.
Portrait of female. 5 MERCHANT'S BANK Portland, Me. View of the Portland Custom House. FIVE 5 Female with basket.	10 Two soldiers throwing up a breast work, officer giving orders. MONUMENT BANK, Charlestown, Mass. X Portrait of Washington. X TEN Same as fives.	Two winged females holding figures 20, two cupids. Spread eagle and shield. ORONO BANK. Orono, Me. 20 Female with sheaf of wheat.
Female reclining on bales of goods; ships, &c., in distance. 10 Portrait of female. MERCHANT'S BANK Portland, Me. Steamboat. 10 Train of cars.	L Bunker Hill Monument. FIFTY MONUMENT BANK, Charlestown, Mass. 50 Surrender of Cornwallis at Yorktown. 50	50 Female in frame with sickle. 50 Two females seated; ship, factory buildings; train of cars crossing bridge. ORONO BANK, Orono, Me. Engine and tender. 50 Boy gathering corn.

100 Sailor seated with flag in hand. | Female and cupid over a city; water and vessels in the distance. ORONO BANK, Orono, Me. Cogwheel and cylinder. | 100 Female Portrait. 100

20 Female. | XX Eagle. XX BIDDEFORD BANK, Biddeford, Me. | 20 Ship.

50 Male figure with spear in right hand. | Female seated with rake; male seated with scroll. THOMASTON BANK, Thomaston, Me. 50 | 50 Cupid in sea-boat. 50

Indian lying behind rock watching two deers. ONE | ONE Woodman cutting a tree, buffalo. LA GRANGE BANK, Lima, Ind. | ONE Portrait of Female.

FIFTY Female. FIFTY | 50 Man and horse. 50 BIDDEFORD BANK, Biddeford, Me. | FIFTY Female. FIFTY

100 Male figure seated. | Spread eagle on branch of a tree; train of cars, canal boats, bridge, &c. in distance. THOMASTON BANK, Thomaston, Me. 100 | 100 Female seated with rake.

TWO Two females holding aloft sheaf of grain and sickle. | Vig. Man with sheaf of grain on shoulder, boy loading a sled to which a horse is attached; on right stacks of grain, and on left house. LA GRANGE BANK, Lima, Ind. | 2 Woodman felling a tree; buffalo.

The figures 100 with the words "one hundred" running across. Portrait. | Horses, wagon, wharf and shipping. BIDDEFORD BANK, Biddeford, Me. | The figures 100 with the words "one hundred" running across. Portrait.

1 Washington. | Female 1 Female COMMERCIAL BANK Bath, Me. | 1 Franklin.

V FIVE | LA GRANGE BANK, Lima, Ind. Vig. Cattle and sheep; on right steamboat in distance, on left in distance cattle and house. | 5 Same as on Twos.

1 Washington. | Female. 1 Female. THOMASTON BANK, Thomaston, Me. | 1 Franklin.

2 Male Head. | Female with Horn of plenty. 2 Female with scales. COMMERCIAL BANK Bath, Me. | 2 Male Head.

1 | Factory and train of cars. 1 BIDDEFORD BANK, Biddeford, Me. | 1 Female.

2 Male portrait. | Female. 2 Female. THOMASTON BANK, Thomaston, Me. | 2 Male portrait.

3 Washington beside a horse. | Female Head. 3 Girl's Head. COMMERCIAL BANK Bath, Me. | 3 Blacksmith.

2 | Aurora and the hours. 2 BIDDEFORD BANK, Biddeford, Me. | 2 Steamship.

3 Washington and his horse. | Female. 3 Female. THOMASTON BANK, Thomaston, Me. | 3 Vulcan with hammer.

F I 5 V E | Female, with factory, locomotive, ships, in back ground. Large V and Indian. COMMERCIAL BANK Bath, Me. | 5 Head of Washington.

3 | Female seated. 3 BIDDEFORD BANK, Biddeford, Me. | 3 Head. THREE

Spread eagle on shield; ship and manufactories in distance. FIVE | Large V, female and child. THOMASTON BANK, Thomaston, Me. | 5 Female with basket of flowers.

X Indian with bow. | Vessels, steamboat in Harbor. X COMMERCIAL BANK Bath, Me. | 10 Female with sheaf of wheat.

5 | Man ploughing with horses. Female, cupid, V. BIDDEFORD BANK, Biddeford, Me. | 5 Female.

Vulcan seated, cars in distance. TEN | X THOMASTON BANK, Thomaston, Me. | 10 Farmer seated.

20 Female with a Book. | XX Eagle. XX COMMERCIAL BANK Bath, Me. | 20 Ship.

10 | Two ships under sail. Ship and X BIDDEFORD BANK, Biddeford, Me. | TEN Head of Washington. TEN

20 Full length female figure with helmet and spear. | 2 Female seated. 0 THOMASTON BANK, Thomaston, Me. XX | 20 Female seated. 20

50 Figure. | Male and Female with Horn of Plenty. COMMERCIAL BANK Bath, Me. 50 | 50 Cupid in a boat. 50

One Hundred and figures 100. Male head.	Wharf scene, covered waggon, team, &c., with ships in back ground. COMMERCIAL BANK Bath, Me.	Same as on the left. Male Head.
100 Sailor with American flag.	MARINE BANK. Damariscotta, Me. 100 ONE Female with Cupid. HUNDRED Cog Wheels.	Female.
ONE Compt's die.	Drove of sheep, dog, &c.; man on horseback; mill and trees in distance. LEONARDSVILLE BANK, Leonardsville, N. Y. Agricultural Implements.	1 Cattle, telegraph and railroad.
500 Man and boy with guns.	500 Laborers with ship building and factory in back ground. COMMERCIAL BANK Bath, Me.	500 500
1 Portrait of Washington.	Female 1 Female BRUNSWICK BANK Brunswick, Me.	1 Franklin.
2 Compt's die. TWO	Horses, cattle and sheep; boy, trees, fence and house in distance. Title of Bank. Dog, key and safe.	TWO Male, female, boy, girl, dog, hen and chickens.
1 Webster	Ships on the stocks. MARINE BANK Damariscotta, Me. Eagle.	1 Sailor.
2 Male Portrait.	Female 2 Female with scales BRUNSWICK BANK Brunswick, Me.	2 Male Portrait.
Compt's die. 3	Two females and a male at work making cheese. Title of Bank. THREE Fish.	3 Pig pen, pigs and chickens.
2 Female	MARINE BANK Damariscotta, Me. Ship under full sail, and a small steamship.	2 Franklin.
3 Washington and his horse.	Female 3 Female BRUNSWICK BANK Brunswick, Me.	3 Blacksmith with hammer.
FIVE Blacksmith, hammer and anvil; factories in distance.	Title of Bank. Man tending large machinery. 5 Arm. 5	5 Compt's die. V across five
3 Sailor with quadrant; small ship	Spread eagle; ship on right, and ship on left MARINE BANK Damariscotta, Me. Indian head.	3 Female with spy-glass
5	View of water falls, factory and buildings. BRUNSWICK BANK Brunswick, Me.	5
Liberty erect with pole, cap, shield and eagle.	X Title of Bank. Indian on shield; eagle at top, horse each side; steamboat in distance on right; cars, factory and canal boat on left. TEN TEN	10 Compt's die.
5 Washington.	John Adams Spread Eagle Jefferson MARINE BANK, Damariscotta, Me. Steamer.	5 Ship under sail.
10 TEN	Vig. View of College buildings and chapel. BRUNSWICK BANK Brunswick, Me.	10 TEN
XX Farmer, tree and scythe.	Title of Bank. Spread eagle on half of the globe. 20 Compt's die. 20	20 Sailor seated with telescope.
Indian and female; globe surmounted by an eagle between; State arms underneath. 10	Portrait of Jackson 10 MARINE BANK, Damariscotta, Me. Sloop.	Female. 10
20 Female erect with spear.	Female seated with rake in right hand between 2 and 0. BRUNSWICK BANK Brunswick, Me. XX	20 Female seated. 20
ONE Indian seated by fig. 1.	Female seated; cars, factory and house in distance. 1 MILLBURY BANK, Millbury, Mass	1 Blacksmith with anvil.
20 Figure of Justice.	Female with extended arms; Cupid on either side. MARINE BANK. Damariscotta, Me. Steamship.	20 Female with sheaf of grain.
50 Figure erect with spear in left hand.	Male and female. BRUNSWICK BANK Brunswick, Me. 50	50 Cupid in a boat with skill 50
2 Catching wild bull.	Females tending machines. MILLBURY BANK, Millbury, Mass.	2 Franklin.
50 Female. 50	Two females seated; ship on right, and on left is rail cars and buildings MARINE BANK. Damariscotta, Me, Locomotive.	50 Boy gathering corn.
100 Male seated with shovel.	Spread eagle on branch of a tree; train of cars in background. BRUNSWICK BANK Brunswick, Me. 100	100 Female figure sitting with rake in left hand.
3 Man cutting down a tree.	Steamship at sea. MILLBURY BANK, Millbury, Mass.	THREE on 3. 3

ONE Brig Sailor reefing, anchor, cap-stan, cordage, &c; ship, brig and sloop in the distance, CITY BANK, Bath, Me. 1 ONE State Arms ONE	2 Eagle standing above the rising sun; female, anchor, &c. NEW CASTLE BK., New Castle, Me. TWO DOLLARS. 2 Same as ones.	3 Maine Logging scene. TRADER'S BANK, Bangor, Me. Portrait of Washington. 3 3
2 Train of cars, factories in distance. CITY BANK, Bath. Me. TWO Sailor on rail of ship, spy glass in hand	The word three and figures. Female seated with sword. NEW CASTLE BK. New Castle, Me. THREE DOLLARS. 3 Three mechanics; man and two horses in background.	FIVE Maine Logging scene. FIVE DOLLARS. TRADER'S BANK, Bangor, Me. Male Portrait. 5
3 State Arms. 3 Ship and steamship in full sail; schooner in distance. CITY BANK, Bath, Me. 3 THREE 3	FIVE Five females, liberty cap, &c. NEW CASTLE BK., New Castle, Me. 5 FI 5 VE 5 FIVE	X TEN TRADER'S BANK, Bangor, Me. Three female figures sitting holding dividers, sickle and sextant. 10 Ship under full sail, city and shipping in the distance.
5 Ship-yard—Ships building. Shield dog, and safe; anchor on left; fact'ies in distance. CITY BANK, Bath, Me. 5 FIVE	Letter X and words ten dollars. Female bathing. NEW CASTLE BK., New Castle, Me. Ship building, &c.; men at work. 10 Washington.	State Arms, on the left two Indians and child, on the right female, three children and globe. 20 Male Portrait. TRADER'S BANK, Bangor. Maine. TWENTY—curved. 20
Goddess of liberty, shield, eagle, &c. 10 Man seated, anvil, boxes; train of cars, hills, lake, buildings, &c. CITY BANK, Bath, Me. 10 Portrait of female.	XX Signing the Declaration of Independence. NEW CASTLE BK., New Castle, Me. TWENTY DOLLARS. 20 Washington.	Male Portrait. 50 State arms with eagle on top, Indian and tents on left, sailor on right. TRADER'S BANK, Bangor. Me. FIFTY 50
20 CITY BANK, Bath, Me. Sailor, two girls, anchor, cog wheels, bbls, &c., tall chimney, hills and town, one shore of lake, light-house, &c. 20 Stream trees &c.; woman & child bathing.	50 Portrait of Jackson. Ship under full sail; ship, steamer, schooner and boat at left; city on right. NEW CASTLE BK., New Castle, Me. Guinea hens. 50 Two sailors, flag, anchors, &c.	C TRADER'S BANK. Bangor Me. Male Portrait. 100 Three female figures seated, on the left a temple
50 Men load of hay, hills in distance. CITY BANK, Bath, Me. Three females; on left town and hills, bridge; train of cars going out. 50 Ship and brig; city in distance.	Goddess of Liberty, eagle, shield, pole and cap. NEW CASTLE BK., New Castle, Me. – Spread Eagle. 100 100 State Arms. Three Indians, four white men, globe, &c., house in background.	ONE Female Indian erect, with bow and arrows and quiver. FOX RIVER BANK, Green Bay, Wis. Vig. Deer, Indian lodges, stream, trees, and Indians in canoe. Compt's die. 1 Female seated, with figure 1, &c.
Female erect holding oval portrait, in left hand a winged wand 100 CITY BANK Bath, Me. Signing declaration of independence. 100	1 State Arms. ONE DOLLAR, in part circle. Eagle on an arch, three females sitting, ship on left, cars on right. TRADER'S BANK, Bangor, Me. 1 ONE	Female portrait. 2 Train of cars, canal, &c. FOX RIVER BANK, Green Bay, Wis. Vig. Female reclining on bale of merchandize, bbl., &c.; on right ships, city, &c. Compt's die. 2 Female Indian. TWO
ONE Aerial figure and female reclining on the ground. NEW CASTLE BK., New Castle, Me. ONE DOLLAR 1 Ship under full sail. Ship and steamboat in distance.	2 Spread eagle, streamship on left, sail-ship on right. State Arms. TRADER'S BANK, Bangor, Me. TWO 2 2	FIVE Female portrait. FIVE FOX RIVER BANK, Green Bay, Wis. Female and shield, and words "Agriculture and commerce" over shield; on right train of cars, &c.; on left steamboats, team and wagon, &c. Compt's die. 5 Female erect and figure 5, on left large building.

Left	Centre	Right
Washington. 1	Farm yard scene, farmer and drover. BK. OF SOMERSET, Skowhegan, Me. Man plowing.	1 Goddess of Liberty, globe and Declaration of Independence.
Men washing sheep. 2	2 Title of Bank.	TWO Female. TWO
1 Female with tablet.	Female portrait. BANK of THE STATE of MAINE, Bangor, Maine. State Arms.	ONE Female in a nearly nude state.
Cattle, sheep, etc. 2	Maine logging scene in winter. Title of Bank. Female with scales, etc.; ship.	2 Jefferson.
Scene in a farm yard. 3	3 Title of Bank.	THREE Female with basket of flowers. THREE
2 Portrait of female.	Title of Bank. State Arms; with agricultural implements and products.	2 Portrait of female.
Clay. 3	Boot and Shoe manufacturing scene. Title of Bank.	3 State Arms.
5 Portrait of Washington. FIVE	View of City of Bath. Title of Bank.	5 Indian. FIVE
3 Female gathering flowers.	A man watering horses at a trough, and woman feeding swine; farmhouse and buildings. Title of Bank. State Arms.	3 Boy gathering corn.
Train of cars; city in distance. 5	Head of Webster. Title of Bank. FIVE	5 and FIVE Large 5, eagle and Goddess of Liberty; head of Washington and "FIVE."
Eagle, shield anchor, etc. FIVE	V Title of Bank.	5 Girl.
Female seated with sickle and figure 5. FIVE	Title of Bank. State Arms.	Female seated and holding out figure 5. FIVE
Franklin. 10	Blacksmith shoeing a horse; train of cars in distance. Title of Bank. Blacksmith & locomotive.	10 Vulcan.
10 Portrait of Washington. TEN	View of the City of Bath. Title of Bank.	10 Head of Indian.
Ship, brig, and schooner. X	Portrait of Gen. Taylor. Title of Bank.	10 State Arms. 10
TWENTY Jackson. 20	Vig. Landscape; locomotive in background; city, train of cars, etc., in distance; farmer plowing, cattle, etc. Title of Bank. Load of hay.	20 Female churning.
Man and anvil, train of cars and village in background. TEN	X Title of Bank.	10 Man holding a handle of wheat.
20 20	Title of Bank. Female seated, eagle and globe and word "America" thereon. State Arms.	20 Washington.
Goddess of Liberty, crown and wreath. 50	Indians and whites trading. Title of Bank. Man cradling grain.	50 Male portrait. FIFTY
FIFTY Female. FIFTY	50 Male and horse. 50 Title of Bank.	FIFTY Female. FIFTY
50 Med. head. 50	Title of Bank. State arms, female on either side; in distance steamboat and train of cars.	50
Goddess of Liberty. 100	Spread eagle; U. S. capitol; steamship in distance. Title of Bank. Agricultural implements.	100 Male portrait.
ONE HUNDRED and figures 100. Portrait.	Covered wagon, shipping, etc. Title of Bank.	Same as on left side. Portrait.
C	Shipping; city in the distance. Title of Bank. State Arms.	100 Spread eagle.
Female, cars, etc. 1	1 SAGADAHOCK BK., Bath, Me.	1 Female.
Indian paddling canoe. 500	500 Title of Bank.	500 Female.
	FREEMEN'S BANK, Augusta, Me. This Bank uses the old Perkins' Stereotype Plate, which has the denomination printed in fine letters all over the bill.	

The word "one" and two cupids. Bust of a Female.	Shield—Indian seated on left and woodchopper on right. LUMBERMAN'S B'K, Old Town, Me. Dog.	1 Female seated with pole and cap.

TWO Bust of a Female.	Spread eagle; ships in the distance. 2 LUMBERMAN'S B'K, Old Town, Me. Agricultural implements.	TWO Sailor. Female seated.

3 Female erect surrounded with wreath with names of the States.	Neptune with sea-car, &c. LUMBERMAN'S B'K, Old Town, Me. Horn of Plenty, safe and key.	3 Large 3, sailor, mechanic, and farmer. THREE

FIVE Large figure 5, female seated, and portrait of Washington. FIVE	Milk-maid and cows. LUMBERMAN'S B'K, Old Town, Me. Horn of Plenty and anvil.	5 FIVE FIVE

Vulcan, with sledge and anvil; train of cars in distance. TEN	X LUMBERMAN'S B'K, Old Town, Me.	10 Man erect, with sickle and sheaf of wheat.

20 Female seated.	XX Spread Eagle. XX LUMBERMAN'S B'K, Old Town, Me.	20 Ship.

FIFTY. Female with wreath. FIFTY	50 Man and horse 50 LUMBERMAN'S B'K, Old Town, Me.	FIFTY. Female. FIFTY.

100 Eagle. 100	C Wild horses and chariot. 100 LUMBERMAN'S B'K, Old Town, Me.	C Washington. C

1 State arms. ONE	CENTRAL BANK, Hightstown, N. J. Train of cars passing under bridge.	ONE Male portrait.

2 Man, peach basket trees, &c.	State arms. Train of cars passing under bridge. CENTRAL BANK, Hightstown, N. J.	TWO TWO

3 Portrait.	State arms. Men, oxen, load of hay, &c. CENTRAL BANK, Hightstown, N. J.	3 3

FIVE State arms. FIVE	Train of cars passing under bridge CENTRAL BANK, Hightstown. N. J.	V Man, peach basket trees, &c.

TEN State arms.	CENTRAL BANK, Hightstown, N. J. Railroad scenery.	X Male portrait.

20 State arms.	Mall portrait, on either side of which is a female, ship, sheaf of wheat, &c., on left; on right train of CENTRAL BANK, Hightstown, N. J.	20 XX

50	CENTRAL BANK, Hightstown, N. J. Market house, shipping, &c. State arms.	L Male portrait.

C 100	Same as 50's. CENTRAL BANK, Hightstown, N. J.	C State arms.

ONE State Arms.	GROCER'S BANK Bangor, Me. Cupid rolling silver dollar; steamboat and city in distance.	1 Head of Webster.

2	Train of cars 2 GROCER'S BANK Bangor, Me.	2 TWO Head of Franklin.

3 Two horses.	GROCER'S BANK Bangor, Me. 3 For dealer trading with Indians.	3 Eagle and shield. Train of cars.

FIVE Washington.	GROCER'S BANK Bangor, Me. Spread eagle, steamer and Capitol at Washington in distance.	5

X	GROCER'S BANK Bangor, Me. X Female seated, anchor, bales, &c; on right steamship, on left ship.	10 Train of cars.

50 Head of Washington. 50	GROCER'S BANK Bangor, Me. Spread eagle; steamship on right, ship on left.	50

C	GROCER'S BANK Bangor, Me. Water Nymphs C	100 Indian erect, spear, bow, quiver of arrows, &c.

ONE Auditor's die	BANK OF CHESTER, Chester, Ills. Large red 1 in centre of note.	1 Liberty surrounded by stars.

Auditor's die Fig. 2; word TWO each side. Franklin.	BANK OF CHESTER, Chester, Ills. 2	2 Female.

3 Female.	BANK OF CHESTER, Chester, Ills. 3 Large 3 in fancy star 3	3 Auditor's die.

5 Female seated with shield and eagle.	Auditor's die. BANK OF CHESTER, Chester, Ills. 5	V 5

ONE	Vessels. 1 BELFAST BANK. Belfast, Me.	ONE Female. ONE
2 TWO 2	Ship and other vessels. 2 BELFAST BANK, Belfast, Me.	TWO Female. TWO
THREE	Reaping scene. 3 BELFAST BANK, Belfast, Me.	THREE Steamer. Figure 3, and word "Three."
FIVE	Female holding drapery over a figure 5. V BELFAST BANK. Belfast, Me.	5 Ship under sail.
The word "Five" and letter "V."	Female holding rake and sickle; sheaf of grain, machinery, &c. Large V with female. BELFAST BANK, Belfast, Me.	5 Washington
X	Signing the Declaration of Independence. X BELFAST BANK, Belfast, Me.	X Locomotive and car.
Female seated; train of cars and canal in distance. 1	Large figure 1, and five male figures. GEORGE'S BANK, Thomaston, Me.	1 Female and sheaf.
Farmers washing sheep. 2	Large figure 2, and five male figures. GEORGE'S BANK, Thomaston, Me.	TWO Female with wreath. TWO
Farmers and cattle; load of hay, &c. 3	3 GEORGE'S BANK. Thomaston, Me.	The word three and figure 3. Female with basket of flowers. THREE.

FI 5 VE	Female with rake and sickle, various emblems representing Commerce, Agriculture, Mechanic Arts &c. V and Indian female. GEORGE'S BANK, Thomaston, Me.	5 Head of Washington
X Indian with bow.	Steamboat and vessels. X GEORGE'S BANK, Thomaston, Me.	10 Female with sheaf of grain.
20 Minerva.	2 Female. 0 GEORGE'S BANK, Thomaston, Me. XX	20 Female seated with horn of plenty, &c. 20
50 Female with spear.	Female with rake, and male with sledge. GEORGE'S BANK, Thomaston, Me. 50	50 Cupid in sail boat. 50
100 Male with sledge.	Spread eagle; train of cars and canal in distance. GEORGE'S BANK, Thomaston, Me. C 100 C	100 Female with rake, &c.
1 Compt's die.	Female seated by silver dollar, anchor, house, etc HOLLISTER BANK, Buffalo, N. Y. Child's head.	1 Bank building.
2 Compt's die. 2	Lovers at a well; barn in distance. HOLLISTER BANK, Buffalo, N. Y. Child's head.	2 Bank building.
100 Two men loading wagon with sheafs; man holding horse.	WAMESIT BANK, Lowell, Mass. ONE HUNDRED Female bathing	100 Squaw and female.
D.	WAMESIT BANK, Lowell, Mass. Three females in clouds with quadrant, sickle, compass and cornucopia.	Female erect with shield and spear. 500

ONE Auditors' die Squaw in canoe.	Drove of cattle and sheep and drover on horseback. BANK OF AURORA, West Aurora, Ills. Dog.	1 Female with tablets.
TWO Female and figure 2.	Two Indians on horseback; cars in distance. BANK OF AURORA, West Aurora, Ills. Child's head.	2 Auditor's die TWO
THREE on 3, supported by three men.	Indian, squaw and papoose in canoe. BANK OF AURORA, West Aurora, Ills. Loaded boat.	3 Auditor's die
FIVE Auditor's die V, and three females.	Mechanic, sailor and farmer with implements. BANK OF AURORA, West Aurora, Ills. Female.	5 Large 5, two Indians, water fall, cars and bridge.
Female erect with vase of flowers, pole and cap. ONE	1 Woodman felling a tree; buffalo. CRESCENT CITY B'K. Evansville, Ind.	1 Male Portrait.
2 Med. head and word two.	CRESCENT CITY B'K. Evansville, Ind. Female seated; train of cars on left, and woodman felling a tree; buffalo.	2 Male portrait.
FIVE Male portrait.	CRESCENT CITY B'K, Evansville, Ind. 5 Female in clouds, with sheaf of wheat and sickle and letters FIVE across lap. 5	FIVE Woodman felling a tree, buffalo.
1 Farmer sharpening scythe.	Cupid rolling silver dollar on railroad track; train of cars, steamboat, and city in distance. BANK OF THE CAPITOL, Indianapolis, Ind. Pig.	1 Male portrait. ONE
5 Male portrait. FIVE	Five silver dollars, and five cupids. BANK OF THE CAPITOL, Indianapolis, Ind. Agricultural implements.	5 Large figure 5, and five females.

1 Country road wagon, horses, load of hay, men, &c.; houses, &c. in distance.	Vig. Man and female on either side of a shield on which is inscribed figure 1, and word one; on left steamboat, and on right, drover, drove of hogs and a negro. ROCK RIVER BANK, Beloit, Wis.	1 Compt's die.
THREE Female seated with quadrant, spread eagle, standing on frame.	3 Vig. Indian and boy feeding horse; Indians seated on left. CITY BANK, Kenosha, Wis.	3 Compt's die. THREE
TEN Indian princess.	FARMINGTON BK., Farmington. N. H. Vig. Female Indian seated with left arm up lifted; on left a deer, trees &c. Men loading hay.	X Horses. X
2 Indian with gun seated on rock.	Vig. Man, woman and child, gun leaning against a rock, house and trees on right, houses, trees and a stream on left. ROCK RIVER BANK, Beloit, Wis.	2 Compt's die.
1 State arms. ONE	Male portrait. Female portrait. Vig. Female seated on plough, sheaf of wheat, &c., train of cars on right, house, &c. on left in distance. FRANKLIN BANK, Zanesville, O.	1 Male portrait.
20 Man seated with gun, train of cars on right.	FARMINGTON BK., Farmington, N. H. Vig. Female on the back of an eagle, soaring in clouds.	20 Indian female reclining.
Female seated holding figure 3, sheaf of wheat on left. Compt's die.	ROCK RIVER BANK, Beloit, Wis. Portrait of female.	Female seated holding figure 3; masts and bbls., bales, &c. on right. 3
3 State arms. THREE	Female head. Portrait of male. Female head. FRANKLIN BANK, Zanesville, O.	3 Male portrait. THREE
L Female seated, portrait of Washington; eagle, train of cars, &c.	FARMINGTON BK., Farmington, N. H.	50 Female portrait.
5 Female portrait. 5	ROCK RIVER BANK, Beloit, Wis. Vig. Female seated, shield, &c., in background falls, &c.	5 Compt's die
5 State arms. FIVE	Portrait of Henry Clay. Female portrait. Large figure 5 whole length of note. FRANKLIN BANK, Zanesville, O.	5 Male portrait. FIVE
Female feeding an eagle from cup. 100	FARMINGTON BK., Farmington, N. H. Train of cars, depot, steamboat, &c. on right. Dog.	100 100
5 Male portrait	Vig. Train of cars and group of seven persons; on right, in distance, is cabin and trees; on left, men loading wagon. BK OF NEWBERRY, S. C. Tree.	5 Female portrait.
10 State arms. TEN	Male portrait. Female with sickle, sheaf of wheat, frame with steamboat, &c. FRANKLIN BANK, Zanesville, O.	10 Male portrait. TEN
ONE 1	(Old Plate.) Vig. Farmer sowing seed. 1 INDIAN HEAD B'K, Nashville, N. H.	1 Ships. ONE
Male portrait. 10	Vig. Three females and cupid floating in water. BK. OF NEWBERRY, S. C. Tree.	10 Female with sheaf of grain on shoulder.
ONE 1 Female seated with right arm resting on figure 1; owl, &c.	FARMINGTON BK. Farminston, N. H. Vig. Spread eagle; on left, steamship; on right, Capitol at Washington.	1 ONE Female seated, liberty pole and cap, shield, globe, &c.
1 1	(New Plate.) INDIAN HEAD B'K, Nashua, N. H. Indians welcoming white men to shore.	1 Indian female and papoose.
20 Female with basket of flowers.	Vig. Male, apparently a soldier, female and child; houses, &c. on right and left. BK. OF NEWBERRY, S. C. Tree.	20 Male portrait.
Female reclining with scales in right hand. 2	Vig. Drove of cattle and sheep, two men, horse and dog. FARMINGTON BK., Farmington, N. H. Man ploughing.	2 Female erect pole, cap and shield.
TWO 2	(Old Plate.) Spread eagle on rock, train of cars on right. 2 INDIAN HEAD B'K, Nashville, N. H.	2 TWO Schooner and sloop.
1 Compt's die. ONE	Vig. Indian and horse on right buffaloes, train of cars, &c. CITY BANK, Kenosha, Wis. Safe.	1 Indian female seated and child.
Mermaid holding horn out of which water is running. 3	Vig. Two men ploughing with horse and oxen; road, train of cars, horses, cows, &c., in distance is city on left, on right is a church, &c. FARMINGTON BK., Farmington, N. H.	3 Female portrait.
TWO Indian Princess.	[New Plate.] INDIAN HEAD B'K, Nashua, N. H. Mechanic seated with sledge hammer, anvil, &c; train of cars and large building on left.	2 Female Portrait.
2 Compt's die. TWO	Vig. Large public building; men and women, horses and carriages, &c., in front CITY BANK, Kenosha, Wis.	2 Locomotive and tender.
FIVE Female seated, pole and cap, shield, flowers, &c.	FARMINGTON BK., Farmington, N. H. 5	5 Blacksmiths at work, horses, men, &c.
THREE 3	(Old Plate.) Sailor standing on wharf; ships, drays, &c. 3 INDIAN HEAD B'K, Nashville, N. H.	3 THREE. Train of cars.

3 Female seated.	[New Plate.] INDIAN HEAD B'K. Nashua, N. H. 3 Indian in canoe. 3	3 Figure 3, sailor, mechanic, and farmer.

Spread eagle; ships, &c., in distance. FIVE	[Old Plate.] Large letter V, and female and cupid. INDIAN HEAD B'K. Nashville, N. H.	5 Girl with basket of flowers.

5	[New Plate.] INDIAN HEAD B'K. Nashua N. H. Indian reclining on shield, on which is inscribed word "Enterprise;" eagle, deers, Indians in canoe, &c.	5 Figure 5, and five females surrounding it

TEN	[Old Plate.] Male seated with mechanical implements. X INDIAN HEAD B'K. Nashville, N. H.	10 Man with sheaf of grain.

10 Female Indian seated.	[New Plate.] INDIAN HEAD B'K. Nashua, N. H. Train of cars; depot, steamer, &c., on left.	X Indian female seated.

20 Full length figure of a female.	Female seated between figures 2 and 0. INDIAN HEAD B'K, Nashville, N. H.	20 Female seated. 20

50 Full length female; pedestal, &c.	Vig. Male and female seated; flowers, &c. INDIAN HEAD B'K, Nashville, N. H.	50 Cupid in sail-boat. 50

100 Male seated with sledge hammer.	Spread eagle on branch of tree; train of cars on left, canal boat, &c., on right. INDIAN HEAD B'K, Nashville, N. H.	100 Female seated with flowers.

500	Indians in canoe. 500 INDIAN HEAD B'K, Nashville, N. H. D D	500 Female holding scales.

Spread eagle and ship. 1000	1000 INDIAN HEAD B'K, Nashville, N. H. M M	1000 Female.

ONE 1	Farmer sowing, two horses and man on right. 1 MANCHESTER BK., Manchester, N. H.	1 Ship. ONE

TWO 2	Spread eagle, with wheels, cogwheels &c., on ground; on left train of cars in distance. 2 MANCHESTER BK., Manchester, N. H.	2 TWO Schooner and sloop.

THREE 3	Sailor standing by bales; vessels, wharf scene &c., on right; ships masts and building on left. 3 MANCHESTER BK., Manchester, N. H.	3 THREE Train of Cars.

FIVE	Female seated and in the act of raising drapery from off a figure 5. V MANCHESTER BK., Manchester, N. H.	5 Ship.

The word FIVE and letter V.	Female seated surrounded by mechanical and agricultural implements and products, on right vessels &c.; on left man, wagon, horses, building, &c. V and Female. MANCHESTER. BK., Manchester, N. H.	5 Head of Washington.

10 X 10	Male erect, behind him oxen. 10 MANCHESTER BK., Manchester, N. H.	TEN Female erect.

20 Female seated.	XX Eagle. XX MANCHESTER BK., Manchester, N. H.	20 Ship.

FIFTY Female. FIFTY	50 Man and Horse. 50 MANCHESTER BK., Manchester. N. H.	FIFTY Female. FIFTY

One Hundred and 100. Portrait.	Wharf scene, wagons, horses, shipping, &c. MANCHESTER BK Manchester, N. H.	Same as left Portrait.

Female figure holding scales of Justice. 1	Drove of cattle and sheep with man on horseback. LEWISTON FALLS BANK. Lewiston, Me.	1 Dairy maid churning.

TWO Same as right	Vig. Female feeding an eagle; horn of plenty in foreground; ship in the distance. LEWISTON FALLS BANK, Lewiston, Me.	TWO Cupid, fig. 2, female erect supporting 2

3	View of Lewiston Falls on the Androscoggin river. LEWISTON FALLS BANK. Lewiston, Me.	3 Female and 3

5 Large V, with five male and female figures in and around it.	Vig. Ornamental figure 5, with five female figures around it; ship, steamer, locomotive, and factories in the distance. LEWISTON FALLS BANK, Lewiston, Me.	5 Large figure 5, with five male and female figures in and around it.

X	View of Lewiston Falls on the Androscoggin river. LEWISTON FALLS BANK, Lewiston, Me.	10 Cotton mill.

Fountain. XX	Vig. Spread eagle and shield; steam ship and building in distance. LEWISTON FALLS BANK. Lewiston, Me.	20 Head of Female.

Goddess of liberty feeding an eagle. 50	Vig. Female resting on cotton bale, and linen wheel in foreground; manufacturing village in distance. LEWISTON FALLS BANK. Lewiston, Me.	50 Female, globe, shield, and Declaration of Independance.

Marble worker at labor. 100	Vig. National capitol. LEWISTON FALLS BANK, Lewiston, Me.	100 Cupid and dolphin.

5 Bridge, canal-boat, and village in distance.	Vig. Female seated on trunk of a tree with tub; steam-boat on right; house, &c., on left. Treasurers' die. BANK OF SCOTTS-VILLE, Scottsville, Va. Quails.	5 Portrait of Washington.

6 Female soaring in the clouds, and another seated.	Vig. Two females seated on right side of a frame, on which is agricultural implements; on right a large building; on left train of cars. Tres's die. BANK OF SCOTTS-VILLE, Scottsville, Va.	6 Portrait of Henry Clay.

7 Male, female seated, and two boys and lamb sheaf of grain.	Tres's die. Vig. Female seated, with pole and cap, and two cupids and easel; on right rain of cars, on left ships, masts, &c. BANK OF SCOTTS-VILLE, Scottsville, Va.	7 Male portrait.

9 Male portrait	Vig. Harvest scene, farmers mowing; on right, in distance, houses, &c.; on left men loading hay, &c. BANK OF SCOTTS-VILLE, Scottsville, Va.	9 Treasurer's die,

1 Farmer seated under tree; sythe hanging on limb.	Tobacco plantation; two men, one holding leafs of tobacco; hogshead, etc. PEOPLES BANK, Bowling Green, Ky.	1 1

5 V	Farmer and drover bargaining for ox. PEOPLES BANK, Bowling Green, Ky.	5 Female.

Female with cornucopia. X	JEFFERSON CO, BK, Watertown, N. Y. Figs. 10, words Ten Dollars on three red dies. Horse.	10 Compt's die.

XX Female gathering wheat.	JEFFERSON CO, BK, Watertown, N. Y. Figs. 20 and words Twenty Dollars on three red dies. Compt's die.	20 Female with flowers.

Train of cars, water and hills in the distance.	1 An angel lifting a canopy, revealing an eagle resting on a globe. 1 ORANGE BANK, Orange, N. J.	

– Female head.	2 Train of cars; water and hills in the distance. 2 ORANGE BANK, Orange, N. J.	

Half length female figure.	3 Train of cars; water and hills in the distance. 3 ORANGE BANK, Orange, N. J.	

FIVEFIVE Head.	5 A man working a cider mill, another seated. The words "Orange Cider," and figure "5" on the mill. 5 ORANGE BANK, Orange, N. J.	FIVE 5 FIVE

TEN TEN Head. TEN	10 Female resting on a globe, with shield and eagle. 10 ORANGE BANK, Orange, N. J.	TEN DOLLARS

TWENTY Head. TWENTY	20 Figure of Justice, with a picture of Washington in her left hand; an eagle at her feet. 20 ORANGE BANK, Orange, N. J.	TWENTY

50 Head. 50	50 State arms. 50 ORANGE BANK, Orange, N. J.	50 Head. 50

Head. 100 Head.	100 Female in a chariot drawn by two horses, and enveloped in clouds. 100 ORANGE BANK, Orange, N. J.	Head. 100 Head.

1 General Taylor.	Brig under sail. Spread eagle. Ship at anchor. KENDUSKEAG BK. Bangor, Me, Bee Hive.	1 Female seated and supporting figure 1.

2 Female seated with pole and cap.	Head of Marshall. Ship under full sail. Head of Clay. KENDUSKEAG BK. Bangor, Me. Horse.	2 Female seated.

3 Female portrait.	Female portrait. Dog & iron chest. Female portrait. KENDUSKEAG BK. Bangor, Me. Steamer.	3 Harrison.

FIVE Male and female. 5	Head of Columbus. Figure in the air with horn of flowers. Portrait of Franklin. KENDUSKEAG BK. Bangor, Me. Vessel.	5 FI 5 VE 5

10 Washington.	Female seated. Loading hay, two men, oxen an. cart; in distance train of cars. 10 KENDUSKEAG BK. Bangor, Me, Eagle.	TEN Female with sickle.

50 Vulcan with sledge, anvil &c.	KENDUSKEAG BK., Bangor, Me. Eagle and globe; female seated on right and Indian on left. 50	50

100 Portrait of La Fayette. 100	100 KENDUSKEAG BK., Bangor, Me. Female seated, a child and dog at her feet—plough, sheaf, &c. behind.	

Female with sheaf of wheat. Figure 5 and words "FIVE" twice.	BK. OF BERKELEY, Martinsburgh, Va. 5 Three dogs hunting a stag.	5 Portrait of female. 5

Horse and oxen before a loaded wagon; three men.	10 Train of cars coming around a curve. BK. OF BERKELEY Martinsburgh, Va.	- 10

20 Med. head. 20	BK. OF BERKELEY, Martinsburg, Va. Vig. Farm yard scene; two females, cows, fowls, &c.; on right, a house.	20 Female Portrait.

	AUGUSTA BANK, Augusta, Me. This Bank uses the old Perkin's Stereotype plate, which has the denomination printed in fine letters all over the bill.	

Left	Centre	Right
1	Cupid rolling silver dollar on railroad track, train of cars, and city in distance. Mechanical implements. BANK OF WATERBURY, Waterbury, Vt.	1 Female, shield, and Declaration of Independence.
Goddess of Liberty, and eagle, drinking from cup. 2	BANK OF WATERBURY, Waterbury, Vt. Two cupids, two silver dollars; train of cars, village, cows, &c., in distance.	2 Female Indian.
THREE Female erect with pole and cap.	Farming scene; two males and female, dog, basket, &c.; in distance, men loading hay. BANK OF WATERBURY, Watorbury, Vt.	3 Portrait of Washington.
FIVE A General erect, with sword in hand.	BANK OF WATERBURY, Waterbury, Vt. Female reclining, with pole and cap eagle, globe &c., steamship, and ship on left.	5
10 Spread eagle, U. S. Capitol on right; and steamer on left.	BANK OF WATERBURY, Waterbury, Vt.	X Farming implements and products.
TWENTY Female seated with pole and cap, flowers, &c.	Two men, horse, dog, and drove of cattle and sheep. BANK OF WATERBURY. Waterbury, Vt.	20 Male Portrait
50 50	BANK OF WATERBURY, Waterbury, Vt. Boy reclining with compass in right hand, engaged on chart; on right 2 men and 2 horses before cart.	50 Female erect with pole and cap, shield and scroll in right hand.
Female seated on rock. 100	BANK OF WATERBURY, Waterbury, Vt. Large public building, horses, carriages, &c., in front.	100 Train of car
ONE Drovers and Cattle. 1	(Old Plate.) 1 Horse and two horsemen in the distance. 1 MECH. & MAN. BK. Trenton, N. J. Train of cars.	ONE Drovers and Cattle. 1

Left	Centre	Right
ONE Male Portrait. 1	(New Plate.) Same as old plate. MECH. & MAN. BK. Trenton, N. J. Train of cars.	ONE Drovers and Cattle. 1
2 Washington. 2	2 Horse terrified by a train of cars; buildings in the distance. 2 MECH. & MAN. BK. Trenton, N. J.	2 on Medallion. Liberty reclining on a figure 2; cars in distance.
3 Atlas upheaving the world. 3	(Old Plate.) 3 Two cavaliers; farm-house in distance. 3 MECH. & MAN. BK. Trenton, N. J. Canal lock.	3 Female reclining on a cog wheel, with ship in distance. 3
3 Male Portrait, 3	(New Plate.) 3 Same as the above. 3 Title of Bank. Canal Lock.	Precisely same as above.
FIVE Shield with Liberty on right, and eagle on left; and motto "E Pluribus Unum." 5	(Old Plate.) 5 Eagle and shield, Justice on left, Liberty on right; train of cars and bridge in distance. Title of Bank. Casks, shipping, &c.	FIVE Female feeding an eagle.
FIVE Male Portrait. 5	Same as above. 5 Title of Bank. Casks, &c.	Precisely the same as above.
Indian springing a bow; landscape in distance. 10	10 Mechanic with anvil, &c.; two females, offering the one fruit; the other, money; shipping in distance. Title of Bank. Head of a horse.	X Franklin. 10
Female feeding an eagle; stars of America around. 20	XX State Arms. XX Title of Bank. Eagle feeding its young.	20 Three figures typifying home and plenty; hive, wheat, water mill, &c., in distance. 20
FIFTY 50 Mechanic, anvil, &c.	L Beehive, flowers &c. L Title of Bank.	Same as on left of twenty. 50

Left	Centre	Right
Same as tens. 100	100 Benjamin Franklin seated. 100 Title of Bank.	Full length statue of Washington. 100
1 Washington.	Female. 1 Female. WHITE RIVER BK., Bethel, Vt.	1 Male Portrait
2 Male Portrait.	Female. 2 Female. WHITE RIVER BK., Bethel, Vt.	2 Male Portrait.
3 Washington and his horse.	Female. 3 Female. WHITE RIVER BK., Bethel, Vt.	3 Vulcan the Blacksmith.
Spread eagle, on shield; village and ship in distance. FIVE	Large V, female and child. WHITE RIVER BK., Bethel, Vt.	5 Little girl with basket.
Vulcan the blacksmith seated, factory and building in distance. TEN	X WHITE RIVER BK., Bethel, Vt.	10 Man tying up bundle of grain.
20 Female seated.	XX Eagle. XX WHITE RIVER BK., Bethel, Vt.	20 Brig.
FIFTY Female erect. FIFTY	50 Man and Horse. 50 WHITE RIVER BK., Bethel, Vt.	FIFTY Female erect. FIFTY
The figures 100 with the words "one hundred" Portrait of Harrison.	Wharf scene, wagons, horses, men, vessels, &c. WHITE RIVER BK., Bethel, Vt.	Same as on the left. Male Portrait,

1 ONE State Arms. | Locomotive and train of cars turning a curve. BORDENTOWN BANKING CO., Bordentown, N. J. | 1 Male portrait.

5 FIVE | 5 Floating female with horn of plenty; ships, etc. V Title of Bank. | Indian with bow and arrow.

100 Female. | Title of Bank. Male. C Female. | 100 Portrait.

TWO 2 State Arms. TWO | Two horses, one man riding and one leading other horse crossing railroad track; locomotive and two cars in the distance. 2 Title of Bank. | TWO Male portrait 2

TEN Small Indian with bow and arrow. | X Shield, three plows, and horse head, female sitting either side. Title of Bank. | 10 10

Female seated; at her feet is a figure 1. ONE | Female seated with agricultural implements and products; in distance is train of cars and canal lock. GREAT FALLS BK., Somersworth, N. H. Female. | 1 Female portrait.

5 State Arms. FIVE | A female sitting on a log with a bucket in her lap; two sheafs; locomotive and cars. Title of Bank | 5 Head of Washington

20 Male portrait | Floating female with horn of plenty; ships, etc. Title of Bank | XX

2 Female portrait | Female seated with mechanical implements around; train of cars, boat on stocks, and steamer in distance. Title of Bank. Dog's head. | 2 Female portrait.

10 Male portrait | Title of Bank. Two Indian figures and child. State Arms. Female, three children and globe. Locomotive. | TEN Milkmaid. TEN

Indian. 1 | Two ships and one steamship. RICHMOND BANK, Richmond, Me. | 1 Female.

THREE Farmer with sheaf of grain and sickle. THREE | Two females seated. Title of Bank. Bull. | 3 Female erect

50 Male portrait | Title of Bank. Female sitting arm resting on money chest. State Arms. Sheaf and two sheep. Locomotive. | 50 50

2 Head of Washington. | Spread eagle. Title of Bank. Dog's head. | 2 Female.

Two females erect; one with sword and balances FIVE | Large figure 5 and female; 4 Cupids sporting around it. Title of Bank. Eagle and shield. | 5 Two females seated—one with scales shield between them FIVE

100 Male portrait | Title of Bank. Female fig. and horn of plenty. State Arms. Female handing $100 bill to other fig. | C Locomotive and cars.

3 Three persons supporting a globe. | Train of cars. Title of Bank. | 3 Angel.

Female erect in clouds. 10 | Female with key in left hand, is seated between 1 and 0; canal lock and train of cars in distance. Title of Bank. Agricultural implements. | 10 Female portrait.

1 ONE | Agricultural scene; man, boy, horses, plow, etc. FARMERS' BANK of WANTAGE, Deckertown, N. J. | Milkmaid, pail on head, cows, etc. ONE

5 Foul anchor. | Title of Bank. FIVE Sailor, ships and steamboats. DOLLARS | 5 Female.

20 Female with spear; globe, behind her. | 2 Female. 0 Title of Bank. XX | 20 Female reclining. 20

2 2 | Shield, three plows and horse's head, female seated on each side. 2 Title of Bank | TWO Female erect with staff and cap of Liberty.

10 Male portrait | Milkmaid and cows. Title of Bank. | 10 Female.

50 Female with spear; pedestal. | Male and female seated. Title of Bank. 50 | 50 Cupid in a sail-boat. 50

3 3 | Man with hammer leaning on anvil; locomotive, foundry, etc. THREE Title of Bank. | Female erect with sickle, sheaf of grain, etc.

Sailor, anchor, etc. FIFTY | Steamship. Title of Bank. | 50 Female holding a spy-glass.

100 Vulcan the blacksmith. | Spread eagle on branch of tree; train of cars, canal-boat, lock, etc. Title of Bank. 100 | 100 Female seated.

Shed, flowers on the roof; two women, one churning, one turning cheese, poultry and cattle, part in the water. | ONE Oxen, cart and hay; man lying, and man with fork on his shoulder. LAMOILLE CO. BK., Hyde Park, Vt. | 1 Mechanics' arm.

TWO 2 | Spread eagle on rock; train of cars on left in distance. 2 LIME ROCK BANK, East Thomaston, Me. | 2 TWO Schooner.

ONE Indian with bow, spear, &c. | Agricultural scene, cattle, &c. Female seated with sickle. BANK of ROYALTON, Royalton, Vt. | The word ONE and figure 1. Man seated with agricultural implements and ONE on half shield.

TWO Woods, stream and Indian creeping with gun. | LAMOILLE CO. BK., Hyde Park, Vt. Woman, eagle, sword, &c. Geese. | 2 Two deers, one feeding; rocks, meadow, &c.

THREE 3 | Sailor, bales, casks, &c.; wharves, drays, &c., on right, and on left vessels, warehouses, &c. 3 LIME ROCK BANK, East Thomaston, Me. Medallion. Medallion. | 3 THREE Train of cars.

Two females embracing each other. 2 | Two farmers, one seated; female seated, load of hay in distance. BANK of ROYALTON Royalton, Vt. | 2 Head of Jefferson.

THREE | LAMOILLE CO. BK., Hyde Park, Vt. Cattle and sheep. Female bathing. | 3 Lady with veil.

5 Ship on stocks, water and skiff. 5 | Head of female. Lime and kilns; quarry on right, with casks and cooper, on left horse, men vessel, &c. Head of child. LIME ROCK BANK, East Thomaston, Me. | 5 Steamship. 5

Blacksmith and anvil. 3 | Three females seated representing Agriculture, Manufactures and Commerce. BANK of ROYALTON Royalton, Vt. | 3 Head of Henry Clay.

V Woman blowing horn, table and crockery load hay in distance, man on load, man with rake, another with scythe sitting. | LAMOILLE CO. BK., Hyde Park, Vt. Wild horses running. | 5

5 Female seated; top sails of vessel in background. | State Arms. LIME ROCK BANK, East Thomaston, Me. Safe, dog, and key. | 5 Female

Large figure 5 and five females. 5 | Head of Hon. Jacob Collamer. BANK of ROYALTON Royalton, Vt. | 5 Female seated with globe quadrant &c.

Santa Claus driving four reindeers. TEN | Female with hand over her eyes. LAMOILLE CO. BK., Hyde Park, Vt. | 10 Village scene, coaches, load of hay, riding horseback, driving cattle, &c.

TEN Steamer and ship. TEN | Farmer with team; house in distance. State Arms. Beehive and flowers. LIME ROCK BANK, East Thomaston, Me. | 10 Farmer with rake and jug; load of grain, house, &c. 10

10 Female seated with sheaf of wheat. | Man washing sheep; factories in distance. BANK of ROYALTON Royalton, Vt. | 10 Colossal figure holding corn in right hand and X in left.

TWENTY 20 Three dogs. | Indian tent, squaw and two Indians, houses, train of cars. Portrait of Webster. LAMOILLE CO. BK., Hyde Park, Vt. Dog | 20 XX 20

10 Justice with sword and scales; spread eagle on a safe. | Ship under full sail at sea. Large X, with ten dollars on both stems. LIME ROCK BANK, East Thomaston, Me. | Medallion head of female.

Mercury seated between 2 and 0 XX | Drover and drove of cattle and sheep. BANK of ROYALTON Royalton, Vt. | 20 Female churning.

L | LAMOILLE CO. BK., 50 Hyde Park, Vt. Two females, train of cars, ship, bundle of grain, &c. Head of Washington. | FIFTY. Two soldiers, one seated with pipe.

20 Female in partly nude state seated; wave, &c. | XX Eagle. XX LIME ROCK BANK, East Thomaston, Me. | 20 Ship.

Female feeding a horse. 50 | A farmer's family reclining in hay field; load of hay &c. BANK of ROYALTON Royalton, Vt. | 50 Head of Webster.

100 Jackson. | LAMOILLE CO. BK., Hyde Park, Vt. Female seated, rooster, two cows, &c.; trees and shed | 100 Clay.

FIFTY Full length female, with wreath on head. FIFTY | 50 Man and horse. 50 LIME ROCK BANK, East Thomaston, Me. | FIFTY Full length female. FIFTY

100 Head of Fillmore. 100 | BANK of ROYALTON Royalton, Vt. Female seated crowning an eagle with wreath; small head of Washington on left of vig. | 100 Load of straw drawn by oxen; man on horseback.

ONE 1 | Farmer ploughing and farmer sowing; trees, &c. 1 LIME ROCK BANK, East Thomaston, Me. | 1 Ship. ONE

Same as on right. Bust of Male. | Wharf scene, wagon, men loading dray, vessels, &c. LIME ROCK BANK, East Thomaston, Me. | The words one hundred across figure 100. Male portrait.

COBBOSSEECONTEE BANK, Gardiner, Me. This Bank uses the old Perkins Stereotype Plate, which has the denomination printed in fine letters all over the bill.

1 Medallion head with one on it. 1 — 1 Vig. Indians hunting buffaloes. 1 — QUEBEC BANK, Quebec, Canada. 1 — Large figure 1 and female on it.

50 Wharf scene, steamboat, ships, &c. 50 — 50 Vig. Female seated and two others soaring in the air; griffin on eagle; bbls, boxes, &c on right. 50 — QUEBEC BANK, Quebec, Canada. — 50

3 Female with veil. — Farm scene; milk-maid and two cows, one lying down. — PRINCETON BANK, Princeton, N. J. — 3 Portrait of Washington.

1 ONE 1 — 1 Vig. Two females on either side of a shield, surmounted by a crown and lion, train of cars in distance. 1 — QUEBEC BANK, Quebec, Canada. — 1 ONE 1

100 Wharf scene, steamboat, ships, &c. 100 — C Vig. Male and female figures seated in a car drawn by sea horses. C — QUEBEC BANK, Quebec, Canada. — 100 Ship in full sail. 100

V Woman with scales; eagle, &c. V — PRINCETON BANK, Princetown, N. J. — 5 Death of Gen. Mercer. 5 — Eagle. — 5 Portrait of Madison. 5

TWO — 2 British coat of arms. 2 — QUEBEC BANK, Quebec, Canada. — 2 Female portrait with helmet. 2

Female seated, holding figure 1, sheaf of wheat. 1 — MOLSON'S BANK, Montreal, Canada. — Vig. Steamship and other vessels. — Female seated, holding figure 1; bbls., bales and ships masts. 1

10 Washington. 10 — Portrait of female. Two females, one standing and the other seated; small ship in distance. 10 — PRINCETON BANK, Princeton, N. J. — Pump, pony, and boy. — X Madison. X

2 Female erect with spear, globe, &c. — Vig. Male and female seated, male with scroll in right hand and rod in left. — QUEBEC BANK, Quebec, Canada. 2 — 2 Female with pail.

Large figure 2, portrait of Prince Albert, and two figure ones. — MOLSON'S BANK, Montreal, Canada. — Vig. Female seated; on right men loading hay, train of cars, houses, &c. — 2 Portrait of Queen Victoria.

20 Madison. 20 — Female portrait. State Arms. 20 — PRINCETON BANK, Princeton, N. J. — Man and cow. — XX Male portrait. XX

Female portrait with helmet. — 4 Vig. River scene, ships, steamboat, city, &c. 4 — QUEBEC BANK, Quebec, Canada. — Female and dolphin — Female portrait with helmet.

Three females, with anchor, sheaf of wheat, &c. CINQ. — 5 MOLSON'S BANK, Montreal, Canada. — Vig. Female seated, with tub, two cows, one lying down; in distance cows trees, house, &c. — Agricultural implements. — 5 FIVE 5

50 Male portrait. 50 — Female portrait. Female in car. 50 — PRINCETON BANK, Princeton, N. J. — Pony and boy at a pump. — 50 Male portrait. 50

5 Farmer and agricultural implements. 5 — 5 Vig. Two winged monsters on either side of a shield on which is a key. 5 — QUEBEC BANK, Quebec, Canada. — Portrait of Queen Victoria.

20 Indian in frame. TWENTY — Vig. Steamship and five vessels, all under way. — MOLSON'S BANK, Montreal, Canada. — Man on horseback. — 20 Man erect, with whip; house and steamboat in distance.

100 Male portrait. 100 — Female portrait. Female holding cup to an eagle. 100 — PRINCETON BANK, Princeton, N. J. — Eagle. — 100 Male portrait. 100

5 Female with shield on which is figure 5. 5 — 5 Vig. Two males on either side of a shield on which is a bull; ship on right; and schooner, train of cars, &c., on left. 5 — QUEBEC BANK, Quebec, Canada. — 5 Three cupids. 5

50 Country road, drove of cattle, load of hay, horses, men, &c. — MOLSON'S BANK, Montreal, Canada. — Portrait of Queen Victoria. — 50 — 50 Train of cars, village in distance.

1 One in med. head. 1 — Word one and figure 1. Female with child in arms, &c. Word one and figure 1. — SALEM BANKING CO., Salem, N. J. — 1 One on med. head. 1

10 Medallion Head. — Vig. Naval scene, ships of war, &c. X — QUEBEC BANK, Quebec, Canada. — Portrait of Queen Victoria.

1 Soldiers raising a breastwork. — PRINCETON BANK, Princeton, N. J. — State arms; in distance on right, steamship; on left, train of cars. — 1 Head of a boy.

3 Med. head. 3 — 3 Shipping. 3 — SALEM BANKING CO., Salem, N. J. — 3 Washington 3

XX Ships, &c. 20 — QUEBEC BANK, Quebec, Canada. — 20 Vig. Three figures, 2 males and 1 female; village on left, and man on horseback on right. 20 — XX Yacht. 20

2 — 2 — Drover buying cattle. Picture of Buck. — PRINCETON BANK, Princeton, N. J. — Eagle — 2 Head of a girl.

5 Female holding goblet to an eagle. — V Female reclining against iron chest; stag in distance, &c. V — SALEM BANKING CO., Salem, N. J. — 5 Two female figures.

Portrait of Franklin.	10 Two female figures; tree, sheep, &c. 10 SALEM BANKING CO., Salem, N. J. Eagle.	Portrait of Washington.
TWENTY	20 Female erect resting on anchor. 20 Female figure. SALEM BANKING CO., Salem, N. J. Eagle.	Portrait of Franklin.
Portrait of Washington.	50 Female; ocean scene. SALEM BANKING CO., Salem, N. J. Eagle.	50 Two females.
100 State arms. 100	Three females; eagle, cars, ship, &c. SALEM BANKING CO., Salem, N. J. Steamboat.	C Portrait of Washington.
Large figure 1, which covers the whole end of the bill. ONE	Female bathing. ONE. State Arms. HUNTERDON CO. BANK. Flemington, N. J. Locomotive	1 ONE Female
2 Train of cars 2	HUNTERDON CO. BANK, Flemington, N. J. Cheese press, two females and man at work. 2 2	2 Bridge and drove of cattle. 2
THREE Loading hay; two men and a horse; men, &c.	HUNTERDON CO BANK. Flemington, N. J. Three Dollars. Head of dog.	3 Milkmaid
5	Large V, word "Five;" man with sickle in hand, sheaf of wheat in and around it. HUNTERDON CO. BANK. Flemington, N. J. Quails.	Letter "V" and word "Five." Female head FIVE
Figure 10, word Ten and letter X. Rustic female	View of the State House. HUNTERDON CO. BANK Flemington, N. J.	Figure 10, word Ten and letter X. Female.

Cattle scene XX	Treasurer's die. HUNTERDON CO. BANK, Flemington, N. J. Fish	20 Female.
ONE Female seated, with arm resting on figure 1.	1 Vig. Female seated, with bbls., bales, quadrant, cornucopia, &c.; on right steamship and vessels, on left city, train of cars, canal, boat, &c, MANUFACTURERS' BANK, Macon, Geo. Female seated.	Figure 1 and word one. Female erect, with figure 1 and shield.
2 Two mermaids. Steamship.	Vig. Female reclining on bale of goods, spinning wheel, &c.; on left city, bridge, &c. MANUFACTURERS' BANK, Macon, Geo. Agricultural implements.	2 Portrait of female.
THREE Female erect, with pole, cap, and shield.	Vig. Three females seated, with sickle, quadrant, &c. 3 MANUFACTURERS' BANK, Macon, Geo. Cogwheels, &c.	3 Sailor, mechanic, and farmer, and figure 3. THREE
5 FIVE FIVE	Vig. Two females on either side of a bust and shield, the one on left crowning bust with wreath; ship on right. Male portrait. MANUFACTURERS' BANK, Macon, Geo. Dog.	FIVE Five female figures, and a figure 5.
10 Spread eagle and motto E Pluribus Unum. TEN	Vig. Two females on either side of a shield surmounted by an eagle, at foot of shield motto "Prosperity and liberty;" on right steamship and train of cars, on left large building and man plowing MANUFACTURERS' BANK, Macon, Geo. Mechanic.	10 Portrait of Male.
20 Male portrait.	Vig. Female seated, portrait of Washington, spread eagle, shield, &c; on left steamer and ship and on right large building and train of cars. MANUFACTURERS' BANK, Macon, Geo. Cornucopia and anvil.	20 Female seated between figures 2 and 0.
ONE on 1 State Arms.	BK OF NEW JERSEY, New Brunswick, N. J. Portrait of Columbus and words one dollar.	ONE on 1. Shipping, bridge and cars.
Female Portrait with figure 2 and word TWO twice over on top border.	BK of NEW JERSEY, New Brunswick, N. J. State Arms.	Female Portrait with figure 2 and word TWO twice over on top border.

Heavy ornamental engraving with figure 3 the middle and word THREE round the top.	BK. of NEW JERSEY, New Brunswick, N. J. State Arms enclosed in a heavy ornamental border with words THREE DOLLARS round the top.	Heavy ornamental engraving with figure 3 the middle and word THREE round the top
5 Female Bust with sickle and wheat.	A large ornamental V with the word FIVE across it. BK of NEW JERSEY, New Brunswick, N. J Anvil, &c.	Word FIVE letter V and figure 5. State Arms.
Same as on right. Female Portrait.	A large ornamental X with word TEN across it BK. of NEW JERSEY New Brunswick, N. J. Figure of Commerce, Shipping, &c.	Word TEN letter X and figures 10. State Arms.
XX Female bust with sickle and wheat.	A large ornamental 20 with word TWENTY across it. BK. of NEW JERSEY New Brunswick, N. J.	20 State Arms.
50 State Arms.	BK. of NEW JERSEY. A large ornamental letter L with female figure enclosed and word FIFTY across it. New Brunswick, N. J.	50
100 State Arms.	A kneeling Female figure with sickle and sheaf of wheat; farm houses and mowers on right; railroad cars on left, the whole surrounded by a large ornamental letter C. BK. of NEW JERSEY New Brunswick, N. J.	100 C
1 Head of female.	PEOPLE'S BANK, Milwaukee, Wis. Vig. Three horses, two standing in background, one running in foreground, boys and dog in pursuit.	1 State Arms.
2 2	Vig. Dairy maid with pail, two cows, one standing and one lying down; house and cattle in distance. 2 on right. PEOPLE'S BANK, Milwaukee, Wis	2 State Arms. TWO
Female with sickle. 3 3	PEOPLE'S BANK. Milwaukee, Wis. Female with liberty pole and cap in right hand, left resting on shield; eagle at right hand. Locomotive.	3 State Arms THREE

Left	Centre	Right
ONE Medallion Head. ONE	Female figure seated supporting figure 1. Water; mill in distance. Female figure seated supporting figure 1. TRENTON BANKING COMPANY, Trenton, N. J. Stm. Engine and coal cars.	ONE Medallion Head. ONE
TWO A seated female with cornucopia, &c. TWO	Medallion head and 2. Dairy maid and cows; farm house in distance. TRENTON BANKING COMPANY. Trenton, N. J.	TWO Male portrait TWO
3 Three cherubs with bunches of grapes. 3	3 View of Old Trenton Bridge. 3 TRENTON BANKING COMPANY, Trenton, N. J. Row Boat.	3 Three cherubs with bunches of grapes. 3
5 Milk maid and pail.	TRENTON BANKING COMPANY, Trenton, N. J. View of Trenton State House.	5 5 in ornamental engraving.
Ornamental Die. Male portrait Ornamental Die.	10 Figures of Agriculture, Labor and science, with heads of cattle in distance. 10 TRENTON BANKING COMPANY. Trenton, N. J.	Ornamental Die. Male portrait Ornamental Die.
20 Male portrait 20	State Arms of N. J., water mill on left agriculture on right in distance. TRENTON BANKING COMPANY, Trenton, N. J	20 Male portrait 20
50 Male portrait 50	50 Shield with the words "liberty and prosperity" on base; figure of agriculture on left, and Minerva on right, holding a shield with the word FIFTY thereon. 50 TRENTON BANKING COMPANY, Trenton, N. J.	50 Male portrait 50
10 0 Male portrait 100	Medallion Head, State Arms of N. J. Medallion Head. TRENTON BANKING COMPANY. Trenton, N. J.	100 Male portrait 100
1 Cattle and swine.	Farmer ploughing. MORRIS CO. BANK. Morristown, N. J. Man with sheaf of wheat.	1 Female figure with vase of fruit.

Left	Centre	Right
2 Mower.	Cattle and sheep. MORRIS CO. BANK. Morristown, N. J. Dragon and Key.	TWO Female churning.
3 Shield with female figure on each side. THREE	Man topping corn in a circle. MORRIS CO. BANK, Morristown, N. J. Oval die with 3.	3 Female holding scales.
5 Blacksmith.	Shield with horses head. Female, Cap of liberty and pole on left, and one with cornucopia on right. MORRIS CO. BANK, Morristown, N. J. Eagle.	5 Figure of liberty leaning on shield containing the figure 5.
Female holding cap and pole in left and cornucopia in right hand. 10	X Same as 5's. X MORRIS CO. BANK, Morristown, N. J. Sheaf of wheat, bee-hive, &c.	10 Female with right arm on shield, in a circle. 10
Train of cars. Female with right arm on shield surmounted by an eagle, left holding scales. Hogsheads, shipping in distance. 20	XX Same as 5's. XX MORRIS CO. BANK, Morristown, N. J Sheaf of wheat, bee-hive, &c.	A half naked female figure with right arm resting on pillar. 20
1 Female portrait. ONE	UNION BANK, Dover, N. J. 1 Figure of America reclining on shield; goods on left; steamboat on right. 1	Full length female. ONE
Ornamental work. Med. head with word two thereon. Ornamental work.	Small med. head and word 2. Coat of arms of N. J., supported by two female figures; Small med. head and word 2. bridges and cars on left in distance. UNION BANK, Dover, N. J.	TWO Figure of America. TWO
THREE Male portrait. THREE	Female figure apparently flying, typifying plenty; ships in distance. UNION BANK, Dover, N. J.	3 3
FIVE Male portrait FIVE	UNION BANK, Dover, N. J. V State Arms supported by two females; cars in distance on left; steamship on right.	5 FIVE

Left	Centre	Right
TEN Female portrait. X	X Mechanic with hammer, anvil, &c. buildings and cars on right. UNION BANK. Dover, N. J.	X 10
20 Farmer and Plough. XX	XX Large vig. of cars, track, and telegraph wires. UNION BANK Dover, N. J.	20
Full length figure of Justice 50	50 Female figure of science seated, balances, &c.; factory and water-mill in distance. 50 UNION BANK, Dover, N. J. State arms supported by two females.	Full length figure of Justice. 50
Compt's Die. 1	Indian with spear and horse; train of cars. STATE BANK. Madison, Wis.	1 Mechanic seated; buildings in distance.
Compt's Die. 2	STATE BANK, Madison, Wis. Three females, one with lyre; another seated painting, and middle one with tablet.	2 Train of cars.
FIVE Compt's Die. FIVE	STATE BANK, Madison, Wis. View of the Capitol building of Wisconsin.	5 Indian reclining; huts in background.
Cow and calf. 1	Cupid rolling silver dollar; village, cars, and steamboat in distance. State Arms BANK of COMMERCE Milwaukee, Wis.	1 Female head.
2 Bust of female.	State Arms. Two cupids and two silver dollars; landscape and cars in distance. BANK of COMMERCE Milwaukee, Wis.	Horses. 2
5 A large letter V, and five figures around it.	State Arms. Five cupids and five silver dollars; cupids all apparently employed. BANK of COMMERCE Milwaukee, Wis.	5

1
Female kneeling.
State arms, with female on either side; buildings in distance. 1
STATE BANK,
New Brunswick, N. J.
ONE
Female bust.
ONE

Word two in ornamental work.
Female bust.
TWO
2 Same as ones.
STATE BANK,
New Brunswick, N. J.
Train of cars.
2

3
Female bust
Same as Ones.
STATE BANK,
New Brunswick, N. J.
3
Female Indian.
THREE

FIVE
Cattle and farmers in a circle.
5
Portrait of Washington. State Arms supported by two females, the one on left seated. Portrait of Franklin.
STATE BANK,
New Brunswick, N. J.
Railroad cars.
FIVE
Cattle and farmers in a circle.
5

TEN
Venus in a sea shell, and ship in distance.
10
10 Same as Fives. 10
STATE BANK,
New Brunswick, N. J.
Schooner.
TEN
Venus in a sea shell, and ship in distance.
10

20
State arms supported by two females, the one on left seated.
20
20 Male figure seated, with torch in left and scroll in right hand; eagle on left, with miniature of Washington round its neck. 20
STATE BANK,
New Brunswick, N. J.
Figure of Agriculture.
XX
A shield supported by figure of agriculture on right, commerce on left shipping &c., in distance.
20

50
Female Portrait.
FIFTY.
State arms supported by two females seated; train of railroad cars, shipping, &c., in distance.
STATE BANK,
New Brunswick, N. J.
50
A ship and shipping.

100
Stone cutter.
Same as Fifties.
STATE BANK,
New Brunswick, N. J.
Figure of Agriculture.
100
Blacksmith.

On this end the words five hundred dollars and portrait of Washington.
Same as Fifties.
STATE BANK,
New Brunswick, N. J.
500
Female Portrait.

1
Portrait of McDonough
BK. OF VERGENNES
Vergennes, Vt.
Agricultural scene—[illegible] ploughing, cattle, &c., spires in the distance.
1
ONE and 1.

2
Man on horseback, cattle drinking, farm-house, &c.
BK. OF VERGENNES
Vergennes, Vt.
Eagle.
2
2

3
Hunting scene—dogs and birds.
BK. OF VERGENNES
Vergennes, Vt.
Train of cars; horses frightened.
3
3

The word "five," letter "V," and figure "5."
Medallion head.
FIVE
BK. OF VERGENNES
Vergennes, Vt.
Man with rake on his shoulder, little girl running to meet him· female and boy rural scenery, &c.
V
5

X
X
Three females, one with cornucopia, one with wings, and the other with quadrant
BK. OF VERGENNES
Vergennes, Vt.
10

Portrait of Washington
20
XX
BK. OF VERGENNES
Vergennes, Vt.
Steamship.
XX
Horses and colt running.

Three figures two seated; on left, factories, &c., on right, canal boat and lock.
50
L Man ploughing. L
BK. OF VERGENNES
Vergennes, Vt.
Clasped hands.
50
Female with ballances; eagle and shield; tiers of bbls.
50

100
Female soaring in clouds with scroll in left and; an eagle on left.
100
100 Female seated with key in left hand. 100
BK. OF VERGENNES
Vergennes, Vt.
Eagle.
Same as on left of 500.
100

Three females with anchor; party sitting; party standing.
ONE
Train of cars; village in the distance.
MERCHANT'S BK.
Burlington, Vt.
State arms
1
Female with spy-glass, sitting beside a bale; ships in the distance.

Female head.
2
Female sitting by a bale; haying scene, and train of cars in the distance.
MERCHANT'S BK.,
Burlington, Vt.
State Arms.
2
Engine, depot, &c.

Portrait of McDonough.
3
Female seated with a basket containing ears of corn, melons, fruit, &c., by her side; lake, sails, village, mountains, &c., in the distance.
MERCHANT'S BK.,
Burlington, Vt.
State arms.
3
Female portrait.

Portrait of Madison.
5
[First Plate.]
Three females with basket of fruit, trident and spear; ship in background.
MERCHANT'S BK.,
Burlington, Vt.
State Arms.
5
Sailor with spy glass.

FIVE
Female with spear, shield and branch.
FIVE
[Second Plate.]
5 Female with horn of plenty and trident, sitting beside barrels, and sheaf of grain; bridge, cars, village and ship in the distance.
MERCHANT'S BK.,
Burlington, Vt.
State Arms.
5
Portrait of Harrison.

TEN
Female with spear, standing beside a globe.
10 Female, globe, book; factory in the background.
MERCHANT'S BK.,
Burlington, Vt.
State Arms.
10
Portrait of Franklin.
TEN

20
Female seated with spear, standing beside a [illegible]
Female seated between figures 2 and 0.
MERCHANT'S BK.,
Burlington, Vt.
XX
20
Small figure of a female
20

50
Female with spear and shield.
Male and female seated; horn of plenty.
MERCHANT'S BK.,
Burlington, Vt.
50
50
Cupid in a sail boat.
50

100
Male seated.
Eagle upon a branch; bridge, and train of cars passing over it.
MERCHANT'S BK.,
Burlington, Vt
C C
100
100
Female with rake, and horn of plenty.

B'K of WINTHROP,
Winthrop, Me.
This Bank uses the old Perkin's Stereotype plate, which has the denomination printed in fine letters all over the bill.

1 — BANK OF RACINE, Racine, Wis. — 1
Country road, with oxen load of hay &c, — Vig. Man watering horse; female feeding pigs; house &c., in distance. — State arms.

State Arms. — Title of Bank. — 5
Indian with gun, &c. — Vig. Man, woman, and child. — Female with bundle of straw on her back.

ONE — State arms. RACINE CO. BANK. Racine, Wis. — 1
Goddess of liberty with spear in left hand. — Portrait of Washington cupid on either side. — Female child with basket.

2 — Vig. Locomotive and train of cars; steamboat on right; city in distance on left. — 2
Female Portrait. 2 — BANK OF RACINE, Racine, Wis — State arms.

1 — STATE BANK OF WISCONSIN, Milwaukee, Wis. — 1
Portrait of Webster. — Vig. Farming scene at noon. — State Arms.

TWO — State arms. RACINE CO. BANK, Racine, Wis. — 2
Little girl. 2 — Two females and male reclining, the female on right has sickle in right hand and sheaf of wheat in left; anvil, sledge, &c.; train of cars on left, vessel on right. Clasped hands. — TWO

3 — BANK OF RACINE, Racine, Wis. — 3
Three cupids encircled with large figure 3 — Vig. Man watering horse; dogs, pigs, child, &c. — State arms

2 — STATE BANK OF WISCONSIN, Milwaukee, Wis. — 2
Female Portrait. — Vig. Female reclining on bale of goods, barrels, &c., ship on right; factory, &c., on left. — State Arms.

3 — State arms. RACINE CO. BANK. Racine, Wis. — 3
Sailor with left hand on rudder block. — Female seated, with blacksmith on right and sailor on left, in distance on left ship; city on right.

5 — Vig. Harvest scene; wagon, loading grain; female with child; men, basket, pitchers. &c., — State Arms. 5
Washington. FIVE — BANK OF RACINE, Racine, Wis. — Male portrait FIVE

5 — Vig. Three females in water, cupid, &c. — Male Portrait. 5
5 — STATE BANK OF WISCONSIN, Milwaukee, Wis. — State Arms.

FIVE — RACINE CO. BANK, Racine, Wis. — FI 5 VE
State arms. 5 — FI 5 VE. Three cows standing in water, train of cars, farm house, &c. — Blacksmith, sailor and farmer.

1 — Vig. Three females in water; Cupid, &c. — 1
Man leaning against a tree with a drum; man sitting on a log; others in background. — BK. OF MILWAUKEE, Milwaukee, Wis. — State arms.

10 — Vig. Land and water scene, train of cars running to the left, one crossing bridge in distance. — 10
Male portrait — STATE BANK OF WISCONSIN, Milwaukee, Wis. — State Arms.

Two females standing. — Cupid rolling silver dollar on railroad track, cars, city, &c. in distance. — 1
1 — WEST RIVER B'K. Jama'ca, Vt. — Female seated clasping figure 1 in her arms.

2 — Three females—one with balances; two ships on right, &c. — 2
Man with a gun; trees, dog, &c. — BK. OF MILWAUKEE, Milwaukee, Wis. — State arms.

1 — Horses and colt; hills and houses in distance. — 1
Bust of female. — CITY BANK Of Racine, Wis. — ONE State arms.

Two men bearing Goddess. — Two Cupids and two silver dollars; cars cattle, &c. in distance. — 2
2 — WEST RIVER B'K, Jamaica, Vt. Cow and calf. — Female churning.

5 — Vig. Children in bed asleep; Santa Claus with toys on his back. Large figure 5 encircled with title of the Bank. — 5
State arms. — Female portrait.

2 — CITY BANK Of Racine, Wis. — 2
State arms. Deer by the brink of a lake. — Pioneer with gun and dog; tree behind him. — Girl seated with sickle and sheaf of wheat.

Female sitting holding scales; sheaf of grain. — Three cupids and three silver dollars. — 3
3 — WEST RIVER B'K, Jamaica, Vt. Man ploughing. — State arms. THREE

State Arms. Male standing with American flag, female sitting at his feet anchor, bale, barrels, &c. — WISCONSIN MARINE AND FIRE INSURANCE CO. Milwaukee, Wis. Vig. Female sitting, resting right arm on anchor; ships on right and left. — 2 Female Portrait.

THREE State arms. Bust of female. — CITY BANK Of Racine, Wis. Man preaching to Indians. — 3 Female with a sheaf of wheat over her shoulder.

Female head. V — Five cupids and five silver dollars. WEST RIVER B'K. Jamaica, Vt. — 5 Sailor and Indian seated; five on shield between them.

State Arms. Three female figures reclining each side the [illegible] THREE — Title of Bank. Vig. St. George on horse, and the dragon. — 3 Female Portrait.

Indian seated on a rock, gun by his side. State arms. — Train of cars, men, women and children. CITY BANK Of Racine, Wis. — 5 Boy gathering corn.

X Goddess erect holding trumpet. Female seated holding liberty cap; eagle, &c. — Goddess and cherub holding portrait of Washington between them. WEST RIVER B'K, Jamaica, Vt. — 10 Stonecutter at work.

1 Mechanic and female. ONE	Cattle and drovers. MOUSUM RIVER BANK, Sandford. Me.	1 Train of cars.	Compt's die. Female with flowers	BADGER STATE BK., Janesville, Wis. Vig. Traveller and man watering horse; child and dog.	3 Flower girl.	ONE Milkmaid. ONE	[Old Plate.] 1 Long ornamental figure 1 enclosing a full length Female figure. FARMERS and MECHANICS BANK. Rahway, N. J.	View of Town. 1 ONE
2 Female seated engaged in warping.	Two females at work at looms in factory. MOUSUM RIVER BANK. Sandford, Me. Eagle	2 Bust of child.	Compt's die. Indian with gun.	BADGER STATE BK., Train of cars. Bee-hive.	5 Female with grain over her shoulder.	ONE Figure of Liberty leaning on an ornamental figure 1, with word ONE in center.	[New Plate.] 1 Long ornamental figure 1 enclosing a full length female figure. FARMERS and MECHANICS BANK. Rahway, N. J.	Banking House. 1
5 Female seated, cows and buildings in background.	Woodcutters, one seated on a stump, and one felling a tree; team and driver in background. MOUSUM RIVER BANK, Sandford. Me. State Arms	5 Portrait of female.	1 Sailor leaning on a capstan, bale and hogshead alongside ship in background.	Female leaning upon a shield containing an anchor, two vessels on each side in the background. JANESVILLE CITY BANK, Janesville, Wis.	1 State arms. ONE	Milkmaid and cows. 2	[Old Plate.] Ornamental figure 1 enclosing a full length female figure. FARMERS and MECHANICS BANK, Rahway, N. J.	2 Female Head.
10 Anchor, cask, boxes, &c.; masts of ship in background.	Train of cars. MOUSUM RIVER BANK, Sandford, Me. State Arms.	10 Female reaper seated.	2 2	JANESVILLE CITY BANK, Janesville, Wis. Female on each side of a shield containing a figure 2, horn of plenty scattering fruit between them; ship on right and locomotive on left. Female head.	2 State arms. 2	TWO Female Portrait. TWO	[New Plate.] 2 Ornamental figure 2 enclosing a full length female figure. FARMERS and MECHANICS BANK, Rahway. N. J.	Banking House. 2
20 Indian leaning against rock; has a rifle.	Female seated, bale of goods, cask, wheel, &c. factories in background. MOUSUM RIVER BANK, Sandford, Me.	20 Equestrian statue of Washington.	5	Indian queen resting against a globe, flags, shield, with stars and stripes; American eagle resting with outstretched wings upon the globe; horn of plenty, &c.; State Arms on right JANESVILLE CITY BANK, Janesville. Wis.	5 Miniature of female. FIVE	THREE Female Portrait, THREE	3 Ornamental figure 3 enclosing a full length figure, the word THREE at top and small figure 3 at bottom. FARMERS and MECHANICS BANK, Rahway. N. J.	Banking House. 3
L 50	Ships sailing; view of town on left in distance. MOUSUM RIVER BANK, Sandford, Me.	50 Female reclining; ships in distance.	ONE Compt's die.	DANE CO. BANK, Madison, Wis. Female reclining upon a rock viewing lake with city on opposite side; cars passing around lake shore. 1	1 ONE	Banking House. 5	Ornamental figure 5 enclosing a full length figure of Washington. FARMERS and MECHANICS BANK, Rahway, N. J	FIVE 5 Male and female supporting a small ornamental 5.
C Portrait of Webster.	Loose horses, galloping and prancing; farm houses in distance. MOUSUM RIVER BANK, Sandford. Me.	100 Blacksmith, sledge, anvil and forge.	TWO Compt's die.	DANE CO. BANK, Madison, Wis. Two females; cars on the right and steamboat on left in the background. Safe.	TWO 2	Oval Die, Female. Oval Die.	10 Two females supporting a shield. FARMERS and MECHANICS BANK. Rahway, N. J. Railroad cars.	TEN Female resting on pillar and shield. TEN
Compt's die. Female with sickle and grain.	BADGER STATE BK., Janesville, Wis. Vig. Male and female; child on man's shoulder.	1 Indian sitting.	3 Compt's die.	DANE CO. BANK, Madison, Wis. Three females joining hands. 3	3	20 Female Portrait. 20	20 Male figure resting on book with torch in hand; eagle &c. FARMERS and MECHANICS BANK, Rahway, N. J. A	20 Female Portrait. 20
Compt's die. Horse frightened by locomotive.	BADGER STATE BK., Janesville, Wis. Haying scene.	2 Dog and safe.	FI5VE Compt's die.	Indian, squaw and child; female and child; between them a shield with word five thereon. DANE CO. BANK. Madison, Wis. Eagle.	5 Med. head.	50 Farmer with axe and sickle. 50	50 Country scene, 50 beehive, plough sheaf of wheat &c. FARMERS and MECHANICS BANK. Rahway, N. J.	50 Female figure; plow, sheaf of wheat. 50

Left end	Centre	Right end
C Indian Female C	100 Mail fe-ure, leaning on an ox; plow, cattle, &c. 100 FARMERS and MECHANICS BANK, Rahway, N. J. Ship.	Figure of Justice 100
50 Female Portrait.	Female reclining with liberty cap and pole; eagle on right; globe on left; shipping in distance. STATE BANK, Elizabethtown, N. J. Sheaf of wheat and plow.	FIFTY Full length female figure leaning on anchor; ships in distance.
State arms. TWO 2	BANK OF GALENA, Galena, Ill. Locomotive and cars.	2 Female portrait.
500 Female Portrait. 500	500 Two females supporting shield; shipping on left and building on right. FARMERS and MECHANICS BANK, Rahway, N. J. Head of Female.	500 Woman churning; country scene in distance.
100 Portrait of Male. 100	Female reclining on bales and other articles of commerce; ship on left and steamer on right in distance. 100 STATE BANK, Elizabethtown, N. J. Dog.	Full length figure of Liberty. 100
3 Cattle, drovers, load of hay, &c.	Female. 3 Man with sickle and bundle of grain. BANK OF GALENA, Galena, Ill.	3 State arms.
ONE Portrait of Male. ONE	Medallion head. Shield with female figure on either side, the one holding liberty cap and pole, the other a cornucopia. Medallion head. STATE BANK, Elizabethtown, N. J.	ONE Portrait of Male. ONE
500 Male Portrait	Shield supported by two females, the one on right holding liberty cap and pole, one on left ears of corn; steamship and railroad cars on right and factory on left. STATE BANK, Elizabethtown, N. J. Female.	500
5 Female portrait.	Female with arm resting on bale; right of vignette, load of hay. State arms. BANK OF GALENA, Galena, Ill.	5 Portrait of Webster.
2 Medallion Head. 2	Male Portrait. Shield with Female figure on either side, the one on right holding a sickle. Male Portrait. STATE BANK, Elizabethtown, N. J.	TWO
1	BANK OF NAPERVILLE, Naperville, Ill. Vig. A rafting scene with a hut, man, boy woman and child.	Female holding the figure one. Auditor's die. ONE
1 Auditor's die. ONE	Man on horseback and drove of cattle and sheep going towards the left. 1 MERCHANTS' AND DROVERS' BANK, Joliet, Ill. Two sheep.	Female with spear and shield supporting a figure 1. ONE
3 Medallion Head. 3	Male Portrait. Shipping, steamer, buildings in distance. Male Portrait. STATE BANK, Elizabethtown, N. J.	3 Medallion Head. 3
2 Hunter with gun and dog.	Cattle, sheep, &c., farmer and drover. BANK OF NAPERVILLE, Naperville, Ill. Peacock.	2 TWO Auditor's die.
2 Auditor's die. TWO	Farmers at lunch; female with basket seated; load of hay and farm houses in distance. MERCHANTS' AND DROVERS' BANK, Joliet, Ill. Two sheep.	2 Two men and drove of cattle. TWO
Circular Die. Female Portrait. Circular Die.	[Old Plate.] 5 Two females supporting an ornamental figure 5, and three boys representing Cupid, Mercury and Love. 5 STATE BANK, Elizabethtown, N. J.	Circular Die. Female Portrait. Circular Die.
1 State arms.	Vig. Female sitting and supporting figure 1; cars to the right and steamboat to the left. BANK OF PERU, Peru, Ill. Shield with bale of goods and anvil.	1 Head of Jackson.
THREE Auditors die. Figure three supported by a sailor, farmer and mechanic.	3 Man and boys with dog, washing sheep. MERCHANTS' AND DROVERS' BANK, Joliet, Ill. Ox.	3 Spread eagle, shield and bale. THREE
5 Female Portrait.	[New Plate.] Neptune driving sea-horses in a shell car with Female seated therein; mermaid &c. in the water; steamer in distance. STATE BANK, Elizabethtown, N. J. 5 and Cupid.	5 Portrait of Girl.
TWO Full length Indian, with bow and arrows in his hand.	State arms. Two females sitting with figure 2 between them. BANK OF PERU, Peru, Ill. Steamboat.	2 Head of Webster.
5 Large V supported by three men and two females.	Auditor's die. Female and shield with steamboat on left, and locomotive and cars on the right. MERCHANTS' AND DROVERS' BANK, Joliet, Ill. Ox.	5 Portrait of Washington. FIVE
Circular Die. Female Portrait. Circular Die.	10 Two females supporting shield; steamer on right and church on left. 10 STATE BANK, Elizabethtown, N. J. 10.	Oval Die. Female Portrait. Oval Die.
Head of Lewis Cass. State arms.	3 Man with rake, and woman with distaff, shield between them. BANK OF PERU, Peru, Ill. Two sheep.	THREE Full length female figure flowers and anchor in her hands.
5 Pig pen, pigs and fowls.	AM. EXCHANGE BK Raleigh, Ills. Spread eagle and shield; lighthouse and ships in distance on right; man plowing and house on left.	5 Auditor's die
20 Shield and eagle with outstretched wings. 20	Female figure reclining; scene representing agriculture on right; railroad cars and shipping on left. STATE BANK, Elizabethtown, N. J. Mechanic and anvil.	20 Female Portrait.
1 Portrait of Franklin.	BANK OF GALENA, Galena, Ill. Two drovers with cattle and hogs.	1 State arms.
Man on horse, and man with hog.	Men at work—harvesting, cradling, gathering and loading wagon with sheafs. AM. EXCHANGE BK Raleigh, Ills.	10 Auditor's die

Female bust | BANK OF WATERTOWN, Watertown, Wis. | 1
1 | Vig. Female reclining in a sea shell; water scene. | Compt's die

TWO | BANK OF WATERTOWN, Watertown, Wis. | 2
Vig. Indian and female reclining on globe, spread eagle between them.
Female figure erect. | 2 | Compt's die.

3 | Vig. Man on horseback; boys, sheep, and load of hay in distance. | 3
BANK OF WATERTOWN, Watertown, Wis.
Compt's die. | Three Cherubs.

5 | Vig. Two farmers inspecting drove of cattle. | Female bust. | 5
BANK OF WATERTOWN, Watertown, Wis.
5 | Compt's die

1 | Female sitting down; cars and load of hay in background. | 1
ONE | FARMERS' & MILLERS' BANK, Milwaukee, Wis.
Head of Henry Clay. | Eagle. | State Arms.

Portrait of female. | Two men reposing under a tree; hay-field in the background. | 2
FARMERS' & MILLERS' BANK, Milwaukee, Wis.
2 | State Arms.

5 | FARMERS' & MILLERS' BANK, Milwaukee, Wis. | 5
Locomotive.
Female sitting down by a shield; State House in background.
5 | State Arms.

ONE | Harvest scene; laborers (with woman and children) reposing; dog in front; load of grain and horses in distance. | 1 | ONE
Drovers, oxen, and sheep. | Ox.
ONE | McLEAN CO. BANK, Bloomington, Ill. | Auditor's die.
Hog.

2 | Drove of cattle and sheep; man on horseback. | TWO
Spread eagle and shield. | McLEAN CO. BANK, Bloomington, Ill.
Auditor's die | Pig. | Female figure, with small mirror

Female sitting with scales and sheaf of wheat. | 1 | Ploughman, horses, &c. | 1
CENTRAL BANK, Peoria, Ill.
Auditor's die | Sheaf of grain and plough | Female with liberty cap.

Auditor's die | Railroad train. | 3 | Female.
3 | CENTRAL BANK, Peoria, Ill.
THREE | Bale of goods, &c. | THREE

Auditor's die | Female, hand resting on portrait of Washington; spread eagle resting on shield. | FIVE
V with five human heads. | CENTRAL BANK, Peoria, Ill. | Figure 5 with five human heads.
Dog.

State arms. | Female seated, resting arm on bale of goods and hand on cornucopia; vessels on left, and cars in distance. | 1
BANK OF ELGIN, Elgin, Ill.
ONE | 1 | Portrait.

TWO | Plough boy unhitching his team from plough; river, steamboat, &c. in distance | 2
BANK OF ELGIN, Elgin, Ill. | State arms.
Portrait of Washington. | Cornucopia, &c. | TWO

5 | State arms. Train of cars, and telegraph poles; city and buildings in background. | 5
BANK OF ELGIN, Elgin, Ill.
Portrait. | Anchor. | 5

1 | Shipping, ships, steamboat, pilot boat and city. | 1
EXCHANGE BANK OF DARLING & CO., Fond du Lac, Wis. | Compt's die.
Farmer seated; scythe hanging on limb of tree. | Capital $50,000. | ONE

2 | Western steamboat; bluffs, &c. | 2
Title of Bank.
Compt's die. | Capital $50,000. | Squaw.

Hunter load ing gun; deer at his feet. | Indian portrait; female instructing children on right; house in distance; on left squaw and papoose | 3
Title of Bank.
THREE | Capital $50,000. | Compt's die.

Compt's die. | Washing sheep; house in distance. | 100
BANK OF VERNON, Vernon, N. Y.
Cattle. | Female shearing.

1 | Vig. Harvest scene; cradlers, &c. | 1
Compt's die. | FARMERS' AND TRADERS' BANK, Charlestown, Ill | Washington
ONE | Two sheep. | ONE

2 | Sailor sitting with back to barrels; ship on right. | 2
Compt's die. | FARMERS' AND TRADERS' BANK, Charlestown, Ill. | Frank Pierce
TWO | Dog. | TWO

3 | Locomotive and train of cars. | 3
Compt's die. | FARMERS' AND TRADERS' BANK, Charlestown, Ill. | Clay.
THREE | Shield with rising sun. | THREE

5 | Two females, one crowning bust of Washington with laurel wreath. | 5
FARMERS' AND TRADERS' BANK, Charlestown, Ill. | Webster.
Compt's die. | Barrels and bales of goods. | FIVE

State Arms. | 1 | Vig. Female sitting; barrels, &c.; ship on right; factory, canal, cars, &c., on left. | Figure 1, with one running across it.
Male sitting resting right arm on figure 1. | CHICAGO BANK, Chicago, Ills. | Female sitting with pole, liberty cap, &c.

State Arms. | 2 | Vig. Indian reclining, with bow and arrow, quiver, &c.; deers in water, on right; eagle flying, &c. | Steamship.
Two mermaid figures. | 2
Steamship. | CHICAGO BANK, Chicago, Ills. | Ships, &c.

Deer. | State Arms. | Vig. Spread eagle, shield, &c.; steamship on right; ship on left. | 3
3 | CHICAGO BANK, Chicago, Ills.
Buffalo. | Farming implements. | Female sitting, &c.

5 | Female Portrait | State Arms | Female portrait. | 5
CHICAGO BANK, Chicago, Ills.
Spread eagle, shield, &c. | Barrell, bale, &c. | Female.

Left end	Centre	Right end
Female reclining, with sickle in right hand State Arms.	2 BANK OF AMERICA, Chicago. Ills. St. George and the Dragon.	2 Female Portrait.
American eagle, two mermaids. Steamship.	[New Plate.] 1 Vig. Train of cars building, &c. MARINE BANK, Chicago. Ill. Barrel, bale, &c.	Figure 1, with one running across it.
XX Female erect with shield and spear.	Female seated by shield, sheafs, &c.; lighthouse and ships in distance. WEST RIVER BANK Jamaica, Vt. TWENTY	20 Female representing Agriculture.
Female sitting, with sickle in right hand State Arms.	3 BANK OF AMERICA, Chicago. Ills. Vig. Female sitting, with eagle, &c.	3 Female Portrait.
Male with American flag; female, bale, anchor, &c.	MARINE BANK, Chicago. Ill. Vig. Ships at sea.	2 State arms.
Justice. FIFTY	Female and eagle soaring. WEST RIVER BANK Jamaica, Vt. FIFTY	50 Jackson.
Compt's. Die. Harvestman, sharpening cradle.	1 Indian and white man, with upright shield between. JEFFERSON COUNTY BANK, Watertown, Wis. Bull	1 Blacksmith.
3 Female standing inside of circle; shield, &c.	American eagle. Vig. Neptune riding in car, sea nymphs, &c. MARINE BANK, Chicago, Ill. Safe.	3 Female portrait. THREE
Female giving eagle drink. 1	Cherub rolling silver dollar; city, cars, bridge and train of cars in distance. ADAMS BANK, North Adams. Mass.	1 Indian seated with fig. 1.
THREE Indian warrior.	Compt's. Die. American officers; Indian Chiefs in council. JEFFERSON COUNTY BANK, Watertown, Wis. Female.	3 Indian mother and child sitting.
Three female figures, &c. FIVE	[Old Plate.] Vig. Steamship, ships, &c. at sea. MARINE BANK, Chicago, Ill.	5 State arms.
Two females 2	Two cherubs and two silver dollars; cars in distance. ADAMS BANK, North Adams, Mass.	2 Sailor and Indian on either side of TWO on shield.
5 Large V., with group of male and female figures.	Compt's. Die. Locomotive and train of cars. JEFFERSON COUNTY BANK, Watertown, Wis. Cornucopia	5 Washington. FIVE
FIVE Indian standing with spear, &c.	[New Plate.] American eagle. Vig. Two females standing, male in centre barrel, bale, &c.; ship on right; sheaf of wheat, &c. on left. MARINE BANK, Chicago, Ill. Dog.	FIVE Five female figures encircled with large figure 5
100 Man seated.	Eagle on tree: canal and cars in distance. MAHAIWE BANK, Gt. Barrington, Mass. 100	100 Female with rake.
1	Vig. Indian on horseback, in chase of Buffaloes. Portrait of Jenny Lind. STOCK SECURITY BANK, Danville, Ills.	ONE Indian with bow; female with sickle.
American eagle. Two mermaids. Steamship.	10 Vig. Steamship, ships, &c. at sea. MARINE BANK, Chicago, Is. Female sitting.	10 Sailor standing, barrels, &c.
1 Auditor's die	Blacksmith shoeing horse; one man sitting and one standing. STATE BANK OF ILLINOIS, Shawneetown, Ill.	1 Train of cars coming down grade.
2 Female instructing children, by use of globe.	STOCK SECURITY BANK, Danville, Ills. Vig. Cattle; man ploughing, and two men in distance. Anvil.	2 Naked figure, sitting with child.
1 ONE	BANK of ELKHART. Elkhart, Ind. Portrait of Washington, and words "one dollar" at top.	1 ONE
2 Auditor's die TWO	STATE BANK OF ILLINOIS. Shawneetown, Is. Cattle and sheep; three men, one on foot and one on horseback.	2 Portrait of lady.
FIVE Female with bucket in hand.	STOCK SECURITY BANK, Danville, Ills. Horses frightened at Locomotive. Female bathing.	5 Locomotive.
5 FIVE	BANK of ELKHART, Elkhart, Ind. Female bust. Duck.	5 FIVE
3 Plank road scene.	Cattle and sheep; one cow in water; church in distance on right. Auditor's die. STATE BANK OF ILLINOIS, Shawneetown, Is.	3 Blacksmith.
ONE Man standing with American flag; barrel, bale, &c.	[Old Plate.] Vig. Ships at dock, warehouse, &c. MARINE BANK, Chicago, Ill. Steamboat.	1 State arms.
D Female and horse.	ROCKLAND BANK, Roxbury, Mass. 500 Female reclining, eagle, globe; ship and steamship in distance.	500 500
Auditor's die Portrait of S. A. Douglass.	STATE BANK OF ILLINOIS, Shawneetown, Is. English horse market; train of cars and church steeple in distance.	5

1 · Portrait of Washington. | BANK of NORTHERN ILLINOIS, Waukegan, Ill. Three horses, with farm-house and grounds in background. | 1 · Compt's die.	V · 5 | Indian; two Squaws and papoose in canoe. SALEM BANK, Ind. | 5 · State Arms.	Auditors' die | 1 BANK OF PIKE CO., Griggsville, Ills. Train of cars; bills and another train in distance. 1 | 1
Compt's die. · TWO | BANK of NORTHERN ILLINOIS, Waukegan, Is. Four sea nymphs bathing. | 2 · Portrait of female.	ONE · Female with bow and arrow, | Man chopping wood, one gold dollar leaning against a stump; horse and wagon in the distance. CENTRAL BANK, Indianapolis, Ind. | 1	2 | Hunter shooting a deer; dog, trees and stream of water. 2 BANK OF PIKE CO., Griggsville, Ills. | 2 on TWO. · Auditor's die
1 · head of Washington. · ONE | Indian reclining on left arm; another Indian coming out of a copse. SOUTHERN BANK, Terre Haute, Ind. Secured, &c. | 1 · State Arms. · ONE	3 | Three men, with sythe sledge, and spy glass. Three one dollar gold pieces to correspond with denom. Ships, barrels, boxes, &c., in distance. 3 CENTRAL BANK, Indianapolis, Ind. | 3 · Female.	THREE · Washington · DOLLARS · THREE | 3 Female portrait. BANK OF PIKE CO., Griggsville, Ills. | 3 · Auditors' die
2 · head of Clay. · TWO | Train of cars; depot, steamboat, &c., in distance. SOUTHERN BANK, Terre Haute, Ind. Secured, &c. | 2 · State Arms. · TWO	5 | Five persons and five one dollar gold pieces; cars in the distance. V and female with sheaf of wheat. CENTRAL BANK, Indianapolis, Ind. FIVE |	5 · Auditor's die | 5 5 Indian head. BANK OF PIKE CO., Griggsville, Ills. | 5 · Two cherubs soaring with distaff and sheaf.
Large figure 5; in back ground, train of cars, water fall, Indian, &c · FIVE | Portrait of Webster; Cupid on either side; flowers and scroll. SOUTHERN BANK, Terre Haute, Ind. Secured, &c | FI 5 VE · State Arms · FIVE	X | Female seated between figures 1 and 0, horn of plenty in right hand, key in left resting on the 0. X CENTRAL BANK, Indianapolis, Ind. | 10 · Portrait. · TEN	10 · Head of Liberty surrounded by stars. | Farmer and mechanic. 10 BANK OF PIKE CO., Griggsville, Ills. | 10 · Auditor's die
State Arms. · Female X · TEN | SOUTHERN BANK, Terre Haute, Ind. Word ten, and figures 10, across. Traveler on horse, watering him at trough; herdsman, sheep, cows &c. Secured, &c. | 10 · Indian leaning on a tree, ship in distance.	1 · ONE | Cupid and gold dollar; train of cars, steamboat and village in the back ground. BANK OF MOUNT VERNON, Mount Vernon, Ind., Man mowing. | A large figure 1 and goddess of Liberty.	X · Compt's die. | View of church, buildings and trees. DANE CO. BANK, Madison, Wis. | 10 · Med. head.
1 · State Arms. | SALEM BANK, Ind. Female portrait in circle, with words "one dollar" at top. | 1 · Female with sheaf of wheat; ships in distance.	THREE · Portrait of Henry Clay. | Three females and figure 3. BANK OF MOUNT VERNON, Mount Vernon, Ind., Man plowing. | A large figure three with female small 3 and word Three.	TWENTY · Female with shield. · Wisconsin. | DANE CO. BANK, Madison, Wis. 2 Female portrait. 0 | TWENTY · Compt's die.
Portrait of a girl; words two dollars on the upper margin of the circle. · 2 | SALEM BANK, Ind. Female with sheaf of wheat on her shoulder. | Same as on left.	State Arms · Letter V surrounded by five human figures. | Large 5 surrounded by five human figures; ships and factory in distance. BANK OF MOUNT VERNON. Mount Vernon, Ind., 5 | Large 5, Washington and word Five thereon	5 · Cars, bridge falls and houses. | Steamboat St. Croix. ST. CROIX RIVER BANK, Grand Rapids Wis. Indian. | 5 · Compt's die.
5 · V 5 V | Female and two cows; in the distance, fence and country scene. SALEM BANK, Ind. Female bathing. | 5 · State Arms.	State Arms · Portrait of Martha Washington, · TEN | BANK OF MOUNT VERNON, Mount Vernon. Ind. TEN X DOLLARS | 10 · Portrait of Washington. · TEN	Liberty and X. | Train of cars and canal boat; bills, bridge and city in distance. ST. CROIX RIVER BANK, Wis. Spread eagle. | 10 · Compt's die.

Left end	Centre	Right end
5 FIVE	Two negroes and a white man at work, pressing cotton with machinery. RIVER BANK, Memphis, Tenn.	5 on FIVE.
10	Hunter shooting a deer; dog, trees and stream of water. 10 RIVER BANK, Memphis, Tenn.	X TEN
20 Liberty surrounded by stars.	RIVER BANK, Memphis, Tenn. Figs. 20 and words Twenty Dollars on three red dies.	20 Two cherubs soaring with distaff and sheaf.
5 State arms. 5	BK. OF ROCKVILLE, Rockville, Ind. Five cupids and five silver dollars. Loading hay.	5 Female seated with right elbow on globe, in her lap a copy of the Declaration of Independence.
10 State arms. 10	BK. OF ROCKVILLE, Rockville, Ind. Female seated with right hand extended towards a group of nine children. Man plowing with two horses.	10 10
1 Plank road, with cattle, &c.	Farm scene; horses, &c., feeding. UNION PLANK ROAD COMPANY, Michigan City, Ind. Steamboat.	1 Female seated with telescope in hand; vessel in distance.
2 Plank road with cattle, &c.	Train of cars. UNION PLANK ROAD COMPANY, Michigan City, Ind. Sheaf of grain plow, &c.	2 Female with tablet surrounded by mechanical implements
Sailor leaning on bales, hogshead &c. with Am. flag in right hand quadrant at foot. FIVE	Female reclining on bales, &c.; shipping in distance. UNION PLANK ROAD COMPANY, Michigan City, Ind. Eagle on limb.	5 Large figure 5 with female seated in it.
Auditor's die	Female farm, house, cattle, &c. 1 CITY BANK, Chicago, Ill.	1 Indian seated.
Mercury holding bag of coin and wand. TWO	Three females bat hing and cupid. CITY BANK, Chicago, Ill.	2 Auditor's die
Female.	3 CITY BANK, Chicago, Ill. 3 Female riding on the water in a shell; ships, &c. 3 Auditor's die. 3	Female
5 Auditor's die	CITY BANK, Chicago, Ill. Ocean scene; steamer and four ships.	5 Female supporting an ornamental figure 5.
1 Compt's die. ONE	Farming scene. INDIANA STOCK BANK, Laporte, Ind. Sheaf of grain and plow.	One and figure 1 across. Female and figure 1.
2 Compt's die. TWO	Farming scene; gathering corn. INDIANA STOCK BANK, Laporte, Ind. Barrels, &c.	2 Two females embracing each other.
5 Compt's die. FIVE	Farming scene; making hay. INDIANA STOCK BANK, Laporte, Ind. Dog.	FIVE Five females and 5.
10 Compt's die. TEN	Female reclining on iron chest; train of cars, cattle, &c. INDIANA STOCK BANK, Laporte, Ind. Steamboat.	10 Indian girl with bow and spear.
1 Plank Road scene, horses cattle men, and load of hay.	Two horses and Man; locomotive and train of cars in the distance. BANK OF INDIANA, Mich. City, Ind. Countersigned numbered and registered.	1 State Arms.
2 Same as on Ones.	Four cows, three standing up and one laying down, also three sheep, two laying down and one standing up. BANK OF INDIANA, Mich City, Ind. Same as the Ones.	2 State Arms.
Three females, anchor, &c. FIVE	One female seated, two cows; house and trees in the distance. BANK OF INDIANA, Mich. City, Ind. Same as Ones.	5 State Arms.
1 ONE Portrait of Thos. Jefferson.	Indian, wife and child on left of American shield, American woman, three children and globe on right. FAYETTE CO. BANK, Connersville, Ind. Locomotive and two cars.	1 Man on horse driving cattle and sheep. ONE
TWO 2 Portrait of Washington.	Harvest scene, 2 cradlers, 3 gathering the grain. 2 horses and wagon. FAYETTE CO. BANK, Connersville Ind. Eagle with wings extended	2 Portrait of Franklin.
3 Head of Daniel Webster. THREE	Head of Washington and eagle; three females in a sitting position. FAYETTE CO. BANK, Connersville, Ind. 2 Farmers.	3 Head of John Adams.
Female Portrait. 5	Cattle; farmer plowing in the distance with 2 cattle and 1 horse. FAYETTE CO. BANK, Connersville, Ind. Female reclining on an anchor.	5 Portrait of Washington. FIVE
10 Portrait of Martha Washington. TEN	Locomotive with train cars; houses behind. FAYETTE CO. BANK, Connersville, Ind. Mechanics Arms.	X Female with sickle, ocean scene behind. 10
20 Portrait of Gen. Pierce	View of the Court House. FAYETTE CO. BANK, Connersville, Ind. Female Portrait	XX Two female Indians, one reclining with sheaf of wheat and sickle.
10 Portrait of Hancock. TEN	BANK OF MONTICELLO, Monticello, Ind. Female reclining and soaring on eagle. Loading grain on wagon	10 Female Portrait.
5 Bust of a Female. FIVE	INTERIOR BANK, Griffin, Geo. Farm scene, plowman, &c. on the right in distance train of cars, on left, house, etc.	FIVE Female feeding horse.

ONE 1 Farmer plowing. ONE	Two females seated, one with sickle; on right cows, on left a building with large steeple. BK. OF POULTNEY, West Poultney, Vt. Agricultural Implements.	1 ONE Female seated with tub at her feet. ONE
TWO 2 Farmer barefooted with sheaf of wheat on left shoulder. TWO	Two females, one seated the other erect, the one erect has pail in her arms; on right outhouse and female milking cow; on right farm house and trees. BK. OF POULTNEY, West Poultney, Vt. Horse.	2 TWO Female erect with two pails at her feet. TWO
V 5 Female seated within large letter V FIVE	Two females on either side of a frame, on which is tree, cow, &c., surmounted by head of reindeer. At bottom words "Vermont, Freedom and Unity." BK. OF POULTNEY, West Poultney, Vt. Dog's Head.	5 V Female seated within large figure 5 FIVE
TEN Female with scroll on which is figure 10. TEN	[Old Plate.] X Spread eagle and shield; agricultural implements and products. X BK. OF POULTNEY, West Poultney, Vt. Female Head.	10 Washington TEN
Male Portrait with spectacles on.	[New Plate] Train of cars; village in distance. Portrait of female. BK. OF POULTNEY, West Poultney, Vt. Frame—with cow, tree and surmounted by a deer's head.	10 Indian female seated with pole and cap and shield.
20 Male with sledge on right shoulder; cog wheel, anvil, &c.	BK. OF POULTNEY, West Poultney, Vt. Train of cars; village in distance. Dog's Head.	20 Factory buildings, men, horse and wagon, &c.
ONE Horse and cart, man on horse, male and female slave.	MECHANICS' SAVINGS' BANK, Savannah, Geo. One dollar crossing ornamental die.	1 Blacksmith with hammer on his shoulder, anvil, &c.
TWO Female with liberty pole and cap, cask and vessel.	MECHANICS' SAVINGS' BANK, Savannah, Geo. Two dollars crossing ornamental die.	2 Female seated, horn of plenty at her feet, cars and bale.
V Portrait of boy.	MECHANICS' SAVINGS' BANK, Savannah, Geo.	5 Blacksmith reclining on anvil, hammer on shoulder, bale in rear, cars and factories.

TEN Male portrait.	Vig. Span of horses attached to dray of cotton; sampler with baskets of samples of cotton. MECHANICS' SAVINGS' BANK, Savannah, Geo.	10 Man gathering rice, boy and horse.
XX Male portrait.	Vig. Ship builders, ship on stocks, small boat, &c MECHANICS' SAVINGS' BANK, Savannah, Geo. Gems.	20 Portrait of girl.
L Sailor and shipbuilder.	MECHANICS' SAVINGS' BANK, Savanah, Geo. Vig. Milk maid with pail on her head; farm-house, cows, &c.	50 H. Clay.
C	MECHANICS' SAVINGS' BANK, Savannah, Geo. Vig. Two females, liberty pole and cap, horn of plenty; wheat, railroad cars, and vessels in distance.	100 State arms.
1 Female leaning on a figure 1. 1	(Old Plate.) ONE Female horn of plenty, plow, schooners, &c. ONE SKOWHEGAN BANK Bloomfield, Me.	1 Eagle. 1
Female head. ONE 1	[New Plate.] SKOWHEGAN BANK Bloomfield, Me. Man ploughing with two horses.	1 Indian.
2 Female and eagle. 2	[Old Plate.] 2 Same as ones, old plate. 2 SKOWHEGAN BANK Bloomfield, Me.	2 Female with scales. 2
Two females. 2	[New Plate.] SKOWHEGAN BANK Bloomfield, Me. Haying scene.	2 Indian.
3 Eagle. 3	[Old Plate.] 3 Same as ones, old plate. 3 SKOWHEGAN BANK Bloomfield, Me.	3 Female. 3

Boy's head. 3	[New Plate.] SKOWHEGAN BANK Bloomfield, Me. Female with milk pail and cows.	3 Indian.
5 MAINE Female with horn of plenty. 5	[Old Plate.] SKOWHEGAN BANK Bloomfield, Me.	5 State arms. 5
5 Figure 5, and five females surrounding it.	[New Plate.] SKOWHEGAN BANK Bloomfield, Me. Female; on right steamer, and on left steamers and cars.	5 Indian holding an ear of corn and a letter V.
	The old plate of 10s and 20s are the same in every particular as the old plate of 5s, except the denomination.	
Female leaning on bale and sheaf of wheat, scales in her hand. 10	[New Plate.] SKOWHEGAN BANK Bloomfield, Me. State arms, with eagle on top and female on either side; in distance, on right train of cars, on left steamer.	10 Bust of female. TEN
FIFTY. Female. FIFTY	50 Man and horse. 50 SKOWHEGAN BANK Bloomfield, Me.	FIFTY Female. FIFTY
Words one hundred and figures 100. Portrait of Harrison.	Scene on a wharf—wagons, shipping, &c. SKOWHEGAN BANK Bloomfield, Me.	Same as on left. Portrait of Columbus.
1	Female seated, in the act of crowning eagle with wreath; ship on left, and drover, drove of cattle, and sheep, and train of cars on right, in distance. Head of Washington, figure 1, CANAL BANK, Portland, Me.	1 Indian Princess.
	☞ All denominations have on the back of the bill, a locomotive and one passenger car; three men and dog.	

2 | Same as ones. 2 | 2
CANAL BANK, Portland, Me. | Mechanic and work-bench.
2

3 | Same as ones. 3 | 3
CANAL BANK, Portland, Me. | Female Portrait.
3

5 | Same as ones. 5 | 5
Female Indian, seated with pole and cap, and shield.
CANAL BANK, Portland, Me.
5

10 | Same as ones. X | 10
Female partly nude with pen and tablet; cog wheel on left.
CANAL BANK, Portland, Me.
10

20 | Same as ones. 20 | Female with sheaf of grain under left arm.
CANAL BANK, Portland, Me.
XX
20 | 20

50 | Same as ones. 50 | Female Portrait.
CANAL BANK, Portland, Me.
50
50 | Med. Head.

100 | Same as ones. 100 | Female erect with sickle and sheaf of wheat.
CANAL BANK, Portland, Me.
100
100

D | Same as ones. 500 | Female figure erect, with flag; left hand on a warrior's shield.
CANAL BANK, Portland, Me.
500
D

Goddess of Liberty. | ONE Vig. Steamship. | 1
Bust of female.
BK. OF SAVANNAH, Savannah, Geo.
ONE

Sailor. | Med. Head. Female seated, with pole and cap, and shield; spread eagle on right. | 2
Cotton plant &c.
TWO | BK. OF SAVANNAH, Savannah, Geo. | TWO

Three females holding aloft, frame on which is letter V. | 5 Two females seated; on right, cotton plant, wagon and two mules; on left, vessel and steamboat. | 5
FIVE
FIVE | BK. OF SAVANNAH, Savannah, Geo. | 5

10 | Female Portrait. Ship, steamship, &c, in distance; on left, view of city, &c. | 10
Indian Princess seated, with pole, cap and shield.
Female with sheaf of wheat.
BK. OF SAVANNAH, Savannah, Geo.
TEN | TEN

20 | Vig. Spread eagle, with a ship each side. | 20
Justice, with scales and sword. | BK. OF SAVANNAH, Savannah, Geo. | Bust of Webster.

50 | BK. OF SAVANNAH, Savannah, Geo. | FIFTY
Bust of Gen. Oass.
Washington on horseback.
50 | Female bust. | FIFTY

100 | Vig. Coat-of-Arms of Georgia; on the right, a plough and agricultural products; on the left, female reaper, with sheaf and 100 railroad view. | ONE HUNDRED
Genius of Liberty, with liberty pole and cap; rays of light radiating from the head.
BK. OF SAVANNAH, Savannah, Geo.
Spread Eagle.

Deer. | 1 Vig. Female reclining. | 1
State arms. | FARMERS' AND MECHANICS' BANK, Detroit, Mich.
Deer. | Steamboat. | Eagle and shield.

Deer. | 2 Vig. State arms. | 2
State arms. | FARMERS' AND MECHANICS' BANK, Detroit, Mich. | Female with sword and balances.
Deer. | Steamboat.

Deer. | 3 Vig. Woodland scene; water, deers, canoe in water, &c. 3 | THREE
Female figure with bow and arrow, quiver at her back.
State arms. | FARMERS' AND MECHANICS' BANK, Detroit, Mich.
Deer. | Steamboat. | THREE

FIVE | [Old Plate.] 5 Vig. Large figure 5 with female either side; three cupids. 5 | Deer.
State arms.
FARMERS' AND MECHANICS' BANK, Detroit, Mich.
Steamboat. | Deer.

Deer. | [New Plate.] 5 Vig. Large figure 5 with female either side; three cupids 5 | Deer.
State arms. | FARMERS' AND MECHANICS' BANK, Detroit, Mich. | State arms.
Deer. | Steamboat. | Deer.

Deer. | 10 Vig. Female, eagle, and shield. | 10
State arms. | FARMERS' AND MECHANICS' BANK, Detroit, Mich. | Female sitting under canopy.
Deer. | Steamboat. | TEN

5 | Fox chase. | 5
Load of grain, two oxen and one horse in wagon. | BK. OF ROCKINGHAM, Harrisonburg, Va. | Trees Die

X | Two females, one milking, the other feeding poultry. | 10
BK. OF ROCKINGHAM, Harrisonburg, Va.
Trees Die. | Locomotive.

20 | Prairie on fire, six wild horses. | 20
Girl with sheaf of grain on her head.
Portrait of Female. | BK. OF ROCKINGHAM, Harrisonburg, Va.

Female. | 50 Spread eagle on shield, ship in the distance. | 50
BK. OF ROCKINGHAM, Harrisonburg, Va. | Female Portrait.
FIFTY.

Cows. | Cotton field and Planter on horseback, negroes picking cotton. | 5
PLANTER'S BANK of FAIRFIELD, S. C. | Portrait of a female.
FIVE | Palmetto.

X | Agricultural device, with a female, sickle in her left hand; coat of arms. | 10
Drove of Cattle. | PLANTER'S BANK of FAIRFIELD, S. C. | Train of railroad cars.
Plow.

20 Goddess of Liberty.	PLANTER'S BANK of FAIRFIELD, S. C. Palmeto, cotton bales, wheat, plow, &c., railroad cars in the distance on the left, steam ship in the distance on the right.	20 Washington on horseback

25 Two females and cotton-field.	PLANTER'S BANK of FAIRFIELD, S. C.	25 Portrait of Calhoun.

50 Ceres sitting on a cow.	PLANTER'S BANK of FAIRFIELD, S. C. Bust of Calhoun. Cotton Stalk in bloom. Coat of Arms. Female with a wreath.	50 Portrait of Jackson.

C Portrait of Washington.	Capitol at Washington. PLANTER'S BANK of FAIRFIELD, S. C.	100 American Eagle and Shield.

Indian standing erect with bow and arrow.	ONE Vig. Sail vessels; light house in back-ground. BATH BANK, Bath, Me. Dog.	1 Portrait of little girl.

TWO Dog's head.	Vig. Indian paddling canoe accompanied by two squaws, shrubbery and mountains in background. BATH BANK, Bath, Me. Ducks.	2 Female reclining on bale of mdse.

3 Sailor and blacksmith.	3 Vig. Eagle, and female partly disrobed. 3 BATH BANK, Bath, Me. Dog.	3 Large sail vessel, other smaller ones, &c.

FIVE State arms. V	Vig. Large sail vessel; smaller ones on either side. BATH BANK, Bath, Me. Female head.	5 Portrait of Webster.

TEN Portrait of boy.	Vig. Log rolling; three persons, another felling a tree; cattle in background, &c. 10 BATH BANK, Bath, Me Beehive.	TEN Group of three females representing Agriculture, Commerce, &c

XX Sailor seated	Vig. Ship-building; ships on stocks, &c ; factory on left. BATH BANK, Bath, Me. Beehive.	20 Miniature view of little girl.

Female. ONE	Load of hay; horses, barn, men, etc. BK. OF KEWANEE, Kewanee, Ills. Dog's head.	1 ONE Auditor's die

TWO Auditor's die TWO	BK. OF KEWANEE, Kewanee, Ills. Drove of wild horses. Ball.	TWO Female and figure 2. 2

Female seated with eagle and shield. 5	Figure 5 in fancy work with a cherub each side. BK. OF KEWANEE, Kewanee, Ills. Bee-hive.	FIVE Auditor's die FIVE

ONE State Arms. ONE	Cows; and man ploughing. VERMONT BANK. Montpelier, Vt.	1 Portrait of a lady. ONE

2 Head of Franklin. TWO	State Arms, surmounted with a stag's head; lady on left; man on right; fruit, &c., below. VERMONT BANK. Montpelier, Vt.	2 Head of Washington. TWO

THREE Locomotive and cars.	State Arms, with female; churn and pail on the right; man with plough and rake on the left. VERMONT BANK, Montpelier, Vt.	3 Female with bow and arrow.

5 Female with sheaf of wheat and sickle. FIVE	Agricultural scene; hay-maker's and team; female seated on left; farmer's hauling hay, on right. VERMONT BANK, Montpelier, Vt.	5 State Arms; female figure each side. FIVE

10 Lady's Portrait 10	Man ploughing; cattle grazing; cars passing under bridge; and in the distance, on left, village and train of cars. VERMONT BANK, Montpelier, Vt.	10 State Arms; female figure each side. TEN

20 Full length female, holding a spear; globe standing partly behind the female.	2 Female. 0 VERMONT BANK, Montpelier, Vt. XX	20 Female sitting; horn of plenty, and bales. 20

50 Full length female figure holding a spear in right hand; left hand rests on a shield.	Male and female seated. VERMONT BANK, Montpelier, Vt. 50	50 Cupid in a sail-boat. 50

100 Man sitting; holds a scale.	Eagle on a tree, canal boat and cars, in back-ground. VERMONT BANK, Montpelier, Vt. 100	100 Female sitting; holds a rake; fruit, &c.

ONE Medallion figure.	1 Two blacksmiths and anvil. 1 WARNER BANK, Warner, N. H.	ONE Figure of a Girl. ONE

TWO Lady's head resting on her hand, elbows on table. 2	2 Haying scene, Girl standing with rake handing cup of water to two men seated on the ground. 2 WARNER BANK, Warner, N. H.	TWO Lady with a sickle resting over her shoulder. 2

FIVE	Spread eagle standing on a shield. V, female and cupid. WARNER BANK, Warner N. H.	5 Girl with Basket of Flowers in her hand.

TEN	Blacksmith seated hammer in his hand, resting on an anvil, wheel by his side on the ground. X WARNER BANK. Warner, N. H	10 Man tying up a bundle of grain, sickle in his hand.

20 Lady seated looking over shoulder.	XX Eagle. XX WARNER BANK, Warner. N. H.	20 Ship

FIFTY Female. FIFTY	50 Man leading a rearing horse. 50 WARNER BANK, Warner, N. H.	FIFTY Female. FIFTY

ONE HUNDRED and figures 100. Male Portrait	Wharf scene; men loading a covered team wagon, &c. WARNER BANK, Warner. N. H.	ONE HUNDRED and figures 100. Male Portrait.	Female. Portrait of Franklin. Female.	20 Vig. Portrait of Washington, with female on either side, &c. MICHIGAN INS. CO., Detroit. Mich. Fish.	20	20 Medallion head of Ariadne. XX	Vig. Representing Commerce, Agriculture, &c., with portrait of Franklin between. EASTON BANK OF MARYLAND.	TWENTY
ONE Female. ONE	[Old Plate.] Vig. Female sitting on a log; steamboat on right; house in distance on left. 1 MICHIGAN INS. CO., Detroit. Mich.	Female standing. 1	Female standing with pole, liberty cap, shield, &c.	50 Vig. Three females reclining, &c. MICHIGAN INS. CO., Detroit. Mich.	50	50 Large ship, full sail; another ship in distance.	Shield draped with American flag, females with girl and globe on right, Indian Squaw and child on left. EASTON BANK OF MARYLAND.	L 50 L
1 Words one dollar, and figure 1 under.	[New Plate.] MICHIGAN INS. CO., Detroit. Mich. Vig. ONE, with ornamented die work.	1 Words one dollar, and figure 1 under.	Sailor boy, with a flag, anchor, &c., in background. FIVE	5 Female seated, resting her right elbow on the Coat-of-Arms of the U. S. PATRIOTIC BANK, Washington, D. C.	5 Female sitting.	100 Farmers loading wagon with bundles of wheat, boy holding horse.	EASTON BANK OF MARYLAND. Spade, rake, sheaf of wheat, bee-hive and plow.	100 Portrait of Jenny Lind.
TWO Male resting arm on shield, &c. TWO	[Old Plate.] TWO on Medallion head. Vig. Two females sitting; bale of goods, &c.; ship on right. MICHIGAN INS. CO., Detroit, Mich.	2 Female resting her arm on figure 2; cask, &c.	10 Washington standing by his horse	Vig. Same as Five's. PATRIOTIC BANK. Washington, D. C.	10 Female; scales in her left hand, &c	Blacksmith leaning against anvil	Three sheep under tree. 5 BANK OF WINCHESTER, Winchester, Va.	5 Portrait of Chief Justice Marshall. 5
2 TWO 2	[New Plate.] MICHIGAN INS. CO., Detroit. Mich. Vig. TWO DOLLARS, with ornamented die work.	2 2 TWO	Female with a sickle in her right hand. TWENTY	20 Vig. same as 5's. PATRIOTIC BANK. Washington, D. C.	20 Female figure, with U. S., flag in her right hand; staff resting on the ground shield, &c., in her left.	10 Female with cornucopia.	Boy on horse driving cattle and sheep. BANK OF WINCHESTER. Winchester. Va.	10 Head of Female.
Female. 3	3 on Medallion head. Vig. Men, women, children, &c. MICHIGAN INS. CO., Detroit, Mich. Female.	3 Portrait of Washington.	50 Female holding scales; eagle under the scales. 50	Vig. Same as the 5's. 50 PATRIOTIC BANK, Washington, D. C.	Female figure. 50	Female head. 20	BANK OF WINCHESTER Winchester, Va. Railroad and bridge. Female head.	20 Man leaning on box.
Indian in full costume. FIVE	[Old Plate.] 5 Vig. Farmer plowing; dairymaid and house in distance. MICHIGAN INS. CO., Detroit. Mich. Sail vessel.	 5	100 Female figure sitting, holding scales in her left hand; a sword in her left.	Female figure sitting, resting her right elbow on the Coat-of-Arms of the U. S. PATRIOTIC BANK, Washington. D. C.	100 Figure of a man with scythe, &c.; buildings in background	FIFTY Man leaning on sheaf of wheat. 50	Two females spinning under tree; Railroad and bridge in background. BANK OF WINCHESTER. Winchester. Va. Sheaf of wheat.	FIFTY Heads of a man and horse. 50
5 V with word five running across it.	[New Plate.] Secured by individual liability. Vig. FIVE, with ornamented die work MICHIGAN INS. CO., Detroit, Mich.	5, V, Five FIVE	5 Indian girl kneeling, sickle in right hand, female standing behind with bow and arrow.	EASTON BANK OF MARYLAND. FIVE on lathe strip, large medallion V on face of note. Anvil.	5 FIVVE 5	ONE View of steam-mill horse, &c. ONE	Vig. Female reclining on anchor, left arm raised, ship in distance on left. MARINERS' BANK, Wiscasset, Me. Head of Indian.	ONE Ship. ONE
Female standing with pole, liberty cap, &c.	10 Vig. Female reclining, &c. MICHIGAN INS. CO., Detroit. Mich. Eagle.	TEN Full length female.	Large X on medallion shield. Hebe sitting on wheat, holding cup to eagle; ship in distance.	EASTON BANK OF MARYLAND. TEN on lathe strip; Large medallion X on face of note. Justice standing; barrels and ships behind.	10 X 10	2 Bust of female. 2	Vig. Sailor, bales, barrels, &c.; ship on left hand in distance. MARINERS' BANK, Wiscasset, Me. Head of Indian.	2 Ship on stocks, &c. 2

THREE Female with a bundle of wheat under her arm. THREE	3 Vig. Sailor with mallet and chisel; ship building, men at work. 3 MARINER'S BANK, Wiscasset, Me. Head of an Indian.	THREE Sailor with glass in hand THREE	10 X 10	Pair of oxen and male standing by their side. 10 FRANCESTOWN B'K Francestown, N. H.	TEN Female with vase of flowers.	Female. XX	20 Bank building. CITY BANK, Montreal, Canada.	20
Female, scroll, &c FIVE	Head of Washington. Head of Jefferson. Vig. Large ship. MARINERS' BANK, Wiscasset, Me. Head of an Indian.	5 Female, pole, &c.	20 Female sitting.	XX Eagle. XX FRANCESTOWN B'K Francestown, N. H.	20 Ship, sails all set.	50	Bank building. CITY BANK. Montreal, Canada.	50
10 Female with arm raised. TEN	Head of Jefferson. Head of Washington. Vig. Large spread eagle; ships on either side. MARINERS' BANK, Wiscasset, Me. Head of an Indian.	10 Head of Adams. TEN	FIFTY Female. FIFTY	50 Man and horse. 50 FRANCESTOWN B'K Francestown, N. H.	FIFTY Female with vase of flowers. FIFTY	100 Prince Albert.	Bank building. CITY BANK. Montreal, Canada.	100 Queen Victoria.
20 Female bust with bow, &c. 20	Portrait. Portrait. Vig. Spread eagle standing on limb of a tree. MARINERS' BANK, Wiscasset, Me. Head of an Indian.	20 Portrait of Washington. TWENTY	100 Eagle. 100	C Four horses abreast driven by Neptune. 100 FRANCESTOWN B'K Francestown, N. H.	C Head of Washington. C	1 Bust of William 4th. UNE	1 1 LA BANQUE DE LA CITE. Montreal, Canada. Indian with bow. UNE PLASTRE.	1 The City B'k will pay the bearer on demand one dollar. UNE
	☞ The 50s and 100s, are of the old Perkins Stereotype Plate, which has the denomination printed in fine letters all over the bill.		1	Bank building. 1 CITY BANK, Montreal, Canada. Crown, sceptre, &c.	ONE Female. ONE	2 The City B'k will pay the bearer on demand two dollars. DEUX	LA BANQUE DE LA CITE, Montreal, Canada. 2 Indian in canoe. 2 DEUX PIASTRES.	2 Bust of William 4th. TWO
1 Head of Washington	Female sitting. 1 Female sitting. FRANCESTOWN B'K Francestown, N. H.	1 Head of Franklin.	2	Bank building. 2 CITY BANK. Montreal, Canada.	TWO Male and female.	CINQ Lion and Unicorn. PIASTRES	5 Figure sustaining the globe with a lever. 5 CITY BANK, Montreal, Canada.	V Bust of William 4th. V
2 Head of Columbus.	Female 2 Female. FRANCESTOWN B'K Francestown, N. H.	2 Male portrait.	4 Victoria with crown. 4	4 Bank building. 4 CITY BANK, Montreal, Canada.	ONE POUND.	10 Bust of William 4th 10	CITY BANK. Montreal, Canada. DIX Lion and Unicorn. 10	X La Banque de la Cite payera au porteur sur demande Dix Piastres. X
3 Portrait of Washington	Female head. 3 Female head. FRANCESTOWN B'K Francestown, N. H.	3 Vulcan the blacksmith.	5 Bust of a female. FIVE	City arms supported by two Indians. 5 Bank building. CITY BANK, Montreal, Canada.	5	20 La Banque de la Cite payera au porteur sur demande Vingt Piastres. XX	VINGT Bust of William 4th; Lion on right, Unicorn on left. CITY BANK. Montreal, Canada.	TWENTY
Letter V with word Five running across it.	Female with sickle and rake, sheaf of grain; steam engine, store house, and shipping in the distance. V and Indian. FRANCESTOWN B'K Francestown, N. H.	5 Head of Washington.	TEN 10 TEN	Bank building. CITY BANK. Montreal, Canada.	10	ONE	ONE and fig. ure 1. Female Figure spinning; wheel and buildings in rear. ONE and fig. ure 1. CITY BANK, Toronto, Canada. 1	Victoria.

TWO 2 Female figure, Agriculture and Commerce in rear. 2 CITY BANK, Toronto, Canada 2 Victoria.	20 Female sitting. XX Eagle XX SALMON FALLS BK., Rollinsford, N. H. 20 Ship.	2 Eagle and shield. 2 Three female figures. TWO ROCHESTER BANK, Rochester, N. H. Dog, key and chest. 2 Female; Goddess of Liberty, with shield and trident. 2
Lion and Unicorn. 5 Figure sustaining the globe with a lever. CITY BANK Toronto, Canada. V Bust of William 4th. V	FIFTY Female standing. FIFTY 50 Man and Horse 50 SALMON FALLS BK., Rollinsford, N. H. FIFTY Female standing. FIFTY	THREE Stone cutter 3 Female reclining; eagle; globe; ships in distance. ROCHESTER BANK, Roohester, N. H. Female and bee-hive. THREE Blacksmith. 3
10 Bust of William 4th. 10 10 CITY BK. 10 Toronto, Canada. Lion and Unicorn. X Female Figure. X	ONE HUNDRED and figures 100. Portrait of Harrison, Loading baggage wagon, horses shipping at wharf. SALMON FALLS BK., Rollinsford, N. H. ONE HUNDRED and figures 100. Portrait.	5 Franklin. 5 Drover on horse, with cattle and sheep. ROCHESTER BANK, Rochester, N. H. Deer. 5 Washington. 5
20 Female Figure. XX 20 Bust of William 4th, Lion and Unicorn. 20 CITY BANK, Toronto, Canada. TWENTY	ONE Female portrait. Man sitting holding sledge; train of cars, factory, &c. in background. 1 FRANKLIN CO. B'K. St. Alban's Bay, Vt. Cog-wheel, bale, &c. Female standing behind pillar. ONE	10 Female head. TEN Female with key on right; chest on left. ROCHESTER BANK, Rochester. N. H. 10 Female head. TEN
1 Washington. Female 1 Female SALMON FALLS BK., Rollingsford, N. H. 1 Franklin.	TWO Female and shield, spear in right hand, branch in left. Female reclining on bale of goods; canal boat, train of cars, town, shipping, &c. in background. FRANKLIN CO. B'K, St. Alban's Bay, Vt. Safe. 2 Female sitting. TWO	20 Minerva; Goddess of wisdom, with spear and helmet; an owl and globe. Female sitting with rake; between 2 and 0. ROCHESTER BANK, Rochester. N. H. XX 20 Female reclining 20
2 Columbus. Female 2 Female SALMON FALLS BK., Rollingsford, N. H. 2 Portrait.	FIVE Female Indian, bow, spear, &c. in right hand, quiver of arrows on back. 5 Female portrait, eagle, shield, &c.; steamer, sail vessel, train of cars, factory &c. in background FRANKLIN CO. B'K, St. Alban's Bay, Vt. Steamer. FIVE Sailor, capstan, hogshead, &c	50 Goddess of wisdom, with spear and helmet. Female with rake; man sitting, roll in hand; fruits piled between them. ROCHESTER BANK, Rochester, N. H. 50 50 Cupid in sail boat. 50
3 Washington and horse. Female Portrait. 3 Female Portrait. SALMON FALLS BK., Rollinsford, N H. 3 Vulcan at his forge.	10 Portrait of Franklin. 10 Steamboat; wharf buildings, sail vessels, &c. in background. FRANKLIN CO. B'K, St. Alban's Bay, Vt. Horn of plenty. 10 Locomotive and cars. 10	100 Workman sitting; roll in his hand. Spread eagle; canal and boat, and railroad cars. ROCHESTER BANK, Rochester, N. H. 100 100 Female sitting with rake.
Eagle on rock with wings extended. FIVE Large V, Female and Cupid. SALMON FALLS BK., Rollingsford, N. H. 5 Female Portrait.	20 Locomotive. 20 Female, sheaves of grain, &c FRANKLIN CO. B'K, St. Alban's Bay, Vt. Sail vessel. 20 Steamship. 20	500 Indian paddling a canoe. 500 ROCHESTER BANK, Rochester, N. H. 500 Justice, with sword and scales.
Vulcan the Blacksmith. TEN X SALMON FALLS BK. Rollingsford, N. H. 10 Reaper.	ONE Figure of Justice, holding sword and balance. Train of cars. ROCHESTER BANK, Rochester, N. H. Carding machine. ONE Washington standing by his horse. ONE	1000 Eagle on cliff; sea and ship in distance. 1000 ROCHESTER BANK, Rochester, N. H. 1000 Indian female warrior with bow and arrow.

Left	Centre	Right
1 Head of Washington.	Cows, woman milking, another woman seated. STRAFFORD BANK, Dover, N. H.	1 Female scales and Eagle.
2 Head of Franklin.	Dog and safe. STRAFFORD BANK, Dover, N. H	2 Eagle.
3 Female bust.	Female, plough, sheaf and sickle; cars in distance STRAFFORD BANK, Dover, N. H.	3 Med. head.
5 Indian female seated.	STRAFFORD BANK. Dover, N. H. Fame with trumpet; globe and eagle. 5 5	5 Female leaning on a column.
10 Head of Judge Marshall.	Female leaning on bale of goods; men loading hay. 10 STRAFFORD BANK. Dover, N. H.	TEN Female with a sheaf. 10
20 Locomotive & building.	Female with her arms extended; boy on each side. STRAFFORD BANK. Dover, N. H.	20 Female, sickle and sheaf
50 Female holding sickle. 50	Two females; ship, buildings and cars in the distance. STRAFFORD BANK. Dover, N. H.	50 Man standing among corn.
100 Sailor with hat in hand, holding a flag	STRAFFORD BANK, Dover, N. H. Female and cherub in a cloud over city.	100 Ship. 100
500 Female.	STRAFFORD BANK, Dover, N. H. FIVE HUNDRED Three females; cars and vessel in the distance.	500 500
M Two females; ships, buildings and cars in distance. 1000	STRAFFORD BANK. Dover, N. H. ONE THOUSAND	1000 1000
1 Portrait of John Jay.	View of the U. S. Capitol. ROCKINGHAM B'K, Portsmouth, N. H. American eagle.	1 Sea nymph.
TWO Steamship.	Portrait of Taylor, Portrait of Fillmore. ROCKINGHAM B'K, Portsmouth, N. H.	2 Brigantine.
3 Portrait of Henry Clay.	ROCKINGHAM B'K, Portsmouth, N. H. Portrait THREE of DOLLARS Daniel Webster.	3 Portrait of John C. Calhoun.
5 Sailor leaning on a capstan.	View of war ships, near the Navy Yard, Portsmouth, N. H. ROCKINGHAM B'K, Portsmouth, N. H.	5 Portrait of Mrs. Crittenden.
10 Portrait of girl.	View of a ship of the line, and merchant ship under sail. ROCKINGHAM B'K, Portsmouth, N. H.	10 Blacksmith near a forge.
Figure of a female representing Young America. 20	ROCKINGHAM B'K, Portsmouth, N. H. Portrait of Daniel Webster.	20 American eagle.
Sailor holding the American flag FIFTY.	Steamship of the Collins' line. ROCKINGHAM B'K. Portsmouth, N. H.	50 Figure of a female with horn of plenty, &c.
American eagle on a shield. 100	Portrait of Washington. ROCKINGHAM B'K. Portsmouth, N. H.	100
1	Stream of water and load of straw; mill in the distance. 1 CONNECTICUT RIVER BANK, Charlestown, N. H. Bundle of grain.	1 Justice with sword and scales.
2	Eagle on an old tree. 2 CONNECTICUT RIVER BANK, Charlestown, N. H. Ox.	2 Head of Washington.
Man representing agriculture, surrounded by axe, sickle, plough; harrow with the motto "Enterprise." THREE	Head. 3 Head. CONNECTICUT RIVER BANK, Charlestown, N. H. Man shearing a sheep.	THREE Minerva with helmet and spear leaning on her shield.
5 Female seated holding United States flag.	Female and eagle. CONNECTICUT RIVER BANK, Charlestown, N. H. Bundle of grain.	5 Bull.
10 Stream of water; load of straw; mill in the distance.	Two females seated. CONNECTICUT RIVER BANK. Charlestown, N. H Bull.	10 Eagle, bale, barrel and shield.
1 Female erect left arm resting on bucket	EXCHANGE BANK, Springfield, Vt. Male Portrait. One dollar above.	1 Mechanic reclining holding hammer in right hand; houses in background.
TWO 2 TWO Male Portrait TWO	EXCHANGE BANK, Springfield, Vt. Masons at work building house, man on ladder, with hod of bricks.	TWO 2 TWO Portrait of Gen. Jackson TWO
THREE 3	EXCHANGE BANK, Springfield, Vt. Picture of a Mechanic, hammer resting on his shoulder.	THREE 3
Figure 5 and medallion head, Portrait of Webster.	Portrait of Washington, on right two females, one seated the other standing, on left three females, one in center holds a sickle. EXCHANGE BANK, Springfield, Vt.	Figure 5 and medallion head. Male Portrait

10 Medallion head. Portrait of Franklin. Medallion Head.	Shield and letter X in center; on right woman children and globe, on left Indians. EXCHANGE BANK, Springfield, Vt. TEN TEN	Double Medallion head. 10 Head Portrait of Henry Clay TEN on right Double Medallion head. X Head

XX 20	EXCHANGE BANK, Springfield, Vt. Two horses, eagle overhead, tree, cow and sheaf of wheat in background, stm boat on right; cars and houses on left.	20

L 50	EXCHANGE BANK, Springfield, Vt. Large spread eagle resting on a limb of a tree; train of cars on right; house and small boat on left. 50	50

State Arms. 1	Three men, one sitting and two standing; rock, &c. BANK of CASTLETON Castleton, Vt. ONE Load of hay.	1 On this end,—One strip of lathe work and figure 1.

State Arms. TWO	2 Female and infant; sheaf of grain, &c. BANK of CASTLETON Castleton, Vt. Female swimming.	On this end—Two strips of lathe work and figure 2.

FIVE State Arms.	BANK of CASTLETON Castleton, Vt. Man on horse, sheep and dog. Dog and safe.	On this end—Five strips of lathe work and figure 5.

State Arms. On this end—One strip of Lathe work and letter X.	Three men standing. BANK of CASTLETON Castleton, Vt. TEN	10 Seminary and grounds.

On this end—Two strips of lathe work and and XX.	Engine and train of cars passing under a bridge; Two men standing, one with a wheelbarrow. BANK of CASTLETON Castleton, Vt. TWENTY.	20 State Arms.

ONE Female figure.	AMOSKEAG BANK. Manchester, N. H. Vig. Indian reclining on frame, and motto "[illegible]" spread eagle, lake, mountains, and deer in background.	1 Portrait R. H. Ayer.

2 Portrait R. H. Ayer.	AMOSKEAG BANK, Manchester, N. H. Vig. Female on each side Coat-of Arms, of New-Hampshire; steamboat, train of cars, &c., in background.	2 Two females.

3 Male Portrait.	AMOSKEAG BANK. Manchester, N. H. Vig. Three females seated.	3 Small female figure reclining. Large figure 3, supported by three laborers.

5 Portrait R. H. Ayer	AMOSKEAG BANK, Manchester, N. H. Vig. Female seated; horn of plenty; books, owl, &c; steamboat and merchandise on left; safe, harrow, rake, and train of cars on right.	5 Large figure 5, supported by 5 females.

Female figure reclining holding scales. 10	AMOSKEAG BANK, Manchester, N. H. Vig. Female reclining on safe; Pastoral scene on right; steam engine and merchandise on left; and commercial scene in background.	10 Portrait of Frank Pierce.

20 Figure of Mercury between figures 20.	AMOSKEAG BANK, Manchester, N. H. Harvest scene; railroad bridge; train of cars; church, &c., in background.	20 Portrait of Frank Pierce.

Male Portrait. 50	Vig. Female seated; hat in lap, beside dog; cattle in background. AMOSKEAG BANK, Manchester, N. H.	50 Portrait of Frank Pierce

100 Male portrait 100	Female with wand; cupids and dolphin sporting. AMOSKEAG BANK, Manchester, N. H.	100 Male portrait

Mountainous native scene, Indian in canoe. 500	500 AMOSKEAG BANK Manchester, N. H.	500 Female holding scales.

ONE 1	Vig. Locomotive and train of cars. DANBY BANK, Danby, Vt.	1 Portrait of Gen. Taylor.

2 2	Vig. Man and boy with horses and plow. DANBY BANK, Danby, Vt.	2 Maid with milk pail.

FI V VE FI V VE	Vig. Locomotive and Train of cars. DANBY BANK Danby, Vt.	V Portrait of Washington.

10 X	Vig. Scene, Commerce—Female standing and one sitting holding liberty cap; train of cars and ship in distance. DANBY BANK, Danby, Vt.	TEN Figure of America.

TWENTY Female figure representing Agriculture.	XX Vig. Blacksmith seated train of cars and factory in the distance. DANBY BANK, Danby, Vt.	XX 20

50	Vig. Same as tens. 50 DANBY BANK, Danby, Vt.	Justice.

1 Medallion head with wreath around it.	Train of cars. CHESHIRE BANK, Keene, N. H. Ox.	1 Woman with plow, sheaf of wheat and cornucopia.

TWO Engine and cars. TWO	Ox-cart load of grain; man on horseback; agricultural implements; mill house in distance. CHESHIRE BANK, Keene, N. H. Fort and ship.	2 Fancy medallion head.

THREE 3 DOLLARS	Spread eagle on a branch; train of cars and canal boats and locks in distance. CHESHIRE BANK, Keene, N. H. Ploughing with horses.	3 Man shearing a sheep, woman standing by.

5 Eagle and shield, which bears the word five.	Medallion head. 5 Medallion head. CHESHIRE BANK, Keene N. H. Plow.	5 Woman with bow and arrow.

10. Head of Washington. | Medallion head of Franklin. X Medallion head. CHESHIRE BANK, Keene, N. H. Ox. | 10. Woman with cornucopia.

10. Female seated. 10. | [Old Plate.] X Train of cars X. Title of Bank. | 10. 10.

10. X. 10. | [First Plate.] Oxen, man, &c. 10. RAIL ROAD BANK, Cumberland, R. I. | TEN. Female with cornucopia in left hand.

20. Roman soldier. | Female with one hand resting on 2 and the other on 0. CHESHIRE BANK, Keene, N. H. XX | 20. Small female with cornucopia, &c. 20.

20. Female standing, holding scales. 20. | [Old Plate.] XX Engine and cars. XX. Title of Bank. | XX.

X. | [Second Plate.] Signing the declaration of independence. X. RAIL ROAD BANK. Woonsocket, R. I. | 10. Train of cars building with steeple.

50. Roman soldier. | Male and female figures seated, with cornucopia between them. CHESHIRE BANK, Keene, N. H. 50 | 50. Cupid in a sail-boat. 50.

Three females—one above the other, and anchor. TWENTY. | [New Plate.] 20 Eagle. Title of Bank. | 20. Engine. 20.

20. Female seated with book on lap. | XX Eagle. XX. RAIL ROAD BANK, Cumberland, R. I. | 20. Ship.

ONE DOLLAR. | [Old Plate.] Eagle and figure 1. Railroad scene; engine and train of cars. CENTRAL RAIL ROAD AND BANKING CO. OF GEORGIA. Savannah, Geo. | 1. Blacksmith's arm holding a sledge-hammer.

Group; Vulcan, Ceres, and Mercury. 50. | L Engine and cars. L. Title of Bank. | 50. Engine and cars on a bridge. 50.

FIFTY. Female holding flowers in one hand and a wreath in the other. FIFTY. | 50 Man and horse. 50. RAIL ROAD BANK, Cumberland, R. I. | FIFTY. Female with a barometer in one hand and flowers in the other. FIFTY.

1. Engine and cars. | [New Plate.] Stone Quarry; one man seated and two standing. Title of Bank. | 1. Female seated.

ONE HUNDRED. | 100 Engine and cars. 100. Title of Bank. | ONE HUNDRED.

ONE HUNDRED and figures 100. Portrait of Harrison. | Wharf scene with men putting barrels into a large covered wagon, shipping, &c., in distance. RAIL ROAD BANK, Cumberland, R. I. | ONE HUNDRED and figures 100. Male Portrait.

2. Two blacksmiths striking upon an anvil. | Engine and train of cars. Title of Bank | 2. Female seated with wheat.

ONE. 1. | Farmer sowing grain and man and horses harrowing. 1. RAIL ROAD BANK, Cumberland, R. I. | 1. Ship. ONE.

Water and trees and an Indian in a canoe. 500. | 500. RAIL ROAD BANK, Woonsocket, R. I. | 500. Female holding scales and sword.

Three females one above another with anchor. FIVE. | Title of Bank. Train of Cars. | 5. Watch dog. 5.

TWO. 2. | Spread eagle on a bale, grers, &c., cars and man plowing in distance. 2. RAIL ROAD BANK, Cumberland, R. I. | 2. TWO. Schooner and sloop.

ONE. Female. | Man ploughing with span of horses. WINCHESTER B'K. Winchester, N. H. | 1. Female.

Schooner under full sail. 5. Engine and cars. | [Old Plate.] 5 View of rising sun surmounted by an eagle; on right, female seated with cap of liberty; on left, female erect with scales. 5. Title of Bank. | Steamboat. 5. Ship under full sail.

THREE. 3. | Wharf scene with Sailor, bales boxes shipping, storehouses, &c. 3. RAIL ROAD BANK, Cumberland, R. I. | 3. THREE. Train of cars.

Blacksmith. TWO. | Female. WINCHESTER B'K. Winchester, N. H. | 2. Reaper.

10. Sailor leaning upon a bale. TEN. | [New Plate.] Title of Bank. Engine and passenger car. | 10. Geo. Washington on horseback. TEN.

Large V and word FIVE. | Wharf scene with female sitting among agricultural implements and merchandise holding sickle and rake. Large V and figure with bow and arrow. RAIL ROAD BANK, Woonsocket, R. I. | 5. Portrait of Washington.

Man cradling grain. THREE. | Railroad cars. WINCHESTER B'K. Winchester, N. H. Man and plow. | 3. Cattle and swine.

Female. FIVE	Female reclining. WINCHESTER B'K, Winchester, N. H Shearing sheep.	5 Group of females.	1 Washington.	Female 1 Female UNION BANK, Swanton Falls, Vt.	1 Franklin.	20 Female seated, book in left hand, right hand on a box.	XX Eagle. XX UNION BANK, Swanton Falls, Vt.	20 Ship, with buildings in the distance.
10 Female. TEN	Female. WINCHESTER B'K, Winchester, N. H.	10 Female. TEN	1 Farmer with sickle and sheaf of grain; cars and canal-boat in distance.	Portrait of Washington. UNION BANK, Swanton Falls, Vt. Large figure 1, with words one dollar running across it,	1 Indian with bow sitting down; huts and canoe in distance.	FIFTY Female with wreath of flowers on her head and in her hands. FIFTY	50 Man and horse. 50 Title of Bank.	FIFTY Female with flowers in her left hand FIFTY
20 Female.	2 Female. 0 WINCHESTER B'K, Winchester, N. H. XX	20 20	2 Portrait of Columbus.	Portrait of female with flowers. 2 Portrait of female with sword and scales. UNION BANK, Swanton Falls, Vt.	2 Male portrait.	Fig. 100 with words one hundred across. Harrison.	Covered wagon, wharf, ships, warehouses, truck-men, &c Title of Bank.	Same as on left end. Columbus.
50 Female.	Male and female. WINCHESTER B'K. Winchester, N. H. 50	50 Cupid in sailboat. 50	2 Female sitting down with sword and scales; cars in distance.	Portrait of Franklin. UNION BANK. Swanton Falls, Vt. TWO 2 DOLLARS	2 Female sitting down with cap of liberty on a pole; church and houses in distance.	ONE State arms. ONE	Vig. Ploughman ploughing with oxen and girl by his side. ASCUTNEY BANK, Windsor, Vt. Steam engine.	ONE Head of Washington. 1
100 Male figure.	Spread eagle on branch of tree; cars and canal boat in distance. WINCHESTER B'K. Winchester, N. H. 100	100 Female.	3 Washington standing beside his horse.	Portrait of female. 3 Portrait of girl. UNION BANK. Swanton Falls, Vt.	3 Man standing with sleigh.	TWO Head of Franklin. Two on head	2 Vig. Blacksmith; rail road train in distance. ASCUTNEY BANK, Windsor, Vt. Wheelbarrow, plough and sheaf of grain.	2 State arms. TWO
FIVE	Female seated; quadrant, sheaf, bbls. &c., anchor; in distance, city, bridge, canal, boats, ships, steamer, &c. Treas. Die. BK. OF THE OLD DOMINION, Alexandria, Va. Bbls., bales, &c.	5 Washington. FIVE	3 Indian sitting down with bow; hut in distance.	UNION BANK, Swanton Falls, Vt. III 3	3 Sailor sitting on bale of goods; steam ship in distance.	THREE Medallion head. State arms.	Vig. Two horses and man crossing in front of railroad train; on left, fig. 3. 3 ASCUTNEY BANK. Windsor, Vt. Man's arm, with hammer anvil and tools.	3 Female head. 3
10 Female seated, with spear and twig, shield.	Treas. Die. Female reclining on bale; ships and town on right; on left, train of cars, canal lock, boats, &c. Title of Bank. Safe.	10	FIVE	Female kneeling against a shield. V UNION BANK, Swanton Falls, Vt.	5 Ship.	Head with five upon helmet. Head of J. Q. Adams	5 Vig. Man on horse-back, driving sheep, with dog; mill in distance; on left, fig. 5, with the word five on top. ASCUTNEY BANK. Windsor, Vt. Eagle.	
Treas. die. Two Mermaid's Steamship.	20 Train of cars; depot, steamboat, &c., in background. Title of Bank. Deer.	20 Male portrait TWENTY	Five on V. Drover on horseback with cattle and sheep. 5	Title of Bank. FIVE 5 DOLLARS	Five on V. 5	X Franklin. TEN	Signing of the Declaration of Independence. Jefferson. Title of Bank.	X John Adams. TEN
FIFTY Female with names of States on wreath, round her. 50	Treas. Die. Female on either side of a shield, surmounted by an eagle; train of cars, steamship on right; on left buildings and man ploughing, &c. Title of Bank. Dog's head.	50 Female erect with spear and shield.	X Indian with bow and arrows.	Steamboat and sail vessels; wharf and buildings in distance. X Title of Bank	10 Female with sheaf of grain under her arm, and hat in her hand.	FIFTY Female seated; steam-boat and sloop in distance. 50	Man with gun and two Indians. Head and word "Fifty" on helmet, either side. Title of Bank.	FIFTY Female seated. 50

1 Full length female.	One man mowing, another whetting his scythe in foreground, two raking in the distance. 1 ORANGE CO. BANK, Chelsea, Vt.	1 Eagle with shield and arrows. ONE
2	Man and boys washing sheep, factories in distance. 2 ORANGE CO. BANK. Chelsea, Vt.	Figure 2 and word TWO. Female with wreath. Figure 2 and word TWO.
3 Officers on horseback.	Blacksmith at work at his forge. 3 ORANGE CO. BANK, Chelsea, Vt.	3 Indian female with bow and arrow.
FIVE Figure 5 and eagle.	Man and oxen. 5 ORANGE CO. BANK, Chelsea, Vt.	5 Horse.
10 Blacksmith at work. TEN	Man on horseback, one on ground with dog near by. X Portrait of Female ORANGE CO. BANK, Chelsea, Vt.	10 Man and machinery; train of cars in distance.
Steamboat. XX Rail cars.	Three females seated, one holding scales; small eagle ship in distance. 20 ORANGE CO. BANK. Chelsea, Vt.	XX Female full length.
FIFTY Female with wreaths of flowers. FIFTY	50 Man and Horse. 50 ORANGE CO. BANK. Chelsea. Vt.	FIFTY Female with horn of plenty. FIFTY
100 Vulcan the blacksmith.	[Old Plate.] Spread eagle, rail road and canal. C ORANGE CO. BANK, C Chelsea, Vt. 100	100 Female.
ONE HUNDRED and figures 100. Portrait.	[New Plate.] Horses, wagons, and shipping. ORANGE CO. BANK, Chelsea. Vt.	ONE HUNDRED and figures 100. Portrait.

Washington. 1	State Arms with females. PEOPLES BANK, N. Providence, R. I.	1 ONE Female with sickle, wheat &c.
Med. head. TWO 2	Two females, wheat, sickles &c.; ship in background. PEOPLES BANK, N. Providence, R. I.	2 Female, eagle and shield.
5 Eagle and female.	Three females. PEOPLES BANK, N. Providence, R. I. The denomination across the bill in red letters.	5 Locomotive.
X F. Pierce. 10	State Arms. PEOPLES BANK, N. Providence, R. I.	10 Telegraph wires, cattle, &c.
20 Female with spear.	2 Female. 0 PEOPLES BANK, N. Providence, R. I. XX	20 20
50 Female with spear, &c.	Female figure with rake. Male figure with scroll in right hand. PEOPLES BANK, N. Providence, R. I. 50	50 Cupid in sailboat. 50
100 Male figure with scroll and staff.	Eagle on branch of tree, train of cars and canal in distance. PEOPLES BANK, N. Providence, R. I. 100	100 Female, rake &c.
Indian in canoe. 500	5 0 0 PEOPLES BANK, N. Providence, R. I. D D	500 Female, scales, sword, &c.
Eagle, ship in background. 1000	1 0 0 0 PEOPLES BANK, N. Providence, R. I. M M	1000 Female indian with bow & arrow.

ONE Girl and dog. 1	1 An Indian with bow and arrows. ONE NASHUA BANK, Nashua. N. H.	1 Girl with rake. ONE
2 Milkmaid with pail and stool.	Reapers. TWO NASHUA BANK, Nashua, N. H.	2 Girl knitting TWO
THREE Full length figure of Justice with scales and sword.	3 Rail road cars and workmen with pick and wheelbarrow. THREE NASHUA BANK, Nashua, N. H.	3 Washington standing by the side of horse. THREE
V 5	Eagle on limb of a tree, loaded canal boats, locomotive and cars in the distance, on right large V. NASHUA BANK, Nashua, N. H.	5 Portrait of girl with sprig in left hand.
TEN Head of Washington. 10	Female and Steamship Mercury. NASHUA BANK, Nashua. N. H	10 Head of Lafayette. X
	☞ The other larger bills, 20s, 50s and 100s, are from the general plate of the New England Bank Note Co., Boston; for a description of which turn to page 149, and see description of 20s, 50s and 100s on the Lime Rock Bank, East Thomaston, Maine.	
ONE Portrait of Washington. 1	Milkmaid sitting and cows. 1 BATTENKILL BANK Manchester, Vt.	1 Portrait of Lady Washington. ONE
2 State arms. TWO	Stone cutters. 2 BATTENKILL BANK Manchester, Vt.	TWO Head of Franklin. TWO on Medallion head.
5 State arms. FIVE	Portrait of De Witt Clinton. 5 Portait of Abby Hutchinson. BATTENKILL BANK Manchester. Vt.	5 Medallion head. 5

FIVE
State arms.
FIVE
BATTENKILL BANK
Manchester, Vt.
Female Large V Female
and man
with sickle.
5
Medallion
head,

FIVE
Statue of Washington; cloak wrapped about him.
FIVE
[Second Plate.]
FARMER'S BANK,
Orwell, Vt.
5 Vig. Two females. 5
V
Canal boat about passing a lock.
FIVE
Female erect
FIVE

50
Female Head
ELMWOOD BANK.
Cranston, R. I.
View of Elmwood Village.
50.
Figures 50 supported by three men representing agriculture, manufacture and commerce.

10
State arms,
TEN
Signing declaration of independence.
Portrait of Washington and large X.
BATTENKILL BANK
Manchester, Vt.
X
Female bust.

FIVE
Female; sheaf of grain; sickle plough, rake, hoe, &c.
V
[Third Plate.]
V Neptune in chariot, pursuing an angel upon the sea; ship. fig. 5 on right
FARMER'S BANK,
Orwell, Vt.
Horse head.
FIVE

1
ONE
Webster.
PETERBOROUGH BANK,
Peterborough, N. H.
Spread Eagle and shield.
1
Washington
ONE

TWENTY
State arms.
TWENTY
20 Two men, with oxen, loading hay, and three oxen in background.
BATTENKILL BANK
Manchester, Vt.
20 Eagle. 20
20
Goddess of Liberty with eagle and shield.

TEN
Franklin.
TEN
FARMER'S BANK,
Orwell, Vt.
X
Cottage scene; shearing a sheep, with family around.
Eagle.
TEN
Austin.
10

TWO DOLLARS
2
Horses running, man on horseback in distance.
PETERBOROUGH
Peterborough, N. H.
2
TWO DOLLARS

50
State arms.
50
Man on horseback, and dog, driving sheep; mill in the distance.
BATTENKILL BANK
Manchester, Vt.
50 Female head. 50
50
Goddess of Liberty sitting; train of cars and buildings in distance.
FIFTY

XX
Eagle; Stars and Stripes.
20
FARMER'S BANK,
Orwell. Vt.
Sheaf of grain; plough and harrow.
Horse.
20
Steam ferry boat and canoe, with two men.
20

THREE
Men Loading Hay.
3
on Three.
PETERBOROUGH BANK.
Peterborough, N. H.
THREE

1
Franklin.
ONE
[First Plate.]
1 Vig. Two females; one sitting and one standing; harvest scene.
FARMER'S BANK,
Orwell, Vt.
Female reclining; bundle of wheat.
1
Female sitting.
ONE

FIFTY
50 FARMER'S BANK. 50
Orwell, Vt
Vig. Sheep, ships, and mountain in the distance; man making fence.
Dog's head, safe, and key.
FIFTY

FIVE
PETERBOROUGH BANK,
Peterborough, N. H.
Drove of sheep, and dogs, man on horseback, mill in distance.
FIVE
5
Pierce.

1
Three Cupid's.
ONE
[Second Plate.]
1 Vig. cattle. 1
FARMER'S BANK,
Orwell, Vt.
Arm and hammer.
1
Female leaning against a monument.
ONE

1
Head of Webster.
ONE
View of Elmwood Village.
ELMWOOD BANK,
Cranston, R. I.
Elm Tree.
ONE
Large figure 1 with maiden supporting it.

Ship on stocks,
Word "Ten" letter "X," and figures "10."
PETERBOROUGH BANK,
Peterborough, N. H.
Female and safe, cotton mill in distance.
10
Woman drawing water, steamboat in distance.

TWO
Indian, gun, dog, &c.
2
2 2
FARMER'S BANK,
Orwell, Vt.
Cupid riding a Reindeer.
TWO
Man, sheaf of grain, &c.
TWO

2
View of Elmwood village.
Head of Franklin Pierce.
ELMWOOD BANK,
Cranston, R. I.
Elm Tree.
II
Female supporting large figure 2.

20
Three female figures.
PETERBOROUGH BANK,
Peterborough, N. H.
XX
Clay.

3
Cattle.
THREE
FARMER'S BANK.
Orwell, Vt.
Female in sitting posture; agricultural implements.
Girl churning.
Female in sitting posture; agricultural implements.
Plough, rake and grain.
3
Goddess of Liberty.
THREE

FIVE
Figure representing a man eating, woman talking and dog watching; high bluff of land water in distance.
5 View of Elmwood village.
ELMWOOD BANK,
Cranston, R. I.
Elm Tree.
5
Figure of Justice with scales.
FIVE

50
Signing Declaration of Independence.
PETERBOROUGH BANK,
Peterborough, N. H.
50
Jackson

5
Eagle and serpent.
5
[First Plate.]
V Vig. Female seated; V
one arm resting on sheaf of grain; agricultural scene.
FARMER'S BANK,
Orwell, Vt.
Man's head.
5
Female reclining against a monument
V

TEN
Female supporting large X.
10
ELMWOOD BANK,
Cranston, R. I.
View of Elmwood Village.
Elm Tree.
10
Letter X covered with vines; female with pail and cow.

1 Winged female with trumpet and wreath,
Another female figure reclining and eagle.
1
LANGDON BANK,
Dover, N. H.
Cupid rolling a silver dollar; village, train of cars, steamboat, in background.
1

Hunter resting on gun, game near him. 2	LANGDON BANK, Dover, N. H. Interior of shoe manufactory. Two horses.	2 Factory.	3 Female reclining, with shield in left hand, she holds grain.	Vig. Female, shield, anchor, sheaf of wheat, plough, &c.; female holds sickle in left hand; cars and bridge on right. CENTREVILLE BK., Warwick, R. I.	3 Indian reclining.	20 Woman with spear and globe.	2 Female sitting. 0 NEW IPSWICH B'K, New Ipswich, N. H. XX	20 20
Man standing with sheaf of grain on left arm; female figure in sitting posture. 3	Three cupids and three silver dollars. LANGDON BANK, Dover, N. H. Load of hay.	3 Man resting on plow. THREE	5 Male Portrait.	CENTREVILLE BK., Warwick, R. I. Vig. Horse, boys, and dog; the boys are trying to catch the horse; one boy is laying on ground.	5 Male Portrait.	50 Woman with helmet, pillar.	Woman and man seated, flowers between them. NEW IPSWICH B'K, New Ipswich, N. H. 50	50 Cupid in sail boat. 50
Goddess of Liberty with scroll and shield.	5 LANGDON BANK, Dover, N. H. Winged female with wreath and trumpet. Portrait of Jackson. Cupid	5 Female with sheaf and sickle, plow and basket of fruit.	10 Male Portrait.	CENTREVILLE BK., Warwick, R. I. Vig. Blacksmith shoeing a horse; two men on left, one seated on log; wagon and wheel on right.	10 Male Portrait.	100 Man seated hand on sword and scroll.	Eagle on branch of tree, cars and canal boat in distance. NEW IPSWICH B'K, New Ipswich, N. H. 100	100 Woman with flowers.
Portrait of female. TEN X	Female and nine cupids and ten gold dollars. LANGDON BANK, Dover, N. H.	10 Female, globe, and shield.		☞ The 20's., 50's., and 100's., are of the Perkin's stereotype plate, which has the denominations prints, in fine letters, all over the bill.		Indian in canoe. 500	5 0 0 NEW IPSWICH B'K, New Ipswich, N. H. D D	500 Woman with scales.
XX Female portrait.	Harvest scene LANGDON BANK, Dover, N. H Cow and calf.	20 Sheaf of wheat. Female portrait.	Spread eagle, shield, Capitol at Washington. 1	1 NEW IPSWICK B'K, New Ipswick, N. H. 1	1 Milkmaid seated with pail.	1 Portrait of Washington.	Female. 1 Female. PEOPLE'S BANK, Derby Line, Vt.	1 Portrait of Franklin.
Military officer, with left foot resting on gun carriage. FIFTY	Goddess of Liberty, globe, eagle, ship, and steamboat. LANGDON BANK. Dover, N. H. Plowing scene.	50 Portrait of Washington. 50	Farmer, man and sheep; mills in distance. 2	Heads of Hancock and Adams. NEW IPSWICH B'K, New Ipswich, N. H.	TWO Woman with wreath. TWO	2 Male portrait.	Female with horn of plenty. 2 Female PEOPLE'S BANK, Derby Line, Vt.	2 Male portrait.
100 Goddess of Liberty, shield, fruit, and grain.	Winged female. Portrait of Webster. Cupid. LANGDON BANK, Dover, N. H.	100 Female portrait.	Man on horseback; another with scythe cattle. 3	NEW IPSWICH B'K, New Ipswich, N. H.	THR3EE Girl with flowers on shoulder. THREE	3 Washington standing by his horse.	Child. 3 Child. PEOPLE'S BANK, Derby Line, Vt.	3 Blacksmith with hammer and anvil.
1 Indian reclining, looking over rock.	Vig. Dog, safe and key; bags of money. CENTREVILLE BK., Warwick, R. I. Shield and anchor.	1 Farmer erect, with sheaf of wheat, and scythe. shoes hanging on handle of scythe	Woman in the air holding shield, eagle beyond. 5	5 NEW IPSWICH B'K, New Ipswich, N. H.	5 State Arms.	Eagle on shield with manufacturing village in distance. FIVE	Large V with female with horn of plenty and a child. PEOPLE'S BANK, Derby Line, Vt.	5 Child with basket.
2 Female seated, with scales and sword.	Vig. Large eagle and shield. CENTREVILLE BK., Warwick, R. I. Wheel and rollers.	2 Female with spy-glass; ships on left, in distance.	Declaration of independence; numerous heads. X	X NEW IPSWICH B'K, New Ipswich, N. H.	10 Locomotive, man with wheelbarrow	Blacksmith with hammer and anvil. TEN	X PEOPLE'S BANK, Derby Line, Vt.	10 Reaper with bundle of grain and sickle.

Left	Centre	Right
20 Man with helmet and spear, globe and an owl at his feet.	2 Female. 0 PEOPLES' BANK, Derby Line, Vt. XX	20 Female. 20
XX Portrait of an Indian, bow in right hand, left hand over right shoulder drawing arrow from quiver.	Female and Indian seated on either side of view of sunrise, wigwams, ship and city in back ground. BANK OF LYNDON, Lyndon, Vt. Woodman chopping tree.	20 Portrait of S. Houston.
FIFTY Female standing, with wreaths and flowers. FIFTY	50 Man and horse. 50 VILLAGE BANK, Smithfield, R. I.	FIFTY Female standing. FIFTY
50 Man with helmet and spear standing beside a broken column.	Vig. Female holding a rake sitting, man sitting, holding a scroll, foot resting on an anchor. PEOPLE'S BANK, Derby Line, Vt. 50	50 Cupid in a sail boat. 50
50 Spread Eagle	3 cows lying down, 1 standing, 2 in background, 1 drinking. BANK OF LYNDON, Lyndon, Vt.	50 FIFTY DOLLARS. Portrait of Webster.
Figures 100, and words ONE HUNDRED across. Portrait.	Shipping, baggage, wagon, &c. VILLAGE BANK, Smithfield, R. I.	Figures 100, and words ONE HUNDRED across. Portrait
100 Man sitting, holding a scroll; foot resting on an anchor.	Vig. Eagle on a branch of a tree, train of cars, locks and two canal boats. PEOPLE'S BANK, Derby Line, Vt. 100	100 Female sitting holding a rake.
C Indian seated with gun and dog, warming his hands at a fire on ground.	2 male and 1 female Indians near wigwam watching and pointing to the approaching train. City, rail road bridge with cars on it, another train coming. BANK OF LYNDON, Lyndon, Vt. Ducks.	100 Portrait of Clay.
1 Nude female. 1	BANK OF ORLEANS, Irasburg, Vt. 1 Safe and dog.	1 Ox. 1
ONE Male Portrait	[First Plate.] BANK OF LYNDON, Lyndon, Vt. Eleven Indians in council; a chief addressing them. Ducks.	1 Portrait of Webster.
1 Female with liberty cap; emblem of Liberty.	Vig. Cupid holding silver dollar; churches and steamboat in the distance. VILLAGE BANK, Smithfield, R. I.	1 Female figure, emblem of com. and manufacture.
ONE Head of Washington. ONE	1 Blacksmith's shop. 1 BANK OF ORLEANS, Irasburg, Vt.	ONE Female. ONE
ONE	[Second Plate.] Large Spread Eagle. BANK OF LYNDON, Lyndon, Vt. Female bathing.	ONE Three females, anchor, sickle, sheaf of grain.
2 Farmer with a cradle, seated on sheaves of grain.	Vig. Two silver dollars; two boys (nude;) mountain and train of cars in background. VILLAGE BANK, Smithfield, R. I.	2 Female in round miniature.
2 Man with sledge on his shoulder. 2	BANK OF ORLEANS, Irasburg, Vt. 2	2 Milkmaid and two cows. 2
TWO Two females holding aloft sheaf of grain	Three Indians in a canoe, one a female; hills, trees, &c. BANK OF LYNDON, Lyndon, Vt. Dog.	2 Male Portrait
THREE Standing female figure, with a spear and emblems of the arts.	Vig. Three silver dollars, and three Cupid's. VILLAGE BANK, Smithfield, R. I.	3 Bust of a sailor, with part of an oar in his hand.
TWO Female. 2	2 Family group. 2 BANK OF ORLEANS, Irasburg, Vt.	TWO 2
Word THREE and figure 3. Man on horseback.	Cattle Scene, 4 cattle, 1 standing 3 lying down, 3 sheep 1 standing 2 lying. BANK OF LYNDON, Lyndon, Vt.	3 Little Girl shading her eyes with left hand.
5 Letter V., with 5 persons around it.	Vig. Five silver dollars, and five Cupid's. VILLAGE BANK, Smithfield, R. I.	5 Head of a female and a horse.
3 Man with axe, oxen and cart. 3	BANK OF ORLEANS, Irasburg, Vt. 3 Man shearing sheep.	3 Two males, female and three children.
V Train of cars	Wild horses running. BANK OF LYNDON, Lyndon, Vt. 5 5	5 Portrait of Jackson.
Standing female, with flowers and lens in her hand. TEN	Vig. Railroad cars depot; shipping and wharf scene. VILLAGE BANK, Smithfield, R. I.	X Indian female in sitting posture.
THREE Man with scythe. Word three and figure 3 across.	3 Female, eagle, anchor, &c. BANK OF ORLEANS, Irasburg, Vt. (There is imitations of this plate.)	THREE Sailor. Word three and figure 3 across.
Large number of cattle and men entering and fording a river. 10	BANK OF LYNDON, Lyndon, Vt. Head of Washington.	10 Man on horseback and boy on foot driving sheep.
20 Female seated, with a book.	XX Eagle. XX VILLAGE BANK, Smithfield, R. I.	20 Ship.
5 Cattle. 5	BANK OF ORLEANS. Irasburg, Vt. Ox.	5 Workmen and boiler. 5

Left end	Centre	Right end
FIVE	Female V BANK OF ORLEANS, Irasburg, Vt.	Ship.
X Agricultural scene — load of grain and man on horseback. X	BANK OF ORLEANS, Irasburg, Vt. X	X Two men and a woman in field. X
X	Signing the declaration of independence. X BANK OF ORLEANS, Irasburg, Vt	10 Train of cars and man with wheel barrow.
20 Female sitting, book in left hand, right hand on a box.	XX Eagle. XX BANK OF ORLEANS, Irasburg, Vt.	20 Ship, with buildings in the distance.
FIFTY Female with wreath of flowers on her head and in her hands FIFTY	50 Man and horse. 50 BANK OF ORLEANS, Irasburg, Vt.	FIFTY Female with flowers in her left hand FIFTY
100 Female with cornucopia. 100	100 100 BANK OF ORLEANS, Irasburg, Vt. 100 100	100 Waterfall and eagle. 100
Figures 100, with words one hundred across. Portrait of Harrison.	Covered wagon, wharf, ships, warehouses, truckmen &c. BANK OF ORLEANS, Irasburg, Vt.	Same as on left end. Portrait of Columbus.
1	Farming scene—haying and harvesting. 1 BRANDON BANK, Brandon, Vt. Wheels and shafts, representing the mechanic arts.	1 Female with sickle in left hand and a head of grain in right hand ONE
TWO	Washing sheep. 2 BRANDON BANK. Brandon Vt. Bundle of grain, plough.	2 Blacksmith, hammer in hand; anvil.
3	Horses ploughing; house, steamboat and other vessels in the distance. 3 BRANDON BANK, Brandon, Vt. Train of cars.	3 Man chiselling marble, with mallet and chisel in hand.
FIVE	Farming scene—oxen ploughing, drove of cattle; cars moving in distance. 5 Seal of State. BRANDON BANK, Brandon, Vt. 5	5 Full length female with a flag. Three cherubs representing Agriculture, Mechanics, &c.
TEN	Farming scene—oxen and cart with load of grain; house in the distance. X BRANDON BANK, Brandon, Vt, Dog's head.	10 Two female figures erect.
20 Full figure of a female.	2 Female. 0 BRANDON BANK, Brandon, Vt. XX	20 Female reclining. 20
50 Male figure standing.	Female and male seated. BRANDON BANK, Brandon, Vt. 50	50 Cupid in a sail-boat. 50
Figures 100, and words one hundred, Male figure sitting.	Large spread eagle on a limb of a tree; cars, canal, and boats in distance. BRANDON BANK, Brandon, Vt. 100	Same as on left end. Female sitting
1 A man sitting cutting a log, gold dollar, a hat, traveling wagon in distance.	ASHUELOT BANK, Keene, N. H. 1	1 Female leaning on a fig. 1, sheaf at her feet.
TWO Female with spear, cap of liberty and scroll; shield at her feet.	ASHUELOT BANK, Keene. N. H. 2 Milkmaid sitting with pail, cows; two gold dollars; man reclining with rake.	2 2
State arms. 3	ASHUELOT BANK, Keene, N. H. Farmer sitting with scythe, sailor sitting with spy glass, blacksmith sitting, and three gold dollars.	3 Female portrait.
5 Large figure 5, with five images with scales, shield, spear, & cap of liberty.	ASHUELOT BANK, Keene, N. H. Three cupids, five gold dollars; sportsman sitting on right, female Indian sitting on left.	5 Female portrait reading.
Large X, with figures 10 across it.	ASHUELOT BANK, Keene, N. H. Harvest scene; males, female, dog, &c.; female sitting with a casket.	X Two females.
One figure with spear, shield, and helmet, and another with scales and sword. 20	Female in the clouds holding a shield; the American eagle flying with its back fastened to the shield. ASHUELOT BANK, Keene, N. H. Bull.	20 Two females, one with sword the other with sickle.
Female with spear, shield and helmet, and a book and globe at her feet. 50	Two men, boy and dog driving a flock of sheep across a stream, man in the foreground pushing a sheep into the stream. ASHUELOT BANK, Keene, N. H. Sheep, plough, rake, &c.	50 Female portrait.
Male with arms extended, sitting between two cupids riding on the back of an eagle. C	100 ASHUELOT BANK, Keene, N. H. A man shearing sheep; factory in the background.	100 Washington
ONE Cattle. 1	[Old Plate.] 1 WAKEFIELD BANK. 1 Wakefield, R. I. Indian in a canoe. Bird feeding her 4 young in a nest.	1 ONE ONE ONE ONE 1
ONE	[New Plate.] Schooner, large Sloop, steamboat, and ship. 1 WAKEFIELD BANK. Wakefield, R. I.	ONE Female Indian with bow and arrow. ONE
TWO Men reaping; furnace, factory and smokestacks in background. TWO	[Old Plate.] Portrait of Washington. 2 WAKEFIELD BANK. Wakefield, R. I.	TWO Ship at sea 2
2 TWO 2	[New Plate.] Ships and schooner. 2 WAKEFIELD BANK. Wakefield, R. I.	TWO Female drawing water at a spring with pail and rope TWO

Rail road engine and cars. 3 Schooner and ship in the distance. | (Old Plate.) 3 Dairywoman churning. 3 WAKEFIELD BANK, Wakefield, R. I. | THREE Cattle. 3

THREE | Girl with bonnet in right hand and sheaf of grain in left; on left man reaping. 3 WAKEFIELD BANK, Wakefield, R. I. | THREE Steamboat. Word THREE and figure 3.

5 Mechanic with vice, anvil and tools; female figure and emblems of commerce. V | (Old Plate.) WAKEFIELD BANK, Wakefield, R. I. Archimedes lifting the world. FIVE | 5 Female sitting with cattle on her right and sheaf on her left. FIVE

Word FIVE and large letter V. | (New Plate.) Female sitting, emblems of manufactures, commerce, and agriculture; factory and locomotive on left. V WAKEFIELD BANK, Wakefield, R. I. | 5 Portrait of Washington.

Indian with a drawn bow and arrow. 10 | (Old Plate.) X Jupiter with his car and horses. X WAKEFIELD BANK, Wakefield, R. I. Female with a sheaf of wheat. | 10 Farmer with his scythe in his field. TEN

X | (New Plate.) Signing the declaration of Indepence. X WAKEFIELD BANK, Wakefield, R. I. TEN | 10 Rail road cars.

20 Farmer plowing with pair of horses, 20 | 20 Milkmaids with pails, and laborers, some standing and others sitting 20 WAKEFIELD BANK, Wakefield, R. I. | Small ship. XX

50 Female Portrait. 50 | Woodman with axe, and hunter with gun, seated on either side of a frame on which is a bull; on right in distance ships' masts and sails. 50 WAKEFIELD BANK, Wakefield, R. I.

100 Female figure reclining with a cap of liberty in right hand. 100 | C Ships, &c. C WAKEFIELD BANK, Wakefield, R I. 100 100 | 100 Justice with scales. 100

100 Man sitting. | (New Plate.) Eagle on branch of tree; cars, canal boats, &c., in background WAKEFIELD BANK, Wakefield, R. I. C ONE HUNDRED 100 C | 100 Female sitting.

3 Head of Washington. THREE | Farmers plowing with two horses. BANK OF CHARLOTTE N. C. Hornet's nest on the branch of a tree. | 3 Man and head of a horse.

Tree over hanging a wagon, loaded and drawn by two oxen and horse; hornets nest on tree. | 4 Spread eagle. BANK OF CHARLOTTE, N. C. | 4 Figure reclining with pole and cap; factories in distance.

Man leaning against an anvil, sledge by his side. | Mecklenberg declaration inside of a shield. Train of cars. BANK OF CHARLOTTE, N. C. Same as 3s. | 5 Med. with head of female. FIVE

TEN A female figure, full length, with a wreath and very light drapery, her thighs very plainly seen on examination. | Mechanic and farmer, horse's head and a tree with the Declaration of Mecklenberg; in distance foundry. BANK OF CHARLOTTE, N. C. Same as 3s. | 10 Med. head of soldier. X

Male portrait 20 Female portrait. | Blacksmith's shop; man shoeing horse, and a man at forge. BANK OF CHARLOTTE, N. C. Same as 3's. | Female portrait. 20 Male portrait

FIFTY Med. head; shield with 20th May, 1775 on it FIFTY | BANK OF CHARLOTTE, N. C. Fox chase Same as threes | 50 Female with grain on her end.

Man and sheep. | 1 Man and horse; cattle and sheep. 1 FAR., & MECH., BK., Burlington, Vt. Dog and safe. | Black smith

1 Figure of mason. | Portrait of female FAR. & MECH., BK., Burlington, Vt. Bee-hive. | 1 ONE Word one and figure 1

Two dollars. Sheep. Two dollars. | 2 Harvest scene; two full length figures and dog. 2 FAR., & MECH., BK., Burlington, Vt. | Two dollars. Cattle. Two dollars.

2 2 | Train of cars; river and mountains in distance. FAR., & MECH., BK., Burlington, Vt. Steamer. | 2 2

THREE Milkmaid. 3 | 3 Blacksmith seated, with sledge-hammer; cars in distance. FAR. & MECH., BK., Burlington, Vt. Dog and safe. | THREE Reaper and dog. 3

3 THREE 3 | Female seated; fruit and grain lying around; vessels in distance. FAR. & MECH., BK., Burlington, Vt. Eagle. | 3 THREE 3

5 Eagle. | Steamer and vessels. FAR., & MECH., BK., Burlington, Vt. Sheaf of wheat. | Head of female. 5

Female and child seated on a plough; reaper's in distance. 10 | 10 FAR. & MECH., BK., Burlington, Vt. Eagle. | Steamboat and vessels. 10

20 Female. | Steamer and vessels. FAR. & MECH., BK., Burlington, Vt. Wheat. | Blacksmith. 20

FIFTY Female reaper. | Spread eagle. FAR. & MECH. BK., Burlington, Vt. Locomotive. | 50

100 Head of Washington. 100 | Spread eagle. FAR. & MECH., BK., Burlington, Vt. Dog and safe.

V Male portrait. 5	FIVE Vig. Large FIVE wagon and horses, steam-boat, houses, &c. MERCHANTS' AND MECHANICS' BANK. Wheeling, Va.	5 Male portrait. V
5	BANK OF NEW ENGLAND, East Haddam, Conn. Ship building. Female	FIVE 5
10 Male portrait.	BANK OF CHESTER, Chester, S. C. Portrait of John C. Calhoun. Same as Fives.	10 Male portrait.
5 Bust of Washington. V	Medallion head and figure 5. Medallion head and figure 5. Vig. Harvest scene; bundles of grain; urchin sleeping. Title of Bank.	5 Male portrait. V
X	View of Goodspeed's Landing. Male portrait on right. BANK OF NEW ENGLAND, East Haddam, Conn. TEN	10
Sailor holding American flag; female in sitting position; casks, anchor, bale of goods, horn of plenty. TWENTY	Train of cars. BANK OF CHESTER, Chester, S. C. Same as Fives.	20 Portrait of female.
5 Male portrait. 5	Female portrait. Vig. Dog and safe. Female portrait. Title of Bank.	5 Male portrait. 5
20	View of Goodspeed's Landing. BANK OF NEW ENGLAND, East Haddam, Conn.	20 Head of D. Webster.
50 Female.	Horses; buildings in the distance. BANK OF CHESTER, Chester, S. C. Same as Fives.	50 Portrait of W. R King.
X Portrait of Washington. 10	TEN Vig. Mechanic reclining on an anvil; house in background. TEN Title of Bank.	10 Male portrait. X
5 Train of cars. 5	B'K OF HAMBURG, Hamburg, S. C. Eagle. Female seated; cars in distance on left. Eagle.	5 Steamboat and two Indians in canoe. 5
100 Portrait of female.	Capitol at Washington. BANK OF CHESTER, Chester, S. C. Same as Fives.	100 Eagle.
50 Medallion head. 50	Med. head. Vig. male figure in standing position. Med. head. Title of Bank.	50 Medallion head. 50
10 Female supporting state arms. TEN	Two oxen, plow and yoke, figure leaning against an ox. Male portrait. Female seated on bale of goods spinning; wheel behind her. B'K OF HAMBURG, Hamburg, S. C	10 Military figure supporting state arms. TEN
ONE Word one and figure 1. ONE	Minature view of farmer mowing, and steamboat; on left, female; in distance on left train of cars, city, steamboat, &c; on right, two male figures, trees, &c. 1 SHAWNEE BANK. Attica, Ind.	Word one and figure 1. Bridge, canal, boats, and village in distance.
100 Cattle shrubbery, &c. 100	Med. head. Vig. Harvest scene, houses and shrubbery in background. Med. head. Title of Bank.	100 Cattle. 100
20 Female with pitcher. 20	Farm house, wagon and team, oxen and trees. B'K OF HAMBURG, Hamburg, S. C.	20 Man shearing a sheep, horse behind him. 20
3	Indian shooting buffalo; horse at his side. 3 SHAWNEE BANK, Attica, Ind.	THREE 3 Train of cars
1 [illegible] of male. ONE	BANK OF NEW ENGLAND, East Haddam, Conn. View Goodspeed's landing	ONE Female. ONE
Female holding sheaf and sickle. 50	50 Train of cars; bbls., boxes, and steamboat in distance. 50 B'K OF HAMBURG, Hamburg, S. C.	Female with cornucopia. 50
FIVE Two Indians erect.	5 Milkmaid and two cows; cattle, houses and steamboat in distance. SHAWNEE BANK, Attica, Ind.	5 Man resting on axe, trees, &c.
2 Male portrait	BANK OF NEW ENGLAND. East Haddam. Conn. View Goodspeed's landing.	TWO 2
100 Milkmaid. C	Figure of Liberty. Ship taking in freight from boats; bridge; steamboats to left. Figure of Liberty B'K OF HAMBURG, Hamburg, S. C.	C Reaper and dog. 100
X Indians abo't to slay white man, squaw pleading for his life to chief.	SHAWNEE BANK, Attica, Ind. X	10 Female seated with sickle; shield, on her right miniature view of steamboat.
3	BANK OF NEW ENGLAND. East Haddam, Conn. Steamboat Granite State. THREE	3 3
5 Portrait of Jefferson.	Surrender of Lord Cornwallis. BANK OF CHESTER, Chester, S. C. Palmetto tree, cotton on each side of it.	5 Portrait of Washington.
ONE Female seated holding quadrant; spread eagle and anchor.	Indian with spear and horse viewing train of cars on prairie, CHEROKEE INS. and BANKING CO., Dalton, Geo.	1 State arms.

Two females, one erect with spear, the other kneeling holding stalks of wheat.	2 Steamboat and other vessels. CHEROKEE INS. and BANKING CO., Dalton, Geo.	2 State arms.

TWO Indian erect; bow and spear in right and left hand raised to his head.	Vig. Locomotive and train of cars. Title of Bank. Two horses standing.	2 Ship under fore and top sail.

Med. head and word five Locomotive and tender. FIVE	Indian and female reclining on either side escutcheon or arms of the State of Virginia. Title of Bank. Female bathing.	5 Med. head.

Indians viewing progress of civilization. FIVE	Portrait of Wahington. CHEROKEE INS. and BANKING CO. Dalton, Geo.	5 State arms.

FOUR Female; right hand resting on a shield, and holding a spear; left holding a sprig of laurel.	Vig. Group of haymaker's at rest, with provision basket, dog, &c.; loaded wagon with four horses, in the distance. Title of Bank. Ship on stocks.	4 Portrait of Prince Albert. FOUR

TEN Male and female and two children, one holding a sheep, &c.	Title of Bank. Large die containing the word ten, figures 10, and letter X.	10 Female with sickle. 10

TEN DOLLARS X Two Indians, one erect, the other kneeling.	Large X with female Indian and child on left; and female and two children on right. CHEROKEE INS. and BANKING CO., Dalton. Geo.	10 State arms.

20 TWENTY Female sitting; scroll in left hand; right resting on shield; spear laying upon shoulder.	Title of Bank. Vig. Female holding a hay-rake in right hand; left hand resting on figure 0, which, with figure 2 at her right hand, is wrought in fancy lettering. Crown.	20 DOLLARS Female sitting; balances in right hand; rod in left.

X Med. head and word ten thereon. 10	Med. head and word Ten.	Female reclining, representing Agriculture. Title of Bank.	Med. head and word Ten.	Word Ten in ornamental Italics.

Coat of Arms of S. Carolina. 5 Coat of Arms of Kentucky.	5 Locomotive and tender with portion of a car. 5 SOUTH WESTERN RAIL ROAD BANK, Charleston, S. C. Ship under full sail.	Coat of Arms of N. Carolina. 5 Coat of Arms of Tennessee

40 FORTY Female Portrait.	Title of Bank. Vig. British Coat-of-Arms, with female figure on each side; right hand holds a trident, and left hand figure, a . word. Ships on stocks.	40 DOLLARS Two Female standing.

TEN Female erect, holding word and balances. 10	Med. head and word ten.	Indian seated and gazing on vacancy. Title of Bank.	Med. head and word ten.	TEN

Coat of Arms of S. Carolina. 10 Coat of Arms of Kentucky.	10 Locomotive and tender with portion of a car. 10 SOUTH WESTERN RAIL ROAD BANK, Charleston, S. C. Ship under full sail.	Coat of Arms of N. Carolina. 10 Coat of Arms of Tennessee.

5 Male portrait. FIVE	MANUFACTURERS' AND FARMERS' BK. Wheeling, Va. Vig. Interior of a glass work establishment; hands at work.	5 Female treading the neck of a tyrant. 5

TEN Male and female and two children, one holding a sheep.	Title of Bank. Large die containing word ten, figures 10, and letter X.	10 Female with sickle in hand. 10

Coat of Arms of S. Carolina. 20 Coat of Arms of Kentucky.	20 Ship under full sail, [illegible] at on right, and boat on its left in fore-ground, a perspective of Charleston in back-ground left of ship. 20 SOUTH WESTERN RAIL ROAD BANK, Charleston, S. C. Locomotive and train.	Coat of Arms of N. Carolina. 20 Coat of Arms of Tennessee.

X TEN	MANUFACTURERS' AND FARMERS' BK. Wheeling, Va. Vig. Group of seven persons; three males and four females; commerce, agriculture, &c.; harbor and lighthouse in distance	10 State arms.

20 Portrait of Washington. 20	Med. head.	Instructor and pupil. Title of Bank.	Med. head.	20 Med. head. 20

Coat of Arms of S. Carolina. 50 Coat of Arms of Kentucky.	50 Vig. Same as 20. 50 SOUTH WESTERN RAIL ROAD BANK, Charleston, S. C. Locomotive train.	Coat of Arms of N. Carolina. 50 Coat of Arms of Tennessee.

State arms—Justice trampling upon the neck of a tyrant. 5	B'K OF WHEELING, Wheeling, Va. Vig. Large letter V and the word FIVE.	5 Medallion Head.

Med. head. 50 Med. head,	50 Group of three females representing Agriculture, Commerce, &c. 50 Title of Bank. Steamboat.	Med. head. 50 Med. head.

Coat of Arms of S. Carolina. 100 Coat of Arms of Kentucky.	100 Vig. Same as 20. 100 SOUTH WESTERN RAIL ROAD BANK, Charleston, S. C. Locomotive and train.	Coat of Arms of N. Carolina. 100 Coat of Arms of Tennessee.

10 State arms—Justice trampling upon the neck of a tyrant.	B'K OF WHEELING, Wheeling, Va. Large letter X and words TEN DOLLARS. Female—Justice and Commerce.	10 Locomotive and cars. 10

5 Hunter dipping water from a brook with his hand.	UNION BANK, Sandusky, Ohio. Head of E. F. Osborn.	V Webster and Calhoun in library, books, papers, &c., lying around. FIVE

ONE Mariner with quadrant.	Vig. Ship yard; two vessels on the stocks, &c. WESTMORLAND BK. Bend of Petticodiac, New Brunswick Cask and bale.	1 Portrait of Queen Victoria. ONE

Male portrait FIVE Male portrait	NORTH-WESTERN BANK, Wheeling, Va. Suspension bridge. Locomotive.	5 Med. head.

Scene—wine harvest—10 figures, four males and six females.	Head of E. F. Osborn. UNION BANK, Sandusky, Ohio.	10

5 | Three female figures, middle figure with reap hook in left hand. State Arms. | FIVE
Female, sheaf of wheat in left hand.
MERCHANTS BANK, Lynchburg, Va.
Merchandise

6 | Tunnel, Rail road cars. State Arms. | 6
6 | MERCHANTS BANK, Lynchburg, Va. | Blacksmith with hammer raised.

7 | Female figure, reclining on money chest; Deer in distance. State Arms. | 7
7 | MERCHANTS BANK, Lynchburg, Va. | Bust of a Male.

E[illegible] | State Arms. 8 male figures—mechanics in shirt sleeves. | 8
Female figure, Eagle, &c. | MERCHANTS BANK, Lynchburg, Va. | 8

9 | Female figure; train and buildings in distance. State Arms. | 9
Rail road. | MERCHANTS BANK, Lynchburg, Va. | Female, banner, &c.

Three female figures; right is reclining posture. State Arms. | X
10 | MERCHANTS BANK, Lynchburg, Va. Merchandise | Female staff in left hand.

20 20 XX | State Arms. 3 vessels; steam boat in distance. MERCHANTS BANK, Lynchburg, Va. | 20

50 | State Arms. Eagle; vessel in distance. | 50
Female figure, grain in left hand. | MERCHANTS BANK, Lynchburg, Va. | Canal and bridge. FIFTY

C | Sheafs of grain; female, milking pail in lap on left; State Arms on right; rail road train &c., in distance. | C
100 | MERCHANTS BANK, Lynchburg, Va. | Female, wheat in left hand. 100

1 | NORTHERN BANK OF ALABAMA. Female portrait. | 1
Parents playing with child. | Portrait of Jefferson.

Catching a wild horse. | NORTHERN BANK OF ALABAMA. Female portrait. | 2
2 | Portrait of Adams.

5 | NORTHERN BANK OF ALABAMA. | 5
Portrait of W. R. King. | 5 Spread Eagle. 5 | Portrait of J. C Calhoun

10 | Bridge over a river, locomotive and train of cars having crossed. NORTHERN BANK OF ALABAMA. | 10
Portrait of Henry Clay. TEN | Portrait of Webster. TEN

20 | NORTHERN BANK OF ALABAMA. | 20
Portrait of Jackson. | Two female viewing the Huntsville Springs and water works. | Portrait of Gen. Taylor.

Indian with gun on right leg. | Negro driving four oxen with a load of cotton, cotton field in the distance with pickers. | 50
50 | NORTHERN BANK OF ALABAMA. | Portrait of M. Fillmore.

Portrait of B. Franklin. | Capitol at Washington with the extension. | 100
100 | NORTHERN BANK OF ALABAMA. | Portrait of Washington.

Word one and figure 1 | Drove of cattle and wagon; houses. | 1
Locomotive. | DANDRIDGE BANK, Dandridge Tenn. | Female seated on bale, ship in distance.

2 | Two men cutting grain; harvester's in the distance. | 2
Female leaning on bucket; cattle and house in distance. | DANDRIDGE BANK, Dandridge, Tenn. | Female and Eagle.

5 V | State House. | 5
Polk's portrait. 5 | DANDRIDGE BANK, Dandridge, Tenn. | Clay's portrait.

10 | Two females—one with sickle in right hand; ships in distance. | 10
Female Indian, &c. | DANDRIDGE BANK, Dandridge, Tenn. | X

20 | XX Female on either side of 20.
Female with sheaf, sickle, &c.; train crossing bridge, in distance. | DANDRIDGE BANK, Dandridge, Tenn.

1 | SOUTHERN BANK OF TENNESSEE, Memphis, Tenn. Female portrait | 1
Shield with cotton plant, on right of shield female teaching with globe, &c.; on left, Indians. | Farmer and hands, harvest scene.

2 TWO | Female sitting in fig. 2; on left man ploughing, on right hay field. Female portrait. | II
Cotton plant, bale of cotton, hogshead of tobacco and harrow in frame. | SOUTHERN BANK OF TENNESSEE, Memphis, Tenn. | Female with sheaf and sickle in left hand and bunch of wheat in right. TWO

3 | SOUTHERN BANK OF TENNESSEE. Memphis. Tenn. | 3
Indians on a rock overlooking a river, with city in the distance, and [illegible] with vessels on the river. | Kentucky coat of arms. Three. Safe. Three. | Head of Jackson.

5 | Battle of New Orleans. | FIVE
Head of Jackson. | SOUTHERN BANK OF TENNESSEE, Memphis, Tenn. | Male portrait.
FIVE | Cupid in sail boat.

Minerva with spear, shield, &c. | 10 Goddess of liberty reclining with children drawing locomotive with cars in distance on the right, and ship at anchor on left in rear. | X
TEN | Title of Bank. Game cock. | Head of J. K. Polk. TEN

Auditors die | Indian female, western hunter, seated—three cupids, and five gold dollars | 5
Figure 5 surrounded by five females. | BANK OF NEW ORLEANS, La. Safe. | Female portrait. FIVE

Left	Centre	Right
TEN Female erect with pole, cap and shield. 10	Auditors die. Female seated with sheaf of wheat, cornucopia of flowers and coin, compass, quadrant, etc., laying around; in distance factories, bridge, train of cars, ships, steamboats, &c. BANK OF NEW OR-LEANS, La. Two sheep.	10 Blacksmith, etc. TEN
Auditors die. Mercury seated on bale of cotton, right arm resting on 2, and left hand supporting 0 on knee TWENTY	Train of cars; steamboat and depot in background. BANK OF NEW OR-LEANS, La. Agricultural implements.	20 Figure of Hope erect, left hand on anchor. TWENTY
50 Marine God and Goddess with dolphin tails. Auditors die	State arms of N Jersey with female on either side, motto "Prosperity and Liberty." In background factories, steamship, train of cars etc. BANK OF NEW OR-LEANS. La. Deer.	50 Head of Franklin. FIFTY
100 Neptune in a shell on the sea; steamboat in distance. One Hundred	Auditors die. Steamboat under way with the name Crescent City, on the wheel house. BANK OF NEW OR-LEANS. La.	100 Female seated on plow, with sickle, sheaf of wheat, fruits &c. One Hundred
500 [illegible] seat- [illegible]undred	Auditors die. Female seated on bale of goods with eagle; ship and steamer in the background. BANK OF NEW OR-LEANS, La.	500 Head of female. 500
1 Female figure [illegible] and word "One."	SOUTHERN B'K OF KENTUCKY. Russelville, Ky. Vig. Female with dividers, &c., mechanical implements around. [illegible]	1 Indian. ONE
2 Cattle and drovers.	(New Plate.) Vig. Milkmaid, cows, &c. Title of Bank. Plough, rake, sheaf, &c.	2 Two cherubs
2 Female with flowers. TWO	(Old Plate.) Spread eagle. 2 Title of Bank. Agricultural implements.	Female figure of Justice. TWO
3 Female head. 3	Vig. Female, eagle, globe, &c. Title of Bank Steamboat.	3 Three female figures. THREE
5 Female head. 5	Vig. Man on horseback with negroes at work. Title of Bank Eagle.	5 Female figure.
10	Vig. Female figure with ears of corn, plough, &c. Title of Bank. Female head.	10
Sailor, flag, female figure &c.	20 Vig. Farmer, tobacco hhd., &c. Title of Bank.	20 Female head. 20
50 Hunter, gun, and dog.	Title of Bank. Vig. Female head.	50 Female figure, with flag, shield, &c.
100 Washington on horseback.	Vig. Female head, with wreath, scythe, &c. 100 Title of Bank.	ONE HUNDRED
Hill in the distance; man on horseback, driving flock of sheep, assisted by a dog. ONE	Portrait of Judge White. FARMER'S BANK OF TENNESSEE	1 Female portrait; left hand resting on shield.
2 Bucket and well, with female drawing water.	FARMER'S BANK OF TENNESSEE. Man ploughing in distance; group of cows, &c.	2 Female binding grain. 2
FIVE Man—left arm resting on bundle of grain. 5	5 Mule team; wagon loaded with cotton; driver walking, and two negroes lying on top of cotton. MINER'S & MAN., BANK. Knoxville, Tenn.	5 Female head.
Three figures; center, one female with Liberty Cap on pole. X	10 Stag chased by three hounds; forest, &c. MINER'S & MAN. BANK, Knoxville, Tenn.	
TWENTY Portrait.	MINER'S & MAN., BANK, Knoxville, Tenn Drove of cattle, and three men on horseback.	20
Manufacturing establishment; smoke in the distance, and laborer in shirt sleeves. 50	MINER'S & MAN., BANK, Knoxville, Tenn 50 Child with rabbits. 50	Square, compass, globe, anvil, hammer and sheaf of grain; three naked boys. (mythological scene.)
	B'K. OF MONTREAL AND BRANCHES. Canada. These notes all have the place from which they are issued printed in the same manner as we have shown in the second description of the ONE.	
Female in a large figure 1.	(Old Plate.) B'K. OF MONTREAL AND BRANCHES, Canada. Steamer towing. FIVE SHILLINGS. City Arms.	Female in a large figure 1.
MONTREAL City arms supported by two Indians, the female seated.	[New Plate.] B'K. OF MONTREAL AND BRANCHES, Canada. FIVE SHILLINGS. ONE DOLLAR.	Steamship and shipping, and large figure 1. MONTREAL
Female figure in large figure 2. 2	(Old Plate.) B'K. OF MONTREAL AND BRANCHES. Canada. Female seated. 2 Female standing. TEN SHILLINGS. City Arms	Female figure in large figure 2. 2
Same as on Ones.	[New Plate.] Title of Bank. TEN SHILLINGS. TWO DOLLARS.	Female shipping and figure 2, and horn of plenty.
4 DOLLARS Female.	Royal Arms with motto. B'K. OF MONTREAL AND BRANCHES. Canada. City Arms.	4 DOLLARS Female.
City Arms supported by two Indians, the female seated.	B'K. OF MONTREAL AND BRANCHES. Canada. TWENTY SHILLINGS. FOUR DOLLARS.	Female holding [illegible] sickle, lamb at her feet; large 4 resting on [illegible] of another lamb

5 Female bust. FIVE

B'K. OF MONTREAL AND BRANCHES, Canada. Large V. with female, figure 5 on either side. City Arms

Bust of female. FIVE

City Arms supported by two Indians, the female seated. 5

B'K. OF MONTREAL AND BRANCHES. Canada. TWENTY-FIVE SHILLINGS. FIVE DOLLARS.

Indian erect, one seated and two on horseback in distance, and 5.

---

10 Female. TEN

B'K. OF MONTREAL AND BRANCHES, Canada. TWO POUNDS TEN X SHILLINGS currency

10 Female. TEN

City Arms supported by two Indians, female seated. 10

B'K. OF MONTREAL AND BRANCHES, Canada. FIFTY SHILLINGS. TEN DOLLARS

Steamboat prospective with large 10

---

50 Bust of Her Majesty. 50

B'K. OF MONTREAL AND BRANCHES, Canada. A large ship in full sail and galliott. TWELVE POUNDS TEN SHILLINGS. City Arms.

50 Bust of Prince Albert. 50

---

100 Female figure representing Justice. 100

B'K. OF MONTREAL AND BRANCHES, Canada. Queen Victoria seated. TWENTY-FIVE POUNDS. City Arms.

100 Female representing Commerce. 100

Head of Jackson. 1

CITIZENS BANK OF NASHVILLE AND MEMPHIS. Tennessee. Large steamboat; city in the distance.

1 Bust of female. 1

---

2 Bust of male.

Title of Bank. Wagon with cotton bales drawn by oxen, driven by a negro; cotton plant; farm house and negro picking cotton in distance.

2 Indian reclining on a bank, gun in right hand.

Indian with gun, right foot on the ground, left knee resting on a rock. 3

3 Man sitting on bale, right arm resting on hogshead tobacco; tobacco plants in foreground; farm house and negroes working tobacco in distance. Title of Bank.

3 Bust of Jackson.

---

5 Locomotive with train. FIVE

Title of Bank. Small spread eagle. Female with cap in right hand, left hand resting on shield. Sheaf with agricultural implements.

5 Bust of Jackson.

---

10 Bust of Jackson.

Battle of New Orleans; Jackson and staff on horseback. Title of Bank.

10 Cotton plant

Bust of Jackson. 20

Title of Bank. Female sitting on bale, helmet on her head, left hand resting on shield with coat of arms.

20 Bust of male

---

50 Small head of Washington. L

Title of Bank. Female reclining, on her left, shield, U. S. flags, &c.; left elbow resting upon the shield, and small spread eagle perched upon it; on the left locomotive and train in the distance; on the right ocean steamer in the distance.

50 Small head of Jackson. L

Three female figures with globe resting on them, each with one hand raised above her head supporting the globe. 100

100 Large spread eagle standing on a shield. Title of Bank. Steamboat.

Bust of Jackson. C

---

1 State Arms. ONE

Female with sheaf, sickle and plow; female head on right, male head on left; town in distance. CITY BANK. Cleveland, Ohio.

1 Male portrait

---

3 State arms. THREE

Male head in centre; female head on each side. CITY BANK.

3 Male head. THREE

---

5 State arms. FIVE

Title of Bank under vig. Head of Henry Clay on the left; female head on the right. Female seated.

5 Portrait of male. FIVE

---

10 State arms. TEN

CITY BANK. Cleveland, O. Male portrait. Vig. Female seated with sheaf of wheat, wreath, &c. Agricultural implements.

10 Portrait of Harrison. TEN

---

5 Bust of male. 5

5 Two females, one seated at the feet of the other; grain and farming tools in rear of one, ship in rear of other 5 COMMERCIAL BANK Columbia, S. C. State arms.

5 Bust of male. 5

X Washington's bust. X

10 Arms of South Carolina, surmounted by spread eagle, a female on either side. 10 COMMERCIAL BANK Columbia, S. C.

X Lafayette's bust. X

---

20 Male bust in uniform. 20

20 XX surmounted by eagle; female, bale of cotton, water, and sloop on left; female, barrel, water, and schooner on right. 20 COMMERCIAL BANK Columbia, S. C.

20 Male bust in uniform. 20

---

50 Head of male 50

Female with left hand resting on an urn; an eagle before her resting upon the clouds. COMMERCIAL BANK Columbia, S. C. State arms. 50

---

100 Female seated on rock, her left hand on a harp. 100

100 Two female figures, the right hand one standing, the left hand one seated, is winged, and holds a wreath in her left hand; water in the distance in the rear; in front a standard, globe, &c. 100 COMMERCIAL BANK Columbia, S. C.

100 Female with sword and balances. 100

Three females seated around a shield, eagle on top; ship in distance. 5

FIVE on medallion shield. PLANTERS BANK OF TENNESSEE.

5 Medallion head

Med. head. FIVE Medallion head.

FIVE Waggoner and dog. FIVE PLANTERS BANK OF TENNESSEE. Small head.

Same as other end.

10

Female reclining supporting a shield; Indian reclining behind shield. PLANTERS BANK OF TENNESSEE. Medallion head

10

Med. head. TEN Med. head.

10 Farmer and girl talking; loading wagon with hay in background. 10 PLANTERS BANK OF TENNESSEE. Indian head.

Same as the other end.

Left end	Centre	Right end
Manufactures and Commerce, two females sitting on ground, sailor and mechanic standing behind; city in the distance.	20 Med. head. PLANTERS BANK OF TENNESSEE.	20
20 Med. Head. 20	Train of cars, hills, &c.; a train of cars, city and bridge in distance. WINDHAM CO., BK. Brooklyn, Conn. Two men; one with spade.	20 Female with flowers.
50 Head. FIFTY	State Arms and two horses; factory, cars and steamboat in background. COMMERCIAL B'K., Burlington, Vt.	50 Head of Female. FIFTY
20 Med. head. 20	20 Large Med. head. 20 PLANTERS BANK OF TENNESSEE.	Same as the other end.
50 Female erect, with helmet and shield.	Male and female seated. WINDHAM CO., BK., Brooklyn, Conn. 50	50 Cupid in a sail-boat. 50
100	COMMERCIAL B'K., Burlington, Vt. Three Females, anchor, sickle, &c.; train cars, vessels and city at distance. 100	100
50 Med. head. 50	Med. heads. Woman with distaff; steamboat in distance. Med. heads. PLANTERS BANK OF TENNESSEE.	Same as the other side.
100 Male figure sitting.	Large eagle on a tree; with canal and boats, and railroad with cars, in background. WINDHAM CO., BK., Brooklyn, Conn. C C 100	100 Female figure with rake, sitting load of hay in the distance.
ONE	Vig. Sailing vessels. 1 FRONTIER BANK, Eastport, Me.	ONE Female. ONE
100 Three females representing Arts, Commerce and Science. 100	Med. head of Franklin. Farmer's boy sleeping; sheafs of wheat rake, &c behind him. Med. head of Franklin. PLANTERS BANK OF TENNESSEE.	Same as the other end.
1 Head of Washington. ONE	Train of cars. COMMERCIAL B'K., Burlington, Vt. State Arms	1 Head of Female 1
2	Vig. Persons engaged with sheep; shrubbery and houses in the background; large figure "2" across the note and miniature view of four persons. FRONTIER BANK, Eastport, Me.	TWO Miniature view of female. TWO
ONE Mechanic erect, with arms folded; buildings in distance.	Two cows with no horns; one standing, the other laying down; mill on right. WINDHAM CO., BK., Brooklyn, Conn. Agricultural implements.	1 Female Portrait.
TWO Head of Franklin TWO	Three females and eagle. COMMERCIAL B'K., Burlington, Vt. State Arms	TWO Girl with rake and boquet of flowers. TWO
3	Vig. Farmers, farming implements, cattle, &c.; vig. on upper left corner. 3 FRONTIER BANK, Eastport, Me.	Figure 3 and word Three. Minature of Female. THREE
Little girl, with sheaf of grain on head; harvesting scene in distance. 2	Farmer, sailor, and blacksmith, apparently talking; 2 horse and man on right. WINDHAM CO., BK., Brooklyn, Conn.	2 Female with pole and cap; word Liberty, at her feet; building and train of cars on left.
THREE Eagle, ship, and female. THREE	Indian with spear and horse; cars in distance. COMMERCIAL B'K., Burlington, Vt. State Arms	3 Indian and female with sickle and sheaf of grain.
Vig. Female in representation of agriculture, commerce, &c.; shipping, houses, &c. Letter V and word Five.	Large V and female. FRONTIER BANK, Eastport, Me.	5 Head of Washington.
3 Male portrait.	Loading hay, two horses and four men; house in distance. WINDHAM CO., BK., Brooklyn, Conn.	3 THREE 3
5 Head. State Arms.	Vessels, steamboat and city. COMMERCIAL B'K., Burlington, Vt. Eagle.	5 Head of Washington. FIVE
X Indian with bow and arrow.	Vig. Steam boat; sail-vessels, &c. X FRONTIER BANK, Eastport, Me.	10 Female with sheaf of grain; forest in back ground.
FIVE 5 FIVE Head of Washington.	Title of Bank Two men; one with no hat, horse and buildings in background.	5 FIVE
Head. State Arms. TEN	TEN on Head. Declaration of Independence. COMMERCIAL B'K., Burlington, Vt. Blacksmith arm and anvil.	X TEN on Head. 10
20 Minature view of female.	XX Vig. Spread eagle. XX FRONTIER BANK, Eastport, Me.	20 Shipping.
10 Two females. TEN	View of the Capitol at Washington. WINDHAM CO., BK., Brooklyn, Conn.	10 Female portrait.
TWENTY	COMMERCIAL B'K., Burlington, Vt. Mechanics, 2 females sitting, city at distance. Anchor, anvil, &c.	20 Farmer, two females, dog and oxen.
FIFTY Female standing erect FIFTY	50 Vig. Man holding wild horse. 50 FRONTIER BANK, Eastport, Me.	Same as on opposite end.

Figure "100," with word "ONE HUNDRED" across.
Male portrait.

Vig. Large covered wagon; horses, persons, &c.; shipping in background.
FRONTIER BANK, Eastport, Me.

Figure "100," with word "ONE HUNDRED" across.
Portrait of Columbus.

ONE
Cotton, barrel and farming implements.
ONE

Vig. Large ship under weigh; on right small vessels, on left steamboat and fort in distance.
COMMERCIAL AND AGRICULTURAL B'K
Galveston, Texas.
Wheelbarrow, plough, sheaf of wheat, &c.

1
Portrait of Washington.

THREE
Cotton, barrel and farming implements.
THREE

Vig. Large ship under weigh; on right small vessels, &c.; on left steamboat and fort in distance.
Title of Bank.
Wheelbarrow, plough, sheaf of wheat, &c.

3
Portrait of Washington.

5
Cotton, barrel and farming implements.
FIVE

Vig. Portrait of Washington and two females, reclining one on either side; on right, bale of goods, barrel, ship and steamboat; on left sheaf of wheat and farmer mowing in background.
Title of Bank.
Barrels and bales of goods, small boats in distance.

5
Female portrait.

1
ONE
Portrait of John Hancock.

MERIDEN BANK, Meriden, Conn.
Farmer ploughing with oxen and horse.
Elephant.

1
Train of cars

ONE
Portrait of Lafayette.
ONE

Blacksmith seated, anvil, &c.; factories in distance
MERIDEN BANK, Meriden, Conn.
Locomotive.

1
Two Indians, one holding spear.

TWO
Portrait of Franklin.

Group of persons separated by a shield; child with hand on globe, &c.
MERIDEN BANK, Meriden, Conn.
Blacksmith's arms, anvil, &c.

2
Female portrait.

3
Indian viewing factories, &c.
THREE

Train of cars
MERIDEN BANK, Meriden, Conn.
Horse.

3
Blacksmith with hammer resting on anvil, &c.

5
Washington.
5

Female holding sickle and sheaf of grain; village in the distance.
MERIDEN BANK, Meriden, Conn.
Arms, anvil, &c.

5
Goddess of Liberty.

Goddess of Liberty.

10 Female, sickle, sheaf of grain; village in distance.
MERIDEN BANK, Meriden, Conn.
Eagle.

TEN
Youth hammering an anvil.
10

20
XX
20

20 Female 20 seated on bales, leaning against cask, sheaf of grain at her feet; vessels in the distance.
MERIDEN BANK Meriden, Conn.

TWENTY

50
Female leaning on rock, &c.: Steamboat in distance.
50

50
MERIDEN BANK Meriden, Conn.

FIFTY

C
Washington.
C

100 100 Man pouring water; bales, &c.; vessel in distance.
MERIDEN BANK Meriden, Conn.

ONE HUNDRED

FIVE
Female
FIVE

B'K OF COMMERCE. Georgetown, D. C.
Portrait of Washington, surmounted by spread eagle; female on either side; sickle, cornucopia and anchor.
Female

5
Liberty resting on coat of arms of U. S.; spread eagle.

X
Cars crossing viaduct in the distance and a sloop in foreground.
TEN

B'K OF COMMERCE, Georgetown, D. C.
Same as 5's.

10
Female

20
Canal boat passing under a bridge.
TWENTY

B'K OF COMMERCE, Georgetown, D. C.
Same as 5's.

20
Female.

50
Female Figure.
FIFTY

B'K OF COMMERCE. Georgetown, D. C.
Same as 5's.
Female and anchor.

50
Shipping, city in the distance.

100
Female with sheaf of wheat.
100

B'K OF COMMERCE Georgetown, D. C.
Same as 5's.
Female and anchor.

100
Large ship sails spread.

FIVE
Med. head of Washington.
FIVE

BK OF W'SHINGTON Washington, D. C.
Two female figures, one standing and one sitting, both leaning on figure 5.

Ship under sail.
5

Female standing, in her right a sword and her left hand resting on a shield.

10 Head of Washington 10 surrounded by flags and trophies; quadrant, &c.
BK OF W'SHINGTON Washington, D. C.

X
TEN
10

XX
Head of Washington.
XX

20 Two females one seated, and one kneeling; ship and steamboat in background.
BK OF W'SHINGTON Washington, D. C.

20
Female leaning on pole with pails.

FIFTY
Head of Washington.
FIFTY

50 Farmer seated on plough, lighting a pipe, cattle in the background.
BK OF W'SHINGTON Washington, D. C.

50
Female seated with pole and cap.

100
Female seated with cornucopia and wheat.
HUNDRED

... of Washington supported on right by sailor with anchor, and on left by figures representing agriculture and mechanics.
BK OF W'SHINGTON Washington, D. C.

HUNDRED
A representation of Washington monument.

1

Male Portrait; on left Female with three children, on right Female with lamb, Men shearing sheep, Railroad cars in distance.
PICKAWAY CO B'K., Circleville, Ohio.

1
ONE DOLLAR in semi-circle.

3
Scene, Wine Harvest.

Male Portrait.
PICKAWAY CO. B'K., Circleville, Ohio.

3
3

5
Hunter kneeling by brook drinking from his hand.

PICKAWAY CO. B'K., Circleville, Ohio.
Male Portrait.

V
Library scene Calhoun seated, Webster standing by his side.
FIVE

Harvest scene, group of ten figures.

Male Portrait.
PICKAWAY CO. B'K., Circleville, Ohio.

X
TEN

1 Agricultural scene. 1 WINDHAM BANK. Windham, Conn. Indian female figure. Froggs.	3 Male portrait. 3 Wine harvest—men, women and children. FRANKLIN BANK, of Portage Co., Ohio. 3	5 Title of Bank. V Scene reaping—two men, negro and two horses; barn in distance. V 5
2 WINDHAM BANK, Windham, Conn. 2 Head of Washington. Large figure 2, Indian male with gun on left, white female with sheaf of wheat on right. 2 Froggs.	FI V VE FRANKLIN BANK, of Portage Co., Ohio. V Library scene; Webster and Clay hour talking. Hunter on his knees, drinking out of his hand. Male portrait. FIVE	X 10 Female between 1 and 0, with basket and plow at her feet; on right man plowing with two horses, farm house in distance; on left man plowing with two oxen. Female loosely dressed standing; sheaf. TEN Title of Bank. TEN
3 Manufacturing scene; state arms, cotton, and wheat. Female head. 3 Med. head. WINDHAM BANK, Windham, Conn. THREE Froggs.	Males, females, spinning wheel, and agricultural and other implements. Male portrait. TEN FRANKLIN BANK, of Portage Co., Ohio 10	XX Title of Bank. 20 Female seated on log; train of cars; wheat; cattle and house in distance. Sailor leaning on rail of ship. 20
5 WINDHAM BANK, Windham, Conn. 5 Train of cars Large V, with female figure and wheat inside, and female head on either side. FIVE Froggs.	1 Male head Female with sheaf and sickle, plough, &c.; train of cars on a viaduct. 1 State Arms. ONE MAHONING CO., BK., Youngstown, Ohio. Male head.	Med. head. Medallion head. Med. head. FIVE UNION BANK, Tenn. FIVE Med. head. 5 Med. head.
X WINDHAM BANK, Windham, Conn 10 TEN Two females; state arms, steamboat, railroad. 10 X Froggs.	3 Female head Male head Female head 3 State Arms. Male head. MAHONING CO., BK., Youngstown, Ohio. THREE THREE	10 Med. head. Female seated with right arm resting on figure 10. Med. head. X Female. Female. X UNION BANK, Tenn. 10
FIVE V Ship in full sail 5 Sailor and mechanic; U. S. flag, bales, &c. BANK of COMMERCE Fredericksburg, Va. State arms.	5 Head of Clay Female head 5 State Arms. Head of Corwin. FIVE MAHONING CO., BK., Youngstown, Ohio. FIVE	Med. head. 10 Female feeding an eagle in a goblet. 10 Med. head. TEN UNION BANK, Tenn. TEN Med. head. Med. head.
X BANK of COMMERCE Fredericksburg, Va. X Female figure in sitting posture with reaping hook in right hand, and sheaf of wheat on shoulder, with left hand over it. TEN 10 10 State arms.	10 Male head Female with sickle and sheaf of wheat, shield; steamboat in distance. 10 State Arms. Male portrait TEN MAHONING CO., BK., Youngstown, Ohio. TEN	Med. head. Med. head. Med. head. Med. head. Med. head. 20 UNION BANK, Tenn. 20 Double med. head. Double med. head.
XX BANK of COMMERCE Fredericksburg, Va 20 Head of Washington and words twenty dollars on either side. XX 20 Spread eagle 20 State arms.	1 NEW CASTLE CO. BANK. Cantwell's Bridge, Del. Female bathing. ONE Blacksmith's shop—two smiths shoeing horse, farmer with hand on horse's back; two men at anvil in background. Milkmaid and churn. ONE	20 (Imitations of this plate.) 20 Two females, two eagles, &c.; steamboat on either side. Female with distaff in hand. UNION BANK, Tenn. Female with a distaff. 20 20
Vig. Male portrait; on right female and three children, on left, Lady and Lamb, man shearing sheep, and train of cars in distance. 1 1 FRANKLIN BANK, of Portage Co, Ohio. One dollar [illegible]	2 Farmer ploughing with two horses; farm-house in distance. 2 Bridge and train of cars; yacht in foreground. Title of Bank. 2	50 Head of Indian. Female seated; wheel behind her; bridge in distance. Head of Indian. 50 Steamboat. Steamboat. 50 UNION BANK, Tenn. 50

100 — Full length figure of Justice. — 100
Female resting on a globe, cupid in front and steamboat on right and left.
UNION BANK, Tenn.
Steamboat and bridge in distance.
Same as the other end.

1 — Compt's dis. — ONE
Man watering three horses from trough by side of well; goat, kid and sheep; cattle and house in distance.
OSHKOSH COMMERCIAL BANK, Oshkosh, Wis.
ONE — Female seated with shield.

Head of Franklin.
20 Female seated on a rock; left hand resting on a stalk of corn, right resting on a cornucopia. 20
BANK OF SMYRNA, Smyrna, Del.
Double med. head.
Head of Washington.

1 — Male portrait — ONE
Pasture two horses, running, negro boy and dogs, mules standing and reclining.
FARMER'S BANK OF KENTUCKY.
Bee Hive.
1 — Female Portrait. — ONE

2 — Farmer's family scene.
Title of Bank.
Indians on horseback hunting buffaloes.
2 on TWO. — Compt's dis. — TWO

Lathe work with statue in niche.
Med. 50. State arms with female on either side, representing Agriculture and Commerce. Med. 50.
BANK OF SMYRNA. Smyrna, Del.
Male portrait.
Same as left.

2 — Female Portrait. — TWO
FARMER'S BANK OF KENTUCKY.
Indian on horseback; Prairie Buffaloes in distance.
2 Bee Hive. 2
2 — Male Portrait — TWO

3 — THREE
Indian family contemplating the progress of civilization.
Title of Bank around Compt's dis.
Fig. 3 on DOLLARS — Female with flowers in her apron.

100 — State arms with female on either side. — 100
Female portrait. Country scene; two men loading hay; pair of oxen to wagon.
BANK OF SMYRNA, Smyrna, Del.
Steamboat.
100 — Ship under sail. — 100

5 — Male Portrait — 5
Drove of cattle and hogs, 2 Drovers and dog, river, covered bridge, rail road bridge, cars in distance.
FARMER'S BANK, OF KENTUCKY.
Bee Hive.
5 — Female Portrait. — 5

5 — FIVE — Compt's dis.
Title of Bank.
Prairie scene—Indians and horse; train of cars, buffaloes and rising sun in distance.
5 on FIVE — Squaw and papoose.

ONE — Female feeding an eagle. — ONE
WOODBURY BANK, Woodbury, Conn.
Two females seated, pole and cap; oxen and wagon at a distance on the left; on right, sheaves of grain and rake.
1 — Female Indian seated

10 — Male Portrait — 10
Female reclining against hogshead tobacco plant, negroes cutting tobacco, wagon on left and steam boat on right in distance. Female 2 Portrait.
FARMER'S BANK, OF KENTUCKY.
Bee Hive.
X — TEN — 10

1 — One and head of female. — 1
Man reaping, child, dog, and 1 agricultural 1 implements in the foreground.
BANK OF SMYRNA. Smyrna, Del.
Female.
1 — One and head of female. — 1

Large female standing, holding pole and Liberty cap in right hand; left hand resting on a large American shield.
WOODBURY BANK, Woodbury, Conn.
Man tending machinery.
2 — Portrait of Jenny Lind

Female Portrait. — Male Portrait
20 White man standing by two horses geared, cart; negro breaking hemp; hemp shock in background; cabin, locomotive and cars in distance.
FARMER'S BANK OF KENTUCKY.
Bee Hive.
20

TWO — Female seated in large figure 2. — TWO
Female seated with child in her arms; shipping in the distance.
2 on med. head each side
BANK OF SMYRNA. Smyrna, Del.
State arms.
TWO — Same as left. — TWO

3
Three females—one seated, the other reclining; globe, compass in left hand, scroll and quadrant. THREE
WOODBURY BANK, Woodbury, Conn.
3 — Female tending a machine.

Three female figures on rock with anchor in the centre.
50 Portrait in frame, on the ground on each side agricultural implements.
FARMER'S BANK OF KENTUCKY.
Bee Hive.
50 — Male Portrait — 50

3 — Drove of cattle. — 3
Med. Three. Shipping—three men in small boat; town in distance. Med. Three.
BANK OF SMYRNA, Smyrna, Del.
3 — Head of Washington. — 3

5 — Two men walking; one with rake on shoulder, the other with a fork; man, boy and house in the distance, on the right
Man on horseback, with dog driving sheep; mill in distance.
WOODBURY BANK. Woodbury, Conn.
Fish.
5 — Female; house and church spire in distance.

100 — Male Portrait — 100
Three female figures; steamboat and town in distance. Female Portrait.
FARMER'S BANK OF KENTUCKY.
Bee Hive.
ONE HUNDRED

5 — Head of female. — 5
Med. Five. Country scene—male and female; four reapers in distance. Med. Five.
BANK OF SMYRNA. Smyrna, Del.
5 — Head of female. — 5

10 — X
Female reclining on a chest; factory in the distance; sheaf of grain and two sheep on the right. 10
WOODBURY BANK, Woodbury, Conn.
TEN — Two females; one standing blindfolded, holding a pair of balances; the other seated, holding a harp.

100 — Ships and other vessels — 100
BASS RIVER BANK, Beverly, Mass.
Wheels and bales.
C — Female shearing.

10 — Female with rake in hand. — 10
Med. X. Woodsman seated on a log with his left hand on his dog's head. Med. X.
BANK OF SMYRNA. Smyrna, Del.
10 — Drove of cattle. — 10

20
Male and female Indian, with a child on left of shield; on right, female with three children and globe; sheaf of grain at her feet. XX
WOODBURY BANK, Woodbury, Conn.
TWENTY — Female seated, with her left hand on shield.

1 — Female seated with large figure 1; train of cars and steamboat in distance. — 1
SPRINGFIELD B'K.
Springfield, O.
Portrait of Clay. — Secured by the pledge of stock - and view of rising sun — Female portrait.

Female seated on bale. — Cupid and fig. 3. Portrait of Washington. Cupid and fig. 3. — Female seated, cornucopia at her feet.
SPRINGFIELD B'K,
Springfield, O.
THREE — Same as ones — THREE

(First Plate.)
5 FIVE — Female on either side of shield, on which is a view of rising sun, &c., surmounted by an eagle; steamer, train of cars, factories man ploughing, &c., in distance. — 5 FIVE
Cattle and sheep. — Title of Bank. Same as ones. — Train of cars

5 — V
Hunter kneeling by stream to drink; woodland scenery. — SPRINGFIELD B'K, Springfield. O — Vig. Webster and Calhoun conversing in a library; books, globe papers, & scattered around.
Maleportrait — FIVE

(First Plate.)
10 — Female on left of shield, on which is a view of rising sun, steamboat, &c.; steamboats, steamer, ships, train of cars, &c. — 10
Spread eagle — Spread eagle
TEN — Title of Bank. Same as ones. — TEN

(Second Plate.)
Group of males and fem les, ten in cumber. — Male portrait. — 10
SPRINGFIELD B'K.
Sprigfield. O. — X

ONE — MYSTIC BANK, Mystic, Conn. — Male figure erect.
Ship. — 1 1 Vig. Indian in canoe going over rapids.
ONE — Locomotive and tender. — ONE

2 — 2 Vig. female seated with wand; ship on left; State Arms on right 2 — Female warrior with spear, right hand resting on shield on which is figure 2.
Female, sickle and grain; figure 2 on left.
MYSTIC BANK,
Mystic, Conn.
TWO — State Arms. — TWO

THREE — 3 Beehive. 3 Vig. Indian and native American on either side of a shield, eagle at top of shield ship on right.
Female and mechanical tools.
MYSTIC BANK,
Mystic. Conn.
3 — Female grain and sickle. — 3

5 — V Vig. Female with balances 5 representing industry. — FIVE
Female with rake.
MYSTIC BANK,
Mystic, Conn.
5

10 — X Vig. Female with grain, leaning on pillar vessel on right X
Launching a ship.
MYSTIC BANK,
Mistic, Conn. — 10
10 — Canal lock, &c.

TWENTY — MYSTIC BANK. Mystic. Conn. — Indian with bow & arrow.
Vig. Archimedes raising the world. XX — 20

1 — Female 1 Female — 1
BK OF HALLOWELL,
Hallowell, Me.
Washington. — Franklin.

2 — Female 2 Female — 2
BK OF HALLOWELL.
Hallowell. Me.
Columbus. — Portrait

3 — Female Portrait. 3 Female Portrait. — 3
BK OF HALLOWELL,
Hallowell. Me.
Washington and horse. — Vulcan at his forge.

Eagle on rock with wings extended. — Large V, Female and Cupid. — 5
BK OF HALLOWELL,
Hallowell, Me.
FIVE — Female Portrait.

Vulcan the Blacksmith. — X — 10
BK OF HALLOWELL
Hallowell, Me.
TEN — Reaper.

ONE — Vig. Whaling scene. — ONE
Small boy, anvil and hammer.
UNION BANK,
New London, Conn.
ONE — Arm, hammer and anvil.

TWO — Vig. Milkmaid, seated with cattle. — TWO
Female, shield, liberty pole, cap and eagle.
UNION BANK
New London, Conn.
TWO — Steamboat.

THREE — Vig. Milkmaid; one cow standing, and one reposing in front of her. — THREE
Same as Two's.
UNION BANK.
New London, Conn.
THREE

FIVE — Vig. Farmer's loading hay. — FIVE
Large ship.
UNION BANK,
New London, Conn.
FIVE — Machinery.

TEN — Vig. View of river, upon which is large ship, steamboat and other vessels. — TEN
Male portrait.
UNION BANK.
New London, Ct.
TEN

20 — Vig. Stone cutter's at work. — 20
Male portrait.
UNION BANK,
New London, Ct.
TWENTY

50 — Vig. Ship carpenter; ship building on left; ships and view of city on right. — 50
Male portrait.
UNION BANK,
New London, Ct.
FIFTY

100 — Vig. Group of three male figures. — 100
Portrait of Washington.
UNION BANK.
New London. Ct.
100

1 — 1 Vig. Whaling scene. 1 — 1
Groton monument. — Female seated, wand in right hand key in left.
WHALING BANK,
New London, Ct.
1 — Ship, barrel, anchor, &c. — 1

TWO — 2 Vig. same as ones. 2 — TWO
Hunter, gun in right hand dog at his feet. — Female, sheaf of wheat, sickle, plow, rake, &c.
WHALING BANK
New London. Ct
TWO — Steamboat. — TWO

THREE | 3 Vig. same as ones. 3 | WHALING BANK. New London, Ct. | Blacksmith's arm and hammer. | Female; on right state arms, on which is eagle standing, on left scales, barrels, &c. | 3 | 3

5 | Locomotive and cars. | FIVE | OCEAN BANK. Stonington, Conn. | V V | Female seated resting upon State Arms of Connecticut, steam ship and ship on right also vessels on left. | 5 | Female Portrait.

Two females supporting letter X. | X Vig. view of ship yard; ship carpenter at work. X | CONNECTICUT B'K. Bridgeport, Ct. | 10 | Female portrait. | TEN

FIVE | 5 | WHALING BANK. New London, Ct. | Vig. same as ones. | Three circular dies with words five dollars running across | Indian in canoe. | 5 | Female giving eagle drink. | V

Sailor seated by his right foot is a coil of rope, flag on left, also hat raised aloft in left hand. | TEN | Large spread eagle on American shield, &c. | OCEAN BANK. Stonington, Conn | Locomotive and Tender. | 10 | Large ship.

Washington and his horse. | 20 | Vig. Group of three females; ship on right. | CONNECTICUT B'K. Bridgeport, Ct. | State arms. | 20 | Female and shield, liberty pole and cap.

TEN | Female seated, circle on her lap, in right hand sprig of flowers. | 10 | TEN Vig. same as TEN ones. | WHALING BANK. New London, Ct. | Cupid seated on reindeer. | TEN | Female resting on stone pillar, upon which is engraved letter X. | X

Female reclining sheaf of grain on left and in right hand sickle. | XX | 20 OCEAN BANK 20 | Stonington, Conn. | View of sea, large ship; light house on right in distance; sail vessel in distance on left. | Female sitting upon barrel with wand in left hand, ship on right. | XX

Female with sword and balances. | FIFTY | CONNECTICUT B'K. Bridgeport, Ct. | Female seated, before her is winged figure holding wand; on right is Neptune in his car drawn by sea serpents. | State arms. | 50 | 50

20 | XX Female seated giving eagle drink. 20 | WHALING BANK. New London, Ct. | Ship. | TWENTY

Three females on a rock; spy glass, anchor &c. | 100 | View of city of New York and Brooklyn with shipping. | OCEAN BANK. Stonington, Conn. | Eagle. | 100 | Female reclining on bale of goods, ships on right, also one on left.

Two females, farming implements on left, ship on right. | CONNECTICUT B'K, Bridgeport. Ct. | Eagle holding shield on which is figures 100. | Three cupids | 100

FIFTY | WHALING BANK. New London Ct. | L Vig. same as ones. L | Indian and canoe. | 50 | Female seated, sheaf of wheat on right, on left scroll on which is engraved figures 50. | 50

Portrait of of Washington. | Female, sickle and grain. | Male portrait. | CONNECTICUT B'K, Bridgeport. Conn. | 1 Vig. Female supporting figure 1. 1 | 1 | Female with arms extended.

ONE 1 ONE | 1 Fort, ships, &c. 1 | STONINGTON B'K. Stonington. Ct. | Figure 1 and word One. | Small figure 1. | Small figure 1.

100 | Vig. same as ones. 100 | WHALING BANK, New London. Ct. | Indian and canoe. | 100 | Male portrait | 100

2 | [First Plate.] | View of wharf, steamboat, large ship and other vessels. | CONNECTICUT B'K. Bridgeport, Conn. | State arms. | 2 | Male portrait.

TWO 2 TWO | 2 Catching seals; ships in distance on left. 2 | STONINGTON B'K, Stonington. Ct. | 2 | 2 | 2

1 | 1 | OCEAN BANK. Stonington, Conn. | 1 | Locomotive and cars. | Steamboat. | 1 | Female seated holding spy-glass; ship on left.

TWO | Female seated on globe, holding liberty pole and blowing trumpet. | [Second Plate.] | Vig. Two females seated; factories on the right, ship on left; cog-wheel, anvil and vice between them. 2 | CONNECTICUT B'K, Bridgeport, Ct. | TWO | Two females, Eagle at top of a shield. | TWO

3 CONNECTICUT 3 | [First Plate.] | 3 Whaling scene, ship on right; men in small boat on left. 3 | STONINGTON B'K. Stonington Ct. | 3 | 3 THREE 3

Sailor seated upon bale of goods with American flag on left, anchor on right. | TWO | Steam ship and other vessels | OCEAN BANK, Stonington, Conn. | State Arms. | 2 | Female Portrait.

3 | Locomotive and cars. Large figure 3 | CONNECTICUT B'K, Bridgeport, Ct. | State arms. | 3 | Female.

Figures, anvil, sledge &c. | 3 | [Second Plate.] | 3 Locomotive and Train Cars. 3 | STONINGTON B'K, Stonington. Ct. | Steam Boat. | Female reclining wand in right hand key in left; building on right. | Sail vessel. | 3

Group of three females supporting figure 3. | 3 Ships. 3 | OCEAN BANK. Stonington, Conn. | Steam ship. | 3 | Sailor, spy glass &c.; vessel on right.

5 | Farmer at work. | 5 | CONNECTICUT B'K. Bridgeport. Ct. | Vig. Female with grain on ornamental V. | 5 | Female Portrait. | FIVE

4 | Female with Liberty pole and cap, also State Arms on right. | 4 | 4 View of Ocean with large ship; ship in distance on right, sail vessel in extreme distance on left. 4 | STONINGTON B'K. Stonington. Ct. | FOUR | Vessel. | FOUR

Chariot in which is seated a female; American shield, &c., in right hand Liberty pole and cap, representation of Neptune and car. [New Plate.] STONINGTON B'K, Stonington. Ct. 5 Large ornamental letter V in which is a female; Eagle, Liberty Pole and cap on left; Globe at her feet. 5	5 Portrait of Barnum. Same as three. PEQUONNOCK B'K., Bridgeport, Ct. V V 5 Portrait of Jenny Lind.	X Female portrait. 10 Three females seated; ship on right. FARMER'S BANK, Bridgeport, Ct. Sheaf of wheat, plow, &c. 10 Male portrait.
5 Male Portrait. 5 [Old Plate.] 5 Chariot drawn by Sea horses in which is seated a female. 5 STONINGTON B'K, Stonington. Ct. Locomotive and cars. FIVE DOLLARS	Female gathering wheat X PEQUONNOCK B'K., Bridgeport, Ct. Vig. Shield, on either side sailor and Indian; eagle at top of shield. 10 Female with flowers.	Female with compass. 20 Vig. Group of figures, supporting figure 20. FARMER'S BANK, Bridgeport, Ct. Dog's head. 20 Male portrait.
10 [New Plate.] Whaling scene. STONINGTON B'K, Stonington, Ct. X 10	20 Two Indians, canoe, &c. Vig. Harvest scene. PEQUONNOCK B'K., Bridgeport. Ct. XX 20 Two females seated, balances, shield &c.	Male portrait. 50 Vig. Female Indian seated; steamship on right; flags, shield, eagle, sale, locomotive and cars, on left. FARMER'S BANK. Bridgeport, Ct. Locomotive and tender. 50 Female holding Ameri. flag.
10 Sheaf of Wheat. 10 [Old Plate.] STONINGTON B'K, Stonington. Ct. Neptune and chariot drawn by sea horses. Locomotive and cars. TEN	FIFTY Mechanic, sailor and 2 females; city on right. PEQUONNOCK B'K., Bridgeport, Ct. Harvest scene, man erect, dog by his side two females seated one holding sickle; also oxen grain &c., Indian with bow and arrow, in shield on right. 50	100 Portrait of Washington. 100 FARMERS' BANK, Bridgeport, Ct. Vig. Sailor standing erect holding American flag. 100 Male portrait 100
20 Portrait of Washington. 20 STONINGTON B'K. XX Chariot in which is seated a female holding key in left hand drawn by lions. XX Locomotive and cars. TWENTY	100 Two Indian with bow and arrow. Vig. Sailor seated amid Nautical instruments; view of sea and ships on left. PEQUONNOCK B'K., Bridgeport, Ct. 100 C	1 Female seated with mechanical tools, &c.; building on right. B'K OF COMMERCE, New London, Ct. Vig. Ship carpenter at work; view of city. Ship on stocks. 1 Boy's head
50 50 STONINGTON B'K, 50 View of ocean upon which is a large ship, also vessel in distance on right; sail vessel in extreme distance on left. FIFTY	Four Cupid's holding figure 1 1 Vig. Mechanic seated; by his side mechanical tools; farmers at work, on left. FARMER'S BANK. Bridgeport, Ct. Locomotive and tender. 1 Male portrait.	2 Female portrait. Vig. View of ocean, upon which is a large ship and other vessels. B'K OF COMMERCE, New London, Ct. Locomotive and tender. 2 Two Cupids and 2.
ONE Farmers loading wagon PEQUONNOCK B'K., Bridgeport, Ct. ONE ONE One male and two female Indians over-looking precipice city in distance. ONE	Female; sheaf of wheat. 2 Vig. Female seated; on right, farmers at work; and locomotive and cars in distance. FARMER'S BANK, Bridgeport, Ct. Steamship. 2 Male portrait.	3 Cooper at his work. Vig. Girl seated, by her side basket of corn; also view of village and river B'K OF COMMERCE, New London, Ct. 3 View of church.
2 PEQUONNOCK B'K., Bridgeport. Ct. Mechanics at work; view of shipyard. 2 2 Two female Indians; one seated the other erect.	3 Male portrait. Vig. Horses and hogs; one horse drinking out of trough; female on left, feeding hogs; farm houses in background. FARMER'S BANK. Bridgeport. Ct. Locomotive and tender. 3 Female with wreath of flowers.	5 Train of cars; another train crossing bridge in distance. BK OF COMMERCE, New London, Conn. Eagle. 5 Female.
Portrait of P. T. Barnum 3 PEQUONNOCK B'K., Bridgeport, Ct. Vig. Country seat of P. T. Barnum. 3 3 3 Portrait of Jenny Lind	5 Male portrait. Mechanic and large letter V; also, mechanical tools. FARMER'S BANK, Bridgeport, Ct. Eagle. 5 Female with sword and balances.	10 Cooper at work. Vig. Whaling scene. BK OF COMMERCE, New London, Conn. 10 Female seated, ship on left.

50 — Same as on right end of ones. — B'K OF COMMERCE, New London, Ct. — Vig. Female seated in ornamental die, vases, &c. on left; bale of goods, anchor, wand, quadrant, &c. on right. — 50 — Sailor, in left hand quadrant, right hand resting on capstan; ship on right; steamship on left. — 50

5 — Portrait of Clay. — 5 — BRIDGEPORT B'K, Bridgeport, Ct. — Vig. Same as ones. — Female head. — 5 — Male portrait. — 5

20 — Train of cars leaving depot. — Female seated with arms [illegible], balances in right hand with cap of liberty in left hand; on left cupid [illegible] melon, small eagle; on right youth seated, bales of cotton, horn of plenty. — Title of Bank. — Steamship. — 20 — Female seated, sickle in hand; sheaf of wheat.

[illegible] female seated, globe on her right, upon which is an eagle, with American flag across its wing. — 100 — Female portrait. — B'K OF COMMERCE, New London, Ct. — Steamboat. — 100 — Anchor, bales, etc.

TEN — Washington on horse back. — BRIDGEPORT B'K, Bridgeport, Ct. — Female portrait. — Vig. Large spread eagle. — Female portrait. — Steamship. — 10 — View of church.

50 — Female portrait. — 50 — Two females seated, wheel and anvil; ship on left; buildings on a bridge on right. — Title of Bank. — Engine and tender. — 50 — Boy standing with fishing pole in right and fish in left hand, fish on the ground.

(1s and 2s are alike.)

Female erect with grain in right hand, and sickle in left. — ONE — Med. head and fig. 1. — Vig. View of sea upon which is two ships; light-house in distance on right. — Med. head and fig. 1. — NEW LONDON B'K, New London, Ct. — ONE DOLLAR

20 — Locomotive and cars. — XX — Med. head on which is twenty. — Vig. [illegible] scene. — Med. head on which is twenty. — BRIDGEPORT B'K, Bridgeport, Ct. — Steamboat. — 20 — Sculptor. — XX

100 — Male with cap in hand and flag. — Title of Bank. — Angel bearing a female up over a city. — Three spools of cotton and wheels. — 100 — Ship. — 100

FIVE — Female; eagle on right, scales, barrels, &c., on left. — 5 — 5 Vig. Indian and native American seated between the arms of one of the States, upon which is standing an eagle; also ship on right. 5 — NEW LONDON B'K, New London, Ct. — 5 — Beehive. — 5

50 — Female seated. — BRIDGEPORT BK, Bridgeport, Ct. — Vig. View of the City of Bridgeport. — FIFTY. — 50 — Figure soaring in air.

1 — Sailor leaning on capstan. — BRIDGEPORT CITY BANK, Conn. — ONE 1 DOLL 1 AR — Vig. Portrait of Washington. — 1 — Female.

X CONNECTICUT. X — 10 Vig. View of harvest field and reaper sitting under a tree. 10 — NEW LONDON B'K, New London, Ct. — 10 — 10

100 — Portrait. — 100 — Female seated, mechanical tools, &c. — Med. head on which is fig. 100 — BRIDGEPORT B'K, Bridgeport, Ct. — Locomotive and tender. — 100 — City of Bridgeport. — 100

2 — Female. — Vig. View of Ocean on which is two large ships; steamship between other vessels in distance. — BRIDGEPORT CITY BANK, Conn. — 2 — Portrait of Calhoun.

XX — XX — 20 Vig. Farmer preparing for work; sail vessel on left. 20 — NEW LONDON B'K, New London, Ct. — 20 — 20

Female portrait. — 1 — Male with cradle on right arm, sheaf of wheat on left shoulder, &c. — BANK of the SOUTH COUNTY, Wakefield, R. I. — 1 — Male portrait.

5 — Female portrait. — BRIDGEPORT CITY BANK, Conn. — Vig. Catching horses three men, one flat on ground, one with hat in hand and one by horses side; dog, two horses and farm house in backgrou'd. — 5 — Webster.

ONE — Farmer at work. — Vig. View of the city of Bridgeport. — BRIDGEPORT B'K, Bridgeport, Ct. — Beehive. — 1 — Female portrait.

TWO — Female seated. — Two blacksmiths, one seated with sledge over shoulder; anvil, &c. — Title of Bank. — 2 — Female portrait. — TWO

Two horses; farmer feeding hogs. — 10 — Female portrait. — BRIDGEPORT CITY BANK, Conn. — 10 — Female portrait.

TWO — Female holding American flag. — Vig. Same as One. — BRIDGEPORT B'K, Bridgeport, Ct. — Eagle. — 2 — Female artist.

5 — Female portrait. — 5 — Title of Bank. — Mechanic seated in large V; houses, &c., in distance. — 5 — Female portrait. — 5

XX — Female with wheat. — BRIDGEPORT CITY BANK, Conn. — Large ornamental die with figure 20 engraved, also the words twenty dollars running across it. — Ornamental die with twenty at top also figure 20.

3 — Female Indian. — Vig. Female reclining on bale; goods, ships on right and left. — BRIDGEPORT B'K, Bridgeport, Ct. — Locomotive and tender. — 3 — Portrait of Daniel Webster.

10 — Male seated. — Female seated; bbl., anvil, rake, &c. — Female portrait. — Title of Bank. — Dog and safe. — 10 — Three females erect.

Female with vase, flowers. — 50 — BRIDGEPORT CITY BANK, Conn. — Ornamental Die on which is figure 50 and the word FIFTY DOLLARS across it. — 50 — Female, eagle, shield.

Left end	Centre	Right end
1 Milk maid and cattle.	FAR. & MECH. BK., Hartford, Conn. Vig. Blacksmith, arm and hammer.	1 Spread eagle.
Full length female, with pole and cap.	1 Vig. Milkmaid seated, with cattle. FAR. & MECH. BK., Hartford, Ct.	ONE Cupid, anvil and hammer. ONE
2 Mechanic and anvil; mechanical tools; bridge, locomotive and cars on right.	FAR. & MECH. BK., Hartford, Ct. Vig. Two in ornamental die. Portrait of Washington.	2 Farmer, view of farm on left.
Full length female with grain and sickle.	Shield; Indian on right; female with sickle on left. FAR. & MECH. B'K., Hartford, Conn.	2 Female with sheaf and sickle.
3 Ship under full sail.	Farmer and blacksmith on either side of shield; cars on right; view of farm on left. FAR. & MECH. B'K., Hartford, Conn.	3 Female.
Female seated, with pole and cap; shield with figure 3 on left.	Eagle with wings extended. FAR. & MECH. BK., Hartford, Ct.	Two females; one reclining, the other soaring in air between them, is figure 3.
5 Sculptor or engraver. V	Med. head, five across V's. Med. head, five across. Interior of a blacksmith's shop. FAR. & MECH. BK., Hartford, Ct.	V Cattle. 5
10 Farmer seated; by his side sickle, rake, etc. X	Female clasping book; mechanical implements; steamboat in distance. Med head and ten on either side. FAR. & MECH. B'K., Hartford, Conn.	X 10 on med. head. 10
TWENTY	20 Group of 8 male figures. FARMERS AND MECHANICS BANK, Hartford, Ct.	20 Two females one with sickle and grain.
Full length female with wand in her left hand, shield in right on which is engraved medal head.	Family group, woman seated, by her side a little boy, man coming towards him with rake on his shoulder in front of him is a little girl, by her side is dog in attitude of barking. Figures 50 at left of vig. Title of Bank Barrels, bales, &c.	50
100 Mechanical implements. 100	Bank Building. FAR. AND MEC BK., Hartford, Ct., Horse.	100
ONE Medal. Head ONE	(First Plate.) EXCHANGE BANK, Hartford, Ct. Two females, view of river; steamboat and sail vessel on left, locomotive and cars on right; medal. head with word ONE on either side.	ONE Full Length Female. ONE
ONE Small male fig., anvil and hammer. 1	[Second Plate.] Rail Road Depot, cars passing through. EXCHANGE BANK, Hartford, Ct. Barrels, &c.	ONE DOLLAR
TWO Indian reclining on shield. TWO	(First Plate.) Med. Head, with word TWO across. Med. Head, with word TWO across. A female on either side of a shield. EXCHANGE BANK, Hartford, Ct.	Medallion Head with word TWO across.
Full length female, right hand resting on shield. TWO	[Second Plate.] 2 Locomotive and Cars. EXCHANGE BANK, Hartford, Ct.	2 Female with pole and cap on right; Eagle standing on shield.
THREE Locomotive and cars. THREE	Female seated with pole and cap, before her two youthful artists; shipping on left; cars on right. EXCHANGE BANK, Hartford, Ct.	3 Two farmers farming implements on their shoulders, farm house on right
Female with starry drapery holding pole and cap; eagle and American shield on right.	5 View of public buildings in Hartford. EXCHANGE BANK, Hartford, Ct. Locomotive and tender.	5
Full length female with spear. TEN	X Vig. Three females, eagle, &c.; bridge, locomotive and cars on right; ship on left. EXCHANGE BANK, Hartford, Ct. Steam-ship.	X Female with pole and cap resting on shield
20 View of city, bridge, railroad and cars.	EXCHANGE BANK, Hartford, Ct. Vig. Three female figures; sickle, anchor and quadrant. XX	20 Large ship, view of city and shipping.
50 Man under large tree; church on right; building on left. FIFTY	EXCHANGE BANK, Hartford, Ct. Vig. River scene; view of city in distance. Eagle.	FIFTY 50
100 Sculptor.	Vig. Group of female figures, eagle between them; waterfalls in background. EXCHANGE BANK, Hartford, Ct. Head of female.	100 Spread eagle, shield, &c. 100
1 Head of Washington. 1	Vig. Train of cars and two horses. BK OF BL'CK RIVER Proctorsville, Vt Fish.	ONE Female head. ONE
TWO Female holding scale and sword. TWO	Vig. Farmers scene, two oxen, cart, and men loading hay. BK OF BL'CK RIVER Proctorsville, Vt. Boxes and bbl's.	2 Female in a sitting posture with a staff.
THREE Female seated on plow holding a sickle and sheaf of wheat. THREE	Train of cars, female with sickle in hand, two Indians, Steamboat in distance. BK OF BL'CK RIVER Proctorsville, Vt. Female head.	3 Female head. 3
FIVE Head of B. Franklin. FIVE	Man ploughing with two oxen and horse. BK OF BL'CK RIVER Proctorsville, Vt. Eagle.	5 Female head. 5
10 Wharf scene with vessels in the ocean	Female head. Indian female and child. BK OF BL'CK RIVER Proctorsville, Vt. Engine.	10 Two females holding scales; Seal of State; Freedom and Unity. TEN
TWENTY Male portrait. TWENTY	20 Two Females, one with basket of fruit; XX between. BK OF BL'CK RIVER Proctorsville, Vt. Wheelbarrow and sheaf of grain.	

Female erect holding staff with Flag of our Union; Eagle.
BK OF BL'CK RIVER
Proctorsville, Vt.
L Three females
50

10
Sailor resting on bale of goods; hat in right hand, Quadrant in left; ship on right
Female resting her left arm on bale of goods, wand in right hand; vessel on left; Locomotive and cars on right.
STATE BANK,
Hartford, Ct.
State Arms.
10
Female seated with sickle and grain.

Female, liberty pole, and cap.
Figure 4
4 Vig. Ships storming a fort. 4
HARTFORD BANK,
Hartford, Ct.
Dog, safe, and key.
Female with sword
Figure 4

ONE
Blacksmith seated on a boiler.
ONE
Vig. Man ploughing with two horses; river and steamboat on left.
STATE BANK,
Hartford, Ct.
State arms.
1
Female seated; factories in background.

TWENTY
Female resting her arm on barrel, wand in right hand; vessel on right.
XX
20 View of Park and Public Building. 20
STATE BANK.
Hartford, Ct.
State Arms.
TWENTY
Blacksmith, anvil and hammer.
XX

FIVE
Med. head; five across.
Vig. Sailor erect, with flag; view of harbor and shipping
Med. head; five across.
HARTFORD BANK,
Hartford, Ct.
Eagle.
5
5 on med. head.
5

1
Female resting on ornamental pillar; mechanical tools, &c. around her.
Vig. View of Trinity College, Hartford.
STATE BANK,
Hartford, Ct.
1
Female and sheaf of grain.

50
Female seated, factories in back ground.
Locomotive and Train of cars. 50
STATE BANK.
Hartford, Ct.
State Arms.
FIFTY
Female, sword and balances.
50

TEN
Med. head, and fig. 10 on it.
Vig. Railroad and train of cars.
Med. head, and fig. 10 on it.
HARTFORD BANK,
Hartford Ct.
Mechanics, arm and anvil.
TEN
Steamboat and row-boat.
TEN

TWO
Female Indian with bow and arrows, liberty pole and cap; hands resting on shield.
Vig. Same as second plate of ones.
STATE BANK,
Hartford Ct.
State Arms.
2
Female with basket of flowers.

100
Female seated with anvil and hammer
100
Vig. Large spread eagle on American shield.
STATE BANK,
Hartford, Ct.
State arms.
100
Male figure holding cornucopia.
100

XX
XX
20 Vig. Female 20 seated, with figure 20 on right; vessel on left.
HARTFORD BANK,
Hartford, Ct.
20
20

TWO
Female seated on chest holding sword and balances.
Locomotive and Tender.
2 Female and sailor seated female with sickle and grain, sailor holding Quadrant.
STATE BANK,
Hartford, Ct.
State Arms.
2
Farmer and Basket of Corn.

1
ONE
Female portrait.
HARTFORD BANK,
Hartford, Ct.
Vig. Two females and eagle; portrait of Washington, ship on left.
1
Portrait of Jenny Lind.

L
L
50 Vig. Female 50 seated; view of canal in distance.
HARTFORD BANK,
Hartford, Ct.
L
L

THREE
Female seated; American shield, &c.
Same as 2d Plate of Ones.
STATE BANK,
Hartford, Ct
3
State Arms.
THREE

1
Med head.
1
Med. head; one across.
Signing the Declar ation in Indepen dence.
Med head; one across.
HARTFORD BANK,
Hartford, Conn
Female and anchor.
1
Med head
1

C
C
HARTFORD BANK,
Hartford, Ct.
100 Vig. Female 100 seated on rock; wood scene.
C
C

3
Female, anvil and hammer.
Two females, one holding sword and scales; the other reclining with pole and cap; Eagle and State Arms on left; ship in distance.
STATE BANK,
Hartford, Ct.
Horn of Plenty, bales, &c.
3
Male figure holding cornucopia.

2
Med. head.
2
Med. head; two across.
View of river, steam-boat and ship; city on right.
Med. head; two across.
HARTFORD BANK,
Hartford, Ct
Dog's head.
2
Med. head.
2

ONE
Railroad bridge, cars and vessel.
ONE
Vig. View of Public building in Hartford,
CITY BANK,
Hartford, Ct.
1
ONE
Female seated, eagle and shield on right.

5
Female on either side of State Arms; Locomotive and cars on left; steamship on left.
Female Portrait.
STATE BANK,
Hartford, Ct.
Sail Vessel.
5
Female in ornamental figure 5.

TWO
Female portrait.
TWO
2 Vig. Sailor reclining, nautical implements, &c.; view of sea and three vessels.
HARTFORD BANK,
Hartford, Ct.
2
Female seated in fig. 2, factory and locomotive on left.
TWO

TWO
Two men, farming implements on their shoulders, dog at their side.
Vig. Same as ones.
Med. head TWO across.
CITY BANK,
Hartford, Ct.
2
Female in figure 2 with sword and balances.
TWO

5
Sailor seated on bales of goods; Quadrant in right hand.
FIVE
State Arms; female on right; flags on left.
STATE BANK,
Hartford, Ct.
Horn of Plenty, Bales &c.
5
Female seated; mechan. tools, &c.
FIVE

THREE
Two females seated, above them sailor and mechanic; view of city and mountain in distance.
HARTFORD BANK,
Hartford, Ct.
Vig. Anchor, anvil, and sheaves.
3
Male
Two females, cattle, dog, &c.

THREE
Two females and city in distance.
CITY BANK,
Hartford, Ct.
Vig. Shield, group of Indians on left; group of females on right, globe, &c.
Eagle
3
Female.

5 | Female seated; deer on a shield; sheep on right. | 5
Female, sheaf of wheat and sickle. | CITY BANK, Hartford, Ct. Dog's head. | Female seated, locomotive, factory and cars on left. FIVE

10 X 10 | Indian head, 10 and X. MERCANTILE BK., Hartford, Ct. | TEN Two female Indians; one seated with sickle and grain; the other with bow and arrow.

Medallion head. Portrait of Washington. | Vig. Man on horse, drove of sheep; mill on left. Fig. 1 on shield. CONN. RIVER BANKING CO. Hartford, Ct. Eagle. | ONE Full length female. ONE

---

10 | Female with pole and cap, shield on right. Vig. Farmers loading grain. CITY BANK, Hartford, Ct. | 10 Female, Indian and squaw.

ONE Washington. ONE | Vig. Banking house. FAIRFIELD CO. BK. Norwalk, Ct. | Figure 1 on shield.

2 Portrait of Washington. 2 | Vig. Head of Franklin in ornamental die, on either side a female; steamboat and ships on right; farming scene on left. Title of Bank | 2 Female seated in fig. 2, railroad cars and factory on left.

---

20 Cattle. TWENTY | Vig. Female reclining on rock; canal locks, railroad and city in distance. CITY BANK, Hartford, Ct. | 20 Med. head. XX

TWO Male portrait. TWO | 2 Milkmaid seated with cattle. FAIRFIELD CO. BK. Norwalk, Ct. | 2

3 Portrait of Franklin. 3 | Vig. View of ocean, steamship and other vessels. Title of Bank. Barrels, bales and goods. | THREE Female erect with spear in right hand. THREE

---

50 Med. head. FIFTY | Med. head 50 on it. Vig. Man on either side of a shield, ship above it. CITY BANK, Hartford, Ct. | 50 Two female Indians, one with sickle and grain, the other with bow & arrow.

THREE Female. THREE | View of sea, on which is two ships; Light house on right. FAIRFIELD CO. BK. Norwalk, Ct. | 3

5 5 | Portrait of Gen. Taylor, with title of bank above and below it. Two females soaring in air | 5

Female giving eagle drink. C | Vig. horse on either side of shield, eagle at top; bridge, train of cars and factory on left. CITY BANK, Hartford, Ct. | 100 Med. head. 100

Female with sword and ballances. FIVE | Vig. Steamship and other vessels. FAIRFIELD CO. BK. Norwalk, Ct. | 5

TEN | Portrait of Washington, with title of bank above and below it. Indian group looking over precipice; view of city and river below. Locomotive and tender. | Letter X on American shield.

Figure 1, and one running across. Female portrait. | MERCANTILE BK., Hartford, Ct. Vig. Female seated; safe, sheep &c. | 1 Sailor seated; spy-glass in left hand.

Female with shield, liberty pole and cap. | 10 Female with cornucopia. FAIRFIELD CO. BK. Norwalk, Ct. | 10

I I | 50 Vig. Female 50 seated with wand, right hand resting on shield; steamboat on left; anchor on right. Title of Bank. | L L

TWO DOLLARS | MERCANTILE BK., Hartford, Ct. 2 | 2 View of ocean; steamship and other vessels. 2

TWENTY Female Indian with bow & arrow | Vig. Train of cars, wharf, steamboat and depot in the back-ground. FAIRFIELD CO. BK. Norwalk, Ct. | XX Female between 2 & 0

C C | 100 100 Vig. Three females, two seated, one standing holding spear in her hand. Title of Bank. | C C

---

3 Female portrait. | Vig. Shield and figure 3; eagle at top of shield; on either side, a horse; steamboat on right; canal, bridge, cars and factories on left. 3 MERCANTILE BK., Hartford, Ct. | THREE

50 Male portrait. FIFTY | Drove of cattle. FAIRFIELD CO BK. Norwalk, Ct. | 50 Male portrait.

1 Portrait of Washington. ONE | 1 Vig. Female seated on barrel; cars on left. 1 PHENIX BANK, Hartford, Ct. Locomotive and cars. | Full length female. ONE

FIVE | 5 Three females seated, with cornucopia, sickle, and quadrant. MERCANTILE BK., Hartford, Ct. | 5 Sailor.

Med. head and figure 100. | Two horses alarmed at [illegible] FAIRFIELD CO BK., Norwalk, Ct. | Same as the other end.

ONE Full length female hand resting on shield. | [New Plate.] 1 ONE 1 PHENIX BANK, Hartford, Ct. Safe. | ONE Blacksmith at work.

2 — Portrait of Washington — TWO
Vig. Two females seated, one holding sickle; grain on left; ship on right. 2
PHENIX BANK, Hartford, Ct.
Steam propeller.
TWO — Sculptor at work. — TWO

TWENTY DOLLARS
20 Vig. Two females seated, one with grain. 20
20 20
PHENIX BANK, Hartford, Ct.
20
CONNECTICUT

FIVE — Sailor with glass; anchor at his feet. — FIVE
NORWICH BANK, Norwich, Conn.
Three cherubs one with flag; grain, rake, etc., on right; sheep on left; vessels in distance.
Female bathing.
5 — Eagle on shield. — FIVE

---

2 — Male portrait.
PHENIX BANK, Hartford, Ct.
TWO
2 — Head of sailor.

FIFTY DOLLARS
50 Vig. Female seated, with wand in right hand; river vessels and houses on left; barrels, &c., on right. 50
50 50
PHENIX BANK, Hartford, Ct.
L
CONNECTICUT

X CONNECTICUT X
X Vig. River, on which is sail-boat; also, man on horse. X
NORWICH BANK, Norwich, Ct.
Female, grain and sickle.
10 10

---

3 — Portrait of Gen. Taylor. — THREE
Vig. Group of mechanics; ship building on left, vessels on right.
PHENIX BANK, Hartford, Ct.
Mechanic's arm and anvil.
3 — Female — THREE

ONE HUNDRED
100 Vig. Female seated overlooking sea, on which is ship. C
100 100
PHENIX BANK, Hartford, Ct.
C
CONNECTICUT.

XX CONNECTICUT XX
20 Vig. Female seated, left hand extended; under it is engraved figure 20; vessel on left. 20
NORWICH BANK, Norwich, Ct.
Steamboat.
20 20

Male portrait.
Group of figures drawing a chariot. 5 on left. 5
PHENIX BANK, Hartford, Ct
State Arms.
Female and sword. — FIVE

ONE — Female, shield, eagle, liberty pole and cap. — ONE
1 Female seated; farming implements, &c.; bridge, locomotive and cars on right. 1
NORWICH BANK, Norwich, Ct
Barrels, Goods, &c.
ONE — Female drawing water from a well; steamboat on left.

CONNECTICUT
L Vig. An ox. L
NORWICH BANK, Norwich, Ct
Steamboat.
50 50

---

5 V 5
PHENIX BANK, Hartford, Ct.
Vig. Three females seated; one with sickle, the other with quadrant.
FIVE
5 V 5

Female. — ONE — Female.
View of Norwich Bank Building, female pole and cap on right; vessel on left.
NORWICH BANK, Norwich, Ct.
Eagle.
Female. — ONE — Female.

Washington and C.
Vig. Signing the "Declaration of Independence."
NORWICH BANK, Norwich, Ct.
Eagle.
100 — Female.

Male portrait.
Vig. Female and figure 5 on shield; female on left, holding triton; cupid and snakes at top of shield; eagle, &c., on left.
PHENIX BANK, Hartford, Ct.
Sword and balances.
Female holding balances; anchor and figure 5 at her feet. — FIVE

---

2 — Two Cupids in Ornamental fig 2.
Spread Eagle on limb of tree; vessels on right; steamboat on left
NORWICH BANK, Norwich, Ct.
Bank Building.
2 — Two figures in Ornamental fig 2.

D — 500
NORWICH BANK, Norwich, Ct.
Group of females on right; Indian, squaw and child on left; between them the Arms of one of the States.
500 — Portrait of Daniel Webster.

---

5 — Five across V — 5
PHENIX BANK, Hartford, Conn.
View of a river and steamboat; town in distance.
FIVE — 5 — FIVE

TWO — Female seated in Ornamental fig. 2, sword in left hand, Balances in right.
NORWICH BANK, Norwich, Ct.
Three females, between them the Arms of one of the States, eagle at top of shield.
Eagle.
Fig. 2 on American shield. — Female seated in Ornamental fig. 2; City on left.

Figure 1 and word ONE. — 1
CHARTER OAK B'K. Hartford Ct.
1 Soldiers under a large oak tree. 1
ONE
1 — Figure 1 and word ONE. — ONE

---

10 — Portrait of Washington. — 10
Female seated, letter X on shield. Female seated with horn of plenty, letter X on shield.
PHENIX BANK, Hartford, Ct.
Female seated; view of ocean; ship on right; goods and ships on left.
10 — Female with pole and cap. — 10

CONNECTICUT
Figure 4. Figure 4.
Group of females seated. Grain, sickle, &c.; one resting arm on chest, key in her right hand; eagle on left, building on right; vessels in distance.
NORWICH BANK, Norwich, Ct.
Figure 4. Figure 4.

---

2 — TWO 2
CHARTER OAK B'K, Hartford, Ct.
2 Vig. Same as Ones. 2
2 — Locomotive and Train Cars.

---

10 X 10
PHENIX BANK, Hartford, Ct.
Vig. Locomotive and train of cars.
10 X 10

5
Five females supporting figure 5; vessels on right.
NORWICH BANK, Norwich, Ct.
Bank Building.
5

Soldiers under a large oak tree. — 3
CHARTER OAK B'K Hartford, Ct.
THREE in ornamental Die Title.
2 — THREE 3

Left end	Centre	Right end
FIVE Soldiers under a large oak tree.	CHARTER OAK B'K. Hartford, Ct FIVE in Ornamental Die.	5 5
1 Man resting on safe; factories in background.	[Second Plate.] Vig. Drove of cattle; two men on horseback; one man sitting by a tree; public house on left. THAMES BANK, Norwich, Ct. Man and horse.	1 Man on horse
100 Male portrait 100	100 Vig. Female on either side of a shield holding balances and spear, eagle at top of shield; ships on right; bridge on left. 100 on right. THAMES BANK, Norwich, Ct. C	100 Group of cupids in circular die. 100
X Same as Fives.	CHARTER OAK B'K, Hartford, Ct Ornamental Die in which is figures 10, letter X, and word TEN. X each side.	10 X
2	Vig. Female overlooking sea, on which is seen ships; anchor at her side, light-house on right. fig 2 on right. THAMES BANK, Norwich, Ct. Female Indian.	TWO View of ocean, steamship and ships; female in ornamental figure 2. TWO
ONE Female and balances, state arms, eagle, &c. ONE	1 Vig. Female with wand in right hand, ship on left. 1 MERCHANTS' B'K, Norwich, Ct.	1 Female seated with pole and cap; ship on left. 1
Deer 1	Masons at work. 1 ONE B'K OF HARTFORD COUNTY, Hartford, Ct Female, anchor, &c.	1
THREE Three cupids in large figure 3. THREE	3 Vig. Two females on either side of a shield, one with liberty pole and cap, and one with grain; steamboat on right; bridge, locomotive, and train of cars on left. 3 THAMES BANK, Norwich, Ct. Indian, bow, and arrows.	THREE Three figures in large figure 3. THREE
Female erect with spear in left hand; right hand resting on shield, on which is figure 2. TWO	2 Vig. Female seated; state arms, anvil and cogwheel on right; ship on left. 2 MERCHANTS' B'K, Norwich, Ct.	Female head with wreath 2 Female head
Two cherubs TWO	Interior of a machine shop; mechanics at work. Ornamental Die with word TWO and fig. 2. B'K OF HARTFORD COUNTY, Hartford, Ct. Locomotive and Cars.	2
5 Female Indian seated with tomahawk. FIVE	5 Vig. Five cupids in ornamental figure 5 5 THAMES BANK, Norwich, Ct. Female head.	5 Female seated in letter V; wand in right hand; bale of goods on right. FIVE
FIVE Portrait of Washington. FIVE	(First Plate.) 5 Vig. Whaling scene. 5 MERCHANTS' B'K, Norwich, Ct.	Female soaring in air with wand in right hand. 5
3 [illegible] Rail [illegible] Cars pass through	Three Male Figures. Two females on right. B'K OF HARTFORD COUNTY, Hartford Ct Eagle.	3
5 Male portrait	Vig. Two figures, sailor and farmer; farmer with sickle, grain, &c.; sailor with spyglass, capstan, and anchor at his feet; sheep on left. THAMES BANK, Norwich, Ct.	5 Female Indian.
5 Male portrait FIVE	[Second Plate.] Vig. Locomotive and train of cars. MERCHANTS' B'K, Norwich, Ct	5 Sailor seated with spy glass, steam boat on left.
FIVE	Cars passing through a tunnel. Female portrait. B'K OF HARTFORD CO., Hartford, Ct. Female bathing	5
V Female. V	Ship. Vig. Female seated emptying water out of pitcher; liberty pole and cap on left. FIVE THAMES BANK. Norwich, Ct. Cupid. Mech's arm.	Five dollars running across three circular dies.
TEN Portrait of Washington. TEN	[First Plate.] 10 Vig. Whaling scene. 10 MERCHANTS' B'K, Norwich, Ct.	Female erect with spear; state arms on right. 10
X	Female 10 B'K OF HARTFORD CO, Hartford, Ct. Two females seated, one looking up to man; dog on right, cattle on left. TEN	
X Male head. X	Vig. View of Greenwich Falls in Connecticut. Med. head. Bee-hive. THAMES BANK. Norwich, Ct. Machinery.	X TEN X
10 Male portrait.	[Second Plate.] Vig. Whaling scene. MERCHANTS' B'K, Norwich, Ct.	10 Male portrait. X
⋈ ⋈	B'K OF HARTFORD CO., Hartford, Ct. 20 Vig. U. S. Capitol. TWENTY	20
10 Portrait of D. Webster.	Vig. View of ocean in storm and boat putting off. THAMES BANK, Norwich, Ct.	10 Two females, one seated with spyglass and one standing.
Two winged figures and urn. Portrait of General Harrison.	L Vig. Man seated with horn of plenty, safe, lions and scales on right; ship, bale of goods, &c. on left L MERCHANTS' B'K, Norwich, Ct Sail vessel.	50 Launching a ship. 50
ONE Female supporting figure 1 ONE	[First Plate.] 1 Vig. Female seated; mechanical tools on right; farming implements on left. THAMES BANK, Norwich, Ct. Female head.	1 Female head
XX Male portrait XX	Vig. Three females seated; beehive, farming implements, &c. THAMES BANK, Norwich, Ct. TWENTY	20 Male portrait 20
A collection of vessels.	C Vig. Female seated, eagle on her lap; ships on left. C MERCHANTS' B'K, Norwich, Ct Steamboat.	100 Shearing sheep. 100

Left	Centre	Right
1 Female seated on bale of goods, with arms extended. 1	View of City Rail Road Depot and Train of Cars. QUINEBAUG BANK, Norwich, Ct. Cogwheel.	1 Medallion Head.
Indian erect with bow, arrow, and tomahawk. TWO	Vig. Three females and cupid bathing. UNCAS BANK, Norwich, Ct. Horse.	2 State die.
Female head. 20	State Capitol. BK OF MONTPELIER Montpelier, Vt. Plough.	20 Head of Pierce.
2 Two Cupids in fig. 2.	Female Indian reclining, bow and arrows by her side; steamboat on left. QUINEBAUG BANK, Norwich, Ct. Locomotive and Tender.	2 Female seated, child by her side holding sickle.
3	Vig. Indian with gun overlooking river. State die. UNCAS BANK, Norwich, Ct. Steamboat.	THREE Full length female.
50 Female. 50	Two females; ship factories and railroad cars in distance. BK OF MONTPELIER Montpelier, Vt.	50 Young man harvesting corn.
3 Female sheaf of wheat and sickle.	Two females seated: locomotive and cars on right, buildings and vessels on left. QUINEBAUG BANK, Norwich, Ct. Cogwheel.	3 Three figures in fig. 3.
5	Vig. Three cattle in water, one reposing; sheep on left. State die. UNCAS BANK, Norwich, Ct.	5 Female Indian. FIVE
100 Sailor with flag in one hand and hat in the other.	BK OF MONTPELIER Montpelier, Vt. Female and cupid over a city.	100 Female head 100
5	Spread Eagle, grain mechanical implements, &c., by his side; ships on right; sheep on left. QUINEBAUG BANK. Norwich, Ct. Female.	5
Three females on rock: anvil, grain, &c., between them. TEN	Vig. Spread eagle on American shield. UNCAS BANK, Norwich, Ct. Indian head.	10 State die.
1 Female.	SHETUCKET BANK, Norwich, Ct. Vig. Three figures man, woman, and child.	1 Sailor.
TEN Female, sword, and balances. TEN	10 Female soaring in air. QUINEBAUG BANK, Norwich, Ct. Eagle.	10
1 1	BK OF MONTPELIER Montpelier, Vt. Female seated and two cows, one standing and the other lying down. Steamboat.	1 Female.
2 Female and flowers.	Vig. Milkmaid seated with cattle; farmhouse and trees in background. SHETUCKET BANK, Norwich, Ct.	2 State die.
20 Indian. 20	XX XX Representation of raising the Globe. QUINEBAUG BANK, Norwich, Ct.	TWENTY
2 Horse, train of cars in distance.	BK OF MONTPELIER Montpelier, Vt. Female portrait. 2	2 Female. TWO
3 Load of hay, clover, and cattle; view of street, buildings, &c., in distance.	Title of Bank Vig. Farmers resting from work. Eagle.	3 Female
50 50	QUINEBAUG BANK, Norwich, Ct. Female, American shield, eagle, liberty pole and cap.	50 Male Portrait 50
Female and 3 THREE	3 Female head. BK OF MONTPELIER Montpelier, Vt	3 Female seated, bales, &c.
Female reclining, sailor holding flag; bale goods, anchor, &c. by his side. FIVE	Vig. View of ocean, steamship and other vessels. SHETUCKET BANK, Norwich, Ct.	5 Child.
100 Female with grain, leaning. 100	QUINEBAUG BANK, Norwich, Ct. ONE HUNDRED	100 Male Portrait 100
State capital. 5	5 BK OF MONTPELIER Montpelier, Vt.	5 Washington.
10 Mason at work; building on left.	Vig. Horses, farm house and cottages. SHETUCKET BANK, Norwich, Ct.	10 State die.
Indian with gun overlooking precipice. 1	UNCAS BANK, Norwich, Ct. Vig. Cotton factories and two females at work.	1 State die.
State capitol 10	BK OF MONTPELIER Montpelier, Vt	TEN Female with sickle.
20 Cupid's die. 20	Female on either side of shield on which is eagle, etc. 20 on right and left. N. Y. STATE BANK, Albany, N. Y. Secured &c.	XX Canal scene, buildings, etc. 20

1 Male portrait. 1 | Vig. Public park in New Haven. 1 1 CITY BANK, New Haven, Ct. 1 Eagle. 1 | 1 Female Indian. 1	Fig. 1 on American shield. River, steamboat, row boat and city in distance, | 1 N. H. CO. BANK, New Haven, Ct. View of sea, ship and other vessels. Dog, Safe and Key. 1 | ONE Female erect with spear.	1 Train of cars. | Ship on stocks. CITY BANK, Manchester, N. H. ONE | 1
TWO | 2 Vig. Same as ones. CITY BANK. New Haven. Ct. Farming implements. | 2 Portrait of General Taylor.	TWO Sailor leaning on Capstain, spyglass in hand TWO | N. H. CO. BANK, New Haven, Ct. View of River; two ships, steamboat and smaller vessels. 2 2 Dog, Safe and Key. | Medal Head and figure 2 Ship.	2 Female and eagle. | Blacksmith at forge. CITY BANK. Manchester. N. H. 2 | TWO
THREE | 3 Vig. Same as ones. 3 CITY BANK, New Haven, Ct. Locomotive and tender. | 3 Three females supporting figure 3.	3 Female grain and sickle. THREE | N. H. CO. BANK. New Haven, Ct. Farming scene, man on horse. 3 3 Dog, Safe and Key. | THREE Milkmaid.	3 Female. | Mechanic, forge, factorys, cars, &c. CITY BANK, Manchester, N. H. 3 | 3
5 State arms. FIVE | Vig. Same as ones CITY BANK, New Haven, Ct. Eagle. | 5 Large eagle. FIVE	5 Mechanic at work. | N. H. CO. BANK, New Haven, Ct. Large spread Eagle on limb of tree, ships on right, steamboats and vessels on left. 5 Dog, key, safe 5 | 5 Female Portrait.	FIVE Female, | Three mechanics. CITY BANK, Manchester, N. H. | FI 5 VE 5
X Portrait of Daniel Webster. TEN | [New Plate.] Vig Same as ones. CITY BANK, New Haven, Ct. Bee-hive. | 10 Male portrait. 10	X Bolls Head TEN | [First Plate. N. H. CO. BANK, New Haven. Ct. Cattle, Man Plowing with oxen and horse; men at work. Dog, key and safe. | Medal Head and fig. 10. Male Portrait	Gen. Stark. TEN | X CITY BANK, Manchester, N. H. | 10 Indian and two squaws, factorys in distance.
10 X | [Old Plate.] Vig. Same as ones. CITY BANK, New Haven. Ct. Females head. | 10 X	10 Sailor seated; bale of goods, &c. | N. H. CO., BANK. New Haven. Ct. Vig. Female seated on chest; small child and dog on right; plough and sheaf of grain, shield, &c., on left. Eagle. | 10 Portrait.	20 | CITY BANK, Manchester, N. H. Three females. | 20 F. Pierce.
20 Portrait of H. Clay. XX | Vig. Same as Ones. CITY BANK, New Haven. Ct. Indian. | 20 Portrait of Gen. Taylor. XX	XX 20 | N. H. CO., BANK. New Haven, Ct. Vig. State Arms; American group on right; Indian, squaw and papoose on left. Dog, safe and key. | XX 20	L 50 | CITY BANK, Manchester, N. H. Franklin. | 50 Harvest scene, male and 2 females cattle, dogs, &c.
50 Female. 50 | Vig. Same as Ones CITY BANK, New Haven, Ct. Female Indian. | 50 Medallion Head, the word Fifty engraved at top.	50 View of city and cars crossing bridge; load of hay on left. | N. H. CO., BANK. New Haven, Ct. Vig. Three females with sickle, quadrant, and cornucopia. Dog, safe and key. | 50 View of river and ship; city in distance.	C | Indian, squaw, and papoose on left of shield; female and three children with book and globe. CITY BANK. Manchester. N. H. | 100 Washington.
100 Portrait of Washington. | CITY BANK, New Haven, Ct. Vig. Same as Ones. | 100 Male Portrait	Group of figures; two females seated, spinning wheels by their side; sailor and mechanic above them; city in distance. | N. H. CO. BANK. New Haven, Ct. C The vig. extends on both ends and across lower margin of note. C Anchor and mechanics implements; oxen | Three figures Two females seated; one with sickle; man standing with pitchfork in right hand; dog on right	D Suspension bridge, canal boats. 500 | Safe, female, ship on stocks, grain, sheep, &c. CITY BANK, Manchester, N. H. Mermaid. | 500 Two males and 1 female.

1 QUINNIPIACK BK., New Haven, Ct. 1 Sailor, capstan, etc. Male portrait. Vig. Indian, squaw and pappoose in a canoe. ONE	2 Vig. same as ones. 2 MECHANICS' BANK, New Haven, Ct Mechanics and mechanical implements. 2 Banking house.	TWO View of Ocean steamship and other vessels. 2 Female floating in air. MERCHANT BANK, New Haven, Ct Female feeding an Eagle. TWO Female Bathing.
Male portrait. QUINNIPIACK BK., New Haven, Ct. 2 2 Vig. Same as ones. Two Cupids in large 2.	3 3 Vig. Female seated on bale of goods, vessel on either side. 3 Female with triton. Female MECHANICS' BANK, New Haven, Ct. 3 Banking house. 3	3 Vig. Three females with quadrant, liberty pole and cap, grain, &c. 3 Two male figures. MERCHANTS' B'K, New Haven, Ct. THREE Shells Male portrait.
Portrait of Webster. QUINNIPIACK BK., New Haven, Ct. 3 Beehive, etc. Three cupids in figure 3. Vig. Same as ones. THREE	5 Vig. Female seated; eagle on globe, flag across his back. 5 Mechanic's arm. Ship. MECHANICS' BANK, New Haven, Ct. V Bank building. 5	View of public square in New Haven. 5 FIVE Sailor and mechanic, sailor with flag, mechanic seated, anchor at his feet. MERCHANTS' B'K, New Haven, Ct. 5 Barrels, bales, goods, &c.
5 Vig. Same as ones. 5 QUINNIPIACK B'K, New Haven, Conn. Anchor, bales, goods, etc. Female.	5 Group of five American Presidents; two flags and eagle at top. 5 Mechanics Arm. Large Ship. MECHANICS' BANK, New Haven Ct. V 5	TEN Vig. Public square in New Haven. 10 Train of cars. MERCHANTS B'K, New Haven, Ct. TEN Female bathing. Sailor.
Vig. Same as ones. 10 Male portrait. QUINNIPIACK B'K, New Haven, Ct. 10 Male and female. TEN	10 Sailor seated holding flag; ship on left. X Female Indian. MECHANICS' BANK, New Haven, Ct. Female seated with sword and balance safe and shield. 10 Mechanic's Arm.	20 Vig. Three females; building in background. 20 MERCHANTS' B'K, New Haven, Ct. XX Eagle. XX
20 QUINNIPIACK B'K, New Haven, Ct. 20 Vig. same as ones. Mechanic, anvil, and cogwheel. Female in a shell.	Three females overlooking precipice, one holding sword and balance. 20 MECHANICS' BANK, New Haven, Ct. 20 Banking House. Female.	L and Fifty MERCHANT'S B'K, New Haven, Ct. 50 Floating female Vig. Group of Indians overlooking precipice; view of city below. Female. female floating
50 QUINNIPIACK B'K, New Haven, Ct. 50 Female and mechanical implements. Ship. Vig. same as ones.	Artist at work, building on right. 50 Male figure the word Franklin engraved on pillar. MECHANICS' BANK, New Haven, Ct. 50 Male Portrait State Arms.	C MERCHANTS' B'K, New Haven, Ct. 100 Vig. Sailor reclining, quadrant in left hand, coil of rope, capstan, &c. on right; river, ships, &c. on left. Ship Eagle Male portrait.
Vig. same as ones. 100 QUINNIPIACK B'K, New Haven, Ct. 100 Vessel.	Female Erect with sword and balances. State Arms. 100 100 Female feeding an eagle. MECHANICS' BANK, New Haven, Ct 100 Portrait of Washington. 100	Female with sheaf of wheat. 1 Ship on stocks. 1 DOVER BANK, Dover, N. H. ONE 1 Sailor.
1 1 Vig. Female seated; ships on right. 1 1 Portrait of Franklin. MECHANICS' BANK, New Haven, Ct. Portrait of Washington 1 Banking house. 1	Full length female with pole and cap, starry drapery across her shoulder. 1 Floating female with cornucopia. 1 MERCHANTS' BANK, New Haven, Ct. Female.	Female seated on bale of goods with sheaf of wheat; cars, factory in distance. 2 Ship on stocks. 2 DOVER BANK, Dover, N. H. TWO 2 Cattle

Left	Center	Right
Female reclining factories in distance. 3	3 Ship on stocks. DOVER BANK, Dover, N H. Washington.	THREE Stone cutter
10 Male portrait.	SLATER BANK, N. Providence R. I. View of Pawtucket falls State arms.	10 X
First Sabbath. 20	Vig. City, depot, and cars. NEW HAVEN BK., New Haven, Ct. Beehive.	20 Female.
Washington	Ship on stocks and female, either side 5 DOVER BANK, Dover N. H. Wheels.	5 Two females.
1 First Sabbath.	(First Plate) Female seated; Female ship on right. NEW HAVEN B'K, New Haven, Ct. Bee-hive.	1 Sailor at work.
FIFTY Female erect, holding flag and spear.	NEW HAVEN B'K, New Haven, Ct. Vig. Female and child; steamboat on right; vessels on left. 50 50 Beehive.	50 First Sabbath.
TEN	Female illustrating industry. X Ship on stocks. DOVERBANK, Dover, N. H.	10 Blacksmith at his forge
1 First Sabbath.	[Second Plate.] Vig. Council of Indians. NEW HAVEN B'K, New Haven, Ct.	1 Beehive.
100 First Sabbath.	NEW HAVEN B'K, New Haven, Ct. Female and Indian on either side of globe, eagle at top; female holding grain, Indian gun, letter C between them. Beehive,	100 Mechanic and tools, sledge on his shoulder.
20 Female.	XX Eagle. XX DOVER BANK, Dover, N. H.	20 Ship sailing.
Female and sheaf of wheat. 2	Vig. Two females seated; cars and canal scene on right; ships on left. NEW HAVEN BK., New Haven, Ct. Beehive.	2 First Sabbath.
1 Two females, one with sword and balances, one with shield and spear.	Vig. Female on either side of state arms. WATERBURY BANK Waterbury, Ct. Goods, cog-wheels, &c.	1 Two females erect, with wand, sickle, and grain.
FIFTY Female. FIFTY	50 Man and horse. 50 DOVER BANK, Dover, N. H.	FIFTY Female. FIFTY
3 First Sabbath.	Vig. Large ship. NEW HAVEN BK., New Haven, Ct.	3 Female Indian.
2 Female.	Vig. Female and eagle, liberty pole and cap, shield, horn of plenty, &c. WATERBURY BANK Waterbury, Ct. Farming implements.	2 Male portrait
Word one hundred and figure 100. Male portrait.	Wharf scene—loading wagon, men, horses, shipping, &c. DOVER BANK, Dover, N. H.	Same as on left Male portrait.
5 Female seated on globe; hand is extended, holding sickle and grain. FIVE	[First Plate.] Cupid Cupid and grain. Female reclining on bale of goods; ship on either side. NEW HAVEN BK., New Haven, Ct. Beehive	5 First Sabbath.
3 Mechanic and anvil.	Title of Bank. Vig. Female seated, one foot resting on globe, left hand resting on shield, which stands upright on a safe, arm around eagle's neck, right hand holding pole and cap, cornucopia at her feet; farming scene on left; factories and cars on right. Cornucopia, bale, etc.	3 Mechanic at work.
1 Minerva with shield, spear sprig and laurel.	View of Pawtucket falls SLATER BANK, N. Providence, R. I. State Arms.	1 Male portrait
Drover selling cattle. Beehive.	[Second Plate.] Female portrait. NEW HAVEN BK., New Haven, Ct.	5 First Sabbath.
5 Three figures—females scattering flowers.	Vig. Female and spread eagle; steamship in distance on right; miniature portrait of Washington; factories, bridge, and cars on left. WATERBURY BANK Waterbury, Ct. State arms.	5 Female with wand and sickle; man in full armor and 5.
TWO Female holding figure 2.	View of Pawtucket falls SLATER BANK, N. Providence, R. I. State arms.	2 Male portrait.
10 Female artist at work.	[First Plate.] Vig Female and mechanic representing trade and industry; ship on right; bridge, locomotive and cars on left. NEW HAVEN BK., New Haven, Ct. Beehive.	10 First Sabbath.
10 Female, sword, and balances.	Female seated between figures 10, key in left hand; cornucopia, safe, bridge, railroad cars on left; grain on right. Title of Bank. Dog's head, and collar marked Fidelity.	10 Female, hand resting on capstan, &c.
V	View of Pawtucket falls. Male portrait. SLATER BANK, N. Providence, R. . State arms.	5 Female with roll of cloth
Beehive. 10	[Second Plate.] NEW HAVEN BK., New Haven, Ct. Vig. Three figures; blacksmith shoeing horse. Ships	10 First Sabbath.
20 Female 20	Female seated between figures 20, rake in right hand. WATERBURY BANK Waterbury, Ct. Imp. and products	20 Female 2 0

100 — Portrait of Washington.
Vig Female seated; bridge, locomotive, and cars on right; canal scene on left.
WATERBURY BANK
Waterbury, Ct.
Bale of goods, cogwheel, &c.
100 — Female.

1 — Male Portrait.
CITIZENS' BANK,
Waterbury, Ct,
Male Portrait, train of cars on right; factories on left.
1 — Male Portrait.

2 — Female.
CITIZENS' BANK,
Waterbury, Ct.
Portrait of Aaron Benedict; cars on right; factories on left.
2 — Female, olive branch in left hand.

5 — Bee Hive.
CITIZENS' BANK.
Waterbury, Ct.
Portrait of J. M. L. Scovil: cars on right; factories on left.
5 on each side.
5 — Bale of goods machinery, &c.

1 — Female, and balances. — ONE
[First Plate.]
Mechanic and tools: factories, bridge and rail road cars on left.
WINSTED BANK,
Winsted, Ct.
Female Bathing.
1 — Two females sickle and grain.

1 — Portrait of Webster. — 1
[Second Plate.]
Train cars, City in distance.
WINSTED BANK.
Winsted, Ct.
Machinery.
Figure 1 on American shield. — Male Portrait — ONE

2 — Portrait of Gen. Taylor. — TWO
Two men, one on horse, the other trying to get horse off track, cars coming towards them.
WINSTED BANK,
Winsted, Ct.
Mechanic's arm, &c.
2 — Female, wheat and sickle. — 2

THREE — Female, shield, liberty pole and cap. — THREE
Vig. Male figures; view of city on right.
WINSTED BANK,
Winsted, Ct.
Dog, safe, and key.
Figure 3, and word three on either side. — Female. — THREE

FIVE 5 HALF
[First Plate.]
Group of Indians overlooking precipice, view of city below. — Female Anchor, &c.
WINSTED BANK,
Winsted, Ct.
Landing Hay.
5 — Female seated with pole and cap; eagle and shield on right.

5 — Female. — FIVE
[Second Plate.]
Two females seated with liberty pole and cap, scroll, &c., river steamboat and vessels on left.
WINSTED BANK,
Winsted, Ct.
Machine.
5 — Dairymaid. — FIVE

Med. head, and figure 10 — View of city, bridge, and train of cars passing over it; load of hay on left.
WINSTED BANK,
Winsted, Ct.
Vig. Three females holding compass; sickle and quadrant.
Farming implements.
Med. head, and figure 10 — River and ship; city in distance on left.

20 — 20
WINSTED BANK,
Winsted, Ct.
Vig. Group of figures on either side of a shield; farm-house in distance on right.
Locomotive and tender.
20 — 20

1 — Female Indian with [illegible] and [illegible].
Female blowing trumpet; eagle on right; flags on left.
EAST HADDAM B'K.
East Haddam, Ct.
Farming implements.
1 — Female artist at work.

TWO — Female and child, flag, liberty pole and cap.
Vig. Squaw with horn of plenty at her feet, flags, safe, shield, eagle at top of globe; steamship on right; cars and factory on left.
EAST HADDAM B'K,
East Haddam, Ct.
Cogwheels, &c.
2 — Ship. — TWO

3 — Female with sword and balances.
Portrait of Washington. Male portrait.
Vig. Female seated among merchandise; vessels on right
EAST HADDAM B'K.
East Haddam, Ct.
Beehive.
3 — Female, sickle and grain. — THREE

5 — Female. — 5
Vig. Large spread eagle.
EAST HADDAM B'K,
East Haddam, Ct.
Steamboat
5 — Female with sword and balances; shield, safe, eagle, &c.

X — Washington. — 10
EAST HADDAM B'K,
East Haddam, Ct.
10
Vig. Female seated; factories and cars on left.
Steamship & merchandise.
X — Male portrait — 10

XX — Male portrait. — XX
XX XX
Vig. Female seated; ship on right.
EAST HADDAM B'K.
East Haddam, Ct.
Vessels, &c.
20 — Washington. — 20

1 — State die.
[First plate.]
HULBURT BANK,
West Winsted, Ct.
1 Large ornamented Die, with One Dollar, running across it. 1
1 — Male portrait

Wild horses — ONE
[Second Plate.]
Girl
HULBURT BANK,
West Winsted, Ct.
1 — Male portrait

TWO
HULBURT BANK,
West Winsted, Ct.
2 Vig. Harvest farm house scene; female blowing trumpet, calling farmers to lunch. Female in circular die; cattle on right; on left. 2
TWO — Cane.

3 — Male portrait
Vig. Shield and Indian on right, with tomahawk; Female on left, with wand; steamboat, vessel, and city in distance, on left.
HULBURT BANK,
West Winsted, Ct.
Female bathing.
3 — Male portrait

Drove of cattle. — V
State die.
HULBURT BANK.
West Winsted, Ct.
Geese.
5 — Spread eagle — Ox.

X — Male portrait
HULBURT BANK,
West Winsted, Ct.
Vig Group of Indians; view of city and cars crossing bridge, and also cars passing through tunnel.
TEN
10 — State die.

Female with compass. — 1
Vig. Flying female blowing horn; flag on left; eagle and globe on right.
BANK OF NORTH AMERICA,
Seymour, Ct.
Farming implements.
1 — Portrait of General Humphrey.

Indian female with bow and arrows — 2
Vig. Large spread eagle on American shield.
Title of Bank.
Beehive.
2 — Portrait of General Humphrey.

3 — Female representing industry.
Title of Bank.
3 Vig. Farmer seated; farming scene and bridge on right; houses on left.
Locomotive.
3

Left	Centre	Right
5 Male portrait	Vig. Puddling in an iron mill Title of Bank. Eagle.	5 Portrait of General Humphrey.
TEN TEN X	Large spread eagle on globe; flags with the names of different States on either side. HATTERS' BANK, Bethel, Ct.	X Portrait of Webster.
C View of cars crossing bridge; city in distance; head of bay on left	Title of Bank. Vig. Three females holding quadrant, sickle, and compass, cornucopia between them. 100	100 View of river and ship; city in distance.
10	Train of cars, bridge and city on left; steamboat and vessel right. Portrait of Gen. Humphrey. Title of Bank	10 Indian reclining on rock, gun in hand.
20 Two men with guns.	XX Portrait of Washington. XX Horses on right, cattle on left. HATTERS' BANK, Bethel, Ct. X X	20 Two soldiers, one seated with gun and pipe, the other standing holding gun.
Four cupids supporting figure 1. ONE	Vig. Horses; cars on the left. CENTRAL BANK, Middletown, Ct.	1 Female.
Portrait of Gen. Humphrey. 20	Title of Bank. Vig. Female resting on state arms; steamship and vessels on right; vessels on left.	20 Female.
50 Eagle and figures 50.	Drove of cattle and sheep. HATTERS' BANK, Bethel, Ct.	50 Male portrait
Eagle and shield. 2	CENTRAL BANK, Middletown, Ct. Vig. Train of cars.	2 Male portrait
Vig. Female, shield, liberty pole, and cap, starry drapery around her hip; U. S. Capitol in 50	Title of Bank. 50	50 Female Indian.
1 Washington	State Arms; eagle at top; two females on right; one on left with pole and cap. SOUTHPORT BANK, Southport, Conn.	1 Martha Washington
3 Female and basket of flowers.	Vig. Farmer seated; farming scene and bridge on right; buildings on left. CENTRAL BANK, Middletown, Ct.	3 Female artist; anvil and hammer on left.
100 Female with rake and sickle.	Title of Bank. Vig. Portrait of General Humphrey.	100 Female; ship on right; mechanical tools, factories, and cars on left.
Two and figure 2. Large ship and shipping in distance.	Vig. Three male figures; view of city on right. SOUTHPORT BANK, Southport, Ct.	2 Female Indian and child.
4 FOUR 4	CENTRAL BANK Middletown, Ct. Vig. Female with triton riding on sea in shell; on either side ship.	4 FOUR 4
ONE ONE	Three females binding hats; hatter on left pressing hats. HATTERS' BANK, Bethel, Ct.	ONE Milkmaid pail on her head; farmhouse on right, cattle on left.
THREE THREE	Train of cars. Vig. Group of Indians, looking down upon a city. SOUTHPORT BANK, Southport, Ct.	3 Two farmers and dog; two men and farm-house in back-ground.
Three females on a rock; anchor, spyglass, &c. FIVE	Large ship; vessel on right; steamship on left. CENTRAL BANK, Middletown, Ct.	5 Male portrait
TWO Female binding hats.	Two horse team, boy on one horse, man attaching team to plow. HATTERS' BANK, Bethel, Ct	2 Mechanic and mechanical implements; [illegible] on his back.
5 Head-quarters of Gen. Washington, at Newburgh FIVE	Vig. Female reclining on chest; State Arms on right. 5 5 SOUTHPORT BANK, SouthpOrt, Ct.	5 Portrait of Jenny Lind
Washington. X	Females seated; eagle at top of globe, flag across eagles neck. CENTRAL BANK, Middletown, Ct.	TEN Female, sword and balances.
3 Portrait of Washington.	Two females, Cornucopia between them; one seated with pole and cap; view of river and vessel, bridge, locomotive and cars on right. HATTERS' BANK, Bethel, Ct.	3 Man pressing hats.
10	Vig. View of ocean; steamship and other vessels. X SOUTHPORT BANK, Southport, Ct. Eagle.	10 X, 10, Ten.
Indian with gun looking over precipice. 25	Female seated on bale of goods; steamship on right; mechanical implements, Depot and cars on left. CENTRAL BANK, Middletown, Ct Female Head.	25 Washington on horseback
FIVE and fig. 5. FIVE FIVE	Train of cars; telegraph and bridge. HATTERS' BANK, Bethel Ct.	FIVE Man pressing hats.
Female with shield, liberty pole, and cap.	50 Vig. Female seated with grain; cars crossing bridge on right; farming implements and canal scene on left. SOUTHPORT BANK, Southport, Ct.	50 Mechanic and mechanical tools, sailor holding flag.
Female with grain. 50	Ship Carpenters at work. CENTRAL BANK, Middletown, Ct.	50 Portrait of Franklin.

1 Male portrait. ONE Stone Quarry; view of city and cars crossing bridge. MIDDLESEX CO B'K Middletown, Ct. Machinery. 1 Female.	3 Female, quadrant and anchor, circle on shield. Vig. Man plowing with horse and cattle. State die. Title of Bank. THREE 3	Female and shield, liberty pole and cap; starry drapery across her lap. 1 Vig. Bank building, carriage, &c.; lady and gentleman on horseback. STAMFORD BANK. Stamford, Ct. Goods, &c. 1 Female.
Female, liberty pole and shield; starry drapery across her shoulder. TWO Male portrait with female each side; steam boat and vessel on right; farmers at work on left. 2 2 MIDDLESEX CO. B.K. Middletown, Conn. Mechanics arms. TWO Two Indians with spear and arrows. TWO	5 Train of cars. State die. Title of Bank. FIVE 5	TWO Female. TWO Vig. Group of figures on either side of shield. STAMFORD BANK, Stamford, Ct. Females head. 2 Female, sheaf of wheat and sickle. 2
3 Portrait of Franklin. 3 Signing the Declaration of Independence. Spread Eagle on shield. MIDDLESEX CO. B'K, Middletown, Ct. 3 3 Goods, &c. Fig. 3 on American shield. Female pole and cap eagle at top of shield.	X Title of Bank. TEN State die. 10 State arms; two females, and factories in distance.	THREE Portrait of Washington. THREE Female portrait. Female portrait. Vig. River on which is row boat; train of cars crossing bridge. STAMFORD BANK, Stamford, Ct. Eagle. 3 Female. THREE
5 Washington. 5 Milkmaid seated with cattle. 5 MIDDLESEX CO. B'K, Middletown, Ct. Female Bathing. FIVE Female. FIVE	XX 20 Title of Bank. Vig. Three females; one with harp and two engraving on tablet. 20 State die.	5 Female. FIVE Vig. Three females with cornucopia, wand, sword and balances, overlooking precipice. STAMFORD BANK, Stamford, Ct. Farming implements. 5 Female Indian liberty pole and shield
10 Vessel, train cars crossing bridge. TEN Two Horses and train cars. 10 MIDDLESEX CO. B'K, Middletown, Ct. Steamship. TEN Large ship. TEN	ONE View of town ONE Male Portrait. Vig. Puddling in an iron mill. Male Portrait. IRON BANK, Falls Village, Conn. Locomotive and cars. ONE Mechanic's arms. ONE	10 Male portrait. Vig. Female Indian seated, horn of plenty at her side, flags, safe, shield, &c.; eagle on globe; train of cars on left, steamboat on right. STAMFORD BANK. Stamford, Ct. Eagle. 10 Female.
20 20 20 20 Vig. Female giving eagle drink. MIDDLESEX CO. B'K, Middletown, Ct. A TWENTY	2 TWO Locomotive and cars. 2 Vig. View of falls and town. 2 IRON BANK, Falls Village, Conn. Cog wheel 2 Female, sword, and balances.	XX Washington XX Female seated, elbow on State Arms; steamship and vessel on right; farming implements on left. 20 on either side of vig. Title of Bank. Horse's head. 20 Cattle and sheep. 20
50 50 50 50 Vig. Spread eagle. MIDDLESEX CO B'K. Middletown, Ct. FIFTY	3 Farmer with scythe. Two milkmaids seated; one milking cow, and one with pail on her lap; farm house on right; vessels on left. IRON BANK, Falls Village, Conn. Bee hive. 3 Mechanic at work.	50 Two females with rakes. 50 L Vig. Indian female reclining; sailor pointing to ship in distance. L STAMFORD BANK, Stamford, Ct. Eagle. 50 Male portrait. 50
1 Female, arm resting on pillar; farm house and cattle on right. State die. Vig. Harvest scene. BANK OF LITCHFIELD CO., New Milford, Ct. Dog & safe. ONE Ocean. 1	5 Mechanic at work. Puddling in an iron mill. IRON BANK, Falls Village, Conn. Building and trees. 5 Portrait of Franklin.	1 State arms. 1 1 Vig. Landing of the Pilgrims. 1 LANDHOLDERS B'K. Kingston, R. I. State arms. Female figure on large figure 1.
Two and figure 2. View of cattle, telegraph and rail road. Title of Bank. Vig. Farmers loading grain. State die. 2	10 Portrait of Washington. Vig. Puddling in an iron mill. Male portrait. Male portrait. IRON BANK, Falls Village, Conn. Steamboat. 10 Male portrait.	TWO Head of Washington. TWO 2 Female figure. 2 Figure of Justice. 2 LANDHOLDERS B'K, Kingston, R. I. State arms. 2 Female sitting, sheaf of wheat &c. 2

3 Female head. 3 3 Vig. Train of cars; houses in back-ground. 3 LANDHOLDERS B'K, Kingston, R. I. State arms. THREE Head. 3	V Indian with bow and arrow. Interior of a Blacksmith shop, man shoeing horse. SAUGATUCK BANK, Westport, Conn. 5 State Die.	3 Three cupids in figure 3. Vig. Drove of cattle and sheep; mill in background vessel in distance. DANBURY BANK, Danbury, Conn. Farming tools. 3 Female in figure 3.
FIVE Female figure 5 V LANDHOLDERS B'K, Kingston, R. I. 5 Ship under sail.	TEN Indian. 10 Shoemaker shop, men at work and female binding shoes. 10 SAUGATUCK BANK, Westport, Conn. X Jackson	5 Female. [First Plate.] Vig. Female seated liberty pole across her lap, eagle and shield on right. DANBURY BANK, Danbury, Conn. Bank building. 5 Med. head.
10 X 10 Pair of oxen with a man standing by an ancient plow. 10 LANDHOLDERS B'K. Kingston, R. I. TEN Female figure with cornucopia of fruits and flowers.	ONE Mechanic &c 1 Indian looking down upon city. PAHQUIOQUE BANK Danbury, Conn. 1 Female	Male portrait FIVE American shield. [Second Plate.] DANBURY BANK, Danbury, Conn. U. S. Capitol. 5 Female. 5 5
20 Female sitting, right hand upon a book. XX Eagle. XX LANDHOLDERS B'K, Kingston, R. I. 20 Ship under sail.	Female indian, farming scene in distance. 2 PAHQUIOQUE BANK Danbury, Conn. 2 Vig. Two oxen; farm house on right. Indian's head. 2 Eagle.	10 Portrait of Washington. Vig. Farming scene—farmers at work. DANBURY BANK, Danbury, Conn. Bank building. 10 Female.
FIFTY Female figure with wreath of flowers in right hand. FIFTY 50 Man and horse. 50 LANDHOLDERS B'K. Kingston, R. I. FIFTY DOLLARS FIFTY Female figure standing globe in her right hand, flowers at her right. FIFTY	5 FIVE Female PAHQUIOQUE BANK Danbury, Conn. 5 Vig. Wild horses. 5 FIVE 5 FIVE Female Indian.	20 Female seated with sword and balances 20 20 Vig. Three females with wand sickle and grain; ship and American shield on right; cars on left. DANBURY BANK, Danbury, Conn. Eagle. 20
Words one hundred running across figures 100. Male portrait Dray cart, into which men are rolling barrels, horses, shipping, &c. LANDHOLDERS B'K, Kingston, R. I. Words one hundred running across figures 100. Male portrait	1 Female with hands upraised holding sickle. ONE [First Plate.] Male portrait. Bakers at work. DANBURY BANK, Danbury, Conn. Farming implements. 1 Female and basket of flower.	50 Med. head. DANBURY BANK, Danbury, Conn. Female blowing trumpet; globe and eagle on right; flags on left. 50 Med. head.
1 Dogs head. SAUGATUCK BANK, Westport, Conn. 1 Drove of sheep, boy on right. 1 ONE State Die.	ONE Large monument. [Second Plate.] DANBULY BANK, Danbury, Conn. Three figures, Farmer, Mechanic and Sailor representing industry. 1 Male portrait	Female resting arm on library, cars, vessel, canal, &c. 1 Large figure 1 with five heads in miniature view on it. BLACKSTONE B'K. Uxbridge, Mass. 1 Female with sheaf.
2 Train of cars. SAUGATUCK BANK, Westport, Conn. 2 2 State Die TWO Village scene	Man resting on sofa. 2 [First Plate.] DANBURY BANK, Danbury, Conn. 2 Male portrait. 2 TWO Large monument.	Washing sheep; houses in distance 2 Large figure 2, with five heads on it. BLACKSTONE B'K Uxbridge, Mass. TWO Portrait of female. TWO
3 Female View of Westport village. SAUGATUCK BANK, Westport, Conn. 3 Portrait of Daniel Webster.	2 Female with arms extended. 2 [Second Plate.] Vig. Farmers at lunch; Horses on right. DANBURY BANK, Danbury, Conn. Horse. 2 Farmer gathering corn	Farming scene 3 Large figure 3 across the bill. BLACKSTONE B'K. Uxbridge, Mass. Fig. 3, word three. Female with basket of flowers. THREE

Left	Centre	Right
1 Head of Washington.	Female 1 Female. MECHANICS' AND TRADERS' BANK, Portsmouth, N. H.	1 Head of Franklin.
2 Head.	Female 2 Female. MECHANICS' AND TRADERS' BANK, Portsmouth, N. H.	2 Head.
3 Washington, full length.	Female head and bust. 3 Female head and bust. MECHANICS' AND TRADERS' BANK, Portsmouth, N. H.	3 Vulcan, full length.
Eagle resting on United States shield and an anchor. FIVE	A large V. with female figure and child. MECHANICS' AND TRADERS' BANK, Portsmouth, N. H.	5 Female figure and basket.
Male figure seated on machinery; cars at distance. TEN	X MECHANICS' AND TRADERS' BANK, Portsmouth, N. H.	10 Male figure with sheaf in hand.
20 Female figure seated.	XX Eagle. XX MECHANICS' AND TRADERS' BANK, Portsmouth, N. H.	20 Ship with sails partly furled.
FIFTY Female figure holding a wreath. FIFTY	50 Man and horse 50 MECHANICS' AND TRADERS' BANK, Portsmouth, N. H.	FIFTY. Female figure holding horn of plenty. FIFTY
Figures 100 and words one hundred. Head of Harrison.	Wagon with horses and goods; ship at a distance. MECHANICS' AND TRADERS' BANK, Portsmouth, N. H.	Figures 100 and words one hundred. Head and bust of male.
1 Head of Wm. Penn. ONE	Female figure and bale; men loading hay wagon on right. DELAWARE CITY BANK, Del.	1 Locomotive, train of cars, and bridge. ONE
2 Head of J. Quincy Adams. TWO	Female figure with sickle and sheaf of wheat in left hand, and bunch of grain in right, plow in background. DELAWARE CITY BANK, Del.	2 Steamboat. TWO
3 Head of Wm. Penn. 3	Three females in a sitting posture, the one on the left with sickle and sheaf of wheat. DELAWARE CITY BANK, Del.	Goddess of Liberty. THREE
5 Medal. Head Washington. 5	(Old Plate.) State Arms, ship in background. DELAWARE CITY BANK, Del. Bee Hive.	5 Canal Boat Train of cars in the distance. 5
5 Head of Female.	[New Plate.] DELAWARE CITY BANK, Del. State Arms; mill, &c., in background. Chickens.	5 Medal. Head J. M. Clayton.
TEN Man and woman in a sitting posture; man with hammer in right hand, woman with sheaf of wheat. 10	Two female figures one has her left hand on a cogwheel; ship-building in background. DELAWARE CITY BANK, Del. Bee Hive.	10 Medal. Head Washington. 10
20 Medal. Head Washington. 20	Man Plowing. DELAWARE CITY BANK, Del. Bee Hive.	TWENTY Washington on horseback. TWENTY
ONE 1	Agricultural scene; farmer sowing; another in the distance harrowing. 1 SOUTH BERWICK BANK. South Berwick, Me.	1 Ship. ONE
1 Farmer sharpening scythe.	SOUTH BERWICK BANK. South Berwick, Me. Female seated, holding vase; vessels in the distance.	1 Blacksmith, forge, anvil, &c.
TWO 2	Spread eagle; iron castings, cannon balls, machinery, &c. 2 SOUTH BERWICK BANK, South Berwick, Me.	2 TWO Schooner rigged boat.
2 Med. portrait of Franklin.	SOUTH BERWICK, BANK, South Berwick, Me. 2 Female seated, having a child in her lap; hogsheads, compass, quadrant, &c. 2	2 Med. head of female
THREE 3	Sailor; hat in hand, reclining against bales; in the distance are vessels, warehouses, dray, horses &c. 3 SOUTH BERWICK BANK, South Berwick, Me.	3 THREE Train of cars
Med. portrait of Lafayette. 3	Female figure seated; sickle in right hand; train of cars, ship and steamer in the distance SOUTH BERWICK BANK. South Berwick, Me.	3 Med. portrait of a female.
5 Blacksmith and anvil. FIVE	Vig. Figure of Mercury, sheaf of grain, anchor &c.; vessel in the distance. V SOUTH BERWICK BANK, South Berwick, Me.	5 Child kneeling. FIVE
Vig. Two females seated; vessels on their right; wagon on their left. 5	SOUTH BERWICK BANK, South Berwick, Me.	5 Med. of Washington.
X Indian and bow.	Steamer, sail-boat, &c. X SOUTH BERWICK BANK, South Berwick, Me.	10 Female figure; bonnet in right hand; sheaf of grain under left arm.
10 Portrait of Hancock. TEN	SOUTH BERWICK BANK. South Berwick. Me.	10 Spread eagle, shield, olive branch, and arrows; ships approaching on either hand. TEN
Steamer. XX Train of cars.	Three female figures seated. 20 SOUTH BERWICK BANK South Berwick, Me	XX Milkmaid; pail in her right hand; cricket in her left hand.
20 Figure of Justice.	Female figure seated; arms extended; Liberty cap and staff in left hand; balance in right; a child on each side; fruit, bales, &c. SOUTH BERWICK BANK, South Berwick, Me	20 Female with sheaf of grain on her back.

50 — Bust of female, with sickle in her right hand; hat on her head. — 50
Two females seated; factories, train of cars and ship in background.
SOUTH BERWICK BANK, South Berwick, Me.
50 — Boy gathering corn.

1 — Female seated blowing trumpet.
Goddess of liberty seated on globe; eagle on her right and small figure with cornucopia on her left.
B'K OF N. AMERICA. Providence, R. I.
Female and anchor.
1 — Male portrait.

ONE — Female erect writing in book resting on ornamental figure 1. — ONE
1 Vig. Two females, one kneeling, the other standing; bales, ship, and steamer on right; fruit, tree, wagon, &c., on left.
MECH'S & MAN. BK. Providence, R. I.
ONE — Female erect with sickle beside ornamental fig. 1. — ONE

100 — Sailor with flag and staff in right hand; left hand raised, holding his hat.
SOUTH BERWICK BANK, South Berwick, Me.
Female and Cupid in the clouds.
100 — Med. head of female. — 100

TWO
B'K OF N. AMERICA, Providence, R. I.
2 Goddess of liberty leaning upon shield
TWO
Dog's Head.
2 — Word TWO upon Medal. Head.

2
Vig. Two females representing Justice and Liberty; ornamental figure 2 between them.
MECH'S & MAN. BK., Providence, R. I.
2 — Female seated with sheaf of grain.

ONE — Two females erect, one with sickle and sheaf. — ONE
Steamship, sail vessels &c.; man in boat pulling toward steamship.
ATLANTIC BANK. Providence, R. I.
Female Head
1 — Spread eagle on shield. — ONE

FIVE — Female seated; pole, cap, &c.
Fig. 5 with word five running across it. Vig. Sailor in boat; city in extreme distance.
B'K OF N. AMERICA. Providence, R. I.
Steamship.
5 — Portrait of Franklin.

TWO — Female portrait in circular die. — TWO
2 Vig. Female with compass and book; cog wheel and anvil on right; plough, yoke, screw, hammer, &c., on left.
MECH'S & MAN. BK. Providence, R. I.
2 — Female seated, child beside her, cornucopia at her feet. — 2

2 — TWO — Small figure with cornucopia.
ATLANTIC BANK, Providence, R. I.
Female seated with left arm resting on shield; on her right, sheaf of wheat, fruit, and cars crossing viaduct in distance; on left ship and steamboat.
Head of Female.
2 — TWO — Small figure with cornucopia.

TEN — Female seated with battle axe in left hand, pole with liberty cap in right.
B'K OF N. AMERICA, Providence, R. I.
10 Vig. Three male figures, 10 representing commerce, agriculture and mechanics; ship on their left in distance; locomotive and town on their right.
Clasped hands.

Portrait of Webster. — 3
MECH'S & MAN. BK., Providence, R. I.
3 Vig. Figure 3 resting on book; two females reclining, one with arm on book on right; one female seated on left with wand in hand; factory in distance behind her.
3 — 3

Large V with word FIVE running across it. Two figures seated. — 5
ATLANTIC BANK. Providence, R. I.
Steamship and three vessels, largest of which is in the foreground.
Female Head
FIVE — Sailor seated among bales; ship in distance. — 5

50 — Indian female seated with bow and arrows.
B'K OF N. AMERICA, Providence, R. I.
State arms.
50
50 — Female seated.

5
Vig. Figure 5, Justice standing behind it holding scales; on either side of the 5 are two female figures, locomotive and factory on right of vig.; ships, bales, &c., on left.
Title of Bank.
Dog's head.
5 — Head of boy

10 — Large X with figures 10 upon it; light house on right, two sailors, one with spyglass other in boat.
ATLANTIC BANK. Providence, R. I.
Large ship under full sail.
Female Head
10 — Female erect standing on rock, ship below under sail.

100 — Small figure holding cornucopia. — 100
B'K OF N. AMERICA, Providence, R. I.
Vig. Spread eagle upon shield; sailing vessels on right, steamship on left
100 — Small figure holding cornucopia. — 100

5 — Female seated in large V. — FIVE
5 Vig. Large 5 with five figures around it. 5
MECH'S & MAN. BK. Providence, R. I.
5 — Female with sheaf of grain seated in large figure 5. — FIVE

Female seated with sword in right hand, balances in left. — 50 — FIFTY
Female seated with sheaf and sickle; sailor with spy glass and quadrant on right; Artisan with hammer in hands on left.
ATLANTIC BANK, Providence, R. I.
Female seated.
50 — Sailor erect

500 — Spread eagle on shield. — 500
Vig. Goddess of liberty seated, with her left hand on shield. D
B'K OF N. AMERICA. Providence, R. I.
Anchor in shield.
500 — Figure erect with left hand on shield, at whose feet is a female with globe and compass.

X — Bales, cog-wheels, &c. — X
MECH'S & MAN. BK., Providence, R. I.
Vig. Large Indian with bow, arrow, and quiver, reclining upon shield; three deers, woods, and water, on his right; deer, Indians in canoe, and soaring eagle on his left.
10 — Female portrait.

Female seated; locomotive, steamship and vessel in distance. — 100 — Sailor seated [illegible] bales, &c.
ATLANTIC BANK, Providence, R. I.
Sailor in circular shield, on either side small figure.
Female Head
100 — Female erect holding sheaf on her head with right hand, sickle in left.

Female soaring in the air, olive branch in left hand, sword in right. — 1000
B'K OF N. AMERICA, Providence, R. I.
Vig. Portion of the globe showing the continent of North America, and extending in a half circle across the face of the note.
Female soaring in the air, strewing flowers with right hand, cornucopia in her left. — 1000

10 — Farmer sowing grain. — TEN
Vig. Jupiter erect, with anchor, shield, sheaf, bags, bales and barrels; ship and steamer in distance, on right; coaches, factory, &c., on left. On right of vig., divided by a small space, is a scene on canal.
MECH. & MAN. BK., Providence, R. I.
10 — Ship and other vessels sailing by a light house. — TEN

Indian erect with bow and arrow. — ONE
1 View of railway station; two boats upon the water before it steamer. 1
B'K OF N. AMERICA. Providence, R. I.
Dog's Head.
Medal. Head with word ONE across.

1 — Female seated resting her arm on shield.
MECH'S & MAN. BK., Providence, R. I.
Vig. Santa Claus in sleigh drawn by deers.
1 — Female leaning on ornamental figure 1, sickle in her right hand

XX — Portrait of female.
MECH. & MAN. BK., Providence, R. I.
Vig. Female kneeling beside globe; quadrant, compass, paper, &c. before her; sailing vessel and steamship on her right.
20 — Bales, anchor, &c.

Steamer. Vig. Three females representing liberty, justice and learning; ship on right; eagle on left. 20 XX XX Female erect, with pail under right arm; stool in left hand. Locomotive and cars. MECH. & MAN. BK., Providence, R. I.	Male portrait. WOOSTER BANK. Danbury, Conn. 5 U. S. Capitol 5 State die. Female. 5	TWENTY B'K OF DELAWARE, Wilmington, Del. 20 2 Female figure. 0 Gen. Taylor. XX
50 MECH. & MAN. BK., Providence, R. I. 50 Vig. Scene in a boiler yard: men working on boiler in background; in foreground, man seated with tools in his hands, leaning on piece of steamer's pipe. 50 Female portrait.	1 Vig. Harvest scene. 1 State Arms. S'TH ROYALTON B'K South Royalton, Vt. ONE House. Portrait.	FIFTY Figure 50 and female head. Two ships and whale boat out. Figure 50 and female head. B'K OF DELAWARE, Wilmington, Del. Engine and cars. FIFTY
50 Vig. Harvesting scene; loading wagon with hay; farm-house in view. 50 L Female kneeling, with sword and balance. Steamer and schooner. MECH. & MAN. BK., Providence, R. I.	2 S'TH ROYALTON B'K South Royalton, Vt. 2 State Arms. Vig. Locomotive and cars. Portrait. TWO House. 2	100 Female; in background, engine and cars; shot tower. 100 Brig. B'K OF DELAWARE. Wilmington, Del. Railroad train. Female holding anchor.
100 MECH. & MAN. BK., Providence, R. I. 100 Vig. Female seated with pole and liberty cap; eagle behind her; globe, ship, and steamship on left. Ornamental fountain. 100	Vig. Cattle and swine; houses in distance. Portrait. 5 State Arms. S'TH ROYALTON B'K South Royalton, Vt Female seated in a large figure 5. FIVE House.	1 Locomotive and train of cars; another train crossing bridge, water vessel &c., in background 1 CONTINENTAL B'K, Providence, R. I. Anchor, bales; &c. Spread eagle. Portrait of Female.
100 C Vig. Four horses drawing chariot through the air, in which is seated figure with torch. 100 C Spread eagle. Portrait of Washington. 100 MECH. & MAN. BK., Providence, R. I. C	10 Vig. Female feeding swine; man seated on trough holding three horses. 10 State Arms. Portrait. S'TH ROYALTON B'K South Royalton, Vt. TEN House. TEN	Same as Ones. Portrait of Webster. 2 CONTINENTAL B'K, Providence, R. I. 2 Sheaf and Plow. Spread eagle and shield.
Vig. Indian paddling canoe, forests in the background. 500 MECH. & MAN. BK., Providence, R. I. Female with sword and scales. 500 D D	1 State arms: locomotive and ship in background. 1 B'K OF DELAWARE, Wilmington, Del. Female figure. Ship.	Three females upon rock, one erect with hand on anchor, stock. CONTINENTAL B'K, Providence, R. I. 3 Child seated upon the shoulder of a man, at whom woman behind is gazing. Female seated, leaning on bale; ship in background. THREE 3 3
MEC. AND MANUFACTURERS' B'K, Providence, R. I. 1000 Spread eagle upon a rock, overlooking the sea, on which a ship is dimly seen. Indian maiden seated. 1000	2 Spread eagle on a tree, ship and steamboat in background. 2 B'K OF DELAWARE, Wilmington, Del. Half of the State Arms. Other half State Arms.	5 Surrender of Lord Cornwallis. 5 CONTINENTAL B'K, Providence, R. I. Indian with gun, seated upon rock. Sheaf and Plow. Portrait of Washington.
ONE WOOSTER BANK, Danbury, Conn. 1 Vig. Farmer, Mechanic and Sailor representing industry. Large monument. State die.	5 State arms. 5 Dog, key, and safe. B'K OF DELAWARE, Wilmington, Del. FIVE V Chartered 1795. V	Male portrait CONTINENTAL B'K, Providence, R. I. 10 10 Goddess of liberty with eagle and globe. Medal. Head. X Male portrait.
State die. WOOSTER BANK, Danbury, Conn. TWO 2 2 Male portrait. 2 Large monument.	X Female with sheaf of wheat, sickle, &c. 10 B'K OF DELAWARE, Wilmington, Del. Female Two harvest men, with dog. 10	20 Ornamental figures 20, with winged females on either side, two small figures in the middle of large 2 & 0. 20 Female seated with spool factory in background. Female seated in shell with trident. CONTINENTAL B'K, Providence, R. I.

50 Ship under sail. Female seated leaning on bale, barrels, &c.; ship on right, factory in distance on left. CONTINENTAL B'K, Providence, R.I. 50 Portrait of Fillmore.	D Mason at work, level in his hand Vig. View of the Capitol at Washington. BLACKSTONE CAN'L BANK, Providence, R. I. 500 Locomo[illegible]	50 Female erect, leaning upon shield; spear in right hand. Vig. Male and female seated; cornucopia between. Title of Bank. 50 50 Cupid in sail boat. 50
100 Female portrait. Vig. Spread eagle on rock, large ship on either side. CONTINENTAL B'K, Providence, R. I. 100 Female erect holding tablet on pillar, cogwheels, &c. around.	M Two large ships under full sail. Vig. Large steamship under full sail at sea; ships on either side. BLACKSTONE CAN'L BANK. Providence, R. I. 1000 Anchor, bales, bbls., &c.; ship in background.	100 Vulcan seated upon a rock. Vig. Spread eagle upon limb of a tree; train of cars, canal and boats in background. Title of Bank. 100 100 Female seated; cornucopia beside her; rake in right hand.
500 Portrait of Henry Clay. Vig. Steamship under full sail, ships on either side. CONTINENTAL B'K, Providence, R. I. 500 Sailor on ship's deck, with spy glass in hand.	ONE Female supporting ornamental fig. 1. ONE 1 Vig. Female seated upon bale; sledge, anvil, cog-wheel, fire, &c., on right; bbl, sheaf, and rake, on left. 1 SMITHFIELD LIME ROCK BANK, Providence, R. I. State arms. ONE Portrait of Washington. ONE	1 Female seated; cars in distance. Vig. Spread eagle upon rock, overlooking sea; large ship on either side. 1 PHENIX BANK, Providence, R. I. Phenix. 1 Female seated; spy-glass in hands.
1 Portrait of Washington. 1 1 Vig. Winged figure with trumpet, globe and eagle on her right, flags on left. BLACKSTONE CANAL BANK, Providence, R. I. State arms. 1 Medallion head. 1	TWO Female and child in ornamental fig. 2. TWO Vig. Spread eagle upon rock overlooking sea; two ships on right, one on left. Title of Bank. State arms. 2 Farmer with cradle and sheaf of grain.	2 Vig. Three females, one on right with sword; one on left with cornucopia; ships in distance on right. 2 PHENIX BANK, Providence, R. I. Phenix. 2 Vulcan with sledge on right shoulder.
2 Male portrait. Vig. Female seated upon bale, figure at her feet; locomotive, canal, &c. in distance on right of vig.; ships, town, &c. on left. BLACKSTONE CANAL BANK, Providence, R. I. State arms. 2 Indian girl seated with shield, pole and liberty cap.	Three females erect supporting figure 3. Vig. Sailor seated among bales, with spy-glass in his left hand; ship in distance on left of vig. Title of Bank. 3 Wild horse upon the prairie fleeing from locomotive.	3 Female seated, with pen and scroll. Vig. Female reclining on bale; ships on right, under sail. 3 PHENIX BANK, Providence, R. I. Phenix 3 Portrait of Henry Clay.
5 Female seated, olive branch in left hand, spear in right. Vig. State arms, female figure on either side, schooner, locomotive and cars in distance on right; bales, barrels, steamboat and ship on left. BLACKSTONE CANAL BANK, Providence, R. I. Sale and cogwheels. 5 Female seated, spindle in right hand wand in left.	FIVE Portrait of female with compass and book. 5 5 Vig. Large 5 with five cupids around it. 5 Title of Bank. State arms. FIVE	FIVE Female with sheaf of grain in left arm. 5 Vig. Spread eagle upon shield. 5 PHENIX BANK, Providence, R. I. Phenix. 5 Goddess of Liberty, with shield, liberty pole and cap.
10 Female portrait. Vig. Mechanic seated, sledge hammer resting on his left shoulder; factories, &c., on right. 10 BLACKSTONE CANAL BANK, ProvidenCe, R. I. State arms. TEN Indian erect with bow and spear in her right hand.	5 5 Vig. Mechanic seated on ground, surrounded with wheel, tools, &c.; hay-making in distance. 5 Title of Bank Dog's head. FIVE Goddess of Liberty erect FIVE	X Portrait of Washington 10 10 Vig. Female seated; liberty pole and and cap on her lap; her right hand upon shield; her left upon cornucopia; spread eagle on right. PHENIX BANK, Providence, R. I. Phenix. 10 Female seated, reclining on bale.
50 FIFTY 50 50 Vig. Female seated, reclining upon bale; ships in background. BLACKSTONE CANAL BANK, Providence. R. I. State arms. 50	X 10 Vig. Female seated upon ground, corn, fruit, &c.; vessels upon stream in distance on left. Title of Bank. Spread eagle. 10 Mason at work, level in his hand.	20 State Arms, female with sickle on right; and cars crossing bridge; plow, corn, grain, scenery, &c., on left. Title of Bank. Steamboat 20 Portrait of Fillmore.
100 HUNDRED 100 100 Vig. Female seated beside anchor, hogshead, &c., with horn of plenty. 100 BLACKSTONE CANAL BANK, Providence, R. I. Steamship. ONE HUNDRED.	20 Female erect; spear in left hand; small globe at her feet. Vig. Female seated between ornamental figures 2 and 0. Title of Bank. XX 20 Female seated; cornucopia, &c. 20	50 Portrait of Gen. Taylor. FIFTY Female seated, arm resting on bale; farm scene loading hay, locomotive and cars in distance on right. Title of Bank. Locomotive and Tender. 50 Female bearing sheaf of grain.

C

Female leaning upon anchor, resting against bale. Schooner and steam-boat in distance on right; city with ships at wharfs in distance on left.

Title of Bank.

Spread eagle.

100

Portrait of Franklin.

RHODE I.

20 Vig. Ship sailing, 20 shore, on which is anchor upright, and motto in scroll, "In God we hope."

Title of Bank.

Anchor.

TWENTY

Female with liberty cap.

50

Man ploughing with a span of horses; train of cars on right; house on left.

Cupid and figures. 50.

CLAREMONT BANK, Claremont, N. H.

FIFTY

Female with horn of plenty.

Large ship under sail at sea.

D

PHENIX BANK, Providence, R. I.

Figures 500 on Circular shield.

Head of Female.

Sailor seated on bale, spy-glass in right hand.

500

RHODE ISLAND

50 Vig. Ship passing 50 of light house; sloop sailing ahead of her.

Title of Bank.

Anchor on shield.

FIFTY

100

Female representing commerce.

CLAREMONT BANK, Claremont, N. H.

Man with a sledge on his shoulder, factory in distance, cars crossing bridge; three cows drinking at the river.

100

Goddess of Justice.

Spread eagle.

1 Portrait of female 1 harp on right; book, scroll and globe on left.

EAGLE BANK, Providence, R. I.

State Arms.

Portrait of Washington.

RHODE ISLAND

100 Vig. Spread 100 eagle upon anchor leaning against rock, overlooking sea, on which ship is seen; upon the rock is a scroll and motto; "In God we hope."

Title of Bank.

Anchor upon shield.

ONE HUNDRED

Portrait of female.

Spread eagle.

Portrait of Indian female.

1 Portrait of female 1 with trident in left hand; quadrant, anchor, bale, &c., on right; antique vase, painter's pallet, &c. on left.

ROGER WILLIAMS BANK, Providence, R. I.

Portrait of female with cornucopia.

Spread eagle on limb.

Portrait of Indian with bow and arrows.

TWO

Locomotive and cars crossing bridge.

TWO

2 Portrait of female, resting 2 left arm, on pail; agricultural implements around.

EAGLE BANK, Providence R. I.

State Arms.

TWO

Steamboat.

TWO

Female.

1

CLAREMONT BANK, Claremont, N. H.

State Arms.

1

Portrait of Webster.

Portrait of two females.

Male portrait.

Portrait of farmer with sickle.

2 Vig. Portrait of female with left arm 2 resting on pail; scythe, rake, and pitcher on right; sieve, sheaf of grain, &c. on left.

Title of Bank.

Portrait of three females.

Portrait of Washington.

Portrait of young girl seated.

Spread eagle on limb of tree.

3 Two females 3 seated; safe and ship on right; steamer in distance on left.

EAGLE BANK, Providence, R. I.

State Arms.

Portrait of Female.

2

Two cows.

TWO

CLAREMONT BANK, Claremont, N. H.

2 Two females seated on each side of a frame on which is a vessel.

2

Male portrait.

5 Vig. Female reclining, with right 5 hand upon anchor, overlooking sea on which is dimly seen a ship.

Title of Bank.

Spread eagle.

State die.

FIVE

5 Female seated V on small globe spread eagle by her side on left.

EAGLE BANK, Providence, R. I.

Anchor.

RHODE ISLAND

THREE

Female seated on a bale.

CLAREMONT BANK, Claremont, N. H.

3 3

Portrait of Washington.

THREE

Female seated on a bale.

Three females erect, supporting shield.

Vig. Shepherd boy reclining watching sheep; 5 village in distance.

Title of Bank.

5 5

Spread eagle.

FIVE

Female erect with sickle in right hand.

5

5

Title of Bank

Vig. Large V. in centre of note; on right female seated, bales, barrel, &c., at her back; river and sloop in background before her; on left man reclining, two men seated on rocks, dray, with man and two horses, in background on his right.

Female seated.

5

5

5

Blacksmith shoeing horse; jackass tied to anvil, train of cars in background.

Letter V. and female.

CLAREMONT BANK, Claremont, N. H.

Wheels, bales, &c.

FIVE

Figure Five surrounded by five females.

Male portrait.

10 Vig. Neptune 10 seated with trident.

Title of Bank.

Spread eagle upon limb of a tree.

TEN

10 Vig. Neptune in X car, drawn by two horses.

EAGLE BANK, Providence, R. I.

Anchor.

RHODE ISLAND

X

Female reclining on bale; city on left.

Letter X and female.

CLAREMONT BANK, Claremont, N. H.

10

Two females.

Female seated holding up fig. 10.

10

Title of Bank.

Vig. Mercury seated upon clouds; bag in outstretched left hand.

Female seated holding up figure 10.

10

X

X

Title of Bank.

Vig. Large X in centre of note; on right goddess of Liberty reclining, eagle behind her, globe, ship, and steam-ship on her left; on left of X female seated on bale, resting on hogshead, anchor, bale, and ship on her left; steamship in distance on her right.

Dog.

X

X

20

Drove of Cattle XX

CLAREMONT BANK, Claremont, N. H.

Sheaf of wheat and farming implements.

20

Female holding sheaf and horn of plenty.

TWENTY

20

Vig. State arms, on right of which is farmer seated on sheaf of grain, with sickle in hand; in distance behind him man on horse and man driving swine; on left of vig. female seated; steamer in distance.

Title of Bank.

Female seated.

20

Portrait of female.

50 Title of Bank. 50
Female seated in shell with trident; ship on either side.
Indian.
Sailor standing erect; ship on either side.

Female supporting 50, holding sickle in right hand.
50 Portrait of Henry Clay. 50
Female seated supporting 50.
MERCHANTS BANK, Providence, R. I.
50 State arms. 50

XX Map—same as ones. 20 Figure of Justice.
Elephant.
DEEP RIVER BANK, Deep River, Ct.
TWENTY 20 TWENTY

100 Vig. Female portrait. 100
Two ships under sail one after the other, schooner in distance.
Title of Bank.
Indian seated upon rock, gun in right hand.

ONE HUNDRED
100 Female seated 100
ships on right; schooner in extreme distance on left.
MERCHANTS' B'K, Providence, R. I.
Ship.
ONE HUNDRED

FIVE BANK OF RALEIGH, Raleigh, Ills. 5
Male portrait
FIVE, V, and red 5.
Cattle, horse, fence, etc., cars and city in distance.
Auditor's die
Dog's head.
FIVE

D Vig. Female seated holding roll of goods and stick with left hand; bale, barrels, cog wheels and church in extreme distance on right; steamboat and factories on left. 500
Medallion head.
Title of Bank.
Medallion head.

Vig. Large ship under full sail in the foreground; sailing vessel on right; steamship and vessel in extreme distance, on left.
Portrait of Franklin
500
500
MERCHANT'S BK., Providence, R. I.

10 Two horses, man, plow and dog; cars, bridge and house in distance. 10
TEN on X.
BANK OF RALEIGH, Raleigh, Ills.
Auditors' die
TEN
Milkmaid, cow, etc.; cars in distance.
Beaver.

Female erect holding sickle in her right hand.
Large steamship under sail at sea; three sailing vessels on right; two left.
Female representing Justice.
1000 Title of Bank. 1000

MERCHANT'S BK., Providence, R. I.
Vig. Female seated, with right arm resting on cog wheel; steamship on right; locomotive and depot on left.
1000
1000
ONE THOUSAND

1 Vig. Female seated reclining on bale; ship on right; factories in distance on left. 1
Sailor erect on ship's deck, holding spyglass
B'K OF COMMERCE, Providence, R. I.
Female erect holding tablet in left arm, pen in left hand.

1 Large ship at sea under sail; ship in distance on left. 1
Portrait of Franklin.
MERCHANTS' B'K, Providence, R. I.
Sailor erect, holding spyglass in left hand, hat in right.
ONE State Arms.

ONE ONE
Washington.
ONE
Word and figure 1.
Map of Conn. on which is seen words New Haven, Hartford, Norwich, Deep River, and L. I. Sound; globe and ship on left, factory, on right.
1
DEEP RIVER BANK, Deep River, Ct.
ONE

Indian seated upon rock, rifle resting upon right leg.
B'K OF COMMERCE, Providence, R. I.
2
2 Vig. Large ship under sail at sea, another large vessel following her; schooner on left. 2
Female with sheaf of grain under right arm.
2

2 Spread Eagle on limb of tree; cars crossing bridge over canal on left; canal scene on right. 2
Portrait of Washington.
MERCHANTS' B'K, Providence, R. I.
Female erect representing Justice with scales and sword.
TWO State Arms.

Head.
TWO
Head.
2 Same as ones. 2
DEEP RIVER BANK, Deep River, Ct.
2
TWO

3 Vig Spread eagle upon shield, overlooking sea, upon which ship is dimly seen 3
Female seated, holding sickle in right hand; bundle of grain in left.
BK., OF COMMERCE, Providence, R. I.
Indian seated, holding gun in right hand.

Vulcan erect sledge over right shoulder; left hand on cog wheel
Indian and female seated; miniature view of city between them, over which is globe with spread eagle upon it.
3
Portrait of Indian female holding bow in right hand.
3 Title of Bank.

Three heads or portraits on this end.
3 Same as ones. 3
DEEP RIVER BANK, Deep River, Ct.
3
THREE

FIVE Vig. Portrait of Henry Clay. 5
Large steamship in foreground; vessels on either side, in distance.
BK., OF COMMERCE, Providence, R. I.
Female seated, holding cornucopia.
Ornamental star.

Three females upon rocks, one erect with hand upon anchor stock
Vig. A number of ships opposite a city.
5
MERCHANTS' B'K, Providence, R. I.
Portrait of female.
FIVE

Same as 3s.
5 Same as ones 5
DEEP RIVER BANK, Deep River, Ct.
5
Head
FIVE
Head.

Vig. A number of vessels upon water opposite a city.
TEN
Female seated holding scales in left hand, sword in right.
B'K OF COMMERCE, Providence, R. I.
10

Sailor standing erect holding aloft a flag; at his feet a female reclines against a cornucopia, bale, anchor, &c.
Vig. Female seated resting left arm on shield, representing state arms; ship and steamship on right; ships in extreme distance on left.
10
Indian female seated, holding shield, liberty pole and cap with right hand.
MERCHANTS' B'K, Providence, R. I.

TEN 10 Eagle. 10
TEN
Female figure of Minerva.
Map same as on ones.
DEEP RIVER BANK, Deep River, Ct.
TEN 10 TEN

50 Vig. Female seated, resting left arm upon cog wheel; ship on right; cars leaving station on left. 50
Small cupid with cornucopia under left arm.
BK OF COMMERCE, Providence, R. I.
Small figure holding sheaf under right arm.
State arms.

1. 100 | BK., OF COMMERCE, Providence, R. I. | 100 | Vig. Female leaning upon anchor, resting against bale; brig and steamboat on right; city, with vessels laying at wharfs.
2. 100 C 100 | 100 State Arms in shield; barrels and factories in distance on right; bales, boat with two men in it, and ships on left. 100 | C C | UNION BANK, Providence, R. I. | 100 | C Rhode Island. C
3. XX | Ship upon the stocks. | Vig. Scene upon a wharf, men loading dray, before which is two horses. | TRADERS' BANK, Providence, R. I. | Locomotive. | 20 | Indian erect extending hand to female seated on left. | XX
4. D | Vig. Female seated, with either hands resting on pillar; spread eagle, locomotive, and train crossing viaduct, on right; town and vessels upon water, in distance on left. | Portrait of Washington | 500 | BK., OF COMMERCE, Providence, R. I.
5. 500 D 500 | 500 Ships upon water opposite a city; light house upon left. 500 | UNION BANK, Providence, R. I | D D | State Arms. | 500 Rhode Island 500
6. FIFTY | Vig. Same as 20s. | TRADERS' BANK, Providence, R. I. | Cattle standing in water. | 50 | Scene in a shoemaker's shop, two men at work. | 50
7. BK., OF COMMERCE, Providence, R. I. | 1000 | Vig. Large steamship in foreground; ships on either side. | 1000
8. 1 | Portrait of Female. | Female reclining supporting ornamental figure 1. | 1 | TRADERS' BANK, Providence, R. I. | Deer. | ONE | Sailor erect gazing down upon female seated at his feet.
9. ONE HUNDRED | TRADERS' BANK, Providence, R. I. | Vig. Female erect holding wreath and wand in right hand; bag in left; her right foot upon a small globe; C each side. | 100 | Samson overcoming the lion. | 100
10. Female seated, holding scales in left hand; sword in right. | 1 | Vig. Female reclining upon bale; ships on right; schooner on left. | UNION BANK, Providence, R. I. | State Arms. | 1 | Female seated, holding spy-glass; ship on left.
11. ONE | Scene upon wharf, ship, steamboat, &c. | ONE | Three females one seated receiving cornucopia; Griffin standing upon safe on left; schooner, &c., locomotive and train in distance on right | TRADERS' BANK, Providence, R. I. | Clasped hands. | ONE | Female seated with staff and liberty cap, ship on left. | ONE
12. 1 | Female seated beside anvil, holding sledge in right hand. | Vig. Indian seated upon rocks, rifle in right hand; steamboat upon water and city in distance on right. | WHAT CHEER B'K, Providence, R. I. | Sheaf and plough. | 1 | Female portrait.
13. TWO | Female seated upon rocks; pail at her feet. | TWO | Vig. Three females reclining; one on right, with sword and scales; one on left, with cornucopia; ships in distance on right. | UNION BANK, Providence, R. I. | State Arms. | 2 | Ship under sail. | TWO
14. TWO | ...mer erect ...h sheaf of grain and ...ake, female with pail ...ted at his feet. | 2 | 2 Female reclining upon State Arms, spread eagle upon right, bales &c., on left. | TRADERS' BANK, Providence, R. I. | Ox. | 2 | Sailor erect leaning upon binnacle spy glass in his left hand.
15. 2 | Female holding tablet upon pillar with left arm, pen in right hand. | Vig. Three horses running loose in a field; farm house on left in distance. | WHAT CHEER B'K, Providence, R. I. | Spread eagle. | 2 | Female portrait.
16. Three females upon rock; one erect with left hand upon anchor stock. | Vig. Large ship sailing at sea, off light-house; vessel in distance on left. | UNION BANK, Providence, R. I. | State Arms. | 3 | Portrait of Washington.
17. St. George fighting the Dragon. | 2 | 2 Neptune seated in his car, drawn by two sea-horses, winged figure with cornucopia soaring above. | TRADERS' BANK, Providence, R. I. | Cupid on Horse. | 2 | Hercules combating with many headed dragon.
18. Female portrait. | 5 | Vig. State arms, eagle surmounting it, female with sword and scales on right, female with cap and staff on left; ship in distance on right; steamboat on left. | Title of Bank. | Steamboat. | 5 | Indian seated with gun in right hand.
19. Female holding sheaf of grain in left arm. | 5 | Vig. Female seated upon plough, with left arm on sheaf with sickle; bunch of grain in right hand; cars crossing viaduct on right; bridge on left. | UNION BANK, Providence, R. I. | State Arms. | 5 | Steamboat.
20. 3 | Drovers and cattle. | 3 | Indian chief, dog beside him. | Vig. Two Indians, waterfall in background, forest scene around. | TRADERS' BANK, Providence, R. I. | Large goblet. | 3 | Washington with his hand upon white horse.
21. 10 | Portrait of D. Webster. | Vig. Cattle, one lying down, two standing in water; sheep on left. | WHAT CHEER B'K, Providence, R. I. | Indian head. | 10 | Anchor, bales, ship, &c.
22. X | Portrait of Franklin. | 10 | Vig. Large steamship in foreground; sailing vessels on either side. | UNION BANK, Providence, R. I. | State Arms. | 10 | Female seated, resting left arm on scroll on pillar; pen in right hand.
23. V | Ship launching. | V | 5 Vig. Sheaf of grain and agricultural implements in foreground; locomotive and bridge in distance on left; waterfall and city on right. 5 | TRADERS' BANK, Providence, R. I. | Steamboat. | V | Female seated among bales, &c. | V
24. FIFTY | Female in clouds holding bag in left hand, wand in right. | Vig. Three females floating upon water; cupid in centre with wings extended. | WHAT CHEER B'K, Providence, R. I. | 50 | Portrait of H. Clay.
25. 50 L 50 | 50 Female reclining upon tablet with 50 upon it; ship on stocks upon left, wharf in distance on right. 50 | UNION BANK, Providence, R. I. | L Rhode Island. L
26. Ten Dollars. | Vulcan seated beside anvil, figure beside and behind him. | 10 | X Vig. Mammoth ox standing looking to left of of note. X | TRADERS' BANK, Providence, R. I. | Spread eagle. | TEN | Drover and cattle. | 10
27. 100 | Henry Clay seated with his dog beside him. | Vig. Female seated between two pillars, eagle and shield at her feet; in distance on right cars crossing bridge; town and ships on left in distance. | WHAT CHEER B'K, Providence, R. I. | 100 | Female seated holding spy-glass; ship on left.

1
Vig. State arms; Indian on left, man with axe in left hand on right. 1
PAWTUXET BANK,
Providence, R. I.
Plough and sheaf.
1
Bull's head.

1
Men in boat, sloops in distance
1
(Old Plate.)
1 Female seated beside steam engine factory with water-wheel in distance on left. 1
Title of Bank.
State Arms.
1
Steamboats upon river.
1

50
Female seated; cornucopia in left hand.
50
Steam- Vig. Steam boat. Head of boat Washington in circular shield, surmounted by eagle on half globe; female on either side; vessels in distance.
AMERICAN BANK.
Providence, R. I.
State Arms.
50
Same as left end.
50

2
Vig. Spread eagle behind shield, female on left, holding portrait of Washington, staff and cap; cars in distance; steamship in distance on right. 2
Title of Bank.
State arms.
TWO
Large ship under sail at sea; vessel on either side.

Male portrait
2
(New Plate.)
View upon East River, large steamer sailing to right of note, ships, sloop, mail steamboat, &c.
AMERICAN BANK,
Providence, R. I.
2
Female seated resting right arm upon shield

100
Female erect holding balances in right hand; sword in left
100
100 Vig. Two females; one with wings, wreath and book seated on right; the other standing with sword and scales; sun breaking through dark clouds over their heads 100
AMERICAN BANK,
Providence, R. I.
State Arms.
100
Same as left end.
100

THREE
Farmer erect with sheaf under left arm, female with pail at his feet.
3
Vig. Ornamental figure 3, medallion head on either side.
PAWTUXET BANK,
Providence, R. I.
State arms.
3
Portrait of Indian girl with bow and arrow in hands.

2
Spread eagle grasping arrows and shield in talons.
2
(Old Plate.)
2 Three females seated representing commerce, agriculture, &c. 2
AMERICAN BANK,
Providence, R. I.
State Arms.
Same as on left.

500
Male portrait
Vig. Indian girl seated upon ground; on left shield, spread eagle upon globe, drum, flags liberty pole and cap, battle axe, &c.; on right ship in distance.
Title of Bank
State arms.
500
D

Steamboat and three sailing vessels; city in distance.
FIVE
Vig. Female with sheaf of grain seated in large ornamental V.
PAWTUXET BANK,
Providence, R. I.
State arms.
5
Sailor erect, leaning upon binnacle, spy glass in left hand.

3
3
AMERICAN BANK,
Providence, R. I.
Scene in a factory; females at work with machines, &c. 3
3
Male portrait

1000
Vig. Spread eagle upon shield. Male portrait
AMERICAN BANK,
Providence, R. I.
State arms.
1000
M

10
X
10
Yoke of oxen, male figure erect beside them. Large ornamental 10.
PAWTUXET BANK,
Providence, R. I.
TEN
Female erect holding horn of plenty in left hand, spade in right.

3
Portrait of Washington.
3
Portrait of female. Vig. Indian in canoe, paddling past high rocks; forest scenery around. Portrait of male.
AMERICAN BANK,
Providence, R. I.
State Arms.
3
Male portrait
3

1
Hunter with rifle in hand, dog beside him.
LIBERTY BANK,
Providence, R. I.
1 Vig. Large horse running in foreground; boys trying to stop him, one with cap in hand on right; factory in distance; one boy fallen down, one running, on left; dog and horses in distance. 1
1
Portrait of child.

20
Female seated, book on her lap, left hand resting upon it.
XX Spread eagle standing upon rock. XX
PAWTUXET BANK,
Providence, R. I.
20
Large sized ship under sail.

5
Male portrait
Vig. Nautical view; large steamship in foreground; sailing vessels on either side.
AMERICAN BANK,
Providence, R. I.
Spread Eagle.
5
Female seated in large ornamental figure.
5

2
Female portrait.
LIBERTY BANK,
Providence, R. I.
Vig. Drover buying cattle of farmer; sheep and two men on left.
2

50
Female erect resting left arm upon shield, spear in right hand.
Vulcan seated beside female holding rake on left; cornucopia between them
PAWTUXET BANK,
Providence, R. I.
50
50
Cupid in sailboat.
50

5
Portrait of Washington.
5
5 Vig. Washington crossing the Delaware. 5
AMERICAN BANK,
Providence, R. I
State Arms.
5
Portrait of Franklin.
5

5
Full length sailor looking to right of note.
LIBERTY BANK,
Providence, R. I.
5 Vig. Landing of Roger Williams on Slate Rock. 5
5
Female portrait.

100
Vulcan seated with sledge in left hand.
Spread eagle upon limb of tree; cars on left crossing canal, canal scene on right.
PAWTUXET BANK,
Providence, R. I.
100
100
Female seated with rake in right hand, grain in left.

Male portrait
10
AMERICAN BANK,
Providence, R. I.
X Vig. State Arms; on right, resting right arm upon it female with liberty pole and cap; steamship in distance on left; female seated with sickle in right hand; locomotive &c., in distance.
10

10
Anchor leaning upon bales; ship in background.
Vig. Goddess of Liberty with pole and cap, shield; spread eagle on left. Portrait of Indian girl with bow and quiver
LIBERTY BANK,
Providence, R. I.
Spread eagle.
10
Portrait of Washington.
TEN

1
Female erect holding tablet upon pillar with left arm, pen in right hand.
(New Plate.)
Female seated resting arm upon shield and quiver; view of niagara falls upon left; trees in background upon right.
AMERICAN BANK,
Providence, R. I.
1
Male portrait

10
Med. head.
10
TEN Vig. Locomotive and train of cars; forest scenery in background. TEN
AMERICAN BANK,
Providence, R. I.
State Arms.
10
Med. head.
10

50
Male portrait
Vig. Spread eagle upon shield, scroll in beak, "E pluribus unum" upon it; vessels on right; cars and city in distance on left.
LIBERTY BANK,
Providence, R. I.
Spread eagle.
50
Indian seated resting right hand upon shield, with pole and cap; quiver on her shoulder.

100	Vig. Surrender of Lord Cornwallis to George Washington. LIBERTY BANK, Providence. R. I.	100 Spread eagle upon shield looking to left of note.

2 Blacksmith leaning over anvil. TWO	GROCERS' AND PRODUCERS' BANK. Providence, R. I. Female seated in large ornamental 2.	2 Portrait of little girl. TWO

Eagle resting on United States shield and an anchor. FIVE	A large V, with female figure and child. WOONSOCKET B'K, Cumberland, R. I.	5 Female figure and basket.

ONE Female portrait. ONE	1 Vig. Spread eagle upon limb, cars crossing canal on left, canal scene on right. 1 CITY BANK, Providence, R. I. Steamship.	ONE Farmer shearing sheep, woman standing behind him. ONE

5 male.	State Arms; Indian seated upon right, farmer with sickle upon left; canoe upon river on right; cars in distance on left. Title of Bank.	Figure 5 with word FIVE. Portrait of Sailor.

Male figure seated on machinery; cars at distance. TEN	X WOONSOCKET B'K. Cumberland, R. I.	10 Male figure with sheaf in hand.

Female standing erect in large ornamental figure 2.	2 Vig. Scene upon the ocean; capturing whale in foreground, boat and ship in background. 2 CITY BANK, Providence, R. I.	TWO Cupid in sail boat. TWO

10 Large X with 10 on it; vissel on right light house on left.	GROCERS' AND PRODUCERS' BANK. Providence, R. I. State Arms, eagle upon globe surmounting it; female on either side.	10 Large ship at sea.

20 Female figure seated.	XX Eagle. XX WOONSOCKET B'K. Cumberland, R. I.	20 Ship with sails partly furled.

5 Poitrait of female with sheaf in hand. 5	5 Vig. Female with shield, eagle, &c., seated in ornamental V, covering centre of note. 5 CITY BANK, Providence, R. I.	FIVE Female seated with staff and cap in left hand. V

50	Title of Bank. Two females seated; one on left supporting shield with sheaf upon its face; one on right holding wand in left hand; portrait of Franklin on right; steamboat vessel &c., on right in distance, wagon crossing bridge cars &c., on left in distance.	50 State Arms. 50

FIFTY Female figure standing globe in her right hand, flowers at her right. FIFTY	50 Man and horse. 50 WOONSOCKET B,K, Cumberland, R. I. FIFTY DOLLARS	FIFTY Female figure with wreath of flowers in right hand. FIFTY

10 Female seated with grain in left hand. X	Vig. Ships, steamboat and other vessels. X CITY BANK, Providence, R. I. Ship under sail.	10 Female with shield and scales in right hand, barrels in rear. X

100	Female seated supporting shield, with arm and hammer upon it; cars, steamship, &c., on right. GROCERS' AND PRODUCERS' BANK, Providence, R. I.	100 Boy with basket seated among sheep cars in distance upon left. 100

Figures 100 and words one hundred. Head of Harrison.	Wagon with horses and goods; ship at a distance. WOONSOCKET B'K, Cumberland. R. I.	Figures 100 and words one hundred. Head and bust of male.

50 Female with left hand resting upon shield, right arm upon the neck of eagle. FIFTY	CITY BANK, Providence. R. I. Vig. Large steamship under full sail	50 Female seated, sickle in right hand, horn of plenty in left, sheaf, boxes &c. FIFTY

D Small Cupid holding cornucopia. 500	Title of Bank Large steamboat sailing past city in background. 500	Farmer erect sharpening scythe, canal bridge in distance. 500

1 Head of Washington.	Female. 1 Female. MONANDOCK BANK, East Jeffrey, N. H.	1 Head of Franklin.

100 Male portrait 100	Vig. Ship building; ship on stocks; ship at wharf on right; sloop under sail in distance on left. CITY BANK, Providence, R. I. Cornucopia, anchor, wand, &c.	100 Portrait of female holding dish of fruit. 100

ONE 1	Agricultural scene; farmer sowing; another in the distance harrowing. 1 WOONSOCKET BK, Cumberland, R. I.	1 Ship. ONE

2 Head.	Female. 2 Female. MONANDOCK BANK, East Jeffray, N H.	2 Head.

	The 500s and 1000s of the City Bank are of the same plate as the Mechanics' and Manufacturers' Bank of Providence. For a description of which see page 205.	

TWO 2	Spread eagle; iron castings, cannon balls, machinery, &c. 2 WOONSOCKET B'K, Cumberland, R. I.	2 TWO Schooner rigged boat.

3 Washington, full length.	Female head and bust. 3 Female head and bust. MONANDOCK BANK, East Jeffroy, N. H.	3 Vulcan, full length.

1 Two cattle one standing other lying down. ONE	GROCERS' AND PRODUCERS' BANK, Providence, R. I. Vig. Two females seated, one on right holding bale of goods upon her lap; factories in distance behind her; steamboat in extreme distance on left.	1 Female on either side of state arms.

THREE 3	Sailor; hat in hand, reclining against bales; in the distance are vessels, warehouses, dray, horses &c. 3 WOONSOCKET B'K, Cumberland, R. I.	3 THREE Train of cars.

Spread eagle; city and vessels in distance. FIVE	Large V, female and Cupid. MONANDOCK BANK, East Jeffrey, N. H.	5 Portrait of a girl.

Left end	Centre	Right end
Vulcan seated; train of cars, &c., in distance. TEN	X MONANDOCK BANK, East Jeffrey, N. H.	10 Farmer with sheaf of wheat and sickle.
XX Female. XX	Vig. Three females seated, with bee-hive on the right, and sheaf of grain on the left. 20 ARCADE BANK, Providence, R. I. Pie.	20 Drover and cattle. 20
10	BK., OF AMERICA, Providence, R. I. Vig. Female seated, holding American shield; Liberty pole and cap laying across lap; United States Capitol in back-ground.	10
20 Female sitting, right hand upon a book.	XX Eagle. XX MONANDOCK BANK East Jeffrey, N. H.	20 Ship under sail.
Full length male figure.	50 Vig. Figures, globe, ship, scroll, &c. ARCADE BANK, Providence, R. I. State arms.	50 Male portrait. 50
20 Locomotive, &c.	Vig. Female seated, holding scales in right hand; pole and liberty cap in left; small figure on either side. BK., OF AMERICA, Providence, R. I. Steamship.	20 Female with sickle and grain.
FIFTY Female. FIFTY	50 Man and horse. 50 MONANDOCK BANK, East Jeffrey, N. H.	FIFTY Female. FIFTY
100 Portrait. 100	100 Vig. Man on horseback. 100 ARCADE BANK, Providence, R. I. State arms.	100 Portrait. 100
50 Portrait of female with sickle. 50	Vig. Two females seated; factories and cars crossing bridge on right; ship in distance, on left. BK., OF AMERICA, Providence, R. I. Locomotive.	50 Boy holding ears of corn in either hand.
Words one hundred running across figures 100. Male portrait	Dray cart, into which men are rolling barrels, horses, shipping, &c. MONANDOCK BK. East Jeffrey, N. H	Words one hundred running across figures 100. Male portrait
500	Vig. Indian paddling a canoe. 500 ARCADE BANK, Providence, R. I.	500 Female with a sword and scales.
100 Full length sailor; American flag in right arm; cap in left hand.	BK., OF AMERICA, Providence, R. I. Vig. Female and Cupid soaring in air, above city. Cog-wheel, &c.	100 Large ship under full sail. 100
ONE	1 View of Arcade city of Providence. 1 ARCADE BANK. Providence, R. I. State Arms.	Beehive. Portrait of Female. American shield.
1000	Vig. Eagle standing upon a rock overlooking the sea, upon which a ship is dimly seen. 1000 ARCADE BANK, Providence, R. I.	1000 Indian girl seated upon a rock, with bow and arrows.
Female portrait. 1	MARKET BANK, Cupid rolling silver dollar on railroad track; cars, steamboat and city in distance. Bangor, Me. Cow and calf.	1 Female Indian seated.
TWO	2 Same as Ones. 2 ARCADE BANK, Providence, R. I. State Arms.	Beehive. Female seated with liberty pole and cap. Shield.
1 Male portrait	Vig. Female seated between two pillars; shield, spread eagle, cars crossing bridge on right; anchor, &c.; city in the distance on left. BANK OF AMERICA, Providence, R. I.	1 Female bearing sheaf on shoulder.
Female reclining with scales in right hand. 2	Two cupids and two silver dollars; cupids apparently in an engagement; train of cars, cattle, hills, city, &c. in distance. MARKET BANK, Bangor, Me. Two horses.	2 Bull's head.
THREE	3 Same as Ones. 3 ARCADE BANK, Providence, R. I. State Arms.	Female with sickle sheaf of grain, &c. THREE
2 Female holding tablet on pillar.	Vig. Female reclining upon bales; ships on right; vessel on left. BK., OF AMERICA. Providence, R. I	2 TWO Male portrait
THREE Female seated, fruits, &c.	Three cupids and three silver dollars, all engaged at some art. MARKET BANK, Bangor, Me.	3 3
Female with her right hand resting on desk, and her left holding a pen.	5 Vig. Same as ones. 5 ARCADE BANK, Providence, R. I. State arms.	Eagle on limb
3 Female seated, holding sword and scales.	Vig. Portrait of Indian girl in ornamental shield, surrounded by drums &c. BK., OF AMERICA, Providence, R. I. Spread eagle between sig.	3 Ship under full sail.
5 Cattle. 5	Five silver dollars and five cupids. MARKET BANK, Bangor, Me. Man plowing with two horses;	5 Cattle; man seen on right
Male portrait 10 Male portrait	10 Vig. Same as ones. 10 ARCADE BANK, Providence, R. I. State arms.	Male portrait TEN Male portrait
5	Vig. Spread eagle upon shield, looking to left. Portrait of Washington BK., OF AMERICA, Providence, R. I. Steamship.	5 State Arms.
Female feeding horse. X	Two men, horse, dog and drove of cattle and sheep. MARKET BANK, Bangor, Me.	10 Boy's head.

Female portrait. 20
Drove of cattle and sheep; man on horseback.
MARKET BANK, Bangor, Me.
20 Female churning.

TEN
Vulcan seated, anvil, sleigh, &c.; train of cars and buildings in distance. X
WHITE MOUNTAIN BANK, Lancaster, N. H.
10 Farmer with sheaf on his knee.

Two males and one female anvil and hammer. 50
L Train of cars. L
MECHANICS' BANK, Augusta, Ga.
Mechanic's Arm.
Steamboat, snake in form of a circle inside of which is building with three pillars and man. 50

---

50 State arms.
Female seated; barrels, bales, anchor, &c.; steamship on right, and ship on left.
MARKET BANK, Bangor, Me.
50 Sailor with left hand on capstan; masts, blocks, &c.

---

20 Female.
XX Eagle. XX
WHITE MOUNTAIN BANK, Lancaster, N. H.
20 Ship sailing.

Nude female erect, standing in smoke, fig. in clouds; horses in water. 100
100 Vig. Same as 50's. 100
MECHANICS' BANK, Augusta, Ga.
Mechanic's Arm.
100 Male in car drawn by two horses; a figure soaring in clouds. 100

Ornamental fountain. C
Female reclining on safe two females, cows, haystack, on right; train of cars, vessel, buildings, &c. on left.
MARKET BANK, Bangor, Me.
100 State arms.

FIFTY Female erect with wreath. FIFTY
50 Man and horse. 50
WHITE MOUNTAIN BANK, Lancaster, N. H.
FIFTY Female erect. FIFTY.

Male portrait. 1
BUTCHERS & DROVERS' BANK, Providence, R. I.
Drove of cattle, hogs, &c.; two men on horseback; cars crossing viaduct in distance.
1 Female portrait.

V Dog's head. V
Man on horseback, driving cow and sheep; boy holding gate open; cattle, trees, &c. in distance; at right of vig. Trea's die.
FAIRMONT BANK, Fairmont, Va.
5 Men loading wagon with hay.

Word one hundred and figure 100. Male portrait
Wharf scene—loading wagon, men, horses, shipping, &c.
WHITE MOUNTAIN BANK, Lancaster, N. H.
Same as on left. Male portrait.

---

2 Male portrait TWO
Title of Bank.
Drove of oxen and sheep; man on horseback; trees, etc., in distance.
2 Female portrait. TWO

X Train of cars coming down grade, house in background, two indians in foreground.
Indian crouching behind rock with gun, watching two deers. Trea's die.
FAIRMONT BANK, Fairmont, Va.
TEN Dog's head.

ONE Portrait of Washington. ONE
Spread eagle on limb of tree; train of cars and buildings in distance. 1
MECHANICS' BANK, Augusta, Ga.
Mechanic's arm, anvil, &c
ONE

Small figure 5. 5
Vig. Three females floating through water, supporting Cupid.
BUTCHERS' & DROVERS' BANK, Providence, R. I.
Ox.
5 Male portrait.

1
Female seated; train of cars, sloop, and steam boat on right; on left canal, lock, &c. Large 1, and five men.
WHITE MOUNTAIN BANK, Lancaster, N. H.
1 Female seated with head on her hand.

TWO Female portrait. TWO
2 Mechanic seated, left arm on anvil. 2
MECHANICS' BANK, Augusta, Ga.
Eagle.
TWO

---

10 Drovers, cattle, hay, &c.
Vig. Two females seated on either side of state arms, steamship on the right, locomotive and cars on the left.
Title of Bank.
Beehive.
10 Portrait of Andrew Jackson.

2
Man and two boys; two sheep in water; drove on left, and buildings on right. Large 2 and five men.
WHITE MOUNTAIN BANK, Lancaster, N. H.
TWO Female seated. TWO

---

5 Female at spinning wheel. V
Female reclining on fig. 5; medall. Head on either side; scow and buildings in distance.
MECHANICS' BANK, Augusta, Ga.
Mechanic's arm.
V Female with rake and twig 5

50
Vig. Female reclining on bale of goods. Portrait of Henry Clay.
BUTCHERS' & DROVERS' BANK, Providence, R. I.
50 Anchor on a bale of goods.

3
Man on horseback, cattle, dog, and man; load of hay entering barn, likewise three men; in distance city. 3
WHITE MOUNTAIN BANK, Lancaster, N. H.
Word three and figure 3. Female erect with basket of flowers. THREE

---

10 Indian seated 10
Eagle on trunk of tree Medall. Head on either side; steamboat on left.
MECHANICS' BANK, Augusta, Ga.
Mechanics arm.
X Indian seated X

Indian looking in distance. 100
Vig. Steamship and other vessels.
BUTCHERS' & DROVERS' BANK, Providence, R. I.
100 Male portrait.

FIVE
Spread eagle on shield; city and ships in distance. Female, cupid, and letter V.
WHITE MOUNTAIN BANK, Lancaster, N. H.
5 Little girl with flowers.

---

20 Female; ship in distance. XX
Female in car drawn by two horses on water; Medall. Head on either side; ship's masts in distance.
MECHANICS' BANK, Augusta, Ga.
Mechanic's Arm.
XX Same as 5's. 20

---

1 1
STATE BANK, Providence, R. I.
Vig. Female seated, resting upon state arms; ship and steamship on right; sailing vessels in distance on left
Dog, safe, and ke
1 View of house and trees.

2 Vig. Locomotive and cars. Female portrait. STATE BANK, Providence, R. I. State arms. 2 View of house and trees.	1 Medal. Head with word ONE. 1 1 State arms with female on either side of it; globe, and cars crossing bridge in distance on right; plow and sheaf on left. 1 MOUNT VERNON BANK. Providence, R. I. ONE Portrait of female with grain in hand ONE	50 Ships sailing 50 Statue of Washington full length. 50 50 MT. VERNON BANK. Providence, R. I. Face. 50 Face.
3 View of house and trees. STATE BANK. Providence, R. I. Vig. Female resting upon State Arms, with steamships and ship on right; ships on left. Eagle. 3 Female portrait.	1 Female feeding horse. Female seated resting arm upon shield with word ONE upon it; bales, &c., on right; bales anchor and ships upon left. Title of Bank. State Arms. 1 Ship under sail with flag flying.	Cupid soaring in air bearing basket of flowers upon his head. 100 Vig. Female seated holding key in right hand, and receiving cornucopia from winged figure on right; griffin standing upon safe on left. MT. VERNON BANK. Provida nce, R. I. Spr d eagle. C 100
5 View of house and trees. Vig. Female resting upon State Arms, with steamship and ship on right; ships on left. STATE BANK, Providence, R. I. Locomotive; 5 Portrait of Washington.	2 Female with pole and liberty cap. 2 Shield surmounted by bee hive; male figures on either side; one on right with rifle, ship in distance; one on left with axe, schooner and cars in extreme distance; 2 on left. Title of Bank. 2 Medal. Head.	1 Male portrait WESTMINSTER B'K, Providence, R. I. Vig. Country scene; one man seated on left, one standing on right. 1 Beehive.
10 Three females upon a rock; one erect with hand upon anchor. TEN 10 Vig. Female resting upon State Arms, with steamship and ship on right; ships on left STATE BANK. Providence, R. I. 10 View of house and trees.	3 Female erect with hand upon capstan Title of Bank. Blacksmith shoeing horse locomotive and mule on left. Anvil,, sledge, &c. 3 Female Portrait.	2 Male portrait WESTMINSTER B'K, Providence, R. I. 2 Vig. Two females seated; town in distance on right. 2 2 Female portrait.
Sailor holding flag aloft, with anchor, bale of goods and female reclining. 20 Vig. Cupid, ...; female seated upon a safe, with vessel and locomotive on the right; sheaf of wheat and plow on left. STATE BANK, Providence, R. I State Arms. 20 View of house and trees.	5 Female Portrait. Title of Bank. Indian girl seated; quiver, shield, &c., rainbow on left. 5 Female seated, scroll in right hand, wand in left.	5 Male portrait Vig. View of city of Providence; cars leaving railway station; water in background, WESTMINSTER B'K, Providence, R. I. 5 Male portrait
50 Female portrait. STATE BANK, Providence, R. I. Vig. Female resting upon state arms; steamship on right; ship on left. 50 Female portrait.	5 V 5 Female standing erect with cornucopia pole and cap. FIVE Title of Bank. FIVE 5 Drover and Cattle. 5	TEN Large steamship, vessels on either side. Vig. Two male portraits. WESTMINSTER B'K. Providence, R. I. 10 Brig sailing.
View of house and trees. 100 Vig. Spread eagle, American shield, &c. STATE BANK. Providence, R. I. State Arms. 100 Female portrait.	10 Portrait of Female. Title of Bank. Female seated, cornucopia in left arm which rests upon shield. coin around her; nine small figures in front of her. 10 Male portrait	20 Vig. Farming scene; farmer on horse drinking out of trough; two figures on right; sheep on left. Female portrait. WESTMINSTER B'K. Providence, R. I. 20 Male portrait.
500 Indian female with bow and arrow. STATE BANK, Providence, R. I. Vig. Female seated; on her left, female seated, with sheaf of grain; and on her right, railroad in extreme distance; man with spade. Eagle. 500 500	TEN Portrait of Washington. TEN Female erect with hands holding an anchor. 10 Title of Bank. 10	50 Male portrait. WESTMINSTER B'K, Providence, R. I. Male portrait. Vig. Female seated holding spy-glass; ship in distance on left. Male portrait. 50 Female portrait.
M 1000 STATE BANK, Providence, R. I Vig. Female seated upon bale; figure kneeling at her feet; cars crossing bridge; canal scene on right; ship and town on left. ONE THOUSAND A 1000 1000	XX Portrait of Franklin. 20 Vig. Lafayette standing erect, cane and hat in right hand. MT. VERVON BANK, Providence, R. I 20	100 WESTMINSTER B'K, Providence R. I. Vig. A number of horses running in a field. 100 Male portrait.

FIVE HUNDRED WESTMINSTER B'K, Providence, R. I. Vig. Eagle surmounting a globe; Indian seated with rifle on left; female seated with sickle and grain on right. Male portrait. 500 Male and female seated in foreground; two figures in background, one with a sickle, the other sharpening scythe.	FIFTY 50 Vig. Female standing erect resting left hand on shield; anchor on right; ship on left. WEYBOSSET BANK, Providence, R. I. L 50 State arms. 50	10 Mechanics Arm and sledge. Two females with State Arms between them, with eagle resting upon State Arms. Title of Bank. 10 Portrait of Washington.
RHODE Female erect with basket upon arm. ISLAND. Vig. Indian paddling in a canoe. WEYBOSSET BANK, Providence, R. I. State arms. 1 ONE	Spread eagle upon rock. 100 100 WEYBOSSET BANK, Providence, R. I. Vig. Female reclining on state arms. 100 Male portrait 100	20 Male portrait Mechanic with tools and pieces of machinery. MECHANICS' BANK, Providence, R. I. State Arms. 20 Portrait of Franklin.
1 Female portrait. WEYBOSSET BANK, Providence, R. I. Vig. Meeting of the pilgrims with the Indians. Head of Indian. 1 Male portrait.	500 Vig. Female reclining upon bales; ships on right; vessel on left. Portrait of Millard Fillmore. WEYBOSSET BANK, Providence, R. I. Female Indian head. 500	FIFTY Female with wreath. FIFTY 50 Man and Horse. 50 MECHANICS' BANK, Providence, R. I. FIFTY Full length female, Globe, Rule, &c FIFTY
2 TWO WEYBOSSET BANK, Providence, R. I. Vig. Sailor seated upon bale, holding flag in right hand; ships on either side. Spread eagle TWO State arms.	Mechanic, anvil, cog-wheel, sledge, &c. ONE Vig. Spread eagle American shield, &c. MECHANICS' BANK, Providence, R. I. State arms. 1 Male portrait	Words one hundred and figures 100 Male portrait. Vig. Market scene; shipping on left. MECHANICS' BK., Providence, R. I. Words one hundred, and figures 100. Male portrait.
RHODE ISLAND. Vig. Female seated raising lid of chest with right hand. WEYBOSSET BANK, Providence, R. I. Spread eagle. Star with fig 2 upon it. Star with fig 2 upon it.	ONE 1 Two Eagles with State Arms in centre. 1 MECHANICS' BANK, Providence, R. I. ONE	Female seated, with farmer at work in distance. 500 500 D MECHANICS' BK., Providence, R. I. 500
2 Female portrait. WEYBOSSET BANK, Providence, R. I. Vig. Elliott preaching to the Indians. 2 Male portrait	2 Male portrait Female resting upon State Arms, schooner in distance on right, and buildings on left. Title of Bank Blacksmith's Arm. 2 Male portrait	1000 THOUSAND Vig. In upper left corner of note, which is vacant—a classical name. MECHANICS' BK., Providence, R. I. Locomotive and cars. 1000 Ship. 1000
5 Female Indian with shield, pole, and liberty cap. Portrait of Washington. Vig. Ship under full sail. Portrait of Madison. WEYBOSSET BANK, Providence, R. I. State arms. 5 Female seated resting arm upon scroll upon pillar.	TWO 2 Two Eagles with State Arms in centre. 2 MECHANICS' BANK, Providence, R. I. TWO	1 Drummer, two men seated. JACKSON BANK, Providence, R. I. 1 Large Portrait Gen. Jackson. 1 1 Blacksmith erect beside anvil.
Spread eagle upon rock overlooking the sea. TEN 10 10 WEYBOSSET BANK, Providence, R. I. Vig. Cornucopia, wand with wings on it, barrel, &c.; ship in distance on left. Washington full length.	FIVE 5 Woman, eagle resting on Globe on left. 5 MECHANICS' BANK, Providence, R. I. Cogwheel. FIVE	2 View of battle field, throwing up entrenchments. JACKSON BANK, Providence, R. I. 2 Same as one. 2 2 Soldier erect holding flag beside cannon
X Portrait of Harrison. 10 Female portrait. Vig. Dog, safe; bag of coin. Female portrait. WEYBOSSET BANK, Providence, R. I. Spread eagle. 10 Portrait of Henry Clay. X	FIVE 5 Two Eagles with State Arms in centre. 5 MECHANICS' BANK, Providence, R. I. FIVE	5 Scene upon prairie, Indians hunting buffalo. JACKSON BANK, Providence, R. I. Vig. Small portrait of Jackson 5 Country scene, two children, oxen in foreground, man felling tree on right of them.

X — Vig. Jackson and staff on horseback overlooking battle field of New Orleans — 10 Portrait of Gen. Taylor. — JACKSON BANK. Providence, R. I. Spread eagle. — Portrait of Gen Scott.	50 — 50 Same as ones. L — RHODE ISLAND. BANK OF BRISTOL. Bristol, R. I. 50	1 — Vig. Group of females, representing milking scene. Steamboat. — 1 Locomotive and cars. — Female bathing. ONE — EXCHANGE BANK, Providence, R. I. State arms. — ONE
C — Vig. View of Harbor of N. Y. ships and steamships sailing off city. — 100 C — JACKSON BANK. Providence, R. I. State Arms. — Portrait of President Jackson.	1 — Cupid rolling silver dollar; locomotive and city in distance on right. — 1 Ornamental Fountain. — ATLAS BANK. Providence, R. I. Goddess of liberty. — Santa claus with bag of toys on back.	ONE — Male portrait with cupid on either side. — ONE Female supporting ornamental fig. 1 — EXCHANGE BANK, Providence, R. I. State arms. — Vig. Boy, sheep, dog, basket, &c.; cars crossing bridge. ONE — 1
ONE — 1 Vig. Indian seated upon ground, bow in right hand 1 — RHODE ISLAND. 1 — BANK OF BRISTOL, Bristol, R. I.	Hunter leaning upon rifle. — ATLAS BANK. Providence, R. I. — 2 2 — Female seated, dog and pail beside her on right; cattle on left. — Female with sheaf of grain.	2 — TWO Vig. Female seated holding key in right hand, receiving cornucopia from winged figure on right, safe and griffin on left. — 2 Vessel and steamboat on river opposite town. — EXCHANGE BANK, Providence, R. I. State arms. — Female with state arms on right, scales on left. TWO
II — 2 Vig. Same as ones 2 — RHODE ISLAND 2 — BANK OF BRISTOL, Bristol, R. I.	3 — Female floating on water; cupids on left and sea monster. — 3 Indian girl seated. — ATLAS BANK. Providence, R. I. — Cupid astride of sea monster.	2 — Male portrait. Vig. Two females; mechanic, safe and anvil; ship on right; cars on left. — 2 Portrait of Daniel Webster. — EXCHANGE BANK, Providence, R. I. State arms. — TWO
3 — 3 Same as ones. 3 — RHODE ISLAND III — BANK OF BRISTOL, Bristol, R. I.	FIVE — Locomotive and cars; Depot on left. — 5 Portrait of Female. Female erect with spear and shield, globe at feet. — ATLAS BANK, Providence, R. I. Dog's Head. — 5	Female seated on bales, with cornucopia; 5 at her feet. — EXCHANGE BANK, Providence, R. I. Large V; female seated, sheaf, etc. — 5 FIVE — Female portrait.
V — 5 Same as ones. 5 — RHODE ISLAND. 5 — BANK OF BRISTOL, Bristol, R. I.	Sailor leaning upon capstan, spy glass in hand. — Artisan seated beside machinery; factories on right in distance. — 10 10 — ATLAS BANK. Providence, R. I. Loading Hay. — Female seated upon anchor, ship in distance.	Vig. Human figure with sickle in right hand; plough, rake, &c. on right; sheaf of grain on left. 10 — 10 Two male figures supporting female with wreath of flowers. 10 — EXCHANGE BANK, Providence, R. I. State arms.
X — 10 Same as ones. 10 — RHODE ISLAND 10 — BANK OF BRISTOL. Bristol, R. I.	Sailor boy in attitude of rowing. — State Arms surmounted by eagle, female with sword and scales on right, female with spear and cornucopia on left, locomotive on right in distance; steamboat on left. — 20 Goddess of liberty with pole cap and shield beside globe. 20 — Title of Bank.	Female soaring in air, with ear of corn in left hand. — 50 Male portrait. 50 — Female soaring in air, sickle in right hand, grain in left. FIFTY — EXCHANGE BANK, Providence, R. I. State arms. — FIFTY
XX — 20 Same as ones 20 — RHODE ISLAND. 20 — BANK OF BRISTOL. Bristol, R. I.	Female with spear and shield. — ATLAS BANK, Providence, R. I. — 50 50 — Female with sword and scales reclining upon shield, view upon it; Cupid soaring on right. — Indian girl seated upon ground, forest scenery in distance.	100 Cupid. — EXCHANGE BANK Providence, R. I. Vig. New York Crystal Palace. — 100 Cupid C — State arms. — Male portrait.
30 — 30 Same as ones. 30 — RHODE ISLAND. XXX — BANK OF BRISTOL, Bristol, R. I.	Female portrait. — Vig. Female resting arm upon shield; safe, sheaf, plough, and cars in distance on right; large steamship on left. — 100 100 — ATLAS BANK, Providence, R. I. — Atlas propping up globe.	Sailor sitting upon bale of goods with spy glass; also ship in rear. — EXCHANGE BANK. Providence, R. I. Vig. Male portrait with cupid on either side. — 500 D Female with sword in right hand, scales in left, cars on left. 500 — State arms.

M | Steamship Humboldt. Male Portrait | 1000
EXCHANGE BANK, Providence, R. I.
State Arms.
Sailor throwing the lead.

THREE | Portrait of Franklin, with female on either side; on right a sheaf of wheat, &c., on left steamboat, and ship. | 3
Female erect with cap of liberty.
State Arms.
THREE | SUSSEX BANK, Newton, N. J. | 3

NATIONAL BANK, Providence, R. I.
Male portrait | 2 Vig. Female and safe on left; locomotive and safe on right. 2 | Portrait of Franklin.
Dog, safe and key.

Five Vig. Five shillings. Group shillings. of three females in representation of three kingdoms, arts and sciences.
Figure of Minerva.
BANK OF NEW BRUNSWICK, St. John, N. B.
Two children.
FIVE SHILLINGS

---

5 | 5 Two females one reclining on a sheaf with sickle in her left hand; the other on a shield containing a plow in its centre, her left hand on a cornucopia 5 | FIVE
Female. 5
Title of Bank.
Portrait of Washington.

---

2 | NATIONAL BANK, Providence, R. I. | 2
Vig. Two females; ships on right; also, female with wand in right hand; American shield and public buildings on left.
Spread eagle, shield, &c. | Spread eagle and shield.

Figure of Minerva. | ONE ONE | ONE
Same as five shillings.
BANK OF NEW BRUNSWICK, St. John, N. B.
Two children.

TEN | 10 Two sloops of war in an engagement. 10 | NEW JERSEY
SUSSEX BANK, Newton, N. J.
Male Portrait with hat on

THREE | 3 Vig. Large spread eagle, on a rock, overlooking the sea. 3 | THREE
NATIONAL BANK, Providence, R. I.
State Arms.

Figure of Minerva. | TWO TWO | TWO
Same as five shillings.
BANK OF NEW BRUNSWICK, St. John, N. B.
Two children.

TWENTY | 20 Female seated on sheaf of wheat, sickle in right hand; farming utensils on her left. XX | NEW JERSEY
Title of Bank.

FIVE | 5 Vig. Large spread eagle on a rock, overlooking the sea. 5 | FIVE
NATIONAL BANK, Providence, R. I.
State Arms.

Figure of Minerva. | V 5 | FIVE
Same as five shillings.
BANK OF NEW BRUNSWICK, St. John, N. B.
Two children.

---

50 | 50 Female seated with sickle in right hand; left hand resting on sheaf of wheat; and two cows at her right. 50 | FIFTY
Horses head.
50 | Title of Bank.
Portrait of Jefferson.

---

5 | 5 Vig. Steamboat and sail boat on right; ship and row-boat on left. 5 | Indian with left hand holding on tree, over looking precipice.
Indian upon rock, with bow in left hand. | NATIONAL BANK, Providence, R. I. | 5

Figure of Minerva. | TEN TEN | TEN
Same as five shillings.
BANK OF NEW BRUNSWICK, St. John, N. B.
Two children.

---

1 | Spread eagle, overlooking sea; ships on right, and ships on left. | 1
Female reclining on ornamental pillar. | NATIONAL BANK, Providence, R. I. | Female Indian with shield, liberty pole, cap, &c.
State Arms.

[New Plate.]
10 | Vig. Large spread eagle standing on anchor; cog-wheel and vessels on right; vessels on left. | 10
Male portrait | NATIONAL BANK, Providence, R. I. | Portrait of Washington
State Arms.

Figure of Minerva. | 25 25 | TWENTY-FIVE
Same as five shillings.
BANK OF NEW BRUNSWICK, St. John, N. B.
Two children.

---

1 | Vig. Spread eagle with ships on right and left. | 1
Female gathering flowers | NATIONAL BANK, Providence, R. I. | Sailor with spy-glass.
State Arms.

Soldier erect with flag in right hand. | Male Portrait. | 50
FIFTY | NATIONAL BANK, Providence, R. I.

ONE | Female seated with pail on her lap; cows on left and right of her. 1 | Large fig. 1, whole length of note.
State Arms.
1 | SUSSEX BANK, Newton, N. J.

ONE | NATIONAL BANK Providence, R. I. | 1
Spread eagle, American shield, &c. | Vig. Naval engagement. | Spread eagle, American shield, &c.
1 | State Arms. | ONE

Female, shield, liberty pole and cap; starry drapery across her lap; U. S. Capitol in rear. | Portrait of Washington. | 1000
NATIONAL BANK, Providence, R. I.
1000

---

2 | Two females with eagle in centre; anchor and ship on right; cornucopia on left. | 2
Washington.
2 | SUSSEX BANK, Newton. N. J. | Female with pole and cap; figure 2.

---

2 | Vig. Large ship, with vessel on right; steamship on left in distance. | 2
Spread eagle overlooking sea, with ships on left. | NATIONAL BANK Providence, R, I. | Spread eagle, American shield; ship on right.
State arms.

ONE | Vig. Scene upon water; sailing vessels &c. 1 | ONE
HOPE BANK, Warren, R. I. | Indian girl erect with bow and arrows.
ONE

2 TWO 2 — Vig. Ships sailing upon water, &c. 2 — HOPE BANK, Warren, R. I. — TWO Female drawing water from a well. TWO	ONE — EAGLE BANK, Bristol, R. I. — Vig. Indian chief squaw, and child upon back, gazing below them from rock. Eagle. — 1 Female seated, eagle beside her on shield.	III 3 III — Vig. Female and state arms. — PROVIDENCE BANK Providence, R. I. 3 — Full length figure of female in ornamental fig. 3.
THREE — Vig. Farmers reaping grain; female with sheaf under left arm, on right. 3 — HOPE BANK, Warren, R. I. — THREE Steamboat. THREE with figure 3 across it.	Goddess of liberty erect with pole and cap in right hand; shield 2 — Spread Eagle. — Vig. Female reclining upon cornucopia. — EAGLE BANK, Bristol, R. I. Female swimming. — 2 Female soaring in air, holding ornamental figure	3 Female seated on bale of goods with figure 3 in right hand; cornucopia in left; bridge and water in distance. — PROVIDENCE BANK Providence, R. I. — Vig. same as second description of ones. — THREE Lighthouse and rocks seen through large ornamental 3; female seated reclining on rocks in front of 3.
FIVE — Vig. Female raising drapery from shield, upon which is figure 5. V — HOPE BANK, Warren, R. I. — 5 Ship at sea with signals flying.	Goddess of liberty erect with pole and cap in right hand; shield eagle — 5 Vig. Farmer driving drove of sheep, mill in distance. — EAGLE BANK, Bristol, R. I. — FIVE Indian erect resting hand on tomahawk	5 Female with horn of plenty. FIVE — Vig. Ornamental figure 5, supported by female on right; cupid and sickle; cupid in centre of five; female on left with sword and balances; cupid with cornucopia. 5 — Title of Bank. State Arms. — FIVE Female erect with sword and balances FIVE
Five with V running across it. — Vig. Female with rake in left hand, sickle in right; ship, canoes, &c. on right; men, team, &c. on left. V and Indian queen. — HOPE BANK, Warren, R. I. — 5 Portrait of Washington.	50 Female erect leaning on a rock, cornucopia. 50 — 50 EAGLE BANK, Bristol, R. I. — FIFTY	FIVE Large ornamental V; female seen through V; females on right and left; factory in distance. 5 — PROVIDENCE BANK Providence, R. I. — Vig. Female seated on bale of goods holding state arms; bridge and train of cars in distance; on left steamer and ship in distance. — FIVE Shield surmounted by two cupids; in centre of shield figure 5 and V.
10 X 10 — Pair of oxen with a man standing by an ancient plow. 10 — HOPE BANK, Warren, R. I. — TEN Female erect holding cornucopia in left hand, barometer in right.	C Portrait of Washington. C — 100 Vig. figure 100 pouring water from vessel; ship on right. — EAGLE BANK, Bristol, R. I. — ONE HUNDRED	10 Indian female with bow in hand, quiver on back. TEN — Vig. Cupid holding $10 gold piece; chest, money and keg on right; on left horn of plenty, barrels, &c. — PROVIDENCE B'K, Providence, R. I. State Arms. — TEN Female erect with helmet on head, spear in hand; left arm resting on shield, which rests on column. TEN
50 Vessel and steamboat sailing. — Vig. Farming scene, loading waggon with grain, man with rake in right hand on right. 50 — HOPE BANK, Warren, R. I. — L Female kneeling with sword and scales.	ONE 1 ONE — Vig. Man seated on rock; ship under full sail on right. — PROVIDENCE BANK Providence, R. I. State arms. — 1 State arms; Indian on left; female on right. 1	10 — PROVIDENCE BANK Providence, R. I. — Vig. same as five above, with words "ten dollars" on right and left of vignette. 10 — 10
50 Female erect arm resting upon shield on pillar. — Vig. Male and female seated, cornucopia between them. — HOPE BANK, Warren, R. I. 50 — 50 Cupid in a sailboat. 50	1 Female sitting on bale of goods, with distaff in left hand. — Vig. State arms supported by female reclining on ground, with left arm resting on bale of goods; factory and cars on right in distance, on left steamers and ships in distance. — PROVIDENCE BANK Providence, R. I. — ONE Female seated, holding roll of goods.	Female seated resting on shield, key in left hand, cornucopia in right. 20 Spread eagle. — XX Vig. Female with XX right arm resting on stone column, in left hand bunch of wheat; on left packages of goods, sloop, and rocks in distance on right. — Title of Bank. Spread eagle. — Female seated, pole and cap; ship in distance on left. 20 Spread eagle
100 Spread Eagle. 100 — C Vig. Mercury in car with torch, drawn by four horses. 100 — HOPE BANK, Warren, R. I. — C Portrait of Washington. C	Full length figure of female standing in large ornamental 2 which reaches from bottom to top of bill. — Vig. State arms, with female seated on left holding liberty pole and cap; ship in distance; cogwheel and anvil on right. — PROVIDENCE BANK Providence, R. I. State Arms. — TWO 2 TWO	FIFTY — Vig. State arms surmounted by wreath; female on right with spear and shield, helmet on head; bridge and cars in distance; female on left with pole and cap, bales of goods. — PROVIDENCE BANK Providence, R. I. — 50 State arms; Indian with bow on left; female on right. 50
100 Vulcan seated, hammer and scroll. — Vig. Spread eagle upon branch of tree; canal scene on right; train of cars crossing bridge on left. — HOPE BANK, Warren, R. I. 100 — 100 Female with rake, seated beside cornucopia.	Large ornamental figure 2 with female seated within; pail behind her. — PROVIDENCE BANK Providence, R. I. — Vig. same as second description of ones. — 2 Female seated on bale of goods, holding figure 2 in right hand; cornucopia in left; bridge and water in distance	ONE HUNDRED — Vig. Same as fifty. — PROVIDENCE BANK Providence, R. I. — 100 Same as fifty 100

D Medallion head with figures 500 running across.	Vig. Female holding keys, &c., in right hand, with cherubs, all floating in clouds, over-guarding a city. PROVIDENCE BANK Providence, R. I. 500	500 Med. head with figures 500 running across. 500
100 Female; steeple, man and a pair of horses in distance. 100	C Steamboat filled with passengers; ship and sloop on left. C Title of Bank. Ornamental star.	100 Three females seated.
1 Cupid, flowers, &c. 1	1 Farmers implements; city on right, and cars on left. TRADERS' BANK, Newport, R. I.	ONE Man erect, with axe in right hand, and sickle in left; sheaf, plow, &c. ONE
1000	Vig. Same as 500s. PROVIDENCE BANK Providence, R. I. 1000	Large letter M with one thousand running across. Med. head with figures 1000 running across.
American shield in which is figure 1. Spanish dollar.	Vig. State arms on either side, male figure; locomotive and cars on left; Indian huts and canal on right. AQUIDNECK BANK, Newport, R. I. Old stone mill.	1 Female sitting upon figure 1.
2	Vig. Farmers washing sheep.; 4 men 2 on right. TRADERS' BANK, Newport, R. I.	TWO Female sitting, holding wreath of flowers. TWO
1 Female seated on bale; ship in distance. 1	Female seated with left arm on shield; pole and cap, eagle, coin, &c. CITIZENS' UNION BANK, Scituate, R. I. Head of female.	1 Female seated with sickle and sheaf on right shoulder. ONE and fig. 1.
2 Express wagon. 2	AQUIDNECK BANK, Newport, R. I. Death of King Philip. Old Stone Mill.	2 Spanish and American Dollar.
2 TWO 2	Vig. Ships on sea. TRADERS' BANK, Newport, R. I.	TWO TWO
TWO Male in grain field. TWO	2 Naval engagement; ships of war men in boat, &c. 2 Title of Bank. Anchor and word "hope" on shield.	2 Male portrait
FIVE Two Spanish and three American dollars.	AQUIDNECK BANK. Newport, R. I. Vig. Steamboat ferry, and view of the city of Newport on left. Old stone mill.	5 Cars, Indians and ornamental figure.
3 Med. head. 3	3 Vig. Female sitting; building, safe, horn of plenty, &c., on right; man plowing with horses and sheaf of grain on left. TRADERS' BANK, Newport, R. I.	3 Female bathing.
3 Same as 1's.	Fame in clouds blowing trumpet; eagle, globe, &c. CITIZENS' UNION BANK, Scituate, R. I.	3 Three Cupids and fig. 3.
10 State arms on either side of a female.	AQUIDNECK BANK. Newport, R. I. Letter X and figures 10 across; on left lighthouse, on right sailor with spy-glass; man in boat.	10 Indian looking at the sea on which a vessel is dimly seen.
THREE Beehive. THREE	Vig. Female sitting; in right hand sickle; in left rake; sheaf of grain and vessels on right; locomotive and building on left. THREE TRADERS' BANK, Newport, R. I.	Word Three and figure 3. Farmers gathering grain. Word Three, and figure 3.
5 Female seated with sheaf of grain.	Figure 5, and five females; ship on right; building on left. CITIZENS' UNION BANK. Scituate, R. I. Agricultural implements.	5 Indian Princess.
20 Female child. 20	AQUIDNECK BANK. Newport, R. I. Old mill; Indian squaw and papoose in a canoe.	20 Female. 20
FI V VE	Vig. Female sitting; sickle in right hand, holding rake in left; vessels, sheaf of grain, on right; building, &c., in background, on left. Large letter V in which is sitting an Indian female. TRADERS' BANK, Newport, R. I.	5 Portrait of Washington.
10 Washington. 10	William Tell and boy on right; man on horseback surrounded by six others. X X CITIZENS' UNION BANK, Scituate, State Arms.	10 Military officer on horse back. 10
50	Large steamship. Portrait of Webster. AQUIDNECK BANK, Newport, R. I. State arms.	50 Ship under sail.
FIVE	Vig. Female kneeling, with arms extended. TRADERS' BANK, Newport, R. I.	5 Vessel.
20 Spread eagle 20	20 Washington on horse-back, receiving gift from a female supporting pole and cap of liberty. 20 Title of Bank. Dog, &c.	20 Lafayette. 20
C Two females and shield; steamship on right.	ONE HUNDRED 100 Head of Columbus. 100 Old mill. AQUIDNECK BANK. Newport, R. I	C
X Indian with bow and arrow.	Vig. Scene on river; steamboat, vessels, &c. TRADERS' BANK, Newport, R. I.	10 Female, sheaf of grain; and in her right hand, hat.
FIFTY	L Agricultural scene, buildings load of hay, laborers with rakes, forks, &c. L Title of Bank. Engine and car.	50 Man and cattle. 50
1	Female seated; train of cars on right; man on horseback, and canal scene on left. Group of male figures. In large 1. TRADERS' BANK. Newport, R. I.	1 Female and sheaf of wheat.
10 X 10	Vig. Man and oxen. 10 TRADERS' BANK. Newport, R. I.	TEN Full length female.

20 Female sitting.	XX Eagle. XX TRADERS' BANK, Newport, R. I.	20 Ship, &c.

FIFTY Female with wreath. FIFTY	50 Man and Horse. 50 R. I. UNION BANK, Newport, R. I.	FIFTY Full length female, Globe, Rule, &c FIFTY

100 Small spread eagle. 100	C Vig. Man in chariot 100 with four horses abreast driving through air, clouds beneath. Title of Bank.	Letter C. Portrait of Washington Letter C.

FIFTY Female erect with wreath of flowers in right hand, and flowers in left. FIFTY	50 Man and horse. 50 TRADERS' BANK, Newport, R. I.	FIFTY Female, globe, square &c.; elbow resting on ornamental pillar. FIFTY

Words one hundred and figures 100 Male portrait.	Vig. Market scene; shipping on left. R. I. UNION BANK, Newport, R. I,	Words one hundred, and figures 100. Male portrait.

ONE Med. head. ONE	1 Vig. View of factory, river, &c.; female Indian and canoe; small deer on right. 1 NEWPORT BANK, Newport. R. I. State arms.	1 1

Words one hundred, and figures 100. Male portrait	Vig. Wharf scene; loading wagon; men, horses, shipping, &c. TRADERS' BANK, Newport, R. I.	Words one hundred, and figures 100. Male portrait

ONE 1	Agricultural scene; farmer sowing; another in the distance barrowing. 1 COMMERCIAL BANK Bristol, R. I.	1 Ship. ONE

TWO Med. head. TWO	2 Vig. 2; on either side a female, one with liberty pole and cap, the other with sword and balances; railroad cars and bridge and view of view of city in distance. 2 Title of Bank. State arms.	2 2

Female child on ornamental die.	1 Ships and sea scene. R. I. UNION BANK, Newport, R. I. Clasping hands.	1

TWO 2	Spread eagle; iron castings, cannon balls, machinery, &c. 2 Title of Bank.	2 TWO Schooner rigged boat.

5 Med. head with five across it. V	Vig. Steamship and other vessels. NEWPORT BANK, Newport, R. I. State arms	FIVE View of Ocean House Newport. FIVE

Wharf scene.	2 Portrait of Gen. Green. R. I. UNION BANK, Newport. R. I. Clasped hands.	2

THREE 3	Sailor; bat in hand, reclining against bales; in the distance are vessels, warehouses, dray, horses &c. 3 Title of Bank.	3 THREE Train of cars.

10 Med. head. TEN	Vig. Large spread eagle upon shield; United States Capitol on right; steam ship, &c., on left. NEWPORT BANK, Newport, R. I. State arms.	Deer, &c. 10 Buffalo.

Indian with bow and arrow, horse on right and dog on left	5 Vig. Winged female cupid and anchor. R. I. UNION BANK, Newport, R. I. Clasped hands.	5

Spread eagle; city and vessels in distance. FIVE	Large V, female and Cupid. Title of Bank.	5 Portrait of a girl.

50 Med. head. 50	Vig. View of sea and rising sun, vessels, &c.; cupid on right; female with sword and balances on left. NEWPORT BANK, Newport. R. I. State arms.	FIFTY Female in ornamental figure, with shield in left hand, and spear in right hand. 50

TEN	Vulcan seated, anvil, sledge, &c.; train of cars and buildings in distance. X R. I. UNION BANK, Newport. R. I.	10 Farmer with sheaf on his knee.

Vulcan seated; train of cars, &c., in distance. TEN	X Title of Bank.	10 Farmer with sheaf of wheat and sickle.

100 Med. head. 100	View of city in distance, shipping, &c. NEWPORT BANK, Newport, R. I. State arms.	100 Spread eagle 100

10 X 10	(Old Plate.) Vig. Man with oxen. 10 R. I. UNION BANK, Newport. R. I.	TEN Female figure with cornucopia of fruits and flowers.

20 Female sitting, with book.	XX Eagle. XX Title of Bank.	20 Ship under sail.

ONE State Arms on either side a female one with scales and the other with shield. 1	Female reclining on State Arms; Neptune in chariot drawn by sea monsters. EXCHANGE BANK, Newport, R. I.	1 Two figures one holding wand. 1

20 Female.	XX Eagle. XX R. I. UNION BANK, Newport, R. I.	20 Ship sailing

FIFTY Female. FIFTY	50 Man and horse. 50 Title of Bank.	FIFTY Female FIFTY

TWO Female seated; ship on left. TWO	2 Female with wand; ship in distance on left. 2 EXCHANGE BANK. Newport, R. I.	Indian with bow and arrow. TWO

Female seated, one looking at sea with eagle seated upon her lap. 3	3 Vig. Steamboat. 3 EXCHANGE BANK, Newport, R. I.	THREE Female erect with balances, eagle on left and miniature portrait of Washington. 3

TEN Female seated with wand in left hand, looking up to male figure. 10	10 Vig. Ship. 10 B'K OF R. ISLAND, Newport, R. I. State Arms.	TEN Old Stone Mill. X

Words one hundred running across figures 100. Male portrait	Dray cart, into which men are rolling barrels, horses, shipping, &c. FALL RIVER UNION BANK, Tiverton, R. I.	Words one hundred running across figures 100. Male portrait

FIVE Female, sheaf of wheat and sickle. 5	5 Female, eagle and miniature of Washington. 5 EXCHANGE BANK, Newport, R. I.	FIVE Flying female with wand. 5

FIFTY	State Arms. B'K OF R. ISLAND; Newport, R. I. 50	50 L

500	500 D Vig. Female sitting, sheaves of rain at her feet; load of grain and men reaping in distance. FALL RIVER UNION BANK, Tiverton, R. I.	500

10 Cupid with scroll figure 10 engraved. 10	Ships. Bust of Com Perry. Female sitting, on right State Arms upon which is engraved an eagle and shield; ship &c., on left. Title of Bank.	X Female State Arms on right upon which is mounted an eagle. 10

100 DOLLARS	State Arms. B'K OF R. ISLAND, Newport, R. I. 100	100 Letter C.

5 Male portrait.	Vig. A building, which was the residence of Thomas Jefferson. MONTICELLO B'K, Charlottesville, Va. Dog's head.	Trea's die and letter V. Figure 5 and three urchins, one holding flag which forms the top of the 5.

TWENTY	XX Neptune and female riding in sea car. XX EXCHANGE BANK, Newport, R. I	20 Cupid and basket of flowers. 20

1	Man on horseback, boy standing with left hand over cow, three other cows standing around on left of man, dog houses in distance. Large figure 1, view of sea monster standing on rock on right. FALL RIVER UNION BANK, Tiverton, R. I. Steamboat and vessel.	ONE Full length figure of Indian with bow and arrow. 1

Train of cars.	Vig. Same as Trea's die fives. MONTICELLO B'K, Charlottesville, Va. Spread eagle.	10 Male portrait.

50 Eagle feeding her young. 50	Female seated with wand in right hand. Same as on left. Indian and native American seated, between them the arms of one of the States, upon which is mounted an eagle. Title of Bank.	50 Eagle feeding her young. 50

2	Train of Cars; Depot and men on right; on left pier steamship, sail vessels, &c. Large figure 2, with portrait of female on right Title of Bank	2 Washington standing beside horse, battle in distance. TWO

20 Milkmaid seated; cows on right.	Trea's die. Same as 5s. MONTICELLO B'K, Charlottesville, Va. Horse.	Male portrait.

ONE State arms, upon which is mounted an eagle ONE	1 Vig. View of water and large ship; also smaller vessels, row-boats, &c. 1 BANK OF RHODE ISLAND, Newport, R. I. Head of female.	ONE Bust of Commodore Perry. 1

FI V VE	Vig. Indian in canoe; sloops and other sail-vessels in distance on right; on left, house, trees, &c.; large letter V, extending across bill. FALL RIVER UNION BANK, Tiverton, R. I. Dog and safe.	5 Spread eagle holding shield in talons, on which is figure 5.

Indian on rock, gun by his side. 1	Boy reclining watching flock of six sheep; village in distance. CITY BANK, Augusta, Ga. Dog's head.	1 Female portrait.

2 Man seated; on right public buildings; on left scrolls of paper. TWO	2 Vig. Female seated with wand in right hand; building on right, and holding key in left hand. 2 B'K OF R ISLAND, Newport, R. I. Steamboat.	2 Female seated near safe; eagle on left; also small portrait of Washington. TWO

X	Vig. Blacksmith sitting on boiler, blowing bellows; forge, anvil, and bench with tools at right; wheel on left, large ornamental X extending across bill. Title of Bank.	TEN Large portrait of Washington. TEN

TWO Hunter with dog and gun.	St. George and the Dragon CITY BANK, Augusta, Ga. Dog's head.	2 Indian princess seated.

Female reclining on anchor, looking over the sea. 3	3 Catching Buffaloes. 3 B'K OF R. ISLAND, Newport, R. I. Head of Female.	3 Launching a vessel. 3

20 Female sitting; right hand resting on chest; open book on lap.	XX Vig. Spread eagle standing on rock. XX FALL RIVER UNION BANK, Tiverton, R. I.	20 Two ships, one in fore ground, one in distance.

Word five in part circle. 5 Word five in part circle.	Large building surrounded by trees; man on horseback. CITY BANK, Augusta, Ga.	Same on the end as on left

FIVE Female seated with eagle on her lap. 5	5 Man seated with mechanical tools &c., ship on left. 5 B'K OF R. ISLAND, Newport, R. I. Head of Lion.	FIVE View of city in distance. Male raising the world. 5

FIFTY Full length figure of female in right hand wreath, and bunch of flowers in left. FIFTY	50 Vig. Man and horse; horse rearing. 50 FALL RIVER UNION BANK, Tiverton, R. I.	FIFTY Full length figure of female. FIFTY

Female blowing horn for farmers to come to lunch.	CITY BANK, Augusta, Va. Ten X Dollars.	10 Male gathering fruit; baskets, &c.

Left end	Centre	Right end
20 XX 20	Two oxen before load of straw; man with fork walking by his side, and man asleep on top of load. CITY BANK, Augusta Ga Ducks.	20 Three Dogs. XX
100 Ship	POCASSET BANK, Tiverton, R. I. C Vig. Indian queen on raft; C on right.	100 Man whetting his scythe.
Figures 100 and words one hundred. Head of Harrison.	Wagon with horses and goods; ship at a distance. Title of Bank.	Figures 100 and words one hundred. Head and bust of male.
50 Dog's Head. L	CITY BANK, Augusta, Ga. Spread eagle on globe; names of a few States on flags, &c.	50
500 Ship of war under full sail; ship in distance.	POCASSET BANK, Tiverton, R. I. D Vig. Indian Queen on raft.	500
ONE	1 Vig. Portrait of Washington; bales, locomotive and ships on right; scene on wharf, men and dray and steamboat on left. 1 WASHINGTON B'K, Westerly, R. I. Arm and hammer.	Med. head. ONE
100	Female soaring in clouds with eagle, sword, balances, &c. Letter C with word ONE above and word HUNDRED below it. Title of Bank.	100 Three females one above the other; one leaning on anchor.
Vig. Indian Queen on raft 1000	POCASSET BANK, Tiverton, R. I. M	1000 Indian seated smoking pipe, canoe on left, dog on right, squaw and wigwam, &c.
TWO	2 Vig. Same as ones. 2 WASHINGTON B'K, Westerly, R. I. Arm and hammer.	Med. head. TWO
ONE	Indian queen of Pocasset, crossing river on raft. Figure 1 with one running across. POCASSET BANK, Tiverton, R. I. Steamboat.	1 Silver dollar
1 Head of Washington.	Female. 1 Female. NEW ENGLAND COMMERCIAL BANK Newport, R. I.	1 Head of Franklin.
THREE Female seated, eagle on her lap, grain in right hand. 3	3 Vig. Portrait of Washington, locomotive, bales, barrels, and sloop. 3 WASHINGTON B'K, Westerly, R. I. Spread eagle.	THREE Female seated with grain and sickle. 3
Figure 2, with two running across.	POCASSET BANK, Tiverton, R. I. Vig. Same as ones. Clasped hands.	2 Two silver dollars.
2 Head.	Female. 2 Female. Title of Bank.	2 Head.
FIVE	5 Vig. Same as threes. 5 WASHINGTON B'K, Westerly, R. I. Spread eagle.	FIVE Female erect, hand upon shield, with balances. V
FIVE Five silver dollars.	5 POCASSET BANK, Tiverton, R. I. Vig. in centre of right end, same as ones. State arms.	Figure 5 with five running across. FIVE
3 Washington full length.	Female head and bust. 3 Female head and bust. Title of Bank.	3 Vulcan, full length.
X Goddess of Liberty, hand upon state arms, pole and cap. 10	10 Vig. Same as 5s. 10 WASHINGTON B'K, Westerly, R. I. Cupid upon deer.	Female erect, scroll in right hand. X
10 Stonecutter at work; men hoisting in distance.	POCASSET BANK, Tiverton, R. I. Vig. in lower right corner same as ones.	10
Eagle resting on United States shield and an anchor. FIVE	A large V, with female figure and child. Title of Bank.	5 Female figure and basket.
TWENTY	XX Vig. Same as 5s. XX WASHINGTON B'K, Westerly, R. I. Spread eagle.	20 Mercury soaring in air. 20
20 Indian queen on raft.	Twenty dollars. 20 Vig. Female soaring with sword in right hand; river scene, steamboat, &c. POCASSET BANK, Tiverton, R. I. State arms.	20
Male figure seated on machinery; cars at distance. TEN	X Title of Bank.	10 Male figure with sheaf in hand.
FIFTY	L Vig. Same as 5s. L WASHINGTON B'K, Westerly, R. I. Female seated, with sickle, &c.	50 Portrait of Franklin. 50
50	POCASSET BANK, Tiverton, R. I. Vig. Scythe hanging in tree, female standing; man sitting, dog lying down, water scene, steamboat, &c. 50	50 Indian queen on a raft. 50
FIFTY Female figure standing globe in her right hand, flowers at her right. FIFTY	50 Man and horse. 50 Title of Bank	FIFTY Female figure with wreath of flowers in right hand. FIFTY
ONE HUNDRED	C Vig. Same as 5s. C WASHINGTON B'K, Westerly, R. I. Ship under sail.	100 Justice with sword and scales. 100

1 — Female seated train of cars and vessel on right, canal scene on left. 1 — COCHECHO BANK, Dover, N. H. — 1 — Female resting arms on fence — 1

---

20 — Female seated, with sword and scales; eagle standing on safe. — Three human figures; centre female with outstretched arms. — COCHECHO BANK, Dover, N. H. — Steamer. — 20 — Female with sheaf of wheat on shoulder.

ONE — Two indians erect. — ONE — Vig. Female reclining on horn of plenty. — Portrait of Washington. — PAWCATUCK BANK. Pawcatuck, Ct. — Bales and barrels. — 1 — Two females: one erect; the other kneeling with grain.

---

1 — Indian on rock with gun. — Two females at work on machines. — COCHECHO BANK, Dover. N. H. — Building. — 1 — Mason at work.

---

50 — Female with sickle. — 50 — Two females seated; on right, ship; on left, factories and cars. — COCHECHO BANK, Dover, N. H. — 50 — Boy gathering corn.

TWO — Portrait of Gen. Taylor. — TWO — Vig. State Arms; eagle surmounting it; two females on right, seated; Goddess of Liberty on left. — PAWCATUCK BANK, Pawcatuck, Ct — Weaving loom. — 2 — Female with sickle and sheaf. — 2

---

2 — Man forcing sheep in water, another man erect; boy driving flock; buildings on right. 2 — Title of Bank. — TWO — Female seated. — TWO

---

100 — Sailor with flag, and swinging his hat. — COCHECHO BANK, Dover, N. H. — Female and cherub over town; cherub scattering flowers. — Machinery. — 100 — Female portrait. — 100

THREE — Female seated feeding eagle. — THREE — Vig. State arms; female and three children on right; Indian squaw and papoose on left. — PAWCATUCK BANK. Pawcatuck, Ct — 3 — Farmer with rake, dog, &c.; town background.

Sailor seated on bale with flag. — TWO — Female on either side of a frame surmounted by eagle, on which is seen plow, steamboat and buildings in distance. — Title of Bank. — Building. — 2 — Female with sheaf of wheat over shoulder.

---

1 — Vig. Two indians on horseback, train of cars in distance. — American silver dollar — NIANTIC BANK, Westerly, R. I. — 1 — 1 — Portrait of Webster. — ONE

FOUR — Stonecutter at work. — Vig. Planing machine, man standing beside it. — PAWCATUCK BANK. Pawcatuck. Ct. — 4 — Girl reaping; farmhouse in background.

---

3 — Man on horseback; cows and men; load of hay entering barn. 3 — COCHECHO BANK, Dover, N. H — Word three and figure 3. — Female with basket of flowers. — THREE

Figure 2 with word two across it. — Female seated holding ornamental figure 2. — Vig. Drover and cattle. — NIANTIC BANK, Westerly, R. I. — Clasped hands. — 2 — Farmer sharpening scythe.

FIVE 5 FIVE — Vig. Indian, squaw, and child on precipice overlooking city. — Portrait of two females. — PAWCATUCK BANK. Pawcatuck. Ct. — Female swimming. — 5 — Goddess of Liberty; eagle upon shield behind her

---

3 — Female seated, with sword and balances. — THREE — Cattle and hogs; buildings in distance. — COCHECHO BANK. Dover, N. H. — Building. — 3 — Male portrait — THREE

V — Indian queen seated with bow and arrows. — Vig. Indians and squaw in a canoe. — NIANTIC BANK, Westerly, R. I. — Moonlight scene. — 5 — Farmer carrying basket of corn.

---

10 — Locomotive crossing bridge; city in distance. — PAWCATUCK BANK, Pawcatuck, Ct. — Vig. Three females representing Commerce, Agriculture, and Science. — Hand and hammer. — 10 — Ships sailing in front of city.

FIVE — Eagle on shield; city and ships in distance. — Large V, female and Cupid. — COCHECHO BANK, Dover, N. H — 5 — Girl with basket of flowers or fruit.

Ship under full sail. — Figure 3 with word three running across it. — Vig. Two females seated, canal boat and factory on right; bales, steamboat and sloop on left. — NIANTIC BANK, Westerly, R. I. — State arms. — III — Large fig. 3 in centre of which is lighthouse, female seated in th 3.

Female erect resting upon column, right hand upon shield. — TWENTY — PAWCATUCK BANK, Pawcatuck, Ct. — Vig. Blacksmith seated, anvil, &c.; city in background. On left of vignette is 20 with words twenty dollars across it. — 20 — XX

Female seated, at work on machine. — 10 — Ships, steamship, &c.; city on left. — COCHECHO BANK, Dover, N. H. — 10 — Female portrait.

---

10 — Ornamental X with figs. 10 and lighthouse on its left; sailor with glass in hand on right. — NIANTIC BANK, Westerly, R. I. — Vig. Goddess of liberty and justice reclining on right of shield; spread eagle; ship in distance on left. — Dog. — 10 — Female erect, light house above her.

---

50 — Portrait of John Adams. — PAWCATUCK BANK, Pawcatuck, Ct. — Vig. Winged female seated on clouds, female soaring on either side. — Steamship. — 50

TEN — Vulcan seated, with sledge and anvil; train of cars and buildings in distance. X — COCHECHO BANK, Dover, N. H. — 10 — Farmer with sheaf and sickle.

Figures 50 upheld by three full length figures representing commerce, agriculture and mechanics. — NIANTIC BANK, Westerly, R. I. — L Vig. Portrait of Henry Clay. L — FIFTY — 50 — Indian hunter upon brink of precipice looking down upon ship at sea.

CALAIS BANK. Calais, Me.

This Bank uses the old Perkin's Stereotype plate, which has the denomination printed in fine letters all over the bill.

V Hunter drinking out of his hand.	CHAMPAIGN CO. BK. Urbana, Ohio. Male portrait.	FIVE Library scene Webster and Calhoun. FIVE
Six females and four males.	Male portrait. CHAMPAIGN CO. BK. Urbana, Ohio.	X 10
Figure 5 with a cupid on either side. Female portrait.	BK. OF GEORGETOWN, Georgetown, S. C. V State Arms.	FIVE 5 Dollars.
10	BANK OF GEORGETOWN, Georgetown, S. C. X	10 Female portrait.
ONE Goddess of liberty erect, shield beside her.	WARREN BANK, Warren, R. I. Indian reclining upon shield, bow and arrows in hand; eagle soaring on left. ONE ONE	1 Female portrait.
2	WARREN BANK, Warren, R. I. Goddess of liberty seated, holding wreath over spread eagle on shield on right; pole, cap and portrait of Washington in right hand. TWO	2 Ornamental fountain
3 Mercury in air, with cornucopia and bag of coin. THREE	WARREN BANK, Warren, R. I. Vig. Goddess of liberty with wreath and scales; spread eagle upon shield.	3 Female seated with cornucopia, &c. THREE
5 5	WARREN BANK, Warren, R. I. Vig. Ship building, ship on stocks, &c, vessels at wharf. FIVE Cars FIVE	5 Cupid astride of dragon.
10	Vig. Farming scene; loading hay in distance; farmers reclining in foreground. WARREN BANK, Warren, R. I. TEN Wheels, etc. TEN	X Sea horses. TEN

20 Female figure seated.	XX Eagle. XX Title of Bank.	20 Ship with sails partly furled.
FIFTY Female erect with wreath. FIFTY	50 Man and horse. 50 WARREN BANK, Warren, R. I.	FIFTY Female erect FIFTY.
Word one hundred and figure 100. Male portrait.	Wharf scene—loading wagon, men, horses, shipping, &c. WARREN BANK, Warren, R. I.	Same as on left Male portrait.
1 Portrait of female.	NEWARK CITY BK., Newark, N. J. Vig. Machinist and heavy turning lathe.	1 Female reaper.
2 Portrait of female.	NEWARK CITY BK., Newark, N. J. Vig. Stone-cutters at work.	TWO Female with small globe.
3 Leather dresser.	NEWARK CITY BK., Newark, N. J. Three females reclining, representing liberty, agriculture and art.	3 Arm-hammer, and anvil.
V Fireman.	Two females, one seated; horn of plenty. NEWARK CITY BK., Newark, N. J.	5 Locomotive and tender.
10 Farmer resting.	NEWARK CITY BK., Newark, N. J. Three females representing music, poetry, and painting.	10
50 Canal boat. 50	State Arms; cars in distance. 50 NEWARK BANKING COMPANY Newark, N. J.	Justice full length. FIFTY

100 State Arms. 100	Spread eagle; cars on left; factory on right. 100 Title of Bank.	Full length female. 100
500 Female, eagle and shield.	Agricultural scene; cars on righ.. Title of Bank.	500 State Arms. 500
1 Boy with rake, fork, and canteen; and dog.	AUBURN BANK, Auburn, Me. Train of cars, load of hay, men, cattle, &c.; in distance train of cars on bridge, city, &c.; in extreme distance city, bridge, water, &c.	1 Two females, one engaged at table, the other with hoe in hand; chickens, &c.
Female reclining with scales. 2	Two men, horse, dog, cattle, and sheep. 2 AUBURN BANK, Auburn, Me. Loading hay.	Female erect with sword and scales.
Male portrait 3	Wharf scene—train of cars, depot, horses and carts, canal boats, vessels, men, buildings, steamboat, &c. AUBURN BANK, Auburn, Me. Cow and calf.	3 Male portrait
V Female portrait.	Five gold dollars with three cupids above them; hunter seated on right; Indian female on left; cars in distance. AUBURN BANK, Auburn, Me.	5 Female portrait.
Female portrait. 10	Female seated; on her right is ten gold dollars; in front of her nine cupids making offering to her; steamboat and cars in distance. AUBURN BANK, Auburn, Me.	X Female seated with sheaf.
20 XX	View of large public building; horses, carriages, mules, females, &c., in front. AUBURN BANK, Auburn, Me. Female seated.	20 Female portrait.
Female erect leaning on anchor; ship in storm in distance. FIFTY	Spread eagle; U. S. Capitol on right, and steamship on left. AUBURN BANK, Auburn, Me.	50 Female reclining with balances, &c.

C Portrait of a boy. 100 Blacksmith shoeing a horse, forge, &c.; a jackass tied to anvil; locomotive on left. AUBURN BANK, Auburn, Me. Two horses. 100 Portrait of Webster.	V RHODE ISLAND V 5 Five dollars. V MERCHANTS' BANK Newport, R. I. V FIVE	Three females on a cliff overlooking the ocean, one resting right hand upon anchor, one with sheaf of wheat under her arm. TWO Female seated resting one arm upon the State Arms of R. I. an ocean scene with ships in the background. Title of Bank. Mechanic Emblems. 2 Medal. head of Franklin.
1 RHODE ISLAND 1 1 One Dollar. 1 MERCHANTS' BK., Newport, R. I. 1 1 ONE 1	RHODE ISLAND 5 5 View of State House. MERCHANTS' BANK Newport, R. I. FIVE	5 Male Figure resting one arm upon a short column palm, ters pallet, &c., at her feet. Female seated on a safe, child playing with a dog at her feet; cars with ship in the distance at the right agricultural emblems on the left. Title of Bank. Sheaf of wheat, plow, &c. 5 Female fig. resting right arm on shield, pole with cap of liberty in her hand, bunch of arrows at her back.
1 View of paper mill and eagle. MERCHANTS' BK., Newport, R. I. Cupid supporting figure 1.	5 Female portrait. FIVE Female reclining with wand in right hand; steamship on right, and locomotive and bridge on left. MERCHANTS' BANK Newport, R. I. 5 Group of females supporting figure 5.	10 Male seated. Female seated with agricultural implements at her left; Female in Medallion; on right, blacksmith shop in background on right. Title of Bank. Dog beside a Safe. 10 Three females erect.
1 Sailor and capstan. Female reclining and supporting figure 1; train of cars on right; steamboat on left. MERCHANTS' BK., Newport, R. I. 1 Female seated on safe, pole, liberty cap and figure 1.	X RHODE ISLAND X 10 Words ten dollars. X MERCHANTS' BANK Newport, R. I. X TEN	20 Train of cars entering a city, seen in the background. Female seated with extended arms, scales in one hand, pole with cap of liberty in the other child upon each side. Title of Bank. Steamship. 20 Female with sheaf of wheat and sickle in her hand.
2 RHODE ISLAND 2 Two Dollars. 2 MERCHANTS' BK., Newport, R. I. 2 TWO	10 Tritons supporting cornucopia. Steamship. Female with spear reclining on state arms, sheaf of grain, safe, plow, and rake; cars in distance on right; steamship on left. MERCHANTS' BANK Newport, R. I. 10 Spread eagle TEN	50 Female Portrait. 50 Two female figures seated; view of factories; cars and ship in the background. Title of Bank. Locomotive. 50 Man picking corn in a field.
2 View of a stone mill. MERCHANTS' BK., Newport, R. I.	RHODE ISLAND 50 Title of Bank. Med. head of Com. Perry. FIFTY	100 Sailor with American flag. Title of Bank. Female with child scattering flowers over a city. Mechanic emblems. 100 Ship under sail. 100
TWO Indian with bow and arrow. Farmers washing sheep. MERCHANTS' BK., Newport, R. I. 2 Two females	50 Four females globe, &c. View of steamship and ship. MERCHANTS' BANK Newport, R. I. 50 Locomotive.	ONE Sailor erect with spy-glass and hat in hand. Female seated on plow with sheaf and sickle; locomotive and cars crossing bridge on right. 1 RHODE ISLAND CENTRAL BANK, East Greenwich, R. I State Arms. Ship under full sail. ONE
3 RHODE ISLAND 3 3 Three Dollars. 3 MERCHANTS' BK., Newport, R. I. 3 THREE	Train of cars. MERCHANTS' BANK Newport, R. I. 100 Ship. Female portrait. 100	TWO Two females standing together. Ornamental shield, female with pail, pole and liberty cap on right; man with rake seated on plow on left. Title of Bank. State Arms. 2 Female holding cornucopia in right hand resting left upon anchor.
3 Female with anchor. Three male figures, and three gold dollars; scythe and sheaf of grain on left; ship and factory on right. MERCHANTS' BK., Newport, R. I 3 Female giving eagle drink.	1 Female seated upon bale of goods with spool of yarn factories in the background. Three females seated, centre one lower than other two, ships in the distance on the right. COVENTRY BANK, Anthony Village, R. I State Arms. 1 Washington on horseback	THREE Female kneeling over fruit right arm upraised Shield scenery upon it, man with axe seated on right; Indian presenting ear of corn on left. Title of Bank. State Arms. Female figure of Justice with sword and scales. THREE

5 Portrait of Female	Title of Bank 5 Man bearing child upon his shoulder, at which woman is gazing. 5	5 Portrait of Washington.	10 Mason at work with level on a wall, bucket and trowel at his feet.	Vig. Spread eagle upon limb of a tree; locomotive and cars crossing bridge over canal on left; canal boat and lock on right. RHODE ISLAND EXCHANGE BANK, East Greenwich, R. I. Female head.	10 Washington on horseback	2 Factory girl at work.	NORTHFIELD B'K, Northfield. Vt. Blacksmith's shop; Blacksmith shoeing horse.	2 Female head.
10 Portrait of Female.	Large steamship sailing at sea; vessels on right, vessel on left. Title of Bank. Spread eagle.	10 Male portrait	20 Portrait of Webster. TWENTY	RHODE ISLAND EXCHANGE BANK. East Greenwich, R. I. Female with sheaf and sickle seated between sailor and blacksmith, ship behind sailor State Arms.	20 Cupid seated on back of sea monster. TWENTY	3	Horse market. Female head. NORTHFIELD B'K, Northfield, Vt.	3 Dairy maid milking.
20 Female seated raising lid of chest with right hand.	XX Eagle. XX RHODE ISLAND CENTRAL BANK, East Greenwich, R. I.	20 Ship under sail.	Figures 50 supported by three males erect, representing Commerce, Agriculture and mechanism.	Title of Bank. Portrait of girl; Cupid with cornucopia on either side. State Arms.	50 Portrait of Franklin.	5 Indian	Train of cars. NORTHFIELD B'K, Northfield, Vt.	5 Female head
FIFTY Female erect with flowers in hand. FIFTY	50 Man and horse 50 RHODE ISLAND CENTRAL BANK, Greenwich, R. I	FIFTY Female erect with flowers in left hand. FIFTY	Figure 1 with word one running across. Train of cars.	Vig. Indian seated with bow; hoe, plow, sheaf of wheat, &c. on left. SUSQUEHANNA VALLEY BANK, Binghampton, N. Y.	Same as on left. Compt's die.	10 Female head.	Load of hay, train of cars and packet boat. NORTHFIELD B'K. Northfield, Vt. State Arms.	10 Vulcan.
100 Female holding bag of coin in hand; at extreme end of bill is words Rhode Island run. "P" 100	RHODE ISLAND CENTRAL BANK, Greenwich, R. I.	100 Spread eagle upon rock overlooking sea. 100	Female with flowers; birds flying on left. 2	Compt's die. Vig. Shield with word Excelsior, on right of which is a female, three children, globe, &c.; on left Indian, squaw and child. Title of Bank.	2	20 Henry Clay sitting, dog at his feet.	Cow and sheep, church in background. NORTHFIELD B'K, Northfield. Vt.	20 Male portrait.
Female seated, supporting figure 1. 1	1 Vig. Females working; looms in factory. 1 RHODE ISLAND EXCHANGE BANK, East Greenwich. R. I. Spread eagle.	Female seated supporting the figure 1. 1	5 Indian head.	Title of Bank. Compt's die. Vig. Two females seated on right of a shield, on which is agricultural implements; on right public building, on left train of cars.	Figure 5, a V and word Five. Female with arm resting on pail.	50 Vulcan, sledge on right shoulder, wheel in left hand.	NORTHFIELD B'K. Northfield, Vt. Men on horseback, watering horse at trough; two boys and dogs.	50 Male portrait.
2 Female working at machine, drawing in warp.	Vig. Goddess of liberty and female with sickle seated on either side of state arms; steamship on right; locomotive on left. RHODE ISLAND EXCHANGE BANK, East Greenwich, R. I.	2 Locomotive and train of cars.	Head of Webster. 10	Vig. Female seated with sickle sheaf of wheat, plow &c., train of cars and canal lock in distance. Bridge, canal boat, horse, village and spire in the distance. Title of Bank.	Figure 10, a letter X and word Ten. Compt's die.	100 Vulcan.	NORTHFIELD B'K, Northfield, Vt. Elliott preaching to the Indians.	100 Portrait of Gov. Paine.
3 Sailor erect holding American flag; bale, anchor and female reclining at his feet.	RHODE ISLAND EXCHANGE BANK, East Greenwich, R. I. Vig. Locomotive and train of cars crossing a bridge; town in distance.	3 Female holding sheaf of grain under her arm.	BROOME COUNTY Goddess of liberty, eagle, shield, liberty pole and cap.	TWENTY DOLLARS. Compt's die. Three females, one with wings, represented as soaring, the others in the act of receiving gift from her. Title of Bank.	20 STATE OF N. Y.	Child and chickens. 3	PAHQUIOQUE B'K, Danbury, Ct. Drover and cattle.	3
Indian with rifle seated on rock looking to right of note. 5	Vig. Female gathering corn; village, with boats on water in front of it in distance. RHODE ISLAND EXCHANGE BANK, East Greenwich, R. I. Sheaf and plough.	5 Portrait of female.	1 Portrait of Frank Pierce	Farmer sitting; oxen. NORTHFIELD B'K, Northfield, Vt. Beehive.	1 Train of cars	TEN Three cupids, anvil, hammer, grain, globe, &c.	PAHQUIOQUE B'K, Danbury, Ct. Child with rabbits. TEN	10 Franklin.

Left	Centre	Right
Female head. State arms.	INDIANA BANK. Madison, Ind. Harvest maid, with sickle, in reclining posture; railroad train crossing a bridge in distance.	1 Flower girl.
Female head. State arms.	INDIANA BANK, Madison, Ind. Milkmaid and cows.	3 Figure 3 and three cupids.
Head of Fillmore State arms.	INDIANA BANK. Madison, Ind. Locomotive and railroad train; town or city in distance.	5 Figure 5 supported by a female figure
Head of Gov. Wright. State arms.	INDIANA BANK, Madison, Ind. Railroad trains crossing the Susquehanna River on Pennsylvania Railroad Bridge.	10
ONE Portrait of Pierce.	Cupid rolling silver dollar on railroad track; cars, steamboat and city in distance. STATE BANK, Augusta, Me.	1 Indian female seated
2 Male portrait	Two cupids and two silver dollars, cupids apparently in an engagement; train of cars, cattle, bills. city, &c. in distance. STATE BANK, Augusta, Me	2 Indian female erect with bow and spear.
Male portrait Figure 3 surrounded by sailor mechanic and farmer.	Three cupids and three silver dollars, all engaged at some art. STATE BANK, Augusta, Me.	3 Cupid astride a sea monster.
5 Male portrait	View of the Maine State House. STATE BANK. Augusta, Me	5 Figure 5 surrounded by 5 females.
X Male portrait	Vig. Same as 5ves, STATE BANK, Augusta. Me	10 State Arms Sailor on right, farmer on left.

Left	Centre	Right
Mercury ed between 3 and 0. XX	State Arms surmounted by an eagle; female on either side; on right in distance, train of cars and buildings; on left steamboat and vessels. Title of Bank.	20 Female reclining on cornucopia. TWENTY
Portrait of Webster. L	Train of cars leaving Depot, horses before carriage rearing; men, &c. STATE BANK, Augusta, Me.	50 Same as 10's
Portrait of Washington. C	Spread eagle on shield; U. S. Capitol on right and steamship on left. STATE BANK, Augusta, Me.	100 Female seated; bales, &c., building in distance.
Eagle on shield. 1	PAWTUCKAWAY BANK, Epping, N. H. Horses with shield and Indian, shield surmounted by an eagle; steamboat, rail cars, and factories in distance.	1 Indian squaw and papoose.
Female 2	PAWTUCKAWAY BANK, Epping, N. H. On right two female figures, one kneeling with a sickle in hand; portrait of Washington, milkmaid and cows on left.	2 TWO 2
State arms. 5	PAWTUCKAWAY BANK, Epping, N. H. Large V and word five.	5 Portrait.
Female portrait. 10	PAWTUCKAWAY BANK, Epping, N. H. Shield; on left Indians; on right women and children studying globe.	10 X 10
Portrait of Webster. XX	PAWTUCKAWAY BANK. Epping, N. H. Farming scene; sheaf of grain.	20 Two female figures.
Portrait of Cass. 50	PAWTUCKAWAY BANK, Epping, N. H. Female figure and iron chest; ship building, sheep &c., on right	50 Female holding globe in right hand, staff in left.

Left	Centre	Right
Word one, and figure 1.	Ship under full sail; ship, steamboat and pilot-boat; city in distance. ONE OCEAN BANK, Kennebunk, Me.	1 Female with arm on American shield.
2	OCEAN BANK, Kennebunk, Me. Foundry; workman pouring out heated metal. TWO	2 Ship under full sail; steamboat in distance.
3	OCEAN BANK. Kennebunk, Me. Three persons in boat, one man rowing; female with spy-glass. Word three and figure 3.	3 Blacksmith with hammer sitting; buildings in background.
FIVE 5 FIVE	OCEAN BANK. Kennebunk, Me. State Arms. Ship-yard; 2 vessels on stocks.	5 FI V VE 5
10 Tree; load of hay; train of cars on bridge with arches.	OCEAN BANK, Kennebunk. Me. Three females representing arts, agriculture and commerce.	10 Ships; city in back ground.
TWENTY	OCEAN BANK. Kennebunk, Me. Two male figures standing, one with quadrant; Two females sitting and holding tablet; one with dividers; spinning wheel and anchor, sea, light-house, mountain and city in background.	TWENTY 20 TWENTY
FIFTY Five female figures, two sitting and three reclining; one with liberty cap and pole.	OCEAN BANK, Kennebunk, Me. L 50 L	50 Man with spy-glass; boy with quadrant.
Liberty, with cap and pole in left hand; right on Am. shield; eagle.	100 Three female figures, left one representing agriculture, with horn of plenty; middle one with wings, joining hands with first; reaching an apple to third, which has quadrant in one hand OCEAN BANK. Kennebunk. Me	100
	YORK BANK. Saco, Me. This Bank uses the old Perkins Stereotype Plate, which has the denomination printed in fine letters all over the bill.	

1	Female seated; train of cars, sloop, and steam boat on right; on left canal, lock, &c. Large 1, and five men. MEDOMAK BANK, Waldoboro, Me.	1 Female leaning head on her hand
ONE Bust of male ONE	Interior of a blacksmiths' shop; two men at work at anvil, forge, &c 1 MEDOMAJ BANK, Waldoboro, Me.	ONE Female. ONE
2	Man and two boys; two sheep in water; drove on left, and buildings on right. Large 2 and five men. MEDOMAK BANK, Waldoboro. Me.	TWO Female seated. TWO
TWO Female. 2	2 Harvest scene; two men seated, one handing female drink; loading hay in background. 2 MEDOMAK BANK. Waldoboro. Me.	TWO Female. 2
3	Man on horseback, cattle, dog, and man; load of hay entering barn, likewise three men; in distance city. 3 MEDOMAK BANK, Waldoboro, Me.	Word three and figure 3. Female erect with basket of flowers. THREE
THREE Farmer sharpening scythe. Word Three, and figure 3.	3 Female seated, entwining wreath around eagles' neck; flowers, fruits, &c. 3 MEDOMAK BANK, Waldoboro. Me	THREE Sailor with hat in hand; horse and cart; ships, &c. Word three, and figure 3.
FIVE Portrait of Webster.	MEDOMAK BANK, Waldoboro. Me. Three females in clouds; one with quadrant; the middle one with sickle. Incorporated in 1836.	5 Female leaning on railing.
Word five, letter V, and figure 5. Female seated, right arm on shield; left hand pointing.	Train of cars; buildings, sloop, &c. MEDOMAK BANK, Waldoboro, Me. Incorporated in 1836.	5 Ship; steam boat on left.
10 Female portrait.	State arms on shield; Indian, squaw and papoose on right; female and three children on left, with globe, &c. MEDOMAK BANK, Waldoboro', Me. Same as fives.	10 Female portrait.

20 Jenny Lind. TWENTY	Steamship and ship; men in boat, view of New York City and Governor's Island. MEDOMAK BANK, Waldoboro', Me. Same as fives.	20 Female portrait.
50 Female seated with sheaf and sickle; train of cars in distance on bridge.	State arms surmounted by an eagle; sailor and ship on right; Indian and huts on left. MEDOMAK BANK. Waldoboro', Me.	50 Female portrait.
100 Female with sheaf and sickle.	MEDOMAK BANK. Waldoboro', Me. Female reclining, at her back eagle; city, train of cars, harvesting, &c., on left.	100 Incorporated in 1836.
1 Female holding tablet and pencil.	Females working at looms. SANDY RIVER B'K, Farmington, Me. Eagle.	1 Portrait of Webster.
2 Male and female sitting.	Man standing against a fence with pipe in his mouth, another man lying on the ground. SANDY RIVER B'K Farmington, Me. Eagle.	2 Sailor with spyglass.
3 Female sitting and holding sheaf of grain.	Woman and cows in front cows, trees, &c., in background. SANDY RIVER B'K, Farmington, Me. Beehive.	3 Female portrait.
5 H. Clay and his dog.	Cattle grazing, sheep to left of cattle. SANDY RIVER B'K, Farmington, Me. State Arms.	5 Female portrait.
10 Female sitting leaning on a shield.	Vig. Same as 5's. SANDY RIVER B'K, Farmington, Me.	10 Currier at work on his leather.
20 Portrait of Pierce.	Men and women on a raft, buildings in left background, village on right, &c. SANDY RIVER B'K, Farmington, Me. Man and cow.	20 Portrait of Webster.

Male portrait 1	Saw mills. 1 Saw mills, dam, lumber raft, &c. VEAZIE BANK, Bangor, Me.	1 Male portrait
Male portrait 2	Ship. 2 Ship. VEAZIE BANK. Bangor, Me.	2 Male portrait
Male portrait 3	Washington on horseback. 3 Washington on horseback. VEAZIE BANK, Bangor, Me.	3 Male portrait
Male portrait 5	Eagle on promontory; ship in distance. Letter V and Indian girl seated. Same as on left side. VEAZIE BANK, Bangor, Me.	5 Male portrait
Likeness of Gen. Jackson 10	Saw mills. X Saw mills, dam, &c. VEAZIE BANK, Bangor, Me.	10 Male portrait
20 Female sitting; right hand resting on book; open book on lap.	XX Vig. Spread eagle standing on rock. XX VEAZIE BANK. Bangor, Me.	20 Two ships, one in foreground, one in distance.
FIFTY Full length figure of female in right hand wreath, and bunch of flowers in left. FIFTY	50 Vig. Man and horse; horse rearing. 50 VEAZIE BANK, Bangor, Me.	FIFTY Full length figure of female. FIFTY
Words one hundred running across figures 100. Male portrait	Dray cart, into which men are rolling barrels, horses, shipping, &c. VEAZIE BANK, Bangor, Me.	Words one hundred running across figures 100. Male portrait
500	500 D Vig. Female sitting, sheaves of grain at her feet; load of grain and men reaping in distance. VEAZIE BANK, Bangor, Me.	500

Group of statuary. 1000	THOUSAND Engine and cars. VEAZIE BANK, Bangor, Me.	1000 Ship 1000
FIVE Hunter drinking from brook: gun by his side.	BANK OF MARION. Marion, Ohio. Male portrait FIVE	5 Library scene with J. C. Calhoun seated and D. Webster erect. FIVE
C	Female reclining on a bale: portrait of Franklin on right, ships in distance. MYSTIC RIVER B'K, Conn. Dog and Safe.	100
Cattle. 1	1 Vig. Farmers cutting grain. 1 BANK OF RUTLAND, Rutland, Vt. Eagle.	ONE Female sitting, with rake, &c. 1
Four Male and six Female figures representing the Arts and Sciences.	Male Portrait. B'K OF MARION, Marion, Ohio. TEN	X 10
1 Auditor's die ONE	Capitol at Washington; eagle, steamer, &c. 1 ALTON BANK, Alton, Ill. Steamboat.	ONE Female standing with shield, &c.
Female churning. 2	Portrait of Hamilton. Portrait of Washington. Vig. Farmers sowing grain. BANK OF RUTLAND, Rutland, Vt. Sheaf of wheat.	2 Farmer picking corn.
1 Portrait of Washington.	View of ship-yard. MYSTIC RIVER B'K, Conn.	1 Groton. Girls head.
TWO Sailor, windlass, &c.	Auditor's die. Female and eagle; railroad and steamboat in the distance. ALTON BANK, Alton, Ill. Horn of plenty and anvil.	2 Female portrait.
Lafayette, full length; York Town monument. V	5 Female sitting with eagle, &c. 5 BANK OF RUTLAND, Rutland, Vt. Arm and hammer.	V Sheep shearing. V
2 Groton.	MYSTIC RIVER B'K, Conn. Female feeding swine, three horses drinking, and man.	2 Portrait of Cass.
THREE Large fig. 3, with mechanic, sailor and farmer. Auditor's die	Eagle on top of a shield, with a female figure sitting on each side; man plowing, railroad and steamboat, and factories in the distance. ALTON BANK, Alton, Ill. Bull.	3 Female portrait. THREE
10 Cattle, &c. 10	Washington. Franklin. Female sitting with sickle and sheaf, cattle, &c. BANK OF RUTLAND, Rutland Vt. Female and sheaf.	10 Sheaf of corn, plow, &c. 10
3 Groton. Portrait of Clay.	MYSTIC RIVER B'K. Conn. Ships, &c.; city in distance.	3 Portrait
5 Female portrait. FIVE	Auditor's die. Female and eagle. ALTON BANK, Alton, Ill. Dog	FIVE Large figure 5 with five females.
Washington full length.	20 Vig. Three female figures sitting. 20 BANK OF RUTLAND, Rutland, Vt. Washington.	20 VERMONT 20
Female portrait 5	MYSTIC RIVER B'K, Conn. Ships.	5 Groton. Portrait of Webster.
1 Compt's die	BK OF SHEBOYGAN Sheboygan, Wis. 1 Blacksmith, hammer, anvil; city in distance. 1	1 Woodcutter.
50 VERMONT 50	50 State arms. 50 and two females. BANK OF RUTLAND, Rutland, Vt. Washington.	50 Female with scales, full length. 50
Female sheaf of wheat. X	10 10 MYSTIC RIVER B'K Conn. Portrait of Fillmore.	Female with sheaf of wheat. X
TWO TWO TWO 2 Locomotive.	Yacht scene—various male and female figures on the beach. BK OF SHEBOYGAN Sheboygan, Wis.	2 Compt's die. TWO TWO TWO
Mother and three children and grape vine. ONE	Male portrait; Girl with pet lamb and man shearing sheep on right. B'K OF MARION, Marion, Ohio.	1 One Dollar, in part circle
20	Whaling scene. Indian Queen. MYSTIC RIVER B'K, Conn.	20 Cooper and barrel.
3 THREE 3	3 Ship yard scene; men at work. BK OF SHEBOYGAN Sheboygan, Wis.	3 Compt's die
3 Wine harvest	Male portrait B'K OF MARION, Marion, Ohio,	3 3
50	MYSTIC RIVER B'K, Conn. Female reclining on a bale of goods, city and ship in distance. Eagle.	50 Groton. Female head.
5	American shield; on right female instructing children, house in distance; on left Indian, squaw and child. 5 BK OF SHEBOYGAN Sheboygan, Wis.	5 on FIVE Compt's die.

1 ONE PHENIX VILLAGE BANK, Phenix, R. I. View of bridge, water falls, houses and trees. Male portrait ONE 1 1 ONE	X 10 X Head of Washington. Same as ones. Head of Clay. Title of Bank. Dog and safe. X 10 X	TEN Full rigged vessel. TEN £10 currency. 10 British coat of arms, &c. 10 Title of Bank Lion. TEN
2 TWO Title of Bank. Vig. Same as ones. 2 2 2	20 Head of Washington 20 20 Same as ones. 20 Title of Bank. Dog and safe. 20 Head of Clay 20	25 Same as tens 25 £25 currency. 25 British coat of arms, &c. 25 Title of Bank. Lion. TWENTY-FIVE
3 THREE Title of Bank. Vig. Same as ones. 3 THREE 3 THREE	50 Head of Washington. 50 50 Same as ones. Title of Bank. Dog and safe. 50 Head of Clay 50	ONE DOLLAR 1 Squaw contemplating progress of civilization; railroad and canal boat in distance; city in extreme distance. NEWARK BANKING COMPANY Newark, N. J. Eagle. 1 Portrait of Franklin.
FIVE 5 Title of Bank. Man tending large machinery. 5 5 Male portrait	100 Head of Washington. 100 Same as ones. 100 Title of Bank. Dog and safe. 100 Head of Clay 100	2 Portrait of Washington. 2 2 Two females, sheaf of wheat and ships in distance. Title of Bank. 2 Female entwined in figure 2
X TEN Men at work in an Iron Mill. X Title of Bank. 10, X and Ten. Male portrait	Word shillings and figure 5 across. Sail vessel; lighthouse in distance. Word shillings and figure 5 across. FIVE British FIVE coat of arms, or lion and unicorn fighting for the crown. COMMERCIAL BANK OF N.-B. St. John. N. B. Lion. Same as on left. View of two persons; harvest scene. Same as on left.	TWO 2 Ornamental figure 2, with two females entwined. Title of Bank Implements of war. Ornamental die. Portrait of Washington. Ornamental die.
50 on red die Title of Bank. View of factories, cars, water, hills, etc. 50 on red die	Seven and sixpence Female erect with vase of flowers, &c. 7 | 6 7|6 British 7|6 Check. coat of arms, &c. Check. 7|6 7|6 Title of Bank. 7 6 CHECK 7 6	3 Female with pole and cap; eagle and shield; ship in distance. Title of Bank Miniature; train of cars Three females on ornamental figure 3; one representing liberty, justice, &c. THREE
100 and C on red die. Title of Bank. Male portrait 100 and C on red die.	ONE Sail vessel. ONE £1 currency. 1 British coat of arms, &c. 1 Title of Bank. Lion. ONE	3 Ornamental figure 3, with three females. Title of Bank. Arms of the State of New Jersey; ship in distance
Head of Clay. 1 Female figure sitting; city in distance, cows, &c. Female head. NORTHERN BANK OF KENTUCKY. Lexington. Ky. 1 Head of Washington	2 Same as ones 2 £2 currency. TWO British coat TWO of arms, &c. Title of Bank. Lion. TWO	5 Med. head, with V on it. 5 Title of Bank. Female seated on bale of goods, with arm resting on shield 5 Med. head, with V on it 5
5 Head of Clay. 5 Title of Bank. 5 Same as ones 5 Dog and safe. 5 Head of Washington 5	FIVE Female seated, holding spear, shield, &c; vessel in distance. FIVE £5 currency. 5 British coat of arms, &c. 5 Title of Bank. Lion. FIVE	5 Female with scales, seated on a barrel; cars in distance. Goddess of Liberty resting on American shield. Ornamental figure, with two females and cherub. Title of Bank. FIVE DOLLARS

5 Female with balance, anchor and shield.	Arms of the State of New Jersey; ship in distance. Ornamental figure 5, with two females and cherub. Title of Bank.	Ornamental die. Portrait of Washington. Ornamental die.

TEN Girl with sheaf of grain on her head, basket on her arm; boy sitting with keg in his lap dog team and load of grain TEN	X Mythological scene; the goddess Mercury descending from her car in the clouds with her attendants; one drinking from a vase. X B'K OF CALEDONIA, Danville, Vt. Dove with a motto in its beak.	TEN DOLLARS

500	Female seated among sheafs of grain, pointing to reapers and workmen loading grain. 500 D GRANITE STATE BK Exeter, N. H.	500

10 Med. head, with X on it. 10	Med. head. View of blacksmith shop; one at bellows and one at anvil; cars in distance. Med. head Title of Bank.	Med. head. TEN Med. head.

	The 20's 50's and 100's are of the General Plate of the N. E. Bank Note Co., for a description of which see Land Holder's Bank, R. I., page 202.	

Farmer, sailor and blacksmith. 3	3 BANK OF WASHINGTON, North Carolina. Female swimming.	3 Portrait of Washington.

20 Med. head, with Twenty on it. 20	Med. head, with two cherubs on left, and one on right. Title of Bank.	20 Med. head, with Twenty on it. 20

Word one and figure 1. Bust of female.	Harvest scene—farmers at lunch; female with child; men loading hay, and farm-house in distance. GRANITE STATE BK Exeter, N. H.	1 Female with pole and cap, seated on safe, right hand on figure 1.

Portrait of Washington. 4	Shield; Indian, squaw and papoose on right of shield; mountain in distance; on left of shield female and three children studying globe; horses in distance. Title of Bank. Anvil.	FOUR Portrait of Mrs. Washington.

50 State Arms.	NEWARK CITY BK. Newark, N. J. L	FIFTY Male figure, and two females seated; agricultural scene.

2 Bust of female.	State arms surmounted by an eagle, female on either side. GRANITE STATE BK Exeter, N. H.	2 Two females erect, one with sickle and sheaf.

5 FIVE	BANK OF WASHINGTON, North Carolina. Three females with quadrant, anchor and sickle. Train of cars Eagle	5 Female 5

100 Two Indians.	State Arms Title of Bank. One hundred.	Two females, one seated, the other erect. 100

FIVE Letter V with three males and two females	Milkmaid seated and two cows; three cows and farm house in distance. GRANITE STATE BK Exeter, N. H.	FIVE 5 and five females

TEN Female, hogshead, &c., train of cars in distance. 10	Head of Washington surmounted by an eagle; on left female, anchor and ship; on right female with horn of flowers. Title of Bank. Boxes and barrels.	X 10

ONE Female writing on desk, the desk representing a large figure 1 ONE	1 Man with sheaf on his left shoulder, and cradle on his right arm, shoes dangling from the snaith, on the right in the distance a farm house and trees and a flock of sheep before it. 1 B'K OF CALEDONIA, Danville, Vt. Spread eagle.	ONE

10 State Arms.	Drove of cattle and sheep; man on horseback GRANITE STATE BK Exeter, N. H.	10 Female seated with sheaf and cornucopia.

20 Male portrait.	Indian seated, plow, &c.; in distance mountains and river. BANK OF WASHINGTON, North Carolina.	XX Indian female, female with sheaf and sickle.

TWO Female with bundle of grain in her left hand raised over head forming top of figure 2, Cupid with sickle &c., TWO	2 Man plowing with a span of horses; ship and steamboat on left and farm house on the right in the background. 2 Title of Bank. Sheaf of Grain and Agricultural Implements.	TWO

20 State arms.	Female seated with portrait of Washington, and with her left hand crowning eagle with a wreath; anchor, hogshead, &c.; in distance factory and steamboat. GRANITE STATE BK Exeter, N. H.	20 Female seated between 2 and 0.

Word fifty running up. Five female figures.	BANK OF WASHINGTON, North Carolina. FIFTY	50 Bridge, telegraph wire and poles, cattle, trees, &c.

THREE Large figure supported by a female and two Cupids. THREE	3 Two men on horseback with drove of cattle and sheep; a covered bridge and sloop. 3 B'K OF CALEDONIA, Danville, Vt. Horse.	THREE

50 Female holding wreath over eagle; in her left hand scales	Female seated holding in right hand emblems of wisdom; state arms on left also safe and coin; on right train of cars, bridge, and steamboat. GRANITE STATE BK Exeter. N. H.	50 50

Small figure of Washington and figures 100. Three male figures, flag, windlass, anvil, &c.	BANK OF WASHINGTON, North Carolina. 100 100	100 River scene Palmetto trees, cotton growing and in baskets.

FIVE Commerce sitting on a bale of goods in a large V. 5	A large figure 5, supported by five winged Cupids 5 B'K OF CALEDONIA, Danville, Vt. Indian's Head.	FIVE

100 State arms.	100 Female seated leaning on bales and looking at ships in distance; on her right train of cars, &c. GRANITE STATE BK Exeter. N. H.	100 100

Two Indians, one kneeling the other erect.	1 Vig. Farming scene, farmer sharpening scythe. HOPKINTON BANK. Westerly, R. I. Stockholders private property holden.	1 Scene upon coast of sea.

1 Portrait of Washington.	(Old Plate.) Female portrait 1 Female portrait. HOPKINTON BANK, Westerly, R. I.	1 Portrait of Franklin.

2 Male portrait	Female. 2 Female. HOPKINTON BANK, Westerly, R. I.	2 Male portrait

Goddess of liberty erect with spear and shield. TWO	Vig. Locomotive and train passing under bridge. HOPKINTON BANK, Westerly, R. I. Stockholders private property holden.	2 State arms. TWO

3 Washington full length.	Female head and bust. 3 Female head and bust. Title of Bank.	3 Vulcan, full length.

  3	Drover on horseback and boy driving swine. State arms. HOPKINTON BANK, Westerly, R. I.	3 Locomotive and tender.

Eagle resting on United States shield and an anchor. FIVE	A large V, with female figure and child. Title of Bank.	5 Female figure and basket.

Goddess of liberty in large figure 5. FIVE	Stockholders private property holden. Three male figures erect, with their coats off. HOPKINTON BANK, Westerly, R. I Wheelbarrow, &c.	5, V, Five Portrait of Washington.

  TEN	Vulcan seated, with sledge and anvil; train of cars and buildings in distance. X Title of Bank.	10 Farmer with sheaf and sickle.

TEN	Goddess of liberty seated, receiving sheaf of grain from one of three figures, representing commerce, agriculture and mechanics. Ten, X, 10. HOPKINTON BANK, Westerly, R. I.	10 Indian girl erect; female with sickle at her feet.

20 Female figure seated.	XX Eagle. XX Title of Bank.	20 Ship with sails partly furled.

FIFTY Female erect with wreath. FIFTY	50 Man and horse. 50 Title of Bank.	FIFTY Female erect FIFTY.

Word one hundred and figure 100. Male portrait.	Wharf scene—loading wagon, men, horses, shipping, &c. Title of Bank.	Same as on left Male portrait.

ONE 1	Agricultural scene; farmer sowing; another in the distance harrowing. 1 MANUFACTURERS BANK, Saco, Me.	1 Ship. ONE

TWO 2	Spread eagle; iron castings, cannon balls, machinery, &c. 2 Title of Bank.	2 TWO Schooner rigged boat.

THREE 3	Sailor; hat in hand, reclining against bales; in the distance are vessels, warehouses, dray, horses &c. 3 Title of Bank.	3 THREE Train of cars.

FIVE	Female resting upon her left knee, lifting veil from figure 5. Title of Bank,	5 ship.

Female seated, holding rake in left hand and sickle in right, ships, buildings &c. in backgro'd.	Large V and Indian. Title of Bank.	5 Portrait of Washington.

10 X 10	Vig. Man with oxen. 10 Title of Bank.	TEN Femal figure with cornucopia of fruits and flowers,

20 Female.	XX Eagle. XX Title of Bank.	20 Ship sailing.

FIFTY Female. FIFTY	50 Man and horse 50 Title of Bank.	FIFTY Female. FIFTY

Words one hundred and figures 100 Male portrait.	Vig Market scene; shipping on left. Title of Bank.	Words one hundred, and figures 100. Male portrait.

Female seated, men loading hay in distance. 500	5 0 0 D Title of Bank.	500

1 ONE	Female reclining on horn of plenty; pole and cap, eagle and shield. STATE BANK; Newark, N. J. State Arms.	1 ONE

2 Goddess of liberty and justice.	Two females seated; ship on left; train of cars and factory on right. STATE BANK, Newark, N. J. Eagle.	2

3 Female and ornamental figure 3.	Three females seated; cars on left and ship on right. STATE BANK, Newark N. J. State Arms.	3

5 Ship; water in commotion.	View of banking house and church. STATE BANK, Newark, N. J. Eagle.	5 5

10 Female with cornucopia.	Vig. Same as 5's. STATE BANK, Newark, N. J. Head of Horse.	10 X

FIFTY / Cooper at work. / L — 50 Female seated, agricultural scene on left; blacksmith shop on right. 50 / STATE BANK, Newark, N. J. / State Arms. — FIFTY / Female seated. / 50

Portrait of Jefferson. / 50 — Ceres sitting by cornucopia; ship under sail in distance on left. / WEARE BANK, Hampton Falls, N. H. / Man ploughing with two horses. — 50 / Female churning.

TEN / Train of cars on a curve approaching. / TEN — Female sitting between 1 and 0; lake and steamer in the distance. / BANK OF BURLINGTON, Burlington, Vt. / Dog, key and safe. — TEN / Young vulcan at the anvil. / X

Figure of Justice. / 100 — C Female reclining on anchor; ship in distance. / STATE BANK, Newark, N. J. / State Arms. — ONE HUNDRED

1 / Female seated with arms uplifted on bale; bbl. &c. ships in distance. / ONE — Boy reclining watching flock of six sheep; in distance. Compt's. die on fig. 1. / BANK OF BELOIT, Beloit, Wis. — 1 / Female erect with flag and shield.

20 / Sheaf of grain. / 20 — 20 Female sitting holding sword in right hand, left resting on pillar, with lion reclining at her left. 20 / BANK OF BURLINGTON, Burlington, Vt. / Indian in canoe. — TWENTY

500 / Female seated; ship, &c. in distance. — State Arms; train of cars on left; Steamboat on right. / STATE BANK, Newark, N. J. / Agricultural Implements. — D

2 / 2 — Four males seated on female with child, basket, &c; in distance men loading wagon with hay, two oxen before wagon; horse &c. Compt's. die on fig. 1. / Title of Bank. — 2 / Washington on horseback.

50 / Ship. / 50 — 50 Female sitting; right hand pointing to vessel; left around a pillar. 50 / BANK OF BURLINGTON, Burlington, Vt. / Spread eagle. — 50 / Ship. / 50

ONE / Female head. / 1 — Man on horseback with drove of cattle and sheep, &c. / WEARE BANK, Hampton Falls, N. H. — 1 / Portrait of Gov. Baker. / ONE

Three females one above the others; an chor on which topmost female has right hand. / THREE — 3 St. George fighting the Dragon. / BANK OF BELOIT, Beloit, Wis. — 3 / Compt's. Die

100 / Portrait of Hamilton. / 100 — 100 Female sitting and feeding eagle from urn. 100 / BANK OF BURLINGTON, Burlington, Vt. / Steamboat. — 100 / Eagle. / 100

Portrait of Gov. Baker. / 2 — Man plowing with two horses. / WEARE BANK, Hampton Falls, N. H. / Loading hay. — 2 / Female with basket of fruits, sickle, sheaf of grain, sittin on a plough.

5 / Compt's Die. — Female seated with sheaf of grain within a large ornamental V. / BANK OF BELOIT, Beloit, Wis. — 5 / Female with 5 in a figure 5.

ONE — Water scene; ship in distance. 1 / ST. STEPHENS' BK. St. Stephen, N. B. ONE DOLLAR. — ONE / ONE

Goddess of Liberty feeding eagle. / 3 — Husbandman sitting, with sheaf of grain and a cradling scythe lying near; mowing and loading grain in the background. / WEARE BANK, Hampton Falls, N. H. / Cow and calf. — 3 / Portrait of Gov. Baker.

ONE / Female head. / ONE — Milkmaid with pail and cows. / BANK OF BURLINGTON, Burlington, Vt. / Locomotive and tender. — 1 / Portrait of female. / ONE

ONE — Vessels, steamboat, &c. 1 / ST. STEPHENS' BK., St. Stephen, N. B. ONE DOLLAR. — ONE / Female Indian seated, with bow and arrow.

FIVE / Justice standing with sword and scales; Mars sitting with spear and shield, book and globe near. — Two trains of cars. / WEARE BANK, Hampton Falls, N. H. — 5 / Portrait of Gov. Baker. / FIVE

TWO / Portrait of female. / TWO — Two females in sitting posture, one with sickle and sheaf; steamboat and sail vessel in distance. / BANK OF BURLINGTON, Burlington, Vt. / State arms. — 2 / Female in sitting posture with sheaf and sickle. / 2

2 / TWO / 2 — Ships on and before the wind. 2 / ST. STEPHENS' BK., St. Stephen, N. B. TWO DOLLARS. — TWO / Female and domestic utensils. / TWO

Boy standing with sheaf of grain under his arm, and farm girl sitting leaning on pail. / X — Two men with horse and dog, among a drove of cattle part of them laying down. / WEARE BANK, Hampton Falls, N. H. — 10 / Man sitting on plough. / X

THREE / Goddess of liberty with shield and eagle on right. / THREE — Drover on horseback, with cattle and sheep. / BANK OF BURLINGTON, Burlington, Vt. / Safe, dog and key. — 3 / Female / THREE

THREE — Harvest scene; male and female reapers. 3 / ST. STEPHENS' BK., St. Stephen, N. B. THREE DOLLARS. — THREE / Steamboat. / THREE

Man sharpening a cradling scythe / 20 — Ganymede and the eagle ship under sail in the distance; cornucopia lying in front. / WEARE BANK, Hampton Falls, N. H. / Two horses — XX / Portrait of Washington.

5 / Portrait of female. / FIVE — Side view of spread eagle on a branch; factory and cars in the distance. / BANK OF BURLINGTON, Burlington, Vt. / Carding machine. — FIVE / Female in sitting posture, right hand elevating liberty cap. / FIVE

V / Steamboat and other vessels and bills. / 5 — Two Indians; one seated and smoking; 5 the other reclining; a fire, trees, waterfall, &c. 5 / SAINT STEPHENS' BANK, St. Stephen, N. B. FIVE DOLLARS. / River scene; men in boats &c. — V / Male in field with sheaf and sickle. / 5

10 X 10 Indian in canoe; in background, vessels, men, hills, &c. SAINT STEPHENS' BANK, S. Stephen, N. B. TEN DOLLARS Eagle. 10 Ship on stocks. 10	50 FIFTY 50 50 Female seated upholding large 50; safe, casks, cornucopia, &c.; two ships on left. MIDDLETOWN B'K, Middletown, Ct. Spread eagle. FIFTY	100 PASSUMPSIC BANK, St. Johnsbury, Vt. Female and eagle soaring in the air. Dog and safe. 100 Female with basket of flowers.
5 Female erect on rock, with spear and shield; ship in distance. FIVE 5 British Coat-of-Arms. Figure 5, with word Five pounds above it; and word Currency below. ST. STEPHENS' BK., St. Stephen, N. B. FIVE POUNDS. Steamboat and other vessels. FIVE	100 HUNDRED 100 C Sailor with spyglass, compass leaning against bales, hhds. in rear; ship and steamer on left. MIDDLETOWN B'K, Middletown, Ct. Horse. ONE HUNDRED	ONE Ships on the ocean. 1 Figure 1 and eagle; in left Indian seated; on right, sailor seated, holding quadrant; in distance ship. EXETER BANK. Exeter, R. I. Female with sickle and sheaf. ONE Female seated; left arm resting on State Arms. 1
X Beehive. X 10 Same as five pound note. Figures 10, and word Ten pound above, and word Currency below. ST. STEPHENS' BK., St. Stephen, N. B. TEN POUNDS. Dog, safe and key. TEN	ONE PASSUMPSIC BANK, St. Johnsbury, Vt. Cattle and sheep. 1 1 Blacksmith and anvil.	TWO Female seated, right arm resting above figure 2. 2 2 Cupid holding figure 2, in front of a block of stone. 2 EXETER BANK, Exeter, R. I. Eagle and small urn. Female erect left arm resting on stone pillar. TWO
ONE 1 Dog and safe. 1 MIDDLETOWN B'K, Middletown, Ct. Ship. ONE	TWO PASSUMPSIC BANK, St. Johnsbury, Vt. Man with sledge on his shoulder; factory and cars in distance. 2 State arms. 2 Two females.	3 Portrait of Washington. 3 3 Female giving eagle drink. 3 EXETER BANK, Exeter, R. I. 3 3 Portrait of De Witt Clinton.
TWO Three milkmaids and two cows; vessels and cottage. MIDDLETOWN B'K, Middletown, Ct. Cogwheel and cylinder. TWO	THREE PASSUMPSIC BANK, St. Johnsbury, Vt. Female with horn of plenty, barrels, &c.; ships, factories and train of cars. 3 Head of dog. 3 Head of Webster.	FIVE Female seated, holding eagle. V 5 Female seated, with sickle; cows standing, and farm-house in distance. 5 EXETER BANK, Exeter, R. I. Indian in canoe. FIVE
THREE 3 Three females seated; one with Mercury's wand, and leaning on shield. 3 MIDDLETOWN B'K. Middletown, Ct. State arms. THREE	5 PASSUMPSIC BANK. St. Johnsbury, Vt. Drove of cattle and sheep; man on horseback. 5 FIVE Indian erect with bow and spear.	10 Female erect and State Arms. 10 TEN Agricultural implements; beehive, cornucopia, tree, sheaf of wheat, linen wheel, &c. TEN EXETER BANK, Exeter, R. I. Cupid on the back of a deer. 10
5 FIVE 5 5 Female resting on anchor and bale of goods; schooner and steamboat on right; city and shipping on left. 5 MIDDLETOWN B'K, Middletown, Ct. Agricult[illegible] implements. 5 Portrait of H. Clay. V	TEN PASSUMPSIC BANK. St. Johnsbury, Vt. Train of cars. X Boy's head. 10 Female with pole and cap.	ONE Male portrait. Farming scene. WORTHINGTON BK. Cooperstown, N. Y. 1 State arms.
10 TEN 10 10 Female, agricultural products and implements around her; on left canal boat and lock; on right cars and bridge. 10 MIDDLETOWN B'K, Middletown, Ct. Locomotive. 10 Washington. 10	20 PASSUMPSIC BANK, St. Johnsbury, Vt. Female seated on sheaf of grain; men loading grain in distance. 10 Female with scales and sword.	TWO DOLLARS State arms. Man plowing with oxen; little girl on right with pail and jug. WORTHINGTON BK. Cooperstown, N. Y. 2 Male portrait.
TWENTY 20 Two winged figures and two cupids upholding large 20. MIDDLETOWN B'K, Middletown, Ct. Steamship. 20 TWENTY 20	Eagle upon shield, bale and barrel, with anchor, sheaf of grain, &c.; falls and factory in distance. 50 PASSUMPSIC BANK, St. Johnsbury, Vt. Imp. and products 50 Female with sheaf and sickle.	FIVE State arms. Farming scene; men at work. WORTHINGTON BK. Cooperstown, N. Y. 5 Male portrait.

Shield, female, starry drapery, liberty pole and cap.
Eagle. 1 Indian viewing the improvement of the white man.
PRODUCERS' BANK, Woonsocket, R. I.
Female bathing.
1 Mechanic's arm, anvil and hammer.

TWO Franklin. TWO
Liberty, Justice and truth: eagle at top of shield; bridge and cars on right: ship on left.
PRODUCERS' BANK, Woonsocket, R. I.
Dog, safe and key.
TWO Female with rake. TWO

3 Washington.
PRODUCERS' BANK, Woonsocket, R. I.
Two horses and train of cars.
Farming implements.
3 Female.

5 Locomotive. FIVE
Horse on either side of shield; eagle at top; steamboat on right; factories, canal scene and cars crossing bridge, on left.
PRODUCERS' BANK, Woonsocket, R. I.
5 Drove of cattle.

X Female. 10
Female seated between figures 10; farming scene on either side. Letter X on shield.
PRODUCERS' BANK, Woonsocket, R. I.
Machinery.
10 Two female Indians with sickle, bow, and arrows.

Female with liberty pole and cap. TWENTY
20 Man ploughing with oxen; little girl on right.
PRODUCERS' BANK, Woonsocket, R. I
20 Female, grain, and sickle.

Female with wand; right hand holds med. head, which rests on pillar.
50 Spread eagle on American shield.
PRODUCERS' BANK, Woonsocket, R. I.
50 Washington.

100 Man seated instructing a little child.
PRODUCERS' BANK, Woonsocket, R. I.
C
100 Med. head 100

500 Artist at work.
Washington. Two females on either side of a beehive.
PRODUCERS' BANK, Woonsocket, R. I.
Machinery.
500 Portrait of Mrs. Washington

1 Milkmaid.
Register's die. Lion and unicorn on either side of the crown.
NIAGARA DISTRICT BANK, St. Catharines, Ca.
1 ONE

2 Prince Albert.
NIAGARA DISTRICT BANK, St. Catharines, Ca.
Register's die. 2
2

5 Ship building
NIAGARA DISTRICT BANK, St. Catharines, Ca.
Portrait of the Queen of England.
Register's die. 5

1 Female with basket of flowers. ONE
Cupid rolling silver $; train of cars, &c., in background.
UNION BANK, Augusta, Ga.
1 Female figure with left hand resting on shield and surrounded by names of the States.

2 Portrait of Female.
Two Cupids and two silver dollars
UNION BANK, Augusta, Ga.
2 Sailor with quadrant, casks, &c.

Female and two cows. 5
Female Portrait
UNION BANK, Augusta, Ga.
5 FIVE 5

TEN X
Two females; between them a shield on which is a cotton plant and a horses head for a crest; horn of plenty, bales, &c.
UNION BANK, Augusta, Ga.
10 Female head and bust.

20 Head of Washington.
Train of cars.
UNION BANK. Augusta, Ga.
20 Female with pole and cap; shield, &c.

50. Sailor with quadrant, casks, &c.
State Arms surmounted by an eagle; on either side a female, motto "Independence."
UNION BANK, Augusta, Ga.
50 Female with maps, books, compass &c., around her

100 Female seated on anchor
Female reclining against bales; behind bales, an eagle with U. S. shield suspended from neck by a chain, motto "E Pluribus Unum," in distance steamboat with masts and ship.
UNION BANK, Augusta, Ga.
100 State Arms Indian on left and sailor on right, ships masts in distance.

Word one and figure 1.
Vig. Train of cars.
1
CITIZENS' BANK, Sanbornton, N. H.
1 Two females Indian grain, sickle, &c.

2 Female with quadrant, anchor at her side; eagle at top of shield on left.
Vig. Group of three females, with quadrant, chart, spy-glass, globe, liberty pole and cap.
CITIZENS' BANK, Sanbornton, N. H.
2 Female with shield and balances.

3 Indian with tomahawk and bow.
Vig. Drove of wild horses.
CITIZENS' BANK, Sanbornton, N. H
3 Squaw and pappoose.

FIVE
CITIZENS' BANK, Sanbornton, N. H.
Vig. Droveofcattle, man plowing on left; farmers at work on right.
5 Two horses; cars on left.

TEN Female right hand resting on shield.
Puddling in an Iron Mill. 10
CITIZENS' BANK, Sanbornton, N. H.
TEN Mechanic.

1 View of Street men and cattle load of hay, town in distance.
Drovers, cattle, and sheep.
LAKE SHORE B'K, Dunkirk, N.Y.
1 State Arms

2 Sailor leaning on capstan.
LAKE SHORE B'K, Dunkirk, N. Y.
Catching wild horse.
2 State Arms.

5 Female artist and implements.
Landing of the pilgrims.
LAKE SHORE B'K, Dunkirk, N. Y.
5 State Arms

ONE	BANK OF GOSHEN, Goshen, Ind.	ONE
	Vig. One dollar in circular die.	
Auditor's die	Spread eagle.	ONE

20	Three females with wand, cornucopia, sword and balances; vessels on right.	20
Female.	ST. ALBANS' BANK, St. Albans, Vt.	Female artist; around her mechanical tools.

50	Male and female seated.	50 Cupid in boat.
Female with spear.	Title of Bank. 50	50

3	BANK OF GOSHEN, Goshen. Ind.	3
	Auditor's Circular die. Circular die. die.	
3		3

50	ST. ALBANS' BANK, St. Albans, Vt.	50
Female.	Portrait of Washington.	Train of cars village in background.

100	Vig. Spread eagle upon branch of tree; canal scene on right; train of cars crossing bridge on left.	100
Man with staff, anchor.	Title of Bank. 100	Female with rake, seated beside cornucopia.

5	BANK OF GOSHEN, Goshen, Ind.	5
	Auditor's die and five circular dies in semicircle below it.	
V		V

100	U. S. Capitol at Washington.	100
Soldiers with fife and drum	ST. ALBANS' BANK St. Albans, Vt.	Portrait of Webster.

	Female seated; train of cars and vessel on right, canal scene on left. 1	1
1	MISSISQUOI BANK, Sheldon, Vt	Female resting arm on fence

X		X
	Ten dies in semi circle.	
TEN	Auditor's die. Title of Bank.	TEN

	Female seated; train of cars, sloop, and steam boat on right; on left canal, lock, &c. Large 1, and five men.	1
1	PITTSFIELD BANK, Pittsfield, N. H.	Female leaning head on her hand.

	Man forcing sheep in water, another man erect; boy driving flock; buildings on right. 2	TWO Female seated.
2	Title of Bank.	TWO

1	ST. ALBANS' BANK, St. Albans, Vt.	1
View of Street, cattle and men, load of hay; town in distance.	Vig. Selling Cattle.	

	Man and two boys; two sheep in water; drove on left, and buildings on right. Large 2 and five men.	TWO Female seated.
2	Title of Bank	TWO

	Man on horseback; cows and men; load of hay entering barn. 3	Word three, and figure 3. Female with basket of flowers.
3	Title of Bank	TH 3REE

2	ST. ALBANS' BANK, St. Albans, Vt.	2
Sailor leaning on capstan, merchandise and anchor on right, ships masts on left.	Vig. Catching Horse.	Mechanic and tools.

	Man on horseback, cattle, dog, and man; load of hay entering barn, likewise three men; in distance city. 3	Word three and figure 3
		Female erect with basket of flowers.
3	Title of Bank.	THREE

	Eagle on shield; city and ships in distance. Large V, female and Cupid.	5
FIVE	Title of Bank.	Girl with basket of flowers or fruit.

3	ST. ALBANS' BANK, St. Albans, Vt.	3
	Blacksmith's shop; men at work, smith shoeing horse.	Female and grain.
	Squaw.	

Spread eagle; city and vessels in distance.	Large V, female and Cupid.	5
FIVE	Title of Bank.	Portrait of a girl.

	Vulcan seated, anvil, sledge, &c.; train of cars and buildings in distance. X	10
TEN	Title of Bank.	Farmer with sheaf on his knee.

Three females on a rock with anchor spy-glass, &c.	Three females and Cupid.	5
FIVE	ST. ALBANS' BANK, St. Albans, Vt.	Female.
	Eagle.	

Vulcan seated; train of cars, &c., in distance.	X	10
TEN	Title of Bank.	Farmer with sheaf of wheat and sickle.

20	XX Eagle. XX	20
Female sitting, with book.	Title of Bank.	Ship under sail.

10	Train of cars; view of river and town; cars crossing bridge.	10
Male portrait	ST. ALBANS' BANK. St. Albans, Vt. Farming implements.	Farmer gathering grain.

20	2 Female. 0	20 Female seated.
Female with spear.	Title of Bank XX	20

FIFTY	50 Man and Horse. 50	FIFTY
Female with wreath.	Title of Bank.	Full length female, Globe Rule, &c.
FIFTY		FIFTY

Left end	Centre	Right end
100 Eagle. 100	C Horses and Chariot, Female. 100 Title of Bank.	C Washington C
2 TWO 2	Vessels, &c. 2 Title of Bank.	TWO Female drawing water. TWO
ONE Early settlers.	Vig. Coal Quarry. OCOEE BANK, Cleaveland, Tenn.	1 1
1 RHODE ISLAND 1	1 Spread eagle on rock, olive branch and arrows in talons. 1 FREEMANS' BANK, Bristol, R. I. ONE	1 ONE 1
THREE	Female with hat in right hand and sheaf in left; farmer reaping, with man behind him with grain in his arms. 3 Title of Bank.	THREE Steamship. TH 3REE
TWO Male portrait.	Two Squaws and Indian in canoe. OCOEE BANK, Cleaveland, Tenn. Female Bathing.	2 Male portrait.
2 RHODE ISLAND 2	2 2 Same as ones. Title of Bank. TWO	2 TWO 2
FIVE	Female lifting drapery from a shield on which is figure 5. V Title of Bank.	5 Vessel.
5 Male portrait.	View of Bridge Telegraph and Railroad. OCOEE BANK, Cleaveland, Tenn.	5 Male portrait.
3 RHODE ISLAND 3	3 3 Same as ones Title of Bank. THREE	3 THREE 3
Large V and word FIVE.	Wharf scene with female sitting among agricultural implements and merchandise holding sickle and rake. Large V and figure with bow and arrow. Title of Bank	5 Portrait of Washington.
X	Depot and train of cars, also another in distance. Male portrait. OCOEE BANK, Cleaveland, Tenn.	TEN View of street, load of hay, vehicles, &c.
FIVE	Spread eagle on shield; city and ships in distance. Female, cupid, and letter V. Title of Bank.	5 Little girl with flowers.
Vulcan with anvil, hammer, &c. TEN	X Title of Bank.	10 Female with sickle and grain.
TWENTY 20 XX	Vig. Farmer and yoke of cattle. Male portrait. OCOEE BANK, Cleaveland, Tenn. Female.	20 Mechanic and tools.
Male figure seated on machinery; cars at distance. TEN	X Title of Bank.	10 Male figure with sheaf in hand.
20 Female sitting; right hand resting on book; open book on lap.	XX Eagle. XX Title of Bank.	20 Ship.
1 Auditors' die	Sailor, female and mechanic; cars, city, steamboat and ship in distance MISSISSIPPI RIVER BANK, Oxford, Ills. Sea monsters.	ONE Man carrying figure 1.
FIFTY Female erect with wreath of flowers in right hand, and flowers in left. FIFTY	50 Man and horse. 50 Title of Bank.	FIFTY Female erect holding cornucopia in left hand, barometer in right. FIFTY
FIFTY Female figure standing globe in her right hand, flowers at her right. FIFTY	50 Man and horse. 50 Title of Bank.	FIFTY Female figure with wreath of flowers in right hand. FIFTY
TWO Female seated on fig. 2.	Steamboat; city and schooner in distance. Title of Bank. Man.	2 Auditor's die
Words one hundred, and figures 100. Male portrait	Vig. Wharf scene; loading wagon; men, horses, shipping, &c. Title of Bank	Words one hundred, and figures 100. Male portrait
Figures 100 and words one hundred. Head of Harrison.	Wagon with horses and goods; ship at a distance. Title of Bank.	Figures 100 and words one hundred. Head and bust of male.
5 Auditor's die	Man feeding pigs; chickens, fence, pig pen, etc. Title of Bank. Head.	5 5 on shield, female each side.
ONE	Sea view with shipping, &c. 1 SMITHFIELD UNION BANK, Woonsocket. R. I.	ONE Female Indian with bow & arrow. ONE
ONE …man and …ing	Indians pointing to the improvements of the white man. OCOEE BANK, Cleaveland, Tenn. Female bathing	1 1
TEN Auditor's die TEN on 10.	Cattle and horses; men, bridge and city in distance. Title of Bank. Spread eagle.	10 TEN on X. Millmaid, cow, etc.

Left end	Centre	Right end
1 ONE on fig. 1	GREENWICH BANK East Greenwich, R. I. Sailor reclining with implements; ships in distance. 1 Stockholders, etc. 1	1 Train of cars
1 ONE	ONE ONE KENTUCKY STOCK BANK, Columbus, Ind. ONE DOLLAR.	1 State arms.
FIVE Vig. Farm-house scene.	HOOSIER BANK, Logansport, Ind. Register's die.	5 Two females seated, one with sickle, above them a man holding pitchfork; dog on right; yoke of cattle on left
2 TWO DOLLARS	Man, female, boy, girl, dog hen and chickens. 2 on shield on right is female instructing children; on left is Indian, squaw and papoose. GREENWICH BANK East Greenwich, R. I. Red 2. Red 2.	2 Squaw and female.
5 5	KENTUCKY STOCK BANK, Columbus, Ind. Coat of arms.	5 5
Word one and figure 1. Female instructing children.	Female bathing. One and figure 1. Vig. Justice with sword and scales, bridge and cars left. CENTRAL BANK, Alabama.	1 Agriculture.
5, V & FIVE. State Arms. FIVE	Signing Declaration of Independence. Washington GREENWICH BANK East Greenwich, R. I. Red 5. Arm. Red 5	5 on med. head. Male portrait
Two females, one kneeling.	1 Two females on right of shield, on which is farming utensils; factory in distance; on left, cars and bridge. LYNN MECHANICS' BANK, Lynn, Mass.	1 Female.
2 TWO 2	Vig. Gathering sugar cane. CENTRAL BANK, Alabama.	2 Gathering cotton; vessels in distance.
ONE Mechanic and sailor with flag, quadrant and [illegible] right	1 Large ship. B'K OF COMMERCE. Belfast, Me.	1 Man chopping a tree. ONE
Female with flowers. 2	State Arms with eagle at top; horse each side; cars, bridge, city and building in distance. Title of Bank.	2 Female with cornucopia.
FIVE Female with shield seated in figure 5.	Vig. Battle of New Orleans CENTRAL BANK, Alabama.	Word five and letter V. View of cattle, telegraph and railroad. FIVE
TWO Two females with arms extended, holding grain	Vig. Steamship. B'K OF COMMERCE. Belfast, Me.	2 TWO
3 Fremont.	Man watering three horses from trough by side of well; goat, kid and sheep; cattle and house in distance. Title of Bank.	3 Two cherubs soaring with distaff and sheaf.
10 X 10	Vig. Female reclining; eagle on left; cars crossing bridge in distance. CENTRAL BANK, Alabama.	10 X 10
3 Sailor seated with quadrant and spyglass, compass by his side, steamship and vessel on right. 3	Farmer and sailor on either side of a shield, representing commerce and industry. B'K OF COMMERCE, Belfast, Me. Geese.	3 Female seated on merchandise.
5 Justice	Title of Bank. Three females sculpturing bust of Washington.	5 on FIVE. Female seated.
20 Female artist.	XX Liberty and eagle. CENTRAL BANK, Alabama.	20 Cars.
V FIVE	Vig. Spread eagle, on either side flags with the names of the different States. B'K OF COMMERCE, Belfast, Me. Geese.	5 Female.
X Five cupids, globe and anvil.	Title of Bank.	10 Five cherubs with rake and tablets.
50 Cupid Mechanic.	SLATER BANK, N. Providence, R. I. Lovers at the well. State Arms.	50 Cupid. Portrait of Slater.
X Dog's head.	Ship building. BANK of COMMERCE Belfast, Me. Female head.	10 TEN
1 Female, representing agriculture; cars crossing bridge on right.	Register's die. Vig. Commercial scene; milkmaid seated with pail on her lap, farm house in background. HOOSIER BANK, Logansport, Ind.	1
Letter C. Portrait of Slater.	Liberty and Eagle. SLATER BANK, N. Providence, R. I. State Arms.	100 Female Manufacturer.
TWENTY Indian with bow and arrow, and boat near him; vessel in distance.	XX Two females with scroll, liberty pole and grain, cornucopia at their feet; cars crossing bridge on right; vessels on left. BANK of COMMERCE Belfast, Me. Female head.	20 Bridge.
2 Female with quadrant, anchor at her side; spread eagle at top of shield on left.	HOOSIER BANK, Logansport, Ind. Register's die.	2 Forest scene men chopping trees.
500 Portrait.	Fame, viz., Female blowing trumpet SLATER BANK. N. Providence, R. I State Arms.	500 Mechanic.

1 | Goddess of Liberty with cap and shield and eagle. | 1 Female with cornucopia. STARK BANK, Bennington, Vt. | 1 | Head of Gen. Stark.

2 | Head of Abby Hutchinson. | 2 | Train of cars; city and mountains in distance. STARK BANK, Bennington, Vt. Nymph bathing. | 2 | Head of Gen. Stark.

FIVE | Head of Gen. Stark. | 5 Drover on horseback with dog, driving sheep; mill in distance. STARK BANK, Bennington, Vt. Wheelbarrow and sheaf. | 5 | Head of Washington.

X | STARK BANK, Bennington, Vt. Head of Gen. Stark. Winged female with cornucopia; female with quadrant. State arms and two females. | 10

20 | Female with sheaf, sickle, &c. | Head of Gen. Stark supported by Liberty, Justice, and Truth; ship in background. STARK BANK, Bennington, Vt. | 20 | Head of Webster.

Female seated. | 50 | Signing the Declaration of Independence. STARK BANK, Bennington, Vt. | 50 | Head of Gen. Stark.

Female. | 5 | Family on a raft. BK. OF KANAWHA, Malden, Va. | 5 | Female in figure 5.

10 | Female. | Milkmaid seated with cattle. BK., OF KANAWHA, Malden, Va. | 10 | Washington on horse. | TEN

20 | Locomotive. | 20 | Manufactories and view of town. BK., OF KANAWHA, Malden, Va. | 20 | Washington.

3 | Female grain and sickle. | BANK OF YANCEYVILLE, North Carolina. Vig. Interior of a tobacco factory. | 3 | Male portrait.

4 | BANK OF YANCEYVILLE, North Carolina. Vig. Same as 3s. IV | 4 | Male portrait.

V5V | Mechanic and tools. | BANK OF YANCEYVILLE, North Carolina. Vig. State arms of North Carolina; ship on right; bridge and cars on left. | 5 | Washington.

X | Male portrait. | BANK OF YANCEYVILLE, North Carolina. 10 Vig. Female, sickle and grain; farm house in background; cars crossing bridge on left. | TEN

20 | Faust, Guttenburgh, and Schoffer; manufacturing. Portrait of Washington. BANK OF YANCEYVILLE, N. C. | XX | Male portrait.

L | Mechanic and mechanical tools. | BANK OF YANCEYVILLE N. C. FIFTY. | 50 | Male portrait.

ONE | Man on horse. | MARINE BANK OF GEORGIA. Portrait of Female. One. | 1 | ONE

2 | Goat and anchor, two sailors one with spy glass. | MARINE BANK OF GEORGIA, Male Portrait. TWO | 2 | 2

FIVE | Group of figures, liberty, &c. | MARINE BANK OF GEORGIA, Male Portrait. FIVE | FIVE | 5

MARINE B'K OF GA. | X | 10 | Male portrait. Jasper rescuing the American prisoners. MARINE BANK OF GEORGIA. TEN | 10

20 | XX | MARINE BANK OF GEORGIA. Vig. Coat of arms; male figure on either side. | 20 | Male portrait.

50 | L | MARINE BANK OF GEORGIA, Vig. General Oglethorpe in council with the Indians. Male portrait. | 50

100 | C | MARINE BANK OF GEORGIA. Male figure with [illegible]; view of [illegible] and ship, city in distance. Male portrait | 100

1 | ONE | Compt's Die. | Vig. Wild Horses. UNADILLA BANK, Unadilla, N. Y. | 1 | Child and rabbits.

2 | Drover and Cattle. Compt's Die. UNADILLA BANK, Unadilla, N. Y. | 2 | Female Portrait.

5 | Two men, one a stone cutter; masons at work in background. UNADILLA BANK, Unadilla, N. Y. | 5 | FIVE | Compt's. Die.

1 | Female | ONE | 1 Female Indian, shield, merchandise, compass, artists' tools, etc.; ship on right. BK. OF THE STATE OF GEORGIA. 1 | Female with cornucopia. | ONE

TWO | Female Indian, artists tools, merchandise &c. | TWO | Med. head and Two on it. Med. head and Two on it. Female on either side of a shield, BK., OF THE STATE OF GEORGIA. | 2 | Female with sword and scales in figure 2. | TWO

Liberty resting her hand on shield.	5 Floating female with cornucopia. BK., OF THE STATE OF GEORGIA.	5 Canal and bridge. 5

20 Washington. 20	Med. head and figures 20. Med. head and figures 20. Signing the Declaration of Independence. Title of Bank. 20 20	20 Female seated with book; vill in background. DOLLARS

2 Man Woman and dog.	Head of Franklin. Farmer with pipe seated on plow, yoke of cattle on right, farm house on left. SOMERSET CO. B'K. Somerville, N. J. Farm implements.	2

TEN Ship. TEN	10 Female seated on merchandise, holding scales; cars, wharf and ship on left; houses in background. BK., OF THE STATE OF GEORGIA.	X Liberty, eagle and shield.

XX 20	Title of Bank. Shield, female with sword and balances, seated on merchandise; cars crossing bridge on left. TWENTY.	20 Man plowing with two horses.

Indian with bow and arrow. THREE	3 Harvest scene farmers at lunch. SOMERSET CO. B'K. Somerville, N. J.	THREE. Female THREE

TWENTY Female with wand, seated on merchandise. 20	20 Spread eagle; farm scene on left; light-house and vessels on right. BK., OF THE STATE OF GEORGIA.	20 Female, grain and sickle.

50 50	Title of Bank. Female. Shield on either side a female.	50

5 Female.	SOMERSET CO. B'K. Somerville, N. J. Vig. Same as One. FIVE in circular Die. Farming Implements.	5 Franklin. 5

Female with cornucopia. 50	BK., OF THE STATE OF GEORGIA. Words Fifty Dollars, and figures 50	50 Sailors' head.

100 C	United States Capitol. Title of Bank.	100

10 Washington. 10	Vig. Drove of cattle and sheep; man on horseback; public house on left. SOMERSET CO. B'K. Somerville, N. J. Farming implements.	10 Female with spear and balances; eagle and small portrait of Washington

C Female, grain, and sickle.	BK., OF THE STATE OF GEORGIA. Words One Hundred Dollars, and figures 100	100 Vessel.

1 Deer.	B'K OF THE NORTH-WEST. Foudulac, Wis. Man, woman, and child.	1 State die. ONE

XX Female. XX	SOMERSET CO. B'K. Somerville, N. J. 20 Vig. Man plowing with two horses, also man with spade on his shoulder, Female,	20 Two farmers with cradle and grain.

ONE Two lovers. ONE	Interior of blacksmith's shop, with men at work. 1 on med head on either side. AUGUSTA INS. AND BANKING CO., Augusta, Geo.	ONE 1 on med. head. ONE

2 State die. TWO	B'K OF THE NORTH-WEST, Fondulac, Wis. Raft scene.	2 Female with grain on her shoulder.

50 Two females with wand and spyglass seated on merchandise	SOMERSET CO. B'K. Somerville, N. J. Vig. Two females seated, with cornucopia and wand steamboat on right; anchor and vessel on left. 50	50 Male portrait.

2 Washington. TWO	2 Horse and train of cars; houses in background. 2 Title of Bank.	Portrait of Clay. Liberty in figure 2; cars and factory on left.

3 Female with spyglass seated on merchandise vessel on left.	Train of cars, group of male and female figures. B'K OF THE NORTH-WEST. Fondulac, Wis.	3 State die. THREE

Female erect with sword, cornucopia at her feet. HUNDRED	SOMERSET CO B'K. Somerville N. J. 100 Vig. Two females with flag overlooking the sea, on which is seen a ship in distress; eagle on right. 100	

FIVE Male portrait FIVE	Title of Bank. Med. head and fig. 5. Med. head and fig. 5. Two females on a rock; cars on right; vessels on left. V V	FIVE Female with cornucopia. FIVE

5 State die. FIVE	Cattle and sheep; buildings in background. B'K OF THE NORTH-WEST. Fondulac, Wis.	5 Farmer sharpening his scythe.

5 Letter V, and five. FIVE	Catching cattle with the lasso AGRICULTURAL BK. Mount Sterling, Ind	Letter V, five and figure 5. FIVE FIVE

10 Male portrait 10	Med hd and fig. 100. Spread eagle on shield; vessels on left. Med hd and fig. 100. Title of Bank. X X Dog's head.	TEN Female with sword and balances. TEN

ONE Male portrait ONE	1 Female on either side of Unicorn with horn of plenty, liberty pole and cap, cars and factories on the left. SOMERSET CO. B'K, Somerville, N. J.	Female with wreath of flowers. ONE

10 X 10	battle at New Orleans AGRICULTURAL BK. Mount Sterling, Ind.	10 Bull's head TEN

ONE Indian. 1 Harvest scene. 1 BURLINGTON COUNTY BANK, Medford, N. J. ONE Two females, one with sickle and grain.	3 View of Clifton House at Niagara Falls. Vig. Same as ones. ZIMMERMAN BANK Elgin, Ca. 3 Queen Victoria.	1 Female. NEW YORK AND VIRGINIA STATE STOCK BANK, Evansville, Ind. ONE and figure 1 1 Male portrait
TWO Cattle. TWO 2 Liberty in large figure 2. 2 BURLINGTON COUNTY BANK, Medford, N. J. 2 Milkmaid.	Female with grain and sickle. FIVE 5 Vig. Same as ones. ZIMMERMAN BANK Elgin, Ca. 5 Train of cars; village in background.	2 Female with scales seated on merchandise, cars on left. Title of Bank. 2 Female.
THREE Man seated on rock. State arms. 3 Vig. Female representing agriculture; cars crossing bridge on right. 3 BURLINGTON COUNTY BANK, Medford, N. J. THREE Female drawing water from a well; steamboat in distance.	10 Vig. Same as ones. Portrait of Prince Albert ZIMMERMAN BANK Elgin, Ca. 10 Female with grain.	THREE Female giving eagle drink. THREE Title of Bank. THREE Figure of Justice. THREE
5 Letter V on medal. head. FIVE 5 Vig. Cattle and teaming; view of town; bridge and coach in back-ground. 5 BURLINGTON COUNTY BANK, Medford, N. J. 5 Letter V on medal head. FIVE	20 View of Clifton House at Niagra. ZIMMERMAN B'K, Elgin, Ca. Vig. Same as Ones. 20 Female with spy-glass seated on merchandise ship on left.	FIVE 5 FIVE Title of Bank. 5 FIVE on letter V. 5
10 Franklin. 10 10 Three female figures representing Agriculture, Science and Art. 10 BURLINGTON CO. BANK, Medford, N. J. X Franklin. X	1 Cow, female, sickle, and grain. Interior of a cotton factory. DODGE COUNTY B'K, Beaver Dam, Wis. 1 Compt's die.	10 X 10 Title of Bank. Female. 10 X 10
20 Male portrait XX 20 Interior of a manufactory, men at work, houses in foreground. 20 BURLINGTON CO. BANK. Medford, N J. 20 Male portrait XX	Female and sheaf of grain. 2 Farmer cutting corn. DODGE COUNTY B'K. Beaver Dam, Wis. 2 Compt's die.	XX Title of Bank. Vig. Female with scroll and spear on either side of shield. 20
50 Male portrait 50 50 William Penn, treating with the Indians. 50 BURLINGTON CO. BANK. Medford, N. J. 50 Male portrait 50	5 Farmer carrying corn. Elliott preaching to the Indians. DODGE COUNTY B'K, Beaver Dam, Wis. 5 Compt's die.	L Female with shield and balances, artists tools, &c. Title of Bank. 50 Spread eagle. L 50
100 Washington. 100 100 Signing the Declaration of Independence 100 BURLINGTON CO. BANK, Medford, N. J. 100 Male portrait 100	5 Man drinking from a brook STARK CO. BANK, Canton, Ohio. Male portrait. Webster and Calhoun conversing together. V FIVE	V Man drinking from a brook. IRON BANK, Ironton, Ohio. Male portrait. 5 Calhoun and Webster conversing. FIVE
1 View of the Clifton House at Niagara Falls. View of the great bridge at Niagara Falls, and cars passing over. ZIMMERMAN BANK Elgin, Canada. 1 Female and mechanical implements	Ten figures, male and female. Male portrait STARK CO. BANK, Canton, Ohio. X TEN	Group of 10 figures, male and female. Male portrait. IRON BANK, Ironton, Ohio. 10 X

Register's die. / Squaw with bow and arrows. Cattle and sheep. B'K OF FONDULAC Fondulac, Wis. 1 / Female and grain.	Same as on five shillings note. ONE ONE Same as Five Shilling note. CHARLOTTE CO. B'K. St. Andrews, N. B. ONE POUND Same as Five Shillings note. ONE	Large figure 5, in centre of which is portrait of Washington. Female reclining on sheaf with sickle; in distance men loading wagon with sheafs and city. BANK OF BELLOWS FALLS, Bellows Falls, Vt. Agricultural implements. 5 / State arms.
Register's die / Female. Title of Bank. Harvest scene and train of cars. 2 / Indian with gun.	Same as on Five Shilling note. THREE THREE Same as Five Shilling note. CHARLOTTE CO. B'K, St. Andrews, N. B. THREE POUNDS Same as Five Shilling note. THREE	Large X with portrait of female and portrait of Franklin. Man on horseback, drove of cattle and sheep. BANK OF BELLOWS FALLS. Bellows Falls, Vt. 10 / Female with sword and scales.
Milkmaid and cattle. Man and two horses; house on right; train of cars on left. Register's die. B'K OF FONDULAC. Fondulac, Wis. 3 / Farmer with cradle and grain.	Same as Five Shilling note. FIVE Vig. Same as Five Shilling note. FIVE CHARLOTTE CO. B'K. St. Andrews, N. B. FIVE POUNDS Same as Five Shilling note FIVE	Female with horn of plenty, pole and cap. / 20 BANK OF BELLOWS FALLS. Bellows Falls, Vt. 20 Female seated with sickle, cows and house on left. 20 Cupid on back of reindeer. 20 / Sheaf. / 20
5 / Hunter with dog. B'K OF FONDULAC, Fondulac, Wis. Reg. die Female Indian, horn of plenty at her feet; steamship and vessel on right; shield, flags, safe, eagle at top of globe, and cars on left. 5 / Dog, safe, and key.	Same as on Five Shilling note. TEN TEN Vig. Same as Five Shilling note. CHARLOTTE CO. B'K. St. Andrews. N. B. TEN POUNDS Same as Five Shilling note TEN	50 / State arms. / 50 Title of Bank. 50 Male seated with pole, mechanical implements; ship on left. 50 Spread eagle. 50 / Two men and cattle. / 50
B'K OF NEWBURY, Wells River, Vt. The 1s, 2s, 3s, 5s, and 10s, are a special stereotype plate with the words "Wells River," in fine letters throughout the upper part of the notes and the denomination in the same manner on lower half	5 / Vulcan with hammer, anvil, forge &c. / Word shillings and letter V. ONE ONE Female seated with sword and scales, lion on right; steamboat on left in distance. CENTRAL B'K OF N BRUNSWICK, Fredericton. N. B. Wharf scene—bales boxes ... men, shipping, &c ONE DOLLAR	1 / Milkmaid. / ONE Harvest scene. SUGAR RIVER B'K. Newport. N. H. 1 / Locomotive.
20 / Female with spear. 2 Female. 0 Title of Bank XX 20 / Female seated. / 20	ONE / Male seated with gun and dog. / ONE 1 British Coat of Arms. 1 CENTRAL B'K OF N. BRUNSWICK. Fredericton. N. B. ONE POUND Steamboat. 1 / Circular Die and word ONE repeated several times therein. / 1	2 / Eagle on top of shield; female on right with quadrant. 2 Harvest scene; man on horse. SUGAR RIVER B'K, Newport. N. H. 2 / Squaw and pappoose.
50 / Female with spear. Male and female seated. Title of Bank. 50 50 / Cupid in boat. / 50	FIVE / Male portrait / FIVE 5 St George fighting the Dragon. 5 CENTRAL B'K OF N. BRUNSWICK. Fredericton. N. B. FIVE POUNDS Lion on a crown. FIVE / FIVE / FIVE	THREE SUGAR RIVER B'K. Newport, N. H. Commerce, Agriculture, and Manufacture. 3
100 / Man with sleigh, anchor Vig. Spread eagle upon branch of tree; canal scene on right; train of cars crossing bridge on left. Title of Bank. 100 100 / Female with rake, seated beside cornucopia.	Female with spear supporting ornamental fig. 1. / ONE 1 Female seated with left arm on bale, spinning wheel on her right; city, bridge, &c. in distance. BANK OF BELLOWS FALLS. Bellows Falls, Vt. Cars 1	FIVE FIVE Sailor, mechanic, and farmer offering grain to Liberty; eagle on her right. SUGAR RIVER B'K. Newport, N. H. 5 / Eagle and Liberty; shield and figure 5.
Ornamental column with figure of female with spear thereon. FIVE SHILLINGS — FIVE SHILLINGS Female seated on boxes, bales, &c.; ship on right and left. CHARLOTTE CO. B'K, St. Andrews, N. B. Female seated, anchor, bales, vessels, &c. FIVE SHILLINGS	2 Train of cars; depot, steam-boat &c. on left. Cupid and fig. 2. BANK OF BELLOWS FALLS, Bellows Falls. Vt. Ox and a tree. TWO / Female seated on bale, horn of plenty at her feet.	X / Two men with rakes. SUGAR RIVER B'K. Newport, N. H. Spread eagle and shield; on either side vessels. 10 / Two females, one kneeling with sickle and grain

Figure of Justice with shield. 20 Little girl; man plowing with oxen. SUGAR RIVER B'K, Newport. N. H. 20 Female, grain, and sickle.	X State Arms. Portrait of Washington; milk maid with pail, and cattle on right; two females representing agriculture on left. Title of Bank. 10 Portrait of Jenny Lind.	3 Washington and horse. Female. 3 Female. WARWICK BANK, Warwick. R. I. 3 Male.
Liberty with starry drapery and shield. Three females. SUGAR RIVER B'K, Newport, N. H. 50	XX Male portrait. State Arms. Liberty and eagle. Title of Bank. 20 Male portrait.	FIVE Female holding her treasure. V WARWICK BANK, Warwick. R. I. 5 Female.
Female giving eagle drink. 100 Shield with portrait of Washington, eagle at top; on either side Liberty, Truth, and Justice. SUGAR RIVER B'K, Newport, N. H. 100 Male head. 100	Drovers and cattle. 1 State die. BK. OF SYRACUSE, Syracuse, Ind. Scene. 1 Bridge.	10 X 10 Man standing side of an ox. 10 WARWICK BANK, Warwick, R. I. TEN
2 TWO 2 Farming scene, female in large fig. 2. BANK OF CLAIBORNE, Tazewell, Tenn. 2 Two farmers with rakes on their shoulders; dog at side, boy, dray, and house in background.	5 State Die. Drove of wild horses. BK. OF SYRACUSE, Syracuse, Ind. Dog. 5 Male portrait.	20 Female sitting, with book. XX Eagle. XX WARWICK BANK, Warwick. R. I. 20 Ship under sail.
3 Secured by public stock, &c. THREE BANK OF CLAIBORNE, Tazewell, Tenn. Truth, deer, shield, grain and sheep on right. THREE Two Cupids in figure 3.	ONE Portrait of Washington. ONE 1 Smiths at a forge. 1 WARWICK BANK, Warwick, R. I. ONE Female. ONE	Woman and three little children on left. ONE B'K OF COMMERCE, Cleveland, Ohio. Male Portrait. Girl, lamb, man, sheep. ONE DOLLAR in part circle
FIVE Female with shield in figure 5. Secured, &c. Three Cupids farming, figure 5, sheep, grain, rake, &c.; view of ship on left. BANK OF CLAIBORNE, Tazewell, Tenn. Letter V, figure 5 and five. Squaw and Pappoose.	1 Bust of Washington Female. 1 Female. WARWICK BANK, Warwick, R. I. 1 Bust of Franklin.	3 Man Woman and two children. Grape Scene making wine Male Portrait. BK. OF COMMERCE. Cleveland. Ohio. 3 3
ONE Man seated CAMBRIDGE VALLEY BANK, North White Creek, New-York. Interior of a blacksmiths' shop; mechanic and tools. 1 State arms.	TWO Female. 2 2 Female portrait, two men seated. 2 WARWICK BANK, Warwick, R. I. TWO Female. 2	Figure 5, woman and three children on left, man drinking from brook. B'K OF COMMERCE, Cleveland. Ohio. Male Portrait. Calhoun and Webster talking. V FIVE
Word two and $ mark. Female drawing water from a well; steamboat on left. Title of Bank. Horse on either side of a shield; eagle at top; cars crossing bridge and view of city on right; building on left 2 State Arms	2 Male portrait Female horn of plenty. 2 Female holding balances. WARWICK BANK Warwick. R. I. 2 Male portrait	Group of ten fig. male and female. Male Portrait. B'K OF COMMERCE, Cleveland, Ohio. TEN X
5 State Arms. Title of Bank below vig. Drovers and cattle; also, farm-house. 5 Two females, with bow, grain and sickle	THREE Man with scythe. 3 3 Female and eagle. 3 WARWICK BANK, Warwick, R. I. THREE Mariner. 3	5 Male portrait Six oxen drawing a load of cotton, negro driver; in distance, house and trees, and negroes picking cotton. FARMERS AND EXCHANGE BANK. Charleston. S. C. 5 Portrait of Calhoun

10
Male portrait.
FARMERS' AND EX. BANK,
Charleston, S. C.
River scene; ships, steamers, etc; houses, &c., in distance.
10
Negroes picking cotton; houses and trees in the distance.

TWENTY
Vig. Indian and female on either side of shield.
MANUFACTURERS' BANK,
Birmingham, Ct.
20
Mechanic seated, factories on left

II
Indian chief's head.
Truck wagon and two-horse team; train of cars on left.
BANK OF FAYETTEVILLE,
Fayetteville, N. C.
TWO
2
2

20
Load of cotton, two negroes on top; man in front, cart and horse, men, trees, &c.
FARMERS AND EXCHANGE BANK,
Charleston, S. C.
XX
20
Portrait of Washington.

50
Three dogs, barking at birds.
Vig. Three female figures, agriculture, liberty and art.
MANUFACTURERS, BANK.
Birmingham, Ct.
Locomotive.
50
Female reaping.

V
5
Liberty, Agriculture, and Commerce between them figure 5; cars on left.
5
BANK OF FAYETTEVILLE,
Fayetteville, N. C.
FIVE
Female, sickle, grain, and cornucopia.

50
Same as 20s.
FARMERS' AND EXCHANGE BANK,
Charleston, S. C.
L
50
Webster.

C
Little girl and dog.
Vig. Wild horses.
MANUFACTURERS' BANK,
Birmingham, Ct.
100
Machinery, female at work.

X
Male portrait
10
Two females; Liberty, Agriculture and Commerce; ships on left.
X
BANK OF FAYETTEVILLE,
Fayetteville, N. C.
10
Washington.
X

C
Vessels, &c.; small boat in front of a ship.
C
FARMERS AND EXCHANGE BANK.
Charleston, S. C.
100
Female erect with rake; haymaking in background.

MERCHANTS BANK.
Massillon, Ohio.
For a description of the first plate of the Merchants' Bank see Springfield Bank, Ohio, page 186.

XX
Cars, wharf, and city in distance.
XX
20
Vig. Same as tens.
BANK OF FAYETTEVILLE,
Fayetteville, N. C.
20
Male portrait

1
Washington.
ONE
Vig. View of river and town.
MANUFACTURERS' BANK
Birmingham, Ct.
1 Locomotive 1
1
Ship.
ONE

Woman, and three children on left.
1
Male portrait.
Female and dog: man shearing sheep; also cars.
MERCHANTS BANK,
Massillon, Ohio.
One dollar in part circle.

ONE and figure 1.
Gen. Taylor.
TIPPECANOE BANK,
Winamac, Ind.
State Die.
Woodmen chopping tree; men in background, cooking, representing early settlers.
1

2
Male portrait
TWO
Vig. Same as ones.
MANUFACTURERS' BANK,
Birmingham, Ct.
2 2
Mechanic's arm and tools.
2
Train of cars, village in background.
TWO

3
Man, woman, and children; grape scene—making wine.
Male portrait.
MERCHANTS BANK
Massillon, Ohio.
3
Three and figure 3.

Five and letter V.
TIPPECANOE BANK,
Winamac, Ind.
Home in the Western country.
State Die.
5
Male portrait

THREE 3 THREE
Male portrait.
THREE
Vig. Same as ones.
MANUFACTURERS' BANK.
Birmingham, Ct.
3 3
Steamboat.
3
Agriculture, female, grain and sickle.
THREE

V5V
Man drinking from brook.
MERCHANTS BANK.
Massillon, Ohio.
Male portrait.
Five and letter V.
Calhoun and Webster conversing together.
FIVE

X
Female seated between figure 10; farming implements, &c; farming on right.
TIPPECANOE BANK,
Winamac, Ind.
State Die.
10
Agriculture female with sickle, seated on shield

5
Female.
FIVE
Vig. Man plowing with horse and oxen,
MANUFACTURERS' BANK
Birmingham, Ct.
Spread eagle.
5
Blacksmiths at work
FIVE

Group of ten figures, male and female.
Male portrait.
MERCHANTS BANK,
Mas..n. Ohio.
X
10

5
Female portrait.
MOHAWK BANK
Schenectady, N. Y.
Indian in canoe going over rapids.
Canal lock
5
Compt's die.
FIVE

10
Female and cornucopia.
TEN
Vig. Liberty, Justice and truth on either side of shield; eagle on top of shield.
MANUFACTURERS' BANK,
Birmingham, Ct.
X Machinery. X
10
Mechanic's arm, anvil, hammer, &c
TEN

ONE
Liberty and shield.
1 Floating female with cornucopia; view of ocean and ships.
BANK OF FAYETTEVILLE.
Fayetteville, N. C,
ONE

TEN
Male portrait
MOHAWK BANK,
Schenectady, N. Y.
Indian in canoe going over rapids.
Loading hay.
10
Female portrait.
Compt's die

1	AMERICA BANK, Trenton, N. J.	ONE
State arms.		
1	1 Large Die 1	Male portrait ONE

TWO	AMERICA BANK, Trenton, N. J.	2
State arms		Male portrait
2	Die 2 Die	TWO

3	AMERICA BANK, Trenton, N. J	3
State arms.		Webster.
THREE	Die Die Die	THREE

FIVE	AMERICA BANK, Trenton, N. J.	V
Male portrait	Die Die Die Die Die	Washington.
State arms.	FIVE	5

TEN	AMERICA BANK, Trenton, N. J.	Three females, anchor, sickle, and grain.
State arms.	X	

Sailor with flag and quadrant; mechanic seated on merchandise; vessel below.	XX	State arms.
	AMERICA BANK, Trenton, N. J.	20

50		L
Depot and train of cars; also cars crossing bridge in distance.	AMERICA BANK, Trenton, N. J.	State arms.

	Spread eagle on shield; on either side, flags with the names of the different States.	100
C	AMERICA BANK, Trenton, N. J.	State arms.

3	FARMERS' BANK. Elizabeth City, N. C.	3
Eagle, liberty starry drapery and shield.	Vig. Three females.	

IV	FARMERS' BANK, Elizabeth City, N. C.	4
	4 Two sailors and female with spy-glass in boat. IV	

FIVE	FARMERS' BANK, Elizabeth City, N. C. 5	5
Two Indians.	FIVE	Female and Indian on either side of shield.

6	Spread eagle on limb of tree factories on right cars crossing bridge on left. 6	6
Male portrait	Title of Bank. SIX	Female with grain and and sickle, farmhouses and church spires in background.

7	Harvest scene.	7
Eagle at top of shield anchor and female with quadrant on right.	FARMERS' BANK, Elizabeth City, N. C.	Female.

8	Eagle at top of shield on either side of shield.	8
Little girl and dog.	FARMERS' BANK, Elizabeth City, N. C	Washington.

X	State Die. Spread eagle and shield, ship on left.	10
Female and child also harvest scene.	FARMERS' BANK, Elizabeth City, N. C.	Male portrait

20 XX	Shield, view of bridge and canal female on either side representing agriculture and commerce. 20	XX
20	FARMERS' BANK, Elizabeth City, N. C.	XX

50	Female and eagle, cars crossing bridge, city in distance.	50
	FARMERS' BANK, Elizabeth City, N. C.	

100	FARMERS' BANK. Elizabeth City, N. C.	100
Milkmaid seated with cattle.	ONE HUNDRED.	Shield, Justice and truth.

Secured, &c. ONE DOLLAR in part circle	Truth; factories on shield, grain and sheep on right.	1 ONE
1	BANK OF MIDDLE TENNESSEE, Lebanon, Tenn.	Artist and tools.

Secured, &c.	Indian and sailor on either side of shield; eagle at top. ship on right.	2
2	BANK OF MIDDLE TENNESSEE, Lebanon, Tenn.	Washington.

Secured, &c.	3 Spread eagle on shield ship on left.	3
Male portrait	BANK OF MIDDLE TENNESSEE, Lebanon, Tenn.	Male portrait

FIVE Secured, &c.	Portrait of Clay. Spread eagle and shield vessels on either side.	5
FIVE	BANK OF MIDDLE TENNESSEE. Lebanon, Tenn.	Male portrait

Male portrait	Two trains of cars, another crossing bridge in distance.	1
1	HOPE BANK, Warren, R. I.	Female portrait

Male portrait	Two cherubs with swords and two silver dollars; cars, hills and steamboat in distance.	2
2	HOPE BANK, Warren, R. I.	Female portrait.

3	Milkmaid milking cow; another lying down.	3
Male portrait THREE	HOPE BANK, Warren, R. I.	Female portrait

Soldier with sword.	Male and female portrait. 5	Justice erect
FIVE	HOPE BANK, Warren, R. I.	FIVE

Female portrait.	Bales and barrels. Female seated representing Commerce; ship in distance.	10
X	HOPE BANK, Warren, R. I.	Indian princess.

Left	Center	Right
1	COMMERCIAL BANK Memphis, Tenn. Three females. State die. ONE	1
Large die and Two Dollars in semi-circle. Female's head. Farm house, &c.	TWO DOLLARS. B'K OF WARSAW, Warsaw, Ind. State die.	Large die and Two Dollars in semi-circle. Female's head. Cattle, &c
TEN Med. head. TEN	Title of Bank. Med. head and Ten. Two females, with pole and scroll; cars on right, vessels on left. Med. head and Ten.	X Female. 10
2 State die.	COMMERCIAL BANK Memphis, Tenn. Two females with scroll, liberty pole, and cap; cars on right; steamboat and vessels on left. 2 Vessel and building.	2
5 Indian looking over precipice; sail boat below.	B'K OF WARSAW, Warsaw, Ind. Four dies in semi-circle. Female's head.	5 State die.
20 Washington. 20	Title of Bank. Med. head and figs. 20. Female Indian reclining on shield; steamship on right; merchandise and artists' tools around her. Med. head and figs. 20.	20 Female 20
State die.	COMMERCIAL BANK Memphis, Tenn. Two sailors and female in row boat; female with spyglass. Large letter V and word five.	5 5
1 Farming implements. ONE	Vig. Train of cars. BANK OF CHATTANOOGA, Chattanooga, Tenn. Steamboat.	1 Female with sword and balances.
50 Med. head. 50	Med. head and figures 50. Two females, Agriculture and Commerce. Med. head and figures 50. Title of Bank.	Female with cornucopia. 50
X TEN	COMMERCIAL BANK Memphis, Tenn. Female teaching child; little girl running to meet her father, dog barking at her. Shells.	10 State die.
2 State die. 2	Vig. Female on either side of a male portrait—representing commerce and agriculture; locomotive on right; vessel on left. BANK OF CHATTANOOGA. Chattanooga, Tenn. Temple,	2 Commerce and Agriculture. TWO
100 Med. head. 100	C Spread eagle on branch of tree. C Title of Bank.	Female erect with liberty pole and cap.
ONE	Male, female, boy, girl, dog, etc. 1 E. B. HINCKLEY & CO.'S BANK OF GRANT CO., Platteville, Wis.	1 Compt's die.
3 View of telegraph and bridge, cars passing through.	Vig. Steamboat. BANK OF CHATTANOOGA. Chattanooga, Tenn. Female bathing.	3 View of cattle, telegraph and railroad.
Secured, &c. Little girl and dog.	FIVE, letter V, and figure 5. female giving eagle drink. BANK OF MEMPHIS, Memphis, Tenn.	5 FIVE
2 TWO	Title of Bank. 2 Drove of cattle and sheep; boy in water; man on horseback; house in distance.	2 Compt's die.
Female with wand holding shield, on which is med. head.	BANK OF CHATTANOOGA, Chattanooga, Tenn. Vig. Three females. 5 Locomotive.	5
Secured, &c. 10	BANK OF MEMPHIS, Memphis, Tenn. Female reclining; eagle on right; view of cars crossing bridge and city in distance.	X Male portrait
5 Compt's die.	Men at work in mine. Title of Bank.	5 5
X Group of five female figures, one holding liberty pole.	BANK OF CHATTANOOGA, Chattanooga, Tenn. TEN	10 Gathering cotton.
Secured, &c. Male portrait	20 Public building. BANK OF MEMPHIS, Memphis, Tenn.	20 Spread eagle on shield.
X Compt's die.	Title of Bank. Man plowing with two oxen.	10 Agricultural implements. TEN
TWENTY	Title of Bank. Vig. Mechanic, sailor and two females; city and lighthouse on right. 20	20 Two females seated, one with sickle, man holding fork, dog at his side; cattle and grain on left.
Word five, figure 5 and letter V.	B'K OF TAZEWELL, Tazewell, Tenn. Vig. Farmers at lunch, load of hay and houses in background. 5 Blacksmith's shop, smith shoeing horse.	5
1 State die.	B'K OF WARSAW, Warsaw, Ind. Large die and one dollar in semi-circle. Girl's head.	1 Bridge.
FIVE Med. head. FIVE	Med. head and fig. 5. Liberty and Agriculture on either side of fig. 5; view of village on right and left. Med. head and fig. 5. PLANTERS BANK OF the STATE of GEO. Savannah, Geo.	FIVE Female. FIVE
10 Male portrait. TEN	Vig. Capitol at Washington. B'K OF TAZEWELL, Tazewell, Tenn.	X Female giving to eagle drink.

Left	Centre	Right
Sailor, mechanic and two females, representing industry, art and commerce.	B'K OF TAZEWELL, Tazewell, Tenn 20 Vig. Milkmaid seated with cattle.	20
1 Child and rabbits.	Drovers and cattle. STAFFORD BANK, Stafford Springs, Ct.	1 Locomotive.
3 Female figure.	Scene in blacksmith's shop; man shoeing horse, &c. MERCANTILE BANK Providence, R. I.	3 Male figure.
Letter L on shield. 50 L	B'K OF TAZEWELL, Tazewell, Tenn. Secured &c. Vig. Public Building.	50
Farmer with scythe, village in distance. TWO	STAFFORD BANK, Stafford Springs, Ct. Drove Wild horses.	2 Child holding hen and chickens.
5 Sailor leaning on capstan.	Steamship, sailing vessels, &c. MERCANTILE BANK Providence, R. I.	5 Female reaper with bundle of grain.
ONE Farmer seated under tree; scythe hanging on limb.	Man watering three horses from trough by side of well; goat, kid and sheep; cattle and house in distance. COMMERCIAL BANK OF NEW JERSEY, Perth Amboy, N. J.	1 Sailor seated with telescope.
3 Female.	STAFFORD BANK, Stafford Springs, Ct. 3 Three Cupids anvil, hammer, grain, globe, compass and square. 3	3 Portrait of Franklin.
10	Rural scene—cows; church in the distance. MERCANTILE BANK Providence, R. I.	10 Portrait of female.
TWO Female feeding fowls.	Steamship and other vessels. Title of Bank.	2 Indian female seated.
5 FIVE	5 STAFFORD B'K, 5 Stafford Springs, Ct. Female on either side of portrait of Webster representing Commerce and Agriculture.	5 FIVE
20 Anchor, boxes, barrels, &c.	Ships, &c., sailing MERCANTILE BANK Providence, R. I.	20 Train of cars; village in the distance.
5 Ship.	Title of Bank. Whaling scene.	5 Sailor.
Farm yard scene. 5	STAFFORD BANK, Stafford Springs, Ct. FIVE Female.	5 Female.
50 Jupiter (God of Thunder) in his chariot.	MERCANTILE BANK Providence, R. I.	50 Man with arms full of corn stalks.
1 Blacksmith with sledge.	Man watering three horses from trough by side of well; goat, kid and sheep; cattle, trees and house in distance. RICHMOND BANK, Alton, R. I. Stockholders, etc.	1 Jenny Lind.
5	Female and grain on her head, harvesting in the background. 5 Dogs chasing Deer. STAFFORD BANK, Stafford Springs, Ct. FIVE	5 FIVE
Portrait of Columbus.	MERCANTILE BANK Providence, R. I. Head of Franklin; on either side cupid. Head of Washington; on either side cupid. 100	100
2 Female erect and another kneeling.	State Arms; two females on right, factories in distance; train of cars on left. RICHMOND BANK, Alton, R. I. Stockholders, etc.	2 Two cherubs soaring with distaff and sheaf.
TEN Farmer sickle and grain. 10	STAFFORD BANK, Stafford Springs, Ct. X Spread eagle on shield, cornucopia on left; view of ocean and ships. X	10 Man and horse. X
500 Portrait of Webster.	MERCANTILE BANK Providence. R. I. Figures of mechanic and sailor, bale of goods; ship in distance.	500 Portrait of Washington.
5 5 in red. Ruling machine.	Three females, one in centre with wings; one on right has quadrant; the other cornucopia. RICHMOND BANK, Alton, R. I. V in red.	5 5 in red. Stockholders etc.
1 Portrait of female.	MERCANTILE BANK Providence, R. I. Figure of sailor; ships in distance.	1 Female figure.
1 Double R. R. track, locomotive and cars.	An Indian with a long spear and horse; railroad cars in the distance. BK. OF NASHVILLE. Nashville. Tenn	1 Two women, one in a stooping position, with a reaphook in one hand and sheaf of wheat in the other
1 Washington.	STAFFORD BANK. Stafford Springs. Ct. Man talking to a stone cutter, masons at work in background. Female.	1 Fig. 1 and word ONE.
2 Figure of mechanic.	MERCANTILE BANK Providence, R. I. Train of cars, male and female figures.	2
Word Two, and figure 2. Two men loading a wagon with sheafs of wheat; two oxen and a horse attached.	Large western steamboat, mountain scenery in the distance. BK. OF NASHVILLE, Nashville, Tenn.	2 TWO

Left	Centre	Right
3	River, with several steam-boats in view, and a magnificent view of the Nashville suspension bridge. BK. OF NASHVILLE, Nashville, Tenn.	3 Goddess of Justice, with scales in right hand; a woman sitting by her side, playing on a harp.
V Man drinking from brook.	Male portrait. FOREST CITY BANK, Cleveland, O.	5 Webster and Calhoun conversing. FIVE
Two males and two females.	5 Anchor. 5 CITIZENS BANK. Woonsocket, R. I.	Female and eagle. FIVE
5 Man with spade, female with sheaf, two children with lamb.	Justice with sword and scales; 5 in circle; locomotive crossing bridge in distance. BK OF NASHVILLE, Nashville, Tenn.	5 State Arms and Compt's die
Group of ten figures, male and female.	Male portrait. FOREST CITY BANK, Cleveland, O.	10 10
10 Female. TEN	1 Female. 0 CITIZENS BANK, Woonsocket, R. I.	10 Female. TEN
Two females, one erect with spear, the other kneeling with sheaf.	X Spread eagle. 10 BK OF NASHVILLE, Nashville, Tenn.	Female with a small ball, bird and staff.
1 Washington.	Female. 1 Female. CITIZENS BANK. Cumberland. R. I.	1 Male.
20 Female with spear.	2 Female. 0 CITIZENS BANK, Woonsocket, R. I. XX	20 Female 20
1 Female.	Portrait of Washington. Spread eagle on shield, ship on left. LAGRANGE BANK, Lagrange, Geo.	Word ONE and fig. 1. Squaw and papoose
1 ONE	CITIZENS' BANK, Woonsocket, R. I. Female seated with wheat in her hand; town in the distance.	1 ONE
50 Female with spear.	Male and female seated. CITIZENS BANK. Woonsocket, R. I. 50	50 Cupid in boat. 50
2 Females Head.	Shield, female with sword and balances seated on merchandise, cars crossing bridge on left, cotton plant and basket on right. LAGRANGE BANK. Lagrange. Geo.	2 Female in fig 2. Female giving eagle drink.
2 Male.	Female. 2 Female. CITIZENS BANK. Cumberland, R. I.	2 Male.
100 Man with sledge. anchor	Vig. Spread eagle upon branch of tree; canal scene on right; train of cars crossing bridge on left. CITIZENS BANK, Woonsocket. R. I. 100	100 Female with rake, seated beside cornucopia.
FIVE Female.	Two females representing commerce and Agriculture. Train of Cars. LAGRANGE BANK, Lagrange. Geo.	Word FIVE, fig. 5, and letter V. Female with scroll and scales seated on merchandise cars on left.
2 Eagle.	Two females. CITIZENS BANK, Woonsocket. R. I.	2 Bull's head. TWO
Figure of Liberty, leaning on figure 1. ONE	BANK OF EAST TENNESSEE, Knoxville, Tenn. Train of cars. Cornucopia and cotton bales.	1 Male portrait.
Figure of Justice. TEN	10 Liberty and eagle. LAGRANGE BANK, Lagrange, Geo	10 X 10
3 Washington and horse	Female. 3 Female. CITIZENS BANK, Cumberland, R. I.	3 Blacksmith with sledge.
ONE	1 Two horses with plough and driver. 1 BANK OF EAST TENNESSEE, Knoxville, Tenn Beehive and agricultural implements.	ONE Portrait of Gen. Taylor. ONE
Female and three children. 1	Male portrait. FOREST CITY BANK, Cleveland, Ohio	Female and dog farmer shearing sheep, cars in distance ONE DOLLAR
3 Train of cars. 3	CITIZENS BANK, Woonsocket, R. I. Three females.	3 Cabin. THREE
Figure 1 on shield. ONE 1	BANK OF EAST TENNESSEE, Knoxville, Tenn. Circular die, One Dollar, and male portrait.	1 Sailor, mechanic and female.
3 Man, woman and two children, grape scene, making wine.	Male portrait. FOREST CITY BANK Cleveland, O.	3 3
Eagle. FIVE	V CITIZENS BANK, Cumberland, R. I.	5 Female with basket of flowers.
TWO	Two females and mechanic reclining; train of cars in distance. Title of Bank. Train of cars and steamship in distance. Shield, flags, cannon, balls, &c.	2

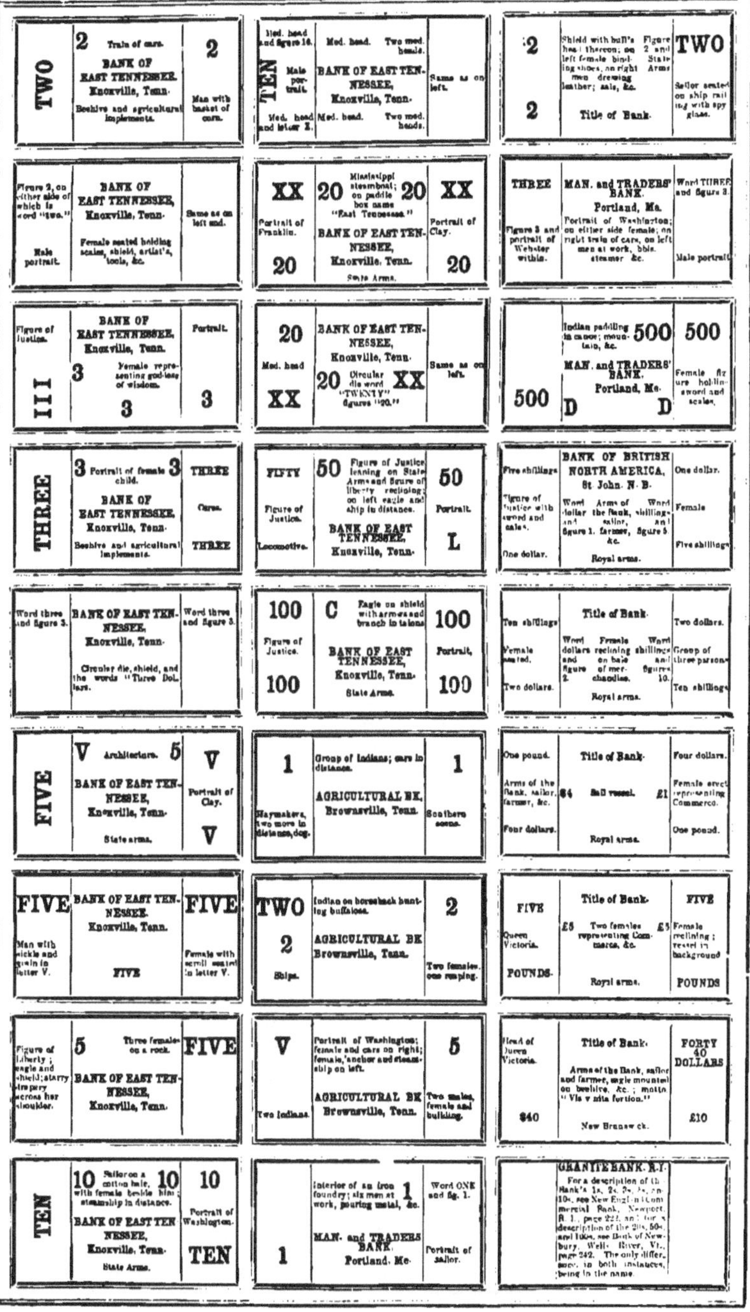

TWO
2 Train of cars.
BANK OF EAST TENNESSEE. Knoxville, Tenn.
Beehive and agricultural implements.
2
Man with basket of corn.

Med. head and figure 10.
TEN
Male portrait.
Med. head and letter X.
Med. head. Two med. heads.
BANK OF EAST TENNESSEE, Knoxville, Tenn.
Med. head. Two med. heads.
Same as on left.

2
2
Shield with bull's head thereon; on left female binding shoes, on right men dressing leather; sails, &c.
Figure 2 and State Arms
Title of Bank.
TWO
Sailor seated on ship railing with spy glass.

Figure 2, on either side of which is word "two."
Male portrait.
BANK OF EAST TENNESSEE, Knoxville, Tenn.
Female seated holding scales, shield, artist's, tools, &c.
Same as on left end.

XX
Portrait of Franklin.
20
20 Mississippi steamboat; on paddle box name "East Tennessee." 20
BANK OF EAST TENNESSEE, Knoxville, Tenn.
State Arms.
XX
Portrait of Clay.
20

THREE
Figure 3 and portrait of Webster within.
MAN. and TRADERS' BANK. Portland, Me.
Portrait of Washington; on either side female; on right train of cars, on left men at work, bbls. steamer &c.
Word THREE and figure 3.
Male portrait.

Figure of Justice.
III
BANK OF EAST TENNESSEE, Knoxville, Tenn.
3 Female representing goddess of wisdom.
3
Portrait.
3

20
Med. head
XX
BANK OF EAST TENNESSEE, Knoxville, Tenn.
20 Circular die word "TWENTY" figures "20." XX
Same as on left.

500
Indian paddling in canoe; mountain, &c. 500
MAN. and TRADERS' BANK. Portland, Me.
D D
500
Female figure holding sword and scales.

THREE
3 Portrait of female child. 3
BANK OF EAST TENNESSEE, Knoxville, Tenn.
Beehive and agricultural implements.
THREE
Cars.
THREE

FIFTY
Figure of Justice.
Locomotive.
50 Figure of Justice leaning on State Arms and figure of liberty reclining; on left eagle and ship in distance.
BANK OF EAST TENNESSEE, Knoxville, Tenn.
50
Portrait.
L

Five shillings.
Figure of Justice with sword and scales.
One dollar.
BANK OF BRITISH NORTH AMERICA, St. John. N. B.
Word dollar and figure 1. Arms of the Bank, sailor, farmer, &c. Word shillings and figure 5.
Royal arms.
One dollar.
Female
Five shillings.

Word three and figure 3.
BANK OF EAST TENNESSEE, Knoxville, Tenn.
Circular die, shield, and the words "Three Dollars.
Word three and figure 3.

100
Figure of Justice.
100
C Eagle on shield with arrows and branch in talons
BANK OF EAST TENNESSEE, Knoxville, Tenn.
State Arms.
100
Portrait.
100

Ten shillings.
Female seated.
Two dollars.
Title of Bank.
Word dollars and figure 2. Female reclining on bale of merchandise. Word shillings and figures 10.
Royal arms.
Two dollars.
Group of three persons.
Ten shillings.

FIVE
V Architecture. 5
BANK OF EAST TENNESSEE, Knoxville, Tenn.
State arms.
V
Portrait of Clay.
V

1
Haymakers, two more in distance, dog.
Group of Indians; cars in distance.
AGRICULTURAL BK, Brownsville, Tenn.
1
Southern scene.

One pound.
Arms of the Bank, sailor, farmer, &c.
Four dollars.
Title of Bank.
$4 Sail vessel. £1
Royal arms.
Four dollars.
Female erect representing Commerce.
One pound.

FIVE
Man with sickle and grain in letter V.
BANK OF EAST TENNESSEE. Knoxville, Tenn.
FIVE
FIVE
Female with scroll seated in letter V.

TWO
2
Ships.
Indian on horseback hunting buffaloes.
AGRICULTURAL BK Brownsville, Tenn.
2
Two females, one reaping.

FIVE
Queen Victoria.
POUNDS.
Title of Bank.
£5 Two females representing Commerce, &c. £5
Royal arms.
FIVE
Female reclining; vessel in background
POUNDS

Figure of Liberty; eagle and shield; starry drapery across her shoulder.
5 Three females on a rock.
BANK OF EAST TENNESSEE, Knoxville, Tenn.
FIVE

V
Two Indians.
Portrait of Washington; female and cars on right; female, anchor and steamship on left.
AGRICULTURAL BK Brownsville, Tenn.
5
Two males, female and building.

Head of Queen Victoria.
$40
Title of Bank.
Arms of the Bank, sailor and farmer, eagle mounted on beehive, &c.; motto "Vis v nita fortior."
New Brunswick.
FORTY 40 DOLLARS
£10

TEN
10 Sailor on a cotton bale, with female beside him; steamship in distance. 10
BANK OF EAST TENNESSEE, Knoxville, Tenn.
State Arms.
10
Portrait of Washington.
TEN

1
Interior of an iron foundry; six men at work, pouring metal, &c. 1
MAN. and TRADERS BANK. Portland, Me.
Word ONE and fig. 1.
Portrait of sailor.

GRANITE BANK. R.I.
For a description of the Bank's 1s, 2s, 3s, 5s, and 10s, see New England Commercial Bank, Newport, R. I., page 22[illegible], and for a description of the 20s, 50s, and 100s, see Bank of Newbury, Wells River, Vt., page 242. The only difference, in both instances, being in the name.

ONE — View of Essex and the Conn River at Essex. — ONE
Eagle, ships, &c.
SAYBROOK BANK, Essex, Ct.
ONE
Bust of female.
1 — Female, ships, bales of goods, &c. — 1

2 — Ship building — 2
Train of cars, three females, ship, &c. 2
SAYBROOK BANK, Essex, Ct.
Agricultural implements, &c.
TWO — View of Essex and Conn. River at Essex. — TWO

THREE
Female, bale, hhd., ship, &c. 3
SAYBROOK BANK, Essex, Ct.
Beehive.
THREE

5
Female, bale of goods, shipping, &c. 5
SAYBROOK BANK, Essex, Ct.
Steamboat.
5 — Female with mallet, &c.

10 — Indian, liberty cap, shield, &c.
Man, woman, bales, train of cars, anvil, nautical instruments, shipping, &c. X
SAYBROOK BANK, Essex, Ct.
Fish.
10 — Female bust.

20 — Wash'ngton on horseback
Two females, bale, train of cars, steamboat, state arms, and horn of plenty.
SAYBROOK BANK, Essex, Ct.
Elephant.
20 — Female resting on bale, shipping, &c.

ONE — Female portrait. — ONE
1 Farming plowing with two horses.
MERRIMACK CO. BK Concord, N. H.
Bell.
1 — Female portrait.

TWO — Washington — TWO
Deers, Indians in canoe, hills, trees, &c.; on a rock on left, in words "Penny Cook, 1728."
MERRIMACK CO. BK Concord, N. H.
Agricultural implements.
2 — Indian female with bow.

5 — Female erect with sword and scales.
Female soaring with eagle; shield, pole and cap, and horn of flowers.
MERRIMACK CO. BK Concord, N. H.
Deer.
5 — Farmer with sheaf on his knee.

10 — Female.
Female seated, with eagle; pole, cap and sheaf; shield on safe, &c.
MERRIMACK CO. BK Concord, N. H.
Agricultural implements
10 — Female on either side of a shield. — 10

20 — Female erect
Female seated on plow, with sickle, sheaf, &c.; on right, train of cars; on left, canal scene. 20
MERRIMACK CO. BK Concord, N. H
Bull.
20 — Figure with spear, shield and owl.

50 — Female seated; sheaf, plow, &c., on her right.
Train of cars; two men in foreground.
MERRIMACK CO. BK Concord, N. H.
Agricultural implements and products.
50 — Female seated, with spear and shield; ship on left.

100 — Vulcan seated with sledge.
Spread eagle on branch of tree; cars and canal in background.
MERRIMACK CO. BK Concord, N. H.
100
100 — Female with rake.

1 — ONE — State arms.
COLUMBIA CO. BK. Portage City, Wis.
Railroad train.
ONE — Portrait of Penn.

2 — State arms.
Rural scene—cattle, sheep, land, water.
COLUMBIA CO. BK. Portage City, Wis.
2 — Female.

5 — State arms. — FIVE
Chariot of the Sun.
COLUMBIA CO. BK. Portage City, Wis.
5 — Train of cars

ONE — Farmers boy with ears of corn in left hand holding cornstalk in right. — ONE
1 Deck of ship with sailor at wheel steering. 1
COMMERCIAL B'K. Providence, R. I.
ONE — Portrait of Indian female with bow in hand, quiver on back. — ONE

2 — Male portrait
COMMERCIAL B'K, Providence, R. I.
Man-of-War and other vessels.
2 — Commercial scene sailor with quadrant, right hand on capstan.

THREE — Female with basket of grapes in right hand. — THREE
3 Two females sitting, at right orange tree, team and wagon in distance; on left bale of goods, ship and steamer in distance.
COMMERCIAL B'K, Providence, R. I.
THREE — Sailor on deck of ship with telescope; ship in distance. — THREE

5 — Female seated holding roll of cloth in left hand, machinery on right. — 5
Vig. Steamboat Boston. 5
Three medallion in frame with words "Five Dollars" running across.
Title of Bank.
Cupid mounted on Stag.
FIVE

5 — Male portrait
COMMERCIAL B'K, Providence, R. I.
Commercial scene group of three sailors; one seated with spyglass.
5 — Child's Head

10 — Ship under full sail. — 10
Female seated left arm resting on vase; in right hand pitcher pouring water in basin; spread eagle on left.
COMMERCIAL B'K, Providence, R. I
Anchors, barrels, and ship in distance.
10 — Shield with view of mill on left; female with pole and cap on right; Indian with rifle. — X

10 — Interior of a blacksmith shop, smith at work.
COMMERCIAL B'K, Providence, R. I.
Commerce and Manufacture shield with anchor and hope, female on right, female with scroll and scales on left.
10 — Male portrait

20 — Female erect with pole and cap, shield with view of mill on right. — 20
20 Neptune in car drawn by sea horses; on right ship in distance. 20
COMMERCIAL B'K, Providence, R. I.
Indian in canoe.
20 — Female seated with sword and balances, resting with left arm on column. — 20

50 — Female with cornucopia in right hand on left arm resting on shield with view of house. — 50
Title of Bank.
Shield; view of machinery on shield, eagle surmounting; on right female with sword and balances, on left female with spear and helmet, bridge and ship in distance. 50
FIFTY
FIFTY

100 — Female erect with hands supporting anchor on right. — 100
100 Shield with eagle holding small shield in talons on large shield; on left female seated with pole and cap; ship in distance, on right cog wheel, anvil, &c. 100
Title of Bank.
Female reclining.
100 — Female erect holding anchor on right. — 100

Full length statue of Washington. — 500
500 500
COMMERCIAL B'K, Providence, R. I.
Female supporting shield in right hand, pole and cap in right, on left spread eagle, all resting on globe.
Spread swan feeding young swans.
Full length figure of female, left arm resting on column in right hand scroll. — 500

Auditor's die — 1 — ONE
RAIL ROAD BANK Decatur, Ill.
Train of cars; canal, river, village, &c.
Clasped hands.
ONE — 1 — ONE

2
Vig. Same as ones.
RAIL ROAD BANK, Decatur, Ill.
Child's head.
2 — Auditor's die

5
RAIL ROAD BANK, Decatur, Ill.
Vig. Same as ones.
V — Auditor's die — FIVE

1 — Male erect, barrels, &c.
Two females reclining with eagle and shield; cars on right; steamboat on left.
PENINSULAR BANK Detroit, Mich.
Plow, sheaf of wheat, &c.
1 — Vessel under full sail.

2 — Two female portraits
Female reclining, sheaf of wheat, country scene, &c.
PENINSULAR BANK Detroit, Mich.
2 — Female sitting. — TWO

THREE — Female, pole, liberty cap, &c.
Female sitting, barrels, &c.; ship on right; cars and factory on left.
PENINSULAR BANK Detroit, Mich.
Safe.
3 — Floating figure. — THREE

FIVE — 5 — FIVE
Female reclining on bale of goods, barrel, &c.; vessels on right; cars on left.
PENINSULAR BANK Detroit, Mich.
Safe.
5 — Female sitting; male with shield figure 5, safe, &c.

TEN — Indian standing with bow and arrow.
10 Female sitting, pole, liberty cap, spread eagle, &c.
PENINSULAR BANK Detroit, Mich.
Plow, sheaf of wheat, &c.
TEN — Squaw and papoose. — TEN

5 — FIVE — State arms.
Eagle on shield. 5
UNION BANK of LA. New Orleans, La.
5
Figure 5 and full length portrait of Washington.

10 — State arms. — Ten Dollars
View of a Western steamboat loaded with cotton.
UNION BANK of LA. New Orleans, La.
TEN — Female feeding an eagle — 10

Female with spear. — TWENTY
State arms. Signing Declaration of Independence.
UNION BANK of LA. New Orleans, La.
Eagle.
XX — Bust of a female. — 20

50 — Female figure.
State arms. Marion dining with the British officer.
UNION BANK of LA. New Orleans, La.
Female seated.
50 — Farmer seated with sheaf of wheat by his side. — FIFTY

100 — State arms.
View of the Capitol at Washington as enlarged.
UNION BANK of LA. New Orleans, La.
Figure of Justice seated.
100 — Spread eagle and shield. — 100

Figure of Justice and a female seated at her side. — $500
State arms. Female with pole and cap crowning an eagle with wreath, shield, anchor, and a portrait of Washington.
UNION BANK of LA. New Orleans, La.
Sailor seated.
500 — Female with sickle and sheaf. — 500

5 — Auditor's die; pelican feeding her young. — 5
FIVE Mechanic seated and resting arm on anvil, holding in left hand a sledge; factories and a stream of water in the background.
MECH. & TRADERS' BANK. New Orleans, La.
Steamship
5 — Female with a sheaf. — 5

10 — Train of cars. — TEN
Auditor's die. Female seated, globe on her right; in distance sea, ship, and steamship.
MECH. & TRADERS' BANK, New Orleans, La.
Mechanical implements, &c.
10 — Female seated.

20 — Sailor boy holding the end of an oar — XX
Auditor's die. Female seated on a rock; cupids sporting with a dolphin.
MECH. & TRADERS' BANK, New Orleans, La.
Plow, sheaf, &c.
20 — Portrait of Franklin. — XX

50 — Sailor with spyglass. — FIFTY
Auditor's die. Mechanic seated with hammer and chisel in hands; in background men at work on boiler; foundry; vessel on right.
Title of Bank
Mechanic's arm and hammer.
50 — Female seated, left arm on a screw wheel. — 50

Auditor's die — Female seated. — 100
100 Female seated on an eagle in full flight.
Title of Bank.
Interior of a blacksmith's shop; anvil, screw wheel, and the hand of a mechanic with hammer.
100 — Vulcan with sledge. — 100

NORTHERN BANK, Hallowell, Me.
This Bank uses the old Perkin's Stereotype plate, which has the denomination printed in fine letters all over the bill.

ONE
Inside of a weaving room; females and looms 1 on left. 1
BANK OF KENT, Coventry, R. I.
ONE — Male Portrait — ONE

2
Man driving cows; factory and village, 2
BANK OF KENT, Coventry R. I.
State arms.
TWO — Head of Franklin. — TWO

5
Forest and factory standing back. 5
BANK OF KENT, Coventry R. I.
State arms.
FIVE — Head of Washington — FIVE

10 — X — 10
Yoke of oxen and man. 10
BANK OF KENT, Coventry, R. I.
State arms.
TEN — Female erect

20 — Female seated
XX Eagle. XX
BANK OF KENT, Coventry, R. I
20 — Ship, &c.

FIFTY — Female erect — FIFTY
50 Man and horse. 50
BANK OF KENT, Coventry, R. I.
FIFTY — Female erect — FIFTY

100 — Eagle — 100
C Horses and men in a chariot, in the clouds. 100
BANK OF KENT, Coventry, R. I
C — Head of Washington. — C

ONE — Bust of Washington. — ONE | 1 Interior of a Blacksmith shop. 1 — ANDROSCOGGIN BK Topsham, Me. | ONE — Female — ONE

TWO — Female — 2 | 2 Farming scene. 2 — ANDROSCOGGIN BK Topsham, Me. | TWO — Female. — 2

THREE — Man sharpening a scythe — 3 | 3 Female and eagle. 3 — ANDROSCOGGIN BK Topsham, Me | THREE — Sailor. — 3

5 — Blacksmith at work at anvil. — FIVE | Mercury erect with right hand on shield on which is figure 5; anchor, sheafs, bales, &c.; ship and man plowing on right; train of cars, buildings, &c. on left. V — ANDROSCOGGIN BK. Topsham, Me. | 5 — Female seated with sheaf — FIVE

FIVE — Two females. — V | FIVE Female seated with right hand on shield on which is 5; ships' masts in background. FIVE — ANDROSCOGGIN BK Topsham, Me. | 5 — Eagle. — 5

FIVE | Spread eagle on shield; buildings and vessel in distance. V, female, and cupid. — ANDROSCOGGIN BK Topsham, Me. | 5 — Girl with basket of flowers.

10 — Farmer sowing. — TEN | Vig. Same as first five, with the exception of the figures. Canal scene. — ANDROSCOGGIN BK Topsham, Me. | 10 — Female, &c. — TEN

TEN — Man pouring water from an urn. — TEN | TEN Female seated with key in right hand. TEN — ANDROSCOGGIN BK. Topsham, Me. | 10 — Head of Indian. — 10

Vulcan seated; anvil, &c. around him; in distance buildings, train of cars, &c. — TEN | X — ANDROSCOGGIN BK. Topsham, Me. | 10 — Farmer with sheaf on his knee.

20 — XX — 20 | 20 Female with sickle in left hand, seated, bale, bbls. &c.; ship in distance. 20 — ANDROSCOGGIN BK. Topsham, Me. | TWENTY

50 — Female leaning on rock; steamboat in distance. — 50 | 50 — ANDROSCOGGIN BK. Topsham, Me. | FIFTY

C — Portrait of Washington. — C | 100 Man seated pouring water from an urn; ship in distance. 100 — ANDROSCOGGIN BK. Topsham, Me. | ONE HUNDRED

1 — Med. Head. — 1 | 1 Female seated with right hand on eagle and left on shield safe by her side. — BANK OF CUMBERLAND Portland, Me. | Large figure 1 and full length female.

2 — Med. Head. — 2 | 2 Female seated on safe with cornucopia &c., farmer plowing on right; building &c., on left. — BANK OF CUMBERLAND, Portland, Me. | Large figure 2 and full length female.

3 — Med. Head. — 3 | Figure 3 and three cupids therein. Sportsman, female and child seated, train of cars on right; log house on left. — BANK OF CUMBERLAND, Portland Me. | Large figure 3 and full length female.

5 — Female seated with sledge; cog wheels &c., buildings in distance. | Female seated with sprig in left hand; eagle, shield, sheaf, train of cars, &c., on right, town ocean and vessels on left. — BANK OF CUMBERLAND. Portland, Me. | 5 — Portrait of Washington

Sailor with flag; bale, bbl., anchor and quadrant — TEN | Shield on which is figure 10; on right farmers seated with sickle, and man on horseback, and negro driving drove of pigs; on left female, rudder, safe and steamboat. — BANK OF CUMBER LAND. Portland, Me. | 10 — Female Portrait.

XX — Male portrait — 20 | 20 Vessels sailing, &c. XX — BANK OF CUMBERLAND, Portland, Me. | 20 — Male portrait — XX

50 — Male portrait — FIFTY | Steamboat, schooners, sloops, &c; Female seated with spear and shield. — BANK OF CUMBERLAND, Portland, Me. | 50 — Male portrait — FIFTY

100 — Portrait of Van Buren. — 1.0 | C Ship under full sail on ocean, two vessels in background. C — BANK OF CUMBERLAND. Portland, Me. | 100 — Male portrait — 100

500 — Portrait of Van Buren. — 500 | Vig. Same as hundreds. 500 — BANK OF CUMBERLAND. Portland. Me. | 500 — Portrait of Jackson. — 500

1000 — Portrait of Jackson. — 1000 | Vig. Same as 20's. Female seated with spear and shield. — BANK OF CUMBERLAND. Portland, Me. | 1000 — Portrait of Van Buren — 1000

ONE — 1 | Farmer sowing. 1 — HIGH STREET B'K, Providence, R. I. | 1 — Ship. — ONE

1 — Portrait of Washington. | Female. 1 Female. — HIGH STREET B'K. Providence, R. I. | 1 — Portrait of Franklin.

TWO — 2 | Eagle on a rock. 2 — HIGH STREET B'K, Providence, R. I. | 2 — TWO — Vessels.

2 — Male portrait | Female. 2 Female. — HIGH STREET B'K, Providence, R. I. | 2 — Male portrait

THREE — 3 | Sailor with hat in hand; bales of merchandise, shipping, &c. 3 — HIGH STREET B'K. Providence, R. I. | 3 — THREE — Train of cars

3 Washington on his horse	Female. 3 Female. HIGH STREET B'K, Providence, R. I.	3 Male figure.

Female figure seated.	5 Steamship and other vessels. Title of Bank. Pelican.	5 Sailor erect; ship in distance.

Two men bearing a female on their shoulders. 500	500 Portrait of 500 Mrs. Washington Title of Bank. Pelican.	Female seated holding basket of flowers; at her feet the letter D. 500

FIVE	Eagle on shield and anchor; buildings, vessels, &c. V, female and child. HIGH STREET B'K, Providence, R. I.	5 Girl with basket of flowers.

10 Male bust. 10	X Female seated, left arm resting on an escutcheon. Title of Bank.	Roman senator in robes with casque. TEN

Figures 1000 supported by two nymphs. Portrait of Washington.	Sea view—steamship and three ships. Title of Bank. Pelican.	1000

FIVE	Female. 5 HIGH STREET B'K, Providence, R. I.	5 Ship.

10 Female seated with spear and branch.	Triton in his car conducting a female. Title of Bank. Farmer leaning on plough	10 Ship.

V FI V VE V	Cattle scene; steamboat in distance. PEOPLES' BANK OF S. C.	5 Male portrait

10 X 10	Man and oxen. 10 HIGH STREET B'K, Providence, R. I.	TEN Female.

20 View of the Cathedral and adjoining buildings in N. O. TWENTY	20 2 Female. 0 Title of Bank	20 Female seated between 2 and 0.

Word Capital and figures 1,000,000, supported by three females as a pedestal. TEN	PEOPLES' BANK OF S. C Blacksmith beside an anvil, right hand holding hammer, left resting on cog wheel.	10 Female figure, head partially covered.

TEN	Vulcan seated; factory and cars in distance. X HIGH STREET B'K, Providence, R. I.	10 Farmer with sheaf on his knee.

20 Female bust. 20	Title of Bank. Female seated, bale, cask, &c.; view of city in distance.	XX Female seated, pail at her feet.

Female seated with sickle. 20	20 PEOPLES' BANK OF S. C. Portrait of W. R. King of Ala.	20 Stone mason at work, tools &c., at his feet.

20 Female.	XX Eagle. XX HIGH STREET B'K, Providence, R. I.	20 Ship.

FIFTY A bust. 50	L Child seated holding an escutcheon; coin around him. Title of Bank.	FIFTY Roman bust. 50

50 Two female figures seated, surveying a cotton field and negroes at work with railroad cars in dist.	PEOPLES' BANK OF S. C. Portrait of John C. Calhoun.	50 Blacksmith standing beside his anvil hand resting on the handle of his sledge, anchor and cog wheel near him.

FIFTY Female erect FIFTY	50 Man and horse. 50 HIGH STREET B'K Providence, R. I.	FIFTY Female erect FIFTY

50 Female bust.	Female seated resting left arm on an escutcheon; on right the head of a bird appearing; cornucopia by her side. Title of Bank. Steamboat.	50 Female erect and three children playing around her.

Collin's steamer under full head of steam and sails set; ship in distance. C	C PEOPLES' BANK OF S. C. Game cock crowing.	100 Male portrait

Figures 100 and words one hundred. Male portrait	Wharf scene men loading wagon; shipping, &c HIGH STREET B'K Providence, R. I.	Figures 100 and words one hundred Male portrait

100 100	C Three ships under way, with all sail set. C Title of Bank.	100 Female with pole and cap 100

1 ONE Male portrait	Three Females with compass, sickle and quadrant in their hands, anchor on right, cornucopia between the two on left. Secured, &c. B'K OF MEMPHIS, Memphis, Tenn.	1 Female with left hand on shield.

5 Female holding sickle in right hand. FIVE	LOUISIANA STATE BANK, New Orleans, La. Female seated, right arm resting on a bird	5 Eagle in the act of flying away from a vase on which is a shield.

100 Public building 100	Head of Washington surmounted by an eagle, with female on either side, city, steamboat, &c., in distance. Title of Bank. Pelican.	100 View of town and steamboats. 100

Secured, &c. TWO Male portrait	Train of cars. B'K OF MEMPHIS, Memphis, Tenn.	2 Female with globe in right hand, bird perched upon it, spear in left resting on ground.

1 Compt's die.	Blacksmith shop, three men at work, and two more at work in background. PASSAIC CO. BANK, Paterson, N. J.	1 Male portrait
Female seated on rock, with pole and cap. 10	Indian female crowning bust with wreath; on right of bust, female with pole and cap. bbl., bale, ship, &c.; sheaf, fruit, &c., on left of Indian female STATE CAPITAL BK. Concord, N. H.	X Man seated with rake; left arm resting on frame on which is "Ten."
Female seated with sword in right hand. TWENTY	Man with two horses (white and black); farmhouse on right; train of cars, water, &c., on left. WALDOBORO BANK Waldoboro', Me. Steamboat.	20 Female seated about to look through spyglass; vessel in distance.
2 Compt's die.	PASSAIC CO. BANK, Paterson, N. J. Large machinery, machinist standing, &c.	2 Male portrait
XX XX	STATE CAPITAL BK Concord, N. H. Harvest scene; man, female and child; man with sickle—another sharpening scythe, and one reclining on ground; loading wagon on right.	20 Female barefooted, with sheaf of grain.
50 50	WALDOBORO BANK Waldoboro', Me. Ship yard; men at work, buildings in background. Dog, key, and safe.	50 Man sharpening scythe, steamboat in distance.
ONE Schooner. ONE	1 Female seated representing Agriculture and Commerce; train of cars, steamboats, &c., in distance. 1 NORTH KINGSTON BANK. Wickford, R. I. Spread Eagle, &c.	ONE Female. ONE
50 Blacksmith shoeing horse, colt present; anvil, &c.; steam engine.	STATE CAPITAL BANK, Concord, N. H. FIFTY	50 Female feeding horse from apron.
100 Henry Clay seated, dog by his side.	WALDOBORO BANK Waldoboro', Me. Female seated in a shell with trident; ships in background. Indian.	100 Female milking cow, one lying down, girl on right
TWO Vessels, &c. TWO	2 Two females seated; wharf scene and vessel on left; steamboat on right, and ship at the females back. 2 NORTH KINGSTON BANK, Wickford, R. I. Arm, hammer, &c.	TWO Female seated with shield on which is anchor. TWO
100 Portrait of Frank Pierce	STATE CAPITAL BK. Concord, N. H. Farmer, wife and children in sitting posture; farm houses; load of grain, dog, &c. One Hundred	Large letter "C." Cupid astride of a sea monster.
Two men carrying female on their shoulders. ONE	Agricultural scene; man reaping, and female with sheaf in her arms. WOODSTOCK BANK, Woodstock, Vt. Female.	1 State Arms. ONE
THREE Vessels, and men in row-boats. 3	3 Male and female in car drawn by two sea horses; ships and steamboat in distance. 3 NORTH KINGSTON BANK, Wickford, R.I. Schooner.	THREE Female seated with torch book, eagle and portrait Washington. 3
1 Indian seated on rock, gun beside him.	Two horses and a colt; farm houses in distance. WALDOBORO BANK Waldoboro', Me. Beehive.	1 Spread eagle
Man with sheaf of grain on his knee.	2 Female seated on plow with sheaf and sickle; train of cars on right. 2 WOODSTOCK BANK, Woodstock, Vt. Sheaf, plow, &c.	Milkmaid erect.
Female reclining on bale with scales in right hand. 1	STATE CAPITAL BK. Concord, N. H. Female reclining with pole and cap; eagle and motto "E Pluribus Unum," on right; in distance on left, steamer and ship.	1 Female with sickle, leaning on ornamental figure 1.
TWO William Penn (full length) with scroll in hand	Indian seated on rock with gun in right hand; city, steamer, steamboat, &c., in distance. WALDOBORO BANK Waldoboro', Me. Spread eagle.	2 Vessel at sea TWO
Female with horn of plenty at her feet, figure 3 on shield. THREE	Forest scene with deers. WOODSTOCK BANK, Woodstock, Vt. Man plowing	3 Indian Queen
2	STATE CAPITAL BK. Concord, N. H. Male at work on chart with compass; on right, three men, two horses and cart. TWO	2 Female sporting with a swan in water.
THREE	Man-of-war with sails set; in distance steamship and vessel. 3 WALDOBORO BANK Waldoboro', Me. State arms.	THREE
5 Portrait of Washington.	State Arms; on either side female and cupid. WOODSTOCK BANK, Woodstock, Vt. Sheaf, plow, &c.	5 Female Portrait.
THREE Female erect with pole, cap and scroll in hands; shield scales, &c.	STATE CAPITAL BK. Concord, N. H. Milkmaid seated, with pail on lap; five cows on her left.	3 Female portrait.
5 FIVE	Three females floating in water, supporting a cupid. 5 WALDOBORO BANK Waldoboro', Me. Head of sailor.	5 Female portrait.
10 Med. head and word TEN. Some cars	State Arms, on left female seated with pole and cap; on right eagle. WOODSTOCK BANK, Woodstock, Vt. Bull.	10 Male and female; male shearing sheep; mill in back ground.
5 Female portrait.	STATE CAPITAL BK. Concord, N. H. Five females, figure 5 between two of them, &c. on left, vessel, &c.; on right building, locomotive and tender.	5 Figure 5 surrounded by five human figures.
10 Female portrait. TEN	WALDOBORO BANK Waldoboro', Me. X Spread eagle on rock at sea; ship on right and left.	10 TEN
50 Female erect with spear and shield.	Female and eagle soaring in clouds with shield between them. WOODSTOCK BANK, Woodstock, Vt. Man plowing with two horses. Some dog's head	50 Female erect with hand on capstan.

ONE Soldier with gun. / Indians hunting buffalo. GREEN BAY BANK, Oconto Wis. / 1 ONE Compt's die.	2 Two females seated. / Drover and cattle. LAKE BANK, Wolfborough, N. H. / 2 Male portrait	7 Farmer seated, scythe hanging on a tree. / Three females reclining one in center holds liberty pole and cap, one on right has a compass. B'K OF CLARENDON, Fayetteville, N. C. / 7 SEVEN 7
TWO 2 Compt's die. / Backwood's scene—men at work clearing. GREEN BAY BANK. Oconto Wis. / 2 Female; cows and calf.	3 Man with grain cradle. / Farmer ploughing with horses; buildings and cars in distance. LAKE BANK, Wolfborough, N. H. / 3 Female churning.	8 8 / Woodmen at work one is seated, one chopping down a tree and one choping a tree on the ground. Man and oxen on right in back-ground. B'K OF CLARENDON, Fayetteville, N. C. / 8 8
5 Portrait of Washington. / State Arms supported by two females. B'K OF WOODSTOCK. Woodstock, Vt. / 5 Coat of Arms	Large V, surrounded by five persons. 5 / LAKE BANK, Wolfborough, N. H. Steamboat. / 5 Head of female. 5	TEN Farmer reclining, female seated, two children, a sheep and sheaf of wheat. / Large letter X, word TEN and figures 10. Steamboat under way, hills in back-ground. B'K OF CLARENDON, Fayetteville, N. C. / TEN
V Female—Goddess of Liberty. V / 5 U. S. Capitol, 5 BANK OF THE METROPOLIS. Washington. D. C. / U Eagle. S	Portrait of female. X / LAKE BANK, Wolfborough, N. H. Ten gold dollars; nine cherubs; female seated. / 10 Head of Frank Pierce 10	1 Auditor's die / LAFAYETTE BANK, Bloomington, Ills. American shield; on right female instructing children; on left Indian, squaw and papoose. / 1 Girl's head.
X Female—Goddess of Liberty. X / 10 U. S. Capitol. 10 BANK OF THE METROPOLIS, Washington, D. C. / U Eagle. S	Female with balances and sheaf of wheat. XX / Shoe and boot manufacturers. LAKE BANK, Wolfborough, N. H. / 20 Portrait of Jackson.	2 TWO / Man watering three horses from trough by side of well; goat, kid, sheep, trees and house. LAFAYETTE BANK, Bloomington, Ills. Auditor's die / 2 TWO
The 20s are the same as 10s all through, with the exception of the denomination.	Female seated. 50 / Portrait of Washington. Capitol on right; winged female on left. LAKE BANK, Wolfborough, N. H. / 50 Portrait of Webster.	Female feeding fowls. THREE / LAFAYETTE BANK, Bloomington, Ills. Drover on horseback, and cattle; boy in water; trees and farm house in distance. Three Doll's Three Doll's / 3 Auditor's die
L Goddess of Liberty. L / 50 U. S. Capitol. 50 BANK OF THE METROPOLIS, Washington, D. C. / U Eagle. S	Portrait of Cass. 100 / Harvest scene; haying; team hauling hay; female with child seated; pitcher, basket, &c. LAKE BANK, Wolfborough, N. H. / 100 Indian seated.	FIVE Train of cars / Southern scene—men, horses, mules, wagons, houses and trees. LAFAYETTE BANK, Bloomington, Ills. Spread eagle. / 5 Auditor's die
Letter C. Goddess of Liberty. Letter C. / 100 U. S. Capitol. 100 BANK OF THE METROPOLIS. Washington, D. C. / U Eagle. S	5 / Large letter V and a female with a scroll. Two females one erect other seated. The one erect holds a scroll in right hand, and liberty pole and cap in left B'K OF CLARENDON, Fayetteville, N. C. / 5 5	[New Plate.] L 50 / Cattle, and drovers driving them in the water; houses and trees in back-ground; a church in extreme distance. FARMERS' BANK OF READING, PA. Locomotive. / 50 Female erect with vase of flowers.
1 Man seated with scythe. / LAKE BANK, Wolfborough, N. H. Indian seated; deer; sailing vessel and steam-boat. / 1 Female seated with pails	6 6 / Large raft floating down river, man in boat holding up two birds, another raft on the right. B'K OF CLARENDON, Fayetteville, N. C. / 6 Squaw and female.	C Two female figures; one reclining. / [New Plate.] FARMERS' BANK OF READING, PA. / 100 Male and female; two boys, dog and a hen.

1	CANAJOHARIE BK., Canajoharie, N. Y. Compt's. die.	1
	The vig., extends the whole width and ends of the note. Vig. Hop scene, gathering hops; two horses attached to wagon; numerous male and female figures at work; trees, &c	

2	CANAJOHARIE BK., Canajoharie, N. Y.	2
Portrait of Calhoun.	Vig. Same as ones, only a different view with farm houses, &c.	Compt's. die.

3	CANAJOHARIE BK., Canajoharie, N. Y.	3
	Compt's. die.	
Shearing sheep.	3	Two men gathering corn.

5	CANAJOHARIE BK., Canajoharie, N. Y.	5
Compt's. die.	Five farmers at work, gathering hay; two oxen before hay wagon.	Clay.

X	CANAJOHARIE BK., Canajoharie, N. Y.	10
Two females, one churning; cars in distance on left.	X Portrait of a girl. X	Compt's. die.

1	Ship on stocks. Winged female seated holding fig. 1. Vessel men, bbls., &c.	1
Female with sickle.	PISCATAQUA EXCHANGE BANK, Portsmouth, N. H.	Female.
1	Male Portrait.	1

Large figure 2; Portrait of Washington and ship on stocks within.	Farmer plowing with two horses; houses, and steamboat in distance. PISCATAQUA EXCHANGE BANK. Portsmouth, N. H.	Large figure 2, Portrait of Franklin and vessels within.

3	Vessels in stocks, men at work, &c.; sloop and city in distance.	3
Sailor erect with quadrant	PISCATAQUA EXCHANGE BANK.	Farmer whetting scythe.
THREE	Portsmouth, N. H.	THREE

5	Male Portrait. Letter V, and female with sheaf within. Portrait of Washington.	5
Med. Head.		Ship on Stocks.
5	PISCATAQUA EXCHANGE BANK. Portsmouth, N. H.	5

10	Med. Head of Franklin. Large letter X and portraits of 10 of the Presidents of the U. S. Med. Head.	10
Female seated, shield, &c		Ship on Stocks.
10	PISCATAQUA EXCHANGE BANK, Portsmouth, N. H.	10

20	Portrait of Wm. Penn. Female seated with tub on knee; two cows; female milking &c. Portrait of Franklin.	20
Portrait of Washington.		Vessel on stocks.
20	Title of Bank. Spread Eagle.	20

100	Vessels. Two females seated; buildings on right, ship on left. Vessel on stocks.	100
Washington.	PISCATAQUA EXCHANGE BANK.	Male portrait
100	Portsmouth, N. H. Agricultural Implements.	100

ONE	1 on med. head. Female seated with book in hand; anvil, sleigh, &c.; in distance on left ship. 1 on med. head.	ONE
Male seated supporting the world with a lever,	MECHANICS' BANK. Newark, N. J.	Male figure seated with tablets.
1		1

1	Mechanic seated; anvil &c.; train of cars, buildings, hills, &c., in distance	1 ONE
Female with sheaf.	MECHANICS' BANK. Newark, N. J. Arm.	

TWO	MECHANICS' BANK. Newark. N. J.	TWO
Male supporting the world.	2 on med. head. Female seated with child in her arms; basket, sheafs of wheat; farmers mowing in background. 2 on med. head	Female seated with book
2	Arm.	2

2	Three males apparently in conversation; view of city in distance on right.	TWO 2
Two farmers with rakes; two in distance and house.	MECHANICS' BANK, Newark, N. J. Arm.	

THREE	3 Three females seated; trees on right; ship in distance on left. 3	Full length female with sickle.
Male supporting the world, &c.	MECHANICS' BANK. Newark, N. J.	
3	Arm.	3

3	Frame surmounted by an eagle; two females on right and female on left; ship, train of cars crossing bridge, in distance.	THREE 3
Portrait of Jenny Lind.	MECHANICS' BANK. Newark, N. J. Arm.	

5	Med. head and fig. 5. Train of cars, man leaning on fence. Med. head and fig. 5.	V
Blacksmith at work.	MECHANICS' BANK. Newark. N. J.	Sailor with hat in hand; masts in distance.
V	Arm.	5

X	Med. head and letter X. Man seated on log with left hand on dog's head, trees, &c. Med. head and letter X.	10
Canal scene; buildings in distance.	MECHANICS' BANK, Newark, N. J.	Brig.
X	Arm.	10

20	20 Female seated with sword, in left hand scales, lion on right, steamboat on left. 20	20
Sheaf.	MECHANICS' BANK, Newark, N. J,	Ship.
20	Arm.	20

50	50 Female seated arm resting on shield, on which is anchor; ship on left. 50	50
Beehive.	MECHANICS' BANK, Newark, N. J.	Eagle.
50	Arm.	50

100	100 Shield on which is figures 100, on either side of which female; reaping scene and steamboat in distance. 100	ONE HUNDRED
Plough, &c.	MECHANICS' BANK Newark, N. J.	
100	Arm.	

500	Med. head and figs. 500. Female reclining looking up; steamboat on right; building on left. Med. head and figs. 500.	500
Female erect supporting shield on which is med. head.	MECHANICS' BANK. Newark, N. J.	Female erect with sword,
	Arm.	500

1000	1000 Female seated on bale of goods, right arm resting on shield. 1000	
Two med. heads and figures 1000.	MECHANICS' BANK, Newark, N. J.	Same as on left end.
M	Arm.	

Male portrait.	EXCHANGE BANK OF COLUMBIA, S. C	5
5	Bust of Calhoun, and female seated.	Female portrait.

Portrait of Calhoun.	Female seated, with liberty pole and cap in right hand; left hand resting on shield.	10
10	EXCHANGE BANK OF COLUMBIA. S. C	Female portrait.

Three female figures grouped around an anchor. TWENTY Female seated; on her right, city in the distance; on the left, rail road in distance. EXCHANGE BANK OF COLUMBIA, S. C. Fire Engine 20 Male portrait	X TEN on Med. Head. 10 Man and boy seated; man is drawing; mill on right; Med. Head and word TEN on either side. WILMINGTON AND BRANDYWINE B'K. Delaware. 10 Man seated drawing. X	Portrait of Washington. 20 Two females reclining; ship on right. Two cupids, beehive, and figs. 20. FARMERS BANK OF DEL. Male portrait
50 Large anchor and chain; mules, and bale of cotton. Engine and train of cars. EXCHANGE BANK OF COLUMBIA, S C 50 Male portrait	20 Portrait of Washington. 20 Two females seated, shield, eagle, &c.; Med. Head and word TWENTY on either side. WILMINGTON AND BRANDYWINE B'K, Delaware. 20 Male portrait 20	50 Sailor erect with American flag. 50 FARMERS BANK OF DEL. Four cupids with baskets, sheaf of wheat, sickle, &c.; house in background. 50 Med. head and figs. 50. 50
100 Portrait of female. Three graces and a cupid. EXCHANGE BANK OF COLUMBIA, S. C Farming tools. 100 Female erect	50 Ship under weigh. 50 Female seated, plow, barrel, bale of goods, &c.; portrait of Washington on left; portrait of Lafayette, vessels, &c., on right. WILMINGTON AND BRANDYWINE B'K. Delaware. Cupid. 50 Steamboat and small boat. 50	100 Med. head and word Hundred. 100 FARMERS BANK OF DEL. View of the landing of Columbus; boats on right; Indians on left in background. Female erect with shield and pole. 100
ONE View of steamboat; building houses, trees, &c. Cupid rolling silver dollar on railroad track; cars, steamboat and city in distance. MER. & MECH. BK., New Albany, Ind. Loading hay. ONE State arms. ONE	100 Female seated, shield &c. 100 Cars and People, Steamboat on left in distance. WILMINGTON AND BRANDYWINE B'K, Delaware. Ship. 100 Female seated, letter C, eagle, shield, &c. 100	1 Portrait of Washington. Female. 1 Female. BANK OF BRATTLEBORO. Brattleboro, Vt. 1 Portrait of Franklin.
2 State arms. TWO Two Cupids, and two silver dollars; Cupids apparently in an engagement; locomotive and tender on right; cars on left; in extreme distance, city, hills, &c. MER. & MECH. BK. New Albany, Ind Man reaping. TWO Female portrait. TWO	Male portrait ONE Female seated and figure 1. 1 FARMERS BANK OF DELAWARE. Three cupids reclining. Female standing with sickle. ONE	2 TWO 2 Female 2 Female BANK OF BRATTLEBORO, Brattleboro. Vt. TWO Female. TWO
Same as on right. State arms FIVE Five Cupids, and five silver dollars; Cupids representing arts and sciences. MER. & MECH. BK., New Albany, Ind. Agricultural implements and products. 5 Word FIVE in part circle. Large figure 5, female, eagle, portrait of Washington, &c. thereon	Male portrait TWO Female with sickle, figure 2 and cupid. 2 FARMERS BANK OF DEL. Female seated and sheep. Female standing with sickle. TWO	3 Washington and his horse Female. 3 Female. BANK OF BRATTLEBORO. Brattleboro, Vt. 3 Male figure
1 Female portrait. ONE Sailor reclining, coil of rope, anchor, windlass, horn, &c. Ships on left in distance. WILMINGTON AND BRANDYWINE B'K, Delaware. Wheelbarrow, &c. 1 Mechanic. ONE	Male portrait 3 Three females, eagle, figure 3, &c. 3 FARMERS BANK OF DEL. Male reclining. Female erect with scales. THREE	FIVE Female. 5 BANK OF BRATTLEBORO, Brattleboro, Vt. 5 Ship.
2 TWO Female seated on barrel, scales, &c. Sailor and Indian, eagle, shield, &c; Ship on right in distance, tents on left. WILMINGTON AND BRANDYWINE B'K, Delaware. Arm, anvil, &c. 2	Male portrait 5 Drove of cattle, man on horse, &c. 5 FARMERS BANK OF DEL. Female erect. Male portrait	10 X 10 Man and oxen. 10 BANK OF BRATTLEBORO, Brattleboro, Vt. TEN Female.
FIVE Farmer reclining with sickle. FIVE Three men erect, one holds a pole; village and water on right. WILMINGTON AND BRANDYWINE B'K, Delaware. Locomotive. 5 Female, sheaf of wheat, &c.	Portrait of Franklin. 10 Two females, sheep, shield, &c. 10 FARMERS BANK OF DEL. Double med. head. Portrait of Wm. Penn.	20 Female. XX Eagle. XX BANK OF BRATTLEBORO, Brattleboro, Vt. 20 Ship.

FIFTY	50 Man and horse. 50	FIFTY
Female erect	BANK OF BRATTLEBORO, Brattleboro, Vt.	Female erect
FIFTY		FIFTY

Figures 100 and words one hundred	Wharf scene, men loading wagon; shipping, &c	Figures 100 and words one hundred
Male portrait	BANK OF BRATTLEBORO. Brattleboro, Vt.	Male portrait

	Female seated, steamer in the distance. Large figure 1 and portrait of five men.	1
1	FRANKLIN BANK, Chepachet, R. I.	Female with sheaf of wheat.

ONE	Vessels. 1	ONE
		Female.
	FRANKLIN BANK, Chepachet, R. I.	ONE

	Agricultural scene. Large 2, and portraits of five men.	TWO
		Female.
2	FRANKLIN BANK. Chepachet, R. I.	TWO

2	Vessels. 2	TWO
TWO		Female.
2	FRANKLIN BANK. Chepachet, R. I.	TWO

	Agricultural Scene. 3	Word THREE and fig. 3.
		Female.
THREE	FRANKLIN BANK, Chepachet, R. I.	THREE

THREE	Man with sickle cutting grain; on right female with sheaf of wheat. 3	THREE
		Steamer.
	FRANKLIN BANK, Chepachet, R. I	Word THREE and fig. 3

	Eagle on shield and anchor; buildings, vessels, &c. V, female and child.	5
FIVE	FRANKLIN BANK Chepachet, R. I.	Girl with basket of flowers.

FIVE	Female. 5	5
	FRANKLIN BANK. Chepachet, R I.	Female.

X	Steamer and sailing vessels. X	10
Indian with a bow,	FRANKLIN BANK, Chepachet. R. I.	Female holding bonnet, and sheaf of wheat.

10	Oxen and man erect. 10	TEN
X		
10	FRANKLIN BANK, Chepachet, R. I.	Female.

Vulcan seated, anvil, &c. around him; in distance buildings, train of cars, &c.	X	10
TEN	FRANKLIN BANK, Chepachet, R. I.	Farmer with sheaf on his knee.

20	XX Eagle. XX	20
Female seated, with book on lap.	FRANKLIN BANK, Chepachet, R. I.	Ship.

Steamer.	Figure of a female seated with spear and balances; eagle on left. 20	XX
XX		
Female.	FRANKLIN BANK, Chepachet, R. I.	Female.

FIFTY	50 Man and horse. 50	FIFTY
Female.		Female.
FIFTY	FRANKLIN BANK. Chepachet, R. I.	FIFTY

50	Agricultural scene. 50	L
Vessels.	FRANKLIN BANK, Chepachet, R. I.	Female.

100	C Fairies. 100	C
Eagle.		Washington.
100	FRANKLIN BANK. Chepachet. R. I.	C

Words One Hundred, and figures 100.	Wharf scene; men loading wagon with bbls.; horses, drays, men, shipping, &c.	Same as on left.
Portrait of Harrison.	FRANKLIN BANK, Chepachet. R. I.	Male portrait

Female portrait.	1 Female representing Commerce with implements.	1
1	CORN EX. BANK, Waupun, Wis.	Compt's die

Male portrait	Spread eagle and shield. 2	2
2	CORN EX. BANK, Waupun, Wis.	Compt's die.

Compt's die.	Three females and fig. 3; factories in distance. 3	3
3	CORN EX. BANK, Waupun, Wis.	Male portrait

5	CORN EX BANK, Waupun, Wis.	5
		Compt's die.
Female portrait	Farmers, etc., in cornfield.	FIVE

5	CITY BANK, Philadelphia, Pa.	5
Portrait of a boy		Portrait of a girl.
5	Signing of the "Declaration of Independence."	5

Female erect with vase of flowers.	Two females seated on either side of a shield; in centre of shield, a ship; the female on the left holds a scroll.	X
10	CITY BANK, Philadelphia, Pa.	Sailor at the helm.

50	CITY BANK, Philadelphia, Pa.	50
Large anchor, box, barrel and bale of goods	Portrait of Washington.	Beehive and flower bushes.
	State arms.	

	CITY BANK Philadelphia, Pa.	
100	Female reclining, and eagle; on left, train of cars crossing a bridge; view of a harbor and city in distance.	100
	100.	

5 Two men at work on a locomotive boiler. MECH. BANK OF PITTSBURGH, PA. 5 Female portrait.	5 Portrait of Prince Albert V Two females, cupids, and three ornamental 5s. COMMERCIAL BANK M. D., Montreal, Canada. National arms. 5 Same as ones V	X 10 Floating female. COM. BANK. M. D., Kingston, Ca. 10 Miniature view of shipping.
X Carpenter sawing a board; bench at his back. MECH. BANK OF PITTSBURGH, PA. Portrait of Washington 10 Man in shirt sleeves erect houses in background.	10 Portrait of Queen Victoria. COMMERCIAL BANK M. D., Montreal, Canada. National arms. 10 TEN	20 Portrait of Queen Victoria. Female seated dividing the figures 20, rake in her right hand. COM. BANK, M. D., Kingston, Ca. 20 Portrait of Prince Albert
Word "twenty" in part circle running up. Blacksmith erect; anvil and sledge; building in distance. MECH. BANK OF PITTSBURGH, PA 20 Three figures reclining; one on left is Mercury; the middle one holds pole and cap. 20	1000 COMMERCIAL BANK M. D., Montreal, Canada. Portrait of the Empress of France. ONE THOUSAND	Portrait of Queen Victoria surrounded by the lion and unicorn. COM. BANK, M. D., Kingston, Ca. 50 50
FIFTY Female erect with sword. 50 Sailor, farmer and mechanic; farmer holds a sickle and sheaf of wheat; man and horse and anvil on right; sheaf on left. MECH. BANK OF PITTSBURGH, PA. 50 Boy and rabbits.	1 Farm boy standing erect, holding sickle and bundle of grain. COM. BANK, M. D. Kingston, Ca. Female reclining; figure 1, cornucopia, &c. 1 1 Sailor standing erect.	100 Miniature of female, representing the Arts and Sciences. C COM. BANK, M. D., Kingston, Ca. 100 British arms 100
Two men rest; in distance, two masons at work. 100 C Mechanic, farmer, wheel, tree, horse, &c.; in background, bridge and buildings. MECH. BANK OF PITTSBURGH, PA. 100	2 Justice and Liberty erect COM. BANK, M. D., Kingston, Ca. Two females seated, cornucopia at their feet. 2 2 Two females standing erect, in representation of Agriculture and Commerce.	5 Portrait of Wm. Penn. CONSOLIDATION BANK. Phila., Penn. Steamer Quaker City under way, and view of Phila. Harbor. Portrait of Female Child. 5 Portrait of Governor Pollock.
Farmers loading wheat; yoke of oxen, horse, &c. MECH. BANK OF PITTSBURGH, PA. 500 500 Female Indian erect.	4 Female portrait. QUATRE Locomotive and train of cars; city in the background; trees, houses, load of hay, &c. COM. BANK, M. D., Kingston, Ca. 4 Female portrait. FOUR	10 Female on a platform working a mechanical instrument. A Drove of Cattle and drovers driving them to the water; house and trees in background and church in the extreme distance. CONSOLIDATION BANK, Phila., Penn. Portrait of a Female Child 10 Sailor seated with spy glass.
Farmer standing with scythe, &c. 1000 M Interior view of an iron mill, and men at work. MECH. BANK OF PITTSBURGH, PA 1000 Female portrait.	FIVE Portrait of Queen Victoria. 5 Large figure 5 enclosing female, the whole surrounded by four cupids. 5 COM. BANK, M. D., Kingston, Ca. British arms. FIVE Portrait of Prince Albert	20 Interior view of a blacksmith shop. CONSOLIDATION BANK, Phila., Penn. Raft floating down a river, man in boat holding up two birds on the right, another raft in background, trees, hills, &c. 20 Workman dressing leather.
1 Portrait of Prince Albert 1 1 Female erect holding a robe; canoe, &c. 1 COMMERCIAL BANK M. D., Montreal, Canada. National arms. 1 Portrait of Queen Victoria in ornamental frame. 1	V 5 Mercury seated, representing Commerce, Justice, &c., lion at his feet. COM. BANK, M. D., Kingston, Ca. 5 Portrait of female.	50 Cattle, telegraph poles and wires; cars and bridge in background. CONSOLIDATION BANK, Phila., Penn. The Globe or the world, and an eagle surmounting it. Portrait of a boy. 50 Woodman erect, hand resting on axe.
2 Portrait of Prince Albert 2 2 Two females seated cornucopia; ship on left; sheaf of wheat and plough on right. 2 COMMERCIAL BANK M. D, Montreal, Canada National arms. 2 Same as ones 2	10 Portrait of Queen Victoria. X Female seated in position to divide the figures 10, supporting cornucopia and key. X COM. BANK, M. D., Kingston, Ca. 10 Portrait of Prince Albert	100 Female with liberty pole and cap, left hand resting on a shield, eagle sitting on the ground. Title of Bank C 100 Female erect holding sickle in right hand, and grain in left. 100 Sailor, blacksmith and anchor.

Steamboat. 1 Female Portrait, sheaf of wheat, &c. 1 Female and red fig. 1. UNION BANK OF DELAWARE. Cars. Arm.	2 Signing the Declaration of Independence. 2 Portrait of Washington. JEWETT CITY B'K, Jewett City, Conn. Portrait of Martha Washington. TWO Spread Eagle. TWO	THREE Portrait of Jackson. Indian hunter behind a rock watching two deers. 3 THREE 3 CENTRAL BANK OF ALA.
2 UNION BANK OF DELAWARE. Two female reclining; safe, &c.; steamboat on left. Farmer seated; dog, sheaf of wheat, &c. 2	TWO 2 Female, anchor, and hope; cars in distance on right; on left spinning wheel, factory, &c. 2 Female, scales, eagle, reel, portrait of Washington, &c. Female reclining on anchor. JEWETT CITY B'K, Jewett City, Conn. TWO House, cattle, plow, trees, &c.	V CENTRAL BANK OF ALA. V Two white men and one colored, one of the white men is seated on a barrel, the other is reclining against an anvil; steamboat on right; a city on left.
5 UNION BANK OF DELAWARE. Figure 5, and five cupids. Train of cars, house, &c. 5	Female, scales, eagle, horn of plenty, casks &c. 3 Two females and one male; horn of plenty, cars, ship, safe, &c. 3 JEWETT CITY B'K, Jewett City, Conn. Agricultural Implements.	X Slaves at work in a cotton field; houses in background. 10 CENTRAL BANK OF ALA. TEN Portrait of Washington.
10 X Farmers at work in corn-field. X 10 Train of cars. Sheaf of wheat, &c. UNION BANK OF DELAWARE. X Steamboat. X	5 Two females, horn of plenty, goods, shipping, steamboat, &c. 5 Female, scales, eagle, horn of plenty, casks &c. Female, scales, &c. JEWETT CITY B'K, Jewett City, Conn. FIVE Dog, safe, &c. FIVE	20 20 XX Large spread eagle and American flag. Indian queen and tent. Portrait of Franklin. CENTRAL BANK OF ALA XX
Ship. 20 View of harbor and village. 20 Farmer erect dog and pitchfork. UNION BANK OF DELAWARE. 20 Pump. 20	5 Female with scales and rod; eagle and portrait of Washington. Figure 5; two females, Cupid with scales, eagle &c., surrounding the figure. 5 Two Heads. JEWETT CITY B'K, Jewett City, Conn. FIVE 5	L CENTRAL BANK OF ALA. 50 Slave with basket of cotton; other slave on left Female reclining with liberty pole and cap; shield, scroll, &c. Female reclining.
50 State Arms; steamship on right; cars and bridge on left. 50 Male portrait Male portrait 50 UNION BANK OF DELAWARE. 50	XX JEWETT CITY B'K, Jewett City, Conn. 20 View of manufacturing village. Three children seated. TWENTY Washington on horseback	C Indians in a canoe; trees and hills in background. ONE 100 CENTRAL BANK OF ALA. C HUNDRED C
100 100 Spread eagle, shield &c. 100 100 Female with pitcher and rake. Portrait of Washington UNION BANK OF DELAWARE. 100 Female Portrait. 100	Female erect, resting right arm on anchor; ship in distance. 50 State arms; on left female erect with horn of plenty at her feet; on right female erect with key in right hand, and "charter 1831" on left. 50 FIFTY FIFTY Title of Bank. Female seated on rock.	5 Farmers and a load of wheat. 5 CORPORATION OF ALEXANDRIA, D. C. Sailor and blacksmith. Farmer with sheaf of wheat.
1 Man on horseback; dog, flock of sheep, grist mill, &c. 1 Portrait of Gen. Taylor. Cars. JEWETT CITY B'K. Jewett City. Conn. ONE Chartered June, 1, 1831. ONE	1 Load of cotton; slave with two baskets of cotton and man on right. 1 CENTRAL BANK OF ALABAMA. Female portrait, ONE	Drove of horses running across a field. 6 Two females erect with sheaf of wheat. CORPORATION OF ALEXANDRIA. D. C. Sailor leaning against windlass.
ONE 1 Female seated holding eagle with olive leaf; horn of plenty at her feet; ships in distance. 1 Female with scales, eagle and portrait of Washington. JEWETT CITY B'K Jewett City, Conn. Female resting on an anchor; ship in distance. ONE Sheaf, plow, rake, &c.	TWO Train of cars and station house; train of cars and bridge on right. 2 CENTRAL BANK OF ALA. TWO	Farmer sowing. Indians in a canoe; hills and trees in background. 7 CORPORATION OF ALEXANDRIA, D. C. Word seven and figure 7. Female seated.

ONE | GRAYVILLE BANK, Grayville. Ill. Farmer, sailor, and blacksmith; sheaf of wheat, anvil, and man and horse on right. | 1 State arms.	TEN | 10 Drove of cattle and sheep; man on horseback. 10 FARMERS BANK OF N. JERSEY, Mt. Holly, N. J. Deer | TEN	5 State arms. FIVE | Portrait of H. Clay. Five and large figure 5. Female portrait. CANAL BANK OF CLEVELAND, Ohio. | 5 Male portrait FIVE
Farmer erect with scythe. 2 | 2 A deer and three dogs. GRAYVILLE BANK, Grayville, Ill. | 2 State arms.	FIFTY | Female with a sheaf of wheat in her hands. FARMERS BANK OF N. JERSEY, Mt. Holly, N. J. | 17 miles from Phila.	10 State arms. TEN | Male portrait. Female seated; shield and sheaf of wheat. CANAL BANK OF CLEVELAND, Ohio. Locomotive. | X Male portrait TEN
5 Sailor erect; coil of rope, &c. | Farmers at work loading hay. GRAYVILLE BANK, Grayville, Ill. | 5 State arms.	ONE HUNDRED | A Group of three females. FARMERS BANK OF N. JERSEY, Mt. Holly, N. J. | 17 miles from Phila.	X Squaw. | WORCESTER CO. BK Blackstone, Mass. Three females representing Agriculture, Commerce and Manufactures. | 10 Cupid and dolphin.
10 F[illegible] sheaf, &c. | GRAYVILLE BANK, Grayville, Ill. Portrait of Washington. | X State arms.	1 Male portrait | Train of cars; on right a city in distance; on left a man erect. B'K OF KNOXVILLE Knoxville, Tenn. | ONE Two females reclining; shield and scales.	Female giving eagle drink. 3 | BRADFORD BANK, Bradford, Vt. Mechanic, sailor and farmer, with implements; three gold dollars. | 3 Reaper seated by Three
X TEN | WESTERN EX. FIRE & MARINE INS. CO., Omaha City, Neb. Indian seated; plough, sheafs, hills, etc. | 10 X on R.N.	2 Male portrait TWO | Man on horse and boy on foot driving a drove of hogs. B'K OF KNOXVILLE Knoxville, Tenn. | 2 Drove of cattle, telegraph, cars, and bridge.	3 Farmer with scythe. | WALTHAM BANK, Waltham, Mass. Female reclining on bales, barrels, factory in distance. | 3 Mechanic, sailor and farmer with fig. 3.
TWENTY | XX Title of Bank. Three females in clouds with quadrant, sickle, compass and cornucopia. | Word Twenty, letter XX and fig. 20.	3 Male portrait THREE | Two wild horses, one white, the other black; to the right more horses in distance. B'K OF KNOXVILLE Knoxville, Tenn. | 3 Female seated on barrel, train of cars in background.	5 Boy and rabbits. | Drovers and drove of cattle; city on right, in distance. ALLENTOWN BK., Allentown. Pa. Sheaf of wheat, rake &c. | 5 Female portrait.
1 ONE Portrait of Franklin. | Man on horse, dog and drove of sheep, mill in distance. FARMERS BANK OF N. JERSEY, Mt. Holly, N. J. | 1 Portrait of Washington. ONE	1 State arms. ONE | Male portrait. Female, sheaf of wheat, &c. Female portrait. CANAL BANK OF CLEVELAND, Ohio. | 1 Male portrait.	Female erect with sheaf of wheat on her head. 10 | ALLENTOWN BK., Allentown, Pa. Farmer, sailor and blacksmith; farmer seated, and holds sickle and sheaf of wheat; anvil, horse and man on right; sheaf of wheat on left. X on left. | 10 Male portrait.
3 Portrait of Washington. THREE | Two horses (one white and the other black), and a train of cars. FARMERS BANK OF N. JERSEY, Mt. Holly, N. J. | 3 Portrait of Franklin.	2 State arms. TWO | Three men, one seated, two standing; on right ship and steamboat; on left shipyard. CANAL BANK OF CLEVELAND, Ohio. | 2 Male portrait TWO	X Female blowing a dinner horn; table, dishes, &c., men and load of hay on right. | [New Plate.] Farmers loading hay; tree on left. FARMERS' BANK OF LANCASTER, PA. | X TEN X
FIVE DOLLARS | 5 Cow and Calf. 5 FARMERS BANK OF N JERSEY, Mt Holly, N. J. Eagle | FIVE DOLLARS	3 State arms. THREE | Female portrait Male portrait and large figure 3. Female portrait. CANAL BANK OF CLEVELAND, Ohio. | 3 Male portrait THREE	Farmer sowing seed. | [New Plate.] L Large building, people, trees, &c. FARMERS' BANK OF LANCASTER, PA. | 50 Portrait of boy.

5 Three sheep; two laying down one standing. 5 Train of cars, &c.; mining view, iron furnace, &c.; train of cars on left, in distance. ANTHRACITE BK., Tamoqua, Pa. 5 Portrait of Henry Clay.	10 Indian Princess with implements of war. Spread eagle holding the American flag in its talons. PHENIX BANK, Westerly, R. I. Phenix with spread wings 10 Female in a sitting posture, holding scales over eagle, one of whose wing are extended over American Flag.	50 Agricultural scene., team, carts, railway, cars, &c. PEOPLES' EXCHANGE BANK, Wakefield, R. I. TWENTY 50 Cattle. Bull Stock.
X Portrait of Gov. Pollock. TEN 10 Farmers at work, loading hay. ANTHRACITE BK., Tamoqua, Pa. Female bathing. 10 TEN 10	20 TWENTY Female in a sitting posture, with one arm thrown over an eagle, which stands on a segment of the globe, labelled "America." PHENIX BANK, Westerly, R. I. Phenix with spread wings 20	100 Fig. of Male with bag of dollars. Three men washing sheep, village, &c. PEOPLES' EXCHANGE BANK, Wakefield, R. I. 100 Girls with a rake making hay.
20 XX 20 ANTHRACITE BK., Tamoqua, Pa. Portrait of boy. Female reclining with sheaf of wheat and sickle; farmers at work on right; train of cars and bridge on left. 20	Female with sheaf of grain, whose feet rest on the figures below. 50 Three females in a group; one holding scales; ships on the right. PHENIX BANK, Westerly, R. I. Phenix with spread wings 50	1 State Arms. ONE Male portrait. Female with sickle and sheaf; plow, &c.; canal boat in background. BANK OF GEAUGA, Painesville, Ohio. Female Portrait. Male Portrait.
Miners at work and a coal shaft; train of cars in back-ground. FIFTY 50 Portrait of Gov. Pollock. ANTHRACITE BK., Tamoqua, Pa. 50 L	1 Two females sitting by Coat of Arms; steam engine, &c. PEOPLES' EXCHANGE BANK, Wakefield, R. I. ONE 1	3 State Arms. THREE Female portrait. Male portrait. Female portrait. BANK OF GEAUGA, Painesville, Ohio. 3 Male portrait. THREE
100 ONE C HUNDRED. 100 Portrait of a girl, Woodmen at work; yoke of oxen on left, in back-ground. ANTHRACITE BK., Tamoqua, Pa. C Portrait of Webster.	2 Three male figures, cart and horse, farming scene. 2 on right. PEOPLES' EXCHANGE BANK, Wakefield, R. I. TWO 2 2 Female	5 State Arms. FIVE Portrait of Clay. 5 Female. BANK OF GEAUGA, Painesville, Ohio. Female. 5 Male portrait. FIVE
1 Portrait of Washington. 1 Female with sheaf of wheat; right hand uplifted, with stems of wheat therein; plow, female, locomotive, &c. PHENIX BANK, Westerly, R. I. Phenix with spread wings 1 Squaw 1	3 Three male figures sitting, farming scene. fig. 3 on right. PEOPLES' EXCHANGE BANK, Wakefield, R. I. THREE 3 Three men & 3	10 State Arms. TEN Male portrait. 1 Female with sheaf. 0 BANK OF GEAUGA, Painesville, Ohio. Sheaf, plow, &c. 10 Male Portrait. TEN
2 Portrait of J. Q. Adams. 2 Steamship, with a sail vessel before and aft. PHENIX BANK, Westerly, R. I. Phenix with spread wings. 2 Female with paper and dividers. 2	5 Female sitting; steamboat, rail car, steamer, &c. PEOPLES' EXCHANGE BANK, Wakefield, R. I. FIVE 5 5 females & 5	Female with cornucopia in her arms, standing beside ornamental figure 1 ONE Ox in front part of vig.; three oxen on left; two laying down; two cows in water on right, with train of cars crossing bridge in distance; trees, &c. AGRICULTURAL BK. Brownsville, Tenn. Dog's head. 1 ONE [illegible]
3 Female Female figure and Indian chief; the former holding stems of [illegible] in one hand, and sickle in the other; both reclining against a globe, on which stands a spread eagle. PHENIX BANK, Westerly, R. I. Phenix with spread wings 3 Portrait.	10 Female figure with pail and cows, &c. PEOPLE'S EXCHANGE BANK, Wakefield, R. I. 10 TEN	TWO State arms. TWO AGRICULTURAL BK. Brownsville, Tenn. Three cows; one standing and two laying down; three sheep; one standing and two laying down; farm-house in distance on left; two on right. Ox. TWO Female with fig. 2. 2
5 Portrait of Henry Clay. 5 [illegible] and female figure with machinery; ship on right, and locomotive and train on left. PHENIX BANK, Westerly, R. I. Phenix with spread wings 5 Female head. V	20 Four figures, load of hay, team and farming implements. PEOPLES' EXCHANGE BANK, Wakefield, R. I. TWENTY TWENTY 20 Female figure standing.	FIVE Farmer sharpening scythe; farm house in distance. State arms. AGRICULTURAL BK. Brownsville, Tenn. Female in clouds, with sheaf of grain and sickle. FIVE Shepherd and dog with four sheep; bridge, top of farm-house, and trees in distance. 5

1 — Male portrait. Female seated, with sheaf and sickle; train of cars, &c., in distance. Female portrait. — 1
State arms. SENECA CO. BANK, Tiffin, Ohio. Male portrait.
ONE

Two Dollars. Arms of Great Britain or lion and unicorn fighting for the crown. Deux Piastres.
BANK OF BRITISH NORTH AMERICA. Montreal, Ca. $2
Montreal. Arms of the Bank. Ten Shillings.

CINQ. Victoria seated in the royal chair. PIASTRES
BANK OF BRITISH NORTH AMERICA, Kingston, Ca. 5 Two females; lion and unicorn. 5 British arms.
FIVE. Indian chief seated. DOLLARS

3 — Female portrait. Male portrait in top of large figure 3. Female portrait. — 3
State arms. SENECA CO. BANK, Tiffin, Ohio. Male portrait.
THREE — THREE

Four Dollars. Indian seated. Quatre Piastres.
BANK OF BRITISH NORTH AMERICA, Montreal, Ca. 4 Large sail vessel; small one in background. 4 British arms.
Quatre Piastres. Miniature view of female reclining, representing Commerce. Four Dollars

DIX. Miniature view of town or city. PIASTRES
BANK OF BRITISH NORTH AMERICA, Kingston, Ca. 10 Two females reclining, shipping, &c. X British arms.
TEN. Arms of the Bank. DOLLARS

5 — Portrait of Clay. 5 Female portrait. — 5
State arms. SENECA CO. BANK, Tiffin, Ohio. Male portrait.
FIVE — FIVE

FIVE. Monument. DOLLARS
BANK OF BRITISH NORTH AMERICA, Montreal, Ca. 5 Large sail vessel; smaller one in distance. 5 British arms.
CINQ. Her Majesty seated in the royal chair. PIASTRES

VINGT. Female standing erect with spear in left hand; right hand resting on a shield. PIASTRES
BANK OF BRITISH NORTH AMERICA, Kingston, Ca. 20 Female reclining on bale of mdse. 20 British arms.
TWENTY. Miniature view of town or city. DOLLARS

10 — Male portrait. Female seated, with sheaf and sickle between ornamental 1 and 0, steamboat, shield, &c. — 10
State arms. SENECA CO. BANK, Tiffin, Ohio. Male portrait.
TEN — TEN

$10. Tent, canoe, persons, trees, &c. Ten Dollars
BANK OF BRITISH NORTH AMERICA, Montreal, Ca. Female reclining on bale of mdse., representing Commerce; shipping, &c., in background. British arms.
DIX. View of entrance to harbor; houses, vessels, &c. PIASTRES

50. Miniature view of group of three females. PIASTRES
Title of Bank. CINQUANTE Female FIFTY reclining, representing Commerce, Justice, and Agriculture. British arms.
50. Miniature view of Indian canoe, tent, trees, &c. DOLLARS

1 — Male portrait. Female seated, with sheaf and sickle; train of cars, &c., in distance. Female portrait. — 1
State arms. WESTERN RESERVE BANK, Warren, Ohio. Male portrait.
ONE

20. View of public buildings in Montreal. PIASTRES
BANK OF BRITISH NORTH AMERICA, Montreal, Ca. VINGT Group of three females, Agriculture, Commerce, &c. TWENTY British arms.
20. Monument, houses, &c. DOLLARS

1. State Arms. ONE
Female seated on a log with a pail, train of cars, sheaf of wheat &c. 1 BELVIDERE BANK, Belvidere, N. J.
ONE. Female erect. ONE

3 — Female portrait. Male portrait in top of large figure 3. Female portrait. — 3
State arms. WESTERN RESERVE BANK, Warren, Ohio. Male portrait.
THREE — THREE

Cinquante. Arms of the Bank. PIASTRES
BANK OF BRITISH NORTH AMERICA, Montreal, Ca. 50 Steamship. 50 British arms.
FIFTY. View of monument, public buildings. DOLLARS

TWO. Female with scales sword and figure 2. TWO
BELVIDERE BANK, Belvidere, N. J. Farmer at work loading wheat, one holds horse.
2. State Arms.

5 — Portrait of Clay. 5 Female portrait. — 5
State arms. WESTERN RESERVE BANK, Warren, Ohio. Male portrait.
FIVE — FIVE

Portrait of Queen Victoria.
FIVE SHILLINGS. BANK OF BRITISH NORTH AMERICA, Kingston, Ca. 1 Arms of the Bank; or sailor, husbandman, dove, beehive, &c. 1
Portrait of Prince Albert.

THREE. Female erect with liberty pole and cap. 3
Drove of sheep; Man on horse; dog; mill on left in distance. [illegible] on right. BELVIDERE BANK, Belvidere, N. J.
Female erect. THREE

10 — Male portrait. Female seated, with sickle between ornamental figure 1 and 0; steamboat, shield, &c. — 10
State arms. WESTERN RESERVE BANK, Warren, Ohio. Male portrait.
TEN — TEN

TEN Shillings. Portrait of Queen Victoria. TWO DOLLARS
$2 Arms of the Bank; or sailor, husbandman, &c. $2 BANK OF BRITISH NORTH AMERICA, Kingston, Ca.
Portrait of Prince Albert. TEN Shillings.

Male portrait. Portrait of Washington. Male portrait.
5 Two houses, farmers wagon, cattle, horses, trees, &c., hills in background. 5 BELVIDERE BANK, Belvidere, N. J. State Arms.
Portrait of Franklin. Male portrait. Male portrait.

One Dollar. Portrait of Queen Victoria. Five Shillings.
BANK OF BRITISH NORTH AMERICA, Montreal, Ca. Arms of the Bank, or sailor, husbandman, beehive, dove, cornucopia, &c.
Montreal. Portrait of Prince Albert. Une Piastre.

QUATRE. Indian chief seated. PIASTRES
Title of Bank. 4 Female reclining representing Commerce; bale of merchandise, anchor, shipping, &c. 4 British arms.
FOUR. Female surrounded by shrubbery, &c.; farming implements at her feet. DOLLARS

Horse head. Male Figure standing in front of fig. 1. X
10 Female seated on rock with arm around eagles neck; men in boat in distance. 10 BELVIDERE BANK, Belvidere N. J.
Flowers. Female, Bust of Washington on pedestal with eagle and shield at bottom. 10

Left end	Centre	Right end
Female head. Male erect.	20 Three females, two seated, one erect. 20 BELVIDERE BANK. Belvidere, N. J.	TWENTY
TWO Two Indians reclining, one smoking, falls in back ground. TWO	2 Three females, two erect and one seated, plow, &c., ship on stocks, &c. 2 CRANSTON BANK. Cranston, R. I. Cattle.	TWO Washington TWO
5 State arms, FIVE	Portrait of Gen. Taylor. Large figure 5 and word five at top. Female portrait SMITHFIELD EXCHANGE BANK. Greenville, R. I.	5 Med. head 5
Female erect with cornucopia. 50	50 Three females seated on bales &c, one smile looking toward vessels; on right sheafs of grain; farm house, rake, &c., on left. 50 Title of Bank. State Arms.	Female erect with sheaf of grain and sickle. 50
THREE	Farmer in field of wheat. Spread eagle, shield, &c. 3 CRANSTON BANK. Cranston, R. I. Old fashioned cars and locomotive.	THREE Portrait of Female. 3
X	Signing Declaration of Independence. X SMITHFIELD EXCHANGE BANK. Greenville, R. I.	10 Train of cars, man with wheelbarrow
FIVE State arms. 5	5 Figure 5 surrounded by five females; house, cars, and ships in distance. SOUTHERN BANK. New Orleans, La. Plough and sheaf.	FIVE 5
5 Franklin.	Female. Three females seated; vessel on right, eagle on left. Cupid CRANSTON BANK. Cranston, R. I. River scene, &c.	5 Washington and his horse
20 Female with book on lap.	XX Eagle. XX SMITHFIELD EXCHANGE BANK. Greenville, R. I.	20 Ship.
10 Male with pediment; globe, bbl., and ship.	State arms. Whites trading with Indians; wigwams in distance. SOUTHERN BANK. New Orleans, La. Man seated with sledge; steamer in background.	10 Portrait of female with flowers in hand. TEN
X Indian in act of shooting with bow.	Steamboat, vessel, &c., buildings on right. X CRANSTON BANK. Cranston, R. I.	10 Female with hat and sheaf.
FIFTY Female erect FIFTY	50 Man and horse. 50 SMITHFIELD EXCHANGE BANK. Greenville, R. I.	FIFTY Female erect FIFTY
20 XX Female seated with pole and cap	State arms. Spread eagle; public building on right; steamship on left. SOUTHERN BANK, New Orleans, La.	20 Female in a reclining posture, pair of scales in her hand. TWENTY
20 Female seated with book on lap.	XX Eagle. XX CRANSTON BANK, Cranston, R. I.	20 Ship
Figures 100 and words one hundred across. Portrait of Harrison.	Wharf scene, &c. SMITHFIELD EXCHANGE BANK, Greenville, R. I.	Same as on left. Male portrait.
FIFTY State arms. Two sea monsters.	50 Female with pole and cap, and flag partly around her; eagle over her right shoulder, and globe over her left; ship and steamship in distance. Title of Bank. Cogwheels, bale, &c.	50 Head and bust of Washington. 50
FIFTY Female. FIFTY	50 Man and horse. 50 CRANSTON BANK. Cranston, R. I.	FIFTY Female erect FIFTY
1 State arms. ONE	Male portrait. Female, sheaf of wheat, &c. Female portrait. SANDUSKY CITY BANK, Sandusky, Ohio.	1 Male Head.
State arms. Male head and bust. 100	Female reclining on a box; plough before her; on right two females and two cows; on her left steamer and other evidences of civilization, foundry, ship, &c., a cluster of fruits partly over the woman. Title of Bank American shield.	100 Indian woman seated with child. 100
Words ONE HUNDRED, and figures 100. Portrait of Harrison.	Wharf scene, loading wagon with bbls. men, horses, shipping, &c. CRANSTON BANK. Cranston, R. I.	Same as on left. Male portrait
3 State arms. THREE	Female portrait. Male portrait and large figure 3. Female portrait SANDUSKY CITY BANK. Sandusky, Ohio.	3 Male portrait THREE
500 Head and bust of a female	State arms. Female and eagle soaring in the air, horn of plenty, the contents of which she is scattering, shield in claws of eagle. SOUTHERN BANK. New Orleans, La.	500 Steamship; ship in back ground.
ONE Washington. 1	Milkmaid seated, cows, &c. 1 SMITHFIELD EXCHANGE BANK. Greenville, R. I.	1 Portrait of elderly female. ONE
5 State arms. FIVE	Portrait of H. Clay. Five and large figure 5. Female portrait SANDUSKY CITY BANK. Sandusky, Ohio.	5 Male portrait FIVE
1 Portrait of Washington	Female 1 Female CRANSTON BANK. Cranston, R. I.	1 Portrait of Franklin.
2 State arms. TWO	Stone cutters at work, &c. 2 SMITHFIELD EXCHANGE BANK Greenville, R. I.	TWO Franklin. Med. head and word two
10 State arms, TEN	Male portrait. Female seated; sickle and sheaf of wheat. SANDUSKY CITY BANK. Sandusky, Ohio.	X Male portrait TEN

Left end	Centre	Right end
ONE	Vessels, &c. 1 CUMBERLAND B'K Cumberland, R. I.	ONE Female Indian. ONE
TWO Fame seated on globe (on which is fig. 2) blowing trumpet and holding pole and cap.	State arms; farmer on left and sailor on right; Ships in distance on right, and mill, trees, &c., in distance on left. MERCANTILE BANK Bangor, Me.	2 Ship at sea. TWO
TWO Girl blowing horn standing at a table. Harvesters in distance.	Cattle and coat of arms of Indiana. FARMERS' BANK OF WESTFIELD, Ind.	2 TWO
2 TWO 2	Vessels, &c., 2 CUMBERLAND B'K. Cumberland, R. I.	TWO Female with rope in hand. TWO
3 Med. head. 3	Spread eagle with shield, arrows, &c. MERCANTILE BANK Bangor, Me.	3 Female seated with hands uplifted, vessels in distance.
5 Indian with rifle in hand kneeling down looking at vessel in distance.	Harvest scene; boy and sled with horse attached; man with bundle of wheat on his shoulder. FARMERS' BANK OF WESTFIELD, Ind.	5 Coat of arms of Indiana.
THREE	Farmers reaping, on right female with hat in hand and sheaf under arm. 3 CUMBERLAND B'K, Cumberland, R. I.	THREE Steamboat with masts. Word THREE and fig. 3.
FIVE 5	State arms; female seated on either side; town on left; vessels on right. 5 MERCANTILE BANK Bangor, Me.	5 Indian princess seated with pole, cap, shield, and quiver.
	STATE BANK, Camden, N. J. The 1's and 2's are nearly all withdrawn from circulation, and there has not been any issued for three years.	
FIVE	Female raising drapery from a fig. 5 on shield. V CUMBERLAND B'K. Cumberland, R. I.	5 Vessel.
10	Steamboat and sloop and steamboat to right; on left vessels; in foreground end of pier with men, bbls, &c. X MERCANTILE BANK Bangor, Me.	10 Female seated with pen and tablets pedestal and cog-wheel.
5 Male portrait V	Medal. Head. Harvest scene. Reaper reclining. Medal. Head. STATE BANK, Camden, N J.	V Male portrait 5
10 X 10	Man, oxen and plow. 10 CUMBERLAND B'K, Cumberland, R. I.	TEN Female erect with horn of flowers in left hand.
20 XX 20	20 Female seated with scales; bbls, bales, sheaf, rake, &c.; vessel in distance 20 MERCANTILE BANK Bangor, Me.	TWENTY
10 Male portrait X	Medal. Head. Liberty and shield, view of river, town, &c. Medal. Head. STATE BANK, Camden, N. J.	X Male portrait 10
20 TWENTY	XX Eagle. XX CUMBERLAND B'K, Cumberland, R. I.	20 Ship.
50 Female erect; steamboat in distance.	FIFTY DOLLARS 50 MERCANTILE BANK Bangor, Me	FIFTY
20 Harvest Scene. XX	Two Medal. Heads. Female reclining with wand. Two Medal. Heads. STATE BANK, Camden, N J.	XX Harvest Scene. 20
FIFTY Female erect FIFTY	50 Man and horse. 50 CUMBERLAND BK. Cumberland, R. I.	FIFTY Female. FIFTY
C Head of Washington. C	100 Male holding jar from which water is running; vessel in distance. 100 MERCANTILE BANK Bangor, Me	ONE HUNDRED
FIFTY	Man plowing. STATE BANK, Camden, N. J. Spread eagle.	50 State Arms. 50
	All other denominations are of the General Plate of the New England Bank Note Co.	
500 500 500	500 Vignette here. 500 MERCANTILE BANK Bangor, Me.	500 D 500
100 Portrait of Franklin. 100	Vig. State Arms. STATE BANK, Camden, N. J. Spread eagle.	C 100 Hundred
Med. head. 1	Fame blowing trumpet and soaring in clouds with globe, eagle, and flags. MERCANTILE BANK Bangor, Me.	1 Sailor seated with spy-glass in left hand.
Oxen and wagon, load of hay; teamster at side, man on load of hay. 1	Coat of arms of Indiana. FARMERS' BANK OF WESTFIELD, Ind.	1 Eagle. ONE
FIVE HUNDRED	500 Two females, Liberty and shield. Title of Bank. 500 D	500 500

Male portrait | 1 | BURLINGTON BK., Burlington, N. J. | Steamboat John Stevens, and view of town. | 1 | Child and rabbits.

2 | Bust of Columbus. | Female. 2 Female. | WATERVILLE B'K, Waterville, Me. | 2 | Male portrait.

FIVE | 5 A naval engagement, men in row-boat, &c. 5 | N. PROVIDENCE BK. N. Providence, R. I. | Beaver. | 5 | Waterfall, building, &c. | 5

2 | Farmer with scythe; church spire in the distance. | BURLINGTON BK., Burlington, N. J. | Farming scene; farmers at work. | 2 | Head of William Penn.

3 | Washington and horse. | Female Bust. 3 Female Bust. | WATERVILLE B'K, Waterville, Me. | 3 | Blacksmith hammer and anvil.

10 and X across. | Female seated, at her side word ten; ship in distance. | Steamer, vessels, row-boat, buildings, hills, &c. | N. PROVIDENCE BK. N. Providence, R. I. | Hope, shield, and anchor. | X | Female seated with sickle, surrounded by grain.

3 | Farmer drinking. | BURLINGTON BK., Burlington, N. J. | Three females, liberty, commerce and manufacture. | 3 | Portrait of Henry Clay.

FIVE | Eagle with spread wings on American flag, steamer on left. | Large V, cupid and female. | WATERVILLE B'K, Waterville, Me. | 5 | Female with basket of flowers.

20 XX 20 | 20 Female seated with scales, sheaf, bbls., bales, &c., on left men plowing; on right ship. 20 | N. PROVIDENCE BK. N. Providence, R. I. | TWENEY

5 | Male portrait | BURLINGTON BK., Burlington, N. J. | Steamboat John Stevens, and view of town in distance. | Locomotive and cars. | 5 | Male portrait

TEN | Male figure seated on car with hammer on knee supported upright; buildings and cars in distance. X | WATERVILLE B'K, Waterville, Me. | 10 | Full length portrait of man with sickle and bundle of wheat.

50 | Female erect; steamboat in distance. | 50 | FIFTY DOLLARS 50 | N. PROVIDENCE BK. N. Providence, R. I. | FIFTY

Male portrait | X | BURLINGTON BK., Burlington, N. J. | Canal scene, and cars crossing bridge; houses on left. | Male portrait | 10

Steamship. | XX | Railroad cars and engine. | Group of three females Faith, Justice, Mercy; ship on right and eagle on left. 20 | WATERVILLE B'K, Waterville, Me. | XX | Full length of female with milk pail and stool.

Words one hundred and figures 100. | Portrait of Harrison. | Wharf scene, loading wagon with bbls., men, houses horses, shipping, &c. | N. PROVIDENCE BK. N. Providence, R. I. | Same as on left. | Male portrait.

20 | Male portrait | 20 | Spread eagle on shield; ship on left. 20 | BURLINGTON BK., Burlington, N. J. | Female with cornucopia | TWENTY

FIFTY | Female full length with wreath in hand and on brow | FIFTY | 50 Man and horse. 50 | WATERVILLE B'K, Waterville, Me. | FIFTY | Full length female with sceptre in one hand and flowers in other. | FIFTY

500 | Indian paddling in a canoe. 500 | N. PROVIDENCE BK N. Providence, R. I. | D D | 500 | Female with scales and sword.

FIFTY | Male portrait | L | BURLINGTON BK., Burlington, N. J. | Factories and train of cars. | 50 | Male portrait

Words ONE HUNDRED and figures 100. | Bust of Harrison. | Market, wagon, men rolling in casks; horse and wagon on right; ship on left. | WATERVILLE B'K, Waterville, Me. | Words ONE HUNDRED and figures 100. | Bust of Columbus.

1000 | Spread eagle on promontory; ship on ocean in distance. 1000 | N. PROVIDENCE BK N. Providence, R. I. | 1000 | Indian female with bow and arrows.

Girl with grain on head; farming scene in the distance. | 100 | BURLINGTON BK., Burlington, N. J. | C State Arms of N. J.; factories on left. | 100 | Portrait of Washington.

ONE | Female leaning on altar. | ONE | 1 Indian erect with gun, dog, and body of a deer; Indian and forest scene on left. 1 | NORTH PROVIDENCE BANK, N. Providence, R. I. | Female portrait. | ONE | Female holding key and eagle. | ONE

TEN | Compt's Die. | Drover on horse back with boy in water and drove of cattle, trees, farmhouse, &c., in distance. | BANK OF BATH, Bath, N. Y. | Safe. | 10 | Male portrait

1 | Bust of Washington. | Female. 1 Female. | WATERVILLE B'K, Waterville, Me. | 1 | Bust of Franklin.

Female with sheaf and sickle. | 2 | Three females seated; eagle on left, vessel on right. 2 | N. PROVIDENCE BK. N. Providence, R. I. | Cars. | TWO | Canal scene buildings in distance. | TWO

TWENTY | Female Portrait. | Goddess of Liberty reclining with pole and cap in right hand; eagle on left. | BANK OF BATH, Bath, N. Y. | Compt's Die. | 20 | Male portrait

ONE 1 Two farmers seated at lunch, female pouring drink; dog; man reaping on left. N. E PACIFIC BANK N. Providence, R. I. State arms. 1 Female erect holding aloft scales.	MANUFACTURERS' BANK, Providence, R. I. There are some few notes out of an earlier emission from 1's to 5's, that are not described, a very few of which are in circulation.	Female seated pointing to farming scene. 500 D 500 MANUFACTURERS' BANK, Providence. R. I. 500
TWO 2 Female seated on left of frame: representing Agriculture and Manufacture; train of cars and steamboat. 2 N. E PACIFIC BANK N. Providence, R. I. State arms. 2 Indian female with bow, &c. 2	1 Female seated with rest on left of shield on which is Hope and anchor; train of cars on right, buildings on left. 1 ONE MANUFACTURERS' BANK, Providence. R. I. Female Portrait.	Raccoon statute, representing human figures. 1000 THOUSAND Train of cars. MANUFACTURERS' BANK, Providence, R. I. 1000 Vessels. 1000
THREE 3 Male and females, six in all, cows, &c.; house on left; vessels on right 3 N. E PACIFIC BANK N. Providence, R. I. State arms 3 Female portrait. 3	2 Same as 1's. 2 MANUFACTURERS' BANK, Providence, R. I. TWO Female Portrait.	Large V, with two females and three scales. 5 5 Local view in New-Orleans; vessels, houses, wharfs, &c. CANAL BANK, New-Orleans, La. Bales and wheels. Large V, with five females entwined. FIVE
FIVE Spread eagle on shield; buildings and vessels in distance. V, female, and cupid. N. E PACIFIC BANK N. Providence, R. I. 5 Girl with basket of flowers.	3 Female erect with hand on capstan. THREE Female reclining with pole and cap in left hand; right arm resting on shield; cornucopia, &c.; steamboat on left; Sheep on right. Title of Bank. 3 Female erect holding aloft scales; sword in left hand.	10 Spread eagle with shield, &c. TEN View of large public building; boats, &c. 10 CANAL BANK, New-Orleans, La. Steamship. TEN Figure of female with pole, cap and shield inside of a wreath around which is names of all the States. 10
TEN Vulcan seated with sledge, anvil, &c.; cars, buildings, &c. in distance. X N. E PACIFIC BANK N. Providence, R. I. 10 Man with sheaf on his knee.	5 Male seated in an arm chair. FIVE FIVE Female seated with pen in right hand and left resting on globe, &c., building, locomotive and tender on left; vessel on right. Title of Bank. 5 Female with spear; globe and owl at her feet.	Ornamental figure 20, supported by 2 marine figures. Steamship. Three females representing agriculture, commerce and manufactures. 20 CANAL BANK, New-Orleans, La. Bales, barrels, &c. Eagle. Goddess of Liberty. TWENTY
20 Female with spear. 2 Female. 0 N. E PACIFIC BANK N. Providence, R. I. XX 20 Female seated. 20	10 View of bridge, coach and four crossing it; buildings in background; canal scene in front. X MANUFACTURERS' BANK, Providence, R. I. TEN Female reclining on cogwheel; pedestal or column in rear. 10	50 Female seated on a barrel; ship and steamship in background. FIFTY Female figure representing manufactures, seated on bale with arm resting on barrel; bale of goods, anchor, ships, &c. CANAL BANK, New-Orleans, La. Pelican feeding her young Female with sword and balances. 50
50 Female erect with spear and shield. Male and female seated. N. E PACIFIC BANK N. Providence, R. I. 50 50 Cupid in a sail boat. 50	TWENTY Female seated with arm around column, pointing to ship on water, behind her sheaf, rake, &c. XX MANUFACTURERS' BANK, Providence, R. I. 20 View of bridge, &c., same as vig. 10's. XX	100 Portrait of Washington. C Steamboat, levee, landing steamboat Eliwan with bales unloading wagon, &c.; locomotive, horses and wagons; numerous male figures; trees, &c. CANAL BANK, New-Orleans, La Steamboat. 100 Female seated on chest with cap and pole; also, cornucopia.
100 Vulcan seated with sledge. Spread eagle on limb of tree; canal scene on right; train of cars on left. N. E PACIFIC BANK N. Providence, R. I. 100 100 Female seated with rake	Rhode Island 50 Canal boat loading with bales of cotton; factory and other buildings in distance; water falls; schooner, men, &c. FIFTY MANUFACTURERS' BANK, Providence. R. I. 50 Male with tablet, resting on screw wheel, &c.	500 Portrait of female, supported by two marine figures. Sea view, with steamship in front; another steamship on left, and a ship on right. CANAL BANK, New-Orleans, La Steamboat 500 Cherub on sea monster. 500
Female seated pointing to farming scene. 500 500 D N. E PACIFIC BANK N. Providence, R. I 500	100 Female. 100 Vig. Same as 50's. MANUFACTURERS' BANK, Providence. R. I 100 Vulcan with sledge; right arm pointing.	1000 Female seated, with helmet and breast-plate on; arm resting on shield; spear in one hand; scroll in the other. Arms of the U. S., with female on either side, representing liberty and plenty; bales, &c.; cars and steamship on right; man plowing, and factories on left. CANAL BANK, New-Orleans La 1000 Steamship. 1000

Left end	Centre	Right end
ONE Mechanic seated. ONE	1 Ferry wharf; view of river and vessels. MECHANICS' BANK, Burlington, N. J.	1 Male portrait ONE
TWO Mechanic and anvil. TWO	2 Female in frame, farming implements on either side. 2 MECHANICS' BANK. Burlington, N. J.	TWO Portrait of Franklin. TWO
THREE Female in fig. 3. THREE	3 Harvest scene; girl boy and dog, farmers at work in distance 3 MECHANICS' BANK. Burlington. N. J.	THREE Male portrait. THREE
Spread eagle.	5 Vig. Five Cupids and fig. 5. 5 MECHANICS' BANK. Burlington, N. J.	Portrait of Washington.
10 View of river, steamboats &c. 10	10 Female between two safes, cars on right. MECHANICS' BANK. Burlington, N. J. TEN	TEN Male portrait TEN
20 Ship. 20	20 Cupid holding wand, dog, safe and key. 20 MECHANIC'S BANK, Burlington, N. J.	20 Male portrait 20
50 Male portrait 50	View of river, steamboat and row boat, also villag . MECHANIC'S BANK, Burlington, N. J.	50 Train Cars. 50
Indian with bow and arrow.	100 Locomotive and train of cars. 100 MECHANICS' BANK, Burlington, N. J.	Washington and his horse. 100
Liberty, female, shield, [illegible] and liberty pole.	Spread eagle. 1 Indian seated viewing the improvements of the white man, CUMBERLAND B'K, Bridgeton, N. J. Female bathing.	ONE Milkmaid. ONE
Liberty. THREE	Spread eagle. Harvest scene; men at work in distance. Figure 3, and word three on either side. CUMBERLAND B'K, Bridgeton, N. J.	Two females, one with sickle and grain.
5 Med. head. FIVE	V Spread eagle on a rock. V CUMBERLAND B'K, Bridgeton, N. J.	FIVE Med. head. 5
10 Cupid and farming implements. 10	Med. head. State arms of N. J. Med. head. CUMBERLAND B'K. Bridgeton, N. J.	X Cupid. X
20 Female soaring in air.	Female seated; safe, flags, eagle at top of shield; ship on right. CUMBERLAND B'K, Bridgeton, N. J. Horse.	20 Man sowing
Liberty and shield.	50 Eagle on limbs of tree. CUMBERLAND B'K. Bridgeton, N. J. Farming implements.	Female representation of Fame, Globe, and figures 50.
ONE Male seated, pitcher by his side.	Indian seated with bow; plough, sickle, sheaf, hut, trees, &c. on left. ASHAWAY BANK, Ashaway, R. I.	1 Female portrait.
2	Two horses (white and black); train of cars on left. ASHAWAY BANK, Ashaway, R. I.	2 Two males erect, and a female seated.
Two females, one erect with spear, and the other kneeling with sprigs of wheat in right hand.	Word Dollars and figure 3. Two females seated, one with sickle; bbl., bales, and vessels in distance on right. ASHAWAY BANK, Ashaway, R. I.	3 Two men with fork and rake, and dog; two males in background coming forward.
Webster. 5	Man on horseback, drove of cattle, boy in water, man with whip; house in background. ASHAWAY BANK, Ashaway, R. I.	5 Squaw and papoose, forest scene in back ground.
Portrait of Indian. X	ASHAWAY BANK, Ashaway, R. I. Female reclining on a box gazing at miniature view of city; sheep on right.	10 Female drawing water from a well steamboat in distance.
1 Coat of Arms and two females. ONE	Head of Franklin. Female, sheaf of wheat, sickle and plough. Head of Washington BK., OF LEBANON, Lebanon, N. H. Man sitting on a plow.	1 Female head
Female sitting with sickle. TWO	Female head. BK., OF LEBANON, Lebanon, N. H. Dog's head.	2 Cow and hogs.
Man sharpening scythe FIVE	V Railroad train. V BK., OF LEBANON, Lebanon, N. H. Sheaf of wheat.	5 Female head
Blacksmith with sledge and anvil. TEN	Female with horn of plenty between 1 and 0; safe, key, female on right. BK., OF LEBANON, Lebanon, N. H. Deer.	10 Two females with sickle; sheaf of wheat, &c
20 Roman warrior, globe, &c.	Female sitting, and large figures 20. BK., OF LEBANON, Lebanon, N. H. XX	20 Lady with horn of plenty; globe, &c. 20
50 Roman warrior.	Two figures seated; horn of plenty. BK., OF LEBANON, Lebanon, N. H. 50	50 Cupid in a sail-boat. 50
100 One Hundred Man sitting; hand on sledge.	Large eagle, wings stretched, railroad trains. BK., OF LEBANON, Lebanon, N. H. 100	100 One Hundred Female sitting; horn of plenty.
20 Male seated, between figures 2 and 0	Compass. die. Female seated; bridge, train of cars, steamer, city, &c CHEMUNG CANAL BANK. Elmira, N. Y. Cog wheels, &c.	20 Female between 2 and 0. TWENTY

Die.	FIVE SHILLINGS.	Die.
Queen Victoria.	BANK OF BRITISH N. AMERICA. Toronto, Ca.	Prince Albert
Die.	Arms of the Bank, or sailor, husbandman, &c.	Die

TWO	Title of Bank.	TWO
Female representing agriculture	2 Two flying griffins, figure 2 between. 2	Portrait of Female.
2	Same as on ones	2

50	Female seated between lion and unicorn.	50
Female figure seated; agriculture.	Title of Bank.	Female seated, armory, &c.; vessel in the background.
FIFTY	Same as on ones.	FIFTY.

TEN SHILLINGS.	$2 Arms of the Bank or sailor, husbandman, &c. $2	Prince Albert.
Queen Victoria.		
TWO DOLLARS.	Title of Bank.	TEN SHILLINGS.

2	Hogs, cattle, drovers, &c.; train of cars and village in distance.	2
Train of cars	Title of Bank	Milkmaid and two cows
TWO	Same as on ones.	TWO

Die.	100 Arms of Great Britain, or lion and unicorn. 100	Miniature of monument, trees, shrubbery, &c.
100	Title of Bank.	
Die.	Flying griffin.	100

QUATRE	Title of Bank.	ONE
Female seated on bale of merchandise shipping, &c	£1 £1	Arms of the Bank
PIASTRES	British arms.	POUND

figure 4.	Female seated holding spear, shield, &c.; lion, implements of war, &c. Fig. 4 on either side.	4
Queen Victoria.	Title of Bank.	Female representing agriculture.
figure 4.	Same as on ones.	4

100	Queen Victoria seated between lion and unicorn.	100
	Title of Bank.	
Miniature view of female seated.	Same as on ones.	Med head.

QUATRE	Title of Bank.	FOUR
Female seated; shipping, &c.	4 4	Arms of the Bank.
PIASTRES	British arms.	DOLLARS

5	5 Lion with his paw upon a shield. 5	5
Queen Victoria.	Title of Bank.	Prince Albert
V	Same as on ones.	V

V	5 Eagle. 5	Vulcan, venus and mars, escutcheon in centre, anvil, &c.
Venus rising from the sea.	MINERAL BANK OF MARYLAND. Cumberland, Md.	V
V	Train of cars.	

CINQ	Title of Bank.	FIVE
Miniature view of house, rural scenery, &c.	5 5	Female seated.
PIASTRES.	British arms.	DOLLARS.

5	Title of Bank.	5
Wild horse.	Queen Victoria; lion and unicorn on either side.	Dog and safe
FIVE	Same as on ones.	FIVE

10	X Female seated resting her arm on a furnace; retorts, mortar, &c. X	
Chemist in his labratory	Title of Bank.	X
10	Eagle.	

CINQ	Title of Bank.	Twenty-five
Same as 5s.	25s. 25s.	Same as 5s.
PIASTRES	British arms.	SHILLINGS

TEN	10 Female representing the Arts and Sciences. 10	TEN
Miniature view of flower girl.	Title of Bank.	Statue of Minerva.
TEN	Same as on ones.	TEN

20	XX Flying figure emptying cornucopia of gold. XX	TWENTY Female seated with wand; male figure in clouds, with cornucopia of gold.
Horse.	Title of Bank.	
20	Dog's head.	XX

DIX	Title of Bank.	TEN
Miniature of Cataract of Niagara.	10 X	Queen Victoria seated in the royal chair.
PIASTRES	British arms.	DOLLARS

10	Steamship; other vessels in distance. 10	
	Title of Bank.	British arms
Sailor with hand on Jack staff.	Bale, bbls. and anchor.	

50	L Female resting on a globe, holding a lighted torch; eagle with head of Washington on its breast. L	50
Canal, railroad, shipping, factories, &c	Title of Bank.	Steamboat.
50	Female head.	50

1	BANK OF UPPER CANADA.	1
Miniature view of lion's head.	1 Female seated half reclining, hand resting on figure 1. 1	Miniature view of female seated, dog, figure 1, &c.
1	St. George and dragon.	1

20	Two female figures; locomotive, vessel, &c., in background.	20
Miniature view of flying griffin.	Title of Bank.	Miniature of Minerva, spear, shield, &c.
TWENTY	Same as on ones.	TWENTY

1	Two females, canal boat and bridge; on right ship and steamboat; on left farmers mowing hay.	1
Female portrait.	ALLEN CO. BANK, Fort Wayne, Ind.	Man chopping down tree.

1	Train of cars and village in distance.	1
	Title of Bank.	
Indian with bow and arrow, &c.	St. George and dragon.	Female seated.

50	L Locomotive and car; shipping, merchandise, &c. L	Miniature view of monument, trees, shrubbery, &c.
Miniature of cupid.	Title of Bank.	
50	Flying griffin.	50

Letter V and word five.	Train of cars; mills, &c., in background.	5
	ALLEN CO. BANK. Fort Wayne, Ind.	
Female and bucket.		Man chopping down a tree.

Female figure seated, holding balances in right hand. 1 — GLOBE BANK Smithfield, R. I. View of a public building. — 1 Male portrait.

1000 Spread eagle standing on rock near water; sail vessel under full sail. 1000 — 1000 GLOBE BANK Smithfield, R. I. M M — 1000 Indian female with bow and arrow.

TEN — Ten on med. head. Train of cars; on left house and trees. Ten on med. head. Title of Bank. Locomotive and tender — 10 Compt's die 10

THE GLOBE BANK. The word TWO in extreme corner and partly lengthwise. — Ocean scene: steamships and sail vessels. — 2 Female with bunch of flowers and grass in left hand.

ONE — 1 Old fashioned train of cars; building with cupola, and other buildings in distance. 1 GEO. R. R. & BANKING CO. Augusta, Geo. — ONE State arms. ONE

Indian warrior holding in left hand belt, in right bow and arrows. TEN — TEN Eagle on limb of tree; canal scene and train of cars in background. Title of Bank. — 10 Indian squaw holding ear of corn in right hand; left hand on an X.

Female seated, with liberty pole and cap in left hand. 3 — GLOBE BANK Smithfield, R. I. Group of hay makers, with female and children sitting and laying on ground; load of hay, with horses in background. — 3 3

1 Bust of young female. — Female with arm over eagle's neck: cornucopia of fruit and flowers; eagle on shield. 1 Title of Bank. — ONE Female figure erect.

TWENTY — XX State arms. XX Title of Bank. Steamboat. — 20 Female holding scale with right hand; shield on left surmounted by an eagle. 20

Water spouting from fountain. 5 — Two steamships and sail vessel. GLOBE BANK Smithfield, R. I. — 5 Female portrait.

TWO — 2 Old-fashioned train of cars. 2 Title of Bank. — TWO

20 Mercury seated, figure 2 and 0. TWENTY — Female seated with pole and cap in hand, on right an eagle: near her is a shield, on which is fig. 20 Title of Bank. — 20 Female with left hand on anchor; on right cornucopia.

Two females standing. 10 — GLOBE BANK Smithfield, R. I. TEN Landscape scene; load of unthrashed wheat. TEN — 10 Female figure standing, ear of corn in right hand, and letter X in left.

2 Female portrait. — 2 Large figure 2, with Mercury seated on left; figure of Justice erect, on right. Title of Bank. — TWO Female seated, leaning on her left hand.

FIFTY — L Old fashioned train of cars and a five story house L Title of Bank. Old fashioned train of cars — [illegible] State arms. 50

20 — GLOBE BANK Smithfield, R. I. Globe with Neptune seated in a shell; steamer and sail vessel in background. — XX Squaw

V Female seated leaning on shield, on which is plow and harrow. — Med figure 5. Man plowing with two horses. Med figure 5. Title of Bank. Cupid astride a deer. — V Drover, cattle and sheep V

Female Indian with bow and spear in hand, quiver on her back. FIFTY — 50 Bust of Washington above the shield of the U. S.; with female on either side, the one on left, placing a wreath on his brow. Title of Bank. — 50 Portrait of Mrs. Washington.

50 — GLOBE BANK Smithfield, R. I. Globe with Heathen God, and two cherubs astride an eagle. L — 50 Portrait of Webster.

5 Train of cars. V — Med head and figure 5. Country inn of two stories with piazza to each; tree on right; train of cars in front. Med head and figure 5. Title of Bank. Locomotive and tender. — FIVE

ONE HUNDRED. — 100 Old fashioned train of cars. 100 Title of Bank. — ONE HUNDRED.

C — GLOBE BANK Smithfield, R. I. Harbor and shipping. C — 100 Female with a bundle of wheat.

FIVE 5 FIVE — Modern train of cars; a building with Grecian front in the distance. Title of Bank — 5 Figure of Justice with scales and sword.

100 Sailor with left hand on capstan. — Female seated, holding shield which is resting on a cornucopia; ship in distance. Title of Bank. Cogwheels and other machinery. — 100 Female holding Am. flag three naked infants near [illegible]

Wild scenery, Indian in canoe. 500 — 500 GLOBE BANK Smithfield, R. I. D D — 500 Female with [illegible]

10 Female erect and leaning on shield of Rhode Island. 10 — Med. X. Steamboat with two upper decks; alligator in foreground. Med. X Title of Bank. Steamboat.

5 Compt's die. 5 — 5 Female, sheaf, cattle and plow. 5 SENECA CO. BANK, Waterloo, N. Y. Female. — Upright figure. FIVE

ONE 1 Two blacksmiths' cutting iron on anvil. 1 ONE
Med. head.
LANCASTER BANK, Lancaster, N. H.
Portrait of female.
ONE
ONE

Sailor boy in act of rowing.
Female soaring in air with eagle.
X
SOWAMSET BANK, Warren, R. I.
Female portrait gazing intently.
10
Vessel on stocks.

FIVE 5 State arms of N. J.; female on either side. 5 FIVE
Female with sword and scales.
FAR. & MER. BANK, Middletown P't, N. J.
Female leaning on ornamental figure 5.
5
V

TWO 2 Female erect, and two other figures reclining. 2 Female.
Female.
LANCASTER BANK, Lancaster, N. H.
2
2

50
SOWAMSET BANK, Warren, R. I.
50
Man with rake, fork, canteen, and dog.
Train of cars, load of hay, men, &c.; city, hills, &c. in distance.
Two females, one with dinner horn; table, dishes, &c.; chickens, &c.

Spread eagle on rock overlooking sea.
10 10
FAR. & MER. BANK, Middletown P't, N. J.
Goddess of Liberty seated.
Plough, rake, &c.
TEN
TEN
X

THREE 3 Female, eagle &c. 3 THREE
Man whetting scythe.
Title of Bank.
Word three and figure 3.
THREE

Female with scroll, pole, and cap, shield, pedestal, &c.
Scene—Whale fishing in Arctic regions.
100
SOWAMSET BANK, Warren, R. I.
Sailor with left hand on capstan; bbls., bales, ships' masts, &c.
100

TWENTY
20 20
FAR. & MER. BANK, Middletown P't, N. J.
XX
Unicorn.
Female seated on bale, water before her; anchor, &c.
XX

5 5 Two females reclining on a shield, on which is figure 5. 5
FIVE
Title of Bank.
Female.
Washington.

ONE 1 Agricultural scene, plowing, oxen, &c. 1 1
Female erect with sword and scales.
FAR. & MER. BANK, Middletown P't, N. J.
Washington.
ONE
1
ONE

Female erect between ornamental 5 and 0.
50 Female reclining on state arms. 50
Female erect with cornucopia.
FAR. & MER. BANK, Middletown P't, N. J.
FIFTY
FIFTY

X Male with staff X X
10
Title of Bank.
Female.
Cupid on deer.
10

1 Title of Bank 1
Farmer carrying sheafs of grain.
Horse running away; boys endeavoring to stop him.
Female portrait.
ONE

100
Female reclining on shield.
FAR. & MER. BANK, Middletown P't, N. J.
Same as 50's.
Female erect feeding eagle from cup.

1
Indian female seated, with left arm pointing; a deer, trees &c. in distance.
1
Ship.
SOWAMSET BANK, Warren, R. I.
Indian reclining supporting figure 1.
1
Vessel.

Unicorn. 2 Mercury. 2 TWO
Eagle on shield.
Title of Bank.
Washington
2
2

1
GLOBE BANK, Providence, R. I.
1
Male supporting the world on shoulders on which is four females, representing the nations; female reclining on left; and male representing time on right; cars and steamship in distance.
Ornamental [illegible] and cupid with [illegible] of plenty.
Same as left.

TWO
Wild horses.
2
Train of cars Steamship.
SOWAMSET BANK, Warren, R. I.
Human figure holding ear of corn and figure 2.
TWO

2
Drover buying cattle.
2
Male and female seated.
FAR. & MER. BANK, Middletown P't, N. J.
Female portrait.
TWO

2
GLOBE BANK, Providence, R. I.
2
Same as ones.
Same as ones
Same as ones

Vessels, &c.
Indians trading with white men.
3
SOWAMSET BANK, Warren, R. I.
Indian princess with bow and arrow.
THREE
Loading hay.

3
FAR. & MER. BANK, Middletown P't, N. J.
3
Drove of cattle, wagon &c.; scene upon road.
Country scene—man on horse which is drinking from trough; female, sheep, &c. around.
Portrait of a little girl.

3
GLOBE BANK, Providence, R. I.
3
Same as ones.
Same as ones
Same as ones

Large view of steamship, ships, &c.
FI5VE
Figure 5, represented by female, eagle, portrait of Washington.
SOWAMSET BANK, Warren, R. I.
V
FIVE

3 3 Female seated upon bale; ships in back ground; water, &c. 3 3
Plough, rake, &c.
Flowers.
FAR. & MER. BANK, Middletown P't, N. J.
3
3

Female seated on rock with trident.
Nautical scene—ships, man of war, steamship, &c.
5
GLOBE BANK, Providence, R. I.
FIVE
5

Left end	Centre	Right end
10 Sailor with hand on capstan; hhls., ships' masts, &c., behind.	Female reclining on bale with wand; city and vessels on right; cars, canal boat, lock, &c., on left. GLOBE BANK Providence, R. I.	10
5 FIVE FIVE	Two females erect; male bust and shield in centre; female on right holds Liberty pole and cap; one on left a wreath; ship on right; sheaf of rice on left. 5 BK. OF SOUTH CAROLINA, Charleston, S. C. Tree, &c.	Cotton bales, anchor, &c. Portrait of Calhoun. Train of cars.
Portrait of female. X	10 Two oxen before hay-cart; boy by side, with pitchfork on his shoulder; another boy laying on top of cart. CUBA BANK, Cuba, N. Y. Ducks and young ones.	TEN Indian hea[d]. Compt's. die
50 Female erect with spear and shield.	Male and female seated. GLOBE BANK, Providence, R. I. 50	50 Cupid in sail boat. 50
Female standing with scales and sword. 10	Eagle, shield and figure ten. BK. OF SOUTH CAROLINA, Charleston, S. C.	Female standing with scales and sword. 10
Two females, one churning; the other turning out cheese; hen and chickens; cows in distance; shed, &c.	Compt's. die. Female with pail; hand resting on hen-roost; two cows, one laying down; hens and rooster; shed, &c; two cows on right, with sheep in distance. CUBA BANK, Cuba, N. Y.	20 XX
100 Vulcan seated with sledge.	Spread eagle on limb of tree; train of cars on left, and canal scene on right. GLOBE BANK, Providence, R. I. 100	100 Female seated with rake.
10 Male and female figures. Steamship.	Steamship under way; shipping on right; shipping on left. 10 BK. OF SOUTH CAROLINA, Charleston, S. C. Trees.	Statute of Calhoun erect. TEN
1 Battle scene, soldier with musket in the act of charging, cannon, drum, soldier lying on the ground, flag, &c.	Auditor's die. Milkmaid seated with flower in her left hand, right hand on pail, two cows on right, farmhouse and trees on left, trees and cows in distance centre HAMILTON CO. B'K, M'Leansboro, Ill.	1 Girl's head.
	The Globe Bank also uses 500's and 1000's, but owing to the POLITENESS of the Cashier of the institution, we are unable to give a description. We believe, however, that they are of the general plate of the New England Bank Note Company.	
TWENTY	20 Female seated on an anchor; shield and words Twenty Dollars; sheaf of rice on right; ship on left. 20 BK. OF SOUTH CAROLINA, Charleston, S. C. TWENTY TWENTY	TWENTY
TWO Farmer giving hay to horse sickle on his shoulder; dog, pitchfork, pigeons, &c.	HAMILTON CO. B'K, M'Leansboro, Ill. Man and boy gathering corn, boy placing it in a wagon, horse before it with colt, corn stalks, dog, &c. Aud. die.	2
Compt's Die. One Dollar, in part circle 1	B'K OF MONTGOMERY, Alabama. Female seated, eagle, train of cars and bridge on right, city and harbor on left in distance.	1 ONE 1
FIFTY Female seated. 50	50 Female erect, with spear and right hand resting on a shield and word Fifty. 50 BK. OE SOUTH CAROLINA, Charleston, S. C	50 Female seated. FIFTY
3 Two male figures, one standing against a tree, the other seated female seated with child in her lap, dog, &c.	HAMILTON CO. B'K, M'Leansboro, Ill. Nine figures male and female applauding the arrival of a train of cars; on right cabin and trees; loading wagon on left; trees, &c.	3 Aud. die.
2	B'K OF MONTGOMERY, Alabama. Three females, one in center holds a sickle, ship on right, bridge and cars on left. Compt's Die.	2
100 Pillar of a building, and words One Hundred. HUNDRED	Female standing with a sickle in right hand; rocks, vase, &c. The title of the Bank is on either side of vig., in a scroll.	100 Pillar of a building, and words One Hundred. HUNDRED
5 Portrait of Girl.	Three boys trying to catch a horse, one with hat raised, another with halter, the other on the ground; dog, cabin and trees on right, horse, colt, fence and trees on left. Aud. Die. Title of Bank. 5	5 Blacksmith working bellows, blacksmiths tools, &c.
8 Compt's Die.	Three men erect, one holds a staff, and represents a farmer. B'K OF MONTGOMERY, Alabama.	3 Cotton plant, barrel, &c.
1 Compt's. die.	CUBA BANK, Cuba, N. Y. Ornamental die work, on which is "One Dollar" in circular form, with portrait of girl at bottom; portrait of Washington on right; woodman felling a tree on left. Cottage.	1 Portrait of female.
5 Indian seated.	5 Female seated; anchor, bale of goods, rudder, &c.; city on left in distance. 5 B'K of CHARLESTON S. Carolina.	Indian walking. 5
5 State Arms. 5	B'K OF MONTGOMERY, Alabama. Group of three females, globe, scroll, building, &c.	5 5
2 Compt's die. 2	Train of cars approaching depot; passengers about to get aboard; train of cars crossing bridge in distance. CUBA BANK, Cuba, N. Y. 2	Ornamental die work, on which is "Two Dollars" in circular form; portrait at bottom. TWO
10 Cars. 10	Med. head. Title of Bank. Med. head. Female seated, safe, money bags, &c.; cars on right.	10 Cars. 10
5 Med. head FIVE	V Eagle standing on a rock; ships on left. V BK. OF SOUTH CAROLINA, Charleston, S. C	FIVE Med. head 5
V Locomotive and cars coming down hill; cabin, trees and hills in distance.	Three men rolling log; two more on right, one of which is felling tree; and still another on left standing by side of oxen; trees, &c. CUBA BANK, Cuba, N. Y. Woodman felling tree.	5 Compt's. die in square form. 5
20 Portrait of Washington. 20	Two females seated, canal and cars on right; Houses and shipping on left. 20 Eagle.	Indian Queen, shield, &c. 20

ONE	Farmer plowing with two horses; man sowing, train of cars in background. 1	1
1	NARRAGANSETT BK Wickford, R. I.	Indian erect with bow and spear.

ONE	Title of Bank.	FOUR
Female reclining.	Three females seated; $4 agriculture, commerce, &c. 1s	Indian Chief seated.
POUND	Arms of Great Britain.	DOLLARS

10	KENTUCKY STOCK BANK, Columbus, Ind.	10
Three dies.	Ten dollars Ten dollars	Three dies.
TEN	Train of cars; two dies on either side.	TEN

	Female on right of a shield on which is an anchor, cupid on left, and ships; on right in background train of cars. 2	2
2	Title of Bank.	Same as one.

Twenty-five	Title of Bank.	FIVE
Arms of the Bank, &c.	Two females seated; $5 shipping, merchandise, &c. £1. 5. 0	Victoria the Royal Chair.
SHILLINGS	Arms of Great Britain	DOLLARS

20	Female portrait; three dies on each side.	20
Three dies.	Title of Bank.	Three dies.
	Twenty Twenty	
TWENTY	Still; four dies each side.	TWENTY

Medallion head.	Spread Eagle on shield buildings and vessels in distance. 3	THREE
3	Title of Bank.	Same as one.

Ten	Title of Bank.	FIFTY
Miniature of three females.	£2. 10. 0 Large beehive, surrounded by shrubbery, etc. $10	Miniature of plow, sheep, vessel, tree, water, &c.
DOLLARS	Arms of Great Britain.	SHILLINGS

ONE	1 Female seated on a bale; factories in background. 1	ONE
Female supporting a figure 1.	TOLLAND CO. BANK, Tolland, Conn.	Portrait of Washington.
ONE		ONE

FIVE	5 Letter V on shield; Indian seated on right, with gun in hand; female on left erect, with spear. 5	FIVE
	Title of Bank.	
	Hope, anchor and shield.	

Ornamental work	1 Large building, and arms of Great Britain. 1	Ornamental work
1	ONE ONE	1
Ornamental work	GORE BANK, Hamilton, Canada.	Ornamental work

TWO	2 Harvest scene. 2	TWO
A cooper at work.	Title of Bank.	Female with grain, and child with sickle.
TWO		TWO

	10 Female seated holding eagle and twig; vessels in distance. X	TEN
	Title of Bank.	
10	Head of Indian.	Full length Female.

2		
Ornamental die, enclosing the words 'Honi Soit Qui Mal Y Pense.'	Two females seated between the lion and Unicorn. TWO TWO	2
2	Title of Bank.	

THREE	3 Farmer boy, with cradle and sheaf of wheat; house in background. 3	THREE
Female figure and cherubs in fig. 3	Title of Bank.	Interior of a blacksmith shop.
THREE	Female head.	THREE

TWENTY	20 Two females seated with wand, cornucopia, &c., on left, wharf scene, vessels, bbls., &c., on right, steamboat; sails of a vessel seen at their back. 20	XX
		Steamboat
	Title of Bank.	20
	Clasped hands	

ONE POUND	4 IV	4
4	Arms of Great Britain, of lion, unicorn, &c.	FOUR DOLLARS
FOUR DOLLARS	Title of Bank.	4

5	Five female figures and figure 5.	5
Female supporting the above figure.	Title of Bank.	
V	Machinery.	Farmer boy

FIFTY	L Female seated receiving horn of plenty from two floating figures; train of cars, bbls, &c. on right; on left, griffin on safe, vessels, &c. L	50
		Steamboat.
	Title of Bank.	50
	Train of cars.	

TEN	A Miniature view of a man mounted on horseback, spearing a dragon. 10	TEN
Miniature view of shipping, bales of merchandise &c.	Title of Bank.	
TEN		

10	Two females; factories in background.	10
	Title of Bank.	
Female with sickle and sheaf.		Indian girl.

Die.	Five Shillings.	Die.
Queen Victoria.	BANK OF B. N. AMERICA, Hamilton, Canada.	Prince Albert.
Die.	Arms of the Bank; or sailor, husbandman, &c.	Die.

Train of cars	BANK OF FULTON, Atlanta, Georgia.	10 X and Ten
X		Two males erect and a female seated; buildings, &c.

50	Male and female	50
	Title of Bank.	Cupid in a sail boat.
Female figure.		50

TEN SHILLINGS	$2 Arms of the Bank; or sailor husbandman, &c. $2	Albert
Victoria		
TWO DOLLARS	Title of Bank	TEN SHILLINGS

Female gathering wheat.	Title of Bank.	20
XX	Male portrait.	Blacksmith, anvil; cars, and city in distance.

100	Spread eagle standing upon a tree; railroad and canal in background.	100
	Title of Bank.	
Vulcan the blacksmith seated.		Female with rake.

1 — Wood-choppers, cattle, and horse. 1 | 1
UNION BANK, Brunswick, Me.
1 | Female with sickle.

TWO | Female holding an eagle. 2 | THOMPSON BANK, Thompson, Conn. Female with sickle and sheaf of wheat, also cows. Bird | 2 | Female holding scales. 2 | TWO | TWO

Female, eagle and shield; factory and steamship in the distance. 3 | 3
MERCHANTS' BK., Bangor, Me.
3 | Sailor.

Locomotive and train of cars. 2 | 2
UNION BANK, Brunswick, Me.
2 | Portrait. 2

THREE | Female with scales; merchandise. 3 | 3 Female feeding an eagle from a cup. 3 | THOMPSON BANK, Thompson, Conn. | THREE | Female, sickle, and sheaf of wheat. 3

Female and merchandise. Large V, female and sheaf of wheat. | FIVE
MERCHANTS' BK., Bangor, Me. Ship
5 | Indian female with bow and arrow.

Three female figures; factories in back ground. 3 | 3
UNION BANK, Brunswick, Me.
3 | Sailor boy.

FIVE | 5 Female and wheel. V | THOMPSON BANK, Thompson, Conn. Fema | FIVE

Farmer, dog and grain. Female and X on right | 10
MERCHANTS' BK., Bangor, Me.
TEN | Female.

Ship building. Large V, female, and sheaf of wheat. | 5
UNION BANK, Brunswick, Me.
5 | Ships.

10 | 10 Two female figures and eagle; ship and canal in background. 10 | THOMPSON BANK, Thompson, Conn. | X | Female. 10

20 | Female figure, with spear and globe. | 2 Female. 0 | MERCHANTS' BK., Bangor, Me. XX | 20 | Female. 20

Vulcan the blacksmith seated. X | 10
UNION BANK, Brunswick, Me.
TEN | Reaper.

TWENTY | 20 Female and lion; steamboat in distance. XX | THOMPSON BANK, Thompson, Conn. Cupid astride deer. | 20 | Female. XX

50 | Female figure. | Male and female seated. | MERCHANTS' BK., Bangor, Me. 50 | 50 | Cupid in a sail boat. 50

20 | Female. | 2 Female. 0 | UNION BANK, Brunswick, Me. XX | 20 | Female 20

50 | Female and anchor; steamboat in distance. 50 | FIFTY DOLLARS 50 | THOMPSON BANK, Thompson, Conn. | FIFTY

100 | Vulcan the blacksmith. | Spread eagle standing on a tree; railroad and canal in background. | MERCHANTS' BK., Bangor Me. 100 | 100 | Female seated.

50 | Female figure | Male and female seated. | UNION BANK, Brunswick Me. 50 | 50 | Cupid in a sail boat. 50

C | Portrait of Washington. C | 100 Neptune, merchandise; ship in distance. 100 | THOMPSON BANK, Thompson, Conn. | ONE HUNDRED

1 | Watering horse from trough; cabin with well; farm scene. | INDIAN RESERVE BANK, Kokomo, Ind. Woodman felling tree. | ONE | Male and female Indian and child.

100 | Vulcan the black smith. | Spread eagle standing upon a tree; railroad and canal in background. | UNION BANK, Brunswick, Me. 100 | 100 | Female seated.

Female, State arms, shipping and railroad. 1 | MERCHANTS' BK., Bangor, Me. | 1 | ONE | Female supporting figure 1. ONE

2 | Indian. 2 | Locomotive and train of cars | INDIAN RESERVE BANK, Kokomo, Ind. Eagle. | 2 | Woodman felling tree. 2

1 | Round die. 1 | 1 Female seated on the ground; eagle and shield; ship in distance. 1 | THOMPSON BANK, Thompson, Conn. | ONE | Female figure. ONE

Sailor, merchandise, and shipping. 2 | MERCHANTS' BK., Bangor, Me. | 2 | 2 | Portrait of female.

Full length Goddess of Liberty. | Shield with Indian on it; spread eagle at top; two horses and steamboat on right; train of cars and factories on left. | INDIAN RESERVE BANK, Kokomo, Ind. | 5 | Woodman felling tree. 5

<table>
<tr>
<td>Block of stores.
1
Female and Merchandise; factory and shipping in background.
CASCO BANK,
Portland, Me.
1
Sailor with quadrant, ships in background.</td>
<td>ONE
Two females with sword, spear, and shield.
Wood-chopper, one gold dollar; log cabin in background.
BRADFORD BANK,
Bradford. Vt.
1
Indian woman.</td>
<td>THREE
Female.
3
3 Interior of a blacksmith's shop. THREE
MECHANICKS' B'K,
Concord, N. H.
3
Female and ships.
THREE</td>
</tr>
<tr>
<td>Block of stores.
2
Female and vegetables; river and village in background.
CASCO BANK.
Portland, Me.
2
Female.</td>
<td>2
Winged female.
Female and eagle.
Farmer boy and milkmaid; also cows; two gold dollars
BRADFORD BANK,
Bradford. Vt.
2
Fountain.</td>
<td>FIVE
Portrait of Van Buren.
5
V Farmers, cattle and sheep. FIVE
MECHANICKS' B'K,
Concord, N. H.
5
Portrait of Jackson.
FIVE</td>
</tr>
<tr>
<td>Block of stores.
THREE
3 Female seated on a bale; steamship and train of cars in background. 3
CASCO BANK.
Portland, Me.
Female and Merchandise.
THREE</td>
<td>Farmer boy with sheaf of wheat, and milkmaid.
5
A hunter and Indian woman, and three cupids; five gold dollars.
BRADFORD BANK,
Bradford, Vt
5
Portrait.</td>
<td>TEN
Portrait of Jefferson.
10
X Farmer sowing seed. X
MECHANICKS' B'K.
Concord, N. H.
10
Portrait of Jackson.
TEN</td>
</tr>
<tr>
<td>Portrait of Fillmore.
5
5 Ships. 5
CASCO BANK.
Portland, Me.
FIVE
Female.</td>
<td>Two females.
10
Coat of arms surmounted; with female each side; steamboat and train of cars in distance.
BRADFORD BANK,
Bradford. Vt.
X
Child and dolphin.</td>
<td>20
Portrait of Franklin.
TWENTY
Female in foreground; harvest scene in background. Canal and boat.
MECHANICKS' B'K,
Concord, N. H.
XX
General Washington
20</td>
</tr>
<tr>
<td>Boy's Head.
5
Landing of the pilgrims,
CASCO BANK.
Portland, Me.
5
Girl's Head</td>
<td>Female,
XX
State arms, farmer and Indian
BRADFORD BANK,
Bradford, Vt.
20
Agricultural imp. & pro'ts</td>
<td>FIFTY
Female.
FIFTY
50 Man and horse. 50
MECHANICKS' B'K,
Concord, N. H.
FIFTY
Female.
FIFTY</td>
</tr>
<tr>
<td>Three female figures and anchor.
TEN
State Arms. Female, sycle, and sheaf of wheat.
CASCO BANK,
Portland, Me.
10
Portrait of Taylor</td>
<td>50
Female reclining; milkmaids and cows; locomotive, shipping, factories in background. Wheels, bals, etc
BRADFORD BANK.
Bradford, Vt.
50
Portrait of Webster.</td>
<td>Words One Hundred and figures 100.
Portrait of Harrison.
Scene on a wharf.
MECHANICKS' B'K,
Concord, N. H.
Words One Hundred and figures 100.
Portrait of Columbus.</td>
</tr>
<tr>
<td>20
Female, eagle, scales and sword.
Female and cherubs
CASCO BANK,
Portland. Me.
20
Female with sheaf of wheat</td>
<td>100
Female with scales
State arms surmounted by an eagle, female on each side.
BRADFORD BANK.
Bradford. Vt.
100
Horses and load of hay.</td>
<td>1
Portrait of Washington.
Female. 1 Female.
BELKNAP CO. B'K,
Meredith, N. H.
1
Portrait of Franklin.</td>
</tr>
<tr>
<td>50
Female and sickle.
50
Two females; factories and ship in background.
CASCO BANK,
Portland. Me.
50
Farmer Boy.</td>
<td>ONE
Portrait of Washington
1
Child's head. Interior of a blacksmith's shop. Child's head.
MECHANICKS' B'K.
Concord, N. H.
1
Portrait.
ONE</td>
<td>ONE
Sailor hoisting a flag.
ONE Female with sword and scales; ship on the stocks.
BELKNAP CO. B'K.
Meredith, N. H
1
Indian girl with bow and spear.</td>
</tr>
<tr>
<td>100
Sailor with flag.
CASCO BANK,
Portland, Me.
One Female and Cupid in the air over a city. Hundred
100
Portrait of Female.</td>
<td>TWO
Ship building.
2
2 Interior of a blacksmith's shop. TWO
MECHANICKS' B'K,
Concord, N. H.
2
Female, eagle and bust of Washington
TWO</td>
<td>TWO
2
Spread Eagle. 2
BELKNAP CO. B'K,
Meredith, N. H.
2
TWO
Sail-boats.</td>
</tr>
</table>

Female. Wood choppers, cattle and horse. 2 BELKNAP CO. B'K, Meredith, N. H. 2 Girl with sheaf of wheat.	50 Vulcan and a female. 50 Cupid in a small boat. Title of Bank. Female. 50 50	100 Shepherd and sheep; village in the distance. 100 Female with sheaf of wheat. Title of Bank. Female. 100
3 Female 3 Flower girl 3 BELKNAP CO B'K, Meredith, N. H. Washington. Vulcan the blacksmith.	100 Spread eagle standing on a tree; railroad and canal. 100 Title of Bank. Vulcan the blacksmith. 100 Female with a rake.	ONE 1 1 ONE B'K OF LOUISVILLE, Kentucky. Full length portrait of Clay in a speaking attitude. Female sitting on a bale. ONE
3 3 Harvest scene 3 3 BELKNAP CO. B'K, Meredith, N. H. Female with flowers. Females raking hay.	1 1 Farmers and cattle. 1 1 Washington. BANK OF MIDDLEBURY, Middlebury, Vt. Head of a Horse. 1 1 1	2 2 2 TWO B'K OF LOUISVILLE, Kentucky. Female with shield. Female leaning on a pedestal sitting. TWO
Spread eagle Large V, female and cupid. 5 Title of Bank. FIVE Flower girl	2 TWO TWO 2 Farmers and cattle. Title of Bank. Three cherubs. 2 Harvest scene. 2	FIVE 5 Eagle with wings extended. 5 FIVE Female sitting in letter V. B'K OF LOUISVILLE, Kentucky. Female sitting in figure 5. 5 Locomotive under headway. 5
Female seated on a rock. Female reclining, Milkmaids, cows; locomotive and factories in background. 5 Title of Bank. V Martha Washington	3 3 Female with her arm resting upon a wheel. 3 3 Male and female. Title of Bank. Farmers and cattle. 3 Female reclining. 3	Washington. 10 Female sitting on a bale, pointing to a ship in the distance; lighthouse in the background. 10 10 Female portrait, with reaper and grain. Female portrait. B'K OF LOUISVILLE, Kentucky. Boone. Eagle with extended wings. 10
10 Cincinnatus standing by his plough. 10 TEN X Title of Bank. 10 Female figure.	5 5 Female, eagle and shield; ship in the distance. 5 Female leaning upon an urn, bearing the name of E. Allen and McDonald; also, winged female with a trumpet. Farmers and cattle. 5 Title of Bank. 5	10 Med. head. Female sitting, with pole and Liberty cap in right hand; river and steamboat in distance. Med. head. X Female figure spinning Female spinning. X B'K OF LOUISVILLE, Kentucky. 10
TEN Capitol at Washington. 10 Title of Bank. Goddess of Liberty. Washington	TEN 10 Vulcan the blacksmith and two females. 10 Child's face. Ten Gold Dollars Title of Bank, X TEN Washington. Child's face	20 Two female figures with ships and cars in the distance. 20 B'K OF LOUISVILLE, Kentucky. Washington. Agricultural implements and grain. Med. head with helmet
20 2 Female. 0 20 Female Female with spear. Title of Bank. 20 20	20 Male and female; sheaf of wheat; canal and reapers in background. TWENTY Washington. 20 Title of Bank. Female bust.	50 Female figure. Female kneeling with sickle in hand; flowers around her. Female figure. 50 Female with horn of plenty. Female with horn of plenty. B'K OF LOUISVILLE, Kentucky. 50 50
FIFTY 50 Man and Horse. 50 FIFTY Female. Title of Bank. Female. FIFTY FIFTY	50 50 Officer mounted. 50 FIFTY Female, eagle and scales; merchandise &c Title of Bank 50	HUNDRED Female with wings, blowing a trumpet; globe and eagle. 100 100 HUNDRED Med. head and helmet B'K OF LOUISVILLE, Kentucky. Med. head and helmet HUNDRED Indian with quiver of arrows. HUNDRED

ONE	Woman swimming. Portrait of H. Clay. Woman swimming.	ONE
Two men standing, two women sitting.	ONE ONE B'K OF KENTUCKY.	Man standing, two women sitting.

FIVE HUNDRED	500 Indian queen 500 with bow in right hand surrounded by a circle composed of the arms of the different States, flags, drums, &c.	FIVE HUNDRED
	B'K OF KENTUCKY. 500	

2	Shepherd reclining; flock of sheep in view.	TWO
Female upholding a globe.	Title of Bank.	Female with sheaf; is shading her eyes with right hand.
TWO	Beehive.	2

5	Portrait of Clay. Female sitting on a bale, holding sheaf of wheat; oxen with wagon load of hay; in the distance locomotive and cars. Portrait of Jefferson.	5
Clay		Washington.
FIVE	B'K OF KENTUCKY. Dog's head.	FIVE

ONE	Wood chopper with axe; house, trees, and dollar gold piece.	1
Steamboat on stocks.	COMMERCIAL BANK OF KENTUCKY.	Male portrait
ONE	State Arms.	ONE

5	Title of Bank.	5
Man gathering corn.		Female with bundle of wheat, encompassed by figure 5.
5	Spread eagle.	5

Henry Clay.	B'K OF KENTUCKY.	Portrait of Shelby.
	5 Hunting scene—hunter, game, &c. 5	
Male figure sitting with scroll in left hand.		Female figure.

THREE	Three men sitting; Farmer, Sailor, and Mechanic; 3 one dollar gold pieces.	3
Male portrait	COMMERCIAL BANK OF KENTUCKY.	Steamboat on stocks.
THREE	State Arms.	THREE

FIVE	5 Female holding pitcher seated on hogsheads; ships in distance. 5	FIVE
Female with sheaf and reap hook.	Title of Bank.	Blacksmith with sledge and anvil.
FIVE	Bust of female.	FIVE

10	Portrait of Boone. Globe with eagle on top, Indian on one side, female on the other. Portrait of Shelby.	10
Washington.	10	Clay.
10	B'K OF KENTUCKY Dog's head.	10

5	Indian woman, three cupids and hunter, and 5 gold dollar pieces.	FIVE
Male portrait	Title of Bank.	View of Harrodsburg Springs.
FIVE	State Arms.	FIVE

10	Female portrait. Female leaning right arm on the Am. ensign, in left hand horn of plenty. Female portrait.	Same on this end as on left.
TEN	Title of Bank.	
10	Plough and sheaf.	

10	B'K OF KENTUCKY.	Indian in a canoe.
Daniel Boone hunting	Woman in a chariot drawn by three horses.	10

10	Steamboat running; small one in the distance. X on right.	TEN
Male portrait	Title of Bank.	Harrodsburg Springs.
TEN	State Arms.	TEN

20	Two females with cotton stock; ship and buildings in the distance.	20
	Title of Bank.	
Washington.	Horse.	Washington.

20	B'K OF KENTUCKY.	20
	Marion offering the British officer sweet potatoes; camp in distance.	
Webster.	Dog's head.	Male portrait

20	Woman reclining; locomotive and vessels, woman and cows in distance.	XX
Harrodsburg Springs.	Title of Bank.	Clay.
TWENTY	State Arms.	TWENTY

Female with cornucopia.	INTERNATIONAL BANK, Raleigh, Ills.	5
	Man watering horses from trough by side of a well; sheep, goat, kid; trees, cattle and house in distance.	Auditor's die
5		5

Portrait of Shelby.	20 Female in the clouds holding flowers in the left hand; ship in the distance. 20	Med. head.
Female figure	B'K OF KENTUCKY.	
Goose.	Agricultural implements and grain.	Female figure.

50	50 Female reclining holding liberty pole and cap in left hand; eagle and globe; ships in the distance.	50
Clay.	Title of Bank.	Crittenden.
FIFTY	State Arms.	FIFTY

Female gathering wheat.	Title of Bank.	10
	Farm scene—farmer and drover bargaining for ox.	Auditor's die
10		10

Female portrait.	Marion offering the British officer sweet potatoes; &c.	50
	B'K OF KENTUCKY.	
50	Dog's head.	Male portrait

100	100 Traders and Indians.	100
Male portrait	Title of Bank.	Male portrait
100	State Arms.	100

1	WINNEBAGO COUNTY BANK, Neenah, Wis.	1
Indian with knee on rock; hand on limb of tree.	Female and male standing beside a well; female has pitcher in her hand, and male a cup about to drink, his foot on trough; barn with horses and load of hay; rail fence, trees, &c., in background.	Compt's die
	Locomotive and tender.	ONE

100	Male portrait. Two females sitting; bbl., anchor, &c.; steamboat in the distance.	100
Male portrait		Portrait of Boone.
	B'K OF KENTUCKY.	Washington.
100	Horse's head.	100

1	A group with a load of hay in view.	1
Female with a scroll and harp.	LAWRENCEBURG BANK OF TENN.	Female with a quiver of arrows at her back; staff in right hand, with shield and eagle beneath it,
	Dog, key, and safe.	

2	Title of Bank.	2
Female seated in canoe, with bow and arrow; trees, tents and canoe.	Two silver dollars; female and cherub; fruit, vegetables, &c.; steamship in distance on right; cabin on left.	Compt's die
	Cornucopia, bales, &c.	

5 — Female seated, bale of goods, &c.; farmers at work and train of cars on right. — Female with sheaf of grain. — Male portrait. — BANK OF THE VALLEY, VA. — Dog's head. — 5 — 5 — 5	VI — 6 — Female with scales, sword, &c.; safe, &c. on right; globe, &c., on left. — 6 — EXCHANGE B'K OF VIRGINIA. — Eagle. — 6 — Cupid and dragon.	V — FIVE Female with a rake. FIVE — 5 — Med. Head. — BANK OF VIRGINIA. — Med. Head. — V — 5
5 — Med. head. Female anchor, figure 5, shield, &c. Med. head — 5 — Female standing. — BANK OF THE VALLEY. VA. — Female. — Boy's head. — 5 — 5	VII — 7 Vig. Same as 6s. — 7 — EXCHANGE B'K OF VIRGINIA. — Eagle. — 7 — Cupid and dragon.	10 — TEN Three females seated. Ship on left in distance. TEN — 10 — Med. Head. — BANK OF VIRGINIA. — Med. Head. — 10 — 10
10 — Female seated; locomotive on right; cows on left. — 10 — Portrait of Washington — BANK OF THE VALLEY, VA. — Indian Queen seated. — Locomotive. — 10	VIII — 8 Vig. Same as 6s. — 8 — EXCHANGE B'K OF VIRGINIA. — Eagle. — VIII	FIFTEEN — Med. Head — Man and boy seated; man is drawing; mill on right in distance. — Med. Head — FIFTEEN — Med. Head and figures 15. — BANK OF VIRGINIA. — Med. Head and figures 15. — Dog's Head. — FIFTEEN — FIFTEEN
10 — Three Cupids. TEN Three Cupids. — 10 — Med. head. — BANK OF THE VALLEY, VA. — Med. head. — Dog's head. — 10 — 10	IX — 9 Vig. Same as 6s. — 9 — EXCHANGE B'K OF VIRGINIA. — Eagle. — IX	20 — Med. Head and figures 20. — Med. Head and figures 20. — XX — Warrior standing, another on the ground. — Two females, one holds a scroll, the other liberty pole and cap. — Med. Head and word TWENTY. — 20 — BANK OF VIRGINIA. — XX
20 — Two females, two Cupids and figure "Twenty." — Portrait of Millard Fillmore. — BANK OF THE VALLEY, VA. — 20 — Indian Queen. — 20	10 — Portrait of Washington — Warrior standing with his left foot placed on another warrior laying on the ground, and who is apparently dead; cars on right; shipping on left; also steamboat. — Male portrait — 10 — Cars, barrels, bales of goods, &c. — Canal, sloop, houses, and shipping. — X — Title of Bank. — X	50 — FIFTY DOLLARS Female seated with liberty pole and cap. — 50 — Med. Head. — BANK OF VIRGINIA. — Med. Head. — 50 — 50
20 — Female erect. Twenty Dollars. Female seated. — 20 — Med. head. — BANK OF THE VALLEY VA. — Med. head. — Boy's head. — 20 — 20	15 — Portrait of Washington — Large ship under way; houses on left in distance. — Male portrait — 15 — Mechanic, anvil, hammer, &c. — EXCHANGE B'K OF VIRGINIA — Warrior erect, &c. — Anchor and shield. — 15	ONE HUNDRED — Washington on a horse. A ONE HUNDRED. G'n. on a horse. — ONE HUNDRED — BANK OF VIRGINIA.
50 — Male and female; Female [illegible]; male holds sickle and [illegible] a [illegible]; men at work in a field on right and house in background. — 50 — Double Medallion head, and word Fifty. — BANK OF THE VALLEY, VA. — Double Medallion head, and word Fifty. — 50 — 50	20 — Portrait of Washington — Indian seated with bow, &c.; ruins of a house in background. — Male portrait — 20 — Ship — EXCHANGE B'K OF VIRGINIA. — Warrior erect, &c. — Indian in a canoe. — XX	Soldier, cannon, and American flag. — 5 Two females, bale of goods, &c., steamboat. — 5 — FIVE — B'K OF WADESBOROUGH, N. C. — Horse. — FIVE — 5
100 — Title of Bank. Female seated; shield, &c. — 100 — Med. head and figure 100. — Med. head and figure 100 — 100 — 100	50 — Portrait of Washington — Two females seated, with key, horn of plenty, &c.; steamboat on right; bbls. and shipping on left. — Male portrait — 50 — Two men, drove of cattle and sheep. — EXCHANGE B'K OF VIRGINIA. — Warrior erect, &c. — 50	10 — BANK OF WADESBOROUGH, N. C. — 10 — Man on horse and slaves at work in a cotton field. — Female reclining. — 10 — 10 — Female, shield, and American flag.
5 — Harbor scene, and city in background. — 5 — Portrait of Washington. — EXCHANGE B'K OF VIRGINIA. — Male portrait — V — V	100 — Same as 10s. — 100 — Male and female. — EXCHANGE B'K OF VIRGINIA. — Man working in a cornfield. — 100 — 100	Sailor, female, anchor, bale of goods, American flag, &c. — 20 Title of Bank. Large Spread Eagle, shield, &c. — Beehive. — 20

Two males and one female; males are carrying the female. THREE
Female reclining; eagle, shield, safe, key, scales, &c.; ship on right; cars on left
COMMERCIAL BK., Wilmington, N. C.
Female and shield.
3 Female erect; scales, sword, &c.

TWENTY
20 Female seated with sickle, a scroll, and word twenty; vessel on left. 20
UNION B'K of SOUTH CAROLINA, Charleston, S. C.
XX
SOUTH CAROLINA

Statue of J. C. Calhoun erect.
Male Portrait. Workmen at work on a dock; shipping, bales of goods, &c.
B'K OF THE STATE OF S. CAROLINA.
ONE Palmetto Tree.

Male and large figure four extending across the note.
4 Female, shield, eagle, &c. 4
COMMERCIAL BK., Wilmington, N. C.
Female and shield
Female erect; scales and large figure four extending across the note.

ONE HUN.
100 Female reclining; man ploughing on right; ship and sloop on right. 100
UNION B'K of SOUTH CAROLINA, Charleston, S. C.
C
ONE HUNDRED

J. C. Calhoun erect.
1 Vig. Cars. 1
B'K OF THE STATE OF S. CAROLINA.
Tree, &c.
Cotton field.

FIVE Female seated and large figure five. FIVE
Female, eagle, shield and figure five. Ornamental V each side
COMMERCIAL BK., Wilmington, N. C.
Female and shield.
FIVE Female seated and figure Five. FIVE

5 Cars 5
Med. head and letter V. Male portrait. Med. head and letter V.
STATE BANK, Charleston, S. C.
Two cupids in a boat.
5 Cars 5

ONE Female erect with sickle. ONE
1 Female reclining with liberty pole and cap. 1
B'K OF THE STATE OF S. CAROLINA.
Female erect and large fig. 1, extending across the note.

Ship and house. 10 [illegible] at work.
Water scene and female representing Liberty in a car; steamship in distance on right; boat in distance on left.
COMMERCIAL BK., Wilmington, N. C.
Female, shield, &c.
10 Female, ear of corn and letter X.

V
STATE BANK, Charleston, S. C.
View of the State Bank in Charleston, corner of East Bay and Broad sts.
5 V

Two on med. head. Locomotive. TWO
Portrait of J. C. Calhoun, and two females seated.
B'K OF THE STATE OF S. CAROLINA.
Tree, &c.
TWO DOLLARS.

---

20 Two females.
Indian Queen, shield, &c.; steamship on [illegible] Female, anchor, &c.
Title of Bank.
20 20

10 Female seated. X
X Cars, trees, &c. 10
STATE BANK, Charleston, S. C.
Male portrait.
X Female seated. 10

TWO Female erect with sickle, &c. TWO
2 Two females, shield, &c., globe and cars in distance on right, and sheaf of grain on left. 2
B'K OF THE STATE OF S. CAROLINA.
Female erect, and large figure 2.

---

50 Two females, one seated, the other [illegible] 50
Female looking over rocks; steamboat, cars, canal and city in distance on right.
COMMERCIAL BK., Wilmington, N. C.
50 Female, eagle, shield, &c.

10 Female, sheaf of wheat. 10
View of harbor, shipping, &c.
STATE BANK, Charleston, S. C.
10 TEN

2 Male portrait
View of the intended State House at Columbia, S. C.
B'K OF THE STATE OF S. CAROLINA.
TWO Portrait of Calhoun.

---

100 [illegible]
Sailor reclining [illegible] anchor, windlass, spy-glass, &c.; vessel on left. 100
COMMERCIAL BK., Wilmington, N. C.
Sailor and blacksmith. Flag and anchor.

Portrait of Franklin.
20 Water scene, female seated in a car. 20
STATE BANK, Charleston, S. C.
Farming implements.
Portrait of Washington.

3 Female with sickle. 3
3 Farmers eating dinner, dog on left, also other farmers at work. 3
B'K OF THE STATE OF S. CAROLINA.
Female standing and large fig. 3.

FIVE
5 Female seated holding sickle; bbl. and ship in distance on right; sloop in distance on left. 5
UNION B'K of SOUTH CAROLINA, Charleston, S. C.
V
SO. CAROLINA

50 Man seated drawing.
STATE BANK, Charleston, S. C.
Indians, shield, cotton plant, female and children; globe, sheaf of wheat on right.
Female in water.
50 Steamboat under way, and men in small boat.

Large figure 4. Male portrait
View of Fort Moultrie.
B'K OF THE STATE OF S. CAROLINA.
Large figure 4. Male portrait.

TEN
X Female seated holding liberty pole ship on right. X
UNION B'K of SOUTH CAROLINA, Charleston, S. C.
TEN DOLLARS

Portrait of Washington
C Female erect and sheaf of grain; man ploughing on right. Figures 100 and cupid
STATE BANK, Charleston, S. C.
C
100

5 Male portrait 5
5 General Marion inviting a British officer to dinner. 5
B'K OF THE STATE OF S. CAROLINA.
5 Male portrait 5

10 Male portrait. Male portrait. 10
Vessels of war sailing in the water.
Female, liberty pole and cap. Female, scales and eagle.
B'K OF THE STATE OF S. CAROLINA.
10 10

FIVE
Two Cupids seated; one drawing, the other reading; sheaf of grain, bee-hive, &c.; sloop on left in distance.
Double Med. head.
Title of Bank.
Eagle and portrait of Washington.
Med. head and figure 5. FIVE on med. head. Med. head, and figure 5.

FIVE
5 Female seated; sickle, plough, and sheaf of grain; cattle on left. 5
MERCHANTS' BANK Newbern, N. C.
FIVE Female, scales, eagle, &c.
V

XX 20 View of a cotton wharf, cars, steamboat, slaves at work, &c. 20 XX
Female, sickle, &c. Negro plowing.
B'K OF THE STATE OF S. CAROLINA.
XX XX

10 Med. head. Barrel, bale of cotton, sheaf of rice, farming implements, and cotton plant. Med. head, and figure 10.
Male portrait
Title of Bank.
10 Arm and hammer.
TEN

Male seated; eagle, shield, &c.
X Female reclining with scroll, eagle, and portrait of Washington. X
10 Male portrait
MERCHANTS' BANK Newbern, N. C.
10 10

50 50 Two females seated; one holds liberty pole and cap, the other shield and spear; steamboat right in distance.
Med. Head.
B'K OF THE STATE OF S. CAROLINA.
50 50

TEN 10 Title of Bank. 10 TEN
Med. head. Large eagle on limb of a tree; cars on right. Med. head.
TEN Arm, anvil, wheel, hammer, &c. TEN

TWENTY
20 Man balancing the globe on end of pole. 20
Two females, one in air with horn of plenty, and other seated.
MERCHANTS' BANK Newbern, N. C.
XX

100 C Female erect, two shields, angel and war general; ship on right in distance, cars on left in distance. C
One hundred
C Male figure ... Female
100 B'K OF THE STATE OF S. CAROLINA. Dollars.

20 Eagle, shield, and ornamental figure 20. Male portrait.
Male portrait
PLANTERS' & MECHANICS' BANK, Charleston, S. C.
20
20 Sword, scales, &c. Male portrait.

100 100 Female seated with liberty pole and cap, shield, eagle, anvil, wheel, &c.; ship on left. 100
Female and eagle.
Female seated with sickle.
MERCHANTS' BANK Newbern, N. C.
100 100

X 10 Steamboat Pike running, sloops &c.; Indian kneeling, and white men in the foreground. 10 X
Male portrait Male portrait
X BK OF THE STATE OF MISSOURI. X

Male portrait
FIFTY DOLLARS
50 Three females, ornamental fig. 50.
50 Male portrait
Title of Bank.
Portrait of Wm. Penn.
FIFTY

5 Farmer seated sharpening his scythe, another farmer erect on right, basket on left. 5
Portrait of Washington
FARMERS' & MECH. BANK, Georgetown, D. C.
Female seated.
5 Eagle. V

Male portrait 20 Two females sitting, iron chest; steamboat in distance. 20 Male portrait
Eagle Eagle
BK OF THE STATE OF MISSOURI.
Male portrait Male portrait

100 100
Portrait of Franklin.
Male portrait. Two females seated, and one standing; one on right holds sickle, &c.; sheep on the ground and ship on left in distance.
Male portrait.
Portrait of Washington
Title of Bank.

10 Canal and boat. Female seated, holding bucket, two others in background and one is milking; house in distance on right; two ships on left. 10
Portrait of Washington
Title of Bank.
Blacksmith at work.

50 B'K OF THE STATE OF MISSOURI.
Female holding portrait of Washington
Female sitting; bridge, rail cars, houses, ships, hills, &c. in distance.
Hunter with dog and gun.
50

POST NOTE
Farming implements and sheaf of grain.
Title of Bank.
Mechanical implements.
500
500 DOLLARS

20 Portrait of Washington. Female shield, eagle horn of plenty, liberty pole and cap. 20
Female erect with basket. Two blacksmiths in shop.
Title of Bank.
20 Plow, sheaf of grain, &c. 20

100 100 Indian on horseback shooting a buffalo, hunters and buffalo in distance 100
Male portrait
Indian portrait.
100
B,K OF THE STATE OF MISSOURI.
Male portrait

Females.
3 Female seated, dog, key, safe, and shield; bee hive on left. 3
Female erect and large figure 3.
MERCHANTS' BANK Newbern, N. C.
THREE

50 Female in the air with a horn; globe and eagle, American colors on left. Ship stocks.
50
Portrait of Washington.
Farmer standing, another in background plowing.
Title of Bank.
50 Wheel, &c.

5 PLANTERS' & MECHANICS' BANK, Charleston, S. C. 5
Figure 5 and word Five.
FIVE Female, ... and eagle.
Dog's head.
5

Large fig. 4 Large fig. 4. Drove of cattle and sheep at a brook. Large fig. 4.
Female with liberty pole and cap.
MERCHANTS' BANK Newbern, N. C.
Female anchor, and large fig. 4.
Large fig. 4. Safe and dog.

1 Carpenter at work, at bench. 1
ARTISANS BANK, Trenton, N. J.
Female portrait
Tress. die.

3 Female with grain and horn of plenty, seated. 3	BK OF CAPE FEAR, N. Carolina. Three males, one with model of boat and one with hammer with his hand resting on anvil; on left ship on stocks; on the right factories and bridge.	3 3

THREE	3 Female seated holding bonnet in left hand; bucket on left. 3 Title of Bank.	Washington. Male portrait

THREE Farmer, dog, fork, &c. THREE	3 Men at work in a corn-field. 3 Title of Bank. Ship.	Female.

Female erect Eagle. 3	3 Female; wheel and monument in background 3 Title of Bank. Two females.	3 Girls head. 3

4 Ship, brig, steamship and steamboats; city in distance,	Female seated on log with pail in her lap; shield with train of cars on it; sheafs of grain on right with cows and trees in distance; trees and farm house on left. Title of Bank.	4

Female seated with sickle and sheaf of grain. Locomotive.	4 Man seated; ship-building in background. Title of Bank.	4 Cooper at work.

4	Female reclining; anchor, &c. ship on left. Large fig. 4. Title of Bank. Sheaf of grain, plow, &c.	FOUR Female erect shield, &c. FOUR

Female erect and eagle. Large fig. 4.	Large fig. 4. Man seated with crock; steamboat on left. Large fig. 4. Title of Bank. Two females.	Large fig. 4. Cupid. Large fig. 4.

5 Male portrait.	Title of Bank. Large V with FIVE on ornamental work across it	5 Two females seated, bale, barrel and sheaf of grain.

Boy, girl, dog, &c. Female and bucket.	5 Five cupids and large figure 5. Title of Bank.	Female and horn of plenty. Eagle. Indian.

Man seated drawing 5	5 Female and cupid in a car, other cupids drawing it. 5 Title of Bank. Indian's head.	Female seated safe &c. 5

Indian with bow and arrow. V	Double med. head. Female seated; ship on left in distance. Double med. head. Title of Bank Two females.	5 Male portrait V

6 VI 6	Scene at sea, clipper ship, water in commotion steamship and other vessels. Title of Bank.	6 6

SEVEN	Shield with Indian seated on right with axe; Indian tents with trees and fire in distance; Female, shield and cornucopia on left; steamboat and city in distance. Title of Bank.	7 VII 7

EIGHT	Train of cars coming under arch; with horses and carriage, on top of arch; telegraph wires and poles, rocks, trees and fence, &c. Title of Bank.	8 8

NINE	Steamship, ship on left; water in commotion. Title of Bank.	9 IX

X 10	Title of Bank. Two Females representing liberty and peace; train of cars on right; steamboat ship and small boat on left.	10 X

Man in corn-field. TEN	10 Miniature view of female, anchor, &c. on right; vase, &c. on left. Title of Bank	Mason at work. TEN

10 Female seated on a log.	Title of Bank. Male, female, and dog: sheaf of grain, &c.	10

TEN	10 Female seated; cars on right. X Title of Bank. Two females	10 Med. head. X

20 Female, sheaf of wheat, sickle, &c. 20	Portrait of Washington. Two females reclining; wagon on right; steamboat and vessels on left. Title of Bank. Eagle.	20 Female with vase.

20 Portrait of female. 20	20 Female holding a goat by the horns. 20 Title of Bank. Bull's head.	20 female erect. 20

female drawing. 50	Female seated, figure fifty, horn of plenty, &c.; on left, two vessels in distance. Title of Bank. Locomotive.	50 Sailor with spy-glass.

50 Medalion head. 50	L Female reclining; ship in distance on right. L Title of Bank.	50 Female with a rake. 50

Female.	100 Male portrait, and a female seated on either side 100 Title of Bank.	Female.

100 Female figure. 100	Cupid and sheep. Female playing on a harp. Cupid, cow and sheep. Title of Bank. Steamboat.	100 Med. head. 100

1 Female seated on stone, with pail	WAUKESHA CO. BK. Waukesha, Wis. 1 Female seated on bale beside silver dollar, anchor, trees, &c. 1 Girl's head.	1 Compt's die

5 Med. head. 5 — 5 5 Eagle, shield, and ship on left in distance. FARMERS' BANK OF VIRGINIA. V V — 5 Med. head. 5

THIRTY — 30 Female reclining, bucket of water, &c. 30 FARMERS' BANK OF VIRGINIA. 30 — RICHMOND

10 Farmer erect with scythe. — Man on horse and slaves at work in a field. Warrior erect and one on ground. CENTRAL BANK, Staunton, Va. Locomotive. — X TEN 10

6 Man and dog. SIX — 6 Woodman seated, and dog, axe, and hat on the ground. 6 FARMERS' BANK OF VIRGINIA. — Male erect. SIX

50 Med. head. 50 — Male and female seated; ship in distance on left. Title of Bank. — 50 Med. head. 50

20 Female, scales and sword. — Warrior erect and one on ground. Milkmaid seated; cows on right; house on left in background. CENTRAL BANK, Staunton, Va. — 20 Train of cars.

Female erect and figure 7. — 7 Female reclining on bale of goods; vessels on left. 7 FARMERS' BANK OF VIRGINIA. — Female erect 7

Male portrait — 50 Female seated, sheaf of wheat, &c. 50 FARMERS' BANK OF VIRGINIA. 50 — Portrait of Washington

50 Female portrait. — Title of Bank. Three females reclining; cars and canal on right. Warrior erect and one on ground. — 50

EIGHT Female seated. VIII — Large fig. 8. Two females and one male; ship in background on right. Large fig. 8. FARMERS' BANK OF VIRGINIA. — EIGHT Female, eagle shield, &c. VIII

FIFTY — 50 Female seated, pole, and shield. 50 FARMERS' BANK OF VIRGINIA. 50 — RICHMOND

5 Portrait of Washington. — Male portrait. Two females reclining; cars and canal on right; shipping on left. Male portrait. BANK OF MOBILE, Mobile, Ala. Steamship. — 5 Med. head.

9 Two cupids erect. — Med. head. Three cupids, two on left and one on right of figure 9; one on right holds sickle. Med. head. FARMERS' BANK OF VIRGINIA. — 9 Female seated.

ONE HUNDRED — 100 Female, shield, plough, &c. 100 FARMERS' BANK OF VIRGINIA. — RICHMOND

10 Female. — Portrait of Washington. Sailor reclining, holds American flag; bale of goods, &c.; ship on left. Portrait of Jefferson. BANK OF MOBILE, Mobile, Ala. Shipping. — 10 Female, scales, eagle, &c.

Female erect by the eagle, liberty pole, and cap. — 10 Man on horse, drove of sheep, and dog; mill in distance. FARMERS' BANK OF VIRGINIA — 10

5 Drovers and Drove of cattle. — Compts. Die. Female seated; sheaf of rice, sickle plow, &c.; cars on right. CENTRAL BANK, Staunton, Va. — 5 Cars. FIVE

20 Two vessels. — Steamboat, vessels, harbor, docks, &c. BANK OF MOBILE, Mobile, Ala. Dog's head. — 20 Cotton plant

Male portrait — 10 Female seated, sheaf of wheat, &c. TEN FARMERS' BANK OF VIRGINIA. — Portrait of Washington.

Registers Die. Male portrait — Female seated, elbow resting on shield; view of falls, Bridge and town. CENTRAL BANK, Staunton, Va. — 6 Female and grain.

50 Steamboat. — BANK OF MOBILE, Mobile, Ala. Angel sounding trumpet; globe, eagle, &c. — 50 Cotton plant

20 Portrait of Washington. 20 — 20 Miniature view of a female; sickle, sheafs of wheat, &c. on right. 20 FARMERS' BANK OF VIRGINIA. XX XX — 20 Med. head. 20

Drove of sheep, man on horse, the horse drinking from trough; load hay in background. Registers Die. CENTRAL BANK, Staunton, Va. — 7

Indian erect, with bow and arrow. 100 — 100 Female standing with scales. 100 BANK OF MOBILE, Mobile, Ala. Eagle. — Male erect 100

Male portrait — 20 Female seated, &c. 20 FARMERS' BANK OF VIRGINIA. — Portrait of Washington.

Registers Die. Beehive. — CENTRAL BANK, Staunton, Va. — 8 Catching horse.

3 — CITY BANK, Lynn, Mass. Yacht race; on the beach various males and females 3 — THREE on 3. Two males.

5 Female and horn of plenty. 5
BK. OF THE STATE OF N. CAROLINA
Men in water.

5 BELVIDERE BANK, Belvidere, Ill. 5
Cattle in foreground; town in background.
Ceres. Auditors die.

50 Female seated, representing Commerce; bales, bbls., &c.; shipping in distance. 50
Bank building.
B'K OF LOUISIANA, New Orleans, La.
Two females representing Justice and Wisdom.
FIFTY Shield.

V 5 Sailor and female seated and figure 5; vessel on left in distance. 5 V
Female seat[illegible] letter V. Female seat[illegible] and fig. 5.
BK. OF THE STATE OF N. CAROLINA.
5 5

ONE Three females reclining, eagle, &c. 1
[illegible] and three children.
BANK OF AUGUSTA, Augusta, Ga.
ONE Train of cars.

100 Train of cars; factories on left; steamboat on right. 100
Indian female with bow, arrows, and spear.
B'K OF LOUISIANA. New Orleans, La.
Female erect with hand on capstan.
Bbls., bales, &c.

TEN Sheaf of [illegible] Sheaf of [illegible] in background. 10
Eagle, shield &c. Female
BK. OF THE STATE OF N. CAROLINA.
10 Female seated. 10

Female erect, Med. Head, &c. 2 Female seated sheaf of wheat, &c. TWO 2
BANK OF AUGUSTA, Augusta, Ga.
TWO

500 View of New Orleans from opposite side of river; ships in distance. 500
Female seated with shield, horn of plenty, pole and cap.
B'K OF LOUISIANA. New Orleans, La.
Portrait of female.
$500 Safe. $500

X 10 Female [illegible] horn; globe and eagle; on left, American flag. 10
Two females and large letter X; anvil and hammer.
Med. head.
BK., OF THE STATE OF N CAROLINA.
X TEN

5 FIVE Female seated holding an eagle; vessels on left, FIVE 5
Female. Beehive.
BANK OF AUGUSTA. Augusta, Ga.
5 Female. 5

ONE THOUSAND 1000 Sailor seated against bales; ships in distance. 1000
B'K OF LOUISIANA, New Orleans, La.
Bank building. 1000

---

20 Female seated bale of goods [illegible], &c; on right farmers at work and train of cars 20
Male portrait. Med. head.
BK., OF THE STATE OF N. CAROLINA
20 20

10 Female seated holding vase of flowers; shipping on right; manufactories on left 10
Portrait of Franklin.
An old man seated, partly supported by a staff reading a book.
BANK OF AUGUSTA Augusta, Ga.
State Arms.

FIVE 5 Female with pole and cap, left arm resting on shield. 5 CINQ
CITIZENS' BANK, New Orleans, La.
Pelican

---

50 Shield and two females; on right, saw mill and vessel; on left barrels and men at work. FIFTY
Med. head. Gen. Washington on a horse.
BK., OF THE STATE OF N. CAROLINA.
50 FIFTY

20 Shield with a miniature view of sunrise, mountain scenery, water, small sail vessels, &c.; a female seated on either side of shield, locomotive and steamboat in distance. 20
Male portrait. Train of cars.
TWENTY Title of Bank. XX
State Arms.

TEN DIX Vig. Same as 5s. TEN
CITIZENS' BANK, New Orleans, La. X
Phœnix. TEN

This Bank uses other denominations, but we were unable to procure a description of them.

20 XX Train of cars crossing a bridge. XX
Male portrait. Military Gen seated holding a book.
BANK OF AUGUSTA. Augusta, Ga.
XX Key. XX

Female with pole and cap; left arm on shield. 20
Phœnix
CITIZENS' BANK, New Orleans. La.
20 VINGT XX

---

1 View of a town. 1
BELVIDERE BANK, Belvidere. Ills.
Female figure, factory, anvil, &c. Auditor's die.

50 Large Spread eagle; sail vessels on either side. Male portrait
Portrait of Washington. BANK OF AUGUSTA. Augusta, Ga. 50
FIFTY State Arms. Male portrait

50 CITIZENS' BANK, New Orleans, La. [illegible] Liberty
L Pelican 50

Indian with gun. Farming scene. 3
BELVIDERE BANK, Belvidere, Ills.
3 Auditor's die.

Steamboat. 10 Two females with pole, cap and shield; portrait of Washington, bales, bbls., and ship on right; sheaf of grain, &c., on left. 10
10 B'K OF LOUISIANA, New Orleans, La.
Steamship. Bank building.
Indian female with ear of corn and letter X

100 C Female with liberty cap and pole, cornucopia, &c. C Cent Piastres
CITIZENS' BANK, New Orleans, La. 100
Phœnix. Cent Piastres

1 — Male portrait — ONE
State Arms; sailor on right; two men on left one is seated.
STATE BANK OF OHIO.
ONE — Full length female.

---

10 — Male portrait — 10
Letter X on shield; female on right; farmers, train of cars on left.
STATE BANK OF OHIO.
TEN — Female with sword and balance. — TEN

ONE — ONE — Compt's die.
Large vessel; ship and steamship on left.
NEW-YORK COUNTY BANK, New-York City, N. Y.
Female bathing.
1 — Portrait of boy.

---

1 — Portrait of Washington — 1
State Arms; farmer reclining with sickle; sheaf on right.
STATE BANK OF OHIO.
Dog's head.
ONE — Full lenght female. — ONE

---

10 — Male Portrait. — TEN
Two females, shield, plow and steamboat; female on right is seated and holds grain; on left anchor and ship in extreme distance.
STATE BANK OF OHIO.
X — Male portrait. — TEN

---

2 — Compt's die. — 2
Coat of Arms of the City of New-York.
Title of Bank.
2 — Portrait of a boy.

---

2 — Male portrait — 2
Shield; Indian and female on either side
STATE BANK OF OHIO.
Dog's head.
TWO — Female — TWO

---

20 — Male portrait. — 20
State Arms, with female on right and houses in distance; on left men on horseback.
STATE BANK OF OHIO.
Dog's head.
20 — Female Indian representing liberty. — XX

V — Soldier with a musket.
State Arms.
Title of Bank.
Ducks.
5 — Compt's die — 5

---

3 — Male portrait — 3
Shield; Indians on right; female on left. 3
STATE BANK OF OHIO.
Mutual Liability.
THREE — Female erect — THREE

---

50 — Male head — 50
State Arms; female on left and steamboat in distance; on right Indian in canoe and figs. 50.
STATE BANK OF OHIO.
Dog's head.
50 — Female artist seated. — 50

---

10 — Men shearing sheep.
Farmers at work loading hay.
Title of Bank.
10 — Compt's die.

THREE — Male portrait — THREE
3 Group of four females; spinning wheel &c.
STATE BANK OF OHIO.
3 — Male head.

---

1 — Girl
Two horses before hay cart; various male and female figures; black smith's shop. *Large* 1. in red on vig.
ORANGE BANK Orange, N. J.
ONE ONE
1 — Head of male

---

20 — XX
Indian in a canoe.
Title of Bank.
Compt's die.
20 — Clay.

Same as on right. — Male Portrait.
STATE BANK OF OHIO.
Group of five male figures.
Figure 5 and words FIVE DOLLARS underneath. — Male head.

---

1 on TWO — Head of male
Title of Bank.
Word TWO in red.
TWO 2 TWO
2 — Female reclining on bales; steamboat and schooner in distance.

---

1 — Female
Bull's head on shield: on right men dressing leather; on left female sewing shoes.
MEDOMAK BANK, Waldoboro, Me.
Incorporated in 1836.
ONE on 1. — Female.

---

5 — Franklin. — 5
Shield; on right two Indians, on left three females city in distance 5
STATE BANK OF OHIO.
FIVE — Full length figure. — FIVE

THREE on 3. — Male portrait
Title of Bank.
3 Female seated with mechanical implements; cars, bridge and factory in distance. Red 3 on vig. 3
THREE
3 — State Arms. — 3

---

1 — Male portrait
Portrait of female; on left female and farming scene; on right female, bale, barrel, steamboat
Title of Bank.
Incorporated in 1836.
1 — ONE — Female with a rake.

FIVE — Female seated within large V. — 5
Franklin. Large ornamental fig. 5, surrounded with cupids.
STATE BANK OF OHIO.
Wheat, &c.
5 — 5

10
Female seated with globe, distaff, quadrant, compass, etc.; ship and steamship in distance X
UNION BANK, Brunswick, Me.
X — Indian seated.

---

2 — Female reaper.
Scene in an Iron Mill; men at work.
Title of Bank.
Incorporated in 1836.
2 — Female with cornucopia.

---

10 — Harrison. — 10
State Arms; Indians on right on horseback; on left woodchopper and hunter; man plowing, cars, &c., in distance.
STATE BANK OF OHIO.
Dogs head.
TEN — Full length female. — TEN

Dear hanging on limb of tree; dog on ground. — THREE
Mechanic, sailor and farmer seated with implements; three gold dollars.
MARTHA'S VINEYARD BANK Edgartown, Mass.
3 — Female seated with fig. 3.

Word Three and fig. — Girl.
Rafting scene—men, women and children on raft.
Title of Bank.
Incorporated in 1836.
3 on Dollars. — Female.

Left	Centre	Right
Reaper. 1	Female reclining; milk-maids, cows, factories, shipping, locomotive, &c., in background. PEOPLES' BANK, Waterville, Me.	1 Female in kneeling posture.
Two females. 2	Female, merchandise and shipping. PEOPLES' BANK, Waterville, Me.	2 Female.
State Arms, reaper and sailor. 3	Milkmaid and cows. PEOPLES' BANK, Waterville, Me. Loading hay	3 Female sitting on a plow, with eagle and sheaf of wheat.
Female feeding an eagle from a cup 5	Indian sitting upon the ground, by the side of a slain deer. PEOPLES' BANK, Waterville, Me.	5 Five female figures and figure 5.
Farmer sharpening a scythe. 10	Scene at a railroad station. PEOPLES' BANK, Waterville, Me.	X Female and ten gold dollars.
Reaper and milkmaid. 20	Cattle and sheep. PEOPLES' BANK, Waterville, Me.	20 Indian woman.
Spread eagle and shield. 1	Portrait of Washington, two females, sickle and sheaf of wheat at the left; milkmaid and cows at the right. ALFRED BANK, Alfred, Me.	1 Female, eagle and shield.
Female. 2	ALFRED BANK, Alfred, Me. Harvest scene.	2 Portrait of Franklin.
Portrait of Webster. Three and 3	Locomotive and train of cars. ALFRED BANK, Alfred, Me.	3 Female seated on a bale.

Left	Centre	Right
V and Five Farmer sitting under a tree	ALFRED BANK, Alfred, Me. Signing of the "Declaration of Independence."	V Female with sickle, and an Indian woman.
State Arms. X, 10, Ten	ALFRED BANK, Alfred, Me. Indian, spread eagle, and two horses: factories and steamboat in background.	10 Female drawing water at a well.
XX Milkmaid.	Man on horseback, farm-house and drove of cattle. ALFRED BANK, Alfred, Me.	20 Female, eagle and shield.
50	Title of Bank. Three female figures. Female	50
1	MARTHA'S VINEYARD BANK, Edgartown, Mass. Shipping. Steamship.	1 Female, globe, and shield.
2	MARTHA'S VINEYARD BANK. Edgartown, Mass. Haymakers at the left, and females preparing dinner at the right; two trains of cars and a city in background.	2
Sailor boy. V	Hunter, Indian woman, three cupids, and five gold dollars. MARTHA'S VINEYARD BANK, Edgartown, Mass.	5 Female reclining; ships in distance.
Female. 10	Goddess of Plenty and cherubs, representing the gathering of the harvest. MARTHA'S VINEYARD BANK, Edgartown, Mass.	10 Ships.
Female. XX	Stonecutters and architect. MARTHA'S VINEYARD BANK, Edgartown, Mass.	20 Sailor.

Left	Centre	Right
Sailor. 50	An Indian with bow and arrow; eagle flying; in the background is a lake; Indians in a canoe, wild deer, &c. MARTHA'S VINEYARD BANK, Edgartown, Mass	50 Two female figures.
C Female with sword and scales.	State arms surmounted by an eagle; female on each side. MARTHA'S VINEYARD BANK, Edgartown, Mass.	100 Spread eagle. 100
	CITY BANK, Columbus, Ohio. For a description of the notes of this, see those of any of the Ohio Independent Banks, they all being nearly alike.	
	MIAMI VALLEY BK. Dayton, Ohio. For a description of this Bank's notes, see Iron Bank, O., page 241, or any other State Stock Bank of that State.	
	COMMERCIAL BK., Cincinnati, Ohio. For a description of the notes of this, see those of any of the Ohio Independent Banks, they all being nearly alike.	
FIVE Two females with sickle, &c. FIVE	Drove of cattle and sheep; man sitting down on left. FARMERS' BANK OF MARYLAND.	FIVE 5 FIVE
Female erect, shield, sword &c. TEN	10 Farmers at work in wheat-field. 10 FARMERS' BANK OF MARYLAND.	TEN Female with sickle and sheaf of wheat. TEN
5 Med. head. 5	Male portrait. Church, monument, and trees. Male portrait. BANK OF CAMDEN, Camden, S. C. Dog's head.	5 Med. head and figure 5. 5
10 Med. head. 10	Med. head and word Ten. Indian Queen, shield, bale of goods, &c.; steamship on right. Med. head and word Ten. BANK OF CAMDEN, Camden, S. C.	10 Med. head. 10

ONE | Blacksmith, anvil, and forge. 1 OAKLAND BANK, Gardiner, Me. ONE | ONE

Female. Portrait of Z. Taylor. | 2 Indian, squaw, and child; plough, sickle, and wheat. 2 CARROLL CO. BANK Sandwich, N. H. | Female. 2

FIVE | Scene in a ship-yard. Female and large V. ROCKLAND BANK, Rockland, Me. | 5 Indian girl.

TWO | 2 Steamboat. 2 OAKLAND BANK, Gardiner, Me. | TWO

3 Locomotive and train of cars. 3 | Indian, squaw, and child; plough, sickle, and wheat. CARROLL CO. BANK, Sandwich, N. H. | THREE Portrait. THREE

TEN | Ships. X ROCKLAND BANK, Rockland, Me. | 10 Sailor.

THREE | Interior of an iron foundry. 3 OAKLAND BANK, Gardiner, Me. | THREE

V Dog and boy. | 5 Vig. Same as 2s. 5 CARROLL CO. BANK, Sandwich, N. H. | V Portrait of female.

Sailor hoisting a flag. | 20 Female reclining; 20 eagle and globe; ships in background. ROCKLAND BANK, Rockland, Me. | Goddess of Liberty.

FIVE Mechanic, sailor, and two females; city and harbor in distance. | OAKLAND BANK, Gardiner, Me. 5 | FIVE Farmer, two females, and a yoke of oxen.

X Female. | 10 Title of Bank. 10 Locomotive and train of cars. | X Female.

20 Female with spear. | 2 Female 0 ROCKLAND BANK, Rockland, Me. XX | 20 Female reclining. 20

X and Ten Girl with a sickle. | OAKLAND BANK, Gardiner, Me. Figures 10 across words Ten Dollars. | 10 Female with horn of plenty.

20 Portrait of Franklin. | CARROLL CO. BANK. Sandwich, N. H. Locomotive and train of cars. | 20 Portrait.

Female feeding an eagle from a cup. 50 | Shipping and merchandise; female seated on a bale. ROCKLAND BANK, Rockland, Me. | 50 Ship; city in distance.

XX Portrait of female. | Figures 20 across words Twenty Dollars, and small figures 20 between words. OAKLAND BANK, Gardiner, Me. Schooner | XX Sailor.

This Bank also uses an old plate, but they are rapidly retiring them from circulation.

100 | Female sitting on the ground; merchandise and shipping in the back-ground. ROCKLAND BANK, Rockland, Me. | 100 Blacksmith, anvil and forge.

Male, female, two children, and a lamb. | OAKLAND BANK, Gardiner, Me. 50 | 50 Sailors.

ONE | Female sitting on the ground, supporting a figure 1; steamboat and train of cars in background. 1 ROCKLAND BANK, Rockland, Me. | 1 Portrait of a female.

CITY BANK, Cincinnati, Ohio. For a description of the notes of this Bank, see of those any of the Ohio Independent Banks, they all being nearly alike.

ONE HUNDRED | Female with spear and shield. | OAKLAND BANK, Gardiner, Me. | 100 ONE HUNDRED

TWO | Spread eagle, Capitol at Washington and steamship. 2 ROCKLAND BANK, Rockland, Me. | 2 Sail-boat.

1 ONE Eagle and shield. | Large building, male and female figures and trees. EXCHANGE BANK OF TENNESSEE, Murfreesboro, Tenn. | 1 Male portrait. ONE

ONE 1 | CARROLL CO. BANK, Sandwich, N. H. Three female figures floating in the air nearly covering the face of the bill. ONE ONE | 1 Portrait.

Steamboat. 3 | 3 ROCKLAND BANK, Rockland, Me. | THREE Fountain. 3

5 | EXCHANGE BANK OF TENNESSEE. Murfreesboro, Tenn. Two females, one reclining. | 5 Female portrait. FIVE

ONE — Female standing, right arm resting on a bucket. | Three farmers and one female in a wheat field; cars in background. SOUTHERN BANK, Beloit Wis. | 1 — State Arms. — ONE

2 — Male portrait — 2 | Male and female seated separated by a miniature view of wood-chopper, rural scenery, &c. STATE BANK OF INDIANA. Public buildings. | TWO — Female seated holding sword and balances. — TWO

FIVE | 5 Female and boy; girl and dog, man entering gate with rake. CLINTON BANK, Clinton, Conn. | 5 — DeWitt Clinton.

3 — State Arms. — THREE | Shield, female and three children on right; Indians on left. SOUTHERN BANK, Beloit Wis. | 3 — Farmer seated; sickle and sheaf of wheat.

3 — Portrait of an American officer. — 3 | State arms, farmer and two females; cart and oxen on right; locomotive and cars on left. STATE BANK OF INDIANA. Dog's head. | 3 — Cass. — 3

TEN — Tree; two men, one on horseback — TEN | Men at work mowing, tying and loading wagon with sheafs. CLINTON BANK, Clinton, Conn. | 10 — Boy's head.

5 | SOUTHERN BANK, Beloit, Wis. Female at a well. State Arms. Hunter erect with hatchet. FIVE | 5

FIVE | Male portrait. Lafayette and implements of war. 5 STATE BANK OF INDIANA. | 5 — Male portrait — 5

Auditor's die — Bull's head. | WARREN CO. BANK, Monmouth, Ills. 5 Drove of wild horses. | 5

TEN — State Arms. — 10 | SOUTHERN BANK, Beloit, Wis. Two horses, eagle, Indian, shield, &c.; ferry-boat on right; cars on left. | 10 — Cars. — 10

5 — Portrait of girl. | State arms surmounted by eagle, female and male on either side. STATE BANK OF INDIANA. 5 | 5 — Female, one arm leaning on 5.

ONE — Male portrait — ONE | Two females, one holding a sword, the other a spear; state arms between them, surmounted by a spread eagle. EXCHANGE B'K OF TENNESSEE, Murfreesboro, Tenn. Cornucopia. | ONE — Compt's die. — 1

1 — Cars, cattle, bridge, telegraph, &c. | Man shearing sheep. BK OF SOUTHERN ILLINOIS, Belton, Ill. | 1 — State Arms

Deer. — 10 — Buffalo. | State Arms surmounted by eagle; female and male on either side. Title of Bank, X | 10 — Squaw holding X and corn.

2 — 2 | Title of Bank, Same as ones. Cornucopia, &c. | Train of cars — Compt's die. — 2

2 — Female with flowers. | Man plowing. Title of Bank. | 2 — State Arms.

20 | State Arms surmounted by eagle; on right mechanic with sledge; on left female with scales; farmer in field and building in distance. 20 Title of Bank. XX | TWENTY — Female erect — TWENTY

III | Same as ones. Compt's die. Title of Bank. Cornucopia. | 3 — Female.

Three on 3. — Female feeding fowls. | Farmers, load of hay, horse and two oxen; steeple of church on left in distance. Title of Bank. | 3 — State Arms

Group of females — 50 | L Cupid in air. L Title of Bank. Canal. | Male; female erect with basket and sheaf of wheat; male seated with sickle; dog on ground. — 50

5 — V | PLANTERS' BK OF TENNESSEE. Three females seated; one playing harp. Locomotive. | 5 — Female seated holding scales in right hand shield and &c. flag in background.

Letter V and word Five. — Farmer seated; scythe hanging on tree. | Drovers and drove of cattle at a brook, some drinking; house in background. B'K OF SOUTHERN ILLINOIS, Belton, Ills. | 5 — State arms.

Female and men harvesting. — 100 | C Farmer ploughing with horses. C STATE BANK OF INDIANA. Locks. | Male picking cotton. — 100

Two female figures, one reclining. | 10 Female with a bucket seated on a log; steamboat on right; house on left. PLANTERS' B'K OF TENNESSEE. | 10 — Cotton plant barrel, &c.

1 — Indian queen seated. | Vig. Female seated, left arm leaning on escutcheon; in right hand scales; locomotive on right; steamboat on left. STATE BANK OF INDIANA. Public building. | 1 — Female standing erect holding shield.

STATE BANK OF OHIO

We have given descriptions of all the Notes of the State Bank of Ohio, except a one, (which has a winged female for vignette,) and a three, (which has cupids and a figure 3 for vignette.)

Male portrait — X | WEEDSPORT BANK, Weedsport, N. Y. Female, eagle and shield. | 10 — Compt's die.

2 — BANK OF BINGHAMPTON, Binghampton, N. Y. — 2. Spread eagle on limb of tree; train of cars, canal, boats, &c. Figure 2 on either side of vignette. Compt's die. Female oval, ed with scroll, spear and globe. Female seated with scales and sword; safe on left.

C — MECH. & FARMERS BK. Albany, N. Y. — 100. Male portrait. One Hundred Dollars. Compt's die. 100. Male and female seated.

Man with child on his knee; female, boy, dog, hen and chickens. — HAVERHILL B'K. Haverhill, Mass. — 5. View of a street. FIVE. Five Dols. Five Dols. Female binding shoes; box of shoes, etc.

FIFTY — Compt's die. Female portrait. 50. BANK OF BINGHAMPTON, Binghampton, N. Y. Horn of plenty and anvil. Indian female erect with bow and arrows. Winged female erect; female seated at her feet, also an eagle.

Female seated with stick and portrait of Washington. 500. — Male portrait. CITY BANK, Philadelphia, Pa. — Shield and letter D bust of female at top, male on right, female at left. 500.

Two men, horse, boy and negro holding bull by nose; cows, etc; barn, trees, etc, in back ground. Word Ten and letter X. — Word Ten and letter X. HAVERHILL BANK, Haverhill, Mass. — 10. Female feeding fowls.

10 on med head. Compt's die. — Male portrait; on right two females; on left three females in clouds; train of cars in distance on right. DEPOSIT BANK, Deposit, N. Y. — 10. Two Indians erect.

M. Shearing sheep. — 1000. Female reclining on shield, on which is a scroll and tree; drapery with stars over the shield. CITY BANK, Philadelphia, Pa. — 1000. M.

Female with flowers in her apron. D. — CONSOLIDATION BK. Philadelphia, Pa. Ornamental portrait of Gen. Scott. D D. Five Hundred Dollars. — 500. Female feeding fowls.

XX. Male portrait. — Compt's die. Three females. DEPOSIT BANK, Deposit, N. Y. Female bathing. — 20.

FIVE. Secured, &c. FIVE. — Portrait of Clay. Eagle on rock with shield; ship on right and ship and steamboat on left. BANK OF MIDDLE TENNESSEE, Lebanon, Tenn. — 5. Male portrait.

1000. Man seated; scythe hanging on tree. — CONSOLIDATION BK. Philadelphia, Pa. Horses drinking from trough by a well; man, goat and kid, sheep, etc. house in background. One Thousand Dollars. — M. Female portrait.

Male Portrait. 20. — View of Falls Village. IRON BANK, Falls Village, Ct. Beehive. — 20. View of factories, etc.

10. Secured, etc. — Man watering horses from trough by the side of well; sheeps, lambs, goats, house, trees, &c. BANK OF MIDDLE TENNESSEE, Lebanon, Tenn. — 10. Male portrait.

FIFTY. Female with distaff and shield; med head on shield and resting on pedestal. — FARMERS' BANK, Amsterdam, N. Y. Men mowing, gathering and loading wagon with wheat. Compt's Die. — 50 on medal lion head. Female.

2. Female with grain on head, and one under her arm. — Female 2 Female. B'K OF UTICA, Utica, N. Y. II. — 2. Compt's die. TWO.

20. Man seated; scythe on tree. — Tobacco field and two men, one holding tobacco in his hand; hhds, &c. BANK OF MIDDLE TENNESSEE, Lebanon, Tenn. — 20. Secured, &c.

100. Man seated; scythe hanging on tree. — FARMERS' BANK, Amsterdam, N. Y. State Arms with two females and cows on right; female and sheaf on left; horn of plenty at bottom. — 100. Portrait of Washington.

10. Train of cars. 10. — X Indian with drawn bow. X. B'K OF UTICA, Utica, N. Y. X. — TEN. Ten one dollar pieces on a column. TEN.

ONE. Female with flowers in apron. — View of a street. HAVERHILL B'K. Haverhill, Mass. One Dollar. One Dollar. — Word one and figure 1. Portrait of Webster.

FIVE. — 5. Female seated with boy leaning on her lap; man entering gate, and little girl running towards him; dog, fence, trees, etc. FARMERS' & MECHANIC'S BANK, Westminister, Md. — 5. Male portrait.

20. Indian. 20. — Train of cars; village in distance. B'K OF UTICA, Utica, N. Y. XX. — 20. Female with scales and sword; lion and key. 20.

Hunter loading his gun; deer at his feet. TWO. — Word Two and $ mark. View of a street. HAVERHILL B'K. Haverhill, Mass. Two Dollars. Two Dollars. — 2. Female gathering wheat.

Word ten and letter X. Man seated; scythe on tree. — BANK OF MONTGOMERY, Ala. Compt's Die. Large red die with figures 10 on it. — 10. Female portrait.

50. Male and female seated. — MECH. & FARMERS B'K. Albany, N. Y. FIFTY DOLLARS. Compt's die. — 50. Male portrait.

3. — View of a street. Word three and figure 3. HAVERHILL B'K. Haverhill, Mass. Three Dols. Three Dols. — 3. Female with cornucopia.

XX. Justice seated; city in distance. — BANK OF MONTGOMERY, Ala. Compt's die. Large red die with figures 20 on it. — 20. Two males standing and female seated.

5 on med head. Treas. die. Train of cars; large chimney, trees houses, sloop, &c., in background. PASSAIC CO. BANK, Paterson, N. J. Dog, key and safe. Five, V, 5. Portrait of a female	5 Female portrait. MAN. & TRA. BANK, Portland, Me. Large letter V, and words Five Dollars. 5 Portrait of Girl.	5 Male portrait. NIAGARA DISTRICT BANK, St. Catherines, Ca. Three men looking at chart on a stone; ship on stocks, shipping and city. 5 and word Five. Royal Arms.
1 Westport. ONE SAUGATUCK BANK, 1 Drove of sheep, boy on right. 1 Connecticut. ONE Man sowing: man ploughing in distance.	10 Female. TEN MAN. & TRA. BANK. Portland, Me. Letter X, and word Ten, shipping on right; haycart trees, city and bridge on left. 10 Female. TEN	20 Female. XX Three females representing Liberty, Agriculture and Commerce. PLANTERS' BANK OF TENNESSEE, Nashville, Tenn. 20 Locomotive and cars.
2 Train of cars. SAUGATUCK BANK, Westport, Conn. 2 Boy asleep on load of hay drawn by two oxen; boy walking with pitchfork in hand. 2 TWO Village scene.	Female with flowers in her apron. 6 MONTICELLO BANK, Charlottsville, Va. View of tobacco plantation; two men, one holding tobacco leaves; both by side of hogsheads. Locomotive. 6 State Arms.	50 Three male figures; anvil, flag, capstan and wheat. PLANTERS' BANK OF TENNESSEE, Nashville, Tenn. Male portrait. L 50 FIFTY
Ship; other vessels and city in background. 50 Female with sheaf and sickle. SAUGATUCK BANK, Westport. Conn. 50 Henry Clay	7 SEVEN 7 MONTICELLO BANK, Charlottsville, Va. Two horses running away from train of cars; trees, &c. 7 State Arms.	100 Washington C State Arms; two females; factories on right, train o' cars on left. 100 PLANTERS' BANK OF TENNESSEE, Nashville, Tenn. ONE HUNDRED
100 Sailor and blacksmith, each with implements of profession. 100 Ship; other vessels and lighthouse in distance. SAUGATUCK BANK, Westport, Conn. 100 Sailor leaning on capstan with quadrant in hand.	8 Man seated; scythe on tree. MONTICELLO BANK. Charlottsville, Va. Three females, representing the Arts and Sciences; house and water in distance. 8 State Arms.	XX Word twenty and two XX. PAHQUIOQUE B'K, Danbury, Conn. State Arms with female on either side. TWENTY 20 Word dollars; an two XX.
TWENTY Compt's die. TWENTY 20 Female seated; scientific apparatus; steamship in distance. 20 BANK OF WHITESTOWN, Whitestown, N. Y. Cattle, trees, etc. XX	Female with cornucopia. 9 MONTICELLO BANK, Charlottsville, Va. Drover and drove of cattle; boy in water; farm house, trees, &c., in distance. 9 State Arms.	On this end is figure 50, $ mark, word fifty, and letter L. PAHQUIOQUE B'K. Danbury, Conn. State Arms, horse on either side and eagle at top; on right train of cars and city; on left building. On this end is figure 50, word dollars and letter L.
10 Auditors' die Rafting scene—men, female and child on raft; man in boat with two birds; other rafts in distance. BK OF SOUTHERN ILLINOIS, Bolton, Ills. 10 Woodcutter.	1 View of Niagara Falls. 1 NIAGARA DISTRICT BANK, St. Catherines, Ca. Five Shil's 1	Male portrait Word one and figure 1. View of stone-yard. BANK OF RUTLAND, Rutland. Vt. One dollar. One dollar. 1 Male portrait
X Hunter and dog by fire. Drove of wild horses. UNION BANK, Swanton Falls, Vt. 10 Girl.	Head of Queen Victoria. 2 NIAGARA DISTRICT BANK, St. Catherines, Ca. Ship on stocks; female reclining on safe on left; on right sheaf of wheat and sheep. 2 Locomotive and tender.	Portrait of Washington. 2 Drover and cattle; boy in water; trees and house in distance. BANK OF RUTLAND, Rutland. Vt. Two dollars. Two dollars. 2 Portrait of Martha Washington.
Cattle and sheep; one of each standing the rest reclining. XX Female portrait. UNION BANK, Swanton Falls, Vt. 20 Hunter drinking from a brook.	FOUR Male portrait. NIAGARA DISTRICT BANK, St. Catherines, Ca. View of N. Y. harbor with steamship and ship. 4 Ship in canal trees, houses, &c.	Female gathering wheat. Word dollars and figure 3. BANK OF RUTLAND, Rutland, Vt. Blacksmith in shop. 3 Female with cornucopia.

500 | Pelican | 500 — CITIZENS BANK, New Orleans, La. — Goddess of Liberty. | 500

50 | Female seated. | 50 — Female, eagle and horn of plenty; letter L on either side. BANK OF MOBILE, Alabama. Indian and Canoe. — FIFTY

500 — Two females conversing; shipping on left; cars on right. CANAL BANK, New Orleans, La. Steamship. — 500

1000 — 1000 Goddess of Liberty. 1000 CITIZENS BANK, New Orleans. La. Pelican. — 1000

ONE HUNDRED — 100 | Sailing vessel. — Two females representing Agriculture and Commerce; on right figures 100. BANK OF MOBILE, Alabama. Sailing craft. — ONE HUNDRED

1000 — CANAL BANK, New Orleans, La. Spread ea le Head of Washington. — 1000

FIVE — 5 Large figure 5, two females, cupid, eagle, etc. 5 BK. OF LOUISIANA. New Orleans, La. — FIVE

Med. head and figures 500. | 500 | Med. head and figures 500. — BANK OF MOBILE, Alabama. Female seated on bale of merchandise; figures 500 on right of vig. — Same as on right end.

1 | Compt's die. — EXCHANGE BANK. Lockport, N. Y. Large die with male portrait and words one dollar in part circle across the top; red figure 1 on either side. — 1 | 1

TWENTY — Man on horseback, going at full speed; 20 on either side. BK. OF LOUISIANA, New Orleans, La. — TWENTY

Med. head and figures 1000. | 1000 | Med. head and figures 1000. — BANK OF MOBILE, Alabama. Neptune seated in a car; schooner; figures 1000 on left of vig. — Same as on right.

2 | Compt's die | 2 — EXCHANGE BANK, Lockport, N. Y. Large die with male portrait and words two dollars across it in part circle; red figure 2 on either side. — 2 | TWO | 2

FIFTY — Female reclining by a grove; 50 on either side. BK. OF LOUISIANA, New Orleans, La. — FIFTY

5 | Portrait of Washington. | 5 — CANAL BANK. New Orleans, La. Large figure 5 surrounded by five females; figure 5 on either side. — 5 | Portrait of Lafayette. | 5

Compt's die. | 3 — EXCHANGE BANK, Lockport. N. Y. Large die with portrait of Washington, and words three dollars in part circle at top; red figure 3 on either side. — Word dollars and figure 3. | 3

ONE HUNDRED — Two females; 100 on either side. BK. OF LOUISIANA, New Orleans, La. — ONE HUNDRED

10 | Columbus. | 10 — Large letter X, medallio heads of Washington and Franklin; four cupids. CANAL BANK, New Orleans, La. — 10 | Male portrait | 10

1 | Washington. | ONE — GRENVILLE CO. BK, Prescott, C. W, Train of cars; cattle in water. — 1 | Man carrying basket of corn.

Die | Portrait of Washington | Die — Female reclining. Eagle and shield, and figures 500. Female and sheep. BK. OF LOUISIANA, New Orleans, La. — FIVE HUNDRED

20 | Male portrait | 20 — Figures 20, two angels and cupid; figures 20 on either side. CANAL BANK, New Orleans, La. — 20 | Female portrait | 20

TWO | Columbus. | 2 — GRENVILLE CO. BK, Prescott, C. W. Wharf scene—men horses, wagons, boxes, barrels, ship and steamer. Beaver. — TWO | Female in figure 2. | TWO

Neptune. | 10 — Female reclining, and eagle with head of Washington on its breast; figure 10 on left of vignette. BANK OF MOBILE, Alabama. Lion. — 10 | Sail vessel. | 10

50 | Jackson. | 50 — Female, figures 50, bales, shipping, etc.; female portrait on either side of vig. CANAL BANK, New Orleans, La. Eagle. — 50 | Lafayette. | 50

Prince Albert. | V and three females. — Steamboat leaving wharf. GRENVILLE CO. BK, Prescott, C. W. Locomotive. — 5 | Large 5, two Indians, water fall, cars and bridge

TWENTY — Female seated holding balances, etc.; Lion with his paw on a key.; XX on either side BANK OF MOBILE, Alabama. — TWENTY

100 | Franklin | 100 — Sailor seated on bale of merchandise; shipping, etc.; figures 100 on left. CANAL BANK, New Orleans, La. — 100 | Washington | 100

Queen Victoria | TEN | 10 — Drove of cattle and sheep; drover on horse. GRENVILLE CO. BK, Prescott, C. W. Bee-hive. — 10 | TEN on X; milkmaid and cows.

10 Female, eagle, key, and safe. TEN View of all the State Arms of the Union; two females on either side; steamship on left; on right men mowing, factories, etc. COMMERCIAL B'K. Troy, N. Y. Portrait. 10 Two females eagle, shield cornucopia, &c. TEN	Figures 100 and $ mark. Large red letter C. MERCANTILE BK. Hartford, Ct. Large die with figures 100, and words one hundred dollars. 100 Large red letter C.	TEN Male portrait Male portrait. View of building, trees and part of street. Male portrait. BANK OF MONT. CO. Norristown, Pa. Dog. 10 Male portrait
20 Male portrait Three men shipyard, &c; ship on stocks on left, and steamboat, ship, and city on right. COMMERCIAL B'K. Troy, N. Y Building small boat. 20 Compt's die	5 Compt's die. 5 5 Two females with ornamental figure 5; two cupids on either side. 5 BUTCHERS' AND DROVERS' BANK. New York City. Wheat, plough, spade. 5 Cattle. 5	500 Female in clouds with cornucopia. UNION BANK, Augusta, Geo. 5 0 0 FIVE HUNDRED DOLLARS. 500 Female in clouds with quadrant.
50 Male portrait Two wild horses alarmed at train of cars; trees, etc. COMMERCIAL B'K. Troy, N. Y. Female and anchor. 50 Compt's die	5 Portrait of Washington. Large letter V with female seated within. 5 TROY CITY B'K. Troy, N. Y Compt's die. Female.	Female gathering wheat. 10 UNADILLA BANK, Unadilla, N. Y. Words ten dollars and figure 10. TEN Female with cornucopia. Compt's die.
L Franklin FIFTY 50 Female seated by shield; male figure in a car drawn by sea monsters. 50 MER. & MECH B'K. Troy, N. Y. Die. Full length male figure	50 Drove of cattle. MARKET BANK, Troy, N. Y. Two females on either side of Washington; on right, steamboat and ship; on left, sheaf and men mowing. 50 Compt's Die.	20 Two females with sheaf &c. UNADILLA BANK, Unadilla, N. Y. TWENTY DOLLARS. Compt's die. XX Milkmaid with tub.
100 Washington. 100 MER. & MECH. B'K. Troy, N Y. 100 100 Vig. Same as Fifties. 100 Three cherubs. 100	TEN Female representing Liberty standing by large X. Compt's die. MANUFACT'RS BK. Troy, N Y Large steamboat; houses and vessels on right and left. Secured, &c. Man sharpening scythe; locomotive in distance 10	1 State Arms. WESTERN BANK, Lockport, N. Y. Miniature view of the horse shoe falls and tower at Niagara Falls ONE ONE 1 Female with flowers in her apron.
1 Steamboat, Vig. Female seated holding a dagger and supporting a silver dollar. State Arms KENOSHA CO. BANK Kenosha, Wis Capital Stock, &c. 1 Female holding large figure 1.	20 Compt's die Two females representing manufactures; factory in distance on right; and steamboat on left. MANUFACT'R'S B'K. Troy, N. Y. Secured, &c. 20 Female seated; factory on right.	1 Female portrait. ONE EDGAR CO. B'K. Paris, Ills. Vig. Rail Road cars; drove of hogs being loaded Beehive. 1 State Arms 1
Vig. River scene, Indian, squaw and child in a canoe. 2 State Arms KENOSHA CO. BANK Kenosha Wis Capital Stock, &c. Female holding large figure 2. TWO	1 Compt's die ONE Vig. Factory, train of cars, horses, canal, boat, houses, trees, &c.; in the distance a train of cars crossing aqueduct NORTHERN BANK Howard, Wis. Capital $50,000, &c. 1 Indian princess seated, figure 1, rainbow, shield, &c	2 Male portrait EDGAR CO. B'K. Paris, Ills. Vig. Prairie scene; wild horses. Load of hay. 2 State Arms. TWO
XX Female gathering wheat. MERCANTILE B'K Hartford, Ct. Sailor at wheel. 20 Female with flowers in her apron.	2 Compt's die TWO Vig. Drove of cattle and sheep, drovers, horse, and dog NORTHERN BANK Howard, Wis Capital $50,000, &c 2 Two Females erect.	3 State Arms. THREE EDGAR CO. B'K. Paris, Ills. Vig. Cattle, sheep, &c. Anvil and horn of plenty. 3 Male portrait
Female with coroncopia. 50 MERCANTILE B'K. Hartford, Ct Male Portrait. FIFTY 50 Ship.	3 Compt's die. THREE Vig. Harvest scene, farmers at lunch, female and children, boy climbing, dog, &c., in distance man, 4 horses, and load of hay. NORTHERN BANK Howard, Wis. Capital $50,000, &c. 3 Figure 3 and three male figures, sailor, farmer, & mechanic.	5 State Arms. 5 EDGAR CO B'K. Paris, Ill. Vig. Indian female, bow and quiver; landscape. Hog. 5 Male portrait FIVE

Female and sailor; bales, anchor, etc. FIVE	5 Train of cars. SOUTHERN BANK of ALABAMA. Eagle.	5 on shield Cotton plant

Three females—Arts and Sciences TEN	Large spread eagle; figure 10 on left. SOUTHERN BANK of ALABAMA. Indian bust.	10 Schooner.

20 Female representing Commerce.	SOUTHERN BANK of ALABAMA. Steamship and other smaller vessels. Car.	20 Female representing Commerce.

50 Female.	Three females—Justice, Commerce, etc. SOUTHERN BANK of ALABAMA. Dogs head.	50 Sailor seated bales of merchandise.

100 Female seated on bale of goods; hhds., etc.	Female seated on bale of goods; hhds., buildings, etc. SOUTHERN BANK of ALABAMA. Bee-hive.	100 Blacksmith arr't; anvil, sledge, cog-wheel, etc.

Female, eagle and globe. 500	SOUTHERN BANK of ALABAMA. Steamship.	500 Washington on horseback

Female with American shield. 1	SOUHEGAN BANK, Milford, N. H. Blacksmith shoeing a horse.	1 Male portrait

Indian female; arms of 20 States for the border. 2	State Arms surmounted by an eagle, female on either side. SOUHEGAN BANK, Milford, N. H.	2 Portrait of Washington

3 Farmer	SOUHEGAN BANK, Milford, N. H. Landscape.	3 Farmer's wife.

Female with scales and sheaf of wheat. 5	Figure 5, surrounded by five females. SOUHEGAN BANK, Milford, N. H. 5	5 Figure 5, and five females.

10 Female churning.	Train of cars SOUHEGAN BANK, Milford, N. H.	X Female seated.

Fancy female head. 20	Farmers nooning. SOUHEGAN BANK, Milford, N. H. Loading hay	20 Fancy female head.

Female figure of Justice.	Boot making device; figs 50 on left. SOUHEGAN BANK, Milford, N. H. Shield, bales, etc	50 Fancy female head.

Female reclining with trident. 100	Arms of the Union; eagle, letter C on shield. SOUHEGAN BANK, Milford, N. H. Liberty.	100 Female representing Agriculture

1	Female seated; factories in distance; fig. 1 on right DERRY BANK, Derry, N. H. Machinery	1 Female with sheaf and basket of fruit.

Indian with bow and arrow. 2	Milkmaid and cattle; fig. 2 on left DERRY BANK, Derry, N. H.	2 Female with sheaf.

3 Sea monsters Steamship	Three females, each leaning on a fig. 1; fig. 3 on left. DERRY BANK, Derry, N. H	3 Three male figures.

Hunter with gun and game. 5	Webster supported by figure of Fame and cupid; 5 on right. DERRY BANK, Derry, N. H.	5 Justice and 5

TEN Justice and Minerva.	Woodcutter and oxen; figures 10 on left. DERRY BANK, Derry, N. H. Loading hay	X Beaver.

XX Female and bales.	Train of cars DERRY BANK, Derry, N. H.	20 Female.

Female and Agriculture. 50	50 Steamship. DERRY BANK, Derry, N. H. Man plowing.	50 Two females

1 Compt's die.	WAVERLY BANK, Waverly, N. Y. Large Die.	1 ONE

2 Compt's die. 2	WAVERLY BANK, Waverly, N. Y. Die. Die. 2 DOLLARS.	2 American shield.

Die. V FIVE	Die. Die. Die. WAVERLY BANK, Waverly, N. Y. Female.	Die. Compt's die 5

1 Figure 1, and words one dollar in part circle.	TRADERS' BANK. Nashville, Tenn. Shield surmounted by an eagle; miniature view of cars, etc., female on either side; ship in distance.	Word one and figure 1. 1

5 Blacksmith, anvil, forge, etc.	TRADERS' BANK, Nashville, Tenn. Drove of cattle, man on horseback, etc., some of the cattle drinking; farm-house, trees, etc., in the background.	5 V 5

Female with cornucopia.	5 State Arms 5 OAK WOOD BANK. North Pepin, Wis.	Female gathering wheat

5 — Vig. Mining scene: loaded coal car, two miners leaning against it; two seated on wheelbarrow upturned; two men at work, and stationary engine in distance on left. — 5
Male portrait. Head of young girl with curls.
FIVE — MAUCH CHUNK BK. Mauch Chunk, Bk. Bear. — FIVE

10 — Title of Bank. — 10
Bust of Washington, Continental soldiers, Indians, and figure of liberty.
Mechanic with hammer and anvil. Figure of Liberty.

XX — ROCKVILLE BANK, Rockville, Conn. — 20
Figures 20, two XX's and words twenty dollars.
Sheep shearing. Boy's head.

10 — Head of young girl. Title of Bank.
Harvest scene: male and female seated; man in act of drinking from pitcher.
Vig. Lumbering scene; man felling tree; another seated; horses dragging a log; saw mill in distance.
TEN DOLLARS.

20 — Title of Bank — 20
Landing of Roger Williams among the friendly Indians.
The Genius of Manufactures and Mechanics. Arms of the United States.

1 — State Arms. — 1
Farm scene; female at table blowing horn; three men in distance.
HACKETTSTOWN B'K, Hackettstown, N. J.
dog. — ONE

20 — Train of cars passing a group of people; some seated, consisting of hunters, hay makers, women, &c. — 20
Man, horse, dog, &c. in field of grain; man with sheaf under right arm.
Young girl erect with glass in her hand.
Title of Bank.
Child's Head.

Design illustrating the tariff protecting American productions.
Title of Bank. American Eagle. — 50
Dairy maid, farmhouse and village church.

TWO — Title of Bank. — 2
An ox and a sheep standing, three cows and two sheep lying down.
Head of girl. Female head.

50 — Vig. Scene on canal; boat locking through; harvest scene and cars on viaduct in background. — 50
Scene upon road, drovers among herd of cattle; hay wagon &c. in distance.
Title of Bank.
Locomotive and train of cars coming round curve; steamboat in distance.

100 — MERRIMACK RIVER BANK, Manchester, N. H. — 100
Female writing on fabrics; village in distance.
Train of cars and village; lake and scenery in distance.

3 — Two oxen before hay cart, boy asleep on top and another walking by the side of oxen. — 3
State Arms.
Ox. — Title of Bank. — 3

C — 100 — Vig. Cupid surrounded by three mermaids floating on water. — C
Woman with basket on left arm feeding chickens.
MAUCH CHUNK BK. Mauch Chunk, Pa. Spread eagle.
Head of female.
100

1 — Two Looms, girls weaving. — 1
ONE — ROCKVILLE BANK, Rockville, Conn.
1 — Female bathing.
Portrait of Webster.

FIVE — Female and Indian on either side of Portrait of Jackson; tents and trees on right, ships and city on left. — 5
Locomotive and train of cars; trees, house, &c.
Title of Bank.
Girl.

1 — River, falls, locks, ruins of old mills, island village and hills in the distance. — 1
Female operative drawing in.
MERRIMACK RIVER BANK Manchester, N. H.
Female portrait.

2 — Agricultural scene; cattle grazing. — 2
ROCKVILLE BANK, Rockville, Conn.
Man on horseback. Ducks. Male portrait.

TEN — Farm scene; men at work mowing, raking and loading wagon; two oxen before wagon. — 10
Title of Bank.
X — Boy.

2 — Title of Bank. — 2
Vig. Same as ones.
Two wheelbarrows up shop? to incoming farmers wagon.
Mill girl with shuttle, and shop boy with hammer and anvil.
TWO

Word three and figure 3. — Agricultural scene; dairy maid with pail, cows, &c. — THREE
Indian girl in door of wigwam.
ROCKVILLE BANK, Rockville, Conn. Dog.
Three female figures with emblems of peace, &c.

XX — Two cows one standing, the other lying down, milkmaid, chickens, cows and sheep; on right in distance trees, shed, &c. — 20
Title of Bank.
Child. Female head.

Three females on a cliff overlooking the ocean, one resting right hand on anchor; one with sheaf under her arm.
Title of Bank. — 3
Vig. Same as ones.
3

FIVE — ROCKVILLE BANK, Rockville, Conn. — 5
5 — Load of hay; boy sleeping on top; boy walking by side of oxen. — 5
Ducks. Female head.

50 — Two boys, one on horse driving sheep, the other holding gate open. — 50
Title of Bank.
Portrait of Washington. Henry Clay.

5 — Title of Bank. — 5
Female seated in large letter V with sheaf.
Indian overlooking the Falls. Portrait of female.

X — ROCKVILLE BANK, Rockville, Conn. — 10
State Arms.
Iron foundry. Girl.

Female with cornucopia. — Sailor reclining on coil of rope; nautical instruments, etc; ships in distance. — 5
B'K OF COMMERCE. Nashville, Tenn.
View of steamer Pacific.
5 — 5 — 5

Farmer erect in field leaning on scythe small village in distance. Compt's Die.
Farmers loading cart with grain; two horses in front. SMITH'S BANK OF PERRY, N. Y. Secured, &c.
1 ONE

5 Female portrait.
Wharf, shipping and building. MARINE BANK, Milwaukee, Wis. Rooster
5 Compt's die

5 FIVE
Tatching scene. B'K OF WILMINGTON, Wilmington, N C. Boxes, bales, &c.
5 Ship sailing.

2 Compt's die. 2
Barn-yard scene—female seated on stool another erect; fowls, cows, haystacks, &c. SMITH'S BANK OF PERRY, N. Y. Secured, &c.
2 Boy and rabbits.

1 Blacksmiths boy at forge. ONE
GLOUCESTER CO. BK Woodbury, N. J. Vig. female on either side of a shield surmounted by horse's head; steamer and cars in distance.
1 ONE Female milking cow; little girl and another cow

6 Horse. 6
Train of cars. B'K OF WILMINGTON, Wilmington, N. C. Schooner.
6 Eagle. 6

5 Little girl and fowls.
SMITH'S BANK OF PERRY N. Y. 5 Male portrait. 5 Secured, &c.
Large 5 and word five on either side. Compt's die. FIVE

3 Horse running away, boys trying to stop him; horse, colt and house in distance.
GLOUCESTER CO. BK, Woodbury, N. J. Female on either side of a shield, surmounted by head of horse.
3 Head of a little girl.

Two sailors and two females on ship; city in distance.
Dairy maid and cows. 7 B'K OF WILMINGTON Wilmington, N. C.
7 7

1 Royal Arms. ONE
EXCHANGE BANK OF TORONTO, Ca. Indian seated on rock with left arm leaning on figure 1; on right, canoe, &c., on left deer, trees, &c.
1 Farmer with sheaf on his knee and sickle.

5 Farmer seated with scythe in hand; village cars, factory, building, &c. in distance.
GLOUCESTER CO. BK Woodbury, N. J.
5 Male portrait

8 Ship sailing.
Jackson between two girls; harvest scene on left; ships and steamboat on right. B'K OF WILMINGTON, Wilmington, N. C. Locomotive.
8 Sailor on ship.

TWO Royal Arms. 2
Harvest field, farmers at work reaping and loading wagon with grain; in distance barn, house, &c. EXCHANGE BANK OF TORONTO, Ca
2 Ships, &c.

10
Cows standing in water; one reclining on bank; sheep on left. Small head of a girl. GLOUCESTER CO. BK Woodbury, N. J.
10 Female portrait

9 Mechanics at work. 9
Female reclining; eagle on right; train of cars and bridge on left; city in distance. B'K OF WILMINGTON, Wilmington, N. C. Ship.
9 Water trees, fruit.

5 Royal Arms. FIVE
View of the ocean, ships, lighthouse &c. EXCHANGE BANK OF TORONTO, Ca
FIVE Female erect leaning on anchor.

20 Farmer, horse, dog, and pigeons.
GLOUCESTER CO. BK Woodbury, N.J. Blacksmith shoeing a horse; man seated on log looking on; man in distance.
20 Female portrait.

X 10
B'K. OF WILMINGTON. Wilmington, N. C. Tatch scene.
10 Girl.

10 Royal Arms. TEN
Two steamships and ship at sea. EXCHANGE BANK OF TORONTO, Ca.
Deer. 10 Buffalo.

Full length male figure with scroll. FIFTY
Drovers and drove of cattle; in distance village, train of cars, building, &c. GLOUCESTER CO. BK, Woodbury, N. J. Bee-hive.
50 Carrier at work.

Twenty and state arms. X X
Steamboat. B'K OF WILMINGTON, Wilmington, N. C. 20
TWENTY 20 XX

1 Sailor, capstan and bale of cotton.
Ships under sail. MARINE BANK, Milwaukee, Wis. Dog
1 Compt's die.

100 Male portrait 100
GLOUCESTER CO. BK, Woodbury, N. J. Signing the Declaration of Independence.
100 Portrait of Washington. 100

50 Die.
Large spread eagle; ships on either side. B'K OF WILMINGTON, Wilmington, N. C. 50
50 Die

2 Farmer with sheaf of grain dog and crow
MARINE BANK, Milwaukee, Wis. Horses, Plough and Farmer. Ducks
2 Compt's die

1 Compt's die ONE
Mechanic seated with sledge and anvil; cars and factories in distance. SENECA CO. BANK, Waterloo, N. Y. Female bathing.
1 Justice.

C Female and eagle; shield.
100 One Hundred. B'K OF WILMINGTON, Wilmington, N. C. C One Hundred C
ONE HUNDRED

1 — Male portrait
Brig, merchant and man of war; light house on left, steamship in distance.
B'K OF CAPE COD. Harwich, Mass.
Codfish.
1 — Female with spy glass seated on cask; ship in distance.

1 — Compt's die.
FLOUR CITY B'K. Rochester, N. Y.
Farming scene.
1 — Man and barrels.

10 — Portrait of girl.
PARK BANK, New York City.
Female seated with nine cherubs, shield, cornucopia and ten gold dollars, locomotive and steamboat in distance.
TEN — Sailor, bales, barrels. Compt's die.

2 — Sailor seated with stars and stripes; anchor, cask, quadrant.
B'K OF CAPE COD. Harwich, Mass.
Landing of Pilgrims at Provincetown.
Codfish.
2 — Portrait of Girl.

TWO — Compt's die. — TWO
Two cherubs; two silver dollars; train of cars and cattle in background.
FLOUR CITY BANK. Rochester, N. Y.
2 — Male portrait

TWENTY — Full length female with sword and scales.
PARK BANK, New York City.
Three females representing agriculture, commerce and manufactures; ship in distance.
Compt's die.
XX — Sailor and Indian seated by shield.

Portrait of female. — 3
B'K OF CAPE COD. Harwich, Mass.
Three sailors, one standing against wharf post, pipe in mouth, another standing at his right; third seated on anchor with spy glass and pipe; casks, ships, &c.
Codfish.
3 — Portrait of Girl.

5 — Male portrait
FLOUR CITY BANK. Rochester, N. Y.
Two flour barrels, sheafs of wheat; men in distance.
5 — Compt's die. — FIVE

FIFTY — Full length female with spear and shield.
PARK BANK. New York City.
Female and eagle in clouds, surrounded by American flag.
Compt's die.
50 — Portrait of Washington

Portrait of a boy. — 4 — FOUR
B'K OF CAPE COD. Harwich, Mass.
Signing Declaration of Independence.
Codfish.
4 — Female seated in sea shell, trident in hand; ships in distance.

X — Two figures carrying sheafs.
Male portrait in frame; winged female on left; cherub on right.
FLOUR CITY BANK. Rochester, N. Y.
TEN — Compt's die

100 — Male portrait
PARK BANK, New York City.
View of the New York City Hall.
Compt's die.
100 — Steamship

5 — Male portrait. — FIVE
B'K OF CAPE COD. Harwich, Mass.
Vig. Signing the first constitution in the cabin of the May Flower in Cape Cod Harbor in 1620.
5 — Male portrait

20 — 20
Compt's die.
Milkmaid seated; cows on left; dog and pail on right.
FLOUR CITY BANK. Rochester, N. Y.
TWENTY — Mechanic; barrels, bales; ship in distance. — TWENTY

500 — Male portrait
PARK BANK, New York City.
Sailor and Indian by side of shield; two females by State Arms, shipping in distance.
Compt's die.
500 — D

10 — Sailor leaning on capstan; casks, bales and shipping
Signing the first constitution on board the May flower, 1620; Indian princes on right, with bow and quiver.
B'K OF CAPE COD. Harwich, Mass.
Codfish.
10 — Portrait of J. Q. Adams — TEN

Sailor by side of shield, bbls. &c. — Compt's die
PARK BANK. New York City
Word one and figure 1. — Red silver dollar — Word one and figure 1.
View of Park Fountain, and the City Hall
Indian on cliff. — ONE

1000 — Sailor event, flag, &c.
PARK BANK, New York City.
Steamship at sea in storm.
Compt's die.
M

20
B'K OF CAPE COD. Harwich, Mass.
Vig. Scene on Marshfield farm; cattle and sheep grazing.
20 — Portrait o Dan. Webster.

TWO — Compt's die. — Spread eagle and shield.
PARK BANK. New York City.
Red silver dollar — Red silver dollar.
View of Park, City Hall, Hall of Records, etc;
2 — Portrait of girl.

1 — Female feeding chickens.
WALWORTH CO. BK. Delavan, Wis.
State die.
1 — Man, horse and dog.

Portrait of female. — 50
B'K OF CAPE COD. Harwich, Mass.
Vig. Sailor standing against vessels rail; steam ships and shipping in distance.
Codfish.
50 — Anchor and chain; box, bales, cask; ships.

Compt's die. — Mexican lassoing wild cattle.
PARK BANK. New York City.
3 Three gold dollars. 3
Steamships and ships at sea.
3 — Drove of cattle, sheep, hogs, &c.; house in distance.

TWO — Smith's shop
WALWORTH CO. BK. Delavan, Wis.
2 Female; bale of goods, houses in distance. 2
2 — State die.

Sailor with flag; female with horn of plenty; bale, anchor, &c.
100 — 100
B'K. OF CAPE COD Harwich, Mass.
Portrait of Washington.
One Hundred.
Female figure of Justice ensign with stars, covering her lap.

5 — Sailor and Indian seated by side of shield; eagle at top.
PARK BANK, New York City.
Five cherubs and five silver dollars.
5
5 — Compt's die — FIVE

5 — Head of female.
Horse Market.
WALWORTH CO. BK. Delavan, Wis
5 — State die.

1 Farmers at lunch. 1 SOMMERSWORTH BANK, Sommersworth, N. H. Load of hay. 1 Sailor.	Laocoon and sons struggling with the serpent. 1000 THOUSAND Train of cars. Title of Bank. 1000 Vessels. 1000	Word five, letter V, and figure 5. Indian figure seated; steamship in distance. Title of Bank. Compt's die. 5 Female reclining; hill &c.
2 Farmers at lunch; dog and sheaf of wheat. 2 Title of Bank. Blacksmith and anvil. 2 Sailor boy pulling oar.	ONE 1 Three male figures; trees village, &c. 1 CHESHIRE CO. B'K, Keene, N. H. ONE	ONE Girl with sheaf of grain on head. Compt's die. 1 Three men, sheaves of grain, sickle, &c. CHEMUNG CO. BANK Horse Heads, N. Y. Two horse's heads. 1 Child's bust and birds.
3 Girls tending looms. 3 Title of Bank. Cattle. 3 Eagle. Train of cars.	TWO CHESHIRE CO. B'K, Keene, N. H. TWO 2 Female feeding fowls. TWO	TWO Compt's die. 2 Horses frightened. CHEMUNG CO. BANK Horse Heads, N. Y. 2 Locomotive.
5 Man plowing with horses. 5 Title of Bank. Man plowing 5 Portrait of Washington.	FIVE DOLLARS FIVE DOLLARS 5 Anvil, plough, anchor, cogwheel, &c. CHESHIRE CO. B'K, Keene, N. H. Dog, key and safe. 5	Compt's die. 3 Dwelling, Railroad, cars canal, boats and bridge. CHEMUNG CO BANK Horse Heads, N. Y. Heads of three horses. 3 Female and dog.
Portrait of a boy. X Drove of cattle. Title of Bank. Horses. TEN TEN X Man cradling wheat.	Word ten, figure 10 and letter X. CHESHIRE CO. B'K, Keene, N. H. Large X. and words ten dollars. Rolling machine. Word ten figure 10 and letter X. Sailor at wheel.	5 Washington. Train of cars crossing bridge; village in distance. CHEMUNG CO. BANK Horse Heads, N. Y. Heads of two horses. 5 Compt's die 5
Female representing liberty, with eagle. XX Artist drawing plans; stone cutters and team in distance. Title of Bank. Bale and machinery. 20 Female head.	XX Female gathering wheat. CHESHIRE CO. B'K, Keene, N. H. Figure 20, across words twenty dollars 20 Female with cornucopia.	1 Man erect with drum, two others seated, one with pipe. Blacksmith shoeing horse; man seated and one erect. ROCK COUNTY B'K, Janesville, Wis. 1 Compt's die
Blacksmith at anvil. 50 Mechanic in a sitting posture, leaning his arm upon a steam boiler; workmen in distance Title of Bank. Safe. 50 Factory building.	Full length female with helmet, spear and shield. 50 50. Ship on stocks. 50 CHESHIRE CO. B'K, Keene, N. H. Fifty dollars. Full length female. 50	Portrait of boy. Compt's die. Men gathering ears of corn; horse, colt, cart and dog. ROCK COUNTY B'K, Janesville, Wis. Dog, key and safe. 2 Portrait of female.
Female figure of Justice. 100 Female with shield, sheaf of wheat and horn of plenty Title of Bank. Anvil, hammer and boiler. 100 Stone cutter at work.	Man sharpening scythe, one gathering wheat, one reclining; female with rake. Word one and figure 1. State Arms. BANK OF HUTSONVILLE, Hutsonville, Ills 1 ONE Indian female seated and child; trees, &c.	Head of girl. Compt's die Group of persons viewing and applauding train of cars; in distance, forest, house, cart, &c. ROCK COUNTY B'K, Janesville, Wis. Dog's head. 3 Female seated with sheaf and sickle.
Female figure representing agriculture; reapers in distance. 500 500 D Title of Bank. 500	2 Compt's die. 2 Horse and oxen before hay cart, two men and boy; trees, spire, &c., in distance. Title of Bank. 2 Female with rake.	5 Compt's die. Cattle, hogs, &c.; town on right. ROCK COUNTY B'K, Janesville, Wis. 5 Henry Clay. 5

5 Woodsman felling trees; oxen in background. LOCKHAVEN BANK. Lockhaven, Pa. Female with sheaf of wheat. Male portrait 5	ONE Sailor, bbl. bales; top of masts of vessels. Schooners and sloops; men fishing; various vessels and lighthouse in distance. B'K OF CAPE ANN, Gloucester, Mass. 1 Boy with rabbits.	2 Two Spanish Dollars. Two silver dollars and female with shield. Title of Bank. Head of a child. 2 State Arms Word two and figure 2
Male portrait TEN TEN LOCKHAVEN BANK. Lockhaven, Pa. DOLLARS Men at work with patent mowing and raking machine drawn by two horses. 10	2 BANK OF CAPE ANN Gloucester, Mass. Vig. Same as ones. 2 Liberty, left arm on shield; train of cars and factory in distance.	III Three silver dollars. Man, two horses, plow and dog; train crossing bridge. Title of Bank. Boats with man and goods 3 State arms THREE
XX 20 LOCKHAVEN BANK, Lockhaven, Pa. Shield with train of cars and rising sun; on right, sheafs and sheep; on left female seated with tub; house in distance. 20 Portrait of Washington	Man with scythe in field; village in distance. 3 Two females; one feeding chickens; the other milking cow, cow, hay-stack, horse, &c. BANK OF CAPE ANN Gloucester, Mass. 3 Female.	FIVE Five silver dollars. State Arms. Two females with sheaf, shield, sickle, etc. Title of Bank. Cornucopia 5 Man carrying basket of corn.
Male portrait 50 LOCKHAVEN BANK, Lockhaven, Pa. State Arms with horse on either side; cars, boats, factories, etc. 50	5 Female with chickens. Vig. Same as ones. B'K OF CAPE ANN, Gloucester, Mass. Figure 5, word five on either side. Indian female, left hand resting on rock.	Female Justice. ONE Female with liberty cap, horn of plenty, sheaf &c; on right train of cars; on left shield surmounted by an eagle. GRAND PRAIRIE BANK, Urbana, Ills. 1 State arms. 1
100 C LOCKHAVEN BANK, Lockhaven, Pa. Female with small tub. 100 Eagle on branch of tree; cars, canal, factories, etc.	10 Female portrait. Launching boat in sea, men apparently going to rescue passengers from ship that has stranded. B'K OF CAPE ANN, Gloucester, Mass. X Shield in cornice work with motto, E Pluribus Unum.	2 State Arms. GRAND PRAIRIE BANK, Urbana, Ills. Load of hay; man driving with fork on shoulder, and man reclining on load. 2 Two men gathering corn.
1 Male portrait WESTERN EXCHANGE FIRE AND MARINE INSURANCE CO. B'K. Omaha City, Nebraska Territory. Three Indians, male and one female and child; prairie scene; train of cars, etc. 1 ONE Female Indian and child.	Spread eagle on shield. 20 B'K OF CAPE ANN, Gloucester, Mass. Large Ship, steamship, and other ships in distance. 20 Sailor seated on rock with telescope.	5 Two men, shearing sheep; boy looking on. GRAND PRAIRIE BANK, Urbana, Ills. Female with sword and scales; eagle, olive branch, etc. 5 State Arms.
2 Portrait of Lewis Cass. Title of Bank. Indian with horse; buffaloes; train of cars; prairie scene TWO 2 Indian reclining.	50 Steamship; ships in distance Female with cornucopia and sheaf of wheat. B'K OF CAPE ANN, Gloucester, Mass. 50 Two males, one holding plan of pillar the other looking at it building a house.	10 Two females supporting sheaf of grain. Female with shield, horn of plenty, etc; State Arms; Indians and wigwams; ship, houses, &c GRAND PRAIRIE BANK, Urbana, Ills 10 10 Girl shading her eyes with her hands
Word dollars and figure 3. Male portrait Title of Bank Indian on horse hunting buffaloes; hills, etc, in background. 3 Milk maid.	100 Three female figures with pole and cap, and horn of plenty, &c. B'K OF CAPE ANN, Gloucester, Mass. C Indian seated on rock with bow.	1 Man seated under tree, scythe hanging on limb of tree. Wagon loaded with bales with two mules and two oxen before it; man on horseback; other figures and wagons in back ground. BANK OF PARIS, Paris, Tenn. 1 Portrait of female.
Figure 5 on med. head. Webster. FIVE Title of Bank. Steamboat with name Omaha on wheel-box; hills and steamboat in background. Figure 5 on med. head. Pierce. FIVE	American dollar and female with sword. 1 E. I. TINKHAM & CO'S BANK, McLeansboro, Ills. State Arms. Train of cars; three cows. ONE Spanish dollar.	FIVE V Female seated reclining on shield; bow and quiver; bales, bbl. etc.; steamer in distance BANK OF PARIS, Paris, Tenn. 5 Man plowing with two horses.

- ONE / State Arms, female and ships. / 1 / Female with sheaf. / MECHANICS BANK, Portland, Me. / ONE / Steamer. / Henry Clay
- 1 / Men, woman and child on timber raft floating down river; another man in boat, other rafts in distance. / ONE / BANK OF TRENTON, Trenton, Tenn. / Compt's die. / Female in dian erect, and a female gathering wheat.
- V / Female in clouds with pole and cap; eagle in front of her; rising sun and motto Excelsior at her back. / Word Five and figure 5 / Male portrait / CITY BANK, Nashville, Tenn. / Same as ones. / Male portrait / 5
- 2 / Cupids. / Three Graces. / MECHANICS' BANK, Portland, Me. / Plough and sheaf. / 2 / Female balancing scales
- Full length female. / BANK OF TRENTON, Trenton, Tenn. / View of a suspension bridge; steamboat, river, houses, trees, hills, &c. / 2 / TWO / Compt's die.
- Female with some branches on head, load of hay and village in distance. / ONE / ELM CITY BANK, New Haven, Conn. / Portrait of Washington. / 1 / Boy with rabbits.
- THREE / Fame seated on a globe blowing trumpet. / Eagle, with steamers and ships in distance. / MECHANICS' BANK, Portland, Me / Dog, key and safe. / 3 / Girl playing a lute
- Female erect with helmet, spear and shield. / FIVE / 5 Men at work in an iron mill. / BANK OF TRENTON, Trenton, Tenn. / 5 / Compt's die.
- 2 / Female with chickens. / ELM CITY BANK, New Haven, Ct. / 2 / Three men by side of a small boat, partly finished; ship on stocks.
- 5 / Female with trident. / 5 / Steamship. / MECHANICS' BANK, Portland, Me. / Locomotive. / 5 / Female portrait.
- 1 / Figure of Mercury with bag of money / HOME BANK, Meriden, Conn. / Drover and farmer bargaining for ox. / 1 / Female figure.
- 3 / Three females with liberty pole and cap, &c. / Three male figures, blacksmith, sailor and farmer; interior of blacksmith shop; horse, anvil and men. / ELM CITY BANK, New Haven, Ct. / 3 / 3
- 10 / Portrait of Washington. / Train of cars. / MECHANICS' BANK, Portland, Me. / Eagle. / 10 / Female indian, shield and liberty cap.
- 2 / Wheelwright and apprentice. / Female figure of manufactures. / HOME BANK, Meriden, Conn. / 2 / Genius of America.
- 5 / Eagle on shield. / View of steamboat Elm City; vessels in distance. / ELM CITY BANK, New Haven, Ct. / Sailing vessels. / 5 / Female.
- 2 Cupids 0 / Fame blowing trumpet; eagle and globe. / MECHANICS' BANK, Portland, Me. / Steamship. / 20 / Roman female.
- 3 / Indian looking over rock / HOME BANK, Meriden, Conn. / Arm and hand with hammer. / 3 / Female feeding chickens.
- 10 / Mower drinking from jug; scythe, fence and field. / Two sailors, one standing; the other seated on box; wharf scene; steamship in distance. / ELM CITY BANK, New Haven, Ct. / 10 / Portrait of female.
- 50 / Sailor with flag. / Female indian, eagle and flag. / MECHANICS' BANK, Portland, Me. / Plough. / 50 / Portrait of female.
- 5 / Justice with scales. / HOME BANK, Meriden, Conn. / Apotheosis of Washington / 5 / Bee-hive.
- 20 / Portrait of Columbus / Large ship, steamships; ships in distance. / ELM CITY BANK, New Haven, Ct. / 20 / Boy with globe and compass.
- Eagle. / 100 / Female portrait. / MECHANICS' BANK, Portland, Me. / Locomotive. / 100 / Sloop, &c.
- 10 / Female holding up counter. / TEN / HOME BANK, Meriden, Conn. / Train of cars. / Female head. / 10 / Female figure.
- Three females representing liberty, justice, and agriculture; field &c / ELM CITY BANK, New Haven, Ct / L 50 L / 50 / Portrait of Franklin.
- Portrait of Franklin. / 500 / State Arms; two females, horse's head, &c. / MECHANICS' BANK, Portland, Me. / 500 / Portrait of female.
- 1 / Male portrait / Shield and view of all the State Arms of the Union; female on either side. / CITY BANK, Nashville, Tenn. / Dogs head with word Fidelity. / 1 / Male portrait
- 100 / ELM CITY BANK New Haven, Ct. / Mechanic and farmer; horse, trees, &c.; factories in distance in lower left corner of note. Cow right. / 10 / Female indian, left hand on rock.

Word one and figure 1. Female seated with shield; farmers binding grain; cable and trees in distance. Female Indian seated; with shield; bow and arrows, tomahawk, cotton bale, etc. NORTHERN BANK of Tennessee. 1 Word one and figure 1. Female erect with pole, shield and eagle. ONE

Female with scales seated 50 Men seated with elbow resting on a column; two men and team of horses. PENNICHUCK B'K. Nashua, N. H. 50 Portrait of Jackson.

2 Two dollars. 2 MECHANICS' BANK, Wilmington, Del. Three blacksmith's at work with their tools; anchor and boiler; on the left of vig. portrait of female; on right portrait of male. 2 TWO 2

2 TWO 2 Vig. Puddling in an iron mill, rolling, &c. NORTHERN BANK of Tennessee. Kegs, lead, shingles, &c. 2 Female seated with sheaf of grain, &c

Portrait of Webster. 100 Cattle, sheep and two men with horse and dog. PENNICHUCK B'K. Nashua, N. H. 100 Hunter with dog, gun and game.

5 Female portrait. MECHANICS' BANK, Wilmington, Del. Ship yard with vessels on the stocks, and men at work; city and sloop in distance. V Eagle V 5 Female feeding chickens.

5 Male portrait V Five boys; three supporting staff with cap of liberty, with a shield; one boy holding sickle, grain, etc. V NORTHERN BANK of Tennessee. Anvil, &c. 5 Male portrait

1 Female head. ONE TRADESMENS' B'K, New Haven. Conn. Battle scene. ONE ONE 1 View of Bank building.

10 Blacksmith at forge. Portrait of female. Sailor seated on anchor smoking pipe, and conversing with two other men. MECHANICS' BANK, Wilmington, Del. Cock. 10 10

Cupid—a fountain of water. 1 PENNICHUCK B'K. Nashua, N. H. Indian female seated. 1 Portrait of Washington.

2 Cows and dairy maids. TRADESMENS' B'K, New Haven, Conn. Blacksmith and anvil; farmer, horse and dog 2 Sailor and shipping.

20 Sailor leaning on capstan; bale, etc.: ship in distance. Five men at work at a puddling furnace MECHANICS' BANK, Wilmington, Del. 20 Figure of Justice.

Female erect with glass in hand. TWO State Arms and eagle; female on either side; cars, factories, steamboat and man plowing in distance. PENNICHUCK B'K. Nashua, N. H. Man plowing with horses. 2 Portrait of Pierce.

3 Landing of R. Williams. TRADESMENS' B'K. New Haven, Conn. THREE 3 DOLLARS 3 3 Female and bale of goods factories in the distance.

50 Farmers at dinner in field. Train of cars; city in distance. MECHANICS' BANK, Wilmington, Del. Steamboat. 50 Female portrait.

Sailor with flag. THREE Title of Bank. Three females seated with sickle, etc. Load of hay. 3 Portrait of Clay.

5 Railroad, steamboat and wharf scene. TRADESMENS' B'K, New Haven, Conn. 5 View of Bank building.

100 C MECHANICS' BANK, Wilmington. Del. Female seated; factories in the distance; on right of vig. male portrait; on left female portrait. 100 C

Sailor, Indian, female, etc. 5 Large V. female within. PENNICHUCK B'K. Nashua, N. H Mechanic seated. 5 Portrait of Chase.

10 Battle field. Farmers resting at noon; two horses attached to plough feeding. TRADESMENS' B'K, New Haven, Conn. 10 View of Bank building

1 Compt's die. 1 Female surrounded by fruit and corn; in distance trees, river, shipping, village, &c CENTRAL BANK OF WISCONSIN. Janesville Wis. Locomotive 1 Portrait of female. 1

Male portrait. X Female seated; cows, milkmaids, engine, ship, etc. PENNICHUCK B'K. Nashua, N. H. 10 Female with liberty cap and declaration of Independence.

20 TWENTY TRADESMENS' B'K. Three blacksmiths with with forge and implements. New Haven, Conn. 20 DOLLARS

2 Compt's die TWO Farm scene; man watering three horses at a trough; female feeding pigs; buildings in distance Title of Bank Steamboat 2 Female with folded hands 2

Indian portrait. XX Female with liberty cap; portrait of Washington; factories and vessels. PENNICHUCK B'K. Nashua. N. H. 20 Dam and water fall.

Interior of blacksmith's shop, with men at work; cottage in distance. 1 MECHANICS' BANK. Wilmington, Del. Portrait of Washington. Fire Engine 1 1

3 Compt's die 3 Title of Bank. Train of cars Agricultural implements. 3 Portrait of Washington. 3

1 ONE — Compt's die.
Drove of cattle; man on horseback, boy in water; trees, house, fence, etc.
BRIGG'S BANK OF Clyde, N. Y.
Safe.
1 — Portrait of female.

3 — Portrait of Gen. Scott.
Cattle and sheep.
PARKE CO. BANK, Rockville, Ind.
Hog.
3 — Portrait of a female.

FIVE — Hunter loading gun.
Liberty surrounded by stars and the implements of war.
CONTINENTAL B'K, Grandville, Ills.
5 — Auditor's die

2 — Compt's die. TWO
Horse and oxen before load of hay; three men and a boy; trees, etc.
Train of cars
BRIGG'S BANK OF Clyde, N. Y.
2 — Canal scene; village in distance.

5 — Female portrait. FIVE
Cattle scene and milkmaid.
PARKE CO. BANK, Rockville, Ind.
Anvil and cornucopia.
5 — Male portrait FIVE

X — Five cupids, globe and anvil.
CONTINENTAL B'K, Grandville, Ills.
Auditor's die
10 — Five cherubs with rake and tablets.

5 — Two men and dog; man and boy behind them; trees and house in distance.
Man plowing with two horses; trees and farm-houses in distance.
BRIGG'S BANK OF Clyde, N. Y.
5 — Compt's die. FI 5 VE

10 — Female portrait. TEN
Stone quarry.
PARKE CO. BANK, Rockville, Ind.
Loading hay.
10 — Portrait of Gen. Scott TEN

1 — Compt's die.
PERRIN BANK, Rochester, N. Y.
Indians hunting buffaloes.
ONE ONE
1 1

TEN — Male, female, two boys, lamb, etc.
Two oxen before hay cart, men loading hay; three men at work in distance. On left of vig. letter X.
Word ten, figs. 10, and letter X.
BRIGG'S BANK OF Clyde, N. Y.
Compt's die.

Word one and figure 1 across. State Arms.
View of large building; horses and carriage in street.
IRON BANK Morristown N. J
One Dollar One Dollar
1 — Train of cars going under bridge; load of hay passing over bridge.

2 — Compt's die. 2
Title of Bank.
The word two running down and repeated six times; on left, conflict between dog and bear, man with uplifted axe; on right, mower at work, house in distance.
TWO TWO
2 2

Female on one knee with sickle and cornucopia. 1
Three men shearing sheep; on left man leading two sheep; barn, &c.; on right, man, trees, &c.
BERGEN CO. BANK, Hackensack, N. J.
One Dollar. One Dollar.
1 — State Arms.

2 — State Arms.
Men at work in iron mill.
IRON BANK,
2 — Two men and dog in foreground, man, hay in background.

5 — Male portrait
Train of cars; two men at work; hills and large body of water in distance.
PERRIN BANK, Rochester, N. Y.
FIVE FIVE
5 — Compt's die 5

2 — Milkmaid; cows, trees house and hills in distance.
Female entwined in figure 2; on left men plowing; on right men mowing.
State Arms.
BERGEN CO. BANK, Hackensack, N. J.
Two dollars Two dollars.
2 — Female entwined in figure 2. Word two and figure 2

3 — State Arms.
IRON BANK, N. J.
View of New York Crystal Palace.
Three dols Three dols
Word three and figure 3. View of cattle, telegraph and railroad

1
View of harbor of New York, with steamer and ship.
ONE
MERCHANTS BANK, Nashville, Tenn.
ONE

Cupids entwined in ornamental figure 3. Figure 3 and with dollars.
Horses, cattle and sheep fence, trees, farm-house, hills, man, &c.
BERGEN CO. BANK, Hackensack, N. J.
Three doll'rs Three doll'rs
Figure 3 and word Three. State Arms.

FIVE
IRON BANK.
5 View of part of the globe with eagle on top.
5 — State Arms

5 — Male portrait
MERCHANTS BANK, Nashville, Tenn.
Word five, letter V, and figure 5 on either side
5 — View of cattle, telegraph and railroad

FIVE — Female seated in ornamental figure 5; shield.
Ornamental fig. 5, with female on either side; village in distance; large V on left.
BERGEN CO. BANK Hackensack, N. J.
Five Dollars. Five Dollars.
5 — State Arms.

2 — Female seated on globe; eagle on the right and a small figure with cornucopia on left.
Male portrait
BANK OF NORTH AMERICA, Providence, R. I.
2

Word one and fig. 1. Milkmaid with tub.
EXCHANGE BANK, Greencastle, Ind.
Circular die with portrait of Henry Clay, and words one dollar in half circle over his head; large figure 1 with the word one twice on each figure.
Word one and fig. 1. Auditors die.

2 — Female portrait. TWO
Farming country, ox in foreground
PARKE CO. BANK, Rockville, Ind.
Canal lock.
2 — Male portrait TWO

100
C View of buildings, country inn, pedestrians, etc.
HAMPDEN BANK, Westfield, Mass.
Dog, safe and building.
100 — Female Med head.

FIVE — Two males erect, one leaning on capstan; two females seated drawing; city in distance.
EXCHANGE BANK, Greencastle, Ind.
V
Auditor's die.
5 — Male figure erect, and two females seated on the ground; dog cattle, sheaf, &c.

V
Utrl.
FARMERS' AND MECHANICS' BANK, Camden, N. J.
Load of hay; woman and boy on top; two horses, man on one; dog, boy and girl; blacksmith shop and men at work.
Dog.
5
FIVE
5

TEN
TEN
Man holding child on his knee; woman, boy, etc.
shearing sheep.
ONTARIO CO. B'K. Phelps, N. Y.
10
Compt's die

Word Ten and letter X.
Portrait of Cass.
Large die with figures 10, and words Ten Dollars across it.
EXETER BANK, Exeter, N. H.
10
Female seated; two men in rear

X
TEN
X
Title of Bank.
Blacksmith shop, four men at work; boy, &c.; man plowing, house and trees in distance.
Dog.
10
Female portrait.

1
Compt's die.
Milkmaid seated with pail; cows, dog, etc; farm house in distance.
B'K OF BELLEVILLE Belleville, Ills.
ONE
Domestic scene of farmer and family.

XX
Portrait of Female.
EXETER BANK, Exeter, N. H.
Large die with figures 20, and words Twenty Dollars running across it.
Word twenty letter XX. and figure 20.
Female portrait.

XX
Two male figures, sailor and blacksmith on board ship.
Title of Bank.
Figure of liberty, right arm resting on shield, on which is portrait of Washington; drapery with stars on it, over the portrait.
Dog.
20
Boy carrying bundle of corn stalks boy and horse behind him.

2
Compt's die.
Drover and boy with cattle; house in distance.
B'K OF BELLEVILLE Belleville, Ills.
2
Two females, one with sheaf and sickle.

Female erect with emblems of liberty
ONE
1 Female seated on a rock; cupids playing with a dolphin.
BANK OF NEW HAMPSHIRE, Portsmouth, N. H.
1
Portrait of female.

50
Female with sheaf and sickle.
Title of Bank.
State Arms with female on either side; ship and cars in distance.
Dog.
50
Shipwright seated; woman with bundle of chips; ship on stocks.

3
Compt's die.
Farmer ploughing with two horses; trees and house in distance.
B'K OF BELLEVILLE Belleville, Ills.
3
Female gathering wheat.

Figure of Justice.
TWO
2 Agricultural scene; laborers seated, load of hay in distance
Title of Bank.
2
Female seated with sheaves and sickle.

Portrait of Washington.
ONE C HUNDRED
Title of Bank.
Boy reclining on load of hay, drawn by two oxen; boy with fork side of oxen.
Dog.
C
100
C

5
Compt's die.
Men hauling hay with two oxen and horse.
B'K OF BELLEVILLE Belleville, Ills.
5
Female with cornucopia

3
Artist with chisel and hammer.
Two ships on the stocks; vessels in distance.
Title of Bank.
3
Figure 3, sailor, farmer and mechanic.

Die.
500
Die.
Title of Bank.
Female seated with sheaf and sickle; houses, trees and men mowing on right; train of cars crossing bridge on left.
Dog.
500
Blacksmith shop; man at forge, anvil, &c.

ONE
ONE
Man seated under tree; scythe hanging on limb.
Portrait of Webster.
EXETER BANK, Exeter, N. H.
Word one and figure 1
ONE

5
Eagle.
V
Helmeted head. Female seated with shield Helmeted head.
Title of Bank.
5
Ship under sail.
V

1
ONE
Compt's die.
Reapers resting from labor; cars and village in distance.
ONTARIO CO. B'K. Phelps, N. Y.
ONE
Man with rake, horse and cart in distance.

TWO DOLLARS
2
Portrait of Cass.
Two females seated representing Commerce and Agriculture; ship in distance.
EXETER BANK, Exeter, N. H.
2
TWO DOLLARS

10
Head of male
X
TEN TEN
X Brig and schooner sailing. X
Title of Bank.
Shield.
TEN TEN TEN TEN
10
Head of male
X

TWO DOLLARS
2
Compt's Die.
2
Drove of Cattle; man on horseback, and boy in water; farm house and trees in background.
ONTARIO CO. B'K. Phelps, N. Y.
2
Female feeding fowls.

THREE
Female binding shoes; two men dressing leather; a bull's head.
EXETER BANK, Exeter, N. H.
3
THREE

TWENTY
Neptune seated; ship in distance.
TWENTY
TWENTY TWENTY TWENTY
TWENTY
Title of Bank.
Shield.
TWENTY TWENTY TWENTY
20
Mercury in clouds.

Word five letter V, and figure 5.
FIVE
Man seated
Man leading horse; oxen to cart; trees, spire, etc. in distance.
ONTARIO CO. B'K. Phelps, N. Y.
5
Compt's die.
FI 5 VE

FIVE
Word Five, letter V, and figure 5. Large V, within which is a female.
EXETER BANK, Exeter, N. H.
5

50
Two helmeted heads.
50
50 Eagle and steamer in distance. 50
Title of Bank.
Shield.
FIFTY

Reaper reclining by sheaves.
HUN DRED.
One hundred One hundred
Title of Bank.
100
Head of male
100

2
Indian squaw in canoe.
CORN EX BANK,
Fairfield. Ills.
Cherub. Compt's Cherub die.
TWO
2
Female with tablets.

TEN
Male, female, boy, girl, dog and chickens.
Female seated with shield pole, cap and eagle; rising sun in distance.
Title of Bank.
10
Woodman felling tree; another seated.

IMPORTERS' & TRADERS' BANK,
New York, N. Y.
The bills of this institution are printed in red and black, and have the denomination in fine letters all over the bills, which effectually prevents their being altered or counterfeited. They are a splendid specimen of art, and reflect great credit on the engravers, Messrs. DANFORTH, WRIGHT, & Co.

3
Female in clouds with sword and branch.
CORN EX. BANK,
Fairfield, Ills.
III Compt's die. III
THREE
3
Female in clouds with flowers.

XX
Female.
Title of Bank
TWENTY
DOLLARS
20
Indian female and child.

ONE
Head of Washington. Ornamental figure 1.
IMPORTERS' & TRADERS BANK,
New York City.
Compt's die.
Secured, &c.
ONE

Male seated eating—female erect and dog; houses in the distance.
CORN EX. BANK,
Fairfield, Ills.
5 FIVE 5
FIVE
Compt's die.
Indian and squaw, dog, canoe and trees.

ONE
Franklin.
Compt's die.
Female and anchor; ship in distance. Word One and figure 1 on either side
NATIONAL BANK,
Albany, N. Y.
1 1
ONE
1
Die with several "ones" on it.
Figure 1.

2
TWO
Title of Bank.
Sailor and sailor boy.
Compt's die.
Secured, etc.
2
TWO

Compt's die.
Drover and drove of cattle; boy in water, farm house, trees, etc.
1
AGRICULTURAL BK.
Marion, Ills.
Word one and figure 1
Female.

TWO
Comp's die.
TWO
Female, eagle, bales and cornucopia; ship in distance.
NATIONAL BANK,
Albany, N. Y.
2 2
TWO
2
Die.
2

5
FIVE
Female seated; shield and eagle.
Title of Bank.
FIVE DOLLARS.
5
Compt's die
FIVE

2
Compt's die.
TWO
Two females representing Agriculture and Commerce; bales, bbl, sheaf, ship, etc.
2
AGRICULTURAL BK.
Marion, Ills.
Word two and figure 2
Female.

Compt's die.
Washington.
3 Female in clouds, with ornamental figure 3, eagle and shield.
NATIONAL BANK,
Albany, N. Y.
3 THREE 3
Word Three and figure 3
3

X
TEN
Two females, one erect, the other kneeling.
NEW YORK
TEN DOLLARS
Title of Bank.
10
Compt's die.

Letter V and word five.
Horses, oxen and sheep, fence, trees and house.
5
AGRICULTURAL BK.
Marion, Ills.
5
Compt's die.

Bales and barrels.
5
Bales and barrels.
Three females representing Agriculture, Commerce and Manufactures; ship in distance
NATIONAL BANK,
Albany, N. Y.
5 FIVE 5
5
Compt's die.
FIVE

50
Female soaring in clouds with cornucopia of flowers.
Title of Bank.
Large 50 in red dies.
Compt's die.
50
Female soaring in clouds.

1
Man watering three horses at trough; sheep, goat and kid; trees and house.
BANK OF MIDDLE GEORGIA,
Macon, Geo.
1
Justice seated; flag.

TEN
Webster.
Female seated with distaff in hand; ship in distance.
NATIONAL BANK,
Albany, N. Y.
X TEN X
10
TEN
Compt's die.

100
New York.
Title of Bank.
Large figures 100 in red die; on right sailor seated, and ship in distance; on left mower on the ground with scythe; trees, etc.
Compt's die.
100

TWO
Female feeding chickens.
State Arms with female on left, and Indian on right.
Title of Bank.
2
Four horses before wagon

1
Female.
B'K OF THE UNION,
Nashville, Tenn.
American flag and shield, with female, three children and globe on right, male and female Indian and child.
Coach.
ONE
Bridge; train of cars and sloop.
ONE

1
Female with sheaf.
And. die
CORN EX. BANK,
Fairfield, Ills.
Cherub. ONE Cherub.
ONE
1
Man with basket of corn.

5
Portrait of Washington with female on either side; sickle, sheaf and locomotive on right; on left shipping.
Title of Bank.
5
Cars passing under arch load of hay on top.

Female entwined in figure 5; shield.
FIVE
B'K OF THE UNION,
Nashville, Tenn.
Male portrait; war implements around it.
5 5
5
Female, eagle, cup and ship.
FIVE

1 — Compt's die. SECOND WARD BK. Female seated; on left steamboat and vessel; on right train of cars crossing a bridge. Milwaukee, Wis 1 — Female seated holding figure 1.	Hunter loading rifle; deer. ONE Two cows before cart; men loading it with hay; men, trees, and haystack in distance. UNION BANK, Frenchtown, N. J. 1 — Registers die.	2 — Compt's die. 2 Hor e, cows and fence; b[illegible] and train of c[illegible] in distance. CROTON RIVER B'K. Southeast, N. Y. Dogs head. TWO — 2 — Male portrait
Female seated in a large figure 2. TWO SECOND WARD BK. View of a landing place with two large steamboats. Milwaukee, Wis 2 — Compt's die.	2 — Washington. Female reclining; shield on which is deer in water; on right sheep and wheat; on left chest and bags of coin. UNION BANK, Frenchtown, N. J. 2 — Registers die	Cattle and sheep, boy on horse trees, &c. V FIVE Eagle. CROTON RIVER B'K. Southeast, N. Y. Locomotive and tender 5 — Compt's die 5
5 Female seated; shipyard; ship in distance. 5 Compt's Die. SECOND WARD B'K. Milwaukee, Wis. 5 — Vessel	Word Three and figure 3. Female feeding chickens. Train of cars; trees, houses, sloop, etc, in distance. UNION BANK, Frenchtown, N. J. 3 — Registers die	10 — Boy with pigeon. Cows, sheep, trees, house, &c. CROTON RIVER B'K. Southeast, N. Y. Dog's head. 10 — Eagle and shield. — Compt's die.
ONE Female feeding fowls. State Arms. CLINTON BANK of NEW JERSEY, Clinton, N. J. 1 — Male portrait	5 — Registers die UNION BANK, Frenchtown, N. J. Portrait of Washington; eagle at top; two females on right, one on left; cars and ship in distance. 5 — Three dogs two birds and trees	Male and female by side of well; fences, etc. load of hay going in barn 20 Compt's die. TWENTY DOLLARS CROTON RIVER B'K. Southeast, N. Y Cow's head. 20 — Milkmaid with pail.
TWO 2 — Head of Franklin. Farmer watering horses at a well; buildings, sheep, goats, &c. Title of Bank. 2 — TWO — Washington	Registers die X UNION BANK, Frenchtown, N. J. Shield on which is cars; sheafs and fruit on right; milkmaid seated on left; in distance farmhouse, cows and trees. TEN — Female reclining; Indian female erect	Hunter loading rifle; deer at his feet. ONE Drover and farmer bargaining for ox; farm yard scene. BANK OF MONROE, Monroe, Wis. 1 — Compt's die — ONE
THREE 3 Three men, farmer, mechanic and tradesman. Title of Bank. 3 — Female head	XX — Drove of cattle. UNION BANK, Frenchtown, N. J. Portrait of Washington; female on either side; on right ship and steamboat in distance; on left sheaf and men mowing. Figures 20 word twenty and two XX. — Reg. die.	Male, female, boy, girl, dog and chickens. TWO Portrait of Washington; milkmaid and cows on right; two females on left. BANK OF MONROE, Monroe, Wis 2 — Compt's die
FIVE 5 — Female with sickle, grain, &c. Title of Bank. Blacksmith standing; anvil and tools. 5 — Girl's head	5 — Med. head. FIVE Train of cars; houses, trees, large chimney and sloop. INDIANA FARMERS BANK, Franklin, Ind. Quails. 5 — Washington	Female feeding chickens. THREE Drover and drove of cattle; boy in water; trees and house in distance. BANK OF MONROE, Monroe, Wis. 3 — Compt's die. — THREE
TEN Female with flowers Title of Bank. Head of Clinton. 10 — Boy's head	10 — Female with sheaf of wheat. TEN Title of Bank. Milkmaid seated with pail; cows, etc. Eagle. 10 on medallion head. — Franklin.	Female gathering wheat. 5 Man watering three horses from trough; sheep goats, trees and house. BANK OF MONROE, Monroe, Wis. 5 — Compt's die.
TWENTY Female seated; eagle, &c. Title of Bank. Horse, flag, etc. 20 — Female with horn of plenty, grapes, &c.	1 — Compt's die. CROTON RIVER B'K. Southeast, N. Y. O N E D O L L A R 1 — Female seated by side of silver dollar bales, anchor and house.	FIVE — Male, boy, female, girl, dog and chickens. SUCK'S BANK. McMinnville, Tenn. Hunter loading rifle; deer at his feet. 5 — Male portrait

Female seated by side of fig. 1. Compt's die. Indian, squaw and child in canoe: wigwams, trees, etc. in distance. BANK OF OLD SARATOGA, Schuylerville, N. Y. Soldier and cannon. 1 Female seated and fig. 1	ONE Female and fig. 1. Compt's die. COMMERCIAL B'K. Saratoga Springs.N.Y. ONE DOLLAR ONE 1 Male reclining; sheep, dog, etc. cars crossing bridge 1	ONE ONE Compt's die. Indian behind rock watching deer; trees, etc. CANASTOTA BANK, Canastota, N. Y. Female bathing. 1 Girl.
2 Compt's die. 2 Indians on horse back viewing train of cars. Title of Bank. Sentinel and cannon. 2 Female and figure 2.	2 Compt's die. TWO Female seated with staff; ships and cars in distance. Title of Bank. Safe. TWO Man sharpening scythe, fig. 2 at his back	2 Compt's die. 2 Shield with Indian on right and female on left; ship city, steamboat, wigwams, trees, &c., in distance. CANASTOTA BANK, Canastota, N. Y. Dog. 2 Two soldiers.
5 Male portrait Female in clouds with shield, pole, cap and eagle. Title of Bank. Sentinel and cannon. 5 Compt's die. 5	5 Eagle. FIVE Title of Bank. Female in clouds with eagle, pole, cap, shield and liberty. Rising sun. Word five and letter V. Compt's die. 5	5 Two Indians on cliff viewing city. Men at work harvesting; two oxen before cart. CANASTOTA BANK Canastota, N. Y. 5 Compt's die. 5
ONE Male portrait. Compt's die. AUBURN EX. B'K. Auburn, N. Y. Red figure 1. Red silver dollar. Red figure 1. Train of cars; load of hay drawn by two horses; men, cows, etc; city and bridges in distance. ONE on 1. Two females, one at table, the other with horn in hand.	Letter X and word Ten. Sailor. TEN Title of Bank Two males and a female; train of cars, steamboat and city in distance. Eagle. TEN Female and letter X. Compt's die.	TEN Two males on cliff. X Load of hay drawn by two horses, female and child on top; blacksmith's shop and men at work; dog, girl and boy. CANASTOTA BANK, Canastota, N. Y. 10 TEN Compt's die.
TWO Compt's die. Two females seated by side of shield Spread eagle. AUBURN EX. B'K. Auburn, N. Y. Red silver dollar. Red silver dollar. TWO 2 Male portrait	20 Washington TWENTY Title of Bank. Female portrait. Female [illegible] blowing trumpet; ship, steamboat and city in distance. Compt's die. Tree. XX Sailor; wharf scene TWENTY	XX Males and females gathering hops. CANASTOTA BANK, Canastota. N. Y. Compt's die. Twenty Dollars 20 Two horses before wagon; two men and dog; men in distance.
Compt's die. THREE Male portrait 3 Cattle, sheep, two men, horse and dog; house in distance. AUBURN EX. B'K. Auburn, N. Y. 3 Man feeding pigs.	FIVE Female. 5 Portrait of female with cupids on either side BANK OF HOWARDSVILLE, Howardsville, Va. Female. 5 die 5	FIVE Large 5; cars crossing bridge; two Indians and water falls. FIVE Two males and a female representing Agriculture, Commerce, &c.; steamboat, train of cars and city in distance. NEW HAVEN BANK New Haven, Ct. Beehive. Letter V, and three females. The first Sabbath preaching.
FIVE Full length figure of Justice. 5 Five cherubs and five silver dollars. AUBURN EX. B'K. Auburn, N. Y. Shield, bales and anvil. 5 Compt's die. FIVE	7 Male portrait SEVEN Title of Bank. Negro harnessing horse; [illegible] cars and trees in distance. Safe. 7 die SEVEN	Female. Letter X, milkmaid; train of cars, cow, etc. Ships at sea. NEW HAVEN B'K. New Haven, Conn. Beehive. 10 Same as 5s.
X Male portrait AUBURN EX. B'K. Auburn, N. Y. 10 Train of cars; steamboat and hills in distance. Indian looking over cliff. Compt's die	8 die. EIGHT Male portrait with Cupid on either side. Title of Bank. Male. 8 Negro with basket of corn.	Same as on right of fives. XX Female reclining; shield pole and cap, etc.; cars, ships and steamship in distance. NEW HAVEN B'K. New Haven, Conn. Beehive. 20 Female.
20 Indian and deer on ground; hills and water in distance. TWENTY AUBURN EX. B'K. Auburn, N. Y. Eagle and shield; on either side is word twenty and figures 20. Compt's die. XX Female Indian reclining; deer in distance.	Canal, boat, lock, horses, men, road, load of hay, etc. 10 Title of Bank Male portrait, with two cupids on either side. Locomotive and tender. 10 die. 10	Boy's head. 500 BRIGHTON MARKET BANK, Brighton, Mass. 500 500 Washington; female on left; Cupid on right.

Left	Centre	Right
1 Auditor's die	Female seated by side of silver dollar; trees house, etc. MORGAN CO. BANK, Jacksonville, Ills. Eagle.	1 ONE Female.
5 Female, male boy, girl, dog and chickens.	Female driving cows home; train of cars and city in distance B'K OF SMYRNA. Smyrna, Del	V 5
Compt's die. Figure 2 with sailor and female.	Two female figures, Justice and Liberty; village on right, cars on left; eagle mounted between the two. COMMERCIAL BANK Glenn Falls. N. Y. Secured, &c.	TWO Figure 2 and female.
2 Auditor's die	Female and cherub, two silver dollars, trees and shield; ship and house in distance. MORGAN CO B'K. Jacksonville, Ills. Beaver.	2 Female and figure 2.
50 Three males supporting figure 50.	View of factories, trees, and houses. MANUFACT'RS B'K, Macon, Geo.	50 Female with roll.
Compt's die. 3	Goddess of Liberty on globe; eagle and shield. COMMERCIAL BANK Glenn Falls, N Y. Secured, &c.	THREE 3 Lighthouse and female seated.
5 Auditor's die	FIVE DOLLARS Portrait of female with cherubs on either side MORGAN CO. BANK. Jacksonville, Ills Man and wheat.	FIVE Train of cars water falls, two Indians and large 5
100 Indian squaw in canoe.	MANUFACT'RS B'K. Macon, Geo Female in clouds with shield, eagle and American drapery.	100 Female with tablets.
Compt's die. Squaw; Indians in canoe; wigwam in distance.	V and letters FIVE — Spread eagle and shield. — V and letters FIVE COMMERCIAL BANK Glenn Falls, N. Y.	5 Female seated with book and pen.
Word Ten and figure 10. Word Ten and figures 10.	MORGAN CO. BANK, Jacksonville, Ills. Man attaching horses to plow, dog on ground, cars in distance. Bales and cornucopia.	10 Letter X; ... maid, ... and cars.
1 ONE Compt's die	CHITTENANGO B'K; Chittenango, N. Y. Female seated by side of silver dollar; red figure 1 on either side. Gold dollar.	1 Female seated with shield and sword.
Compt's die. Large X and sea scene.	COMMERCIAL BANK Glenn Falls, N. Y. Female blowing trumpet; steamboat and ship on right, village, load of hay and trees on left.	X and letters TEN Mechanic seated on a boiler. TEN
50 Female with cornucopia.	CENTRAL R. R. & BANKING CO. Savannah, Geo. Train of cars; trees, houses, sloop and large chimney. Dog's head.	50 Millard Fillmore.
2 Compt's die. 2	Female, cherub and two silver dollars CHITTENANGO B'K, Chittenango. N. Y. Rising Sun.	TWO Large figure 2 and female
ONE	B'K OF CAZENOVIA. Cazenovia, N. Y. Large one in red die. Compt's die.	1 ONE 1
100 Trees, wagon; train of cars crossing bridge; city in distance.	CENTRAL R. R. & BANKING CO Savannah, Geo. Three females in clouds. Locomotive.	100 Ship, city in distance.
Compt's die. 3	Indian, squaw and pappoose in canoe; wigwams and hills in distance. CHITTENANGO B'K. Chittenango, N. Y Bales and cornucopia.	3 Female with figure 3,
TWO DOLLARS	B'K OF CAZENOVIA. Cazenovia, N. Y. Large Two in red die Compt's die.	2 TWO 2
Female with flowers in her apron.	FARMERS' BANK OF TENNESSEE, Knoxville, Tenn Sailor and farmer on either side of a shield.	5 FIVE Word five, letter V, and figure 5.
FIVE	Five Globe Dollars with three females around it, and male at bottom. GLOBE BANK, Providence, R. I. Shield	Word five, and figure 5 5 Word five and figure 5.
FIVE	BK. OF CAZENOVIA, Cazenovia, N. Y. Large five in red die.	5 Compt's die. FI V VE
1 ONE 1	Man watering horses from trough; sheep, goats, trees and house. B'K OF SMYRNA, Smyrna, Del.	1 Washington.
X 10 X	Ten Vig. Dollars Sameness five. GLOBE BANK. Providence, R. I. Shield.	TEN
ONE and 1. Franklin.	MER. & PLANTERS' BANK, Savannah, Geo. Wagons loaded with cotton. State Arms.	ONE and 1. Train of cars
TWO DOLLARS	2 Drover bargaining for ox; negro, boy, horse, cattle, dog, etc. BANK OF SMYRNA, Smyrna, Del.	2 Female feeding fowls.
Compt's die. Mechanic; safe and anvil; two females, steam ship in distance.	1 Female in clouds over city, distributing flowers; view of rising sun. COMMERCIAL BANK Glenn Falls, N. Y. Secured, &c.	ONE Washington. ONE
2 Washington.	MER. & PLANTERS' BANK, Savannah, Geo. Men harvesting wheat. State Arms.	2 Portrait of Martha Washington

1 Man, horse, dog and pigeons.	Farmer selling cattle to drover; man on horseback engaged in conversation with another. FARMERS' BANK, Wickford. R. I. Sloop and schooner.	1 Female portrait.
2 Blacksmith and forge.	Man feeding hogs; two horses on right. FARMERS' BANK, Wickford. R. I. 2	2 Farmer with bundle of corn.
3 Machinist's at work.	FARMERS' BANK, Wickford. R. I. Man on horse; horse drinking, boy and man at right, sheep and house on left; in distance loading wagon withgrain.	3 Female feeding chickens
5 Man erect with jug; man, woman with child seated; dog and basket at right.	FARMERS' BANK, Wickford, R. I. Portrait of Franklin	5 Man cutting down tree; two oxen and children; in background horse and man plowing.
10 Shield on which is anchor, on either side female.	FARMERS' BANK, Wickford. R. I. Men gathering corn; horse, colt, waggon and dog.	10 Female portrait.
20 Sailor by capstan.	FARMERS BANK, Wickford, R. I. Portrait of Washington.	20 Female, seated, sheaf cow, &c.
ONE Mower with scythe seated.	Female seated; dog and pail on right, cow on left. GERMAN BANK, Sheboygan, Wis.	1 Compt's die.
TWO Compt's die.	Women at work on cotton machines. GERMAN BANK, Sheboygan, Wis.	2 Train of cars.
Compt's die. Word three and fig. 3.	GERMAN BANK, Sheboygan, Wis. Three females; ship in distance.	3

5 Steamboat.	GERMAN BANK. Sheboygan, Wis. 5 Compt's die.	FIVE
1 Compt's die	Female seated by side of shield; ship, steamer, light house, &c. in distance. 1 ONTARIO BANK. Utica, N. Y.	ONE Indian on cliff looking at city. ONE
Compt's die. Fig. 3, eagle and female.	Indian reclining, deer on ground; stream of water, hills, &c., in distance. ONTARIO BANK. Utica, N. Y.	3 Train of cars.
FIVE Female erect with sword and balances	5 Female putting wreath of flowers around her hat; dog, pail and cars. ONTARIO BANK, Utica, N. Y.	5 Compt's die. FIVE
Farmer with scythe. Compt's die.	1 Indian and ornamental fig. 1. BANK OF NORWICH, Norwich, N. Y.	Word one and figure 1. Male portrait ONE
TWO Compt's die. TWO	Female on either side of fig. 2 TWO BANK OF NORWICH, Norwich, N. Y.	2 Male portrait
Compt's die. Male portrait	Three females and ornamental fig. 3; factory in distance. Fig. 3 on left. BANK OF NORWICH Norwich, N. Y.	Word three and fig. 3. Mechanic, sailor and farmer in fig 3.
5 Male portrait FIVE	Five females, and fig. 5; shipping, and factories in distance. BANK OF NORWICH. Norwich, N. Y. Loading hay.	5 Compt's die FIVE
Male portrait TEN	Nine cherubs and ten gold dollars; female with cornucopia, shield, &c. BANK OF NORWICH Norwich, N. Y.	10 Agricultural implements. Compt's die.

Word one and figure 1. Royal arms. ONE	PROVINCIAL BANK, Stanstead. Canada. British Coat of Arms.	1 Five shillings Words one dollar and figure 1.
TWO Royal Arms. Word two and 3 mark.	PROVINCIAL BANK Stanstead, Canada. Indian man and boy with horse: Indians and wigwams in distance.	2 Portrait of Queen Victoria
5 Indian family on cliff, viewing factories	PROVINCIAL BANK Stanstead, Canada Ornamental figure 5: in top letters [illegible] at bottom portrait of Prince Albert, and words "one Pound Five."	5 Royal Arms. FIVE
1 View of cattle, telegraph and railroad.	BANK OF FULTON, Atlanta, Geo Farm scene; farmer and drover bargaining for ox.	1 Woodman felling a tree; another seated.
2 Female with spear.	BANK OF FULTON, Atlanta, Geo. Tobacco plantation, two men and hhds.	2 Locomotive.
Hunter loading rifle, deer at his feet. 5	Female reclining, eagle, drapery, &c.; city, train of cars, bridge, &c., in distance. BANK OF FULTON, Atlanta. Geo.	5 Portrait of female.
1 ONE Compt's die. ONE	Female seated on log, with pail by side of shield, on which is cars and rising sun; sheafs on right. MERCHANTS' BANK Madison, Wis. Eagle.	1 Male with distaff; sea scene.
3 Compt's die THREE	Female with sheaf. Three females in clouds, sun rise. MERCHANTS' BANK Madison, Wis. Dog, key, safe, balances.	3 Two cherubs and figure 3.
FIVE Compt's die. Indian female and child; trees, &c.	MERCHANTS' BANK Madison, Wis. Shield with deer in water on it; female reclining on left; sheep, &c on right.	5 View of cattle, telegraph and railroad.

1 ONE Henry Clay. NIAGARA CO. B'K. Lockport, N. Y. Compt's die. ONE	TWO TWO Compt's die. 2 2 MARINE BANK. Oswego, N. Y. Female with wheat. 2 Female with flowers. TWO DOLLARS	3 THREE Compt's die. Wolf's head on shield; on left female binding shoes; on right man dressing leather. Title of Bank. THREE Large figure 3, in top curve is fig. 3.
2 TWO NIAGARA CO. B'K. Lockport, N. Y. 2 Compt's die. Male Portrait. 2 TWO	Compt's die. THREE 3 Ships and other vessels; city in distance. 3 MARINE BANK, Oswego, N. Y. THREE	5 FIVE Title of Bank Three cherubs with lever, &c., breaking stone. 5 5 Compt's die. FIVE
THREE Compt's die. NIAGARA CO. B'K Lockport, N. Y. Stone cutters at work. 3	5 Compt's die. FIVE View of N. Y. Harbor, with a steamer and ship. MARINE BANK, Oswego, N. Y. 5 FIVE	X TEN Title of Bank Five cherubs with globe, anvil hammer, &c. X Word ten, letter X and figure 10. Compt's die.
FIVE Male portrait. 5 NIAGARA CO. B'K. Lockport, N. Y. Female, sheaf, plow, &c; in distance, cars, bridge, canal lock, boat, &c. 5 Compt's die FIVE	10 Sailor [illegible] captain. Three horses drinking from trough; sheep, &c.; farm scene in general. MARINE BANK, Oswego, N. Y. X Ship on stocks. Compt's die.	Female in clouds, small figure 1 to left. Compt's die. OSWEGO RIVER BK. Fulton, N. Y. Indian seated by fig. 1; trees, water fall, hills, &c. in distance 1 Male portrait
X TEN NIAGARA CO. B'K Lockport, [illegible] Mechanic with anvil and hammer; city in distance. X 10 Compt's die.	XX Two sailors and female [illegible] boat. TWE Compt's die. NTY MARINE BANK, Oswego, N. Y. 20	TWO Compt's die. TWO OSWEGO RIVER BK. Fulton, N. Y. Figure 2, with female on either side. Canal Lock. 2 Male portrait
TWENTY NIAGARA CO. BK. Lockport, N. Y. Two cherubs in clouds. Red die with figure 20 and words twenty dollars. Compt's die 20 Sheep.	10 Two In[illegible]. Portrait of Franklin surrounded by five females. FAR. & MECH. B'K. OF GENESEE, Buffalo, N. Y. 10 Compt's die.	5 Male portrait OSWEGO RIVER B'K. Fulton, N. Y. Female reclining; 5 in front of her; ships in distance. 5 5 Compt's die 5
ONE Hunter with dog and gun. Cattle and sheep—some of the cows in water. NATIONAL BANK, Equality, Ills. 1 Auditor's die	Yatch race, various male and female figures. XX Compt's die. Title of Bank. 20 Female seated; cars and factories in distance. TWENTY	X Two girls with sheafs of grain. Men harvesting; man seated on sheafs; farm scene. OSWEGO RIVER BK. Fulton, N. Y. Beehive. 10 Male portrait Compt's die.
5 Machinist with implements. Farmer and drover bargaining for ox; barn yard scene NATIONAL BANK, Equality, Ills. 5 Auditor's die	1 ONE MAN. & TRADERS' BANK, Buffalo, N. Y. Compt's die. Blacksmith anvil and hammer; city in distance. 1	XX Male portrait TWENTY Indian reclining, deer on ground at his back; stream of water, hills, &c. in distance. OSWEGO RIVER BK. Fulton, N. Y. Compt's die. TWENTY Female erect with shield and spear. TWENTY
1 ONE Farmer seated with scythe. Sailor seated. On demand, and one dollar in red die. MARINE BANK, Oswego, N. Y. Compt's die. 1	2 TWO Title of Bank. Compt's die. Ship yard; men at work and ship on stocks. TWO Figure 2, in top curve is figure 2.	Black-smith, sledge and anvil. 1 Ox team, stone quarry, &c. ROCKPORT BANK, Rockport, Mass. Man plowing. 1 Stone cutter &c.

1 — Two Indians on a cliff viewing city. | Various vessels. CITY BANK of Perth Amboy, N. J. Female bathing. | 1 — State Arms. — ONE

Treas. die. — Mower seated with scythe | TEN Portrait of Washington. TEN — Title of Bank. | 10 — Two females, one with flag and shield.

Auditor's die. — 2 | BANK OF QUINCY, Quincy, Ills. Male, female and child; female portrait on either side, and words "two dollars" under both portraits. | 2 — Men gathering corn.

TWO | Female reclining on bales; steamboat in distance. Girl. Title of Bank. Dog. | 2 — Train of cars. — 2

Ornamental work. — Boy's head. — ONE | 1 Female seated on bale with roll of cloth; factories, road, &c., on right; falls and village on left. NEW MARKET BK. New Market, N. H. Mechanical implements. | Ornamental work and figure 1. — Girl's head. — ONE

3 | Wharf scene, city, steamboat and vessels, R. R. Depot, and various male and female figures. Auditor's die. BANK OF QUINCY, Quincy, Ills. | 3 — Sheep.

5 — Factory. | State Arms. Title of Bank. Ducks. | V — Male portrait.

2 — Male portrait. | Farmers harvesting; male, female and child in front; men loading hay cart in background. Girl. Title of Bank. Mechanical implements. | 2 — Female feeding chickens.

5 — Auditor's die. | BANK OF QUINCY, Quincy, Ills. Man on rock with gun, female loading a gun; battle scene in distance. | 5 — Head of female.

100 — C | CITY BANK, Worcester, Mass. City Bank building. | 100 — Portrait of Webster. — 100

5 — Male portrait. | Title of Bank. Declaration of Independence. Eagle. | 5 — Case.

10 — Two horses and plow; man at lunch; farm scene. | BANK OF QUINCY, Quincy, Ills. Auditor's die. | 10 — Male portrait.

D | Title of Bank. City Bank Building. Five Hundred Dollars. | 500 — Clay.

Ornamental work. — 10 | Portrait of Webster. Title of Bank. Farmer and drover bargaining for ox; barn yard scene. Horse. | 10 — Justice.

1 — Male portrait. | Man on horse; men harvesting in distance. BANK OF NEWARK, Newark, Del. Sheep. | 1 — Head of girl.

Figure of Justice. — FIVE | Train of cars, and two men; steamboat and hills in distance; figure 5 on left of vig. FROSTBURG BANK. Frostburg, Md. Mechanical Implements. | 5 — Die. — 5

Ornamental work. — Clay. | Two females with wings, and two cupids entwined in figs. 20 in clouds. Figs 20 on either side vig. Title of Bank. | Ornamental work. — Male Portrait.

Male figure erect. — TWO | 2 Blacksmith shoeing horse, drover seated on log, blacksmith in background. BANK OF NEWARK, Newark, Del. Cock. | 2 — Male portrait.

10 — Two girls with sheafs of grain. | X Spread eagle. X Title of Bank. Two horses. | 10 — Indian on cliff.

Ornamental work. — Female figure of Liberty; U. S. Capitol in distance. | 50 Title of Bank. Large portrait of Washington. | 50 — Head of female.

5 — Washington. | Milkmaid seated with pail, cows, &c.; farm house in distance. BANK OF NEWARK, Newark, Del. | 5 — Chickens.

Female. — XX | Men harvesting; farm scene. Figs. 20 on either side of vig. Title of Bank. | Female. — 20

Spread eagle, shield, etc. — 100 | Ship on stocks. Title of Bank. | 100 — Head of Indian female.

10 — X | Drove of cattle, pigs, &c.; two men on horseback; train of cars, bridge and village in distance. BANK OF NEWARK, Newark, Del. Beehive. | 10 — X

5 — Man with scythe. | Five cherubs and five silver dollars. FARMERS' BANK of Fincastle, Va. Wheat. | 5 — Treas. die. — FIVE

ONE — Head of girl. | Indians hunting buffaloes on the prairie. BANK OF QUINCY, Quincy, Ills. | 1 — Auditor's die.

Man gathering corn. — TWENTY | 20 Head of girl. 20 BANK OF NEWARK, Newark, Del. | Mower sharpening scythe. — TWENTY

3 THREE 3 MERCHANTS' AND PLANTERS' BANK. Savannah, Geo. Steamship; city and vessels in distance. State Arms 3 Clay	X TEN X BK OF COMMERCE, Savannah, Geo. Steamship. State Arms. 10 Indian.	Die. Sheep shearing. L Shield, surmounted by eagle; Justice on right, liberty on left. BANK OF ATHENS, Athens, Geo. 50 Male portrait
5 V State Arms; female on either side. Steamboat. Title of Bank Ducks. 5 V Train of cars	20 View of cattle, telegraph, railroad, etc. B'K OF COMMERCE, Savannah, Geo. Raft of timber floating down the river; boatmen, women and children on it; other rafts in distance. 20 Woodman with axe, trees, logs, &c.	C 100 C Cattle and sheep. BANK OF ATHENS, Athens, Geo. State Arms. 100 Female reclining on bale.
TEN [illegible] portrait Title of Bank. Female seated; houses, trees, &c. in distance. Dog 10 State Arms.	50 Ship, steamship and brig, city in distance; B'K OF COMMERCE, Savannah, Geo. Farmer and drover bargaining for ox; farm yard scene, &c. 50 Cotton plantation.	ONE Female feeding chickens. Drove of cattle and drover; boy in water; trees, and house in distance. SHELBYVILLE BK. Shelbyville, Tenn. 1 Indian female and child; trees, &c.
20 [illegible] on horse Title of Bank. Shield with females on either side, ship and train of cars in distance. State Arms. 20 Shipbuilder; ship on stocks	C Five females in the clouds B'K OF COMMERCE, Savannah, Geo. Large C; and words one hundred dollars. One Hundred 100 Male portrait	2 Man seated with child on his knee, female, boy, dog, hen and chickens. Train of cars; factory, large chimney, sloop and hill in distance. SHELBYVILLE BK. Shelbyville, Tenn. 2 Two males erect, and female seated, house, &c.
50 [illegible] Title of Bank. State Arms, black horse on right; light house on left; eagle at top. Ducks. 50 [illegible]	Die. Factory. 1 Female seated, bales; steamship in distance. BANK OF ATHENS, Athens, Geo. State Arms. 1 ONE	50 THE Die work. View of New York harbor with steamship and ship. BK. OF HARTFORD COUNTY Hartford, Ct. 50 Die work.
[illegible] State Arms. 100 Female seated, men plowing and factories in distance Title of Bank. Ducks C Sailor seated on bale 100	2 Female with sheaf and sickle. Load of cotton bales, drawn by two horses; houses, trees, &c. BANK OF ATHENS, Athens, Geo. Ducks. 2 Male portrait	100 THE C Spread eagle; ship, steamship and steamboat in distance. BK. OF HARTFORD COUNTY Hartford, Ct. 100 $100
1 Negro with basket of cotton. Ship—scene at sea. BK OF COMMERCE, Savannah, Geo. Dog 1 ONE 1	V Men harvesting. Male portrait. BANK OF ATHENS, Athens, Geo. Dog. 5 FIVE 5	5 Cows in water Wild horses, trees, &c. EXCHANGE BANK, Murfreesboro, Tenn. V 5
TWO 2 Blacksmith shop—men at work; man plowing in distance. BK OF COMMERCE, Savannah, Geo. Ducks. 2 Girl.	10 Negro with basket of cotton. BANK OF ATHENS, Athens, Geo. Female seated with mechanical implements; factory and train of cars in distance. Ducks. 10 State Arms.	10 Word ten, let. x and fig. 10. Farmer and drover bargaining for ox; barn, barn yard scene. EXCHANGE BANK, Murfreesboro, Tenn. 10 [illegible]
V Girl. BK OF COMMERCE, Savannah, Geo. Shield on which is State Arms—female bust at top, on right soldier and war like implements; on left female. Female bathing. 5 FIVE 5	Word twenty running across extreme end. XX Four females at work on cotton machine State Arms. BANK OF ATHENS, Athens, Geo. Dog. 20 XX	10 Female portrait. Drover and drove of cattle; boy in water, trees, and house in distance. BANK OF SMYRNA, Smyrna, Del. 10 X

ONE Ship; city in distance and other vessels.	1 Train of cars stopping at station. VILLAGE BANK, Bowdoinham, Me.	1 Wood cutter. ONE

V Male portrait	BANK OF AMERICA, Clarksville, Tenn. Shield with female on either side; ship and train of cars in distance. Ducks.	5 Male portrait

Shield, bust of female, soldier and war implements and female. C	Male portrait. Title of Bank. Letter C with words [illegible] hundred [illegible]	Die. Die.

2 Indians on cliff; city in distance	Two oxen before load of hay, boy on top and another boy with fork. VILLAGE BANK, Bowdoinham, Me. Bee hive.	2 Webster.

X Male portrait	Shield on which is State Arms; female bust at top; soldier and war-like implements on right; female on left. BANK OF AMERICA, Clarksville, Tenn. Female bathing.	10 Female.

TEN Male portrait	Bank building, trees, &c., male portrait on either side. BANK OF MONTGOMERY CO. Norristown, Pa. Dog.	10 Male portrait

THREE Male portrait	Cattle and sheep. VILLAGE BANK, Bowdoinham, Me. Head.	3 State Arms. 3

ONE Head of girl.	State Arms. Female seated resting on shield, on which is fig. 1 FREEHOLD BANKING CO. Freehold, N. J.	1 Male portrait

XX Male portrait	Men at work in Iron mill. Bank building. Title of Bank. Dog's head.	20 Male portrait

V Male portrait	Ship Washington. VILLAGE BANK Bowdoinham, Me. Female bathing.	5 Eagle. FIVE

Female seated by portrait of boy. 2	2 Two oxen before hay cart, boy asleep on top, another boy walking by side. Title of Bank.	2 Girl.

20 XX	CITY BANK. Philadelphia, Pa. Head of Washington on shield; right Indians and female with pole and cap; on left a Continental soldier. Portrait of Penn on right of vignette, and Franklin on left.	20 XX

X TEN X	Spread eagle on globe with flags for every State surrounding it. VILLAGE BANK, Bowdoinham, Me. Ducks.	10 Washington

3	Two horses before hay cart; on top, woman and child; man on one of the horses; boy, girl, blacksmith shop, &c. Male portrait Title of Bank.	Word three and figure 3. Webster.

FIVE FIVE V	Female seated with flowers around her; man plowing on left; buildings on right. SUSSEX BANK, Newton, N. J. Female bathing.	5 V

TWENTY Indian erect, with bow and quiver.	XX Wild horses. VILLAGE BANK, Bowdoinham, Me. Dog.	XX 20

5	Title of Bank. The vig. extends across the whole lower part of the note, and is men shearing sheep on left and men gathering corn right.	5

TEN	Shield on which is letter X—female bust at top; soldier and war implements on right; female on left, and head of female on right of vig. BK OF MIDDLETW'N Middletown, Pa. Ducks.	10 10

1 ONE Compt's die.	Cattle and sheep. BANK OF KENT, Ludingtonville, N. Y.	1 Men gathering corn.

10 Train of cars	Title of Bank. Female in clouds with eagle and sword.	10 Male portrait

Die. Male portrait	20 Milkmaid and two cows; other cows in distance. Title of Bank. Dog.	20 Female head

2 Compt's die. 2	Woodcutters at work. BANK OF KENT, Ludingtonville, N. Y	2 Men gathering corn

XX Female with sickle and sheaf.	Title of Bank. Shield with female on either side; train of cars and ship in distance.	20 Male portrait

50 Male portrait	Female in clouds with sword and eagle. Female with grain. Title of Bank.	50 Male portrait

Female seated by side of portrait of boy. V	Men harvesting. BANK OF KENT. Ludingtonville, N. Y.	5 Compt's die. 5

50 Male portrait	Title of Bank. State Arms.	50 FIFTY 50

10 Portrait of a General.	Spread eagle. BANK OF RUTLAND, Rutland, Vt. Tree and cow.	10 Portrait of a General.

ONE · Indian reclining; deer behind him; gold dollar. · 1 Female erect with fig. 1. · WAMSUTTA BANK, Fall River, Mass. · Indian head.	Man holding fig. 20. · Female reclining on cornucopia with distaff; ship in distance. · 20 Sea-monsters 20 · UNION BANK, Haverhill, Mass. · Steamship.	X · Male portrait. · Man at work in iron mill; anvil and forge. · 10 TEN · Title of Bank. Compt's die.
2 · Male and female seated, two gold dollars; cattle, trees and house in distance. · 2 Female representing Agriculture. · WAMSUTTA BANK, Fall River, Mass. · Squaw seated.	Cherub and dolphin. · Squaw seated; deer and hills in distance. · 50 50 · UNION BANK, Haverhill, Mass. · Justice seated.	TWENTY · Man tending large machinery. Title of Bank. · 20 Compt's die. · Male portrait.
3 · Mechanic, sailor and farmer seated with implements and three gold dollars. · THREE Female portrait. · WAMSUTTA BANK, Fall River, Mass. · Liberty and a squaw.	State Arms. · Indian reclining; deer. · 100 100 · UNION BANK, Haverhill, Mass. · Female representing Agriculture.	Indian princess seated; shield, &c. · HADLEY FALLS BK, Holyoke, Mass. · 50 Portrait of Daniel Webster; female each side; ships and farmer in distance. 50 · 50 Horse 50 · Blacksmith erect.
V · Five gold dollars, three cherubs, hunter and Indian; cars in distance · 5 Farmer with scythe. · WAMSUTTA BANK, Fall River, Mass. · Female portrait.	1 · MISSISQUOI BANK, Sheldon, Vt. Large spread eagle. · 1 Man with scythe. · Female representing Agriculture.	Girl's head. · L Three males supporting 50. · MECHANICS' BANK, Syracuse, N. Y. Cupids and 50. · Compt's die
10 · Nine cherubs, ten gold dollars, female, cornucopia, shield, &c.; cars and steamboat in distance · X WAMSUTTA BANK, Fall River, Mass. Indian head. · Mechanic. · Cherub and dolphin.	Female portrait. · Female in clouds reclining on eagle. · 2 2 · MISSISQUOI BANK, Sheldon, Vt. · Female portrait.	100 · Girl's head. · 100 MECHANICS' BANK, Syracuse, N. Y. Liberty seated. · Compt's die · Stone cutter.
FIFTY · Indian, squaw and papoose seated; city in distance. · 50 Female with shield and spear. · WAMSUTTA BANK, Fall River, Mass. · Female portrait.	Indian head. · Female reclining on a chest; two females and cows on right; cars and ship on left. · 3 3 · MISSISQUOI BANK Sheldon, Vt. · Indian head.	Female with flowers. · B'K. OF BRIGHTON, Brighton, Mass. · 50 Boy running after horses; sheep, cattle, trees, etc. 50 · View of a street and bank building.
Deer and dog. · Female seated on rock; three cherubs sporting in water with dolphin. · 100 HUNDR'D · WAMSUTTA BANK, Fall River, Mass. · Indian head.	1 · MANUFACTURERS' BANK OF Rochester, N. Y. · 1 ONE and fig. 1 on three red dies. Compt's die. · Female.	100 · B'K. OF BRIGHTON, Brighton, Mass. · 100 Street and bank building. · Drover and cattle, boy in water; trees and farm house in distance. · Men dressing leather.
L · Drove of cattle and sheep; man on horseback. · 50 Male portrait · NORTHBOROUGH BANK, Northborough, Mass. Horses. · Female churning.	2 on TWO. · Title of Bank. · 2 Compt's die. · TWO and fig. 2 on three red dies. TWO · Blacksmith, hammer and anvil.	Female erect with shield on which is figs. 500. · B'K. OF BRIGHTON, Brighton, Mass. · 500 State Arms; horse on either side with eagle at top; cars on right; building on left. · Large building.
100 · Blacksmith at work; boy and horse. · 100 Portrait of Z. Taylor. · NORTHBOROUGH BANK, Northborough, Mass. Cows. HUNDRED · Building.	5 on FIVE. · FIVE and fig. 5 on three red dies. · 5 Title of Bank. · Compt's die. Blacksmith. · V	5 · Female in clouds with cornucopia · 5 Liberty erect · BLACK RIVER B'K, Watertown, N. Y. Compt's die.

1 | Man dressing leather.
FARMERS' BANK OF THE STATE OF DELAWARE, Dover, Del.
Three males and female, harvest scene; cars and house in distance.
1 | Washing sheep; houses in distance.

100
View of U. S. Capitol. C
HARTFORD BANK, Hartford, Conn.
100 | Liberty surrounded by stars.

5 | Male portrait | V
Female seated with child; reapers and house in distance. 5 on med. head on either side of vig.
BANK OF MIDDLETOWN, Middletown, Pa.
FIVE

2 | Woodcutter,
Title of Bank.
Deer and tree on shield; on right, sailor, ship in distance; farmer with scythe on left.
Locomotive.
2 | Female erect and another kneeling.

ONE | Compt's die | ONE
Sailor and female seated; sheafs, quadrant, etc.; in distance, ship and house. 1
CITY BANK, Oswego, N. Y.
Secured &c.
ONE | Female seated; factory in distance. | ONE

5 | Reaper seated. | FIVE
5 Spread eagle. 5
BANK OF MIDDLETOWN, Middletown, Pa.
FIVE | Female erect with shield and helmet. | FIVE

50 | [illegible]
BANK OF MIDDLE GEORGIA, Macon, Geo.
50 on three red dies.
Cars.
50 | Sailor seated

ONE
1 on med. head. Eagle on a shield. 1 on med. head.
CUMBERLAND BK., Bridgton, N. J.
1 | ONE on med. head. | 1

20 and word TWENTY. | Male portrait
Female, shield, flag, ship, etc.
NATIONAL BANK, Albany, N. Y.
Compt's die.
20

100 | Three females; cars and city in distance.
Title of Bank.
100 and words one hundred dollars on three red dies.
100 | Two Indians, canoe and deer.

THREE | Justice. | 3
Female seated, eagle, rock, shield, etc.; ships in distance. 3 on med. head on either side of vig.
CUMBERLAND BK., Bridgton, N. J.
THREE | Ship. | THREE

Female. | 50
Female, eagle, globe, ship etc.
NATIONAL BANK, Albany, N. Y.
Compt's die.
50

500 | Five cupids, globe and anvil.
Title of Bank.
Five Hundred on red lathe work.
500 | Five cherubs with rake and tablets.

THREE | Male portrait | THREE
COMMERCIAL B'K, OF WILMINGTON. North Carolina.
Liberty and plenty; ships and trees in distance.
3 | Sailor.

100 | Sailor, ships, etc.
Compt's die. Female, eagle, flag, etc.
NATIONAL BANK, Albany, N. Y.
100 | Male portrait

5 | Squaw and papoose.
View of the Deaf and Dumb Asylum.
HARTFORD BANK, Hartford, Conn.
5 | Male head.

4 | Sailor.
Title of Bank.
Vig Same as 3s.
Red 4 Red 4
4 | Male portrait

3 | Cattle.
Female seated with cornucopia; factories, bridge, canal and cars in distance
MATTAPAN BANK, Dorchester, Mass.
3 | Cattle.

10 | Male portrait
Steamboat "Granite State;" hills and raft.
HARTFORD BANK, Hartford, Conn.
10 | Female.

5 | Compt's die
MECH. & FAR. BK., Albany, N. Y.
Blacksmith seated by anvil, forge, factories, vessels, etc.
FIVE
5 | Agriculture.

100 | Cattle
Spread eagle on shield; U. S. Capitol on right; steamship on right.
CAMBRIDGE MARKET BANK, Cambridge, Mass
100
100 | Tell's head.

XX | Female with cornucopia.
HARTFORD BANK, Hartford, Conn.
Vig. Same as fives.
20 | Male portrait

FIVE on med. head. | Male portrait
NORTH-WESTERN BANK, Wheeling, Va.
View of Suspension bridge; steamboats and houses.
5 | Male portrait

ONE | Sailor hoisting flag.
Steamship and other vessels.
BEDFORD COM BK, New Bedford, Mass.
ONE Female. ONE
1

Female with flowers. | 50
Title of Bank.
Shield on which is a deer; eagle at top, horse on either side; bridge and city in distance on right; building on left.
50 | Indian.

5 | Washington | V
Three females seated; ship in distance. 5 on med. head on either side of vig.
NORTH-WESTERN BANK, Wheeling, Va.
FIVE

2 | Female with flowers.
Female seated with telescope by shield; ship in distance. Fig. 2 on right.
Title of Bank.
Ship and other vessels | TWO

ONE	One on 1. Cattle, sheep and a colt; boy on horse.	1
Blacksmith with anvil; cars in distance.	WOODSTOCK BANK, Woodstock, Vt.	ONE

Treas. die.	NORTHFIELD BK., Northfield, Vt.	5
5	Five gold dollars, three Cupids, hunter and Indian; cars in distance. Cog-wheels, etc.	Male portrait

ONE	Wharf scene—men horses, boxes, bbls., carts, ship, steamship and other vessels. Female.	ONE
First Sabbath.	NEW HAVEN B'K, New Haven, Conn. Bee-hive.	1

TWO	Two females seated with cornucopia; anvil between them; factory in distance.	2
Two children	WOODSTOCK BANK, Woodstock, Vt.	Female portrait.

TEN	Train of cars; steamboat and houses in distance.	10
Treas. die. 10	NORTHFIELD BK., Northfield, Vt. Mechanics arm.	Male portrait

Female entwined in fig. 2	Two females and shield; steamship in distance.	2
Female.	NEW HAVEN BANK New Haven, Conn. Bee-hive.	First sabbath.

Female with scales, bale.	3 Female reclining on cornucopia; ship in distance.	3
THREE	WOODSTOCK BANK, Woodstock, Vt.	Three on 3.

100	ALFRED BANK, Alfred, Me.	100 C
Two females; shield between.		100

3 Female head.	NEW HAVEN BANK New Haven, Conn.	THREE
First sabbath.	Mechanic, sailor and farmer with implements. Beehive.	3

Female erect and captain.	Portrait of Washington surrounded by all the State Arms and implements of war.	20
20	WOODSTOCK BANK, Woodstock, Vt. Bell.	Cupid in sail boat. 20

TWENTY	MERCHANTS' BANK Newport, R. I.	Squaw and female.
Two Indians.	TWENTY Twenty Twenty	20

X Cotton, barrel and farming utensils.	Washington and two females; ship and steamboat on right and farming scene on left.	X
TEN	COMMERCIAL AND AGRICULTURAL BK, Galveston, Texas. Bales and barrels.	Female portrait

	Cherub reclining holding an American coin; cornucopia, box, barrels, &c.	Two males carrying a female.
Female.	WOODSTOCK BANK, Woodstock, Vt. Bell.	100

100 Building.	Spread eagle on branch of tree; cars, bridge, water and factories.	100
100	LANCASTER BANK, Lancaster, Pa.	

20; Cotton, barrel and farming utensils.	Three females by State Arms, eagle on top; trees, cars and ship in distance.	20
TWENTY	Title of Bank. Spread eagle.	Ship.

	Female seated between 1 and 0, with cornucopia and key. Compt's die.	10
10	CHESTER BANK, Chester, N. Y. Scenery, &c.	Men, cattle, and sheep.

100	Man watering three horses from trough by the side of well; sheep, goat, kid, trees, &c.; farm-house in distance.	100
Male portrait	FARMERS' BANK OF SCHUYLKILL CO., Pottsville, Pa.	Male portrait

50 Same as on left of 20s.	Same as twenties. Title of Bank.	50
FIFTY	Spread eagle.	Ship.

ONE Treas. die.	NORTHFIELD B'K., Northfield, Vt. Four males, two females, child, dog; horses, load of grain and men in distance.	1
Cupid and 1.	Boxes, bbls., &c.	Male portrait

50	Three females representing Liberty, Commerce and Agriculture.	FIFTY
Compt's die	WATERTOWN BK AND LOAN CO., Watertown, N. Y. Safe.	Female giving eagle drink. L

100	Title of Bank. Three female representing Agriculture, Commerce and Manufactures	100
Cars, bridge, trees and load of hay	100	City and shipping

	Mechanic seated by a boiler; men at work on boiler in distance. Male portrait	2
Treas. die.	NORTHFIELD BK, Northfield, Vt. Agricultural implements.	Cupid and 2

Ten dollars.	Compt's die.	10
Mechanic, sailor and farmer making offering to Goddess of Liberty; implements, &c	COMMERCIAL B'K, OF CLYDE, N. Y.	Female.

TEN Spread eagle.	Surrender of Burgoyne. 10	Justice.
10	BANK OF OLD SARATOGA, Schuylerville, N. Y. Soldier and cannon.	Compt's die

Treas. die.	Milkmaid seated with pail, cars in distance.	3
3	NORTHFIELD BK, Northfield, Vt. Dog's head.	Male portrait

TWENTY	COMMERCIAL B'K, OF CLYDE, N. Y. 20	20
Two males and two females with tablets and quadrant; city in distance	Compt's die.	Male, two females, dog and cattle.

Two horses, man, dog, plow, etc	Compt's die female each side.	20
XX	BANK OF OLD SARATOGA, Schuylerville, N. Y. Soldier and cannon.	Blacksmith with anvil

1 Wild horses. 1 B'K OF COMMERCE, Carmel, N. Y. Compt's die ONE on 1. Female.	THREE Same as ones. 3 ROCKPORT BANK, Rockport. Mass. Knickerbocker. Eagle. Female reapers	5 Same as ones. 5 Liberty. BLUEHILL BANK, Dorchester, Mass. FIVE Female representing Agriculture.
2 B'K OF COMMERCE, Carmel, N. Y. 2 Compt's die. 2 Horses, load of hay men and barn; load of hay in distance. 2 2 TWO	Man with cradle. Same as ones. 5 ROCKPORT BANK, Rockport, Mass. 5 Female.	X Same as ones 10 BLUEHILL BANK, Dorchester, Mass, Farmer with scythe. Two females.
10 Cattle in pasture; one drinking. 10 B'K OF COMMERCE, Carmel, N. Y. TEN Male portrait TEN and ten dollars across Compt's die.	Soldier with sword. Same as ones. 10 ROCKPORT BANK, Rockport, Mass. TEN Female portrait.	1 MECHANICKS' B'K, Concord, N. H. 1 Female erect with shield and spear. 1 View of a street with bank and other buildings.
20 Cattle and sheep; water in distance. 20 B'K OF COMMERCE, Carmel, N. Y. Male portrait Compt's die, X on TWENTY on left and X on DOLLARS on right. XX	Female. Same as ones. 20 ROCKPORT BANK, Rockport, Mass. XX Cow and calf Male portrait	2 2 MECHANICKS' B'K. Concord, N. H. Justice erect Same as vig. of ones. 2
Female reaper. BK OF CHATTANOOGA, Chattanooga, Tenn. 50 50 50 Female with a dove. 50 Female with cornucopia.	Franklin. Same as ones. 50 ROCKPORT BANK, Rockport, Mass. 50 Shield. Male portrait	3 MECHANICKS B'K, Concord, N. H, 3 Wheels and bales. Safe. 3 Same as ones. 3
MECHANICS' BANK, Worcester. Mass. D Female seated with book and mechanical implements; factories on right and steamboat on left. 500 Dog, key and safe.	Male portrait Same as ones. 100 ROCKPORT BANK, Rockport, Mass. 100 Dog's head. Webster.	5 Same as ones. 5 MECHANICKS' B'K, Concord, N. H. Pierce. Large fig. 5 surrounded by five females.
ONE HUNDRED 100 FARMERS' AND MECHANICS' BANK OF CARROLL CO. Westminster, Md. 100 ONE HUNDRED Milk-maid with a pail. Female	1 View of a street with bank and other buildings. 1 BLUEHILL BANK, Dorchester, Mass. Female portrait. Cows.	TEN MECHANICKS' B'K. Concord, N. H. 10 Same as the vignette on ones. Pierce. X TEN
Blacksmith, sledge and anvil. Team of oxen, stone quarry, &c. 1 ROCKPORT BANK, Rockport, Mass. 1 Man plowing. Stone-cutter.	2 Same as ones. 2 BLUEHILL BANK, Dorchester, Mass. Portrait of a female. Horses. Female.	20 MECHANICKS' B'K, Concord, N. H. 20 TWENTY Same as ones. DOLLARS Female portrait. Male portrait
Sailor and captain; masts, bbls. and bales. Same as ones. 2 ROCKPORT BANK, Rockport, Mass. 2 Loading wagon. Two females.	3 Same as ones. 3 BLUEHILL BANK, Dorchester, Mass. Stone-cutter Female.	9 Southern scene—various male and female figures, horses, wagons, mules, &c. 9 BK OF CLARENDON Fayetteville, N. C. Female with shield. 9

Left	Centre	Right
1 Word one twice and a fig. 1. Compt's die.	BANK OF TROY, Troy, N. Y. Liberty surrounded by stars in red die with words one dollar at top.	1 Same as on left. Die.
50	BK OF HAMBURG, Hamburg, S. C. State Arms, eagle at top, horse each side; steamboat in distance on right; cars and factories on left.	50
View of building, trees and monument. 5	BK OF THE STATE OF GEORGIA, Red die. Savannah, Geo.	5 Squaw.
2 Compt's die. TWO	BANK OF TROY, Troy, N. Y. Red 2 across. Male portrait in red die work with the words two dollars at top.	2 Red 2 across Die.
100 and C in red.	BK OF HAMBURG, Hamburg, S. C. Head of Liberty surrounded by stars.	100 and C in red.
X Red work.	Title of Bank. Vig. Same as on left of 5s	10 Red work.
Compt's die. Red 3 across. 3	BANK OF TROY, Troy, N. Y. Washington in red die work, with words three dollars at top.	3 Red 3 across 3
TEN	X WAVERLY BANK, Waverly, N. Y. Male portrait	10 Compt's die
XX Red work.	Title of Bank. Vig. Same as left of fives.	20 Red work.
5 FIVE in red. FIVE	BANK OF TROY, Troy, N. Y. Three cherubs forming a 5; sheaves, rake, sheep; ship in distance.	FIVE in red. 5 Compt's die. FIVE
TWENTY	XX WAVERLY BANK, Waverly, N. Y. Male portrait	TWENTY 20
3 Sailor standing by capstan, bbls., bales, &c.	View of street with bank and other buildings. BARNSTABLE B'K, Yarmouth, Mass. Ship.	THREE on 3. Male portrait
20 Two males and female with telescope in boat.	CITIZENS' BANK, Sanbornton, N. H. 20	20 Male, two females, dog and cattle.
Female portrait. 20	Female seated on a rock; three cherubs sporting with dolphin in water. CONNECTICUT RIVER BANK, Charlestown, N. H.	20 Two females.
20 TWENTY Male portrait	BARNSTABLE B'K, Yarmouth, Mass. Same as threes.	20 Liberty seated with globe and shield.
L 50 Die	View of the U. S. Capitol CITIZENS' BANK, Sanbornton, N. H.	L 50 Die
Female seated. 50	View of U. S. Capitol. 50 Title of Bank.	Justice.
50 Sailor boy's head.	Same as threes. BARNSTABLE B'K, Yarmouth, Mass. Barrels.	50 Male portrait FIFTY
100 Three females representing the Arts and Sciences.	CITIZENS' BANK, Sanbornton, N. H.	Female giving eagle drink. 100
Soldier with sword. 100	Female seated on bale giving eagle drink, cornucopia and distaff at her feet; ship in distance. Title of Bank.	100 Female representing Agriculture.
100 Male portrait	BARNSTABLE B'K, Yarmouth, Mass. Vig. Same as threes. Ship.	100 Female portrait.
TEN on X. X	BK OF HAMBURG, Hamburg, S. C. Farm scene—male, female, children, well, dog and horse; man watering horse. Ten Dollars on red lathe strip.	10 X
3 THREE	Compt's die. Five females and a male gathering vines WORTHINGTON BK, Cooperstown, N. Y. Male portrait	3
5 Cattle in water.	Drove of horses; man on horse in distance. EXCHANGE BANK, Murfreesboro', Tenn.	V 5
20 XX	Title of Bank. Shield on which is a tree; eagle at top, female on either side, bridge and cars in distance on right; ship and steamboat on left.	20 XX
X TEN	Male portrait Hunter shooting a deer; dog, trees and stream. WORTHINGTON BK, Cooperstown, N. Y.	10 Compt's die
10 10, X and Ten.	Farmer and drover bargaining for ox EXCHANGE BANK, Murfreesboro', Tenn.	10 Female feeding fowls.

Female erect by fig. 1. ONE on 1.	View of Shelburne Falls. SHELBURNE FALLS BANK, Shelburne Falls, Mass.	1 Female churning.
1 Farmer, dog, horse, pigeons, etc.	WASHINGTON CO. BANK, Carolina Mills, R. I. Washington	1 Female feeding fowls.
Justice erect and Minerva seated. Two dollars.	Cattle, sheep and colt; boy on horse. PINE RIVER BANK, Ossipee, N. H. TWO TWO	2 Female with flowers.
2 Farmer with scythe.	Farmers mowing; others loading wagon in distance Title of Bank.	2 Female representing Agriculture.
2 Two mechanics at work on frame of cart.	Man seated; two horses; male portrait on each side of vig. Title of Bank.	2 Washington
3 Man cutting down a tree	3 Blacksmith shop; man shoeing horse; Jackass tied to anvil; cars in distance. PINE RIVER BANK, Ossipee, N. H. THREE THREE	3 Boy's head.
3 Blacksmith; anvil.	View of Shelburne Falls. 3 Title of Bank.	Liberty.
3 Farmers at lunch.	Title of Bank. Female portrait.	3 Blacksmiths at work.
Justice erect FIVE	Ox; house and oxen in distance. PINE RIVER BANK, Ossipee, N. H. FIVE FIVE	5 Female churning.
5 Washington	Mechanic seated with hammer; cars, factory, bridge and cattle in distance. Title of Bank.	5 Female with grain.
5 Soldiers erecting breast work.	Title of Bank. Soldier, shield with head on it; female, two Indians etc.	5 Female; cow, heifer, ducks, etc.
Reaper X	Males and females, vines, etc. PINE RIVER BANK, Ossipee, N. H. Ten Dollars Ten Dollars	10 Franklin.
X	Female seated before shield, reclining on chest; milkmaid and cows in distance on right; cars and ships on left. Two men Title of Bank.	10 Female with shield, cornucopia and knives.
10 Female seated with pole, cap and shield; buildings in distance.	Indians apparently frightened at white men; men in distance on right. Title of Bank.	10
Indian on a cliff.	Female on either side of shield, surmounted by an eagle; steamboat in distance. PINE RIVER BANK, Ossipee, N. H. TWENTY TWENTY	20 Male portrait 20
50 Female with flowers.	View of Shelburne Falls. Title of Bank.	50 Male portrait
5 Med. head. 5	5 on med. head. Eagle on shield; ships in the distance. 5 on med. head. MERCHANTS' BANK Salem, Mass. V Dog's head. V	5 Med. head. 5
FIFTY Washington	L on American shield; eagle at top surrounded by flags. PINE RIVER BANK, Ossipee, N. H. FIFTY FIFTY	50 50
100 Female portrait.	Three females representing Agriculture, Commerce and Manufactures. Title of Bank.	100 Franklin.
10 Med. head. 10	MERCHANTS' BANK Salem, Mass. Indian queen seated, left hand on shield; quadrant, compass, bales, barrel, etc.; steamship in distance. TEN on medallion head on each side of vig. X Steamship. X	X TEN on med. head. 10
100 100	Female seated; letter C; factories and bridge in distance. PINE RIVER BANK, Ossipee, N. H. ONE HUNDRED	100 D. Webster.
Female portrait. 50	Three females representing Agriculture, Commerce and Manufactures. PEOPLES BANK, Waterville, Me.	50 Webster.
	MERCHANTS' BANK Salem, Mass. ☞ This Bank also uses the Perkins' Stereotype Plate, which has the denomination printed in fine letters all over the bill.	
TEN Female feeding fowls.	X Men, horse, dog, cattle and sheep. FAR. & MECH. BK., Rochester, N. Y.	10 Male portrait
Jefferson. 100	Farming scene—men at lunch. PEOPLES BANK, Waterville, Me.	100 Jackson.
ONE Female feeding fowls.	1 Man seated by basket of fruit and cradle; load of hay in distance. PINE RIVER BANK, Ossipee, N. H. ONE ONE	1 Child's head.
20 Indian on ground, dead deer, scenery etc.	AMERICAN BANK, Providence, R. I. Female on eagle soaring in clouds. Red 20.	20 Squaw seated.

Left	Centre	Right
1 Compt's die	BANK OF THE CITY OF LACROSSE, La Crosse, Wis. Scene on Western river with steamboats	1 Augusta House.
2 Compt's die. 2	Drove of cattle and sheep; drovers on horseback; cars and city in distance. MERCANTILE BK., Wis.	2 2
TEN inverted Female feeding fowls.	X Cattle and sheep; dog, man and horse FAR. & MECH. B'K, Rochester, N. H.	10 Male portrait
2 TWO	Title of Bank. Western rafting scene.	2 Compt's die
5 Compt's die 5	Shipping and city. MERCANTILE BK., Wis.	5 5
TWENTY Officer with sword.	20 Female seated; locomotive and factory in distance. FAR. & MECH. B'K, Rochester, N. H.	20 Male portrait
3 Cattle, sheep horse, colt, boy, etc.	Title of Bank. Compt's die. 3	THREE on 3. Train of cars
1 Washington.	Landing of Columbus. B'K OF COLUMBUS, Columbus, Wis.	1 Compt's die.
Two children 50	Farmer seated; others at work in distance. FAR. & MECH. B'K, Rochester, N. H.	50 Washington
5 Two children	Title of Bank. Male portrait, word dollars under it.	5 Compt's die.
2 Male portrait	B'K OF COLUMBUS, Columbus, Wis. Man at work surveying.	2 Compt's die
Fountain. 100	Battle of Niagara. FAR. & MECH. B'K, Rochester, N. H.	100 Large building
1	COMMERCIAL BANK Racine, Wis. Wharf scene—cars, drays, males, females, shipping, etc. Girl.	1 Compt's die
5 Indian on a horse.	Two males, two females and child, dog and Indians. B'K OF COLUMBUS, Columbus, Wis.	5 FIVE Compt's die.
1 on ONE. Cotton plant and barrel	COMMERCIAL BANK OF BRUNSWICK, Georgia. Men drawing logs out of dock; ship on stocks; ship house and steamer in distance.	1 Franklin.
ONE Compt's die. Milkmaid and cows.	COMMERCIAL BANK Racine, Wis. Farmer, horse and dog. Blacksmith, anvil and forge.	1 Sailor with implements.
ONE Liberty and squaw.	ONE on fig. 1. Indian, squaw and papoose seated; city in distance. FAR. & MECH. B'K, Rochester, N. H.	1 Female representing Agriculture.
2 on med. head. Male portrait	Title of Bank. Portrait of Washington, surmounted by eagle; two females on right, cars in distance; female on left, and ship in distance.	2 Vessel, cars and bridge
2 Female.	COMMERCIAL BANK Racine, Wis. Train of cars, men, trees, etc.; cars, bridge and hills in distance.	2 Compt's die.
Females haying. 2	Men at work in boot and shoe manufactory. FAR. & MECH. B'K, Rochester, N. H.	2 Two females.
FIVE on V. Liberty surrounded by stars.	Title of Bank. Rafting scene—males, female and child on raft; man in boat with two birds; other rafts in distance.	5 Cherubs forming fig. 5; sheafs &c.
3 Female portrait.	COMMERCIAL BANK Racine, Wis. Female portrait. Compt's die.	3 Female portrait.
3 Female, eagle, shield, and fig. 3.	Three cherubs and three silver dollars; mechanical and other implements. FAR. & MECH. B'K. Rochester, N. H.	THREE on 3. Female head.
Female erect with distaff and shield on which is lled. Head TEN	Title of Bank. Steamboat, lighter and other vessels.	10, X and Ten Cotton plantation.
1 Compt's die. 1	Indian seated; city in distance. MERCANTILE BK., Lodi Wis.	1 1
Farmer with scythe. 5	5 Milkmaid milking cows; another cow on left. FAR. & MECH. B'K, Rochester, N. H.	5 Franklin.
TWENTY Hunter loading his gun.	Title of Bank. Justice seated on bale; American shield and cotton on right; cars and bridge on left in distance.	20 State Arms. XX

<table>
<tr>
<td>ONE
HUDSON CITY BK,
Hudson, Wis.
Wharf scene—cars, drays, males, females, shipping, etc.
Female portrait.
1
ONE
Compt's die.</td>
<td>5
Compt's die.
FIVE
NORTH WESTERN BANK,
Marquette, Wis.
Mechanic with implements and V; factories in distance.
5
Girl's head.</td>
<td>Squaw and female.
ONE
Males and females; views, etc.
BROWN CO. BA[illegible]
Deper[illegible]
ONE
Farming utensils.
Compt's die.</td>
</tr>
<tr>
<td>2
Farmers mowing.
HUDSON CITY BK,
Hudson, Wis.
Compt's die.
2
Farmers, dog, horse and sheep.</td>
<td>X
Compt's die.
Indians welcoming white men.
Jackson
NORTH WESTERN BANK,
Marquette, Wis.
10
Female portrait.</td>
<td>TEN
Compt's die.
B[illegible]WN CO. BANK,
Depere, Wis.
Female seated with shield and sheaf; ship in distance.
10
Train of cars</td>
</tr>
<tr>
<td>5
Sailor and captain.
HUDSON CITY BK,
Hudson, Wis.
Men at work surveying.
Pigs.
5
Compt's die</td>
<td>1
Indians alarmed at white men.
KATANYAN BANK,
La Crosse, Wis.
1
Compt's die.
1
Farmers; horse drinking, etc.</td>
<td>1
Washington on his horse.
Shepherd reclining; sheep in distance.
BANK OF THE CAPITOL,
Madison, Wis.
1
Compt's die</td>
</tr>
<tr>
<td>1
Four cows and three sheep.
Girl's head.
BANK OF RIPON,
Ripon, Wis.
Farming utensils.
1
Compt's die.</td>
<td>2
Scene in a battle.
2
Compt's die.
KATANYAN BANK,
LaCrosse, Wis.
2
Female feeding fowls.</td>
<td>3
Boy gathering corn-stalks.
Indian seated; city in distance.
Title of Bank.
2
Compt's die.</td>
</tr>
<tr>
<td>2
Compt's die.
Train of cars; city and town.
BANK OF RIPON,
Ripon, Wis.
2
Female feeding fowls.</td>
<td>5
Girl's head.
Girl's head.
Men at work surveying
Girl's head.
KATANYAN BANK,
La Crosse, Wis.
Dog
5
Compt's die.</td>
<td>5
Indian princess.
Title of Bank.
Large V and female.
5
Compt's die.</td>
</tr>
<tr>
<td>5
Farming utensils.
Female portrait.
Men at work surveying.
BANK OF RIPON,
Ripon, Wis.
5
Compt's die.</td>
<td>1
Female portrait.
Compt's die.
Female seated with shield and sheaf; ship in distance.
WAUPUN BANK,
Waupun, Wis.
ONE
Farmer.</td>
<td>ONE
Compt's die.
Steamboat Prairie du Chein and St. Paul.
1
BANK OF PRAIRIE DU CHEIN,
Prairie du Chein, Wis.
Cars.
Indian
ONE</td>
</tr>
<tr>
<td>1
Female seated with fig. 1.
Farmer with dog, mowing.
MILWAUKIE B'K,
Milwaukie, Wis.
Female
1
Compt's die
ONE</td>
<td>TWO
Female with scales, etc.
Compt's die.
WAUPUN BANK,
Waupun, Wis.
Santa Claus in sleigh drawn by reindeers, on roofs of houses.
2
Female portrait</td>
<td>2
Two children
Wild horses.
Title of Bank.
Dog.
2
Compt's die.</td>
</tr>
<tr>
<td>3
Female portrait
Cars, &c.
MILWAUKIE BK,
Milwaukie, Wis.
Man plowing
3
Compt's die.
THREE</td>
<td>Soldier with sword.
THREE
Female and eagle.
Compt's die.
WAUPUN BANK,
Waupun, Wis.
Word Three and fig. 3.
Female portrait.</td>
<td>3
Compt's die.
Rafting scene.
Title of Bank.
Dog's head.
3
Farmers.</td>
</tr>
<tr>
<td>FIVE
Large V, two females and three males.
Compt's die.
Steamer and other vessels.
MILWAUKIE B'K,
Milwaukie, Wis.
Bull
5
Female portrait.
FIVE</td>
<td>Female portrait.
10
Spread eagle; cars, city and shipping in distance
10
BANK OF BELOIT,
Beloit, Wis.
Horse.
Compt's die.</td>
<td>5
Farmer.
Title of Bank.
Compt's die.
Load of hay, cars, city and bridges.
5
Two females.</td>
</tr>
</table>

5 | 5 Mercury seated with cornucopia and wand; safe, lion, etc.; cars, canal scene, vessels, etc., in distance. 5 | Female erect; building in distance.
Compt's die.
5 | MERCHANTS' BANK New York City. Bank building.

FIVE | Compt's die. Sailor seated with telescope; vessels in distance. | 5
Three males; two females and letter V | GROCERS BANK, New York City. | Five females and fig. 5

5 | V 5 and three females; ship-ping, cars, etc., in distance. V | 5
Female, safe, eagle, scales, etc. | Med. head.
FIVE | AMERICAN EX. BK, New York City. Eagle. | FIVE

10 | X Vig. Same as fives. X | Die.
Compt's die. | MERCHANTS' BANK New York City. | 10
10 | Bank building. | Die

Compt's die. | 10 Female on either side of ship; cars, vessels, etc., in distance. | TEN
Sailor erect; capstan, masts, etc. | GROCERS BANK, New York City. Safe. | 10

10 | Female on either side of shield; shipping, city, canal scene, etc. | 10
Same as fives | AMERICAN EX. BK New York City. | Two females, eagle, cornucopia and motto "Excelsior."
TEN | Eagle. | TEN

20 | 20 Vig. Same as fives. 20 | Sea monsters.
Compt's die. | MERCHANTS' BANK New York City. | Vessels.
20 | Die. | Sea monsters.

20 | Compt's die. Female between 2 and 0. | XX
Mercury between 2 & 0. | GROCERS BANK, New York City. City Arms. | Ship and other vessels

TWENTY | 20 Female seated; scientific apparatus; in distance steamship. 20 | Die.
Same as fives | AMERICAN EX. BK, New York City. Eagle. | XX
TWENTY | | Die.

50 | 50 Vig. Same as fives. 50 | Sea monsters.
Compt's die. | MERCHANTS' BANK New York City. | Same as fives
50 | Die. | Sea monsters.

50 | Ships and other vessels; city in distance. | 50
Compt's die. | GROCERS BANK, New York City. | Male portrait
50 | Machinery, etc. | FIFTY

FIFTY | Two Indians and white man. FIFTY on med. head on each side. | FIFTY
Female seated; steamboat. | AMERICAN EX. BK, New York City. | Female seated; acrew-press; buildings in distance.
50 | Capitol. | 50

100 | C Vig. Same as fives. C | 100
Compt's die. | MERCHANTS' BANK New York City. | Boy's head.
100 | Bank building. | 100

Merchandise | 100 Three females seated. | 100
Compt's die. | GROCERS BANK, New York City. |
Cars. | Bbls., bales, etc. | Male portrait

HUNDRED | 100 on med. head. Female on either side shield, eagle at top; cars, shipping, etc. 100 on med. head | ONE HUNDRED
Female. | AMERICAN EX. BK, New York City. |
100 | Capitol |

Die | Figs. 500, with Cupids on each figure. | Same as vig. of fives.
Compt's die. | MERCHANTS' BANK New York City. |
Die. | Bank building. | 500

Steamboat, schooner, buildings, men, etc. | 1 Two females, shield, surmounted by an eagle; cars; shipping, etc. 1 |
ONE | BK OF THE STATE OF NEW YORK, New York City. | Spanish dollar
Compt's die. | |

500 | 500 Cars; steam vessel in distance. | 500
Same as fives | AMERICAN EX. BK, New York City. |
500 | Eagle. |

ONE | Compt's die. View of street, buildings, pedestrians, etc. |
Female seated with fig. 1 | GROCERS BANK, New York City. | 1

II | Vig. Same as ones. 2 | Two spanish dollars lapped.
Compt's die. | Title of Bank. |
TWO | |

1000 | Steamship and other vessels; houses, etc. Figs. 1000 on each side. | ONE THOUSAND
Same as fives | AMERICAN EX. BK, New York City. |
1000 | |

TWO | Compt's die. Female on either side of a fig. 2. | 2
Female seated on bbl. | GROCERS BANK, New York City. Bales and barrels. | Male portrait

 | 3 Vig. Same as ones. | III
Two spanish dollars and one American lapped. | Title of Bank. | Compt's die.
 | | THREE

5 | Three females, ship in distance. | 5
Washington on his horse. | CONNECTICUT B'K, Bridgeport, Conn. Shield, etc. | Liberty.

3 | Compt's die. Female reclining on merchandise; ships, cars, canal scene in distance. |
Mechanic, sailor, farmer and fig. 3 | GROCERS BANK, New York City. | 3
THREE | |

Cupid on a dolphin; building ... Compt's die. | 20 Two females on right of shield; eagle and vessel on left. | 20
 | IRVING BANK, New York City. | Male portrait
TWENTY | Steamship. | TWENTY

Five hundred | MAVERICK BANK, Boston, Mass. | 500
Washington | |
500 | D Winthrop block and a street in East Boston. |

Left end	Centre	Right end
1 Compt's die 1	Female on horse catching buffalo; hunting buffaloes in distance. ONE LEATHER MANUFACTURERS' BANK, New York City. Shield.	Cupid and grindstone. ONE
2 Compt's die. 2	2 TWO Title of Bank. Shield.	Same as vig. of ones. 2
3 Compt's die. 3	3 Cupid and grindstone. 3 Title of Bank. 3	Goat's head. THREE Goat's head.
5 Compt's die. 5	V Vig. Same as ones. 5 Title of Bank. 5	FIVE Female, vessel, cow, sheep, etc. V
10 Compt's die. 10	Cupid and grindstone. X Title of Bank. Steamboat.	Same as vig. of ones. 10
20 Compt's die. 20	20 Vig. Same as ones. TWENTY Title of Bank.	SAFETY Cupid and grindstone. FUND 20
50 Compt's die. 50	50 Title of Bank. 50 Cupid and grindstone.	FIFTY
100 Compt's die. 100	100 Vig. Same as ones. Title of Bank.	100
500 Compt's die. 500	Female with eagle; ships in distance. Title of Bank.	Statue of Washington 500

Left end	Centre	Right end
Die Compt's die. Die.	1000 Cupid and grindstone. 1000 Title of Bank.	1000 Full length Female with anchor.
ONE 1 ONE	GLOBE BANK, Boston, Mass. The title of this Bank is repeated twice on the note—a special plate like Perkins', which has the denomination in fine letters all over the bill.	1 ONE 1
TWO 2 TWO	GLOBE BANK, Boston, Mass. Same as ones.	2 TWO 2
THREE 3 THREE	GLOBE BANK, Boston, Mass. Same as ones.	3 THREE 3
FIVE 5 FIVE	GLOBE BANK, Boston, Mass. Same as ones.	5 FIVE 5
TEN X TEN	GLOBE BANK, Boston, Mass. Same as ones.	10 TEN 10
FIFTY 50 FIFTY	GLOBE BANK, Boston, Mass. Same as ones.	50 FIFTY 50
C 100 C	GLOBE BANK, Boston, Mass. Same as ones.	100 C 100
	GLOBE BANK, Boston, Mass. 500s and 1000s, same as ones except in the denomination	

Left end	Centre	Right end
1 State Arms.	SOUTH ROYALTON BANK, South Royalton, Vt. Female portrait and words One Dollar on a large round die.	1 Eagle.
2 State Arms.	Title of Bank. 2 2 Female.	2 TWO
3 THREE State Arms.	Title of Bank. THREE 3 THREE	3 DOLLARS Female seated with pole, cap and shield; buildings in distance.
THREE	3 Indian princess seated. 3 BANK of the STATE OF NORTH CAROLINA.	THREE Three females; centre one helmeted. THREE
Med. head.	4 Train of cars. Title of Bank.	FOUR Female erect with sickle. FOUR
Female and log. 20	20 Men, saw-mill, sloop, etc. 20 Title of Bank. Female, ship, etc.	Female and dog. 20
5 Justice. V	Med. head on frame; female seated on either side. BANK OF LOUISVILLE, Ky.	V Justice. 5
5 Female with shield, etc.	BANK OF LOUISVILLE, Ky. Male portrait 5	5 Female representing Manufactures.
20 Indians hunting buffaloes.	BANK OF LOUISVILLE, Ky. Female portrait.	20 Man felling a tree; oxen, children, houses, etc.

ONE / Mercury. / Female and State Arms; ships, etc., in distance. / NORTHERN BANK, Providence, R. I. / 1 / Female with sheaf, cow and sickle

Cupid and fig 1. / Anchor. / COMMERCIAL B'K. OF ALABAMA, Selma, Ala. / Head of Wm. R. King. / Cupid and figure 1. / Bee hive.

TEN / BANK OF ASHLAND Ashland, Ky. / Male and female on either side of a shield on which is a head; two Indians on left. / 10 / Female head.

TWO / Female figure of Mechanics and the Fine Arts. / Spread eagle on shield. / NORTHERN BANK, Providence, R. I. / 2 / Farmer carrying stalks

2 / Sailor with quadrant. / Title of Bank. / Two male portraits. / 2 / Female figure of Commerce; bales and shipping

Train of cars another train crossing bridge in distance. / 20 / BANK OF ASHLAND Ashland, Ky. / 20 / Clay.

THREE / Justice. / Steamship and other vessels. / NORTHERN BANK, Providence, R. I. / 3 / Female feeding fowls.

3 / Title of Bank. / Three male portraits. / THREE DOLLARS / 3

ONE / Sailor with flag. / Shipping; navy yard in background. / MARINE BANK, Providence, R. I. / 1 / Anchor and bales.

FIVE V / Dr Kane and party in the Arctic Regions. / NORTHERN BANK, Providence, R. I. / 5 / Milkmaid, cow and calf.

Male portrait / 5 / Title of Bank. / FIVE DOLLARS / Train of cars passing through new country; group of backwoods men. / 5 / Female with glass.

Sailor with flag and female figure of Agriculture. / 2 Whaling scene / MARINE BANK, Providence, R. I. / 2 / Female with glass looking seaward.

X / Hen and chickens. / NORTHERN BANK, Providence, R. I. / Puritans at prayer surprised by Indians. / 10

10 / Female, shield and State Arms. / Steamboat loaded with cotton. / Title of Bank. / 10 / Male portrait

Three females representing Agriculture, Commerce and Manufactures. / Steamship; city in distance. / MARINE BANK, Providence, R. I. / 3 / Female figure of Commerce.

50 / Beaver. / Nooning—farmer, two horses, etc. / NORTHERN BANK, Providence, R. I. / 50 / Dog and game.

20 / Continental soldiers and drummer boy. / Male head. / Steamboat landing and Railroad depot, city view, etc. / Title of Bank. / 20 / 20

5 / Sailor leaning on capstan. / Launch of the Adriatic / MARINE BANK, Providence, R. I. / 5 / Head of Fulton. / FIVE

100 / Deer. / A party of surveyors. / NORTHERN BANK, Providence, R. I. / 100 / Men building railroad.

Sailor with flag, and female figure of Agriculture. / Title of Bank. / Two females supporting State Arms: on right, vessels at sea; on left water works. / 50 / Male portrait

RHODE ISLAND / 10 / X / MARINE BANK, Providence, R. I. / Female, anchor and word "Hope" in a frame; on right, female, vessels, etc; on left female and view of Niagara Falls. / TEN DOLLARS / 10 / RHODE ISLAND / X

500 / Bull. / Horses at trough, and girl filling bucket. / NORTHERN BANK, Providence, R. I. / 500 / Indian.

100 / Portrait of King. / Title of Bank. / 100 / Three sailors shipping in distance.

50 / Fancy female head. / Steamboat landing and railroad depot; city view, etc. / MARINE BANK, Providence, R. I. / 50 / Eagle on a shield.

1000 / Indian on horseback. / Signing the first Constitution on board the May-flower. / NORTHERN BANK, Providence, R. I. / 1000 / Dog and closet.

5 / Continental soldier charging bayonet / Girl's head. Five men at work in Iron Foundry Girl's head. / BANK OF ASHLAND Ashland, Ky. / Machinery. / 5 / Female portrait.

100 / Sailor leaning on capstan. / Fame blowing trumpet; eagle, globe, etc. / MARINE BANK, Providence, R. I. / 100 / Washington

ONE Court House building.	Cattle. BANK OF THE CO. OF ELGIN, St. Thomas, Canada.	1 Hen and chickens.
XX Portrait of girl with curls.	Female representing Agriculture; ship in distance. 20 FREDONIA BANK, Fredonia, N. Y Compt's die.	TWENTY Female erect with spear and shield. TWENTY
5 Male portrait	Title of Bank. Three Indians; cars, hills, etc. Secured &c.	5 Compt's die. FIVE
2 Male portrait	Train of cars. Title of Bank.	2 Court House building.
ONE Male portrait	Girl's head. Loaded wagon two boys, two oxen, etc. TIVERTON BANK, Tiverton, R. I. Ducks.	1 Factories.
10 Three Indians erect, etc.	Title of Bank. Large X across the title. TEN Male portrait. DOLLARS TEN	10 Building. Compt's die.
5 Portrait of the Duke of Wellington.	Horses at trough; man, sheep, etc.; houses in background. Title of Bank. Secured, etc.	5 Court House building
TWO Female seated.	TIVERTON BANK, Tiverton, R. I. TWO Dog.	2 Female seated on grain.
1 Cooper at work. UNE	1 Farmer with plow and scythe; buildings in distance. 1 LA BANQUE DU PEUPLE, Montreal, Canada.	1 Four cherubs and fig 1
10 Male head.	Train of cars going thro' new country; backwoods men in foreground. Title of Bank.	10 Court House building.
3 Steamboat.	TIVERTON BANK, Tiverton, R. I. Female on either side of shield, surmounted by an eagle, on which is view of sunrise, buildings, etc.	3 Train of cars
Ship carpenter seated with tools.	4 Milkmaid seated; female milking cow; vessels in distance. Title of Bank. Dog's head.	4 Blacksmith at work. 4
1 ONE Compt's die.	Female and fig. 1; cars and steamboat in distance. ONE FREDONIA BANK, Fredonia, N. Y.	Indian on cliff. ONE
5 Male portrait FIVE	5 Anchor on shield, surmounted by eagle; female on either side. 5 TIVERTON BANK, Tiverton, R. I. RHODE ISLAND	5 Female portrait. FIVE
50 Blacksmith's apprentice.	Cattle WASHINGTON CO. BANK, Carolina Mills, R. I.	50 Train of cars
TWO Compt's die. TWO	Farmer and milkmaid; two gold dollars; cows, houses, etc. 2 FREDONIA BANK, Fredonia, N. Y.	TWO Two females erect. TWO
X TEN X	TIVERTON BANK, Tiverton, R. I. Female seated on grain; houses, loading hay, etc. distance.	10 D. Webster.
Compt's die.	Female seated, flowers, &c.; factories and men plowing in distance. FARMERS' BANK OF WASHINGTON CO. Fort Edward, N. Y	1 Female shading her eyes with her hand.
Compt's die. THREE Mechanic, sailor, farmer and figure 3	3 Three females representing Agriculture, Commerce and Manufactures; ship in distance FREDONIA BANK, Fredonia, N. Y.	3 Female.
Secured, etc. Compt's die	Three Indians; train of cars, hills &c., in distance. 1 MOHAWK RIVER BANK, Fonda, N. Y.	ONE and 1. Male portrait
2 Compt's die. 2	Farmer seated, girl and horses on right; boy and dog on left. Title of Bank. Tomb of Jane McCrea.	2 TWO
5 Female.	Five females, fig. 5 in centre; ship, fur, factory, locomotive and tender in distance. 5 FREDONIA BANK, Fredonia, N. Y.	5 Compt's die 5
2 Compt's die. 2	Title of Bank. Three Indians; suspension bridge, etc. TWO Train of cars.	2 Male portrait
5 Portrait of a boy.	Female seated on grain; houses, cattle, loading hay, etc., in distance. Title of Bank.	5 Compt's die FIVE
TEN Blacksmith, anvil, hammer, forge, etc. TEN	FREDONIA BANK, Fredonia, N. Y. 10 Nine cherubs making offering to female seated with cornucopia and two gold dollars.	10 TEN Compt's die
Compt's die. Building. 3	Three Indians; cars, hills, etc., in distance. THREE Title of Bank.	3 Male portrait
X Female seated with sword; word TEN on shield.	Two horses before load of hay; man on one of the horses, woman and child on top of hay; boy with rake and girl with flowers; dog; blacksmith with sledge and interior of shop with men at work. Title of Bank.	10 Building, pedestrians etc Compt's [illegible]

Steamboat.	5 Female representing Agriculture. 5	Steamboat.
	FARMERS' & MERCHANTS' BANK, Baltimore, Md.	
5		5

3	Man, three horses at trough; female feeding hogs; houses etc.	3
Female portrait.	BANK OF WADESBOROUGH, Wadesborough, N. C.	Two females.
3	Dog, key and safe.	3

ONE	FARMERS' BANK, Bridgeport, Conn.	1
ONE	Female portrait on large die; words "one dollar." Two females tending looms.	ONE

TEN	10 Female seated; stages, etc. 10	TEN
Shearing sheep.	Title of Bank.	Ship.
TEN		TEN

Fig. 5, cars, bridge, Indians, water, etc.	5 Washington 5	Female seated with sheaf.
	CITIZENS' BANK, Fulton, N. Y.	
Compt's die.	Secured, etc.	5

2	FARMERS' BANK, Bridgeport, Conn.	2
	Milkmaid and boy.	
Washington		Female with rose.

20	20 Female spinning; houses harbor, etc. 20	20
Sheep.	Title of Bank.	Sail vessel.
20		20

20	STATE BANK OF OHIO.	Female with spinning wheel; steamboat in the distance.
Clay.		20

FIVE	FARMERS' BANK, Bridgeport, Conn.	5
	Vigs. in lower right and left corners. Blacksmiths' shop, men, shoeing horse, etc.; farmer, wife and boy at lunch &c.	

FIFTY	Female representing Agriculture. Figs 50 on left, and 50 and L on the right of vig.	Die.
	Title of Bank.	FIFTY DOLLARS
		Die

FOUR	BANK OF FAYETTEVILLE, Fayetteville, N. C.	FOUR
		Indian.
Figure 4.	Men bitching team to plow; man on horseback. 4	FOUR

10	X Female portrait. X	10
	SMITH'S BANK OF PERRY, N. Y.	
Male portrait	Secured &c.	Compt's die.

100	Female reclining on bales; ship, cornucopia, etc Figs. 100 on either side.	ONE HUNDRED
	Title of Bank.	

5	Large V, female therein.	5
	BK of GEORGETOWN Georgetown, S. C.	
Male portrait		Portrait of a Girl.

5	Female seated; shield, house, sheep, etc.	5
	BK OF THE STATE OF INDIANA.	
Male portrait		Male portrait

10	MOLSON'S BANK, Montreal, Canada.	10
Bee hive.	Large X and three Cupids.	Female portrait.
DIX	Steamboat.	TEN

10	Man on horse; reaping scene etc., on right.	10
Female seated; X on a shield.	FAR. & MECH BANK OF KENT CO. Chestertown, Md.	Female portrait
	Machinery.	

10	Four male figures seated; city in distance.	10
	BK. OF THE STATE OF INDIANA.	
Male portrait		Male portrait

1	Indians hunting buffaloes.	1
	BK OF TENNESSEE.	
Boy's head.		Female portrait.

5	Treas. die. Female seated: ship in distance.	FIVE
	BANK OF THE OLD DOMINION, Alexandria, Va.	
Washington		Female with flag; squaw at her side.

20	BK. OF THE STATE OF INDIANA.	20
	Sailor, male and dog; sloop in distance.	
Male portrait		Male portrait

2	Cattle and hogs; village in distance.	2
Female seated with sword and scales	BK OF TENNESSEE.	Liberty erect

10	Steamboat and crocodile. Train of cars.	X
Male portrait	MERCHANTS' BANK Cheraw, S. C.	Ox team.
10	Cherub astride deer.	10

10	Female seated between ornamental 1 and 0.	10
Head of girl with long hair.	PAWTUXET BANK, Providence, R. I.	Female head
TEN		TEN

	Mechanic, sailor and farmer; city in distance. Male portrait.	5
	BK OF TENNESSEE.	
5		Med. head.

20	Female, cows and sheep.	20
	FREDERICKTOWN SAV. INSTITUTION, Frederick, Md.	
Boy and rabbits.	Man seated on plow.	Female.

5	Scene upon the prairie; Indians hunting buffaloes.	5.
	WEYBOSSET BANK, Providence, R. I.	
Female erect beside State Arms.		Male portrait

ONE Female seated.	EXCHANGE BANK OF THE STATE OF GEORGIA, Griffin, Geo. 1 Man on horse; negroes at work in field, buildings, etc., in distance. 1 Ducks.	1 Female seated with sword etc.; locomotive and tender in distance.

Female erect with wand, eagle, etc. 20	20 Female portrait. HIGH STREET BK., Providence, R. I.	20 Franklin.

100 Washington One Hundred	Title of Bank. Capitol of the United States.	100 Liberty seated. One Hundred

2 Two negroes in cotton field.	Title of Bank. TWO on large die.	2 Female seated shading her eyes with her hand.

FIFTY Agricultural products. 50	50 Three females seated; vessel on left. HIGH STREET BK., Providence, R. I.	Word FIFTY and fig 50. Vulcan seated with anvil, hammer, etc; cars on left.

20 Liberty: on left globe.	Female seated with rake, between 2 and 0. BK OF HALLOWELL Hallowell, Me. XX	20 Female with cornucopia, etc. 20

5 Female with grain.	Title of Bank. FIVE on large die. Dog.	5 Male portrait

2 Portrait of a girl.	Fig. 2 on shield; eagle on right and female with pole, cap, bales, etc. on left. TWO MANUFACTURERS' BANK, Providence, R. I.	2 Female portrait.

5 Washington	Man watering three horses at trough; house in background. Female portrait FAR. & MECH. BK. OF KENT CO., Chestertown, Md. Beehive.	5 Cooper at work.

10 Continental soldier with gun.	Title of Bank. X Train of cars X Ducks.	10 Clay.

1 Female and fig. 1; shield, etc.	BANK OF WEST TENNESSEE, Memphis, Tenn. Cupid rolling silver dollar; cars, etc., in distance	1 Squaw with bow and fig. 1; falls, etc., in distance. One Dollar

Compt's die. Farmer seated with scythe.	Female on either side of a shield on which is a ship, plow, etc.; vessels and city in distance. KINGSTON BANK, Kingston, N. Y. Building, &c.	2 Carpenter at his work bench.

FIVE Hunting wild cattle.	AMERICAN BANK, Providence, R. I. Female seated by fig. 5; ships in distance.	5 Farmer feeding hogs.

2 Milkmaid; house in distance. TWO DOL.	Title of Bank. Two Cupids in combat, two silver dollars; cars, etc., in distance.	2 Man seated with rake, plow, etc. TWO DOL.

Compt's die Head.	Indian, globe, city, female, eagle, &c. ALBANY CITY BK, Albany, N. Y.	1

5 Portrait of a girl with curls.	AMERICAN BANK, Providence, R. I. Large spread eagle.	5 Female portrait. V

5 Sailor erect. Five Dollars	Title of Bank. Five Cupids as artisans with five silver dollars.	FIVE Figure 5 surrounded by five females. Five Dollars

2 Compt's die. 2	2 Male, two females, anvil, sledge, etc. 2 ALBANY CITY BK., Albany, N. Y. Houses.	TWO

5 Two girls carrying sheafs.	Five silver dollars and five cherubs, AMERICAN BANK, Providence, R. I.	5 Female portrait.

10 Hunter with gun, dog, etc	Title of Bank. Female reclining on bale: cornucopia, bbl., etc.; shipping, railroad, canal, etc. in distance.	10 Squaw with corn and X. TEN DOL

20 Compt's die 20	20 XX ALBANY CITY BK., Albany, N. Y.	Male, two females, anvil and sledge. 20

100	Female seated holding shield; U. S. Capitol in distance. Washington. NATIONAL BANK, Providence, R. I.	100

20 Mechanic seated with implements; factories in distance. Twenty Dol	Title of Bank. Western steamboat loaded with cotton.	20 Female seated, money bags, hhd. and growing tobacco. Twenty Dol

50 Compt's die. 50	House in die; words Fifty Dollars around it. 50 on right. ALBANY CITY BK., Albany, N. Y.	Same as 20s 50

Three females on rock, anchor, etc. TEN	10 Female resting on State Arms; ship and steamship on right; ships on left. STATE BANK, Providence, R. I.	10 View of house and trees.

50 Mermaid and merman. Steamship Fifty Dol	Title of Bank. Female reclining on bales with cotton plant, hhd, spinning wheel, etc.; factories in distance.	50 Female erect surrounded with border on which is the names of the States. 50

10 10	BANK OF LOUISVILLE, Ky. Female, eagle, shield, etc. Webster on right; Clay on left.	10 10

Webster. 2
STATE BANK OF OHIO.
2
Two horses, two men, canal scene, railroad, etc

FIVE
View of the Natural Bridge: Military Academy and College at Lexington.
BK OF ROCKBRIDGE, Lexington, Va.
Shield.
5 and FIVE. 5 5 and FIVE.

X
Sq
NIAGARA RIVER BANK, Buffalo, N. Y.
View of the Suspension Bridge.
10
Compt's die

Compt's die. Washington
1 Cattle, etc
YATES CO. BANK, Penn Yan, N. Y.
1
Female seated with sword, etc.

X 10 X
Vig. Same as fives
BK OF ROCKBRIDGE Lexington, Va.
anchor and shield.
TEN

20 XX
Title of Bank
Cattle; stream of water, trees, etc.
Compt's die
20 XX

50
Female portrait
Train of cars, etc.
BANK OF RUTLAND Rutland, Vt.
Dog's head.
50
Female portrait.

20 XX
Vig. Same as fives.
BK OF ROCKBRIDGE Lexington, Va.
Horse.
20 XX

L
Title of Bank.
View of the Crystal Palace; pedestrians, horses, carriages, etc.
Compt's die.
50

TEN
Male, female and child.
Sailor seated on anchor, two others erect; ship in distance.
STAMFORD BANK, Stamford, Conn.
CONNECTICUT
10
Clay.

50
Squaw seated
Vig. Same as fives.
BK OF ROCKBRIDGE Lexington, Va.
50
Female seated with pen and tablets; masts, cars, buildings &c.

5
Female portrait.
CATARACT CITY BK Paterson, N. J.
Signing the Declaration of Independence.
5
State Arms.

5
Male portrait
BK OF KNOXVILLE, Knoxville, Tenn.
Female seated representing Manufactures; cars, factories, etc., in distance
Dog.
5
State Arms.
FIVE

ONE
Farmer, female, boy, girl, dog, chickens, &c.
CLINTON BANK, Clinton, Conn.
Train of cars; sloop, hills, trees, etc.
1
Female with sword, book, and scales.

X
State Arms.
CATARACT CITY BK Paterson, N. J.
Penn's treaty with the Indians.
10
Head of Liberty surrounded by stars.

TEN
Male portrait
Female on either side of a shield, on which is eagle, view of sunrise, canal scene, city, etc
Title of Bank.
Ducks.
10
State Arms.
X

Connecticut
Female erect with med. head on shield.
2 Farmer plowing with oxen; railroad, etc.
CLINTON BANK, Clinton, Conn.
2
Female seated with sickle and sheaf.

100
Female with shield and eagle.
BANK OF CHATTANOOGA, TENN.
Words one hundred dollars and figs. 100.
100
Female portrait.

XX
Male portrait
Steamboat, sloops, cars, lighthouse, etc
Title of Bank.
Female bathing.
20
State Arms.
XX

3
THREE
CLINTON BANK, Clinton, Conn.
Yacht race; males, females, etc., on beach
3
Sailor.

20 20 XX
Treas. die
Two men; one with tobacco in hand; hhds., &c.
MERCHANTS' BANK Lynchburg, Va
20

Female and figure
1
Rafting scene; male female and child.
COMMERCIAL BK. OF KENTUCKY.
Words "State of Ky.," on shield.
Female with figure 1
1

20
Cupid and cornucopia.
CITIZENS' BANK, Waterbury, Conn.
Female feeding fowls. 20 Farmer horse dog, etc
20
Cupid and sheaf.

1
Sailor with flag, anchor, etc
BK. OF TENNESSEE.
1 Two females seated, ship, buildings, cars, etc., in distance 1
1
Female with grain.

FIVE
V two females and three males
5 Five females, fig. 5; factory, locomotive and tender on right; steamer, etc., on left.
COMMERCIAL BK. OF KENTUCKY.
State Arms.
FIVE
Pierce.
5

FIFTY
Indian princess.
Compt's die
Female on either side of shield and bust; ship in distance.
BANK OF SARATOGA SPRINGS. Saratoga Springs, N.Y.
50
Female erect

2
Female portrait.
BK. OF TENNESSEE.
Apotheosis of Washington; continental soldier on left; female and two Indians on right.
2
Male portrait

ONE
Female and 1
ONE
RHODE ISLAND EXCHANGE BANK,
East Greenwich, R. I.
View of town, hills, sloop, schooner, etc.
ONE.
ONE
Farmer and figure 1

XX inverted.
Milkmaid and cows.
Title of Bank.
TWENTY DOLLARS on dies.
20 inverted.
Two females on right of a shield, on it agricultural implements and products; cars, building, etc., in distance.

3
Portrait of a girl and boy.
REED'S BANK,
Galesburg, Ills.
Four human figures on a team.
3
Auditor's die

Female each side of fig. 2
2
Title of Bank.
Vig. Same as ones.
Shield and anchor.
TWO
Female entwined in figure 2.

50
Milkmaid; cows and house in the distance.
Title of Bank.
Mechanic erect with anvil and hammer; buildings in distance.
50
Liberty seated.

5
Girl's portrait.
REED'S BANK,
Galesburg, Ills
Female on left of shield; cars steamship, vessel, &c.
Bee-hive.
V
Auditor's die

V
5
Hunter shooting deer.
STATE STOCK BANK
Greneville, Tenn.
5
Female with flowers.

100
Washington
Title of Bank.
Female on either side of a beehive.
100
Martha Washington

5
Female shading her eyes with left hand.
BK OF JEFFERSON,
Dandridge, Tenn.
Milkmaid and cows; chickens, etc.
5
FIVE
5

10
Female with sickle, &c.
Farming scene; man sharpening scythe; reaping, &c.
STATE STOCK BANK
Greneville, Tenn.
Two cherubs with sheaf soaring in clouds.
10

5
Treas. die.
5 Buchanan; female on either side. 5
BANK OF PHILIPI,
Philipi, Va.
V, 5 and words Five dollars blended in one die.
5
Female feeding horse.

3
Farmer with rake, etc.
MASSASOIT BANK,
Fall River, Mass.
Train of cars, harvesting scenes, etc.
3
Two females preparing dinner.

20
Train of cars
STATE STOCK BANK
Greneville, Tenn.
Anchor, anvil, plow, &c.
20
Squaw.

10
Treas. die.
Shield; farmer on left, Indian on right; cars, canal, city, wigwams, canoe, &c., in distance.
BANK OF PHILIPI,
Philipi, Va.
X and TEN
Dog.
TEN

5
Man at work in iron foundry.
View of Falls and village.
IRON BANK,
Falls Village, Conn.
Building and trees.
5
Male portrait

ONE
WINDHAM COUNTY BANK,
Brattleboro, Vt.
Man and three horses at well; goats; sheep, houses, etc.
1
1
Indian apparently asleep.

20
Treas. die.
Cattle and sheep; houses in distance.
BANK OF PHILIPI,
Philipi, Va.
Soldier and cannon.
20
Male portrait

1
Female portrait.
ONE
Cupid rolling silver dollar; cars and city on right.
BK OF TECUMSEH,
Tecumseh Mich.
Two horses.
1
[illegible]

2
Farmer plowing.
TWO
Title of Bank.
Cattle; farming scenes, etc., in distance.
2
Female with sheaf and sickle.
2

50 inverted
Treas. die.
BANK OF PHILIPI,
Philipi, Va.
Female on either side of a shield on which is eagle; cars, factory, steamship, etc.
Horse.
50 inverted.

2
Female head
Two Cupids and two silver dollars; locomotive on right; cattle on left.
Title of Bank.
Cattle.
2
Squaw and papoose.
TWO

5
Indian head
Title of Bank.
Horse on either side of a shield, on which is an eagle, tree, cow, etc.; cars, building, etc. in distance.
Five and 5.
5

1
Boy with pigeons.
REED'S BANK,
Galesburg, Ills,
Man feeding hogs; pig pen, chickens, etc.
Soldier and cannon.
1
Auditor's die

THREE
Indian female.
Three Cupids and three silver dollars.
Title of Bank.
Man plowing.
3
Mechanic, sailor, farmer and 3.

X
Title of Bank
Three females and bust representing the Arts and Sciences.
10
X

2
Female portrait.
REED'S BANK,
Galesburg, Ills.
Female, shield, eagle, &c.
Head of an ox.
2
Auditor's die

FIVE
Indian.
Five Cupids and five silver dollars.
Title of Bank.
Load of hay.
5
Five females and 5.

ONE
Compt's die.
Man plowing with two horses.
FARMERS BANK,
Hudson, Wis.
1
Cattle, rail road, telegraph, etc.

5 on Five.
Three females and bust.
Female portrait.
SAUK CO. BANK,
Baraboo, Wis.
5 on Five.
Compt's die.
FIVE

5
Compt's die.
Two females representing Liberty and Justice on either side of male portrait; cars, bridge, factory, steamer, &c., in distance.
WISCONSIN BANK,
Madison, Wis.
Bull
5
5

2
Compt's die.
Farm yard scene; two men, boy, negro, bull, horse, sheep, cattle, barn, etc
FARMERS BANK,
Hudson, Wis.
2
Female portrait

1
ONE
Farmer, milkmaid, child, cows, houses, etc.
HALL & BROS. BK.,
Eau Claire, Wis.
Eagle.
Indian, fig. 1 female. One.
Compt's die.

10
Male portrait
WISCONSIN BANK,
Madison, Wis.
Compt's die on X.
Indian.
10
Reaper seated, loading wagon in the distance
TEN

3
THREE
FARMERS BANK,
Hudson, Wis.
Bridge; men on rafts, etc.
3
Compt's die.

2
Eagle
Title of Bank.
Squaw, female, shield; buildings, locomotive, etc. on right; Indian scene on left.
Beehive.
Female holding fig. 2.
Compt's die

1
Boy and girl.
Man feeding pigs; pigpen, chickens, etc.
PRODUCERS' BANK,
Janesville, Wis.
One and 1.
1
Compt's die

5
FIVE
Compt's Die.
Large V. farmer seated within.
FARMERS BANK,
Hudson, Wis.
5
Two men with fork and rake, dog, man and boy in distance.

Fig. 3 and female portrait.
Compt's die
THREE
Saw mill; men, horses, logs, etc.
Title of Bank.
Locomotive.
3
Men at work digging, etc

2
Female seated with fig. 2, distaff, etc
Two males and two females husking corn.
PRODUCERS' BANK,
Janesville, Wis.
Beehive.
2
Compt's die

FIVE
Eagle on cliff
Compt's die.
Men propelling raft on river
ST. CROIX VALLEY BANK,
St. Croix Falls, Wis.
Sunset
Five on 5
5, Indians, cars, waterfalls, etc.

FIVE
Compt's die.
Fig. 5 and Justice.
Female on either side of shield on which is arm and hammer.
Title of Bank.
Cornucopia, bales, etc.
5
Hunter and dog

3
Horse, cows, fence, water, cars, bridge, &c.
PRODUCERS' BANK,
Janesville, Wis.
Compt's die.
3
Buchanan.

10
X, female, cows, cars, etc.
Steamboat Eolian.
Title of Bank.
Compt's die.
10
Indian, water etc

Indian, female and fig. 1.
Compt's die.
MERCHANTS' AND MECHANICS' BANK,
Whitewater, Wis.
Two males and two females husking corn; dog, chickens, etc.
ONE ONE ONE
1
Train of cars

FIVE
Drove of horses.
PRODUCERS' BANK.
Janesville, Wis.
Words Five Dollars, fig. 5 and letter V.
Five on 5.
Compt's die
Five on 5.

ONE
Compt's die.
ONE
SAUK COUNTY B'K,
Baraboo, Wis.
Blacksmith shop; shoeing horse; man at forge; farmer, etc.
1
Indian female.

Sailor, female and fig. 2.
Compt's die.
Title of Bank.
Two males; one seated on a basket, the other with scythe; two horses, boy on one of them; hay by barn, dog, chickens, &c.; man on horse, trees, etc., in distance.
TWO Bull TWO
2
Two men gathering corn stalks.

5
Indian with spear
Female on either side of male portrait in clouds.
ARCTIC BANK,
Eau Claire Wis.
Words Five Dollars and V.
5
Compt's die

TWO
SAUK CO. BANK,
Baraboo Wis.
Shield: farmer seated town, etc., on right; Indian, hills, etc., on left.
2
2
Compt's die.
TWO

ONE
Vig. same as the above 2.
WISCONSIN BANK,
Madison, Wis.
Badger
1
Compt's die.
ONE

TEN
Compt's die.
Female, X, and Indian.
Two females on either side of shield on which is canal boat, sheaf, &c; eagle at top; cars, bridge and village in distance.
ARCTIC BANK
Wis.
Rising sun.
10
Eagle on rock
Ten on Dollars.

3
Female with dove
SAUK CO. BANK,
Baraboo, Wis.
Cattle, trees, stream of water, etc.
3
Compt's die.
THREE

TWO
Male portrait with Indian, wigwams and canoe on right; farmer, sheaves, cars, bridge, canal boat, etc., on left.
WISCONSIN BANK,
Madison, Wis.
2
Compt's die.
TWO

20
Compt's die.
20
ARCTIC BANK,
Wis.
Globe with four females representing the four quarters of the globe.
20
Rafting scene.

FIVE | Compt's die. | FIVE | KOKOMO BANK, Hillsdale, Wis. | FIVE Cattle in water; trees, etc. FIVE | 5 | Male head

2 | Farmer, dog and horse. | Female by column; stream-er and house in distance. Compt's die. | MANITOWOC CO. BK. Two Rivers, Wis. | TWO 2 TWO | 2 | Dog watching game.

TEN | Sailor about hoisting flag. | ST. LOUIS BANK, Superior, Wis. | X Indian reclining by dead deer. X | TEN | 10 | Compt's die.

X | Girl's head. | Old man, boy, dog, trees, etc.; sheep in distance. TEN running up and down on each side of vig. | KOKOMO BANK, Hillsdale, Wis. | X, Ten, 10 on each other. | 10 | Compt's die. | TEN

5 | Compt's die. | Horse Sailors on beach; ship and boat in distance. Eagle | MANITOWOC CO BK. Two Rivers, W.s. | 5 FIVE 5 | 5 | Dog, key and safe.

XX | Female head | ST. LOUIS BANK, Superior, Wis. | TWENTY | Large steamboat; another in distance. | 20 | Compt's die.

V | Five cherubs with anvil, globe and sledge. | SHAWANAW BANK Shawanaw, Wis. | Compt's die. | 5 | Five cherubs with tablet and rake.

1 | BK OF PORTAGE, Portage, Wis. | Horse, colt, man with bag of grain; two boys, falls and bridge. | Compt's die and fig. 1. | 1 | Male portrait

1 | Compt's die. | BANK OF OCONTO, Oconto, Wis. | 1 Girl's head. 1 | ONE | ONE | Female erect with flag and shield; Indian seated.

X | Train of cars | SHAWANAW BANK Shawanaw, Wis. | Compt's die. | 10 | Indian seated; plow, cabin, wheat, etc.

2 | Battle scene; old man and female; soldiers in distance. | BK OF PORTAGE, Portage, Wis. | Compt's die and 2. | 2 | Female by column; steamer and houses in the distance. | TWO

3 | Scene in a shipyard. | BANK OF OCONTO, Oconto, Wis. | Female portrait. | 3 | 3 | Compt's die.

5 | Male portrait | OCONTO CO. BANK, Oconto Wis. | 5 on Five | Indian with uplifted tomahawk; female with child kneeling; man with knife. | 5 on Dollars | 5 | Compt's die.

3 | Farming implements. | BK OF PORTAGE, Portage, Wis. | Compt's die and 3. | 3 | THREE | Rafting scene.

5 | Compt's die. | BANK OF OCONTO, Oconto, Wis. | Two females, globe, barrels, bales; house and shipping in distance. | FIVE | 5 | Buchanan

TEN | Compt's die | Laborer and sailor seated on either side of State Arms; steamboat and houses in distance | OCONTO CO. BANK, Wis. | 10 | Female portrait.

5 | Compt's die. | Two Indians on horseback attacked by wild animals. | BK OF PORTAGE, Portage, Wis. | FIVE | 5 | Scene at depot.

10 | Sailor boy. | BANK OF OCONTO, Oconto, Wis. | Compt's die | X TEN | 10 | Scene at depot; locomotive and cars

FIVE | Farmer seated at lunch. | TRADESMENS BK., Chippewa Falls Wis. | 5 Three females with quadrant, sickle, compass and cornucopia. 5 | Five Dollars Five Dollars | 5 | Compt's die. | FIVE

5 | Female head | CLARK CO. BANK. Chippewa Falls Wis. | Two Indians, female and shield; cars and trees in distance. | 5 | Compt's die. | FIVE

1 | Deer. | BK OF MANITOWOC, Manitowoc, Wis. | Scene at depot and on wharf. Bust of Washington on right and Franklin left. | ONE ONE | 1 | Compt's die

10 | Liberty. | Mechanic and farmer. 10 | TRADESMENS BK., Wis. | 10 | Compt's die.

10 | Compt's die. | TEN | CLARK CO. BANK, Wis. | Two Indians, three females, shield with X on it; cars and city in the distance. | 10 | Female head

2 | TWO | Compt's die. | BK OF MANITOWOC, Manitowoc, Wis. | Horse and colt, two boys, man with bag of grain, bridge, falls, etc. | TWO | TWO | Female seated representing Commerce.

1 | Compt's die. | Indians on horseback attacked by wild animals. Female portrait 1 | MANITOWOC CO. BK Two Rivers, Wis. | ONE 1 ONE | 1 | Female, bales, shipping, etc

5 | Washington | ST. LOUIS BANK, Superior, Wis. | FIVE | 5 Scene in ship yard; men at work. 5 | 5 | Compt's die

5 | BK OF MANITOWOC, Manitowoc, Wis. | Female portrait and V. | Male and female on either side of shield, on which is 5; horse, man, boy and steamboat in distance. | 5 | Compt's die. | Wisconsin.

1 — Compt's die. LACROSSE CO. BK. LaCrosse, Wis. Man feeding pigs; pigpen, chickens, etc. Locomotive. 1 — Female holding fig. 1.	5 — Compt's die. BK OF APPLETON, Appleton, Wis. FIVE DOLLARS. Western scene—males and females, wagon, trees, cars, etc. 5	Female head — 1 Compt's die. MENOMONEE BANK Menomonee, Wis. 1 — Indians on horseback killing buffaloes.
2 — Compt's die. LACROSSE CO. BK, LaCrosse, Wis. 2 Horse, cows, bridge, cars, water, etc. Boat. 2	1 — Two females with shield and bale. CITY BK OF BEAVER DAM, Wis. Portrait of girl. ONE ONE 1 — Compt's die.	Cherub and fig. 2. — Indian on horse. Scene in cabin—family at prayer; Indians about entering. MENOMONEE BANK Menomonee, Wis. Duck. Fig. 2 and cherub — Compt's die
3 LACROSSE CO. BK. LaCrosse, Wis. White female showing Indian the progress of civilization; cars, city, etc. 3 3 — Compt's die.	1 — Indians on horseback spearing buffaloes. BK OF SUPERIOR, Superior, Wis. Compt's die. ONE — Four cherubs with fig. 1. — ONE	3 — Farming implements. MENOMONEE BANK Menomonee, Wis. Arctic scene; men fishing boat; dogs, ship, etc. 3 — Compt's die.
FIVE LACROSSE CO. BK, LaCrosse, Wis. Eagle within V. Compt's die. 5 — Reaper seated; men loading wagon in distance.	2 — Compt's die. BK OF SUPERIOR, Superior, Wis. Scene at depot and on wharf. 2 — Sailor boy; ships.	Surveying scene. — FIVE MENOMONEE BANK Menomonee, Wis. Child's head. 5 — Compt's die
1 — Female portrait. Steamboat and town. CITIZENS BANK OF OSHKOSH, Wis. Beaver 1 — Compt's die.	3 BK OF SUPERIOR, Superior, Wis Sailor and Indian on other side of shield, eagle at top; Indian in canoe and ship in distance Girl's head 3 — Compt's die.	ONE — Man supporting the globe on one knee. Female, eagle, globe, flags, etc. GLOBE BANK, Milwaukie, Wis. Cherub and fig. 1. — Compt's die. — ONE
2 — Female portrait. CITIZENS BANK OF OSHKOSH, Wis. Compt's die and 2. Two men at work sawing logs with machine. Indian. 2 — TWO	5 — Indian with spear on horse. BK OF SUPERIOR, Superior, Wis. Compt's die. Scene in the Arctic regions; men fishing boat; dogs, ship, etc. 5	Female on globe with cap, pole and trumpet. — TWO Man supporting the globe; cars and steamer in distance. Head of girl on either side of vig. GLOBE BANK, Milwaukie, Wis. 2 — Compt's die.
1 — Compt's die. B'K OF APPLETON, Appleton, Wis. Steamboat. Female at work. 1 — Webster.	1 — Indians on horses hunting buffaloes. JUNEAN BANK, Milwaukie, Wis. Large Male portrait. 1 — Compt's die. — Wisconsin.	1 — Male portrait BK OF WISCONSIN, Madison, Wis. ONE Battle scene—old man and female; soldiers in distance. ONE ONE ONE 1 — Compt's die
2 — Two men at work; wheel, etc. Horse, colt, man with bag of grain; two boys, falls and bridge BK OF APPLETON. Appleton, Wis. 2 — Compt's die.	5 — Two men at work: wheel, sledge, etc. JUNEAN BANK, Milwaukie, Wis. Male portrait. Compt's die and 5. 5 — Female feeding fowls.	2 — Male, female and child. BK OF WISCONSIN, Madison, Wis. Compt's die. Horse and colt, man and child herd, etc. 2 — TWO
Compt's die. Two men plowing with two horses; dog, fence, etc. THREE BK OF APPLETON, Appleton, Wis. 3 — Female portrait	X — White men in boat; Indians on shore. — TEN JUNEAN BANK, Milwaukie, Wis. Large male portrait. TEN DOLLARS 10 — Compt's die	5 BK OF WISCONSIN, Madison, Wis. Arctic regions—men fishing boat; dogs, ship, etc. 5 5 — Compt's die.

ONE Buchanan. ONE Two females on either side of shield representing Liberty and Justice; cars, bridge, factory, steamer, etc., in distance. BK. OF MONTELLO, Princeton Wis. Badger 1 Compt's die	V 5 Title of Bank. Cattle and sheep, water, trees, houses, etc. Girl's head. FIVE 5 Compt's die. FIVE	2 Female Portrait. Drove of cattle and sheep; drover on horse. MILWAUKEE BANK Milwaukee, Wis. Agricultural impl'ts, &c. 2 Compt's die TWO
2 Milkmaid with pail. BK. OF MONTELLO, Wis. Indian, squaw and papoose in canoe. Female head 2 Compt's die TWO	Five on 5. Compt's die NORTHERN WISCONSIN BANK, Wausau Wis. Two males; one seated on a basket, the other with scythe; two horses, boy on one of them; hay by barn, dog, chickens, &c.; man on horse, trees, etc., in distance. V Dog's head V Five on 5. Female seated holding fig 5.	ONE inverted 1 Shield—on which is Am. shield, shovel, plow, arm pick and motto "E Pluribus Unum," surmounted at top by weasel; mechanic on right; sailor on left. Bank of Fox Lake, Compt's die. Fox Lake, Wis. Figure 1. Indian, female and fig. 1. Male portrait
5 Compt's die. FIVE Man feeding pigs; pigeon, chickens, etc. V each side of vig. WISCONSIN VALLEY BANK, Weyauwega Wis. Words Five Dollars V, and figure 5. 5 Female and horse.	10 Compt's die. TEN Title of Bank. Two males and two females husking corn; dog, chickens, etc. X and eagle. 10 Large X, Ten on it; female etc.	2 Farmer sharpening scythe. Female on either side of an eagle and words "Two Dollars" between. BANK OF FOX LAKE Fox Lake, Wis. Cornucopia, bales, etc. 2 Compt's die
10 Eagle on rock TEN Title of Bank. Compt's die and X. Female seated by cow erect; two cows reclining; man, child, fence, etc. Die. 10 TEN	1 Compt's die. Large ornamental ONE and female; ship, bbls., etc., in distance. KANKAKEE BANK, Black River Falls, Wis Dog's head. 1 Female portrait.	V Cattle, sheep, etc. Female portrait. BANK OF FOX LAKE Fox Lake, Wis. Anchor, bales, bbls, etc. 5 Compt's die.
1 Compt's die. BANK OF WHITEWATER, Whitewater, Wis. Farmers at work, mowing and loading wagon—one in foreground resting. ONE 1 Boy and girl.	2 Compt's die Large ornamental TWO with two females; house in distance. KANKAKEE BANK, Black River Falls, Wis Female. 2 Laborers at work.	1 Female seated with cornucopia. Pigs and fowls. Chickens in pen. MT. HOLLY BANK, Mt. Holly, N.J. One on red die. 1 Treas. Die.
Three on 3. Compt's die. Title of Bank. Female seated with dog and pail, cows, etc. THREE 3 Cars	3 KANKAKEE BANK, Black River Falls, Wis Two males, two horses, boy on one; hay, barn, dog, chickens, etc; man on horse trees in distance. Compt's die and 3 across 3 Female portrait.	TWO DOLLARS 2 Three cherubs. State Arms; cars and factory in distance. MT. HOLLY BANK, Mt. Holly, N.J. Two on red die. 2 Treas. die.
Blacksmith at forge. ONE 1 Justice seated; eagle, shield, etc.; cars, bridge, village and shipping in the distance. CITY BANK OF PRESCOTT, Wis. ONE 1 Compt's die. ONE	5 on Five. Compt's die. 5 on Five. KANKAKEE BANK, Black River Falls, Wis V Two males and two females husking corn; dog, chickens, &c. V Shield. FIVE	5 Henry Clay. MT. HOLLY BANK, Mt. Holly, N.J. View of large building and street. 5 5 5 Treas. die.
2 Three men—one on horse back watering horse from trough; shop, hay wagon, etc. Title of Bank. Compt's die. 2 Eagle. 2 Two horses, boy, girl and duck by trough.	FIVE Blacksmith with sledge, anvil, etc; locomotive and factory. NORTHERN BANK Green Bay, Wis. Compt's die. 5 Train of cars; cars, etc, in distance.	10 Treas. die. Man watering three horses from trough by side of well; goat, kid, sheep, trees and house. MT. HOLLY BANK. Mt. Holly, N.J. X Male portrait
3 3 Cars. Justice. Title of Bank. 3 Compt's die.	10 Large Spread eagle. NORTHERN BANK Green Bay, Wis. ..mpt's die. 10	20 Treas. die. Three men at work with two horses and patent mowing machine; house in distance. MT. HOLLY BANK, Mt. Holly, N.J. 20 Female seated.

Fig. 1 inverted. Female portrait ONE BK OF LOUISVILLE, KY. Female seated—in front large ornamental ONE; barrels, ships, &c., in background. 1 Female with figure 1.	XX Man dressing leather. LYNN MECHANICS' BANK, Lynn, Mass. Male portrait; female and children on right; Indian family on left. 20 Female portrait.	1 Propeller. ONE BANK OF CUMBERLAND, Portland, Me. Sailor and farmer on either side of shield on which is deer and tree. 1
100 Ornamental letter C surrounding sheaf and head of female. ELMWOOD BANK, Cranston, R. I. Two females with scythe and shield. Tree. 100 View of village 100	L Female with dove. Title of Bank. Hunter shooting deer; dog, water, trees, etc. 50 Indian seated.	2 Title of Bank. Female erect, apparently reading to three others seated. 2
ONE State Arms. BK OF COMMERCE, Boston, Mass. 1 Male portrait	C Two medallion heads. Title of Bank. Three females seated and one standing reading to others. 100 Two medallion heads.	3 Steamboat and other vessels. Title of Bank. 3 Liberty.
2 Ship. BK OF COMMERCE, Boston, Mass. 2 Male portrait	500 Male seated with tablets. Washington. Justice and Manufactures seated in alcove; beehive between them. Title of Bank. Machine. 500 Lady Washington.	TWENTY DOLLARS Two females seated with grain and sickle. 20 on either side of vig., and also on each side of title. PHENIX BANK, Hartford, Conn. 20 CONNECTICUT
THREE Sailor, capstan, anchor, etc. BK OF COMMERCE, Boston, Mass. 3 Male portrait	V 5 on Five. BANK OF TRENTON Trenton, Tenn. Henry Clay. V Female portrait. 5 5 5 5 Compt's die.	FIFTY DOLLARS 50 Female seated representing Commerce; boxes, bbls, etc. 50 50 Title of Bank 50 L CONNECTICUT
1 Washington LEE BANK, Lee, Mass. 1 Girl with dove. 1 1 State Arms.	X Henry Clay. BANK OF TRENTON Trenton, Tenn. X Female portrait. X 10 Compt's die.	ONE HUNDRED Female seated holding letter C, ship in distance—C and 100 on each side. 100 Title of Bank 100 C CONNECTICUT
2 Female portrait LEE BANK, Lee, Mass. Three females and bust of Washington. TWO TWO Large fig. 2 and 2 in top.	XX Male portrait BANK OF TRENTON Trenton, Tenn. Large red fancy shield with 20 in centre. 20 Female portrait.	5 Washington's headquarters V Male portrait. V POWELL BANK, Newburgh, N. Y. FIVE 5 Compt's die FIVE
5 Portrait of girl. Female, safe, shield, sheep, sheaf, etc. STATE BANK AT ELIZABETH, N. J. FIVE 5 on head. Male portrait	Five on 5. Female head KITTANNING BK., Kittanning, Pa. Three females representing the Arts and Sciences; bust of Washington. FIVE 5 Male portrait	3 Arm, hammer, anvil, etc. RICHMOND BANK, Alton, R. I. Spread eagle on State Arms, horse either side; steamer on right, factories and cars on left. Stockholders, etc. 3 Two men erect, female seated; factories, etc.
10 Franklin 10 Three females and bust of Washington. Title of Bank. TEN TEN Portrait of girl. TEN	10 Girl with dove Title of Bank. Four females on globe; shield, flag and sword. 10 Male portrait	10 Clay. Title of Bank. Scene in an iron mill—five men at work. X, Stockholders, etc., on right of vig 10 Female feeding fowls.

5 | STROUDSBURG BK
Stroudsburg, Pa.
Men dressing leather.
FIVE | 5
Franklin | | Wm. Penn.

10
Treas. die.
10 | Title of Bank.
Mining scene—two men digging coal in mine.
TEN | X
Female seated, two males behind her.

X
Men dressing leather. | Male portrait with female, cars, sheaf, etc, on right; female, boxes, bbls., men and steamer on left.
MONROE CO. BANK,
Rochester, N. Y. | 10
Compt's die

X
Washington | Man watering three horses from trough by side of well; goat, kid, sheep, trees and house.
Title of Bank. | 10
Lady Washington.

20
20 | Rafting scene—men, women and child on raft; skiff, raft in distance
Treas. die.
Title of Bank.
20 | 20
Male portrait

XX
Bricklayers at work. | Male portrait; Justice, bridge and cars on right; manufactories on left.
MONROE CO. BANK,
Rochester, N. Y.
Compt's die. | 20
Female sewing shoes.

20
View of cattle, telegraph and railroad. | Washington—female, scythe, sheaf, cars, etc., on right; female, anchor, men, boxes, barrels and steamer on left.
Title of Bank. | XX
Two cherubs with sheaf and distaff.
XX

1
Compt's die. | LAKE ONTARIO BK,
Oswego, N. Y.
Female representing Agriculture, sailor and blacksmith with implements, ship city and cars in distance.
Anchor on shield. | ONE
Male portrait

1
Compt's die. | Cars and view of Mathews Hunt & Co.'s Warehouse.
WALLKILL BANK,
Middletown, N. Y.
ONE | 1
Female Portrait

50
Locomotive. | Title of Bank.
Rafting scene; men on raft.
FIFTY | 50
Male portrait

2
Compt's die.
2 | Vessels at sea.
LAKE ONTARIO BK,
Oswego, N. Y.
Anchor on shield. | TWO
Male portrait

2
Compt's die.
TWO | Cattle in water, trees etc.
Title of Bank.
TWO | TWO
Female feeding fowls.

100
Farmer seated at lunch. | Horse on either side of shield, eagle at top; cars, factory and steamboat in distance.
Title of Bank. | C
ONE HUNDRED

V | Scene on wharf; various vessels in distance; men at work on dock; horse cart, etc.
Male portrait
LAKE ONTARIO BK,
Oswego, N. Y.
Anchor on shield. | 5 on Five.
Compt's die.
5

5
Lady Washington.
FIVE | View of cars and saw manufactory.
Title of Bank.
FIVE | FIVE
Compt's die.
FIVE

1
ONE | LAMBERTVILLE BK
Lambertville, N. J.
Sheep shearing scene.
Female head
Treas die. | 1
ONE

1
Compt's die. | Men moulding in iron mill.
MONROE CO. BANK,
Rochester, N. Y.
ONE | 1
Factory.

10
Building. | Bull's head on shield; men dressing leather on right; female sewing shoes on left.
Title of Bank.
TEN | 10
Compt's die

2
TWO | Title of Bank.
Treas. die.
Railroad scene—train of cars, mountains river, etc. | 2
Female head.
TWO DOLLARS

TWO
Compt's die.
2 | Male portrait
Anchor on shield; shipping, city and cars in distance.
MONROE CO. BANK,
Rochester, N. Y.
TWO | 2
View of cattle, telegraph railroad, etc.

XX
Female with dove. | Compt's die with female and children on right; squaw and papoose on left.
Title of Bank.
TWENTY | 20
Male portrait

THREE
3
Girl with a dove. | Title of Bank.
Treas. Die.
Pigs, pen, chickens, etc. | 3
THREE

Compt's die.
3 | Female seated by chest, shield with ship on stocks; sheep, sheaf, &c.
MONROE CO. BANK,
Rochester, N. Y.
THREE | 3
View of canal

500
Justice. | NATIONAL BANK.
Providence, R. I.
Spread Eagle on shield—Letter D on each side of vig. | 500
Goddess of Liberty.

5
Treas. die
5 | Title of Bank.
Interior of iron mill—men at work.
FIVE | 5
Indian boy paddling canoe

5
Male portrait | Milkmaid seated with pail by side of shield on which is cars; sheaf, on right; cable on left.
MONROE CO. BANK,
Rochester, N. Y.
FIVE | 5
Compt's die
FIVE

1000
Farmer erect with scythe. | Train of cars crossing bridge; in background another train and city.
MECHANICS' BK OF
Pittsburg, Pa. | M
Female portrait

Female, cars, &c. 1 1 LONG REACH BANK Bath, Me. 1 Female.	X Capitol at Washington. 10 PEJEPSCOT BANK. Brunswick, Me. Head of Indian. Indian seated	ONE Woodcutter erect beside fallen tree in forest. 1 Female head on die; word One above and Dollar below. COLONIAL BANK, of Canada. ONE
Men washing sheep. 2 TWO LONG REACH BANK, Female. Bath, Me. 2 TWO	Female head Capitol at Washington 20 PEJEPSCOT BANK, Brunswick, Me. XX Indian's head	Indian hunters overlooking deer; cabin and squaws in background. 2 TWO Female portrait. 2 COLONIAL BANK of Canada. 2
Scene in a farm yard. 3 THREE LONG REACH BANK Female with basket of flowers. Bath Me. 3 THREE	50 Vessels and steamer. 50 PEJEPSCOT BANK, Brunswick, Me. Sailor standing with cap in hand. Webster.	3 Three females; one seated—one holds staff, the other flag. 3 St. George and the Dragon. COLONIAL BANK of Canada. Female Portrait.
FIVE Female with rake, grain, machinery, &c. Female Indian seated in V. 5 LONG REACH BANK Bath, Me. F I V V E Washington	C Engine, Depot and cars. 100 PEJEPSCOT BANK, Brunswick, Me. Female seated beside a basket holding sheaf of grain. 100	FOUR COLONIAL BANK of Canada. 4 FOUR Queen Victoria. Justice. 4 4 4
Signing Declaration of Independence. X 10 LONG REACH BANK Bath, Me. X Cars, man, buildings, etc	Five on 5. Steamboat; city and steamboat in distance. 5 ALLEGHANY BANK, Alleghany, Pa. Locomotive and tender. FIVE Female portrait	FIVE 5 5 Farmer seated; female in background; mowing scene. COLONIAL BANK of Canada. 5 Female portrait.
Female and figure 1. Indian seated, holding fig. 1. 1 PEJEPSCOT BANK, Brunswick, Me. One and 1. Female head	X Three cherups with lever sledge, wedge and stone. 10 ALLEGHANY BANK, Alleghany, Pa. Female with love. Head of bull	Scene at depot; cars, people, etc. X 10 COLONIAL BANK of Canada. 10 X X Squaw erect
Two females carrying grain. State Arms with females seated each side. 2 PEJEPSCOT BANK, Brunswick, Me. Female holding a flag with an Indian seated. 2	20 Two females and shield on which is farming implements; cars and factory in distance. 20 ALLEGHANY BANK, Alleghany, Pa. Girls portrait Negro holding bull; sheep, fence etc.	St. George and the dragon. COLONIAL BANK of Canada. 20 Farmers loading hay 20 XX XX Female portrait.
Factory. Ships and steamer. Three and 3 PEJEPSCOT BANK, Brunswick, Me. 3 Head of Indian.	50 View of the wharf at Pittsburg with steamboats receiving and discharging freight. 50 ALLEGHANY BANK, Alleghany, Pa. Female portrait. Indian portrait.	50 Marine view—ships sailing 50 COLONIAL BANK of Canada. St. George and the Dragon. Female portrait.
5 Signing declaration of Independence. 5 PEJEPSCOT BANK, Brunswick, Me. Washington Female head	100 Mexican lassoing wild cattle. C ALLEGHANY BANK Alleghany, Pa Female with sickle and grain Portrait of boy.	100 COLONIAL BANK of Canada. 100 100 C 100 Steamship; sailors in boat. Queen Victoria.

Left end	Center	Right end
5 Male portrait.	Bridge at Coatesville; iron works; mule team; hills in the background. BANK OF CHESTER VALLEY, Coatesville, Pa. FIVE	5 Male portrait.
Female shading her face with her hand. Train of cars.	X Street scene—carriage passing, men and women walking. ATLANTIC BANK, Portland, Me. TEN	10 10
Female with a rose. TWENTY	Family group at supper; Indians looking in at the door; dog barking at them. CASCO BANK, Portland, Me. 20 20	20 Male portrait.
10 Female with sickle and hat; dog; houses in distance.	Title of Bank. Interior of a rolling mill. TEN	10 Wm. Penn.
Loging scene 20	Title of Bank. Words Twenty Dollars and large Twenty running across.	20 Steamship
Female portrait. 50	Signing treaty with the Pilgrims. CASCO BANK, Portland, Me. FIFTY	50 Male portrait.
XX Three smiths at work at anvil.	Title of Bank. Female seated on sheaf with sickle; farm building and men loading hay in distance. XX Geese and goslings.	20 Female shading her eyes with her hands.
50 Sailor seated on barrel.	FIFTY DOLLARS PORTLAND L Title of Bank.	50 Female seated on mechanical implements; cars on right and building on left.
100	Marine view—large steamship, city in background. CASCO BANK, Portland, Me. HUNDRED	100 Male portrait.
50 FIFTY 50	Title of Bank. Oxen before load of hay; driver with fork; man reclining on top of hay. FIFTY	50 Male portrait.
100 Female portrait.	Two females seated; cattle on left; building on right. ATLANTIC BANK, Portland, Me. 100	100 Sailor boy.
Female Portrait. 500	CASCO BANK, Portland, Me. Hunter with gun overlooking rock; female behind him. D D FIVE HUNDRED	500 Male portrait.
100 Buchanan.	Vig. Same as fives. Title of Bank. 100	100 Clay.
500	Blacksmith leaning on anvil; farmer leaning on stick; female with rake on shoulder holding child by hand. D Title of Bank. Dog.	500 Machinist leaning on engine.
M	Wharf scene—steamboat—men on dock, horses, drays, men at work; city in background. Male portrait. CASCO BANK, Portland, Me. 1000	1000 Sailor boy; two sailors in distance; ship seen in offing.
ONE Buchanan.	1 Inside of a factory; girls at work on looms, weaving. 1 ATLANTIC BANK, Portland, Me. ONE Duck.	1 Female seated with sword.
20 Female holding grain in right hand.	VILLAGE BANK, Danvers, Mass. Figures 20, XX, and the word Twenty.	20 Man plowing with two horses.
5	Indian hunter overlooking deer; cabin and squaw in background. 5 BK OF NEW HAMPSHIRE, Portsmouth, N. H. Vessel	5 Female head
Female suspended in the air; steamboat, building, etc. at her feet; buildings, cattle, etc., on right.	TWO DOLLARS White TWO across title. 2 Female bathing.	2 Ship under full sail.
50 Horses and goats at well, man, etc.	VILLAGE BANK, Danvers, Mass. FIFTY	50 Male portrait.
10 Buchanan.	Title of Bank. X Steamship sailing; men in boat. X	X Am. shield.
3 3 on Three	Ship yard scene; men at work. 3 Arm and sledge. ATLANTIC BANK, Portland, Me.	3 State Arms 3
100 Female portrait.	VILLAGE BANK, Danvers, Mass. 100 C	100 Two mechanics erect.
Girl with basket on her head; loading grain in distance. 20	Title of Bank. Steamboat; lighthouse in background.	20 Female with flowers.
5 Mechanic, sailor, flag, etc. Five Dollars	5 Spread eagle. 5 ATLANTIC BANK, Portland, Me. FIVE	FIVE Three females representing Agriculture and Commerce.
D Three females, two seated, one erect with open book.	VILLAGE BANK, Danvers, Mass. Round red die on which is figs. 500 and words Five Hundred.	500 Female holding cornucopia and flowers.
50 Washington	Storm on the coast; sailors in surf boat; ship in distress in distance. Title of Bank.	50 Spread eagle on shield.

Blacksmith, hammer and anvil. ONE | Indian chief, woman and boy. NOROMBEGA BANK Bangor, Me. | 1 1

1 Portrait. ONE | PRAIRIE STATE BK, Washington, Ills. Man and woman each side of shield. | 1 Washington ONE

ONE | SUSSEX BANK, Newton, N. J. Men Loading Hay. | 1 ONE

TWO Female with flag and shield; squaw. | NOROMBEGA BANK Bangor, Me. Indian woman. | 2 Male portrait

3 Female. 3 | Figure 3, and three cupids, Part of Title on each side of vig. | 3 Female 3

TWO | Man seated; Girl and boy playing with dog; ho ses. SUSSEX BANK, Newton, N. J. | 2 Girl seated with horn in hand.

3 Fig. 3, female, eagle and shield. | NOROMBEGA BANK Bangor, Me. Portrait of an Indian. | Three on 3 THREE 3

5 Female portrait. 5 | PRAIRIE STATE BK, Washington, Ills. Female seated with arm resting on shield; fells in background. Farming implements. | 5 Female entwined in fig. 5. FIVE

100 Boys Head. | SUSSEX BANK, Newton, N. J. State Arms, female on either side. | 100 Female portrait.

5 Woodman felling trees. | Indian and State Arms. NOROMBEGA BANK Bangor, Me. | 5 Male portrait

10 Portrait. TEN | THE PRAIRIE STATE Hunter BANK, gun and dog. | 10 Portrait. TEN

1 ONE Compt's die. | Indian family seated. BANK OF UTICA, Utica, N. Y. Canal Locks. | 1 Male portrait

10 X | Female; ship and steamboat in background. 10 NOROMBEGA BANK Bangor, Me. | TEN Indian.

5 Buchanan. | Man and boy plowing with horses; trees, dog and fence in distance. Girl's Head on each side of vig. BK OF CRAWFORD COUNTY, Meadville, Pa. FIVE FIVE | Fig. 5 inverted. Female feeding fowls.

TWO Compt's die TWO | Farmers mowing; men and haying on right. BANK OF UTICA, Utica, N. Y. Two horses. | 2 Female with flag; squaw seated.

3 Compt's die. 3 | 3 Cattle 3 CHEMUNG CANAL BANK, Elmira, N. Y. Indian in canoe. | 3 Canal locks. 3

X 10 | Farmer eating lunch; horses, hay, plow, etc in background. Eagle Childs head Title of Bank. TEN TEN | X Male portrait

Compt's die. 3 | BANK OF UTICA, Utica, N. Y. Three females, seated representing agriculture, Commerce and arts Cow and Calf. | 3 on Three Female portrait

5 Compt's die. 5 | 5 5 Title of Bank. Two females, eagle, shield, cars, shipping, etc. Canal locks. | FIVE Male portrait 5

20 Farming implements and products. | Coal mining scene; men resting; men hewing timber; cars, etc. Title of Bank. TWENTY | 20 Male portrait

5 Male portrait | Female seated leaning on cornucopia and pointing to ship on right. BANK OF UTICA, Utica, N. Y. Anvil, sledge &c. | 5. Compt's die. FIVE

Female erect with pole and cap. 50 | 50 Title of Bank. 50 Compt's die. Boy astride a deer. | Female portrait. 50

50 | Surveying scene. Head of Penn. Title of Bank. FIFTY | 50 Two sailors with boat; sailor boy in front; man-of-war in distance.

10 Two females carrying grain. | Nine cherubs making an offering to female seated beside Cornucopia; ten Gold dollars. BANK OF UTICA, Utica, N. Y. Grain. | 10 Farming implements and products Compt's die

100 Male figure destroying serpents. 100 | 100 Compt's die 100 Title of Bank. Canal locks. | 100 Neptune in car; female resting in air. 100

100 Washington | Title of Bank. Two Beavers knawing limbs of trees. 100 | 100 Farmer feeding pigs; head of horses over fence

20 XX | Farmer seated beside cradle; basket of fruit and grain. Compt's die. BANK OF UTICA, Utica, N. Y. Beehive. | 20 Drove of cattle and hogs

50 Female with chickens. UNCAS BANK, Norwich, Conn. Indian seated resting his head on right hand. 50 Child and rabbits.	Male portrait 1 BURLINGTON BK, Burlington, N. J. 1 Milkmaid with stool in left hand, leaning on cow; cows, sheep, &c. 1 1 Child and rabbits.	Three females representing Liberty, Justice and Agriculture. STAFFORD BANK, Stafford, Conn. TWENTY DOLLARS 20 20 20 Indian seated.
100 C UNCAS BANK, Norwich, Conn. State Arms, female on either side. 100 C	20 Jefferson. Shield—two females on left—Indian on right. FELLS' POINT SAVINGS INSTITUTION, Baltimore, Md. 20 Female head	50 Farmer in act of drinking from mug STAFFORD BANK, Stafford, Conn. FIFTY DOLLARS FIFTY Lathe die. 50 Two females; ship on ocean
Farmer in act of drinking from mug. ONE THAMES BANK, Norwich, Conn. Circular die enclosing female head—"One" over it—"Dollar" beneath. 1 Goddess of Liberty.	50 Marine view—ships sailing, etc. Title of Bank. Bust of female 50 Eagle on shield.	ONE Blacksmith with sledge. 1 Female seated; ship on left; lighthouse, etc, on right. EAST HADDAM BK, East Haddam, Conn. 1 Cars passing over and cattle under arch.
TWO Gleaner with sheaf and sickle. THAMES BANK, Norwich, Conn Henry Clay. 2 State Arms.	X Liberty, eagle and shield. GREENWICH BANK East Greenwich, R. I. View of buildings, trees and park. Stockholders, etc. 10 Female portrait.	2 Buchanan. EAST HADDAM BK, East Haddam, Conn. Two females on either side of anvil; buildings on right. 2 Female portrait.
3 Three females soaring in clouds THAMES BANK, Norwich, Conn. Milkmaid erect holding stool in left hand; shading her eyes with right; boy beside; cows, etc 3 Eagle on shield.	Female with pail. XX Title of Bank. Train of cars coming from under arch; two laborers. Stockholders, etc. 20 Man plowing with two horses.	THREE Female feeding fowls. 3 Inside of factory; females weaving. EAST HADDAM BK, East Haddam, Conn. 3 THREE Farmer shearing sheep.
FIFTY Female with pole and cap. 50 Two Indians and boy; vessels on left in distance and on right a wood. On each side of vig. is a male head and word "Fifty" on it. ALBANY EX. BANK Albany, N. Y. Building. FIFTY Female reclining with mechanical implements. 50	50 Sailor, mechanic, two females, city, lighthouse, chimney, bills etc. Title of Bank. State Arms. 50 Fifty inverted. Plow boy, two females, dog, oxen, sheafs, &c	V Girls' head. EAST HADDAM BK. East Haddam, Conn. View of ship yard; men at work, etc. V V 5 Sailor boy, shield, barrels, etc.
HUNDRED Justice. 100 Two females reclining; eagle, &c.; vessels on left and bridge on right. Figs. 100 on med. head, on each side of vig. Title of Bank. Building. ONE HUNDRED	Farmer erect in act of drinking from mug. 50 CECIL BANK, Port Deposit Md Milkmaid erect holding stool in left hand; shading her eyes with right; boy beside; cows, etc. 50 Female head	C C United states Capitol. SHETUCKET BANK, Norwich, Conn. 100 Female head
Goddess of Liberty erect. FIVE HUNDRED BK OF COMMERCE, Savannah, Geo. Ship in circular die.	100 Farmer erect holding scythe; village in distance. CECIL BANK, Port Deposit, Md. Milkmaid erect holding stool in left hand; right resting on cow; sheep, cows, etc. 100 Female holding flowers.	5 Female portrait. Steamer, ship, yachts, etc. STAMFORD BANK, Stamford, Conn. 5 Webster.
5 Female Portrait. 5 V Female on either side of shield; eagle at top. V BANK OF MIDDLETOWN, Middletown, Pa. 5 Female with grain, &c. 5	1 Washington STAFFORD BANK, Stafford, Conn. Two females beside loom. 1 Female head	Compt's die. 3 BK OF NEWBURGH, Newburgh, N. Y. Figure of Justice. THREE 3

Left end	Centre	Right end
1 Indian on rock. ONE	COMMERCIAL BK OF CANADA, Kingston, Ca. Farming scene; cars and city in distance.	1 Female Indian. ONE
10 Female gleaner.	X Sailor, farmer and blacksmith. Title of Bank.	10 Male portrait
FIVE Female seated with grain and sickle.	5 Washington on horseback with his staff around him. UNION BANK OF Reading, Pa.	5 Male portrait
2 Fowls. TWO	Cattle in water, etc. Title of Bank.	2 Female feeding fowls.
TWENTY Male portrait	CORN E'X BANK, 20 Philadelphia, Pa.	Corn husking scene. 20
10	Miller and farmer beside wagon; two horses, one drinking from trough; mill in background. Male portrait UNION BANK OF Reading, Pa.	X Female. Portrait
5 Engineers surveying land. FIVE	Farming scene; cars and city in distance. Title of Bank.	5 Man with pickaxe, shovel; &c.
50 50	Western steamers, etc. 50 Title of Bank.	FIFTY Milkmaid, erect with stool; cows etc.
1 Auditor's die	CITY BANK, Ottawa, Ills. Milkmaid with stool in left hand, leaning on cow; cows, sheep, &c.	1 Female portrait.
10 Queen Victoria.	Title of Bank. Three sailors, anchor, bales, &c; ship on right.	10 Female portrait.
C 100	Marine view—ships sailing C T tle of Bank. 100	100 Two farmers gathering corn.
Fig. 5, with word Five on each side.	Indian hunters overlooking deer; squaw and wigwam in background. Aud. Die CITY BANK, Ottawa, Ills.	5 Child and rabbits.
1 ONE	United states Capitol. Female head UNION BANK, Concord, N. H.	1 Female portrait
V on Five. Female reaper erect.	JERSEY SHORE BK, Jersey Shore, Pa. Scene on a raft, etc.	5 Men at work in mine.
3 Drove of cattle, load of hay.	CITIZENS BANK, Waterbury, Conn. Interior of a Blacksmith shop.	3 Farmer carrying corn.
2 Male portrait TWO	UNION BANK, Concord, N. H. Medallion head on shield; Indian and two females on shaft; on left soldier.	2 Male portrait TWO
X Male portrait	JERSEY SHORE BK, Jersey Shore, Pa. Female seated on a log beside shield with cars on it; sheafs of grain on right; farm house in distance on left	10 Male portrait
10 Farming scene—male and female with child seated; man standing against tree.	CITIZENS BANK, Waterbury, Conn. X	10 Blacksmith standing beside anvil.
5 Battle scene—female loading gun; Old man gazing at troops below.	Vessels at dock; cars, drays, &c. UNION BANK, Concord, N. H.	5 Male portrait
XX Male portrait	JERSEY SHORE BK, Jersey Shore, Pa. Bull's head on shield; men dressing leather on right; female sewing shoes on left. 20	20 Female portrait.
C Henry Clay and his dog.	CITIZENS BANK, Waterbury, Conn. Landing of the pilgrims.	100 Female portrait
10 Washington	Launching of a steamship; city in background. UNION BANK, Concord, N. H.	10 Female feeding fowls.
3 Bulls head. THREE	WINDHAM COUNTY BANK, Brattleboro, Vt. T H R E E 3 Farmers operating with reaping machine.	3
TEN Washington	BK OF CAZENOVIA, Casenovia, N. Y. TEN in large red die.	10 TEN Compt's die
5 [illegible]	Miller and farmer beside wagon; two horses, one drinking out of trough; mill in background. CORN EXCHANGE BANK, Philadelphia, Pa. Farmer seated on plow	5 Female head
10 Blacksmith at work.	Scene at depot; cars, steamboats, drays, etc. COMMERCIAL BK of Troy, N. Y.	X Compt's die.
Die. 20 Die.	BK OF CAZENOVIA, Casenovia, N. Y. TWENTY in large red die.	20 Franklin.

Left	Centre	Right
1 Indian erect and lone star.	Hunter on horseback catching wild bull. HIDE AND LEATHER BANK, Boston, Mass ONE	1 Sailor.
Male portrait Treas die.	Indian, squaw and papoose in canoe. Large white 3 across the vig. HOBOKEN CITY BK, Hoboken, N. J.	Three across 3. THREE Three dogs.
FIVE	5 Girl milking cow. BK OF ORANGE COUNTY, Goshen, N. Y. Agricultural implements.	Compt's die
TWO	Indian on horse hunting buffaloes. Boston Title of Bank. TWO	2 Head of bull.
FIVE Train of cars. Coal heaver standing with pick; large white V across.	Men heaving coal. View of a yacht sailing. HOBOKEN CITY BK, Hoboken, N. J. Portrait of Buchanan. 5	5 Treas die.
TEN Farmer sharpening scythe.	X Milkmaid seated adorning hat with flowers; cattle on left; dog and pail on right. Title of Bank. Farmer plowing.	10 Compt's die
3 Female with shield, cornucopia, &c	Fig. 3 on die; men dressing leather on right; female sewing shoes on left. Title of Bank. THREE	3
TEN Train of cars with large white X across.	Treas. die. Shipbuilding; two carpenters in the foreground. 10 in white across. HOBOKEN CITY BK, Hoboken, N. J.	10 Girl with horn.
20 Cars passing over arch; cattle, &c.	Title of Bank. Female milking cow; other cattle in distance. Compt's die.	20 Farmers shearing sheep.
V 5	Scene in a leather manufactory; men dressing leather, etc. Title of Bank.	5 5
50 Male portrait	Female nursing child; boy and dog; reapers in background. Letter L across vignette. Treas. die. HOBOKEN CITY BK, Hoboken, N. J.	50 Female portrait.
Washing sheep. 2	Large 2; five men in small circular frame. NORTHAMPTON BK Norhampton, Mass.	TWO Female with wreath. TWO
ONE HUNDRED	Title of Bank. Three females—two seated, one erect reading from book.	100
1 Barrels, bales, ship, &c. 1	ONE DOLLAR 1 Female seated beside bales; ship on left. 1 BK OF BRATTLEBORO, Brattleboro, Vt.	1 Agricultural implements. 1
Farmer on horse; boy, barn, load of hay, plough, &c. 3	Cattle; city, &c. in distance. 3 NORTHAMPTON BK Northampton, Mass.	3 across three. Girl with flowers. THREE
Female seated with book on lap. 500	Title of Bank.	500 Ship in red circular die.
2 Washington on horseback 2	TWO DOLLARS 2 Female seated beside fig. 2; flowers, etc. 2 Title of Bank.	2 Washington on horseback 2
1 Coal diggers in a circular frame.	Two females seated with sickle, wheel, &c., factory on right; cattle on left. FARMERS' & MECH. BANK. Camden, N. J.	1 Blacksmith at work.
Goddess of Liberty erect	Title of Bank. 1000 1000	1000 Cupids with grain between them.
3 Childs head. 3	THREE DOLLARS 3 Female seated beside fig. 3. 3 Title of Bank.	3 Childs head. 3
2 Justice.	Farmer, blacksmith, girl with rake; boy, etc. Title of Bank. Female bathing.	2 Wm. Penn.
Male portrait ONE	HOBOKEN CITY BK, Hoboken, N. J. Treas. die on fig 1. Fig. 1; farmers at lunch; boy playing with dog, &.	1
Compt's die. Men with scythe.	CAYUGA CO. BANK, Auburn, N. Y. Female with sheaf of wheat seated in large letter V.	5 Cattle and hogs.
3 Factory.	Scene in an iron foundry. Title of Bank. Ducks	3 Female with grain, etc.
TWO Boy.	Treas. die and 2. Team of oxen; load of hay, two boys and fig. 2. HOBOKEN CITY BK, Hoboken, N J. Dog.	
Compt's die. Blacksmith.	CAYUGA CO. BANK, Auburn, N. Y. Large ornamental X enclosing figures of justice and liberty.	10 Figure of Justice.
3 THREE	Compt's die. Pigs and fowls in pen and 3 on right. ONTARIO CO. BANK Phelps N. Y. THREE	3 Liberty.

V Male plowing / BK OF CATASAU-QUA, Catasauqua, Penn. Depot, factory, etc. FIVE / 5 Squaw and pappoose.	100 / Title of Bank. HUNDRED Steamboat under way; steamboat and vessel in distance. Compt's die. / 100 Female erect with pole and shield.	TEN Male portrait / ORANGE BANK, Orange, N. J. 10 Boy with birdcost; woman, child, dog, &c.; farmers in the rear. Large white X across vig 10 / 10 Male portrait
10 Female feeding fowls. / Scene in barnyard—farmer and drover bargaining for ox. Title of Bank. 10 / 10 Female with sheaf and sickle.	500 Two females with sheafs of grain. / Drover with cattle, sheep and horse. Compt's die. Title of Bank. Words Five Hundred and figs. 500 across. / 500 and D. Albany. Farmers with load of hay, horses, etc.	Cupid and 5. Male portrait / BANK OF GERMAN-TOWN, PA. Farmer gathering corn; horse, colt and wagon V V / 5 and Cupid. Male portrait
2) Train of cars. / Title of Bank. Female head. / 20 Men at work in coal mine.	2 Cass. / Female, agricultural implements, mirror and grain; cars on left. STATE STOCK BANK Eau Claire, Wis. / 2 Compt's die. Wisconsin.	10 Farmers at lunch. / Male portrait. Boy watering horses; girl standing beside, &c. BANK OF GERMAN-TOWN, PA. / 10 Male portrait
50 Hunter loading rifle. / Men at work in iron mill. Title of Bank. FIFTY / 5) Scene on a canal.	3 Compt's die. Wisconsin / Female reclining on bales; sea and ships in distance. STATE STOCK BANK EauClaire, Wis. / 3 Male portrait	5 Large white V on red ground work Compt's die. / FIVE Goddess of Liberty, eagle, shield, &c. FIVE BANK OF AMERICA, New York City. / 5 Large white 5 on red ground work.
100 Farmer and family. / Title of Bank. Letter C on large red die. / 100 Squaw.	5 Girl in circular frame. / MARATHON CO. BK, Eagle River, Wis. Indian beside dead deer, beckoning to some one in distance. FIVE / 5 Compt's die.	X Red end with white X across the end. Compt's die. / TEN Goddess of Liberty, eagle, shield, &c. TEN BANK OF AMERICA New York City. / 10 White X across red end.
FIVE Washington / Female representing Agriculture with left arm on shield; sheaf of wheat, &c., on right; ship in distance. BANK OF THE IN-TERIOR, Albany, N. Y. FIVE / 5 Compt's die. FIVE	10 Compt's die / MARATHON CO. BK, Eagle River, Wis. Female on each side of anvil; factory on left. TEN / 10 Female portrait.	Female figure hovering over earth; steamboat, houses, cars, &c., beneath her. / Houses, stream of water, &c. FARMERS BANK Orwell, Vt. Farming scene—men gathering corn; large white 1 across / 1
10 Eagle and shield. / Female seated on each side of anvil; buildings in distance. Title of Bank. TEN / 10 Compt's die TEN	2 Henry Clay / WOONSOCKET FALLS BANK, R. I. View of the falls; road and village in distance. / 2 Female portrait.	Two girls under shed; one churning the other making cheese; cattle, etc. on right. / 2 Title of Bank. Man and girl gazing at boy playing with dog; farming scene on right. Large white 2 across. / 2
20 Farmer sharpening scythe. / Title of Bank. TWENTY Compt's die / 20 Female seated on bale holding rake above her.	10 Girl. / WOONSOCKET FALLS BANK, R. I. View of the falls; road and village in distance. / 10 Female feeding fowls.	Stone cutter. 5 / BK OF RUTLAND, Rutland, Vt. 5 Farmer sharpening scythe; agricultural scene in the distance. 5 FIVE Dog. FIVE / 5 Female portrait.
50 Justice. / Farm scene—gathering hops; vines, etc. Compt's die. Title of Bank. FIFTY / 50 Deer in water	Farming scene and 5 across, V / Large white V across note. Train cars. ORANGE BANK, Orange, N. J. / 5 Male portrait	20 Farmer with scythe. / Title of Bank. Marble quarries; oxen drawing load of marble. / 20 Female with sheaf and scythe.

5 — FARMERS' & MERCHANTS' BANK, Baltimore, Md. — 5 — 5 — 5
Portrait of Girl. 5
Vig.—Farming scene—farmer with sickle over his shoulder, female with grain under her arm; sailor with hands in his pocket; ship in distance on left.
Five and 5. Five and 5.

20 — Three male figures erect beneath motto with "Faust, Guttenberg, and Schoeffer, upon it; printers' frames on left; press, &c., on right. — 20
Female seated, dog beside her. Title of Bank. Wm. Penn.

10 — Men reaping. Portrait of Washington — 10
Female and little girl seated; man drinking out of a jug. BANK OF LIMA, Lima, N. Y. Compt's die.

Title of Bank. — 10
Vig. Same as five. Letter X and words Ten Dollars.
10 TEN Milkmaid; cow, calf, ducks, &c.

50 — Title of Bank. — 50
Female shading her eyes with hand. Circular die containing outline map of Penn, N. Y., O., Va., Md., N. J., surmounted by bust of Washington; soldier on right; goddess of liberty, cannon, &c., on left. Sailor seated.

Male portrait — 1 Milkmaid, cattle, sheep, &c. 1 — 1
J. T. RAPLEE'S BK Penn Yan, N. Y.
Compt's die. ONE Female portrait.

20 — Title of Bank. — 20
TWENTY
Female; steamship and buildings in distance. 20 Vig. same as five.

100 — Title of Bank. — 100
State Arms.
Franklin. Scene in an iron mill.

2 — J. T. RAPLEE'S BK, Penn Yan, N. Y. — 2
Compt's die. 2 Two young girls holding flowers. 2
2 Male portrait

Cherub. 50 Surveying scene. 50
Title of Bank.
Female portrait. FIFTY DOLLARS Anchor, bales, bbls., &c.

1 — Drover, farmer, boy, dog, negro, bull, sheep, cows, etc. — 1
BANK OF TRADE, Toms River, N. J.
Treas die. Female portrait.

Two Indians overlooking water fall; deer. Indian camp. V Webster V 5
J. T. RAPLEE'S BK, Penn Yan, N. Y. Compt's die.
Fig. 5, with five on each side. 5
Farmer seated on plow

100 — Sailor boy. Sailors; one looking through telescope; one seated on broken mast; one resting his face on hand; ships in distance on right; men seen in distance on left. — 100
Man with corn stalks. Title of Bank. ONE HUNDRED Female feeding fowls.

2 — Six men at work in stone quarry; cars, city, etc., in distance. — 2
BANK OF TRADE, Toms River, N. J.
Treas die. Female with dove.

X — View at steamboat landing. — 10
BANK OF ST. LOUIS, St. Louis, Mo.
Men dressing leather TEN Male portrait

Farmer loading hay on ox team. Girls portrait 500
Title of Bank.
500 500 Sailor boy; ship on right; sailors on left.

5 — BANK OF TRADE, Toms River. N. J. — 5
View of water, vessels, &c.
Treas die. Boy & girl.

XX — Portrait of Washington with female, scythe, ears sheaf, etc., on right; female, men, boxes, bbls. and steamer on left. — 20
BANK OF ST. LOUIS, St. Louis, Mo.
Male portrait 20 Female portrait

1000 — Farmer plowing; boy at horses head with branch; dog, basket, etc. — 1000
Sailor leaning on capstan; ship in distance. Title of Bank. Maryland
1000 Girl's portrait.

Henry Clay 1 Boy on horse driving sheep; cows, colt, &c. 1
BANK OF LIMA, Lima, N. Y.
Compt's die. Cattle passing under and cars over arch.

Indian in canoe. 500 500
MECHANICS' BANK, New Bedford, Mass.
500 D D Justice.

5 — Girls' head. Man, horse, colt, bridge, two boys; hills in background. — 5
Farmer, dog, horses' head, implements, bird flying, &c. COMMONWEALTH BANK, Philadelphia, Pa. Two sailors pulling rope, etc.
FIVE FIVE FIVE

TWO — BANK OF LIMA, Lima, N. Y. — 2
Compt's die. Anvil; female on either side; cornucopia; factory in rear.
TWO Webster.

1 — Train of cars. Figure of Liberty. — 1
BK OF EUA CLAIRE, Eau Claire, Wis.
Compt's die. Fowls

10 — Title of Bank. — 10
Two females seated representing Agriculture and Commerce; factories and buildings on right; cows, sheep and village in distance on left.
Mechanic and bench. Sailor; ships, houses, etc., in background.

5 — Engine entering depot; cars leaving; two trains in distance. — 5
Compt's die.
BANK OF LIMA, Lima, N. Y.
Male portrait FIVE

2 — BK OF EUA CLAIRE, EuaClaire, Wis. — 2
Goddess of Liberty. Large steamboat.
Compt's die.

V	Female seated with wand pointing at ship on left; cornucopia on right.	5
Compt's die.	MERCHANTS' BK.	
FIVE	New, Orleans, La.	Female portrait.

X	WARREN CO. BANK Warren, Pa.	10
Female reaper.	Med die with letter X, words "Ten Dollars" and figs 10 on it.	Female with flowers in her apron.

FIVE	SOUTHERN BANK, St. Louis, Mo.	5
	Steamship.	Female erect pointing to pillar on which is inscribed "Union"
Male portrait		

TEN	Title of Bank.	10
Compt's die.	Female seated beside grain; ship on left; light-house and promotory on right.	
X		Female portrait.

ONE	1 Farmer seated on grain; reapers on left; loading hay on right.	1
Justice.	BANK OF TORONTO. Toronto, Canada.	Indian seated supporting fig. 1.

10	SOUTHERN BANK, St. Louis, Mo.	
	X Man tanning leather.	Men working at bench.
Girls head.		

Compt's die.	50 Female figure representing minerva pointing at steamer on left; mirror, safe, grain cornucopia, &c. on left.	FIFTY
Female p[illegible].		Statue of Justice with sword and scales.
FIFTY	Title of Bank.	

4	Three females seated representing Agriculture Commerce, and Arts.	FOUR
	BANK OF TORONTO, Toronto, Canada.	Portrait of an Indian Chief.
Farmers and scythe.	City Arms.	

Female seated.	20 Engineers surveying land.	20
	SOUTHERN BANK, St. Louis, Mo.	20
TWENTY	Eagle.	TWENTY

1	ONE DOLLAR	1
Barrels, bales, ship, &c.	1 Female seated beside bales: ship on left 1	Agricultural implements.
1	THOMASTON BANK, Thomaston, Me.	1

5	BANK OF TORONTO, Toronto, Canada.	5
	British Arms.	Female seated, large fig. 5; bales, ships, &c.
Female portrait.	City Arms.	

100	Title of Bank. State Arms; sailor on right and Indian on left.	
C	Girls head.	100

1	BK OF NORWALK, Norwalk, Conn.	1
Female with sewing machine.	Blacksmith's shop. Male portrait	

TEN	BANK OF TORONTO, Toronto, Canada.	10
	City Arms.	
Beaver.		Train of cars

1	Men chopping trees; cabin, horse, &c., in background.	1
Anchor, bales, bbls, &c.	QUEBEC BANK, Quebec, Canada.	Bee Hive surrounded by flowers.
	St. George and the Dragon.	

	Sailors on shore; one looking through telescope; ships, men, etc., in distance. Male portrait.	3
3	BK OF NORWALK, Norwalk, Conn.	Sheep.

10	10 Cattle, sheep, &c. 10	X
Compt's die.	SARATOGA COUNTY BANK, Waterford, N. Y.	Med head.
10	Cornucopia, &c.	X

10	QUEBEC BANK, Quebec, Canada.	10
	TWO POUND TEN.	
Sailor at Capstan.	Yoke of Oxen—man chopping and two children.	

5	Male portrait Two females, shield, &c; ships, houses, etc., in distance.	5
Blacksmith boy.	BK OF NORWALK, Norwalk, Conn.	5

5	WEBSTER BANK, Boston, Mass.	5
	5 Full length figure of Webster. 5	

Compt's die.	2 Farming scene—farmers at lunch; haying in background.	2
Two cherubs	CENTRAL CITY BK, Syracuse, N. Y.	
Female portrait.	Agricultural Implements.	Flower girl.

100 across words One Hundred.	Wharf scene; loading wagons; ships, &c.	Same as on left end.
	HINGHAM BANK. Hingham, Mass.	
Male portrait		Male portrait

5	V Females and fig. 5. V	5
Compt's die.	BK OF DANSVILLE, Dansville, N. Y.	Med head.
FIVE	Eagle.	FIVE

Compt's die.	5 Three females representing Agriculture, Commerce and arts.	5
Two sea nymphs.	CENTRAL CITY BK, Syracuse, N. Y.	Five figures around large V.
Steamship.		

5	WARREN CO BANK Warren, Pa.	5
V	Ornamental fig. 5; female on each side; houses, etc., in distance. Word FIVE each side of vig. running up and down.	FIVE

5	Farmers at lunch. Franklin.	5
Washington	WEST BRANCH BK. Williamsport, Pa.	Canal and boats.
5	Agricultural Implements.	5

FIVE	Female crowning an Eagle with left hand, holding Portrait of Washington; with buildings on left; ships on right.	5
Spread Eagle and Shield.	CENTRAL CITY BK, Syracuse, N. Y.	Five females around fig 5
Compts die.	Agricultural Implem[illegible]	

5 — Farming scene; farmer [illegible] cattle, [illegible] of hay in background. Fig. 5 on right and left. — 5
Comp's die — Female seated.
BROOME CO BANK, Binghampton, N. Y.
FIVE — FIVE

5 — NAUMKEAG BANK, Salem, Mass. — 5
FIVE — Street in Salem. — FIVE
5 — Anchor, etc. — 5

20 — Cattle dealer selling cow to farmer. — 20
BK OF CALEDONIA, Danville, Vt.
Man carrying grain; horse, dog, etc. — Female portrait.
Boy on horseback.

TWENTY — 20 — Indian princess with shield. — 20
BANK OF BINGHAMPTON, N. Y.
Justice erect and Goddess of War seated.
Shield, etc. — Female

100 — CUMBERLAND BK, Bridgeton, N. J. — 100
Washington.
Indian on horse. — Sailor boy.

TEN — Farmer gathering grain; on right men reaping; on left man on horse talking to farmer. — 10
CLINTON BANK, Clinton, Conn.
TEN — Portrait of Boy.

20 — Female seated with vase between 2 and 0. — 20
Compt's die. — Franklin
AUBURN CITY BK, Auburn, N. Y.
TWENTY — Shield. — TWENTY

20 — 20 — Female on either side of shield on which is 20; ship in distance. — TWENTY
Compt's die.
ULSTER CO. BANK, Kingston, N. Y.
20 — Die.

20 — BUNKER HILL BK, Charlest.wn, Mass. — 20
Female, two Indians and old soldier gazing at portrait of Washington. 20 each side.
Anchor, etc. — Jefferson.

BK OF TENNESSEE. — 10
Jackson.
Male portrait — Male portrait

1 — BANK OF THE STATE OF INDIANA — ONE
One Dollar across circular die. — 1
Male portrait — 1 ONE 1 — Male portrait

10 — Female seated with basket; reapers on right; stream; house on left. — 10
Compt's die. — Squaw.
LIVINGSTON CO. BK, Geneseo, N. Y.
10 — Eagle. — 1

20 — Three females representing Justice, Peace and plenty. — 20 — Justice.
Taylor.
BK OF TENNESSEE.
20 — Beehive. — TWENTY

3 — Title of Bank. — 3
3 — Three across large die. — 3
Male portrait — Three. — Male portrait

Med. head. — FARMERS BANK OF VIRGINIA.
10 — TEN
Female seated, [illegible]
Med. head.

50 — BK OF TENNESSEE. — 50
State Arms. — Female offering drink to eagle on shield. — Washington
50 — 50

Indian in canoe. — 500 — 500
BEDFORD COMMERCIAL BANK, New Bedford, Mass.
500 — D — D — Justice.

TEN — Working in an iron foundry; — 10
Compt's die
IRON BANK, Rockaway, N. J.
Bank building. — TEN

Female, sheaf, etc. — 500 — D — 500
MARINE BANK, New Bedford, Mass.
500

500 — MERCHANTS BANK, New Bedford, Mass. — 500
Male and female. — State Arms; female on each side; eagle at top; steamboat on right; houses on left. — Female.
D — Bank Building. — 500

Farmer ploughing with two horses. — L — Indian seated in canoe going through rapids. — FIFTY
Old soldier reading
50 — MOWHAWK BANK, Schenectady, N. Y. — 50
Compt's die. — Cars.

Shipping. — D — 500
MARINE BANK, New Bedford, Mass.
500 — Sailor at helm.

10 — X — Farmer with child on right shoulder, female holding its hand. — X — 10
Female seated, right hand on pail; cattle and trees on left.
BK OF RHINEBECK, Rhinebeck, N. Y. — Compt's die.

XX — BK OF COMMERCE, Fredericksburg, Va. — 20
Female seated beside barrels; ship in distance. — Female, cows, chickens, &c.
Treas. die.

FIVE — Female holding drapery over shield on which is a 5. — V — 5
WARREN BANK, Warren, R. I.
Ship.

Wm. Penn. — QUINSIGAMOND BK Worcester, Mass. — 10
Street in Worcester
TEN — Indian seated.

10 — Large letter X in center; Med. Heads of Washington and Franklin on either side supported by four cherubs. — 10
Banana tree surrounded by barrels, bales, wheat, &c.
Girl's portrait. — BK OF GEORGETOWN, S. C.

ONE 1 — MERCHANTS BANK, Salem, Mass. Has the title, denomination and place of issue in red letters—The words "Merchants' Bank, Salem and "One Dollar" all over the middle part of bill in fine letters. ONE — Sailor boy. ONE 1

50 — Title of Bank. 50 — Three men erect; vessels in distance. Red letter L.

10 inverted. Vig. Same as ones with green X each side. 10 — Train of cars. AETNA BANK, Hartford, Conn. City Arms, deer, water trees, etc. 10 inverted.

TWO — MERCHANTS BANK, Salem, Mass. 2 TWO 2 — Vessel on stock. Same as ones with denomination changed only. TWO

10 — THE LEE BANK, Lee, Mass. 10 — Figure of Justice with sword and scales, seated on box. Two female figures seated; owl, barrels, bust, globe, &c.; at am. ship on left; buildings on right. Female bust.

Female seated painting its reapers and load of hay. 500 D — 500 — MERCANTILE BK, Salem, Mass. 500

FIVE — MERCHANTS BANK, Salem, Mass. 5 FIVE 5 — Vessels. Same as ones with denomination changed only. FIVE

XX — Title of Bank. 20 — Female on either side of anvil; building in distance. Portrait of Indian female. Two children.

Female portrait. Vessels at sea. Large X, word Ten in centre. NEW HAVEN BANK. New Haven, Conn. 10 — Female, cow, &c. Bee hive. First Sabbath.

TEN — MERCHANTS BANK, Salem, Mass. 10 TEN 10 — Vessels. Same as ones with the denomination changed only. TEN

Justice erect. 50 — Title of Bank. 50 — Three females representing Commerce, Manufacturers and Agriculture; vessel in distance. FIFTY — Male portrait.

First Sabbath. Female resting on shield; steamer, ship, cars, bridge, &c., in distance. 20 — XX — NEW HAVEN BANK. Bee hive. Female.

FIFTY — MERCHANTS BANK, Salem, Mass. 50 FIFTY 50 — Steamboat. Same as ones with the denomination changed only. FIFTY

100 — Title of Bank. 100 — Female resting on bale on which is letter C: city, etc., in distance on left. State Arms. Male portrait.

5 — Large steamship; tow-boats in foreground; vessels, city, &c., in distance. 5 — Shield, &c. Male portrait. FIVE — CITY BANK OF NEW HAVEN. Eagle. FIVE

100 — MERCHANTS BANK, Salem, Mass. 100 — Sailor and shipping. Same as ones with the denomination changed only. 100 — 100

ONE across figure 1. 1 — Female, with arm resting on bundle of grain, pointing to St. Aetna in distance; ship, &c., on left of her. 1 — ONE across figure 1. ONE — Sailor with quadrant pointing to seaward; steamer in distance. THE AETNA BANK, Hartford, Conn. ONE across figure 1.

Webster. Four eagles, letter X, medallion head of Franklin and Washington blended together. 10 — Fillmore. CITY BANK OF NEW HAVEN. Bee-hive. 10 — 10

MERCHANTS BANK, Salem, Mass. The plates of the 20's are of the general plate of the N. E. Bank Note Co.

TWO 2 — Vig. Same as ones. 2 — Vessels. AETNA BANK, Hartford, Conn. City Arms; deer, water, trees, etc. TWO — TWO

FIFTY — 50 — Cupid sharpening knife on grindstone. FIFTY — FARMERS' AND MECHANICS' BANK, Detroit, Mich. Steamboat, vessels, bales of goods, &c. Arm and hammer. 50

HIDE & LEATHER BANK, BOSTON. State of Massachusetts. 10 — Title of Bank again and X. Steamship.

3 — AETNA BANK, Hartford, Conn. 3 — Agricultural implements and products. 3 Vig. Same as ones. 3 — Two girls carrying grain. THREE across fig. 3

ONE HUNDRED — 100 — Vulcan, sledge, and anvil; nude female seated on his left; another figure in background. 100 ONE — Male portrait. HUNDRED 100 — Title of Bank. Drove.

XX — Title of Bank. 20 — Title of Bank again and 20 on red die. Old man, boy and dog. Cattle.

FIVE — AETNA BANK, Hartford, Conn. 5 — V and words Five Dollars. Vig. same as ones. CONNECTICUT — 5 — FIVE

5 — COMMERCIAL B'K, Troy, N. Y. 5 — Laborers working; one smoking a pipe, another wheeling a barrow. Compt's die. Farmer with corn. 5 — 5 FIVE

<table>
<tr>
<td>FIVE
Male portrait
Five and green V.</td><td>ONTARIO BANK,
Bowmanville, Canada.
Five and fig. 5. Man sharpening scythe. 5 and Dollars</td><td>5 and green V
FIVE
Bull's head.</td>
<td>Male portrait
5</td><td>View of depot, cars, church, etc.
RAILROAD BANK,
Lowell, Mass.</td><td>5
Five females surrounding fig. 5.</td>
<td>TWO
2
TWO</td><td>Title of Bank.
2 State Arms. 2
TWO DOLLARS
MASS.</td><td>TWO
2
TWO</td>
</tr>
<tr>
<td>10 and green X.
Canal and railroad scene.</td><td>Indian with shield on which is canal scene, sun, steamer, man plowing, etc; bison on right; deer on left.
Title of Bank.</td><td>10 and green X.
Cattle, cars, telegraph, bridge, etc.</td>
<td>10
X</td><td>View of buildings, pedestrians, etc.
Title of Bank.</td><td>X
Male portrait.</td>
<td>X
Portrait of Girl.</td><td>BANK OF UPPER CANADA.
Two females seated, with owl, bust, anchor, etc.; ocean scene on left; building, etc., on right.
Toronto, Canada,</td><td>10
Cattle, telegraph, cars, bridge, etc.</td>
</tr>
<tr>
<td>10
Calhoun.</td><td>MERCHANTS BANK of South Carolina,
Two females with owl, bust, anchor, &c.; ocean scene on left; buildings, etc., on right. Yellow X either side.
Cheraw, S. C.</td><td>10
Sailor with nautical instruments.</td>
<td>ONE
Female resting arm on fence.
ONE</td><td>FARMERS' BANK,
Bangor, Me.
Has the denomination in small words and letters all over the middle part of the bill.</td><td>1
ONE
1</td>
<td>Female with flag and shield; Indian female at her feet</td><td>20 Two shoemakers at work; female at household duties in background.
RANDOLPH BANK,
Randolph, Mass.</td><td>20
Cattle, telegraph; cars on bridge.</td>
</tr>
<tr>
<td>XX
OF SOUTH
Female portrait.</td><td>MERCHANTS BANK
Female on either side of anvil; buildings in distance.
Cheraw, S. C.</td><td>20
CAROLINA
Cars, bridge, etc.</td>
<td>2
Men, horses, carts, buildings, etc.
TWO</td><td>Title of Bank.
Has the denomination same as ones.</td><td>2
TWO
2</td>
<td>FIFTY
Female representing Agriculture.
50</td><td>50 Farmer seated 50 with implements and products; load of hay, buildings, etc., in distance.
Title of Bank.</td><td>50
Female portrait.</td>
</tr>
<tr>
<td>FIFTY
Sailor, State Arms, hh'ds., masts, etc.
FIFTY</td><td>THE MERCHANTS
50
Negroes picking and carrying cotton.
Bank of South Carol'a
Cheraw, S. C.</td><td>50
Cotton weighing scene.</td>
<td>FIVE
Vessel; name Gold Hunter on sail.
FIVE</td><td>Title of Bank.
Has the denomination same as ones.</td><td>5
FIVE
5</td>
<td>100
Female portrait.</td><td>Two females seated; steamer, etc., in distance on left; buildings, monument, etc., on right.
Title of Bank</td><td>100
Train of cars bridge and cars in distance.</td>
</tr>
<tr>
<td>2
TWO</td><td>2 View of levee on Western river; numerous steamboats, produce, etc. 2
ARTISAN BANK,
Trenton, N. J.
Compt's die.</td><td>2
TWO</td>
<td>TEN
Vessel on stocks.
TEN</td><td>Title of Bank.
Has the denomination same as ones.</td><td>10
TEN
10</td>
<td>Two girls with sheafs.
ONE</td><td>Cupid rolling silver dollar on track; cars, steamboat, city, etc., in distance.
WHITE MOUNTAIN BANK,
Lancaster, N. H.</td><td>1
Cattle, sheep, hogs, etc.</td>
</tr>
<tr>
<td>3
THREE</td><td>Interior of an iron foundry; men at work.
ARTISAN BANK
Trenton, N. J.</td><td>3
Compt's die.</td>
<td>100
Justice seated.</td><td>Shoe and Leather Dealers store; horses, wagon, men, wharf and shipping
SHOE & LEATHER DEALERS BANK,
Boston, Mass.</td><td>100
Female portrait.</td>
<td>TWO
Female and squaw.</td><td>2 Santa Claus in sleigh drawn by reindeers over roofs of houses.
Title of Bank.</td><td>2
Cars; bridge, cars, etc, in distance.</td>
</tr>
<tr>
<td>5
State arms.</td><td>ARTISAN BANK,
Trenton, N. J.
View of Suspension bridge, river, steamboats, etc.</td><td>5
Female portrait.</td>
<td>500</td><td>Same as 100s.
Title of Bank.</td><td>500
Cows.</td>
<td>Three across 3.
Female portrait.</td><td>Title of Bank.
Man with scythe; loading hay on left.</td><td>THREE across fig. 3
Male portrait.</td>
</tr>
<tr>
<td>X
TEN</td><td>Mechanic. Female seated on the left of a shield on which is ship building scene.
ARTISAN BANK,
Trenton, N. J.</td><td>10
State Arms.</td>
<td>1
ONE</td><td>MASSACHUSETTS BANK,
Boston, Mass.
State arms; words "One Dollar" across fig. 1 each side.</td><td>1
Massachusetts.
ONE</td>
<td>Female giving eagle drink.
5</td><td>Female seated with spy-glass, shield and wheat; vessels, steamer, lighthouse, etc, in distance.
Title of Bank.</td><td>5
Male portrait.</td>
</tr>
</table>

Left	Centre	Right
ONE Eagle, shield, &c. Compt's die.	DOVER PLAINS B'K, Dover Plains, N. Y. Farmer mowing with cradle; loading grain on left.	1 Deer in water.
C Boy's head.	CITIZENS' BANK. Farmer riding horse; boy on fence.	100 William Penn.
TWO Scene in a blacksmith shop	Milkmaid seated, cows, &c. B'K OF NORWALK. Norwalk, Conn.	2 Male portrait
2 Compt's die. 2	Engine and tender entering depot; train of cars leaving it. DOVER PLAINS B'K.	2 Two children playing with flowers.
5 Male portrait	B'K OF THE STATE OF MISSOURI, St. Louis. Scene in the arctic regions; men pushing boat off ice.	5 Male portrait
	B'K OF NORWALK. TEN Female standing beside pillar. Steamship and vessels.	10 Male portrait
5 Farmer with scythe.	V Drover on horse; drove of cattle, sheep, &c. V DOVER PLAINS B'K	5 Compt's die. 5
FIVE	MECHANICS BANK St. Louis, Mo. Scene in a blacksmith shop. Girl's head. FIVE	5 Farmer carrying corn.
Male portrait 20	B'K OF NORWALK. Indian. Female seated beside eagle, shield, &c. Sailor.	20 20
X Cattle passing under, and cars passing over bridge.	Farmer ploughing with team of horses. DOVER PLAINS B'K.	10 Compt's die. TEN
Girl seated. TEN	MECHANICS BANK. 10 TEN	Cupid. Mechanic's arm and hammer.
Scene in a mill; carrying out grain ONE	B'K OF BLOOMINGTON, Illinois. Compt's die.	1 Male portrait
20	DOVER PLAINS B'K. Drover on horse; drove of cattle, sheep, &c. Compt's die.	20 Milkmaid churning.
Female figure floating in air above stream of water.	Houses, trees, &c. LITCHFIELD BANK, Litchfield, Conn. 1 Cattle, &c.	1
2 Compt's die.	B'K OF BLOOMINGTON. Girl's head.	Cupid supporting figure 2. Farmer and boy ploughing with horse.
5 Female head.	CITIZENS' BANK, Male portrait. Pittsburgh, Pa. Scene in a grist mill; man loading horse with grain; boys fishing in brook.	5 Blacksmith with hammer in hand, standing beside anvil.
Cattle drovers, &c. 2	Cattle drinking out of pond. LITCHFIELD BANK. 2 2	2 Farmers gathering corn.
3 Surveyors measuring ground.	B'K OF BLOOMINGTON. Girl's head. Farmers loading hay. Girl's head.	3 Compt's die.
X Female	Interior of an iron foundry. Buchanan. CITIZENS' BANK.	10 Female standing beside pillar
Female with sickle. 5	V Wood cutters in woods chopping. LITCHFIELD BANK. Anvil.	Sailor. 5
5	B'K OF BLOOMINGTON. Scene in the arctic regions; men pushing boat off of ice. Compt's die.	5 James Buchanan.
Girl seated. TWENTY	CITIZENS' BANK. Robert Morris Coal heavers leaning against cart	20
TEN Mechanic & sailor.	LITCHFIELD BANK. X TEN Female either side of State arms; vessels, trees, cars, &c.	TEN Three females, grain, sickle, anchor, &c.
5 Indian. FIVE V	Lion. Queen Victoria. Unicorn. ST. FRANCIS BANK, Canada West. V	5 Prince Albert CINQ.
50 Battle scene, soldier charging bayonet.	Female head. Blacksmith mending cart; farmer standing beside him with horse. CITIZENS' BANK.	50 Thomas Jefferson
1 Boy's head.	NORTHERN BANK of Kentucky. Drovers, cattle, Sheep, &c.	1 Girl's head.
10 Anchor and bales. TEN X	St. George and the dragon. ST. FRANCIS BANK. X	10 Queen Victoria. DIX.

5 Compt's die FIVE V Fig. 5, five females and words Five Dollars. V STATE SECURITY BANK, Gemekon, Wis. Dog. 5 Eagle in clouds. Wisconsin.	5 Steamboat. Compt's die. Title of Bank. 5 Woodmen with axe in woods.	2 Two children Indian viewing the progress of civilization. Title of Bank. Game. TWO Compt's die
TEN Compt's die. 10 Title of Bank. Female portrait and letter X. Three men, boy, horses, dog, fowls, in front of shop. Eagle. 10 TEN	BUFFALO COUNTY BANK, Indians on horseback killing buffaloes. Beavers knawing trees Northhousen, 1 Compt's die. Wisconsin.	THREE Female head on a 3. Compt's die Title of Bank. Eagle and fig. 3. Oxen before sled drawing load of wood, man and boy, houses and men skating in distance. Indian. 3 THREE
V Compt's die. BANK OF MONEKA, Viroqua Wis. Indians viewing train of cars on prairie. 5 on Five. Indian female.	5 Compt's die. Title of Bank. Indians on horseback killing wild animals. 5 Female seated.	5 Man seated, female erect, dog, houses, etc. Title of Bank. Compt's die. 5 Indian, dog squaw, canoe, etc.
X Compt's die. Female seated on cliff; city, cars, locks, etc., below. Title of Bank. 10 Squaw and papoose.	10 Indian with gun on cliff. Wisconsin. Eagle. Title of Bank. Compt's die. 10 Family at their devotions; Indians entering door.	Continental soldiers. ONE Girl's head. Female seat. ed; vessels in distance. BANK OF NEW LONDON, New London, Wis. ONE ONE 1 Compt's die. Wisconsin.
Portrait of Squaw. 20 NOROMBEJA BANK Bangor, Me Scene in a ship yard; city, vessels, etc., in distance. 20 Squaw.	1 Compt's die. ONE Indian on horseback shooting buffaloes. WAUPACCA COUNTY BANK, Waupacca, Wis. 1 Female portrait.	5 Female erect with steamer and building in distance. Steamboat; city on right and left. Title of Bank. FIVE FIVE 5 Compt's die. Wisconsin.
FIFTY Indian princess erect. 50 Letter L on shield surmounted by eagle and surrounded by warlike implements. Title of Bank. 50 Two females.	Indians on cliff viewing city, etc. 2 Farmer lunching with boy, girl, dog, etc.; horses on right. Title of Bank. 2 Compt's die.	Female seated in chair. FIVE BANK OF THE INTERIOR, Wausau, Wis. Compt's die. Female with eagle, and "America" on globe. 5 Female, cow, calf, fowls, etc.
Figs. 100 in oval. Man with rake, keg, fork and dog. 100 Indian and dead deer. Title of Bank. 100 Female portrait.	3 Cattle in stream of water. Compt's die. Title of Bank. 3 Girl shading eyes with hand.	10 Compt's die. Wisconsin. Title of Bank. Girl's head. Farmers at lunch under a tree; female, horses, etc. 10 Portrait of Girl.
ONE Sheep ONE Hunter shooting deer crossing stream; dogs in pursuit. UNION BANK, Milwaukie, Wis. 1 Compt's die ONE	5 Compt's die. Title of Bank. Farmer and hunter on each side of a shield surmounted by vessel. 5 Female with dove.	Female seated holding shield on which is V and 5. Compt's die Two men, child, anvil, wheel, etc. FRONTIER BANK, Stevens' Point Wis. 5 Sailor seated with pipe.
2 Steamboat discharging. Rafting scenes on river. Title of Bank. 2 Compt's die TWO	1 Indian fishing. ONEIDA BANK, Berlin, Wis. Two men grinding corn; children, dog, horse, etc. Beehive. Fig. 1: Indian on left; female on right. Compt's die	Female soaring above houses, cars, steamboat, etc; on right upper is cattle, houses, etc. Comp's die. Title of Bank. 10 Mechanic at bench.

FIVE 5 View of steamboat, schooner, men, bridge, etc. 5 FIVE Justice. COMMERCIAL BK, Salem, Mass. State Arms. FIVE FIVE	Whaling scene. Male portrait. 2 Title of Bank. TWO Sailor at helm.	X 10 Men at work in mines. X TEN Title of Bank. Webster.
Female and eagle. Word "Twenty" across figs. 20. Female 20 Title of Bank. 20 Franklin.	3 Steamboat "Plymouth Rock," and other vessels. 3 Title of Bank Male portrait Sailor with glass.	TWENTY 20 Indian seated; two Indians in canoe in distance. XX Title of Bank. Red figs. 20. Buchanan.
C Eagle on bale; agricultural products, etc. 100 100 Men and boats. Female representing Agriculture. Title of Bank. 100 100	5 Men at work, cutting down trees; drawing logs, etc. Girls' head. 5 Compt's die. OSBORN BANK, of New London, Wis. Male portrait Wisconsin	50 View of factories, buildings, cars, river, bridge, etc. L Title of Bank. Calhoun. Boy and girl.
Female seated pointing to reapers and load of hay. 500 D 500 Title of Bank. 500	10 Female seated on right of shield on which is vessel, plow, etc.; cars on bridge in distance. 10 Compt's die. Female with sheaf, sickle, cow, etc. Title of Bank. Wisconsin.	Men and three horses at well; goat, kid, sheep, etc. C 100 Title of Bank.
20 XX Eagle. XX 20 LOWELL BANK, Lowell, Mass Female. Ship.	10 Man and boy plowing with two horses. 10 BK OF LA POINTE, La Pointe, Wis. Compt's die Female portrait.	L inverted Red 50 on die; on right, old man, boy, dog, etc; on left milkmaid seated; Steamboat in background. L inverted HUNTERDON CO BK, Flemington, N. J. Male portrait Female portrait with a bonnet on.
Female seated pointing to reapers and load of hay. 500 D 500 Title of Bank. 500	20 Title of Bank. 20 Compt's die. Sailor, farmer and blacksmith conversing; horse and man on right. TWENTY Female with dove.	100 Four females; one erect reading. Red C either side. ONE HUNDRED Title of Bank. Female portrait.
20 Female representing fame blowing trumpet; eagle globe, flag, &c. 20 John Hancock. JOHN HANCOCK BK, Springfield, Mass. TWENTY State arms.	5 Girls' head. Farmer with sack on shoulder horse colt, boys on bridge, etc. 5 Compt's die. Laborers at work; railroad etc. LABORERS' BANK, Markesan Wis. Wisconsin.	5 on Five. Men at work in mine. 5 Two Indians and tent. SHAMOKIN BANK, Shamokin, Pa. Female with dove. 5
Indian female with eagle, globe, &c. 100 on large die. 100 Title of Bank. Farmer with scythe; cars, mill, etc., in distance. 100 Dog's head.	X Laborers resting from work; two erect, and two seated; in distance men at work on logs. Henry Clay. 10 Compt's die Mason at work. Title of Bank. Wisconsin.	10 Buildings, coal train, track, etc. X TEN Title of Bank. Female with flowers. 10
Male portrait Sailor seated with nautical implements; vessels in distance. 1 STONINGTON BK, Stonington, Conn. ONE Vessels.	5 Large V with reaper seated within; on right is old man, boy, dog, etc; on left is female seated with sheaf, sickle; cars, canal, locks, &c. in distance. 5 5 CENTRAL BANK OF PENNSYLVANIA, Hollidaysburg, Pa. Female portrait.	20 Title of Bank. 20 20 Head of Liberty. 20 TWENTY DOLLARS Blacksmith. Female with grain and sickle.

1 — Female with two calves; cars, canal scene, cows, etc., in distance on left. ROCKAWAY BANK, Rockaway, N. J. — 1
Boy and girl. | State Arms.

10 — Title of Bank. Female reclining with quadrant, pole and cap, merchandise, etc.; ocean scene on left; buildings, etc. on right. Cornucopia, &c. — 10
Treas. die. | Letter X Ten on it; milkmaid, cow, cars, etc.

V — BANK OF ALEDO, Aledo, Ills. Train of cars, depot, passengers, etc; on right cars, bridge, etc. Compt's die. — V
Female with cornucopia of flowers. | Female with cornucopia of flowers.

2 — Title of Bank. Train of cars, in front of manufactory. — 2
State Arms. | Man plowing with two horses.

1 — WISCONSIN PINERY BANK, Stevens Point, Wis. Female with child in arms; boy, dog, etc.; in distance man mowing. — 1
Hunter drinking from brook. | Compt's die.

5 — MCKEAN CO. BANK, Smethport, Pa. Two females seated on rock; city on right; cars on left.
Franklin. | Washington, some Dog's Head; other female with sickle, on this end.

5 — Men at work in mine. Title of Bank. — 5
State Arms. | Vessel.

2 — Title of Bank. Compt's die. — 2
Hunter and dog seated by fire in woods. | Milkmaid and cattle.

5 — Title of Bank. 5 FIVE — 5
Loading cart with lumber; canal boat at dock, etc. | Female with bird.

ONE — FAIRFIELD CO. BK, Norwalk, Conn. View of buildings, etc—a general street view. — 1
Male portrait | 1

Female with sickle and dog. — Title of Bank. Mechanic, farmer, horse, buildings, etc. — 3
Three, 3, III | Compt's die. THREE

10 — Title of Bank. Cars. — 10
Franklin. | Female portrait.

TWO — Female with two calves; cars, canal scene, cows, etc., in distance on left. Title of Bank. — 2
Blacksmith | Male portrait

5 — Three females and bust of Washington. Title of Bank. — 5
Boy and rabbits. | Compt's die.

1 — Factories, buildings, cars, river, bridge, etc. MERCHANTS BANK, Paterson, N. J. — 1
State Arms. | Man carrying leather.

THREE — Large fig. 3 on which is Title of Bank, words "Three Dollars," etc. — 3
Male portrait | Female soaring in clouds with quadrant.

XX — HAVERHILL BANK, Haverhill, Mass. TWENTY — 20
General street view in village. | Same as on left end.

2 — Factories, river, &c.; cars and buildings on right. Title of Bank. — 2
State Arms. | Blacksmith with sledge anvil and hammer.

V — BK OF MANASSA, Front Royal, Va. Boy and girl fishing in stream; on right men, load of hay, barn, etc.; on left bridge, houses, etc. — V
5 | Treas die.

50 — Title of Bank. Words "Fifty Dollars" across red figs. 50. — 50
General street view in village. | Indian erect.

V — Female on cliff viewing city, cars, canal, etc. Title of Bank. — 5
Clay. | State Arms.

10 — Title of Bank. Wild horses. — 10
Female with shield. | Treas. die.

20 — MECHANICS BANK, Public buildings, fountains, pedestrians, horses, carriages, etc. St. Louis, Mo. — 20
Boy and girl. | Male portrait

1 — Female with two calves; cars, canal scene, cattle, &c., in distance. SOUTHERN BANK OF GEORGIA, Bainbridge, Geo. — 1
Cattle, telegraph, cars, bridge, etc. | Female with arm resting on railing.

5 — View of steamer, tug, vessels, men in row-boat, city, etc. RAPPAHANNOCK BANK, Tappahannock, Va. American Shield. — 5
Portrait of Girl. | Treas. die.

50 — Three females and bust of Washington. Title of Bank. — 50
Clay. | Steamboat discharging.

2 — Loading wagon with grain; men mowing, etc. Title of Bank. — 2
Man plowing with two horses. | Two cherubs with sheaf, etc., soaring in the air.

ONE 1 Boy on horseback, horse, colt, sheep, cows, etc. 1
MAINE BANK, Brunswick, Me.
Men watching cattle. 1

ONE View of a street in Salem. 1
Indian and dead deer. NAUMKEAG BANK, Salem, Mass. Cars, passengers, etc.
ONE Cars. ONE

Laocoon and serpents. THOUSAND Cars and laborers. 1000
Title of Bank. Vessels.
1000 1000

TWO Santa Claus in sleigh drawn by reindeers over roofs of houses. 2 TWO
MAINE BANK, Brunswick, Me. Cattle, hogs, sheep, etc.
2

FIVE Street view in Salem. 5
Indians. Title of Bank. FIVE
Female.
FIVE Boats, men, etc. Massachu't's

Female seated pointing to reapers and load of hay. 500
D 500
500 PRESCOTT BANK, Lowell, Mass.

Farmer drinking; woman and child; load of grain; farmers mowing; cars, crossing bridge, etc. 3
THREE DOLLARS
MAINE BANK, Brunswick, Me.
3 Three on 3.

50 Man with rake; load of hay, reapers, etc. 50 L
Schooner and steamboat. Title of Bank. Female with sword and scales.

Female soaring above houses, cars, steamboat, etc; on right upper is cattle, houses, etc. State Arms. 1
STOCK SECURITY BANK, Hackensack, N. J.
Anvil. Female with dove.

FIVE MAINE BANK, 5
FIVE 5 FIVE
Franklin DOLLARS Female seated on bale with quadrant, etc., vessels, etc., in distance.
Brunswick,
FIVE State of Maine.

500 Female seated on shield on which is letter D on die; vessel in distance. Figures 500 each side of vig. 500
500 D
500 Title of Bank 500

2 Title of Bank. 2
Two females seated; cattle, sheep, factory, etc.; in distance. State Arms.
Sailor boy. 2

Male portrait Ship yard scene; city in distance. 10
MAINE BANK, Brunswick, Me.
X Male portrait

THOUSAND Female erect in circular frame with cornucopia, etc. 1000
Title of Bank. M
1000

Washington in circular frame surmounted by eagle; soldier and implements of war on right; female with pole and cap on left. State Arms. 5
5 Title of Bank. Indian warrior.

20 Female either side of anvil; building in distance. 20
Title of Bank. Sailor and farmer either side of shield on which is a deer and tree.
Washington.

Letter C. Spread eagle on bale; products, etc. 100 100
Men and boats. Female.
100 SALEM BANK, Salem, Mass. 100

1 Blacksmith shoeing horse; old man by side of horse; man at anvil. 1
ONE B'K OF NEWARK, Newark, N. Y.
Compt's die. Female portrait.

FIFTY 50 Three females seated; eagle, shield, vessel, etc. Fifty on 50.
Agricultural products. Title of Bank. Vulcan seated; cars, buildings, etc., in distance.
50

Indian paddling canoe. 500 in red across light 500. 500
Title of Bank.
500 Justice.
D D

TWO TWO TWO 2 Old man seated under tree with boy and dog; sheep in distance. 2 TWO TWO TWO
Compt's die. Title of Bank. Female with dove.
2

C Eagle on bale; products, etc. 100 100
Men and boats. Title of Bank. Female with sickle and sheaf.
100 100

20 Female seated between fig. 2 and 0. 20
ASIATIC BANK, Salem, Mass. Female.
Female. 20
XX

5 Three females and bust of Washington. 5
Title of Bank. Compt's die
Female feeding fowls. Five Dollars Five Dollars FIVE

10 BANK OF SENECA FALLS, Seneca Falls, N. Y. 10
Drovers, horses, &c.; cars on left. Blacksmith with sledge, &c., beside forge and anvil.
Compt's die. X X

Female seated pointing to reapers and load of hay. 500 D 500
Title of Bank.
500

X Female and two calves; canal scene, cars, cows, etc., in distance. 10
Title of Bank.
Clay. Compt's die

FIVE inverted.	MERCHANTS' AND	5
Sailor seated on bales; female, vessel and steamer above him.	Green tinted V and machinery.	
Green 5 and word Five.	MANUFACT'S B'K., Hartford, Conn.	Female gazing at stars.

5	Five females, fig. 5 and words "Five Dollars" blended together.	5
	BK OF ROANOKE, Salem, Va.	
Male portrait	Indian.	Treas die

Compt's die.	Title of Bank	3
	Indian princess with shield etc; steamer in back ground.	
3		Male portrait

X	MERCHANTS' 10 AND	Two females seated; owl, bust, globe, etc.; steamship, etc., on left; buildings monument, &c., on right.	10
State Arms sailor, bbls., etc.	MANUFACT'S B'K. Hartford, Conn.	Two children with fruit and butterfly

10	Title of Bank.	10
	10 on X. Indian seated viewing the progress of civilization.	
Treas. die.	Dog.	

	NORTH WESTERN BANK, OF GEORGIA, Ringgold, Geo.	10
	Male portrait on pid either side.	
Indian seated viewing progress of civilization.	10	Ten on large X; milkmaid, cow, cars, &c.

20	THE MERCHANTS'	20
Connecticut	Female either side of anvil; one on left has cornucopia of flowers; factories, etc.; in distance on right.	Hartford,
Female seated on safe with sword and scales.	AND MANUFACTUR'S BK	City Arms—deer, tree, water, &c.

XX	20 Female feeding Eagle 20	XX
Compt's die.	CAYUGA CO. BANK, Auburn, N. Y.	Justice.
20	Eagle.	20

Female soaring in clouds with sprig and dagger.	Title of Bank.	Female in clouds with flowers.
	Female with fig. 2 on left and 0 on right.	
20	Clasped hands.	20

5	BK OF ST. JOHNS, Jacksonville, Florida.	5
	Cotton plant.	
Train of cars.		Female with eagle on shield, etc.

50	STATE OF NEW YORK BANK, Kingston, N. Y.	50
	Indian reclining with dead deer.	
Washington.	Compt's die.	Cars.

	Man, woman, child, cows, chickens, fence, houses, etc. Compt's die.	100
	CROTON RIVER BK, South East, N. Y.	
100	Horse.	Letter C, female bust, sheaf, etc.

10	Hunter shooting deer crossing stream; dogs in pursuit.	10
	Title of Bank.	
Indian warrior.		Same as 5s.

ONE	Girl on branch of tree	
Female, sickle, etc.	BK OF LOWVILLE, Lowville, N. Y.	Female enclosed in large ornamental fig. 1.
ONE		

	GLOBE BANK,	Five on 5.
FIVE	Three females around globe; male at bottom.	5
	Providence, R. I.	
	Anchor on shield.	Five on 5.

Same as on right of 5s.	Steamboat "Everglade" and other sailing vessels	20
	Title of Bank.	
Female with dove.		Female with flowers.

TEN	X Boy on horse; cattle, &c.	10
	BK OF WESTFIELD, Westfield, N. Y.	
Blacksmith with sledge, beside anvil.		Compt's die

	Title of Bank.	X
TEN	Same as above fives.	10
	Anchor on shield.	X

V	BK OF COMMERCE, Fernandina, Florida.	5 on Five.
	Vig. Small view of two females on either side of shield, on which is tree and cow.	
Ship.		Male portrait

50	MOUNTHOLLY BK, Mount Holly N. J.	50
Female with flowers.	Drover on horse, boy and drove of cattle; farm house etc., in distance.	State Arms

20	Farmer seated; girl and horses on his left; boy and dog on right.	20
	BK OF AMERICA, Clarksville, Tenn.	
Male portrait	Ducks.	Female portrait.

X	Title of Bank.	10
	Same as 5s.	
Locomotive and tender.		Cotton field; vessel in distance.

ONE	MER. & MECHANICS' BANK, Troy, N. Y.	1
Compt's die	Male portrait; sailor on right; farmer on left.	Man carrying leather.

50	Spread eagle upon shield, surmounting top of globe, words America, &c., on it; flags, etc.	50
	Title of Bank.	
Male portrait	Dog.	Male portrait

XX	Title of Bank	20
	Steamer and other vessels, and 20 on red die in square frame.	
Same as vig. of 5s.		Woodman.

2	Title of Bank	2
	Three men erect; shipping, &c. in distance.	
Compt's die	TWO DOLLARS	

100	Male portrait; Indian seated, tents, etc., on the right; female seated, city, ship, steamboat, etc., on left.	C
		100
Male portrait	Title of Bank.	C

Left	Centre	Right
5 Portrait of Boy.	Two females seated; factories on right; cows, sheep, etc., on left. FARMERS' BANK OF MISSOURI, Lexington, Mo. Dog.	5 Washington.
10 Reaper girl holding sickle and bonnet.	Title of Bank. Two men conversing; one reclining on anvil; the other has his right arm around boy beside him.	10 Female portrait.
V Female kneeling with sheaf and sickle.	Male portrait — Indian hunter crouching behind rocks watching two deers. SHELBYVILLE BK, Shelbyville, Tenn. Dog.	5 Reaper with bundle of grain.
10 Male portrait	Six mules before load of cotton; negro reclining on one of them. Title of Bank. Ducks.	10 Indian seated
XX Farmer bearing bundle of grain.	Scene in a ship yard. Title of Bank. XX	20 Justice.
TEN Man on horseback.	Male portrait. — Milkmaid, pail on her left arm; cows, chickens, &c. Title of Bank.	10 Washington.
20 Male portrait	Title of Bank. Frame containing bust of Washington; male seated on right, locomotive &c; female seated on left, steamboat, &c. XX XX	20 Female portrait.
5 Portrait of Boy	Barn yard scene; negro with two horses, one drinking; woman seated on door step with infant. SOUTHERN BK OF KENTUCKY, Russellville, Ky. Female bathing.	V Girl seated.
Female seated at work on hat. XX	Title of Bank. Cattle and sheep. XX Agricultural Implements.	20 Jackson.
Female seated with sickle in right hand, left resting on portrait of girl. FIFTY	Two men conversing; one reclining on anvil; the other has his right hand round little boy at his side. Title of Bank. L L	50 Female portrait
10 Female seated.	Woman churning; child beside her running toward wagon with hay coming up in background; negro playing with child. Title of Bank Ducks.	10 Female seated holding hammer in left hand.
5 Male portrait	SOUTH WESTERN BK OF VIRGINIA. Female portrait — State Arms. — Female portrait	5 Male portrait
100 Male portrait	River scene—steamboat; three men in small boat. Title of Bank. C C	100 Justice.
X TEN X	State Arms. — Female with liberty pole and cap reclining; right arm resting on shield. BK OF JEFFERSON, Dandridge, Tenn. Dog.	10 Portrait of Boy.
10 10	Female reclining on cornucopia; vessel in distance. — Cornucopia's dis. BANK OF RONDOUT, Rondout, N. Y.	10 Male portrait
1 Female with sheaf and sickle.	MILLVILLE BANK, Millville, N. J. Scene in a glass blowing establishment. Dog.	1 Factory, &c
XX	Yoke of oxen before wagon which two men are loading with hay; two men raking hay, one sharpening his scythe. — State Arms. Title of Bank. Ducks.	20 Female portrait.
FIVE	5 IRON BANK, Morristown, N. J. V Eagle on half of the globe.	5 State Arms
2	Scene in a factory; girls working at looms. — Female portrait. Title of Bank. Ducks.	2 Mechanic.
V Jackson.	MANUFACTURERS' BANK, Macon, Geo. Females at work on cotton Looms. State Arms.	5 Justice
5 Sailor conversing with mechanic on ship.	V Two oxen drawing load of grain; man on top; man with fork upon his shoulder beside the oxen. V CORPORATION OF ALEXANDRIA.	5 Farmer with grain.
3 Portrait of Boy.	Title of Bank. Female seated with infant; child offering birds nest.	3 State Arms. 3
10 Female seated beneath tree; spade, sickle, &c., beside her; men at work in distance.	10 Shoemaker at work; female sewing. Title of Bank.	10 Female head
Two females holding bundle of grain.	Wild horses running on prairie. CORPORATION OF ALEXANDRIA.	6 Sailor leaning on capstan with quarant
5 Female portrait.	Same as ones. Title of Bank.	5 Three Black-smiths at work.
20 Negro carrying basket of cotton; two negroes at work in the background.	Shield enclosing State Arms, surmounted by eagle; sailor seated on right, steamship &c; Indian with bow seated on left. Title of Bank. Ducks.	20 Clay.
Farmer scattering grain from his right hand; man ploughing in distance. 7 on Seven.	Indian in canoe containing squaw and children. CORPORATION OF ALEXANDRIA.	7 Female seated.

Left	Centre	Right
5 Male portrait	Shield containing ship; male seated on right, &c.; female seated with rake; steamboat, river, &c., on left. BK OF CAPE FEAR, Wilmington, N. C.	5 Sailor beside anchor; shipping in background.
L	Title of Bank. Vig. in lower left corner of note—Local view on river; steamboat bridge, &c; cars in background. State Arms.	50 Washington.
5 Male portrait	EXCHANGE BANK of St. Louis, Mo. Local scene; view of iron mountain; mule team, locomotive, cars, men, trees, etc., in foreground.	5 Female portrait.
10 Male portrait	Title of Bank. Shield surmounted by eagle, containing cars &c; sailor seated on right holding fish in his right hand; farmer with spade seated on left.	10 Male portrait
100 Figs. 100 across words "One Hundred." C	Title of Bank. Vig. in large ornamental C. Hunter seated warming his hands at fire, dog on right.	100 Figs. 100 across word Dollars. C
10 Reaper girl seated; dog beside her.	Title of Bank. 10 Male portrait. 10 TEN	10 Bank building.
5 Male portrait	Two females seated; factories, &c., on right; cows sheep, &c, on left. LEWISBURGH BK, Lewisburgh, Pa. Ducks.	5 Male portrait
V	Farmer seated; girl and team of horses on left; boy and dog. boy on his back on right. V BK OF BEAVER CO., New Brighton, Pa. Dog.	5 Franklin.
20 Male portrait	Men at work in iron furnace. Girl seated at table. Title of Bank.	20 Male portrait
10 Male portrait	Title of Bank. Blacksmith with hammer; farmer with scythe; girl with rake; child with fruit. Female bathing.	10 Male portrait
Full length flying female country scene, river, steamboat, locomotive, &c; in background.	Title of Bank Two females seated representing Agriculture and Manufactures factories on right; cows &c., on left.	10
50 Male portrait	Female seated on either side of shield, enclosing ornamental L with spread eagle at top; river and steamboat on right; cars on left. Title of Bank.	50 State Arms.
ONE Portrait of Boy.	BK OF COLUMBUS, Columbus, Geo. Wagon loaded with cotton—six mules before it: another wagon drawn by oxen.	1 Female with sickle and sheaf. 1
ONE Man seated beside … quadrant, &c at his side.	BK OF THE EMPIRE STATE, Rome, Geo. Female seated with State Arms; pole and cap in her left hand. Ducks.	1 Female portrait.
Full length floating female; city and country, locomotive, river, etc., in background.	Male portrait; letter C either side. Title of Bank. 100	100 Bank building.
TWO 2	Title of Bank. Local view; river, bridge, steamboat, locomotive, trees, &c.	2 2
Washington. Sailor erect beside Mechanic seated.	Steamboat "Pennington" country in background; men in boat. Title of Bank.	2 Justice.
10 Sheep.	FAR. & DROVERS' BANK, Waynesburg, Pa. Harvesting scene; man bearing sheaf on shoulder: boy on his knees apparently unhitching team of horses.	10 Female with dove.
V 5 V	Cars passing under bridge with people, horses and carriage on it. Title of Bank. State Arms.	5 Washington.
5 Indian on cliff viewing the progress of Civilization.	Title of Bank. Female seated with infant; child offering her bird's nest; man and woman at work in field. Ducks.	5 State Arms.
20 Female portrait.	Title of Bank. Shield containing a portion of N. Y., Pa., and Va.; farmer seated on right, locomotive, etc.; female with rake seated on left.	20 Female portrait
TEN Girl seated.	Title of Bank. Female seated with infant; child offering birds nest; dog lying; man and woman at work in field. Ducks.	10 State Arms.
X Female seated.	Title of Bank. Farmer seated; girl and horses on his left; boy and dog on right. State Arms.	10 TEN
50	Scene in a rolling mill; men at work. MERCHANTS' AND MANUFACTURERS' BANK of Pittsburg, Pa. Anvil.	50 Portrait of girl.
XX Female seated resting left hand on sledge, right foot on pail.	Local view; cotton factories on river bank; six mules before wagon load of cotton. Title of Bank. Ducks.	20 Scene in a cotton field; men working man on horseback. XX
XX	Figs. 20 across female seated on either side of State Arms; train of cars. Title of Bank. Ducks.	20 Clay.
100 Scene in an iron foundry, men carrying metal, etc.	Title of Bank. Letter C.	100 Men engaged in moulding.

1 Agricultural implements and products Compt's die.	Mowing and harvesting scene; load of hay in distance. BK OF NEWPORT, Newport, N. Y.	ONE Female portrait.

1 Indian with bow and spear supporting fig. 1.	Indian reclining with dead deer. Compt's die. BANK OF THE REPUBLIC McLeansboro, Ills.	ONE Indian on cliff gazing at city beneath.

Cupid, sheaf etc. Female portrait.	10 Title of Bank. 10 X Scene at grist mill; carrying out grain; horses; boys on bridge. X 10 10	Cupid, cornucopia, etc. Male portrait.

TWO Compt's die. TWO	Milkmaid seated; farmer reclining on ground; two gold dollars; cattle on left; farm houses on right. Title of Bank.	2 Cars.

TWO Female feeding fowls.	Title of Bank 2 Compt's die. 2	TWO Farmer feeding hogs.

C Female erect beside pillar.	UNITED Eagle shield, &c. STATES ONE HUNDRED DOLLARS 100 Soldier and two Indians; Washington; goddess of liberty 100 100 100	Large C. Sailor boy.

Compt's die. Cow. Three on 3.	Farmer, sailor and mechanic; three gold dollars, &c. Title of Bank.	3 Cars passing over and cattle passing under arch

5 Compt's die.	Farmer, drover, cattle, sheep, &c. Title of Bank, 5 5	FIVE Large fig. 5 with female, Washington, eagle, &c., enclosed. FIVE

Green D across fig. 500 Howell Cobb. $500	Female on either side of anvil; buildings, &c., in distance. The UNITED STATES 500	Green D across fig. 500. Eagle, shield, ship, &c. $500

5 Clay.	Female seated either side of anvil. Title of Bank.	5 Compt's die. 5

5 Three males, two females and large V.	Compt's die. Indian family seated contemplating city, &c. CRESCENT CITY BK, New Orleans, La. A crescent.	V Five females entwined in fig. 5.

1000 Justice.	Spread eagle. UNITED STATES. M 1000 M	1000 Male portrait.

5 Compt's die. FIVE	Spread eagle. BK OF AMERICA, New Orleans, La. Half of Globe.	[illegible] Men shearing sheep.

10 Blacksmith and forge; cars on right.	Compt's die. Nine cherubs making offering to female; ten gold dollars, &c. Title of Bank. A crescent.	10 Female portrait TEN

Vessels [illegible]	Female seated with hat in lap; dog, bucket, cows, etc. Fig. 5 above word SHILLINGS either side. BANK OF PRINCE EDWARD ISLAND, Charlottetown, P.E.I.	FIVE SHILLINGS

X 10 TEN Compt's die	Spread eagle. Title of Bank, Half of Globe.	10 X Cars passing over and cattle under arch.

TWENTY Female feeding fowls.	Compt's die. 20 Negroes picking and carrying cotton. Title of Bank. A crescent.	20 Martha Washington. TWENTY

£ 0. 6. 8. STERLING	Man plowing with two horses; cars and man harrowing in distance. Fig. 10 above word SHILLINGS either side. Title of Bank. Vessel.	TEN SHILLINGS

TWENTY 20 Compt's die. TWENTY	Spread eagle. Title of Bank. Half of Globe.	TWENTY 20 Two females.

Compt's die Girl FIFTY	50 Female seated on either side of anvil; buildings on right. Title of Bank A crescent.	50 Weighing cotton. FIFTY

£. 0.13.4. stg ONE £. 0.13.4. stg	Female seated with shield, wheat, etc.; vessel, steamer, lighthouse, etc. Fig. 1 above word POUND either side. Title of Bank	ONE POUND

Cattle. 50 Compt's die.	Title of Bank, Spread eagle. Half of Globe.	Train of cars 50 Vessels on stocks

100 Compt's die. Two cherubs. 100	Drove of wild horses. Title of Bank. A crescent.	100 Female portrait. 100

TWO £1. 6. 8. STERLING TWO	£2 Farmer seated with basket of corn cradle, etc.; load of hay, etc., in distance. £2 Title of Bank. Ship.	Same as left end.

100 Compt's die. Boy and girl with grapes.	Title of Bank. Spread eagle. Half of Globe.	100 100

5 5	BK OF POTTSTOWN, Pottstown, Pa. Buchanan on left of title and female portrait on right. V Farmer and boy plowing with two horses. V	5 5

Victoria. Five Pounds £3. 6. 8. STERLING.	British Arms. Fig. 5 above word POUNDS either side. Title of Bank.	Prince Albert Five Pounds £3. 6. 8. STERLING.

1 Compt's die. Wisconsin. Indians on horseback fighting wild animals. Child's head. 1 BANK OF SPARTA, Sparta, Wis. 1 Female feeding fowls.	Compt's die. Two Indians on cliff watching deer; on right is Indians, hut, etc. Portrait of female. BANK OF NORTH AMERICA, Grand Rapids, Wis 5 FIVE 5 5 Laborers at work; one seated smoking.	Red 1. Compt's die. CATARACT BANK, View of Niagara Falls. Lockport, N. Y. Red 1. Female portrait.
Cupid and fig. 2. Man, horse, dog, pigeons, etc. Boy on horse; pony, female, ducks, trough; houses, etc., in distance. Title of Bank. 2 Compt's die. WISCONSIN	Compt's die Two men, two horses, mill, WISCONSIN wagon, chickens, etc. Title of Bank. TEN TEN 10 Female with boquet.	Red 2. Compt's die Red 2. Title of Bank. Pigs, fowls, &c. Fowls. Red 2. Male portrait
Soldiers of the Revolution. THREE 3 Man and boy plowing with two horses. Title of Bank. 3 Compt's die. WISCONSIN	20 Female on either side of shield. Child's head. Dogs pursuing deer. Child's head. Title of Bank. TWENTY 20 Compt's die. WISCONSIN	Red 5. Female beside column; steamer, &c in distance. Title of Bank. Miniature view of the tower and horse shoe falls Red 5. Compt's die. Red V.
FIVE Title of Bank. Surveyors at work, &c. Portrait of boy. 5 Compt's die WISCONSIN	5 Compt's die. 5 5 Indian seated in canoe going over rapids. 5 MOHAWK BANK, Schenectady, N. Y. FIVE Male portrait 5	Female seated, barrel, &c cars and vessel in distance. 1 Fig. 1 with six male heads in centre of it. NORTHAMPTON BK, Northampton, Mass. 1 Female with grain.
Deer. V Buffalo. Compt's die. V Female on globe in clouds with torch, eagle, portrait of Washington, etc. MECHANICS' BANK, Green Lake, Wis. 5 Female portrait.	C Men fishing. 100 Fag's on bale of goods, &c. 100 WORCESTER CO. BK. Blackstone, Mass. 100 Female with sickle and grain. 100	Words one hundred and fig, 100. Male portrait Wharf Scene. Title of Bank. Words one hundred and fig 100. Male portrait
Indian, squaw and child in canoe. 1 Compt's die. RICHLAND COUNTY BANK, Richland Centre, Wis. 1 Female with dove.	5 Female FIVE Female seated; beneath her, upon which she is gazing, train of cars, steamboat and canal boat; town in distance. CUMBERLAND CITY BANK, Cumberland, Md. Female in water. FIVE Female holding pen in hand. FIVE	Word FIVE inverted. V Rafting scene on river; steamboat, &c. etc. Compt's die. HOWARD BANK, Stiles, Wis. 5 Female with sheaf and sickle.
Compt's die. Indian and female on either side of shield; vessel, steamboat, buildings, wigwams, etc., in distance. Title of Bank. 2 Female portrait.	TEN X on 10 Female seated with torch, eagle, portrait of Washington, &c. X on 10 CHEMICAL BANK, New York City. Chemists laboratory. X Compt's die. X	X Compt's die. TEN Steamboats on river and at wharfs. Title of Bank. 10 Sailor seated with glass.
3 Blacksmith at furge. MORRIS COUNTY BK, Morristown, N. J. Female, fig. 3, eagle, shield, &c. Spread eagle. THREE Female with sheaf and sickle. 3	1 Men at work in mine. Two females seated; cows in distance. FAR. & MECHANICS' BANK, Camden, N. J. Bee-hive 1 Three blacksmiths.	FIFTY Grain, &c. 50 50 Three females seated with liberty pole and cap, eagle shield &c; ship in distance. FITCHBURG BANK, Fitchburg, Mass. Fifty on 50. Male seated with mechanical implements.
V Boy, horses, colt, cattle and sheep. Title of Bank 5 Female reclining on bales, masts of vessels in background.	Fig 5 inverted Compt's die. Man with white and black horse; cars, water scene, building, etc. MONROE CO. BANK, Sparta, Wis. Indian. Fig. 5 inverted. Female seated with pail cows, church etc., in distance.	C Sailors and boat. 100 Spread eagle, grain &c. 100 Title of Bank. 100 Female with sickle, grain. 100

1 Mechanic seated with implements; farmers in background. 1
SOUTHERN BANK of ILLINOIS, Grayville, Ills.
Road, cattle, etc. State die.

3 Sailor farmer and blacksmith; factories, vessels, etc., in distance. THREE
State Arms Steamship.
3 HUDSON CO. BANK, Jersey City, N. J. 3

Male portrait PITTSFIELD BANK, Pittsfield, Mass. 5
Two females, spinning wheel, cattle scene on left; buildings on right.
5 Female bathing 5

Female with figure 2. Indian on rock; river, steamboat, city, etc. 2
Title of Bank.
2 State die

State Arms. 5 Two females, shield, cornucopia, &c. 5
Title of Bank Washington
FIVE Beehive FIVE

Female with tridentin band; eagle, sheaf, &c. 20
Twenty on figs 20.
Franklin
20 MACHINISTS' BANK Taunton, Mass.

5 General railroad scene. 5
Title of Bank.
Female and figure 5. State die.

X, 10, two sailors, telescope, lighthouse, etc. 10 View of a large building, etc. 10
Title of Bank.
Compt's die. Female with cornucopia.

5 Negroes rolling hogshead, pigs of lead, bales, etc.; ass, man and dray on left; steamboat on right. V 5
MERCHANTS BANK, of St Louis. Mo.
5 in red. FIVE FIVE Portrait of a Boy.

Webster. Title of Bank. 10
Cattle in water; sheep on the bank of the stream.
10 State die.

50 CENTREVILLE BK., Warwick, R. I. 50
Men gathering and loading cart with corn; cult, etc.
Male portrait Male portrait

10 Title of Bank. 10 in red.
Portrait of girl. X in red. Vig. Same as fives.

X Horse with a bag across his back; two men and boy; wheel, tools, etc. 10 10
ILLINOIS CENTRAL BANK, Newton, Ills.
10 State die.

100 Title of Bank. 100
Horses in fields.
Male portrait Male portrait

20 inverted. Portrait of girl. Title of Bank. 20 in red.
TWENTY Vig. Same as 5s. DOLLARS
20 Twenty in red. 20

20 in red die. TWENTY TWENTY 20 in red die.
Horse, man, sheep, one boy on gate; one driving sheep; large tree.
State die. Title of Bank.

1 Man and woman watering horses at trough. 1
MONTGOMERY CO. BANK, Johnstown, N. Y.
Compt's die. Milkmaid, cow, calf and ducks.

Title of Bank. 50 50 in red.
FIFTY in red.
Vig. Same as fives. 50 in red. Male portrait

2 Female. 2 Female. 2
BANK OF BRATTLEBORO'. Brattleboro, Vt.
Male portrait Male portrait

2 Man and boy plowing with two horses. 2
Compt's die Title of Bank.
2 Fowls.

Male portrait Title of Bank. 100
Figs. 100 in red and words One Hundred across in black.
C in red. Vig. Same as fives. C in red.

Signing Declaration of Independence. X 10
Title of Bank.
X Cars, men, etc.

V Cattle, sheep, etc. 5
Title of Bank. Compt's die.
Clay. V

5 Indian, squaw and papoose in canoe. 5
FRONTIER BANK, Benton, Ills. Auditors' die
Two Indians on rock. 5

Blacksmith seated, sledge, anvil, etc. 10
Title of Bank.
TEN Farmer with sheaf and sickle.

X Man and three horses at well; goats, hide, sheep, houses, etc. 10
Title of Bank.
Washington. Compt's die

Wigwam, two Indians and squaw; cars, city, &c. Auditors' die.
Title of Bank.
10 Indian seated with tomahawk.

5 and V blended. Auditors' die

MERCHANTS' BANK Carmi, Ills. 5 Jackson. 5

FIVE Girl's head FIVE

---

5 Franklin. FIVE

Title of Bank. Portrait, officer, two Indians, and female with pole and cap. FIVE FIVE

5 Auditor's die FIVE

---

5 Two children with grain.

Title of Bank. Female with basket, calves; boat, cars, cows, horses on left.

V State Die.

Illinois. Auditor's die 10

Title of Bank. Steamboat; city, etc., on left; flat boat on right.

10 Female portrait. Ten on Dollars.

---

5 State Die.

Blacksmith, farmer, girl with rake, child, etc. BK OF ALBION. Albion, Ills.

5 Female portrait.

---

10 Female with dove.

Title of Bank. Public square; horses, carriages, man on horse, dog, etc.

X State Die.

---

5 Man shearing sheep.

Emigrant wagon, dog, train of cars; steamboat on right. HIGHLAND BANK, Pittafield, Pa.

5 Auditor's die

10

Farmer seated, two children, one lying down, dog, horses, &c. State Die. Title of Bank.

10 Mechanic at bench.

---

10 Milkmaid, cows, shed, &c. TEN

FARMERS BANK of Chippewa, X Conterelle, Wis Compt's die.

10 Boy beside load of grain, boy on top TEN

---

10 10

Title of Bank. Farmers gathering hay; oxen, wagon, &c.

10 Auditor's die

---

5 Plowman and horses.

OCTORARO BANK, Female with two calves, tree; canal boat, cars, etc., in distance Oxford, Pa. V V V V

V Female with rose.

---

1 Compt's die. 1

Farmer and child at lunch boy playing with dog, &c. EAST RIVER BANK, New York City.

ONE Some have portrait of girl; others Sailor at capstan on this end.

ONE ONE Auditor's die

Milkmaid and cows. CITIZENS BANK, Mt. Carmel, Ills.

One and fig 1 Female with grain.

---

10 Washington

Four females—one erect. Title of Bank. TEN TEN

X Two girls.

---

5 FIVE

Two females reclining; factory on right; sheep and cattle on left. EAST RIVER BANK New York City.

V Compt's die. V

TWO Auditor's die

Spread eagle. Title of Bank. TWO 2 TWO

2 Boy.

---

20 Dolls head.

Title of Bank. Reaper men at work in field of wheat; town in distance. TWENTY

20 Rams head.

XX Compt's die XX

20 Shield surmounted with sloop; farmer and Indian. 20 BANK OF ALBANY, Albany, N. Y. Beaver.

XX in circular die.

Female with fig. 5. Auditor's die

Female with plant; plowman on left; factories on right. Title of Bank. FIVE FIVE

V Girl shading her eyes with hand.

---

1 Clay.

1 Eagle on shield; ocean on right; town on left. NATIONAL BANK, Providence, R. I. ONE

1 Washington

---

50 in circular die.

L Same as 20s. L Title of Bank. Beaver.

50 Compt's die 50

---

10 TEN Auditor's die

Title of Bank. Female on either side of shield surmounted by eagle; steamer on left; cars on right. TEN TEN

10 TEN X

---

1 State Die.

BANK OF CARMI, Carmi, Ills. Bull, trees, houses, &c.

1 Female portrait.

---

100 in circular die.

Compt's die. Same as 20s. Title of Bank. Beaver.

C

---

1 Washington ONE

Female, monument; steamboat in distance. BK of the FEDERAL UNION, Rock Island, Ills. ONE

1 Auditor's die ONE

---

2 State Die.

Title of Bank. Cattle drinking; cattle and farm house in dis.

2 Mechanic seated; factories, &c.

---

100 Compt's die 100

100 N. Y. STATE BANK, Albany N. Y. State arms. Male head.

100

TWO TWO 2 — Female seated in fig. 2; farming scene on right and left. — 2 PEOPLES BK OF KY. Female portrait. — Boy and girl	5 BANK OF St. Louis. — Man with bag; horse, colt, mill, two boys on bridge, etc. — 5 in red. Female head 5 Missouri. — Eagle on shield. — FIVE	5 — MER & MEC. BANK of Wheeling, Va. — 5 Man and three horses at well; goats, kids, etc. 5 — Female head.
THREE THREE THREE — Female seated on plow with sheaf, sickle; cars and canal scene in distance. — 3 Female portrait. THREE — Title of Bank. — Female portrait.	X — Steamboat; city, etc., on left; flat boat on right. — 10 Title of Bank. Female head. — Male portrait.	5 — Female seated with two calves; canal and railroad scene on left. — 5 Title of Bank. Bull's head. — Female with flowers.
TEN TEN X — Female seated between 1 and 0: farming scene on right and left. — 10 Title of Bank. Female portrait. — Man plowing.	20 — Title of Bank. — 20 Man and boy plowing with two horses. Figs. 2 and 0 blended either side. Children and butterfly. — Girls' portrait.	Red TEN inverted. — Title of Bank. — TEN to right of fig. 10. Cattle and sheep on bank; cow in stream. Red TEN inverted. — Male portrait X — Jefferson. Eagle.
TWENTY TWENTY 20 — Female with eagle, pole, cap and motto "Excelsior" above. — 20 Title of Bank. Female with flowers. — 20 on red die. — Clay.	500 in center of black die, with red border. — MECHANICS' BANK. FIVE Male portrait — HUNDRED Missouri. — St. Louis.	Female, cows, sheep, ducks, etc. 10 TEN Title of Bank. X — Red TEN Red TEN — Hunter leaning on gun; deer at his feet.
5 — BULL'S HEAD BK. St. Maries, Ills. — 5 Bull's head. Portrait. — 5 5 — State die.	V — BK OF FAYETTE CO. Uniontown, Pa. — 5 Female seated with calves; canal and railroad scene on left. Clay. — Penn.	Buchanan. — MONONGAHELA VALLEY BANK, McKeesport, Pa. — 5 FIVE 5 — Female, calves, cars, canal scene, etc.
X — Ten Dollars across red 10. — 10 Title of Bank. Bull's head. State die — TEN TEN — Girl's head.	10 — Title of Bank. — X Drovers and cattle in stream; country scene in general. Jackson. — Female head.	10 — State Arms; horse either side; State House and bridge in distance. — 10 Title of Bank. Sailor, shipping, etc. — 10 — Female head.
Steamboat. — 1 LAKE SHOE BANK. Manitowoc, Wis. 1 — One Dollar One Dollar — Compt's die.	20 — Title of Bank. — 20 General reaping scene with "patent reaper;" city in distance. Washington. — Lafayette.	20 — Compt's die. Scene on wharf and at Railroad depot. — 20 BK OF THE CAPITOL Albany, N. Y. Knickerbocker. — 20 — Male with quadrant, globe, bbls, &c.
3 — Males and females on beach, witnessing yacht race. — 3 Title of Bank. Sailors on ship pulling rope. — Three Dol's Three Dol's — Compt's die	2 — Female portrait SOUTHERN BANK of KY. — 2 Female erect by column; steamer. — Husking scene; males, female, donkey, fence, hogs, house, &c. TWO	50 — Steamboat "America" towing canal boats on river. — FIFTY DOLLARS Female portrait. — Title of Bank. FIFTY — Compt's die.
V — Shipping scene; city on left. — 5 Title of Bank. Anchor, bales, masts, etc. — Five Dol's Five Dol's — Compt's die.	3 — Child's head. Vig. Same as above twos. — 3 Title of Bank. Washington — Cock. — 3	500 — Spread eagle on shield, cars, city, vessels, &c., in distance. — D WORCESTER BANK, Worcester, Mass. Med. head — D — Med. head

V | Six mules driven by negro before load of cotton, passing house on road; ox team in background on right. STATE BANK OF FLORIDA, Tallahassee, Florida | 5
City. | State Arms

2 | General reaping scene with "patent reaper". REEDSBURGH BK, Reedsburgh, Wis. | 2
Female portrait. | Compt's die

Female blowing dinner horn, table, etc. | CORN PLANTER'S BANK, Waupaca, Wis. Large red tinted 5. Compt's die. | 5
Female with pail on leore; open gate, etc

10 | Train of cars coming around curve; steamboat and train on left in distance. Title of Bank. | 10
State portrait | State Arms.

3 | Title of Bank. Two men, two horses at trough, mill, bags, wagon, chickens, etc. | 3
Farmer with sheaf and sickle, dog; houses. | Compt's die

Two men in corn field. | Title of Bank. Two men, wagon, mill, horses drinking at trough; chickens, etc. | 10
X | Compt's die.

20 | Title of Bank. Red 20. Two men gathering corn. | 20
Two Indians. | State Arms.

1 | GARDEN STATE BK, Hutsonville, Ills. General drover and cattle scene: cars and buildings on left in distance. | 1
State die. | Female with dove.

Large fig. 1. FARMERS BANK, Garden City, Minnesota. Spread eagle. | 1
Sheep | Female feeding fowls. | Man carrying corn stalks.

5 | Indians hunting buffaloes. CHISACO CO BANK, Taylors Falls, Minn. Indian seated. | V
Female seated in V. | Girls' portrait.

TWO | Man with pitcher; female and dog seated; men reaping on left in distance. Title of Bank. | 2
State Die. Female portrait | Boy and girl

Cupid and 2. | Title of Bank. Boys trying to catch runaway horse. | 2 and cupid
Two males, horse, colt, sheep, dog, etc.

10 | Title of Bank. Rafting scene on Western river. Dog. | X
Ten on X; female on left; cow, etc., on right | Youthful portrait with cap.

5 | Fig. 5 and letter V blended; on left is Indian and sailor on either side of shield on which is eagle, word FIVE and letter V; shipping scene on sailors right, and Indian scene on left of Indian. On right is eagle. Title of Bank running above and below vignette and across 5 and V. Dog's head. | 5
State die.

THREE | Portrait of female. Title of Bank. | 3
Hunter and dog. | Man loading cart; driver, dog, etc.

1 | BK of the STATE OF MINNESOTA, St. Paul, Minn. Large white fig. 1 across face of note with "One Dollar" across. | 1
Youthful figure with cap. | Female with silver dollar.

1 | Western steamboat scene. WINONA CO. BANK, Winona, Minn. | 1 ONE
Two Indians viewing progress of civilization | Female portrait.

5 | Cattle and stream of water. Title of Bank. | 5
Portrait of boy. | Girl's portrait.

Two Cupids and two silver dollars; cars, cattle, etc., in distance. Title of Bank. Clasped hands. | Female portrait. | 2
TWO | Female with roll of cloth. TWO

1 | Western Steamboat scene. Title of Bank. | 1
Two Indians viewing progress of civilization. | Female with dove.

Indians spearing buffaloes. | GOODHUE CO. BK, Cannon Falls, Minn. Beavers knawing limbs. | Red 1. Beehive.

Female portrait. | Title of Bank. Three Cupids and three silver dollars. Locomotive and tender. | 3
3 | Female with pail resting on fence; open gate.

2 | Indian head in frame with female, three children and globe on right; squaw and child on left. Title of Bank. | 2
Portrait of a boy. | Indian princess.

Red 5. | Title of Bank. Indians attacked by wild animals. | 5
Deer. | Female with tub.

Fig. 5 inverted. | Title of Bank. Indians hunting buffaloes. | Same as on left end.
Female with cornucopia of flowers | 5 Female head. 5

Female floating above steamboat, cars, building, etc.; on her upper right country scene. | Two females, spinning wheel; cattle, buildings, etc. Title of Bank. | Small fig. 3 inverted. 3

X | Title of Bank. Eagle. Covered wagon and four horses. Settlers at their devotions; Indians entering door. | Red 10.
Indian on cliff.

1 — Man with two horses; cars and houses in distance. — 1
STATE BANK OF MINNESOTA, Austin, Minn.
Female, column, steamer. — Laborers at work; one smoking; cars, etc.

---

1 — Males and females applauding train of cars. — 1
EXCHANGE BANK, Glencoe, Minn.
1 — Sailor boy, vessel, boat, men, etc.

Auditor's die — Eagle, female, and globe. — Male portrait — 1
Female portrait. — CITY BK OF CAIRO, Cairo, Ills.
ONE — Female portrait.

TWO — Two men, two horses at trough, mill, wagon, boys, chickens, etc. — 2
Title of Bank
Female with sheaf and sickle. — Deer.

---

2 — Title of Bank. — 2
Indians attacked by wild animals.
Girl's portrait. — Dog and game.

Female portrait. — Title of Bank. — 2
Cattle and sheep.
Auditor's die — Male portrait

---

5 — Milkmaid seated, cows, houses, etc. — 5
Title of Bank
City. — Girl's portrait.

---

5 — Indians spearing buffaloes. — 5
Title of Bank.
5 — Female portrait.

---

3 — Horse, cart, colt, dog and three males. — Female portrait. — 3
Title of Bank.
Auditors' die — Female portrait.

---

5 — Woodcutter in forest. — 5
BK OF OWATONNA Owatonna, Minn.
Girl with chickens. — Boy and rabbits.

BANK OF SAINT PAUL. — 1
Western steamboat scene. — Female with sheaf.
1 — St. Paul, Minn. — Beehive.

Auditor's die — Portrait of female. — Country scene; man on horseback, colt, two sheep, dog, &c. — 5
Title of Bank.
5 — Female portrait.

Title of Bank. — 10
Three females. — X TEN DOLLARS X
Secured, etc. — Youthful portrait with cap.

---

2 — Title of Bank. — 2
Man and boy plowing with two horses. — Female portrait.

PITTSBURGH,
THE MERCHANTS' & — 5
General wharf scene. — Indian head.
MANUFACTURERS BK of Pittsburgh, Pa.
5 — Sailors on ship hoisting.

---

1 — Compt's die. — Indians surprised at appearance of white men. — 1
Farmer cleaning scythe; mill, canal and railroad scene in distance.
Female seated; cow, sheaf, sickle, etc. — BK OF JEFFERSON, Jefferson, Wis.

Cupid and fig. 5. — Title of Bank — 5
Hunter shooting deer; dogs in pursuit.
5 — Indian warrior on horseback.

FIVE — Five human figures and five gold dollars. — 5 FIVE
5 — CITY BANK. Oswego, N. Y.
Compt's die. — Implements. — Female feeding eagle.

---

2 — Indians welcoming white men in boat. — Jefferson — 2
Title of Bank.
Compt's die. — Farmer carrying corn stalks.

Large portrait of female. — Title of Bank. — 10
Hunters shooting buffaloes. — Eagle
TEN — X

Man with bag on back; horse, colt, mill; two boys on bridge. — FOND du LAC, — 1
The Farmers and Mechanics' Bank, ONE DOLLAR — Compt's die
1 — ONE ONE — Wisconsin.

---

5 — V Sailors conversing; shipping, etc. — 5
FIVE — BK OF COMMERCE, Erie, Pa
Female head. — DOLLARS — 5

---

3 — THREE Female locomotive, buildings, etc. 3 — THREE
Vulcan. — RAILROAD BANK. Lowell, Mass.
3

FARMERS and MECHANICS' BK — 2
Man erect with horse; wheelwrights at work. — Portrait of Boy.
TWO — FOND du LAC, TWO — Compt's die — Wisconsin.

X — Title of Bank — 10
TEN — DOLLARS
Jackson. — X Steamship. X — Female portrait.

---

10 — BK of the COMMONWEALTH, Robinson, Ill. — TEN
Female blowing dinner horn; table, men, etc. — State Die. — Three females, sheaf, sickle, anchor, etc.

Compt's die. — 1 Human Washington figure floating in air. — 1
BANK OF GENEVA, Geneva, N. Y. ONE
Female head — Female figure holding fig 1.

5 DANVILLE BANK, Danville, Va 5 Cars. 5 Female, cow, calf, ducks, etc.	1 British Arms. View of Suspension bridge; cars, buildings, etc. 1 Victoria. Title of Bank. Prince Albert	1 Sailor steering ship. 1 Female with pen and tablets. MANUFACTURERS' BANK of Brooklyn, N. Y. Compt's die.
X Title of Bank. 10 TEN Female erect with foot on tyrant's throat. Two men, horse, a fe. buildings etc. Mal. head.	Female with sheaf and sickle. 2 British Arms—large view. 2 2 Title of Bank. Arms. TWO	Indian on cliff. Title of Bank 2 2 Mechanic with hammer, anvil, cog-wheel, etc. Compt's die.
Female erect beside column; steamer. Tobacco planter seated by side of that; men at work in field on left. 20 20 Title of Bank. Female portrait.	5 Title of Bank. 5 British Arms Drovers and cattle; house, etc. FIVE V 5	THREE Milkmaid and cows; houses in distance. 3 View of wharves vessels, etc. Title of Bank. THREE Compt's die.
50 on red die. Title of Bank. 50 on red die Female portrait. Two females, spinning wheel etc; buildings on right; cows, sheep, etc., on left. Head of Liberty surrounded by stars.	Female and Indian either side of X. BANK OF FULTON, Atlanta, Geo. 10 10 Train of cars; city, river, etc. Soldier and cannon. Male portrait	5 Title of Bank. 5 Female portrait Mechanic erect in a letter V; anvil, hammer, cog wheel, etc.; buildings, &c., in distance. Compt's die.
1 Man whittling stick beside horse. cow, sheep, boy on gate; boy in distance. 1 Machinist & implements. HOLYOKE BANK, Northampton, Mass. Buildings in background, bridge and buildings in foreground.	Drover and cattle Spread eagle. 20 XX Title of Bank. Temple. Clay.	Spread eagle; buildings, street, etc. Female portrait. 10 10 Title of Bank. Compt's die.
TWO Two females, spinning wheel; cattle scene on left; buildings on right. 2 Same as on right end of 1. Title of Bank. Dog. Female, cow, calf, ducks, etc.	50 Two females seated with view of sunrise on shield. 50 Male portrait Title of Bank. Bank building FIFTY	20 Title of Bank 20 Arm and hammer. 20 Figures 20, winged female on either side; two cupids between 2 and 0 TWENTY Compt's die.
5 V View in street; buildings, church, etc. V 5 Eagle Title of Bank. Female portrait.	100 Title of Bank. 100 Portrait of girl. Sailor, female and mechanic seated; buildings, etc., on right; shipping scene on left Letter C enclosing bust of female & sheaf. Anchor on shield.	50 Three females and winged cupid floating in water. Compt's die. 50 50 Title of Bank. Female with compass, &c.
10 X Settlers at their devotions; Indians entering door; dog. X Ten on X. Clay. Title of Bank. Male portrait	5 Man with bag of grain on his back; horse, colt, mill, etc.; two boys on bridge on left. 5 Female head. BANK OF WESTON, Weston, Va. Treas. die.	100 Cattle and stream of water. 100 Female reclining with sheaf and sickle. Title of Bank. Compt's die
1 INTERNATIONAL BANK OF CANADA, Toronto, Ca. 1 Victoria. View of tower and horse shoe falls. British Arms. Prince Albert	Two Indians on cliff watching deer; Indians and huts on right. Treas. die 10 10 Title of Bank. Female head.	Red end with white 2 2 FAR. and MER. BK, Middletown Pt, N. J. 2 Red end with white 2 Anchor, bales, &c. Two dollars on large ornamental die. Eagle and Shield Female with flowers.

ONE Three females floating in water supporting cupid. SAFETY FUND BK, Boston, Mass. 1 State Arms.	ONE 1 Columbus. 1 BANK OF THE METROPOLIS, Boston, Mass. State Arms. ONE	1 Vessels. Ship yard scene—men at work, etc. BLACKSTONE BANK Boston, Mass. 1 Mechanic with sledge.
2 Female erect beside pedestal; steamer in distance. Scene in the Arctic Regions; men shoving boat; dog, icebergs, etc. Title of Bank, 2 State Arms.	2 State Arms. Head of Franklin. Title of Bank. TWO TWO TWO	Two inverted. Sailor with female, vessels, etc., above him. TWO Title of Bank. 2 Boy and rabbits.
THREE on 3. Scene in Printing office, Faust, Guttenburg and Schoeffer. Title of Bank. Eagle 3 State Arms 3	THREE State Arms. View of the State House, in Boston. Title of Bank 3 THREE	Washington. 3 Shoemakers at work; female attending to household duties in background. Title of Bank. 3 Female, fig. 3
State Arms. 5 Title of Bank Apotheosis of Washington; soldier on left; female and two Indians on right. Red V each side. 5 Dog, key and safe.	FIVE Title of Bank. Signing the Declaration of Independence. 5 State Arms.	5 Female with flowers. Title of Bank. Large public building 5 Cooper at work on bbls
10 Franklin at work at printing case State Arms Two females, owl, buildings, steamer, etc. Title of Bank. Eagle. 10 Sailor with anchor.	TEN Large public building, horses, carriages, pedestrians, &c. Title of Bank. 10 State arms.	X Washington. Title of Bank. State Arms, or Indian and lone star. 10 Female with Ten on shield
50 Boy and rabbits. Female seated by side of shield on which is view of city, vessel on stocks, etc.; 50 and Indian in canoe on right; steamboat on left. Title of Bank. 50 State Arms	Red 20. TWENTY XX Title of Bank. State Arms. Red 20. TWENTY XX	20 Female with dove. Eagle, building and steamer. Title of Bank. 20 Cars.
XX Indian princess. Two females, anvil, building, etc. NAUMKEAG BANK, Salem, Mass. 20 Squaw.	Red 50. State Arms. Title of Bank. Three sailors, one looking through telescope. Red 50. Eagle.	50 Sailor, steamer, &c General railroad scene at depot. Title of Bank. 50 Female portrait
FIFTY Sailor with female, vessels, etc., above him. FIFTY Title of Bank. 50 Indian female; rainbow, falls, etc.	Red C. State Arms. Title of Bank. Anchor, bales, barrels, masts, etc. Red 100. Girls' portrait.	C Female portrait. Female seated by side of shield, safe etc.; steamer on right; cars and steam boat on left. Title of Bank. 100
100 Arm with scimeter. State Arms. Title of Bank. Indian, squaw, boy and papoose on cliff viewing city, etc. 100 Load of grain.	Red 500 Horse Eagle Title of Bank. Ocean scene; vessels, etc. Red 500. State Arms.	500 Ocean scene. D Title of Bank. 500 Franklin.

ONE State of N.Y. Compt's die. Hunters killing buffaloes. J. N. HUNGERFORD'S BANK, Corning, N. Y. ONE Webster.	10 Med. head of Washington. Man with bag, horse, colt, mill, etc.; boys on bridge. BK OF CHAMBERSBURG, Chambersburg, Pa. 10 Printer at his stand.	Red 2. State Arms. State House, seperating the words "State Bank," and small female head on right Red 2. Farmer gathering corn
2 Compt's die. TWO Man and boy plowing with two horses. Title of Bank. 2 Child's head.	20 Two children and butterfly Three Indians reclining, city etc. OXFORD BANK, Oxford, Mass. 20 American shield.	Female portrait Red 5. State House. - State Arms. Title of Bank. Red 5. Female feeding fowls.
Compt's die. 3 Dogs pursuing deer. Title of Bank. 3 Girl's head.	1 Compt's die. Wisconsin. SAUK CITY BANK, Sauk City, Wis. ONE DOLLAR 1 Female reclining with shield, pole cap, eagle &	5 Train of cars. Sea god and goddess in chariot drawn by sea horses and attended by followers. NORTH KINGSTON BANK, Wickford, R. I. State Arms. 5 Cattle.
Five inverted Sailor seated with female, ships, etc. before him. Rafting scene on river; steam boat, etc. Title of Bank. 5 Compt's die. Cogwheels, bale, etc.	2 Portrait of girl. Wisconsin. Title of Bank. Compt's die. Man on load of hay in front of building, man in window; horse, colt, shop, etc. Dog's head. 2 TWO	10 Female with scales, eagle, etc. 10 X Female seated by shield on which is eagle, etc. 10 Title of Bank. Head of lion. TEN Ten coins lapped. TEN
10 X on TEN. 10 STATE BANK of Ohio. Three men—smith, student, farmer; tools, etc. TEN 10 Male portrait	20 XX BROADWAY BANK, Boston, Mass. Machinery, locomotive, etc. 20 Anchor, bales, barrels, etc.	50 Pelican and its young 50 Indian; eagle on shield; male figure on right. Female with wand etc., on either side of vignette. Title of Bank. Steamboat. 50 Pelican and its young. 50
1 Compt's die. Steam mill, carts, boat, etc. H. J. MINER & Co's BANK, Dunkirk, N. Y. 1 Female with flowers.	500 Machinery, locomotive, etc. Title of Bank. Female and swan. 500	100 Female with torch, eagle, Washington, etc. 100 100 Washington. 100 Title of Bank. Eagle. 100 Vessels. 100
2 Compt's die. 2 Locomotive and depot. Title of Bank. 2 Girl.	100 Female with rake, etc. C Med. head. Female reclining on bale with spear; steamboat in distance. Med. head BK OF LOUISVILLE KENTUCKY. C Female with rake, &c.	Washington. Mules before loaded wagon of bales. EASTERN BANK, Eufaula, Ala. 5 Men weighing cotton.
V Woman with wheat. Steamboats and vessels. Title of Bank. 5 Compt's die. Secured, etc.	XX Female portrait. XX Female on rock, cupids and dolphin sporting in water. SUFFOLK BANK, Boston, Mass. TWENTY TWENTY 20 Dog's head. XX	10 Negro picking cotton. Negro loading wagon with bales; mules, cars, steam boat, etc. Title of Bank. 10 Female with dove.
TEN Mechanic with sledge. River and wharf scene—barge and steamboat with tow. Title of Bank. 10 Secured, etc. Compt's die.	Red 1. Cattle, load of hay. STATE BANK, Montpelier, Vt. State House. Red 1. State Arms	20 Female seated with sword and scales. General railroad scene at depot. Title of Bank. 20 Eagle on shield.

ONE — View of Fulton Ferry, City Railroad Station, etc.; New York in distance. — ONE

NASSAU BANK, of Brooklyn, N. Y.

Compt's die — Boy and rabbits.

X — 10 Surveyors at work. — 10

Female — Title of Bank.

TEN — Female feeding fowls.

---

3 — Frame holding map of State of Ohio, with cupids on right. — 3

Title of Bank.

Male portrait — Two children and butterfly

---

2 — Two Cupids and two silver dollars; cattle, locomotive, etc.; in distance. — 2

Compt's die. — Title of Bank.

TWO — Female portrait

---

1 — Carpenter at bench. ESSEX CO. BANK, Newark, N. J. — 1

Boy's head. — Girls' portrait

---

5 — Map of Ohio, with three females and eagle on right; Indian squaw and white man on left. — 5

Agricultural implements and products

Title of Bank.

Female portrait. — FIVE

Compt's die. — Lanuching the Adriatic. — 3

Title of Bank.

3 — Franklin

---

2 — 2 Farmers at rest, one seated, one leaning against fence. 2 — 2

Title of Bank

Girls portrait — Fowls.

---

10 — Battle scene; white man, Indians, etc. — 10

Title of Bank. — Map of Ohio.

Two girls with grain. — TEN

V — Sailor reclining on beach; steamer and vessels in distance. — 5

Title of Bank.

Female — Compt's die

THREE 3 — Title of Bank. — THREE 3

Mechanic, tradesman and sailor.

Anchor, bales, &c. — Girls' head

---

20 — Male portrait — Female seated between 2 and 0. — 20

Arms. — Title of Bank. — Male portrait

20 — Man on plow. — 20

THE STATE BANK OF MICHIGAN.

These notes are printed on what is known as "Lyman's Protection" which consists in grading the portion of the bill covered by the note proper according to the denomination of the bill, thus:—

1s, one third the length of the paper.
2s, one-half the " " "
3s, two-thirds the " " "
5s, three fourths " " "

and are also done in colors.

---

10 — Spread eagle — 10

Title of Bank.

Girl's portrait. — Compt's die.

V on 5 — Title of Bank, — 5

Men in boiler shop.

Two children — Man dressing leather.

---

20 — Title of Bank. — 20

Three females seated with compass, sickle, etc.

Steamboat; Governor's Island indistance. — Ship.

Compt's die.

---

10 — Title of Bank. — 10

Head of sailor. — Four females—one reading.

TEN — Blacksmith.

---

1 — Title of Bank. — 1 Detroit 1 on ONE

State Bank of Michigan.

Eagle on shield: deer either side; steamboat on right; cars on left.

Two children and butterfly — One Dollar.

---

50 — Title of Bank. — 50

Female reclining with shield, flag, etc.; ship in distance.

Washington. — Compt's die. — Female seated and figure 50.

L — Three female figures—liberty, protection, etc. — 50

Title of Bank.

Clay. — Milkmaid and cows.

Red 2. — Title of Bank. — 2

Indians spearing buffaloes.

Spread eagle; steamer, building, etc.; in distance. — Compt's die. — 100

Title of Bank.

100 — Sailor and capstan.

C — Title of Bank. — 100

Four female figures representing the Union.

Sailor. — Webster.

Title of Bank. — 3

Female portrait. — Large white 3.

White word Three. — Man carrying corn stalks.

Cupid and ornamental work — 5 Man and boy plowing with two horses. — 5

BK of LAWRENCE COUNTY, Newcastle, Pa.

Mechanic with sledge. — Girl's portrait.

---

1 — Map of Ohio, Indian seated on left, female on right; wigwams, building, cars, etc., in distance. — 1

BK OF DELAWARE, Delaware, Ohio.

Figure of Justice. — Male portrait

---

5 on red die. — Steamboat 5 — 5

Title of Bank

5 — Anchor, bales, barrels, etc.

Female with pen, tablets, etc. 1
BK of ORANGE CO.,
Chelsea, Vt.
Old man with gun; female loading gun at his back.
ONE 1 Female with pole, cap, &c ONE

TWENTY
XX State Arms.
HONESDALE BANK,
Honesdale, Pa.
20 Male portrait

1 Female portrait.
TRENTON BANKING COMPANY
Trenton, N. J.
Milkmaid erect; boy pointing.
1 Female portrait

2 TWO Cupid.
Eagle.
Title of Bank.
Apotheosis of Washington; soldier on left; female and two Indians on right. Fig. 2 on right of vig.
2 Female, cow, calf, fowls, etc.

FIFTY inverted. FIFTY
Mining scene. Title of Bank.
50 Male portrait

2 Female portrait.
Title of Bank.
Female seated with agricultural implements and products.
2 Scott.

Female portrait. THREE
Title of Bank.
Man and boy plowing with two horses.
3 Agricultural implements and products

100 Mining scene
C Indian seated with left arm resting on shield.
Title of Bank.
100 Male portrait

3 Beehive
Title of Bank.
Female seated with sheaf and sickle.
3 Child's head

Title of Bank. 5
Portrait of boy.
Man with bag, horse, colt, mill etc.; boys on bridge.
5 Female feeding fowls.

1 1
WOOD CO. BANK,
Grand Rapids, Wis.
Compt's die.
Woodcutters in forest at work.
1 Female feeding fowls

5 Boy and girl.
Horse, colt, man with bag on back, mill, wheel, boys on bridge, etc.
Title of Bank.
5 Male head

10 Man, horse, dog, pigeons, etc.
Title of Bank.
Scene in the Arctic Regions; men shoving boat; dog, icebergs, etc.
10 Blacksmith at forge.

2 Compt's die.
Title of Bank.
Raft scene on Western river.
Beehive.
2 Portrait with frilled cap on head.

X Female portrait.
Title of Bank.
Female seated with right arm on rock; factories and man plowing in distance.
10 Children and butterfly,

20 Bull.
Title of Bank.
Large portrait of Washington; cupid either side at bottom
20 Two females one milking cows, etc.

Male portrait 5
Drover on horseback, drove of sheep, dog, mill, etc.
UNION CO. BANK,
Jonesboro, Ills.
5 Auditor's die

XX Female portrait.
Title of Bank.
Female erect reading, two others seated listening.
20 Female portrait.

50 Female, column, steamer, etc.
Title of Bank.
Male, female, horses at trough, etc.
50 Male, female, child, etc.

10 Auditor's die
Oxen before load of hay; men loading hay, etc.
Title of Bank.
10 Male portrait

50 Squaw.
Girl's portrait.
Title of Bank.
50 Female with jars and tablets.

C 100
Title of Bank.
Man and woman either side of shield; girl, dog, oxen, etc.
100 Indian on horse.

5 Male portrait
Female either side of shield on which is ship; building, factories, cars, etc., in background. Red V below.
PHILADELPHIA BK,
Philadelphia, Pa.
5 Male portrait

100 Cattle, telegraph, railroad, etc.
Female seated pointing with right hand to ship.
Title of Bank.
100 Portrait of girl.

III 3
Western steamboat, cars, locomotive, etc.
BANK of FAYETTEVILLE,
Fayetteville, N. C.
3 Male portrait

10 Male portrait
Vig. Same as 5s.
Title of Bank.
Red X.
10 Clay.

Compt's die. Male portrait
Cattle and sheep.
BK of PORT JERVIS,
Port Jervis, N. Y.
3 Sailor.

Left end	Centre	Right end
10 Compt's die.	Two females reclining; spining wheel, sickle, etc.; cattle and factories in distance. BK of PORT JERVIS, Port Jervis, N. Y.	10 Penn.
5 Large fig. 5, two Indians, water fall, etc	Steamboat, "Charleston & Cincinnati Packet;" other steamboats at wharves. MANUFACTURERS' BANK of Kanawha, Va. Eagle.	5 Female with foot on tyrant's neck.
5 Male portrait Five on 5.	PEOPLES' BANK, Baltimore, Md. Train of cars; canal scene, city, and general view of country in background.	5 Cupid with cornucopia. FIVE on 5.
20 Female kneeling with sheaf and sickle.	Compt's die. Eagle on globe; shield, clouds and flags. Title of Bank.	20; old issues has XX.
10 inverted. Female with roll of cloth.	Title of Bank. Train of cars; building in background on right. Dog.	10 inverted. Same as above 5s.
10	Vessels at sea. Female portrait. Title of Bank. Eagle.	10 TEN on large X; milkmaid, cow, etc.
Female with sickle and dog.	50 Interior of blacksmith, shop; four men and boy. Title of Bank. 50 Compt's die 50	50 Female portrait
2 Milkmaid going through gate.	General view of stores, canal scene, horse, cart, bbls., cars, etc. BANK of HORICON, Horicon, Wis. Eagle	2 Compt's die. TWO
20 Female seated with spear and shield.	Cattle; horse looking over fence. Title of Bank. Man and sheaf	20 Blacksmith beside anvil.
5 Agricultural implements and products	Male portrait. Scene in a rolling mill; two men at work, etc. IRON CITY BANK, Pittsburgh, Pa.	5
3 Female portrait.	Corn husking scene—males, females, etc. Title of Bank. Dog.	3 Compt's die. THREE
50 Mechanic holding a lifter.	Sailor, female and blacksmith seated; city, bridge, vessels, etc., in distance. Title of Bank. Schooner	50 Washington.
10 Female portrait.	View of Banking House. 10 Title of Bank.	Pennsylv'a Smith at forge. TEN
ONE Two men, two females, factories, city, etc.	KANKAKER BANK. Kankakee City, Ills. Auditor's die.	1 Male, two females, oxen, dog, etc.
100 Franklin. 100 on Dollars	Male and female at well; barn, load of hay, etc. Title of Bank.	Eagle in clouds. 100 100 on Dollars
Male portrait 20	Title of Bank. Wharf scene, railroad depot, steamboats, vessels, cars, men, horses, carts, etc.	20 Portrait of girl.
2 Farmer with fork, rake, etc.	Title of Bank. Auditor's die Train of cars; load of hay, cows, etc.	TWO Females preparing dinner; fowls, etc.
Red and white V across. V Male portrait.	Steamboat; others to left. ILLINOIS STATE SECURITY BANK, Equality, Ills.	5 Aud. die. Red and white V across.
50	Launch of the Adriatic. Female portrait. Title of Bank.	50 Fowls.
Female FIVE	LANCASTER BANK, Lancaster, Ills. Three cupids forming a fig. 5; sheep, vessels, etc.	5 Auditors' die
Red end, white X across. 10 Aud. die.	Female seated with cupid either side. Title of Bank.	10 Male portrait. Red end, white X across.
100 C	Half length figures of the inventors of printing; press, &c. Male portrait Title of Bank. One Hundred in red.	100 Male portrait
10	Title of Bank. Horse either side of shield on which is eagle, plow, vessel, etc., building, cars, etc., in distance.	10 Auditor's die
ONE Two females. ONE	Steamer and other vessels. ATLANTIC BANK, Providence, R. I. Girls' head.	1 Eagle on rock in ocean. ONE
One Hundred across 100. Male portrait	Wharf scene—men, horses, wagons, carts, etc GLOBE BANK, Providence, R. I.	Same as on left end.
20 Male portrait	Compt's die. Men loading hay; oxen, etc. HUNGERFORDS' BK, Adams, N. Y.	TWENTY Full length figure in Roman costume TWENTY
2 TWO Cupid.	Title of Bank. Female and State Arms; vessels, cars, etc., in distance. Girls' head.	2 TWO Cupid.

Male portrait (Have Lyman's Protection.) 1 1 ONE 1 Title across large fig. 1. MERCHANTS' BANK N. Y. City, Compt's die	TWO WAUKESHA COUNTY BANK, Waukesha, Wis. TWO Compt's die. TWO Corn husking scene—two males, two females, dog, fowls, etc. Female head	Small 5 inverted. 5 Female portrait; on left is Fame with trumpet; on right, Cupid. 5 Female seated, spade, sickle, house etc. BELOIT SAVINGS' BANK, Beloit, Wis. Compt's die.
Male portrait 2 2 Compt's die with word Two above and below and fig. 2 on right. 2 Title across large 2.	1 KOSHKONING BK., Fort Atkinson, Wis. 1 Indian, squaw and papoose in canoe. Compt's die. Female portrait.	10 Two females seated, spinning-wheel; cattle buildings, etc., in distance. 10 Compt's die. Title of Bank. Man on horseback. TEN
Compt's die. Title of Bank. Child's head 3 3	2 Indians on cliff watching deer; Indian scene on right. Female head. 2 Title of Bank Compt's die. Eagle on shield.	Female portrait. Cars. BK. OF GREEN BAY, Green Bay, Wis. 1 Man seated at lunch, two horses, plow, etc. Compt's die. Female portrait
V Child's portrait MERCHANT'S BANK, 5 5 Compt's die.	2 PORTAGE CO, BANK, Jordan, Wis. 2 Compt's die. 2 TWO Scene in Arctic regions—men shoving boat; icebergs, dogs, etc. TWO 2 2	2 Corn gathering scene. Title of Bank. 2 Female beside shield, on which is anchor and word "Forward;" vessels in distance. Compt's die.
5 BANK of THE COMWEALTH, Robertson, Ills. 5 Males, females gathering, press; Indians, etc. Auditors die Loaded team two men, road scene. Team loading.	THREE Title of Bank 3 Arm and hammer. 3 THREE Compt's die.	Youthful portrait with cap. HADLEY FALLS BK., Holyoke, Mass. 1 Hunter killing buffaloes. 1 Dog. Female portrait
Auditor's die Female in clouds with eagle on globe. Male portrait. 1 Portrait of girl. ONE CITY BK OF CAIRO, Illinois. Portrait of girl.	2 Female portrait; on right is Indians viewing progress of civilization; on left is female, calves, ducks, etc. 2 Dog and game. BANK OF ALBANY, Albany, Wis. Compt's die.	Male portrait Title of Bank, 5 Steamship at sea. 5 Indian boy's head. Female portrait.
Female head Cattle, sheep, water. 2 Title of Bank. Auditor's die Male portrait	Cupid and small fig. 3. Title of Bank. Cupid and small fig. 3. 3 Female with 3 dove. 3 3 Compt's die. Squaw and child.	5 Title of Bank. 5 Man on horse, colt, dog, sheep; man on fence. Female beside column; steamer, etc. Boys' portrait.
3 Corn gathering scene. Female portrait. 3 Title of Bank. Auditor's die Female head	5 BANK OF PHŒNIXVILLE, Phœnixville, Pa. 5 Cars. Washington at Valley Forge. Eagle Male portrait Female feeding fowls. Phoenix.	5 Title of Bank. 5 Corn husking scene—males and females in barn. Boy and girl. Female bathing. Male portrait
Auditor's die Female portrait. Man on horse, boy on fence, dog, colt, sheep, etc. 5 5 Title of Bank. Female head	X Man holding horse, sack on back; wheelwrights repairing cart. 10 Clay. Title of Bank TEN inverted Phoenix. Cars.	TWENTY Vig. rural scene, cows and sheep. 20 XX MERCHANTS' BK., Newburyport, Mass. Female erect with sword and scales. Female with sheaf of wheat.

Left end	Centre	Right end
5 Male portrait	BURLINGTON CO. BK Medford, N. J. Drover and farmer bargaining for bull; negro, boy, dog, horse, sheep, barn, etc.	5 Male portrait
ONE	Farm scene—man leaning on gate, woman milking; farm house in distance. Male portrait STATE BANK of IOWA.	1 Man carrying gun.
Red 1. Compt's die.	Man and boy plowing with two horses. Female portrait. STISSING BANK, Pine Plains, N. Y.	Red 1. Indian with gun.
10 Male portrait	Title of Bank. Female, calves, canal scene, cars, etc.	10 Male portrait
2 Military scene—officer, men with implements.	Drovers, cattle, sheep, and hogs. Title of Bank.	2 Boy's head.
2 Compt's die. TWO	Title of Bank. Portrait of boy. Males, horse, colt, cart, etc., in corn field.	Red 2. Indian erect
Large ornamental fig. 1.	NICOLLET CO. BK, Saint Peter, Minn. Raft scene. Gold Dollar.	1 Indian head
3 Female THREE	Husking scene. Title of Bank.	3 Deer crossing stream.
Red 5. Female seated in fig. 5.	Girl's portrait. Man with bag, horse, colt, mill etc.; boy on bridge. Title of Bank.	Red 5. Compt's die FIVE
TWO Female clasping fig. 2.	Title of Bank. Corn husking scene—males, females, etc. Clasped hands.	2 Indian on cliff with gun.
5	Title of Bank. Emigrant train.	5 Portrait of Antoine Le Claire.
Red X. Two females either side of X with cupid either side.	Cow and calf in stream; sheep, house, etc., in distance. Title of Bank. TEN	10 Compt's die.
3 Indian on horse.	Title of Bank. Red die with word THREE in white, and word DOLLARS in black across. Girl's head.	3 Squaw with fish.
10 Cars crossing bridge.	Map of Iowa with steamer "Iowa," farming implements, etc., on left, and female, factory, etc., on right. Title of Bank. Building.	10 Male portrait
20, XX and Twenty.	Two winged females, 20 and two cupids. Girls' figures portraits. Title of Bank. TWENTY Compt's die. DOLLARS	Red 20. Fowls.
5 Washington.	Title of Bank. Woodcutters in forest at work. Dog's head.	5 Female seated within a V
5 Clay.	BK OF ROCHESTER, Rochester, Minn. Five females and fig. 5. Indian.	5 Eagle in clouds above ocean.
FIFTY Grain, fruit, &c. 50	50 Three female fig's, ship, eagle, etc. SALEM BANK, Salem, Mass.	Fifty on 50. Vulcan seated with implements.
Farmer with basket of corn. FIVE	Ship yard scene—vessels on stocks. LAKE MICHIGAN BANK, Harrisburg, Ills.	5 Auditor's die
10 Indian fishing.	Title of Bank. Male portrait	10 TEN on large X; milkmaid, cow, etc.
4 Two females. 4	Male portrait Female with grain, plow, etc. BANK of WADESBOROUGH, Wadesborough, N. C.	4 Female erect FOUR
10 TEN on large X; milkmaid, cow, etc.	Scene on Lake—vessels, lighthouse, men in boat, etc. Title of Bank.	10 Auditor's die
5 Farmer sharpening scythe.	WESTERN BANK, Philadelphia, Pa. Large V.	5 Mason at work on wall
Female with open book.	V BK of INDEMNITY, Gallatia, Ills. Man on rock with gun; female loading gun.	5 Auditor's die
XX 20	Female portrait; female beside column, steamer, etc., on right; female in shell, vessels, etc., on left. MERCHANTS' BANK Nashville, Tenn.	XX 20
10 Indian warrior on horseback.	Title of Bank. Large X.	TEN Female erect with shield on which is med. head.
TEN Sailor, mechanic, farmer, ocean, capstan, etc.	Female with pole, cap and eagle in clouds. Title of Bank. Boy on white horse drinking; black pony; house, etc.	10 Auditor's die

500 Indian paddling a canoe. 500 LAIGHTON BANK, Lynn, Mass. 500 Justice.	Female portrait 10 BUNKER HILL BK., Charlestown, Mass. U. S. Capitol. 10 Female seated in a shell	1000 1000 Female head. Title of Bank. Red M. Female seated with shield, starry drapery, pole and cap across her lap; building in distance. 1000 Female holding glass; ship, water, etc.
1 Box, bale, anchor, ship, etc. 1 1 Female seated, bales, box, barrels, vessels, etc. 1 FALMOUTH BANK, Falmouth, Mass. 1 Agricultural implements, etc. 1	50 Female head Title of Bank. Man with gun; female loading gun. 50 Adams.	Auditor's die ONE Cattle; cars passing over arch. Female seated by safe, shield, etc.; on left men, locomotive, shipping, etc, on right females and cows. KANE COUNTY BK., Geneva, Ill. 1 Male portrait.
2 Man on horse. 2 2 Female seated with fig. 2. 2 Title of Bank. 2 Man on horse. 2	C Boy's portrait. Angel blowing trumpet; eagle, globe, flags, etc. Title of Bank. C 100 Indian on shield.	2 Girls with sheafs. Auditors' die. Milkmaid, cows, dog, pail, etc. Title of Bank. 2 Men washing sheep.
3 Child's head. 3 3 Female and fig. 3 on shield. 3 Title of Bank. 3 Child's head. 3	5 FIVE UNION Eagle. BANK. Female, column, steamer, buildings, etc. Red V. Female head. Philadelphia, Pa. 5 FIVE	Auditors' die Justice. Agricultural scene—man seated—others cradling and loading wagon; farm-house, steamboat and vessel in distance. Title of Bank. 3 Female, churn; cow and barn in distance.
50 Female portrait. 50 Bullock between man with axe, and hunter with gun. Title of Bank. 50 Portrait.	Cupid with sheaf. X Title of Bank. Female in clouds with shield, pole, cap, eagle, etc. Sailors hoisting. TEN. 10 Girl's portrait.	Auditors' die FIVE Washington. Drover, cattle and sheep. Title of Bank. 5 Liberty with fig. 5.
1 BUNKER HILL BK., Charlestown, Mass. Signing Declaration of Independence. Eagle. 1 Milkmaid, cow and calf.	20 Sailor and farmer each side of shield on which is deer and tree UNION Washington. BK., TWENTY. 20 S. C. arms, Cupid, female, soldier, etc.	5 Red tinted V and 5 blended with sailor seated with glass, bales, bbls, etc.; ship in distance on left, and female with cog-wheel, bale, etc. on right, and Mer. and Mech. Bank above and below either vignette. Dog's head. 5 Girl's portrait.
Sailor and Indian either side of a red 2 on red shield surmounted by eagle. 2 Female, column, steamer, etc Title of Bank. 2 Girl's portrait.	50 Female with sledge hammer; factories, etc. Calhoun. Title. Webster. Female and Mercury; ships on right; canal and railroad scene on left. 50 Sailor boy; two sailors and man-of-war in distance.	Red 10. Sailor with quadrant; vessels. MERCHANTS' AND MECHANICS' BK., Wheeling, Va. TEN on red X. Washington. TEN on red X. Red 10. Wheelwright at work.
3 3 Title of Bank. Launch of the Adriatic. 3 Eagle and shield.	100 UNION One Hundred Med. head of Franklin. HUNDRED. Med. head of Washington. Penn's treaty with the Indians. 100 BANK. One Hundred	5 Female, bale, bbls.; factories, vessels, etc., in distance. NORTH-WESTERN BANK of Virginia. Youthful portrait with cap. 5 Mechanic seated, wheel, hammer, etc.; two farmers, house, etc., in distance.
V Female portrait. Landing of William Penn; whites and Indians. Title of Bank. 5 Fowls.	500 Title. 500. Mechanic and boy repairing cart; farmer, horse, etc. Child's head. Red 500. Red D. Goddess of Liberty.	X Female portrait. 10 Title of Bank. Scene in blacksmith's shop. 10 Female with dove 10

1 | R. M. GODDARD & CO.'S BANK, Canton, N. Y. | 1
Compt's die. | Cattle on bank and in stream; buildings in distance. | 1

Twenty in-verted. Man with sheaf. 20 | Title of Bank. Spread eagle; town, etc., in distance. | 20 Female head

20 State Arms. | Title of Bank. Sailor and farmer either side of shield. | 20 Jefferson.

2 Compt's die 2 | Figure of little girl. Title of Bank | 2 Milkmaid, cow, calf, etc.

50 Med. head. 50 | Goddess of Liberty reclining against U. S. Arms; Indian on right; two females on left. Title of Bank. | 50 Man with corn, basket, etc.

50 Madison. | Title of Bank. L Negro woman holding child. L | 50 State Arms.

5 Milkmaid seated with pail; cows, church, etc. | Cow and calf in stream; cattle and house in distance. Title of Bank. | 5 V

100 Blacksmith and anvil. | Title of Bank. C Horses at trough; railroad and canal scene; steamboat, etc. | 100

100 Male portrait | Title of Bank. Female seated with sickle and sheaf. | 100 State Arms

THREE 3 Wm. Penn. | Boys attempting to catch horse; dog, etc. UNION BANK, Concord, N. H. | 3 Blacksmith and implements.

1 State Arms. | COMMERCIAL BK., Salem, Mass. Hunter killing buffalo. | 1 Male portrait

Males, females, anvil, etc. 3 | Building. 3 ALBANY CITY BK., Albany, N. Y. | 3 Compt's die. 3

20 Farmer, horse, dog, pigeons, etc. | Scene in blacksmith's shop; old man and boy hammering. Title of Bank. | 20 Milkmaid, cow and calf.

2 Two Indians, city, etc | Female with cloth pointing to mills and road scene on right; on left village and falls. Title of Bank. Eagle. | 2 Female with spy glass; [illegible]

ONE HUNDRED. | Males, females, anvil, etc. 100 Building. Title of Bank. | 100 C

50 Female seated with sheaf and sickle. | Title of Bank. Cattle, sheep, stream, etc. | 50 Webster.

3 | Two horses before load of hay, man on one, woman and child on top; boy, girl, dog, blacksmith and shop. Title of Bank. | 3 Portrait of officer.

5 ILLINOIS Auditors' die | STATE BANK, New Haven, Ills. Female, eagle, flag, globe, etc. | 5 Boys attempting to catch horse; dog; buildings, horse, cart, etc., in distance.

C Man and boy mending carts. | Title of Bank. Female in clouds with eagle, pole, cap, shield, etc., 100 on left. | 100 Female portrait.

5 Male head. | Two sailors and nautical instruments; vessels, steamer, etc. Title of Bank. | 5 Female with globe, tablets, etc.

10 Farmer whetting cradle in field. | Train of cars; cow and calf and harvest scene. Title of Bank. | 1[illegible] Auditors' die

5 Clay. | LEBANON VALLEY BANK, Lebanon, Pa. Female erect; cow, sheep, etc. Beehive. | 5 Female seated with pole and cap.

5 Washington. | BANK OF THE COMMONWEALTH, Richmond, Va. Two men; hhds. of tobacco, etc. | 5 State Arms.

5 Compt's die. 5 | Female seated on plow holding sheaf and sickle. 5 BANK OF GENEVA, Geneva, N. Y. | Female holding sheaf. 5

TEN Justice. | Title of Bank. Three military men; one on horseback; flag in distance. | 10 Eagle.

10 Male portrait | Title of Bank. Head on shield surmounted by vessel; farmer on left; hunter, dog, etc., on right. | 10 State Arms.

20 Compt's die. TWENTY | Drover on horseback; drove of cattle and sheep. ILION BANK, Ilion, N. Y. | 20 Female with rake; female in distance.

ONE 1 Eagle on limb of tree. 1 — Female with sickle and grain. — LYONS BANK, Lyons, N. Y. — Female erect in large fig. — ONE

1 ONE 1 — CALAIS BANK, Calais. Me. — Male portrait; angel on left; cherub on right. — 1 — Female and fig. 1.

1 — Auditor's die — BANK OF ILLINOIS, New Haven. Ill. — Franklin. — 1 — 1 ONE

TWO 2 Female seated with sickle and wand; factory and canal in distance. 2 — Female seated with safe, scales, eagle, etc. — Title of Bank. — Farmer cradling. — Vulcan seated with implements; ears of corn above and below him. — TWO

2 — Farmer and sailor either side of shield — Saw mill; men seated on load of lumber drawn by two oxen. — Title of Bank. — 2 — Male portrait

3 — Auditor's die — Female seated with arm on a shield on left of a fig. 3, eagle on right. — Title of Bank. — THREE on 3. — Female portrait

5 — Justice, safe, eagle, scales, etc. — FIVE — V Three females amidg 5 cars, ships, farm scene, etc., in distance. V — Title of Bank — Farmer cradling. — 5 — Med. head. — FIVE

3 — Sailor and State Arms. — Ship-yard scene in general. — Title of Bank. — THREE 3 — Male portrait

5 — Female portrait. — Man seated, cradle, fruit, grain; haying scene on right. — Title of Bank. — 5 — Auditors' die

ONE — Stonecutter at work. — ONE — Compt's die. — Blacksmith shoeing horse; mule; locomotive in distance. — CENTRAL CITY BK., Syracuse. N. Y. — 1 — Blacksmith anvil, hammer. — ONE

This Bank also uses the Perkins' stereotype plate which has the denomination printed in fine letters all over the face of the bill.

20 — Male portrait — Female seated leaning on a bale; vessels in distance. — FAR. & MECH. BANK of Kent Co, Md. — 20 — Franklin.

10 — Compt's die. — TEN — Man looking at chart; two stonecutters, etc.; men, horses and cart in distance. — Title of Bank. — 10 — Female head — TEN

Man and boy plowing with two horses. — Female portrait. — BANK OF CHARLOTTE, Charlotte, N. C. — 5 — Female beside column, etc.

Goddess of Liberty. — FIFTY — Title of Bank. — Female reclining in corn field; negro gathering corn. — 50 — FIFTY

Female seated with scales. — Compt's die. — 20 View of N. Y. bay, vessels, etc. — Title of Bank. — TWENTY — Sailor hoisting flag.

10 — Female, cow, calf, etc. — Female head. — Title of Bank. — Three females and cupid floating in water. — 10

100 — Female with sickle and sheaf. — Female seated holding ear of corn; men, boats and village in distance. — Title of Bank. — 100 — Female portrait

Farmer with pitcher, etc. — 20 — UNION BANK, Reading, Pa. — Man cutting a stick; horse, cow, sheep and trees. — 20 — Female with flowers

Girl seated in chair. — TWENTY — Surveyors at work. — Title of Bank. — 20 — Farmer carrying corn stalks.

10 — Horse, colt and cattle running away from cars. — COMMERCIAL AND FARMERS' BANK. Baltimore, Md. — Female seated with horn of plenty; anchor, etc. — 10 — Male portrait

50 — Two men and horse; factories in distance. 50 — Title of Bank. — FIFTY — Milkmaid; boy pointing.

50 — Farmer at lunch; two horses, plow, etc. — Male portrait. — Title of Bank. — FIFTY 50 FIFTY — 50 — Loaded cart with bales negro on top.

FIFTY — Male figure seated with left hand resting on wheel, anvil, hammer, etc., ship in distance, 50 either side. — ESSEX CO. BANK. Keesville, N. Y. — FIFTY

100 — Female with sword and scales. — C Two females and machinery. C — Title of Bank. — Farmer seated with sickle; men reaping in distance.

100 — Female portrait. — Hundred. — Man holding horse; men repairing cart, etc. — Title of Bank. — 100 — Sailor boy. — Hundred.

100 — Milkmaid. — 100 — Washington. — Male figure supporting the globe on lever. — FAR. & MECH BK. of Georgetown, D. C. — 100

ONE Moonlight scene; fishing schooners, etc. 1 BUCKSPORT BANK, Bucksport, Me. Indian crouching with gun. Boy's portrait.	Female representing Commerce. Men in top of 1. 1 WHITE RIVER BK., Bethel, Vt. 1 Female with grain; fence, etc.	3 Two females either side of anvil. 3 MARKET BANK, Boston, Mass. Indian seated on safe. 3
TEN Marine view; ship, schooner and other vessels under sail. X Title of Bank. Female with sheaf. State Arms.	Sheep washing scene. Men in top of 2. 2 on TWO Title of Bank. Female seated. 2 2 on TWO	20 Three females, safe, etc. 20 SAFETY FUND BK., Boston, Mass. State Arms. Clay.
Agricultural scene; female seated pointing to reapers. 500 D 500 MERCHANTS' BK. Portland, Me. 500	Man on horse, cattle, dog, load of hay, etc. 3 3 Title of Bank. 3 Washington on horse.	50 Female on left of view of city, boats, shipbuilding, etc.; 50 on stone and Indian in canoe on right; steamboat in distance. 50 SAFETY FUND BK., Boston, Mass. Boy and rabbits. State Arms.
Indian paddling canoe. 500 500 PEJEPSCOT BANK, Brunswick, Me. 500 D D Female holding scales.	Female seated representing agriculture; boats, village, etc., in distance. Male portrait. 5 COCHECO BANK, Dover, N. H. 5 Indian seated.	C Title of Bank. 100 Four females on globe. One Hundred Dollars. State Arms. Male portrait.
Indian princess. Female reclining on safe; cattle and girls on right; wharf, vessels, bbls., bales, locomotive on right. 500 500 STATE BANK, Augusta, Me. Indian portrait.	C Eagle on bale; horn of plenty, grain, etc. 100 100 Men, vessels, etc. DERBY BANK, Derby, N. H. Female with sheaf and sickle. 100 100	100 Spread eagle, railroad and canal. 100 ADAMS BANK, North Adams, Mass. Vulcan with implements. 100 Female with rake.
2 2 Female seated with fig. 2. 2 2 Man on horse THOMASTON BANK, Thomaston, Me. Man on horse 2 2	FIFTY 50 Three females seated; pole, cap, eagle, scales, ship, etc. FIFTY on 50. Agricultural products, etc. MECHANICKS' BK., Concord, N. H. Vulcan seated by anvil. FIFTY	L CONWAY BANK, Conway, Mass. 50 Hunter warming himself; gun, dog, etc. Female in clouds with sword, scales, eagle, etc. Female binding shoes; child.
FIFTY L 50 VILLAGE BANK, Bowdoinham, Me. Ship yard scene in general. Steamship and schooner Cars, tunnel, bridge, city, etc.	C Eagle on bale; cornucopia, grain, etc. 100 100 Men, vessels, etc. Title of Bank. Female with sheaf and sickle. 100 100	XX Female seated with bale, box, barrel, etc.; yacht and steamship in distance. 20 GRAFTON BANK, Grafton, Mass. Train of cars. Male portrait.
500 General ship yard scene. 500 Old man with musket; female loading gun. LONG BEACH BK., Bath, Me. 500	Same as right. Wharf scene. One Hundred and 100. BANK OF ORLEANS, Irasburgh, Vt. Harrison. Columbus.	Female in clouds with eagle, etc. Male portrait. C Title of Bank. 100 Female binding shoes; child.
50 CARROLL CO. BANK, Sandwich, N. H. 50 Egyptian figure with wings seated beside globe; female, etc. 50 50	100 BANK OF RUTLAND, Rutland, Vt. 100 Indian beside dead deer. C Indian female seated and pointing.	100 Spread eagle on limb of tree; canal and railroad. 100 GREENFIELD BK., Greenfield, Mass. Vulcan with implements. 100 Female with rake.

ONE Two horses; farm-house in distance. 1 PEOPLES' BANK, Derby Line, Vt. ONE Boy gathering corn. ONE	3 Pigs. Wild horses. KANSAS VALLEY BANK Atchison, Kansas. 3 Female portrait.	100 Steamboat "Bay State;" yachts and forts in distance. METACOMET BANK, Fall River, Mass. C Indian in canoe spearing porpoise.
2 Female picking fruit. Man watering three horses female feeding pigs; farm house in distance. Title of Bank. 2 Farmer with scythe.	5 Female with dove. Indian on horseback shooting buffaloes. Title of Bank. 5 Portrait of a farmer.	500 500 Indian, squaw and child in canoe; Indian is spearing porpoise. Title of Bank. D Male portrait
5 Washington. Drove of cattle and sheep. Title of Bank. 5 Train of cars.	10 Title of Bank. Cars. X Steamboat, river, etc. 10	1000 Vig. same as above 100s. Title of Bank. Letter M in die and words "One Thousand" around. Indian.
10 Four small portraits of Ex Presidents. 10 10 Three farmers and female at lunch; horses, etc. Title of Bank X Indian seated	20 Female each side of shield Emigrant train. Title of Bank. 20 Male portrait	3 Male portrait Man pressing horns in comb press; basket of horns, etc. NORTHBOROUGH BANK, Northborough, Mass 3 Farmer, sailor, blacksmith and fig. 3.
Female and eagle. 20 TWENTY on 20. Female FAIRHAVEN BANK Fairhaven, Mass. 20 Franklin.	50 Sailor, capstan, bbls., vessels, etc. Title of Bank. Steamboat; city and boat on left. 50 Male portrait	ONE Female seated under tree; man and boy reclining. CHISAGO CO. BANK., Taylors' Falls, Minn. ONE = 1 1 Female head
FIFTY 50 50 Three females, eagle and shield Title of Bank. 50 Mechanic and factory.	C Male portrait Title of Bank Eagle on shield. 100 Male portrait	Small 2. 2 Emigrant train in motion. Figure of girl. Title of Bank. 2 Eagle on shield.
C Boats and men. 100 Eagle on bale. 100 Title of Bank. 100 Female with sickle. 100	Washington. 3 Steamships and ship at sea. NEW IPSWICH BK., New Ipswich, N. H. 3 Webster.	50 Male portrait BK. OF THE STATE of Indiana. Male portrait. Three men; one seated. 50
Agricultural scene; female pointing to rempers. 500 500 D Title of Bank. 500	50 Man, woman and child. FIFTY Landing of Roger Williams; Indians, etc. BK. OF CALEDONIA. Danville, Vt. 50 Male portrait	100 Male portrait Title of Bank. Two males and two females. 100 Male portrait
10 Female seated on safe with scales and sword. ALTON BANK, Alton, Ill. State Arms on large X. 10 Train of cars	100 Two farmers, woman and babe. Female seated with bales, etc.; factories, dam and village in distance. Title of Bank. 100 Male portrait	500 Indian paddling canoe. 500 MANCHESTER BK., Manchester, N. H. D D 500 Justice.

Left	Centre	Right
1 Drummer and soldiers.	Washington reading paper; man writing on drum head; horse, negro, cannon, men, etc. **WASHINGTON BK.,** Boston, Mass.	1 Portrait with frilled cap.

Left	Centre	Right
TWENTY	20 Street scene. **HAMPDEN BANK,** Westfield, Mass.	TWENTY on 20. Washington.

Left	Centre	Right
1 Man currying leather.	1 **REVERE BANK,** Male portrait. Boston, Mass.	1 State Arms.

Left	Centre	Right
Cupid and 2. 2	Title of Bank. Washington on frame; female, soldier, Indians, TWO either side.	2 and Cupid. 2

Left	Centre	Right
500 Male figure with a stylus and tablet.	Washington. Two females and beehive. **HAVERHILL BANK** Haverhill, Mass.	500 Martha Washington.

Left	Centre	Right
2 Blacksmiths boy at forge.	Male portrait. Stonecutter and man with plan. Title of Bank.	2 State Arms.

Left	Centre	Right
3	Washington on horse; officer submitting plans; other officers, cannon, horses, etc. Title of Bank.	3 Washington.

Left	Centre	Right
Same as right. Harrison.	Scene on a wharf. **BEVERLY BANK.** Beverly, Mass.	One Hundred and 100. Columbus.

Left	Centre	Right
3 Sailor boy, etc.	Title of Bank. Male portrait.	3 State Arms.

Left	Centre	Right
100	Female seated with eagle, shield, flags, etc. Female portrait. **ANDOVER BANK,** Andover, Mass.	100 Female portrait.

Left	Centre	Right
TWENTY. Male and female seated; two children and lamb.	**FALL RIVER BANK,** Fall River, Mass. Word Twenty in a semicircle, Dollars on figs. 20 on a die. Double med. head either side.	20 Male portrait.

Left	Centre	Right
5 State Arms.	Steamship, tug, city, etc. Title of Bank.	5 Male portrait.

Left	Centre	Right
500 Indian princess.	Title of Bank. Three females; ship and cars in distance.	500 500

Left	Centre	Right
L Two girls.	Title of Bank. Boy watering two horses at trough, female with pitcher and pail.	50 Male portrait.

Left	Centre	Right
10 State Arms.	General scene in moulding shop: men, wheels, machinery, etc. Title of Bank.	10 Male portrait.

Left	Centre	Right
M 1000	Title of Bank. Two females seated; shipping and cars in distance.	1000 1000

Left	Centre	Right
C Girls' head.	Steamboat. Title of Bank.	100 Male portrait.

Left	Centre	Right
C Anchor, bale, etc.	Female seated with shield, pole, cap, eagle, etc. **PEMBERTON BANK,** Lawrence, Mass.	100 Eagle.

Left	Centre	Right
Same as right. Harrison.	Scene on wharf. **QUINCY STONE BK.,** Quincy, Mass.	One Hundred and 100. Columbus.

Left	Centre	Right
50 Female with spear and shield.	Male and female seated. **FALL RIVER BANK,** Fall River. 50	50 Cupid in boat. 50

Left	Centre	Right
500 Dorcester Heights.	Landing of the Pilgrims. Title of Bank.	500 Massach'ts D

Left	Centre	Right
500 D	Indian padding in canoe. 500 Title of Bank D	500 Female with sword and scales

Left	Centre	Right
500 Female.	Title of Bank Three females; shipping, cars, etc., in distance.	500 500

Left	Centre	Right
Female seated pointing to reapers. 500	500 D **UNION BANK OF WEYMOUTH AND BRAINTREE.** Weymouth, Mass.	500

Left	Centre	Right
1000	Spread eagle on promontory; ship in distance. 100 Title of Bank.	1000 Indian female with bow and arrows.

Left	Centre	Right
M Shipping. 1000	Title of Bank. Two females.	1000 1000

Left	Centre	Right
Laocoon and sons strangled by serpents. 1000	Train of cars. THOUSAND. Title of Bank.	1000 Vessels. 1000

Left end	Centre	Right end
ONE Beehive.	Drovers on horseback and cattle. HOWARD BANK, Boston, Mass.	1 Portrait of officer.
FIVE HUNDRED	Spread eagle, shield, etc. SHAWMUT BANK, Boston, Mass.	Figs. 500. Male portrait Figs. 500.
FIFTY Head of Liberty surmounted by stars. 50	ASHAWAY BANK, Ashaway, R. I. 50	50 50
2 Youthful portrait with cap.	Med. bust on shield surmounted by eagle; Continental soldier, spear in etc., on right; female with pole and cap on left. Title of Bank.	2 Sailor and captain.
1000	Spread eagle shield and motto "E Pluribus Unum," etc. Title of Bank.	1000 Washington. 1000
1 Two sailors on spar reefing. ONE	LIME ROCK BANK, Providence, R. I. Sailor and Indian either side of State Arms surmounted by eagle.	1 Male portrait
3 THREE	Title of Bank. Three females in clouds; vessels in distance.	3 Portrait of officer.
Figs. 500. Male portrait Figs. 500.	Female either side of Indian on shield. HAMILTON BANK, Boston, Mass.	Figs. 500. Vessels.
2 Oldman with gun; female loading gun.	Girl's head. TITLE. Red 2. Man and boy plowing with two horses.	2
V Man dressing skins	Sailor on beach with anchor, etc.; steamer and vessels in distance. Title of Bank.	5 Female with V on shield.
Female seated pointing to reaping scene. Figs. 500.	500 D LEE BANK, Lee, Mass.	500
Three females erect supporting figure 3.	Vig. sailor seated among bales, with spy glass in his left hand; ship in distance on left of vig. Title of Bank.	3 Wild horse upon the prairie fleeing from locomotive.
10 Female, column, steamer, etc.	Title of Bank.	10 Portrait of officer.
Female seated pointing to reapers. 500	500 D LOWELL BANK, Lowell, Mass.	500
5 5	Vig. Mechanic seated on ground, surrounded with wheel, tools, &c.; hay making in distance. 5 Title of Bank. Dog's head.	FIVE Goddess of Liberty erect FIVE
Cupid on V. Female on safe with sword and scales.	View of Merchant's Bank and other buildings, street scene. MERCHANTS' BK., Boston Mass.	FIVE Fig. 5 on which is eagle, female and Washington. FIVE
Five Hundred. Washington. 500	MAVERICK BANK, Boston Mass. D Winthrop block and a street in Boston.	Figs. 500.
X 10	Vig. Female seated upon ground, corn, fruit, &c.; vessels upon stream in distance on left. Title of Bank. Spread eagle.	10 Mason at work, level in his hand.
Figs. 500. Eagle. Figs. 500.	Sailor, vessels, horse, cart, men, buildings, etc. 500 Title of Bank.	Figs. 500. Ship. Figs. 500.
M	1000 on a shield, surmounted by eagle; female each side; steamboat and cars in distance. NATIONAL BANK, Boston, Mass.	1000 Female with grain.
20 Female erect; spear in left hand; small globe at her feet.	Vig. Female seated between ornamental figures 2 and 0. Title of Bank. XX	20 Female seated; cornucopia, etc. 20
1000 Eagle. 1000	Vig. Same as 500s. Title of Bank.	1000 Female with figs. 1000. 1000
D Washington.	U. S. Capitol. LECHMERE BANK, East Cambridge, Mass.	500 Male portrait
50	Steamship sailing out of harbor, steamboat, sail vessels, etc. LIME ROCK BANK, Providence, R. I.	50 Female portrait
Figs. 500.	Harvest scene; female seated pointing to reapers. 500 D BOYLSTON BANK, Boylston, Mass.	500
D State Arms.	MERCHANTS' BK. FIVE HUNDRED Dollars. Lowell, Mass.	500 Male portrait
Female portrait	Title of Bank. Marine view; man-of-war and other vessels under sail.	100

---

1 | View of Falls, village, factories, etc. | 1
WOONSOCKET FALLS BANK, Woonsocket R. I.
Blacksmiths' boy at forge. | Portrait of female.

Mercury with wand and eagle. | Female portrait. | 20
Title of Bank.
20 | Franklin.

---

20 | Cattle, sheep, stream. | 20
STAMFORD BANK, Stamford, Conn.
Female portrait. | Fillmore.

THREE | 3 Vessel under full sail; lighthouse and steamer in distance. | 3
TRADERS' BANK, Providence, R. I.
Female, anchor, lighthouse, vessel, etc. | Two children with fruit.

FIFTY | 50 Three females seated with pole, cap, scales, book, eagle; ship. | Fifty on 50.
Grain, fruit, flowers, etc.
Title of Bank.
50 | Blacksmith seated with implements.

---

50 | Depot, steamboat landing, wharf, buildings and shipping. | 50
Title of Bank.
Male portrait. | Female portrait.

Indian princess surrounded by flags, drums, etc. | 3 | THREE
Farmer with sickle and sheaf.
BANK OF NORTH AMERICA, Providence, R. I.
3 | THREE

Eagle on bale. | 100 | 100
Men and boats.
Title of Bank.
Female with sickle.
100 | 100

---

100 | Launch of the Adriatic; river, ship-yard, city, etc. | 100
Title of Bank.
Female portrait. | Male portrait.

---

2 | Clay. Ancient Puritans around table. | 2
CITIZENS' UNION BANK, Scituate, R. I.
Sailor with flag, female at his feet. | Male and female seated.

---

5 | Two men tending furnaces. | 5
IRON BANK. Falls Village, Conn.
Man forging iron. | Franklin.

---

50 | STATE BANK. OF TROY, N. Y. | 50
FIFTY | Female portrait; on right female, column, steamer; on left, female, cow, calf, etc. | DOLLARS
50 | Compt's die. | 50

---

5 | Eagle and shield. | 5
COVENTRY BANK, Anthony Village, R. I.
Female seated with pen, scroll, harp, etc. | Indian princess.

---

3 | MERCHANTS' BK., Norwich, Conn. | THREE DOLLARS
Agricultural machine.
Whaling scene. Three on 3 on left; Dollars on 3 on right.
3

---

100 | Indians spearing buffaloes. | 100
COMMERCIAL BK., Troy, N. Y.
Deer. | Compt's Die. | Dog and game.

XX inverted | WARREN BANK, | 20
Male portrait; 20 and word Twenty on red die on left; 20 and word Dollars on red die on right.
Justice on safe. | Warren, R. I. | Female churning.

---

50 | SHETUCKET BANK, Norwich, Conn. | 50
Signing the Declaration of Independence.
Cass. | Webster.

FIVE | Cow and calf in stream; cattle and house in distance. | Female portrait. | 5
Male portrait | Compt's die.
BURNET BANK, Syracuse, N. Y.
5 | 5

FIFTY | Title of Bank. | FIFTY
Male portrait. Fifty and 50 on red die on left; Dollars, and 50 on red die on right.
Girl with sheaf. | Female with pole, cap, scroll, etc.

---

50 | BK. OF NORWALK, Norwalk, Conn. | 50
Male and female harvesters resting; cow, calf, etc.
Male portrait | Female portrait.

Compt's die. | 3 Male portrait. 3 | 3
LAKE SHORE BANK, Dunkirk, N. Y.
Indians hunting buffaloes. | Man cutting tree; two children, oxen, etc.

---

100 | Title of Bank. | 100
Male portrait. C and One Hundred on red die on left; C and Dollars on red die on right.
Farmer with rake, fork, keg, dog, etc. | Portrait of female.

---

20 | HURLBUT BANK, West Winsted, Conn. | XX
Female holding pole and cap in left hand, and frame with 20 on it in right.
Man on horseback. | Soldier with musket.

---

10 | Title of Bank. | 10
Sailor on ship with quadrant.
Anchor, bales, bbls., etc. | Compt's die.

Female seated with agricultural implements; factories, shipping, etc. | Indian girl in V. | 5
LANDHOLDERS' BANK, Kingston, R. I.
V on FIVE | Washington.

XX | BK. OF LITCHFIELD COUNTY, New Milford, Conn. | 20
20 on two stripes of lathe work. | Three females seated with pen, tablet, book, harp, etc. | State Arms.

---

100 | ONEIDA BANK. Utica, N. Y. | 100
Factory, ship, cars, etc. | Male figure seated in clouds with staff, lightning, eagle and shield. C each side. | Cherub with basket of flowers.
100 | 100

Compt's die. Male portrait THREE Bust of Fulton; mechanic seated on right; cars and steamship in distance. FULTON BANK. New-York City. 3 Steamboat.	20 Compt's die. XX Two females, shield, buildings, etc. GENESSEE VALLEY BANK, Geneseo, N. Y. Sheaf. 20 Male portrait TWENTY	3 Dog's head. 3 Female, boy, anvil; rake, plow, etc. STATE BANK, Camden, N. J 3 Dog's head 3
FIVE 5 Girl milking cow. V BK. OF ORANGE CO., Goshen, N. Y. Agricultural tools. Compt's die.	20 XX 20 Female with pole and cap on right of shield; female with sickle on left. Compt's die below. FARMERS' BANK of Washington Co., N.Y. 20 Man with musket.	Female soaring above buildings, river, cars, steamboat, etc; on upper right country scene. Coal train and mine. PITTSTON BANK, Pittston, Pa. 5 Indian.
FIVE Two girls with sheafs. 5 Boy, horses, colt, cows and sheep. BK. OF ORANGE CO., Goshen, N. Y. 5 Compt's die. FIVE	50 Female seated under tree. Title of Bank. Compt's die. 50 Farmer carrying corn stalks.	10 Female seated and dog's head. Title of Bank. Female seated among implements; cars on bridge and factories in distance. 10 Female with sheaf. 10
TEN Man sharpening scythe X Milkmaid seated with hat on lap; dog, cars, etc. Title of Bank. Man plowing. 10 Compt's die.	10 Male portrait TEN X Dales, two horses, canal boat; cars, steamboat, mountains, etc., in distance. X J. T. RAPLEE'S BK., Penn Yan, N. Y. 10 Compt's die.	Men with pick; coal-pit and men shoving coal car. Title of Bank. Men at work with wheelbarrows on dock, horse, cart, coal, etc. 10
20 Cattle, telegraph, arch, cars, etc. Milkmaid milking cow, etc. Title of Bank. Compt's die. 20 Men shearing sheep.	20 Two girls, vase on left. Title of Bank 20 Female erect column, steamer, etc. 20 XX Compt's die. XX 20 Male portrait	Mechanic with sledge. 20 Moonlight scene on canal, men, horses, boat, hills, and distant city. Title of Bank. 20 Female portrait.
3 Female portrait. Compt's die. Fig. 3 on bale; female with distaff on left; two females on right. 3 AUBURN CITY BK., Auburn, N. Y. THREE Female erect with shield, cap, etc.	20 Foundries. IRON BANK, Morristown, N. J. View in rolling mill; men and machinery. 20 State Arms.	BANK OF MUTUAL REDEMPTION. Boston, Mass. ☞ This Bank uses the Perkins' stereotype plate; which has the denomination in fine print all over the face of the bill. They intend shortly to use a different plate
FIFTY Female with battle axe and shield. Compt's die. Title of Bank. 50 FIFTY Female and anchor.	50 Foundries. Title of Bank. Same vig. as 20s. 50 State Arms.	1 Compt's die. 1 One Dollar One twice. 1 Spread eagle. 1 SENECA CO. BANK, Waterloo, N. Y. Steamboat. One Dollar four times. [illegible] Franklin. ONE
TWENTY DOLLARS BK. OF NORWICH, Norwich, N. Y. Female seated on either side of male portrait; sword, spear, bales, steamboat, cars, etc. 20	5 Half length figure of girl. Corn husking scene. YORK COUNTY BK., York, Pa. 5 Blacksmith at forge.	2 Compt's die. 2 Two Dollars. Two Dollars. 2 Female either side of fig 2 on shield; motto "speed the plow" at bottom; vessel in distance. 2 Title of Bank. Canal scene. Two Dollars. Two Dollars. Male figure erect. TWO
FIFTY Boy on horse back; cows, sheep, etc. FIFTY. Compt's die. Title of Bank. 50 Male portrait	Farmer seated holding glass and scythe; women with utensils Jefferson. Males and females and train of cars. Title of Bank. X	3 Compt's die. 3 Title of Bank. 3 Female erect beside monument; sloop, hills, etc., in background. 3 Indian in canoe. 3 Lafayette. 3

1 | Men on horseback; negroes tapping pine trees. | 1
Negroes in cotton field. | TIMBER CUTTERS' BANK, Savannah, Ga. | Sailor reclining on bale.

ONE | Negro boy holding donkey; man and woman gathering corn. Girl's portrait | 1
SOUTHERN BANK of Kentucky. | Sheep.

---

20 | MECHANICS' BANK, Philadelphia, Pa. | 20
XX | Penn. Goddess of Liberty holding bust of Washington; soldier and two Indians looking at it. Franklin. | XX

---

2 | 2 Negro with boy and tobacco leaves. 2 | 2
Girl. | Title of Bank. | Sailor boy.

---

3 | Negro boy watering horses, male and female gathering corn. Girl's head. | 3
Washington. | Title of Bank. Rooster. | 3

---

10 | Two females seated, spinning wheel, sickle, etc; cars, cattle, etc., in distance. State Arms | 10
Male portrait | SOUTH WESTERN BK. OF VIRGINIA. | Male portrait

---

Female soaring above buildings, river, cars, steamboat, etc.; country scene on upper right. | Title of Bank. Raft scene on Western river; steamboat. | 5

---

5 Female leaning on a monument V | Female seated on left of shield; cars and steamboat in distance. BK. OF TENNESSEE. | 5 Female with scales, eagle, etc.

---

5 Female and chickens. | Two females seated spinning, wheel, sickle; cars, cattle, etc., in distance. BANK OF METROPOLIS, Newmarket, Ill. | 5 Auditors' die

---

Farmer drinking 50 | Female erect with stool, etc. CECIL BANK, Port Deposit, Md. | 50 Portrait of female.

State Arms. TWENTY XX | Two females seated; eagle, anchor, globe, etc.; temple of Fame and steamship in distance. MERCHANTS' BK., New Orleans, La. | 20 Female portrait.

Female soaring above buildings, river, cars, steamboat, etc.; on upper right country scene. | Auditors' die. X Title of Bank. | 10 Laborers at work; one lighting pipe

---

100 Farmer with scythe; village, etc. | Milkmaid with stool, cows, sheep, etc. Title of Bank. Steamer. | 100 Female with flowers.

TEN | Female erect leaning on shield; ship in distance; 10 either side. BK. OF LOUISIANA, New Orleans, La. | TEN

---

5 | Man and boy plowing with two horses. Auditor's die. BANK OF GENESEO, Geneseo, Ill. FIVE | 5 Milkmaid, cow and calf

---

X Female portrait. | Man holding bell, sheep, boy holding horse, two men, dog, etc. BANK OF SCOTTSVILLE, Scottsville, Va. | 10 State Arms

---

XX Male portrait TWENTY | Woodcutter seated; oxen, horse, etc., on right, man fishing on left. COMMERCIAL BK. of Kentucky. | XX Steamboat on stocks. TWENTY

---

10 | Man and boy plowing with two horses. BK. OF DELAWARE COUNTY, Chester, Pa. Vessel and lighthouse. | 10 Girl's head.

Hunter loading rifle. XX | 20 Female with pole, cap, eagle, etc. Title of Bank. | 20 State Arms.

---

10 Auditor's die | Man on horse; one on fence, dog, colt, sheep, etc. Male portrait. STATE BANK OF ILLINOIS, Shawneetown, Ill. | 10 Fowls.

---

10 Female with sheaf. | Blacksmith shop, farmer, two horses, plow, rake, etc. FAR. & MECH. BK., Philadelphia, Pa. | 10 Mechanic and lathe.

Statue holding a scroll. | FIVE Angel flying 5 above shields, female on left; officer on right. MERCHANTS' BK., Cheraw, S. C. | V Cars, shipping, etc.

---

5 5 | Girl's portrait. Scene at mill door; man, horse, colt, two boys on bridge. OCOEE BANK, Cleaveland, Tenn. | 5 FIVE

---

20 20 | Title of Bank. Female with bundle of grain. Cogwheels, etc. | 20 Farmer, two horses, plow, blacksmith, anvil, etc. TWENTY

---

500 Male portrait | An oval tablet containing Title of Bank, with words Five Hundred Dollars below. CENTRAL BANK of Alabama. White 500. | 500 Washington.

TEN Female portrait. TEN | Indian seated on cliff viewing river, city, etc. Title of Bank. | 10 Negro in cotton field.

C Vig. same as right of 20. | Mechanic and lathe. Title of Bank. 100 | 100 C 100

Left end	Centre	Right end
ONE Agricultural implements and products ONE	1 Ox, sheep, horse, etc. 1 ONTARIO BANK, Bowmanville, Canada ONE	1 ONE Men shearing sheep.
5 Auditor's die	Title of Bank. Harvest scene; four men, two horses and reaper, sheafs; railroad in distance.	5 Portrait of female.
1 Auditors' die	Female seated with sprig, eagle, etc.; railroad, marine and city scene in distance. BANK OF AMERICA, Mt. Carmel, Ill.	1 Indian princess.
TWO Mechanic with sledge, anvil; locomotive, etc.	Two and 2. Female seated, hat on lap, dog, cows, etc. Title of Bank. TWO	2 TWO 2
5 Male portrait	Train of cars; building in background on right. CLINTON BANK, Westernport, Md.	5 Female erect with scales, etc. FIVE
2 Auditors' die	Winged female with trumpet, globe and eagle. Title of Bank.	2
5 Girls with sheafs	CITY BANK OF BEAVER DAM, Wis. Portrait in round die; word "Dollars" at bottom, and "Five" either side. V V	5 Compt's die.
Woman and three children. ONE	Male portrait. BANK OF THE OHIO VALLEY, Cincinnati, Ohio.	Girl with hat on; man shearing sheep. One Dollar in part circle.
3 Auditors' die	Female in clouds with pole, cap, eagle, shield. Title of Bank.	3
THREE Farmers.	BK. of the REPUBLIC, McLeansboro', Ill. 3 Auditors' die. 3 Cars, load of hay, men, cattle, etc.	Three inverted. Two female preparing dinner; fowls, etc.
3 Males and females making wine.	Male portrait. Title of Bank.	3 3
5 Auditors' die	Spread eagle, shield, etc. Title of Bank.	5
1 ONE Dogs hunting birds.	Milkmaid seated on log; house, steamer, etc. BLOOMINGTON BK., Bloomington, Ind.	1 State Arms
FIVE Hunter drinking from brook; gun by his side.	Title of Bank. Male portrait. FIVE	5 Library scene with Calhoun seated and Webster erect. FIVE
Indian princess. 10	Title of Bank across large 10.	10 Auditors' die
FIVE State Arms.	Horses, cattle, sheep. Title of Bank.	V, 5, Five. Cherubs.
Group of ten human figures, males and females.	Male portrait. Title of Bank. TEN	X 10
Full length figure of Liberty.	20, XX, and word TWENTY. Title of Bank.	20 Auditors' die
1 Auditor's die	Surveying scene—three men by log in foreground, one man in distance at work on railroad, PITTSFIELD BANK, Pittsfield, Ill.	1 Man carrying corn stalks.
3 Compt's die. Wisconsin.	MARATHON Cupid. Cupid. CITY Milkmaid and boy. BK., Marathon City.	3 Female portrait
50 Auditors' die	FIFTY DOLLARS 50 and $ mark. Title of Bank.	FIFTY Female erect with flag and shield.
Two inverted Female with sheaf and sickle.	Title of Bank. Auditors' die. Boys attempting to catch running horse; dog; houses, horse, colt, etc., in distance.	2 2
Girl with chickens. CITY 5	MARATHON Mechanic erect in V; buildings, etc. Boy and rabbits. BANK, Marathon City. FIVE FIVE FIVE	5 Compt's die. Wisconsin
100 Auditors' die	One Hundred Dollars. 100 Title of Bank.	100 Female giving eagle drink; cornucopia, etc.
5 Auditors' die	Title of Bk. FIVE Female head DOLLARS Corn husking scene; males, females, negro, dog, etc.	5 5
Children. ONE	NEWARK BANKING COMPANY, Newark, N. J. Milkmaid under tree, boy pointing.	1 Male portrait
Auditors' die in large red circle.	Title of Bank. Red 500. Head of Liberty.	Red 500.

ONE Queen Victoria. EASTERN TOWNSHIP BANK, Sherbrook, Canada. Falls, mills, bridge, buildings, etc. Indian on cliff. ONE	TEN Auditors' die Battle of New Orleans. Title of Bank. 10 Female portrait	LEWISBURG BANK, Lewisburg, Pa. Boys attempting to catch running horse; dog, horses, etc. Male head. 20 Man carrying corn-stalks.
5 Female with book. Man with sack on back; mill, horse, colt, wheel; boys on bridge. Title of Bank. 5 Man cleaning scythe.	20 Continental soldier. Title of Bank. Soldier, wife and child; country scene in distance. 20 Auditors' die	ONE Female and 1. ONE REAPERS' BANK, Fairfield, Ill. Farmer in field whetting cradle and scythe. 1 Auditors' die
TEN Hunter by fire, dog, etc. Boy watching sheep. Title of Bank. 10 Cars; buildings in distance.	ONE on 1. ONE ONE on 1. Map of Kentucky with State arms on upper corner; on right, hunters in canoe; on left, squaw. COMMERCIAL BK. OF KENTUCKY. Bull. 1 Female with dove.	TWO Man gathering corn. TWO Title of Bank. Large TWO in front of two females; building, ocean scene, etc., in distance. TWO 2 Auditors' die
XX Female, wheel, building, etc. Man plowing with two horses; men harrowing, city, etc., in distance. Title of Bank. 20 Female with spear and XX on shield	2 Female portrait. Vig. Same as above ones. Title of Bank. Dog. TWO TWO TWO	Boy and girl. 3 Man on horse conversing with farmer, another on ground. Title of Bank. Three gold dollars. 3 Auditors' die
FIVE Road scene; drovers, cattle, load of hay, man on horse, etc. BK. OF THE STATE, Equality, Ill. Medallion head. FIVE DOLLARS. Auditors' die. 5 Female beside column; steamer.	3 Boy and rabbits. Vig. Same as above ones. Title of Bank. Canal lock. 3 Youthful figure with cap.	5 FIVE Female with 5 on shield. Patent reaping machine at work in field; city, etc. in distance Title of Bank. 5 Auditors' die
TEN Map of Illinois; female and Indian either side. Title of Bank. 10 TEN DOLLARS. Auditors' die. 10 Mining scene	5 Negro picking cotton. BK. OF LEXINGTON, Lexington, N. C. 5 Two females seated; building in distance. 5 5 Cotton weighing scene.	Auditors' die Steamboat, etc. Raft scene on Western River. OHIO RIVER BANK, Golconda, Ill. 1 Sailor.
XX Auditors' die Female portrait. Title of Bank. Washington on horse; officer submitting plan; officers, tent, cannon, etc. 20 Clay.	10 Female with sickle. Patent reaping machine at work in field; city, etc. in distance. Title of Bank. 10 Female with sickle and sprig.	Auditors' die Agricultural implements and products Boy watching sheep. Title of Bank. 2 Sheep.
1 Auditors' die PATRIOTIC BANK, Hutsonville, Ill. Battle scene. ONE Man and boy with gun.	ONE Compt's die. UNION BANK OF TROY, N. Y. View of large building, street, etc 1 ONE 1	Auditors' die Road scene; drovers, cattle, load of hay, man on horse, etc. Title of Bank. Hunters at fire in woods; deer on horse, dogs, etc. 3 Female with dove.
FIVE on Dollars. Two soldiers. Title of Bank. Battle scene. 5 Auditors' die	2 Compt's die. 2 Title of Bank. Vig. Same as above ones. 2 Male portrait	Auditors' die Female with sickle. Title of Bank. Man with sack, horse, colt, wheel; boys on bridge. 5 Female in field reaping.

Full length statue on dark ground. — 10 Cattle in stream; boy and child on bank. BK. OF NEWPORT, Newport, N. Y. — 10 Compt's die.	TWO Indian princess. — COLUMBIAN BANK, Elizabethtown, Ill. Calhoun. — 2 on TWO. Auditors' die	100 Shield and motto. — Title of Bank. 100 C 100 — 100 Female portrait.
XX Youthful portrait with cap. — Compt's die. Boy on horse, colt, sheep, cattle, etc. Title of Bank. — 20 Cooper at work on barrels.	3 Female with sickle and cornucopia. — Title of Bank. Clay. — 3 Auditors' die	Female erect with sword and scales. ONE — HAMPDEN BANK, Hampden, Mass. General view of street and buildings. — 1 Franklin.
Female holding 50. FIFTY — Horse running; boys attempting to stop; dog, horses, houses, etc. BRIGHTON MARKET BANK, Brighton, Mass. — Female holding 50. FIFTY	5 — Title of Bank. Eagle on shield. Washington. — 5 Auditors' die	TWO Female with sheaf and sickle. — Title of Bank. Vig. Same as above ones. — 2 Washington.
C 100 — Boy and horses at trough; female, pail, ducks, etc. Youthful portrait with cap. Title of Bank. — 100 Female, cow, calf, ducks, etc.	Female with sickle and sprig. 10 — Title Bank. Mah ad. — 10 Auditors' die	5 Youthful portrait with cap. — Title of Bank. Vig. Same as above ones. — 5 Female portrait.
Auditor's die Female gazing at ocean on which is steamer, etc. — BANK OF LASALLE, Lasalle, Ill. Steamboat Illinois. — 1 Boy and rabbits.	TWO DOLLARS — MANUFACTU… 'RS' BANK, Macon, Ga. Boy, horses, colt, cattle and sheep. — 2 Portrait of farmer.	FIFTY DOLLARS — MER. & MAN. BANK, Hartford, Conn. 50 50 Male portrait. — FIFTY DOLLARS
Auditor's die Children with sheafs. — Title of Bank. Stores, canal, cars, boats, horses, carts, men, etc. — 2 Cattle, telegraph, cars, arch, etc.	5 Male portrait — Female in clouds with eagle, canopy, etc. Title of Bank. — 5 Temple with pillars, soldier, etc.	100 Female on rock gazing at ocean on which is steamer, etc. — Title of Bank. Green C. Male portrait — 100 C
Auditors' die Female on safe with sword and scales. — Title of Bank. Jolly raftsmen on Western river; steamboat on left. — 3 Canal and railroad scene.	10 Buchanan. — Title of Bank. Female either side of anvil; buildings, etc. — 10 Calhoun.	ONE on 1 Sailor, quadrant, capstan; steamer. — Schooners, etc. HINGHAM BANK, Hingham, Mass. — 1 Female portrait
5 Auditors' die — BK. OF COMMERCE, Vienna, Ill. Two females seated, one with sickle; vessels in distance. — 5 Sailor with flag.	Negro on load of bales drawn by two horses. 20 — Title of Bank. Male portrait — 20 Female with spear and XX on shield	2 — Title of Bank. Males, female, house, well, dog, horse at trough, etc. — 2 Female portrait.
X Auditors' die — Title of Bank. Sailor with spy-glass; bales, bbls., vessels, etc. — 10 Train of cars.	FIFTY Female with sheaf and sickle — 50 Vessel under sail; lighthouse, vessels, etc. AETNA BANK, Hartford, Conn. — 50 Portrait of female.	3 — Men haying, etc. Title of Bank. — THREE Milkmaid erect, boy pointing.

www.ingramcontent.com/pod-product-compliance
Lightning Source LLC
Chambersburg PA
CBHW021356210326
41599CB00011B/900

* 9 7 8 3 7 4 1 1 9 7 5 1 2 *